Handbook of Research on Cross–Disciplinary Uses of Gamification in Organizations

Oscar Bernardes
ISCAP, ISEP, Polytechnic Institute of Porto, Portugal & University of Aveiro, Portugal

Vanessa Amorim
ISCAP, Polytechnic Institute of Porto, Portugal

António Carrizo Moreira
University of Aveiro, Portugal

A volume in the Advances in Business Strategy and Competitive Advantage (ABSCA) Book Series

Published in the United States of America by
IGI Global
Business Science Reference (an imprint of IGI Global)
701 E. Chocolate Avenue
Hershey PA, USA 17033
Tel: 717-533-8845
Fax: 717-533-8661
E-mail: cust@igi-global.com
Web site: http://www.igi-global.com

Library of Congress Cataloging-in-Publication Data

Names: Bernardes, Oscar, 1978- editor. | Amorim, Vanessa, 1992- editor. |
  Moreira, António Carrizo, editor.
Title: Handbook of research on cross-disciplinary uses of gamification in
  organizations / Oscar Bernardes, Vanessa Amorim, and Antonio Moreira,
  editor.
Description: Hershey, PA : Business Science Reference, [2022] | Includes
  bibliographical references and index. | Summary: "This book looks at the
  field of Gamification for economic and social development while
  providing for further research opportunities in this dynamic and growing
  field with the goal of increasing the understanding of the importance of
  Gamification in the context of organizations' improvements, providing
  relevant academic work,and empirical research findings"-- Provided by
  publisher.
Identifiers: LCCN 2021035415 (print) | LCCN 2021035416 (ebook) | ISBN
  9781799892236 (hardcover) | ISBN 9781799892250 (ebook)
Subjects: LCSH: Gamification--Economic aspects. | Simulation
  games--Psychological aspects. | Simulation games in education. |
  Management games. | Organizational behavior.
Classification: LCC HB144 .H364 2022 (print) | LCC HB144 (ebook) | DDC
  519.3--dc23
LC record available at https://lccn.loc.gov/2021035415
LC ebook record available at https://lccn.loc.gov/2021035416

This book is published in the IGI Global book series Advances in Business Strategy and Competitive Advantage (ABSCA)
(ISSN: 2327-3429; eISSN: 2327-3437)

British Cataloguing in Publication Data
A Cataloguing in Publication record for this book is available from the British Library.

All work contributed to this book is new, previously-unpublished material. The views expressed in this book are those of the
authors, but not necessarily of the publisher.

For electronic access to this publication, please contact: eresources@igi-global.com.

Advances in Business Strategy and Competitive Advantage (ABSCA) Book Series

Patricia Ordóñez de Pablos
Universidad de Oviedo, Spain

ISSN:2327-3429
EISSN:2327-3437

MISSION

Business entities are constantly seeking new ways through which to gain advantage over their competitors and strengthen their position within the business environment. With competition at an all-time high due to technological advancements allowing for competition on a global scale, firms continue to seek new ways through which to improve and strengthen their business processes, procedures, and profitability.

The **Advances in Business Strategy and Competitive Advantage (ABSCA) Book Series** is a timely series responding to the high demand for state-of-the-art research on how business strategies are created, implemented and re-designed to meet the demands of globalized competitive markets. With a focus on local and global challenges, business opportunities and the needs of society, the **ABSCA** encourages scientific discourse on doing business and managing information technologies for the creation of sustainable competitive advantage.

COVERAGE

- Tacit Knowledge
- International Business Strategy
- Differentiation Strategy
- Resource-Based Competition
- Value Chain
- Innovation Strategy
- Core Competencies
- Strategic Alliances
- Competitive Strategy
- Joint Ventures

IGI Global is currently accepting manuscripts for publication within this series. To submit a proposal for a volume in this series, please contact our Acquisition Editors at Acquisitions@igi-global.com or visit: http://www.igi-global.com/publish/.

Titles in this Series

For a list of additional titles in this series, please visit: http://www.igi-global.com/book-series/advances-business-strategy-competitive-advantage/73672

Critical Analysis and Architecture for Strategic Business Planning
James McKee (Independent Researcher, Australia)
Business Science Reference • © 2022 • 289pp • H/C (ISBN: 9781799880738) • US $215.00

Multidisciplinary Perspectives on Cross-Border Trade and Business
Asmat-Nizam Abdul-Talib (University Utara Malaysia, Malaysia) Norhayati Zakaria (University of Wollongong in Dubai, UAE) and Samshul-Amry Abdul-Latif (Universiti Utara Malaysia, Malaysia)
Business Science Reference • © 2022 • 375pp • H/C (ISBN: 9781799890713) • US $225.00

Cases on Digital Strategies and Management Issues in Modern Organizations
José Duarte Santos (Instituto Superior Politecnico, Spain)
Business Science Reference • © 2022 • 365pp • H/C (ISBN: 9781799816300) • US $195.00

Employee Share Ownership and Impacts on Organizational Value and Behavior
Sara Elouadi (Hassan II University, Casablanca, Morocco)
Business Science Reference • © 2022 • 255pp • H/C (ISBN: 9781799885573) • US $215.00

ICT as Innovator Between Tourism and Culture
Célia M.Q. Ramos (University of Algarve, Portugal) Silvia Quinteiro (University of Algarve, Portugal) and Alexandra R. Gonçalves (University of Algarve, Portugal)
Business Science Reference • © 2022 • 319pp • H/C (ISBN: 9781799881650) • US $215.00

Handbook of Research on Big Data, Green Growth, and Technology Disruption in Asian Companies and Societies
Patricia Ordóñez de Pablos (The University of Oviedo, Spain) Xi Zhang (Tianjin University, China) Mohammad Nabil Almunawar (Universiti Brunei Darussalam, Brunei) and José Emilio Labra Gayo (University of Oviedo, Spain)
Business Science Reference • © 2022 • 415pp • H/C (ISBN: 9781799885245) • US $295.00

Driving Factors for Venture Creation and Success in Agricultural Entrepreneurship
Mohd Yasir Arafat (Aligarh Muslim University, Aligarh, India) Imran Saleem (Aligarh Muslim University, Aligarh, India) Jabir Ali (Indian Institute of Management, Jammu, India) Adil Khan (O.P. Jindal University, Raigarh, India) and Hamad Hussain Balhareth (Saudi Electronic University, Saudi Arabia)
Business Science Reference • © 2022 • 356pp • H/C (ISBN: 9781668423493) • US $215.00

701 East Chocolate Avenue, Hershey, PA 17033, USA
Tel: 717-533-8845 x100 • Fax: 717-533-8661
E-Mail: cust@igi-global.com • www.igi-global.com

List of Contributors

Table of Contents

Detailed Table of Contents

Chapter 1

    Demos Parapanos, University of Cumbria, UK
    Eleni (Elina) Michopoulou, University of Derby, UK

Gamification is recognized as the next big thing in marketing by using game design elements in a non-game context. Producing desirable experiences and motivating users to remain engaged in an activity is one of the strengths of gamification. The introduction of digital social networks has become the biggest change regarding digital technology, also leading to the evolution and popularity of gamification. Although it is possible to design games, serious games, or gamified systems without knowing who the target users are, it is more likely to create a more engaging experience when these users are identified first. Taking this into consideration, this chapter will look to identify and present the motivations of individuals when using gamification systems. Identifying the motivations behind gamification usage and acknowledging the interaction between them will help organizations understand their audience and create more engaging experiences.

Chapter 2

    Daniel Cermak-Sassenrath, IT University of Copenhagen, Denmark

A pervasive application of gamification in many areas of everyday life has arguably yet to happen. For instance, despite much commercial interest in and a potentially huge market for successful gamification products in the areas of education and health, much of the excitement is still based on speculation, and reception in parts of the academic community remains sceptical. The chapter aims to collate observations from multiple empirical studies and meta-studies and collect and highlight issues that need to be resolved or mitigated for gamification to progress. Such issues include unclear definitions, a limitation on small sets of elements employed with unclear effects, unintentional side-effects of competition, a confusing variety of operationalizations, the erosion of intrinsic motivation through extrinsic incentives, a disconnect between theoretical understandings and practical realizations, a strong focus on a behaviorist paradigm, studies' mixed, partial, and inconclusive results, a lack of attention to moderating factors, and methodological limitations.

Gamification has created great expectations for education and has become a trend in education. It is not an easy process to integrate gamification into educational environments. The design and development phases of gamification are very important. Therefore, it is necessary to follow a model that will guide the process in gamification designs. Individual differences among students are an important factor affecting their learning performance. In this context, considering student characteristics will increase the effect of gamification in education. Personalized gamification designs that meet the needs and expectations of students will be more effective than one-size-fits-all designs. It can benefit from player/user types in gamification designs to identify individual differences. This chapter aims to discuss player/user types in relation to gamification in the context of education.

Chapter 4

Although gamification has been applied to the e-government domain for the past 20 years, the literature shows that the field still lacks formal definitions to support the design of gamified strategies on these types of platforms and services, and that game element selection is often a subjective matter. This chapter provides a useful taxonomy of game elements to support the design of e-government initiatives, elaborated from the analysis of the literature on gamification frameworks and models applied to this domain. This work was additionally validated by gamification experts from public and private organizations during a series of workshops. A total of 30 commonly used game elements were selected, conceptualized, and classified into six dimensions. Gamification experts agreed that this work contributes to standardizing the game elements employed in e-government services, while the authors also believe this taxonomy can be a useful tool to analyze already existing frameworks.

The chapter examines the researchers' objective to see how gamification has been investigated in various science disciplines during the COVID-19 pandemic and its impact by grouping the findings into central concerns and core issues. The PRISMA approach is used to narrow down the list of relevant articles. The necessity for gamified interventions in the retail, education, and health domains is deliberated in this chapter. The findings suggest that academicians take the chance to collect empirical data and evaluate it in real-time to better understand the impact of gamification in a variety of professions.

Chapter 6

Gamification, a popular tool widely used in various contexts such as marketing, education, and organizations, among others, has demonstrated its potential for engaging, motivating, and achieving behavioral change in the targeted audience. For an ideal gamification system, it is necessary to know how the gamification elements affect human emotions. This chapter conducts a journey through gamified contexts and their psychological impacts on individuals. This chapter gathers up the different threads of gamification in the marketing context. The three important objectives fulfilled by this chapter would be that it provides information about the topic of gamification and the psychological perspectives behind its operation; discusses its application in various marketing contexts, such as digital marketing and online payment sites; and finally, investigates various behavioral outcomes of gamification.

Chapter 7

Advances in digital marketing technologies and the experience and value they provide to consumers have become important factors in market success. Therefore, businesses are focusing much more on the use of innovative technologies such as gamification. Gamification is the use of game design elements and mechanisms in non-game environments to increase the motivation of users to guide their behavior. Gamification elements used in marketing activities have an impact on the attitudes and behaviors of consumers towards brands, products, and services by increasing experience and value for them. Accordingly, this chapter is aimed at evaluating the gamified marketing activities from the perspective of customer value. In this context, the concepts of customer value and gamification are examined, and gamification techniques used in marketing and their effects on consumer value are evaluated. Also, the case study of Starbucks' gamified mobile application is presented from the perspective of customer value.

Recent technological advances have promoted a social change that affects all areas of society, but mainly communication and entertainment, where social networks play a primordial function as they facilitate sociability and the creation of virtual communities. So-called "social media marketing" facilitates direct interaction between brands and markets through the Internet. For this, new communication strategies have been implemented, oriented towards the active participation of the users to increase their engagement. Some of these are inspired by the main product of the entertainment industry, videogames, through gamification. However, not many research studies have focused on classic role-playing games (RPGs), despite being considered the types of games that create the greatest player involvement. This work enquires about the possibilities offered by these games for the implementation of social media marketing strategies. A qualitative research study was conducted in which the engagement strategies utilized by RPG were associated with those utilized in social networks.

Chapter 9

Gamification and health are discussed from a one-sided perspective. Gamification and health studies focus on the use of gamification for health and overlook the perspective on how gamification affects health. This chapter discusses gamification and health in terms of organizations, individuals, and society, and addresses the effects of gamification on health and the use of gamification for health. Existing research on gamification and health addresses gamification practices developed for health and the health effects of gamification separately. Consequently, the aim of this chapter is to contribute to the original research collection organized into gamification studies in health from a holistic perspective.

The psychological health outcomes of video games are drawing increasing interest around the world. There is growing interest in video games as an accessible health intervention for depression and anxiety, both of which are rising health concerns globally. New interaction techniques for video games are becoming increasingly popular, with natural user interfaces (NUIs) becoming more commonplace in game systems. This chapter explores the design of a meditative game, a subgenre of casual games that intends for players to become calm and relaxed, and the evaluation of the NUIs for the game. The purpose of the chapter is to ascertain which NUI is most suitable for meditative games. A meditative fishpond game was designed that accepts two NUIs: touch and eye-tracking. The game was evaluated using a Positive and Negative Affect Schedule. The study found the eye-tracking interface reported a higher positive affect score from users and is therefore most suitable for meditative games.

Stroke is a debilitating condition that impairs one's ability to live independently while also greatly decreasing one's quality of life. For these reasons, stroke rehabilitation is important. Engagement is a crucial part of rehabilitation, increasing a stroke survivor's recovery rate and the positive outcomes of their rehabilitation. For this reason, virtual reality (VR) has been widely used to gamify stroke rehabilitation to support engagement. Given that VR and the serious games that form its basis may not necessarily be engaging in themselves, ensuring that their design is engaging is important. This chapter discusses 39 principles that may be useful for engaging stroke survivors with VR-based rehabilitation post-stroke. This chapter then discusses a subset of the game design principles that are likely to engage stroke survivors with VR designed for upper limb rehabilitation post-stroke.

    Jaana-Maija Koivisto, Häme University of Applied Sciences, Finland
    Elina Haavisto, Tampere University, Finland
    Antti J. Kaipia, Pirkanmaa Hospital District, Finland
    Ira H. Saarinen, Etelä-Pohjanmaa District Hospital, Finland
    Jari Multisilta, Satakunta University of Applied Sciences, Finland

A current concern in the medical field is that nurses leave their careers due to low work motivation. Intrinsic motivation is a key factor that influences satisfaction in the workplace. This study aimed to develop a gamification intervention for implementation in a hospital setting and evaluate its effects on nurses' work motivation. It was hypothesized that nurses' work motivation would improve by the end of the intervention. The study was conducted in a surgical ward at a hospital in Finland. The design was descriptive and quasi-experimental. The study found that continuous feedback from gamification interventions influenced nurses' work motivation. The gamified group offered more positive feedback than the non-gamified group. These findings add to our understanding of the effects of gamification interventions on nurses' work motivation in hospital settings. However, more research is needed to demonstrate the potential of gamification to increase the retention of much-needed human resources.

    Jessica Reuter, GOVCOPP, University of Aveiro, Portugal
    Marta Ferreira Dias, GOVCOPP, DEGEIT, University of Aveiro, Portugal
    Maria José Sousa, Business Research Unit, Instituto Universitário de Lisboa, Portugal

Organisations always seek to maximize the effectiveness of their internal systems. Gamification is a growing trend in work contexts, with employers realizing that many of the elements associated with it can be transferred to a business environment. Understanding the main concepts that make games appealing to society allows us to understand how they can be adapted and used in the professional environment, as well as in organizations. Therefore, besides gamification, game-based learning and serious games can be used in organizations for training and skills development. Understanding how gamification activities affect both extrinsic and intrinsic motivation is critical to understanding how they affect workers and how they can be used to their full potential. This study provides a critical analysis of the use of these tools to increase the motivation and collaboration of individuals in organizations. Playing in groups to learn is a practice that still needs more incentives and diffusion to be widely used in the company context.

    Victor Neto, Centre for Mechanical Technology and Automation (TEMA), Department of
        Mechanical Engineering, University of Aveiro, Portugal
    Henrique Bessa, Centre for Mechanical Technology and Automation (TEMA), Department of
        Mechanical Engineering, University of Aveiro, Portugal
    Ricardo Ferreira de Mascarenhas, RM Consulting, Portugal

It is more important than ever that organizations make the most of their resources, reduce costs, optimize processes, and engage in continuous improvement. A lean philosophy presents itself as a management model that guides companies in this direction, but for the successful implementation of lean methodologies, human resources at all levels need to learn what it is and be engaged with it. Thus, there is a need to develop tools that would transmit the lean theoretical concepts in a practical and involved way. This chapter proposes the development of a tool that is the result of merging gamification and lean philosophy, developing a game for people without knowledge in this area, serving as an introduction to it, and demonstrating some applications of this philosophy. The practical result of the synergy created between strategies of gamification and training in lean methodologies is described.

One of the main challenges faced by tourist destinations is waste management. A poor waste collection and management policy is an additional factor affecting the tourist destination's sustainability within this general problem. These situations are trying to be solved with incentives derived from gamification tools that motivate people to recycle. This study, within the scope of a European project called UrbanWaste, found significant results that suggested that this tool can promote recycling behavior, but what happens when customers come back home? Gamification even makes a habit take root in the people who use it by activating external motivators. This recycling habit emanates from an altruistic feeling and aims to leave a better world for future generations (intrinsic motivation). However, they also recommend the app to show a benevolent image by making the behavior visible (internalized extrinsic motivation) and improving destination branding.

This chapter provides a comprehensive overview of the phenomenon of review bomb, which occurs when an abnormally large amount of information is submitted to a rating system in a very short period of time by an overtly anonymous mass of accounts, with the overall goal of sabotaging the system's proper functioning. Because review bombs are frequently outbursts of social distress from gaming communities, gamification theories have proven useful for understanding the behavioral traits and conflict dynamics associated with such a phenomenon. A prominent case is analysed quantitatively. The methodology is discussed and proposed as a generalized framework for descriptive quantification of review bombs. As a result of the study, considerations for technological improvements in the collection of rating data in systems are proposed too.

Hate speech is increasingly hindering the possibility of raising collective understanding as well as the values of democracy based on mutual respect, tolerance, and equality. For that reason, the main objective of this chapter is to determine how game-based learning favors the acquisition of transversal competences within the framework of 21st century skills for tackling and addressing hate speech. In doing so, a total of four serious games—Bury Me, My Love; Another Lost Phone: Laura's Story; Never Alone; and Life is Strange: Episode 2 "Out of Time"—have been selected to analyze their potential as a learning tool for combating hate speech. To this end, the Octalysis framework serves as a methodology for identifying transversal competences in matters of justice, equity, and emotional intelligence. The main results show that serious games are helpful assets in promoting empathy and other social values and skills that are necessary to combat hate speech in young people.

Chapter 18

Marvin Jammermann, Carl von Ossietzky Universität Oldenburg, Germany
Beybin Elvin Tunc, Carl von Ossietzky Universität Oldenburg, Germany

The aim of this chapter is to explore the connections between the inherent characteristics of gamification and the current need for sustainable integration activities that are based on meaningful social interactions. By highlighting the potential of gamification for creating democratic spaces of social interaction and engaging diverse actors in joyful encounters, it is possible to underline the notion of social change that gamification can induce. In the area of integration, humanitarian organizations can harness the potential of gamification in their integration activities in order to ensure increased social cohesion. Through a critical analysis of existing gamification and integration approaches, the chapter provides arguments for why gamification is perfectly suited to improve integration processes by highlighting the manifold applications of gamification experience in the humanitarian field.

Chapter 19

Sean Fitzpatrick, Griffith University, Australia
Timothy Marsh, Griffith University, Australia

While gamification represents one of the largest technology trends of the last decade, only a limited selection of literature exists that explores the negative outcomes of contemporary gamified services, applications, and systems. This chapter explores the consequences of gamified systems and services, investigating contemporary implementations of gamification and acknowledging the ethical concerns raised by researchers towards contemporary gamified services. This chapter further explores these ethical concerns through a critical instance case study of China's Social Credit System and arrives at informed observations on the potential for gamified cycles of reward and punishment to encourage unethical activity within organisations as well as legitimise ideological objectives that violate fundamental human rights. Recommendations are then made for researchers to explore this potential further, while recognising how gamification may justify the authority and practices of organisations, particularly those engaged in unethical and dehumanising behaviour.

In recent years, communication and digital technologies have widely affected the cultural heritage sector, offering incredible opportunities to enhance the experiential value of heritage assets and improve cultural activities. Furthermore, another trend has gained significant attention: increasing users' engagement through gamification. Several studies have shown the efficacy of gamification for learning achievements, and gaming is also emerging as a useful tool for touristic objectives such as marketing, dynamic engagement with users, and audience development. This chapter aims at presenting two Italian game projects for mobile devices, created to enhance and promote the cultural offer of two peculiar territories. Game design choices, objectives, and outcomes will be discussed to highlight the benefits and limits of these tools and point out the changing practices of cultural institutions and local administrations, which are showing an increasing interest in the exploitation of video games, considering them as strategic marketing tools to promote cultural heritage and tourism.

This chapter presents a novel learning approach for studying ancient Bulgarian history, civilization, and their cultural heritage, namely the Thracian civilization, through storytelling and serious game combinations. The chapter also provides an overview of serious educational games, digital storytelling, and game development tools that can be used to present ancient history and their cultural heritage. The combination of storytelling and serious games successfully helps instructors to motivate student learning, stimulate their curiosity, and make them interested. The authors developed a game editor and a game portal that facilitated the game's development by applying game templates, layout styles, and question pools.

This chapter shows that, contrary to what some researchers claim, setting up the conditions for a "playful environment" is not so simple, in particular when it comes to organizing a new competition for the popularization of science (MT180®). In fact, we will see that popularization does not fit so easily into the "playful environment" desired by the organizers due to the gamified nature of the approach, which gradually colonizes the initial desire to present one's scientific work and pushes some participants to exaggerate their results in order to go as far as possible in the competition. It is therefore feared that the gamification of scientific work, while compatible with neoliberal expectations, will in fact lead to the production of bad science. The question then arises as to whether the need to turn researchers into effective communicators with a view to building the "knowledge society" advocated by international institutions can be achieved through gamified approaches, with the risk of creating an ever-greater distance between (real) scientific knowledge and citizens.

Chapter 23
Grethe Østby, Norwegian University of Science and Technology, Norway
Stewart James Kowalski, Research Institutes of Sweden, Sweden

In this chapter, the authors outline their process for introducing serious games as a course in an Information Security Master Course Program at the Norwegian University of Science and Technology. The process is built on the author's experiences from both participating, coaching, judging, and even arranging serious games and cyber security challenges. With the lack of cultural recipes (or shared experiences) in information and cyber security from previous generations, these recipes must be learned in other environments. Given the efficiency of using exercises for incident response training, the authors suggest that information and cyber security incident response can be learned efficiently through serious games as one type of exercise. The authors suggest that serious games give relevant learning experiences from both developing them and participating in them, and they suggest these learning experiences as part of the course, in addition to necessary instructions.

Chapter 24
Nashwa Ismail, Durham University, UK
Anne Adams, The Open University, UK

This study investigates the enablers and barriers of embedding technology for continuing professional development (CPD) of staff in the police sector. The research team developed an online game called "Child Witness Interview Simulation" (CWIS) to complement existing interview training for police officers and help them gain competency in interviewing children. Within the game design, development, and commercializing phases, the research team came across key themes that define the opportunities and challenges of implementing GBL through a police-based learning approach to CPD. The study identified that the successful implantation of Technology-Enhanced learning (TEL) in CPD falls into two broad categories: organizational, which considers learning outcomes, and individual, which considers learning aims and competency. Therefore, for successful implementation of TEL in CPD, ongoing supportive organizational culture that encourages employees and managers to be committed and motivated to implement TEL in CPD is necessary.

Chapter 25

Cadets, in order to become pilots, apart from successfully passing their flight training program, need to also complete their academic education, where many technical subjects, such as aeronautics, exist. Cadets often face difficulties in comprehending certain concepts in the subject "aeronautics" as well as the applied link between aeronautics and flight safety. To this end, at the Hellenic Air Force Academy, an innovative educational tool is under development so as to facilitate students' understanding of the practical use of aeronautics and its impact on aircraft safety. An important aspect of the proposed educational tool is that it can be easily adopted into the pilots' flight training program and offer a complimentary training experience regarding mid-air crisis scenarios. The new educational tool is based on introducing in-class simulation and problem-based learning, thus combining theory and practice. The aim of this chapter is to describe the development of this educational tool and to demonstrate the way that it can be employed for academic and flight training purposes.

Preface

Topics in gamification have rapidly become a trend recently. The number of peer-reviewed scientific articles on games and gamification has increased dramatically during the last five years, indicating this trend. Games and gamification have become an interest in many domains, such as health, education, software engineering, psychology, social politics, and business.

There is a discussion about terms related to games and gamification. This book covers substantial literature on the impact of games and gamification on different scenarios. However, before discussing the literature, let us take a moment to review what a game is and what gamification is.

There are various definitions of "game," and there is much discussion about the term. According to the Oxford Dictionary, a game can be considered an entertainment or pleasure activity. In general, "game" is related to "play." Hence, a game is defined as "a form of competitive activity or sport played by rules." Here, a game can have characteristic definitions, namely: (1) an activity undertaken for pleasure (to play), (2) led by rules, and (3) and the player tries to achieve a goal (to win).

Some of these criteria have been ignored with recent games, as there are some games with no clear end goal, such as the Sims or World of Warcraft (WoW). Goals in the game are necessary; otherwise, the player will have no targets. Therefore, it must be said that when an objective is not explicitly provided, the game must have goals for progress, which can also be very different per person as the goal is set by themselves. These self-made goals are designed to give players freedom of choice when setting them.

Games also have genres to determine the type of game; developers use them to understand gaming needs and consumers use them to help identify the game's focus to fit their gaming preferences or current mood. Game genres define the interactive and narrative nature of games compared with literature and film, where their genres describe only their narrative. The complexity of the game genre stems from the interactive nature that other artforms lack. Adventure, role-playing (RPG), and even action are examples of extensive genres for the core gameplay mechanics, whereas first-person, third-person, will be the main point of view of the player in the game.

There are game genres that are not used in general, and they serve the purpose of helping to describe the game, but they may be too specific to be used as an identifier, which would be a rare sight. An example is how some websites or game distributors that list games may use genres like action games or turn-based role-playing but not "cooking" as one; this is then usually solved when there are enough cooking games for cooking to be placed under the "simulation game" genre. Unfortunately, this can confuse players looking for games when using many of these game genres.

One of the crucial factors in developing a game is the design. Game development has different areas for creating games, and game design is one of the many vital roles. Game design is the art of creating in-game experiences; they direct the game to the final product by making many choices ranging from mechanics, aesthetics, and dynamics, which are described in the Game Development Lifecycle (GDLC).

GDLC is the game industry's Software Development Lifecycle (SDLC). It was created to adapt to the needs of the multidisciplinary aspect of game development, as the regular SDLC sometimes proved inadequate. There are at least six steps in the GDLC process. It starts with prototyping, where the initial game concept is thought out, along with prototyping for the game mechanics. Next, the pre-production phase involved refining the initial game concept and writing game documents. After the pre-production phase comes the primary production. During this phase, the team will go through milestone checks every specified period. Just before the live release, there will be a beta phase where the team will run public tests for bug fixes and gameplay errors.

The gamification term was introduced in 2002 by Nick Pelling, a British-born videogame developer, as part of his startup, Conundra Ltd. Gamification seeks to apply the art and science of turning customers' everyday interactions into games that serve business goals. The field of gamification is still growing, so there are many opinions related to the gamification definition. According to the Oxford Dictionary, gamification can be defined as applying distinctive elements of gameplay (e.g., point scoring, competition with others, and rules of the game) to other areas of activity.

In recent years, gamification has gained worldwide popularity. Many activities are related to this topic; for example, Gamification Summits are held in the USA, Australia, and other countries. In addition, educational platforms offer courses related to gamification from several well-known universities worldwide.

Gamification is about (1) utilizing elements of a game (not the entire game), meaning it does not necessarily include game techniques, but more about how the game will be played and the idea behind it; (2) the implementation in a non-game environment; and (3) increasing target behavior and engagement. Therefore, most of the benefits of gamification are not limited to a commercial environment. It can also be used for internal purposes, such as improving behavior. Many companies have considered the influence of games in changing people's behavior. For example, LinkedIn, Amazon, and Foursquare are some companies that have included a gaming element in their websites and services.

In addition, gamification is growing in popularity with regard to website optimization. Website optimization is about how to utilize a website to have a better influence on the website visitor's behavior, and gamification is an excellent solution in this matter. After identifying which targeted visitor behavior to encourage, several techniques are applied to achieve this target. Here, gamification can be implemented to stimulate the targeted behaviors. A well-designed game provides a feeling of joy and happiness to the players. They create an environment to ensure the players are involved and want to continue the experience and feelings.

Every time a player wins and receives a reward, the brain produces dopamine. This dopamine creates feelings of joy, fun, and well-being. The dopamine created will be more significant when the levels of challenge, achievement, and satisfaction are greater; hence, the player will feel satisfied. Therefore, it can be said that games create happiness, fun, and enjoyment by offering challenges that can be overcome until they finally produce dopamine.

Because games have been proven to teach knowledge or skills that will be useful in life, gamification using game elements can also increase engagement and target behavior in other areas as well, for example, in promotions, employee productivity, behavior change, loyalty, and education.

This book covers many topics related to games and gamification that fit into today's world. Therefore, this book is suitable for anyone interested in learning more about gamification, games, and their application in various fields.

The book comprises 25 chapters, where every chapter explains different implementations of gamification from a cross-discipline view. It covers all the necessary information about gamification, starting from player/user types for gamification, motivations of different gamification user types, identifying challenges, and gamification application areas. An interesting point of view where gamification could be more beneficial during the COVID-19 pandemic is also written in this book. Several applications of gamification in e-government are also mentioned. In the marketing domain, evaluations of gamification from both the customer value perspective and the psychological view are described. It also covers the implementation of gamification case studies such as in politics, in developing eco-friendly behavior, in the course of information security management programs, in child witness interview simulations in the police sector, and in-flight safety training.

The first chapter, "Let's All Play Together: Motivations of Different Gamification User Types," will attempt to ascertain and present the motivations of people who engage in gamification activities. Recognizing the motives for gamification's use and their interaction will assist companies in better understanding their audience and creating more engaging experiences.

Despite considerable commercial interest and a potentially enormous market for effective gamification products in education and health, much of this knowledge remains speculative. In this context, Chapter 2, "Should I Play or Should I Go? Identifying Challenges for Gamification," purports to examine ambiguous definitions related to a reliance on tiny sets of elements with unknown effects, unintended consequences of competition, a bewildering range of operationalizations, and the loss of intrinsic motivation via extrinsic incentives, among other issues.

The next chapter, "Player/User Types for Gamification," seeks to analyze the individual disparities among students that influence their academic success. Taking student traits into account will amplify the impact of gamification in this scenario. Thus, this chapter aims to discuss player/user types concerning gamification in education.

"How to Gamify E-Government Services? A Taxonomy of Game Elements" presents a useful taxonomy of game features that can be used to aid in the design of e-government projects. It was developed by examining the literature on gamification frameworks and models used in this domain.

The chapter "A View on the Impact of Gamified Services in the Wake of the COVID-19 Pandemic: An Interdisciplinary Approach" covers the researchers' purpose of examining how gamification has been researched in many science fields during the COVID-19 pandemic and its influence using the PRISMA approach to categorize the findings into primary problems and core issues.

It is vital to understand how gamification aspects affect human emotions in order to design an optimal gamification system. "Application of Gamification in Marketing Context: Psychological Perspectives," Chapter 6, takes the reader on a tour of gamified environments and the psychological effects they have on humans. This chapter summarizes the various strands of gamification in the context of marketing.

The following chapter, "Gamification in Marketing: A Case Study From a Customer Value Perspective," examines the relationship between customer value and gamification, as well as the gamification strategies employed in marketing and their effect on consumer value. Additionally, a case study of Starbucks' gamified mobile application is provided from the customer value standpoint.

"Role-Playing Games as a Model of Gamification Applied to Engagement of Online Communities" is the title of Chapter 8, which seeks to implement the opportunities that these games present for implementing social media marketing techniques. A qualitative research study was done to determine the correlation between role-playing games' engagement tactics and those used in social networks.

Chapter 9, "Gamification and Health in a Holistic Perspective," explores the relationship between gamification and health in terms of organizations, individuals, and society, as well as the consequences of gamification on health and the usage of gamification for health.

The effects of video games on mental health are gaining worldwide attention, and natural user interfaces (NUIs) are becoming more common in-game systems. In this context, the chapter "Natural User Interfaces for Meditative Health Games" explores the design of a meditative game, a subgenre of casual games that intends for players to become calm and relaxed, and the evaluation of the NUIs for the game.

"Serious Games Design Principles Using Virtual Reality to Gamify Upper Limb Stroke Rehabilitation: The Importance of Engagement for Rehabilitation," Chapter 11, emphasizes that a stroke limits one's ability to live independently while also lowering one's quality of life. This chapter then discusses a subset of the game design principles that are likely to engage stroke survivors when they use virtual reality for upper limb rehabilitation following a stroke.

Intrinsic motivation is a critical factor in determining job satisfaction. Chapter 12, "The Effects of Gamification on Nurses' Work Motivation," pretends to develop a gamification intervention for implementation in a hospital setting and evaluate its effects on nurses' work motivation.

The next chapter, "Collaborative Learning: Increasing Work Motivation Through Game-Based Learning," demonstrates how organizations can benefit from game-based learning and serious games for training and skill development, providing a critical analysis of the use of these tools to increase motivation and collaboration among individuals in organizations.

It is critical for organizations to maximize their resources, reduce costs, optimize processes, and engage in continuous improvement now more than ever. Chapter 14, "Applying Gamification Strategies to Create Training in Lean Methodologies: A Practical Case," seeks to propose the development of a tool that is the result of fusing gamification and lean philosophy by creating a game for those unfamiliar with the subject, serving as an introduction to it, and demonstrating some of the philosophy's applications.

Chapter 15, "Gamification or How to Make a 'Green' Behavior Become a Habit," establishes that waste management is a significant issue for tourist destinations. This study, conducted as part of a European project called UrbanWaste, discovered significant results indicating that this tool can help increase recycling behavior. However, what happens when customers return home?

"Review Bomb: On the Gamification of the Ideological Conflict," Chapter 16, provides an in-depth examination of the Review Bomb phenomenon, which occurs when an abnormally large amount of information is submitted to a rating system in a short period of time by an overtly anonymous mass of accounts with the intent of undermining the system's proper functioning.

Hate speech is eroding the possibility of collective understanding and undermining the democratic values of mutual respect, tolerance, and equality. In this context, the chapter "Game-Based Learning for the Acquisition of Transversal Skills: Preventing and Addressing Hate Speech" has as its objective to determine how game-based learning favors the acquisition of transversal competencies within the framework of 21st-century skills for tackling and addressing hate speech.

Chapter 18, "The Potential of Gamification for Humanitarian Organizations to Support Integration in Migration Contexts," explores the connections between gamification's inherent characteristics and the current demand for sustainable integration activities built on meaningful social interactions. The chapter demonstrates why gamification is ideally suited to improving integration processes through a critical analysis of existing gamification and integration approaches.

The chapter "The Dehumanising Consequences of Gamification: Recognising Coercion and Exploitation in Gamified Systems" considers the implications of gamified systems and services, examining current gamification implementations and addressing ethical concerns raised by researchers about current gamified services. This chapter examines these ethical concerns in greater detail through a critical case study of China's Social Credit System.

Communication and digital technologies have had a significant impact on the cultural heritage sector in recent years, providing excellent opportunities to increase the experiential value of legacy assets and cultural events. In this perspective, the chapter "Gamifying Cultural Heritage. Education, Tourism Development, and Territories Promotion: Two Italian Examples" aims to present two Italian mobile game projects designed to enhance and promote the cultural offerings of two distinct territories.

"Studying Thracian Civilization Through Serious Games and Storytelling" presents an innovative method for understanding ancient Bulgarian history, culture, and cultural heritage, specifically the Thracian civilization, through the use of storytelling and serious games. Additionally, the chapter discusses serious educational games, digital storytelling, and game production tools.

Chapter 22, "Is the Gamification of Scientific Work a Good Idea? 'Little Lies Between Friends' at MT180®," shows that, contrary to what some researchers claim, setting up the conditions for a "playful environment" is not so simple, in particular when it comes to organizing a new competition for the popularization of science.

"Introducing Serious Games as a Master Course in Information Security Management Programs: Moving Towards Socio-Technical Incident Response Learning" pretends to outline the process of introducing serious games as a course in an Information Security Master Course Program at the Norwegian University of Science and Technology. The process is built on the author's experiences from participating, coaching, judging, and even arranging serious games and cyber security challenges.

The enablers and barriers of embedding technology for Continuing Professional Development (CPD) of staff in the police sector are explored in the chapter "Enablers and Barriers of Integrating Games-Based Learning in Professional Development Programmes: Case Study of Child Witness Interview Simulation in the Police Sector." The research team developed an online game called "Child Witness Interview Simulation" (CWIS) to complement existing interview training for police officers and help them gain competency in interviewing children.

The last chapter, "Embracing Simulations and Problem-Based Learning to Effectively Pair Concepts of Aeronautics With Flight Safety Training," emphasizes that cadets often face difficulties in comprehending certain concepts of the subject "aeronautics" as well as the applied link between aeronautics and flight safety. In this perspective, the chapter seeks to describe the development of this educational tool and to demonstrate the way that it can be employed for academic and flight training purposes.

We hope that this book provides an enjoyable reading experience for readers.

Chapter 1
Let's All Play Together:
Motivations of Different Gamification User Types

Demos Parapanos
https://orcid.org/0000-0001-8720-3334
University of Cumbria, UK

Eleni (Elina) Michopoulou
https://orcid.org/0000-0002-1857-4462
University of Derby, UK

ABSTRACT

Gamification is recognized as the next big thing in marketing by using game design elements in a non-game context. Producing desirable experiences and motivating users to remain engaged in an activity is one of the strengths of gamification. The introduction of digital social networks has become the biggest change regarding digital technology, also leading to the evolution and popularity of gamification. Although it is possible to design games, serious games, or gamified systems without knowing who the target users are, it is more likely to create a more engaging experience when these users are identified first. Taking this into consideration, this chapter will look to identify and present the motivations of individuals when using gamification systems. Identifying the motivations behind gamification usage and acknowledging the interaction between them will help organizations understand their audience and create more engaging experiences.

INTRODUCTION

Gamification has a strong practical impact due to its wide adoption and powerful market growth worldwide (Schöbel, Janson & Söllner, 2020), producing desirable experiences and motivating users to engage in an activity. Digital games are fun, engaging, and popular, leading many organizations (including schools, retail companies and health-care organizations) to consider the use of games to train individuals, engage online customers and connect a global workforce (Dickey, 2005). Games are popular

DOI: 10.4018/978-1-7998-9223-6.ch001

because they are offering pleasure (Zicherman & Linder, 2010) but are considered unproductive, with no or limited valuable outcome. On the other hand, gamification aims to engage users in solving real-world problems and entails value-adding activities and outcomes (Lombriser & Van der Valk, 2011). Hence the element of pleasure in gamification might not be enough to create similar engagement levels as games. The rapid development of digital capabilities and the increased coverage of the internet (da Silva Brito et al., 2018) are propelling the growth of the gaming industry, and even more so the mobile game industry (Kim et al., 2010).

The popularity of video games is empowered by the development of technologies, such as smart mobile devices and internet accessibility, catering for mobile experiences and vibrant on-site communication (Xu, Buhalis & Weber, 2017). The introduction of the first wave of smartphones back in 2006-2007, and the availability of broadband connections, helped mobile gaming to evolve dramatically (Feijoo et al., 2012), and become a multi-billion-dollar media industry overcoming traditional entertainment (such as movie and music) industries, reporting more profits than both of them combined (Bowman, Kowert & Cohen, 2015). The evolution of mobile and portable devices such as laptops, tablet and smart phones offer significant computational power, storage, and portability. Connecting people all over the world with the introduction of digital social network has become the biggest change regarding digital technology (Sooksatit, 2016).

This led to the evolution and popularity of the phenomenon of Gamification. Kirsh (2014, p. 63) defined gamification as "using game-based mechanics aesthetics and game thinking to engage people, motivate action, promote learning and solve problems". Da Silva Brito et al (2018) added to that the importance of motives towards the engagement of the phenomenon in peoples' lives defining gamification as the use of technologies engaged in promoting intrinsic motivations by using diverse characteristics of games in other domains outside the entertainment industry, such as education, marketing, public administration, politics and health. This trend derived from the popularity of games and their intrinsic ability for call to action to solve problems or enable learning in different fields and in people's lives (da Silva Brito, 2018). Considering the success gaming industry has in the society and everyday lives as a form of leisure, and the evolution of information and communication technologies and mobile devices, it becomes clear that gamification will continue to grow (Kapp, 2012).

Surprisingly, more than half of all organizations attempts to utilize gamification are predicted to fail due to the poor understanding of the gamification design process (Morschheuser et al., 2018). Organizations seem to focus on the obvious game mechanics, such as points, badges and leader boards, rather than the subtler and more important game design elements, like balancing competition and collaboration, or defining a meaningful game economy. It is important to recognize that even though people like games, not everyone likes the same kind or style of games. Although it is possible to design games, serious games or gamified systems without knowing who the target users are, it is more likely to create a more engaging experience when these users are identified first. Taking this into consideration, this chapter will look to identify and present motivations of individuals when using gamification systems. Identifying motivations behind gamification usage will help organizations understand their audience and create more engaging experiences.

BACKGROUND

Effective gamification is dependent on internal or external motivation (Post, 2014). It is found that gamification can motivate people to change their behaviors through a balanced mix of reinforcements that can be either extrinsic (like prizes, money, points and badges, penalties trophies,) or intrinsic (like sense of fun and enjoyment, belonging to a group, mastery, and power) (Patrício, Moreira & Zurlo, 2018). The aim of this chapter is to explore the motives of individuals when using gamification by looking into the literature of games, gamification and technology adoption. At the end of the chapter a typology for gamification systems' users is proposed.

Games

Video games are a growing reality of modern age (Bowman, Kowert & Cohen, 2015), probably also as a result of the technology development happening in the last years specially in the mobile industry. In the USA alone around 97% of teens play video games and gaming industry has a revenue of $12 billion per year (Sajid et al., 2018). In 2016, the video game market in the USA was valued more than 17 billion US dollars with three companies, namely Microsoft, Sony and Nintendo, monopolizing the home video game industry (Zhan et al., 2020). Becoming more varied, socially inclusive, and accessible, video game sales now surpass the US$43 billion mark and boast larger revenue streams than digital music and blockbuster films combined (Hemovich, 2021). In Australia, 95% of adolescents have access to at least one game-equipped device in their home such as a tablet, smartphone, or personal computer (PC) (Smith, Gradisar & King, 2015).

Cox (2014) comparing video game revenue with other well-known features of the entertainment industries (such as movie and book industries) revealed that the blockbuster movie of "Harry Potter and the Deathly Hallows" set a box office record by earning $169m in revenue during its opening weekend in 2011, and the book "Harry Potter and the Deathly Hallows" generated $220m in the first 24 hours of release. Interestingly, the same year, a game called "Call of Duty: Modern Warfare 3" eclipsed these records, raise $400m in revenue on just the first day, highlighting the demand gaming industry in enjoying lately. Moreover, Cox (2014) identifies that the video game generated $1bn in revenue within the first 16 days, narrowly overcoming the previous entertainment record set in 2009 by the film "Avatar" within the first 17 days of release. This highlights that the video game industry is nowadays overcoming traditional entertainment industries of movies and books industries, becoming the most popular tool of entertainment at the current years.

These numbers show a lot regarding the popularity and the profitability of video games, but still nothing has been said about the engagement they provide. The average video game player has been playing games for over 12 years, not to mention that more and more people at all ages are playing games. Smith, Gradisar & King (2015) found that Australian adolescents play computer games anywhere between 2 and 18 hours per week. Mintel (2020) announced that in China the number of online game users in 2020 increased by 9% compared with the previous year reaching the number of 540 million. Kapp (2012) reveals that, back in 2012, 26% of people used to playing games were over the age of 50, which is a mere 9% increase from 1999. Since 2011, people were already spending an average of three billion hours a week gaming and this number has only increased (da Silva et al., 2018). Nearly 62 million U.S. internet users, or 27% of the online audience, play at least one game on a social network monthly (Kapp, 2012). Concluding, one can say that video games attract and engage individuals at any stage of their life.

Motivation and Engagement in Games

As video games exhibit progressively expansive game environments, there has been growing interest in employing generative computational algorithms to mitigate the cost of authoring game content (Sorenson, Pasquier & DiPaola, 2011). These computational techniques promise to reduce the involvement of a human designer, thereby enabling smaller development teams to create more content than would otherwise be possible. Consequently, content generated algorithmically is not as fixed content as content generated by hand, it is more readily adapted to the unique preferences of the individual player (Sorenson, Pasquier & DiPaola, 2011), and therefore personalized, promoting individual preferences and creating engagement and sustainability. In a gaming environment if the player uses a weapon frequently, similar weapons are made available, and where a weapon is left unused, it appears less frequently (Sorenson, Pasquier & DiPaola, 2011). This interaction explains that the user is more likely to be engaged with the system as it recognizes their preferences and problem-solving mechanics in the game. The success of this interaction lies in the fact that the user is continually using the system giving more and more information to the platform. This can only be achieved if the user is attached to the system providing data for future activities and tasks; and it is safe to admit that this interaction is what is indeed missing in a relationship between a non-game organization and the user. The outcome of this relationship highlights the importance of engagement between the user and the system through the successful data collection games can achieve.

Although games share in a technological level many aesthetic features with movies and music (Smith, 2006), engagement between the system and the user is a result of the achievement, motivation, and task persistence, as well as meaningful processing on achievement measures (Hoffman & Nadelson, 2010). The entertainment provided to individuals when playing video games is different from the content individuals get when they buy a movie ticket, DVD or CD (Smith, 2006), as the depth of processing and the activation of problem-solving strategies they promote result in promoting and enabling engagement (Hoffman & Nadelson, 2010). The main difference between playing games and watching a movie is the element of control that games provide to the user (Smith, 2006), and therefore they can provide an advanced level of engagement with the user through immersion and interactivity. Smith (2006) adds up that the element of control in a game can cause a user to identify with a mediated character to a greater degree than is possible with characters portrayed in other media, because the user is the protagonist in the game. As a result, games provide a sense of immersion to their audience in a much higher degree than other sources of entertainment.

Key Motives in Games

Gamers return to online game playing if their previous experience has been positive and are motivated to reach a higher goal, to score points against each other, and gain either material or non-material gains such as inclusion to a hall of honour (Xu, Buhalis & Weber, 2017). In order to emphasize on the volunteering element of games, McGuire & Jenkins (2009) clarify that, players are not required to play the game, therefore their first decision is whether to play at all, and even throughout the game, they would continually re-evaluate whether to keep playing; hence players must expect to get something out of their experience. The section below discusses four elements (fun, immersion, social interaction and aesthetics) found to lead to engagement between games and gamers.

The Element of Fun

Fun is desirable in nearly every game and probably the most important outcome, even though sometimes fun defies analysis (Schell, 2010). Fun is an elusive concept, defining it as expectation, engagement and endurability, by adjusting terms such as challenge, fantasy and curiosity (Davis, 2014). It is difficult to describe fun in a game, since it is associated with intrinsic satisfaction to the player (Davis, 2014). However, Richard Bartle (2004) in the gaming literature identified that individuals found the element of "fun" as a motivation to play games; explained that fun has different meaning in the game, based on players' profile classifying these four activities as: 'achieving', 'exploring', 'socialising' and 'imposing upon others. Moore (2011) also explains that there are actions that players perform in a game which are considered fun, and these are the actions the player wants to do more often. Since fun is subjective there are many different features that must go into a game to make it fun (Dunniway & Novak, 2008). Effective application of mechanics for each player profile will create interaction between the user and the system, making it easier to collect valuable information about users' preferences then utilised effectively by the system enhancing the experience and creating engagement.

The Element of Immersion

Many people play games in part to escape from their real world, like any form of popular entertainment. Self-Determination Theory helps towards the understanding of gaming motivations (Ryan, Rigby & Przybylski, 2006) and provides a valuable framework for understanding intrinsic motivation to video games (Siemens et al., 2015). It is proposing that the satisfaction of three basic psychological needs (competence, autonomy and relatedness) (Ryan & Deci, 2000) will result in greater intrinsic motivation and overall enjoyment (Mills et al., 2018). Immersion in games is different from reading a novel or watching a movie, because games allow players to become actively involved in the world they escape into (Klug & Schell, 2006). The different involvement in games than other activities is a result of the flow they provide. The concept of flow was developed by Csikszentmihalyi (1990), based on his observations of the immersion and high levels of enjoyment experienced by a group of artists (Kaye & Bryce, 2012). Flow is a highly enjoyable psychological state that refers to the holistic sensation people feel when they act with total involvement in an activity (Kowal & Fortier, 1999). When entering the flow state while playing an online game, this means that whoever is interested in playing the game, is curious about the game, has full control over the game, and is focused on playing the game with no other distraction.

Sometimes, players experience such a degree of engagement in a game that they ignore other things, or sometimes unconsciously imagine a role of themselves in the game (Roohi & Forouzandeh, 2019). Immersion can be defined as a sensation of being surrounded by a completely different reality taking over all of an individual's attention (Kiili et al., 2012). However, it is not clear what exactly is causing immersion, although there seems to be a some understanding of immersion in the gaming context (Jennett et al., 2008; Roohi & Forouzandeh, 2019). Kiili et al (2012) divided immersion into three components: sensory, challenge-based and imaginative immersion. According to Roohi & Forouzandeh (2019), a player is developing immersion in games through sound and game music. In fact, immersion is critical to game enjoyment, being the outcome of a good gaming experience (Jennett et al., 2008).

The Element of Social Interaction

Although playing video games is often stereotypically conceptualized as a solo and socially isolating activity (de Kort, IJsselsteijn & Poels, 2007), it has become an increasingly social activity which facilitates online and offline interactions amongst existing and new friends (Kaye & Bryce, 2012). Video games, which encourage positive social interaction among players, are beneficial to children's social skill development and socialization (Maitland et al., 2018). Socialising is thus one of the key motivations for playing video games, which are, broadly, played in a social context (Rogers, 2017). The importance of such interactions in shaping the gaming experience is evidenced by the overwhelming participation in virtual communities (such as Active Worlds) and massively multiplayer online games (such as World of Warcraft), and the personal relevance of these communities to those intensively involved in such games (de Kort, IJsselsteijn & Poels, 2007). Rapp (2018) highlights that the social dynamics in World of Warcraft are strongly influenced by design, which actually shapes how players interact with each other and favours the emergence the specific types of social structures. The example of a game like World of Warcraft shows the strength of social interaction as a crucial factor in enjoyment, motivation to play, and game design (Maitland et al., 2018). It is argued that video games can provide opportunities for positive social interactions with other players, through team formation and in-game collaboration (Maitland et al., 2018).

The Element of Aesthetics

Digital games exist in the realm of art and aesthetic experience. The recursive quality of computer games appears to be a central element of its aesthetics that permeates the level of the algorithmic game system, as well as that of the text. For example, music, sound effects and animations, are believed to be crucial components of the video game experience (Andersen et al., 2011). Good aesthetics can make the player more likely to tolerate imperfections in game design and draw a player into a game they might otherwise have ignored (Andersen et al., 2011). Plot animations and pictures, which are used as rewards following important events such as the defeat of a major enemy, clearing a level, or ending a game have as a purpose the motivation of players to advance game stories. By evaluating the importance of aesthetic quality in two games (Refraction and Hello Worlds), Andersen et al (2011) found that animations caused users to play more. Similarly, games like Charades and Quake (both promoting competitiveness), succeed when the various teams or players in the game are defeating each other. For enhancing the sense of accomplishment, the game provides additional aesthetics (i.e. supporting adversarial play and providing clear feedback about who is winning), otherwise the game is rapidly losing interest. This highlights the importance of advanced and appealing aesthetics in game design.

Overview of Gamification

In 2017, the global gamification market was valued at USD 2.17 billion and is estimated to reach USD 19.39 billion by 2023 (Xi & Hamari, 2019). Hofacker et al (2016) points out that the annual global mobile retail purchases are expected to surpass $700 billion and account for 30% of online purchases in 2018. In parallel with the growth of mobile market, interest in gamification has emerged (Hofacker et al., 2016). During recent years, the enhancement of software, via design features borrowed from video games, has become a notable development in many software engineering projects (Morschheuser et al.,

2018). However, after considerable investments in gamification, many gamified business projects have largely failed (especially in the business domain), with 80% of current gamified applications estimated to fail to meet their objectives due to poor design - leading companies to gradually lose confidence in the role of gamification in building strong customer-brand connections (Xi & Hamari, 2020). Hence, this raises several important questions in terms of the effectiveness of gamification in securing consumer engagement (Venkatesh, 2020). The answer can be distilled to the following: it is only through knowing your customer typologies that effective gamified systems can be built.

Understanding of the gamers' behaviour contributes towards engagement with games and will be beneficial for building a gamification strategy for an organization. In the marketing context, the main goal of customer relationship is to engage with a customer who loves the product and is a fan of the brand (Xi & Hamari, 2019), very similar to how games can build a fan base around them. New technologies have been created to inspire people's motivation and help them to develop beneficial behaviour, both individually and collectively, with gamification being the most popular trend in this respect (da Silva Brito et al., 2018).

Gamification aims to increase users' motivations towards activities or use of technology, thereafter, increasing the quality and quantity of these activities (Morschheuser et al., 2018), aiming to address this intrinsic motivation by applying game design thinking to engage people into meaningful and effective activities. Table 1 provides a summary of some of the most prominent gamification definitions.

Table 1. Gamification definitions

Definition	Source
'Gamification is the use of game design elements in a non-game context'	Deterding et al (2011)
"The use of game design elements and mechanisms in non-game contexts to create a sense of playfulness […] so that the participation becomes enjoyable and desirable"	Maedche, Botzenhardt & Neer (2012, p. 186)
"Gamification is a careful and considered application of game thinking to solving problems and encourage learning using all the elements of games that are appropriate"	Kapp (2012, p. 15)
"Gamification is using game-based mechanics aesthetics and game thinking to engage people, motivate action, promote learning and solve problems"	Kirsh (2014, p. 63)
Good gamification design does not start with good game elements (mechanics), but it starts with core drives.	Choo (2015)
"The use of technologies engaged in promoting intrinsic motivations by using diverse characteristics of games in other domains outside the entertainment industry, such as education, marketing, public administration, politics and health. It is an emerging trend derived from the huge popularity of games and their intrinsic ability for call to action to solve problems or enable learning in different fields and in people's lives"	da Silva Brito et al (2018)

Considering these definitions, gamification includes a complex process of understanding human behaviour to encourage activities such as motivation and problem solving. However, gamification is mainly focusing on the motivational power of competitiveness and achievement - such as the introduction of rewards, challenges and contests (Warmelink, 2014). This led many gamification enthusiasts to introduce scoring systems, badges and leaderboards among customers (in their marketing efforts), displaying limited understanding of common characteristics of games and failing to address motivational factors of users with different motivations (Warmelink, 2014). Al-Zaidi (2012) argues that brands are trying to engage individuals by rewarding them with points and badges, while this is not enough to successfully keep individuals hooked (see for instance platforms like Foursquare). Instead, Al-Zaidi (2012) mentions the successful example of Nike+, explaining that the system incorporates other mechanics (such as sharing individuals' faster runs and gaining acknowledgment and the feeling that someone "likes" that rendered photo on Instagram) that promote the feeling of acknowledgment and socialization of the individual.

Key Motives in Gamification

It is necessary to understand how humans behave to understand game dynamics and gamification use. Marczewski (2014) clarifies that it is possible to design gamified systems without considering the target users', but it is unlikely that these systems will provide engaging experiences. Gamification should address intrinsic motivation by applying game design thinking in order to engage people into meaningful and effective activities. Considering that games are just for fun and entertainment, whereas gamification has a certain purpose, suggests that there can be differences in the player profiles between gamers and gamification users. According to Choo (2015), a very important factor of gamification is the "Human-Focused Design" as opposed to the "Function-Focused Design". The Human-Focused Design acknowledges that people in the system have insecurities, feelings, and reasons behind their behaviour. The gamification framework called Octalysis analysed eight core drives that motivate individuals to do what they do (Choo, 2015). These core drives are: Epic Meaning and Calling (feel something bigger), Development and Accomplishment (feel of improvement), Empowerment of Creativity and Feedback (be creative), Ownership and Possession (feel of protecting and improving something belongs to me), Social Influence and Relatedness (influenced by the society), Scarcity and Impatience (feel impatient), Unpredictability and Curiosity (intrigued by the unknown), Loss and Avoidance (scared of losing). It is useful for organizations to examine strategies to identify users' motivations. For example, a game gives the individual the opportunity to be the last man standing to save the world when it comes close to an end enhancing the Epic Meaning and Calling core drive or Nike+ allows users to access short-term accomplishments providing them an indication that they are getting better enhancing the Development and Accomplishment core drive. Users' behaviour will help organizations to identify users' motivations. For example, Kapur (2021), used the eight core drives to discuss the adoption of these eight core drives by the most popular Instant Messaging app (WhatsApp) to explain what mechanic in the app is addressing each core drive.

Marczewski (2014) suggests that for a more gamification-specific taxonomy for user types, four additional motives need to be considered: Relatedness (the desire to socialise); Autonomy (the urge that an individual has to direct his or her own life); Mastery (the desire to get better and better in something that matters); and Purpose (the force to do an activity in the service of something with bigger meaning). These four motivations were used to describe four intrinsically motivated user types: Socialisers, Free Spirits, Achievers and Philanthropists, respectively. Afterwards, a fifth type was suggested; an extrinsically motivated type: The Player, who is actually motivated by the reward (Marczewski, 2014).

The Element of Social Influence (Relatedness)

Human beings inherently have a desire for a social connection. The social interaction facilitated within a system may potentially satisfy this need, such as a sense of recognition, which refers to the social feedback users receive on their behaviour (Hamari & Koivisto, 2015). Marczewski (2014) refers to relatedness as a motive for users to engage with gamification very similarly to the social interaction element games are using. Social influence occurs when behaviour is influenced by the surrounding, and it relates to being frequently rewarded for behaving in accordance with the attitudes, opinions and advice from social channels. It is defined as the degree to which an individual values the importance of others' persistence that he or she should use the new system (Hamari & Koivisto, 2015). Users motivated by social influence are interested in those mechanics of the system that enable them to accomplish this, and they promote and evangelize the internal social network similarly to how gamers follow these mechanics in games. This group values the social engagement of cooperation, and they are more likely to follow cooperative verbs in gamification strategy such as join, share, help, gift exchange and trade. Suggested design elements for this group are guilds or teams, social networks, social comparison, social competition and social discovery. The concepts of social influence, social interaction and relatedness share the same motive of 'Socialising' for the purpose of this chapter.

The Element Self-Efficacy (Autonomy)

Enjoyment, goal orientation and self-efficacy play important roles in determining a person's behaviour (Yi & Hwang, 2003). Self-efficacy influence's goal choices, the amount of effort spent in achieving a goal, and the level of persistence when encountering difficulties (Lee & Mao, 2016). When users' complete tasks and know how well they are doing, it influences their self-efficacy (Lee & Mao, 2016). Self-efficacy is defined as a user's belief in his or her ability to complete a task (Kim, Lee & Bonn, 2017; Adukaite, Zyl & Cantoni, 2016) in a specific situation, which affects the choice of activities, effort and persistence of that individual (Lee & Mao, 2016). Marczewski (2014), identifies that in gamification users' will want to direct their own life, which falls under the self-efficacy definition. Therefore, game mechanics that enhance players sense of autonomy will yield more effective gamified systems for this intrinsically motivated type of player.

The Element of Openness (Mastery)

Individuals positive to 'openness to experience', actively seek out new and varied experiences, and value change. Openness to experience represents an individual's curiosity and willingness to explore new ideas, and open individuals tend to devise novel ideas, hold unconventional values and willingly question authority (Devaraj, Easley & Crant, 2008). Those individuals scoring high in openness are more likely to hold positive attitudes and cognitions towards accepting technology, as they are less threatened by the changes implied in adopting technology (Devaraj, Easley & Crant, 2008). They are looking to learn new things and improve themselves by overcoming challenges. These individuals want to be perfect on the internal learning system. Even though they do this for their own satisfaction, they do not mind showing off. Marczewski (2014) found users in gamification applications have an intrinsic need of self-expression by exploring the game to get the most out of the system for their own enjoyment. This shows us that open people are attracted to online activity to satisfy their curiosity and seek out new forms of adventure. By providing gamified experiences, such as gaining a feeling of mastery, organizations can transform boring tasks into engaging behaviours. Suggested design elements for this group are challenges, certificates, learning new skills, quests, levels or progression and epic challenges.

The Element of Altruism (Purpose)

Altruism represents an individual's willingness to benefit the wellbeing of others on a voluntary basis, without the anticipation of any form of return (Kim, Lee & Bonn, 2016), as well as a form of unconditional kindness without the expectation of a return (Hung, Lai & Chang, 2011). Altruism is a result of individuals helping others by natural instinct and it builds upon interpersonal trust (Iglesias-Pradas, Hernandez-Garcia & Fernandez-Cardador, 2017). Marczewski (2014) found that in gamification users are motivated by purpose. This group of users offer selfless dedication for "the cause" because they enjoy helping and suggested design elements for this group are collection and trading, gifting, knowledge sharing and administrative roles, which appeal to the motivation of altruism. As a motivation altruism is exhibited through individuals' willingness to help others (regardless of getting anything in return), and by providing help and achieving a sense of satisfaction from the action itself (Hung et al., 2011). In general, altruistic behaviour in social media manifests itself through knowledge sharing (Kim, Lee & Bonn, 2016), and it is very evident in platforms such as TripAdvisor. Individuals feel that, if they have previously received information and help in networks, they should now repay that benefit; therefore, they are increasingly motivated to collaboratively participate and contribute to the network (Parra-Lopez et al., 2011). In fact, the tendency of this behaviour is constantly increasing, and it is found that it is a factor that motivates most online review writers: helping others by sharing their own positive experiences, since other travel reviews helped them, and they want to return the favour and save others from negative experiences by warning them (Parra-Lopez et al., 2011). In games, altruistic users often act as guides for other users by sharing knowledge or assisting others to complete tasks and gain achievements.

The Element of Reward

Intrinsic motivation is commonly considered as the most productive force behind individuals' behaviour (Xi & Hamari, 2019) and the exploration of the elements of social influence, self-efficacy, openness and altruism contributes towards the understand of the intrinsic motivation in gamification. Although intrinsic motivation is an important type of motivation, it is not the only type or even the only type of self-determined motivation (Ryan & Deci, 2000). It is often observed that people lack intrinsic motivation towards different activities they would like to undertake (Xi & Hamari, 2019), hence extrinsic motivation should also be taken into consideration when developing gamification strategies to enhance engagement with the user. Extrinsic motivation is defined as the performance of an activity because it is perceived to be instrumental in achieving valued outcomes that are distinct from the activity itself (Hansen & Levin, 2016). In other words, individuals will engage in behaviour that they perceive it will eventually lead to valued rewards (Chang, Hsu & Wu, 2015). From a motivational perspective, rewards are among the most widely accepted motivations (Chang, Hsu & Wu, 2015), either tangible, (monetary bonuses, certificates, prizes and awards), or intangible (skill that is perceived to be more useful or needed in the future or that improves one's special standing) (Hansen & Levin, 2016). Marczewksi (2014) refers to this group of users in gamification as the individuals who want collect rewards from the system. The difference from the previous intrinsically motivated users is the fact that they are extrinsically motivated by the reward itself and they are happy to take advantage of "loopholes" to gain an edge. Suggested design elements for this group are points, rewards, or prizes, leaderboards, badges or achievements, virtual economy and lotteries or games of chance.

Additional Motives for Gamification

There can be significant differences in the individuals' profiles when comparing gamers to gamified application users, because games and gamification are designed from different perspectives. The primary outcome of games is to entertain, whereas gamification seeks to motivate people to change behaviours, develop new skills or perform certain actions; highlighting the importance of extrinsic motivation and the utilitarian design aspects for gamified systems. To explain factors or motivations influencing intention to use a particular technology (such as gamification), many studies have used multiple models and constructs (Maitland et al., 2018; Taherdoost, 2018). However, the concepts of usefulness, ease of use and trust have been consistently found important, robust and relevant to technology acceptance across settings and samples (Herrero & Martin, 2012; Kim & Qu, 2014; Tan et al., 2014). Hence, it is proposed that these concepts should also be examined as motives in gamification.

The Element of Perceived Usefulness

Perceived usefulness is a core construct (Davis, 1989) in explaining behavioural intention (Natarajan, Balasubramanian, & Kasilngam, 2017). Usefulness is defined as the degree to which a person believes that using a particular technology will enhance his or her performance (Kim & Preis, 2016; Chiu et al., 2009). An individual is more likely to form favourable feelings of satisfaction and intent to continued usage when such usage is perceived as useful (Chiu et al., 2009). Yang, Asaad & Dwivedi (2017) found a positive effect between perceived usefulness and customers' intention to engage in gamification, whilst Yoo et al., (2017) found a positive effect on intention to use Gamified Applications. This is to show that a system applying gamification can be perceived as useful and therefore perceived usefulness should be seen as a motivation in this context.

The Element of Perceived Ease of Use

Perceived ease of use (PEOU) is also a key consideration for technology acceptance (Chang, Hajiyev & Su, 2017). Perceived ease of use refers to the degree to which a person believes that using a particular system would be free of effort (Davis, 1989; Venkatesh, 2000; Lu et al., 2015). Perceived ease of use is an element tied to an individual's assessment of the effort involved in the process of using the system (Venkatesh, 2000). The main feature of perceived ease of use is "simplicity", whether in comprehension, interaction, accessibility, or operation (Yang, Asaad & Dwivedi, 2017). Yang, Asaad & Dwivedi (2017) found a positive relationship between perceived ease of use and customers' intention to engage in gamification, and Yoo et al (2017) found a positive relationship between perceived ease of use and intention to use Gamified Smart Tourism Applications. It could therefore be assumed that gamification in organizations must be easy to use, otherwise it could prove a demotivating factor for the user.

The Element of Trust

Recent developments in understanding users' behaviour, in commercial and research contexts, led to heightened interest in trust and its determinants within the digital environment (Hansen, Saridakis & Benson, 2018). For example, it is argued that in trust is an important motivation in the online consumption since users will not shop from seller's website they do not trust (Amaro & Duarte, 2015). Similarly, users will not be engaged in gamification from an organization or a system they do not trust. Trust is defined as the belief that one party will reliably keep its word or promise and fulfil its obligations in an exchange relationship (Chemingui & Lallouna, 2013); or as the willingness of a party to be vulnerable to the actions of another party based on the expectation that the other will perform a particular action important to the trust or irrespective of the ability to monitor or control that other party (Amaro & Duarte, 2015). It is important for the organization to create the feeling of trust with the user at the early stages of the interaction for the user to be engaged in the long term. It could be argued that lack of trust between the user and the organization could work as a demotivator.

The Suggested Gamification Users Classification

In the previous sections the overview of games showed their success of the industry. The concept of 'game' was examined, and gamers' motivational factors that underpin that success were explored, focusing on four elements (fun, immersion, social interaction and aesthetics). Gamification could enable users as gamers to have a sense of engagement, immediate feedback, feeling of accomplishment and success of striving against a challenge and overcoming it (Kirsh, 2014). Due to the different outcomes that gamification and games deliver, it was deemed necessary to explore different motivations from the gamification literature that may create engagement between the system and the user. This yielded five elements (social influence, self-efficacy, openness, altruism and reward). Considering information systems literature, it was found important to add three more motivations (perceived usefulness, perceived ease of use and trust), since they have been used in the past to predict users' behaviour in technology environments and gamification should be seen as such. Due to the similarities in definition of social interaction from the gaming literature and social influence from gamification literature, one motivation was retained named 'socialising'. Looking at gaming, gamification and technology acceptance bodies of knowledge, eleven motivations have been identified in total as key predictors of engagement with gamified systems. Organizations looking into applying gamification to create engagement, should be aware that their target market will fall into one or more of these categories. Table 2 lists the motivation definition and the user type attached to each one of them. Furthermore, it proposes strategies to attract each user type (mechanics are adapted by: Marache-Francisco & Brangier (2013); Aparicio et al., (2012); Chou (2015)).

The typology of gamification users leads to valuable practical implications, as it provides a useful tool for managers to understand their audience to classify users' profiles and promote mechanics that may be more likely to influence users' future decisions. Overall, the chapter provides developers with an overall understanding of users' behaviour, especially based on their personal motivation using the gamified system. The classification suggests that gamification developers should focus on building an experience through their systems that equally satisfies users' intrinsic and extrinsic motivations through mimicking the experience of a gaming system.

The meaning of intrinsic motivation has been explored and defined from the gaming and gamification literature. Gamification developers should investigate mechanics that can enhance fun, immersion, socialising, self-efficacy, openness and altruism as users are likely to be motivated to use the system because of these elements. Motivations associated with extrinsic motivation such as rewards was identified from the gamification literature and elements such as usefulness, ease of use and trust were explored from the technology acceptance literature. It is important to understand the interaction of these categories to create a sustainable eco-system where everyone will be contributing based on their preferences.

Table 2. Motivations and Gamification User types

Motive	Description	User Profile	Proposed Strategies
Fun	These users are engaged with the gamified system because of the experience of fun it promotes	Joker	MDA (Mechanics, Dynamics, Aesthetics)
Immersion	These users are engaged with the gamified system because of the immersion experience it promotes	Absorbed	Profiles, Interactive Avatars, Observer attachment
Socializing	These users are engaged with the gamified system because of the social interaction it allows	Extrovert	Groups, Messages, Chat,
Aesthetics	These users are engaged with the gamified system because of the aesthetics it promotes	Artist	Teamplay
Self-efficacy	These users are engaged with the gamified system as it allows them a freedom of choice and expression	Achiever	Collecting, Prizes, Virtual goods
Openness	These users are engaged with the gamified system as it allows them the feeling of achievement and challenge	Explorer	Alternative activities, Built from scratch
Altruism	These users are engaged with the gamified system as it allows them the feeling of contribution	Giver	Optimal challenge,
Rewards	These users are engaged with the gamified system for the hunting of the outcome	Receiver	Points, Levels,
Usefulness	These users are engaged with the gamified system because of the convenience it promotes	Pragmatist	Offering, Helping
Ease of Use	These users are engaged with the gamified system as it allows them effortless actions	Simplifier	Rewards (Discounts, offers), Reward planning
Trust	These users are engaged with the gamified system as it promotes the feeling of security	Sceptic	Opportunities, Progressive information,

A gamified system should be balanced for all users with every typology helping the system to thrive. Once this structure is established, a thoughtful system of tangible and intangible rewards can be integrated, although it should not be dependent on them to function effectively. Once the organization starts giving someone a tangible reward, then they must provide that reward loop forever (Zichermann & Cunningham, 2011), hence it is advised for the system to avoid having too many users with extrinsic behaviour (rewards), as the eco-system will run the risk of devaluation. Instead, it is proposed for the system to focus on providing intangible rewards (such as badges, points, levelling up) at the early stages of users experience to satisfy the needs of this group. By doing so it will delay overcrowding this group of users. Receivers will still help the eco-system since they will be revealing future rewards for Achievers to desire. Achievers will need pleasant aesthetics to acknowledge their achievements, hence forcing the system to adapt, thus create an environment to attract Artists. Artists' need for nice aesthetics will create an environment which will create an immersive experience for the Absorbed. The interaction between Artists and Absorbed will create a fun eco-system to attract Jokers; users motivated by the element of Fun. Jokers are expected to share the fun and enjoyment they receive in the eco-system, hence socially interact with Extroverts whose main motivation is the socialising. Extroverts as a group will be revealing secrets and information of the system to Simplifiers helping them minimizing their effort in progressing in the system. Furthermore, they might be useful for evangelizing and bringing other categories in the eco-system. Simplifiers will showcase the easiness of the system attracting Pragmatists since making the system easy will make it useful. The eco-system itself then will investigate on how to apply useful materials for users to explore making it interesting for users motivated by openness, attracting the group of Explorers. Explorers will uncover these secrets from the system, for givers then to share with the community in order to help others. Givers will try to help everyone, offering valuable advice and information for the system, contributing towards Sceptics to create trust with the eco-system. Finally, alongside the influence of Givers, the system will reliably keep its promise and fulfil its obligations in the exchange relationship to deliver the rewards promised maximizing the element of trust for Sceptics. These rewards will then attract Receivers creating a circle of influence.

Figure 1. Example of gamification users' interaction

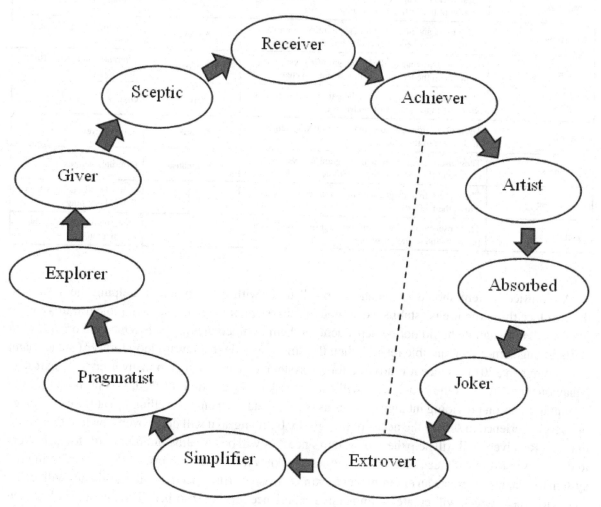

The above figure is an example of users' relationship in a gamified ecosystem, and it is possible to change depending on the scope of the strategy. For example, in this interaction extroverts (motivated by socialising) interact with simplifiers (motivated by ease of use), however it is possible in a different system to interact with Achievers (motivated by self-efficacy) helping that group to achieve tasks. It is important to highlight that the relationships between different users are fluid and the graph above does not propose a linear or circular flow; it rather provides an example of how the different profiles can interact with each other within a gamified system. The relationship between each typology of users is useful to be appreciated when developing a gamified strategy. Gamification is an approach to change or influence the behavior of someone by increasing motivation through persuasive design (Friedrich et al., 2020), which highlights the importance of recognizing this typology of gamification users when developing gamification in organizations. The acknowledgement of users' typology provides a useful tool for gamification developers to understand users' interaction within the system and promote mechanics that more likely enhance users' engagement. It is suggested that gamification developers should focus on building an experience that satisfies users' motivations applying mechanics suitable for all types of users. Examples of game components such as points, rankings, levels or quests that are implemented in a gamified system (Friedrich et al., 2020), however they might not be enough to satisfy the needs of every user.

FUTURE RESEARCH DIRECTIONS

It is worth noting that the proposed typology interaction could change depending on the context of the system. Probably, there might be different interaction if the system is applied for gamification in health context, education context, or tourism context. Each context is addressing different audience with different priorities and reactions. For example, gamification in tourism context might show more characteristics as explorers since tourists are mostly interested in exploring the destination where in education users might show more characteristics as achievers focusing on achieving the tasks provided. Taking this into consideration it worth looking into similarities and differences between each context of application. This will help organizations to develop a typology of users more precisely according to their audience. Gamification is a complex phenomenon, which has only recently begun to be understood. Further research is required to further conceptualize and comprehend the intricacies inherent in the definitions and meanings currently ascribed to it. Patterns of users as they relate to user typology needs further investigation to discover the motivations to use gamification.

CONCLUSION

Gamification has increasingly been used as an essential part of today's services, software and systems to engage and motivate users, as well as to spark further behaviors (Xi & Hamari, 2019). Gamification is used by brands to motivate employees, create healthy competition among teams, generate buzz or social proof, and encourage customer loyalty, implemented with a variety of techniques (some easy to implement, some requiring advanced planning, coding, or technical expertise). The sustainability and success of a gamified system relies on users' continued usage rather than first-time adoption behaviour.

Many gamified applications are failing due to poor game design (Burke, 2013), since they are focusing on points, badges and leaderborads. The creation of an engaging experience is more likely when the users' motives are identified when designing games, serious games and gamified systems (Marczewski, 2014). For a gamified application to be successful, the personal goals of the individual should be identified in the first place. The meaning of gamification user typology is to provide a better understanding of why and how people would use a system and the interaction between them. Gamification can be effective only when players' interests are put first because elements like reward points, achievements and badges do not automatically mean sustained engagement. The identification of gamification users' typology can help organizations to apply the appropriate mechanics to attract and engage individuals for the long-term success of the system.

Summarizing, this chapter explored the concept of gamification, by identifying users' motivations looking into the literature of games, gamification and technology adoption. Eventually, this chapter proposes a typology for gamification systems' users is creating an example of a balanced eco-system where each user contributes as part of a society. It is believed that organizations should acknowledge the motives of their users when they apply gamification to ensure an effective strategy. Section title should be "Conclusion", not "Conclusions". Provide discussion of the overall coverage of the chapter and concluding remarks.

REFERENCES

Adukaite, A., van Zyl, I., & Cantoni, L. (2016). The role of digital technology in tourism education: A case study of South African secondary schools. *Journal of Hospitality, Leisure, Sport and Tourism Education, 19*, 54–65. doi:10.1016/j.jhlste.2016.08.003

Al-Zaidi, Z. (2012). Gamification's march to ubiquity. *The Guardian.* https://www.theguardian.com/media-network/media-network-blog/2012/apr/26/gamification-ubiquity

Amaro, S., & Duarte, P. (2015). An integrative model of consumers' intentions to purchase travel online. *Tourism Management, 46*, 64–79. doi:10.1016/j.tourman.2014.06.006

Andersen, E., Liu, Y.-E., Snider, R., Szeto, R., & Popovic, Z. (2011). Placing a value on aesthetics in online casual games. *Proceedings of the 2011 annual conference on Human factors in computing systems*, 1275–1278. 10.1145/1978942.1979131

Aparicio, A. F., Vela, F. L. G., Sánchez, J. L. G., & Montes, J. L. I. (2012, October). Analysis and application of gamification. In *Proceedings of the 13th International Conference on Interacción Persona-Ordenador - INTERACCION '12, Elche, Spain* (pp. 3-5). 10.1145/2379636.2379653

Bartle, A. R. (2004). *Designing virtual worlds*. New Riders Publishing.

Bowman, N. D., Kowert, R., & Cohen, E. (2015). When the ball stops, the fun stops too: The impact of social inclusion on video game enjoyment. *Computers in Human Behavior, 53*, 131–139. doi:10.1016/j.chb.2015.06.036

Burke, B. (2013). How Gamification Motivates the Masses. *Forbes.* https://www.forbes.com/sites/gartnergroup/2014/04/10/how-gamification-motivates-the-masses/?sh=6f613665c047

Chang, C.-T., Hajiyev, J., & Su, C.-R. (2017). Examining the students' behavioral intention to use e-learning in Azerbaijan? The General Extended Technology Acceptance Model for E-learning approach. *Computers & Education, 111*, 128–143. doi:10.1016/j.compedu.2017.04.010

Chang, Y.-W., Hsu, P.-Y., & Wu, Z.-Y. (2015). Exploring managers' intention to use business intelligence: The role of motivations. *Behaviour & Information Technology, 34*(3), 273–285. doi:10.1080/0144929X.2014.968208

Chemingui, H., & Ben lallouna, H. (2013). Resistance, motivations, trust and intention to use mobile financial services. *International Journal of Bank Marketing*, *31*(7), 574–592. doi:10.1108/IJBM-12-2012-0124

Chiu, C.-M., Lin, H.-Y., Sun, S.-Y., & Hsu, M.-H. (2009). Understanding customers' loyalty intentions towards online shopping: An integration of technology acceptance model and fairness theory. *Behaviour & Information Technology*, *28*(4), 347–360. doi:10.1080/01449290801892492

Choo, Y-K. (2015). The Octalysis Framework for Gamification & Behavioral Design. *Yu-kai Chou: Gamification & Behavioral Design*. https://yukaichou.com/gamification-examples/octalysis-complete-gamification-framework/

Cox, J. (2014). What Makes a Blockbuster Video Game? An Empirical Analysis of US Sales Data. *Managerial and Decision Economics*, *35*(3), 189–198. doi:10.1002/mde.2608

Csikszentmihalyi, M. (1990). Flow: The Psychology of Optimal Experience. New York: Harper Collins.

D'arc da Silva Brito, R., Hernan Contreras Pinochet, L., Luiz Lopes, E., & Aparecido de Oliveira, M. (2018). Development of a gamification characteristics measurement scale for mobile application users. *Internext*, *13*(1), 1–16. doi:10.18568/1980-4865.1311-16

Davis, F. D. (1989). Perceived Usefulness, Perceived Ease of Use, and User Acceptance of Information Technology. *Management Information Systems Quarterly*, *13*(3), 319–340. doi:10.2307/249008

Davis, S. B. (2014). *Constructing a Players-Centred Definition of Fun for Video Games Design*. ResearchGate.

de Kort, Y. A. W., IJsselsteijn, W. A., & Poels, K. (2007). Digital games as social presence technology: development of the Social Presence in Gaming Questionnaire. PRESENCE 2007 Proceedings, 195–203.

Deterding, S., Dixon, D., Khaled, R., & Nacke, L. (2011). From game design elements to gamefulness: defining gamification. In *Proceedings of the 15th International AcademicMindTrek Conference* (pp. 9–15). 10.1145/2181037.2181040

Devaraj, S., Easley, R. F., & Crant, J. M. (2008). How does personality matter?: Relating the five-factor model to technology acceptance and use. *Information Systems Research*, *19*(1), 93–105. doi:10.1287/isre.1070.0153

Dickey, M. D. (2005). Engaging by Design: How Engagement Strategies in Popular Computer and Video Games Can Inform Instructional Design. *Educational Technology Research and Development*, *53*(2), 67–83. doi:10.1007/BF02504866

Dunniway, T., & Novak, J. (2008). *Game Development Essentials: Gameplay mechanics*. Delmar Cengage Learning.

Feijoo, C., Gómez-Barroso, J.-L., Aguado, J.-M., & Ramos, S. (2012). Mobile gaming: Industry challenges and policy implications. *Telecommunications Policy*, *36*(3), 212–221. doi:10.1016/j.telpol.2011.12.004

Friedrich, J., Becker, M., Kramer, F., Wirth, M., & Schneider, M. (2020). Incentive design and gamification for knowledge management. *Journal of Business Research, 106*, 341–352. doi:10.1016/j.jbusres.2019.02.009

Hamari, J., & Koivisto, J. (2015). Why do people use gamification services? *International Journal of Information Management, 35*(4), 419–431. doi:10.1016/j.ijinfomgt.2015.04.006

Hansen, J. M., & Levin, M. A. (2016). The effect of apathetic motivation on employees' intentions to use social media for businesses. *Journal of Business Research, 69*(12), 6058–6066. doi:10.1016/j.jbusres.2016.06.009

Hansen, J. M., Saridakis, G., & Benson, V. (2018). Risk, trust, and the interaction of perceived ease of use and behavioral control in predicting consumers' use of social media for transactions. *Computers in Human Behavior, 80*, 197–206. doi:10.1016/j.chb.2017.11.010

Hemovich, V. (2021). It Does Matter If You Win or Lose, and How You Play the (Video) Game. *Games and Culture, 16*(4), 481–493. doi:10.1177/1555412020913760

Herrero, A., & Martin, H. S. (2012). Developing and testing a global model to explain the adoption of websites by users in rural tourism accommodations. *International Journal of Hospitality Management, 31*(4), 1178–1186. doi:10.1016/j.ijhm.2012.02.005

Hofacker, C. F., de Ruyter, K., Lurie, N. H., Manchanda, P., & Donaldson, J. (2016). Gamification and Mobile Marketing Effectiveness. *Journal of Interactive Marketing, 34*, 25–36. doi:10.1016/j.intmar.2016.03.001

Hoffman, B., & Nadelson, L. (2010). Motivational engagement and video gaming: A mixed methods study. *Educational Technology Research and Development, 58*(3), 245–270. doi:10.100711423-009-9134-9

Hung, S.-Y., Durcikova, A., Lai, H.-M., & Lin, W.-M. (2011). The influence of intrinsic and extrinsic motivation on individuals' knowledge sharing behavior. *International Journal of Human-Computer Studies, 69*(6), 415–427. doi:10.1016/j.ijhcs.2011.02.004

Hung, S.-Y., Lai, H.-M., & Chang, W.-W. (2011). Knowledge-sharing motivations affecting R&D employees' acceptance of electronic knowledge repository. *Behaviour & Information Technology, 30*(2), 213–230. doi:10.1080/0144929X.2010.545146

Iglesias-Pradas, S., Hernández-García, Á., & Fernández-Cardador, P. (2017). Acceptance of Corporate Blogs for Collaboration and Knowledge Sharing. *Information Systems Management, 34*(3), 220–237. doi:10.1080/10580530.2017.1329998

Jennett, C., Cox, A. L., Cairns, P., Dhoparee, S., Epps, A., Tijs, T., & Walton, A. (2008). Measuring and defining the experience of immersion in games. *International Journal of Human-Computer Studies, 66*(9), 641–661. doi:10.1016/j.ijhcs.2008.04.004

Kapp, K. (2012). *The Gamification of Learning and Instruction: Game-based Methods and Strategies for Training and Education.* John Wiley & sons, Inc.

Kapur, M. (n.d.). An Octalysis Analysis of WhatsApp. Retrieved May 28, 2021, from https://yukaichou.com/gamification-guest-posts/octalysis-analysis-whatsapp/

Kaye, L. K., & Bryce, J. (2012). Putting the "Fun Factor" into gaming: The influence of social contexts on experiences of playing video games. *International Journal of Internet Science*, 7(1), 23–37.

Kiili, K., de Freitas, S., Arnab, S., & Lainema, T. (2012). The Design Principles for Flow Experience in Educational Games. *Procedia Computer Science*, *15*, 78–91. doi:10.1016/j.procs.2012.10.060

Kim, C.-S., Oh, E.-H., Yang, K. H., & Kim, J. K. (2010). The appealing characteristics of download type mobile games. *Service Business*, *4*(3), 253–269. doi:10.100711628-009-0088-0

Kim, M., & Qu, H. (2014). Travelers' behavioral intention toward hotel self-service kiosks usage. *International Journal of Contemporary Hospitality Management*, *26*(2), 225–245. doi:10.1108/IJCHM-09-2012-0165

Kim, M. J., Lee, C.-K., & Bonn, M. (2016). The effect of social capital and altruism on seniors' re-visit intention to social network sites for tourism-related purposes. *Tourism Management, 53*, 96–107. doi:10.1016/j.tourman.2015.09.007

Kim, M. J., Lee, C.-K., & Bonn, M. (2017). Obtaining a better understanding about travel-related purchase intentions among senior users of mobile social network sites. *International Journal of Information Management*, *37*(5), 484–496. doi:10.1016/j.ijinfomgt.2017.04.006

Kim, M. J., & Preis, M. W. (2016). Why Seniors use Mobile Devices: Applying an Extended Model of Goal-Directed Behavior. *Journal of Travel & Tourism Marketing*, *33*(3), 404–423. doi:10.1080/10548408.2015.1064058

Kirsh, B. A. (2014). *Game in Libraries: Essays on using play to connect and instruct*. McFarland & Company Inc. Publishers.

Klug, G. C., & Schell, J. (2006). *Playing video games: Motives, Responses and Consequences*. Routledge Taylor and Francis Group.

Kowal, J., & Fortier, M. S. (1999). Motivational Determinants of Flow: Contributions From Self-Determination Theory. *The Journal of Social Psychology*, *139*(3), 355–368. doi:10.1080/00224549909598391

Lee, P. C., & Mao, Z. (2016). The relation among self-efficacy, learning approaches, and academic performance: An exploratory study. *Journal of Teaching in Travel & Tourism*, *16*(3), 178–194. doi:10.1080/15313220.2015.1136581

Lombriser, P., & van der Valk, R. (2011). *Improving the Quality of the Software Development Lifecycle with Gamification*. Springer-Verlag.

Lu, J., Mao, Z., Wang, M., & Hu, L. (2015). Goodbye maps, hello apps? Exploring the influential determinants of travel app adoption. *Current Issues in Tourism*, *18*(11), 1059–1079. doi:10.1080/13683500.2015.1043248

Maedche, A., Botzenhardt, A., & Neer, L. (2012). *Software for people: Fundamentals, trends and best practices*. Springer. doi:10.1007/978-3-642-31371-4

Maitland, C., Granich, J., Braham, R., Thornton, A., Teal, R., Stratton, G., & Rosenberg, M. (2018). Measuring the capacity of active video games for social interaction: The Social Interaction Potential Assessment tool. *Computers in Human Behavior, 87*, 308–316. doi:10.1016/j.chb.2018.05.036

Marache-Francisco, C., & Brangier, E. (2013, October). Process of Gamification. From the Consideration of Gamification to its Practical Implementation. In *CENTRIC 2013, The Sixth International Conference on Advances in Human oriented and Personalized Mechanisms, Technologies, and Services, Venice, Italy* (pp. 126–131). Academic Press.

Marczewski, A. (2014). *Marczewski's Gamification User Types*. E-Learning Industry. https://elearningindustry.com/marczewski-gamification-user-types

McGuire, M., & Jenkins, O. C. (2009). *Creating Games: Mechanics*. Content and Technology. A K Peters, Ltd.

Mills, D. J., Milyavskaya, M., Mettler, J., & Heath, N. L. (2018). Exploring the pull and push underlying problem video game use: A Self-Determination Theory approach. *Personality and Individual Differences, 135*, 176–181. doi:10.1016/j.paid.2018.07.007

Mintel. (2020). *Lifestyles of Gamers - China - October 2020*. Mintel. https://reports.mintel.com/display/1046705/?fromSearch=%3Ffreetext%3Dvideo%2520gamers%2520demographics

Moore, M. E. (2011). *Basics of game design*. Taylor and Francis Group.

Morschheuser, B., Hassan, L., Werder, K., & Hamari, J. (2018). How to design gamification? A method for engineering gamified software. *Information and Software Technology, 95*, 219–237. doi:10.1016/j.infsof.2017.10.015

Natarajan, T., Balasubramanian, S. A., & Kasilingam, D. L. (2017). Understanding the intention to use mobile shopping applications and its influence on price sensitivity. *Journal of Retailing and Consumer Services, 37*, 8–22. doi:10.1016/j.jretconser.2017.02.010

Parra-López, E., Bulchand-Gidumal, J., Gutiérrez-Taño, D., & Díaz-Armas, R. (2011). Intentions to use social media in organizing and taking vacation trips. *Computers in Human Behavior, 27*(2), 640–654. doi:10.1016/j.chb.2010.05.022

Patrício, R., Moreira, A. C., & Zurlo, F. (2018). Gamification approaches to the early stage of innovation. *Creativity and Innovation Management, 27*(4), 499–511. doi:10.1111/caim.12284

Rapp, A. (2018). Social Game Elements in World of Warcraft: Interpersonal Relations, Groups, and Organizations for Gamification Design. *International Journal of Human-Computer Interaction, 34*(8), 759–773. doi:10.1080/10447318.2018.1461760

Rogers, R. (2017). The motivational pull of video game feedback, rules, and social interaction: Another self-determination theory approach. *Computers in Human Behavior, 73*, 446–450. doi:10.1016/j.chb.2017.03.048

Roohi, S., & Forouzandeh, A. (2019). Regarding color psychology principles in adventure games to enhance the sense of immersion. *Entertainment Computing, 30*, 100298. doi:10.1016/j.entcom.2019.100298

Ryan, R. M., & Deci, E. L. (2000). Self-Determination Theory and the Facilitation of Intrinsic Motivation, Social Development, and Well-Being. *The American Psychologist, 55*(1), 68–78. doi:10.1037/0003-066X.55.1.68 PMID:11392867

Ryan, R. M., Rigby, C. S., & Przybylski, A. (2006). The Motivational Pull of Video Games: A Self-Determination Theory Approach. *Motivation and Emotion, 30*(4), 344–360. doi:10.100711031-006-9051-8

Sajid, M. J., Cao, Q., Xinchun, L., Brohi, M. A., & Sajid, M. F. (2018). Video gaming a new face of inducement tourism: Main attractors for juvenile gamers. *International Journal of Scientific Study, 4*(5), 52–56.

Schell, J. (2010). *The art of game design: A book of lenses*. Morgan Kaufmann Publishers.

Schöbel, S. M., Janson, A., & Söllner, M. (2020). Capturing the complexity of gamification elements: A holistic approach for analysing existing and deriving novel gamification designs. *European Journal of Information Systems, 29*(6), 641–668. doi:10.1080/0960085X.2020.1796531

Siemens, J. C., Smith, S., Fisher, D., Thyroff, A., & Killian, G. (2015). Level Up! The Role of Progress Feedback Type for Encouraging Intrinsic Motivation and Positive Brand Attitudes in Public Versus Private Gaming Contexts. *Journal of Interactive Marketing, 32*, 1–12. doi:10.1016/j.intmar.2015.07.001

Smith, B. P. (2006). *Playing video games: Motives, Responses and Consequences*. Routledge Taylor and Francis Group.

Smith, L. J., Gradisar, M., & King, D. L. (2015). Parental Influences on Adolescent Video Game Play: A Study of Accessibility, Rules, Limit Setting, Monitoring, and Cybersafety. *Cyberpsychology, Behavior, and Social Networking, 18*(5), 273–279. doi:10.1089/cyber.2014.0611 PMID:25965861

Sooksatit, K. (2016). Customer Decisions on Hotel Booking via Mobile Phone and Tablet Applications: A Case Study of Luxury Hotels in Bangkok. In e-Consumers in the Era of New Tourism. Managing the Asian Century. Springer. doi:10.1007/978-981-10-0087-4_6

Sorenson, N., Pasquier, P., & DiPaola, S. (2011). A generic approach to challenge modelling for the procedural creation of video game levels. *IEEE Transactions on Computational Intelligence and AI in Games, 3*(3), 229–244. doi:10.1109/TCIAIG.2011.2161310

Taherdoost, H. (2018). A review of technology acceptance and adoption models and theories. *Procedia Manufacturing, 22*, 960–967. doi:10.1016/j.promfg.2018.03.137

Tan, G. W.-H., Ooi, K.-B., Leong, L.-Y., & Lin, B. (2014). Predicting the drivers of behavioral intention to use mobile learning: A hybrid SEM-Neural Networks approach. *Computers in Human Behavior, 36*, 198–213. doi:10.1016/j.chb.2014.03.052

Venkatesh, V. (2000). Determinants of Perceived Ease of Use: Integrating Control, Intrinsic Motivation, and Emotion into the Technology Acceptance Model. *Information Systems Research, 11*(4), 342–365. doi:10.1287/isre.11.4.342.11872

Warmelink, H. (2014). *Online Gaming and Playful Organization*. Routledge. doi:10.4324/9780203781920

Xi, N., & Hamari, J. (2019). Does gamification satisfy needs? A study on the relationship between gamification features and intrinsic need satisfaction. *International Journal of Information Management, 46*, 210–221. doi:10.1016/j.ijinfomgt.2018.12.002

Xi, N., & Hamari, J. (2020). Does gamification affect brand engagement and equity? A study in online brand communities. *Journal of Business Research, 109*, 449–460. doi:10.1016/j.jbusres.2019.11.058

Xu, F., Buhalis, D., & Weber, J. (2017). Serious games and the gamification of tourism. *Tourism Management, 60*, 244–256. doi:10.1016/j.tourman.2016.11.020

Yang, Y., Asaad, Y., & Dwivedi, Y. (2017). Examining the impact of gamification on intention of engagement and brand attitude in the marketing context. *Computers in Human Behavior, 73*, 459–469. doi:10.1016/j.chb.2017.03.066

Yi, M. Y., & Hwang, Y. (2003). Predicting the use of web-based information systems: Self-efficacy, enjoyment, learning goal orientation, and the technology acceptance model. *International Journal of Human-Computer Studies, 59*(4), 431–449. doi:10.1016/S1071-5819(03)00114-9

Yoo, C., Kwon, S., & Chang, B. (2017). Factors Affecting the Adoption of Gamified Smart Tourism Applications: An Integrative Approach. *Sustainability, 9*(12), 2162. doi:10.3390/su9122162

Zhan, C., Li, B., Zhong, X., Min, H., & Wu, Z. (2020). A model for collective behaviour propagation: A case study of video game industry. *Neural Computing & Applications, 32*(9), 4507–4517. doi:10.100700521-018-3686-8

Zicherman, G., & Linder, J. (2010). *Game based marketing*. John Wiley & Sons.

Zichermann, G., & Cunningham, C. (2011). *Gamification by design: Implementing game mechanics in web and mobile apps*. O'Reilly Media.

ADDITIONAL READING

Hulsey, N. (2020). *For play: games in everyday life*. Emerald Publishing.

Mullins, J. K., & Sabherwal, R. (2020). Gamification: A cognitive-emotional view. *Journal of Business Research, 106*, 304–314. doi:10.1016/j.jbusres.2018.09.023

Negruşa, A., Toader, V., Sofică, A., Tutunea, M., & Rus, R. (2015). Exploring Gamification Techniques and Applications for Sustainable Tourism. *Sustainability (Basel, Switzerland), 7*(8), 11160–11189. doi:10.3390u70811160

Parapanos, D., & Michopoulou, E. (2021). *Gamification, Game Mechanics, Game Thinking and Players' Profile and Life Cycle. Gamification for Tourism*. Multilingual Matters. doi:10.21832/9781845418236-004

Xu, F., Tian, F., Buhalis, D., Weber, J., & Zhang, H. (2016). Tourists as Mobile Gamers: Gamification for Tourism Marketing. *Journal of Travel & Tourism Marketing, 33*(8), 1124–1142. doi:10.1080/1054 8408.2015.1093999

KEY TERMS AND DEFINITIONS

Extrinsic Motivation: The motive to act in response to get external outcome.

Fun: The accomplishment of intrinsic satisfaction when fulfilling a task.

Gamification: The use of game mechanics, game elements and game aesthetics for non-gaming or entertainment purposes, to create engagement and contribute towards problem solving.

Gamified Ecosystem: An environment where users and software, work together to form a bubble of life and interactions, following the game-like activities.

Intrinsic Motivation: The motive to act in response to an internal will, only looking to for internal joy.

Reward: The tangible or intangible outcome received when achieving a task.

Video Games: Electronic games that involves manipulating an input device in response to the graphics on a screen.

Chapter 2
Should I Play or Should I Go?
Identifying Challenges for Gamification

Daniel Cermak-Sassenrath
IT University of Copenhagen, Denmark

ABSTRACT

A pervasive application of gamification in many areas of everyday life has arguably yet to happen. For instance, despite much commercial interest in and a potentially huge market for successful gamification products in the areas of education and health, much of the excitement is still based on speculation, and reception in parts of the academic community remains sceptical. The chapter aims to collate observations from multiple empirical studies and meta-studies and collect and highlight issues that need to be resolved or mitigated for gamification to progress. Such issues include unclear definitions, a limitation on small sets of elements employed with unclear effects, unintentional side-effects of competition, a confusing variety of operationalizations, the erosion of intrinsic motivation through extrinsic incentives, a disconnect between theoretical understandings and practical realizations, a strong focus on a behaviorist paradigm, studies' mixed, partial, and inconclusive results, a lack of attention to moderating factors, and methodological limitations.

INTRODUCTION

The idea to fit play with purposes beyond itself, to "leverage aspects of games to achieve something beyond playfulness" (Richter et al., 2015, p. 23), has been proposed and implemented many times, before and after the "digitalisation of society or the massive economic success of computer games" (Fuchs, 2014, p. 136)[1], under a plethora of monikers. One of the recent, most prominent notions is *gamification*. Regardless of when and by whom the notion was first proposed (see, for instance, Hägglund, 2012, p. 8; Tulloch, 2014, p. 318; Yıldırım&Şen, 2019, p. 2), "only around the beginning" of the 2010s (Fuchs, 2014, p. 120) it "gained widespread usage" (Tulloch, 2014, p. 318), and "has become a favoured buzzword of marketers, online strategists, start-up gurus, venture capitalists and digital consultants" (ibid., p. 317). Gamification as a research field is variously seen to be in its "infancy" (Hung, 2017, p. 62; Koivisto&Hamari, 2019, p. 192), as an "emerging" (Sailer&Homner, 2020, p. 101) or "maturing" field

DOI: 10.4018/978-1-7998-9223-6.ch002

(Nacke&Deterding, 2017; Rozman&Donath, 2019, p. 16), or even as a "science" (Landers et al., 2018) or "as a new educational theory" (Biro, 2014 in Dichev&Dicheva, 2017, p. 23).

A pervasive application of gamification in many areas of everyday life is arguably yet to happen. Despite much commercial interest in and a potentially huge market for successful gamification products, for instance, in the areas of education and health, much excitement is still based on speculation, and reception by "many games studies academics and game designers" remains sceptical (Tulloch, 2014, p. 317; see e.g. Fizek, 2014; Raczkowski, 2014; Sailer&Homner, 2020, p. 78). Although "results in general lean towards positive findings about the effectiveness of gamification", Koivisto and Hamari (2019, p. 191) note that "the amount of mixed results is remarkable". The idea and the practices of gamification have attracted and continue to attract a fair amount of criticism: "Ever since its advent[,] gamification has sparked controversy between game designers, user experience designers, game theorists and researchers in human-computer interaction" (Dichev&Dicheva, 2017, p. 2). Bai et al. (2020, p. 2) speculate that Bogost's (2011) well-known description of gamification as "marketing bullshit" "reflects many people's attitudes"; Yıldırımand and Şen (2019, p. 1; see ibid., p. 4) note that "[w]hether [educational] gamification is an organized structure that contributes to student achievement, a simple pontification process or total nonsense is a matter of debate"; and for Tulloch (2018), educational gamification is but "an enactment, and reinforcement tool of neoliberal and market logic" (Kalogiannakis et al., 2021, p. 23).

Gamification is a non-trivial endeavour (Khalil, 2018; Landers et al., 2018, p. 328; Koivisto&Hamari, 2019, p. 199) and is marked by a multiplicity of different implementations; it is a "very diverse" research field "with respect to the focus of the studies and the reported outcomes" (Dichev&Dicheva, 2017, p. 12). An almost Babylonian confusion of understandings, definitions and notions plagues the discourse; Sailer and Homner (2020, p. 78) observe a "conceptual heterogeneity in gamification". Conflicting views and contradictory observations concern central aspects of the idea; for instance, it is demanded that single elements of gamification are tested rigorously in isolation for their effects on, for instance, learners (e.g. Dichev&Dicheva, 2017, p. 10; Ortiz-Rojas et al., 2017), and at the same time it is noted that elements only work meaningfully in combination (e.g. Nacke&Deterding, 2017; Xi&Hamari, 2019, p. 212); it is claimed that empirical gamification research often only measures "motivation and engagement" (Ortiz-Rojas et al., 2017), and at the same time it is also claimed that, in fact, motivation is not measured at all or only by second-hand measures (e.g. Johnson et al., 2016; Dichev&Dicheva, 2017, p. 12); educational gamification is praised as a way to empower learners and to increase their autonomy compared to traditional teaching methods (e.g. Zeng&Shang, 2018, pp. 539–40; Zainuddin et al., 2020, p. 1), while at the same time, much of educational gamification is informed by classic conditioning theories of learning within a behaviourist paradigm (e.g. Landers et al., 2018, p. 331; Baptista&Oliveira, 2019, p. 311); and it is noted that the engagement of learners with gamified learning systems aligns with their academic performance (e.g. Tsay et al., 2018, p. 9; Bai et al., 2020, p. 14) and does not align with their academic performance (Hung, 2017, pp. 61-2; Kalogiannakis et al., 2021, p. 1).

The chapter does not aim to point out faults or shortcomings of researchers, studies or approaches; but it tries to *take stock*: By collating observations from multiple empirical studies and meta-studies, *this study identifies, presents and discusses challenges gamification faces*[2]. The chapter does not exhaustively list experiences or results of gamification, but it collects and highlights issues that need to be resolved or mitigated for gamification to progress. The issues are identified and described, but not weighed or ranked. Therefore, an unsystematic analysis of the discourse in the form of studies and meta-studies is appropriate. The survey includes empirical gamification studies and meta-studies that are identified through online searches using various search engines such as *Google Scholar*, and reviews of empirical studies this author is aware of such as Hamari et al. (2014), Seaborn and Fels (2015), Johnson et al. (2016), Dichev and Dicheva (2017), Majuri et al. (2018), Koivisto and Hamari (2019), and Sailer and Homner (2020).[3]

Each section of the chapter highlights and briefly discusses problematic aspects for gamification to address; these aspects are unclear definitions, a limitation on small sets of elements employed with unclear effects, unintended side-effects of competition, a confusing variety of operalizations, the erosion of intrinsic motivation through the provision of extrinsic incentives, a disconnect between theoretical understandings and practical realizations, a strong focus on a behaviourist paradigm, studies' mixed, partial and inconclusive results, a lack of attention at moderating factors, and methodological limitations[4].

PROBLEMATIC DEFINITIONS

There is a plethora of notions associated with the idea of purposeful play. For the area of education, Majuri et al., for instance, list "serious games, edugames or games for education, game-based learning, and lately, gamification" (2018, p. 12; see e.g. Hung, 2017, p. 57; Bai et al., 2020, pp. 1-2)[5]. Often, the notions of gamification and serious games are seen as complementary: Gamification injects some game elements into an otherwise mundane activity, and serious games are full-fledged games that incorporate some useful (e.g. educational) content (Seaborn&Fels, 2015; see Kalogiannakis et al., 2021, pp. 2–3). In some studies, notions such as gamification, game-based learning and serious games are used synonymously (e.g. Koivisto&Hamari, 2019; da Silva et al., 2019).

The Core Aim of Gamification is Purposeful Use of Play

While the notions and their use vary considerably in the area of gamification, the underlying core idea is clear and stable: To use the playing of games for instrumental purposes. Koivisto and Hamari (2019, p. 191) observe that "utilitarian and hedonic systems are in a state of spiraling convergence" in gamification. They explain that "gamification technology" aims to transfer the "self-purposeful nature of the activity" and the "engagement and enjoyment of [...] playing games [...] into contexts that commonly have a more instrumental purpose" (ibid., pp. 191-2; see Dichev&Dicheva, 2017, p. 25, Landers et al., 2018, p. 331, Kalogiannakis et al., 2021, p. 3).

The notion of gamification does not describe an artefact but a process. Landers et al. define gamification as a "design process [...] intended to augment or alter an existing real-world process using lessons (initially) from the game design research literature to create a revised version of that process that users will experience as game-like" (2018, p. 317; see Bai et al., 2020, p. 2).

What Are Game Elements?

One early, still prominent (Rapp, 2017, p. 649; Albertazzi et al., 2017, p. 192) and brief definition of gamification in the academic discourse is Deterding et al.'s (2011) definition, which focuses on the use of game design elements and game mechanics (Seaborn&Fels, 2015, p. 14) in non-game contexts. It assumes that "single design elements, such as points, badges and leaderboards" can be extracted "from their original gaming context" and implanted "in other environments", with "their effects on players" intact (Rapp, 2017, p. 670). If gamification is to replicate the appeal and, in particular, the motivational thrust of games for instrumental purposes, the challenge arises to identify the core of this appeal; it seems to be a reasonable assumption that "adding elements, such as those found in games" to the gamification initiative, "will create immersion in a way similar to what happens in games" (Dichev&Dicheva, 2017, p. 2).

While Varannai et al. (2017, p. 1) believes Deterding et al.'s (2011) definition to be "the most accurate", and Ekici (2021, p. 33) believes it to be the "simplest definition of gamification", it is not unproblematic. There are several obvious questions inherent in this definition: What is a game? What concretely are "game elements"? Which particular experiences are facilitated by games, and how these can be brought about? The definition might also be paradoxical: If the core of gamification is taken to be that one takes game elements and implants them into something that is not a game, will this what is not a game then be experienced by somebody (else) as a game? Should it (not) be experienced as a game? If it is experienced as a game, does it then cease to be a gamified other?[6]

For all element-centric definitions of gamification an essential question to address is, what are the elements (see Hung, 2017, p. 60)? Bai et al. (2020, p. 2) point out that "[a]lthough game elements are the basic building components of gamification [...], there is no commonly agreed on classification of game elements". Koivisto and Hamari (2019, p. 7) observe "variation" in how "the various affordances [i.e. elements] have been defined and implemented". While Deterding et al. (2011) "propose to define game design elements as those elements that are characteristic of games, i.e. that can be found in many games, and that are significant to the meaning of the game" (Sailer et al., 2017, p. 372), Sailer et al. note that it "is often somewhat arbitrary and subjective" (ibid.), "which building blocks should be identified as characteristic game design elements" (ibid.; see Landers et al., 2018, p. 321).[7]

There are many suggestions discussed in the discourse which game elements to use; for example, Kalogiannakis et al. list a diverse set of "game elements", including "Competition", "progression", Animations and sounds", "time", "Repeat-testing" and "points", to name some (2021, Table 4 on p. 19; see, for instance, Khalil, 2018; Rozman&Donath, 2019, p. 6; factually only small sets of elements are used in the majority of studies, see below); but the disagreements do not only concern a particular selection or set of elements or how characteristic or representative an element is for all games or for some games; but also what elements of games *are*, and if such things *exist at all*. A romantic view of play would explain that a game is not activities, objects or elements. Huizinga (1955, pp. 3–4) asserts that, "whatever else play is, it is not matter". From such a position a game can be seen primarily as a mental construct that only uses rather arbitrary sets of secondary material items and activities (Cermak-Sassenrath, 2015). Such a mental construct could then not simply be taken and transplanted, top-down, into a different context. It could only emerge, freely, distinctly, potentially disruptively.

Limited Sets of Game Elements are Used, with Unclear Effects

In the vast majority of studies, gamification appears to aquire an almost exclusive focus on a rather small set of specific elements[8] and to be characterized by it. Koivisto and Hamari note that "the triad of points, badges and leaderboards" (2019, p. 198) "are often considered to be the blueprint of gamification" (ibid., p. 200). They emphasize that these three elements "continue [...] to dominate the landscape of gamification" (ibid., p. 198) although "[s]everal critical views regarding the prevalence of these elements have been voiced" (ibid., pp. 198–9). They explain that while "the diversity of elements [games] contain is vast [...] in gamification design, this is often ignored and the implementations are reduced to a replication of the blueprint triad" (ibid., p. 204). Werbach and Hunter call the elements of "points, levels and leaderboards" the "trinity of gamification design elements" (2012 in Nacke&Deterding, 2017; see

Khalil et al., 2018, Table 5 on p. 7, Koivisto&Hamari, 2019, p. 191,201, Huang et al., 2020, p. 1887, Ekici, 2021, p. 3336).

Various studies confirm that only a handful of elements are typically employed in gamification implementations. For instance, the study by Zainuddin et al. (2020, p. 9) finds that by far the most often-used elements are points (in 38 of 46 analysed journal articles on educational gamification), leaderboards (33) and badges (33), then levels (21); other elements are much rarer (the most popular of them are trophies (7) and rankings (5); trophies appear to this author to be similar to badges, and rankings to leaderboards or levels). The set of common elements is only rarely extended; for instance, in the case of a health gamification intervention targeted at older adults, adaptive difficulty may be added (Koivisto&Malik, 2020, p. 6).

Usually, studies use multiple elements simultaniously (Bai et al., 2020, p. 9). Bai et al.'s meta-analysis of "24 relevant articles that discuss 30 independent interventions" (ibid., p. 14) finds "[a] majority of the interventions [to] use [...] the combination of badges, leaderboard, and points (n = 8). The next most common combination was badges, leaderboard, levels, and points, which was used by six interventions. Four interventions used the combination of badges and points. Only three interventions used a single type of game element (i.e., points)." (Ibid., p. 9)

Mekler et al. observe that most often "[p]oints, levels and leaderboards" and used, "the poster children of gamification"; they speculate that their popularity is "due to their apparent connection to digital games [...] and due to them being readily applicable to various non-game contexts" (2017; see Koivisto&Hamari, 2019, p. 198, Rozman&Donath, 2019, p. 16). Dichev and Dicheva (2017, p. 10) assert that "[t]his combination [of "points, badges and leaderboards"] in its trivial form can be applied to almost any context, even if there isn't a good reason to do so".

Unclear or Different Effects of Individual Elements or Combinations of Elements

It is often unclear what a game design element is, and which psychological effect it has on players/users (Seaborn&Fels, 2015). Dichev and Dicheva observe that "studies reporting positive results from using a specific combination of game elements do not promote the understanding of the causal effect of the combination, as it is unclear whether the combination or a particular element led to the positive outcome" (2017, p. 19; see Hamari et al., 2014).

While a shared understanding exists that gamification is premised on creating motivation for participants (Kalogiannakis et al., 2021, pp. 22–3; see below), Kalogiannakis et al. find that "a connection between an element or set of them with a specific motivational aspect [...] cannot be generalized" (ibid.). Hanus and Fox (2015) observe that "the effectiveness of various gamification elements ha[s] not been sufficiently tested". Sardi et al. (2017, p. 40) similarly observe a "serious lack of research that provides well-founded and rigorous empirical evidence of the motivation process driven by the core elements of gamification". Koivisto and Hamari (2019, p. 206) conclude that "the link between gamification affordances and resulting psychological states is still unexplored" and that it is thus "unknown through which mechanisms gamification produces the psychological effects it aims to achieve"; and Ekici (2021, p. 3341) finds that "[m]ost of the studies in the review corpus [of gamified flipped learning research] have no explanation as to which game element is used for what purpose".

Empirical gamification studies usually test combinations of multiple elements (e.g., Sardi et al., 2017, p. 40; Majuri et al., 2018, p. 18[9]; discussed briefly above), and "examine [...] the effects of a gamification system as a whole" (Koivisto&Hamari, 2019, p. 201). As Koivisto and Hamari point out, "there is

[then] little possibility of identifying which of the affordances actually produced the effects" (ibid.), and to properly attribute effects to one specific, employed feature (Majuri et al., 2018, p. 18). Kalogiannakis et al. point out the one "cannot presume the effects of each gaming element alone since all studies [in their review] use [...] gaming elements in combinations" (2021, p. 25; see Dichev&Dicheva, 2017, p. 21, Hung, 2017, p. 59, Koivisto&Hamari, 2019, p. 207).

Majuri et al. (ibid.) find in their review that on average, four elements are used; only few studies "examine [...] the effects of one element at a time". In the meta-analysis by Koivisto and Hamari (2019, p. 207), "only 11 of the 66 controlled experimental studies examine [...] the effects of individual affordances". Xi and Hamari (2019, p. 211) observe that "granular research" into the effects of of certain elements on motivation "has been slow to emerge".

To contribute to the understanding of effects of particular elements and combinations of elements, it is thus regularly recommended to rigorously test elements in isolation. For instance, Ortiz-Rojas et al. recommend to use "specific individual gamification elements" in studies "to be able to determine explicit differential effects of these elements on learning performance" (2017, see Landers et al., 2018, p. 330, Dichev&Dicheva, 2017, p. 10). However, a gamified application with a single element is likely to be both boring and unrepresentative of games, and thus, unrepresentative of the phenomenon of gamification. Xi and Hamari (2019, p. 212) explain that experiments on the effects of singular elements are not relevant for applications in the real world because they "can lack external validity as gamification implementations are commonly more nuanced and complex assemblages of stimuli".

While it is regularly recommended to identify effects of a single element when used in gamification (see above), the effects of a combination of several elements can be different from the individual effects of the elements, as Nacke and Deterding (2017) emphasize. It is often unclear how elements interact with each other (see Sailer&Homner, 2020, p. 80). Nacke and Deterding (ibid.) posit that to be able to explain "gameful systems, which are complex combinations and interactions between elements", an understanding of "how each element functions individually" might be insufficient. Attention levelled at individual elements may hinder studies to "cast [...] a more holistic view on how gamification can more broadly affect a full range of intrinsic need satisfaction" (Xi&Hamari, 2019, p. 212; see Dichev&Dicheva, 2017, p. 26).

The identification of effects of particular elements or combinations of elements is further complicated by the impact of moderating factors. The effects of elements are not consistent between participants (Sardi et al., 2017, p. 41, Koivisto and Hamari, 2019, p. 199, da Silva et al., 2019, p. 6). Koivisto and Hamari explain the inconsistent relationship between particular game elements and effects on participants with the substantial influence of moderating factors; the effect being "highly dependent on the nature of the activity, the contextual factors related to it, as well as the specific situation where the system is being used – all in addition to the individual's own personal and demographic characteristics" (2019, p. 199; see ibid., p. 207 and below).

Unintended or Undesirable Side-Effects of Competition

Competition is a central mechanism of many gamification initiatives (Majuri et al., 2018, p. 11, Koivisto&Hamari, 2019, p. 198, Kalogiannakis et al., 2021, p. 22). Da Silva et al. (2019, p. 8) even take an orientation towards competition to be an integral part of the concept of educational gamification. But competition as a mechanism in gamification might be problematic, specifically in educational situations. Rozman and Donath (2019, p. 6) describe the "PBL (Points-Badges-Leaderboards) mechanism" as "a must in e-learning process", but note that it is "difficult to implement it to be effective" and that it "can be even counterproductive".

Kalogiannakis et al. point out that all of the top-four elements used in gamification aim to make gamification interventions more competitve (2021, p. 19; however problematic the element selection or identification might be, see ibid.). Koivisto and Hamari note that a "sense of competition among users" is promoted in gamification through the use of "leaderboards or other means of social comparison" (2019, p. 198; see ibid., p. 206; for a brief discussion on leaderboards see Bai et al., 2020, pp. 15–6). Leaderboards is one of the most popular elements and used often in gamification (Majuri et al., 2018, p. 13, Zainuddin et al., 2020, p. 8). While other popular elements such as points and badges also implicitly promote and enable competition, leaderboards do so explicitly.

While the naming of the top-three elements of gamification varies slightly (see above), they centre on a score or points as a measure of progress (Koivisto&Hamari, 2019, p. 198, Huang et al., 2020, p. 1894; see Albertazzi et al., 2019, p. 201). Sardi et al. (2017, p. 41) conclude that points are the "core component of gamification, particularly in progress visibility and leaderboards".

Negative Effects of Competition

Not all effects of gamification are desirable. Hamari et al. (2014) note that while "[a]ll of the studies in education/learning contexts considered the learning outcomes of gamification as mostly positive [...] at the same time, the studies pointed to negative outcomes which need to be paid attention to", such as increased competition. Hanus and Fox identify as "potential areas for concern' in education gamification "increased social comparison, competition, and reward systems [which] might have detrimental effects over the long term for students' motivation, satisfaction, enjoyment, and engagement with class material" (2015). Specifically, they identify "some common mechanics used in classroom gamification" such as "leaderboards, badges, and competition mechanics" that "may harm" intrinsic motivation, "satisfaction, and empowerment" and lead to "lower final exam scores" (ibid.).[10]

Schunk (2014) notes that competitive in-game performance can be a motivating goal for a player; watching competent players or read a highscore list provides models for self-efficacy. But competition can increase as well as decrease users' (extrinsic) motivations. The same "social features [...] designed to create a competitive environment" which positively and effectively encourage "self-improvement" (Sardi et al., 2017, p. 41), might also act as demotivating factors when "users may actually feel disheartened if they are not able to surpass their fellows or [when] they realize that they do not have in-app friends to connect with" (ibid.; see Bai et al., 2020, p. 16). Competition can have detrimental effects, such as detachment from the subject content and discouragement, for instance, in educational situations (Ekici, 2021, p. 3341; see Koivisto&Hamari, 2019, p. 205). Huang et al. (2020, p. 1894) emphasize that the results of their meta-analysis "minimally call into question the overuse of leaderboards in gamification solutions" because of the problematic effects competition may have on participants. Consequences of negative experiences of competition are not limited to the gamification intervention; disengaged participants might not only reduce their activity within the gamified system, for instance, in education or health, but also lose interest in the domain or subject matter.

While the potentially problematic effects of competition are widely acknowledged in the discourse (see above), there is an arguably surprising number of studies which appear to ignore this fact and to uncritically promote competition. For instance, after summarizing Tulloch's and Randell-Moon's (2018) gamification critique and despite mentioning several times that the creation of "competitive environment[s] is controversial" (Kalogiannakis et al., 2021, p. 25), Kalogiannakis et al. (ibid., p. 23) explain that according to their assessment, "the use of gaming elements such as levels, points, leaderboards, and competition environment, can not only promote students' extrinsic motivation but also positively affects students' behavior and increase their intrinsic motivation even in subjects and concepts that students have difficulty in understanding". Zainuddin et al. claim for educational gamification that "social comparison can explicitly promote social connectivity and a sense of relatedness amongst students" (2020, p. 12); they also note that "badges, points, leader-boards, levels, progress bars, virtual goods and trophies [...] foster [...] a strong social connectivity among students via competition and comparison of points including scores on the leader boards [sic]" (ibid., p. 14). They even report the results of a study that show that "badges did not successfully increase intrinsic motivation" (ibid., p. 13), and of "[o]ther studies [which] claimed that the use of points, badges, levels and leader boards [sic] failed to promote students" sense of community and did not significantly increase students' competence, their need for satisfaction and intrinsic motivation" (ibid.), and still declare that their "findings indicate that the use of game-based elements such as badges, points, trophies, leader boards [sic], avatars and virtual gifts not only promote students' extrinsic motivation but also increases their intrinsic value [sic] for learning" (ibid.). Positive effects of "competitiveness in a gamified [educational] setting" as reported by Kalogiannakis et al. (2021, p. 19) are "increase[d] motivation, incite[d] dedication in the learning process", and the creation of "an enjoyable learning environment"; in addition, it "positively affects students' behavior and helps them overcome negative attitudes towards competition"; it also "favors developing metacognitive abilities, empathy, and promoting teamwork". Sailer and Homner (2020) attempt to mitigate the problematic role of competition in gamification by introducing a distinction between desirable and undesirable competition; after admitting that competition has the potential to not only "enhance" but also to "undermine intrinsic motivation", Sailer and Homner (2020, p. 81; see ibid., p. 103) describe "two types of competition [that] can be distinguished", of which the (desirable) "*constructive* competition [...] encourages cooperation and mutual support". They report this type of "competition" to be conductive to learning within a gamified system (ibid., p. 101, p. 108).

Unsystematic Implementation Strategies

Gamification is a diverse practice. Sailer et al. (2017, p. 371) point out that the use of "many different game design elements [...] can result in very diverse applications". But even one single element can be realized in various ways (see Sailer&Homner, 2020, p. 106), also in combination with other elements (Dichev&Dicheva, 2017, p. 14, Hung, 2017, p. 59). The choice of notion and method or framework lead to diverse "specific designs and realizations of gamification environments" (Sailer et al., 2017, p. 371; see Landers et al., 2018, p. 328). One effect of the variety and diversity of approaches in gamification practice are difficulties to compare or relate them to each other; Nacke and Deterding (2017) note that "many studies are still to some extent comparing apples with oranges, testing different implementations of design elements with different effect measures"[11].

Figure 1. Example – Duolingo user home page interface with gamification elements (Cermak-Sassenrath, 2019)

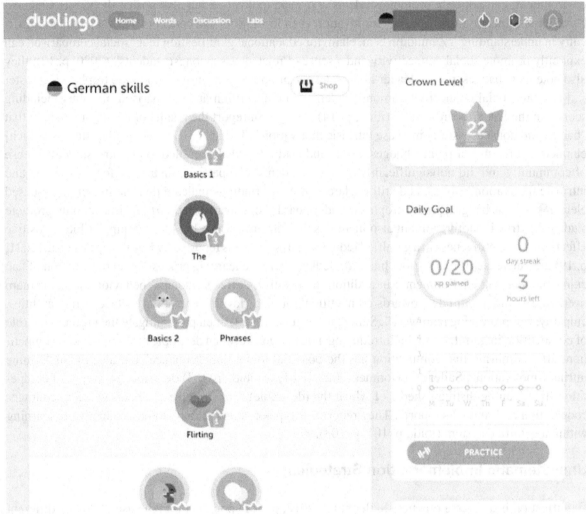

Gamification is applied in various contexts; for example, gamification initiatives include applications as different as *FourSquare*, *Stack Overflow*, *CAPTCHA*s and *Duolingo* (Richter et al., 2015; Figure 1), the *Khan Academy* and *Codecademy* (Hägglund, 2012), an in-house currency at Google, a carpooling game at SAP, the *Foldit* campaign for participants to playfully solve scientific problems, recycling initiatives by Recycle Bank, Opowerl and the Halton Borough Council, a response-time leaderboard at Engine Yard, and gamified annual reviews at Spotify and Living Social (Dale, 2014). Various international companies such as Amazon, Baidu, Expedia, Starbucks and Tencent have integrated "gamified elements into their marketing strategies" (Zhang et al., 2017 in Eisingerich et al., 2019, p. 200).

The aims of gamification also vary; for example, it may be used to facilitate engagement and motivation e.g. in educational gamification or health gamification, to sweeten or "to inject a little fun into mundane activities" (Sardi et al., 2017, p. 31) or into otherwise tedious or boring tasks (Seaborn&Fels, 2015, p. 27; Hanus&Fox, 2015, p. 152; Sardi et al., 2017, p. 31,32,41); "to promote participation, persistence and achievements" (Richter et al., 2015, p. 23); to change behaviour (Aparicio et al., 2012; Nicholson, 2012; Blohm&Leimeister, 2013; Sakamoto et al., 2012 in Seaborn&Fels, 2015; Rapp, 2017, p. 648; see below) which might include "increased participation, improved performance, or greater compliance" (Seaborn&Fels, 2015, p. 28; see Rapp, 2017, p. 670); to function "as an analytical strategy to capture and track data in a system" (Seaborn&Fels, 2015, p. 27); "to create engaging workplaces [...]; facilitate mass-collaboration [...] or encourage knowledge contribution" (Richter et al., 2015, p. 21); "to incentiv- ize repeat usage, increase contributions, and establish user reputations" (ibid.); and to "solve problems" (Kapp, 2012, p. 10 qtd. in Seaborn&Fels, 2015, p. 18).

The heterogenous and fragmented understandings of gamification have yet to lead to a shared and commonly accepted model or framework. For instance, with regard to the concrete selection of elements and their effects in gamification initiatives, Dichev and Dicheva note "the level of understanding of how to promote engagement and learning by incorporating game design elements to be questionable" (2017, p. 3), and emphasize that findings "[f]rom the 14 studies [...] with 14 different combinations of game elements and 15 different gamified activities" (ibid., pp. 20–1) make it "difficult to derive use- ful information on how to gamify a new (different) activity with predictable outcomes" (ibid.). They conclude that for educational gamification, "the process of integrating game design principles within varying educational experiences appears challenging and there are currently no practical guidelines for how to do so in a coherent and efficient manner" (ibid., p. 25), and that "the design of successful gamification applications in education that can sustain the intended behavior changes is still more of a guessing practice than science" (ibid., p. 2).[12]

Intrinsic Motivation and Extrinsic Rewards

In the discourse, the premise and *raison d'être* of gamification is widely accepted to be the facilitation of intrinsic motivation for a target audience (e.g., Hamari et al., 2014, Hanus&Fox, 2015, Dichev&Dicheva, 2017, p. 12, Rapp, 2017, p. 670, Albertazzi et al., 2019, p. 192, Kalogiannakis et al., 2021, p. 3; see Deterding, 2015); if this does not happen, gamification fails.[13,14]

Gamification Relies Essentially on Extrinsic Incentives

Gamification can thus be seen as an attempt to turn away from a reliance on traditional methods of extrinsic motivation such as "rewards or punishments" (Johnson et al., 2016, p. 5). But paradoxically, gamification uses these very methods, and appears to expect them to not function as extrinsic incentives. Gamification *centrally builds on* the use of extrinsic rewards, and such rewards are the functionally effective core of gamification. The use of (extrinsic) rewards is almost synonymous with gamification: "Rewards (e.g. points, achievement badges, and leaderboards) are perceived as a core gamification strategy" (Sardi et al., 2017, p. 32; see Johnson et al., 2016).

Kalogiannakis et al. (2021, p. 20) report that "points and leaderboards, two quite common game compo- nents in our research [on educational gamification] [...] have [...] been criticized for only providing extrinsic motivation", and point out that "[t]hese findings are in line" with previous research (Erdoğdu&Karatas, 2016), "who discovered that although their external students' [sic] motivation significantly increased, their intrinsic did not". Tobon et al. (2020, p. 10) assert that "the most frequent mechanisms [used in gamification] [are] rewards (points, badges, and feedback), challenges, interactivity, and meaningfulness", and specify that the influence gamification has "on online consumer decisions is explained, primarily, by the reward mechanism [...] whether it is symbolic or real". Tohidi and Jabbari posit that competition "in general" is a factor in extrinsic motivation, "because it encourages the performer to win and beat others, not to enjoy the intrinsic rewards of the activity" (2012; see Hanus&Fox, 2015). Dichev and Dicheva (2017, p. 11) note that gamification should not "simply [be] a stream of extrinsic motivators".

The Erosion of Intrinsic Motivation Through the Introduction of External Incentives

The paradoxical situation is, that gamification attempts to facilitate intrinsic motivation with extrinsic rewards. While one could plausibly assume that to introduce external incentives generally increases participants' motivations for an activity, this is not necessarily the case. It is a well-publized observation and widely-accepted fact that extrinsic incentives eventually erode intrinsic motivations (e.g. Deci et al., 2001, Ryan&Deci, 2020).[15] This is explained by the extrinsic incentives being experienced as controlling (instead of informational) by participants, leading to a "loss of intrinsic motivation" (Tsay et al., 2018, p. 2).

Concretely applied to a gamification context, Tobon et al.'s (2020, p. 10) literature review "[shows] that the Reward is the most studied gamification mechanism" and that "this strategy has proven to be effective in stimulating demand in the short term"; but they note that there are "many doubts about its effectiveness in the long term". With reference to Self-Determination Theory (SDT), they expect "extrinsic motivation (when people do something to obtain a reward)" to be "not effective in the long term because without a reward the behavior ceases". With reference to Deci el al. (2001), Ekici (2021, p. 3341) asserts that "reward, incentive and competition used in gamification activities are known to reduce intrinsic motivation". Mekler et al.'s study examines "how points, leaderboards, and levels, – three of the most commonly employed game elements [...], – affect need satisfaction, intrinsic motivation and performance" (2017, p. 526). They find that "in this particular study context, points, levels and leaderboards may have functioned as (effective) extrinsic incentives" (ibid., p. 532), leading neither to "more feelings of competence" nor to increased "intrinsic motivation compared to the plain condition" (ibid.). Tsay et al. (2018, p. 11) observe a "decline of student engagement" in their study "especially towards the end of the two-academic-term teaching period" that they explain with Deci et al.'s (2001) prediction that "that all forms of rewards (extrinsic motivation) eventually erode intrinsic motivation".

Dichev and Dicheva pose the question "[h]ow to balance points and rewards with play and intrinsic engagement?" (2017, p. 10) and assert that "the bulk of theoretical research addressing gamification" (ibid., p. 23) indicates that a focus "on points and rewards rather than on play and intrinsic engagement" (ibid.) in educational gamification "cannot always meet the goal of desired behavior change by catering to the intrinsic values of learners" (ibid.). Summarizing Mekler et al.'s (2015 [sic – apparently 2017]) study, Nacke and Deterding (2017) note that "game design elements do increase performance, but not through intrinsic motivation".

Can the Erosion of Intrinsic Motivations Through Extrinsic Incentives be Mitigated?

There are several possible lines of argument to explain how the erosion of intrinsic motivation through incentive-based gamification can be mitigated: SDT can be wrong about predicting the erosion of intrinsic motivation through the use of extrinsic incentives; or there exist possibilities to turn the extrinsic motivators into intrinsic and thus avoid the detrimental impacts of extrinsic incentives on intrinsic motivation. A third possibility is to create gamification that does not rely on the use of extrinsic rewards as motivational incentives.

Is SDT's claim that intrinsic motivation is regularly eroded through the use of extrinsic incentives disconfirmed by empirical research? Zeng and Shang (2018, p. 537) refer to a study by Filsecker and Hickey (2014) which "investigated the impact of external rewards on the motivation of primary school students playing educational games". Because the study found that "the addition of external rewards did not weaken students' motivation", Zeng and Shang conclude that "the negative impact of using external rewards can be solved in the new generation of learning environments with rich feedback". Kalogiannakis et al. (2021, p. 23) observe "some evidence which indicates that the combination of intrinsic motivation, like enjoyment, enthusiasm, and fun, in combination with external rewards, can affect [i.e. benefit] the acquisition of skills, competence, and improving [sic] the understanding of scientific concepts". Xi and Hamari explain that "beyond [...] optimistic expectations" (2019, p. 210) that gamification can "increase the ability of a system or a service to satisfy intrinsic needs" (ibid.) and thus trigger in an autotelic way (ibid.) "beneficial behaviors [...] there is a dearth of empirical evidence on how different gamification features satisfy different dimensions intrinsic needs" (ibid.). However, they find in their study that "gamification can have a substantially positive effect on intrinsic need satisfaction for services users" (ibid.)[16]. They then plainly state that their "study [...] alleviate [...] the concerns related to the possible negative effect on motivation stemming from the argumentation that gamification would provide extrinsic motivations which many believe to be detrimental for intrinsic motivation (although not much evidence for such doubt has been put forward in prior research [...])" (ibid., p. 217). They go on to assert that gamification does not only not hurt intrinsic motivation, but that it supports and facilitates its emergence; in their study they find "that gamification can have a substantially positive effect on intrinsic need satisfaction for services users, especially the achievement and social-related features", and gamification thus "can satisfy users' intrinsic needs" (ibid., p. 218).

Figure 2. Regulatory styles in human motivation (redrawn from Ryan&Deci, 2000a)

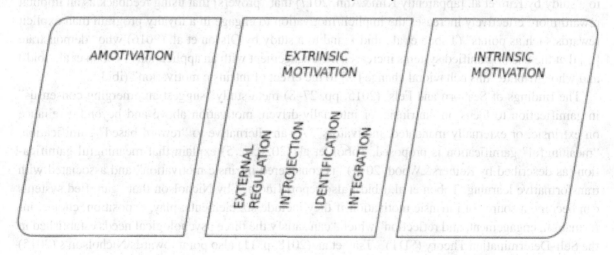

SDT proposes a continuum between amotivation and intrinsic motivation on which motivators are located (Figure 2); can rewards as used in gamification be made to appear to participants as intrinsic motivators? Several gamification studies aim to facilitate the emergence of intrinsic motivations through rewards. Nicholson (2012) subscribes to the idea for gamification "to buil[d] upon intrinsic, or internal, motivation rather than [on] extrinsic, or external, motivation" (Seaborn&Fels, 2015, p. 19). He "outlines a number of core theories that could inform a more intrinsic gamified strategy for meaningful engagement" (ibid.). The main idea appears to be to move the external motivators for the desired outcomes of the intervention along the "continuum of motivation intentionality mediated by internal and external methods of control" from "extrinsic motivation" towards "internally-controlled or autonomous intrinsic motivation" (ibid.).[17] Sakamoto et al. (2012) develop a similar "value-based gamification framework for designers aiming to encourage and harness intrinsic motivation" (Seaborn&Fels, 2015, p. 19). Zichermann (apparently Zichermann&Linder, 2010) propose "to craft extrinsic motivators – external controllers of behavior – such that they feel like or become internalized as intrinsic motivators" (Seaborn&Fels, 2015, p. 17).[18] A number of models are proposed of how to represent external motives "in concrete game elements" (ibid.) which then translate those into intrinsic motivations.

Another approach is to use specific, individualized implementations targeted at particular target audiences, rather than an "ideal gamified system – an optimal combination of game elements, mechanics, and dynamics that always works" (Seaborn&Fels, 2015, p. 28). Seaborn and Fels propose that the design of gamified systems would negotiate the "individual differences in *what* is intrinsically motivating" with "the objectives, requirements, and restrictions of the designer (or client)" (ibid.; see Deterding, 2015, p. 301). Such "gamified systems may need to be selectively designed given the individual makeup of the end-user population or even be designed flexibly and inclusively, allowing for personalization and customization, to accommodate individual users" (Seaborn&Fels, 2015, p. 28).

Tobon et al. claim that "Self-Determination Theory (SDT) and the Technology Acceptance Model (TAM) are the two most common theoretical explanations for *why gamification works*" (2020, p. 1, emph. added); they acknowledge that "[f]rom the point-of-view of Self-Determination Theory, [reward-based] gamification could be considered extrinsic motivation" (ibid., p. 5), but then assert that "these kinds of rewards can become a form of intrinsic motivation" (ibid.). They back up their assertion by reference to a study by Kim et al. [apparently Kim&Ahn, 2017] that "prove[s] that using feedback as an implicit reward more effectively increases the implicit motivation to engage in a loyalty program than explicit rewards such as points" (Tobon et al., ibid.), and to a study by Olsson et al. (2016) who "demonstrate [...] that the use of gamified systems increases the engagement with an application" (Tobon et al., ibid.) and who attribute "this behavioral change [...] to the effect of intrinsic motivation" (ibid.).

The findings of Seaborn and Fels' (2015, pp. 27–8) meta-study "suggest an emerging consensus" in gamification to focus on "intrinsic, or internally-driven, motivation above and beyond a reliance on extrinsic, or externally mandated, motivators". As an alternative to "reward-based" gamification, "meaningful" gamification is proposed. Tobon et al. (2020, p. 5) explain that meaningful gamification (as described by Reiners&Wood, 2015) "is considered intrinsic motivation" and associated with transformative learning. Tobon et al. (ibid.) also report findings by Nicholson that "gamified systems can become a source of intrinsic motivation if they include six elements: play, exposition, choice, information, engagement, and reflection" which "can satisfy the three psychological needs established in the Self-Determination Theory (SDT)". Tsay et al. (2018, p. 11) also point towards Nicholson's (2015) recipe for meaningful gamification.

Disconnect Between Theory and Practice

The discourse on gamification suffers from a disconnect between theory and practice. For educational gamification, Dichev and Dicheva (2017, p. 1) note that "the practice of gamifying learning has outpaced researchers' understanding of its mechanisms and methods".

Limited Understanding of Gamification (and Games)

The both limited and diverse understandings of gamification may reflect the limited and diverse understandings of games (Koivisto&Hamari, 2019, p. 204); to understand and design gamification, arguably, games need to be understood first. It appears, a rather mechanistic and simplistic view of play underlies many current gamification practices (see Nacke&Deterding, 2017); Koivisto and Hamari state that "if we consider the variety and degree of gamification, we can immediately notice" that a broad, universial and historical perspective of pre-digital games is "almost completely absent" (ibid., p. 205; see Dichev&Dicheva, 2017, p. 9).

A lack of theoretical underpinnings is observed in many studies of gamification (Seaborn&Fels, 2015, Koivisto&Hamari, 2019, p. 196, da Silva et al., 2019, pp. 13–4, Tobon et al., 2020, p. 10, Zainuddin et al., 2020, p. 13, Kalogiannakis et al., 2021, p. 14; see also below). Dichev and Dicheva emphasize that the provision of theoretical underpinnings could "help understand the researchers' motivation" and justify "their gamification approach[es]" (2017, pp. 22–3), but that "[w]ithout a theoretical framework backing the design of the studies and the interpretation of their results, it is problematic to select an appropriate gamification structure or to differentiate which of the employed game mechanisms and principles were essential for arriving at successful outcomes" (ibib., p. 25).

Two possible causes of this situation are that the gamification discourse is "dominated by industry publications and frameworks" (Nacke&Deterding, 2017; see Dichev&Dicheva, 2017, p. 25). Also, the uptake of academic insights is lagging; Nacke and Deterding (2017) comment that similar to "much human-computer interaction research [...] most research outcomes are not adopted by practitioners because they are unknown or impractical".

A Strong Focus on a Behaviourist Paradigm

Much of current gamification research is informed by a behaviourist understanding of human motivation. The behaviourist orientation may even become so dominant for it to be seen as an integral part of the idea of gamification (see Baptista&Oliveira, 2019, p. 311). There is wide agreement in the discourse with regard to the essential importance of behavioural changes as the central or main outcome of gamification, and it is openly communicated (e.g. by Dichev&Dicheva, 2017, p. 2; Landers et al., 2018, p. 331; Koivisto&Hamari, 2019, p. 191, p. 199; da Silva et al., 2019, p. 7; Bai et al., 2020, p. 2; Díaz-Ramírez, 2020, p. 1; Koivisto&Malik, 2020, p. 1; Tobon et al., 2020, p. 1; Kim&Castelli, 2021, p. 2). The success of gamification is to be measured by the behavioural effects it produces in users; Koivisto and Hamari (2019, p. 193) explain that "at their core [gamification systems] motivate and support the user toward a given activity or behavior [...] their usefulness is determined on the basis of whether they manage to do so". And successes are indeed reported; Khalil et al. (2018) claim that (educational) gamification has already demonstrated its ability "to achieve desirable outcomes by influencing user behaviors", and

Fadhli et al. (2020, p. 851) report that "the gamification method can [...] be empirically proven to make children conditioned".

Briffa et al. (2020, pp. 223–4) explain that "[g]amification builds on established game-based approaches and an understanding of the nature of humankind, founded on behavioural economics and psychology, to allow system designers to achieve objectives". The mechanism of gamification is to provide "external rewards for tasks and thereby manipulating the users to engage in a real world setting in order to earn rewards" (ibid., p. 224). Landers et al. state that "the goal of gamification scientists is to understand how to best influence human behavior, attitudes, and other states" (2018, p. 318), or simply, to create "interventions intended to influence human behavior" (ibid.; see ibid., p. 331)[19].

Figure 3. A basic model of a behaviourist understanding of gamification (simplified and redrawn from Denny et al., 2018, Figure 1 on p. 2)

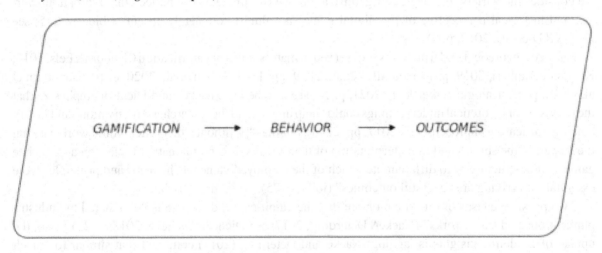

Simplistic and uni-directional understandings of gamification as, for instance, represented in Figures 3 and 4, are criticised by Koivisto and Hamari, who comment that such an "incomplete" (2019, p. 205) "understanding of gamification [...] is reflected in both the theoretical and empirical literature on gamification" (ibid., p. 206) which is understood "as a process within which the implemented elements linearly proceed to affecting psychological states and experiences, and eventually user behavior" (ibid.). They note (ibid., p. 205) that compared to "the main premise behind gamification [...] to affect motivations and behavior [...] significantly less attention has been paid to issues and aspects which precede the effects of gamification".

Figure 4. A model of a behaviourist understanding of gamification (by Huotari&Hamari, 2012; Hamari et al., 2014; Deterding, 2015, redrawn from Koivisto&Hamari, 2019, p. 193)

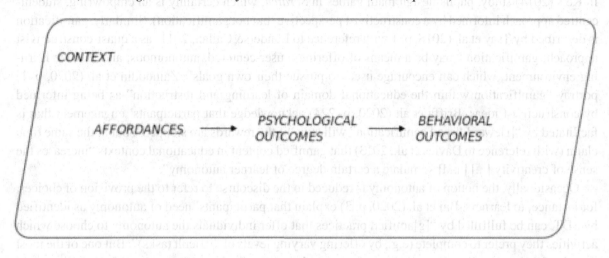

The strong position of the behaviouist paradigm in gamification is reflected in empirical studies. The results reported for gamification centre on behavioural effects, rather than on cognitive or motivational (see Mekler et al., 2017; compare Lieberoth, 2014). Given the focus of and interest in creating, maintaining and increasing intrinsic motivations, it might be surprising that what can be observed in many empirical studies so far is rote reinforcement learning (Johnson et al., 2016, Dichev&Dicheva, 2017, pp. 13–4, Table 7 on p. 15, Tobon et al., 2020, p. 11).

Because gamification is heavily based on such understandings of motivation, one would assume that classic conditioning theories are broadly represented in the gamification discourse and discussed in studies; meta-studies that report on theories used in gamification should pick this up. This appears to happen only rarely. For instance, Bai et al. (2020, p. 3) explain Skinner's operant conditioning theory, and claim that it was a theory "frequently applied in the gamification literature" (ibid., p. 2); and Fadhli et al. (2021, p. 846) reference Skinner (1974) to explain the reward mechanism in gamification. Conditioning theories are absent from Tobon et al.'s meta-study in the section on "Gamification theories" (2020, pp. 5–6; and from Table 3 on p. 5), and from Kalogiannakis et al.'s meta-study in the section "Theories Underpinning Gamification" (2021, pp. 3–4). Kim and Castelli (2021, p. 1) observe a "paucity of research about gamified learning instructional strategies".

Autonomy in Gamification

There exist an overt opposition between the rhetoric and the reality of gamification: While much of gamification clearly follows a behaviourist paradigm and is informed by classic conditioning theories (see above), some studies claim that gamification would increase participants' agency or autonomy. For instance, Zeng and Shang identify "educational games as the main cognitive tools for the learner-centered classroom" (2018, p. 533). They observe that the "[u]nderstanding of educational games has gone from a knowledge container to a knowledge construction tool", and that "students [...] interact with educational games, independently [of teachers] explore and discover", and that "as a result, [a] learner-centered classroom is achieved" (ibid., p. 539) that promotes "active learning and meaning construction" (ibid.,

p. 540). They do not explain how this is to be achieved, and only give a single example (ibid., p. 539): In Ke's (2014) study, pupils design math games in *Scratch*, which certainly is an empowring, student-centred approach informed by a constructivist perspective (but not gamification). Similarly, gamification is described by Tsay et al. (2018, p. 1 with reference to Landers&Callan, 2011) as a quasi-constructivist approach; gamification "may be a means of offering a user-centered, autonomous, and flexible learning environment, which can encourage users to pursue their own goals". Zainuddin et al. (2020, p. 1) portray "gamification within the educational domain of learning and instruction" as being informed by constructivist ideas. Briffa et al. (2020, p. 224) acknowledge that participants' engagement that is facilitated by "[r]eward-based gamification" will stop "if the rewards are stopped", but at the same time claim (with reference to Davies et al., 2013) that gamified content in educational contexts "increases the sense of creativity [...] [and] stimulate a certain degree of learner autonomy".

Occasionally, the notion of autonomy is reduced in the discourse to refer to the provision of choices, for instance, to learners. Bai et al. (2020, p. 3) explain that participants' need of autonomy as identified by SDT, can be fullfilled by "[g]amified practices that offer individuals the autonomy to choose which activities they prefer to complete (e.g., by offering varying levels of difficult tasks)". But one of the most meaningful choices players of a game make is, to play or not to play it. Just to be able to select one of different parts of a game to play is a choice which is not as substantial. The "mere inclusion of user choice in media does not automatically make engaging events" as Wilson (1993) points out; "the inclusion of choice structures does not automatically indicate a new respect for the user's autonomy, intelligence, or call out significant psychic participation'. He goes on to assert that "much interactive media" might be "a cynical manipulation of the user, who is seduced by a semblance of choice", in which the "[t]he missing choices might be more important than the 'choices' offered".

An interesting observation is made by Koivisto and Hamari (2019, p. 205) who note that the introduction of structure into an activity through gamification "may help users to reach set goals", but that it also may limit which paths of action are open to them, which can, in effect, diminish "creative action and thinking". Kalogiannakis et al. (2021, p. 23) observe in their systematic literature review that educational gamification "tries to reorganize learning around measurable rewards systems and competition" and offers but "little autonomy and flexibility". They take "[t]he dominant presence of competition and PBL [points, badges, leaderboards] game elements" to imply "a more goal orientated and reward/points accumulation approach consistent with the promotion of a neoliberal learning agenda" which "arguably shares common attributes with rote learning and memorization"[20].

A behaviourist orientation in gamification may reflect and reproduce behaviourist understandings of application domains, such as education. Dichev and Dicheva (2017, p. 10) observe an "overuse of points, badges and leaderboards" in educational gamification and speculate that "they somewhat parallel the traditional classroom assessment model". This speculation is confirmed by Koivisto and Hamari (2019, p. 200) who describe how the behaviourist orientation of gamification aligns well with "[c]ourse or assignment grades, and other forms of measuring academic performance" which explains the "popularity of education as the main domain for the study of gamification". A conditioning approach to education is shared by Fadhli et al. (2020, p. 846) who formulate that "children and pets are trained through rewards and punishments".

Motivation is Not Assessed

One effect of the common behaviourist approach in gamification studies is a focus on observable outcomes such as performances or results, not on (for instance, learners') motivations. Ekici (2021, p. 3342) finds that while "increased engagement and participation are two main promises of gamification [...] only a few studies in the corpus" of gamified flipped learning research focus on them. Johnson et al. (2016, p. 33) do not find "a single [...] study" in their review, which "capture[s] effects of game design elements on intrinsic motivation as a direct outcome"; they take this to indicate, "together with the fact that the majority of studies focused purely behavioral outcomes [...] that the dominant theoretical and practical logic of the studied health and wellbeing gamification interventions is positive reinforcement". They thus conclude that "the promise of intrinsically motivating health behavior by taking learnings from game design is currently neither explored nor tested". Similarly, Dichev and Dicheva find that motivation is often assessed only indirectly by way of performative measurements; papers in their meta-study "claiming to examine the motivational effects of gamification often report effects on learning outcomes instead" (2017, p. 12; see ibid., p. 21). Dichev and Dicheva report that "the educational benefits of gamification in terms of increasing student motivation or linking this motivation to learning outcomes are still not well understood" (ibid., p. 26) and that thus "the effect of gamification as a motivational tool" has so far not been confirmed by "persuasive evidence" (ibid., p. 12).

Evaluating Engagement, Motivation and Social Aspects

Other (meta-) studies observe that the extant empirical studies in (educational) gamification rarely test impacts on students' learning performance. For instance, Ortiz-Rojas et al. (2017) report that "the majority of available research rather focuses on the evaluation of motivation and engagement" than on "learning performance". Bai et al. (2020, p. 3) review five studies on educational gamification, but "[n] one of [these] reviews have examined the effects of gamification on learner academic performance".

One aspect that is not in the focus of gamification research for far, appears to be the social or collective dimension. Koivisto and Hamari observe that "a large portion of the existing research is aimed at supporting individualistic motivations [...] [with an] emphasis [...] still on individual development and progress". They recommend that "instead of focusing strongly on individual motivation and behaviors, gamification research" could investigate "how to induce and maintain collective and collaborative behaviors" (2019, p. 204, see ibid., p. 206). In Dichev's and Dicheva's (2017, p. 11) meta-study of empirical studies of educational gamification, only three out of 30 studies assess "social outcomes"; with the "majority of empirical works" examining "the impact of [...] gamification on students' engagement, performance, participation or retention" (ibid.). Majuri et al. note that "inducing any sort of social interaction has very rarely been the behavioral goal" of gamification. They take "[t]his finding [...] [to be] in line with the general trend of gamification implementations not being often designed to support collaborative action and cooperation" (2018, p. 14). This observation is supported by them finding only a single one of 128 "empirical research papers" which studied "Cooperation" as a "[b]ehavioral outcome" (ibid., p. 15).

Mixed, Partial and Inconclusive Results

Gamification research appears to continue to produce mixed, partial or inconclusive results (Hanus&Fox, 2015; Seaborn&Fels, 2015). Koivisto and Hamari (2019, p. 191) report that generally, results of studies "lean towards positive findings" with regard to "the effectiveness of gamification", but emphasize that "the amount of mixed results is remarkable". Kalogiannakis et al. (2021, p. 19) believe that the mixed results with regard to "learning outcomes" produced by educational gamification have created "controversy and [cast] doubts over its potential".

Johnson et al. (2016, p. 1) report 59% positive and "41% mixed effects"; of the 24 studies Hamari et al. (2014) review, two are fully positive and 13 are partly positive; Seaborn and Fels emphasize that the "[f]indings concerning the effectiveness of gamification [are] mostly positive (61%), but there [are] a fair amount (39%) of mixed results" (2015, p. 27). A meta-study of educational gamification by Ortiz-Rojas et al. (2017) reports "9 studies [which] show [...] a positive impact of gamification on learning performance, 12 studies [which find] no significant differences and 2 [which] show [...] negative effects". Huang et al. report both mixed results (2020, p. 1875, p. 1876) and positive results (ibid., p. 1893) of "[g]amification research in educational settings" (ibid., p. 1875): They observe that "the application of gamification in education is presently in disarray without conclusive evidence of the overall effects of gamification" (ibid., p. 1876); they then state that as "[t]he primary conclusion from the analyses conducted [...] gamification does appear to have a positive and significant effect on student learning outcomes in formal educational settings" (ibid., p. 1893).

The results of Koivisto's and Hamari's (2019, p. 201) analysis of "66 identified controlled experimental quantitative studies" show "mixed but mainly positive results [...] in nearly half (47.0%)", with only 28.7% of the papers reporting "positive research findings". Xi and Hamari (2019, p. 211) report that "in the business domain, 80% of current gamified applications [are] estimated to fail to meet their objectives due to poor design". Dichev and Dicheva find a large number of studies with inconclusive results in their analysis; and in the 15 studies out of 41 that "present conclusive evidences for the reported outcomes [...] the findings related to the benefits of [educational] gamification are mixed" (2017, p. 18; see ibid., p. 1). Da Silva et al.'s (2019, p. 3) meta-study confirms that studies with a "positive influence in education are still scarce". Mixed results of gamification studies are also reported by Denny et al. (2018), Tsay (2018, p. 3), Xi and Hamari (2019, p. 211), Díaz-Ramírez (2020, pp. 2–3), Zainuddin et al. (2020, p. 2) and Kalogiannakis et al. (2021, p. 21).

There are some specific aspects that participants like and/or dislike about gamification. Hung's (2017, p. 59) unsystematic review finds that "[i]n general [...] studies suggest a positive response to [educational] gamification from the students [...], with most improvements seen in attendance, participation, and motivation", but that "[o]ther studies show a more mixed response, with some students finding the gamification too complex or overly competitive". In a study by Bai et al. (2020, p. 12), results from 32 qualitative studies show "four main reasons why learners enjoy gamification: (a) gamification can foster enthusiasm; (b) gamification can provide feedback on performance [e.g. through scores and leaderboards (ibid., p. 13)]; (c) gamification can fulfill learners' needs for recognition [e.g. through the use of badges (ibid.)]; and (d) gamification can promote goal setting", and "two major reasons for learners" dislike of gamification: (a) gamification does not bring additional utility [i.e. a "concrete reward" (ibid.) such as grade improvement, "to convert badges into tangible marks that count toward actual course grades" (ibid., p. 15)] and (b) gamification can cause anxiety or jealousy ["usually" (ibid., p. 14) for students who do not do well on the gamification intervention (ibid.) and "who failed to get a top position on the [leader]board" (ibid.)]".

Other studies report (often moderate or weak) positive results. For instance, Koivisto's and Malik's (2020, p. 1) review of health gamification shows "[p]ositively oriented results [...] in 10 of 12 studies"; they add, however, that the "results are [...] mostly weak indications of positive effects". Yıldırım and

Şen (2019, p. 1) find that "gamification has a moderately positive [...] effect on student achievement" in their analysis of four studies on student achievement. In a meta-analysis of educational gamification by Sailer and Homner (2020, p. 100), "results indicate [...] significant, small positive effects of gamification on cognitive, motivational, and behavioral learning outcomes". Kim and Castelli (2021, p. 8) observe in their meta-analysis of educational gamification that "the gamification strategy has a moderate, positive effect on engagement behaviors and test scores".

Sailer's and Homner's (2020, p. 106) note that while "the positive effect of gamification on cognitive learning outcomes can be interpreted as stable, results on motivational and behavioral learning outcomes have been shown to be less stable"; in addition, they identify a "substantial amount of heterogeneity [...] in the subsamples [which] could not be accounted for by several moderating factors investigated in this analysis, leaving partly unresolved the question of which factors contribute to successful gamification". They conclude that although "gamification might in fact be effective when it comes to learning [...] the question of which factors contribute most to successful gamification remains partly unresolved, at least for cognitive learning outcomes" (ibid., p. 108).

Unqualified or significant positive effects of gamification are reported as well. Rozman and Donath (2019, p. 16) note that "[a]lmost all [19 analysed] studies show [...] that gamification design/game elements positively affect mentioned factors [of *motivation, (learning) performance, attitude, engagement and social interactions*]". Similarly, "[t]wenty-nine [...] of the 36 papers" in Tobon et al.'s (2020, p. 1) review find "empirical evidence that the inclusion of game elements in non-game activities has a significant [positive (ibid., p. 6)] influence on consumer engagement and online consumer decisions in digital contexts". That the "gamification method is statistically effective in improving students' knowledge, skills, and children's attitudes" is found by Fadhli et al. (2020, p. 845) in their systematic meta-analysis of six studies on educational gamification for children.

Hung (2017, p. 59) lists numerous aspects that can make the interpretation of (positive) results of gamification challenging; for instance, the diversity of specific gamification implementations (see ibid., p. 58), the varying depths of integration with the target domain, the absence of long-term results, and the limitation of most experiences to a small set of (educational) disciplines. Similarly, Dichev and Dicheva note that due to the "relatively small number of (15) papers" in their review of 41 studies that report conclusive albeit mixed results of educational gamification, "and a diverse specter of game elements and activities, the presented outcomes are insufficient to draw definitive conclusions on the effectiveness of gamification on students' engagement, learning or participation" (2017, pp. 18–9; see Kalogiannakis et al., 2021, p. 2).

Even when they find (some) positive effects of various strengths, studies usually recommend to act cautiously when introducing gamification initiatives, for instance, in educational contexts. Briffa et al.'s (2020, p. 140) meta-analysis finds an almost dramatic positive effect of gamification; "students' performance can improve by 50%" (although with "a big amount of variance in the students' results possibly due to sampling errors or confounding covariates"), but they recommend to employ "gamification [...] with caution", and to carefully align gamification mechanics with educational content, to assess contextual factors, and to consider how to embed gamification initiatives within teaching. Kalogiannakis et al. (2021, p. 25) report that "gamification improves the teaching of science education and boosts student motivation, engagement, and learning outcomes", but they also point out that "several issues [...] need to be carefully considered in future studies", such as the lack of longitudinal studies of educational gamification (see below).

The File-Drawer Effect

An issue for gamification research is *publication bias*, also called the *file-drawer effect*. It refers to the phenomenon in academic writing that mostly "favorable results" are published (Bai et al., 2020, p. 8), and negative (or null) results are not (Seaborn&Fels, 2015; Huang et al., 2020, p. 1895). It is an "identified phenomenon related to publication practices on a general level, and thus affects all research" (Koivisto&Malik, 2020, p. 10), not only gamification.

Seaborn and Fels (2015) posit that the file-drawer effect may explain the high number of reports of positive results of gamification (see above). Koivisto and Malik believe "it [...] close to impossible to state" whether publication bias has "affected the reviewed body of literature" and advise that "the possibility of it affecting the findings should be taken into account when evaluating the results of the review" (2020, p. 10; see Koivisto&Hamari, 2019, p. 201).

Other studies offer support for the assumption that the phenomenon does not exist or does not significantly impact the reporting. For instance, using a variety of tests, Yıldırım and Şen show that "publication bias was not found to be a critical issue for [their] [...] study" (2019, p. 10; similarly, Bai et al., 2020, p. 10, Fadhli et al., 2020, p. 850, Huang et al., 2020, p. 1892, Kim&Castelli, 2021, p. 8).

Alignment of Educational Gamification with Academic Performance

An essential question for gamification is how much its results align with intended, real-world outcomes. Studies report indications that support the assumption that gamification does align, and indications that support the assumption that it does not. Bai et al. (2020, p. 2) note that "there is little consensus about whether [educational gamification] contributes to improved academic performance"; they emphasize that "[p]revious studies have reported mixed findings, with some reporting positive effects with varying effect sizes [...], and others reporting no effects [...] or adverse effects on students' exam scores".

For their meta-study of educational gamification, Tsay et al. (2018, p. 9) identify an alignment between "[b]ehavioral engagement and course performance". Bai et al. (2020, p. 14) find an "overall significant positive effect" of medium strength of educational gamification on academic performance, which suggests "that gamification can increase student learning performance". In some initiatives, an assumed alignment of gamification with, for instance, educational performance, has prompted educators to attempt to exchange one for the other. Bai et al. (2020, p. 15) report that in one educational gamification experiment, students' study grades were "determined [...] by the amount of gamification points the students had earned". Bai at al. (ibid.) then speculate that "gamification points earned in a course may also be exchanged for other types of tangible rewards"; they list "access to more useful course information (e.g., exam tips)" and the promotion of students to forum moderators[21].

Other studies' results disconfirm the proposition of a tight alignment of gamification results with, for instance, learners' academic performance. A study by Kalogiannakis et al. (2021, p. 1) finds that "the implementation of gamification has been generally considered successful around user engagement" but indicates that "results vary [...] among individuals" with regard to "impact on learning outcomes". Similarly, Hung (2017, pp. 61-2) notes that the performance of learners in a gamified educational application often does not align with their grades (ibid., p. 59). He also observes that while "learning analytics can give instructors some insights into their courses, such as seeing what resources are accessed most often or which discussion forums are most active", the data does not show "how resources are used or how much thought went into a discussion post", and warns that "[b]asing gamification around superficial measures [...] runs the risk of reifying learning profiles that do not correspond to actual learning" (ibid., p. 61).

One reason why gamification may appear to be uneffective is the missing transfer from the gamified activity to the target activity. While gamification might be effective in promoting certain behaviours, the exhibition of these behaviours might be inconsequential with regard to the intended outcomes. Sailer and Homner point out that, for educational gamification, "[t]he aim [...] is to directly affect behaviors and attitudes relevant to learning" (2020, p. 78); but they also note that the "behavioral learning outcomes [...] were almost exclusively measured during the interventions". They speculate that the "behavior and performance in the immediate situation [...] do [...] not necessarily transfer to situations outside the gamified context" (ibid., p. 107). Similarly, Kim and Castelli (2021, pp. 9–10) observe direct behavioural outcomes of gamification interventions, but no effect beyond the gamified activity. Kalogiannakis et al. (2021, p. 20) emphasize that the impact of educational gamification might be limited to "short-term and immediate effects".

Non-Uniform User Behaviours

Play is praised for its universal appeal which can readily be observed across all contexts, cultures and times; Yıldırım and Şen observe that "people of all ages play games" (2019, p. 1, see Koivisto&Malik, 2020, p. 2); Koivisto and Hamari (2019, p. 191) assert that "[g]ames are especially known for their ability to engage and excite". Dichev and Dicheva (2017, p. 12) even formulate their believe that because "video games are explicitly designed for entertainment, they can produce states of desirable experience and motivate users to remain engaged in an activity with unparalleled intensity and duration". The observations on games' universal attraction and appeal are similarly made about gamification; dela Cruz and Palaoag (2019, p. 264) comment that gamification can be attractive for everybody. Fadhli et al. (2020, p. 851) write that "[t]he gamification method can [...] be used in all forms of topography and demographic forms".

However, experiences of gamification initiatives appear to vary widely between participants; regularly, studies report non-uniform or even erratic user behaviours, and significant variances across application contexts (Hamari et al., 2014; see above). While "in all of the studies", users of gamified applications experienced "engagement and enjoyment", the "same aspects were most often disliked by some respondents in the study" (ibid.). A study by Denny (2013) of "an online multiple-choice question (MCQ)-based learning system" reports that "the number of questions authored [by students] or [the] perceived quality of the learning environment" were uneffected by badges; and that an "interest in viewing, if not collecting, badges was not uniform across students, suggesting that students were motivated for different reasons". Seaborn and Fels (2015, p. 28) find that "similar implementations of gamification in different domains did not necessary impact participants in the same way". Majuri et al. (2018, p. 16) note that the results of qualitative evaluation methods in educational gamification studies are often indicative of "very varying [participant] experiences and outcomes even when the general tendency of the findings would be positively oriented"; usually, "qualitative results contain a mention of e.g. some users benefitting from and being motivated by the gamification while others do not".

A Limited Selection of Popular Audiences

So far, gamification studies have often focused on a few select audiences. Various studies find that certain groups of participants are over- or underrepresented (Dichev&Dicheva, 2017, p. 26; Koivisto&Malik, 2020, p. 2; Tobon et al., 2020, p. 10; Kalogiannakis et al., 2021, p. 5).

Popular audiences picked for gamification interventions appear to be often young adults (Koivisto&Malik, 2020, p. 8). For educational gamification, Higher and Secondary Education are more common application scenarios than Primary Education (Kalogiannakis et al., 2021, p. 21); in one systematic review of educational gamification, Kalogiannakis et al. (ibid., p. 13) report that ten of the 24 included studies involve "students from higher education" and nine from "secondary", and that only five studies focus "on primary education". Dichev and Dicheva (2017, p. 6) find that "the bulk of [educational] gamification studies in the survey period were conducted at university level (44 papers), with less attention to K-12 education (7 papers)". Bai et al. (2020, p. 9) observe in their meta-analysis a fair number of studies which involve school students; they find "[n]ine of the interventions" to be at elementary school level, five "at the high school level", one to involve "a mixture of high school, undergraduate, and postgraduate students", ten to be "carried out with undergraduate students", and three to be "conducted with postgraduate students". However, Fadhli et al. (2020, p. 85) report that for educational gamification, "children of six to ten years of age" are "still very rarely" the target of the "gamification method". Kalogiannakis et al. (2021, p. 6) comment that "it remains unclear whether the lack of studies in primary and secondary education is associated with the education levels, other target group characteristics, such as demographics [...], or to the content area gamification is mostly used, i.e., computer and information courses, which is most usually associated with higher education".

Certain audiences are rarely involved in gamification initiatives. For instance, Koivisto and Malik (2020, p. 2) identify older adults as "[o]ne of the demographic groups that has been given limited attention within the gamification research domain"[22].

A Limited Set of Domains for Gamification

A lot of gamification research and practice was and still is "highly concentrated" (Koivisto&Hamari, 2019, p. 205) on a relatively selective set of domains. In their "review of applied gamification research", Seaborn and Fels (2015, p. 28) observe "a wide range of interest but a largely limited playing field". The most popular domains for gamification are (in this order) "education, health and crowdsourcing" (Koivisto&Hamari, 2019, p. 191; see Albertazzi et al., 2019, p. 197). Other popular domains are sustainability, social behavior and networking, online communities, software development, work/workplace, innovation/ideation, consulting, and marketing/customer loyalty (Hamari et al., 2014, p. 3029; Raczkowski, 2014; Hanus&Fox, 2015, p. 152; Richter et al., 2015, p. 21,36; Seaborn&Fels, 2015, p. 27; Sailer et al., 2017, p. 371; Koivisto&Hamari, 2019, p. 204; Tobon et al., 2020, p. 1). Similar lists of gamification domains are variously reported in the literature (for instance, in Koivisto&Hamari, 2019, p. 192, p. 206; Baptista&Oliveira, 2019, p. 306; da Silva et al., 2019, p. 6).

Educational gamification is often done in but a limited area of academic disciplines or subject areas (see Kalogiannakis et al., 2021, p. 5); the focus is clearly on technical disciplines. Ortiz-Rojas et al. note that "[t]he STEM (Science, Technology, Engineering and Mathematics) domains account for 19 out of 23 studies" in their systematic literature review; within these disciplines, "most studies are related to Computer Science Engineering (11), followed by Technology (4), Mathematics (4) and Sciences (1)"

(2017; see Dichev&Dicheva, 2017, p. 7, Díaz-Ramírez, 2020, p. 2, Huang et al., 2020, p. 1890, Kalo-giannakis et al., 2021, p. 2). Dichev and Dicheva (2017, p. 7) note that "[i]n sharp contrast" to the large number of gamification interventions in computer science and IT education, "gamification experiments targeting activities related to disciplines from humanity and social sciences are extremely limited"; in their review of 51 educational gamification studies, they only identify a single such study.

Nacke and Deterding (2017) comment that the application context of gamification is a "vital aspect of gamification design". They assert that "many scholars have cautioned that not all activities and contexts lend themselves equally to being gamified [...] and systematically studying the moderating effects of different individual and situational contexts is thus very much in need". Koivisto and Hamari (2019, p. 205) believe that "the narrow scope of domains sheds a shadow on the entire field of gamification research", and point out that a "[h]eavy emphasis only in a few domains affords an unbalanced view of how gamification works" because of varying "contextual factors [that] affect the outcomes of the gami-fication in the different domains"; they warn that "applying results from one field to another might not provide similar results". Dichev and Dicheva (2017, p. 19) also emphasize that gamification "success in one educational context does not guarantee that the same mechanism will be motivationally successful in another educational context". Kalogiannakis et al. (2021, p. 22) speculate that "[educational] gamifica-tion seems to have restrictions regarding [its] content it [...] should not be regarded as a universal tool for all content in the curriculum".

Moderating Factors

Some of the mixed results of gamification are explained by being caused by different personalities of various audiences or other moderating factors (e.g. Seaborn&Fels, 2015). Sardi et al. (2017, p. 38) note that "incorporating game mechanics is unlikely to be equally suited to people of all ages". Denny et al. (2018) identify different effects of a gamification intervention on the top-performing quartile of students and on the rest of students. With reference to Bartle's well-known model of player types (1996), Al-bertazzi et al. (2019, p. 192) warn that a single, uniform gamification approach "might not be effective for everyone". Hamari et al. offer as an explanation of the variances between users that "people in fact interact with game-like systems in different manners, and for different reasons" (2014), and with differ-ent experiential results (ibid.). Koivisto and Hamari assert that "engaging large groups of people with varying characteristics and backgrounds [...] is [...] a challenging task" (2019, p. 205, see ibid., p. 204). Studies indicate that moderating factors or variables might play a significant role in gamification, and various such factors are proposed; Tsay et al. (2018, p. 2) offer as examples of "contextual factors [...] the design of the gamified system, player qualities, and the match between the motivational affordances embedded in the system and users' overall goals, interests, and needs" (2018, p. 2) as well as "personal-ity [...], gamer type [...], and attitudes toward game-based learning and experience with games" (ibid., p. 13; see da Silva et al., 2019, p. 7; Landers et al., 2018, p. 324, p. 326). Not many studies focus on moderating variables yet (Koivisto&Hamari, 2019, p. 205, Bai et al., 2020, p. 16).

It appears as if the currently narrow focus in gamification on particular demographics (see above) limits its understanding. Tsay et al. emphasize that "background factors that students bring to a gamified course [...] influence their perception of [it] and [their] participation [in it]" (2018, p. 3). They identify a "lack of systematic examinations of 'what' user background variables to include and 'how' they influence a gamified system" (ibid., p. 4; see Koivisto&Hamari, 2019, p. 206). Tsay et al. add that such disregard can render a system "inappropriate for the players it was designed to support" (2018, p. 2). Sardi et al.

(2017, p. 41) similarly note that most gamification implementations "disregard the demographic characteristics of the targeted users to a significant extent". Majuri et al. advise that "future research should pay more attention to the contextual factors" (2018, p. 17) such as "different learning styles in addition to [users'] personality and demographic characteristics" (ibid., p. 18) in "gamification solutions as well as in study designs" (ibid.).

Dichev and Dicheva (2017, p. 12) note that "motivation is not a unitary phenomenon – different people may have different types and amounts of motivation". With reference to Barata et al. (2014), Hung (2017, p. 59) speculates "that different types of students may be drawn to gamification in different ways, with 'achievers' being the most proactive and engaged, 'disheartened' being those who start strong and lose interest along the way, and 'underachievers' showing low levels of participation, least engagement, and poorer performance". Zichermann (2011) judges the appeal to "specific intrinsic motivators" (Seaborn&Fels, 2015, p. 17) in gamification as too unreliable, "given [the] individual variability in what is intrinsically motivating" (ibid.). Linderoth (2014) similarly observes that "there is no one-size-fits-all relationship between game design and intrinsic interest and enjoyment". Tsay et al. (2018, p. 13) assert that "a gamified course may not be equally effective for all students" and present, qualified as anecdotal evidence, the observation that "mature students did not perceive the usefulness of a gamified course and therefore did not spend much time with the online learning activities".

Moderating factors of gamification do not function in isolation; Nacke and Deterding comment that while "extremely little" is known "about the actual effect of 'player types', and [...] individual differences beyond them", even less is known about "the relative impact of person versus situation on the effects of gamification, let alone potential interaction effects of the two" (2017; see Landers et al., 2018, p. 326, Koivisto&Malik, 2020, p. 2).

Methodological Limitations

The methodological quality of gamifiction studies is regularly questioned. While Bai et al. (2020, p. 14) report that "the quality of the quantitative gamification research studies reviewed in [their] meta-analysis is generally comparable with those published in other disciplines", many other studies point to methodological limitations (e.g., Hanus&Fox, 2015). For instance, "gamification research" is diagnosed to "suffer [...] from a lack of methodological rigor" (Sailer&Homner, 2020, p. 106, see Dichev&Dicheva, 2017, p. 21); studies may provide "mostly moderate or lower quality of evidence" (Johnson et al., 2016) or report "results [...] backed by inconclusive and insufficient evidence" (Dichev&Dicheva, 2017, p. 25); and "measurement instruments" may lack consistency (Koivisto&Hamari, 2019, p. 200).

Methodological limits are occasionally hard to mitigate; Kim and Castelli (2021, p. 10) observe that not all academically desirable evaluation methods can easily be implemented, for instance, "randomized sampling in an educational setting".

A Low Number of Empirical Studies

Various studies point out that the number of empirical studies is low (e.g., Hamari et al., 2014, Lieberoth, 2014, Hanus&Fox, 2015, Richter et al., 2015, Seaborn&Fels, 2015, Johnson et al., 2016, Sardi et al., 2017, p. 31,42, Khalil et al., 2018). Certainly, the number of empirical studies has risen in recent years; Baptista and Oliveira (2019, p. 309) even observe a "burgeoning number of studies, conferences, and books released in recent years", and Kim and Castelli (2021, p. 3) see an exponential increase between

2010 and 2019. However, Sailer and Homner (2020, p. 101) still note that "the number of primary studies eligible for [their] meta-analysis [on educational gamification] [is] rather small".

Small Sample Sizes

One critizism that is often articulated concerns the (small) sample sizes of empirical, quantitative gamification studies (e.g. Dichev&Dicheva, 2017, Table 12 on p. 22, Koivisto&Malik, 2020, p. 10, Koivisto&Hamari, 2019, p. 207). Marín et al.'s study is one of the few studies with a large number of participants; it is conducted in a "programming course" which is "compulsory for first-year engineering students" and employed a sample of over 800 students (over two academic terms; 2018, p. 4:3), half of which "used the gamified platform" and half of which "used the non-gamified platform" (ibid., p. 4:10). Another study with a large sample is conducted by Denny et al. They use a "large first-year anatomy and physiology course" (2018, p. 1) with 2101 enrolled participants (ibid., p. 4); the students "were randomly assigned to one of four groups: 'control', 'points', 'badges' or 'both'" (ibid.). The use of the gamified system "was completely optional, and no course credit was associated with participation", and "701 students [...] logged in [...] and successfully answered at least one question" (ibid., p. 5).

Durations of Interventions

A very apparent issue of gamification research are missing longitudinal studies (see, e.g. Sardi et al., 2017, p. 42). Short study durations "pose an evident threat to the validity of study findings" and increase "the risk of findings being skewed by the novelty of the implementation" (Koivisto&Hamari, 2019, p. 207).

The lack of longitudinal studies is particularly problematic for gamification because motivational theories such as SDT predict that extrinsic incentives do not last (see above). Wu explains that "when the external incentives can no longer keep pace with the users' expectation, they will lose all their motivation to perform the gamified behavior" (2011; see Hung, 2017, p. 62).[23] Without such studies, it is also unknown "whether the positive student responses [to gamification initiatives] also translate to other improvements and/or lead to long-term benefits" (Hung, 2017, p. 59; see above). Sardi et al. (2017) also acknowledge the hope of positive effects through the use of gamified systems in the domain of health, but they also point out that "most of the e-Health applications and serious games investigated have been proven to yield solely short-term engagement through extrinsic rewards".

Seaborn and Fels (2015, p. 28) speculate that "early positive results [of gamification interventions] may be subject to the phenomenon of regression to the mean due to the novelty factor associated with gamified systems". They assert a "lack of comparative and longitudinal study designs, despite the literature suggesting that gamification effects, especially if they rely on extrinsic motivation, may be temporary or even damaging over time". Koivisto's and Hamari's (2014) study "show[s] that the appeal of a gamified system might be due to a novelty effect, and that positive effects such as engagement and interest decrease over time" (Hanus&Fox, 2015, p. 153). Results from the meta-study by Bai et al. "indicate that shorter gamified interventions have greater average effect sizes than longer interventions" (2020, p. 15; see Kim&Castelli, 2021, p. 1). They speculate (ibid.) that this result might be a product of the "novelty effect" (Hamari et al., 2014; Lieberoth, 2014; see Sardi et al., 2017, p. 38), and believe it plausible (Bai et al. ibid.) that "in short-term interventions, learners are excited by the use of gamification, which leads to high participation in the course activities and better learning outcomes in the short term" (ibid.); but once the excitement is over, engagement diminishes[24]. Hamari et al. (2014, p. 3028) note that "[t]he main results" from a study on intra-organizational systems by Farzan et al. (2008) "indicate that gamification has a positive effect on some users for a short time". Hung (2017, p. 62) reports that according to Nicholson (2015), "reward-based gamification, such as using badges and points to reward good behavior" may only exhibit "limited, short-term effectiveness at best".

So far, relatively short study durations of 16 weeks or less are common in empirical gamification research (Ortiz-Rojas et al., 2017, Bai et al., 2020, p. 9, Zainuddin et al., 2020, p. 6,13, Ekici, 2021, p. 3341). There are few gamification studies conducted with relatively long durations. Sardi et al. describe a time duration of six months for health gamification research studies as a "long period" (2017, p. 37); they report that "the [two] longest evaluations of gamified [health] applications reported in the selected papers lasted 6 months" (ibid.). A study on educational gamification by Barata et al. (2017) is repeatedly mentioned in the literature (e.g. by Zainuddin et al., 2020, p. 13) as an example of a study with a long time frame. Another study referenced (by Tsay et al., 2018, p. 12) is a "2-year longitudinal study by Hamari (2015)". Koivisto and Hamari (2019, p. 196) mention unidentified "multi-year experiments" in educational gamification.

Long-term studies are urgently needed to assess long-term effects of gamification (Bai et al., 2020, p. 16, Briffa et al., 2020, p. 238, Zainuddin et al., 2020, p. 13). Such experiments are particularly in demand because there exist a lack of findings as well as a diversity of expectations about long-term effects of gamification. Critics of gamification might wonder how a long-term engagement can be facilitated through, for instance, educational gamification, if the learners are factually uninterested in the subject matter; to care about something might be the primary way to become deeply engaged in it. Temporary initiatives might affect changes through persuasion or distraction, but it might appear questionable how and if learners can be engaged and stay engaged long-term. For the educational domain Dichev and Dicheva (2017, p. 1) assert that "insufficient evidence exists to support the long-term benefits of gamification". Sardi et al. (2017, p. 41) warn that "the noticeable short-term effect [of gamification] on users' motivation and engagement is unlikely to be sustained, as the users' interest and enthusiasm in the game-like features seems [sic] to decrease in the long run".

However, Tsay et al. (2018, p. 2) formulate Nicholson's (2012) expectation that gamification "could potentially result in a long-term and deeper engagement among learners", and Sardi et al. (2017, p. 32) claim that "[g]amification [...] promises a dual improvement consisting of making the activities more pleasant while ensuring people's long-term engagement with tasks perceived to be demotivating". Based on their meta-analysis that reviewed studies with durations of up to six months, Sailer and Homner (2020, p. 104) report that "for cognitive and behavioral learning outcomes [...] gamification can be effective in both the short and long term", and claim that their findings "can weaken the fear that effects of gamification might not persist in the long run and might thus contradict the interpretations presented in reviews".

A Predominance of Quantitative Methods

A large portion of gamification research relies on quantitative measures. Meta-studies variously report quantitative measures or mixed methods to be used most often in gamification research (e.g. Majuri et al., 2018, p. 11,16, Khalil et al., 2018, Table 1, Koivisto&Hamari, 2019, p. 197, Tobon et al., 2020, p. 11, Zainuddin et al., 2020, p. 5, Kalogiannakis et al., 2021, p. 11).

CONCLUSION

This chapter set out to identify, to briefly present and to discuss challenges of gamification. By collating observations from multiple empirical studies and meta-studies, it identified unclear definitions, a limitation on small sets of elements employed with unclear effects, unintendented side-effects of competition, a confusing variety of operalizations, the issue of the erosion of intrinsic motivation through extrinsic incentives, a disconnect between theoretical understandings and practical realizations, a strong focus on a behaviourist paradigm, studies' mixed, partial and inconclusive results, a lack of attention at moderating factors, as well as methodological limitations such as a lack of longitudinal studies.

Although no weighing or ranking was attempted in this chapter, several key issues appear to significantly handicap gamification: One such issue is the opposition between external rewards which essentially make up the core of gamification and their potentially detrimental impact on participants' intrinsic motivation, specifically when gamification is used beyond infrequent, short-term interventions.

Another issue is the behaviourist paradigm which is domimant in much of the gamification discourse as represented in empirical studies. It is tempting to draw a line from this limiting perspective, to the use of a specific set of competitive elements such as scores, badges and leaderboards taken to be characteristic of games, to quantitative evaluation measures.

A third issue is the fragmentary conceptual understanding that pervades much of gamification practice. This review finds that the understanding is limited not only with regard to the operalization of gamification, that is, how to gamify a certain discipline, content, curriculum or domain; but also with regard to conceptual aspects, that is, why does it (not) work? The use of theory appears often sketchy, and sometimes dubious, for example, in cases when SDT is used to explain "why gamification works", and when a small number of empirical studies is employed to declare that problems identified by theory simply do not exist.

So far, the "assumptions underlying the usefulness of gamification in educational context[s]", that it can be "motivating, [...] [and] engaging, [...] [and] improve attendance and participation" (Dichev&Dicheva, 2017, p. 26), have not been "confirmed by the results of the reviewed empirical studies" (ibid., p. 18), and gamification has yet to deliver on the expectations levelled at it. While a "potential to create enhanced learning environments" is apparent, there exists "insufficient evidence that it [...] produces reliable, valid and long-lasting educational outcomes, or [...] does so better than traditional educational models" (ibid., p. 21). For a conclusive verdict, "more empirical studies are necessary to actually demonstrate the effectiveness of such approach" (da Silva et al., 2019, p. 3).

Until then, it is recommended that implementations of gamification which are quasi-mandatory, for instance, for learners or patients to use, should be attempted with great caution. In a large-scale study by Denny et al. (2018, p. 5), just over one-third of students of a course use a "completely optional" gamified system. Koivisto and Hamari (2019, p. 205) acknowledge that "gamification might have positive effects on the users who choose to adopt it" but ask "what will be the effect on the bulk of users who will not adopt the gamification features?" Similarly, Dichev and Dicheva point out an underresearched area of the conditions when *not* to employ educational gamification (2017, p. 21) to "avoid gamification scenarios that can harm learning" (ibid., p. 26).

Not addressed in this study was the question if the challenges pointed out are indicative of shortcomings or faults of the implementations of gamification in particular ways or projects or of conceptual incoherencies or inadequacies. If a conceptual incompatibility between play and purpose exists (see, for instance, Raczkowski, 2014), the identified challenges might be symptoms rather than causes of the mixed results and the sceptical reception of gamification in parts of academia.

The gamut of gamification appears clearly limited by the current conceptual and practical approaches. If gamification is to sustainably progress and mature, the issues identified need to be addressed and resolved or mitigated. After approximately ten years of practical application and 20 years of academic research it cannot be long before gamification conclusively validates itself as a concept and establishes practical applications where it excels, or is abandoned.

REFERENCES

Albertazzi, D., Ferreira, M. G. G., & Forcelli, F. A. (2019). A Wide View on Gamification. *Technology. Knowledge and Learning*, *24*(2), 191–202. doi:10.100710758-018-9374-z

Aparicio, A. F., Vela, F. L. G., Sánchez, J. L. G., & Montes, J. L. I. (2012). Analysis and application of gamification. *Proceedings of the 13th International Conference on Interacción Persona-Ordenador (INTERACCION'12)*. 10.1145/2379636.2379653

Bai, S., Hew, K. F., & Huang, B. (2020). Does gamification improve student learning outcome? Evidence from a meta-analysis and synthesis of qualitative data in educational contexts. *Educational Research Review*, *30*, 100322. doi:10.1016/j.edurev.2020.100322

Baptista, G., & Oliveira, T. (2019). Gamification and serious games: A literature meta-analysis and integrative model. *Computers in Human Behavior*, *92*, 306–315. doi:10.1016/j.chb.2018.11.030

Barata, G., Gama, S., Jorge, J., & Gonçalves, D. (2014). Identifying student types in a gamified learning experience. *International Journal of Game-Based Learning*, *4*(4), 19–36. doi:10.4018/ijgbl.2014100102

Barata, G., Gama, S., Jorge, J., & Gonçalves, D. (2017). Studying student differentiation in gamified education: A long-term study. *Computers in Human Behavior*, *71*, 550–585. doi:10.1016/j.chb.2016.08.049

Bartle, R. (1996). Hearts, clubs, diamonds, spades: Players who suit MUDs. *Journal of MUD Research*, *1*(1), 19.

Biro, G. I. (2014). Didactics 2.0: A pedagogical analysis of gamification theory from a comparative perspective with special view to the components of learning. *Procedia: Social and Behavioral Sciences*, *141*, 148–151. doi:10.1016/j.sbspro.2014.05.027

Blohm, I., & Leimeister, J. M. (2013). Gamification: Design of IT-based enhancing services for motivational support and behavioral change. *Business & Information Systems Engineering*, *5*(4), 275–278. doi:10.100712599-013-0273-5

Bogost, I. (2007). *Persuasive games. The expressive power of videogames*. MIT Pr. doi:10.7551/mitpress/5334.001.0001

Bogost, I. (2011). Gamification is bullshit. *The Atlantic*. Retrieved from https://www.theatlantic.com/technology/archive/2011/08/gamification-is-bullshit/243338

Briffa, M., Jaftha, N., Loreto, G., Pinto, F. C. M., & Chircop, T. (2020). Improved students' performance within gamified learning environment: A meta-analysis study. *International Journal of Education and Research*, *8*(1), 223–244.

Cermak-Sassenrath, D. (2015). Playful computer interaction. In V. Frissen, S. Lammes, M. de Lange, J. de Mul & J. Raessens (Eds.), Playful Identities: The ludification of digital media cultures (pp. 93–110). Amsterdam Univ. Pr. doi:10.1515/9789048523030-005

Cermak-Sassenrath, D. (2019). Current challenges in gamification identified in empirical studies. In R. Ørngreen, M. Buhl, & B. Meyer (Eds.), Proceedings of the 18th European Conference on e-Learning (ECEL 2019) (pp. 119–127). Academic Conferences and Publishing International Limited.

da Silva, R. J. R., Rodrigues, R. G., & Leal, C. T. P. (2019). Gamification in management education: A systematic literature review. *BAR – Brazilian Administration Review*, *16*(2), art. 3.

Dale, S. (2014). Gamification: Making work fun, or making fun of work? *Business Information Review*, *31*(2), 82–90. doi:10.1177/0266382114538350

Davies, D., Jindal-Snape, D., Collier, C., Digby, R., Hay, P., & Howe, A. (2013). Creative learning environments in education-A systematic literature review. *Thinking Skills and Creativity*, *8*(1), 80–91. doi:10.1016/j.tsc.2012.07.004

Deci, E. L., Koestner, R., & Ryan, R. M. (2001). Extrinsic rewards and intrinsic motivation in education: Reconsidered once again. *Review of Educational Research*, *71*(1), 1–27. doi:10.3102/00346543071001001

dela Cruz, C. S., & Palaoag, T. D. (2019). An empirical study of gamified learning application engagement to exceptional learners. *Proceedings IEEA*, *2019*, 263–267. doi:10.1145/3323716.3323762

Denny, P. (2013). The effect of virtual achievements on student engagement. *Proceedings of the SIGCHI Conference on Human Factors in Computing Systems*, 763–72. 10.1145/2470654.2470763

Denny, P., McDonald, F., Empson, R., Kelly, P., & Petersen, A. (2018). Empirical Support for a Causal Relationship Between Gamification and Learning Outcomes. *Proceedings CHI 2018*, paper 331. 10.1145/3173574.3173885

Deterding, S. (2015). The lens of intrinsic skill atoms: A method for gameful design. *Human-Computer Interaction*, *30*(3–4), 294–335. doi:10.1080/07370024.2014.993471

Deterding, S., Sicart, M., Nacke, L., O'Hara, K., & Dixon, D. (2011). Gamification. Using game-design elements in non-gaming contexts. *CHI'11 Extended Abstracts on Human Factors in Computing Systems*, 2425–8.

Díaz-Ramírez, J. (2020). Gamification in engineering education – An empirical assessment on learning and game performance. *Heliyon*, *6*(9, e04972), 1–10. doi:10.1016/j.heliyon.2020.e04972 PMID:32995639

Dichev, C., & Dicheva, D. (2017). Gamifying education: What is known, what is believed and what remains uncertain: A critical review. *International Journal of Educational Technology in Higher Education*, *14*(9), 9. doi:10.118641239-017-0042-5

Eisingerich, A. B., Marchand, A., Fritze, M. P., & Dong, L. (2019). Hook vs. hope: How to enhance customer engagement through gamification. *International Journal of Research in Marketing, 36*(2), 200–215. doi:10.1016/j.ijresmar.2019.02.003

Ekici, M. (2021). A systematic review of the use of gamification in flipped learning. *Education and Information Technologies, 26*(3), 3327–3346. doi:10.100710639-020-10394-y

Erdoğdu, F., & Karatas, F. O. (2016). *Examining the effects of gamification on different variables in science education.* Identifying Turkish Society's Level of Scientific Literacy View Project Identifing Turkish Society's Level of Scientific Literacy View Project. Available online: https://www.researchgate.net/publication/312164266_Examining_the_Effects_of_Gamification_on_Different_Variables_in_Science_Education

Fadhli, M., Brick, B., Setyosari, P., Ulfa, S., & Kuswandi, D. (2020). A meta-analysis of selected studies on the effectiveness of gamification method for children. *International Journal of Instruction, 13*(1), 845–854. doi:10.29333/iji.2020.13154a

Farzan, R., DiMicco, J. M., Millen, D. R., Brownholtz, B., Geyer, W., & Dugan, C. (2008). Results from deploying a participation incentive mechanism within the enterprise. *Proceedings of the Twenty-Sixth Annual SIGCHI Conference on Human Factors in Computing Systems*, 563–72. 10.1145/1357054.1357145

Filsecker, M., & Hickey, D. T. (2014). A multilevel analysis of the effects of external rewards on elementary students' motivation, engagement and learning in an educational game. *Computers & Education, 75*, 136–148. doi:10.1016/j.compedu.2014.02.008

Fizek, S. (2014). Why fun matters: In search for emergent playful experiences. In Rethinking Gamification. Meson Pr.

Fuchs, M. (2014). Predigital Precursors of Gamification. In Rethinking Gamification. Meson Pr.

Hägglund, P. (2012). *Taking gamification to the next level – A detailed overview of the past, the present and a possible future of gamification* (Master's thesis). Umeå University.

Hamari, J. (2015). Do badges increase user activity? A field experiment on the effects of gamification. *Computers in Human Behavior*, 1–10.

Hamari, J., Koivisto, J., & Sarsa, H. (2014). Does gamification *work? – A* literature review of empirical studies on gamification. *Proceedings of the 47th Hawaii International Conference on System Sciences*, 3025–34. 10.1109/HICSS.2014.377

Hanus, M. D., & Fox, J. (2015). Assessing the effects of gamification in the classroom: A longitudinal study on intrinsic motivation, social comparison, satisfaction, effort, and academic performance. *Computers & Education, 80*, 152–161. doi:10.1016/j.compedu.2014.08.019

Huang, R., Ritzhaupt, A. D., Sommer, M., Zhu, J., Stephen, A., Valle, N., Hampton, J., & Li, J. (2020). The impact of gamification in educational settings on student learning outcomes: A meta analysis. *Educational Technology Research and Development, 68*(4), 1875–1901. doi:10.100711423-020-09807-z

Huizinga, J. (1955). *Homo ludens. A study of the play element in culture.* Beacon Pr.

Hung, A. C. Y. (2017). A Critique and Defense of Gamification. *Journal of Interactive Online Learning*, *15*(1), 57–72.

Huotari, K., & Hamari, J. (2012). Defining gamification – A service marketing perspective. *Proceedings of the 16th International Academic MindTrek Conference*, 17–22. 10.1145/2393132.2393137

Johnson, D., Deterding, S., Kuhn, K.-A., Staneva, A., Stoyanov, S., & Hides, L. (2016). Gamification for health and wellbeing: A systematic review of the literature. *Internet Interventions: the Application of Information Technology in Mental and Behavioural Health*, *6*, 89–106. doi:10.1016/j.invent.2016.10.002 PMID:30135818

Kafai, Y. B., & Burke, Q. (2015). Constructionist Gaming: Understanding the Benefits of Making Games for Learning. *Educational Psychologist*, *50*(4), 313–334. doi:10.1080/00461520.2015.112402 2 PMID:27019536

Kalogiannakis, M., Papadakis, S., & Zourmpakis, A.-I. (2021). Gamification in science education. A systematic review of the literature. *Education in Science*, *11*(1), 22. doi:10.3390/educsci11010022

Kapp, K. M. (2012). *The Gamification of Learning and Instruction: Game-based Methods and Strategies for Training and Education*. Pfeiffer.

Ke, F. (2014). An implementation of design-based learning through creating educational computer games: A case study on mathematics learning during design and computing. *Computers & Education*, *73*(1), 26–39. doi:10.1016/j.compedu.2013.12.010

Khalil, M., Wong, J., de Koning, B., Ebner, M., & Paas, F. (2018). Gamification in MOOCs: A review of the state of the art. *Proceedings IEEE Global Engineering Education Conference (EDUCON2018)*. 10.1109/EDUCON.2018.8363430

Kim, J., & Castelli, D. M. (2021). Effects of gamification on behavioral change in education: A meta-analysis. *International Journal of Environmental Research and Public Health*, *18*(7), 3550. doi:10.3390/ijerph18073550 PMID:33805530

Kim, K., & Ahn, S. J. (2017). Rewards that undermine customer loyalty? A motivational approach to loyalty programs. *Psychology and Marketing*, *34*(9), 842–852. doi:10.1002/mar.21026

Klabbers, J. H. G. (2018). On the architecture of game science. *Simulation & Gaming*, *49*(3), 207–245. doi:10.1177/1046878118762534

Koivisto, J., & Hamari, J. (2019). The rise of motivational information systems: A review of gamification research. *International Journal of Information Management*, *45*, 191–210. doi:10.1016/j.ijinfomgt.2018.10.013

Koivisto, J., & Malik, A. (2020). Gamification for older adults: A systematic literature review. *The Gerontologist*, 1–13. PMID:32530026

Landers, R. N., Auer, E. M., Collmus, A. B., & Armstrong, M. B. (2018). Gamification science, its history and future: Definitions and a research agenda. *Simulation & Gaming*, *49*(3), 315–337. doi:10.1177/1046878118774385

Landers, R. N., & Callan, R. C. (2011). Casual social games as serious games: The psychology of gamification in undergraduate education and employee training. *Serious Games and Edutainment Applications*, 399–423.

Lepper, M. R., Greene, D., & Nisbett, R. E. (1973). Undermining children's intrinsic interest with extrinsic reward: A test of the 'overjustification' hypothesis. *Journal of Personality and Social Psychology*, *28*(1), 129–137. doi:10.1037/h0035519

Lieberoth, A. (2014). Shallow gamification: Testing psychological effects of framing an activity as a game. *Games and Culture*, 1–20.

Majuri, J., Koivisto, J., & Hamari, J. (2018). Gamification of education and learning: A review of empirical literature. *Proceedings of the 2nd International GamiFIN Conference (GamiFIN 2018)*, 11–9.

Marín, B., Frez, J., Cruz-Lemus, J., & Genero, M. (2018). An empirical investigation on the benefits of gamification in programming courses. *ACM Trans. Comput. Educ.*, *19*(1), 4:1–4:22.

Mekler, E. D., Brühlmann, F., Opwis, K., & Tuch, A. N. (2013). Do points, levels and leaderboards harm intrinsic motivation? *Proceedings of the First International Conference on Gameful Design, Research, and Applications (Gamification '13)*, 66–73. 10.1145/2583008.2583017

Mekler, E. D., Brühlmann, F., Tuch, A. N., & Opwis, K. (2017). Towards understanding the effects of individual gamification elements on intrinsic motivation and performance. *Computers in Human Behavior*, *71*, 525–534. doi:10.1016/j.chb.2015.08.048

Nacke, L. E., & Deterding, S. (2017). Editorial: The Maturing of Gamification Research. *Computers in Human Behavior*, *71*, 450–454. doi:10.1016/j.chb.2016.11.062

Nicholson, S. (2012). A user-centered theoretical framework for meaningful gamification. *Proceedings Games+ Learning+ Society*, 223–30.

Nicholson, S. (2015). A recipe for meaningful gamification. In *Gamification in education and business* (pp. 1–20). Springer. https://scottnicholson.com/pubs/recipepreprint.pdf

Olsson, M., Hogberg, J., Wastlund, E., & Gustafsson, A. (2016). In-store gamification: Testing a location-based treasure hunt app in a real retailing environment. *Proceedings 49th Annu. Hawaii Int. Conf. Syst. Sci. (HICSS) 2016*, 1634–41. 10.1109/HICSS.2016.206

Ortiz-Rojas, M., Chiluiza, K., & Valcke, M. (2017). Gamification and learning performance: A systematic review of the literature. *Proceedings ECGBL17*.

Raczkowski, F. (2014). Making points the point: Towards a history of ideas of gamification. In Rethinking Gamification. Meson Pr.

Rapp, A. (2017). Drawing inspiration from World of Warcraft: Gamification design elements for behavior change technologies. *Interacting with Computers*, *29*(5), 648–678. doi:10.1093/iwc/iwx001

Reiners, T., & Wood, L. C. (2015). *Gamification in education and business.* Springer International Publishing, School of Information Systems, Curtin University. doi:10.1007/978-3-319-10208-5

Richter, G., Raban, D. R., & Rafaeli, S. (2015) Studying gamification: The effect of rewards and incentives on motivation. In Gamification in Education and Business. Springer.

Rozman, T., & Donath, L. (2019). The current state of the gemification in e-learning: A literature review of literature reviews. *Journal of Innovative Business and Management*, *11*(3), 5–19.

Ryan, R. M., & Deci, E. L. (2020). Intrinsic and extrinsic motivation from a self-determination theory perspective: Definitions, theory, practices, and future directions. *Contemporary Educational Psychology*, *61*, 101860. doi:10.1016/j.cedpsych.2020.101860

Ryan, R. M., & Deci, L. E. (2000a). Intrinsic and Extrinsic Motivations: Classic Definitions and New Directions. *Contemporary Educational Psychology*, *25*(1), 54–67. doi:10.1006/ceps.1999.1020 PMID:10620381

Ryan, R. M., & Deci, L. E. (2000b). Self-Determination Theory and the Facilitation of Intrinsic Motivation, Social Development, and Well-Being. *American Psychologist Association*, *55*(1), 68–78. doi:10.1037/0003-066X.55.1.68 PMID:11392867

Sailer, M., Hense, J. U., Mayr, S. K., & Mandl, H. (2017). How gamification motivates: An experimental study of the effects of specific game design elements on psychological need satisfaction. *Computers in Human Behavior*, *69*, 371–380. doi:10.1016/j.chb.2016.12.033

Sailer, M., & Homner, L. (2020). The gamification of learning: A meta-analysis. *Educational Psychology Review*, *32*(1), 77–112. doi:10.100710648-019-09498-w

Sakamoto, M., Nakajima, T., & Alexandrova, T. (2012). Value-based design for gamifying daily activities. In M. Errlich, R. Malaka, & M. Masuch (Eds.), *Entertainment Computing – ICEC 2012* (pp. 421–424). Springer. doi:10.1007/978-3-642-33542-6_43

Sardi, L., Idri, A., & Fernández-Alemán, J. L. (2017). A systematic review of gamification in e-Health. *Journal of Biomedical Informatics*, *71*, 31–48. doi:10.1016/j.jbi.2017.05.011 PMID:28536062

Schunk, D. H. (2014). *Learning theories – An educational perspective* (6th ed.). Pearson.

Seaborn, K., & Fels, D. I. (2015). Gamification in theory and action: A survey. *International Journal of Human-Computer Studies*, *74*, 14–31. doi:10.1016/j.ijhcs.2014.09.006

Skinner, B. F. (1974). *About behaviorism*. Knopf.

Tang, S. H., & Hall, V. C. (1995). The overjustification effect: A meta-analysis. *Applied Cognitive Psychology*, *9*(5), 365–404. doi:10.1002/acp.2350090502

Tobon, S., Ruiz-Alba, J. L., & García-Madariaga, J. (2020). Gamification and online consumer decisions: Is the game over? *Decision Support Systems*, *128*, 113167. doi:10.1016/j.dss.2019.113167

Tsay, C. H.-H., Kofinas, A., & Luo, J. (2018). Enhancing student learning experience with technology-mediated gamification: An empirical study. *Computers & Education*, *121*, 1–17. doi:10.1016/j.compedu.2018.01.009

Tulloch, R. (2014). Reconceptualising gamification: Play and pedagogy. *Digital Culture & Education*, *6*(4), 317–333.

Tulloch, R., & Randell-Moon, H. E. K. (2018). The Politics of Gamification: Education, Neoliberalism and the Knowledge Economy. *Review of Education, Pedagogy & Cultural Studies, 40*(3), 204–226. doi:10.1080/10714413.2018.1472484

Werbach, K., & Hunter, D. (2012). *For the Win: How Game Thinking Can Revolutionize Your Business.* Wharton Digital Press.

Wilson, S. (1993). *The Aesthetics and Practice of Designing Interactive Computer Events.* online.sfsu.edu/~swilson/papers/interactive2.html

Wu, M. (2011). *The gamification backlash + two long term business strategies.* community.lithium.com/t5/Science-of-Social-Blog/The-Gamification-Backlash-Two-Long-Term-Business-Strategies/ba-p/30891

Xi, N., & Hamari, J. (2019). Does gamification satisfy needs? A study on the relationship between gamification features and intrinsic need satisfaction. *International Journal of Information Management, 46*, 210–221. doi:10.1016/j.ijinfomgt.2018.12.002

Yıldırım, İ., & Şen, S. (2019). The effects of gamification on students' academic achievement: A meta-analysis study. *Interactive Learning Environments.*

Zainuddin, Z., Chu, S. K. W., Shujahat, M., & Perera, C. J. (2020). The impact of gamification on learning and instruction: A systematic review of empirical evidence. *Educational Research Review, 30*(100326), 1–23. doi:10.1016/j.edurev.2020.100326

Zeng, J., & Shang, J. (2018). A review of empirical studies on educational games: 2013–2017. *Proceedings of the 26th International Conference on Computers in Education*, 533-42.

Zhang, C., Phang, C. W., Wu, Q., & Luo, X. (2017). Nonlinear effects of social connections and interactions on individual goal attainment and spending: Evidences from online gaming markets. *Journal of Marketing, 81*(6), 132–155. doi:10.1509/jm.16.0038

Zichermann, G. (2011). *Intrinsic and extrinsic motivation in gamification.* Gamification Co. www.gamification.co/2011/10/27/intrinsic-and-extrinsic-motivation-in-gamification

Zichermann, G., & Cunningham, C. (2011). *Gamification by design: Implementing game mechanics in web and mobile apps.* O'Reilly Media.

Zichermann, G., & Linder, J. (2010). *Game-based marketing: Inspire customer loyalty through rewards, challenges, and contests.* Wiley.

KEY TERMS AND DEFINITIONS

Behaviourism: An educational theory that prioritizes facilitating observable, tangible outcomes over understanding internal, mental operations. It centrally uses conditioning (reward and punishment) to affect behaviour changes. Successful learning is seen as the exhibition of changed behaviour.

Game Elements: Structures, objects, or activities taken to be characteristic of games; it is disputed in the discourse what such elements are, how they are defined, and if they exist.

Incentives: Deci et al. (2001) posit that incentives such as rewards 'have two aspects' that can lead to people to feel either 'feel competent and in control' or to 'feel powerless and incompetent' (Hanus & Fox, 2015). CET explains that '[t]he informational aspect conveys self-determined competence and thus enhances intrinsic motivation', while 'the controlling aspect prompts an external perceived locus of causality (i.e., low perceived self-determination) and thus undermines intrinsic motivation' (Deci et al., 2001).

Moderating Factor: Variables in an evaluation that significantly affect the strength of the relationship of a predictor or independent variable with an outcome or dependent variable. Examples for moderating factors in the context of gamification include learner personalities and preferences, gaming experiences, and the educational content or domains.

Motivation, Extrinsic: SDT divides motivation into two main types, extrinsic and intrinsic motivation. Extrinsic motivation is described as an action that is performed for the sake of achieving a consequential end state or to avoid an unwanted outcome, for example when a student does her homework to avoid punishment from her teacher or parents (Ryan & Deci, 2000a, p. 60).

Motivation, Intrinsic: Intrinsic motivation is described as an action that is performed because of the enjoyment of itself, for example when a student does his homework because he considers it fun or interesting (ibid.). Intrinsic motivation refers to people's inherent desire to seek challenges, explore and learn (Ryan & Deci, 2000b, p. 70).

Rewards: The use of desirable, 'tangible rewards (including material rewards, such as money and prizes, and symbolic rewards, such as trophies and good player awards)' decreases intrinsic motivation, 'because tangible rewards are frequently used to persuade people to do things they would not otherwise do, that is, to control their behavior' (Deci et al., 2001).

ENDNOTES

[1] Fuchs (2014) "present[s] examples" of "predigital gamification" from the areas of "religious practice, music, magic, education, lifestyle, and styles for killing". For a brief account of the history of gamification see, for instance, Fuchs (ibid.) or Bogost (2007).

[2] Many studies and meta-studies the chapter is based on originate from the area of education; it is assumed that observations and findings align with other areas fully or partially (see Majuri et al., 2018, p. 16).

[3] The chapter is substantially revised and extended from a conference article by this author (2019).

[4] The focus is on problems specific to gamification; general problems common to many or all media-based initiatives are omitted from the discussion. For instance, Hung (2017, p. 61) points out that educational gamification requires a substantial effort on the part of the teachers; Sardi et al. (2017, p. 41) observe the same issue in health gamification; costs and required teacher skills are noted by Kalogiannakis et al. (2021, p. 5) also for educational gamification; they also discuss technical issues (ibid., p. 21); and da Silva et al. (2019, p. 3) also mention technical issues and in addition cost factors.

[5] Sardi et al. (2017, p. 32) speculate that one reason for the inflationary introduction and use of terms and notions roughly pertaining to the same idea of purposeful use of play might be that the notion of gamification is severly discredited in some discourses.

6   Deterding et al. appear to make a distinction between "gamification" and "gameful design" (2011; see Koivisto&Hamari, 2019, p. 204); the former simply uses one or several "game elements" such as progress bars (Landers et al., 2018, p. 322), while only the latter aims to turn an activity that was not a game before into something that is experienced as a game by the person interacting with it. The notions of gamification and gameful design appear to fall together at least for some authors; for instance, Koivisto and Hamari describe "the core of what commonly is titled gamification" as "employing game elements into different types of systems and services, *with the goal of affording gameful experiences*" (2019, p. 192, emph. added; see ibid., p. 193). Landers et al. describe gamification as "a design process [...] intended to augment or alter an existing real-world process using lessons (initially) from the game design research literature to create a revised version of that process that *users will experience as game-like*" (2018, p. 317, emph. added; similarly, Xi&Hamari, 2019, p. 211; Briffa et al., 2020, p. 235; Sailer&Homner, 2020, p. 78).

7   Many elements are actually not unique to games (Hamari et al., 2014) or typical for games (such as a progress bar; see Landers et al., 2018, p. 322). For a critical account of which qualities are usually recognized by gamification attempts in games and thus reproduced outside and independent of them see Raczkowski (2014).

8   The notions of game elements, components, mechanics, parts, features and affordances as used by various authors in the discourse on gamification to refer to "the basic building blocks of gamification applications" (Sailer et al., 2017) appear to vary only slightly in their intended meaning and are used here synonymously. Sailer et al. (ibid.) posit that "[g]ame design elements [...] are largely equivalent with game design patterns" – a position that appears not to be pervasively represented in the discourse.

9   This author is only aware of a single article that claims that "empirical research [of educational games] often uses single-factor experiments to discusses [sic] the effects of a certain variable separately" (Zeng&Shang, 2018, p. 537).

10   Hanus and Fox (2015) maintain that their "findings [...] align with existing literature on the negative effects of rewards on motivation (Deci et al., 2001; Lepper et al., 1973; Tang&Hall, 1995) as well as the negative effects of social comparison on motivation and performance in educational settings".

11   For instance, gamification is variously applied to initially boring or interesting tasks (Hamari et al., 2014; Johnson et al., 2016).

12   Attempts have, of course, been undertaken to operationalize definitions and unify the design of gamification, for example the gamification RECIPE by Nicholson (2015).

13   Marín et al. (2018, p. 4:2) add that "[g]amification relies on the argument that many traditional activities (including school activities and traditional learning) are not inherently interesting", which to this author appears to be a dabatable proposition.

14   Sardi et al. (2017, p. 42) include the facilitation of extrinsic motivation in gamification's mission when they state that "[e]xtrinsic and intrinsic motivation should be tuned up to yield a permanent engagement with the [gamified] application".

15   See da Silva et al. (2019, p. 7) and Zainuddin et al. (2020, p. 12) for lists of publications on the relationship between motivation and rewards in educational gamification.

16   For some users; the study sample has considerable limitations (Xi&Hamari 2019, p. 213) and is likely unrepresentative of the general population.

17   Deterding (2015) criticizes Nicholson's model for failing to articulate an "actual method".

18   Rapp (2017, p. 661) identifies and outlines an internalising strategy in *World of Warcraft* that stimulates players "to interiorize new habits" based on "the norms of the guild which they belong to".

19   However, they emphatically reject Klabbers' claim that "'gamifiers' apply a behaviorist approach to managing the workplace, to improve performance" (Klabbers 2018, p. 232 qtd. in Landers et al., 2018, p. 316).

20   For the description of a contrasting, constructivist (or more specifically, constructionist) approach to play in education, see, for instance, Kafai and Burke (2015).

21   Hung (2017, p. 58) reports that projects exist to make badges from gamified educational applications visible within social networks such as *LinkedIn*. Koivisto and Malik (2020, p. 9) discuss the possibility to integrate health gamification with other health-related IT systems.

22   If the audience is "older adults aged [3]55" (Koivisto&Malik 2020, p. 1), the domain is often health-related; Koivisto and Malik find that "[e]leven of the 12 studies" (ibid.) in their review or even all of them (ibid., p. 3) "were conducted in the health domain" (ibid., p. 1).

23   However, Wu outlines "two effective strategies that can lengthen the effective window of your gamification" (2011).

24   From a two-academic term experiment, Tsai et al. (2018, p. 12) report that the novelty effect "did not completely wipe out students' interest in the gamified course" at the start of the second term.

Chapter 3
Player/User Types for Gamification

Necati Taşkın
Ordu University, Turkey

Ebru Kılıç Çakmak
Gazi University, Turkey

ABSTRACT

Gamification has created great expectations for education and has become a trend in education. It is not an easy process to integrate gamification into educational environments. The design and development phases of gamification are very important. Therefore, it is necessary to follow a model that will guide the process in gamification designs. Individual differences among students are an important factor affecting their learning performance. In this context, considering student characteristics will increase the effect of gamification in education. Personalized gamification designs that meet the needs and expectations of students will be more effective than one-size-fits-all designs. It can benefit from player/user types in gamification designs to identify individual differences. This chapter aims to discuss player/user types in relation to gamification in the context of education.

INTRODUCTION

Gamification refers to the *"use of game design elements within non-game context"* (Deterding et al., 2011a). At the same time, *"human-oriented design"* and *"motivational design"* is emphasized for gamification (Berber, 2018; Chou, 2016). In gamification designs, the game mindset must be properly adapted to the context in which it is used (Kapp, 2012). Therefore, it would be beneficial to use a design model to guide the process (Kumar & Herger, 2013). Especially in the context of education, this becomes even more important. Because learning should not happen unplanned. A planned and sequenced process should be followed for instructional design (Seels & Glasgow, 1998). In addition, individual differences of students are an important variable that affects the success of education (Thorndike, 1918). They express various personal characteristics. Ability, learning style, perception and motivation of each person are different.

DOI: 10.4018/978-1-7998-9223-6.ch003

It is not correct to assume that all students have the same characteristics. For a more effective learning, the individual differences of the students should be known, furthermore these differences should be considered in instructional design. So, gamification designs should not be made by "*one size fits all*" approach. As the interests and expectations of each person may differ, gamification design should be carried out considering the characteristics of the target audience (Sezgin, 2020). Individual differences are an important factor affecting the efficiency of gamification (Barata et al., 2017; Mekler et al., 2017). Therefore, the significance of personalized gamification designs has increased (Santos et al., 2021). In gamification design, user preferences should be at the center of the process (Burke, 2014; Marczewski, 2015; Werbach & Hunter, 2015). In this context, player/user types can be used in gamification designs to explain individual differences. This chapter aims to discuss player/user types in relation to gamification in the context of education.

BACKGROUND

The Benefits of Gamification for Education

Gamification originally appeared in the marketing field and later spread to other fields such as healthcare, management, and entertainment (Domínguez et al., 2013). Effective applications of gamification in these areas have revealed the idea of using it in education (Deterding et al., 2011a). According to Lee and Hammer (2011), gamification will encourage students to learn, and it will make education more fun. This situation was likened to "*peanut butter meeting chocolate*" and interpreted as "*two great tastes working together*". Gamification has created great expectations and it has become a trend in education (Surendeleg et al., 2014).

With gamification, it is aimed to facilitate learning by providing motivation and engagement in learning environments (Seaborn & Fels, 2015). Gamification can make significant contributions to engagement and motivation in educational environments (Simões et al., 2013). The inclusion of game elements in learning environments increases student engagement and outcomes related to engagement (Goehle & Wagaman, 2016; Looyestyn et al., 2017; Tenório et al., 2016). Gamification helps students produce quality educational outcomes by increasing their engagement in educational tasks and their interaction with course content (Armier et al., 2016; Cózar-Gutiérrez & Sáez-López, 2016; Darejeh & Salim, 2016). Students have positive attitudes and high satisfaction with gamification (Hew et al., 2016; Kopcha et al., 2016). Also, gamification promotes students' 21st-century skills such as collaboration, communication, and critical thinking (Dicheva et al., 2015; Lee & Hammer, 2011). In addition, gamification creates an opportunity for formative assessment and offers an alternative solution to innovative assessment methods (Taşkın & Kılıç Çakmak, 2017).

Gamification in education can be done without using any technology (Gennari et al., 2016). However, developments in the internet and computer technology have a great role on the popularity of gamification (Deterding et al., 2011b). Today's students live in an era which the internet and computers are used extensively (Prensky, 2016). They also have close ties to digital games. Gamification offers great opportunities for students who are called "*digital natives*". They have grown up with technological possibilities and can use them effectively. The inclusion of gamification in online learning environments increases interaction and encourages students to learn (Castro et al., 2018). The use of gamification in online environments increases students' positive attitudes towards these environments and increases their motivation and social interaction (Domínguez et al., 2013). For this reason, gamification is mostly used to find solutions to the learning performance, engagement, and motivation problems in the online learning environment (Reich et al., 2019). Castro et al. (2018) states that gamification provides an increase in the number of course completions, the session duration, and the number of logins in the online learning environment. In addition, gamification reduces drop-out and increases students' achievement scores. Although it is seen that gamification provides significant benefits, its effect on learning has not been clearly revealed yet (Antonaci vd., 2019; Dichev & Dicheva, 2017; Looyestyn et al., 2017; Seaborn & Fels, 2015). The gamification was used for the first time in the literature in 2008, yet it started to be mentioned towards the end of 2010 (Deterding et al., 2011b). Since gamification became an approach in 2014 (Gartner, 2014), the studies are not yet at the desired level (Antonaci et al., 2019; Dehghanzadeh et al., 2019). The effect of gamification on individuals with different motivation levels is not yet clear (Perryer et al., 2016). Although some studies show that gamification is successful in education, the relationship between gamification elements and learning outcomes is not clear (Dehghanzadeh et al., 2019). Gamification studies have shifted towards designs that prioritize the target audience, compared to previous research (Raitskaya & Tikhonova, 2019). However, little is known about the impact of designs using user types (Nacke & Deterding, 2017). Especially studies on how to make personalized gamification designs by player types in the educational context are limited (Cömert & Samur, 2021). Although the great potential of gamification has made it the target of scientific studies (Koivisto & Hamari, 2019), current research shows that this field needs further expansion (Silva et al., 2019).

There are many studies in the literature pointing to the motivation and engagement-enhancing effect of gamification (Antonaci et al., 2019; Castro et al., 2018; Fitz-Walter et al., 2017; Landers et al., 2015; Tenório et al., 2016; Tsay et al., 2018). Although similar elements are used, there have been studies stating that gamification has a negative effect (De-Marcos et al., 2014; Domínguez et al., 2013; Hanus & Fox, 2015; Kyewski & Krämer, 2018; Toda et al., 2017). Since gamification applications are not simple (Kapp, 2012; Landers et al., 2015), attention should be paid to the design phase for gamification to create the desired effect (Domínguez et al., 2013). Gamification solutions should be designed in a systematic way to meet expectations and goals (Darejeh & Salim, 2016).

When the problem is related to education, the solution is instructional design. The instructional design process begins with the definition of the problem. It ends with the production of a learning system that offers a solution to the problem. Maybe gamification may not be the right way to solve the problem. Therefore, the analysis of the problem is as important as the selection of the gamification elements. The purpose of instructional design is to make learning easier, more efficient, and effective (Morrison et al., 2019). The instructional design describes how to design learning content to teach a subject most effectively. In summary, it is tried to make learning more attractive with instructional design. Therefore, it is necessary to follow a model suitable for the educational context that will guide the process in gamification designs.

Gamification Design

The fact that gamification produces effective results does not mean it will make every context successful (Fitz-Walter et al., 2017; Glover, 2013). Not every game element has the same impact on every context and target audience (Ibáñez et al., 2014). The gamification elements are successful only if they attract the attention of the target audience. If there is no harmony between the problem and the solution, it is not possible for gamification to attract the attention of users.

Thinking that gamification consists of only badges, points and leaderboards causes the psychological structure behind it to be ignored (Landers et al., 2015). According to Zichermann and Linder (2010), *"Gamification is 75% psychology and 25% new technologies"*. Not every element is suitable for every application and randomly added elements will make gamification away from success (Antonaci et al., 2019). Incorrect and unnecessary use of gamification elements may increase cognitive load (Turan et al., 2016) as well as lead to corruption in motivation (Werbach & Hunter, 2015). Using gamification elements is just like preparing meal (Berber, 2018). The desired taste in a meal can only be obtained with the ingredients used in its consistency.

It's easy to use gamification elements as rewards (Kyewski & Krämer, 2018). However, it may have negative effects on the engagement of motivated students (Hanus & Fox, 2015). Extrinsic rewards have positive effects on student performance, but they may also inhibit intrinsic motivation (Cameron et al., 2005; Deci et al., 2001; Pierce et al., 2003). In addition, it is known that for some contexts, there will be no need for intrinsic motivation, and extrinsic motivators will be more effective (Kuo & Chuang, 2016). For example, rewards can be effective when there are simple rules and clear goals (Pink,2009). Therefore, gamification elements sometimes may have positive or negative effects. The leaderboard is a component that can both harm learning outcomes (Hanus & Fox, 2015; Ibáñez et al., 2014) and increases student achievement (Mekler et al., 2017) and engagement (Landers & Landers, 2014). Although badges seem to be a good way to motivate students (Hakulinen et al., 2015) and increase engagement of students (Sitra et al., 2017), Kyewski and Krämer (2018) state that badges do not contribute to motivation. Zichermann and Cunningham (2011) recommend designers to use intrinsic and extrinsic motivation together rather than separating them. Extrinsic rewards need to be put to work together with intrinsic values (Perryer et al., 2016). For successful gamification designs, it is necessary to determine the goals and to define the target audience first (Berber, 2018). Instead of directly using points, badges, and leaderboards, it would be more beneficial to use the design process that shows where to start the design (Kumar & Herger, 2013). Therefore, using a model to guide the process is very crucial for effective gamification design. There are some design models suggested for gamification in the literature.

Gamification Design Models

Burke (2014) proposed a seven-step path for gamification design that includes the player experience. The player experience design process guides the designer step-by-step to the gamified solution. It is a process that involves understanding the players and how to motivate them. This path: (1) Outcomes and success metrics, (2) Target audience, (3) Player goals, (4), Engagement model, (5) Play space and journey, (6) Game economy, and (7) Play, test, and iterate. The design process steps are indicated in Figure 1.

Figure 1. The Player Design Experience Process (Burke, 2014)

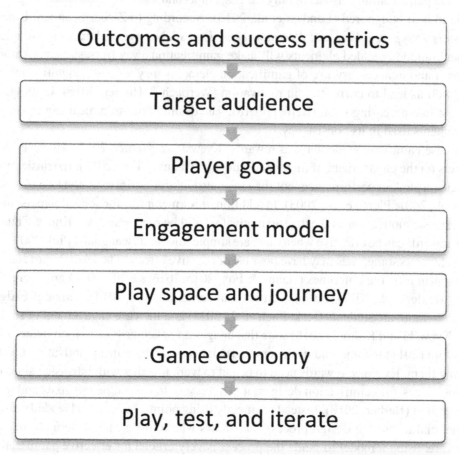

Kumar and Herger (2013) created the *"User Centered Design"* process by putting the user and the goals at the center of the process. The process begins with defining both users and targets. It is followed by motivational theories. It is stated that it is necessary to be familiar with motivation theories in order to produce good mechanics. It tries to create a flow through users, goals, and motivation theories. In the process, it is necessary to manage the goals, monitor the motivation and constantly measure the mechanics. It is stated that entertainment should not be neglected considering the institutional content, legal and ethical issues. Figure 2 shows of the design model.

Figure 2. User Centered Design (Kumar & Herger, 2013).

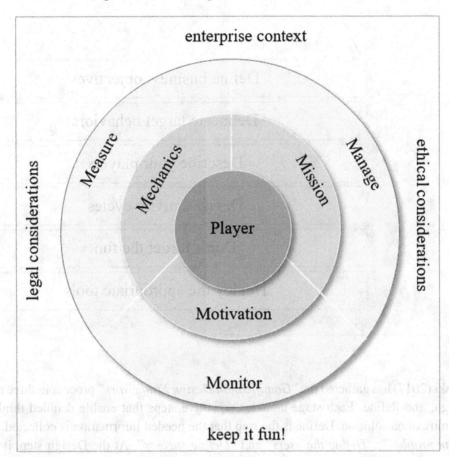

Werbach and Hunter (2012) created the "*D6 Gamification Framework*". Before the gamification design, answers are searched to some questions. Here are the steps of the model; (1) Define business objectives, (2) Delineate target behaviors, (3) Describe your players, (4) Devise activity cycles, (5) Don't forget the fun and (6) Deploy the appropriate tools. According to this model, it is necessary to define why gamification is needed and to set goals. Then the desired behavioral changes and gains should be determined. The gamification solution to be used differs for each target audience. Therefore, the target audience should be analyzed correctly. Then, the activity cycle, activity duration, number of activities, and feedback should be determined. In addition, entertainment must be adapted to the process to attract and motivate the users. The last step is to determine the right tool, software, and platform. The design process steps are indicated in Figure 3.

Figure 3. D6 Gamification Framework (Werbach & Hunter, 2012)

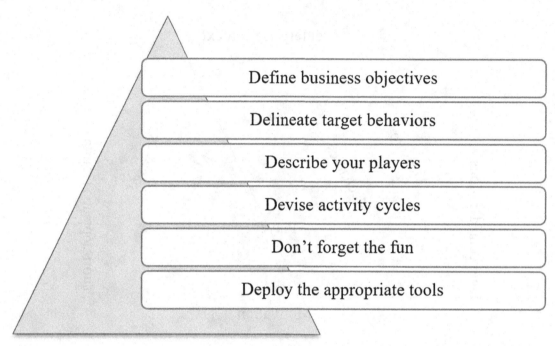

Marczewski (2017) has gathered the *"Gamification Design Framework"* process in three main steps: Define, Design, and Refine. Each stage includes repetitive steps that enable detailed thinking while creating a gamification solution. Define is the step that the needed information is collected. It consists of *"Define the problem"*, *"Define the users"* and *"Define success"*. At the Design step, it is decided what needs to be done for gamification. In gamification design, *"The journey of the user"* between the initial state and the mastery state should be realized in flow. This user journey is structured within the framework of *"Action/Feedback loop"* in the light of *"Behaviors"*, *"Motivations"*, *"Emotions"*, and *"Mechanics"*. The final step of the design process is Refine. This process is repeated until the desired structure is obtained. Figure 4 shows of the design model.

Huang and Hew (2018) developed the GAFCC model, which consists of Goal, Access, Feedback, Challenge, and Collaboration motivation elements. Game design elements such as badges, points, progress bar, individual or team challenges are associated with these five motivational elements. To implement this model, the process steps consisting of examine, decide, match, launch, and evaluate are followed. According to this design model, online learning platforms should be examined in terms of instructional objectives, learner context, and technology affordances. Then it is decided which motivating elements to use. It is decided which gamification strategies will be used by matching motivating elements with game design elements items and learning activities. Finally, design should be evaluated in terms of behavioral, cognitive, and affective aspects.

Figure 4. Gamification Design Framework (Marczewski, 2017)

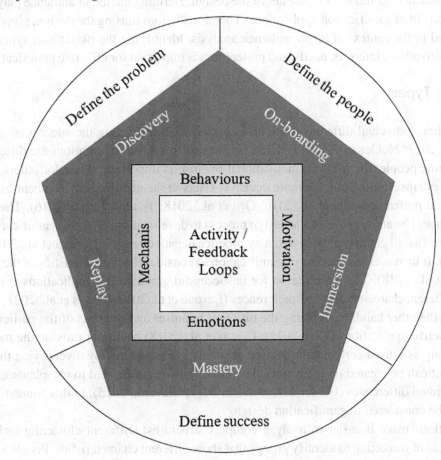

Gamification design models are like instructional design models. ADDIE Model, Dick and Carey Systems Approach Model, Morrison, Ross, and Kemp Model are the most known instructional design models. Instructional design models manage processes for creating high-quality teaching and learning environments (Branch & Kopcha, 2014). Instructional design models generally include the stages of analysis, design, development, implementation, and evaluation. In instructional design models, the process both is the end of one stage and the start of the next. These models involve repetitive stages. Evaluation and updating are continued until the desired performance are reached. In instructional design models, the characteristics and needs of the target audience are important. In the instructional design, the situation of the learners is taken into consideration more than the course content (Morrison et al., 2019). It is necessary to choose the most appropriate strategies and methods for the target audience. In this context, models that consider the target audience should be used for educational gamification designs.

The needs and expectations of users have importance in gamification design. Knowing the target audience is an important phase of gamification design models. It is seen that the step of *"Identifying player/user"* has important in design models and the development phase is shaped around this step. In design models, the importance to the question *"Who are the users?"* is seeking. It is necessary to know this to interact with users. *"Who is the target audience?"* The answer to this question will help to produce long-term and effective solutions. Since gamification is a human-oriented motivation design, the interests of the target audience should be at the center of the design. Defining the target audience plays a key role in the development of gamification applications. Therefore, before starting the design, player/user types are determined in the context of target audience analysis. Identifying the player/user types associated with users' motivations, interests, needs, and preferences is important for effective gamification designs.

Player/User Types

As stated earlier, individual differences are an important factor affecting the success of gamification (Barata et al., 2017; Mekler et al., 2017). Each person's interests and expectations are different (Chou, 2016). For some people, the intrinsic motivational impulse is important, while for others, the stimuli that provides extrinsic motivation are more decisive. Users in the gamified environment have different perceptions and preferences (Jia et al., 2016; Orji et al., 2018; Tondello et al., 2016). Therefore, user preferences should be at the center of the design process to develop more effective gamification applications. One-size-fits-all gamification design may produce negative results (Hamari et al., 2014; Seaborn & Fels, 2015). It increases the success of gamification to consider the characteristics of the target audience (Mora et al., 2018). The main reason for unsuccessful gamification applications is the fact that users have different characteristics and preferences (Lavoué et al. 2018; Santos et al., 2021; Tondello et al. 2017). On the other hand, recognizing the different impulses and interests of the participants helps to create attractive applications (Kim, 2015). Castro et al. (2018) could not provide the motivation of the whole group as it used certain gamification elements. He stated that by diversifying the elements, a greater effect can be created on the results. Therefore, it is recommended to use player/user types to identify individual differences (Gelder & Kovenock, 2017; Gil et al., 2015). In this context, player/user types should be considered in gamification designs.

Classifications make it easier to analyze complex structures. Different clustering techniques are used in the field of marketing to identify groups that show different characteristics. People are clustered geographically (continent, country, region, city), demographic (age, gender, profession, social status, educational status), psychological (attitude, interest, value, lifestyle) or behavioral (Hamari & Tuunanen, 2014). With the player/user types, it is aimed to categorize the skills and characteristics that affect the users' gaming experiences (Cowley et al., 2013). For a gamification design in which individual differences are considered, player types must be determined first (Sezgin, 2020). Researchers have considered player/user from different aspects. Therefore, there are many types of players classified according to different criteria in the literature.

Bateman and Boon (2005) divide the players into four categories in the Myerr–Briggs model as "*Conqueror*", "*Manager*", "*Wanderer*" and "*Participant*". The main goal of a conqueror type player is to win. The manager type deals with games to strategize and organize others. The wanderer is the type of gamer looking for a fun experience. The participant, the last player type of the model, wants to socialize and communicate with other players.

Ip and Jacobs (2005) classified the types of players as "*Hardcore*" and "*Casual*" according to their general game attitude, knowledge, playing and purchasing habits.

Lazzaro (2009) states that games increase engagement by creating positive emotions. Accordingly, users are classified as "*Hard fun*", "*Easy fun*", "*Serious fun*" and "*People fun*" according to the emotions they feel while playing the game.

Fullerton (2008) suggested nine different types based on player satisfaction. "*Competitors*", "*Explorers*", "*Collectors*", "*Achievers*", "*Jokers*", "*Artists*", "*Storytellers*", "*Directors*", and "*Performers*".

Competitors strive to be the best. Explorers are curious and have adventurous characters. Collectors aim to collect in-game items and prizes. Achievers aim to pass all stages and be successful in the game. Jokers do not take the game seriously and their main purpose is entertainment. Artists aim to produce different solutions using different strategies. Directors want to dominate the game and manage it. Storytellers create a new world based on their imaginations within the game. Performers aim to share their in-game experience with other players.

Ferro et al., (2013) developed five types of players. Dominant players like to be at the forefront of the game environment, and they are selfish. Objectivist players are less selfish than dominant players, but they only think about themselves during the process. They want to show their skills and abilities to other users. They progress through their own knowledge and skills without help. Humanists assign themselves a social role in the game and care about the needs of others. They like to take care of other players' problems and solve their problems as well as their own achievements. Inquisitive enjoy doing research and discovering new things. They are inquisitive and like to discover the solution instead of following the instructions. Creatives love to use their experience to develop and create new things.

Götzenbrucker and Köhl (2009) examined the gaming experiences and attitudes of online players and identified four different types of players. Social interaction is important for communicative role-players. Anarchists see themselves differently, they like to exhibit unpleasant behavior in the game. Steady gamers see games as a part of their lives and focus on being successful. Designers focus on the mechanics of games. They like to try new things in-game and design their own game worlds.

Vahlo et al., (2017) examined the digital game preferences of players. They have identified seven types of players: "*Mercenary*", "*Companion*", "*Commander*", "*Adventurer*", "*Patterner*", "*Daredevil*", and "*Explorer*". These types were created based on the game preferences of the players. E.g., the Mercenary enjoys first-person shooter-type games to kill enemies and apply war tactics, while the commander prefers strategy-type games to establish, develop and manage a city or quarters.

Kallio et al., (2011) in the InSoGa model classified the types of players into three main categories of intensity, sociability, and games. In this classification, playing time, continuity, concentration, location, device, type of game, and mode of access are taken into consideration.

Tseng (2011) categorizes the types of players as aggressive, social, and inactive according to motivational elements such as aggression and exploration that reveal the needs of the players to play.

Whang and Chang (2004) classified the players in terms of social behavior. The players are into three types according to the character (1) single-oriented player, (2) community-oriented player, and (3) off-Real world player. Single-oriented players do not consider the wishes of other players in the game and do not think about harming other players. Community-oriented players are social and tend to be successful. Off-Real world-oriented players act to develop an identity in the virtual world and want to be included in a group. It also tend to harm other players in the game.

Nacke et al., (2014) classified players' satisfaction based on neurobiological findings in the BrainHex model. This classification consists of seven different types as seeker, survivor, daredevil, mastermind, conqueror, socialiser and achiever. Seekers are motivated by curiosity and exciting situations. Survivors are motivated by fear and tension. Daredevils enjoy taking risks and seeking excitement. Masterminds like finding solutions to problems and solving puzzles. Conquerors love to deal with difficult situations and complete difficult tasks. For socialisers, other people are a source of excitement and satisfaction. Achievers want to complete tasks to reach the goal and be successful.

Xu (2012) identified five different types of players. Achievers aim to act individually in the game and improve their performance. Active buddies like to form small groups of friends and do activities with this group. Social experience seekers love to socialize and talk about their characters in the game. Team players strive to improve the performance and success of the team. Freeloaders, although they do not quit the game, are not in the active game and do not care about the game process.

Schuurman et al., (2008) analyzed the players according to their motivation sources and classified them into four different types. Overall convinced gamers consider gaming as a part of their identity. Convinced competitive players enjoy the competition, but they are quite reluctant to look different, make new discoveries, or be social. Escapist gamers are motivated by freedom and impersonation. Passtime gamers play games just to pass time.

Although there are different models for player types in the literature (Hamari & Tuunanen, 2014; Sezgin, 2020; Şenocak & Bozkurt, 2020; Cömert & Samur, 2021), the classification created by Bartle (1996) by observing users playing *"Multiplayer Dungeon Games"* is the most well-known and most preferred model in gamification solutions (Hamari & Tuunanen, 2014; Sezgin, 2020). It has been accepted in the field of education (Aldemir et al., 2018; Lopez & Tucker, 2019; Fiş Erümit et al., 2021). Marczewski (2015) introduced a new classification called *"User Type HEXAD"* by expanding and detailing Bartle's (1996) player types. This model is also the first model to classify user types, developed for use in gamification designs. In this context, Bartle's (1996) and Marczewski's (2015) player types of classification are discussed in detail.

Bartle's (1996) Player Types

Bartle (1996) investigated the reasons for players to play a game in MUDs (Multi-user Dungeons), which is multiplayer and includes different mechanics. Players are classified as achievers, explorers, killers, and socializers according to their different behaviors. The player types are indicated in Figure 5.

Figure 5. Player types (Bartle, 1996)

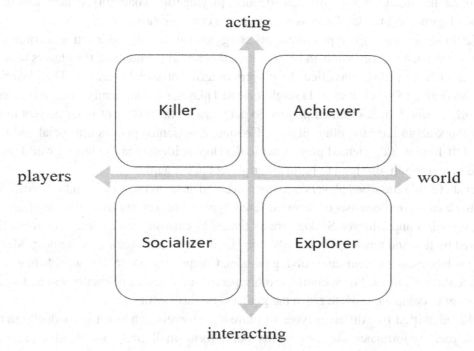

These types of players help to understand the characteristics of the target audience. The achievers focus on the gaming environment. To complete the goals, earn points or level up is their primary goal. They are results-oriented and completing tasks is important to them. Explorers focus on interaction. They try to understand and solve the system that reveals the structure of the game. They aim to learn all the features of the game and discover the hidden places in the game. They want to unlock different places in the game and have different objects or features. Revealing a hidden situation is more important to them than earning points. Other players are important to killers. They aim to defeat and harm other players. It is more important to them than their own success to see other players defeated. Socializers focus on interaction. Winning or losing is secondary to them. It is more important to communicate, chat, shop or interact with other players. Their primary expectation from the game is to have a good time.

Marczewski's (2015) User Types HEXAD

Marczewski (2015) introduced a new classification called "*User Type HEXAD*" by expanding and detailing Bartle's (1996) player types. It is the first model to classify user types for use in gamification designs. In this model, "*Achiever*", "*Socialiser*", "*Philanthropist*" and "*Free spirit*" constitute the four main types of users fed by intrinsic motivation. The "*Player*", who constitutes the main audience, represents the external user type. Apart from these, there is another user type called "*Disruptor*" that tries to distribute the system. Autonomy, competence, and relatedness from Deci and Ryan's (1985) "*Self-Determination Theory*", and autonomy, mastery and purpose from Pink's (2009) "*Drive Theory*", constitute the main structure of the model. The model is indicated in Figure 6.

Figure 6. User Type HEXAD (Marczewski, 2015)

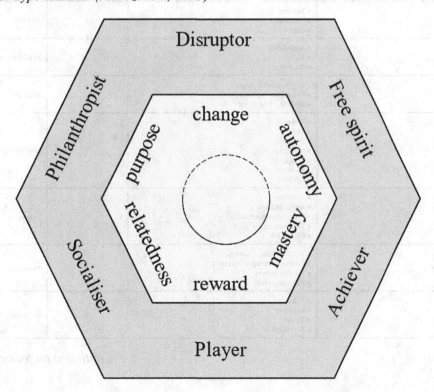

Table 1. Player/User Types

Developer	Player/User Types	Number of Player Type	Classification Criteria
Bateman & Boon (2005)	• Conqueror • Manager • Wanderer • Participant	4	Behaviour
Ip & Jacobs (2005)	• Hardcore players • Casual players	2	Attitude
Lazzaro (2009)	• Hard fun • Easy fun • Serious fun • People fun	4	Emotion
Fullerton (2008)	• Explorers • Collectors • Achievers • Jokers • Artists • Storytellers • Directors • Performers	9	Behaviour
Ferro (2013)	• Dominant • Objectivist • Humanists • Inquisitives • Creatives	5	Behaviour
Götzenbrucker & Köhl (2009)	• Communicative role-players • Anarchists • Steady gamers • Designers	4	Game experience and attitudes
Vahlo et al., (2017)	• Mercenary • Companion • Commander • Adventurer • Patterner • Daredevil • Explorer	7	Game preferences
Kallio et al., (2011)	• Intensity • Sociability • Games	3	Attitude
Tseng (2011)	• Aggressive • Social • Inactive	3	Motivation
Whang & Chang (2004)	• Single-oriented player • Community-oriented player • off-Real world player		Behaviour
Nacke et al., (2014)	• Seeker • Survivor • Daredevil • Mastermind • Conqueror • Socialiser • Achiever	7	Neurobiological
Xu (2012)	• Achievers • Active buddies • Social experience seekers • Team players • Freeloaders	5	Behaviour
Schuurman et al., (2008)	• Verall convinced gamers • Convinced competitive gamer • Escapist gamers • Passtime gamers	4	Motivation
Bartle (1996)	• Achievers • Explorers • Killers • Socializers	4	Behaviour

Continued on following page

Table 1. Continued

Developer	Player/User Types	Number of Player Type	Classification Criteria
Marczewski (2015)	• Achiever • Socialiser • Philanthropist • Free spirit • Player • Disruptor	6	Motivation

Achievers are motivated by mastery. They struggle to overcome all obstacles and complete all missions. They like to solve problems. When faced with a mystery or riddle, they cannot rest until they find the answer.

Socializers are motivated by relatedness. They want to interact and communicate with other players. They want to feel part of the group by trying to make social connections. They enjoy performing team/group activities cooperatively.

Philanthropists are motivated by purpose or meaning. They try to provide others with the opportunities they need to advance without expecting anything in return. They are happy to see, with their help, others achieve their goals.

Free spirits are motivated by autonomy and self-expression. They love to explore. They want to draw their own path by acting according to their own rules. They like to anticipate all the possibilities offered by the system, experience new things, and see what happens because of different experiences.

Players are motivated by rewards earned in various ways. They independently do whatever it takes to earn rewards within the system. They try to collect all the rewards in the system for themselves. They are part of the competitive game. If they are satisfied with what they will achieve at the end of an activity, they act and focus on the target.

Disruptors are motivated by change. They try to disrupt the gamified system either directly or by influencing other players. They want to test the limits of the system. They form the smallest set of user types. Winning or losing is not important to them. Rather than following the rules, they try to show other users that they are different.

Player/user types of developer and classification criteria, mentioned in this chapter, are summarized in Table 1.

SOLUTIONS AND RECOMMENDATIONS

Classifications were generally created by observing individuals playing digital games (e.g Lineage, Tomb Raider, Multi-user Dungeons). "*Game*" and "*Gamification*" are similar in terms of language phonetics and contain many features of games. But they differ from each other in terms of structure. However, gamification is used in non-game contexts. The target audience of gamification does not always consist of individuals who play games. For this reason, it is necessary to discuss the usability of player/user types in determining the characteristics of the target audience for gamification. It does not seem to be suitable for different types of games and especially for gamification (Busch et al., 2016; Kim, 2012; Marczewski, 2015; Sezgin, 2021). On the other hand, Bartle's (1996) player types are the most preferred classification for gamification. This model ignores that individuals' reasons for playing may vary depending on the context and that players' motivations may change over time (Herbert et al., 2014; Yee, 2006). Although Marczewski's (2015) classification was developed for gamification, it is based on Bartle's (1996) classification. For this reason, new classifications can be developed for gamification according to the behavior of individuals in their social life. People are constantly exposed to many different game elements in daily life. For example, people used to collect newspaper coupons in the past, they accumulate shopping points now. Sometimes, people struggle in life to be chosen as the employee of the month, to increase the number of followers, and to get a status. Considering these facts in social life while creating classifications may be more effective in personalizing gamification.

FUTURE RESEARCH DIRECTIONS

Individuals who make up the target audience have different player/user types. In addition, users may be interested in more than one player/user type. For this reason, designs should be made to cover the entire target audience, not according to a single dominant type. It should also be noted that user types are dynamic. The types of players representing users are constantly changing. Therefore, dynamic structures in which user types are constantly analyzed will be more effective than fixed personalization. Today, interest in personalized gamification designs has increased. The personalized gamification designs can also be benefited from player types. It is seen that studies on user types are generally on scale development/adaptation or theoretical foundations. The number of studies on how user types can be adapted to gamification design, which classification is more effective in gamification, or the effect of personalized gamification designs is quite limited. It is predicted that the interest in personalized gamification studies will increase in the future. It is thought that this study will be useful in developing personalized gamification designs focused on user types.

CONCLUSION

Gamification is used as an alternative method in education to increase the engagement, motivation, and learning performance of students. Integrating gamification into educational environments is not an easy process. Therefore, it is recommended to follow a gamification design model. Knowing the target audience is an important phase of gamification design models. Player/user types are used in gamification designs to explain individual differences. Students have different needs and expectations. These individual differences of students are an important factor affecting their learning performance. Using player/user types will help to create a better game feel and cover a wider audience. Therefore, player/user types should be considered in gamification designs. In this context, considering student characteristics will increase the effect of gamification in education. Personalized gamification designs that meet the needs and expectations of students will be more effective than a one-size-fits-all gamification design. The appropriate player/user types of classification should be selected considering the context in which gamification will be used. In the literature, it is seen that users are classified according to criteria such as behavior, attitude, emotion, and motivation. In instructional design, psychological and behavioral classifications are used to reveal the characteristics of the target audience. In this context, when gamification is designed for education, it would be more appropriate to use player/user types that classify users according to their motivation and behaviors. In educational gamification designs, students' learning styles and learning goals should also be considered. Students may sometimes want to learn how to increase their knowledge, get ahead of their peers and get high grades. In addition, each student has a different way of accessing information and learning styles. Learning styles are characteristic features of individuals and affect their success. Some students like individual learning, while others like to learn by discussing with their friends (Jonassen & Grabowski, 1993).

Determining player/user types does not make sense on its own. It is important to reflect the distribution of player/user types towards the gamification design. A balance must be struck between the distribution of player/user type and the game elements used in gamification design. The elements reflecting the player/user type must be selected and the correct mechanics must be created using these elements. If the other steps are not taken correctly, determining the user types will not work alone. Therefore, player/user types must be used within a gamification design model.

REFERENCES

Aldemir, T., Celik, B., & Kaplan, G. (2018). A qualitative investigation of student perceptions of game elements in a gamified course. *Computers in Human Behavior, 78*, 235–254. doi:10.1016/j.chb.2017.10.001

Antonaci, A., Klemke, R., & Specht, M. (2019). The effects of gamification in online learning environments: A systematic literature review. *Informatics (MDPI), 6*(3), 32. doi:10.3390/informatics6030032

Armier, D. D. Jr, Shepherd, C. E., & Skrabut, S. (2016). Using game elements to increase student engagement in course assignments. *College Teaching, 64*(2), 64–72. doi:10.1080/87567555.2015.1094439

Barata, G., Gama, S., Jorge, J., & Gonçalves, D. (2017). Studying student differentiation in gamified education: A long-term study. *Computers in Human Behavior, 71*, 550–585. doi:10.1016/j.chb.2016.08.049

Bartle, R. (1996). Hearts, clubs, diamonds, spades: Players who suit MUDs. *Journal of MUD Research, 1*(1), 19. http://www.arise.mae.usp.br/wp-content/uploads/2018/03/Bartle-player-types.pdf

Bateman, C., & Boon, R. (2005). *21st century game design (game development series)*. Charles River Media.

Berber, A. (2018). *Oyunlaştırma: Oynayarak başarmak*. Seçkin Yayıncılık.

Branch, R. M., & Kopcha, T. J. (2014). Instructional design models. In J. Spector, M. Merrill, J. Elen, & M. Bishop (Eds.), *Handbook of research on educational communications and technology*. Springer. doi:10.1007/978-1-4614-3185-5_7

Burke, B. (2014). *Gamify: How gamification motivates people to do extraordinary things*. Gartner, Inc.

Busch, M., Mattheiss, E. E., Hochleitner, W., Hochleitner, C., Lankes, M., Fröhlich, P., & Tscheligi, M. (2016). Using player type models for personalized game design an empirical investigation. *Interaction Design and Architecture, 28*, 145–163. http://www.mifav.uniroma2.it/inevent/events/idea2010/doc/28_8.pdf

Cameron, J., Pierce, W. D., Banko, K. M., & Gear, A. (2005). Achievement-based rewards and intrinsic motivation: A test of cognitive mediators. *Journal of Educational Psychology, 97*(4), 641–655. doi:10.1037/0022-0663.97.4.641

Castro, K. A. C., Sibo, Í. P. H., & Ting, I.-h. (2018). Assessing gamification effects on e-learning platforms: An experimental case. In L. Uden, D. Liberona & J. Ristvej (Eds.), *Learning technology for education challenges* (pp. 3-14). Springer. 10.1007/978-3-319-95522-3_1

Chou, Y.-K. (2016). *Actionable gamification: Beyond points, badges, and leaderboards.* Octalysis Media.

Cömert, Z., & Samur, Y. (2021). A comprehensive player types model: Player head. *Interactive Learning Environments*, 1–17. doi:10.1080/10494820.2021.1914113

Cowley, B., Charles, D., Black, M., & Hickey, R. (2013). Real-time rule-based classification of player types in computer games. *User Modeling and User-Adapted Interaction*, 23(5), 489–526. doi:10.100711257-012-9126-z

Cózar-Gutiérrez, R., & Sáez-López, J. M. (2016). Game-based learning and gamification in initial teacher training in the social sciences: An experiment with MinecraftEdu. *International Journal of Educational Technology in Higher Education*, 13(2), 2. Advance online publication. doi:10.118641239-016-0003-4

Darejeh, A., & Salim, S. S. (2016). Gamification solutions to enhance software user engagement–A systematic review. *International Journal of Human-Computer Interaction*, 32(8), 618–642. doi:10.1080/10447318.2016.1183330

De-Marcos, L., Domínguez, A., Saenz-de-Navarrete, J., & Pagés, C. (2014). An empirical study comparing gamification and social networking on e-learning. *Computers & Education*, 75, 82–91. doi:10.1016/j.compedu.2014.01.012

Deci, E. L., Koestner, R., & Ryan, R. M. (2001). Extrinsic rewards and intrinsic motivation in education: Reconsidered once again. *Review of Educational Research*, 71(1), 1–27. doi:10.3102/00346543071001001

Deci, E. L., & Ryan, R. M. (1985). *Instrinsic motivation and self-determination in human behavior.* Springer. doi:10.1007/978-1-4899-2271-7

Dehghanzadeh, H., Fardanesh, H., Hatami, J., Talaee, E., & Noroozi, O. (2019). Using gamification to support learning English as a second language: A systematic review. *Computer Assisted Language Learning*, 1–24. doi:10.1080/09588221.2019.1648298

Deterding, S., Dixon, D., Khaled, R., & Nacke, L. (2011a). From game design elements to gamefulness: Defining "Gamification". *Proceedings of the 15th International Academic MindTrek Conference*, 9-15. 10.1145/2181037.2181040

Deterding, S., Sicart, M., Nacke, L., O'Hara, K., & Dixon, D. (2011b). Gamification. using game-design elements in non-gaming contexts. *CHI '11 Extended Abstracts on Human Factors in Computing Systems*, 2425-2428. doi:10.1145/1979742.1979575

Dichev, C., & Dicheva, D. (2017). Gamifying education: What is known, what is believed and what remains uncertain: A critical review. *International Journal of Education Technology in Higher Education*, 14(1), 9. doi:10.118641239-017-0042-5

Dicheva, D., Dichev, C., Agre, G., & Angelova, G. (2015). Gamification in education: A systematic mapping study. *Journal of Educational Technology & Society*, 18(3), 75–88. https://scinapse.io/papers/2187022131

Domínguez, A., Saenz-De-Navarrete, J., De-Marcos, L., Fernández-Sanz, L., Pagés, C., & Martínez-Herráiz, J.-J. (2013). Gamifying learning experiences: Practical implications and outcomes. *Computers & Education*, *63*, 380–392. doi:10.1016/j.compedu.2012.12.020

Ferro, L. S., Walz, S. P., & Greuter, S. (2013). Towards personalised, gamified systems: an investigation into game design, personality and player typologies. In *Proceedings of The 9th Australasian Conference on Interactive Entertainment: Matters of Life and Death* (p. 7). ACM. 10.1145/2513002.2513024

Fiş Erümit, S., Şılbır, L., Erümit, A. K., & Karal, H. (2021). Determination of player types according to digital game playing preferences: Scale development and validation study. *International Journal of Human-Computer Interaction*, *37*(11), 991–1002. doi:10.1080/10447318.2020.1861765

Fitz-Walter, Z., Johnson, D., Wyeth, P., Tjondronegoro, D., & Scott-Parker, B. (2017). Driven to drive? Investigating the effect of gamification on learner driver behavior, perceived motivation and user experience. *Computers in Human Behavior*, *71*, 586–595. doi:10.1016/j.chb.2016.08.050

Fullerton, T. (2008). Working with dramatic elements. In *Game Design Workshop: A playcentric approach to creating innovative games* (pp. 97-128). CRC Press.

Gartner. (2014). *Gartner's 2014 hypecycle for emerging technologies maps out evolving relationship between humans and machines*. https://www.gartner.com/newsroom/id/2819918

Gelder, A., & Kovenock, D. (2017). Dynamic behavior and player types in majoritarian multi-battle contests. *Games and Economic Behavior*, *104*, 444–455. doi:10.1016/j.geb.2017.05.008

Gennari, R., Melonio, A., & Torello, S. (2016). Gamified probes for cooperative learning: A case study. *Multimedia Tools and Applications*, *76*(4), 4925–4949. doi:10.100711042-016-3543-7

Gil, B., Cantador, I., & Marczewski, A. (2015). Validating gamification mechanics and player types in an e-learning environment. In *Design for teaching and learning in a networked world* (pp. 568–572). Springer. doi:10.1007/978-3-319-24258-3_61

Glover, I. (2013). *Play as you learn: Gamification as a technique for motivating learners*. In J. Herrington, A. Couros & V. Irvine (Eds.), *Proceedings of EdMedia 2013--World conference on educational media and technology* (pp. 1999-2008). Association for the Advancement of Computing in Education (AACE). https://www.learntechlib.org/primary/p/112246/

Goehle, G., & Wagaman, J. (2016). The impact of gamification in web based homework. *PRIMUS (Terre Haute, Ind.)*, *26*(6), 557–569. doi:10.1080/10511970.2015.1122690

Götzenbrucker, G., & Köhl, M. (2009). Ten years later. Towards the careers of long-term gamers in Austria. *Eludamos (Göttingen)*, *3*(2), 309–324. https://www.eludamos.org/index.php/eludamos/article/view/vol3no2-12/143

Hakulinen, L., Auvinen, T., & Korhonen, A. (2015). The effect of achievement badges on students' behavior: An empirical study in a university-level computer science course. *International Journal of Emerging Technologies in Learning*, *10*(1), 18–29. doi:10.3991/ijet.v10i1.4221

Hamari, J., Koivisto, J., & Sarsa, H. (2014). Does gamification work?--A literature review of empirical studies on gamification. *2014 47th Hawaii International Conference on System Sciences (HICSS)*, 3025-3034. 10.1109/HICSS.2014.377

Hamari, J., & Tuunanen, J. (2014). Player types: A meta-synthesis. *Transactions of the Digital Games Research Association, 1*(2), 29–53. doi:10.26503/todigra.v1i2.13

Hanus, M. D., & Fox, J. (2015). Assessing the effects of gamification in the classroom: A longitudinal study on intrinsic motivation, social comparison, satisfaction, effort, and academic performance. *Computers & Education, 80*, 152–161. doi:10.1016/j.compedu.2014.08.019

Herbert, B., Charles, D., Moore, A., & Charles, T. (2014). An Investigation of Gamification Typologies for Enhancing Learner Motivation. *2014 International Conference on Interactive Technologies and Games*, 71-78. 10.1109/iTAG.2014.17

Hew, K. F., Huang, B., Chu, K. W. S., & Chiu, D. K. (2016). Engaging Asian students through game mechanics: Findings from two experiment studies. *Computers & Education, 92*, 221–236. doi:10.1016/j.compedu.2015.10.010

Huang, B., & Hew, K. F. (2018). Implementing a theory-driven gamification model in higher education flipped courses: Effects on out-of-class activity completion and quality of artifacts. *Computers & Education, 125*, 254–272. doi:10.1016/j.compedu.2018.06.018

Ibáñez, M.-B., Di-Serio, A., & Delgado-Kloos, C. (2014). Gamification for engaging computer science students in learning activities: A case study. *IEEE Transactions on Learning Technologies, 7*(3), 291–301. doi:10.1109/TLT.2014.2329293

Ip, B., & Jacobs, G. (2005). Segmentation of the games market using multivariate analysis. Journal of Targeting. *Measurement and Analysis for Marketing, 13*(3), 275–287. doi:10.1057/palgrave.jt.5740154

Jia, Y., Xu, B., Karanam, Y., & Voida, S. (2016). Personality-targeted gamification: a survey study on personality traits and motivational affordances. *CHI '16: Proceedings of the 2016 CHI Conference on Human Factors in Computing Systems*, 2001-2013. 10.1145/2858036.2858515

Jonassen, D. H., & Grabowski, B. L. (1993). *Handbook of individual differences, learning, and instruction*. Routledge., doi:10.4324/9780203052860

Kallio, K. P., Mäyrä, F., & Kaipainen, K. (2011). At least nine ways to play: Approaching gamer mentalities. *Games and Culture, 6*(4), 327–353. doi:10.1177/1555412010391089

Kapp, K. M. (2012). *The gamification of learning and instruction: Game-based methods and strategies for training and education*. Pfeiffer.

Kim, B. (2015). Understanding Gamification. *ALA TechSource, 51*(2). Advance online publication. doi:10.5860/ltr.51n2

Koivisto, J., & Hamari, J. (2019). The rise of motivational information systems: A review of gamification research. *International Journal of Information Management, 45*, 191–210. doi:10.1016/j.ijinfomgt.2018.10.013

Kopcha, T. J., Ding, L., Neumann, K. L., & Choi, I. (2016). Teaching technology integration to K-12 educators: A 'gamified' approach. *TechTrends, 60*(1), 62–69. doi:10.100711528-015-0018-z

Kumar, J., & Herger, M. (2013). *Gamification at work: Designing engaging business software*. The Interaction Design Foundation. doi:10.1145/2468356.2468793

Kuo, M.-S., & Chuang, T.-Y. (2016). How gamification motivates visits and engagement for online academic dissemination – An empirical study. *Computers in Human Behavior, 55*, 16–27. doi:10.1016/j.chb.2015.08.025

Kyewski, E., & Krämer, N. C. (2018). To gamify or not to gamify? An experimental field study of the influence of badges on motivation, activity, and performance in an online learning course. *Computers & Education, 118*, 25–37. doi:10.1016/j.compedu.2017.11.006

Landers, R. N., Bauer, K. N., Callan, R. C., & Armstrong, M. B. (2015). Psychological theory and the gamification of learning. In T. Reiners & L. Wood (Eds.), *Gamification in education and business* (pp. 165–186). Springer., doi:10.1007/978-3-319-10208-5_9

Landers, R. N., & Landers, A. K. (2014). An empirical test of the theory of gamified learning: The effect of leaderboards on time-on-task and academic performance. *Simulation & Gaming, 45*(6), 769–785. doi:10.1177/1046878114563662

Lavoué, E., Monterrat, B., Desmarais, M., & George, S. (2018). Adaptive gamification for learning environments. *IEEE Transactions on Learning Technologies, 12*(1), 16–28. doi:10.1109/TLT.2018.2823710

Lazzaro, N. (2009). Why we play: affect and the fun of games. In A. Sears & L. A. Jacko (Eds.), Human-computer interaction: Designing for diverse users and domains (pp. 156-175). CRC Press, Taylor & Francis Group. doi:10.1201/9781420088885.ch10

Lee, J. J., & Hammer, J. (2011). Gamification in education: What, how, why bother? *Academic Exchange Quarterly, 15*(2), 146. https://mybrainware.com/wp-content/uploads/2017/11/Gamification_in_Education_What_How_Why.pdf

Looyestyn, J., Kernot, J., Boshoff, K., Ryan, J., Edney, S., & Maher, C. (2017). Does gamification increase engagement with online programs? A systematic review. *PLoS One, 12*(3), e0173403. Advance online publication. doi:10.1371/journal.pone.0173403 PMID:28362821

Lopez, C. E., & Tucker, C. S. (2019). The effects of player type on performance: A gamification case study. *Computers in Human Behavior, 91*, 333–345. doi:10.1016/j.chb.2018.10.005

Marczewski, A. (2015). Even Ninja Monkeys Like to Play: Gamification, game thinking and motivational design. Gamified UK.

Marczewski, A. (2017). *A revised gamification design framework*. Gamified UK: Thoughts on gamification and more. https://www.gamified.uk/2017/04/06/revised-gamification-design-framework/

Mekler, E. D., Brühlmann, F., Tuch, A. N., & Opwis, K. (2017). Towards understanding the effects of individual gamification elements on intrinsic motivation and performance. *Computers in Human Behavior, 71*, 525–534. doi:10.1016/j.chb.2015.08.048

Mora, A., Tondello, G. F., Nacke, L., & Arnedo-Moreno, J. (2018). Effect of personalized gameful design on student engagement. *2018 IEEE Global Engineering Education Conference (EDUCON)*, 1925-1933. 10.1109/EDUCON.2018.8363471

Morrison, G. R., Ross, S. J., Morrison, J. R., & Kalman, H. K. (2019). *Designing effective instruction.* John Wiley & Sons.

Nacke, L. E., Bateman, C., & Mandryk, R. L. (2014). BrainHex: A neurobiological gamer typology survey. *Entertainment Computing, 5*(1), 55–62. doi:10.1016/j.entcom.2013.06.002

Nacke, L. E., & Deterding, S. (2017). The maturiting of gamification research. *Computers in Human Behavior, 71*, 450–454. doi:10.1016/j.chb.2016.11.062

Orji, R., Tondello, G. F., & Nacke, L. E. (2018). Personalizing persuasive srategies in gameful systems to gamification user types. *CHI '18: Proceedings of the 2018 CHI Conference on Human Factors in Computing Systems, 435*, 1-14. 10.1145/3173574.3174009

Perryer, C., Celestine, N. A., Scott-Ladd, B., & Leighton, C. (2016). Enhancing workplace motivation through gamification: Transferrable lessons from pedagogy. *International Journal of Management Education, 14*(3), 327–335. doi:10.1016/j.ijme.2016.07.001

Pierce, W. D., Cameron, J., Banko, K. M., & So, S. (2003). Positive effects of rewards and performance standards on intrinsic motivation. *The Psychological Record, 53*(4), 561–578. doi:10.1007/BF03395453

Pink, D. H. (2009). *Drive: The surprising truth about what motivates us.* Penguin Group, Inc.

Prensky, M. (2016). *Education to better their world: Unleashing the power of 21st-century kids.* Teachers College Press.

Raitskaya, L., & Tikhonova, E. (2019). Gamification as a field landmark in educational research. *Journal of Language & Education, 5*(3), 4–10. doi:10.17323/jle.2019.10688

Reich, J., & Ruipérez-Valiente, J. A. (2019). The MOOC pivot. *Science, 363*(6423), 130–131. doi:10.1126cience.aav7958 PMID:30630920

Santos, A. C. G., Oliveira, W., Hamari, J., Rodrigues, L., Toda, A. M., Palomino, P. T., & Isotani, S. (2021). The relationship between user types and gamification designs. *User Modeling and User-Adapted Interaction, 31*(5), 907–940. Advance online publication. doi:10.100711257-021-09300-z

Schuurman, D., De Moor, K., De Marez, L., & Van Looy, J. (2008). Fanboys, competers, escapists and time-killers: a typology based on gamers' motivations for playing video games. *DIMEA '08: Proceedings of the 3rd international conference on Digital Interactive Media in Entertainment and Arts*, 46-50. 10.1145/1413634.1413647

Seaborn, K., & Fels, D. I. (2015). Gamification in theory and action: A survey. *International Journal of Human-Computer Studies, 74*, 14–31. doi:10.1016/j.ijhcs.2014.09.006

Seels, B., & Glasgow, Z. (1990). *Exercises in instructional design.* Merrill Pub.

Şenocak & Bozkurt, A. (2020). Oyunlaştırma, oyuncu türleri ve oyunlaştırma tasarım çerçeveleri. *Açıköğretim Uygulamaları ve Araştırmaları Dergisi, 6*(1), 78-96. https://hdl.handle.net/11421/24971

Sezgin, S. (2020). Digital player typologies in gamification and game-based learning approaches: a meta-synthesis. *Bartın University Journal of Faculty of Education, 9*(1), 49-68. https://dergipark.org.tr/en/pub/buefad/issue/51796/610524

Silva, R. J. R., Rodrigues, R. G., & Leal, C. T. P. (2019). Gamification in management education: A systematic literature review. *BAR - Brazilian Administration Review, 16*(2), e180103. Advance online publication. doi:10.1590/1807-7692bar2019180103

Simões, J., Redondo, R. D., & Vilas, A. F. (2013). A social gamification framework for a K-6 learning platform. *Computers in Human Behavior, 29*(2), 345–353. doi:10.1016/j.chb.2012.06.007

Sitra, O., Katsigiannakis, V., Karagiannidis, C., & Mavropoulou, S. (2017). The effect of badges on the engagement of students with special educational needs: A case study. *Education and Information Technologies, 22*(6), 3037–3046. doi:10.100710639-016-9550-5

Surendeleg, G., Murwa, V., Yun, H. K., & Kim, Y. S. (2014). The role of gamification in education - a literature review. *Contemporary Engineering Sciences, 7*(29-32), 1609–1616. doi:10.12988/ces.2014.411217

Taşkın, N., & Kılıç Çakmak, E. (2017). Öğrenci Merkezli Öğrenme Ortamlarında Oyunlaştırmanın Alternatif Değerlendirme Amaçlı Kullanımı. *Bartın Üniversitesi Eğitim Fakültesi Dergisi, 6*(3), 1227–1248. doi:10.14686/buefad.333286

Tenório, T., Bittencourt, I. I., Isotani, S., Pedro, A., & Ospina, P. (2016). A gamified peer assessment model for on-line learning environments in a competitive context. *Computers in Human Behavior, 64,* 247–263. doi:10.1016/j.chb.2016.06.049

Thorndike, E. L. (1918). Individual differences. *Psychological Bulletin, 15*(5), 148–159. doi:10.1037/h0070314

Toda, A. M., Valle, P. H., & Isotani, S. (2017). The dark side of gamification: An overview of negative effects of gamification in education. In *Researcher links workshop: higher education for all* (pp. 143–156). Springer.

Tondello, G. F., Orji, R., & Nacke, L. E. (2017). Recommender systems for personalized gamification. In *Adjunct publication of the 25th conference on user modeling, adaptation, and personalization* (pp. 425-430). 10.1145/3099023.3099114

Tondello, G. F., Wehbe, R. R., Diamond, L., Busch, M., Marczewski, A., & Nacke, L. E. (2016). The gamification user types hexad scale. *CHI PLAY '16: Proceedings of the 2016 Annual Symposium on Computer-Human Interaction in Play,* 229-243. 10.1145/2967934.2968082

Tsay, C. H.-H., Kofinas, A., & Luo, J. (2018). Enhancing student learning experience with technology-mediated gamification: An empirical study. *Computers & Education, 121,* 1–17. doi:10.1016/j.compedu.2018.01.009

Tseng, F.-C. (2011). Segmenting online gamers by motivation. *Expert Systems with Applications, 38*(6), 7693–7697. doi:10.1016/j.eswa.2010.12.142

Turan, Z., Avinc, Z., Kara, K., & Goktas, Y. (2016). Gamification and education: Achievements, cognitive loads, and views of students. *International Journal of Emerging Technologies in Learning, 11*(7), 64-69. doi:10.3991/ijet.v11i07.5455

Vahlo, J., Kaakinen, J. K., Holm, S. K., & Koponen, A. (2017). Digital game dynamics preferences and player types. *Journal of Computer-Mediated Communication, 22*(2), 88–103. doi:10.1111/jcc4.12181

Werbach, K., & Hunter, D. (2015). *The gamification toolkit: Dynamics, mechanics, and components for the win.* Wharton School Press.

Whang, L. S.-M., & Chang, G. (2004). Lifestyles of virtual world residents: Living in the on-line game "Lineage". *Cyberpsychology & Behavior, 7*(5), 592–600. doi:10.1089/cpb.2004.7.592 PMID:15667054

Xu, Y., Poole, E. S., Miller, A. D., Eiriksdottir, E., Kestranek, D., Catrambone, R., & Mynatt, E. D. (2012). This is not a one-horse race: Understanding player types in multiplayer pervasive health games for youth. In *Proceedings of the ACM 2012 conference on computer supported cooperative work* (pp. 843-852). ACM.

Yee, N. (2006). Motivations for play in online games. *Cyberpsychology & Behavior, 9*(6), 772–775. doi:10.1089/cpb.2006.9.772 PMID:17201605

Yee, N., Ducheneaut, N., & Nelson, L. (2012). Online gaming motivations scale: Development and validation. *CHI '12: Proceedings of the SIGCHI Conference on Human Factors in Computing Systems,* 2803-2806. 10.1145/2207676.2208681

Zichermann, G., & Cunningham, C. (2011). *Gamification by design: Implementing game mechanics in web and mobile apps.* O'Reilly Media, Inc.

Zichermann, G., & Linder, J. (2010). *Game-based marketing: Inspire customer loyalty through rewards, challenges, and contests.* John Wiley & Sons.

ADDITIONAL READING

Cömert, Z., & Samur, Y. (2021). A comprehensive player types model: Player head. *Interactive Learning Environments,* 1–17. doi:10.1080/10494820.2021.1914113

Fiş Erümit, S., Şılbır, L., Erümit, A. K., & Karal, H. (2021). Determination of player types according to digital game playing preferences: Scale development and validation study. *International Journal of Human-Computer Interaction, 37*(11), 991–1002. doi:10.1080/10447318.2020.1861765

Hamari, J., & Tuunanen, J. (2014). Player types: A meta-synthesis. *Transactions of the Digital Games Research Association, 1*(2), 29–53. doi:10.26503/todigra.v1i2.13

Santos, A. C. G., Oliveira, W., Hamari, J., Rodrigues, L., Toda, A. M., Palomino, P. T., & Isotani, S. (2021). The relationship between user types and gamification designs. *User Modeling and User-Adapted Interaction, 31*(5), 907–940. Advance online publication. doi:10.100711257-021-09300-z

Taşkın, N., & Kılıç Çakmak, E. (2020). Adaptation of modified gamification user types scale into Turkish. *Contemporary Educational Technology*, *12*(2), ep268. doi:10.30935/cedtech/7942

Tondello, G. F., Mora, A., Marczewski, A., & Nacke, L. E. (2019). Empirical validation of the gamification user types hexad scale in English and Spanish. *International Journal of Human-Computer Studies*, *127*, 95–111. doi:10.1016/j.ijhcs.2018.10.002

KEY TERMS AND DEFINITIONS

Gamification Design: To produce solutions through gamification within a plan.
Gamification Design Model: Steps to guide the gamification design process.
Personalized Gamification: Gamification customized to users' personal characteristics.
Player/User Types: Classifications that group users according to their characteristics, such as their behavior, motivation, attitude, or emotions.

Chapter 4

How to Gamify E–Government Services?
A Taxonomy of Game Elements

Ruth S. Contreras-Espinosa
https://orcid.org/0000-0002-9699-9087
University of Vic-Central University of Catalonia, Spain

Jose Luis Eguia-Gomez
Polytechnic University of Catalonia, Spain

ABSTRACT

Although gamification has been applied to the e-government domain for the past 20 years, the literature shows that the field still lacks formal definitions to support the design of gamified strategies on these types of platforms and services, and that game element selection is often a subjective matter. This chapter provides a useful taxonomy of game elements to support the design of e-government initiatives, elaborated from the analysis of the literature on gamification frameworks and models applied to this domain. This work was additionally validated by gamification experts from public and private organizations during a series of workshops. A total of 30 commonly used game elements were selected, conceptualized, and classified into six dimensions. Gamification experts agreed that this work contributes to standardizing the game elements employed in e-government services, while the authors also believe this taxonomy can be a useful tool to analyze already existing frameworks.

INTRODUCTION

E-government represents a way of providing services to the citizens via online platforms, while the so-called e-participation facilitates the communication between citizens and the public administration. The latter is divided between political participation, where citizens engage in public affairs with the aim of influencing political outcomes (Brady, 1999), and civic participation, where citizens act for the public good (Thiel, 2017). In general, the success of these platforms is dependent on the goals and ob-

DOI: 10.4018/978-1-7998-9223-6.ch004

jectives of participation, and it is for this reason that gamification has been a useful strategy applied to e-government (Hollebeek, 2011). Moreover, gamification has been successfully used in other domains such as healthcare (Johnson et al., 2016), education (Nah et al., 2019), and transportation (Yen et al., 2019), among others, where game elements were integrated into platforms or services.

Gamification in the context of civic engagement is a possible means to positively influence active participation on online civic platforms (Coronado Escobar & Vasquez Urriago, 2014). On the other hand, according to Ryan et al. (2006), gamification is also useful as part of the motivational design and can influence the behavior of the users based on the incentives they receive. Thus, counting with information regarding motivators contributes to effective gamification design. Consequently, one of the main goals of gamification in e-government services is to increase user motivation and engage citizens as active players through measures that facilitate activities such as taking part in the public conversation, giving feedback to possible local government decisions, or actively meeting common objectives. However, gamification is still a relatively emergent area of scientific inquiry and there is still a lack of understanding of how such goals could be materialized (Hassan, 2016).

In their literature review, Contreras-Espinosa and Blanco (2021) revealed that the majority of works focused on the inclusion of gamification in e-government services does not follow any methodology in order to quantify the impact of the implementation of game elements and that the selection of these elements is rather a consequence of the expectations of the designer. For example, Bista et al. (2013) proposed the implementation of game elements over an online community for young people transiting from parental support towards economical emancipation in an e-government interaction and service called Next Step. This initiative from the Australian Department of Human Services enabled transactions between citizens and the management of the service itself. The designers and authors of this work included basic game elements such as points and rankings, but they did not conduct a previous analysis to select them, or any post-analysis to evaluate their impact. Thus, game elements were selected based on the preference and expectations of the designers, rather than according to the objectives of the implementation. In another example, Blazhko et al. (2017) addressed citizen stimulation to understand available open government data. This service provided the citizens with different types of information to teach them about a variety of concepts and indicators, such as pollution, death rates, etc. The main goal was to improve citizen information levels to encourage and facilitate informed decision-making during elections or other democratic processes like referendums. To motivate the users, the researchers gamified the service including elements such as points, rankings, and rules. However, this work was also characterized by a lack of formal criteria to determine which elements to implement, and which indicators could be useful to assess their performance. These examples highlight the present demand for a taxonomy or any other tools that can help designers select the most appropriate game elements for public services.

Public officers and servants are interested in using gamification in e-government services, but they do not count with the time or resources to understand the differences and similarities among game elements, which is a crucial step in order to decide which elements would be appropriate for each case (Al-Yafi & El-Masri, 2016). Furthermore, a clear definition of the individual game aspects and their differences is still missing (Thiel, 2017), while gamified e-participation tends to be misunderstood in practice, diminishing its potential (Hassan, 2016). With the aim to contribute to filling this gap, the authors present in this chapter the first approximation to a taxonomy of game elements appropriate for e-government services, elaborated with the collaboration of, and approved by, gamification experts from public and private organizations. The contributions of this chapter include: (1) a novel taxonomy, providing details on the concept, comprehensibility, use, and scope of game elements, and (2) a proposal on how to organize game elements semantically, to be used by public officers and servants, designers, or other stakeholders.

BACKGROUND

Defining Gamification

Playing games has increasingly become a widely visible form of leisure with demonstrated affordances for human engagement, flourishing and skills development (Hassan & Hamari, 2020). Gamification is thus understood as the introduction of game elements to non-gaming contexts to generate motivation and engagement (Deterding et al., 2011) and bring about positive experiences to potential users, consequently affecting their behavior and cognitive processes (Hollebeek, 2011). Gamification is about the design of systems, services, and processes towards inducing engaging, positive psychological experiences such as enjoyment or gamefulness (Huotari & Hamari, 2017). These experiences can be translated into a behavioral engagement and employed to elicit participation in different contexts such as education (Kalogiannakis et al., 2021), health (van Gaalen, 2021), production management (Warmelink et al., 2020), or Smart City Urban Planning (Aguilar et al., 2020), among others.

In the field of e-participation, gamification appears to have the potential to increase citizen engagement with the common good and societal decision-making (Opromolla et al., 2015). It has been used to provide special incentives for citizens (May Saßmannshausen et al., 2021) towards public participation (Romano et al., 2021) and to improve e-government services (Contreras-Espinosa & Blanco-M, 2021), leading to new research and practical work on gamified e-participation. Incorporating gamification has become increasingly normalized because users have come to expect that most of the websites, applications, and systems they use are gamified in one way or another, as they experience in other contexts (Sgueo, 2017).

Gamification commonly applies game mechanics, and authors such as Peng et al. (2012) and Hamari and Tuunanen (2014) make a distinction between 3 categories of gamification mechanics and game design which are directly related to gaming motivation: (1) the immersion-related, (2) the achievement-related and (3) the social-related dimensions. Immersion-related features pursue to immerse the user in a self-directed activity and include storytelling, avatars, or role-play as game mechanics. On the other hand, achievement-related features seek to increase the user's sense of accomplishment and include challenges, badges, missions, leaderboards, goals, or progression metrics. Finally, social-related features pursue to enable user social interaction and include collaboration and cooperation structures.

Gamification Frameworks

Gamification of e-participation induces increased user engagement with the government, as intended from its introduction to e-participation (Devisch et al., 2016). To facilitate the design of gamified systems, several studies have proposed different gamification frameworks. The most well-known include:

- **Mechanics-Dynamics-Aesthetics** (Hunicke et al., 2004): a model composed of (1) the game mechanics, which are the basic actions that players can undertake in a game, responses, algorithms, stored data, etc.; (2) game dynamics, the run-time behavior of the previously defined mechanics in response to the player input and the interaction between other types of mechanics; and (3) game aesthetics, the emotional responses produced in the player.

- **Six Steps to Gamification** (Werbach & Hunter, 2012): a model based on six stages, as follows: (1) define the objectives that you want to achieve; (2) delineate the target behaviors that you expect from the users; (3) describe your players' profile (interest, what drives them); (4) devise activity loops (the process that the users have to follow); (5) don't forget the fun (think what make your users return), and (6) deploy the appropriate tools (how the interaction will be measured, score systems, badge assignation, etc.).
- **Gamification Model Canvas** (Jiménez, 2013): a flexible and agile tool that enables representing in a single page all the necessary elements, tasks, and expected results of the gamified environment.
- **GAME** (Marczewski, 2013): a framework with four components: (1) Gather what information will be collected; (2) Act on the information you have, design the best solution for your goals and the experience of your users based on the information that you have; (3) Measure user activity and goals, iterate improvements; and (4) Enrich your solution over time to match the changes in society. This methodology evolved into the RAMPS Motivation Model and, later, into the User Types Hexad Scale, which is employed to identify the types of users.
- **Octalysis** (Chou, 2015): focuses on human design rather than on functional design. This framework is depicted as an octagon shape, which represents the core drivers. According to the author, the right side of the octagon reflects intrinsic motivation factors, and the left side, the extrinsic motivation.

Some of these frameworks aim to help designers choose which game elements should be employed in gamified strategies. Thiel (2017) mentioned that the different core drivers of the Octalysis model were associated with the game elements used in initiatives and projects such as mySidewalk, which uses points and rewards, equivalent in the Octalysis as accomplishment and ownership; or Love Your City, which uses points, profile, and statistics. However, using frameworks is not an easy task since many of them present limitations, ranging from their purpose (Dichev & Dicheva, 2017), to the number of definitions of game elements used, or a lack of knowledge or common understanding of the set of elements that can be used by gamified systems (Mora et al., 2015), which can confuse inexperienced designers who wish to gamify experiences (Savignac, 2017). Additionally, the lack of general frameworks to help us understand and define gamification (Hollebeek, 2011), as well as initiatives that could serve as a starting point for successful implementation, hinder the use of gamification in public services and applications.

The first drawback encountered by designers is choosing which game elements are appropriate for the target users, but the absence of conventions on element naming, or the lack of consensus on which elements belong to gamification are other issues found in the literature, as different synonyms are often used to designate the same item (Koivisto & Hamari, 2019). In general, the most frequently employed gamification elements are points, badges, and leaderboards (Hamari et al., 2014; Koivisto & Hamari, 2019; Rigby, 2015; Warmelink et al., 2020). This pattern is also observed in the literature on e-government services (Contreras-Espinosa & Blanco-M, 2021; Koivisto & Hamari, 2019). Point (score) constitutes the main game element, as designers consider it as the basic metric on which other aspects are built upon. It quantifies user progress, and without this element, it is unreasonable for the user to obtain badges, arrive at levels, or progress on leaderboards (Contreras-Espinosa & Blanco-M, 2021).

Motivation

Intrinsic motivation is an internal motivational drive to behave in a certain way for the sake of the behavior itself and the internal reward it provides (Hassan, 2016). Extrinsic motivation, on the other hand, is the pursuit of a behavior conditioned by some other external reason (Rigby, 2015). During the design of a service, both motivational affordances are used with the intention of affecting the intrinsic and extrinsic motivation of the users. In consequence, this can affect the directional expression of the motivation in terms of a behavioral change or increased engagement of the user with the service (Coronado Escobar & Vasquez Urriago, 2014; Koivisto & Hamari, 2019).

Gamification based on providing rewards or badges is effective for a quick behavioral change, but it only lasts for as long as the rewards are available (Rigby, 2015), while the Organismic Integration Theory emphasizes the negative correlation between intrinsic and extrinsic motivations (Deci & Ryan, 2004). When gamification is introduced as a reward mechanism, the long-term levels of intrinsic motivation are adversely affected (Rigby, 2015). Thus, if the goal is to induce a long-term change, then rewards may be less adequate (Hamari et al., 2014) because it would constitute an instability to replace intrinsic rewards for behaviors with an increasing dependency on extrinsic rewards.

According to Rigby (2015), sustained engagement is a consequence of the fulfillment of three basic needs, as proposed in the Self-Determination Theory, a motivation theory. The first is represented by the core psychological needs in intrinsically motivated behavior: free choice and the potential to behave in accordance with one's wishes. The second basic need is the drive to learn new skills to the point of excellence. Finally, the third need is the feeling of belonging to a community. Nevertheless, the perception of the psychological experiences provided by gamification and that lead to intrinsic motivation remains a subjective matter.

MATERIALS AND METHODS

In a first phase, and after compiling the frameworks and game elements found in the literature, the authors analyzed the terminology and classification provided by other researchers in relation to the gamification frameworks used in e-government services and selected the most commonly used game elements: Reputation, Competition, Cooperation-Team, Social interaction, Progress bar, Reward-Prize, Level, Badge, Point, Leaderboard-Ranking, Mission, Puzzle, Goal, Customization, Emotion, Vote, User profile, Player roles, Stories, Avatar, Rule, Lifetime, Economy, Imposed Choice-Action, Forum, Chat, Share, Post, Emoticons-Emojis, and Location tagging. Based on the methodology of Toda et al. (2019), a semantic analysis was applied to define a conglomerate of game elements that could be used to gamify e-government initiatives, and evaluated them based on the following characteristics:

- Concept: description of every game element.
- Comprehensibility: the consensual concept of game elements, as agreed by the experts.
- Use: examples to understand the use of each game element, as reported in the literature.
- Scope: the representation of a set of game elements in a taxonomy. The selected set aims to cover the needs for e-government services.

This phase focused on conceptualizing and defining the game elements. The first compilation of elements present in the literature was validated by 22 gamification experts working in practical European research projects during a first session (Workshop 1). The participants were selected based on the following criteria: (1) familiarity with the subject matter and relevant experience in gamification and e-government services, (2) reputation of the expert and the institutions or companies in which they work, and (3) the creation of a heterogeneous group. Expert participants worked in ACCIÓ (n=3), VALORTEC program (n=2), EMPENTA program (n=2), La Salle - Ramón Llull University (n=2), KIC Innoenergy (n=1), the Germans Trias i Pujol Research Institute (n=1), University of Lleida (n=1), Pompeu Fabra University (n=1), University of Turin (n=1), University of Milano-Bicocca (n=1), University of Helsinki (n=1), and Tecnológico de Monterrey (n=1), while five of them worked in private companies.

In another session (Workshop 2), the expert participants reviewed a second proposal, extended from the first draft with the addition of dimensions to group the selected game elements. The experts agreed that this second proposal constituted a useful tool to support stakeholders when choosing the most appropriate game elements to implement with gamification strategies in e-government services.

In a third round, the concepts were analyzed at a semantic level and discussed with the experts in order to produce final definitions, groups, and dimensions of game elements. Finally, practical examples from the literature were added, discussing the advantages and disadvantages of employing them in every case.

This process resulted in the final version of the taxonomy that the authors present in this chapter. The whole methodological process is described in Figure 1.

Figure 1. Methodological process

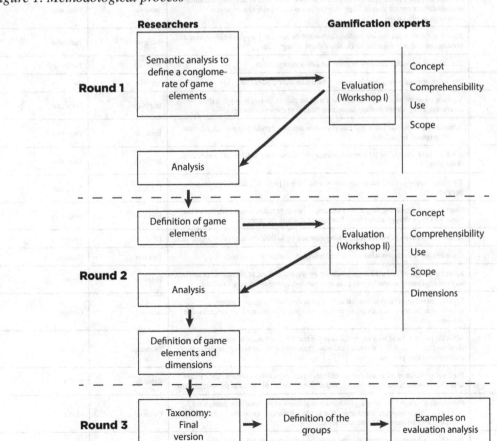

RESULTS

Table 1. Game element taxonomy

Game element	Concept	Motivation	Dimension
Reputation	Related to the titles, classification, or status that a player may gain and accumulate. Represents a social status that does not reflect the players' skills. Used to create a hierarchy within the game environment or the communities.	Intrinsic	Social
Competition	When two or more players compete against each other towards a common goal. Related to tasks in which citizens have to cooperate. Though it is the opposite of cooperation, both elements can be used together.	Intrinsic	Social
Cooperation-Team	The combined action of a group of players, especially when efficient and effective.	Intrinsic	Social
Social interaction	The interaction with other players, especially for pleasure.	Intrinsic	Social
Progress bar	Allows players to locate themselves (and their progress) within a game with progress bars, maps, steps.	Extrinsic	Achievement
Reward-Prize	A positive consequence for a player as a result of a given behavior or action which is desirable, such as the return of lost items when found.	Extrinsic	Achievement
Level	Hierarchical game layers, providing a gradual way for players to obtain new advantages upon advancing. Examples: character levels, skill levels.	Extrinsic	Achievement
Badge	Elements that symbolize the rewards given to players for their achievements, such as acing a skill. Badges help players feel recognized for their efforts.	Extrinsic	Achievement
Point	Unit used to measure player performance. Examples: scores, number of kills, experience points.	Extrinsic	Achievement
Leaderboard-Ranking	Related to the visual information provided by the game environment to the players, where they can see their completed actions or tasks, or overall stats.	Extrinsic	Achievement
Mission	Provides the player with a goal or a purpose to perform tasks, such as receiving discounts after obtaining a certain score in a task. Also known as quests, side-quests, to-dos, milestones, or objectives.	Intrinsic	Particular
Puzzle	Related to the activities that are implemented within the service. They can be considered as learning challenges or cognitive tasks. Also present through quizzes.	Intrinsic	Particular
Goal	The object of a person's ambition or effort; an aim or desired result.	Intrinsic	Particular
Customization	The action of modifying something to suit a particular individual or task.	Intrinsic	Particular
Emotion	Visual or sound stimulation. Related to the use of the players' senses to improve their experiences using Virtual Reality, Augmented Reality, or dynamic interfaces.	Intrinsic	Particular
Vote	Action through which an individual expresses their support or preference towards a certain motion, proposal, or candidate.	Intrinsic	Particular
User profile	A collection of settings and information associated with the characteristics and preferences of the player.	Intrinsic	Particular
Player roles	The player assumes or acts out in a particular role that was previously defined by the game designer.	Intrinsic	Imaginary
Stories	Order of events happening, i.e., choices influenced by player actions, such as strategies the player uses to go through a level (stealth or action), that also influence the ending.	Intrinsic	Imaginary
Avatar	Allows personalization. For instance, players may adapt it to their actual physical appearance.	Intrinsic	Imaginary
Rule	Statement that tells players what is or is not allowed in a particular situation.	Extrinsic	Context
Lifetime	Related to time itself and used to push forward the players' actions. In e-government services, it can be represented as deadlines (e.g., to use coupons), countdown timers, or clocks.	Extrinsic	Context
Economy	Concept related to any transaction that may occur in the platform (i.e., exchange, crowdfunding, market, etc.). Example: trading points in exchange for advantages related to the content, etc.	Extrinsic	Context
Imposed Choice-Action	When the player is faced with an explicit decision that they must make to advance. Example: show the players two different options and make them choose one or another, blocking their progress until they pick one.	Extrinsic	Context
Forum	Players may exchange ideas and discuss different topics, especially important public issues, with other players, in one space that acts as a repository for the messages in the form of a list.	Extrinsic	Media
Chat	Players talk to others who are using the service or platform at the same time through the exchange of typed messages in one space that acts as a repository for the messages, and with others that may be interested in the same topic.	Extrinsic	Media
Share	When players broadcast content on social media to their friends, groups, or specific individuals. Players enjoy sharing content with their connections.	Extrinsic	Media

Continued on following page

Table 1. Continued

Game element	Concept	Motivation	Dimension
Post	When players post ideas or information and discuss issues in messages entered into a service or platform, such as a discussion group or online forum.	Extrinsic	Media
Emoticons-Emojis	Emoticons (punctuation marks, letters, and numbers used to create pictorial icons) are a display for players to express an emotion or sentiment. Emojis (pictographs of faces, objects, and symbols) have the same objective, but they represent faces with various expressions, as well as buildings, animals, food, objects, and more.	Extrinsic	Media
Location tagging	The process through which a player attaches location information in the form of geographical metadata. Geo-tags may be used in digital output, for example, as tweets or posts updates on social media.	Extrinsic	Media

Taxonomy

The main goal of a taxonomy is to identify, classify, and give names to elements according to their characteristics. In this work, the authors propose a taxonomy that includes a list of the selected game elements, the concept definitions, the type of elicited motivation (extrinsic or intrinsic), and the dimension they can be ascribed to (Table 1).

Dimensions

The extended taxonomy (Table 1) includes a classification using six different dimensions, as agreed with the gamification experts, to group the selected game elements: Social, Achievement, Particular, Imaginary, Context, and Media. The definition of each dimension is displayed in Table 2.

Table 2. Game element dimensions

Dimension	Description
Social	Related to the interactions between players and the game environment. Without social elements, players may feel isolated or unable to interact with others. Examples: Reputation, Competition, or Cooperation-Team.
Achievement	Reveals the situation of the player and can be used to provide feedback. The absence of this dimension may result in the players feeling lost, due to a lack of clear feedback from the system in relation to their actions. Examples: Points or Levels.
Particular	Related to the player using the game environment. The lack of these elements can make players feel demotivated because the service does not adapt to them. Examples: Missions or User profile.
Imaginary	Reveals the habitat or fictional space in which the game takes place through storytelling that connects player experiences to the context. Fictional elements can be employed to provide context or create an immersive experience. Players may complete tasks following stories that may influence their game experience. Examples: Player roles, Stories, or Avatar.
Context	Related to the environment in which the gamification is being implemented. Game elements can be represented as properties. The lack of these elements makes the game environment feel boring. Examples: Economy or Lifetime.
Media	Related to the interactions of players with social media and other technologies to chat, share, post, write, etc. With media elements, players may express to public administrations or others what they feel, think, vote, etc. Examples: Post or Location tagging.

Examples of Use

Two examples of services and platforms found in the literature are described in the following paragraphs to illustrate the analysis and evaluation of the selected game elements with the proposed taxonomy.

Thiel and Fröhlich (2017) created an interface with game elements to evaluate the impact of gamification to motivate citizens to improve their city. The gamified application enabled reporting issues in the city to the public administration, such as damages or improvements required in public services or various areas. The game elements used in this mobile application are shown in Table 3.

Table 3. Game elements in Thiel and Fröhlich (2017) following the proposed taxonomy

Game elements included	Dimension
Social interaction	Social
Point Leaderboard-Ranking	Achievement
Mission Goal User profile	Particular
N/A	Imaginary
Rule Lifetime Economy	Context
Post Emoticons-Emojis Location tagging	Media

With the help of the taxonomy, it is possible to observe that this service presents 12 game elements that cover 5 different areas, with very solid Particular (3), Context (3), and Media (3) dimensions, including game elements within the Achievement (2) and Social (1) dimensions, while the Imaginary items are completely absent.

In this application, the element Social interaction (Social dimension) enables users to interact with other citizens and discuss and notify where they encountered issues in the city, such as cracks and bumps in the road, for instance. Points (or meters traveled) are assigned based on app and user activity, a Leaderboard provides a visualization of the tasks the citizen has completed, and the Ranking promotes competition among the users by displaying and comparing their progress (Achievement dimension). Missions are employed to provide the user with purpose and motivation to perform the tasks to achieve the Goal, i.e., reporting the problems encountered in the city, and citizens count with a User profile that displays their personal information and characteristics (Particular dimension). The application counts with a set of Rules the users need to follow, their actions are pushed forward thanks to the Lifetime element and, throughout the process, users can get rewards that they can trade in the application store for available products through transactions, representative of the Economy element (Context dimension). Users may Post, use Emoticons to express how they feel, and include Location tagging in their reports (Media dimension).

Some of the elements present in this example seem to be commonly used, such as Ranking (Achievement dimension), present in the applications described by Kazhamiakin et al. (2016) and Lindley and Coulton (2015), or Post (Media dimension), which also appears in the services described by Bianchini et al. (2016) and Devisch et al. (2016).

The application described by Rodrigues et al. (2019) focuses on two key aspects: competition and reward. It was designed to help the public administration promote events for citizens, cultural festivals, or seminars taking place in the city and to stimulate tourism. On the other hand, the application allows users to point out anomalous situations they may encounter across the city, see reports by other citizens, and confirm that such situations are solved. The prototype required establishing communications between a mobile application and a central web server that acted as the provider of all the necessary information for the correct operation of the app. This initiative was based on a gamification framework specifically designed for Smart Cities and included the game elements compiled in Table 4.

Table 4. Game elements in Rodrigues et al. (2019) following the proposed taxonomy

Game elements included	Dimension
Competition	Social
Progress bar Reward-Prize Point	Achievement
Mission Goal Puzzle Vote	Particular
Stories	Imaginary
Rule Imposed Choice-Action	Context
Location tagging	Media

According to the presented taxonomy, this second example includes 12 game elements that represent the 6 areas, with robust Particular (4) and Achievement (3) dimensions, and elements ascribed to Context (2), Social (1), Imaginary (1) and Media (1).

This gamified application is focused on Competition (Social dimension) and uses a Progress bar to display the evolution of the users, that gain Points and Rewards based on their participation and actions (Achievement dimension). Citizens are rewarded upon Mission completion and challenge or Puzzle fulfillment at specific touristic places, while they are also encouraged to pursue a clear Goal, i.e., to report anomalous situations within the city, and exercise their capacity to Vote, rate events, and participate in city hall decisions (Particular dimension). In addition, the gamified environment takes advantage of the element Stories (Imaginary dimension). A series of Rules and Imposed Choice-Action govern the application, for instance, by forcing the user to choose an action to continue using the system (Context dimension). Location tagging is also a useful element in this environment, for example, to produce localized reports (Media dimension).

Some of the game elements included in this example seem to be commonly used as well, such as Stories with characters (Imaginary dimension), that are employed in the works of Devisch et al. (2016)

and Kazhamiakin et al. (2016), or Location tagging (Media dimension), described in Devisch et al. (2016), Gnat et al. (2016) and Olszewski et al. (2016).

DISCUSSION

The taxonomy presented in this chapter is a first step to standardizing the game elements employed in e-government services, and the dimensions included here might constitute an additional tool to support their design. Designers, public officers and servants, as well as researchers, might benefit from this taxonomy to use and extract appropriate game elements and analyze already existing systems with the concepts described here.

This proposal is also aligned with the suggestions made by Koivisto and Hamari (2019), who state that gamification studies should pay more attention to various types of feedback and explore and incorporate the definition of universal taxonomies, as well as the recommendations of Hassan and Hamari (2020) to develop a broader understanding of practices in gamification. The proposed taxonomy contributes to simplifying the game element repertoire, as there is no consensual classification and some applications only employ the most popular and basic elements: points, leaderboards, and missions.

As previously mentioned, the **Social dimension** is related to the interactions between citizens and the social aspects of the game environment. These elements connect people and can have an influence on their behavior in relation to a task and, therefore, they must be employed carefully. Regarding the elements included in this dimension, **Reputation** represents the social status the citizens can achieve within the service or platform. The best citizens, or those who participate most, obtain a better reputation and a high status, but users that do not have a good reputation may experience a lack of acknowledgment and conclude that their actions are not meaningful (Dignan, 2011). **Competition** contributes to active environments in which citizens try to beat other users in order to obtain a prize. Nevertheless, to design an optimal competition, it is important not to tie it exclusively to reward-based activities (Papadopoulos et al., 2016). In contrast to Competition, Cooperation is seen as a positive addition to e-government environments, although it is not easy to apply. **Cooperation-Team** constitutes the combined action of a group of players to complete tasks together. The absence of actions in the group may lead to segregation, which may result in the user abandoning the platform. The use of this element may encourage citizens to share actions, information, and work together, and it can be helpful for social connectivity, to overcome group challenges, and for activities that include remote or direct competition (Foxman & Forelle, 2014). Finally, **Social interaction** refers to the interaction with other users, especially for pleasure, though it may also be somehow enforced by the service through the activities assigned.

The **Achievement dimension** must always be present in any gamified environment so that the users receive feedback on every action, for instance, through Points, Levels, or Badges. The absence of this dimension may result in users feeling lost or frustrated because their actions and interactions are not being overtly recognized, which may lead to unexpected outcomes, such as the undertaking of actions that were not foreseen by the designers. **Progress bars** are considered a highly relevant element when learning something since a perceived lack of progression might lead users to a feeling of frustration and anxiety (Dignan, 2011). Another basic and highly relevant element within this dimension is **Reward-Prize**. Motivations for gameplay include the addition of extrinsic rewards, such as vouchers or coupons for reduced garbage collection charges, parking, or entrance fees to public amenities (Crowley et al., 2012). On the other hand, if this element is tied to a financial reward from a private company, the perception of gamification as a controlling activity is greater than if the same element merely leads to a badge or listing on a leaderboard (Deterding, 2011). **Level** is also considered a significant element and represents the relative position in relation to others using the service or platform. Toda et al. (2019) highlighted that the lack of levels may make the users think that they did not advance at all in their skills or their actions. **Badges, Points**, and **Leaderboard-Ranking** are pillars, and they are present in almost all gamified platforms and services as interconnected elements. For some users, a point system attached to public status is important enough to them to perform a dull task, but for others a leaderboard is meaningless and the task itself needs to be transformed through gameful activities to provide that connection (Nicholson, 2012). Therefore, it is crucial to remember that the use of a scoring system with points requires a deeper connection with the activity to establish a meaningful connection with the experience. In addition, providing multiple streams to achieve points within the gamification system can allow users to select those methods most meaningful to them (Nicholson, 2012). Badges are features that similarly reward users, and Ranking systems can be based on badges that unlock promotions or new features. Leaderboard-Ranking may be included in other services, in which each check-in made by the users leads to accumulating points. In addition, users may receive free products or discounts, normally after repeated check-ins at the same place or service (Crowley et al., 2012).

The **Particular dimension** is related to the citizen using the environment. The lack of this type of element can make the citizen feel demotivated because the service does not provide enough context for the user. Missions or Puzzles are examples of intrinsic motivation elements that the user might not perceive as game elements because their format masks their gamified nature. **Missions** provide the citizen a goal or a purpose to perform tasks and are also known as quests, side-quests, to-dos, milestones, or objectives. The mission breaks down the goal and provides a set of related tasks designed to achieve it. It can include different levels, and players may be rewarded upon completion of each level or mission (Shah, 2012). **Puzzles** are represented through challenges, i.e., activities that are implemented within the service, and they can be considered as learning challenges or cognitive tasks. The **Goal** is a basic game element present in all environments with a gamification strategy, and without it, the user may feel lost or confused. On the other hand, designers should be cautious not to encourage undesired actions. For instance, the inclusion of too many simultaneous goals may lead users to pursue several of them without attempting to complete them accurately. Therefore, it is paramount to identify what the organization intends to achieve with gamification in order to delimit this element. For example, the goal may be to increase adoption rates, to encourage employee learning, to improve brand awareness, or to shorten processes (Shah, 2012). **Customization** is another intrinsic motivation game element, and it is the action of modifying something to suit a particular individual or task. **Emotion**, or Sensation according to Toda et al. (2019), is considered to be a highly relevant intrinsic motivator. It is related to the use of the senses, such as visual or sound stimulation, to improve the experience of the user through Virtual Reality, Augmented Reality, or dynamic interfaces. It is noteworthy that major privacy issues may arise, nonetheless, while the user is interacting, for example, with Augmented Reality markers in public and providing sensitive personal information such as username access (Contreras-Espinosa et al., 2021). This problem can be solved by informing the user about what personal data is used and what type of processing is performed (Kotsios, 2015), as well as by considering user privacy during service design, which entails delegating data storage and management to certified services (Perera et al., 2016). **Vote** represents an action, such as emitting an online comment or clicking on an icon to participate in city hall decisions. Voting could be seen as the consequence of the capacity to decide. By voting, citizens essentially decide on a concrete matter, but they often do so on a single occasion (Thiel et al., 2016). In e-platforms, citizens are encouraged to participate and actively select, through their vote, the options to be implemented by the administration. The aim is not only to collect input from the users, but to involve citizens in decision-making and receive qualified proposals, ideas, and requests from them (Bohøj et al., 2011). The last element ascribed to this dimension is **User profile**. Platforms must capture and manage user profiles in order to provide users with adapted services and relevant information (Zaoui et al., 2014). All this information collected by e-government platforms may be useful to detect behavioral patterns that enable personalizing missions, establishing the difficulty degree of the game, or choosing which type of rewards should be given to the users.

The **Imaginary dimension** is responsible for revealing the game environment and may include storytelling that connects with the experiences of the user and the context. This dimension is not commonly considered when designing e-government environments. This occurs because public administrations do not usually differentiate between narrative in different layers and storytelling. If designed correctly, this dimension can help the user focus on the content because fictional elements can provide an immersive experience. Consequently, citizens may complete tasks following **Stories**, and this can have a positive influence on their game experience. Stories are instruments to materialize a narrative, and they can powerfully do so in a stylish manner, by using text, music, audio-visuals, or other technologies. They may affect user engagement because they can be employed to provide additional information or context to the physical reality (e.g., provide historical information about a certain location in services devoted to promoting touristic places), or provide alternative explanations for tasks that the user must solve. **Player roles** and a compelling narrative to encourage user participation are key factors that improve both the process and the results (Abu-Shanab & Al-Sayed, 2019). Lastly, despite **Avatar** is not a common game element when designing e-government environments, it can constitute a robust tool to connect the user with the storytelling.

The **Context dimension** is related to the environment in which the gamification is being implemented. These game elements can be represented as properties and their absence makes the game environment feel boring. Gartner Group (2011) identified a series of principles required for the successful engagement of users, including clear **Rules**, which improve gamification success. **Lifetime** is also a key success factor for gamified platforms and affects and determines user expectations (Abu-Shanab & Al-Sayed, 2019). For instance, knowing the remaining lifetime affects how players organize their activities. **Economy** is the element represented by any transaction that may occur in the platform (e.g., exchange, crowdfunding, etc.), and these can be connected with blockchain. Last, the **Imposed Choice-Action** element provides options for the user, who is forced to make a decision, although it is crucial that designers include absolutely clear information about each option.

The **Media dimension** is related to the interactions of the citizens with social media and other technologies. It is necessary to allow the user to participate in **Forums, Chat, Share, Post**, send **Emoticons-Emojis**, or perform **Location tagging**. The implementation of these technologies will allow not only the improvement of spatial planning processes but also the development of an open geoinformation society that will create smart cities (Gnat et al., 2016).

Despite the main focus in application design typically lies on gamification and technology, the authors of this work are particularly concerned about how citizen privacy might be invaded when applying gamification due to the current use of ICT (Information and Communications Technology) and consider that this issue should be addressed when designing smart cities and e-government platforms. A smart city is a complex space that surrounds connected objects, and the technology employed is destined to produce data in the cloud (Internet), where intelligence is managed and analyzed to help organize the city, make better decisions, and improve citizen well-being (IOT Magazine, 2017). In these spaces, it is common to find ICT at the service of citizens. Indeed, e-government is defined as the process of utilizing ICT as a tool to improve the efficiency and quality of public services and government management (Michel, 2005), which affects the procedures to handle sources of information and citizens as the receptors of such services. While the concept of privacy is determined by social and national cultural values, and despite the relevance a society places on privacy may vary (Kurbalija, 2014), legal and privacy issues should not be neglected during the design of this type of application.

CONCLUSION

This work proposes a taxonomy of game elements as a tool to analyze and evaluate gamified systems. The authors, with the help of gamification experts, developed the details on the concept, comprehensibility, use, and scope of the selected game elements. Game elements were organized semantically and classified into six dimensions, which constitutes an additional useful supporting tool for public officers and servants, designers, or other stakeholders when implementing gamified strategies. Lastly, the authors introduced examples of use to demonstrate the utility of this taxonomy for the analysis and evaluation of game elements and included suggestions pertaining to each dimension. The main limitation of this ongoing work resides in the fact that the proposed taxonomy could not be validated by a larger number of experts due to time constraints.

The main conclusions of this study are being implemented in the development of the CO3 project platform to be tested in three city pilots in Athens, Paris, and Turin. This European research project aims at assessing the benefits and risks of technologies in the co-creation, co-production, and co-management of public services with citizens and public administrations and includes gamified strategies to engage citizens through a platform that includes a variety of services. Despite some of the main results and phases of the CO3 project have been previously published, with an extensive literature review on gamified e-government services (Contreras-Espinosa & Blanco-M, 2021), a first draft of the gamification strategy to use in the pilot projects (Frisiello et al., in press), or a participatory design-oriented approach to engage stakeholders in the definition of public services augmented by technologies and gamification in the Athens pilot (Pautasso et al., 2021), it is still necessary to provide more details on the concept, comprehensibility, and use of the game elements employed in the CO3 project.

It is paramount to evaluate the proposed taxonomy with a group of persons interested in using gamification in e-government services and, as future lines of work, the authors plan to test it with public officers and servants. As additional steps, the authors also contemplate analyzing user perception regarding this taxonomy to further improve the description of game elements and study the challenges of gamification in e-government from a legal perspective.

The authors firmly believe that this work can help as a first tool to provide effective guidance to public officers and servants, designers, or other stakeholders aiming at designing e-government services.

REFERENCES

Abu-Shanab, E. A., & Al-Sayed, M. R. (2019). Can Gamification Concepts Work With E-Government? *Journal of Information Technology Research*, 12(3), 44–59. doi:10.4018/JITR.2019070103

Aguilar, J., Díaz, F., Altamiranda, J., Cordero, J., Chavez, D., & Gutierrez, J. (2020). Metropolis: Emergence in a Serious Game to Enhance the Participation in Smart City Urban Planning. *Journal of the Knowledge Economy*. Advance online publication. doi:10.100713132-020-00679-5

Al-Yafi, K., & El-Masri, M. (2016). Gamification of e-Government Services: A Discussion of Potential Transformation. In *Proceedings of the Twenty-second Americas Conference on Information Systems* (pp. 1-9). Academic Press.

Bianchini, D., Fogli, D., & Ragazzi, D. (2016). TAB sharing: A gamified tool for e-participation. In *Proceedings of the International Working Conference on Advanced Visual Interfaces - AVI '16* (pp. 294–295). ACM Press. 10.1145/2909132.2926071

Bista, S. K., Nepal, S., & Paris, C. (2013). Data abstraction and visualisation in next step: Experiences from a government services delivery trial. In *Proceedings International Congress on Big Data* (pp. 263–270). IEEE. 10.1109/BigData.Congress.2013.42

Blazhko, O., Luhova, T., Melnik, S., & Ruvinska, V. (2017). Communication model of open government data gamification based on Ukrainian websites. In *Proceedings of 2017 4th Experiment at International Conference: Online Experimentation* (pp. 181–186). IEEE. 10.1109/EXPAT.2017.7984367

Bohøj, M., Borchorst, N. G., Bødker, S., Korn, M., & Zander, P. (2011). Public deliberation in municipal planning: Supporting Action and Reflection with Mobile Technology. In *Proceedings of the 5th International Conference on Communities and Technologies - C&T '11* (pp. 88–97). ACM Press. 10.1145/2103354.2103367

Brady, H. (1999). Political Participation. In J. P. Robinson, P. R. Shaver, & L. S. Wrightsman (Eds.), *Measures of Political Attitudes* (pp. 737–801). Academic Press.

Chou, Y. K. (2015). *Gamification & Behavioral Design*. Available at: https://yukaichou.com/gamification-examples/octalysis-complete-gamification-framework/

Contreras-Espinosa, R. S., & Blanco-M, A. (2021). A Literature Review of E-government Services with Gamification Elements. *International Journal of Public Administration*, 1–17. Advance online publication. doi:10.1080/01900692.2021.1930042

Contreras-Espinosa, R. S., Blanco-M, A., & Eguía-Gómez, J. L. (2021). Implementation Barriers to Augmented Reality Technology in Public Services. *International Journal of Interactive Mobile Technologies*, 15(3), 43–56. doi:10.3991/ijim.v15i13.22667

Coronado Escobar, J. E., & Vasquez Urriago, A. R. (2014). Gamification: an effective mechanism to promote civic engagement and generate trust? In *ICEGOV '14: Proceedings of the 8th International Conference on Theory and Practice of Electronic Governance* (pp. 514-515). ACM Press. 10.1145/2691195.2691307

Crowley, D. N., Breslin, J. G., & Corcoran, P. (2012). Gamification of Citizen Sensing through Mobile Social Reporting, In *Proceedings of the 2012 IEEE International Games Innovation Conference* (pp.1–5). IEEE. 10.1109/IGIC.2012.6329849

Deci, E., & Ryan, R. (2004). *Handbook of self-determination research*. University of Rochester Press.

Deterding, S. (2011). Situated motivational affordances of game elements: A conceptual model. In *CHI 2011* (pp. 1–4). ACM Press.

Deterding, S., Dixon, D., Khaled, R., & Nacke, L. (2011). From game design elements to gamefulness: defining gamification. In *Proceedings of the 15th International AcademicMindTrek Conference on Envisioning Future Media Environments - MindTrek* (pp. 9). ACM Press. 10.1145/2181037.2181040

Devisch, O., Poplin, A., & Sofronie, S. (2016). The Gamification of Civic Participation: Two Experiments in Improving the Skills of Citizens to Reflect Collectively on Spatial Issues. *Journal of Urban Technology, 23*(2), 81–102. doi:10.1080/10630732.2015.1102419

Dichev, C., & Dicheva, D. (2017). Gamifying education: What is known, what is believed and what remains uncertain: A critical review. *International Journal of Educational Technology in Higher Education, 14*(9), 9. Advance online publication. doi:10.118641239-017-0042-5

Dignan, A. (2011). *Game Frame. Using games as a strategy for success*. Free Press.

Foxman, M., & Forelle, M. (2014). Electing to Play: MTV's Fantasy Election and Changes in Political Engagement Through Gameplay. *Games and Culture, 9*(6), 454–467. doi:10.1177/1555412014549804

Frisiello, A., Nhu Nguyen, Q., Chiesa, M., Contreras-Espinosa, R. S., & Blanco-M., A. (in press). Conceptual design of a Gamification strategy applied to Commoning. In *XII Congress of the Italian Society of Ergonomics "Gentle Ergonomics"*. Academic Press.

Gartner Group. (2011). *More Than 50 Percent of Organizations That Manage Innovation Processes Will Gamify Those Processes*. Retrieved from https://www.gartner.com/newsroom/id/1629214

Gnat, M., Leszek, K., & Olszewski, R. (2016). The Use of Geoinformation Technology, Augmented Reality and Gamification in the Urban Modeling Process. In O. Gervasi & ... (Eds.), Lecture Notes in Computer Science: Vol. 9787. *Computational Science and Its Applications. ICCSA 2016*. Springer. doi:10.1007/978-3-319-42108-7_37

Hamari, J., Koivisto, J., & Sarsa, H. (2014). Does gamification work? A literature review of empirical studies on gamification. In *47th Hawaii International Conference on System Sciences (HICSS)* (pp. 3025-3034). IEEE. 10.1109/HICSS.2014.377

Hamari, J., & Tuunanen, J. (2014). Player types: A meta-synthesis. *Transactions of the Digital Games Research Association, 1*(2).

Hassan, L. (2016). Governments Should Play Games: Towards a Framework for the Gamification of Civic Engagement Platforms. *Simulation & Gaming, 48*(2), 249–267. doi:10.1177/1046878116683581

Hassan, L., & Hamari, J. (2020). Gameful civic engagement: A review of the literature on gamification of e-participation. *Government Information Quarterly, 37*(3), 1–21. doi:10.1016/j.giq.2020.101461

Hollebeek, L. (2011). Exploring customer brand engagement: Definition and themes. *Journal of Strategic Marketing, 19*(7), 555–573. doi:10.1080/0965254X.2011.599493

Hunicke, R., LeBlanc, M., & Zubek, R. (2004). MDA: A formal approach to game design and game research. In *Proceedings of the Challenges in Games AI Workshop, Nineteenth National Conference of Artificial Intelligence* (*vol. 4*, pp. 1-9). Academic Press.

Huotari, K., & Hamari, J. (2017). A definition for gamification: Anchoring gamification in the service marketing literature. *Electronic Markets*, 27(1), 21–31. doi:10.100712525-015-0212-z

Jiménez, S. (2013). *Gamification Model Canvas*. Available at: https://gecon.es/wp-content/uploads/2017/07/GMC-Evolution_vDef.pdf

Johnson, D., Deterding, S., Kuhn, K.-A., Staneva, A., Stoyanov, S., & Hides, L. (2016). Gamification for health and wellbeing: A systematic review of the literature. *Internet Interventions: the Application of Information Technology in Mental and Behavioural Health*, 6, 89–106. doi:10.1016/j.invent.2016.10.002 PMID:30135818

Kalogiannakis, M., Papadakis, S., & Zourmpakis, A.-I. (2021). Gamification in Science Education. A Systematic Review of the Literature. *Education Sciences*, 11(22), 2–36. doi:10.3390/educsci11010022

Kazhamiakin, R., Marconi, A., Martinelli, A., Pistore, M., Fondazione, G. V., & Kessler-Trento, B. (2016). A Gamification Framework for the Long–term Engagement of Smart Citizens. In *Proceedings of the IEEE 2nd International Smart Cities Conference: Improving the Citizens Quality of Life, ISC2 2016* (pp. 1–7). IEEE. 10.1109/ISC2.2016.7580746

Koivisto, J., & Hamari, J. (2019). The rise of motivational information systems: A review of gamification research. *International Journal of Information Management*, 45, 191–210. doi:10.1016/j.ijinfomgt.2018.10.013

Kotsios, A. (2015). Privacy in an augmented reality. *International Journal of Law and Information Technology*, 23(2), 157–185. doi:10.1093/ijlit/eav003

Kurbalija, J. (2014). *An Introduction to Internet Governance* (6th ed.). Diplo Foundation.

Lindley, J., & Coulton, P. (2015). Game of Drones. In *Proceedings of the 2015 Annual Symposium on Computer-Human Interaction in Play - CHI PLAY '15* (pp.613–618). ACM Press. 10.1145/2793107.2810300

Magazine, I. O. T. (2017). *Four Essential Elements for Smart City Success*. Available at: https://www.iotnow.com/2017/10/05/68412-four-essential-elementssmart-city-success/

Marczewski, A. (2013). *Gamification: a simple introduction. Tips, advice and thoughts on gamification*. Andrzej Marczewski.

May Saßmannshausen, S., Radtke, J., Bohn, N., Hussein, H., Randall, D., & Pipek, V. (2021). Citizen-Centered Design in Urban Planning: How Augmented Reality can be used in Citizen Participation Processes. In *Designing Interactive Systems Conference 2021 (DIS '21)*, (pp.250-265). ACM Press. 10.1145/3461778.3462130

Michel, H. (2005). e-Administration, e-Government, e-Governance and the Learning City: A typology of Citizenship management using ICTs. *The Electronic Journal of E-Government*, 3(4), 213–218.

Mora, A., Riera, D., Gonzalez, C., & Arnedo-Moreno, J. (2015). A literature review of Gamification design frameworks. In *7th International Conference on Games and Virtual Worlds for Serious Applications (VS-Games)* (pp.1–8). IEEE. 10.1109/VS-GAMES.2015.7295760

Nah, F. F. H., Zeng, Q., Telaprolu, V. R., Ayyappa, A. P., & Eschenbrenner, B. (2014). Gamification of Education: A Review of Literature. In F. F.-H. Nah (Ed.), Lecture Notes in Computer Science: Vol. 8527. *HCI in Business. HCIB 2014*. Springer. doi:10.1007/978-3-319-07293-7_39

Nicholson, S. (2012). A User-Centered Theoretical Framework for Meaningful Gamification. *Games+Learning+ Society, 8*(1), 223–230.

Olszewski, R., Turek, A., & Łączyński, M. (2016). Urban Gamification as a Source of Information for Spatial Data Analysis and Predictive Participatory Modelling of a City's Development. In *Proceedings of the 5th International Conference on Data Management Technologies and Applications – DATA* (pp. 176-181). 10.5220/0006005201760181

Opromolla, A., Ingrosso, A., Volpi, V., Medaglia, C. M., Palatucci, M., & Pazzola, M. (2015). Gamification in a Smart City context. An analysis and a proposal for its application in co-design processes. In *Proceedings of the international conference on games and learning alliance* (pp. 73-82). 10.1007/978-3-319-22960-7_8

Papadopoulos, P. M., Lagkas, T., & Demetriadis, S. N. (2016). How revealing rankings affects student attitude and performance in a peer review learning environment. In *Communications in Computer and Information Science* (pp. 225–240). Springer International Publishing. doi:10.1007/978-3-319-29585-5_13

Pautasso, E., Frisiello, A., Chiesa, M., Ferro, E., Dominici, F., Tsardanidis, G., Efthymiou, I., Zgeras, G., & Vlachokyriakos, V. (2021). The Outreach of Participatory Methods in Smart Cities, From the Co-Design of Public Services to the Evaluation: Insights From the Athens Case Study. *International Journal of Urban Planning and Smart Cities, 2*(1), 59–83. doi:10.4018/IJUPSC.2021010105

Peng, W., Lin, J. H., Pfeiffer, K. A., & Winn, B. (2012). Need satisfaction supportive game features as motivational determinants: An experimental study of a self-determination theory guided exergame. *Media Psychology, 15*(2), 175–196. doi:10.1080/15213269.2012.673850

Perera, C., McCormick, C., Bandara, A. K., Price, B. A., & Nuseibeh, B. (2016). Privacy-by-Design Framework for Assessing Internet of Things Applications and Platforms. In *Proceedings of the 6th International Conference on the Internet of Things*. 10.1145/2991561.2991566

Rigby, C. S. (2015). Gamification and motivation 4. In S. P. Walz & S. Deterding (Eds.), *Gameful world: Approaches, issues, applications* (pp. 113–138). The MIT Press.

Rodrigues, M., Monteiro, V., Novais, P., & Analide, C. (2019). Getting Residents Closer to Public Institutions Through Gamification. In *Ambient Intelligence – Software and Applications –, 9th International Symposium on Ambient Intelligence. ISAmI2018 2018* (pp. 33-39). Springer. 10.1007/978-3-030-01746-0_4

Romano, M., Díaz, P., & Aedo, I. (2021). Gamification-less: May gamification really foster civic participation? A controlled field experiment. *Journal of Ambient Intelligence and Humanized Computing*. Advance online publication. doi:10.100712652-021-03322-6

Ryan, R. M., Rigby, C. S., & Przybylski, A. K. (2006). The Motivational Pull of Video Games: A Self-Determination Theory Approach. *Motivation and Emotion, 30*(4), 344–360. doi:10.100711031-006-9051-8

Savignac, E. (2017). *Gamification of Work: The Use of Games in the Workplace*. Wiley Publishing. doi:10.1002/9781119384564

Sgueo, G. (2017). *Gamification, participatory democracy and engaged public (S)*. University of Vienna. https://papers.ssrn.com/sol3/papers.cfm?abstract_id=3045361

Shah, A. (2012). Gamification: It's all about Processes. *Cognizant 20-20 Insights*, 1-4.

Thiel, S-K. (2017). Let's play Urban Planner: The use of Game Elements in Public Participation Platforms. *PlaNext - Next Generation Planning, 4*, 58–75. doi:10.24306/plnxt.2017.04.005

Thiel, S.-K., & Fröhlich, P. (2017). Gamification as Motivation to Engage in Location-Based Public Participation? In G. Gartner & H. Huang (Eds.), *Progress in Location-Based Services 2016*. Springer. doi:10.1007/978-3-319-47289-8_20

Thiel, S-K., Reisinger, M., Röderer, K., & Fröhlich, P. (2016). Playing (with) Democracy: A Review of Gamified Participation Approaches. *eJournal of eDemocracy and Open Government, 8*(3), 32-60.

Toda, A. M., Klock, A. C. T., Oliveira, W., Palomino, P. T., Rodrigues, L., Shi, L., Bittencourt, I., Gasparini, I., Isotani, S., & Cristea, A. I. (2019). Analysing gamification elements in educational environments using an existing Gamification taxonomy. *Smart Learning Environments, 6*(1), 16. Advance online publication. doi:10.118640561-019-0106-1

van Gaalen, A. E. J., Brouwer, J., Schönrock-Adema, J., Bouwkamp-Timmer, T., Jaarsma, A. D. C., & Georgiadis, J. R. (2021). Gamification of health professions education: A systematic review. *Advances in Health Sciences Education: Theory and Practice, 26*(2), 683–711. doi:10.100710459-020-10000-3 PMID:33128662

Warmelink, H., Koivisto, J., Mayer, I., Vesa, M., & Hamari, J. (2020). Gamification of production and logistics operations: Status quo and future directions. *Journal of Business Research, 106*, 331–340. doi:10.1016/j.jbusres.2018.09.011

Werbach, K., & Hunter, D. (2012). *For the Win: How Game Thinking Can Revolutionize Your Business*. Wharton Digital Press.

Yen, B. T. H., Mulley, C., & Burke, M. (2019). Gamification in transport interventions: Another way to improve travel behavioural change. *Cities (London, England), 85*, 140–149. doi:10.1016/j.cities.2018.09.002

Zaoui, I., Elmaghraoui, H., Benhlima, E., & Chiadmi, D. (2014). Towards a Personalized E-Government Platform. *International Journal of Computer Science: Theory and Application, 2*(2), 35–40.

Chapter 5
A View on the Impact of Gamified Services in the Wake of the COVID–19 Pandemic:
An Interdisciplinary Approach

Sebastian Joy Panattil

ⓘ https://orcid.org/0000-0001-6277-2362

Cochin University of Science and Technology, India

Anoop George

Cochin University of Science and Technology, India

Manu Melwin Joy

Cochin University of Science and Technology, India

ABSTRACT

The chapter examines the researchers' objective to see how gamification has been investigated in various science disciplines during the COVID-19 pandemic and its impact by grouping the findings into central concerns and core issues. The PRISMA approach is used to narrow down the list of relevant articles. The necessity for gamified interventions in the retail, education, and health domains is deliberated in this chapter. The findings suggest that academicians take the chance to collect empirical data and evaluate it in real-time to better understand the impact of gamification in a variety of professions.

INTRODUCTION

The COVID-19 pandemic has swept the globe, infecting every region. As policymakers struggle with revised lockdown policies to combat the virus's spread, national economies and companies are experiencing adverse consequences. According to the International Monetary Fund, the global economy will contract to 4.9% in 2022. This will mark the fault lines which were initially papered over by 2021's

DOI: 10.4018/978-1-7998-9223-6.ch005

projected growth rate of 6%. The downturn faced immediately in the aftermath of the pandemic in 2020 where the IMF predicted a negative growth of -3.2%, according to the officialdoms, is the worst since the Great Depression of the 1930s (*World Economic Outlook Update, July 2021*, 2021). Shoppers remained at home, causing retail footfall to plummet to new lows. Since the first lockdown, the number of pedestrians has decreased even further. The hospitality industry has closed its doors all over the world. The experts say that international travel and tourism will not recover to pre-pandemic heights up until 2025. Because of all these, most of the governments have recently begun to offer a substantial economic assistance program to their residents and enterprises, primarily in the form of wage grants, money allotments to lesser income families, and reductions in taxes and rent drops for businesses (Açikgöz & Günay, 2020). No doubt that these actions have helped all sectors and people for their existence. Even if we can't stop harmful viruses from advancing, we can plan to mitigate their effect on various economic sectors. The COVID-19 has pushed the idea of working from home into the mainstream, and social isolation has converted the new normal. Consumers' instinct buying habits have been influenced by their ability to do something at home. All these also led to changes in consumer behavior. Understanding more about how we can adapt to these changes to survive or develop the business is a need and a concern.

One of the behavioral effects of the lockdowns during the COVID-19 pandemic is a massive rise in Internet and social media use (Donthu & Gustafsson, 2020). There is also a dramatically altered fulfillment of needs and aspirations such as greater happiness, higher participation, and general well-being, resulting in a higher probability of misfits employed in organizations. People are becoming more linked across the world as a result of digital technologies. In most countries, online shopping has become more popular. The truth is that innovative digital technology has become a requirement rather than an option. The adoption of innovative technologies by various sectors helped them to survive during the pandemic to a greater extent. Gamification has been one of the most critical and innovative technological developments. Gamification is the method of adding game-like features to a service in order to support users' overall value development (Huotari & Hamari, 2012). Gamification's main goal is to encourage desired user activity. Understanding psychology theories is a necessary and unavoidable building block in the development of good gamification since motivation and behavior are explored in psychology. Gamification may be encompassed in a variety of situations from the past years. They include topics such as business, fitness, well-being, productivity, learning, and development, sports, finances, entertainment, crowdsourcing, etc., to name a few. We also see gamification strategies that are more organized around concepts of intrinsic motivation instead of just driven by external influences in early 2019.

Gamification is gaining importance across various sectors and also being in the interest of both industrialists and academicians. We can also find research papers which are empirically proved that gamification has positive significance in multiple areas (Majuri et al., 2018a) and has been published globally by IGI Global, Sage Publications, and Springer, etc. However the research that focuses on the influence of gamification on different verticals during the COVID-19 pandemic has been overlooked. This is an area that needs to be addressed as it could provide both academicians and managers with many inferences and possible coping mechanisms for such situations in the future. Therefore, the mission is to check how gamification has been studied during the COVID-19 pandemic in interdisciplinary branches of science and the effect it now has by highlighting the results into central topics and core issues. For this, the relevant empirical papers that match with the context are being identified by looking at various journals. The PRISMA methodology is expanded to identify the relevant works of literature, which is detailed in the methodology part. The working principles and theories were explained, which back up the relevance of the literature. Basically, the chapter will cover three areas like retail, education, and health, where gamification helped make things far better during the pandemic. It also details how gamification could make positive significance on these verticals.

We chose to adopt these three domains as they represent both personal and commercial domains of interest, both equally disrupted in the wake of the pandemic. In the case of retail, e-commerce platforms have had to adapt to the sudden upheaval brought about by pandemics by way of disrupted supply lines resulting in longer delivery timelines. In the case of learning and education, there was a seismic change in terms of the traditional classroom learning format being replaced by more modern remote learning technologies and platforms. With more people having to turn to a work-from-home lifestyle due to the shutting down of offices and establishments going remote, there was an upheaval in the lifestyles of people, and their personal schedules were thrown astray. With the increased threat of Covid infections rising, people were finding it difficult to maintain a healthy lifestyle. The need for services that helped people and organizations across these domains through the pandemic has been in demand. The following sections will detail existing service platforms that seek to engage users and bring about changes in behavioral patterns by adopting gamification mechanisms into the core service. In a way, this chapter seeks to take inspiration from the writing of the ancient Greek historian Herodotus, who wrote about a society called the Lydians who survived an eighteen-year famine by playing a dice game called Mancala (McGonigal, 2011). An eighteen-year-long famine coped with by just playing a dice game seems too far-fetched. But Herodotus details the manner in which this society did so. The Lydians played the dice game every alternate day while they worked and scavenged for food the next day. This way, they were able to keep their minds off of their hunger and famine. Playing the dice game together also brought them together as a community and helped them develop stronger social bonds. In a way, this pandemic has disrupted our social connections and means of bonding, and we, as authors, seek to identify ways in which we as a society can cope with this pandemic that has wreaked such havoc across the globe.

METHODOLOGY

The PRISMA approach(PRISMA, 2021) was used to determine which articles to include in the analysis in order to satisfy the objectives. The universe was comprised of all works reported in Scopus and Google Scholar between 2020 and 2021, which included the terms "gamification*pandemic" and "gamification*covid." There were 7492 papers found in this search. In order to find suitable articles for the study, the following criteria were used.

- The papers that were not either research articles or review articles are excluded.
- The articles which were not from the retail, health & well-being and education sectors were excluded.
- The duplicate articles are eliminated.
- Papers published in a language other than English are excluded.
- Papers that were published before 2020 are not considered for the study.
- The articles with only abstracts, tutorials, and posters are all excluded.

and therefore the number of articles was reduced to 88. The three authors made the final selection of research articles from these 88 articles in order to avoid discrepancies that emerged and were resolved by screening the complete document. Finally, 27 relevant articles across the three verticals were selected, from which the majority of articles were from IGI global, Sage Publications, and Springer. A detailed flow diagram highlighting the procedure of selecting the final 27 research articles relevant to the theme of the chapter is shown in Figure 1.

Figure 1. PRISMA Flow Diagram

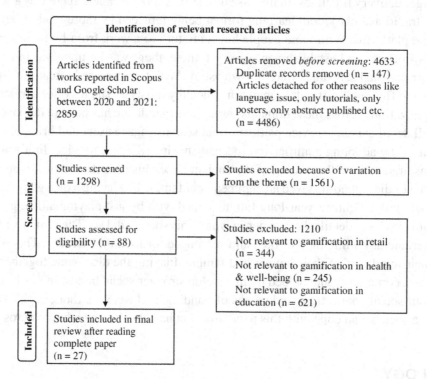

PANDEMIC EFFECT ON RETAIL

Since we're in the midst of a COVID-19, estimating the long-term repercussions on financial, behavioral, or social implications is extremely challenging, as these components have still not been examined extensively in the prior. Today communities are more accessible than before; people depend on imports of critical things like food, fuel, and diagnostic supplies instead of obtaining them locally; but there are few measures to plan for pandemic breakouts. Many firms have been forced to shut down as a result of the COVID-19 pandemic, causing severe disruptions in various industries. As people remain at home and economies closed down due to the COVID-19 pandemic, several reputed brands in various sectors are expected to go bankrupt (Trucker, 2020). Short-term difficulties confront retailers and firms, including those relating to health and safety, distribution network, labor, working capital, customer needs, sales, and promotion. A further effect of the lockdowns during COVID-19 is a massive surge in Internet and social media traffic. Prior studies have found that those who are lonely are much more likely to use social media and, in certain situations, prefer it to physical communication (Nowland et al., 2017).

The article "Effects of COVID-19 on business and research "by (Donthu & Gustafsson, 2020) shares that the COVID-19 has ramifications not only for the economy but for the entire society. The study results also claim that there are significant changes in how firms and consumers conduct themselves. The research article, "Impact of COVID-19 on Consumer Behavior: Will Old Habits Return or Die?" from (Sheth, 2020), looks at how the COVID-19 has impacted various parts of human livelihoods that ranges from individual mobility to online shopping. Since of the COVID-19 pandemic's fear of infection, customers are opting to purchase from a residence instead of stepping out now because people believe it is a safer option. As a result, customer behavior and attitudes have altered, and the pandemic has influenced consumer buying behavior (Laato et al., 2020). Numerous sectors, particularly in the tourist and hospitality industries, have vanished. Surprisingly, electronic communication, digital media, and internet shopping are all seeing exceptional growth at the very same period. Understanding what mechanisms can lead to dealing with reported unusual behavior is important for retail services for at least three reasons: initially, to be able to more effectively respond to parallel circumstances in the forthcoming days; second, to assist presently struggling retail services in dealing with the continuing pandemic; and lastly, to deliver insight about advanced gamification concepts.

Need For Gamification In Retail

The COVID-19 virus's long-term socioeconomic and health effects are indeed uncertain. The one and only chance of recovery are for present worldwide efforts to limit the virus and its effects to be effective. And according to the researcher's perspective, wise retailers are considering how to incorporate design thinking methods to innovation over and done with gamification(Patrício et al., 2020) and apply into their operations for making plans appropriately. Shoppers' online channel decision is mainly driven by contextual impacts, with one of the contextual elements, the COVID-19 pandemic, being successful in converting shopper intents into online food delivery activity. Approximately forty-six percent of shoppers were purchasing online for the first time throughout that time frame, and seventy-one percentage stated they intend to keep online purchasing after the outbreak because of the anxiety and uncertainty surrounding the COVID-19 pandemic(*COVID-19 Spurring Impulse Spending, Reveals Survey*, 2020).

E-commerce platforms like Amazon show that game mechanics such as points and badges can have a positive influence on behavioural intentions among the target user groups (García-Jurado et al., 2019). During the pandemic, this has a substantial effect on sales purchases in e-tailing, with sales anticipated to reach 6.5 trillion US dollars in 2023(Hashem, 2020).In retail outlets, arousing the sensory experiences with light, sound, scent, feel, and engagement with salesmen as well as other shoppers improves the customer experience. These features, however, don't really encourage consumers to purchase online; instead, comfort, value benefits, enjoyment, and fun are heavily favored to win the consumer experience(Karać & Stabauer, 2017). In the online purchasing journey, an interactive and engaging user interface can lead to a flow scenario by creating a more delightful retail experience. There have been numerous studies that show that gamification is a component of the gradual shift from accessibility and toward a more holistic view to user experience leading to purchase intention (Brühlmann, 2018; García-Jurado et al., 2019; Hamari & Koivisto, 2014).

Gamification For Purchase Journey

Gamification is now being deployed in a number of sectors(Rapp et al., 2019), including retailing and marketing, to boost engagement and retention, leading to increased revenue. Gamification technologies can be employed on retail internet sites for a variety of goals, including content production, conversion optimization, and user loyalty promotion. Multinational businesses, such as Amazon, Flipkart, and eBay, are capitalizing on the good qualities of game elements by incorporating them into their web and mobile applications to increase user involvement(Moin & Rahman, 2019). Whatsoever in both multinational and local retail businesses, the shopper purchase journey consists of three stages. They are before purchase, during purchase, and after purchase. The pre-buy component involves all interactions between the consumer and the retailer prior to making a purchase, and often includes need awareness, exploration, and evaluation. Gamification can assist customers in better identifying their own requirements and searching for acceptable product possibilities at this level. All buyer transactions that take place during the purchase phase, such as selecting, obtaining, and transaction, are included in the purchase phase. All buyer engagements with the retailer after the sale has been accomplished, including usage and intake, post-purchase involvement, and customer information, are included in the after purchase phase. Gamification is frequently used to determine the buyer's follow-up services and also to maintain the loyalty scheme. Gamification's support should so aid the consumer in obtaining the required goods and finishing the transaction. Many retailers, as per (Roggeveen & Sethuraman, 2020), use gaming features during the pandemic to keep customers engaged even during the purchasing process. Figure 2 represents the game mechanics applied in these three stages of the purchase journey along with its working principle

Figure 2. Purchase journey and the relevant game mechanics

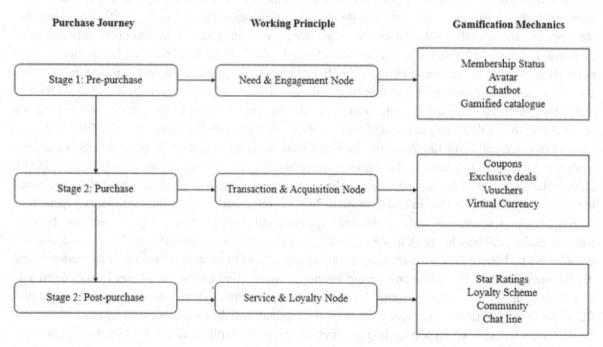

During the pre-purchase stage game mechanics like avatars and animated chatbots can bring a human effect to the interactions between the consumer and the retail service. In the purchase stage, coupons, virtual currency can help improve user perceptions of transactional value from the retail service. Finally in the post purchase stage, mechanics like community, loyalty schemes can help build long lasting relationships both with the retail service and fellow consumers.

The Scope For Future Studies

The majority of the research papers the authors had shortlisted are based on a well-defined theoretical foundation, allowing the researchers to create narrow research questions that can help advance the theory. Flow theory, Technology Acceptance Model and Uses, Self-Determination Theory (SDT), and Uses and Gratification Theory (UGT) are some of the most common theories associated with retail and COVID-19. Whatsoever the papers linking pandemic and gamification in retail are very limited even though the scope is very high. Future studies can also incorporate the effectiveness of individual game mechanics on three stages of the purchase journey in e-tailing, considering the pandemic situation.

GAMIFICATION AND LEARNING AND EDUCATION DURING THE PANDEMIC

With the advent of the COVID-19 pandemic, the field of education and learning had to undergo a forceful, seismic change in terms of the delivery model. In order to comply with government and various health body recommendations and protocols with regards to social distancing, physical classrooms were replaced with remote virtual classrooms where teachers and students interacted using various online meeting platforms like Google Meet, Zoom, Microsoft Teams, and Cisco's Webex. The domain of education and learning was one that had to undergo this change in a swift manner (Almarzooq et al., 2020). Although the usage of such platforms to ensure the continuance of learning in a remote manner were also available to the various stakeholders in the domain prior to the pandemic, the litmus test for such platforms came when the entire domain of education and learning had to switch to such a mode for every aspect of learning delivery. The availability of modern communication technologies has made it possible for educators to deliver their courses through such distance learning platforms, and it has provided students with easy access to information and encourages the development and sharing of knowledge. However, the challenge to identify ways to boost students' motivation and involvement remain, and it becomes more important in the wake of the pandemic. As a result, a lot of effort has gone into developing innovative teaching tactics that boost students' interest and commitment while simultaneously maximizing their information acquisition (Nieto-Escamez & Roldán-Tapia, 2021). Gamification involves a method of educational training that blends gaming dynamics into educational programs and is becoming increasingly popular. Many studies have demonstrated that it is more effective than traditional education techniques at enhancing knowledge, skills, and satisfaction (Majuri et al., 2018b; O'Connell et al., 2020). Platforms like ChemDraw, used for chemistry drawings have incorporated game mechanics of community and competition with a view to enhance student learning and skill development with regards to organic chemistry (Fontana, 2020).

Theoretical Background for Gamification in Education and Learning

Most gamification studies are posited on the Self Determination Theory (Ryan & Deci, 2000a), which bats for the satisfaction of intrinsic needs of autonomy, competence, and relatedness (Ryan & Deci, 2000b) which according to the theory when satisfied by a given system tends to result in better engagement outcomes for the users of the system (Wee & Choong, 2019; Xi & Hamari, 2019). In an educational context, when these needs of students are fulfilled, the students are seen to have improved performance and learning outcomes. Autonomy refers to the need for individuals to feel in control of their behaviors and goals. This need can be satisfied by providing them with a sense of volition that initiating certain actions that will result in significant change. For example, when a student partakes in a particular assignment that allows him to take charge of their own actions is an example of a learning system that satisfies their need for autonomy. Competence refers to the need for gaining mastery or expertise over a particular skill set. A learning system that enables and constantly reinforces this need is one that will find considerable improvements in the skill levels of the users over a period of time. Relatedness refers to the need for people to connect and develop a sense of belonging with each other in a community or a group setting. Another theory that is often relied upon in gamification studies is the Goal Setting Theory. The theory puts forward the argument that individuals need to be challenged, with indicators of progress provided by way of feedback mechanisms and (Locke & Latham, 2006). In the context of learning, the student's performance is influenced by four factors: their commitment to the goal, the feedback they receive, the activity's complexity, and the situational limitations (Landers, 2014; Locke & Latham, 2006). The development of learning systems enhanced with gamification features has been seen in the wake of the COVID-19 pandemic. These systems are developed with the aim of mitigating the shortcomings of the remote learning environments necessitated by the pandemic. Staying true to these foundational theories seen in gamification studies and applied in gamified learning environments, these systems seek to provide students with collaborative environments to review key concepts (da Silva Júnior et al., 2020), to ensure a sense of wellness and class community (Fontana, 2020) and to motivate and engage the students (Pakinee & Puritat, 2021).

Need for Gamification in Learning and Education

With the onset of the COVID-19 pandemic, the stakeholders of the learning and education domain have had to adapt quickly to the changes brought about by social distancing measures and lockdowns across the world. The traditional methodology of curriculum delivery through classical structures like physical classrooms has had to be replaced with virtual platforms. Students and teachers have had to carry on with their individual roles by trying to keep themselves and others motivated to learn. It is pertinent to have learning systems that motivate students to initiate learning-related behaviors by providing them with clear and defined goals while constantly reinforcing their skill development activities by employing dynamic feedback mechanisms and by providing a platform for them to connect with each other while being socially distant, could be vital in ensuring that learning outcomes and program objectives are met (Nieto-Escamez & Roldán-Tapia, 2021). Literature has shown that gamified learning solutions developed especially in the context of the COVID-19 pandemic have shown to have superior learning outcomes when compared to traditional curriculum delivery methodologies. By implementing these solutions, students would be enabled to take ownership and control of the learning process, which in turn enhances their motivation to further their learning outcomes in many scenarios (Oe et al., 2020). Therefore gamification should be strategically implemented in the curriculum to assist students' learning by making the learning process appealing, fair, and engaging (Syakur et al., 2020; Whitton & Langan, 2019). Designers of learning systems should incorporate learning from such studies in order to aid the design of learning systems to cater to the post COVID-19 learning and education environments.

Scope for Future Studies

Research in the field of learning and education in the wake of COVID-19 could do well to look at the social support mechanisms incorporated in gamified learning platforms. This could prove to be especially useful in an environment where students and teachers are becoming increasingly isolated. Also, future studies could investigate the effect of specific gamification features like instant feedback on the motivation levels of both teachers and students using a gamified learning and education platform.

HEALTH AND WELLNESS DOMAIN IN THE WAKE OF COVID-19

The havoc caused by the pandemic had thrown the healthcare sector into disarray. With resources stretched, healthcare providers, pharmaceutical companies, and governments were seen to be looking for ways to find a cure and manage the spread of the COVID-19 virus. With a world already facing a plethora of health-related problems due to rapidly changing lifestyles (Johnson et al., 2016), the COVID-19 pandemic further exacerbated the problem. In the domain of healthcare, there are a plethora of platforms and information systems that seek to deliver healthcare solutions and interventions to users who face hindrances in availing healthcare resources (Lenihan, 2012). By implementing gamification features into healthcare platforms, designers of such platforms are able to drive long-term behavior change. Gamified healthcare services seek to provide users with a variety of solutions that range from health and wellness awareness (DeSmet et al., 2014; Gao et al., 2015; Middelweerd et al., 2014), physical rehabilitation and disease management (Martínez-Pérez et al., 2013; Theng et al., 2015) and training of healthcare service providers (Chon et al., 2019; de Ribaupierre et al., 2014; Gupta et al., 2021; Ricciardi & Paolis, 2014; Wang et al., 2016). There have been several applications of game mechanics like challenges, rules, transparency, feedback and reward in gamified health awareness campaigns such as Booster Buddy, Flu Busters and Land of Secret Gardens (Mat Zain et al., 2021).

Need for Gamification in Health and Wellness

Since the COVID-19 pandemic hit the world, governments and healthcare stakeholders have been trying to raise awareness among people with regards to the importance of social distancing, personal hygiene, and health management. There have been studies that look into the efficacy of gamification features applied in a healthcare-related context (Alahäivälä & Oinas-Kukkonen, 2016; DeSmet et al., 2014). In the context of the COVID-19 pandemic, the need for Health and Behaviour Change Support Systems (HBCSS) (Alahäivälä & Oinas-Kukkonen, 2016; Mettler, 2015; Oinas-Kukkonen & Harjumaa, 2009) that facilitate health-oriented behavioral changes and results, are the need of the hour. HBCSS are defined as socio-technical information systems with psychological and behavioral effects meant to develop, change, or maintain attitudes, behaviors, or a compliance act without the use of pressure or manipulation (Oinas-Kukkonen, 2013). With present treatment options involving symptom-based management and the efficacy of certain vaccines yet to get global acceptance, healthcare service providers are looking to implement and promote healthcare practices to manage and prevent the spread of the disease. This prevention of the disease requires established protocols that involve social distancing, sanitizing, and hygiene-related measures. Governments and healthcare stakeholders have been working hard to create awareness about the importance of practicing various preventive measures to combat the spread of the virus. In the present scenario, health and behavior change support systems that promote such health awareness campaigns have been researched with encouraging results among the selected sample of respondents (Mat Zain, 2020; Mat Zain et al., 2021).

Theoretical Background for Gamification in Health and Wellness

Gamified HBCSS use social support, social influence, and user feedback mechanisms to bring about behavioral change among users (Al-Ramahi et al., 2016; Myneni & Iyengar, 2016; Taiminen & Taiminen, 2016). The use of these mechanisms strongly supports the satisfaction of the intrinsic need of relatedness, which can be afforded by incorporating online social network interactions and online communities (Fu et al., 2009; Tolks et al., 2019; Xi & Hamari, 2019). Research has shown that feedback that is suited to the characteristic of each user (Imbeault et al., 2011). In order to satisfy the relatedness need, some HBCSS applications are seen to incorporate interaction and collaboration among users on popular social media platforms while other applications had their own online exclusive social network (AlMarshedi et al., 2015; Cafazzo et al., 2012; Patricio et al., 2020).

In this period of social distancing and isolation, the need for relatedness cannot be stressed enough. Gamified HBCSS that address this need would help users enjoy engaging in the system's health-related behaviors sought to be afforded. As the world looks for a cure, it is up to every individual to support each other in their efforts to combat the virus and its spread.

Scope for Future Studies

Future studies in the domain of gamified HBCSS could seek to investigate the effect of individual game mechanics that cater specifically to or a combination of the intrinsic needs of autonomy, competence, and relatedness. Also, longitudinal studies could investigate the effect of COVID-19 prevention awareness programs perpetuated through a gamified HBCSS.

CONCLUSION

The researchers used the PRISMA approach to find relevant papers that linked COVID-19 and gamification in this chapter. The 27 articles have been chosen for review and insight into many fields such as retail, learning, and health. The scarcity of research articles in these fields is a major stumbling block. As a result, the researchers recommend academics take advantage of opportunities to collect empirical data and analyze it to better understand the impact of gamification in real-time across many fields. This chapter also discusses the scope of future research in these areas.

ACKNOWLEDGMENT

This research received no specific grant from any funding agency in the public, commercial, or not-for-profit sectors.

REFERENCES

Açikgöz, Ö., & Günay, A. (2020). The early impact of the Covid-19 pandemic on the global and Turkish economy. *Turkish Journal of Medical Sciences*, *50*(SI-1), 520–526. doi:10.3906ag-2004-6 PMID:32283904

Al-Ramahi, M., El-Gayar, O., & Liu, J. (2016). Discovering Design Principles for Persuasive Systems: A Grounded Theory and Text Mining Approach. *2016 49th Hawaii International Conference on System Sciences (HICSS)*, 3074–3083. 10.1109/HICSS.2016.387

Alahäivälä, T., & Oinas-Kukkonen, H. (2016). Understanding persuasion contexts in health gamification: A systematic analysis of gamified health behavior change support systems literature. *International Journal of Medical Informatics*, *96*, 62–70. doi:10.1016/j.ijmedinf.2016.02.006 PMID:26944611

AlMarshedi, A., Wills, G. B., & Ranchhod, A. (2015). The Wheel of Sukr: A Framework for Gamifying Diabetes Self-Management in Saudi Arabia. *Procedia Computer Science*, *63*, 475–480. doi:10.1016/j.procs.2015.08.370

Almarzooq, Z. I., Lopes, M., & Kochar, A. (2020). Virtual Learning During the COVID-19 Pandemic. *Journal of the American College of Cardiology*, *75*(20), 2635–2638. doi:10.1016/j.jacc.2020.04.015 PMID:32304797

Brühlmann, F. (2018). *Gamification From the Perspective of Self-Determination Theory and Flow*. 10.31237/ doi:osf.io/6kauv

Cafazzo, J. A., Casselman, M., Hamming, N., Katzman, D. K., & Palmert, M. R. (2012). Design of an mHealth App for the Self-management of Adolescent Type 1 Diabetes: A Pilot Study. *Journal of Medical Internet Research*, *14*(3), e70. doi:10.2196/jmir.2058 PMID:22564332

Chon, S.-H., Timmermann, F., Dratsch, T., Schuelper, N., Plum, P., Berlth, F., Datta, R. R., Schramm, C., Haneder, S., Späth, M. R., Dübbers, M., Kleinert, J., Raupach, T., Bruns, C., & Kleinert, R. (2019). Serious Games in Surgical Medical Education: A Virtual Emergency Department as a Tool for Teaching Clinical Reasoning to Medical Students. *JMIR Serious Games*, *7*(1), e13028. doi:10.2196/13028 PMID:30835239

COVID-19 spurring impulse spending, reveals survey. (2020). *Retail Customer Experience*. https://www.retailcustomerexperience.com/news/covid-19-spurring-impulse-spendingreveals-survey/

da Silva Júnior, J. N., de Sousa Oliveira, J. M., Winum, J.-Y., Melo Leite, A. J. Junior, Alexandre, F. S. O., do Nascimento, D. M., Silva de Sousa, U., Pimenta, A. T. Á., & Monteiro, A. J. (2020). Interactions 500: Design, Implementation, and Evaluation of a Hybrid Board Game for Aiding Students in the Review of Intermolecular Forces During the COVID-19 Pandemic. *Journal of Chemical Education*, *97*(11), 4049–4054. https://doi.org/10.1021/acs.jchemed.0c01025

de Ribaupierre, S., Kapralos, B., Haji, F., Stroulia, E., Dubrowski, A., & Eagleson, R. (2014). Healthcare Training Enhancement Through Virtual Reality and Serious Games. In M. Ma, L. C. Jain, & P. Anderson (Eds.), *Virtual, Augmented Reality and Serious Games for Healthcare 1* (pp. 9–27). Springer. doi:10.1007/978-3-642-54816-1_2

DeSmet, A., Van Ryckeghem, D., Compernolle, S., Baranowski, T., Thompson, D., Crombez, G., Poels, K., Van Lippevelde, W., Bastiaensens, S., Van Cleemput, K., Vandebosch, H., & De Bourdeaudhuij, I. (2014). A meta-analysis of serious digital games for healthy lifestyle promotion. *Preventive Medicine*, *69*, 95–107. https://doi.org/10.1016/j.ypmed.2014.08.026

Donthu, N., & Gustafsson, A. (2020). Effects of COVID-19 on business and research. *Journal of Business Research*, *117*(January), 284–289. https://doi.org/10.1016/j.jbusres.2020.06.008

Fontana, M. T. (2020). Gamification of ChemDraw during the COVID-19 Pandemic: Investigating How a Serious, Educational-Game Tournament (Molecule Madness) Impacts Student Wellness and Organic Chemistry Skills while Distance Learning. *Journal of Chemical Education*, *97*(9), 3358–3368. https://doi.org/10.1021/acs.jchemed.0c00722

Fu, F.-L., Su, R.-C., & Yu, S.-C. (2009). EGameFlow: A scale to measure learners' enjoyment of e-learning games. *Computers & Education*, *52*(1), 101–112. https://doi.org/10.1016/j.compedu.2008.07.004

Gao, Z., Chen, S., Pasco, D., & Pope, Z. (2015). A meta-analysis of active video games on health outcomes among children and adolescents: A meta-analysis of active video games. *Obesity Reviews*, *16*(9), 783–794. https://doi.org/10.1111/obr.12287

García-Jurado, A., Castro-González, P., Torres-Jiménez, M., & Leal-Rodríguez, A. L. (2019). Evaluating the role of gamification and flow in e-consumers: Millennials versus generation X. *Kybernetes*, *48*(6), 1278–1300. https://doi.org/10.1108/K-07-2018-0350

Gupta, A., Lawendy, B., Goldenberg, M. G., Grober, E., Lee, J. Y., & Perlis, N. (2021). Can video games enhance surgical skills acquisition for medical students? A systematic review. *Surgery*, *169*(4), 821–829. https://doi.org/10.1016/j.surg.2020.11.034

Hamari, J., & Koivisto, J. (2014). Measuring flow in gamification: Dispositional Flow Scale-2.). . *Computers in Human Behavior*, *40*, 133–143. doi:10.1016/j.chb.2014.07.048

Hashem, T. N. (2020). Examining the Influence of COVID 19 Pandemic in Changing Customers' Orientation towards E-Shopping. *Modern Applied Science*, *14*(8), 59. https://doi.org/10.5539/mas.v14n8p59

Huotari, K., & Hamari, J. (2012). Defining Gamification—A Service Marketing Perspective. *Proceedings of the IADIS International Conference Interfaces and Human Computer Interaction 2012, IHCI 2012*, 3–5. doi:10.1145/2393132.2393137

Imbeault, F., Bouchard, B., & Bouzouane, A. (2011). Serious games in cognitive training for Alzheimer's patients. *2011 IEEE 1st International Conference on Serious Games and Applications for Health (SeGAH)*. doi:10.1109/SeGAH.2011.6165447

Johnson, D., Deterding, S., Kuhn, K.-A., Staneva, A., Stoyanov, S., & Hides, L. (2016). Gamification for health and wellbeing: A systematic review of the literature. *Internet Interventions: the Application of Information Technology in Mental and Behavioural Health*, *6*, 89–106. https://doi.org/10.1016/j.invent.2016.10.002

Karać, J., & Stabauer, M. (2017). Gamification in e-commerce a survey based on the octalysis framework. *Lecture Notes in Computer Science, 10294*, 41–54. doi:10.1007/978-3-319-58484-3_4

Laato, S., Islam, A. K. M. N., Farooq, A., & Dhir, A. (2020). Unusual purchasing behavior during the early stages of the COVID-19 pandemic: The stimulus-organism-response approach. *Journal of Retailing and Consumer Services, 57*(July), 102224. https://doi.org/10.1016/j.jretconser.2020.102224

Landers, R. N. (2014). Developing a Theory of Gamified Learning: Linking Serious Games and Gamification of Learning. *Simulation & Gaming, 45*(6), 752–768. https://doi.org/10.1177/1046878114563660

Lenihan, D. (2012). Health Games: A Key Component for the Evolution of Wellness Programs. *Games for Health Journal, 1*(3), 233–235. https://doi.org/10.1089/g4h.2012.0022

Locke, E. A., & Latham, G. P. (2006). New Directions in Goal-Setting Theory. *Current Directions in Psychological Science, 15*(5), 265–268. https://doi.org/10.1111/j.1467-8721.2006.00449.x

Majuri, J., Koivisto, J., & Hamari, J. (2018a). Gamification of education and learning: A review of empirical literature. *CEUR Workshop Proceedings, 2186*(GamiFIN), 11–19.

Majuri, J., Koivisto, J., & Hamari, J. (2018b). *Gamification of education and learning: A review of empirical literature.* Academic Press.

Martínez-Pérez, B., de la Torre-Díez, I., & López-Coronado, M. (2013). Mobile Health Applications for the Most Prevalent Conditions by the World Health Organization: Review and Analysis. *Journal of Medical Internet Research, 15*(6), e2600. https://doi.org/10.2196/jmir.2600

Mat Zain, N. H. (2020). GAMEBC Model: Gamification in Health Awareness Campaigns to Drive Behaviour Change in Defeating COVID-19 Pandemic. *International Journal of Advanced Trends in Computer Science and Engineering, 9*(1.4), 229–236. doi:10.30534/ijatcse/2020/3491.42020

Mat Zain, N. H., Johari, S. N., Abdul Aziz, S. R., Ibrahim Teo, N. H., Ishak, N. H., & Othman, Z. (2021). Winning the Needs of the Gen Z: Gamified Health Awareness Campaign in Defeating COVID-19 Pandemic. *Procedia Computer Science, 179*, 974–981. https://doi.org/10.1016/j.procs.2021.01.087

Mettler, T. (2015). Health Behaviour Change Support Systems: Past Research and Future Challenges. *Management Research*, 12.

Middelweerd, A., Mollee, J. S., van der Wal, C. N., Brug, J., & te Velde, S. J. (2014). Apps to promote physical activity among adults: A review and content analysis. *The International Journal of Behavioral Nutrition and Physical Activity, 11*(1), 97. https://doi.org/10.1186/s12966-014-0097-9

Moin, M. T., & Rahman, M. A. U. (2019). *Eliminating laundering of virtual currency.* Academic Press.

Myneni, S., & Iyengar, S. (2016). Socially Influencing Technologies for Health Promotion: Translating Social Media Analytics into Consumer-facing Health Solutions. *2016 49th Hawaii International Conference on System Sciences (HICSS)*, 3084–3093. doi:10.1109/HICSS.2016.388

Nieto-Escamez, F. A., & Roldán-Tapia, M. D. (2021). Gamification as Online Teaching Strategy During COVID-19: A Mini-Review. *Frontiers in Psychology, 12*, 648552. https://doi.org/10.3389/fpsyg.2021.648552

Nowland, R., A. Necka, E., & Cacioppo, J. T. (2017). Loneliness and social internet use: Pathways to reconnection in a digital world? *Perspectives in Psychological Science, 13*(1,2), 70–87.

O'Connell, A., Tomaselli, P. J., & Stobart-Gallagher, M. (2020). Effective Use of Virtual Gamification During COVID-19 to Deliver the OB-GYN Core Curriculum in an Emergency Medicine Resident Conference. *Cureus, 12*(6), e8397. https://doi.org/10.7759/cureus.8397

Oe, H., Takemoto, T., & Ridwan, M. (2020). Is Gamification a Magic Tool?: Illusion, Remedy, and Future Opportunities in Enhancing Learning Outcomes during and beyond the COVID-19. *Budapest International Research and Critics in Linguistics and Education (BirLE) Journal, 3*(3), 1401–1414.

Oinas-Kukkonen, H. (2013). A foundation for the study of behavior change support systems. *Personal and Ubiquitous Computing, 17*(6), 1223–1235. https://doi.org/10.1007/s00779-012-0591-5

Oinas-Kukkonen, H., & Harjumaa, M. (2009). Persuasive Systems Design: Key Issues, Process Model, and System Features. *Communications of the Association for Information Systems, 24*. doi:10.17705/1CAIS.02428

Pakinee, A., & Puritat, K. (2021). Designing a gamified e-learning environment for teaching undergraduate ERP course based on big five personality traits. *Education and Information Technologies, 26*(4), 4049–4067. https://doi.org/10.1007/s10639-021-10456-9

Patricio, R., Moreira, A., Zurlo, F., & Melazzini, M. (2020). Co-creation of new solutions through gamification: A collaborative innovation practice. *Creativity and Innovation Management, 29*(1), 146–160. https://doi.org/10.1111/caim.12356

Patrício, R., Moreira, A. C., & Zurlo, F. (2020). Enhancing design thinking approaches to innovation through gamification. *European Journal of Innovation Management*. doi:10.1108/EJIM-06-2020-0239

PRISMA. (2021). *PRISMA- Transparent reporting of systematic reviews and meta-analyses.* http://prisma-statement.org/PRISMAStatement/PRISMAStatement

Rapp, A., Hopfgartner, F., Hamari, J., Linehan, C., & Cena, F. (2019). Strengthening gamification studies: Current trends and future opportunities of gamification research. *International Journal of Human Computer Studies, 127*(November), 1–6. doi:10.1016/j.ijhcs.2018.11.007

Ricciardi, F., & Paolis, L. T. D. (2014). A comprehensive review of serious games in health professions. *International Journal of Computer Games Technology, 2014*(9), 9. https://doi.org/10.1155/2014/787968

Roggeveen, A. L., & Sethuraman, R. (2020). Customer-Interfacing Retail Technologies in 2020 & Beyond: An Integrative Framework and Research Directions. . *Journal of Retailing, 96*(3), 299–309. doi:10.1016/j.jretai.2020.08.001

Ryan, R. M., & Deci, E. L. (2000a). Self-Determination Theory and the Facilitation of Intrinsic Motivation, Social Development, and Well-Being. *The American Psychologist*, 11.

Ryan, R. M., & Deci, E. L. (2000b). Intrinsic and Extrinsic Motivations: Classic Definitions and New Directions. *Contemporary Educational Psychology, 25*(1), 54–67. https://doi.org/10.1006/ceps.1999.1020

Sheth, J. (2020). *Impact of Covid-19 on consumer behavior: Will the old habits return or die?* doi:10.1016/j.jbusres.2020.05.059

Syakur, A., Susilo, T. A. B., Wike, W., & Ahmadi, R. (2020). Sustainability of Communication, Organizational Culture, Cooperation, Trust and Leadership Style for Lecturer Commitments in Higher Education. *Budapest International Research and Critics Institute (BIRCI-Journal): Humanities and Social Sciences, 3*(2), 1325–1335. doi:10.33258/birci.v3i2.980

Taiminen, H., & Taiminen, K. (2016). Usage of Facebook-and Anonymous Forum – Based Peer Support Groups Online and Their Influence on Perceived Social Support Types in Weight Loss. *2016 49th Hawaii International Conference on System Sciences (HICSS)*, 3094–3103. doi:10.1109/HICSS.2016.389

Theng, Y.-L., Lee, J. W. Y., Patinadan, P. V., & Foo, S. S. B. (2015). The Use of Videogames, Gamification, and Virtual Environments in the Self-Management of Diabetes: A Systematic Review of Evidence. *Games for Health Journal, 4*(5), 352–361. https://doi.org/10.1089/g4h.2014.0114

Tolks, D., Sailer, M., Dadaczynski, K., Lampert, C., Huberty, J., Paulus, P., & Horstmann, D. (2019). ONYA—The Wellbeing Game: How to Use Gamification to Promote Wellbeing. *Information, 10*(2), 58. doi:10.3390/info10020058

Trucker, H. (2020). Coronavirus bankruptcy tracker: These major companies are failing amid the shutdown. *Fobes.* www.forbes.com/sites/hanktucker/2020/05/03/%0Acoronavirus-bankruptcy-tracker-these-major-companies-are-failing-amid-theshutdown/#%0A5649f95d3425

Wang, R., DeMaria, S. J., Goldberg, A., & Katz, D. (2016). A Systematic Review of Serious Games in Training Health Care Professionals. *Simulation in Healthcare, 11*(1), 41–51. https://doi.org/10.1097/SIH.0000000000000118

Wee, S.-C., & Choong, W.-W. (2019). Gamification: Predicting the effectiveness of variety game design elements to intrinsically motivate users' energy conservation behaviour. *Journal of Environmental Management, 233*, 97–106. https://doi.org/10.1016/j.jenvman.2018.11.127

Whitton, N., & Langan, M. (2019). Fun and games in higher education: An analysis of UK student perspectives. *Teaching in Higher Education, 24*(8), 1000–1013. https://doi.org/10.1080/13562517.2018.1541885

World Economic Outlook Update, July 2021: Fault Lines Widen in the Global Recovery. (2021, July). *IMF.* https://www.imf.org/en/Publications/WEO/Issues/2021/07/27/world-economic-outlook-update-july-2021

Xi, N., & Hamari, J. (2019). Does gamification satisfy needs? A study on the relationship between gamification features and intrinsic need satisfaction. *International Journal of Information Management, 46*, 210–221. https://doi.org/10.1016/j.ijinfomgt.2018.12.002

KEY TERMS AND DEFINITIONS

Badges: Badges are a great method for a gamified system to socially promote the product offerings of a gamified service. Badges can indicate goal completion and consistent play advancement inside the system.

Community: A group of people who have a common interest, purpose, or objective and who learn to acquaint themselves with one another over time through a gamified information system.

Engagement: Engagement is a desirable, if not necessary, user response to information system mediated stimuli or tasks. When an information system captivates and holds a user's attention and interest, he is said to be engaged.

Game Mechanics: Game mechanics are made up of rules and feedback loops that are designed to emulate the fun that is derived from traditional forms of game playing. They are the building elements that can be used to gamify any context that isn't a game.

Gamified Health Behaviour Change Support Systems (HBCSS): A gamified HBCSS is one which incorporates gamification features into an information system that provides users with tools to modify and change their health related behavior to achieve the desired health related outcomes.

Leaderboards: The purpose of a leaderboard is to make simple comparisons. It is an ordered list with a score beside each user's name. It is also used a form of ranking system in gamified systems.

Levels: Levels are used to show progress in most games, though they are not always used in this way. Levels are a way for players to keep track of where they are in a game over time.

Points: Points refer to a quantifiable value gained by the user of a gamified information system for completing specific tasks. Designers of gamified systems must value and track every move that the players make, even if the scores are only accessible to the designer. It allows the designer to see how players interact with the system, plan for results, and make adjustments as needed.

Virtual Currency: Virtual currency is a sort of digital currency, although it may not necessarily have all of the properties of real money. In the context of gamification, virtual currency refers to both nonstandard virtual money used while playing the game and a money point system with some monetary worth.

Chapter 6
Application of Gamification in a Marketing Context:
The Psychological Perspectives

Ebina Justin M. A.
Cochin University of Science and Technology, India

Manu Melwin Joy
Cochin University of Science and Technology, India

ABSTRACT

Gamification, a popular tool widely used in various contexts such as marketing, education, and organizations, among others, has demonstrated its potential for engaging, motivating, and achieving behavioral change in the targeted audience. For an ideal gamification system, it is necessary to know how the gamification elements affect human emotions. This chapter conducts a journey through gamified contexts and their psychological impacts on individuals. This chapter gathers up the different threads of gamification in the marketing context. The three important objectives fulfilled by this chapter would be that it provides information about the topic of gamification and the psychological perspectives behind its operation; discusses its application in various marketing contexts, such as digital marketing and online payment sites; and finally, investigates various behavioral outcomes of gamification.

INTRODUCTION

Gamification is a popular term that emerged in digital platforms and is now applied in several contexts (Kamel et al., 2017). In concrete language, gamification transfers the structure of games to a new context, encouraging customers to earn from attributes such as timely feedback and challenges. The game design elements, which are the backbone of gamification, helps to fulfill different psychological needs. Studying how game elements interact with human emotions is necessary to know the psychological mechanisms behind gamification (Zhang, 2008). The expected outcome from most gamified platforms is 'user motivation' (Tang & Zhang, 2019). Game design elements that satisfy the essential psychological

DOI: 10.4018/978-1-7998-9223-6.ch006

needs of 'intrinsic motivation' are identified as points, badges, and leader boards fulfill the competence need, profile building and options to select avatars satisfies the autonomy need, and team activities and friendly competitions contribute to the relatedness need (Sailer et al., 2017). It is also identified that providing rewards without a meaningful link to psychological needs can undermine intrinsic motivation (Lopez & Tucker, 2019). Another essential outcome expected from the application of gamification is 'user engagement.' The three kinds of engagement identified are behavioral, emotional, and cognitive engagement (Fredricks, 2004). Mere reward distribution or badge allocation contributes only to the behavioral engagement of the user. In order to fetch cognitive engagement outcomes, the gamified system must be capable of contributing to user development (Da Rocha Seixas et al., 2016).

The purpose of most gamified applications is to enable consumers to alter their behavior. The pair of pathways through which gamification affects behavioral change is the informational and affective pathways (Cardador et al., 2017). Informational pathways provide frequent and adequate feedback about one's performance and affective pathway, making the tasks more enjoyable. The change that comes from a see-feel situation is better than a change that comes from an analysis-think situation (Kumar & Raghavendran, 2015). The success of any gamified application depends on how it measures and communicates the user experience (Hamari, 2013). As we see in the practice, gaming under relevant scientific and methodological support conditions has the most efficient mechanism that can be applied in education, marketing, human resource management, and productivity improvement. Researchers suggest that gaming illustrations should inspire employees and customers in marketing to fetch the best results (Vinichenko et al., 2016).

Designing organizational tasks as different game levels and integrating with different game elements can help people achieve their goals without a forced mechanism (Mochocki, 2011). Different game elements like frequent feedback, rewards, and recognition motivate employees to contribute their best to the organization. Many researchers like (Lazzaro 2008) supported it, who states that "Video games lead the design of interactive systems that realize behavioral changes. When we incorporate the essence of a game into an activity design, the activity becomes more fun, providing emotional consequences to the user. Full-fledged games often incorporate points, badges, and leader boards to reward users, based on simulations of real-world scenarios like gamification systems. The various complex design elements that make this game attractive are rarely exploited instead. Gamification is also used in certain behavioral experiments to motivate people to behave in certain 'desirable' ways by exploiting different elements of the game. (Linehan et al., 2015). The role of gamification is to attain the desired behavior from the users without pressurizing or controlling them. When the game elements and mechanics are utilized in a non-game context, the fun and entertainment aspect is expected to be embedded.

This chapter gathers up the different threads of gamification in the marketing context. The essential objectives of this study are to provide the reader's insights about the topic gamification and conduct a literature review of the topic in the marketing context. This chapter is organized into two different sections, which fulfill the stated two objectives of the study. Section 1 deals with the overview of gamification and the psychological perspectives behind its functioning. Section 2 illustrates important themes identified from the literature review of gamification in the marketing context; In addition, this section also elucidates two gamified contexts: The application of gamification in digital marketing and online payment sites.

METHODOLOGY

This chapter aims to provide readers an insight into the topic of gamification and to conduct a literature review of the topic in the marketing context. We have reviewed the articles published on gamification within a period of 2000 – 2020. Only peer-reviewed articles published either in SCOPUS indexed journals or journals included in either SCOPUS or ABDC journal quality list are used for the review. Section 1 elucidates the general nature of gamification, and the articles published on gamification without any emphasis on specific context were used for this review. However, section 2 reviews articles published only within the marketing context. The articles published on gamification in the marketing context were analyzed and coded based on their output variables. Based on these codes, essential themes in which most published articles were identified and demonstrated in this section. The review identified that most articles on gamification in the marketing context examined the topics of customer engagement, intention to use/ perform, brand image, and data generation. The topics are further elucidated in section 2.

1. GAMIFICATION

In the area of Human Engagement, gamification has now become possibly the best technique (HCI). It refers to the conversion of systems, services, institutions, and activities to provide similar experiences, motivations, and competencies to those found in good games (Huotari and Hamari, 2017). As per (Dicheva et al., 2015), the most prominent game mechanisms discovered in their study were points, badges, and leader boards. Due to their apparent connection to digital games and their ease of handling to several different contexts, points, levels, and leader boards have become the most prominent advocates of gamification (Hamari et al., 2013). According to (Zagal et al., 2005), all three are used to record and provide feedback on game behavior, thus categorizing them as goal metrics. They act as excellent, meaningful, constructive feedback. According to (Przybylski et al. 2010), they constitute an excellent aspect of digital games' motivational appeal since they allow users to fulfill their drive for expertise. As per the findings of (O'Donovan et al., 2013), leader boards were reported to be highly motivating, followed by points and ranks, whereas progress bars, final prizes, and badges were the least motivating. A new scale has been validated by (Eppmann et al., 2018) to assess the users' gaming experience. Both practitioners and academics can benefit from it. It can be used to measure the user experience when they are interacting with the gamified system (Eppmann et al., 2018).

Definitions

- According to (Kapp 2012), "Gamification uses game-based mechanics, aesthetics and game thinking to engage people, motivate action, promote learning, and solve problems."
- Gamification enhances services through gameful experiences to support value creation (Huotari & Hamari,2017).
- (Zichermann and Cunningham, 2011) defined *gamification* as "the process of game-thinking and game mechanics to engage users and solve problems."
- However, the most commonly used definition, provided by (Deterding, Dixon et al.,2011), is "the use of game design elements in non-game contexts".

- Thus, gamification is an umbrella term focusing on game elements instead of full-fledged games to improve user experience and engagement in non-game contexts (Deterding, Sicart et al., 2011) including education.

Although previous work on gamification has investigated both psychological outcomes and outcomes as behaviors, outcomes are dependent on desirable cognitive triggers, primarily because they regard psychological outcomes as processes of cognitive motivation. When studied in gamification, emotional processes focus primarily on aesthetic experiences as positive influences (e.g., fun) or more global phenomena in the general sense. While it is crucial to ensure that most gamified experiences are generally fun, designers must understand how positive and negative emotions can help people achieve the desired goals. Recognizing the multiple perspectives of emotion, we consider it a variable intensity mental state that exhibits evaluative (i.e., positive or negative) responses to stimuli in the dynamic environment. Cognition refers to mental activities related to acquiring and applying knowledge, including processes such as attention, learning, language processing, problem-solving, and memory (Lee & Jin, 2019).

The Millennials generation is the primary spectator and target of gamification. They value freedom, joy, and intensely hate restrictions, unable to imagine life without the Internet. They were born into a world of technology, and that also influenced their behavior. I was offended that it could take a long time because they can gather all the necessary information in a short time over the Internet. A key feature that sets the Millennials generation apart from the rest of the world is their excessive reliance on games. An essential characteristic of the game's "flow" is that it acts as an intermediary between most gamified applications and the behavioral intentions represented by the Millennials generation. While previous generations love the usefulness and fun derived from applications (GarcíaJurado et al., 2019), `social networking/interconnection between people is another critical factor that can motivate the Millennials generation, and most of them of gamified applications use this element (Trees, 2015). While some managers have been skeptical of the interactive and entertainment programs used for gamification, gamification is proven successful when applied in the proper format and context (Trees, 2015). Millennials prefer to use flexible working hours because they want to benefit from their work and be more involved in decision-making. Managing and motivating these employees using traditional methods is problematic (Jain & Dutta, 2019). Gamification cannot help here. Often, the latest gaming technology in a business is nothing like regular gaming. For example, the 'game-storming approach' (a combination of games and brainstorming) is helpful (Veretehina 2015).

The 'MDE' Framework: The MDE framework of gamification includes 'mechanics', 'dynamics', and 'emotions' as interdependent aspects. "MDE" seeks to describe the psychological mechanisms that achieve gamified emotional outcomes (Robson et al., 2015).

- Mechanics refers to the "design" aspect of a gamified system. Mechanics include Installation Mechanism: The context of the environment, e.g., single or multiplayer objects that can be used within the game. Structure of Rules: Objectives Allowed actions and constraints. Example: time limit, success criteria. Progression Mechanism: Compensation and enhancements used to influence player behavior. Examples: points, badges, and leader boards.
- Dynamics states that the behavior of the player is not entirely under the control of the designer. The way each player responds to the gamed context is influenced by the personality and context factors of the individual. Each element interacts with each player differently. Combining the

game's structure and mechanics creates an experience that players can play, ultimately leading to player engagement.

- Emotions refer to the feelings of players that is derived as the outcome of the gamified application.

Some of the unintended consequences of gamification arise through' dynamics', and sometimes it may even fail. The MDE framework suggests that rather than concentrating only on the definition of rules, designers should consider the mechanics and dynamics in the design process (Plangger et al., 2016).

Gamification is a widely used concept in the market to foster customer engagement and to attain behavioral changes. Its utilitarian and hedonic features influence the customer experience and help attract and retain the customers (Naqvi et al., 2021). The following section reviews and analyzes gamification's application specifically in the marketing contexts.

2. THEMES IDENTIFIED FOM ARTICLES ON GAMIFICATION IN THE MARKETING CONTEXT

Many studies examine different behavioral outcomes of gamification in the marketing context. In the first part of the section, we have conducted a literature review of gamification in the marketing context and found many articles on this topic. Only peer-reviewed articles are selected for this review. The studies under this category were examined and coded; the studies were again classified under different themes based on the given codes. The four critical themes identified from this process are customer engagement, intention to use/ perform, brand image, and data generation. The second part of this section elucidates two gamified contexts: The application of gamification in digital marketing and online payment sites.

1. **Customer engagement:** Many studies in the literature give evidence to suggest that the application of gamification boosts customer engagement. Customer engagement is a mediator between gamified applications and many behavioral outcomes (Abou Shouk & Soliman, 2021)). Three critical aspects of gamification concerning customer engagement are motivational affordance, gameful experience, and value realization (Hammedi & Poncin, 2019). In order to provide good customer experiences and achieve engagement, the designers should emphasize the content of gamified applications rather than concentrating on the game elements or mechanics (Harwood & Garry, 2015). The factors of gamification that contribute to customer engagement are identified as interconnection, mastery, goals, levels, and rewards. Rewarding people for their ability, creativity, observation, and commitment can help maintain an emotional attachment (Kankanhalli et al., 2012). Even providing an option for social connection between the customers, like publically exhibiting the name of winner for any games In addition, or providing exclusive access for some of them to some meetings or seminars can boost customer engagement (Moise & Cruceru, 2014). Furthermore, it is found that 'hope' and 'autonomy' have a positive relationship with customer engagement, whereas 'compulsion to participate in any application cannot impact engagement and even have a negative impact (Eisingerich et al., 2019). Different researchers have used different types of motivation (Extrinsic or intrinsic motivation) to explain engagement derived from gamification, but most researchers consider it intrinsic motivation.

2. **Intention to use/ perform:** Many studies regarding gamification in marketing examines its effectiveness in creating a sense of intention to use the service among the users. A study by (Whittaker et

al., 2011) found that the gameful experience derived from a gamified application creates a continuous intention to use the service and stimulates behavioral intentions to perform sustainable energy behavior and service volunteer activities (Bowser et al., 2013). It is also found that encouraging the customers to participate in a gamified loyalty program conducted by the shop positively influences their purchase intention (Wen et al., 2014). The two essential mediators between motivational affordances and purchase intention were 'enjoyment' and 'flow.' In addition, customers who are more familiar with games exhibited higher purchase intention in gamified services. In addition, the interaction with a gamified application help users reduces their emotional anxieties to a certain extend (Li & Guo, 2021). However, gamified systems can reap their potential benefits when the users actively interact with the system; the reason for the failure of gamification in some situations was the passive involvement of users in the system (Hamari, 2013).

Similarly, the gamified interventions designed with due consideration to game mechanics and frameworks are found to become more successful than others. Likewise, gamification can be applied when the target group is the younger generation, and extrinsic and intrinsic rewards can enrich the customer experiences (Bittner & Shipper, 2014). Many other studies have also explored the possibility of gamification in promoting environmental and economic behaviors from the users (AlSkaif et al., 2018).

3. **Brand image:** Apart from continuous intention to use the gamified service, it is proved that gamification is found to have a positive relationship with brand image (Nobre & Ferreira, 2017). Companies have been using gamification as a tool for different motives like employee motivation and customer engagement (Raj & Gupta, 2018). There is a dearth of scientific evidence in the literature to prove this relationship. Brand engagement is the positive customer experience they derive while dealing with a particular brand, which ultimately encourages them to stay connected with the brand (Xi, N & Hamari, 2019). Later it is found that it can be used to influence the brand attitudes of the customers. It can also drive the consumers to become more loyal and faithful towards the organization. Since gamification can positively influence brand equity through brand image, it can be viewed as a good tool in managing the brand (Xi N & Hamari, 2020). Among different elements of gamification, the fun and storytelling method used in the brand apps has a strong positive correlation with the perception of customers towards the brand image (Lee & Jin, 2019). Despite many studies, researchers state that there is more scope for future researchers to examine the impact of gamification in this context.

4. **Data generation:** Despite continuously engaging the customers with different challenges and entertainment, it also helps firms collect frequent and valuable data on consumers' opinions and interactions. Some scholars support the view that gamification is an extension of the organization's 'Customer relationship management function, which collects customer opinions and feedback and tries to attract them by providing discounts and rewards' (Moise, 2013). Despite this perspective, the data collected from a gamified marketing application can be used to understand customer behavior and perspective, which can be used to decide the marketing strategy and provide personalized offers. It is suggested that future studies on this topic should cover outcomes In-game outcomes, Intra-organizational level outcomes, firm practical level outcomes, and transformative level outcomes (Wünderlich et al., 2020).

Application of Gamification in Digital Marketing

In the present world, where marketing has experienced a drastic shift to e-marketing, gamification is one of the relevant research topics that has captured attention among practitioners and researchers (Noorbehbahani et al., 2019). At some point, the existing marketing tools become outdated and can no longer be appropriate to engage customers. Gradually firms attempt to make a shift to embrace the latest technologies. Presently, enterprises of all sizes and industries are approaching different gamification strategies to crack the competition. It is not easy to engage and retain customers through an online channel for an extended period. When gamification is incorporated into mobile marketing, it contributes to fun and interactivity. Amid the tight competition between the retail companies, it becomes necessary for companies to use differentiated strategies like gamification to reap success. The most crucial objective of gamification in marketing is to increase user engagement and persuade them to participate without any forcing mechanism. Initially, the discussion on gamification was confined only to the human-computer interaction perspectives; then, the concept was disseminated to other areas like service marketing. Despite the immense scholarly attention received in service marketing, plenty of topics within the context remain unexplored.

Furthermore, the application of gamification in the service marketing context had experienced a drastic increase from 2017 (Hamid & Kuppusamy, 2017). The service marketing perspectives view game mechanics as services and games as service systems (Huotari & Hamari, 2011). Apart from the retail section, gamification is widely used in fitness training institutions and apps (Feng & Hsieh, 2020). They use both intrinsic and extrinsic rewards. Around the world, the concept is used by any organization irrespective of its size, starting from grocery stores to multinational corporations (Aleksandrovna, 2020). The vital game elements used in the digital marketing context are feedback, levels, progress bars, rewards, similar to those in any other area. The four essential aspects of gamification identified by (Huotari & Hamari, 2017) are 'affordances, psychological mediators, goals of gamification and the context of gamification.' The outcome derived from gamification may sustain for the short term or long term depending on the design structure (Helmefalk & Marcusson, 2019). When the gamification design copied from some application is utilized in another context, without customizing the design factors to suit the purpose, it fails in attaining the desired outcome. The design should be customized to the context and the purpose to avoid the failure of the gamified application.

The mobile marketing industry experienced dramatic growth of approximately ten times that of traditional markets between 2010 and 2015. Mobile marketing has many gamified applications, but research by (Hofacer et al., 2016) states that this topic has not achieved any potential benefits and has not covered many vital areas. Gamification can digitally enhance the retail experience. Customers can then purchase online and use the service for an extended period (Insley & Nunan, 2014). It not only shows designers the untapped possibilities of gamifying mobile marketing applications, but it is also a challenge and an opportunity. The importance of gamification in digital marketing can be understood from the finding that the perceived usefulness and fun of gamification positively affect consumers' brand attitudes and intention to use services (Yang et al., 2017). In addition to the gaming elements already mentioned, the accuracy and frequency of feedback, social links, and site attractiveness are vital factors that make gaming effective in digital marketing (Conaway & Garay, 2014). Granting the player some elemental privileges to give the player more options for selection and determining the player's strategy can help make the application more attractive. The feeling of empowerment between players can also be created using the same techniques that give the best player a mediation position among other users (Moise & Cruceru, 2014).

Research on gaming marketing has dealt with various themes, such as gaming ethics, in the context of marketing (Thorpe & Roper, 2019). We suggest that gamification needs to be regulated and controlled by an informal code of conduct to maintain the game's outcome for a long time. Gamification is also being applied in tourism marketing as an innovative tool that enables deeper relationships with visitors. Players generally start with information retrieval and reach the fundamental simulation level (Xu Weber & Buhalis, 2013; Xu Tian et al., 2016). Communication interventions designed for gaming applications have been very successful in tourism (Yılmaz & Coşkun, 2016). In addition to all these areas, gaming is also widely applied to crowdsourcing technology. Crowdsourcing involves getting work, information, or opinions from many people, a recent topic of interest (Sigala, 2015). Some studies explain the function of gaming from an implicit motive point of view. Others have suggested alternative mechanisms that work to obtain changes in user behavior (Mitchell et al., 2017). It is predicted that gamification will enter into all its unexplored or less explored areas like finance, large-scale collaborations, and collective intelligence (Park & Bae, 2014).

Application of Gamification in Online Payment Sites

With the advent of virtual marketplaces and online shopping sites, online payment methods have increased. Various online payment methods such as digital cash and electronic wallets have been integrated to help consumers make transactions in the virtual market convenient and with themselves (Chen & Nath, 2008). With online transactions, India's future looks very promising with a positive reaction. This improves the country's credit rating and increases investment (Brahma & Dutta, 2018). Encourage customers to move to home banking as bankers can offer lower-cost transactions because the cost per transaction performed by banking customers online is significantly lower from outside point banking. (Fenu & Pau, 2015). Some of the factors that motivate people to choose mobile payment systems are convenience, ease of use, discount, cashback, these. We need to know more about what drives users to make more online payments (Thakur & Srivastava, 2014). The potential advantages of gamification, like any other sector, force the e-banking sector to incorporate game elements into their designs to attract and retain users (Rodrigues et al., 2016b). One of the main uses of gamification is to enhance users' engagement and motivation (Darejeh & Salim, 2016). The application of gamification in mobile banking applications can contribute to improving its usage. Gamification is driven by the premise that ubiquitous modern technology converges as "an informed, connected, empowered, and active consumer" and that experience leads to customer engagement and consequently positive relationships (Harwood & Garry, 2015).

By stimulating different visual and voice senses through mobile applications, different browsing experiences are created for users (Tarute, Nikou & Gatautis 2017). It is no surprise that the adoption of gamification on online payment websites is accelerating. Facilitate customer engagement Payment apps gamified design promotes the use of mobile payment apps. The continued use of applications promotes user motivational behaviors, keeps users loyal to their devices, increases user value and satisfaction, and promotes engaging motivational behaviors (Kim & Wachter, 2013). In contrast, turning off the design can reduce utilization. For example, mobile banking has many advantages, such as ubiquitousness and instantaneously, but some users do not prefer mobile transactions (for example, most offices have low demand for mobile payments). Considering a significant amount of time and money required to develop a mobile payment system (Zhou, Lu & Wang, 2010), ensuring that mobile users use the payment system is paramount. Attention should be paid to developing and designing the system for appropriate payment services (Kim et al., 2010).

CONCLUSION

Gamification applications are designed with due consideration to human emotions and need satisfaction to enjoy a higher chance of success in the long term. The unique experience derived from playing a game can be called 'gamefulness .' Games are not the only source that can create gamefulness (Huotari & Hamari, 2017). Applying game elements in another context like work or learning can also create 'gamefulness,' which helps users enjoy it (Kirillov, et al., 2016). Gamification elements capture user attention and engagement by generating human motivation to use the service further (Darejeh & Salim, 2016). The 'Mechanics Dynamics and Emotions framework' (MDE) explains how the game elements interact with human emotions (Ruhi, 2015). Mechanics are the game design structure, dynamics refers to the interaction of mechanics with human emotions, and emotions represent the inner feelings of users derived from the interplay with game elements (Robson et al., 2016).

The concept of gamifying banking applications has widely used customer engagement and creates a sense of continuous intention among customers. Increasing user satisfaction will boost customer reuse intention and loyalty. High customer satisfaction will also enable e-service providers and their users to sustain a long-term relationship (Chen, Yen, & Hwang, 2012). Gamification helps create experientially based Customer Engagement and consequential positive relational outcomes. As a result, gamification has seen substantial adoption by firms in recent years, with an estimated 70 percent of Global 2000 firms having at least one gamified application (Harwood & Garry, 2015).In order to test the impact of gamification on the number of daily sessions (web traffic) opened on a website application, researchers from Romania used a Multiple Regression model based on data collected with Google analytics. After one year since it was implemented and launched, they concluded that the gamification instruments proved valuable by keeping users in the application and that they come back, share content and positively influence the number of web traffic sessions. Nevertheless, gamification cannot replace aggressive marketing, given that the number of users has not increased as expected (Maican et al., 2016). Apart from its application in different fields like education, work, and marketing, gamification can even solve social issues (Volkova, 2013).

An investigation conducted by researchers to provide empirically generated insights into a gamification approach to online customer engagement suggests that engagement is achieved at a behavioral level, manifesting in the performance and completion of tasks, collection of points and badges, and some attainment of rewards. Indeed, where the game tasks are tied to existing modes of interaction with the brand through its Web site, this may increase traffic through the experience environment. Additionally, they find out that the lack of positive social and firm interaction concerning the game mechanics is problematic insofar as the length of time customers are prepared to spend within the experience environment is limited and, we posit, may be a contributory factor as to why adverse outcomes such as subversion of the game mechanics have emerged as outcomes (Harwood & Garry, 2015)..

The objective of most gamified applications is to provide enjoyment and ease of use (Rodrigues et al., 2016). However, inappropriate designing and rhetorical gamification lead to the system's failure (Landers, 2018). Personality difference of the users also influences the success of gamified systems in motivating individuals. Characteristics of the players determine how game mechanics affect human emotions. Users' perception towards gamification and player type are also critical factors that influence the effectiveness of gamified applications (García et al., 2017). Despite many articles published in different peer-reviewed journals, the concept still deserves much more attention from researchers.

LIMITATIONS AND FUTURE RESEARCH DIRECTIONS

We have not focused on any gamification outcomes, which is both a limitation and a strength of this chapter. Instead, the chapter examines publications on gamification in marketing without concentrating on any specific objective, such as customer engagement, intention to use the application or brand image, which will also be worth the literature. The majority of studies on the intention to use gamified applications is conducted from the perspective of managers; nevertheless, future researchers may investigate gamification's adoption from the perspective of users both quantitatively and qualitatively (Abou-Shouk & Soliman, 2021). This can assist in bringing out the application's true efficacy. From a practical standpoint, creating gamification as a combination of intrinsic motivational incentives (avatars, narratives, choices, and connectedness) and extrinsic motivational incentives (points, rewards, and leader boards) will assist to maintain the application's flow and pleasure. From the perspective of researchers, it will be worthwhile to investigate the impact of both intrinsic and extrinsic motivational incentives on various outcomes (Bittner & Shipper, 2014).

REFERENCES

Abou-Shouk, M., & Soliman, M. (2021). The impact of gamification adoption intention on brand awareness and loyalty in tourism: The mediating effect of customer engagement. *Journal of Destination Marketing & Management*, *20*, 100559. doi:10.1016/j.jdmm.2021.100559

Aleksandrovna, M. S. (2020). *Impact of gamification in marketing on consumer behavioural intentions* [Doctoral dissertation]. St. Petersburg University.

AlSkaif, T., Lampropoulos, I., Van Den Broek, M., & Van Sark, W. (2018). Gamification-based framework for engagement of residential customers in energy applications. *Energy Research & Social Science*, *44*, 187–195. doi:10.1016/j.erss.2018.04.043

Bittner, J. V., & Shipper, J. (2014). Motivational effects and age differences of gamification in product advertising. *Journal of Consumer Marketing*, *31*(5), 391–400. doi:10.1108/JCM-04-2014-0945

Bowser, A., Hansen, D., He, Y., Boston, C., Reid, M., Gunnell, L., & Preece, J. (2013, October). Using gamification to inspire new citizen science volunteers. In *Proceedings of the first international conference on gameful design, research, and applications*, (pp. 18-25). 10.1145/2583008.2583011

Brahma, A., & Dutta, R. (2018). Cashless Transactions and Its Impact-A Wise Move Towards Digital India. *International Journal of Scientific Research in Computer Science, Engineering and Information Technology, 3*(3), 14–28.

Cardador, M. T., Northcraft, G. B., & Whicker, J. (2017). A theory of work gamification: Something old, something new, something borrowed, something cool? *Human Resource Management Review*, *27*(2), 353–365. doi:10.1016/j.hrmr.2016.09.014

Chen, L., & Nath, R. (2008). Determinants of mobile payments: An empirical analysis. *Journal of International Technology and Information*, *17*(1), 9–20.

Chen, S. C., Yen, D. C., & Hwang, M. I. (2012). Factors influencing the continuance intention to the usage of Web 2.0: An empirical study. *Computers in Human Behavior*, *28*(3), 933–941. doi:10.1016/j.chb.2011.12.014

Conaway, R., & Garay, M. C. (2014). Gamification and service marketing. *SpringerPlus*, *3*(1), 1–11. doi:10.1186/2193-1801-3-653 PMID:25392812

Da Rocha Seixas, L., Gomes, A. S., & De Melo Filho, I. J. (2016). Effectiveness of gamification in the engagement of students. *Computers in Human Behavior*, *58*, 48–63. doi:10.1016/j.chb.2015.11.021

Darejeh, A., & Salim, S. S. (2016). Gamification Solutions to Enhance Software User Engagement—A Systematic Review. *International Journal of Human-Computer Interaction*, *32*(8), 613–642. doi:10.1080/10447318.2016.1183330

Deterding, S., Dixon, D., Khaled, R., & Nacke, L. (2011, September). From game design elements to gamefulness: defining "gamification". In *Proceedings of the 15th international academic MindTrek conference: Envisioning future media environments* (pp. 9-15). 10.1145/2181037.2181040

Deterding, S., Sicart, M., Nacke, L., O'Hara, K., & Dixon, D. (2011). Gamification. using game-design elements in non-gaming contexts. In CHI'11 extended abstracts on human factors in computing systems, (pp. 2425-2428). ACM.

Dicheva, D., Dichev, C., Agre, G., & Angelova, G. (2015). Gamification in education: A systematic mapping study. *Journal of Educational Technology & Society*, *18*(3), 75–88.

Eisingerich, A. B., Marchand, A., Fritze, M. P., & Dong, L. (2019). Hook vs. hope: How to enhance customer engagement through gamification. *International Journal of Research in Marketing*, *36*(2), 200–215. doi:10.1016/j.ijresmar.2019.02.003

Eppmann, R., Bekk, M., & Klein, K. (2018). Gameful experience in gamification: Construction and validation of a gameful experience scale. *Journal of Interactive Marketing*, *43*, 98–115. doi:10.1016/j.intmar.2018.03.002

Feng, W., Tu, R., & Hsieh, P. (2020). Can gamification increases consumers' engagement in fitness apps? The moderating role of commensurability of the game elements. *Journal of Retailing and Consumer Services*, *57*, 102229. doi:10.1016/j.jretconser.2020.102229

Fenu, G., & Pau, P. L. (2015). An analysis of features and tendencies in mobile banking apps. *Procedia Computer Science*, *56*(1), 26–33. doi:10.1016/j.procs.2015.07.177

Fredricks, J. A., Blumenfeld, P. C., & Paris, A. H. (2004). School engagement: Potential of the concept, state of the evidence. *Review of Educational Research*, *74*(1), 59–109. doi:10.3102/00346543074001059

García, F., Pedreira, O., Piattini, M., Cerdeira-Pena, A., & Penabad, M. (2017). A framework for gamification in software engineering. *Journal of Systems and Software, 132*, 21–40. doi:10.1016/j.jss.2017.06.021

García-Jurado, A., Castro-González, P., Torres-Jiménez, M., & Leal-Rodríguez, A. L. (2019). Evaluating the role of gamification and flow in e-consumers: Millennials versus generation X. *Kybernetes, 48*(6), 1278–1300. doi:10.1108/K-07-2018-0350

Hamari, J. (2013). Transforming homo economicus into homo ludens: A field experiment on gamification in a utilitarian peer-to-peer trading service. *Electronic Commerce Research and Applications, 12*(4), 236–245. doi:10.1016/j.elerap.2013.01.004

Hamid, M., & Kuppusamy, M. (2017). Gamification implementation in service marketing: A literature. *Electronic Journal of Business & Management, 2*(1), 38–50.

Hammedi, W., Leclercq, T., & Poncin, I. (2019). Customer engagement: The role of gamification. In *Handbook of research on customer engagement* (pp. 164–185). Edward Elgar Publishing. doi:10.4337/9781788114899.00014

Harwood, T., & Garry, T. (2015). An investigation into gamification as a customer engagement experience environment. *Journal of Services Marketing, 29*(6–7), 533–546. doi:10.1108/JSM-01-2015-0045

Helmefalk, M., & Marcusson, L. (2019). Gamification in a servicescape context: A conceptual framework. *International Journal of Internet Marketing and Advertising, 13*(1), 22–46. doi:10.1504/IJIMA.2019.097894

Hofacker, C. F., De Ruyter, K., Lurie, N. H., Manchanda, P., & Donaldson, J. (2016). Gamification and mobile marketing effectiveness. *Journal of Interactive Marketing, 34*, 25–36. doi:10.1016/j.intmar.2016.03.001

Huotari, K., & Hamari, J. (2011). "Gamification" from the perspective of service marketing. *Proc. CHI 2011 Workshop Gamification.*

Huotari, K., & Hamari, J. (2017). A definition for gamification: Anchoring gamification in the service marketing literature. *Electronic Markets, 27*(1), 21–31. doi:10.100712525-015-0212-z

Huotari, K., & Hamari, J. (2017). A definition for gamification: Anchoring gamification in the service marketing literature. *Electronic Markets, 27*(1), 21–31. doi:10.100712525-015-0212-z

Insley, V., & Nunan, D. (2014). Gamification and the online retail experience. *International Journal of Retail & Distribution Management, 42*(5), 340–351. doi:10.1108/IJRDM-01-2013-0030

Jain, A., & Dutta, D. (2019). Millennials and gamification: Guerilla tactics for making learning fun. *SA Journal of Human Resource Management, 6*(1), 29–44.

Kamel, M. M., Watfa, M. K., Lobo, B., & Sobh, D. (2017). Is enterprise gamification being cannibalized by its own brand? *IEEE Transactions on Professional Communication, 60*(2), 147–164. doi:10.1109/TPC.2017.2656598

Kankanhalli, A., Taher, M., Cavusoglu, H., & Kim, S. H. (2012). *Gamification: A new paradigm for online user engagement*. Academic Press.

Kapp, K. M. (2012). *The gamification of learning and instruction: game-based methods and strategies for training and education*. John Wiley & Sons.

Kim, C., Kim, C., Mirusmonov, M., & Lee, I. (2010). An empirical examination of factors influencing the intention to use mobile payment. *Computers in Human Behavior*, 26(3), 310–322. doi:10.1016/j.chb.2009.10.013

Kim, Y. H., Kim, D. J., & Wachter, K. (2013). A study of mobile user engagement (MoEN): Engagement motivations, perceived value, satisfaction, and continued engagement intention. *Decision Support Systems*, 56(1), 361–370. doi:10.1016/j.dss.2013.07.002

Kirillov, A. V., Vinichenko, M. V., Melnichuk, A. V., Melnichuk, Y. A., & Vinogradova, M. V. (2016). Improvement in the learning environment through gamification of the educational process. *International Electronic Journal of Mathematics Education*, 11(7), 2071–2085.

Kumar, H., & Raghavendran, S. (2015). Gamification, the finer art: Fostering creativity and employee engagement. *The Journal of Business Strategy*, 36(6), 3–12. doi:10.1108/JBS-10-2014-0119

Landers, R. N. (2019). Gamification misunderstood: How badly executed and rhetorical gamification obscures its transformative potential. *Journal of Management Inquiry*, 28(2), 137–140. doi:10.1177/1056492618790913

Lazzaro, M. (2008). *Game usability: Advice from the experts for advancing the player experience*. Morgan Kaufmann.

Lee, J. Y., & Jin, C. H. (2019). The role of gamification in brand app experience: The moderating effects of the 4Rs of app marketing. *Cogent Psychology*, 6(1), 1576388. doi:10.1080/23311908.2019.1576388

Li, M., Xu, D., Ma, G., & Guo, Q. (2021). Strong tie or weak tie? Exploring the impact of group-formation gamification mechanisms on user emotional anxiety in social commerce. *Behaviour & Information Technology*, 1–30. doi:10.1080/0144929X.2021.1917661

Linehan, C., Kirman, B., & Roche, B. (2015). Gamification as behavioral psychology. In *The gameful world: Approaches, issues, applications* (pp. 81–105). MIT Press.

Lopez, C. E., & Tucker, C. S. (2019). The effects of player type on performance: A gamification case study. *Computers in Human Behavior*, 91(October), 333–345. doi:10.1016/j.chb.2018.10.005

Maican, C., Lixandroiu, R., & Constantin, C. (2016). Computers in Human Behavior Interactivia. ro e A study of a gami fi cation framework using zero-cost tools. *Computers in Human Behavior*, 61, 186–197. doi:10.1016/j.chb.2016.03.023

Mitchell, R., Schuster, L., & Drennan, J. (2017). Understanding how gamification influences behaviour in social marketing. *Australasian Marketing Journal*, 25(1), 12–19. doi:10.1016/j.ausmj.2016.12.001

Mochocki, M. (2011). Reality is Broken: Why Games Make Us Better and How They Can Change the World. Jane McGonigal. 2011. New York: Penguin Press, ss. 388. Czasopismo ludologiczne Polskiego Towarzystwa Badania Gier, 239.

Moise, D. (2013). Gamification-The new game in marketing. *Romanian Journal of Marketing*, (2).

Moise, D., & Cruceru, A. F. (2014). The use of gamification in events marketing. *International Journal of Economic Practices and Theories, 4*(2), 185–190.

Naqvi, M. H., Guoyan, S., & Naqvi, M. H. A. (2021). Measuring the Influence of Web Features in the Online Gamification Environment: A Multimediation Approach. *Wireless Communications and Mobile Computing, 2021,* 2021. doi:10.1155/2021/3213981

Nobre, H., & Ferreira, A. (2017). Gamification as a platform for brand co-creation experiences. *Journal of Brand Management, 24*(4), 349–361. doi:10.105741262-017-0055-3

Noorbehbahani, F., Salehi, F., & Zadeh, R. J. (2019). A systematic mapping study on gamification applied to e-marketing. *Journal of Research in Interactive Marketing, 13*(3), 392–410. doi:10.1108/JRIM-08-2018-0103

O'Donovan, S., Gain, J., & Marais, P. (2013). A case study in the gamification of a university-level games development course. In *Proceedings of the South African Institute for Computer Scientists and Information Technologists Conference* (pp. 242-251). 10.1145/2513456.2513469

Park, H. J., & Bae, J. H. (2014). Study and research of gamification design. *International Journal of Software Engineering and Its Applications, 8*(8), 19–28.

Plangger, K., Kietzmann, J., Robson, K., Pitt, L., & McCarthy, I. (2016). Experiences with gamification: The MDE framework. In *Marketing Challenges in a Turbulent Business Environment* (pp. 491–491). Springer. doi:10.1007/978-3-319-19428-8_125

Przybylski, A. K., Rigby, C. S., & Ryan, R. M. (2010). A motivational model of video game engagement. *Review of General Psychology, 14*(2), 154–166. doi:10.1037/a0019440

Raj, B., & Gupta, D. (2018, September). Factors Influencing Consumer Responses to Marketing Gamification. In *2018 International Conference on Advances in Computing, Communications and Informatics (ICACCI)* (pp. 1538-1542). IEEE. 10.1109/ICACCI.2018.8554922

Robson, K., Plangger, K., Kietzmann, J. H., McCarthy, I., & Pitt, L. (2015). Is it all a game? Understanding the principles of gamification. *Business Horizons, 58*(4), 411–420. doi:10.1016/j.bushor.2015.03.006

Robson, K., Plangger, K., Kietzmann, J. H., McCarthy, I., & Pitt, L. (2016). Game on: Engaging customers and employees through gamification. *Business Horizons, 59*(1), 29–36. doi:10.1016/j.bushor.2015.08.002

Rodrigues, L. F., Oliveira, A., & Costa, C. J. (2016). Does ease-of-use contributes to the perception of enjoyment? A case of gamification in e-banking. *Computers in Human Behavior, 61,* 114–126. doi:10.1016/j.chb.2016.03.015

Rodrigues, L. F., Oliveira, A., & Costa, C. J. (2016b). Playing seriously - How gamification and social cues influence bank customers to use gamified e-business applications. *Computers in Human Behavior, 63,* 392–407. doi:10.1016/j.chb.2016.05.063

Ruhi, U. (2015). Level Up Your Strategy: Towards a Descriptive Framework for Meaningful Enterprise Gamification. *Technology Innovation Management Review, 5*(8), 5–16. doi:10.22215/timreview/918

Sailer, M., Hense, J. U., Mayr, S. K., & Mandl, H. (2017). How gamification motivates: An experimental study of the effects of specific game design elements on psychological need satisfaction. *Computers in Human Behavior, 69*, 371–380. doi:10.1016/j.chb.2016.12.033

Sigala, M. (2015). Gamification for crowdsourcing marketing practices: Applications and benefits in tourism. Advances in crowdsourcing, 129-145.

Tang, J., & Zhang, P. (2019). Exploring the relationships between gamification and motivational needs in technology design. *International Journal of Crowd Science, 3*(1), 87–103. doi:10.1108/IJCS-09-2018-0025

Tarute, A., Nikou, S., & Gatautis, R. (2017). Mobile application driven consumer engagement. *Telematics and Informatics, 34*(4), 145–156. doi:10.1016/j.tele.2017.01.006

Thakur, R., & Srivastava, M. (2014). Adoption readiness, personal innovativeness, perceived risk and usage intention across customer groups for mobile payment services in India. *Internet Research, 24*(3), 369–392. doi:10.1108/IntR-12-2012-0244

Thorpe, A. S., & Roper, S. (2019). The ethics of gamification in a marketing context. *Journal of Business Ethics, 155*(2), 597–609. doi:10.100710551-017-3501-y

Trees, L. (2015). Encouraging millennials to collaborate and learn on the job. *Strategic HR Review, 14*(4), 118–123. doi:10.1108/SHR-06-2015-0042

Veretehina, S. V. (2015). Automated personnel evaluation system. *Personnel and Intellectual Resources Management in Russia, 4*(5), 72-77.

Vinichenko, M. V., Melnichuk, A. V., Kirillov, A. V., Makushkin, S. A., & Melnichuk, Y. A. (2016). Modern views on the gamification of business. *Journal of Internet Banking and Commerce*.

Volkova, I. I. (2013). Four pillars of gamification. *Middle East Journal of Scientific Research, 13*, 149–152.

Wen, D. M. H., Chang, D. J. W., Lin, Y. T., Liang, C. W., & Yang, S. Y. (2014, June). Gamification design for increasing customer purchase intention in a mobile marketing campaign app. In *International conference on HCI in business* (pp. 440-448). Springer. 10.1007/978-3-319-07293-7_43

Whittaker, L., Mulcahy, R., & Russell-Bennett, R. (2021). 'Go with the flow' for gamification and sustainability marketing. *International Journal of Information Management, 61*, 102305. doi:10.1016/j.ijinfomgt.2020.102305

Wünderlich, N. V., Gustafsson, A., Hamari, J., Parvinen, P., & Haff, A. (2020). The great game of business: Advancing knowledge on gamification in business contexts. *Journal of Business Research, 106*, 273–276. doi:10.1016/j.jbusres.2019.10.062

Xi, N., & Hamari, J. (2019, January). The relationship between gamification, brand engagement and brand equity. *Proceedings of the 52nd Hawaii International Conference on System Sciences*. 10.24251/HICSS.2019.099

Xi, N., & Hamari, J. (2020). Does gamification affect brand engagement and equity? A study in online brand communities. *Journal of Business Research, 109*, 449–460. doi:10.1016/j.jbusres.2019.11.058

Xu, F., Tian, F., Buhalis, D., Weber, J., & Zhang, H. (2016). Tourists as mobile gamers: Gamification for tourism marketing. *Journal of Travel & Tourism Marketing, 33*(8), 1124–1142. doi:10.1080/10548 408.2015.1093999

Xu, F., Weber, J., & Buhalis, D. (2013). Gamification in tourism. In Information and communication technologies in tourism, (pp. 525-537). doi:10.1007/978-3-319-03973-2_38

Yang, Y., Asaad, Y., & Dwivedi, Y. (2017). Examining the impact of gamification on intention of engagement and brand attitude in the marketing context. *Computers in Human Behavior, 73*, 459–469. doi:10.1016/j.chb.2017.03.066

Yılmaz, H., & Coşkun, İ. O. (2016). New toy of marketing communication in tourism: Gamification. In e-Consumers in the Era of New Tourism (pp. 53-71). Springer.

Zagal, J. P., Mateas, M., Fernández-Vara, C., Hochhalter, B., & Lichti, N. (2007). Towards an ontological language for game analysis. *Worlds in play: International perspectives on digital games research, 21*, 21.

Zhang, P. (2008). Technical opinion Motivational affordances: Reasons for ICT design and use. *Communications of the ACM, 51*(11), 145–147. doi:10.1145/1400214.1400244

Zhou, T., Lu, Y., & Wang, B. (2010). Integrating TTF and UTAUT to explain mobile banking user adoption. *Computers in Human Behavior, 26*(4), 760–767. doi:10.1016/j.chb.2010.01.013

Zichermann, G., & Cunningham, C. (2011). *Gamification by design: Implementing game mechanics in web and mobile apps*. O'Reilly Media, Inc.

Chapter 7
Gamification in Marketing:
A Case Study From a Customer Value Perspective

Umit Basaran
Zonguldak Bulent Ecevit University, Turkey

ABSTRACT

Advances in digital marketing technologies and the experience and value they provide to consumers have become important factors in market success. Therefore, businesses are focusing much more on the use of innovative technologies such as gamification. Gamification is the use of game design elements and mechanisms in non-game environments to increase the motivation of users to guide their behavior. Gamification elements used in marketing activities have an impact on the attitudes and behaviors of consumers towards brands, products, and services by increasing experience and value for them. Accordingly, this chapter is aimed at evaluating the gamified marketing activities from the perspective of customer value. In this context, the concepts of customer value and gamification are examined, and gamification techniques used in marketing and their effects on consumer value are evaluated. Also, the case study of Starbucks' gamified mobile application is presented from the perspective of customer value.

INTRODUCTION

Technology and globalization emerge as the most effective factors in the transformation of the marketplaces where businesses operate. Changes in communication technologies allow societies to become global. The fact that digital technologies have become an important part of consumers' lives causes the demand for these technologies and technology-based services to increase rapidly. Therefore, businesses are beginning to benefit intensely from digital and interactive marketing techniques within the framework of developments in technology and changes in consumer demands. Gamification applications included in these techniques constitute one of the most up-to-date marketing activities. Gamification technique is carried out by using video game elements such as game mechanics and dynamics in non-game environments to improve user experience and interaction (Deterding et al., 2011c, p. 2425; Simoes et al., 2013, p. 346). This technique is used by businesses to integrate game technology and game design methods

DOI: 10.4018/978-1-7998-9223-6.ch007

into web pages, services, consumer communities, created contents and marketing campaigns to attract users and increase their participation (Deterding et al., 2011a, p. 10).

Gamification in marketing brings benefits such as increasing the number of visits to the website, improving the effectiveness of ads, increasing sales, providing feedback from customers, and collecting primary data (Noorbehbahani et al., 2019, p. 393). The main purpose of using gamification in marketing can be summarized as increasing the value created for the customer (Huotari and Hamari, 2012, p. 19). In this way, customer participation and loyalty are increased by establishing a connection between the brand and the consumer (Hamari et al., 2014, p. 3025). In customer-oriented gamification applications, marketers increase customer efficiency and experience, reveal repurchasing intention, educate customers about the usage of the product or service, or create new products and services with customers (Burke, 2014, p. 63; Helmefalk and Marcusson, 2019, p. 128).

Marketers use gamification as gamified marketing practices in mobile applications and websites. In these gamification activities, it is seen that different game mechanics such as collecting points, leveling, earning badges, gaining virtual products or gifts, and different game dynamics such as gaining rewards, achieving status, achievement, competing, self-expression are used (Blohm & Leimeister, 2013, p. 276; Simoes et al., 2013, p. 348). In addition, the motivation factors underlying consumers' use of gamification vary as intellectual curiosity, social reputation, achievement, cognitive stimulation, and self-determination (Blohm & Leimeister, 2013, p. 276; Hamid & Kuppusamy, 2017, p. 40).

Based on this information, it seems important to examine how businesses can design effective gamification applications that will enable them to create added value for their customers and increase their income. Therefore, the purpose of this chapter is threefold: a) to present a conceptual framework for the use of gamification technique in marketing from the customer value point of view, b) to review the literature to determine the effects of the use of gamification technique in marketing on creating customer value and its consequences in terms of consumer behavior, c) to explain the issues covered in the chapter through a case study within the scope of the practice of an business using the gamification technique. Accordingly, in this chapter, a literature-based conceptual study and a case study are carried out with an exploratory research approach.

Firstly, it is planned to examine customer value management in detail and reveal the importance of customer value in marketing and gamified marketing activities. Secondly, it is aimed to determine the principles and issues that should be considered to design effective gamification techniques in marketing and evaluate the examples of various gamification practices used in marketing. Thirdly, it is proposed to discuss the antecedents and effects of these practices on customer value and consumer behavior. Lastly, it is designed to examine a gamified marketing application as a case study from the customer value point of view. For these purposes, the concept of customer value will be discussed comprehensively within the framework of perceived customer benefits and costs. Then the gamification technique will be reviewed extensively within the framework of basic game mechanisms and dynamics, and the applications of gamification in marketing will be emphasized. Afterward, evaluations will be made on the effectiveness of gamification in influencing consumer experience and increasing customer value and consumers' behavioral intentions in the marketing context. Finally, Starbucks' gamified mobile application is analyzed through a case study from the perspective of customer value.

BACKGROUND

Conceptualizing Customer Value

Customer value has a driving force on customer loyalty (Mulcahy et al., 2015; El-Adly, 2019; Molinillo et al., 2020), customer satisfaction (Mulcahy et al., 2018; Hsu & Chen, 2018b; Huang et al, 2019; Mulcahy et al., 2021), customer attitude (Hamari & Koivisto, 2015; Hsu et al., 2017), customer engagement (Itani et al., 2019), and purchase intention (Gan & Wang, 2017). Therefore, it provides a competitive advantage to the company. According to Zeithaml (1988, p. 14), customer value is conceptualized as

the consumers' overall assessment of the utility of a product based on perceptions of what is received and what is given.

Customer value is also defined as an interactive and relative experience preferred by the consumer (Holbrook, 1996, p. 138). Customer value is the benefits the customer receives in response to the price paid in addition to other purchase-related costs (McDougall & Levesque, 2000, p. 304). Benefit is defined as the advantage or gain obtained by the consumer because of the performance of a product or service (Lovelock & Wright, 2002, p. 6). Accordingly perceived benefit is expressed as the perceived gain obtained by the consumer as a result of the use of certain functions or features provided by the product or service (Park et al., 2011, p. 166). The sacrifices or costs perceived by the consumers also have an important factor in the formation of customer value. Perceived cost refers all the elements that the consumer must give up in order to obtain a product or service (Zeithaml et al., 2018, p. 451) and includes all the costs that a consumer encounters while making a purchase.

Based on this information, it can be said that customer value concept is a multi-dimensional and complex construct (Sheth et al., 1991; Babin et al., 1994; Mathwick et al., 2001; Sweeney & Soutar, 2001; Gallarza & Saura, 2006; Lee et al., 2014; Gordon et al., 2018). The incorporation of customer value into gaming and gamification literature is based on Huatori and Hamari's (2012; 2017) definition of gamification as a value-creating interaction. Within the game and gamification literature, hedonic and utilitarian value distinction (Hamari & Koivisto, 2015; Hsu & Lin, 2016; Hsu & Chen, 2018b; Tanouri et al., 2019; Molinillo et al., 2020) and the concept of experiential value (Mulcahy et al., 2015; Hammedi et al., 2017; Eppmann et al., 2018) are the most mentioned customer value concepts. According to Mathwick et al. (2001), experiential value consists of four dimensions: entertainment, customer return on investment (CROI), aesthetics and service excellence. Mulcahy et al. (2015) adopt Mathwick et al.'s (2001) experiential value dimensions for electronic games. As a result of the study, it was found that these experiential value dimensions are effective on different components of consumer-based brand equity (brand awareness, brand image, perceived quality and brand loyalty). On the other hand, Hammedi et al. (2017) conceptualize experiential value of gamified services in terms of entertainment, escapism, challenges, and social dynamics. Tanouri et al. (2019) consider customer return on investment and service excellence constructs as utilitarian value dimensions and aesthetics and playfulness constructs as hedonic value dimensions. Hsu et al. (2017) and Hsu & Chen (2018a) expand the scope of customer value construct for online gamification context and consider information value, transaction value and social value in addition to experiential value. Accordingly, Whittaker et al. (2021) analyze the customer value of gamified app with ecological, economic, emotional, functional, and social value. In addition to these findings, research indicate that customer value of gamified marketing activities is closely related to customer engagement (Lucassen & Jansen, 2014; Hammedi et al., 2017; Yang et al., 2017; Xi & Hamari, 2020; Whittaker, 2021).

Figure 1. "Value get, value give" framework. Source: Itani et al., (2019)

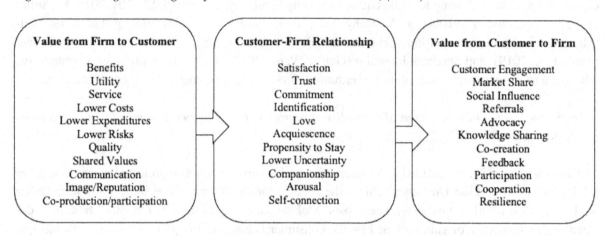

Customer engagement emerges through the interactive and co-creative customer experiences that the consumer has with the brand, product or service (e.g., a gamified app) (Brodie et al. 2011: 260). Therefore, if customers experience high customer value and become engage to brand, product or service, their brand loyalty or behavioral intentions also increase (Sigala, 2015b; Hammedi et al., 2017; Jang et al., 2018; Xi & Hamari, 2020; Whittaker, 2021). These relationships among constructs are illustrated in Figure 1. The framework asserts that a customer will return certain benefits of customer value to the firm through engagement behaviors (e.g., market share, participation, co-creation) related to the firm (Itani et al., 2019, p. 80).

The Use of Gamification in Marketing

Gamification is accepted as a system in which game thinking and game mechanics are used to motivate and engage users (Zichermann, 2011). In the marketing context, gamification is the integration of game dynamics and mechanics into companies' websites, mobile applications, products, services or brands, and marketing campaigns to gain customer participation, engagement, and loyalty (Bunchball, 2010). The gamification system differs from standard digital games. The games contain content that motivates users to participate in an activity of unparalleled intensity and duration and is specifically designed to entertain users (Kovacevic et al., 2014, p. 316). From this point, gamification is the integration of game dynamics in non-game environments (WTM, 2011). According to Deterding et al. (2011a, p. 10) gamification is

the use of game design elements in non-game contexts.

Huotari & Hamari (2012, p. 19) define gamification from a service marketing perspective as *a process of enhancing a service with affordances for gameful experiences in order to support user's overall value creation.*

Gamification has four basic components namely, game, elements, non-game context and design (Deterding et al., 2011a; 2011b; 2011c). Werbach and Hunter (2012, p. 78) argue that gamification consists of three game elements. These are dynamics, mechanics and components. Game mechanics are concerned with the functional elements of a game. Game dynamics is about the interaction of the player with the game mechanics. They are the basic processes that advance the action and ensure player participation (Werbach & Hunter, 2012, p. 79; Wrona, 2012, p. 96). The most important game dynamics are restrictions such as limitations and forced exchanges; emotions such as curiosity, competitiveness, and happiness; narrative as a coherent and ongoing story; the progress of the players; social interactions that produce feelings of friendship, status, and altruism. Game mechanics include challenges, competition, cooperation, feedback, rewards and win situations. Game components are more specific forms that mechanics or dynamics can take, such as achievements, avatars, badges, gifts, leaderboards, levels, points, and virtual goods (Werbach & Hunter, 2012, p. 80; Patricio et al., 2018, p. 502). Table 1 demonstrates that game elements are often interchangeable. For example, levels and leveling may refer to ranks achieved by points or denote stages or areas in the game. In this case, progression is seen as a key factor and varies according to its application to the person or environment (Seaborn & Fels, 2015, p. 20).

Table 1. Game element terminology

Term	Definition	Alternatives
Points	Numerical units indicating progress	Experience points, score
Badges	Visual icons signifying achievements	Trophies
Leaderboards	Display of ranks for comparison	Rankings, scoreboard
Progression	Milestones indicating progress	Levelling, level up
Status	Textual monikers indicating progress	Title, ranks
Levels	Increasingly difficult environments	Stage, area, world
Rewards	Tangible, desirable items	Incentives, prizes, gifts
Roles	Role-playing elements of character	Class, character

Source: Seaborn, K., & Fels, D. I. (2015).

Gamification results from the use of game design elements (Huotari & Hamari, 2017, p. 25). Table 2 indicates that game design elements are defined at five levels distinguished game interface design patterns, game design patterns or mechanics, game design principles or heuristics, game models and game design methods (Deterding et al., 2011a, p. 12). Gamification design features are classified according to dimensions related to achievement, immersion, and social interaction (Xi and Hamari, 2020, p. 405). Gamification features related to immersion include game mechanics such as avatars, storytelling, narrative structures, role-playing mechanics. Achievement-related features involve game mechanics such as badges, challenges, missions, goals, leaderboards, progress metrics. Features related to social interaction contain game mechanics such as team, group and competition (Hamari et al, 2014, p. 3034; Hamari & Tuunanen, 2014, p. 44; Koivisto & Hamari, 2014, p. 181; Koivisto & Hamari, 2019, p. 199).

Table 2. Levels of game design elements

Level	Description	Example
Game interface design patterns	Common, successful interaction design components and design solutions for a known problem in a context, including prototypical implementations	Badge, leaderboard, level
Game design patterns and mechanics	Commonly reoccurring parts of the design of a game that concern gameplay	Time constraint, limited resources, turns
Game design principles and heuristics	Evaluative guidelines to approach a design problem or analyze a given design solution	Enduring play, clear goals, variety of game styles
Game models	Conceptual models of the components of games or game experience	MDA (Mechanics, Dynamics, Aesthetics); challenge, fantasy, curiosity; game design atoms; CEGE (Core Elements of the Gaming Experience)
Game design methods	Game design-specific practices and processes	Playtesting, playcentric design, value conscious game design

Source: Deterding, S., Dixon, D., Khaled, R., & Nacke, L. (2011a).

Gamification uses game elements for purposes other than entertainment (Deterding et al., 2011a, p. 12). Therefore, when game elements are considered to gamify a system, a stock market board, decision support systems, loyalty programs and other services that include levels, points and progression criteria are also gamification (Huotari & Hamari, 2012, p. 19). Loyalty programs, which form the basis of gamification technique, have been used in marketing for many years. Most current frequent flyer programs implemented by businesses are operated with elements of game mechanics such as points systems (air miles) or status levels (frequent flyer status). Innovation regarding the use of gamification in marketing includes combining such game design elements with information technology-based services (Blohm & Leimeister, 2013, pp. 276-277). Therefore, gamification in marketing leverages the latest innovations in games, loyalty programs and behavioral economics (Zatwarnicka-Madura, 2015, p. 1461). The game design methods most used by marketers are progressions, levels, rewards, collectibles, memberships, and points (Hamari & Lehdonvirta, 2010, p. 27). One of the most important indicators pushing businesses to use gamification is Foursquare's success in using scores and badges to motivate user activity and retention. After that, companies became more interested in gamification technology to increase human-computer interaction and elevate the consumer experience (Sigala, 2015a, p. 136). Because gamified marketing activities allow the company to enhance the cognitive, emotional and social experience of the marketing offer associated with the gamification technique (Lee and Hammer, 2011, pp. 3-4). The use of gamification in marketing offers businesses the opportunity to show customers how important they are and their dispositions. At the same time, by providing fun and pleasure to customers, brand love can be created, and customers' behaviors and social attitudes can be changed (Wrona, 2012, p. 104). Table 3 shows some examples of gamification pratices created by companies in different industries.

Table 3. Examples of the gamification in marketing

Industry	Company	Description	Game Elements
Airline & Transportation	American Airlines	Gamified mobile application indicates the current elite status of customers.	Progress bar points Levels (gold, platinum, executive platinum)
	Turkish Airlines	As part of the gamified marketing campaign, national flags with QR codes have been placed on digital bus stops for the London 2012 Summer Olympics. Users who scan the code can win tickets.	Physical rewards Badges
Retail & Hospitality	Shopkick	Gamified shopping application that offers users rewards for both online and in-store shopping activities such as entering stores, scanning items, making in-app or in-store purchases, and submitting invoices.	Virtual currency Rewards Contests
	Starwood SPG program	Through the partnership with the Foursquare gamified mobile application, customers are given the opportunity to earn 250 bonus points per check-in and free accommodation.	Point system Badges
	Marriott My Hotel	As a gamified internal marketing activity, the purpose of the social media game is to attract new staff for job vacancies and engage users in various parts of the hotel.	Point system Levels Virtual goods
Food & Beverage	Starbucks	The gamified mobile application provides customers with the opportunity to collect star points for every purchase they make and earn free items.	Progress bars Leveling Rewards
	4foods	Through the gamified mobile application, customers create and share the sandwiches they want. Sandwich posts are ranked on the leaderboard according to their popularity.	Leaderboard Relatedness
Destination	Foursquare	Gamified mobile application allows users to check-in at physical locations and earn special discounts and rewards from certain retailers.	Badges Leaderboard Reward with real world offers (discounts)

Source: Xu, F., Weber, J., & Buhalis, D. (2014).

Gamified marketing methods can be easily realized through websites and smart phones. Gamified websites and gamified applications try to increase the interaction between marketing programs and users by activating the motivations of the consumers (Noorbehbahani et al., 2019, p. 400). These techniques aim to help businesses take advantage of crowdsourcing effects to build a customer database and increase customer loyalty (Sigala, 2015a, p. 142). For example, TripAdvisor has gamified the website experience by turning website functions into game tasks to attract new users and increase the motivation of travelers to use and interact with the website. Game tasks include activities such as reading reviews, contributing content, or interacting with others (Sigala, 2015b, p. 192). Online fashion retailer ASOS also gamifies the shopping experience on its website through the fashion bingo activity. With this activity, users are asked to match celebrities with clothes and Pinterest competitions are held for customers to win prizes. To encourage customers to participate in this retailing game, the company uses strategies such as flash sales and leaderboards that give early bird exclusivity to sales (Insley & Nunan, 2014, p. 343). Similarly, Starbucks applies gamification techniques through its loyalty program called Starbucks Rewards to increase customer engagement and ensure customer loyalty. When customers use Starbucks' mobile app for their shopping, they receive stars with every purchase. Thereby, customers can earn reward points for free drinks in the future. With its gamified mobile application, Starbucks provides incentives to stimulate the sense of achievement in consumers and instills the idea that they will be rewarded if they remain loyal to the company (Hwang & Choi, 2020, p. 365). Developed by Nike, the Nike Plus gamified mobile app is designed as a complex step counter. The app offers runners challenges that allow them to compete with themselves and other runners. Runners are also encouraged to share their results on social media. This social loop increases the motivation of the user and validates his use of the program (Agnieszka, 2014, p. 61). The Nike Plus app generates benefits such as intensifying ties with customers and encouraging them to purchase more sports equipment (Zichermann & Cunningham, 2011, p. 96; Zatwarnicka-Madura, 2015, p. 1463).

MAIN FOCUS OF THE CHAPTER

Customer Value in Gamified Marketing Practices

Based on the definition by Huotari & Hamari (2017, p. 25) gamification in marketing has three dimensions namely motivational affordances, gameful experience and users' overall value creation. The concept of affordance refers to any feature of the gamification system that allows the game experience to emerge (Huotari & Hamari, 2012, p. 19). Motivational affordances are considered as features designed to support the motivational needs of users and to influence their psychological states (Zhang, 2008, p. 145; Huotari & Hamari, 2017, p. 26; Hammedi et al., 2019, p. 170). The gameful experience refers to voluntary and intrinsically motivated experience customers live when they are interacting with the gamified setting (Huotari & Hamari, 2017, p. 26; Hammedi et al., 2019, p. 170). Lastly, value creation indicates the behavioral outcomes generated by gamification when customers recombine game elements provided by companies to form their gameful experience and engage with the brand, product, or service (Hamari et al., 2014, p. 3026; Huotari & Hamari, 2017, p. 27; Hammedi et al., 2019, p. 171). Therefore, studies investigating the relationship between the use of gamification in marketing and consumer behavior focus on the impact of gamification on consumers' motivations (Bittner & Shipper, 2014; Hsu & Chen, 2018b; Jang et al., 2018; Xi & Hamari, 2019) and the effects of gamified marketing methods on consumers' perceptions, experiences, attitudes, and behaviors (Poncin et al., 2017; Yang et al., 2017; Hsu & Chen, 2018a; Xi & Hamari, 2020).

Motivation refers to an individual's preference for participating in an activity and the intensity of effort or persistence in that activity (Garris et al., 2002, p. 451). Gamification is a persuasive technology that uses game design elements to induce people to perform a challenging and complex task, achieve a particular goal or act in a certain way by activating individual motivations in non-gaming environments (Chorney, 2012; Blohm & Leimester, 2013; Bittner & Shipper, 2014; Conejo et al., 2019; Patricio et al., 2021). Table 4 highlights user motives revealed by different game design elements. In the gamification literature, existing studies on the factors that determine users' motivation consider the distinction between intrinsic and extrinsic motivation within the scope of self-determination theory (Ryan et al., 2006, p. 346; Seaborn & Fels, 2015, p. 19; Xi & Hamari, 2019, p. 211; Xi & Hamari, 2020, p. 450). This theory proposes that human motivation is intrinsically or extrinsically motivated. Accordingly, the motivational factor changes depending on whether the activity is performed for its own sake or for reasons other than itself (Ryan & Deci, 2000a, pp. 56-60; Koivisto & Hamari, 2019, p. 193).

Table 4. Game-design elements and motives

Game-design elements		Motives
Game mechanics	**Game dynamics**	
Documentation of behavior	Exploration	Intellectual curiosity
Scoring systems, badges, trophies	Collection	Achievement
Rankings	Competition	Social recognition
Ranks, levels, reputation points	Acquisition of status	Social recognition
Group tasks	Collaboration	Social exchange
Time pressure, tasks, quests	Challenge	Cognitive stimulation
Avatars, virtual worlds, virtual trade	Development/organization	Self-determination

Source: Blohm, I., & Leimeister, J. M. (2013).

Intrinsic motivation describes the natural disposition towards assimilation, mastery, interest, and exploration. Therefore, it is crucial for the cognitive and social development of an individual (Ryan & Deci, 2000b, p. 70). According to self-determination theory, people have three basic psychological needs, namely competence, autonomy, and relatedness, associated with intrinsic motivation (Ryan & Deci, 2000b, p. 68). On the other hand, extrinsic motivation is represented by behaviors that are instrumental for consequences such as gaining a reward or social approval, avoiding punishment, or achieving a valuable outcome (Ryan & Deci, 2017, p. 14). When playing games, people commonly experience mastery, social interaction, cooperation, competition, enjoyment, immersion, or flow and all of these are characteristics of intrinsically motivated human behavior (Kim & Ahn, 2017; Jang et al., 2018; Xi & Hamari, 2019; Whittaker et al., 2021). Therefore, gamification combines extrinsic and intrinsic motivations. Because it allows to gain a sense of mastery, achievement, autonomy, enjoyment or belonging while using external rewards such as levels, points, badges, leaderboards to increase user participation (Muntean, 2011, p. 326; Richter et al., 2015, p. 24). Table 5 illustrates the interaction of the extrinsic motivation elements provided by gamification and the intrinsic motivations of consumers. The asterisks indicate the primary desire fulfilled by a particular game mechanic, while the plus signs show other motives influenced by that game mechanic (Bunchball, 2010).

Table 5. The interaction of basic human desires and game play

Game Mechanics	Human Desires					
	Reward	**Status**	**Achievement**	**Self-Expression**	**Competition**	**Altruism**
Points	*	+	+		+	+
Levels		*	+		+	
Challenges	+	+	*		+	+
Virtual Goods	+	+	+	*	+	
Leaderboards		+	+		*	+
Gifting & Charity		+	+		+	*

Source: Bunchball (2010)

Self-determination theory (Deci & Ryan, 1985) encompasses many different theories in psychology regarding human motivations (Ryan & Deci, 2017, p. 19). To reveal the differences between these theories, the distinction between extrinsic motivation driven by extrinsic rewards or pressure from the environment and other individuals, and intrinsic motivation driven by the interest and pleasure an individual experiences from the activity, is considered (Vassileva, 2012, p. 186). The theory of planned behavior (Ajzen, 1991), like the self-determination theory, encompasses both intrinsic and extrinsic motivations. Extrinsic motivations or rewards are the focus of Skinner's (1969) reinforcement theory and the expectancy value theory (Eccles et al., 1983). Intrinsic motivations are in the focus of the needs-based theories of Maslow (1943), Alderfer's (1969) ERG (existence – relatedness – growth) theory, the acquired needs theory (McClelland, 1965), cognitive evaluation theory (Deci & Porac, 1978), as well as Bandura's (1997) self-efficacy theory and the goal setting theory (Locke & Latham, 1990). The social comparison theory (Festinger, 1954), the personal investment theory (Maehr & Braskamp, 1986) and the equity theory (Adams, 1965) consider the interplay of intrinsic, extrinsic, and social motivators. According to Tobon et al. (2020), main gamification theories are self-determination theory (Deci & Ryan, 1985), technology acceptance model (Davis, 1989), theory of planned behavior (Ajzen, 1991), flow theory (Csikszentmihalyi, 1975) and social comparison theory (Festinger, 1954).

Based on these motivational theories, it can be said that by offering gamified services, businesses try to foster additional user value in terms of specific user experiences (Eppmann et al., 2018, p. 98; Wolf et al., 2020, p. 353). Current studies indicate that gamification is positively related to customer value (Hammedi et al., 2017, p. 653; Hsu et al., 2017, p. 202; Hsu & Chen, 2018b, p. 129; Tanouri et al., 2019, p. 133; Mulcahy et al., 2020, p. 383; Whittaker et al., 2021) and customer experience (Insley & Nunan, 2014, p. 345; Harwood & Garry, 2015, p. 540; Sigala, 2015b, p. 202; Poncin et al, 2017, p. 325). Gamified services allow consumers to achieve experiences such as immersion, achievement, and social interaction (Xi & Hamari, 2020, p. 452). Among these experiences, immersion is positively associated with autonomy intrinsic need, while achievement and social interaction are positively related with autonomy, relatedness and competition intrinsic needs (Xi & Hamari, 2019, p. 216). For gamified mobile apps, motivational user experiences comprise of self-development, social connectedness, expressive freedom, and social comparison (Wolf et al, 2020, p. 353). Based on different studies, various motivational affordances used in gamification applications and systems can be grouped by their type, into achievement/progression-oriented (such as, points, badges, leaderboards, challenges, quests), social-oriented (such as, cooperation, competition, customization, peer-rating), immersion-oriented (such as, in-game rewards, avatars, storytelling), real world-related (such as, location data, check-ins, financial reward) and miscellaneous (such as, reminders, warnings, penalties, virtual object) elements (Koivisto & Hamari, 2019, p. 199).

The benefits that consumers derive from gamified marketing activities can be classified into three categories. Epistemic benefits allow users to acquire information and increase understanding of the environment. Social integrative benefits enable users to strengthen their relationships with others. Personal integrative benefits relate to strengthening the credibility and social status of users among others (Jang et al., 2018, p. 251). In addition, the factors driving the use of gamification can be similarly divided into three categories. These factors consist of utilitarian benefits expressed as usefulness and ease of use, hedonic benefits expressed as enjoyment and playfulness, and social benefits considered as recognition and social influence (Hamari & Koivisto, 2015, p. 421).

Focusing on the experiences consumers obtain in relation to gamified marketing practices, according to Sigala (2015b, p. 202), experiential values gained from gamified service are customer ROI (return on investment), social value and enjoyment/immersion. Customer ROI refers to the aspects of the gamified service that enable the consumer to make the purchasing decision easier and save time. Furthermore, dimensions of experiential value in electronic games are playfulness, customer return on investment (CROI), aesthetics and service excellence. From these dimensions, playfulness and CROI represent active value, while aesthetics and service excellence reflect reactive value (Mulcahy et al., 2015, p. 262). According to Eppman et al. (2018, p. 109) gameful experience consumers feel when they engage with gamified applications consist of enjoyment, absorption, creative thinking, activation, absence of negative effect and dominance. In a similar way, there are four different experiential value dimensions revealed by gamification mechanics, defined as challenge, entertainment, social dynamics, and escapism. In Figure 2, these four types of experiential value are categorized according to two dimensions: intrinsic/extrinsic and active/reactive (Hammedi et al., 2017, p. 654).

Figure 2. Gamification: Experiential value typology
Source: Hammedi, W., Leclerq, T. and Van Riel, A.C.R. (2017).

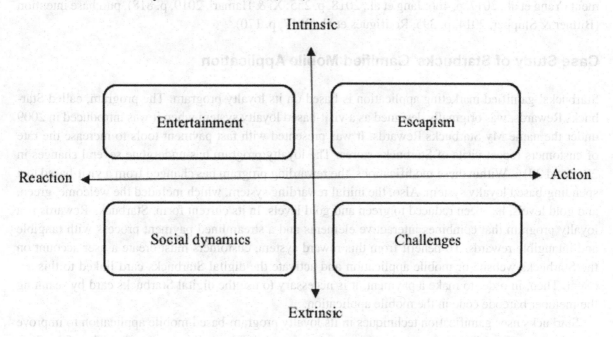

Based on the flow theory, research on a sustainable marketing gamified app show that flow has a direct significant impact on value-in-behavior consists of five dimensions, functional, economic, emotional, social, and ecological value. Flow is defined as the state where people feel intense involvement in an activity and the experience itself involves high enjoyment. Flow can also be stated as the optimal experience. Because it occurs when an activity is optimally stimulating and pleasurable and influencing the individual's intrinsic motivation to engage (Csikszentmihalyi, 1990). Flow can be conceptualized as a hierarchical and multidimensional structure. Therefore, it is measured via the nine dimensions proposed as autotelic experience, challenge/skill balance, unambiguous feedback, clear goals, sense of control, action-awareness merging, concentration on task, loss of self-consciousness, and time transformation (Whittaker et al., 2021). To encourage health and well-being behaviors gamified apps and serious games can create enjoyment, social and transformative value consists of three dimensions – knowledge, distraction, and simulation (Mulcahy et al., 2021, p. 234). Also, informational and emotional social support provided by the gamified apps have a positive association with value consisting of utilitarian and hedonic dimensions. This indicates that social support creates a valuable transformative gamification service experience for users (Tanouri et al., 2019, p. 127). Gamified website services' perceived mobility, hedonic features and utilitarian features positively influence user experience and user experience has a positive effect on consumers' information value, experiential value, social value and transaction value (Hsu & Chen, 2018a, p .125). Similarly, the experience of entertainment, interaction, trendiness, intimacy and novelty that gamified marketing activities provide to the consumer has a positive and significant effect on hedonic and utilitarian value (Hsu & Chen, 2018b, p. 129).

Finally, looking at the effects of gamification on consumers' behavioral outcomes, it is seen that gamification is positively related to brand attitude (van Reijmersdal et al., 2012, p. 38; Yang et al., 2017, p. 466), brand awareness (van Reijmersdal et al., 2012, p. 38; Lucassen & Jansen, 2014, p. 198), brand/customer loyalty (Hsu & Chen, 2018a, p. 125; Hwang & Choi, 2020, p. 372), brand/customer engagement (Yang et al., 2017, p. 466; Jang et al., 2018, p. 255; Xi & Hamari, 2019, p. 818), purchase intention (Bittner & Shipper, 2014, p. 395, Rodrigues et al., 2017, p. 170).

Case Study of Starbucks' Gamified Mobile Application

Starbucks' gamified marketing application is based on its loyalty program. The program, called Starbucks Rewards, was originally designed as a visit-based loyalty system when it was introduced in 2009 under the name My Starbucks Rewards. It was presented with fast payment tools to increase the rate of customers repeat visits of Starbucks stores. The loyalty program has undergone several changes in 2012 and 2016. Within these modifications, the rewarding program has changed from a visit-based to a spending-based loyalty system. Also, the initial rewarding system, which included the welcome, green, and gold levels, has been reduced to green and gold levels. In its current form, Starbucks Rewards is a loyalty program that combines interactive elements and a streamlined payment process with tangible and intangible rewards. To benefit from this reward system, customers must create a user account on the Starbucks website or mobile application and activate the digital Starbucks card linked to this account. Then, in order to make a payment, it is necessary to use the digital Starbucks card by scanning the member barcode code in the mobile application.

Starbucks uses gamification techniques in its loyalty program-based mobile application to improve consumers' coffee drinking experience, create more customer value and increase sales. Therefore, Starbucks Rewards members can earn and accumulate stars that can be redeemed for Starbucks Rewards benefits at participating Starbucks stores in the United States. As a Starbucks Rewards member, customers may be eligible for additional benefits such as birthday reward, free refills of coffee and tea, early or extended access to certain promotions and offers, personalized offers and coupons, double star day (Starbucks Rewards, 2020). In its gamified loyalty marketing program, Starbucks uses game mechanics like progression, points, levels, badges, rewards, challenges and gifting as extrinsic motivators. These extrinsic motivators reveal members' intrinsic motivations or provide them benefits such as achievement, autonomy, competence, relatedness, altruism, and enjoyment. Figure 3 shows the displays of the Starbucks gamified mobile application.

Figure 3. Starbucks Gamification Mobile Application Screenshots
Source: Source: App Store Preview (2021)

In this case study, it is evaluated which intrinsic motivations are triggered by the different game mechanics used in Starbucks' gamified mobile application. In addition, the value components that customers can obtain from Starbucks through these game mechanics and intrinsic motivations are emphasized. The study is based on transaction, information, experiential and social value dimensions which are the customer value components recommended by Hsu et al. (2017) and Hsu and Chen (2108a). In the study, the economic value is added to these customer value components. Accordingly, transaction value states that customers can make their purchases more efficiently, easily, and conveniently through the gamified application. Information value means that the gamified mobile application increases the knowledge of the customers about the company, products, and services, and provides novel and interesting information to the customers. Experiential value indicates that customers feel great, happy, and fulfilled through the stars, awards, badges they achieve, levels they reach and challenges they overcome in the gamified application. Social value refers to the social status and self-esteem that customers gain by sharing and comparing the stars and rewards they achieve and levels they attain through the gamified application with their social environment.

Starbucks' gamified mobile application features a star points system that works with the member barcode and digital Starbucks card to enhance customer value and experience and increase customer engagement, along with a progress bar that displays the stars customers collect and their progress between different star levels. In addition, there is a reward system consisting of different star levels that allows them to earn free products and incentives, challenge system that allow customers to earn bonus stars and double stars on certain days by completing certain tasks, and a Starbucks gift card feature that allows them to send and receive electronic gifts. In addition, customers can customize menu items and order ahead through the app. The app allows customers to access information about brand new products and services, bonus star and double star offers, and store locations. Customers also can earn a member-only game play by making a purchase through the gamified app. For example, between October 4-24, 2021, members can play Starbucks Starland: 50th Anniversary Edition game to earn exclusive prizes, free food and drinks, and more. Table 6 and 7 presents a conceptual framework regarding the effects of different game mechanics and application-specific features used in Starbucks' gamified mobile application on customers' intrinsic motivational factors and perceived customer value components.

Table 6. Starbucks' Gamified Mobile App Game Mechanics, Members Intrinsic Motivations and Customer Value Components

Starbucks' Gamified Mobile App Game Mechanics (Extrinsic Motivation)	Intrinsic Motivations (Benefits)	Customer Value
Points - Members can collect stars with almost every purchase	Achievement Collection Convenience Efficiency Social comparison	Experiential value Social value Transaction value
Progression - Members can check their star balance and track their progression between star levels	Achievement Competence Exploration Social comparison	Experiential value Information value Social value
Levels - Members can reach 25 stars – 50 stars – 150 stars – 200 stars – 400 stars levels	Achievement Competence Exploration Mastery Social comparison Social status	Experiential value Information value Social value
Rewards - Members can redeem stars for free drinks, food and more - They can get a free drink or food of their choice on their birthday - They can have free coffee or tea refills while they are in the store - They can win instant prizes in Starland game - They can win grand (raffle) prizes in Starland game	Achievement Autonomy Competence Economy Enjoyment Immersion Mastery Social comparison	Economic value Experiential value Social value Transaction value
Badges - Member can collect badges in Starland game (e.g. The Big Spender, The Regular, etc.)	Achievement Collection Competence Enjoyment Immersion Mastery Social comparison Social status	Experiential value Social value
Challenges - Members must use their stars within 6 months - They can earn bonus stars with regular opportunities - They can earn twice the stars in special days	Achievement Competence Economy Exploration Social comparison Stimulation	Economic value Experiential value Information value Social value Transaction value
Gifting - Members can send and receive digital Starbucks gift card	Altruism Social interaction	Experiential value Social value

The purchases made by Starbucks customers using the mobile application allow them to earn a certain number of points depending on the monetary amount they spend. These points are called stars. For example, when customers pay with their digital Starbucks card in the app, they will earn 2 stars for every 1 US Dollar they spend. Therefore, customers must add money to their digital Starbucks cards using any payment option and scan the member barcode in the app before paying in-store (Starbucks Rewards, 2021). This system, which allows customers to pay with digital Starbucks cards and collect star points by scanning member barcodes, offers them the opportunity to make their purchases more easily and pay faster. In addition, customers reach different levels by accumulating the stars they collect and can compare the star points with the people in their social environment. With the star balance and the progress bar indicators on the home page of the gamified app, customers view and track their progression and compare them with others.

The application consists of different levels. When customers reach certain levels with their stars, they are awarded with a variety of different incentives. For example, at 25 stars level, customers can redeem their stars for customizing their drink with espresso shot, syrup or sauce, or a dairy alternative option. At 400 stars level, they may redeem their stars for packaged coffee item or a select merchandise item with a value up to 20 US Dollars. In addition, every year on their birthday customers may receive complimentary handcrafted beverage or food item or ready-to-drink bottled beverage. Moreover, customers can receive free refills of hot or iced brewed coffee or tea at stores. For this, customers must scan the member barcode in the app before purchasing their beverage and when they request a refill (Starbucks Rewards, 2020). This reward system provides cost savings to customers with awards at different levels. It also allows customers to choose from different prizes. Rewards consisting of different products or options might make the purchasing activities of customers more enjoyable.

Starbucks' gamified app has a few restrictions, challenges, and different opportunities for their members. First, stars expire six months after the calendar month in which they were earned. The oldest collected stars will be used first for redemptions. Members may occasionally earn additional bonus stars through Starbucks promotional offers. For this, they must fulfill the campaign conditions. For example, packaged coffee products purchased using the app within a certain period of time can earn customers an extra 5 bonus stars. Additionally, Starbucks may offer special occasions where members will earn double the stars for their purchase. Members can send Starbucks gift cards via message or email in the app using certain payment methods. They also have the option to register the gift card they receive for use with Starbucks gamified mobile app.

Table 7. Starbucks' Gamified Mobile App Specific Features, Members Intrinsic Motivations and Customer Value Components

Starbucks' Gamified Mobile App Features	Intrinsic Motivations (Benefits)	Customer Value
Streamlined payment method - Members can save time and collect rewards when they pay with the app at stores	Convenience Efficiency	Transaction value
Digital Starbucks card - Members can check Starbucks card balance, add money to card, view past purchases and transfer balances between cards (e.g., gift card)	Convenience Economy Efficiency Exploration	Economic value Information value Transaction value
Member barcode - Members must scan the QR code	Convenience Efficiency	Transaction value
User account - Members must create an account by giving information about first and last name, email address and password	Autonomy Convenience Efficiency	Experiential value Transaction value
Order ahead - Members can place their orders and then pick up them from the store without waiting in line.	Autonomy Convenience Efficiency	Experiential value Transaction value
Order customization - Member can customize their order and track an estimated pickup time	Autonomy Convenience	Experiential value Transaction value
Inbox - Members can get messages about brand new products and services, promotions and offers	Exploration	Information value
Stores - Members can explore nearby stores, get directions and working hours, and view store facilities	Exploration	Information value
Offers - Members can earn bonus stars with regular opportunities - They can earn twice the stars in special days	Achievement Competence Economy Exploration Stimulation	Economic value Experiential value Information value Transaction value
Starland game: 50th anniversary edition - Members can win instant and grand prizes - They can collect badges	Achievement Collection Competence Enjoyment Immersion Mastery Social comparison Social status	Experiential value Information value Social value Transaction value

Starbucks Starland game is designed for the 50th anniversary to encourage customers to use the gamified mobile application even more. The game integrates gamification techniques with augmented reality. Members can earn one game play per order by making a purchase through the mobile app and up to two game plays per day. The game features a combination of an instant win game and a trivia game. In the instant win game, players can explore iconic Starbucks locations to instantly win prizes and raffle tickets for a chance to win grand prizes. In the trivia game, players can unlock trivia questions about Starbucks history, coffee farming and industry expertise and iconic Starbucks locations to win prizes, and collect badges based on their game activity (Starbucks Stories & News, 2021). Instant win prizes include bonus stars, gift cards, free brewed and handcrafted drinks, free bakery items. Raffle prizes consist of free drinks for 50 days, 50 weeks or 50 months and a trip to a Starbucks Reserve Roastery in Seattle, Chicago or New York. These periodic games for members can contribute to the reinforcement of motivations such as achievement, competence, mastery and enjoyment provided by the gamified application. Members can also increase their social status and interactions by sharing icons such as raffles and badges they earn, or rewards such as instant and grand prizes they win.

Based on the issues discussed in the Starbucks' gamified mobile app case study, it is anticipated that the game elements and other features provided to customers/members will primarily increase the perceived transactional value of customers as these characteristics allow them to make their purchasing and payment transactions more effectively, easily, and quickly. In addition, rewards, incentives, and prizes such as free menu or merchandise items obtained through redeeming the stars earned in the application or seasonal games can contribute to the economic value. It is thought that elements such as leveling, rewarding, progression and earning badges will enhance the experiential value by increasing the level of enjoyment and immersing customers more deeply in the flow. The fact that customers have the opportunity to choose among different options for the rewards they win and to individualize their orders will also increase their experience. Customers' perception of social value will also increase as they can use their mastery information about the number of stars they earn, the levels they reach, the rewards they win, the badges they collect or the challenges they achieve to raise their social status. Finally, the gamified app also enriches the information value perceived by customers by providing them continuous information about the stars they have, the rewards they earn, offers and promotions they can benefit, new products and services they will experience, and stores they can visit.

SOLUTIONS AND RECOMMENDATIONS

This chapter considers the scope of gamification activities used in marketing and their impact on consumer behavior by reviewing the Starbucks' gamified mobile app case. It carries out this evaluation from the perspective of customer value, which is an important determinant of the market success of businesses and allows them to gain competitive advantage. With the developments in technology, there are great transformations in digital, online, and mobile marketing applications. In this changing environment, increasing the experience and value provided to customers seems to be one of the crucial factors for businesses to stand out from the competition. Gamification technique enables consumers to gain more experience and value from marketing activities. The intrinsic motivation of the consumers to participate in the activities carried out by the company regarding the product, service or brand can be increased through gamification. In addition, attitudinal and behavioral patterns of consumers such as customer loyalty, brand awareness, positive customer attitude, purchase intention can be revealed. The relationships between these variables are illustrated in Figure 4, which is adapted from Hammedi et al.'s (2017, p. 653) conceptual framework.

Figure 4. Conceptual framework
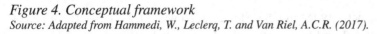
Source: Adapted from Hammedi, W., Leclerq, T. and Van Riel, A.C.R. (2017).

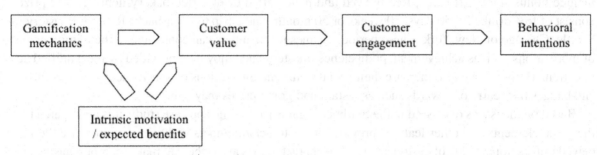

Based on a literature review on the scope and impact of gamification activities in marketing and a case study of Starbucks' gamified mobile application, this conceptual framework is expected to provide a broad perspective. According to self-determination theory, gamification design elements and mechanics such as points, badges, rewards, progression or leaderboards act as an external motivation and they trigger intrinsic motivation or reveal benefits such as achievement, competition, enjoyment, mastery, and social interaction. Therefore, customers may make an inference about customer value after gaining benefits and experiencing gamification elements. It should be noted that the customer value obtained by users has a multi-dimensional and complex structure such as experiential value, hedonic value, utilitarian value, social value, information value, or transaction value. As a result of the gamified experience, customer engagement of the user, who achieves high customer value, also increases. This customer engagement is reflected in the customer's loyalty to the brand, repurchase intention, and positive word-of-mouth communication towards the brand.

Empirical studies in the literature and statistics on the business world also support the issues resolved in the case study. Hwang & Choi (2020) confirm that Starbucks' bingo game based gamified mobile loyalty program increases consumer loyalty which in turn enhanced consumer participation intention and app download intention. Kim & Ahn (2017) reveal that gamification elements (e.g., graphical feedback) added to Starbucks' loyalty program can be effective on increasing intrinsic motivation to participate in the program. Xin et al. (2018) state that the point system used as a game element in My Starbucks Rewards program affects the purchasing motivation of customers. Hyeuk (2016) finds out that the intervening conditions of Starbucks' branded mobile app such as convenience, usefulness, having fun and saving cost exercise significant influence on brand engagement. Li (2018) demonstrates that elements such as locatability, transaction convenience, economic benefits, and gamification provided by Starbucks' mobile application are treated as pull factors for customers to use the application. Moreover, Starbucks gamified application is the second most used mobile payment app for point-of-sale transactions in the US, right after Apple Pay (Emarketer, 2021). According to one study, 6.9 percent of respondents using the Starbucks app visit Starbucks more than once a day, compared to only 0.7 percent of non-app users (Statista, 2019a; 2019b). Based on this further information, in technological competitive market environment, it is crucial for companies to utilize gamification techniques, that are compatible with consumers' intrinsic motivations and include experiential, transactional, informational, and social benefits, in their marketing activities.

FUTURE RESEARCH DIRECTIONS

With the intensive use of gamification technique, it is an important issue to understand the success factors of this technology in the marketing activities of companies. Through an exploratory research approach, this study evaluates the examined issues with literature review and case study analysis. Therefore, the chapter constitutes the preliminary study of the empirical research that will be conducted in the future on the effects of Starbucks' gamified mobile application on customers' perceived customer value. Customer value is the most important way for companies to increase the lifetime value of their customers. Customers, whose relationship and interaction with the product, brand and service is increased, become more loyal to company and their offerings. As gamified marketing activities enrich the customer experience, they also allow to increase the value created by the company. For this reason, customer value dimensions should be analyzed in detail in order to obtain customer engagement, which is one of the most important outputs of gamification. Therefore, in terms of future studies, it is thought that analyzing the relationships between different customer value components (e.g., transactional, hedonic, utilitarian, experiential, social value) and customer engagement dimensions (e.g., cognitive, emotional, social) with empirical research in a multi-dimensional manner will make an important contribution to the literature and practice. Considering the gamification technique differentiates the user's experience with the product, service, or brand, it can be stated that scale development studies regarding the dimensions of customer experience should also be increased.

CONCLUSION

In recent years, with the developments in online gaming technologies, gamification has become the latest marketing activity used by companies to increase customer experience and value and to ensure customer engagement. Gamification is not a technology used only in the field of marketing. In addition to health and education, it is also used in other business areas such as increasing employee participation. The purpose of gamification is to motivate users or consumers to perform a challenging and complex task, achieve a particular goal or act in a certain way. Thus, gamification refers to the use of game design elements in non-game environments.

With the increase in the use of gamification technique in the field of marketing, the intensity of conceptual and empirical studies on the subject is also increasing. In this chapter, the use of gamification technique in marketing is discussed from the perspective of customer value. Firstly, a general evaluation of the importance of customer value in marketing, gamification technique and its design elements are presented. Then, it is mentioned how gamification applications are used in the context of marketing. Finally, based on this presented framework, a comprehensive case study of Starbucks' gamified mobile app is provided, in line with the conceptual and empirical studies carried out on gamified marketing activities, from the perspective of customer value.

The literature review and case study indicate that different game elements can activate different internal motivations of customers and enable them to enrich their experience and value. In the context of marketing, gamification activities are frequently used in the field of mobile and online marketing as gamified websites and gamified applications. The most important advantage of gamification in marketing is increasing customer engagement through improving the experience and value of customers. Therefore, gamified marketing activities can be used to create positive brand equity (brand loyalty, brand awareness, brand image) by increasing customer experience, value, and engagement.

REFERENCES

Adams, J. S. (1965). Inequity in social exchange. *Advances in Experimental Social Psychology, 2,* 267–299. doi:10.1016/S0065-2601(08)60108-2

Agnieszka, W. S. (2014). Gamification as a new trend in marketing. *Marketing and Management of Innovations, 4,* 57–64.

Ajzen, I. (1991). The theory of planned behavior. *Organizational Behavior and Human Decision Processes, 50*(2), 179–211. doi:10.1016/0749-5978(91)90020-T

Alderfer, C. P. (1969). An empirical test of a new theory of human needs. *Organizational Behavior and Human Performance, 4*(2), 142–175. doi:10.1016/0030-5073(69)90004-X

App Store Preview. (2021). *Starbucks iPhone screenshots.* Retrieved October 10, 2021, from https://apps.apple.com/us/app/starbucks/id331177714?_branch_match_id=981323254902129837&utm_source=Web&utm_medium=marketing

Babin, B. J., Darden, W. R., & Griffin, M. (1994). Work and/or fun: Measuring hedonic and utilitarian shopping value. *The Journal of Consumer Research, 20*(4), 644–656. doi:10.1086/209376

Bandura, A. (1997). *Self-efficacy: The exercise of control.* W. H. Freeman and Company.

Bittner, J. V., & Shipper, J. (2014). Motivational effects and age differences of gamification in product advertising. *Journal of Consumer Marketing, 31*(5), 391–400. doi:10.1108/JCM-04-2014-0945

Blohm, I., & Leimeister, J. M. (2013). Gamification: Design of IT-based enhancing services for motivational support and behavioral change. *Business & Information Systems Engineering, 5*(4), 275–278. doi:10.100712599-013-0273-5

Brodie, R. J., Hollebeek, L. D., Juric, B., & Ilic, A. (2011). Customer engagement: Conceptual domain, fundamental propositions, and implications for research. *Journal of Service Research, 14*(3), 252–271. doi:10.1177/1094670511411703

Bunchball. (2010). *Gamification 101: An introduction to the use of game dynamics to influence behavior.* Retrieved from June 20, 2021, from http://jndglobal.com/wp-content/uploads/2011/05/gamification1011.pdf

Burke, B. (2014). *Gamify: How gamification motivates people to do extraordinary things.* Bibliomotion, Inc.

Chorney, A. I. (2012). Taking the game out of gamification. *Dalhousie Journal of Interdisciplinary Management, 8*(1), 1–14. doi:10.5931/djim.v8i1.242

Conejo, G. G., Gasparini, I., & da Silva Hounsell, M. (2019). Detailing motivation in a gamification process. In *Proceedings of 19th International Conference on Advanced Learning Technologies* (pp. 89-91). Washington, DC: IEEE Computer Society.

Csikszentmihalyi, M. (1975). Play and intrinsic rewards. *Journal of Humanistic Psychology*, *15*(3), 41–63. doi:10.1177/002216787501500306

Csikszentmihalyi, M. (1990). *Flow: The psychology of optimal experience*. Harper & Row Publishers, Inc.

Davis, F. D. (1989). Perceived usefulness, perceived ease of use, and user acceptance of information technology. *Management Information Systems Quarterly*, *13*(3), 319–340. doi:10.2307/249008

Deci, E. L., & Porac, J. (1978). Cognitive evaluation theory and the study of human motivation. In M. R. Lepper & D. Greene (Eds.), *The hidden costs of reward: new perspectives on the psychology of human motivation* (pp. 149–176). Lawrence Erlbaum Associates.

Deci, E. L., & Ryan, R. M. (1985). *Intrinsic motivation and self-determination in human behavior*. Springer. doi:10.1007/978-1-4899-2271-7

Deterding, S., Dixon, D., Khaled, R., & Nacke, L. (2011a). From game design elements to gamefulness: Defining gamification. In *Proceedings of the 15th International Academic MindTrek Conference: Envisioning Future Media Environments* (pp. 9-15). New York, NY: Association for Computing Machinery. 10.1145/2181037.2181040

Deterding, S., Dixon, D., Khaled, R., & Nacke, L. (2011b). Gamification: Toward a definition. In *Proceedings of CHI 2011 Gamification Workshop* (pp. 12-15). New York, NY: Association for Computing Machinery.

Deterding, S., Sicart, M., Nacke, L., O'Hara, K., & Dixon, D. (2011c). Gamification: Using gamedesign elements in non-gaming contexts. In *Proceedings of CHI Conference on Human Factors in Computing Systems* (pp. 2425-2428). New York, NY: Association for Computing Machinery. 10.1145/1979742.1979575

Eccles, J. S., Adler, T. F., Futterman, R., Goff, S. B., Kaczala, C. M., Meece, J. L., & Midgley, C. (1983). Expectancies, values, and academic behaviors. In J. T. Spence (Ed.), *Achievement and achievement motivation: Psychological and sociological approaches* (pp. 75–146). W. H. Freeman and Company.

El-Adly, M. I. (2019). Modelling the relationship between hotel perceived value, customer satisfaction, and customer loyalty. *Journal of Retailing and Consumer Services*, *50*, 322–332. doi:10.1016/j.jretconser.2018.07.007

Emarketer. (2021). *How the Starbucks app is energizing mobile payment use*. Retrieved October, 6, 2021, from https://www.emarketer.com/content/how-starbucks-app-energizing-mobile-payment-use

Eppmann, R., Bekk, M., & Klein, K. (2018). Gameful experience in gamification: Construction and validation of a gameful experience scale. *Journal of Interactive Marketing*, *43*, 98–115. doi:10.1016/j.intmar.2018.03.002

Festinger, L. (1954). A theory of social comparison processes. *Human Relations*, *7*(2), 117–140. doi:10.1177/001872675400700202

Gallarza, M. G., & Saura, I. G. (2006). Value dimensions, perceived value, satisfaction and loyalty: An investigation of university students' travel behaviour. *Tourism Management, 27*(3), 437–452. doi:10.1016/j.tourman.2004.12.002

Gan, C., & Wang, W. (2017). The influence of perceived value on purchase intention in social commerce context. *Internet Research, 27*(4), 772–785. doi:10.1108/IntR-06-2016-0164

Garris, R., Ahlers, R., & Driskell, J. E. (2002). Games, motivation, and learning: A research and practice model. *Simulation & Gaming, 33*(4), 441–467. doi:10.1177/1046878102238607

Gordon, R., Dibb, S., Magee, C., Cooper, P., & Waitt, G. (2018). Empirically testing the concept of value-in-behavior and its relevance for social marketing. *Journal of Business Research, 82,* 56–67. doi:10.1016/j.jbusres.2017.08.035

Hamari, J., & Koivisto, J. (2015). Why do people use gamification services? *International Journal of Information Management, 35*(4), 419–431. doi:10.1016/j.ijinfomgt.2015.04.006

Hamari, J., Koivisto, J., & Sarsa, H. (2014). Does gamification work? A literature review of empirical studies on gamification, In *Proceedings of the 47th Hawaii International Conference on System Sciences* (pp. 3025-3034). Washington, DC: IEEE Computer Society. 10.1109/HICSS.2014.377

Hamari, J., & Lehdonvirta, V. (2010). Game design as marketing: How game mechanics create demand for virtual goods. *International Journal of Business Science and Applied Management, 5*(1), 14–29.

Hamari, J., & Tuunanen, J. (2014). Player types: A meta-synthesis. *Transactions of the Digital Games Research Association, 1*(2), 29–53. doi:10.26503/todigra.v1i2.13

Hamid, M., & Kuppusamy, M. (2017). Gamification implementation in service marketing: A literature review. *Electronic Journal of Business & Management, 2*(1), 38–50.

Hammedi, W., Leclercq, T., & Poncin, I. (2019). Customer engagement: The role of gamification. In L. D. Hollebek & D. E. Sprott (Eds.), *Handbook of research on customer engagement* (pp. 164–185). Edward Elgar Publishing. doi:10.4337/9781788114899.00014

Hammedi, W., Leclerq, T., & Van Riel, A. C. R. (2017). The use of gamification mechanics to increase employee and user engagement in participative healthcare services: A study of two cases. *Journal of Service Management, 28*(4), 640–661. doi:10.1108/JOSM-04-2016-0116

Harwood, T., & Garry, T. (2015). An investigation into gamification as a customer engagement experience environment. *Journal of Services Marketing, 29*(6/7), 533–546. doi:10.1108/JSM-01-2015-0045

Helmefalk, M., & Marcusson, L. (2019). Gamification in a servicescape context: A conceptual framework. *International Journal of Internet Marketing and Advertising, 13*(1), 22–46. doi:10.1504/IJIMA.2019.097894

Holbrook, M. B. (1996). Customer value - A framework for analysis and research. *Advances in Consumer Research. Association for Consumer Research (U. S.), 23,* 138–142.

Hsu, C. L., & Chen, M. C. (2018a). How does gamification improve user experience? An empirical investigation on the antecedences and consequences of user experience and its mediating role. *Technological Forecasting and Social Change, 132*, 118–129. doi:10.1016/j.techfore.2018.01.023

Hsu, C. L., & Chen, M. C. (2018b). How gamification marketing activities motivate desirable consumer behaviors: Focusing on the role of brand love. *Computers in Human Behavior, 88*, 121–133. doi:10.1016/j.chb.2018.06.037

Hsu, C. L., Chen, Y. C., Yang, T. N., & Lin, W. K. (2017). Do website features matter in an online gamification context? Focusing on the mediating roles of user experience and attitude. *Telematics and Informatics, 34*(4), 196–205. doi:10.1016/j.tele.2017.01.009

Hsu, C. L., & Lin, C. C. (2016). Effect of perceived value and social influences on mobile app stickiness and in-app purchase intention. *Technological Forecasting and Social Change, 108*, 42–53. doi:10.1016/j.techfore.2016.04.012

Huang, C. K., Chen, C. D., & Liu, Y. T. (2019). To stay or not to stay? Discontinuance intention of gamification apps. *Information Technology & People, 32*(6), 1423–1445. doi:10.1108/ITP-08-2017-0271

Huotari, K., & Hamari, J. (2012). Defining gamification – A service marketing perspective. In *Proceedings of the 16th International Academic MindTrek Conference* (pp. 17-22). New York, NY: Association for Computing Machinery. 10.1145/2393132.2393137

Huotari, K., & Hamari, J. (2017). A definition for gamification: Anchoring gamification in the service marketing literature. *Electronic Markets, 27*(1), 21–31. doi:10.100712525-015-0212-z

Hwang, J., & Choi, L. (2020). Having fun while receiving rewards?: Exploration of gamification in loyalty programs for consumer loyalty. *Journal of Business Research, 106*, 365–376. doi:10.1016/j.jbusres.2019.01.031

Hyeuk, C. (2016). Consumer brand engagement by virtue of using Starbucks's branded mobile app based on grounded theory methodology. *International Journal of Asia Digital Art and Design, 19*, 91–97.

Insley, V., & Nunan, D. (2014). Gamification and the online retail experience. *International Journal of Retail & Distribution Management, 42*(5), 340–351. doi:10.1108/IJRDM-01-2013-0030

Itani, O. S., Kassar, A. N., & Loureiro, S. M. C. (2019). Value get, value give: The relationships among perceived value, relationship quality, customer engagement, and value consciousness. *International Journal of Hospitality Management, 80*, 78–90. doi:10.1016/j.ijhm.2019.01.014

Jang, S., Kitchen, P. J., & Kim, J. (2018). The effects of gamified customer benefits and characteristics on behavioral engagement and purchase: Evidence from mobile exercise application uses. *Journal of Business Research, 92*, 250–259. doi:10.1016/j.jbusres.2018.07.056

Kim, K., & Ahn, S. J. G. (2017). The role of gamification in enhancing intrinsic motivation to use a loyalty program. *Journal of Interactive Marketing, 40*, 41–51. doi:10.1016/j.intmar.2017.07.001

Koivisto, J., & Hamari, J. (2014). Demographic differences in perceived benefits from gamification. *Computers in Human Behavior, 35*, 179–188. doi:10.1016/j.chb.2014.03.007

Koivisto, J., & Hamari, J. (2019). The rise of motivational information systems: A review of gamification research. *International Journal of Information Management, 45*, 191–210. doi:10.1016/j.ijinfomgt.2018.10.013

Kovacevic, I., Zecevic, G., & Veljkovic, S. (2014). "Gamification" concept: Theoretical framework and destination marketing management practice. *Ekonomika Preduzeca., 62*(5-6), 315–322. doi:10.5937/ekopre1406315K

Lee, J. J., & Hammer, J. (2011). Gamification in education: What, how, why Bother? *Academic Exchange Quarterly, 15*(2), 1–5.

Lee, M. R., Yen, D. C., & Hsiao, C. Y. (2014). Understanding the perceived community value of Facebook users. *Computers in Human Behavior, 35*, 350–358. doi:10.1016/j.chb.2014.03.018

Li, C. Y. (2018). Consumer behavior in switching between membership cards and mobile applications: The case of Starbucks. *Computers in Human Behavior, 84*, 171–184. doi:10.1016/j.chb.2017.12.042

Locke, E. A., & Latham, G. P. (1990). *A theory of goal setting & task performance*. Prentice-Hall, Inc.

Lovelock, C., & Wright, L. (2002). *Principles of service marketing and management*. Pearson Education Inc.

Lucassen, G., & Jansen, S. (2014). Gamification in consumer marketing – Future or fallacy? *Procedia: Social and Behavioral Sciences, 148*, 194–202. doi:10.1016/j.sbspro.2014.07.034

Maehr, M. L., & Braskamp, L. A. (1986). *The motivation factor: A theory of personal investment*. Lexington Books.

Maslow, A. H. (1943). A theory of human motivation. *Psychological Review, 50*(4), 370–396. doi:10.1037/h0054346

Mathwick, C., Malhotra, N., & Rigdon, E. (2001). Experiential value: Conceptualization, measurement and application in the catalog and internet shopping environment. *Journal of Retailing, 77*(1), 39–56. doi:10.1016/S0022-4359(00)00045-2

McClelland, D. C. (1965). Toward a theory of motive acquisition. *The American Psychologist, 20*(5), 321–333. doi:10.1037/h0022225 PMID:14323512

McDougall, G. H. G., & Leveque, T. (2000). Customer satisfaction with services: Putting perceived value into the equation. *Journal of Services Marketing, 14*(5), 392–410. doi:10.1108/08876040010340937

Molinillo, S., Japutra, A., & Liebana-Cabanillas, F. (2020). Impact of perceived value on casual mobile game loyalty: The moderating effect of intensity of playing. *Journal of Consumer Behaviour, 19*(5), 493–504. doi:10.1002/cb.1831

Mulcahy, R., Russell-Bennett, R., & Iacobucci, D. (2020). Designing gamified apps for sustainable consumption: A field study. *Journal of Business Research, 106*, 377–387. doi:10.1016/j.jbusres.2018.10.026

Mulcahy, R., Russell-Bennett, R., & Rundle-Thiele, S. (2015). Electronic games: Can they create value for the moderate drinking brand? *Journal of Social Marketing, 5*(3), 258–278. doi:10.1108/JSOCM-06-2014-0043

Mulcahy, R. F., Russell-Bennett, R., Zainuddin, N., & Kuhn, K. A. (2018). Designing gamified transformative and social marketing services: An investigation of serious m-games. *Journal of Service Theory and Practice*, *28*(1), 26–51. doi:10.1108/JSTP-02-2017-0034

Mulcahy, R. F., Zainuddin, N., & Russell-Bennett, R. (2021). Transformative value and the role of involvement in gamification and serious games for well-being. *Journal of Service Management*, *32*(2), 218–245. doi:10.1108/JOSM-05-2019-0137

Muntean, C. I. (2011). Raising engagement in e-learning through gamification. In *Proceedings 6th International Conference on Virtual Learning ICVL* (pp. 323-329). Bucharest: Bucharest University Press.

Noorbehbahani, F., Salehi, F., & Zadeh, R. J. (2019). A systematic mapping study on gamification applied to e-marketing. *Journal of Research in Interactive Marketing*, *13*(3), 392–410. doi:10.1108/JRIM-08-2018-0103

Park, J., Snell, W., Ha, S., & Chung, T. L. (2011). Consumers' post-adoption of m-services: Interest in future m-services based on consumer evaluations of current m-services. *Journal of Electronic Commerce Research*, *12*(3), 165–175.

Patricio, R., Moreira, A. C., & Zurlo, F. (2018). Gamification approaches to the early stage of innovation. *Creativity and Innovation Management*, *27*(4), 499–511. doi:10.1111/caim.12284

Patricio, R., Moreira, A. C., & Zurlo, F. (2021). Enhancing design thinking approaches to innovation through gamification. *European Journal of Innovation Management*, *24*(5), 1569–1594. doi:10.1108/EJIM-06-2020-0239

Poncin, I., Garnier, M., Mimoun, M. S. B., & Leclercq, T. (2017). Smart technologies and shopping experience: Are gamification interfaces effective? The case of the Smartstore. *Technological Forecasting and Social Change*, *124*, 320–331. doi:10.1016/j.techfore.2017.01.025

Richter, G., Raban, D. R., & Rafaeli, S. (2015). Studying gamification: The effect of rewards and incentives on motivation. In T. Reiners & L. C. Wood (Eds.), *Gamification in education and business* (pp. 21–46). Springer. doi:10.1007/978-3-319-10208-5_2

Rodrigues, L., Costa, C., & Oliveira, A. (2017). How does the web game design influence the behavior of e-banking users? *Computers in Human Behavior*, *74*, 163–174. doi:10.1016/j.chb.2017.04.034

Ryan, R. M., & Deci, E. L. (2000a). Intrinsic and extrinsic motivations: Classic definitions and new directions. *Contemporary Educational Psychology*, *25*(1), 54–67. doi:10.1006/ceps.1999.1020 PMID:10620381

Ryan, R. M., & Deci, E. L. (2000b). Self-determination theory and the facilitation of intrinsic motivation, social development, and well-being. *The American Psychologist*, *55*(1), 68–78. doi:10.1037/0003-066X.55.1.68 PMID:11392867

Ryan, R. M., & Deci, E. L. (2017). *Self-determination theory: Basic psychological needs in motivation, development, and wellness*. The Guilford Press. doi:10.1521/978.14625/28806

Ryan, R. M., Rigby, C. S., & Przybylski, A. (2006). The motivational pull of video games: A self-determination theory approach. *Motivation and Emotion*, *30*(4), 344–360. doi:10.100711031-006-9051-8

Seaborn, K., & Fels, D. I. (2015). Gamification in theory and action: A survey. *International Journal of Human-Computer Studies, 74*, 14–31. doi:10.1016/j.ijhcs.2014.09.006

Sever, N. S., Sever, G. N., & Kuhzady, S. (2015). The evaluation of potentials of gamification in tourism marketing communication. *International Journal of Academic Research in Business & Social Sciences, 5*(10), 188–202. doi:10.6007/IJARBSS/v5-i10/1867

Sheth, J. N., Newman, B. I., & Gross, B. L. (1991). Why we buy what we buy: A theory of consumption values. *Journal of Business Research, 22*(2), 159–170. doi:10.1016/0148-2963(91)90050-8

Sigala, M. (2015a). Gamification for crowdsourcing marketing practices: Applications and benefits in tourism. In F. J. Garrigos-Simon, I. Gil-Pechuan, & S. Estelles-Miguel (Eds.), *Advances in crowdsourcing* (pp. 129–145). Springer. doi:10.1007/978-3-319-18341-1_11

Sigala, M. (2015b). The application and impact of gamification funware on trip planning and experiences: The case of TripAdvisor's funware. *Electronic Markets, 25*(3), 189–209. doi:10.100712525-014-0179-1

Simoes, J., Redondo, R. D., & Vilas, A. F. (2013). A social gamification framework for a K-6 learning platform. *Computers in Human Behavior, 29*(2), 345–353. doi:10.1016/j.chb.2012.06.007

Skinner, B. F. (1969). *Contingencies of reinforcement: A theoretical analysis.* Appleton-Century-Crofts.

Starbucks Rewards. (2020). *Starbucks rewards terms of use.* Retrieved October 16, 2021, from https://www.starbucks.com/rewards/terms#about-starbucks-rewards

Starbucks Rewards. (2021). *Cash or card, you earn stars.* Retrieved October 16, 2021, from https://www.starbucks.com/rewards

Starbucks Stories & News. (2021). *Celebrate 50 years of Starbucks with the Starland: 50th anniversary edition game.* Retrieved October 17, 2021, from https://stories.starbucks.com/press/2021/starbucks-starland-50th-anniversary-edition/

Statista. (2019a). *Frequency of visits to Starbucks by those who use the app in the United States as of October 2019.* Retrieved October 17, 2021, from https://www.statista.com/statistics/1083426/starbucks-app-users-visit-frequency/

Statista. (2019b). *Frequency of visits to Starbucks by those who do not use the app in the United States as of October 2019.* Retrieved October 17, 2021, from https://www.statista.com/statistics/1083461/starbucks-non-app-users-visit-frequency/

Sweeney, J. C., & Soutar, G. N. (2001). Consumer perceived value: The development of a multiple item scale. *Journal of Retailing, 77*(2), 203–220. doi:10.1016/S0022-4359(01)00041-0

Tanouri, A., Mulcahy, R., & Russell-Bennett, R. (2019). Transformative gamification services for social behavior brand equity: A hierarchical model. *Journal of Service Theory and Practice, 29*(2), 122–141. doi:10.1108/JSTP-06-2018-0140

Tobon, S., Ruiz-Alba, J. L., & Garcia-Madariaga, J. (2020). Gamification and online consumer decisions: Is the game over? *Decision Support Systems, 128*, 113167. doi:10.1016/j.dss.2019.113167 van Reijmersdal, E. A., Rozendaal, E., & Buijzen, M. (2012). Effects of prominence, involvement, and persuasion knowledge on children's cognitive and affective responses to advergames. *Journal of Interactive Marketing, 26*(1), 33–42. doi:10.1016/j.intmar.2011.04.005

Vassileva, J. (2012). Motivating participation in social computing applications: A user modeling perspective. *User Modeling and User-Adapted Interaction, 22*(1-2), 177–201. doi:10.100711257-011-9109-5

Werbach, K., & Hunter, D. (2012). *For the win: How game thinking can revolutionize your business.* Wharton Digital Press.

Whittaker, L., Mulcahy, R., & Russel-Bennett, R. (2021). 'Go with the flow' for gamification and sustainability marketing. *International Journal of Information Management, 61*, 102305. doi:10.1016/j.ijinfomgt.2020.102305

Wolf, T., Weiger, W. H., & Hammerschmidt, M. (2020). Experiences that matter? The motivational experiences and business outcomes of gamified services. *Journal of Business Research, 106*, 353–364. doi:10.1016/j.jbusres.2018.12.058

Wrona, K. (2012). Gamification and games, their potential for application in marketing strategies. *Transactions of the Institute of Aviation, 227*(6), 93–105. doi:10.5604/05096669.1076720

WTM. (2011). *World travel market global trends report 2011.* Retrieved September 20, 2021, from http://www.toposophy.com/files/1/files/onsite_global_trends_v3_lo.pdf

Xi, N., & Hamari, J. (2019). The relationship between gamification, brand engagement and brand equity. In *Proceedings of the 52nd Hawaii International Conference on System Sciences* (pp. 812-821). Honolulu, HI: Creative Commons. 10.24251/HICSS.2019.099

Xi, N., & Hamari, J. (2020). Does gamification affect brand engagement and equity? A study in online brand communities. *Journal of Business Research, 109*, 449–460. doi:10.1016/j.jbusres.2019.11.058

Xin, O. W., Zuo, L., Iida, H., & Aziz, N. (2018). Gamification effect of loyalty program and its assessment using game refinement measure: Case study on Starbucks. In Computational science and technology (pp. 161-171). Springer Nature Singapore Pte Ltd.

Xu, F., Weber, J., & Buhalis, D. (2014). Gamification in tourism. In Z. Xiang & I. Tussyadiah (Eds.), *Information and communication technologies in tourism 2014* (pp. 525–537). Springer.

Yang, Y., Asaad, Y., & Dwivedi, Y. (2017). Examining the impact of gamification on intention of engagement and brand attitude in the marketing context. *Computers in Human Behavior, 73*, 459–469. doi:10.1016/j.chb.2017.03.066

Zatwarnicka-Madura, B. (2015). Gamification as a tool for influencing customers' behaviour. *International Journal of Economics and Management Engineering, 9*(5), 1461–1464.

Zeithaml, V. A. (1988). Consumer perceptions of price, quality, and value: A means-end model and synthesis of evidence. *Journal of Marketing, 52*(3), 2–22. doi:10.1177/002224298805200302

Zeithaml, V. A., Bitner, M. J., & Gremler, D. D. (2018). *Services marketing: Integrating customer focus across the firm.* Mc-Graw Hill Education.

Zhang, P. (2008). Motivational affordances: Reasons for ICT design and use. *Communications of the ACM, 51*(11), 145–147. doi:10.1145/1400214.1400244

Zichermann, G. (2011, January). *A long engagement and a shotgun wedding: Why engagement is the power metric of the decade.* Paper presented at The Gamification Summit, San Francisco, CA.

Zichermann, G., & Cunningham, C. (2011). *Gamification by design implementing game mechanics in web and mobile apps.* O'Reilly Media, Inc.

ADDITIONAL READING

Berger, A., Schlager, T., Sprott, D. E., & Herrmann, A. (2018). Gamified interactions: Whether, when, and how games facilitate self–brand connections. *Journal of the Academy of Marketing Science, 46*(4), 652–673. doi:10.100711747-017-0530-0

Dymek, M. (2018). Expanding the magic circle – gamification as a marketplace icon. *Consumption Markets & Culture, 2*(6), 590–602. doi:10.1080/10253866.2017.1361153

Garcia-Jurado, A., Castro-Gonzalez, P., Torres-Jimenez, M., & Leal-Rodriguez, A. L. (2019). Evaluating the role of gamification and flow in e-consumers: Millennials versus generation X. *Kybernetes, 48*(6), 1278–1300. doi:10.1108/K-07-2018-0350

Hamari, J., & Koivisto, J. (2014). "Working out for likes": An empirical study on social influence in exercise gamification. *Computers in Human Behavior, 50*, 333–347. doi:10.1016/j.chb.2015.04.018

Hassan, L., & Hamari, J. (2020). Gameful civic engagement: A review of the literature on gamification of e-participation. *Government Information Quarterly, 37*(3), 101461. doi:10.1016/j.giq.2020.101461

Kamboj, S., Rana, S., & Drave, V. A. (2020). Factors driving consumer engagement and intentions with gamification of mobile apps. *Journal of Electronic Commerce in Organizations, 18*(2), 17–35. doi:10.4018/JECO.2020040102

Rahi, S., & Ghani, M. A. (2018). Does gamified elements influence on user's intention to adopt and intention to recommend internet banking? *International Journal of Information and Learning Technology, 36*(1), 2–20. doi:10.1108/IJILT-05-2018-0045

Robson, K., Plangger, K., Kietzmann, J., McCarthy, I., & Pitt, L. (2015). Game on: Engaging customers and employees through gamification. *Business Horizons, 59*(1), 29–36. doi:10.1016/j.bushor.2015.08.002

KEY TERMS AND DEFINITIONS

Customer Engagement: A state of being involved in product, service or brand derived from interactive customer experience.

Customer Experience: Internal and subjective customer responses such as feelings and cognitions aroused by the stimuli associated with a product, service, or brand.

Customer Value: An assessment that the customer derives from their judgment between what is expected and what is received regarding the outputs, benefits or utility of a product or service.

Gamification: The usage of game design elements and mechanics in non-game environments to motivate users to perform a task or act in a certain way.

Gamified Apps: Mobile applications containing game design elements and mechanics to engage and retain customers.

Gamified Websites: Web pages containing game-like features, mechanics, and user interface elements that try to increase the interaction between marketing programs and customers by activating users' motivations.

Self-Determination Theory: It proposes that human motivation is driven by intrinsic or extrinsic factors in performing an activity. It also states that people have three basic psychological needs, which are related to intrinsic motivation: competence, autonomy, and relatedness.

Chapter 8
Role–Playing Games as a Model of Gamification Applied to Engagement of Online Communities

Jose-M Jimenez-Pelaez
Nebrija University, Spain

Juana Rubio-Romero
Nebrija University, Spain

ABSTRACT

Recent technological advances have promoted a social change that affects all areas of society, but mainly communication and entertainment, where social networks play a primordial function as they facilitate sociability and the creation of virtual communities. So-called "social media marketing" facilitates direct interaction between brands and markets through the Internet. For this, new communication strategies have been implemented, oriented towards the active participation of the users to increase their engagement. Some of these are inspired by the main product of the entertainment industry, videogames, through gamification. However, not many research studies have focused on classic role-playing games (RPGs), despite being considered the types of games that create the greatest player involvement. This work enquires about the possibilities offered by these games for the implementation of social media marketing strategies. A qualitative research study was conducted in which the engagement strategies utilized by RPG were associated with those utilized in social networks.

INTRODUCTION

The generalization and expansion of social media marketing in the last decade has facilitated the direct and segmented communication of brands with their clients (Hubspot, 2021), and has also structured new communication strategies based on the leading role of the virtual community (Gómez-Carreño, 2021). In

DOI: 10.4018/978-1-7998-9223-6.ch008

this context, a need has appeared to search for mechanisms and strategies that promote the participation of social network users, to obtain a greater degree of engagement (Xi & Hamari, 2019).

Likewise, videogames have expanded and become more popular in the last few decades, to become one of the main leisure activities and industries (Asociación Española de Videojuegos [AEVI], 2021). Their success has caught the interest of sectors that are far from related to pure entertainment, becoming inspired by their keys to their success when implementing strategies that connect with their interests (Oliveira et al., 2021). Gamification was thus born, a strategy which applies the mechanics and dynamics of games to non-entertainment areas, such as marketing (Deterding et al., 2011).

In general terms, gamification strategies are inspired on the design and mechanics present in videogames (Sailer et al., 2020), in which in most cases, the participation of the user is limited to the control or guidance of a specific, previously designed element, to overcome the different challenges provided by the game. On the other hand, gamification strategies do not tend to consider other types of games in which the participation and involvement of the player is indispensable for their development (Koivisto & Hamari, 2019), such as role-playing games.

Role-playing games have become one of the most successful genres of videogames (AEVI, 2021). Without a doubt, they are the inheritors of the classic role-playing games which became popular as board games in the 1970s, although they have always been part of the act of playing. Since their introduction, the classic role-playing games have evolved and still have supporters, but their use is presently low.

This chapter will delve into the classic role-playing games to discover what they can contribute to gamification: the possible application of their dynamics and mechanics to promote the participation and involvement of the participants in the current context of social networks. This is due to their high participative and cooperative value (Murray, 1999), and their possible contribution when designing new gamification tactics and strategies in social networks.

As a result, the present study intends to broaden the perspective of gamification in which most of the studies consulted focus on, as the most studied elements in the gamification strategies are the points, the classification tables, and the badges (Klock et al., 2020), when other role-playing game elements and tactics are more effective than these components, especially if the objective is to improve engagement and promote user participation.

Therefore, the objectives of our study are: to inquire about the role of games in the new digital culture, and gamification as a social and commercial communication strategy; to delve into the design and mechanics present in this type of classic/analog role-playing game to promote the participation and involvement of the participants; to relate the communication strategies followed by community managers with that of role-playing game game masters; to show the way to other modalities and areas of interest associated with the use of classic role-playing games. To address these objectives, the starting question raised is if the structure of the classic role-playing games can become similar to the present conversations found in social media, and if this the case, to inquire if the strategies utilized in the role-playing games can be applied to also promote the participation in communications established in social networks.

BACKGROUND

Game and Gamification: The Apogee of Leisure

Various studies, such as those conducted in Spain by Sigmados, Ipsos and the Spanish Association of Software Distributors and Publishers, "Videogame Industry Annual", and Women Play, Consume, Participate" (AEVI, 2020 & 2021), or those conducted in other countries such as the United States, by the Entertainment Software Association (ESA), highlight the current expansion, importance, and reach of videogames in our society, as an everyday leisure activity.

This interest in games is not new, since it has always been there, as part of the culture and history of humanity. Games have attracted the attention of many thinkers in many eras and have played different roles, according to the value given to them by each culture and society. It is starting in the 19th Century that the interest in games was lost (Huizinga, 2008), coinciding with the exaltation of what was useful and their systematization and discipline (creation of clubs, championships, etc.).

According to Callois (1986), it is possible to understand the qualities and defects of a society through the games which predominate within it, given that the activity of entertainment creates a defined social structure and model. Starting with this concept, authors such as Murray (1999) reflected on the current rise of videogames, in the context of technologization and the rise of entertainment. Scolari (2013) also echoed this sentiment in his book "Homo Videoludens", which title brings homage and is a parallelism of the evolution of leisure and entertainment found in human society since Huizinga (1938) defined the term "Homo Ludens".

Authors such as Csíkszentmihalyi (1990) or Esnaola (2009) focused their research studies on the recreational experience. Esnaola herself attested that the recreational experiential attitude was a pre-requisite for adapting ourselves to a technological environment that is permanently changing. This is especially true when immersion and the participation propitiated by these technologies are already part of ways of being in the world, at the same time that they favor the attainment of the flow state (Csíkszentmihalyi, 2007). This is an optimum state of intrinsic motivation, experienced by the person who is immersed in whatever he or she is doing. Mihaly Csíkszentmihalyi postulates that with the practice of games such as chess, tennis, or poker, it is easy to enter into a state in which a person is completely absorbed by an activity, pushing his or her skills and abilities to the extreme, while experiencing an enormous satisfaction and fulfillment due to this.

The social and economic repercussion of videogames in our society has motivated authors such as McGonigal (2011) to try to adapt elements that are present in videogame design for their adoption in other non-entertainment spheres, with the main objective being to motivate and influence the behavior of individuals (Deterding et al., 2011). This is known as gamification.

Even though only a decade has passed since the appearance of the term gamification, the idea of utilizing the reasoning and mechanics present in games to resolve problems and motivate individuals has long been applied to society (Zichermann & Cunningham, 2011). This practice has been developed in business to improve the engagement and the loyalty of clients, at the same time that it has motivated workers and providers to reach higher levels of performance (Bunchball, 2010).

Staring from the first gamification strategies applied, it was observed that for example, the use of re-enforcement facilitated the loyalty of individuals and increased their motivation to acquire products and services (Zichermann & Linder, 2010; Cortizo et al., 2011). The social aspect was also highlighted, as it favored the appearance of collaborative and competitive behaviors between users (Bunchball, 2010), and had a close relationship with the social structure and paradigm of the social web (McGonigal, 2011). In this manner, it is not only possible to make the user perceive tedious and/or boring tasks as attractive (Cortizo et al., 2011), but also that their participation is voluntary (Lee & Hammer, 2011). On the other hand, the research studies consulted indicated that the game mechanics and elements associated with the achievement or consecution of objectives, and those related with the social interaction between participants, had a significant effect on the engagement of the consumer with the brand (Xi & Hamari, 2020).

Thus, if the most studied and utilized elements in the gamification mechanics are points, classification tables and badges (Hamari et al., 2020), then all the elements and mechanics present in the game that allow social interaction, or are related with the representation of achievements and advances, are more effective on the motivation of the participants, given that they are associated with the intrinsic human needs, such as competence, autonomy and social interaction (Ryan & Deci, 2000; Sailer et al., 2017).

This classification of the gamification elements according to their aim: immersion, achievement, or social interaction, is more common to research studies on gamification (Koivisto & Hamari, 2019) than the ones proposed previously, which were centered on the figure of the game designer, as the focus was placed on mechanics, dynamics, and aesthetics (MDA model) offered by the game (Werbach & Hunter, 2012; Ramírez, 2014; Teixes, 2015). As for the relationship with the MDA model, Werbach and Hunter (2012) compared the archetype of the game design with the creation of natural language, referring to grammar as the present but not visible structure (aesthetic), where the verbs (dynamics), and nouns (mechanics) are the solid matter that make language a reality.

Despite the agreement of various authors on the difficulty of designing effective gamification strategies, if they are applied correctly, they can help to align the interests of the businesses with the intrinsic motivations of the clients/players, amplified with the mechanics and rewards, which allows the users to enter into this dynamic, bring friends, and remain within it (Zichermann & Cunningham, 2011).

Brand Communities, the Rise of the Relational

As indicated by Currier (2008), in the 1940s and 1950s, brands discovered that if they presented convincing messages to people who watched television or listened to the radio, they could influence their purchasing behaviors and decisions. The audiences consumed advertising passively as mere receivers (Howe, 2008). But the arrival of the new communication technologies revolutionized this panorama, and the success of social networks has radically disrupted the manners in which brands communicate with their consumers, who have acquired a main role and transformed into "prosumers": consumers and producers of content.

The progressive introduction of personal computers into the homes in the 1980s and 1990s greatly expanded the capacities of humans (Murray, 1999), and the development of the Internet promoted the social evolution and propagation of other technologies, such as videogames. Castells (2001) refers to the profound social modification derived from the technological revolution, and Lasen (2014) highlights the effects derived from this broad dissemination and personalization, until reaching the point of reshaping numerous aspects of everyday life.

The malleability of these communication technologies led to the adoption of a new paradigm known as Web 2.0 (O'Reilly, 2017), which was a fundamental aspect in the emergence of participative culture, present in the nucleus of the Internet since its beginnings (Brabham, 2013). The users/consumers were placed at the center of communication (Cobo & Pardo, 2007), and exponentially increased their possibilities of collective thought and social influence (Levy, 1994). Along this line, Fumero (2007) defined

Web 2.0 as a Network turned into a social space which favored the establishment of virtual communities of users and which had been constructed from the start of the global deployment of telecommunication networks (Castell, 1997). These virtual communities of users, which tended to be ruled by ethical principles and values (Himanen, 2004), did not stop growing, and kept on increasing in number with every generational change (Fumero, 2007), until arriving at the so-called digital natives (Prensky, 2001).

Such is the case, that for adolescents, the creation of a profile in a social network is an authentic rite of passage, playing a primordial function in their social insertion, especially when referring to the increase in their social capital and achievement of recognition (Rubio-Romero et al., 2019). And when specifically referring to virtual brand communities, the youth show a broad following of brands through social networks (Rubio-Romero & Barón-Dulce, 2019).

Social networks made possible the change of the brand-client relationships into conversations, which became susceptible to certain compromises (Fernández-Gómez & Gordillo-Rodríguez, 2015). Such is the case that a company's efforts are mainly directed towards promoting the participation of the users, who are becoming increasingly avoidant and demanding with the brands. However, brands know that humans are relational beings, and therefore constantly seek contact with other humans around them (Fernández-Gómez & Gordillo-Rodríguez, 2015). Therefore, marketing in Social Networks opens a way to effectively penetrate into a market that has increasingly become more competitive (Gómez-Carreño & Palacios-Alvarado, 2021) and increasingly susceptible to conversational marketing (Hubspot, 2021).

Since the appearance of social networks at the start of the 21st Century, they have been considered by marketing strategists as indispensable communication tools, to the point of stating that not being in them signifies their lack of importance and subsequent disappearance (Kaplan & Haenlein, 2010). And this concept has become more important, as an increasing number of companies, independently of their size or capital, are utilizing them (Shen et al., 2020), and have been forced to progressively increase the budget for this medium (Michaelidou, 2014). This is mainly because this is where the consumers are, which helps in increasing the relationship of the brands with their clients (Gómez-Carreño & Palacios-Alvarado, 2021), converse with them, and even turn them into collaborators.

Fournier (1998) has long declared the relationships between consumers and brands at the level of personal relationships, and Fernandez (2013) mentioned that consumers accept brands as part of their relationships, contributing to their humanization. Presently, businesses not only seek to exploit the relationship between users and brands, but also promote the relationships between the consumers themselves, thus contributing to the creation of authentic communities, brand communities (Muniz & O'Guinn, 2001), which fundamentally revolve around specific interests and/or values.

Muniz and O'Guinn (2001, p. 412) define a brand community as "a specialized, non-geographically bound community, based on a structured set of social relations among admirers of a brand". McAlexander, Schouten and Koenig (2002, in Fernández-Gómez & Gordillo-Rodríguez, 2015), assert that the products are bought and consumed in specific social contexts, and point out that individuals tend to establish relationships with others who consume the same products or identify themselves with the same brands, so that they share values and attitudes (García, 2005).

These communities, around a brand, create a series of opportunities but also risks, which should be considered by the companies that promote them.

These opportunities range from supporting the communication strategy to increasing their commercial development, and therefore, the value of the brand (Gode et al., 2016), given that it facilitates the appearance and introduction of brand extensions (Fernández-Gómez & Gordillo-Rodríguez, 2015), and increases the ability to obtain feedback and contribute with suggestions to improve the development of products and other marketing aspects (McAlexander et al., 2000 cited in García, 2005). The community users themselves become "evangelists" within their social group (McAlexander et al., 2000 cited in García, 2005), and could even assist the consumers in the use of the products (Fernández-Gómez & Gordillo-Rodríguez, 2015).

However, this ability to persuade becomes a problem when rumors or criticisms about the products or negative attitudes towards the company are disseminated. The communities can swiftly develop and extend different types of protests, boycott, or rejection in regard to specific actions or decisions by the business, interpreted as wrong or far from the authentic spirit of the brand (Fernández-Gómez & Gordillo-Rodríguez, 2015). In this sense, the prosumers and the members of the brand communities interact in real time with them and want to receive immediate responses to their doubts and consultations. In the end, they seek a closer and faster relationship with the product providers and services they are interested in (Cornellá & Rucabado, 2006).

Therefore, in a scenario where advertising and brands have ceded part of their power to the users, who are integrated into virtual communities with others who are similar, they have had to re-define their communication strategies, being aware that a community is something that can be facilitated and supported, but not something that could be created or controlled (Cothrel & Williams, 1999). This demands the need to rely on professionals who are responsible for communicating with potential consumers and for safeguarding the reputation of the company in digital media, such is the case of community managers (Soengas et al., 2015).

ROLE-PLAYING GAMES AS A MODEL OF ENGAGEMENT AND PARTICIPATION STRATEGIES

Method

Three main questions are asked about gamification and engagement strategies within the context of role-playing games, which will guide the research study.

Research Quest One: Can role-playing games be considered tools of interest for the implementation of gamification strategies and communicative engagement due to their high participative and co-operative value?

Research Quest Two: Can the mechanics and dynamics of conventional role-playing games help improve the involvement of Social Media users, given their creative and interactive potential?

Research Quest Three: What is the relationship between the actions of the game master from a role-playing game and the community manager in businesses?

To answer these questions, and to achieve the research objectives, the following methodological process was followed:

In first place, a selection was made of the role-playing games that were best evaluated by the players of these types of games. For this, an open poll was conducted among the community of players from La Mazmorra de Pacheco (Pacheco's Dungeon), a YouTube channel focused on role playing games with one of the largest community of followers at the international level (82,500 subscribers); in this poll, the subscribers were asked to name the best role-playing games. With more than 2,500 votes received, the most-voted titles were the following: Dungeons & Dragons, Call of Cthulhu, Vampire: The Masquerade, Pathfinder, Fate and Steam States.

Next, a study was made of the game rules from the game rulebooks from the 6 most-voted games; all the strategies and recommendations proposed in these rulebooks were subjected to the assessment of the game masters according to the importance provided to maintain the interest and participation of the players. This allowed us to create a list and select the strategies that were common to all of these role-playing games. In total, 20 tactics were extracted which addressed the relationship of the game master with the community, whose aim was to create engagement and improve the player's loyalty to the game.

Afterwards, this information was compared with the opinion of the experts consulted, from both role-playing games, and social networks. Six in-depth qualitative interviews were conducted: 3 to role-playing game game masters, and 3 to community managers.

The community manager sample was composed of the following: the Director of the Digital Production Section at TBWA (EP1); a member of the management team from AERCO (Spanish Association of Online Community Managers), who also worked as a community manager (EP2); the Communication Strategies manager at the communication agency Territorio Creativo (EP3).

As for the individuals selected from the role-playing game sphere, we counted with the participation of the Director from the main role-playing game publisher in Spain, Nosolorol (EP1), and the two main influencers of the role-playing games in Spain (EP2 and EP3), with all of them also veteran game masters of role-playing games.

All the interviews began by openly raising the subject of strategies utilized for the management and promotion of community participation, which facilitated the free and spontaneous speech of the interviewees. Afterwards, we delved into matters that were specifically related with the research objectives. The interview ended with the validation by the interviewees of the list of 20 tactics extracted from the review of the rulebooks from the selected role-playing games.

The interviews were conducted in person in Madrid (Spain) and lasted between 45 and 60 minutes. All of them were recorded for their posterior analysis.

Characteristics of the Role-Playing Games According to Game Masters

The game masters and designers of the role-playing games consulted indicated three basic characteristics of the analog role-playing games which fostered engagement and the participation of the players.

In first place, they highlighted the immersion of the participants in the game narrative, which they defined as "putting yourself in the character's shoes", interpreting the role, which requires imagination and creativity, and which must be fed and encouraged by the person who directs the game, and which is built upon during gameplay.

In second place, they mentioned teamwork, the cooperation of all those involved to arrive at an agreed-upon narrative that considered all the individual differences. This is a type of game to have fun, where the collaborative experience must exceed the competitive one, pointing out its strong social character: "and it is also social; the people who play role-playing games are creating, at that moment, a shared history" (EP6).

In third place, the experts pointed to the system of rules that preside every type of game. In the case of the analog role-playing games, the rules are established in what the experts called a "social contract" between the group of players, as proposed by the game master, who becomes their keeper and guarantor. The rules are the limits that the game design establishes, which does not impede the players themselves from deciding if they are acceptable or not, while trying to change them. Thus, there are no pre-defined options (choose A or B), but on the game itself, it is decided if an option belongs or not in the game, according to the rules of the game: "the rules will serve to decide if this can happen or not, but nothing stops you from trying" (EP4). The only condition is that all the players know the rules of the game when providing play proposals, so that these make sense and provide coherence to the general structure of the narrative.

For this, the role-playing game experts defined the role-playing game as an interaction between all the players during game play, which highlights its profoundly dialogic character: "the role-playing game, in the end, is a conversation. Playing a role-playing game is conversing in this group, which is trying to recreate or tell a combined history, as there is truly a very broad range of actions; a defined set of options is not available" (EP4).

This turns the role-playing games into a collaborative experience.

Construction of a Fictional Universe and Functions of the Game Master

One of the most addicting aspects of the role-playing games is without a doubt the creation of their own universe within the context of a world that is co-created by all the players, in which each one can project oneself through an avatar in this shared work of fiction. This is how an expert expresses this aspect: "the most addicting aspect is feeling the sensation of having an avatar, so to speak, in a fictional or relatively fictional world, a projection of their idea of self, 'I'm going to be this character and I'm going to act like this' and feeling as the avatar does for a period of time" (EP5).

Thus, two connections are produced in the role-playing game: personal (player and avatar), and social (between the different avatars), aside from a direct interaction between the game master and the players, both of which have clearly-defined roles. The person who guides the game plays the role of "coach" before the role of omnipotent game master, thus becoming another participant in the game experience. His or her main role should be more centered on the involvement of the players in the game, rather than a mere a keeper of the rules; all the efforts made should be oriented towards the participation of the players on the description of narrative elements of the game and the characters.

The classic role-playing games have evolved towards a shared narrative authorship, thus increasing the degree of participation and the co-creation between the players. Even though the rules are a key aspect of the game (without rules there is no game, just as without law there is not society), there is a great amount of freedom when applying them to the role-playing games, as pointed out by one of our experts: "the rules of the game normally serve to determine the results of the actions, but freedom is on a higher plane, in the plane of actions" (EP4).

The analog role-playing game, just as the digital (videogames) emphasizes the interactions and participation of the players, which is stimulated by their mechanics from the start of the game: "the game should include mechanics that make it unnecessary for the game master to try to make the participants play, but instead the game mechanics should entail that the players participate" (EP4). But even though this is the case for videogames and analog games, the latter have the particularity that they deal with authentic brainstorming, which makes the game experience be more direct and personalized.

In role-playing games, the player's success is fundamentally derived from his or her intervention in the narration of the game, so that the player is placed above the person who directs the game. One of the game designers stated: "when you have a successful (die) throw, the player narrates what is happening;

it is not about 'I succeeded and now you tell me what happens', but the games determines that I, as a player, have to say what happens because I was successful in a throw" (EP4).

But for the game to work, the game master becomes a fundamental figure. Aside from outlining the rules of the games and being the guarantor of the "social contract" between the players when they have to comply with them, the main role is to motivate the players to participate/talk, to have them make detailed descriptions about the players and each of the elements that participate in the game narrative: "the role-playing games, if well-played, can potentially promote participation, but not by themselves, you have to know how to play them" (EP5).

Thus, the person who guides the role-playing game has three different functions: motivate the participation, guarantee the compliance of the game rules, and establish consensus: "the first thing is that everyone plays what they want to play, that everyone agrees on what they want to play, a social contract stating that we are going to play this, that everyone is informed, that their expectations coincide and are clear" (EP6).

This is why it is important to know the players well, to motivate their participation given their personal characteristics: "You have to know each player, and the good thing is that in a role-playing game, the game master can look after each one on every occasion. I don't think this can be done in any other game" (EP6).

Role Playing Games and Gamification

Playing role-playing games is practicing gamification in itself, given that the role-playing game is an experience inherited from role playing, which is closer to the area of psychology and education than the game itself. Thus, a role-playing game would therefore be *role playing* with an added set of rules, which turns it into a game, because, as we have highlighted, a game cannot exist without rules.

Gamification, as pointed out by Werbach and Hunter (2012), must combine the elements and designs present in games, with a purpose and an objective that goes beyond the game. When applying role-playing game design to gamification strategies, we must apply them to other areas and for specific aims, as proposed by Teixes (2015): "gamification is the application of resources from games (design, dynamics, elements, etc.) into non-entertainment contexts, to modify the behavior of the individuals, to act on their motivation, for the execution of specific objectives" (pg. 18).

The role-playing game experts consulted considered that playing a role-playing game was, within itself, gamification; it would be then, "gamification within gamification", as the fact that no constrained rules exist, as in other types of games, creates their understanding of this as a manner of gamifying the rules of the game so that "they are fun" (EP4). In fact, as previously mentioned, the rules of the role-playing games have evolved so that the players are now involved in their creation, so that they are fun within themselves: "There was a moment in time in which the main worry was that the rules be realistic, then that they would be at the service of the story, and not act as an obstacle, and now, without saying that these two things are no longer important, there is a general worry that they are fun to play with" (EP4).

It could be said, then, that the role-playing game is role playing designed as a fun experience, and thus they move away from the therapeutic aspect… "really, the role-playing techniques are being applied, and the only thing we have to do is to add the component of the mechanics, which gives it the aspect of a game, and perhaps this could serve us to make the experience more fun, result in learning, and lead to the use of the advantages of role-playing" (EP4).

The role-playing games mesh with the innate nature of humans, and this makes them perfectly adaptable to numerous gamification experiences, as long as the objectives are clear. One of the experts stated: "it is very natural, all of them are born role players, all the children role play, they play being mom and dad, Cowboys and Indians, and this is role playing. It is easy to give it another meaning, set objectives to your game, which are the external objectives you want, design values, design a subject, create a complete group dynamic [...] I think this makes it an easily-attainable tool, very moldable and very useful" (EP6).

Presently, gamification starting with games is conducted in many fields. It is obvious that the fields of education, health, and psychology occupy privileged spaces, as they have ample experience. But in companies, especially when referring to the management of teams, the role-playing games have also been widely accepted when gamifying experiences with different objectives:

"The team-building techniques are increasingly being utilized in the business sector for strategies of team management and to provide training on specific competences" (EP4).
"Many businesses are dedicated to making live role-playing games to promote good relations within businesses" (EP5).

The areas of marketing and communications, although less present in the discourse of our interviewees, were also mentioned spontaneously, mainly highlighted within the context of social networks, where interaction is primordial: "...many strategies are being utilized in marketing, for example, in social networks, which are fundamental marketing channels, the impact of the publications are based on the interactions achieved, so that promoting the interaction of individuals is almost mandatory" (EP4).

Communication Objectives of the Community Managers in Social Networks

Business communications in social networks, whose responsibility lies on the community managers, seek three basic objectives:

- Capture the attention of the users.
- Know the clients in-depth.
- Obtain interactions with the contents they publish.

These three objectives absolutely overlap, although the strategies which substantiate them are inspired by other sources.

Those responsible of social media, and the community managers interviewed, were unanimous when confirming the importance of creativity for capturing the attention of the clients. They considered indispensable that the subjects on which their publications were based, be relevant for their target audience, be coherent with the brand, that they "surprise", and get attention at the formal and content levels. This creativity has many times solidified in the imitation of good practices from some brands: observing what works and what doesn't, or through trial and error.

It is also fundamental to know the users well, and therefore, psychology is another fundamental source of inspiration. When connecting with clients, it is necessary to feel empathy and understand the desires and concerns of humans. "We all like to appear more intelligent", our experts pointed out, "projecting ourselves according to the desires that others value the most" (EP1).

The third objective sought, to obtain the interaction and participation of the users, points directly to the game, as it is the most "fun" and "simple" way to obtain interaction. Gamification, on the other hand, has tools, such as the mechanics of the challenge or rewards, which are highly useful, as they test the player's intelligence and luck; this facilitates the participation of the users and becomes a source of motivation for the co-creation of content: "people really like it when we propose a challenge that is complicated, that is easy to understand by the user, that does not require much effort and that is not boring when doing it…many game mechanics appear" (EP3).

Playing is an insight in itself, as an expert expressed: "because playing is an insight; if you play a board game, role-playing games, or games as such, you are contributing ideas, and applying them to the digital experience, but in the end it's the same" (EP3).

For community managers, it is very important to create synergies between associated brand communities (for example, the successful strategy implemented between the PlayStation and McDonald's brands), and personalized conversations. The objective of personalizing communication is to achieve higher-quality and stronger engagement with the users, as one of the experts comments: "Talking (conversing) for us is the main aspect for achieving better engagement, and for increasing the number of fans who become more involved with us […] they love it when you answer their questions and do something more specific for them; they feel special" (GD3).

Marketing in Social Networks and Gamification: Tactics and Strategies of Community Managers

The experts in communication management in social networks consider that gamification is as naturalized as are games, although until the present, no one had mentioned this, and therefore it absolutely overlaps in their work: "I believe that gamification has always been present in all of human history, hidden in some way […] Gamification is as simple as rewarding someone's participation, even in a publication" (EP1).

The need is highlighted to differentiate gamification from the ad-hoc creation of games and/or applications, which is known as serious games. While serious games require a great investment that on many occasions is not recovered, gamification is simply the application of game mechanics to marketing actions, which only demands creativity and knowledge of the target to whom the actions are directed: "what we do is to take everyday games and try to digitalize them. This works very well, because we have all been children and have had experiences with basic games, such as what color do you see? Or the dress, the "stop" gif, that kind of thing… questions, answers, hints, having to search, check someplace, all of this works. This is what works the most, in fact, if you have a game that does not bore people, questions are the typical thing" (EP3).

Thus, gamification promotes and boosts universal human feelings and desires such as: "pleasure", "entertainment", "coping", "being children again", "showing others how smart one is…", "showing that I'm better than the others…". The competitive aspects become more explicit in the gamification of marketing than that verified in gamification of role-playing games, which are more centered on collaboration than competition.

The use of challenges is one of the main tactics utilized by community managers to interact with their clients and push them towards participation: "if we know a secret about some videogame, we give them a wink so that the user participates when trying to guess certain things, which for them is an added gift" (EP3). Aside from the challenge, this idea is strongly associated with the strategy of the mystery, "resolve some conflict…", which is very fruitful in role-playing games.

Whatever mechanics utilized in gamification, the most important aspect is that they respond to a previously-planned strategy, aside from its execution for being attractive: "well-planned and well-executed, this always gives good results" (EP2).

And the social networks are considered as the ideal terrain for bringing gamification to practice, in that they are conversation spaces *par excellence* in the digital society. However, the experts consulted were aware that users in general are not given to participation, so that one cannot abuse these types of strategies: "in the end, the user is becoming comfortable, and if you ask for far too many requisites for doing something, he or she will not do it, because I think that it's a very comfort-driven society now" (EP3).

It is clear that this also depends on the type of target for which these types of gamification techniques are implemented. In their opinion, it does not work with every type of community: "it depends on the community; in communities aged from 35-45 years old, it frequently works, but this is not the case with the younger ones; don't ask them to make much effort through points, you are not going to achieve it" (EP3). Therefore, it is necessary to plan the strategies well, and to adapt them to the type of target we want to reach.

Similarities and Differences Between the Figures of the Game Masters in Role-Playing Games and the Community Manager

As observed, these two profiles had some similarities. A fundamental, structural one, is that both professionals perform their activity in a conversational environment. This is because both role-playing games and social networks are dialogic contexts within which, beyond the existence of previous grammar (dynamics, in the case of the role-playing games, and strategic planning, in the case of marketing), the fundamental aspect is interaction, with both demanding prior knowledge about the interests of the speaker (players/clients) to obtain their involvement.

Both types of professionals also coincided in that internal motivation was much stronger than the external one, which entails the in-depth knowledge of human desires and a respect for the differences, in light of the personalization of the experience. In spite of this being this way, it was observed that the marketing professionals appealed much more to the competition resources, as compared to the game masters who granted more value to collaboration.

These results, derived from the spontaneous discourse of the 2 collectives interviewed, were complemented with their assessment of 20 tactics extracted from the role-playing game rulebooks. The experts were asked to assess these tactics according to their suitability for motivating their communities in social networks. These tactics were the following:

1 Understand the audience
2 Give something to every member of the community
3 Keep the rhythm from slowing down
4 Not forgetting rewards
5 Promote mystery and intrigue
6 Involve the members of the community as much as possible
7 Meet the expectations of the community
8 Do the work ahead of time
9 Not abuse the power
10 Promote the trust between the audience and the community managers

11 You should not try to please everyone the same
12 Consider the direct suggestions from the community and try to incorporate them
13 Not intimidate or force the audience to participate
14 Not direct the conversations or select content subjectively
15 Obtaining attention requires one to seem interested in what one is telling
16 The audiovisual supports are useful
17 If the members feel frustrated, the community managers must avoid frustration
18 Avoid that the dramatic or emotional load of the community increase
19 One should not be responsible for solving all the problems
20 Maintain an internal consistency

The results indicated many similarities in the assessments made by both sets of professionals: all the tactics proposed, except for two (Keep the rhythm from slowing down, by the community manager, and avoiding frustration, by the game masters), were marked as amenable to being implemented in the sphere of social networks.

Next, they were asked to point out 10 tactics they considered to be more suitable for their application to a communication strategy in social networks. The following were selected:

Tactic 1: Understand the audience
Tactic 2: Give something to every member of the community
Tactic 3: Involve the members of the community as much as possible
Tactic 4: Meet the expectations of the community
Tactic 5: Not abuse the power
Tactic 6: You should not try to please everyone the same
Tactic 7: Consider the direct suggestions from the community and try to incorporate them
Tactic 8: Not intimidate or force the audience to participate
Tactic 9: Not direct the conversations
Tactic 10: Maintain internal consistency

Lastly, they were asked to vote (Table 1) on the most valuable tactics when implementing gamification strategies in social networks.

Table 1. Prioritization of tactics in social media and role-playing games

RPG*			SOCIAL MEDIA			VOTES		ROLE-PLAYING GAME TACTICS
EP6	EP5	EP4	EP3	EP2	EP1			
1	1	1	1	1	1	6	1	Understand the audience
1	1	1	1			4	2	Give something to every member of the community
	1	1				2	3	Keep the rhythm from slowing down
1		1				2	4	Not forgetting rewards
1	1	1				3	5	Fomentar el misterio y la intriga
1	1	1				3	6	Involve the members of the community as much as possible
1		1	1	1		4	7	Meet the expectations of the community
1			1	1	1	4	8	Do the work ahead of time
	1	1	1			3	9	Not abuse the power
1	1		1		1	4	10	Promote the trust between the audience and the community managers
	1			1	1	3	11	You should not try to please everyone the same
	1	1	1	1		4	12	Consider the direct suggestions from the community and try to incorporate them
1		1	1			3	13	Not intimidate or force the audience to participate
			1	1		2	14	Not direct the conversations or select content subjectively
		1			1	2	15	Obtaining attention requires one to seem interested in what one is telling
			1	1	1	3	16	The audiovisual supports are useful
					1	1	17	If the members feel frustrated, the community managers must avoid frustration
					1	1	18	Keep the dramatic or emotional load of the community from increasing
					1	1	19	One should not be responsible for solving all the problems
1	1	1	1	1	1	6	20	Maintain internal consistency

*RGP= Role-Playing Games
Source: The authors

As we can observe, both types of professionals considered that "understanding the audience" and "maintain internal consistency" were indispensable tactics for performing their work well.

These are followed, in second place, by: "Give something to every member of the community", "Meet the expectations of the community", "Do the work ahead of time", "Promote the trust between the audience and the community managers", and "Consider the direct suggestions from the community and try to incorporate them".

In third place, we find "Not abuse the power", "One should not be responsible for solving all the problems", and "Not intimidate or force the audience to participate".

Lastly, it should be highlighted that "Involve the members of the community as much as possible", and "Promote mystery" were well-assessed tactics in the area of role-playing games, and not values from the community managers; this is the contrary to what was found with "use of audiovisual supports", unanimously valued by the community managers, and not valued by the game masters.

SOLUTIONS AND RECOMMENDATIONS

After the analysis of the information collected in the interviews conducted, RQ3 is confirmed, as it is corroborated that the activity of a role-playing game master is similar to that of a community manager in his or her work managing social networks. The main objective of both is to know their community in order to make proposals that fit with their interests and motivate their co-creation of a common discourse.

Likewise, and as extracted from the social media experts consulted mentioned, gamification has been applied to marketing strategies in social networks for some time (Oliveira et al., 2021), not only confirming the RQ2 hypothesis, but statements from authors such as Xi and Hamari (2019) or Gómez-Carreño (2021). The use of challenges, rewards, public recognition, and rankings are considered common and very effective for involving and promoting the participation of users in social networks; which at the same time supports the many studies on gamification that focus on these elements (Koivisto & Hamari, 2019; Klock et al., 2020). Also, the role-playing game masters, and overall the community managers, are constantly seeking new manners of participation, which they research through trial and error tests.

The experts consulted confirmed that the mechanics and dynamics of conventional role-playing games allow for a great involvement of the participants, due to the actions and decisions made within the game, which require creativity, improvisation, and the interaction of the players. For this, role-playing games have been defined by professionals in this area as that which allow the interaction between all the participants while playing the game, highlighting their profound dialogic character, as Murray (1999) had already forecasted. This defines the role-playing game as a very complete collaborative entertainment experience, also considering it as a practice of gamification in itself, "gamification within gamification": as there is a lack of constrained rules as in other types of games, this would be the manner in which to gamify the rules of the game to make them more "fun", thereby becoming part of the game experience itself.

For the two collectives investigated, active listening and coherence were fundamental, and for this "understanding the audience" and "maintaining internal consistency" were the two unanimously-selected tactics. While the social media experts considered strategic planning as fundamental, and that their publication capture the attention of the audience, so that great value was placed on the tactics "Do the work ahead of time" and the "Use of audiovisual supports". The main objective of the role-playing game experts was that the players have fun and participate in the creation of the game, at the same time that they must ensure that the rules of the game are followed; thus, as their tactics of interest, they highlighted "Give something to every member of the community" (personalization), "Promote mystery", and "Involve the members of the community as much as possible".

Therefore, we can consider that role-playing games are tools that must be in mind for the implementation of gamification strategies, given their high participative and collaborative value, thus answering the last research question of this chapter (RQ1).

FUTURE RESEARCH DIRECTIONS

In light of our results, three future lines of research are proposed, which would of interest to continue delving into the work initiated:

Research line One. Develop a quantitative empirical study centered on the specific performance of the two collectives investigated, through the analysis of specific cases and the measurement of their effectiveness.

Research line Two. Delve into the differences in the actions performed on the communities from the two universes investigated, considering specific variables such as the influence of the gender differences in professional performance.

Research line Three. Conduct research on the perspective of the users to discover which tactics are strongly valued by the role-playing game players, and which gamification strategies are more motivational for the participation of social network users.

CONCLUSION

The results of the research study confirm that the mechanics and dynamics of the classic role-playing games can be utilized in the design of gamification strategies to promote the participation and engagement of social network users.

The experts consulted confirmed that it is possible to extract mechanics, elements, and strategies that are present in the classic role-playing games. The dialogue between the game master and the players is ratified as a technique that could be applicable to other communication environments such as Social Media, due to its effectiveness in increasing the participation and engagement of individuals. Also, all the individuals interviewed corroborated that the activity of the Game Master and Community Manager was similar with respect to the maintenance of a constant dialogue with the community of individuals who are able to construct a history that is common to all of them.

The opinions collected from the spheres of role-playing games and social media were similar in their suitability of considering and applying game elements beyond the leisure sphere to favor and promote the participation of their communities. All the experts interviewed coincided in their affirmation that the game was an important part and a reflection of current society, and therefore, it should be present in communication actions that are performed, because they believed that it increased the probability of user participation. This is a key element for all the individuals who participated in the present research study, as they considered that the objective of social media and role-playing games was the same: their activity depends on the user's participation.

To achieve this aim, both figures acted similarly, and highlighted active listening as a key tactic, as it was considered as an indispensable element for knowing their audience and for providing them with what they needed to make them more involved in the communication they were creating. They also considered fundamental the maintenance of consistency and coherence in the story that is told to the audience, even if the story is fictitious or if it corresponds to the development of a brand.

These two tactics, active listening and consistency in the narrative, along with the other 18 tactics ratified by the Social Media professionals, come from role-playing game rulebooks, published before the development of Web 2.0 and the peak of online communities.

Therefore, the classic role-playing games not only serve as the basis for the development of videogames called RPG or MMORPG, from which elements such as avatars or experience points are extracted and applied to gamification strategies, but can also be studied and applied to enrich the design of a gamified project. This is especially true given their creative and participative character, which are important when constructing the promoting dialogue within a community of individuals.

REFERENCES

Asociación Española de Videojuegos. (2021). *Anuario de la Industria del Videojuego*. http://www.aevi. org.es/web/wpcontent/uploads/2021/04/AEVI_Anuario_2020.pdf

Asociación Española de Videojuegos. (2021). *Las Mujeres Juegan, Consumen, Participan*. http://www. aevi.org.es/descargables/informe-las-mujeres-juegan-consumen-participan/

Brabham, D. C. (2013). *Crowdsourcing*. The MIT Press. doi:10.7551/mitpress/9693.001.0001

Bunchball. (2010). *Gamification 101: An introduction to the use of game dynamics to influence behavior*. https://www.bunchball.com/sites/default/files/downloads/gamification101.pdf

Castells, M. (1997). *La era de la información, Vol. Nº 1 La sociedad Red*. Alianza Editorial.

Castells, M. (2001). *La Galaxia Internet*. Plaza & Janes. doi:10.1007/978-3-322-89613-1

Cobo, C., & Pardo, H. (2007). *Planeta Web 2.0. Inteligencia colectiva o medios fast food*. Grup de Recerca d'Interaccions Digitals, Universitat de Vic.

Cornellá, A., & Rucabado, S. (2006). *Futuro presente: 101 Ideas-Fuerza para entender las próximas décadas*. Deusto.

Cortizo, J. C., Carrero García, F., Monsalve Piqueras, B., Velasco Collado, A., Díaz del Dedo, L. I., & Pérez Martín, J. (2011). Gamificación y docencia: Lo que la Universidad tiene que aprender de los videojuegos [Paper presentation]. VII jornadas internacionales de innovación universitaria, España.

Cothrel, J., & Williams, R. (1999). Understanding on line communities. *Strategic Communication Management*, (Feb), 16–21.

Csikszentmihalyi, M. (2007). *Aprender a fluir*. Editorial Kairós.

Currier, J. (2008). *Gamification Game Mechanics is the new marketing*. https://blog.oogalabs. com/2008/11/05/gamification-game-mechanics-is-the-newmarketing/

Deterding, S., Dixon, D., Khaled, R., & Nacke, L. (2011). *From game design elements to gamefulness: Defining gamification* [Paper presentation]. 15th International Academic MindTrek Conference: Envisioning Future media Environments, Finland.

Esnaola, G. (2009). Videojuegos en redes sociales: Aprender desde experiencias óptimas. *Comunicación (Cartago)*, *1*(7), 265–279.

Fernández, J. D. (2013). *Principios de estrategia publicitaria y gestión de marcas. Nuevas tendencias de Brand Management*. McGraw-Hill.

Fernández-Gómez, J. D., & Gordillo-Rodríguez, M. T. (2015). Aproximación teórica al branding relacional: De las teorías de Fournier a las brand communities. *Revista Mediterranea de Comunicación*, *6*(1), 131–152. doi:10.14198/MEDCOM2015.6.1.08

Fournier, S. (1998). Consumers and their brands: Developing relationship theory in consumer research. *The Journal of Consumer Research*, *24*(4), 343–353. doi:10.1086/209515

Fumero, A., Roca, G., & Sáez, F. (2007). *Web 2.0*. Fundación Orange España.

García, P. (2005). Comunidades de marca. El consumo como relación social. *Política y Sociedad*, *42*(1), 257–272.

Gode, B., Manthiou, A., Pederzoli, D., Rokka, J., Aiello, G., Donvito, R., & Singh, R. (2016). Social media marketing efforts of luxury brands: Influence on brand equity and consumer behavior. *Journal of Business Research*, *69*(12), 5833–5841. doi:10.1016/j.jbusres.2016.04.181

Gómez-Carreño, E., & Palacios-Alvarado, W. (2021). Revisión de literatura sobre Marketing en Redes Sociales. *Revista de Ingenierías Interfaces*, *4*(1), 1–16.

Himanen, P. (2004). *La ética del hacker y el espíritu de la era de la información*. Destino.

Howe, J. (2008). *Crowdsourcing, How the Power of the Crowd is Driving the Future of Business*. Random House Business Books.

Hubspot. (2021). *Tendencias en Redes Sociales*. https://offers.hubspot.es/tendencias-redes-sociales-2021

Huizinga, J. (2008). *Homo Ludens*. Alianza Editorial.

Kaplan, A. M., & Haenlein, M. (2010). Users of the world, unite! The challenges and opportunities of Social Media. *Business Horizons*, *53*(1), 59–68. doi:10.1016/j.bushor.2009.09.003

Klock, A. C., Hamari, J., Gasparini, I., & Pimenta, M. S. (2020). Tailored gamification: A review of literature. *International Journal of Human-Computer Studies*, 144.

Koivisto, J., & Hamari, J. (2019). The rise of motivational information systems: A review of gamification research. *International Journal of Information Management*, *45*, 191–210. doi:10.1016/j.ijinfomgt.2018.10.013

Lasén, A. (2014). *Las mediaciones digitales de la educación sentimental de los y las jóvenes. Jóvenes y comunicación. La impronta de lo virtual*. Fundación de Ayuda contra la Drogadicción.

Lee, J. J., & Hammer, J. (2011). Gamification in education: What, How, Why bother? *Academic Exchange Quarterly*, *15*(2), 1–5.

Lévy, P. (1994). *Inteligencia colectiva: por una antropología del ciberespacio*. Centro Nacional de Información de Ciencias Médicas.

McGonigal, J. (2011). *Reality is broken. Why games make us better and how they can change the world*. Random House.

Michaelidou, N., Siamagka, N. T., & Christodoulides, G. (2011). Usage, barriers and measurement of social media marketing: An exploratory investigation of small and medium B2B brands. *Industrial Marketing Management*, *40*(7), 1153–1159. doi:10.1016/j.indmarman.2011.09.009

Muniz, A. M. Jr, & O'Guinn, T. C. (2001). Brand community. *The Journal of Consumer Research*, *27*(4), 412–432. doi:10.1086/319618

Murray, J. H. (1999). *Hamlet en la Holocubierta. El futuro de la narrativa en el ciberespacio*. Paidos.

O'Reilly, T. (2007). What is Web 2.0: Design Patterns and Business Models for the Next Generation of Software. *Communications & Stratégies*, *1*, 17–37.

Oliveira, W., Pastushenko, O., Rodrigues, L., Toda, A. M., Palomino, P. T., & Hamari, J. (2021). Does gamification affect Flow experience? A systematic literature review. *Proceedings of the 5th International GamiFIN Conference 2021 (GamiFIN 2021)*.

Prensky, M. (2001). Digital Natives, Digital Immigrants. *On the Horizon*, *9*(5), 1–6.

Ramírez, J. L. (2014). *Gamificación. Mecánicas de juegos en tu vida personal y profesional*. SCLibro.

Rubio-Romero, J., & Barón-Dulce, G. (2019). Actitudes de los jóvenes hacia las comunidades virtuales y su vínculo con las marcas. Una aproximación a través de los estudiantes universitarios de comunicación y de marketing de la Universidad Nebrija. adComunica. *Revista Científica de Estrategias. Tendencias e Innovación en Comunicación*, (18), 41–62.

Rubio-Romero, J., Jiménez, J. M., & Barón-Dulce, G. (2019). Digital social networks as spaces for sociability among adolescents. Case study: Escolapios school in Aluche. *Mediterranean Journal of Communication*, *10*(2), 85–99.

Ryan, R. M., & Deci, E. L. (2002). Overview of self-determination theory: An organismic dialectial perspective. Handbook of self-determination research, 3-33.

Sailer, M., Hense, J. U., Mayr, S. K., & Mandl, H. (2017). How gamification motivates: An experimental study of the effects of specific game design elements on psychological need satisfaction. *Computers in Human Behavior*, *69*, 371–380.

Scolari, C. A. (2013). *Homo Videoludens 2.0. De Pacman a la gamification*. Laboratori de Mitjans Interactius (Universitat de Barcelona).

Shen, C. W., Luong, T. H., Ho, J. T., & Djailani, I. (2020). Social media marketing of IT service companies: Analysis using a concept-linking mining approach. *Industrial Marketing Management*, *90*, 593–604.

Soengas, X., Vivar, H., & Abuin, N. (2015). Del consumidor analógico al digital. Nuevas estrategias de publicidad y marketing para una sociedad hiperconectada. *Revista Telos*, *101*, 115–124.

Teixes, F. (2015). *Gamificación. Motivar jugando*. Editorial UOC.

Werbach, K., & Hunter, D. (2012). *For the Win: How Game Thinking Can Revolutionize Your Business*. Wharton Digital Press.

Xi, N., & Hamari, J. (2020). Does gamification affect brand engagement and equity? A study in online brand communities. *Journal of Business Research*, *109*, 449–460.

Zichermann, G., & Cunningham, C. (2011). *Gamification by Design: Implementing Game Mechanics in Web and Mobile Apps*. O'Reilly Media, Inc.

Zichermann, G., & Linder, J. (2010). *Game-based marketing. Inspire customer loyalty through rewards, challenges and contests*. John Wiley & Sons.

Chapter 9
Gamification and Health in a Holistic Perspective

Selin Ögel Aydın
Istanbul Vocational School of Health and Social Sciences, Turkey

ABSTRACT

Gamification and health are discussed from a one-sided perspective. Gamification and health studies focus on the use of gamification for health and overlook the perspective on how gamification affects health. This chapter discusses gamification and health in terms of organizations, individuals, and society, and addresses the effects of gamification on health and the use of gamification for health. Existing research on gamification and health addresses gamification practices developed for health and the health effects of gamification separately. Consequently, the aim of this chapter is to contribute to the original research collection organized into gamification studies in health from a holistic perspective.

INTRODUCTION

Gamification is a field of research and practice that aims to use the power of games to ensure participation, improve user experience and maintain participation by replacing extrinsic motivation with intrinsic motivation by using game design elements in non-game contexts (Deterding et al., 2011; Huotari & Hamari, 2012). Gamification has become a used application in different fields, such as education, health, management, marketing, finance (da Silva, 2021). Organizations use gamification for reasons such as creating brand loyalty, increasing the frequency of purchases, and creating customer satisfaction. Different industries have been using game elements to achieve their business goals. The emergence of gamification as a trend in different sectors attracts the attention of academics, educators and practitioners in various fields. Gamification provides several benefits, especially to organizations, such as cheaper technology, personal data monitoring and the prevalence of the gaming environment, along with the digital transformation. Through the digital transformation in recent years, gamification has created new opportunities that can benefit even industries previously unrelated to gaming. Particularly in the health field, gamification is increasingly recognized as a valuable tool to encourage continued use of a system or to encourage certain health behaviors. Gamification aims to encourage physical activity, smoking

DOI: 10.4018/978-1-7998-9223-6.ch009

cessation, health education, improvement of mental health, healthy eating habits and similar systems that can positively affect human health. Considering the health effects and the use of gamification for health, it is necessary to develop methods that support the quality of human life, healthy nutrition, reduction of environmental pollution, or all issues that need to be raised.

Studies on gamification have focused on proposing theoretically grounded frameworks for designing gamified systems or demonstrating the positive effects of gamification (AlMarshedi, Wills & Ranchhod, 2015; Hamari et al., 2017; Matallaoui et al., 2017; Patrício, Moreira & Zurlo, 2020). It is seen that the negative aspects of gamification are considered only as side notes (Johnson et al., 2016). Some researchers have begun exploring the negative aspects of gamification (Hyrynsalmi et al., 2017; Toda et al., 2017; Yang & Li, 2021).

Gamification is an issue that needs to be addressed in line with its intended use because besides the benefits that organizations give to the individual and society by using gamification, there are also damages. Organizations must consider consumer benefit and social interests besides their own benefit. This chapter addresses gamification and health from the perspective of the organization, individual and society, and to evaluate the health effects of gamification and the use of gamification for health. Studies mention the negative and positive effects of gamification for health (Ahtinen et al., 2013; Reynolds et al., 2013). As a result, research still lacks a comprehensive overview of the undesirable side effects of gamification in health. For this reason, it is important to consider the use of gamification for health and the positive and negative aspects of gamification practices in terms of individual and public health.

In this section, the use of gamification in the field of health is discussed in general terms. First, the definition and conceptual framework of gamification were drawn. In this context, the academic history of gamification was presented. Since this section covers gamification and health, the concept of gamification was not associated with any theory. On the other hand, the literature on gamification was evaluated within the scope of health. Afterwards, the gamification and health behavior literature was systematically reviewed. In this context, the positive and negative aspects of gamification on health were included without making any comparisons. In the conclusion, suggestions for future research were made and recommendations were given to practitioners.

BACKGROUND

Concept of the Game and Gamification

The concept of game defines as a type of interaction with rules in which players compete against one another (Salen & Zimmerman, 2004). The game is an activity that makes it attractive to distance oneself from one's current conditions and to enter a temporary realm of activity with its own inclinations (Huizinga, 2014). Games have their own times and social groups, although players can be observed to reflect their real lives within games (Consalvo, 2009; Michael & Chen, 2005; Susi et al., 2007). Fullerton (2019) defines games as closed, official systems that place players in a structured conflict and produce unequal outcomes. Schell (2014) takes this one more step to add the concept of problem-solving to the definition of game, defining a game as a problem-solving activity with a fun attitude. Today, mobile devices facilitate easy access to games, and gaming behavior has become more widespread thanks to these devices (Korn et al., 2012; Mekler et al., 2013; Zichermann & Cunningham, 2011). Individuals or groups can cooperate or compete in game activities (Knaving & Björk, 2013). Games can have one or multiple rules and players who join a game to reach a certain goal accept these rules as they are, whereas some players try breaking these rules (Deterding et al., 2011; Von Ahn & Dabbish, 2008).

People take part in activities that they enjoy. Entertainment is a well-known phenomenon to everyone, and is one of the basic human needs. Everyone can enjoy different entertainment experiences (Altarriba, 2014; Huizinga, 2014). Researchers have shown that humans played games, and have discovered the complex relationships between our brains, our nervous systems and how we play (Zichermann & Cunningham, 2011). When they feel happy, people can undertake complicated tasks and be more creative in problem-solving (Anderson, 2011; Isen, 2001). Games put people in a mental state that rarely exists, with each game having its own rules. Entertainment and games can provide extrinsic motivation to people, different from extrinsic motivation. These results from the fact that the psychological needs of human beings and their behavioral patterns connected with each other (Altarriba, 2014; Consalvo, 2009; Ryan & Deci, 2000).

Recognizing the psychological effect of entertainment on people, Volkswagen used entertainment to motivate people, they would not normally do in a campaign called "The Fun Theory," which was based on the belief that people can motivate to undertake an activity by making it more fun. A product that offers entertainment generates a pleasurable feeling in its users. Products that offer a wide range of emotions can motivate users and increase their motivation to use a product (Arrasvuori et al., 2011). According to Norman (2004), positive emotions are important in generating interest among people and encouraging them to learn new things (Norman, 2004).

The concept of "gamification" is not as old as the concept of game, but used more frequently. The term "gamification" contains the concept of game thanks to the institutionalization of video games and their adaptation to daily activities (Chatfield, 2010). According to another view, it results from the fact that the motivational effects of games, which have entertainment as their primary purpose, can adapt to non-game products and/or services to create fun and engaging applications (Zichermann & Cunningham, 2011; Flatlą et al., 2011). Bartle (2011) use the concept of "gamifying" to refer to turning a non-game thing into a game, while Zicherman and Cunningham (2011) define gamification as the "usage of game principles and the way of thinking in a game to draw users' attention and to solve problems". Gamification attracts people via an entertaining interaction and motivates them to take the desired action (Hamari et al., 2014). Deterding et al. (2011) argue that gamification cannot limit to the narrow boundaries of serious games or simulations. Gamification is a "gaming" application that is like serious games (Patrício et al., 2018). Gamification does resemble serious games, but it is not exactly a game. Gamification involves using game elements, such as rewards, scores and leaderboard, meaning that it has pre-defined rules and goals, but lacks the aspect of "playing".

Werbach and Hunter (2012) explain the concept of gamification using a model with three categories, being dynamic mechanics and components, that take a pyramid-shaped structure containing elements of gamification. Gamification comprises a player motivation, and game dynamics and the application of these components. In gamification, as motivating the player in the system to be created is the main element, the player or the user takes precedence over everything else. Accordingly, player motivation is an essential element in a system to be created on the basis of gamification. The concepts of intrinsic motivation and extrinsic motivation are important in the psychological analysis of gamification. Intrinsic motivation refers to a mental state springing from the person himself/herself, whereas the effects of the surrounding environment and the system influence extrinsic motivation (Zichermann & Cunningham, 2011).

In a sense, gamification replaces extrinsic motivation with intrinsic motivation, and to this end, user skills should be taken into account, and users should be able to move to higher levels as they gain more experience. The potential applications of gamification are many. By using a game-like approach, game elements such as gameplay, fun, challenges, rules, transparency, and rewards can address almost any real-world problem (Pereira et al., 2014).

The Effect of Gamification on Health Behavior

Some of the health problems the world is facing are high blood pressure, high blood sugar, obesity, high cholesterol, cancer and mental distress. These health problems are caused by poor water quality, air pollution, tobacco use, physical inactivity, stress, malnutrition, unhealthy nutritional content or excessive food consumption (Stevens et al., 2009; Johnson et al., 2016). These existing health risks and the resulting diseases are affected by some situations that people are exposed to (for example, poor quality water, air pollution, or unhealthy food ingredients that are not informed) and the individual health behaviors of people. It is possible to say that people's health behaviors are directly or indirectly affected.

Health behavior includes personal attributes, personality characteristics, behavioral patterns, actions, and habits that relate to health maintenance, health restoration, and health improvement (Gochman, 1982). Health behavior change is a complex and difficult to achieve process (Cugelman, 2013), potentially influenced by different factors such as emotion, social influences or knowledge about a health condition (Michie et al., 2005). To prevent or reduce diseases, the World Health Organization (2015) forces organizations, researchers, and politicians to act with holistic physical, mental and social well-being in mind (Carlisle & Hanlon, 2008; Johnson et al., 2016; Hanratty & Farmer, 2012; Huppert & So, 2013; Marks & Shah, 2004; Schulte et al., 2015). However, many organizations and politicians try hiding their role in increasing health problems by emphasizing individual responsibility by using "choice" and "balance" narratives (Dorfman & Yancey, 2009). Kraak et al. (2009) recommend preparing a code of conduct and establishing a transparent accountability mechanism to guide industry activities. Dorfman and Yancey (2009) argue that what the industry should do goes beyond running healthy election campaigns and create healthier foods because they should also create healthier environments and communities.

A need is obvious to develop methods to help people develop health behaviors. Co-creating new solutions through gamification can be a solution method, considering that it has an aspect that can affect variables such as motivation, behavior, attitude, intention (Patricio et al., 2020). Gamification is gaining interest in health field, as mental health (Boendermaker et al., 2015; Hall et al., 2013; Li, Theng & Foo, 2016; Savulich et al., 2017; Wagner & Minge, 2015), about physical activities for health (Hammedi et al., 2017; Edney et al., 2019; Fortunato et al., 2019; Sanders et al., 2019; Fang et al., 2019; Ahn et al., 2019; Harrison et al., 2019; Kurtzman et al., 2018; Mitchell et al., 2017; van Mierlo et al., 2016) for healthy eating (Berger and Schrader, 2016; Chow et al., 2020; Jones et al., 2004; Buller et al., 2009; Nour et al., 2018; Dassen et al., 2018); weight management (Chung et al., 2017; Lee & Cho, 2017); health management practices (Bock et al., 2019); education for health (Sousa, et al., 2019; Holzmann et al., 2019; Azevedo et al., 2019; Belogianni et al., 2019; Dassen et al., 2018; van Lippevelde et al., 2016; González et al., 2016; Block, et al., 2015); treatment of chronic diseases (Allam et al., 2015; AlMarshedi et al., 2016; Cechetti et al., 2019); healthcare (Maher et al., 2015). Using gamification in the healthcare field combines with badges, leaderboard, points, and challenges (Miller et al., 2014) and can increase users' health management motivation and interest through entertainment (Karahanna et al., 2018).

Gamification in the Health as a Positive Perspective

Promote healthy lifestyles to prevent disease, support self-management of treatments, and raising public awareness are increasingly being accomplished through applications and information technologies. Gamification, one of these systems, is a purpose-built system for enjoyment and participation, and its ability to motivate is high, so it is important to use gamification for serious purposes, like health (Deterding, 2015).

Gamification is gaining acceptance in healthcare practices (Tuah et al., 2021). Gamification has elements of engaging and motivating users to achieve and maintain sustainable behavior change (Alahäivälä & Oinas-Kukkonen, 2016). Therefore, gamification design is an effective way for healthcare organizations to change individuals' healthcare management behaviors and improve healthcare management performance (Yang & Li, 2021). The purpose of applying gamification in the health is to empower users to make lasting positive changes in certain health behaviors through higher motivation levels (Stepanovic & Mettler, 2018).

Persuasive technology used in gamification revolves around the application of certain design principles or features that drive targeted behaviors and experiences. Some authors have suggested that many game design elements can pair with established behavior modification techniques (Cheek et al., 2015; Cugelman, 2013; King et al., 2013). Gamification has the ability that encourages users to make sound decisions and activate the desired behavior for the benefit of their health and wellness (Pereira et al., 2014). Gamification increases the fun, engagement and compliance of individuals (e.g. consumers, patients, healthcare professionals) (Lenihan, 2012). The application of gamification in health-related contexts intends to promote wellness and consequently reduce the potential negative outcomes associated with unhealthier/risky behaviors (Pereira et al., 2014). Among the areas where gamification uses as health-related contexts are physical activity, diet and weight loss, personal hygiene, hand hygiene for healthcare workers, gamification for work environments, medication/medical treatment, health behavior changes (Pereira et al., 2014; Villasana et al., 2020).

The use of gamification for health differentiates and develops with digitalization. The innovations that come with digitalization are affecting the way clinicians and patients manage their health concerns. Gamification with digital media and technologies is used as a tool to improve patient health literacy, which can affect clinical and patient outcomes (Davaris et al., 2021). Medical practice includes routines boring, repetitive and/or painful for both practitioner and patient. Thus, with gamification, healthcare professionals can take part and collaborate more effectively (Pereira et al., 2014). Technology interventions such as sensor-related technologies, games, virtual reality, applications on smartphones such as e-Health and m-Health can promote learning, increase motivation, and promote cognitive and behavioral change (Király et al., 2015; Ebert et al., 2017; Von Der Heiden, et al., 2019). In addition, social media platforms, which have taken an important place in our lives with digitalization, also encourage the use of gamification for health. Gamification and social network platforms help people increase and sustain their physical activity levels to improve their overall health (Monteiro-Guerra et al., 2019; Rubin et al., 2020; Neupane et al., 2021). The fact that gamification enables interaction and information sharing with social media encourages and motivates participants to change physical activity and diet-related behaviors through gamification principles such as competitions, challenges and rewards (Goodyear et al., 2021). Gamified health mobile applications are innovative approaches to self-management and risk factor reduction. Davis et al. (2021) reported that gamified health mobile apps resulted in greater improvement in physical activity, HbA1C and diabetes self-management enhancement, and more physical activity motivation compared to a neutral content control app, and heart failure knowledge also improved significantly.

Gamification is effective in many areas related to health. Mental health, one of these areas, has been discussed in the literature. Building on past literature, researchers have explored the intervention of digital technologies for mental health support (Brown et al., 2016; Naslund et al., 2017; Lau et al., 2017; Alqithami et al., 2019). The game and gamification approach to improving mental health, in which it uses various participation processes in engaging with individuals as education, motivation, and health support (Hall et al., 2013; Boendermaker et al., 2015; Wagner & Minge, 2015; Li, Theng & Foo, 2016; Fleming et al., 2017; Savulich et al., 2017). Using gamification for mental health, especially with technological progress, the use of devices and applications has gained great importance in supporting personal development in various fields such as loss of interest or pleasure, decreased motivation, poor concentration, anxiety, depression, and stress reduction (Ibrahim et al., 2021). Some of these applications are used to change the behavior of users in the processes of reducing alcohol consumption or preventing addiction, where strong will and mental health are needed (Wróblewski et al., 2020).

Using serious games and gamification for treating serious mental illness has a high level of applicability and acceptability among users and providers alike, depending on key features of the operation and logic of designs (Fitzgerald & Ratcliffe, 2020). Because gamification is an effective approach to engage individuals in emotionally sensitive issues and foster positive health-related behavior change, it is a way to overcome the perceived unpleasant nature of discussions about death and dying and to encourage improved care planning behaviors (Liu et al., 2021). Based on gamification principles, psychosocial and cognitive areas targeted according to deficiencies in various psychiatric disorders, cognitive behavior therapy, cognitive training and rehabilitation, behavior change, social motivation, attention development and biological feedback provided (Vajawat et al., 2020). By integrating multiple gamification elements, lifestyle interventions involving family members that increase motivation to improve mental health are effective (Blok et al., 2021).

The effects of gamification on health have been studied in different age groups as well. One of them is elderly people. Using gamification techniques to support the elderly has proven beneficial in improving both the physical, cognitive, social and emotional state and well-being of the elderly person (Martinho et al., 2020). Although gamification applications used for elderly health vary according to the environment, physical and cognitive abilities of people, feedback, progress, rewards and social interaction development emphasize as frequently used game design elements. Autism is not a mental illness, but cognitive activities can be supported because it is a neurological disease due to developmental delay of the brain. The use of behavior modification techniques and gamification-driven mobile health applications in adults with autism spectrum disorder shows promising results in harnessing the strengths of autism and increasing physical activity (Lee, 2021).

One of the studies conducted in different age groups is addresses pre-school children, children and adolescents. The results of this study shows that games and/or gamification are used to improve health indicators in educational settings and be effective with school-based interventions to promote physical activity in preschool children, children and adolescents (Saucedo-Araujo et al., 2020). In the gamification studies on children, there are also studies on nutrition, which is very important for the health and development of children. More specifically, gamification can increase children's fruit and vegetable intake and promote healthy eating behaviors by improving their nutritional knowledge and attitudes. It can also help promote food research to increase children's acceptance of new foods and reduce picky eating behaviors (Chow et al., 2020). In addition, it is necessary to look at the issue of eating and drinking preferences, dietary habits and healthy nutrition from a broad perspective. Because gamification has the purpose of strengthening motivation to perform a (boring) task. Quantification, including self-monitoring, data analysis, and chart layout, provides a 'rational' basis for dietary habits, while gamification provides the emotional support needed to maintain motivation and continue dieting (Maturo & Setiffi, 2016).

Gamification is used for different effects in different periods. One of these periods is the Coronavirus (COVID-19) pandemic. In this period, people had to overcome different difficulties. Gamification used in overcoming these difficulties has made significant positive contributions to human health. During the COVID-19 pandemic, gamification applications used in health awareness campaigns (Zain et al., 2020; Zain et al., 2021), mental health and academic obstacles for students (Fontana, 2020), physically active during lockdown (Yang & Koenigstorfer, 2020). Despite being recognized as effective measures to curb the spread of the COVID-19 pandemic, social distancing and house arrest have created a mental health burden in older adults who consider being more vulnerable to psychosocial pressures. Innovative approaches such as gamification are beneficial to improve the physical and mental health of the elderly, thus preventing/reducing psychosocial tension during pandemics (Ammar et al., 2021). In addition, gamified digital tools have helped increase vaccination knowledge, motivating vaccine benefits and vaccine purchases, and ultimately raise awareness of vaccine coverage (Montagni et al., 2020).

The use of gamification in the field of health provides important contributions to human health in many ways. The use of gamification and contributions in health differs. Researchers have shown promising results showing that gamification can positively affect various health-related impact measures (Johnson et al., 2016; Sardi et al., 2017).

Gamification in the Health as a Negative Perspective

The purpose of gamification design is to develop personal interest and then to encourage motivation and individual behavior. However, gamification design can also have negative effects on users (Yang & Li, 2021). Epstein et al. (2021) stated that not all gamification interventions work for all participants in all contexts and may even lead to negative behaviors. While the use of digital technologies such as gamification is promising for a healthy life, it does not guarantee success. The results of applications that require user experience vary depending on the availability of technology, knowledge and expectations of users. These results can be negative due to excessive promise of better results, poor use of technology, deficiencies in the renewal of designs, misrepresentations, etc. (Davaris et al., 2021). With regard to gamification, there are ethical concerns about harm and deception. (Thorpe & Roper, 2019).

The use of gamification does not guarantee the desired effect. Gamified solutions can only induce behavior when users are rewarded (Bui et al., 2015). For this reason, when those involved in gamification move away from the main purpose of the system, productivity losses may occur (Thiebes et al., 2014). A health management application can only be used to gain success and rewards in gamification rather than for health management purposes (Knaving & Björk, 2013; Silpasuwanchai et al., 2016; Hyrynsalmi et al., 2017). The use of gamification applications may result in different results than the designers intended. If users get bored with the gamification design, they may not be able to reduce or even stop using it (Yang & Li, 2021). The fact that a task given in gamification is too simple can cause gamified solutions to be demotivating (Augustin et al., 2016).

Gamification provides a racing environment due to its structure. For this reason, the approaches carried out with the aim of winning may differ and even cause negative behaviors towards the competitors. All these points need to be considered when designing gamification. Gamification, which is lucrative for a single person, can offer competing interests against teamwork, thus preventing the team from achieving its best performance (Marlow et al., 2016). Gamification design features mainly include visibility of success, competition, and interaction. If only a single user participates in gamification, these design features cannot function or influence the user. Gamification design elements can be effective when a large number of users participate in a gamification application (Du et al., 2020; Suh & Wagner 2017). The inclusion of social functions in gamification design (such as health gamification) facilitates user interaction and competition and encourages users to participate. Although interaction and competition increase, social contexts such as social media can become a burden for users, tire users and lead to exhaustion of the main purposes of gamification (Maier, et al., 2015; Cao et al., 2018; Yang & Li, 2021). In addition, the mutual circulation of information and data among users can lead to feelings of invasion of personal privacy and social overload, making gamification design a source of stress for users and invasion of the user's privacy and personal life because of reveal information about the users' health data and related health information (Kim & Werbach, 2016; Xiao & Mou, 2019; Yang & Li, 2021).

Despite the high potential of gamification to increase physical activity, health, and well-being, the quantified feedback of gamified systems has been shown to create an addiction that can harm motivation (Hamari et al., 2014; Attig & Franke, 2019). For example, gamification may involve basic elements such as "leveling up", adding points to an overall score or variable, or providing words of encouragement when a user engages in physical activity. Feedback can also refer to smaller elements of the experience, such as playing sound effects or animations in response to smaller target points or cues, or negative reinforcement when a user misses a day's physical activity. While daily physical activity is personally rewarding for maintaining a healthy lifestyle, real-world exercise does not provide any assurance that what is being done contributes to a long-term goal (Rubin et al., 2020).

Gamification is frequently used in areas related to dietary habits such as eating and drinking preferences, nutrition, and calorie intake. This use causes a number of negative consequences as well as health-improving effects. Gamification focuses on the experiential dimensions of food (and often experiential dimensions outside of the food itself), and both are extremely important when it comes to consumer attitudes and thoughts about eating. Tackling the 'eat more' environment strictly at the nutritional level is a losing proposition, and one needs to be mindful of how marketing strategies such as gamification introduce new challenges to public health (Elliott, 2015). Gamification has negative effects that encourage unhealthy foods that can lead to unhealthy eating behavior among children (Chow et al., 2020). Gamification-based diet practices are based on a reductionist approach to obesity and weight loss, when obesity is framed as an individual problem and weight loss is viewed as individual motivation. Such framing tends to obscure the social determinant of health and the social and political causes of obesity (Maturo & Setiffi, 2016).

While there are many gamification applications designed for health, it is not possible to determine whether these applications are purely entertainment or actually improve health behavior. Incorrect approaches to gamification are not only insufficient to increase the motivation and participation of users, but also cause undesirable side effects that can eliminate the positive effects of gamified systems and even harm their users (Hyrynsalmi et al., 2017; Toda et al., 2017). There is still no clear evidence that gamification applied in m-Health practices can effectively help the management of diseases such as diabetes type 1 (Alsalman et al., 2020). Davis et al.(2021) noted in their study that there was no greater benefit than usual care from using gamified health mobile apps for blood pressure or body mass index, or for heart failure self-management, medication adherence, or atrial fibrillation information. Therefore, it is stated that these practices have limitations in terms of efficacy or applicability in elderly patients at high risk for cardiovascular diseases, lack of knowledge, and limitations to confirm their potential, such as self-management, risk factor reduction, and encourage nurses to recommend such practices. In the use of gamification in elderly health, there are risks and associated negative effects (Martinho et al., 2020).

Although gamification has many positive effects on mental health, there are challenges associated with game-based digital interventions in psychiatry (cost-benefit analysis, cultural humility and sensitivity, infrastructure, internet connectivity issues, impact on conventional psychiatric practice, legal and ethical concerns, policy, research, special population, technological "mindedness") and the negative consequences these challenges can have (Vajawat et al., 2020). As organizations become more educated about the deep psychological mechanisms that support user engagement, such as gamification, they design systems that are increasingly persuasive. At the same time experiences can attract users in more complex ways and be more subtle, but more powerful in persuading users to buy. Psychology-based research shows this potential, and companies have the economic motivation to follow, adopt and use such developments. For instance, the use of gamification in pro-drinking practices that support or even encourage alcohol consumption and the high popularity of these practices creates an indirect incentive to alcohol consumption (Ghassemlou et al., 2020; Wróblewski et al., 2020). Using gamification as a marketing tool can lead people to unconscious consumption, which can lead to physiological and psychological consequences that harm human and public health (Thorpe & Roper, 2019).

SOLUTIONS AND RECOMMENDATIONS

This chapter, present an framework that draws on previous research and synthesises the gamification and health. Wiht this framework opens up interesting avenues for future research. There appears to be a clear research gap in understanding what gamification is without being evaluated from a single perspective, and a multifaceted perspective is recommended for future work.

Gamification applications used for health do not always give the expected results. However, different areas where gamification is used can adversely affect health. Evaluating gamification in the context of health requires looking at both gamification practices for health and the effects that gamification can have on health. In this chapter, the effects of gamification on health are present from different perspectives.

The purpose of this study is not to encourage users to avoid gamified solutions. Instead, it is calling on researchers, practitioners, organizations, and even decision-makers to deal with the dark side of gamification and to honestly investigate and be aware of the negative effects of gamification's everyday solutions, especially on individual and public health.

FUTURE RESEARCH DIRECTIONS

Although support for the behavioral effect of gamification is solid, Hamari et al. (2017) argue that understanding the mechanism of gamification to reach the suggested motivating experience is still unclear. The methodological problems common to many gamification studies are particularly highlighted, including studies that do not involve comparison groups or validated criteria, short treatments, single time point measurements. It is important to eliminate these problems and to carry out applications by considering the whole of society.

CONCLUSION

Using applications and information technologies such as gamification has become widespread in health-related contexts and in many areas. Widespread use of gamification does not mean it is perfect. For this reason, it has become necessary to deal with all aspects of the use of gamification, especially in health. In this chapter, the use of gamification in health and its effects on individual and public health when used outside the field of health are discussed. Gamification has been evaluated in terms of individual and public health by considering health with a holistic approach. It has been stated that gamification has both positive and negative effects on health.

This study deals with the existing knowledge about the positive and negative effects of gamification when it comes to health, with a literature study. A systematic literature review was used to collect the articles and focused on existing literature studies on gamification and health. It is seen that the negative effects of gamification on health are handled less than the positive effects.

The positive effects of gamification on health are discussed in some titles. These topics can be listed as follows: promoting a healthy life (physical activity, healthy nutrition); support for boring health related situations with digitalization; creating health awareness; creating motivation-enhancing competition with social media integration; protecting, supporting, promoting mental health; contributions to physical activity, cognitive development and well-being in different age groups; uses of gamification for health in periods such as pandemics.

In addition to the positive effects of gamification on health, the negative effects of gamification can be divided into those that are related to the limits of gamification and that are directly harmful. The limitation may be due to the complexity of the technology and software engineering fields that design gamification. For example, inefficient tools, processes, and methods can be major causes of adverse effects. Human nature tends to test these changes and find their vulnerabilities. At the same time, the reinforcement of motivation by gamification with a reward system can lead users to different areas and cause them to move away from the main purpose (health). In some age groups (elderly), the positive effects of gamification in some areas used for health cannot be proven, but it is also seen that it has negative effects. Apart from these, the use of gamification in areas such as marketing causes people to be motivated about over-consumption. For this reason, it is also known that gamification designs make interventions that may threaten human health. The use of gamification should be carried out not only in the field of health, but also in areas of use other than health, considering the health of the individual and the community.

Although it has positive and negative effects, the common output that can be expressed for gamification is that it has a side that affects human and public health.

REFERENCES

Ahn, S. J., Johnsen, K., & Ball, C. (2019). Points-based reward systems in gamification impact children's physical activity strategies and psychological needs. *Health Education & Behavior*, *46*(3), 417–425. doi:10.1177/1090198118818241 PMID:30678507

Ahtinen, A., Mattila, E., Välkkynen, P., Kaipainen, K., Vanhala, T., Ermes, M., Sairanen, E., Myllymäki, T., & Lappalainen, R. (2013). Mobile mental wellness training for stress management: Feasibility and design implications based on a one-month field study. *JMIR mHealth and uHealth, 1*(2), e11. doi:10.2196/mhealth.2596 PMID:25100683

Alahäivälä, T., & Oinas-Kukkonen, H. (2016). Understanding persuasion contexts in health gamification: A systematic analysis of gamified health behavior change support systems literature. *International Journal of Medical Informatics, 96,* 62–70. doi:10.1016/j.ijmedinf.2016.02.006 PMID:26944611

Allam, A., Kostova, Z., Nakamoto, K., & Schulz, P. J. (2015). The effect of social support features and gamification on a Web-based intervention for rheumatoid arthritis patients: Randomized controlled trial. *Journal of Medical Internet Research, 17*(1), e3510. doi:10.2196/jmir.3510 PMID:25574939

AlMarshedi, A., Wills, G., & Ranchhod, A. (2016). Gamifying self-management of chronic illnesses: A mixed-methods study. *JMIR Serious Games, 4*(2), e5943. doi:10.2196/games.5943 PMID:27612632

AlMarshedi, A., Wills, G. B., & Ranchhod, A. (2015). The Wheel of Sukr: A framework for gamifying diabetes self-management in Saudi Arabia. *Procedia Computer Science, 63,* 475–480. doi:10.1016/j.procs.2015.08.370

Alqithami, S., Alzahrani, M., Alzahrani, A., & Mostafa, A. (2019). Modeling an augmented reality game environment to enhance behavior of adhd patients. In *International conference on brain informatics* (pp. 179-188). Springer. 10.1007/978-3-030-37078-7_18

Alsalman, D., Ali, Z. M. B., Alnosaier, Z. F., Alotaibi, N. A., & Alanzi, T. M. (2020). Gamification for diabetes type 1 management: A review of the features of free Apps in Google Play and App Stores. *Journal of Multidisciplinary Healthcare, 13,* 425–432. doi:10.2147/JMDH.S249664 PMID:32523349

Altarriba, F. (2014). The revolution of fun. *Documento de trabajo. Disponible en.*

Ammar, A., Bouaziz, B., Trabelsi, K., Glenn, J. M., Zmijewski, P., Müller, P., Chtourou, H., Jmaiel, M., Chamari, K., Driss, T., & Hökelmann, A. (2021). Applying digital technology to promote active and healthy confinement lifestyle during pandemics in the elderly. *Biology of Sport, 38*(3), 391–396. doi:10.5114/biolsport.2021.100149 PMID:34475622

Arrasvuori, J., Boberg, M., Holopainen, J., Korhonen, H., Lucero, A., & Montola, M. (2011). Applying the PLEX framework in designing for playfulness. In *Proceedings of the 2011 Conference on Designing Pleasurable Products and Interfaces* (pp. 1-8). 10.1145/2347504.2347531

Attig, C., & Franke, T. (2019). I track, therefore I walk–Exploring the motivational costs of wearing activity trackers in actual users. *International Journal of Human-Computer Studies, 127,* 211–224. doi:10.1016/j.ijhcs.2018.04.007

Augustin, K., Thiebes, S., Lins, S., Linden, R., & Basten, D. (2016). Are we playing yet? A review of gamified enterprise systems. In PACIS (p. 2). Academic Press.

Azevedo, J., Padrão, P., Gregório, M. J., Almeida, C., Moutinho, N., Lien, N., & Barros, R. (2019). A web-based gamification program to improve nutrition literacy in families of 3-to 5-year-old children: The nutriscience project. *Journal of Nutrition Education and Behavior, 51*(3), 326–334. doi:10.1016/j.jneb.2018.10.008 PMID:30579894

Bartle, R. (2011). *Gamification: Too much of a good thing.* Digital Shoreditch.

Belogianni, K., Ooms, A., Ahmed, H., Nikoletou, D., Grant, R., Makris, D., & Moir, H. J. (2019). Rationale and design of an Online educational program using game-based learning to improve nutrition and physical activity outcomes among university students in the United Kingdom. *Journal of the American College of Nutrition, 38*(1), 23–30. doi:10.1080/07315724.2018.1476929 PMID:30071183

Berger, V., & Schrader, U. (2016). Fostering sustainable nutrition behavior through gamification. *Sustainability, 8*(1), 67. doi:10.3390u8010067

Block, G., Azar, K. M., Block, T. J., Romanelli, R. J., Carpenter, H., Hopkins, D., Palaniappan, L., & Block, C. H. (2015). A fully automated diabetes prevention program, Alive-PD: Program design and randomized controlled trial protocol. *JMIR Research Protocols, 4*(1), e3. doi:10.2196/resprot.4046 PMID:25608692

Blok, A. C., Valley, T. S., & Abbott, P. (2021). Gamification for family engagement in lifestyle interventions: A systematic review. *Prevention Science, 22*(7), 1–14. doi:10.100711121-021-01214-x PMID:33786746

Bock, B. C., Dunsiger, S. I., Ciccolo, J. T., Serber, E. R., Wu, W. C., Tilkemeier, P., Walaska, K. A., & Marcus, B. H. (2019). Exercise videogames, physical activity, and health: wii heart fitness: A randomized clinical trial. *American Journal of Preventive Medicine, 56*(4), 501–511. doi:10.1016/j.amepre.2018.11.026 PMID:30777705

Boendermaker, W. J., Boffo, M., & Wiers, R. W. (2015). Exploring elements of fun to motivate youth to do cognitive bias modification. *Games for Health Journal, 4*(6), 434–443. doi:10.1089/g4h.2015.0053 PMID:26421349

Brown, M., O'Neill, N., van Woerden, H., Eslambolchilar, P., Jones, M., & John, A. (2016). Gamification and adherence to web-based mental health interventions: A systematic review. *JMIR Mental Health, 3*(3), e39. doi:10.2196/mental.5710 PMID:27558893

Buller, M. K., Kane, I. L., Dunn, A. L., Edwards, E. J., Buller, D. B., & Liu, X. (2009). Marketing fruit and vegetable intake with interactive games on the internet. *Social Marketing Quarterly, 15*(1), 136–154. doi:10.1080/15245000903038316

Cao, X., & Sun, J. (2018). Exploring the effect of overload on the discontinuous intention of social media users: An SOR perspective. *Computers in Human Behavior, 81*, 10–18. doi:10.1016/j.chb.2017.11.035

Cechetti, N. P., Bellei, E. A., Biduski, D., Rodriguez, J. P. M., Roman, M. K., & De Marchi, A. C. B. (2019). Developing and implementing a gamification method to improve user engagement: A case study with an m-Health application for hypertension monitoring. *Telematics and Informatics, 41*, 126–138. doi:10.1016/j.tele.2019.04.007

Chatfield, T. (2011). *Fun Inc. Why gaming will dominate the twenty-first century.* Pegasus Communications.

Chow, C. Y., Riantiningtyas, R. R., Kanstrup, M. B., Papavasileiou, M., Liem, G. D., & Olsen, A. (2020). Can games change children's eating behaviour? A review of gamification and serious games. *Food Quality and Preference*, *80*, 103823. doi:10.1016/j.foodqual.2019.103823

Chung, A. E., Skinner, A. C., Hasty, S. E., & Perrin, E. M. (2017). Tweeting to health: A novel mHealth intervention using Fitbits and Twitter to foster healthy lifestyles. *Clinical Pediatrics*, *56*(1), 26–32. doi:10.1177/0009922816653385 PMID:27317609

Consalvo, M. (2009). *Cheating: Gaining advantage in videogames*. MIT Press.

Cugelman, B. (2013). Gamification: What it is and why it matters to digital health behavior change developers. *JMIR Serious Games*, *1*(1), e3139. doi:10.2196/games.3139 PMID:25658754

da Silva, T. P. (2021). Why Gamification Is Not the Solution for Everything. In *Handbook of research on solving modern healthcare challenges with gamification* (pp. 20–33). IGI Global. doi:10.4018/978-1-7998-7472-0.ch002

Dassen, F. C., Houben, K., Van Breukelen, G. J., & Jansen, A. (2018). Gamified working memory training in overweight individuals reduces food intake but not body weight. *Appetite*, *124*, 89–98. doi:10.1016/j.appet.2017.05.009 PMID:28479405

Davaris, M. T., Bunzli, S., Dowsey, M. M., & Choong, P. F. (2021). Gamifying health literacy: How can digital technology optimize patient outcomes in surgery? *ANZ Journal of Surgery*, *91*(10), 2008–2013. doi:10.1111/ans.16753 PMID:33825300

Davis, A. J., Parker, H. M., & Gallagher, R. (2021). Gamified applications for secondary prevention in patients with high cardiovascular disease risk: A systematic review of effectiveness and acceptability. *Journal of Clinical Nursing*, *30*(19-20), 3001–3010. doi:10.1111/jocn.15808 PMID:33872436

Deterding, S. (2015). The lens of intrinsic skill atoms: A method for gameful design. *Human-Computer Interaction*, *30*(3-4), 294–335. doi:10.1080/07370024.2014.993471

Deterding, S., Dixon, D., Khaled, R., & Nacke, L. (2011). From game design elements to gamefulness: Defining "gamification". In *Proceedings of the 15th International Academic MindTrek Conference: Envisioning Future Media Environments* (pp. 9-15). 10.1145/2181037.2181040

Du, H. S., Ke, X., & Wagner, C. (2020). Inducing individuals to engage in a gamified platform for environmental conservation. *Industrial Management & Data Systems*, *120*(4), 692–713. doi:10.1108/IMDS-09-2019-0517

Ebert, D. D., Cuijpers, P., Muñoz, R. F., & Baumeister, H. (2017). Prevention of mental health disorders using internet-and mobile-based interventions: A narrative review and recommendations for future research. *Frontiers in Psychiatry*, *8*, 116. doi:10.3389/fpsyt.2017.00116 PMID:28848454

Edney, S., Ryan, J. C., Olds, T., Monroe, C., Fraysse, F., Vandelanotte, C., Plotnikoff, R., Curtis, R., & Maher, C. (2019). User engagement and attrition in an app-based physical activity intervention: Secondary analysis of a randomized controlled trial. *Journal of Medical Internet Research*, *21*(11), e14645. doi:10.2196/14645 PMID:31774402

Elliott, C. (2015). 'Big Food' and 'gamified' products: Promotion, packaging, and the promise of fun. *Critical Public Health*, *25*(3), 348–360. doi:10.1080/09581596.2014.953034

Epstein, D. S., Zemski, A., Enticott, J., & Barton, C. (2021). Tabletop board game elements and gamification interventions for health behavior change: Realist review and proposal of a game design framework. *JMIR Serious Games*, *9*(1), e23302. doi:10.2196/23302 PMID:33787502

Fang, Y., Ma, Y., Mo, D., Zhang, S., Xiang, M., & Zhang, Z. (2019). Methodology of an exercise intervention program using social incentives and gamification for obese children. *BMC Public Health*, *19*(1), 1–10. doi:10.118612889-019-6992-x PMID:31159776

Fitzgerald, M., & Ratcliffe, G. (2020). Serious games, gamification, and serious mental illness: A scoping review. *Psychiatric Services (Washington, D.C.)*, *71*(2), 170–183. doi:10.1176/appi.ps.201800567 PMID:31640521

Flatla, D. R., Gutwin, C., Nacke, L. E., Bateman, S., & Mandryk, R. L. (2011). Calibration games: Making calibration tasks enjoyable by adding motivating game elements. In *Proceedings of the 24th Annual ACM Symposium on User Interface Software and Technology* (pp. 403-412). 10.1145/2047196.2047248

Fleming, T. M., Bavin, L., Stasiak, K., Hermansson-Webb, E., Merry, S. N., Cheek, C., Lucassen, M., Lau, H. M., Pollmuller, B., & Hetrick, S. (2017). Serious games and gamification for mental health: Current status and promising directions. *Frontiers in Psychiatry*, *7*, 215. doi:10.3389/fpsyt.2016.00215 PMID:28119636

Fontana, M. T. (2020). Gamification of ChemDraw during the COVID-19 Pandemic: Investigating how a serious, educational-game tournament (molecule madness) impacts student wellness and organic chemistry skills while distance learning. *Journal of Chemical Education*, *97*(9), 3358–3368. doi:10.1021/acs.jchemed.0c00722

Fortunato, M., Harrison, J., Oon, A. L., Small, D., Hilbert, V., Rareshide, C., & Patel, M. (2019). Remotely monitored gamification and social incentives to improve glycemic control among adults with uncontrolled type 2 diabetes (idiabetes): Protocol for a randomized controlled trial. *JMIR Research Protocols*, *8*(11), e14180. doi:10.2196/14180 PMID:31746765

Fullerton, T. (2019). *Game design workshop: A playcentric approach to creating innovative games*. AK Peters/CRC Press.

Ghassemlou, S., Marini, C., Chemi, C., Ranjit, Y. S., & Tofighi, B. (2020). Harmful smartphone applications promoting alcohol and illicit substance use: A review and content analysis in the United States. *Translational Behavioral Medicine*, *10*(5), 1233–1242. doi:10.1093/tbm/ibz135 PMID:33044528

Gochman, D. S. (1982). Labels, systems and motives: Some perspectives for future research and programs. *Health Education Quarterly*, *9*(2-3), 167–174. doi:10.1177/109019818200900213 PMID:7188305

González, C. S., Gómez, N., Navarro, V., Cairós, M., Quirce, C., Toledo, P., & Marrero-Gordillo, N. (2016). Learning healthy lifestyles through active videogames, motor games and the gamification of educational activities. *Computers in Human Behavior*, *55*, 529–551. doi:10.1016/j.chb.2015.08.052

Goodyear, V. A., Wood, G., Skinner, B., & Thompson, J. L. (2021). The effect of social media interventions on physical activity and dietary behaviours in young people and adults: A systematic review. *The International Journal of Behavioral Nutrition and Physical Activity, 18*(1), 1–18. doi:10.118612966-021-01138-3 PMID:34090469

Hall, M., Caton, S., & Weinhardt, C. (2013, July). Well-being's predictive value. In *International Conference on Online Communities and Social Computing* (pp. 13-22). Springer. 10.1007/978-3-642-39371-6_2

Hamari, J. (2017). Do badges increase user activity? A field experiment on the effects of gamification. *Computers in Human Behavior, 71*, 469–478. doi:10.1016/j.chb.2015.03.036

Hamari, J., Koivisto, J., & Sarsa, H. (2014, January). Does gamification work?--A literature review of empirical studies on gamification. In *2014 47th Hawaii International Conference on System Sciences* (pp. 3025-3034). IEEE.

Hammedi, W., Leclerq, T., & Van Riel, A. C. (2017). The use of gamification mechanics to increase employee and user engagement in participative healthcare services: A study of two cases. *Journal of Service Management, 28*(4), 640–661. doi:10.1108/JOSM-04-2016-0116

Harris, M. A. (2019). Maintenance of behaviour change following a community-wide gamification based physical activity intervention. *Preventive Medicine Reports, 13*, 37–40. doi:10.1016/j.pmedr.2018.11.009 PMID:30510892

Harrison, J. D., Jones, J. M., Small, D. S., Rareshide, C. A., Szwartz, G., Steier, D., Guszcza, J., Kalra, P., Torio, B., Reh, G., Hilbert, V., & Patel, M. S. (2019). Social incentives to encourage physical activity and understand predictors (STEP UP): Design and rationale of a randomized trial among overweight and obese adults across the United States. *Contemporary Clinical Trials, 80*, 55–60. doi:10.1016/j.cct.2019.04.001 PMID:30954675

Holzmann, S. L., Schäfer, H., Groh, G., Plecher, D. A., Klinker, G., Schauberger, G., Hauner, H., & Holzapfel, C. (2019). Short-term effects of the serious game "fit, food, fun" on nutritional knowledge: A pilot study among children and adolescents. *Nutrients, 11*(9), 2031. doi:10.3390/nu11092031 PMID:31480257

Huizinga, J. (2014). *Homo ludens ils 86*. Routledge. doi:10.4324/9781315824161

Huotari, K., & Hamari, J. (2012). Defining gamification: A service marketing perspective. In *Proceeding of the 16th international Academic MindTrek Conference* (pp. 17-22). 10.1145/2393132.2393137

Hyrynsalmi, S., Smed, J., & Kimppa, K. (2017, May). The dark side of gamification: How we should stop worrying and study also the negative impacts of bringing game design elements to everywhere. In GamiFIN (pp. 96-104). Academic Press.

Ibrahim, E. N. M., Jamali, N., & Suhaimi, A. I. H. (2021). Exploring gamification design elements for mental health support. *International Journal of Advanced Technology and Engineering Exploration, 8*(74), 114–125. doi:10.19101/IJATEE.2020.S1762123

Johnson, D., Deterding, S., Kuhn, K. A., Staneva, A., Stoyanov, S., & Hides, L. (2016). Gamification for health and wellbeing: A systematic review of the literature. *Internet Interventions: the Application of Information Technology in Mental and Behavioural Health, 6*, 89–106. doi:10.1016/j.invent.2016.10.002 PMID:30135818

Jones, B. A., Madden, G. J., Wengreen, H. J., Aguilar, S. S., & Desjardins, E. A. (2014). Gamification of dietary decision-making in an elementary-school cafeteria. *PLoS One, 9*(4), e93872. doi:10.1371/journal.pone.0093872 PMID:24718587

Karahanna, E., Xu, S. X., Xu, Y., & Zhang, N. A. (2018). The needs–affordances–features perspective for the use of social media. *Management Information Systems Quarterly, 42*(3), 737–756. doi:10.25300/MISQ/2018/11492

Kim, T. W., & Werbach, K. (2016). More than just a game: Ethical issues in gamification. *Ethics and Information Technology, 18*(2), 157–173. doi:10.100710676-016-9401-5

Király, O., Urbán, R., Griffiths, M. D., Ágoston, C., Nagygyörgy, K., Kökönyei, G., & Demetrovics, Z. (2015). The mediating effect of gaming motivation between psychiatric symptoms and problematic on-line gaming: An online survey. *Journal of Medical Internet Research, 17*(4), e88. doi:10.2196/jmir.3515 PMID:25855558

Knaving, K., & Björk, S. (2013). Designing for fun and play: Exploring possibilities in design for gamification. In *Proceedings of The First International Conference on Gameful Design, Research, and Applications* (pp. 131-134). 10.1145/2583008.2583032

Korn, O., Schmidt, A., & Hörz, T. (2012). Assistive systems in production environments: Exploring motion recognition and gamification. In *Proceedings of the 5th International Conference on Pervasive Technologies Related to Assistive Environments* (pp. 1-5). 10.1145/2413097.2413109

Kurtzman, G. W., Day, S. C., Small, D. S., Lynch, M., Zhu, J., Wang, W., Rareshide, C. A. L., & Patel, M. S. (2018). Social incentives and gamification to promote weight loss: The LOSE IT randomized, controlled trial. *Journal of General Internal Medicine, 33*(10), 1669–1675. doi:10.100711606-018-4552-1 PMID:30003481

Lau, H. M., Smit, J. H., Fleming, T. M., & Riper, H. (2017). Serious games for mental health: Are they accessible, feasible, and effective? A systematic review and meta-analysis. *Frontiers in Psychiatry, 7*, 209. doi:10.3389/fpsyt.2016.00209 PMID:28149281

Lee, D. (2021). Knowledge gaps in mobile health research for promoting physical activity in adults with autism spectrum disorder. *Frontiers in Psychology, 12*, 12. doi:10.3389/fpsyg.2021.635105 PMID:33841267

Lee, H. E., & Cho, J. (2017). What motivates users to continue using diet and fitness apps? Application of the uses and gratifications approach. *Health Communication, 32*(12), 1445–1453. doi:10.1080/10410236.2016.1167998 PMID:27356103

Lenihan, D. (2012). Health games: A key component for the evolution of wellness programs. *Games for Health Journal, 1*(3), 233–235. doi:10.1089/g4h.2012.0022 PMID:26193441

Li, J., Theng, Y. L., & Foo, S. (2016). Exergames for older adults with subthreshold depression: Does higher playfulness lead to better improvement in depression? *Games for Health Journal, 5*(3), 175–182. doi:10.1089/g4h.2015.0100 PMID:27135146

Liu, L., Zhao, Y.-Y., Yang, C., & Chan, H. Y.-L. (2021). Gamification for promoting advance care planning: A mixed-method systematic review and meta-analysis. *Palliative Medicine, 35*(6), 1005–1019. doi:10.1177/02692163211005343 PMID:33775174

Maher, C., Ferguson, M., Vandelanotte, C., Plotnikoff, R., De Bourdeaudhuij, I., Thomas, S., Nelson-Field, K., & Olds, T. (2015). A web-based, social networking physical activity intervention for insufficiently active adults delivered via Facebook app: Randomized controlled trial. *Journal of Medical Internet Research, 17*(7), e4086. doi:10.2196/jmir.4086 PMID:26169067

Maier, C., Laumer, S., Weinert, C., & Weitzel, T. (2015). The effects of technostress and switching stress on discontinued use of social networking services: A study of Facebook use. *Information Systems Journal, 25*(3), 275–308. doi:10.1111/isj.12068

Marlow, S. L., Salas, E., Landon, L. B., & Presnell, B. (2016). Eliciting teamwork with game attributes: A systematic review and research agenda. *Computers in Human Behavior, 55*, 413–423. doi:10.1016/j.chb.2015.09.028

Martinho, D., Carneiro, J., Corchado, J. M., & Marreiros, G. (2020). A systematic review of gamification techniques applied to elderly care. *Artificial Intelligence Review, 53*(7), 4863–4901. doi:10.100710462-020-09809-6

Matallaoui, A., Koivisto, J., Hamari, J., & Zarnekow, R. (2017). How effective is "exergamification"? A systematic review on the effectiveness of gamification features in exergames. *Proceedings of the 50th Hawaii International Conference on System Sciences.* 10.24251/HICSS.2017.402

Maturo, A., & Setiffi, F. (2016). The gamification of risk: How health apps foster self-confidence and why this is not enough. *Health Risk & Society, 17*(7-8), 477–494. doi:10.1080/13698575.2015.1136599

Mekler, E. D., Brühlmann, F., Opwis, K., & Tuch, A. N. (2013). Do points, levels and leaderboards harm intrinsic motivation? An empirical analysis of common gamification elements. In *Proceedings of the First International Conference on Gameful Design, Research, and Applications* (pp. 66-73). 10.1145/2583008.2583017

Michael, D. R., & Chen, S. L. (2005). *Serious games: Games that educate, train, and inform* (1st ed.). Thomson Course Technology.

Michie, S., Johnston, M., Abraham, C., Lawton, R., Parker, D., & Walker, A. (2005). Making psychological theory useful for implementing evidence based practice: A consensus approach. *BMJ Quality & Safety, 14*(1), 26–33. doi:10.1136/qshc.2004.011155 PMID:15692000

Miller, A. S., Cafazzo, J. A., & Seto, E. (2016). A game plan: Gamification design principles in mHealth applications for chronic disease management. *Health Informatics Journal, 22*(2), 184–193. doi:10.1177/1460458214537511 PMID:24986104

Mitchell, R., Schuster, L., & Drennan, J. (2017). Understanding how gamification influences behaviour in social marketing. *Australasian Marketing Journal, 25*(1), 12–19. doi:10.1016/j.ausmj.2016.12.001

Montagni, I., Mabchour, I., & Tzourio, C. (2020). Digital gamification to enhance vaccine knowledge and uptake: Scoping review. *JMIR Serious Games, 8*(2), e16983. doi:10.2196/16983 PMID:32348271

Monteiro-Guerra, F., Rivera-Romero, O., Fernandez-Luque, L., & Caulfield, B. (2019). Personalization in real-time physical activity coaching using mobile applications: A scoping review. *IEEE Journal of Biomedical and Health Informatics, 24*(6), 1738–1751. doi:10.1109/JBHI.2019.2947243 PMID:31751254

Naslund, J. A., Aschbrenner, K. A., Araya, R., Marsch, L. A., Unützer, J., Patel, V., & Bartels, S. J. (2017). Digital technology for treating and preventing mental disorders in low-income and middle-income countries: A narrative review of the literature. *The Lancet. Psychiatry, 4*(6), 486–500. doi:10.1016/S2215-0366(17)30096-2 PMID:28433615

Neupane, A., Hansen, D., Fails, J. A., & Sharma, A. (2021). The role of steps and game elements in gamified fitness tracker apps: A systematic review. *Multimodal Technologies and Interaction, 5*(2), 5. doi:10.3390/mti5020005

Norman, D. A. (2004). *Emotional design: Why we love (or hate) everyday things*. Basic Civitas Books.

Nour, M. M., Rouf, A. S., & Allman-Farinelli, M. (2018). Exploring young adult perspectives on the use of gamification and social media in a smartphone platform for improving vegetable intake. *Appetite, 120*, 547–556. doi:10.1016/j.appet.2017.10.016 PMID:29032184

Patricio, R., Moreira, A., Zurlo, F., & Melazzini, M. (2020). Co-creation of new solutions through gamification: A collaborative innovation practice. *Creativity and Innovation Management, 29*(1), 146–160. doi:10.1111/caim.12356

Patrício, R., Moreira, A. C., & Zurlo, F. (2018). Gamification approaches to the early stage of innovation. *Creativity and Innovation Management, 27*(4), 499–511. doi:10.1111/caim.12284

Patrício, R., Moreira, A. C., & Zurlo, F. (2020). Enhancing design thinking approaches to innovation through gamification. *European Journal of Innovation Management*.

Pereira, P., Duarte, E., Rebelo, F., & Noriega, P. (2014). A review of gamification for health-related contexts. In *International Conference of Design, User Experience, and Usability* (pp. 742-753). Springer. 10.1007/978-3-319-07626-3_70

Reynolds, L., Sosik, V. S., & Cosley, D. (2013). When Wii doesn't fit: How non-beginners react to Wii fit's gamification. In *Proceedings of the First International Conference on Gameful Design, Research, and Applications* (pp. 111-114). 10.1145/2583008.2583027

Rubin, D. S., Severin, R., Arena, R., & Bond, S. (2020). Leveraging technology to move more and sit less. *Progress in Cardiovascular Diseases*. PMID:33129794

Ryan, R. M., & Deci, E. L. (2000). The darker and brighter sides of human existence: Basic psychological needs as a unifying concept. *Psychological Inquiry, 11*(4), 319–338. doi:10.1207/S15327965PLI1104_03

Salen, K., Tekinbaş, K. S., & Zimmerman, E. (2004). *Rules of play: Game design fundamentals*. MIT Press.

Sanders, I., Short, C. E., Bogomolova, S., Stanford, T., Plotnikoff, R., Vandelanotte, C., Olds, T., Edney, S., Ryan, J., Curtis, R. G., & Maher, C. (2019). Characteristics of adopters of an online social networking physical activity mobile phone app: Cluster analysis. *JMIR mHealth and uHealth*, 7(6), e12484. doi:10.2196/12484 PMID:31162130

Sardi, L., Idri, A., & Fernández-Alemán, J. L. (2017). A systematic review of gamification in e-Health. *Journal of Biomedical Informatics*, 71, 31–48. doi:10.1016/j.jbi.2017.05.011 PMID:28536062

Saucedo-Araujo, R. G., Chillón, P., Pérez-López, I. J., & Barranco-Ruiz, Y. (2020). School-based interventions for promoting physical activity using games and gamification: A systematic review protocol. *International Journal of Environmental Research and Public Health*, 17(14), 5186. doi:10.3390/ijerph17145186 PMID:32709132

Savulich, G., Piercy, T., Fox, C., Suckling, J., Rowe, J. B., O'Brien, J. T., & Sahakian, B. J. (2017). Cognitive training using a novel memory game on an iPad in patients with amnestic mild cognitive impairment (aMCI). *The International Journal of Neuropsychopharmacology*, 20(8), 624–633. doi:10.1093/ijnp/pyx040 PMID:28898959

Schell, J. (2008). *The art of game design: A book of lenses*. CRC Press. doi:10.1201/9780080919171

Silpasuwanchai, C., Ma, X., Shigemasu, H., & Ren, X. (2016). Developing a comprehensive engagement framework of gamification for reflective learning. In *Proceedings of the 2016 ACM Conference on Designing Interactive Systems* (pp. 459-472). 10.1145/2901790.2901836

Sousa, P., Martinho, R., Reis, C. I., Dias, S. S., Gaspar, P. J., Dixe, M. D. A., Luis, L. S., & Ferreira, R. (2020). Controlled trial of an mHealth intervention to promote healthy behaviours in adolescence (TeenPower): Effectiveness analysis. *Journal of Advanced Nursing*, 76(4), 1057–1068. doi:10.1111/jan.14301 PMID:31880009

Stepanovic, S., & Mettler, T. (2018). Gamification applied for health promotion: Does it really foster long-term engagement? A scoping review. In *Proceedings of the 26th European Conference on Information Systems* (pp. 1-16). AIS.

Stevens, K. (2009). Developing a descriptive system for a new preference-based measure of health-related quality of life for children. *Quality of Life Research: An International Journal of Quality of Life Aspects of Treatment, Care and Rehabilitation*, 18(8), 1105–1113. doi:10.100711136-009-9524-9 PMID:19693703

Suh, A., & Wagner, C. (2017). How gamification of an enterprise collaboration system increases knowledge contribution: An affordance approach. *Journal of Knowledge Management*, 21(2), 416–431. doi:10.1108/JKM-10-2016-0429

Susi, T., Johannesson, M., & Backlund, P. (2007). *Serious games: An overview*. Academic Press.

Thiebes, S., Lins, S., & Basten, D. (2014). Gamifying information systems-a synthesis of gamification mechanics and dynamics. In *Proceedings of the 20th European Conference on Information Systems*. AIS.

Thorpe, A. S., & Roper, S. (2019). The ethics of gamification in a marketing context. *Journal of Business Ethics*, *155*(2), 597–609. doi:10.100710551-017-3501-y

Toda, A. M., Valle, P. H., & Isotani, S. (2017, March). The dark side of gamification: An overview of negative effects of gamification in education. In *Researcher Links Workshop: Higher Education for all* (pp. 143-156). Springer.

Tuah, N. M., Ahmedy, F., Gani, A., & Yong, L. N. (2021). A survey on gamification for health rehabilitation care: Applications, opportunities, and open challenges. *Information (Basel)*, *12*(2), 91. doi:10.3390/info12020091

Vajawat, B., Varshney, P., & Banerjee, D. (2020). Digital gaming interventions in psychiatry: Evidence, applications and challenges. *Psychiatry Research*, 113585. PMID:33303223

Van Lippevelde, W., Vangeel, J., De Cock, N., Lachat, C., Goossens, L., Beullens, K., Vervoort, L., Braet, C., Maes, L., Eggermont, S., Deforche, B., & Van Camp, J. (2016). Using a gamified monitoring app to change adolescents' snack intake: The development of the REWARD app and evaluation design. *BMC Public Health*, *16*(1), 1–11. doi:10.118612889-016-3286-4 PMID:27494932

Villasana, M. V., Pires, I. M., Sá, J., Garcia, N. M., Zdravevski, E., Chorbev, I., Lameski, P., & Flórez-Revuelta, F. (2020). Promotion of healthy nutrition and physical activity lifestyles for teenagers: A systematic literature review of the current methodologies. *Journal of Personalized Medicine*, *10*(1), 12. doi:10.3390/jpm10010012 PMID:32121555

Von Ahn, L., & Dabbish, L. (2008). Designing games with a purpose. *Communications of the ACM*, *51*(8), 58–67. doi:10.1145/1378704.1378719

Von Der Heiden, J. M., Braun, B., Müller, K. W., & Egloff, B. (2019). The association between video gaming and psychological functioning. *Frontiers in Psychology*, *10*, 1731. doi:10.3389/fpsyg.2019.01731 PMID:31402891

Wagner, I., & Minge, M. (2015). The gods play dice together: The influence of social elements of gamification on seniors' user experience. In *International Conference on Human-Computer Interaction* (pp. 334-339). Springer. 10.1007/978-3-319-21380-4_57

Werbach, K., & Hunter, D. (2012). *For the win: How game thinking can revolutionize your business*. Wharton Digital Press.

Wróblewski, M., Klingemann, J. I., & Wieczorek, Ł. (2020). Review and analysis of the functionality of mobile applications in the field of alcohol consumption. *Alcohol Drug Addict*, *33*(1), 1–18. doi:10.5114/ain.2020.95977

Xiao, L., & Mou, J. (2019). Social media fatigue-Technological antecedents and the moderating roles of personality traits: The case of WeChat. *Computers in Human Behavior*, *101*, 297–310. doi:10.1016/j.chb.2019.08.001

Yang, H., & Li, D. (2021). Understanding the dark side of gamification health management: A stress perspective. *Information Processing & Management*, *58*(5), 102649. doi:10.1016/j.ipm.2021.102649

Yang, Y., & Koenigstorfer, J. (2020). Determinants of physical activity maintenance during the Covid-19 pandemic: A focus on fitness apps. *Translational Behavioral Medicine, 10*(4), 835–842. doi:10.1093/tbm/ibaa086 PMID:32926160

Zain, N. H. M., Johari, S. N., Aziz, S. R. A., Teo, N. H. I., Ishak, N. H., & Othman, Z. (2021). Winning the Needs of the Gen Z: Gamified Health Awareness Campaign in Defeating COVID-19 Pandemic. *Procedia Computer Science, 179,* 974–981. doi:10.1016/j.procs.2021.01.087

Zain, N. H. M., Othman, Z., Noh, N. M., Teo, N. H. I., Zulkipli, N. H. B. N., & Yasin, A. M. (2020). GAMEBC model: Gamification in health awareness campaigns to drive behaviour change in defeating COVID-19 pandemic. *International Journal of Advanced Trends in Computer Science and Engineering, 9*(4).

Zichermann, G., & Cunningham, C. (2011). *Gamification by design: Implementing game mechanics in web and mobile apps.* O'Reilly Media, Inc.

ADDITIONAL READING

Adrián, S. R., & Elena, P. G. M. (2019). Active methodologies in health. Scientific production on gamification in health sciences. *Science for Education Today, 9*(3).

Alexandre Peixoto de Queirós, R., & Marques, A. J. (Eds.). (2021). *Handbook of research on solving modern healthcare challenges with gamification.* IGI Global. doi:10.4018/978-1-7998-7472-0

Garett, R., & Young, S. D. (2019). Health care gamification: A study of game mechanics and elements. *Technology. Knowledge and Learning, 24*(3), 341–353. doi:10.100710758-018-9353-4

Marston, H. R., & Hall, A. K. (2016). Gamification: Applications for health promotion and health information technology engagement. In Handbook of Research on Holistic Perspectives in Gamification for Clinical Practice (pp. 78-104). IGI Global.

Nacke, L. E., & Deterding, C. S. (2017). The maturing of gamification research. *Computers in Human Behaviour,* 450-454.

Nyström, T. (2021). Exploring the darkness of gamification: You want it darker? In *Intelligent Computing* (pp. 491–506). Springer. doi:10.1007/978-3-030-80129-8_35

Schmidt-Kraepelin, M., Thiebes, S., Stepanovic, S., Mettler, T., & Sunyaev, A. (2019). Gamification in health behavior change support systems-A synthesis of unintended side effects. In *Proceedings of the 14th International Conference on Wirtschaftsinformatik* (pp. 1032-1046).

Segura-Robles, A., & Parra-González, M. E. (2019). Active methodologies in health. Scientific production on gamification in health sciences. *Science for Education Today, 9*(3), 223–237. doi:10.15293/2658-6762.1903.13

KEY TERMS AND DEFINITIONS

Autism Spectrum Disorder (ASD): A spectrum of psychological conditions characterized by widespread social interaction and communication anomalies and severely limited attention and excessively repetitive behavior.

Coronavirus (COVID-19): Virus that causes respiratory symptoms (fever, cough, shortness of breath) to develop in China's Wuhan Province in late December 2019.

Diet: Regulation of the types and amounts of foods to be consumed for treatment or protection.

Disease: Interruption or deviation of the normal structure and functions of any part, organ, or system of the body, manifested by a series of characteristic signs and symptoms, with known or unknown possibilities for recovery and changes in the body.

E-Health: A relatively new healthcare application powered by electronic processes and communication.

Gamification: Use of game elements to convert extrinsic motivation to intrinsic motivation in non-game contexts.

HbA1c: Amount of blood sugar (glucose) bound to hemoglobin in the blood.

Hygiene: All of the activities for a healthy life and the measures taken for cleaning.

M-Health: An acronym for mobile health, a term used for medical and public health practices powered by mobile devices.

Chapter 10
Natural User Interfaces for Meditative Health Games

Ifeoluwapo Fashoro

iD https://orcid.org/0000-0002-1791-4744
Nelson Mandela University, South Africa

Sithembile Ncube
Nelson Mandela University, South Africa

ABSTRACT

The psychological health outcomes of video games are drawing increasing interest around the world. There is growing interest in video games as an accessible health intervention for depression and anxiety, both of which are rising health concerns globally. New interaction techniques for video games are becoming increasingly popular, with natural user interfaces (NUIs) becoming more commonplace in game systems. This chapter explores the design of a meditative game, a subgenre of casual games that intends for players to become calm and relaxed, and the evaluation of the NUIs for the game. The purpose of the chapter is to ascertain which NUI is most suitable for meditative games. A meditative fishpond game was designed that accepts two NUIs: touch and eye-tracking. The game was evaluated using a Positive and Negative Affect Schedule. The study found the eye-tracking interface reported a higher positive affect score from users and is therefore most suitable for meditative games.

INTRODUCTION

Mental health is integral to individual and community health. The World Health Organization (WHO) describes mental health as a state of well-being in which individuals realize their abilities, cope with stress in their life, are productive and contribute positively to their community (World Health Organization, 2018). Mental health is the presence of psychological, social and affective well-being (Everymind, n.d.; Simon & Durand-Bush, 2014), thus positive mental health is synonymous with well-being. The WHO stresses that mental health in essence goes beyond the absence of mental disorders and encompasses

DOI: 10.4018/978-1-7998-9223-6.ch010

the ability of individuals to "think, emote, interact with each other, earn a living and enjoy life" (World Health Organization, 2018). Mental health is therefore critical to the effective functioning of every society.

Growing concerns regarding mental health have led to its inclusion in the United Nations' Sustainable Development Goals as Goal 8: Good health and well-being (United Nations, 2015). There has been a reported 13% rise of mental health conditions in the last decade, with 20% of children and adolescents (between ages 10 and 19) currently living with mental health conditions worldwide (World Health Organization, n.d.). Depression affects approximately 264 million people globally and is said to be one of the main causes of disability worldwide (World Health Organization, 2019). The COVID-19 pandemic has exacerbated concerns relating to public mental health and is predicted to have a long-term impact (Javed et al., 2020; Kim et al., 2020; Nabavi, 2021; Nguse & Wassenaar, 2021). Depression and anxiety have notably increased due to the pandemic (Nabavi, 2021).

Individuals suffering from mental health conditions face many barriers to seeking help such as lack of resources, lack of trained health-care providers and the social stigma associated with mental conditions (Pine, Sutcliffe, et al., 2020; World Health Organization, 2020). Vast disparities exist between the need for mental health interventions and availability of interventions worldwide. The WHO reports that between 76% and 85% of people with mental health conditions receive no treatment in low and middle-income countries (World Health Organization, 2019). This disparity has been aggravated by the COVID-19 pandemic and the lockdown response of most national governments. People who previously had access to mental health interventions before lockdown enforcements, have less access to physicians, medication and even friends and family for support (Nabavi, 2021; Nguse & Wassenaar, 2021).

Traditional mental health interventions, such as cognitive behavioral therapy, are proven to be very effective but can be costly and time consuming. Cost-effective and accessible solutions to mental health are required. Digital therapies and mental health tools have been developed to overcome barriers to traditional mental health interventions (Pine, Sutcliffe, et al., 2020). These digital alternatives have proven to have positive outcomes for treating depression and anxiety (Pine, Fleming, et al., 2020). Examples of such digital tools include mobile apps, Internet-mediated video-based psychotherapy, artificial intelligence (AI), virtual reality and video games (Aboujaoude et al., 2020; Cohen et al., 2021).

Over the last few decades, there has been an increasing interest in the ability of video games to improve users' well-being. Studies have shown how video games can help users relieve stress, regulate emotions, overcome post-traumatic stress disorder and enter a mindfully meditative state (Carras et al., 2018; Jones et al., 2014; Sliwinski et al., 2015). Mindfulness is a practice that promotes one's awareness of self and has positive influences on both mental and physical health (Rybak, 2013). In recent studies, psychological health outcomes have been a major focus for research on video games with a particular interest in their capacity for intervention in depression and anxiety (Fleming et al., 2017; Kowal et al., 2021; Pine, Fleming, et al., 2020; Poppelaars et al., 2021).

Video games have also been studied in relation to affective well-being (Agrawal et al., 2018; Jagoda & McDonald, 2019; Johannes et al., 2021). Affective well-being describes the balance between one's positive (pleasant emotions) and negative (unpleasant emotions) affect and one's overall satisfaction with life (Simon & Durand-Bush, 2014). Video games have been found to improve positive affect and players' well-being. Casual video games are suggested as an accessible intervention to lower anxiety similar to other low cost and accessible interventions like meditation, deep breathing, massage, and exercise (Fish et al., 2018; Pine, Sutcliffe, et al., 2020). Casual video games are easily accessible, fun, simple to learn, require short amounts of time to play and require no prior knowledge or skill (Pine, Fleming, et al., 2020). Meditative games are often classified as casual video games and fit into the category of accessible interventions that can be used for mental health interventions. Meditative games, also known as mindful games, have grown in popularity in recent years. These games have no definitive goals and are explorative in nature with the aim of inducing mindfulness in players (Sliwinski et al., 2015).

A concurrent development in the video game industry is the use of Natural User Interfaces (NUIs), which have been seen in other electronic devices such as mobile phones and tablets. These interfaces replicate real world interaction techniques for digital systems and are a steadily emerging trend in video games (Bowman et al., 2017). Video games drive the early adoption of NUIs in broader society and are usually a testing ground for these interfaces (University of Melbourne, n.d.). NUIs make gameplay feel natural by mimicking interaction skills that are used daily.

As awareness of mental health increases, there is a need to consider users' well-being as more people play video games and adapt to the trend of NUIs in tandem. There have been several studies done on NUIs in work-like tasks, but little research has been done on NUIs in the context of video games (University of Melbourne, n.d.), particularly relating to mental health. Specifically, there is a dearth of information available on which NUIs provide the most positive affect for users in meditative games. Studies have shown that the delivery platform or interfaces used for video games for health play a role in their effectiveness (Kim et al., 2014; Vara et al., 2016).

The purpose of this chapter is to ascertain which NUI technique is most suitable for application in meditative video games that intend to make players calm and relaxed through the development of a meditative game that different types of NUIs. The most suitable technique is measured by analyzing the positive affect users report when using NUIs. The efficacy of these NUI techniques is investigated using a new meditative game called 'Lumiere'.

The book chapter is structured as follows: The next section discusses a brief history of video games and their relation to health. This is followed by a section that delves into mindfulness and flow in video games and how they impact mental health. Meditative games are described, and a review of some meditative games is presented. Natural user interfaces are discussed in the next section, which is followed by the description of the development and evaluation of the proposed meditative game. The chapter ends with concluding thoughts and further research opportunities.

VIDEO GAMES AND HEALTH

The use of video games in health is far from a new concept. Despite having often been associated with negative health consequences, video games have been found to be very useful for therapeutic purposes. Games for health benefits have been reported since the early 1980s, with video games being historically used in health for pain management, physiotherapy, and occupational therapy (Griffiths, 2005). In 1996, an immersive virtual reality game for pain reduction in burn patients was co-created by Hunter Goffman and David Patterson in collaboration with Sam Sharar M.D. (UW Human Photonics Lab, n.d.). The game allowed patients' wounds to be cared for while experiencing less pain and less trauma. This immersive virtual reality game, SnowWorld, distracted patients from the pain with a psychologically cooling atmosphere. Kato (2010) studied video games tailored towards health outcomes. The study listed video games in health care including a diabetes intervention game created in 1995 called Packy and Marlon, where children manage the insulin levels of their characters through an adventure. Other games listed in Kato's study are those tailored towards medical education such as games to improve surgery skills and games to educate on cancer care. Most notable on the topic of psychological health are anxiety management games played on the Nintendo Gameboy device (Kato, 2010).

In a 2012 study by Primack et al. (2012), 38 articles on positive, clinically relevant health consequences of video games were reviewed. A total of 195 positive health outcomes were examined. Each of these 195 health outcomes were classified among combinations of the following seven categories: physical therapy, psychological therapy, health education, disease self-management, distraction from discomfort, physical activity, and clinician skills. The most notable outcomes observed from this study were in intervention games related to psychological therapy, which contributed to 69% of the 195 positive health outcomes, and games related to physical therapy, which contributed to 59% of the positive health outcomes. The Primack et al. (2012) study highlights the variety of research that supports the existence of positive health benefits for games, especially the various psychological health benefits of playing video games.

In more recent studies, the psychological health outcomes have indicated a larger focus for research on video games, specifically related to intervention in depression and anxiety which are identified as rising health concerns globally (World Health Organization, 2017). Global Health has recognized depression as the leading cause of disability around the world (Friedrich, 2017). These studies provide motivation for incorporating interventions for depression and anxiety in video games. Carras et al. (2018) reviewed literature on the use of commercial video games as a therapy and found that these games have positive outcomes in improving cognitive status in the elderly, treating anxiety during cancer treatments and before operations, treating depression and post-traumatic stress disorders, improving symptoms of schizophrenia and prevention of intrusive memories post-trauma. Pine, Fleming, et al. (2020) reviewed articles on the effects of casual video games on anxiety and depression, and this review revealed that casual games have been reported to reduce anxiety, depressive mood, or stress-related symptoms.

In June 2020, the United States Food and Drug Administration (FDA) approved the first ever prescription only video game treatment, EndeavorRx, as a digital therapy for children with ADHD (Anderson, 2020). The game was originally licensed from a University of California, San Francisco neuroscientist, Adam Gazzaley. EndeavorRx is designed to challenge a child's brain during treatment by focusing on multiple tasks at a time. The treatment provided by EndeavorRx refutes the negative side effects and stigmatization of video games and thus provides good motivation to further research on the effectiveness of digital health interventions (Pandian et al., 2021). Innovations such as EndeavorRx are part of over a decade of video games created as scientifically proven health interventions.

MINDFULNESS AND FLOW IN VIDEO GAMES

Video games are becoming more prolific and accessible to individuals through a variety of devices, which allows games to be readily available to serve as tools for teaching mindfulness and improving psychological well-being (Cruea, 2020). Cruea concludes that the state of flow induced by video games is useful in allowing players to achieve mindfulness through relaxation, enhanced concentration, improved mood, reduced stress, and greater empathy. Mindfulness and flow can be experienced in a variety of games.

Mindfulness is described as one's awareness of their internal states and surroundings (Rybak, 2013). Mindfulness has been reported to have a positive impact on psychological well-being (Sliwinski et al., 2015). This concept is an important aspect of therapeutic interventions and can be incorporated in activities like cognitive behavioural therapy, mindfulness stress reduction, and mindfulness meditation.

Mindfulness can be used to avoid destructive mental states and habits by focusing on present thoughts and emotions without prejudice (Mindfulness, n.d.).

Csikszentmihalyi (2014) describes the concept of flow as a state reported by individuals when completely immersed in an activity to the point of forgetting about everything but the activity itself including time, and even fatigue. Flow has been identified as fundamental to positive psychology (Chen, 2007).

Video games have been observed to be particularly adept at inducing flow because they meet the preconditions for flow studied by Csikszentmihalyi: perceived challenges or opportunities for action; clear proximal goals and immediate feedback about progress made; intense and focused concentration on the present moment; merging of action and awareness; loss of reflective self-consciousness; a sense that one can control one's actions; distortion of one's sense of time; and experience of the activity as intrinsically rewarding (Chen, 2007; Lopez & Snyder, 2012).

This flow inducing aspect of video games makes them desirable and effective as a means of achieving mindfulness. There is extensive research supporting the merits of mindfulness practices, such as meditation, as a means of nurturing one's mental health and improving overall well-being (Flett et al., 2019; Rybak, 2013). Though a state of flow can be achieved through many games, there are some games that are specifically designed as tools to improve one's skills associated with achieving mindfulness (Siegel et al., 2009). Games designed with the aim to improve skills to achieve mindfulness are classified as meditative games. Examples of these games are PLAYNE, SoundSelf and Deep VR and they are discussed and reviewed in the next section.

MEDITATIVE GAMES

Recent studies in video games use the term meditative to describe games that have a similar set of characteristics relating to meditation. One of the most established definitions of the term meditation is from the American Psychological Association (APA) Dictionary of Psychology which states that meditation is "profound and extended contemplation or reflection in order to achieve focused attention or an otherwise altered state of consciousness and to gain insight into oneself and the world" (Meditation, n.d.). The Dictionary of Psychology further explains that meditation is also used to provide relaxation as well as relief from stress. Thus, the term meditative means 'involving meditation'.

Johnson (2018) uses the term 'Meditative game' to describe the game Mountain and comments on how traditional game play is subverted with the player imagining what it is like to be a mountain. Chang (2011) comments on the rise of 'Zen gaming' where the term zen is used to describe an easily achievable meditative experience. Chang (2011) ascribes the game Flower as being a meditative experience, with the incorporation of Zen Buddhist art in the game's aesthetics. Sliwinski et al. (2015) use the term 'Mindful gaming' to describe games that enable users to enter a mindfulness or meditative state. These games generally have no goal, are explorative and have an audio-visual experience that induces meditation.

For the purposes of this chapter, a meditative game is defined as a game that requires focused attention to make a user calm or relaxed. This definition encompasses the ideas that have been discussed in studies of video games where the term meditative is used to describe a game (Johnson, 2018; Sliwinski et al., 2015). Synonyms observed for the term meditative include 'games for meditation', 'mindful games' and 'zen games'. Three games that can be described as meditative games are reviewed based on how players interact, and the user interfaces adopted in the game. Common themes and distinct practices used to create a meditative experience for users are identified from the review.

PLAYNE – The Meditation Game

PLAYNE is a game that is designed to improve a player's mental well-being by teaching a specific meditation technique and encouraging players to build a habit of mindfulness (Shrikumar, 2018). The game includes a meditation activity where the player is instructed to close their eyes and focus on their breathing while listening to the game audio. The landscape of the player's game is altered with the frequency of the player's meditation. PLAYNE uses standard keyboard and mouse controls but can also be played with virtual reality using motion tracking support.

SoundSelf

SoundSelf is described as a 'technodelic', a combination of the two terms technology and psychedelic. Rather than engaging the mind with competition or problem solving as with most video games, the technodelic game actively disengages the player's unconscious habits of self-centeredness and allows them to enter a dissociated trance-like state through technology. SoundSelf is available on computer and can be experienced by itself, although the experience is designed to be best used with virtual reality. The game helps a user achieve a meditative state by reacting to breathing and sounds from voice input with audio-visual feedback designed to shift you into a meditative state. This is modelled after a meditative use of sound called 'vocal toning'. Vocal toning is a form of vocalizing that uses the natural voice to express sounds ranging from cries, grunts, and groans to humming on the full exhalation of the breath (Snow et al., 2018).

The screens are designed as moving psychedelic screens with strobing tunnels-of-light and unusual shapes. Though SoundSelf responds to users input through voice and breathing, the game itself does not measure a user's meditative state. Studies on SoundSelf have measured the users meditative state using heart rate monitors and a Positive Affect Negative Affect Schedule. It should be noted that the strobing effects may negatively affect users with epilepsy, migraines and similar conditions triggered by flashing lights.

Deep VR

Deep VR is a meditative virtual reality game controlled by breathing. The purpose of this game is to teach emotional regulation techniques through deep breathing to combat anxiety in an immersive and relaxing experience (Van Rooij et al., 2016). Deep VR allows players to navigate through a serene underwater atmosphere. Movement is controlled by slow, deep breathing which soothes and relieves anxiety in the player. This breathing is measured using a custom controller developed for use with the game that works as a waistband connected to the game. The custom game controller reacts to breathing by measuring diaphragm expansion and is specifically designed to be able to track deep breathing. This deep breathing provides biofeedback data for the game that allows a user to move around through controlled breathing. When a user is practicing deep meditative breathing, the environment becomes easier to navigate and this deep breathing pattern is what allows the player to move freely in the game. When a user is not practicing deep meditative breathing, the environment becomes more difficult. The slow-moving underwater environment with visual cues gently encourages the player to slow their breathing and relax. Deep VR can be played for therapeutic or aesthetic reasons, and does not require the use of arms, legs, or hands.

Table 1 provides a summary of the interaction objectives and the respective NUIs identified in the games reviewed.

Table 1. Summary of evaluated systems

Game	NUIs	Interaction objectives
PLAYNE	Motion Sensing	Manipulate the game environment through motion
SoundSelf	Voice control, Motion Sensing	Use voice to generate visualizations
Deep VR	Custom breathing controller	Move around in water through deep breathing

Based on the review of the three games, there are common themes associated with the development of meditative games. Meditative games are generally modelled after real world meditation practices such as the use of vocal toning in SoundSelf and deep breathing in Deep VR. Movement is optional and players are often not given explicit goals or scores in these types of games. Meditative games may involve the use of NUIs such as motion sensors and touch screens. NUIs associated with meditative games are typically low effort interfaces that do not require the player to exert themselves.

NATURAL USER INTERFACES

Natural User Interfaces have become increasingly popular in the field of Human-Computer Interaction. NUIs are interfaces that provide a new way to interact with computers using familiar interaction techniques such as touch, voice or gestures (Mortensen, 2020). Lee Son et al., (2018) found many related definitions of an NUI that in some way originate from a definition by (Blake, 2012) that states: "A natural user interface is a user interface designed to reuse existing skills for interacting directly with content". These interfaces adapt to user needs and preferences, rather than the user adapting to the limits of technology (Mortensen, 2020). NUIs are fun, easy and natural to use.

Wigdor and Wixon (2011) provide guidelines for the creation of NUIs in their book 'Brave NUI World'. Wigdor and Wixon caution designers to avoid attempting to mimic the real world with their interfaces but to look at the creation of experiences that allow a user to feel comfortable, masterful, and an expert at what they are doing. The overall guidelines for the design of an NUI can be summarized as a focus on designing for a user experience that is natural to a user rather than focusing on the interface being intrinsically natural. Other specific guidelines given by Wigdor and Wixon are that the designer of an NUI must:

- "Create an experience that, for expert users, can feel like an extension of their body."
- "Create an experience that feels just as natural to a novice as it does to an expert user."
- "Create an experience that is authentic to the medium—do not start by trying to mimic the real world or anything else."
- "Build a user interface that considers context, including the right metaphors, visual indications, feedback, and input/output methods for the context."
- "Avoid falling into the trap of copying existing user interface paradigms."

With this in consideration, NUIs and how suitable they may be for use in meditative games can be explored.

Touch

A touch screen is a visual display used to control a range of devices such as smartphones, video game consoles, and tablet computers (Gray, 2014). Touch screens are commonplace particularly with the proliferation of smartphones. The "swipe and tap" gesture is now highly intuitive to most people (Bowman et al., 2017). The swiping of a digital book on an iPad is similar to turning the page of a physical book. This is a great example of NUIs becoming natural to the users. Example devices with touch screens used to control games are the Nintendo Wii U GamePad, Nintendo DS, Nintendo 3DS, Nintendo Switch, and PlayStation Vita. Games that commonly use touch as a user interface are strategy games, puzzle games, and casual games.

Motion Sensing

There are a variety of motion sensors available in modern devices such as accelerometers, gyroscopes and magnetometers (Christiansen & Shalamov, 2017). Motion sensing, though not physically connected to the user, imitates real-time activities in the physical environment that involve action and reaction, where the user makes a motion and then receives feedback from the system (Mortensen, 2020). Motion sensor controllers have been increasingly integrated into console gameplay through devices such as the Nintendo WiiMote, the PlayStation Move, the Xbox Kinect, and the Nintendo Switch JoyCons. Other devices that use motion sensing include the Leap Motion Controller, Intel RealSense, and virtual reality gear such as the HTC Vive. According to Bowman et al. (2017), users appear to favor NUIs for sports games that require simulating simple movements from respective disciplines such as Nintendo Wii sports games and Xbox Kinect sports games.

Eye-Tracking

Eye-tracking uses natural eye movements to achieve a goal. The user's gaze becomes the source of input for the device. The device most often used to measure eye movement is known as an eye-tracker (Duchowski, 2017). The Tobii EyeX eye-tracker is a powerful ocular tracking device that is integrated into over 140 games. The device can be integrated into games because of the support available for use with popular game development engines like Unity and Unreal Engine (de Araújo et al., 2020). Eye-tracking can also be used to measure attention (Cox et al., 2006).

The NUIs selected for this study are touch and eye-tracking. Motion sensing will not be adopted because it is more suited for sporting games that require a range of movement from the player.

RESEARCH METHODOLOGY

The project from which this paper is derived used a Design Science Research (DSR) methodology. DSR is a set of analytical techniques and perspectives for conducting Information Systems research involving two activities, creation of new knowledge through the design of innovative artefacts and the analysis of the artefact's performance (Vaishnavi et al., 2017). The five steps of the DSR methodology were followed iteratively to design and develop and evaluate the meditative game. These steps are problem awareness, suggestion, development, evaluation and conclusion.

The problem awareness and suggestion steps were performed through a literature review and an extant systems review. The sections above present some of the findings from these reviews. The development step is described in the Game Concept and Development section and the evaluation is discussed in the Evaluation section below. The final step presents conclusions which is done in the Conclusion section.

The different iterations of the game are not presented in this paper. The paper focuses on the final iteration.

GAME CONCEPT AND DEVELOPMENT

Lumiere is 'a meditative game where you control a firefly interacting with a fishpond'. It is a simulation game that works with multiple NUIs such as touch and eye-tracking and allows users to control a firefly that interacts with a fishpond and the fish inside. Features and elements incorporated in the game include:

- the main character, a glowing firefly,
- AI fishes flocking to simulate real fish behavior, and
- visual feedback when the firefly hovers over a fish

In Lumiere, the sole gameplay interaction is movement of the fishes and firefly. This allows for the game to be compatible with a variety of NUIs such as eye-tracking technology and gesture control. The aesthetic of Lumiere incorporates stylized 3D character models with light emitting creatures.

The review of the meditative games, PLAYNE, SoundSelf and DEEP VR revealed some repeated themes that were selected for incorporation into the development of Lumiere. These themes were used to determine the functional and non-functional requirements of the game. Common themes found in meditative games can be summarized as follows:

- Meditative games do not have a focus on competitive score tracking.
- Meditative games encourage exploration and free movement.
- Meditative games often incorporate nature in their aesthetics and gameplay.
- Common interaction methods in meditative games are:
  - Movement – The meditative games studied, allowed for users to move freely around their screen.
  - Object interaction – Object interaction in meditative games is often seamlessly incorporated with movement and does not require much additional effort from the player.
  - Menu interaction – The meditative games studied provided menu interaction that was minimal, easy to access, and comfortable to interact with.

The functional and non-functional requirements for the game are presented in Table 2 and Table 3 below.

Table 2. List of functional requirements for the proposed game

ID	Description
FR1	User should be able to view the home screen.
FR2	User should be able to view game instructions.
FR3	User should be able to view the main game scene.
FR4	User should be able to move the cursor within the main game scene.
FR5	User should be able to open the menu.
FR6	User should be able to select and use at least two NUIs in game.
FR7	User should be able to end session.

Table 3. List of non-functional requirements for the proposed game

ID	Description
NR1	The game should have calming visuals.
NR2	The game should have relaxing music.
NR3	The game should have a simple user interface.
NR4	The game should incorporate elements of nature

The game was designed using Unity which is a cross platform game development engine by Unity Technologies that can be used to create both 2D and 3D games (Unity, n.d.). Unity can be used to create games for Windows, Mac, Linux, mobile, web, and consoles. The code for the game was written using C# which is the standard programming language in Unity. Adobe Photoshop was used for image editing to make elements for the game menu. Adobe Photoshop is versatile at creating high quality images with layers representing each component of the image. These layers can be exported with each layer as an individual element that can be used in Unity. The NUIs for the game development were selected based on their compatibility with the Unity game development engine and their availability during development time. The first targeted NUI is touch which is available for use on many laptops. The second targeted NUI is eye-tracking using a Tobii Eye-X device.

Touch screen interfaces are integrated in a variety of laptops as an input device. Touch screens are targeted for interaction through a user's fingers or a stylus. Unity's standard input was used for touch which also simulates using a mouse. This provides a fall back in case a touch interface does not work as intended during practice and allows for quicker testing by replicating touch through mouse controls in development.

The Tobii Eye-X was chosen as the NUI used for eye-tracking. The Unity game development engine provides access to eye-tracking capabilities using the Tobii Application Programming Interface (API). The Tobii API provides methods and classes that incorporate gaze tracing elements within the game such as a user's gaze position on screen, a users' presence in front of a computer, and a user's head position.

Development Method and Roadmap

The Game Development Software Engineering (GDSE) process lifecycle was employed in the development of the game (Aleem et al., 2016). The GDSE process includes aspects unique to the creation of games. Phases of the GDSE in order of execution consist of concept design, design, implementation, testing, and deployment. These steps are similar to both the design process lifecycle and the system development lifecycle (Aleem et al., 2016). The requirements determination of the GDSE process required additional factors to be considered that may not usually be considered in the creation of other systems. This includes emotion, gameplay, and aesthetics.

The development was done in five iterations that brought the elements of the game design together and addressed the functional and non-functional requirements.

Phase 1: Development with Primitives

During the first phase of development, the game movements were created using basic 3D objects such as cubes to represent the fish. A fish flocking algorithm was coded to simulate the behavior of fish in a pond. The movement of the main character was coded to follow the mouse constantly. The overhead game camera was also coded to follow the player as they move around the simulated fishpond. This addressed the functional requirements **FR3** and **FR4** by creating a main game environment and allowing the player to move their cursor within the game. Figure 1 shows primitive cubes representing fish to create a flocking algorithm.

Figure 1. Phase 1 showing the development of the game using primitive objects

Phase 2: Adding Models

In Phase 2, the primitive shapes were replaced with koi fish models obtained from the Unity Asset Store. The fish models can be seen in Figure 2. The fish models are animated to look like they are swimming when they move forward. In this phase, the main character model was created using a textured primitive sphere and particle effects, to give the character a simple look that feels like a firefly hovering above the pond. In Figure 3, the game view from the main camera is shown. The center of the screen shows the firefly main character with a green texture and some particles trailing behind as the character moves around. An underwater terrain was also created during this phase. This addressed the non-functional requirement **NR4**.

Figure 2. The simulated fishpond scene with koi fish models visible

Figure 3. The game view from the main camera showing the fishpond from above

Phase 3: Cursor and Interactions

During this phase, it was decided that there would not be a cursor implemented for the touch interface as the touch interface controls simply require the user to touch the screen to move. If the mouse is being used, the default mouse cursor will be visible.

Object interactions within the game occur through collisions between the firefly's extended collision capsule and the collision capsule of the fish. Figure 4 shows the extended collision capsule of the firefly. Upon collision with a fish, a particle effect attached to the fish is set off that gives a sparkling effect.

Figure 4. The collision capsule of the firefly extending to the water

Phase 4: Menus and NUI Incorporation

During development, it was noted that creating the menu options to change NUI controls might interfere with users' interaction with the pond. Therefore, all the menu options were implemented on the home screen. Figure 5 shows the menu home screen.

Figure 5. Menu mock-up

The main menu allows players to read the instructions for using each device to ensure they are ready to begin a session. Figure 6 shows the instruction screen for the touch screen interface of the game and Figure 7 shows the instructions screen for the eye-tracking interface.

Figure 6. Touch Interface Instructions

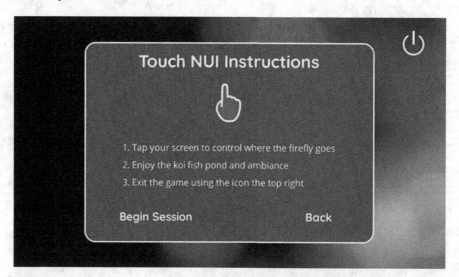

Figure 7. Eye-tracking interface instructions

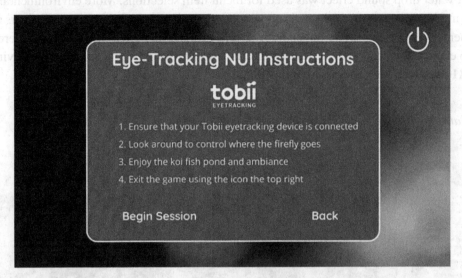

The mock-up image files were created in Adobe Photoshop and exported to Unity, then rearranged to create the game's main menu. The menu items were animated using the LeanTween animation library that allows for smooth quick animations to be coded to objects in games. Figure 8 depicts the final main menu screen for the game. This phase addressed the functional requirements **FR1**, **FR2**, **FR5**, **FR6**, and **FR7**, and the non-functional requirement **NR3**.

Figure 8. Main Menu Screen fully implemented in Unity

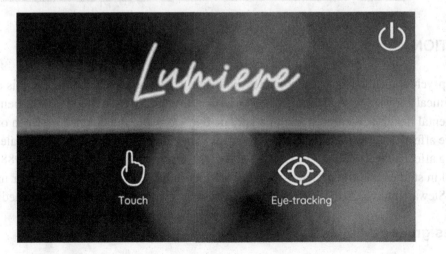

Phase 5: Aesthetics and Sound

Sounds used in the game include royalty free background music and free sound effects. The music incorporates calming string music with ambient background sounds that reinforce the water theme in the game. A water drop sound effect was used for menu item selections. More environmental elements were added into the game using a free environmental package that contains a variety of plants and rocks. These elements were placed in the underwater terrain to make the environment more interesting and attractive to explore. Figure 9 shows the overall terrain design after the placement of the environmental objects. **NR1** and **NR2** were addressed in this phase.

Figure 9. Game environment viewed from Unity Scene mode

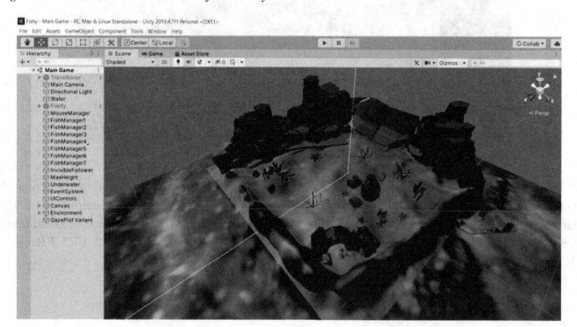

EVALUATION

Affect is a psychological construct that relates to mental states involving feelings and is an important aspect of clinical knowledge on mental illness (Díaz-García et al., 2020). Affective well-being is one way in which mental health is measured and this is done by measuring the balance between one's positive and negative affect. The Positive and Negative Affect Schedule (PANAS) is one such scale widely used for assessing affective well-being. The PANAS scale was developed by Watson et al., (1988). It has been widely used in studies relating to depression and anxiety in adults and for screening for mental illness (Taggart & Stewart-brown, 2015). This scale was used in the evaluation of Lumiere as a meditative game.

Study Design

The evaluation process was designed as a balanced study with eight participants where each participant played the game using one NUI, then the other NUI. Half of the participants began with the touch interface and followed that session by using the eye-tracker interface. The other half of the participants started with the eye-tracking interface and then played the game using the touch interface. Participants were divided into two groups to avoid a bias of users reporting their perspectives according to the order they experienced the NUIs. The eye-tracking interface was calibrated for each user's eyes before beginning their session. The experiment took place in an isolated sunroom providing natural lighting and a calm environment for the participants. After each study, participants completed a questionnaire to collect data on the evaluation metrics. During the study, the following equipment was used:

- Touch screen laptop running Windows 10
- Laptop running Windows 10 and compatible with Tobii Eye-X
- Tobii Eye-X eye-tracker

Participants

The study had 8 participants: 3 females and 5 males, and their ages ranged from 22 years old to 29 years old. Participation in the study was voluntary. Participants were selected based on the following criteria:

- Be willing to travel to the location of the principal investigator at their own cost.
- Understand the risks COVID-19 posed and be willing to meet in person for the evaluation study. Measures were taken to adhere to COVID-19 protocols such as observing social distance, wearing masks, and sanitizing devices and surfaces between evaluations.
- Should not have any known comorbidities.
- Be willing to give about an hour of their time.
- Have access to a smartphone with internet connectivity for communication purposes.
- Are familiar with playing games on a touch screen.
- Have heard about meditative or zen games or have an idea about games that are intended for positive mental health outcomes.

Positive and Negative Affect Schedule (PANAS)

Positive Affect (PA) is related to positive emotions and high energy and can be reflected in an individual's feelings of enthusiasm, activeness, and alertness. Negative Affect (NA) is associated with negative emotions such as distress but also encompasses a range of mood states associated with displeasure such as anger, guilt, fear, and nervousness.

PANAS consists of two 10-item mood scales that observe PA and NA. The PANAS questionnaire requires participants to rate their current feelings and mood using the 20 adjectives on a five-point Likert Scale. Table 4 provides a list of the positive and negative adjectives used in the scale. The scale ratings are: Very slightly or not at all, A little, Moderately, Quite a bit, and Extremely. When calculating PA, NA, and an overall PANAS score, each rating on the scale is given a corresponding numerical value from 1 (Very slightly or not at all) to 5 (Extremely). The result of summing the total PA scores gives a value between 10 and 50, where a higher score would indicate more positive affect. Similarly, the result of summing the total NA scores gives a value between 10 and 50, where a lower score indicates less negative affect and a higher score indicates more negative affect.

Table 4. PANAS Descriptors

PA Adjectives	NA Adjectives
Active	Afraid
Alert	Ashamed
Attentive	Distressed
Determined	Guilty
Enthusiastic	Hostile
Excited	Irritable
Inspired	Jittery
Interested	Nervous
Proud	Scared
Strong	Upset

Results

Table 5 shows the sum of the scores from the PANAS questionnaire for the study participants. The PA and NA sums were separated for each corresponding NUI. Averages and standard deviations were also obtained for affect scores.

Table 5. PANAS questionnaire PA and NA sums for Touch and Eye-Tracking NUIs

Interface	Touch		Eye-tracking	
Participant	PA Sum	NA Sum	PA Sum	NA Sum
P1	33	15	35	12
P2	22	10	24	10
P3	19	13	34	12
P4	33	16	47	12
P5	40	16	42	20
P6	33	11	35	10
P7	30	11	35	10
P8	29	10	34	10
Averages	29.88	12.75	35.75	12
Standard Deviation	6.69	2.60	6.67	3.38

Figure 10 shows a radar chart for the sums of the PANAS descriptors for each of the NUIs. The ten descriptors on the right half of the chart are the PA descriptors. The remaining ten descriptors on the left of the chart are the NA descriptors. The size of the area of the graphs within each half of the radar chart visually indicate the amount of PA and NA reported.

Figure 10. Affect sums for each PANAS descriptor

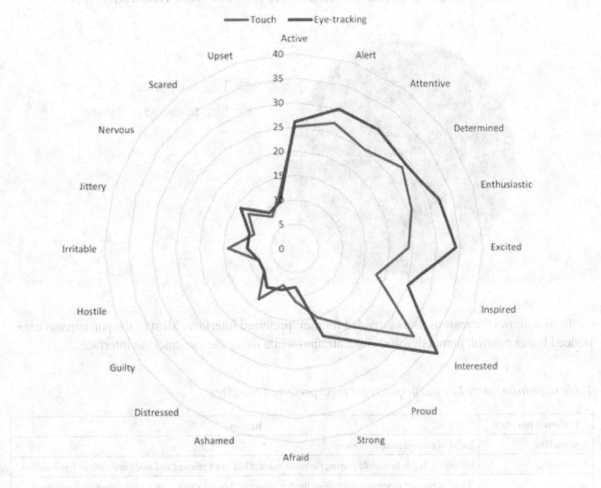

PANAS Descriptor Radar Chart for Touch Interface vs Eye-Tracking

Preferred Interface

Users were asked which interface they preferred and why. Figure 11 below shows that in this study, 7 out of 8 participants (87.5%) preferred the eye-tracking interface over the touch interface for the meditative game.

Figure 11. Preferred NUI selection among participants

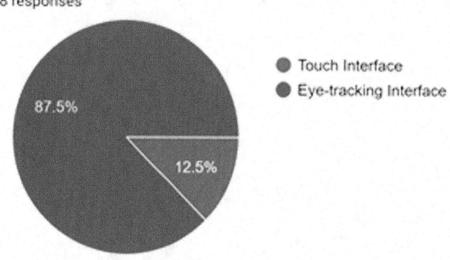

Which user interface did you prefer for the game?
8 responses

87.5%

12.5%

● Touch Interface
● Eye-tracking Interface

Table 6 shows the reasons users provided for their preferred interface. Most of the participants experienced better control, immersion and concentration while using the eye-tracking interface.

Table 6. Reasons stated by participants for their preferred interface

Preferred Interface	Reason
Eye-tracking	Easier to use and more responsive
Eye-tracking	Having my hands free while playing the game made it feel more relaxing and made interactions feel effortless.
Eye-tracking	It was interesting to use and controlling the dot felt better. I could also see the whole screen, so it was much easier to notice the fish going in and out of the screen.
Touch	Easy to use
Eye-tracking	Something I am not used to. Pretty cool.
Eye-tracking	This interface to me was more interesting. It brought a new level to the game. I felt more invested and immersed in the world with the eye-tracking interface.
Eye-tracking	I found it quite exciting to try out the eye-tracking because I'd never used it before, and I felt that it helped with the flow of the game (felt a bit more like I was floating around with the fish compared to the touch interface cause with the touch I had to be more focused and persistent about catching the fish
Eye-tracking	The focus and control needed for eye movements would serve a meditative function in a more effective manner than touch interface.

The PANAS scores indicate that both NUIs gave a high PA score and a low NA score. The PA score for the eye-tracking interface was higher with a PA score average of 35.75 ± 6.67, where the PA score average for the touch interface was 29.88 ± 6.69. The standard deviations for these scores were very similar, indicating that the variance in the average results was similar. This indicates a similar level of consistency among participants for their PA scores related to each interface. The NA scores were generally low with an average of 12.75 ± 2.60 for the touch interface and an average of 12 ± 3.38 for the eye-tracking interface.

There was a larger PA recorded for the eye-tracking interface than the touch interface as seen in Figure 10. Overall, the highest rated PA descriptors for both interfaces were 'Interested' and 'Excited'. The graph appears to indicate a higher NA score for the touch interface, though the NA scores were both generally low. The highest rated NA descriptors for the touch interface were 'Distressed', 'Irritable', and 'Nervous'. The highest rated NA descriptors for the eye-tracking interface were 'Nervous' and 'Distressed'. It should be noted that though these were the higher NA descriptors, the overall NA scores were quite low.

DISCUSSION

The study revealed that both NUIs are efficacious in producing PA while playing Lumiere. Although, the eye-tracking interface had higher PA scores, players rated both interfaces highly. This high rating could be explained in relation to user interface embodiment, which is the degree to which a user's body interacts with the game (Kim et al., 2014; Vara et al., 2016). Embodied interfaces such as the touch screen and eye-tracker used in this study, elicit emotional responses from the user and provide a greater sense of presence and engagement (Vara et al., 2016).

The higher score for the eye-tracking interface might also be due to a higher immersion and embodiment of the player while using this interface. The player's body and cognition are involved to a higher degree in playing the game while using eye-tracking, thus producing a higher emotional experience and making it more enjoyable to players. This is supported by the comments by one of the participants, which says "The focus and control needed for eye movements would serve a meditative function in a more effective manner than touch interface". The findings of this study are consistent with other studies that found that embodied interfaces can make games more enjoyable, enhance mood and generate feelings of well-being in users (Kim et al., 2014; Vara et al., 2016). One participant commented about the immersion experience of the eye-tracker, stating "I felt more invested and immersed in the world with the eye-tracking interface." This is similar to other studies on eye-tracking devices and immersion in video games, where it was found that eye-tracker provide a more immersive experience for players (Antunes & Santana, 2018; Smith & Graham, 2006).

FUTURE RESEARCH DIRECTIONS

Further research could include a wider variety of NUIs such as voice recognition and gesture recognition. The evaluation study could also be redesigned as a multi-phase study to test players' affect prior to playing the game and after playing the game to determine changes in affect. Other proxies for mental health could also be included in the evaluation by employing questionnaires that measure other aspects of mental health. Mindfulness and meditation could be measured by incorporating devices that measure breathing, heart rate and brain activity to the evaluation study.

Limitations

This study was hampered by the effects of the current COVID-19 pandemic as the availability of users to test the game throughout the creation and evaluation process was limited due to restrictions to mitigate the pandemic. Working from home to adhere to social distancing regulations prevented adequate access to research equipment and technology that could have been integrated into this study. Under normal circumstances, there would have been more types of NUIs available for testing and equipment that could be used to measure the meditative state of users. A personal fitness tracker was available during the study, however, the results and variability of heart rate from the fitness tracker was deemed unreliable upon observed daily use and was thus removed from the study.

CONCLUSION

Mental health is important to a well-functioning society, however, individuals suffering from mental health conditions face many challenges in accessing traditional interventions. The COVID-19 pandemic has impacted public mental health and worsened access to interventions due to lockdown strategies implemented by many governments globally. Consequently, alternative mental health interventions such as video games are being adopted. Meditative games are a genre of video games that are purposed to help with focused attention, calmness, and relaxation. These games have been proposed as a way of helping people with conditions such as depression and anxiety. Many of these games employ NUIs as a way of making gameplay easy, fun and intuitive for the user.

The purpose of the study was to ascertain which of the two NUIs was best suited for the game since the type of interface design is a critical variable to the efficacy of games. A meditative game, Lumiere was designed and evaluated using the PANAS scale to determine the effectiveness of two NUIs in achieving the purpose of the game. The game was designed based on common design theme ascertained during the evaluation of existing meditative games.

To measure the effectiveness of meditative games in eliciting positive affect in users, the PANAS scale is an immediately accessible tool that also reflects the broad psychological state of the player. The game implemented two NUIs, touch screen and eye-tracking. Based on the evaluation study, which used affect as a proxy for mental health, although both interfaces had high positive affect score and low negative affect score, the eye-tracking interface produced better positive affect results than the touch screen interface.

The results of the study show that the designed game is effective in producing positive affect in players and can therefore be used as an alternative intervention for managing mental health. This study also highlighted common themes in meditative games by evaluating three meditative games which could be used as guidelines for game designers. Meditative game designers should also seek to implement user interfaces with higher embodiment than the touch screen such as the eye-tracker. This would ensure users are more present and engaged while playing the game and increase the efficacy of the meditative games.

REFERENCES

Aboujaoude, E., Gega, L., Parish, M. B., & Hilty, D. M. (2020). Editorial: Digital Interventions in Mental Health: Current Status and Future Directions. *Frontiers in Psychiatry, 11*(February), 10–12. doi:10.3389/fpsyt.2020.00111 PMID:32174858

Agrawal, V., Duggirala, M., & Chanda, S. (2018). Journey: A game on positive affect. *CHI PLAY 2018 - Proceedings of the 2018 Annual Symposium on Computer-Human Interaction in Play Companion Extended Abstracts,* 373–379. 10.1145/3270316.3271532

Aleem, S., Capretz, L. F., & Ahmed, F. (2016). Game development software engineering process life cycle: A systematic review. *Journal of Software Engineering Research and Development, 4*(1), 6. Advance online publication. doi:10.118640411-016-0032-7

Anderson, M. (2020, August). Prescription-strength gaming: ADHD treatment now comes in the form of a first-person racing game. *IEEE Spectrum, 57,* 9–10. doi:10.1109/MSPEC.2020.9150542

Antunes, J., & Santana, P. (2018). A study on the use of eye tracking to adapt gameplay and procedural content generation in first-person shooter games. *Multimodal Technologies and Interaction, 2*(2), 23. Advance online publication. doi:10.3390/mti2020023

Blake, J. (2012). *Natural User Interfaces in. NET.* Manning Publications Company.

Bowman, N. D., Pietschmann, D., & Liebold, B. (2017). The golden (hands) rule: Exploring user experiences with gamepad and natural-user interfaces in popular video games. *Journal of Gaming and Virtual Worlds, 9*(1), 71–85. Advance online publication. doi:10.1386/jgvw.9.1.71_1

Carras, M. C., Van Rooij, A. J., Spruijt-Metz, D., Kvedar, J., Griffiths, M. D., Carabas, Y., & Labrique, A. (2018). Commercial video games as therapy: A new research agenda to unlock the potential of a global pastime. *Frontiers in Psychiatry, 8*(JAN), 1–7. doi:10.3389/fpsyt.2017.00300 PMID:29403398

Chang, A. Y.Alenda Y. Chang. (2011). Games as Environmental Texts. *Qui Parle, 19*(2), 56. Advance online publication. doi:10.5250/quiparle.19.2.0057

Chen, J. (2007). Flow in Games. *Communications of the ACM, 50*(4), 31–34. doi:10.1145/1232743.1232769

Christiansen, K. R., & Shalamov, A. (2017). *Motion Sensors Explainer.* Retrieved June 20, 2020, from https://www.w3.org/TR/motion-sensors/

Cohen, K. A., Stiles-Shields, C., Winquist, N., & Lattie, E. G. (2021). Traditional and Nontraditional Mental Healthcare Services: Usage and Preferences Among Adolescents and Younger Adults. *The Journal of Behavioral Health Services & Research, 48*(4), 537–553. Advance online publication. doi:10.100711414-020-09746-w PMID:33474642

Cox, A. L., Cairns, P., Berthouze, N., & Jennett, C. (2006). The Use of Eyetracking for Measuring Immersion. *CogSci 2006 Workshop: What Have Eye Movements Told Us so Far, and What Is Next.*

Cruea, M. D. (2020). Gaming the Mind and Minding the Game: Mindfulness and Flow in Video Games. In Video Games and Well-being. doi:10.1007/978-3-030-32770-5_7

Csikszentmihalyi, M. (2014). Flow and the Foundations of Positive Psychology. In *Flow and the Foundations of Positive Psychology*. doi:10.1007/978-94-017-9088-8

de Araújo, F. M. A., Fonseca Ferreira, N. M., Mascarenhas, V. T. O. C., Adad Filho, J. A., & Viana Filho, P. R. F. (2020). *Eye Tracking in Framework for the Development of Games for People with Motor Disabilities*. doi:10.1007/978-981-15-1465-4_25

Díaz-García, A., González-Robles, A., Mor, S., Mira, A., Quero, S., García-Palacios, A., ... Botella, C. (2020). Positive and negative affect schedule (Panas): Psychometric properties of a venezuelan Spanish version in medical students. *BMC Psychiatry*, *20*(56), 301–315. doi:10.118612888-020-2472-1 PMID:32039720

Duchowski, A. T. (2017). Eye Tracking Techniques. In *Eye Tracking Methodology*. Springer International Publishing., doi:10.1007/978-3-319-57883-5_5

Everymind. (n.d.). *Understanding mental health and wellbeing*. Retrieved August 4, 2021, from https://everymind.org.au/mental-health/understanding-mental-health/understanding-mental-health-and-wellbeing#:~:text=Mental health is a positive,a state of overall wellbeing.

Fish, M. T., Russoniello, C. V., & O'Brien, K. (2018). Zombies vs. Anxiety: An Augmentation Study of Prescribed Video Game Play Compared to Medication in Reducing Anxiety Symptoms. *Simulation & Gaming*, *49*(5), 553–566. doi:10.1177/1046878118773126

Fleming, T. M., Bavin, L., Stasiak, K., Hermansson-Webb, E., Merry, S. N., Cheek, C., Lucassen, M., Lau, H. M., Pollmuller, B., & Hetrick, S. (2017). Serious games and gamification for mental health: Current status and promising directions. *Frontiers in Psychiatry*, *7*(JAN). Advance online publication. doi:10.3389/fpsyt.2016.00215 PMID:28119636

Flett, J. A. M., Hayne, H., Riordan, B. C., Thompson, L. M., & Conner, T. S. (2019). Mobile Mindfulness Meditation: A Randomised Controlled Trial of the Effect of Two Popular Apps on Mental Health. *Mindfulness*, *10*(5), 863–876. doi:10.100712671-018-1050-9

Friedrich, M. J. (2017). Depression Is the Leading Cause of Disability Around the World. *Journal of the American Medical Association*, *317*(15), 1517. doi:10.1001/jama.2017.3826 PMID:28418490

Gray, L. (2014). *How Does a Touch Screen Work?* Gareth Stevens Publishing.

Griffiths, M. (2005, July). Video games and health. *British Medical Journal*, *331*, 122–123. doi:10.1136/bmj.331.7509.122

Jagoda, P., & McDonald, P. (2019). Game Mechanics, Experience Design, and Affective Play. In The Routledge Companion to Media Studies and Digital Humanities (pp. 174–182). Routledge. doi:10.4324/9781315730479-17

Javed, B., Sarwer, A., Soto, E. B., & Mashwani, Z. (2020). The coronavirus (COVID-19) pandemic's impact on mental health. *The International Journal of Health Planning and Management*, *35*(5), 993–996. doi:10.1002/hpm.3008 PMID:32567725

Johannes, N., Vuorre, M., & Przybylski, A. K. (2021). Video game play is positively correlated with well-being. *Royal Society Open Science, 8*(2), 202049. Advance online publication. doi:10.1098/rsos.202049 PMID:33972879

Johnson, M. R. (2018). How to talk about videogames. *Information Communication and Society, 21*(12), 1862–1865. Advance online publication. doi:10.1080/1369118X.2017.1409787

Jones, C. M., Scholes, L., Johnson, D., Katsikitis, M., & Carras, M. C. (2014). Gaming well: Links between videogames and flourishing mental health. *Frontiers in Psychology, 5*(MAR), 1–8. doi:10.3389/fpsyg.2014.00260 PMID:24744743

Kato, P. M. (2010). *Video Games in Health Care: Closing the Gap.* doi:10.1037/a0019441

Kim, A. W., Nyengerai, T., & Mendenhall, E. (2020). Evaluating the Mental Health Impacts of the COVID-19 Pandemic in Urban South Africa: Perceived Risk of COVID-19 Infection and Childhood Trauma Predict Adult Depressive Symptoms. *Psychological Medicine,* 1–13. doi:10.1017/S0033291720003414 PMID:32895082

Kim, S. Y., Prestopnik, N., & Biocca, F. A. (2014). Body in the interactive game: How interface embodiment affects physical activity and health behavior change. *Computers in Human Behavior, 36,* 376–384. doi:10.1016/j.chb.2014.03.067

Kowal, M., Conroy, E., Ramsbottom, N., Smithies, T., Toth, A., & Campbell, M. (2021). Gaming Your Mental Health: A Narrative Review on Mitigating Symptoms of Depression and Anxiety Using Commercial Video Games. *JMIR Serious Games, 9*(2). Advance online publication. doi:10.2196/26575

Lee Son, T., Wesson, J., & Vogts, D. (2018). Designing a Natural User Interface to Support Information Sharing among Co-Located Mobile Devices. *South African Computer Journal, 30*(2). Advance online publication. doi:10.18489acj.v30i2.440

Lopez, S. J., & Snyder, C. R. (2012). The Oxford Handbook of Positive Psychology. In The Oxford Handbook of Positive Psychology (2nd ed.). doi:10.1093/oxfordhb/9780195187243.001.0001

Meditation. (2020). In *APA Dictionary of Psychology*. Retrieved from https://dictionary.apa.org/meditation

Mindfulness. (2020). In *APA Dictionary of Psychology*. Retrieved from https://dictionary.apa.org/mindfulness

Mortensen, D. H. (2020). *Natural User Interfaces – What are they and how do you design user interfaces that feel natural?* Retrieved July 20, 2021, from Interaction Design Foundation website: https://www.interaction-design.org/literature/article/natural-user-interfaces-what-are-they-and-how-do-you-design-user-interfaces-that-feel-natural

Nabavi, N. (2021). Covid-19: Pandemic will cast "a long shadow" on mental health, warns England's CMO. *BMJ (Clinical Research Ed.),* (June), n1655. Advance online publication. doi:10.1136/bmj.n1655 PMID:34183352

Nguse, S., & Wassenaar, D. (2021). Mental health and COVID-19 in South Africa. *South African Journal of Psychology. Suid-Afrikaanse Tydskrif vir Sielkunde, 51*(2), 304–313. doi:10.1177/00812463211001543

Pandian, G. S. B., Jain, A., Raza, Q., & Sahu, K. K. (2021). Digital health interventions (DHI) for the treatment of attention deficit hyperactivity disorder (ADHD) in children - a comparative review of literature among various treatment and DHI. *Psychiatry Research, 297*, 113742. doi:10.1016/j.psychres.2021.113742 PMID:33515870

Pine, R., Fleming, T., McCallum, S., & Sutcliffe, K. (2020). The effects of casual videogames on anxiety, depression, stress, and low mood: A systematic review. *Games for Health Journal, 9*(4), 255–264. doi:10.1089/g4h.2019.0132 PMID:32053021

Pine, R., Sutcliffe, K., McCallum, S., & Fleming, T. (2020). Young adolescents' interest in a mental health casual video game. *Digital Health, 6*, 1–7. doi:10.1177/2055207620949391 PMID:32944270

Poppelaars, M., Lichtwarck-Aschoff, A., Otten, R., & Granic, I. (2021). Can a Commercial Video Game Prevent Depression? Null Results and Whole Sample Action Mechanisms in a Randomized Controlled Trial. *Frontiers in Psychology, 11*(January), 1–17. doi:10.3389/fpsyg.2020.575962 PMID:33510666

Primack, B. A., Carroll, M. V., McNamara, M., Klem, M., King, B., Rich, M., Chan, C. W., & Nayak, S. (2012). Role of video games in improving health-related outcomes: A systematic review. *American Journal of Preventive Medicine, 42*(6), 630–638. doi:10.1016/j.amepre.2012.02.023 PMID:22608382

Rybak, C. (2013). Nurturing Positive Mental Health: Mindfulness for Wellbeing in Counseling. *International Journal for the Advancement of Counseling, 35*(2), 110–119. doi:10.100710447-012-9171-7

Shrikumar, K. (2018). *PLAYNE – The Meditation Game*. Vismaya.

Siegel, R. D., Germer, C. K., & Olendzki, A. (2009). Mindfulness: What is it? where did it come from? In Clinical Handbook of Mindfulness (pp. 17–35). New York, NY: Springer New York. doi:10.1007/978-0-387-09593-6_2

Simon, C. R., & Durand-Bush, N. (2014). Differences in psychological and affective well-being between physicians and resident physicians: Does high and low self-regulation capacity matter? *Psychology of Well-Being, 4*(1), 1–19. doi:10.118613612-014-0019-2

Sliwinski, J., Katsikitis, M., & Jones, C. M. (2015). Mindful gaming: How digital games can improve mindfulness. Lecture Notes in Computer Science, 9298, 167–184. doi:10.1007/978-3-319-22698-9_12

Smith, J. D., & Graham, T. C. N. (2006). Use of eye movements for video game control. *International Conference on Advances in Computer Entertainment Technology 2006*. 10.1145/1178823.1178847

Snow, S., Bernardi, N. F. N. S.-K., Moran, D., & Lehmann, A. (2018). Exploring the Experience and Effects of Vocal Toning. *Journal of Music Therapy, 55*(3), 381. doi:10.1093/jmt/thy003 PMID:29800304

Taggart, F., & Stewart-brown, S. (2015). *A Review of Questionnaires Designed to Measure Mental Wellbeing*. Retrieved July 27, 2021, from - website: https://warwick.ac.uk/fac/sci/med/research/platform/wemwbs/research/validation/frances_taggart_%0Aresearch.pdf%0D

United Nations. (2015). *Transforming our world: the 2030 Agenda for Sustainable Development*. Retrieved April 4, 2019, from Sustainable Development Goals Knowledge Platform website: https://sustainabledevelopment.un.org/post2015/transformingourworld

Unity. (n.d.). *Developer Tools*. Retrieved August 7, 2021, from https://unity.com/developer-tools

University of Melbourne. (n.d.). *Social play in immersive gaming environments*. Retrieved July 20, 2021, from https://cis.unimelb.edu.au/hci/projects/social-play/

UW Human Photonics Lab. (n.d.). *Virtual Reality Pain Reduction*. Retrieved June 10, 2021, from https://depts.washington.edu/hplab/research/virtual-reality/

Vaishnavi, V., Kuechler, B., & Petter, S. (2017). *Design Science Research in Information Systems*. http://www.desrist.org/design-research-in-information-systems/

Van Rooij, M., Lobel, A., Harris, O., Smit, N., & Granic, I. (2016). DEEP: A biofeedback virtual reality game for children at-risk for anxiety. In *Conference on Human Factors in Computing Systems – Proceedings*. Association for Computing Machinery. 10.1145/2851581.2892452

Vara, M. D., Baños, R. M., Rasal, P., Rodríguez, A., Rey, B., Wrzesien, M., & Alcañiz, M. (2016). A game for emotional regulation in adolescents: The (body) interface device matters. *Computers in Human Behavior*, *57*, 267–273. doi:10.1016/j.chb.2015.12.033

Watson, D., Clark, L. A., & Tellegen, A. (1988). Development and Validation of Brief Measures of Positive and Negative Affect: The PANAS Scales. *Journal of Personality and Social Psychology*, *54*(6), 1063–1070. doi:10.1037/0022-3514.54.6.1063 PMID:3397865

Wigdor, D., & Wixon, D. (2011). Brave NUI World: Designing Natural User Interfaces for Touch and Gesture. In *Brave NUI World*. Morgan Kaufmann Publishers Inc. doi:10.1016/C2009-0-64091-5

World Health Organisation. (2018). *Mental health: Strengthening our response*. Retrieved June 29, 2021, from https://www.who.int/news-room/fact-sheets/detail/mental-health-strengthening-our-response

World Health Organisation. (2019). *Mental Disorders*. Retrieved June 29, 2021, from https://www.who.int/news-room/fact-sheets/detail/mental-disorders

World Health Organisation. (2020). *Depression*. Retrieved June 29, 2021, from https://www.who.int/news-room/fact-sheets/detail/depression

World Health Organisation. (n.d.). *Mental Health*. Retrieved June 29, 2021, from https://www.who.int/health-topics/mental-health#tab=tab_2

World Health Organization. (2017). *Depression and Other Common Mental Disorders Global Health Estimates*. WHO.

ADDITIONAL READING

Bach, D. (2021). *Mind games: How gaming can play a positive role in mental health*. Retrieved June 12, 2021, from https://news.microsoft.com/features/mind-games-how-gaming-can-play-a-positive-role-in-mental-health/

Bedal, L. (2016). *User Experience as Embodied Experience: Considerations for UX Designers*. Retrieved July 30, 2021, from https://uxdesign.cc/user-experience-as-embodied-experience-considerations-for-ux-designers-b66813b08adf

Cowley, B., Charles, D., Black, M., & Hickey, R. (2008). Toward an understanding of flow in video games. *Computers in Entertainment*, *6*(2), 1–27. doi:10.1145/1371216.1371223

Granic, I., Lobel, A., & Engels, R. C. M. E. (2014). The benefits of playing video games. *The American Psychologist*, *69*(1), 66–78. doi:10.1037/a0034857 PMID:24295515

Mandal, S. P., Arya, Y. K., & Pandey, R. (2012). Mental Health and Mindfulness: Mediational Role of Positive and Negative Affect. *SIS Journal of Projective Psychology & Mental Health*, *19*(2), 150–159.

Poppelaars, M., Lichtwarck-Aschoff, A., Kleinjan, M., & Granic, I. (2018). The impact of explicit mental health messages in video games on players' motivation and affect. *Computers in Human Behavior*, *83*, 16–23. doi:10.1016/j.chb.2018.01.019

Rajkumar, R. P. (2020). COVID-19 and mental health: A review of the existing literature. *Asian Journal of Psychiatry*, *52*(March), 1–5. doi:10.1016/j.ajp.2020.102066 PMID:32302935

Villani, D., Carissoli, C., Triberti, S., Marchetti, A., Gilli, G., & Riva, G. (2018). Videogames for Emotion Regulation: A Systematic Review. *Games for Health Journal*, *7*(2), 85–99. doi:10.1089/g4h.2017.0108 PMID:29424555

KEY TERMS AND DEFINITIONS

Affect: An experience or expression of emotion which could be positive or negative.
Affective Well-Being: Emotional wellness. A healthy balance between negative and positive emotions.
Flow: The state of being fully engrossed in an activity; deep concentration.
Gameplay: The way a game is played.
Meditative: Having to do with the act of meditation; causing calmness and relaxation.
Meditative Game: A game that requires focused attention to make a user calm or relaxed.
Mindfulness: A state of awareness characterized by being focused on your current feelings and senses.
User Interface: The aspect of a device that links the human and device for communication.

Chapter 11
Serious Games Design Principles Using Virtual Reality to Gamify Upper Limb Stroke Rehabilitation:
The Importance of Engagement for Rehabilitation

Robert Herne
Murdoch University, Australia

Mohd Fairuz Shiratuddin
Murdoch University, Australia

Shri Rai
Murdoch University, Australia

David Blacker
Perron Institute, Australia

ABSTRACT

Stroke is a debilitating condition that impairs one's ability to live independently while also greatly decreasing one's quality of life. For these reasons, stroke rehabilitation is important. Engagement is a crucial part of rehabilitation, increasing a stroke survivor's recovery rate and the positive outcomes of their rehabilitation. For this reason, virtual reality (VR) has been widely used to gamify stroke rehabilitation to support engagement. Given that VR and the serious games that form its basis may not necessarily be engaging in themselves, ensuring that their design is engaging is important. This chapter discusses 39 principles that may be useful for engaging stroke survivors with VR-based rehabilitation post-stroke. This chapter then discusses a subset of the game design principles that are likely to engage stroke survivors with VR designed for upper limb rehabilitation post-stroke.

DOI: 10.4018/978-1-7998-9223-6.ch011

INTRODUCTION

Stroke affects an individual's ability to live independently, because it impairs their ability to perform basic activities such as eating, dressing, washing and walking (Ploderer et al., 2017). Given the impact a stroke has on someone's life and independence, rehabilitation is important. Engagement with the rehabilitation process has been recognised as playing a crucial part in stroke rehabilitation, increasing a stroke survivor's recovery rate and positive outcomes of their rehabilitation (MacDonald et al., 2013). Gamification is considered to be important with the engagement process. According to Patricio et al. (2020):

Gamification is the process of making activities more game-like in non-game contexts to encourage users' motivation and engagement in a particular task.

Patrício et al. (2018) also stated that:

Effective gamification approaches attempt to encourage users' engagement, amusement, and enjoyment toward various activities.

Because of the importance of gamification, this chapter discusses various Serious Games (which form the basis of VR) Design Principles using VR to enable the gamification of stroke rehabilitation for improved engagement. The chapter begins with a background discussion of stroke, rehabilitation, Serious Games, VR and the use of VR for stroke rehabilitation. The chapter then provides a discussion of game design principles that may be applicable in the design of VR for gamified stroke rehabilitation, with the aim of making it more engaging. The chapter concludes by discussing an application of the principles to upper limb rehabilitation post-stroke. This research identified which of the game design principles discussed are likely to engage stroke survivors with VR designed for upper limb rehabilitation post-stroke.

BACKGROUND

Stroke

The Stroke Foundation of Australia (*What is a stroke — Stroke Foundation - Australia*, 2021) provides this layperson definition of stroke:

Your brain is fed by blood carrying oxygen and nutrients through blood vessels called arteries. A stroke happens when blood cannot get to your brain because of a blocked or burst artery. As a result, your brain cells die due to a lack of oxygen and nutrients.

Physical impairments potentially caused by a stroke include impaired movement of limbs (Norman, 2014). Having upper limb impairment means that one arm is likely to be paralysed or suffer from limited movement. A paralysed arm curls upwards into a wing with a clenched fist. Having only one good arm makes tasks that require or are much easier to perform with two arms very difficult. This can include simple domestic tasks such as opening a jar or using a telephone.

Stroke Rehabilitation

Intensive rehabilitation after a stroke is crucial to minimise long-term effects, improve rehabilitation results and decrease the responsibility placed on carers and health care systems (Langstaff et al., 2014).

Physical Rehabilitation

Physical rehabilitation includes rehabilitation of both the upper and lower limbs, including motor skills, gait and balance. Conventionally, a course of physiotherapy is used in the physical rehabilitation of stroke survivors. Other methods used for physical rehabilitation include Serious Games (see the section "Stroke Rehabilitation and Serious Games" for an in-depth discussion of this) and VR (see the section "Stroke Rehabilitation and Virtual Reality").

Rehabilitation and Engagement

Engagement with the rehabilitation process has been recognised as playing a crucial part in stroke rehabilitation, increasing a stroke survivor's rate of rehabilitation and rehabilitation outcomes (MacDonald et al., 2013). If they are not engaged, they may fail to attempt rehabilitation and lose what movement they have remaining. Therefore, stroke survivor engagement with their rehabilitation is critical. To engage is defined as (*Oxford Dictionary of English*, 2010): "occupy or attract (someone's interest or attention)."

Stroke Rehabilitation and Serious Games

Serious Games are a method of making users engage with activities that have defined purposes (Bruno & Griffiths, 2014), and this is why they are used for rehabilitative purposes. Burke et al. (2009) performed a study into optimising the engagement level of Serious Game-based upper limb stroke rehabilitation. They identified two important game design principles for this: *meaningful play* and *challenge*. Their research did not state whether other principles were tested and were found to not be engaging. Lohse et al. (2013) determined six principles of effective game design that have an empirical basis for increasing motivation and engagement with physical rehabilitation interventions. These were: reward, difficulty and challenge, feedback, choice and interactivity, clear goals and mechanics and socialisation. The actual application and testing in settings such as stroke rehabilitation were not discussed.

Virtual Reality

Virtual Reality (VR) is defined by Henderson et al. (2007) as: "a computer-based, interactive, multisensory simulation environment that occurs in real-time. VR presents users with opportunities to engage in activities within environments that appear, to various extents, similar to real-world objects and events." VR can be used to play a Serious Game. Two main types of VR exist: *immersive* and *non-immersive*.

Immersive

Immersive VR utilises a head-mounted display (HMD) (Kourtesis et al., 2019), which presents the game world to the user. While immersive VR has been used in both neuroscientific and neuropsychological research settings, the use of HMDs in both research and clinical settings has concerns related to motion, cyber and VR sickness (Kourtesis et al., 2019).

Non-Immersive

Another type of VR is Desktop VR (Kalawsky, 1993), also known as non-immersive VR. According to Pimentel and Teixeira (1995), it is "a subset of traditional virtual reality systems. Instead of a head-mounted display, a large computer monitor or projection system is used to present the virtual world." Because of cybersickness concerns with HMDs (Garcia-Agundez et al., 2019; Kourtesis et al., 2019), non-immersive Desktop VR is more suitable for stroke rehabilitation.

Stroke Rehabilitation and Virtual Reality

Previous studies have used Serious Games and VR as a means of delivering stroke rehabilitation with promising results. Types of stroke rehabilitation include upper limb, balance and cognitive rehabilitation.

Effectiveness of VR Therapy

The effectiveness of VR therapy for stroke rehabilitation has been evaluated by previous systematic reviews and standard research studies. A systematic review by Viñas-Diz and Sobrido-Prieto (2016) found that VR therapy being beneficial for upper limb rehabilitation is strongly supported. However, further research would be required to properly determine what changes in the brain occur, which type of VR is most effective, whether training remains for a long time and how often and how intense the use of the therapy should be. Another systematic review by Aminov et al. (2018) found that VR can have a highly positive effect on body structure and function and level of activity outcomes for stroke survivors. Lee et al. (2019) found that VR was effective for rehabilitating lower and upper limb function post-stroke.

VR Therapy vs Conventional Therapy

There is currently no consensus on whether virtual reality therapy is more effective than conventional therapy. Regardless, VR therapy may have other benefits that this section will also discuss. A systematic review by Howard (2017) found that VR rehabilitation was more effective than conventional rehabilitation for physical improvement. Three reasons for this have been hypothesised: excitement, physical fidelity and cognitive fidelity. Future research would need to be performed to determine whether these are actually the cause. Alternatively, a systematic review by Laver et al. (2017) found that for upper limb rehabilitation, outcomes from VR-based therapy were no higher than traditional therapy. While the therapy may not have any advantages by itself, the engagement aspects may still have an impact.

In-Home Rehabilitation Using VR

In-home VR therapy is an area that is increasing in popularity due to accessibility, which in turn means that the rehabilitation can be engaged with more regularly and for longer periods. Fluet et al. (2019) examined using an in-home stroke rehabilitation system for hand movement rehabilitation over 12 weeks. The system utilised the Leap Motion controller. The study concluded that a 12 week in the home virtual rehabilitation system is feasible and that the motivational enhancement could increase overall motivation, adherence to the program and motor skill improvement outcomes.

The Problem of Engagement

The sizeable problem is that users are often not engaged by Serious Games, particularly in comparison to non-Serious Games (Dele-Ajayi et al., 2016). As Serious Games form the basis of VR-based rehabilitation, the problem extends to this as well. This raises the question of what specifically can be done to make Serious Games and VR (including Desktop VR) designed for rehabilitation engaging for its users. In this case: these are stroke survivors.

GAME DESIGN PRINCIPLES

Performing an investigation into what game design principles potentially support stroke survivor engagement with Desktop VR-based Serious Games designed for rehabilitation would ensure stroke survivors achieve the greatest benefit from such rehabilitation. Since these are not known, a good basis is to review the literature on what game design principles are engaging for healthy individuals so that their engagement level for stroke survivors can be examined. Game design principles that engage healthy individuals cannot be guaranteed to also engage stroke survivors since they have suffered cognitive disability.

Principles suggested by Rabin (2010), Oxarart et al. (2014), Desurvire and Wixon (2013), McDaniel et al. (2010), Martey et al. (2014), O'Brien and Toms (2008), Brockmyer et al. (2009) and Whitton (2011) are discussed. Many of the principles suggested by the researchers are interrelated and were therefore placed into 13 logical groupings. This was so that they could be analysed in the context of their relationships with one another. This means that when making game design considerations for them that they could be targeted as groups. The principles were logically grouped (see Figure 1 in the section "Game Design Principle Groupings") based on their definitions (see "Game Design Principle Groupings" for these definitions) and the logical relationships between them. Consideration was given to how these design principles could be targeted by similar or the same design aspects of a Desktop VR stroke rehab program.

General Game Design Principles

The general game design principles include, but are not limited to: *fun, a safe environment, improvisation, emotional connection, coolness, delight* and different types of sound, graphics and music.

Rabin (2010) believes that games should be fun to play, be initiated in safe circumstances, and be improvisational (i.e. a player should be able to figure out how to play the game without assistance). These may be interpreted as principles of game design. Oxarart et al. (2014) say that practising a skill under safe circumstances and several times is a key game design principle.

Desurvire and Wixon (2013) discussed the principles of "PLAY", which includes a list of gameplay areas: game usability, gameplay, game mechanics, game immersion, emotional connection, coolness and delight. They also stated that when users are not faced with unintentional difficulties with the tools used to play the game, they will concentrate and focus on the game. This ties in with Rabin's design principle that games should be improvisational (i.e. a game's interface should be intuitive and transparent to the

239

point that a player can focus on the game). A game with a complicated user interface would suffer a detraction from interest and immersion while also creating the artificial challenge.

Martin (2012) stated that the sensory aspects of games like music and graphics improve Serious Game learning outcomes. In addition, Jeong and Kim (2007) discovered that stroke survivor motivation was increased by music. Based on this, engagement with Serious Game-based stroke rehabilitation is likely to be supported by sensory and visual components.

Dark play, meaning the use of inappropriate or unethical actions in games, was studied by Buijs-Spanjers et al. (2019) as a principle in designing a Serious Game. The research found that its inclusion did not impact the effectiveness of Serious Games. The research also found that a more realistic take on another person's point of view may be more important in Serious Games for improving player empathy.

Visual aspects include graphics, which could be 2D or 3D and low or high-fidelity, along with whether the view is first (through the player character's eyes) or third person (i.e. from above and behind the player character). Sensory aspects include sound and music. Sounds could be used as feedback, such as a clicking sound indicates a button press has been successful. Sound can also be ambient in that it exists in the background to help users feel as though they have a presence in a virtual world. The ambient sound could be wind in a desert, the sound of lapping waves by a lake or the sound of a fire burning in the kiln of an Atlantean potter's shop. Music, like sound, could also be used as feedback (such as a fanfare ditty in response to a user successfully completing a task) or as ambience (such as establishing an ominous tone in an abandoned place).

Story is often considered an important part of game design, with a good storyline being likely to capture a player's interest and immerse them within the game. McDaniel et al. (2010) have discussed the place of serious storytelling in Serious Games. They discussed using story as a method for creating immersion or presence in Serious Games, just as in non-Serious Games. Further research is required to determine whether Serious Games having a storyline would increase the engagement of stroke survivors.

Principles Relating to Engagement

Game design principles relating to engagement include but are not limited to: *involvement, immersion, arousal, attention, interest, identification, enjoyment, effort, flow, presence, interest, motivation, challenge, awareness, novelty,* aesthetic and sensory appeal (i.e. high-fidelity graphics), *perceived control, interactivity, feedback, presence, psychological absorption* and *purpose.*

Martey et al. (2014) stated that engagement in games consists of definitions including involvement, immersion, arousal, attention, interest, identification, enjoyment, effort, flow and presence. O'Brien and Toms (2008) identified interest, motivation, challenge, awareness, novelty, aesthetic and sensory appeal, perceived control and time, interactivity and feedback as key contributors to user engagement. Simões-Silva et al. (2021) also discussed the importance of motivation in game-based rehabilitation. Brockmyer et al. (2009) discussed engagement based on the components of immersion, presence, flow and psychological absorption. Whitton (2011) used the learning game engagement factors: challenge, control, immersion, interest and purpose in her research. Whitton also discussed flow, which occurs when a player is fully immersed in a game and unconsciously ignores anything outside it (Rabin, 2010). A player will feel completely in control of the game and not feel self-conscious (Whitton, 2011). Flow is caused by a balance between player challenge and skill, avoiding player frustration and boredom (Rabin, 2010). Challenges will need skill to complete, with rules being understandable (Whitton, 2011). In addition, flow theory dictates that goals should always be clear and attainable, and feedback should be immediate (Whitton, 2011). Lyons (2015) also discussed the potential usefulness of feedback, challenge and rewards in exergames, of which VR games designed for rehabilitation are a type.

Game Design Principle Groupings

The 39 game design principles discussed in "General Game Design Principles", "Principles Relating to Engagement", and "Stroke Rehabilitation and Serious Games" can be placed into 13 logical groupings (shown in Figure 1). This means that when making game design considerations for them in the design of VR for rehabilitation post-stroke, they can be analysed and targeted as groups. The logic behind these groupings is discussed below.

Figure 1. The 39 game design principles (Herne et al., 2019)

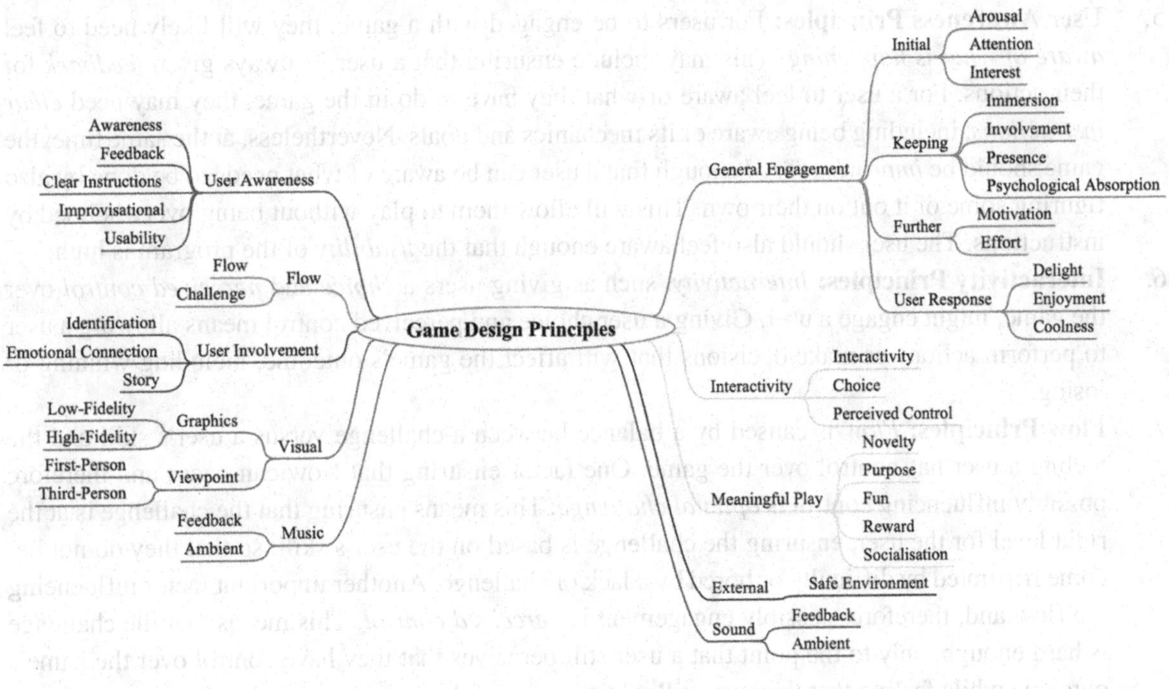

The 13 logical groupings are defined below:

1. **General Engagement Principles — Initial:** The factors that may initially engage a user are *arousal*, *attention* and *interest*. If a game can arouse a user's attention and interest, then the user may initially be engaged enough to play the game.
2. **General Engagement Principles — Keeping:** Once a user has been initially engaged with the system, principles that may keep users engaged include *immersion*, *presence*, *involvement* and *psychological absorption*. A user may be engaged with a game if they feel immersed with and as though they a present in the game world. From this, they may be further engaged if, upon feeling immersed and present in the world, they feel involved with it (such as with its inhabitants or events).

This may cause them to be psychologically absorbed by aspects of the world (such as caring for what happens for a particular character), which may further engage them.

3.   **General Engagement Principles — Further:** These principles that may keep a user engaged with a game may, in turn, make a user feel the *motivation* to keep playing the game and use *effort* to complete the game's goals. *Motivation* and *effort* may engage a user enough to keep them playing further into the game.

4.   **General Engagement Principles — User Response:** Principles that a game may elicit from a user in response to the game (possibly in response to the other aforementioned principles potential influencing engagement) that may cause a user to be continuously engaged are *delight*, *enjoyment* and *coolness*. If a user feels delighted in response to the game, enjoys playing it or feels that it is cool, they may be engaged to the point that all or some of these factors alone are enough to keep them playing the game. The other specific principles outlined below may influence these more general principles.

5.   **User Awareness Principles:** For users to be engaged with a game, they will likely need to feel *aware of what is happening*. This may include ensuring that a user is always given *feedback* for their actions. For a user to feel aware of what they have to do in the game, they may need *clear instructions*, including being aware of its mechanics and goals. Nevertheless, at the same time, the game should be *improvisational* enough that a user can be aware of what needs to be done by also figuring some of it out on their own. This will allow them to play without being overwhelmed by instructions. The user should also feel aware enough that the *usability* of the program is high.

6.   **Interactivity Principles:** *Interactivity*, such as giving users a *choice* and *perceived control* over the game, might engage a user. Giving a user choice and perceived control means allowing a user to perform actions or make decisions that will affect the game's outcome, including winning or losing.

7.   **Flow Principles:** *Flow* is caused by a balance between a challenge versus a user's skill and the feeling a user has control over the game. One factor ensuring that flow can occur and therefore possibly influencing control is *optimal challenge*. This means ensuring that the challenge is at the right level for the user, ensuring the challenge is based on the user's skill, so that they do not become frustrated by difficulty or bored by a lack of challenge. Another important factor influencing the flow and, therefore, possibly engagement is *perceived control*. This means that the challenge is hard enough, only to the point that a user still perceives that they have control over the game's outcome while feeling that they can still win or successfully complete a task.

8.   **Meaningful Play Principles:** Meaningful play was suggested by Burke et al. (2009) as a factor influencing engagement with games. Principles that may encourage meaningful play and therefore engage stroke survivors with a game include *novelty* (i.e., being new, interesting, different or unusual), the game having a *purpose*, being *fun*, offering them in-game *rewards*, and offering socialisation aspects (such as competitive aspects).

9.   **User Involvement Principles:** Three factors that may engage a user with a game by involving them are *identification*, *emotional connection* and *story*. A story may allow a user to feel more involved with the game by including an interesting setting, characters and/or events. These are aspects with which a user may identify and therefore possibly form an emotional connection.

Table 1. Game Design Principle Definitions (Herne et al., 2019)

Principles Grouping	Principles	Definition
General Engagement Principles — Initial	Arousal	"Evoke or awaken (a feeling, emotion, or response) (*Oxford Dictionary of English*, 2010)."
	Attention	"Notice taken of someone or something; the regarding of someone or something as interesting or important (*Oxford Dictionary of English*, 2010)."
	Interest	"Excite the curiosity or attention of (someone) (*Oxford Dictionary of English*, 2010)."
General Engagement Principles — Keeping	Immersion	"Involve oneself deeply in a particular activity (*Oxford Dictionary of English*, 2010)."
	Involvement	"Be or become occupied or engrossed in something (*Oxford Dictionary of English*, 2010)."
	Presence	The feeling of "being there" within a game world (Martey et al., 2014).
	Psychological Absorption	*Psychological absorption* means complete engagement with an experience currently occurring (Brockmyer et al., 2009).
General Engagement Principles — Further	Motivation	"Provide (someone) with a reason for doing something; cause (someone) to have interest in or enthusiasm for something (*Oxford Dictionary of English*, 2010)."
	Effort	"A vigorous or determined attempt (*Oxford Dictionary of English*, 2010)."
General Engagement Principles — User Response	Delight	"Please (someone) greatly (*Oxford Dictionary of English*, 2010)."
	Enjoyment	"Take delight or pleasure in (an activity or occasion) (*Oxford Dictionary of English*, 2010)."
	Coolness	"The quality of being fashionably attractive or impressive (*Oxford Dictionary of English*, 2010)."
User Awareness Principles	Awareness	"Knowledge or perception of a situation (*Oxford Dictionary of English*, 2010)."
	Feedback	"Any information about how a skill was performed and/or the effectiveness with which the skill was performed (Lohse et al., 2013)."
	Clear Instructions	*Clear instructions* are instructions that make it clear how to use a VR-based rehabilitation tool in an unambiguous and easy to understand manner.
	Improvisation	"Performed spontaneously or without preparation (*Oxford Dictionary of English*, 2010)."
	Usability	"The degree to which something is able or fit to be used (*Oxford Dictionary of English*, 2010)."
Interactivity Principles	Interactivity	"The ability of a computer to respond to a user's input. (*Oxford Dictionary of English*, 2010)"
	Choice	"The right or ability to choose. (*Oxford Dictionary of English*, 2010)"
	Perceived Control	This refers to whether you believe you have control over the tool and its outcomes.
Flow Principles	Flow	*Flow* is caused by a balance between player challenge and skill, avoiding player frustration and boredom (Rabin, 2010). This means you will feel the game is not easy enough for you to become bored and not hard enough to cause you to become frustrated.
	Challenge	"A task or situation that tests someone's abilities (*Oxford Dictionary of English*, 2010)."
Meaningful Play Principles	Novelty	"The quality of being new, original or unusual (*Oxford Dictionary of English*, 2010)."
	Purpose	"The reason for which something is done or created or for which something exists (*Oxford Dictionary of English*, 2010)."
	Fun	"Amusing, entertaining, or enjoyable (*Oxford Dictionary of English*, 2010)."
	Reward	"A thing given in recognition of [..] effort or achievement (*Oxford Dictionary of English*, 2010)."
	Socialisation	"The activity of mixing socially with others (*Oxford Dictionary of English*, 2010)."
User Involvement Principles	Identification	"The action or process of identifying someone or something (*Oxford Dictionary of English*, 2010)."
	Emotional Connection	This refers to an emotional connection to a VR-based rehabilitation tool or someone or something within it.
	Story	"A plot or storyline (*Oxford Dictionary of English*, 2010)." Plot is: "the main events of a play, novel, film, or similar work, devised and presented by the writer as an interrelated sequence (*Oxford Dictionary of English*, 2010)."
External Factor	Safe Environment	A *safe environment* means initiating the use of VR-based rehabilitation in what you would consider being safe circumstances.
Visual Principles	Low vs. High Fidelity Graphics	*Low fidelity graphics* refers to graphics that have less detail and realism. Inversely, *high fidelity graphics* refer to graphics with a high level of detail and look more realistic.
	First vs. Third Person View	A *first-person view* is where the player (you) sees the game world through the eyes of the controlled character. A *third-person view* is where the player sees the controlled character from behind.
Sound Principles	Feedback Sounds	*Feedback sounds* are sounds that are played in response to an action to indicate that something has happened in the game or that the game has recognised your input.
	Ambient Sounds	*Ambient sounds* are sounds that give an auditory atmosphere to a game, such as by establishing an outdoor location by having the player hear wind or establishing a laboratory with computer sounds.

Continued on following page

Table 1. Continued

Principles Grouping	Principles	Definition
Music Principles	Feedback Music	*Feedback music* is music that is played in response to an action to indicate that something has happened in the game or that the game has recognised your input. This can take the form of fanfare in response to successfully completing something in a game or music that indicates some event has occurred in-game.
	Ambient Music	*Ambient music* is music that is played in a game to establish atmospheres, such as incidental music in a television program or film.

10. **External Factors:** An external factor that is independent of the game itself, but is determined by the environment in which the game is played is whether it is played in a *safe environment*. This means a stroke survivor may feel more engaged depending on where they are given the intervention. This may mean that if they feel their home is a safer environment than a clinic, they will be more engaged at home. This also means that engagement may be affected by the expectations that are placed on them. If they feel pressure to perform or improve, they may not be engaged as if there were no pressure.

11. **Visual Principles:** Principles related to what the player sees, including *low* or *high-fidelity* graphics and a *first-person* (where the player sees through the game's playable character's eyes) or a *third-person* (where the player sees the game world with the playable character in view).

12. **Sound Principles:** The two principles in this category are *ambient* (sounds played in the background of a game to create atmosphere) and *feedback sounds* (sounds played in response to a player action to help inform them of its impact in the game).

13. **Music Principles:** The two principles in this category are *ambient* (music played in the background of a game to create atmosphere) and *feedback music* (music played in response to a player action to help inform them of its impact in the game).

The 39 principles are defined in Table 1 and were previously used as part of the author's research, with additional specifics added in reference to the VR-based intervention used (Herne et al., 2019). See the section on "Application of Game Design Principles" for a discussion of this research.

SOLUTIONS AND RECOMMENDATIONS

The authors applied these 39 game design principles to desktop VR-based upper limb rehabilitation in a user experience case study to identify which game design principles are likely to engage participants (Herne et al., 2019). Additionally, feedback was gained to determine how the VR intervention could be more engaging concerning the game design principles discussed. This was done so that the VR intervention could be improved and then used in the future to determine whether the important game design principles do engage the participants. This is because the VR intervention's updates will likely support them.

Methodology

We used a multiple case study methodology (see "Multiple Case Study Approach") with an overview shown in Figure 2. The research began with the 39 game design principles defined in "Game Design

Principle Groupings". The game design principles were then evaluated by the participants (see "Questionnaire") in relation to the VR intervention (used by the participants over 12 weeks, see "VR Intervention Using NRS"), with feedback on how to make the VR intervention more engaging also being collected (see "Questionnaire"). The responses to the game design principle evaluation lead to the identification of the game design principles that are likely to engage (see "Results" — "Game Design Principles Responses"). The feedback on the VR intervention led to the determination of necessary improvements to the VR intervention to make it more engaging (see "Results" — "VR Intervention Feedback").

Sir Charles Gairdner Hospital had approved this research: Human Research Ethics Committee (HREC) #2015-114 and Murdoch University Ethics: #2016/088. Written consent was obtained from the participants.

Figure 2. Methodology Flow Diagram

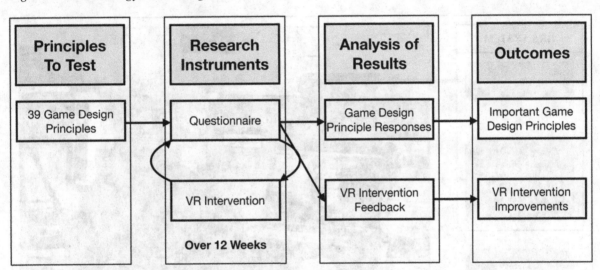

Multiple Case Study Approach

Strokes can be different because of type (a clot or a bleed), location (back or front of the brain), multiple stroke occurrences and severity. This changes their impact. Stroke survivors also differ by age (during the study and at the time of the stroke), lifestyle (employment, health, commitments, etc.) and health (before and after the stroke), creating very different cases. Because of this, a multiple case study approach was utilised to identify what likely engages the participating stroke survivors with desktop VR designed for upper limb rehabilitation rather than universally. Therefore, each stroke survivor is a single case.

"Case study" is a research methodology for when one instance of something is examined in-depth to obtain a deep understanding of it and the complex processes and relationships within it (Oates, 2006). With stroke and stroke survivor cases being very different, the use of a case study allows all factors that will affect this and the rehabilitation to be understood. Because the study aimed to determine what game design principles could make the NRS more engaging, it was, therefore, an exploratory case study. Since multiple case studies were being performed (one for each stroke survivor participant), this study was, therefore, a "multiple case study" (Oates, 2006). Comparable findings from the different cases can solidify their conclusions, with contrasts supporting further interesting conclusions (Oates, 2006).

VR Intervention Using NRS

The research had six stroke survivor participants use a Desktop VR-based upper limb rehabilitation tool, called the Neuromender Rehabilitation System (NRS), for 12 weeks (the same as Fluet et al. (2019)). The NRS has six parts, all designed for different levels of stroke rehabilitation. The NRS is used in-home (improving accessibility), with rehabilitation being monitored and controlled remotely by clinicians (Herne et al., 2019; Murdoch University, 2015). The NRS consists of a personal computer with Windows 10 installed, a standard widescreen monitor, mouse, keyboard and a non-intrusive Microsoft Kinect motion sensor used to track a user's arm movements (see Figure 3).

Figure 3. A Stroke Survivor Using the NRS

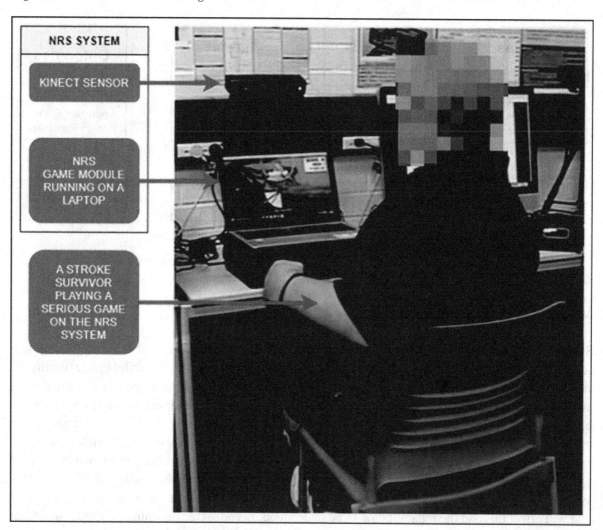

The NRS's rehabilitation Module 3 for upper limb rehabilitation, with its Serious Game "The Wingman", was played by the stroke survivors. The game's goal is for a stroke survivor to use their upper arm to control their flight through a set of rings. The angle between their upper arm with the body determines the elevation of the Wingman onscreen, aiming to enter the centre of the rings that appear during their flight. Movement of the upper arm is achieved by aiming and lowering the elbow. By repeating this movement of the arm, the rehabilitation's goal is to increase the angle of controlled movement that the upper arm and elbow can reach. Three courses are available, differing in the number of rings and visuals, for user selection (beach, forest or temple, see Figure 4). There are also three speed options available to the player: slow (lasting 240 seconds), medium (lasting 180 seconds) and fast (lasting 120 seconds). The timing determines the length between the start and finish line, meaning movement along the course and through the rings is increased with shorter timespans.

Figure 4. NRS — The Wingman's Courses: Beach (Left), Forest (Middle), Temple (Right)

Each stroke survivor has a clinician assigned "angle threshold", which is the angle their upper arm needs to be held to achieve a full 10 points (when the centre of the red ring is entered – Figure 4). Each degree off the threshold results in one less point until no points are given. If a stroke survivor regularly achieves 10 points on a ring, the threshold may be raised to practice moving and holding the arm at a larger angle from their body. The stroke survivor's arm angle (represented by the black bar), in relation to the angle threshold (represented by the blue bar), is shown on the arm angle gauge (the yellow bottom quarter circle, called the arm elevation gauge) at the bottom centre of the game view. Figure 4 shows the blue bar and the black bar are aligned to give maximum points on entry to the ring. The gauge in Figure 5 shows its position when the right arm is being rehabilitated. For the left arm, the gauge would be shown with a left bottom quarter circle.

Figure 5. NRS Data Collection and Analysis Web Portal — Angles and Scores Achieved Over A Session (Left), Angles and Scores Achieved During One Game (Middle), Angles and Scores Achieved Over Multiple Sessions (Right)

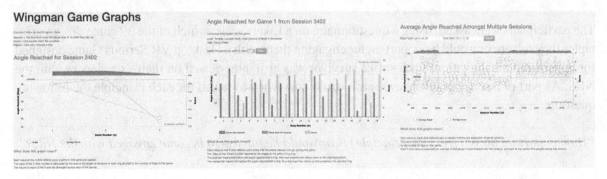

The stroke survivors are provided access to a web portal (shown in Figure 5). Here they can review the angles to which they lifted their arms and scores achieved over time. This can be for a specific game or session while also allowing progress in both to be shown over a specific time period. This feedback is also made visible to supervising rehabilitation clinicians for monitoring and control purposes.

Participant Demographics

Purposive sampling (when an expert decides what cases are selected, or a researcher nominates cases based on their value for a purpose (Ishak et al., 2014)) was used for this case study. The supervising neurologist acted as the case selector for this study, with the criteria being that a survivor's disability could meaningfully be attributed to a stroke. The stroke survivor participant demographics are described in Table 2. "Time Since Stroke" indicates the time elapsed between when a survivor's stroke occurred and when they began the study.

Table 2. Participant Demographics

Participant	Gender	Age	Side-Affected	Time Since Stroke
1	Male	73	Left	6 years, 3 months
2	Female	36	Left	14 years, 4 months
3	Male	63	Left	16 years, 4 months
4	Female	76	Left	5 years, 1 month
5	Male	62	Right	1 year, 3 months
6	Male	72	Right	10 months

Participant 4 was the only stroke survivor involved that did not know how to use a computer, nor did she own or know how to operate a mobile phone. Participant 5 indicated that he was previously a senior IT and business consultant. Participant 2 was the only stroke survivor involved that had played computer games. Over the 12 weeks at home, the stroke survivors could play the game up to 6 times a day for a maximum of 42 times a week. There was also a limit of 3 games per session, with a mandated gap between sessions of at least 3 hours. The supervising therapist mandated these rules to ensure that stroke survivors would not overuse the system and become fatigued, which would be counter-productive to their rehabilitation.

Questionnaire

The participants were asked, using a questionnaire on a Likert scale, which of the 39 game design principles they felt are or would be important for engaging them with a Desktop VR Serious Game designed for upper limb rehabilitation. Each stroke survivor was also interviewed on their experiences with the NRS. As part of a series of interviews, each stroke survivor was asked for each principle the following question:

"How important do you feel [the principle] is or would be for you to become engaged with the NRS?"

They were asked to answer the question on a Likert scale derived from Brown (2010). The values, their definitions and associated scores are described in Table 3.

Table 3. Likert Scale Associated Scores

Likert Value	Associated Score	Definition
Not at All	1	The participant feels that the principle is not at all important for them to become engaged with the system.
Very Little	2	The participant feels that the principle is or would be of very little importance for them to become engaged with the system.
Somewhat	3	The participant feels that the principle is or would be somewhat important for them to become engaged with the system.
To a Great Extent	4	The participant feels that the principle is or would be important to a great extent for them to become engaged with the system.

The definitions of the game design principles given in Table 1 were provided to ensure that the participants properly understood their meaning. Once all answers were obtained from the questionnaires, each principle was given a total score, based on the sum of the associated scores with the Likert scale value each participant gave for that principle. Likert scale values were not used for quantitative analysis because a multiple case study methodology was used. The total scores were then ranked and grouped in importance based on the score groupings described in Table 4. The intention of this was not to perform statistical analysis but to find trends in the participants' answers to establish which principles overall are most likely to engage the participants.

Table 4. Importance Grouping

Group	Total Score	Definition
Warrant the Focus of Further Investigation	24	The principle warrants the focus of further investigation.
Also Important to a Great Extent	21 - 23	The principle is also of importance to a great extent for the stroke survivor participants to become engaged.
High Importance	18 - 20	The principle is or would be of high importance for the stroke survivor participants to become engaged.
Somewhat Important	12 - 17	The principle is or would be somewhat important for the stroke survivor participants to become engaged.
Little Importance	6 - 11	The principle is or would be of little importance for the stroke survivor participants to become engaged.

The principles and questions were provided to the participants at the beginning of the study and were intended to be asked over the last eight weeks of the study. This was so the first four weeks would give them time to familiarise themselves with the system, and so they only had to consider a small number of principles at one time. More specific principles were discussed later to ensure maximum familiarity. The interview breakdown was this:

- **Week 5:** General Engagement Principles — Initial
- **Week 6:** General Engagement Principles — Keeping
- **Week 7:** General Engagement Principles — Further; General Engagement Principles — User Response
- **Week 8:** User Awareness Principles
- **Week 9:** Interactivity Principles
- **Week 10:** Meaningful Play Principles
- **Week 11:** User Involvement Principles; External Factor
- **Week 12:** Visual Principles; Sound Principles; Music Principles

During each interview, participants were also asked the following open question to initiate discussion:

In what ways do you think the NRS could be made more engaging?

Each of the 39 principles was specifically addressed in the following way during the interview during their relevant week:

In what ways could the NRS better support [the principle]?

This information derived from the interviews intended to find how the NRS could be best updated to support the game design principles, as identified as important by the stroke survivors using the Likert scales.

The participants were allowed to answer in the most comfortable form (i.e., in person, over Skype or FaceTime or via email). The reason for this was to ensure that each stroke survivor would give their most informative answers because they felt as comfortable as possible. This was so that the stroke survivors did not become unnecessarily fatigued, which would impact their rehabilitation. While the intention was to answer the questions over 8 weeks, most stroke survivors felt they could answer some earlier and therefore did. This concession was made for the same reasons as the different interview forms.

Results

The complete breakdown of how each participant answered the questions (which was the format they were most comfortable with) is presented below:

- Participant 1 completed the questionnaire over five interviews via FaceTime.
- Participant 2 completed the questionnaire over seven interviews via Skype.
- Participant 3 completed the questionnaire during a single, in-person interview.
- Participant 4 completed the questionnaire over two in-person interviews.
- Participant 5 supplied the questionnaire's answers in a Microsoft Word document via email over eight weeks.
- Participant 6 completed the questionnaire over two in-person interviews.

Game Design Principles Responses

The responses each participant gave for each game design principle are shown in Table 5.

Table 5. Likert Scale Responses (Pre-Test)

Group	Principle	Participant 1	Participant 2	Participant 3	Participant 4	Participant 5	Participant 6	Total Score
General Engagement Principles — Initial	Arousal	Somewhat	Somewhat	To a Great Extent	To a Great Extent	Very Little	To a Great Extent	20
	Attention	Somewhat	To a Great Extent	To a Great Extent	To a Great Extent	To a Great Extent	To a Great Extent	23
	Interest	To a Great Extent	To a Great Extent	To a Great Extent	To a Great Extent	Very Little	To a Great Extent	22
General Engagement Principles — Keeping	Immersion	Very Little	To a Great Extent	To a Great Extent	To a Great Extent	Somewhat	Not at All	18
	Involvement	To a Great Extent	To a Great Extent	To a Great Extent	To a Great Extent	To a Great Extent	Somewhat	23
	Presence	Not at All	To a Great Extent	To a Great Extent	To a Great Extent	Very Little	To a Great Extent	19
	Psychological Absorption	To a Great Extent	To a Great Extent	To a Great Extent	To a Great Extent	Very Little	To a Great Extent	22
General Engagement Principles — Further	Motivation	To a Great Extent	To a Great Extent	To a Great Extent	To a Great Extent	Somewhat	To a Great Extent	23
	Effort	To a Great Extent	To a Great Extent	To a Great Extent	To a Great Extent	Somewhat	To a Great Extent	23
General Engagement Principles — User Response	Delight	Somewhat	Somewhat	To a Great Extent	Very Little	Not at All	Somewhat	16
	Enjoyment	To a Great Extent	To a Great Extent	To a Great Extent	Very Little	Very Little	Somewhat	19
	Coolness	Not at All	Not at All	Very Little	Not at All	Not at All	To a Great Extent	10
User Awareness Principles	Awareness	To a Great Extent	To a Great Extent	To a Great Extent	To a Great Extent	To a Great Extent	To a Great Extent	24
	Feedback	To a Great Extent	To a Great Extent	To a Great Extent	To a Great Extent	To a Great Extent	To a Great Extent	24
	Clear Instructions	To a Great Extent	To a Great Extent	Somewhat	To a Great Extent	To a Great Extent	To a Great Extent	23
	Improvisation	Somewhat	Not at All	To a Great Extent	Not at All	Somewhat	Very Little	14
	Usability	To a Great Extent	To a Great Extent	To a Great Extent	To a Great Extent	To a Great Extent	Somewhat	23
Interactivity Principles	Interactivity	To a Great Extent	To a Great Extent	To a Great Extent	To a Great Extent	To a Great Extent	To a Great Extent	24
	Choice	To a Great Extent	To a Great Extent	To a Great Extent	Not at All	Very Little	To a Great Extent	19
	Perceived Control	To a Great Extent	Somewhat	To a Great Extent	Not at All	To a Great Extent	To a Great Extent	20
Flow Principles	Flow	To a Great Extent	To a Great Extent	To a Great Extent	To a Great Extent	To a Great Extent	To a Great Extent	24
	Challenge	To a Great Extent	To a Great Extent	To a Great Extent	To a Great Extent	To a Great Extent	To a Great Extent	24

Continued on following page

Table 5. Continued

Group	Principle	Participant 1	Participant 2	Participant 3	Participant 4	Participant 5	Participant 6	Total Score
Meaningful Play Principles	**Novelty**	Somewhat	Somewhat	To a Great Extent	Not at All	Somewhat	Not at All	15
	Purpose	To a Great Extent	To a Great Extent	To a Great Extent	To a Great Extent	Very Little	To a Great Extent	22
	Fun	To a Great Extent	To a Great Extent	To a Great Extent	Not at All	Somewhat	Somewhat	19
	Reward	To a Great Extent	To a Great Extent	Somewhat	Not at All	Somewhat	To a Great Extent	19
	Socialisation	Very Little	Somewhat	To a Great Extent	Somewhat	Not at All	To a Great Extent	17
User Involvement Principles	**Identification**	Very Little	Somewhat	Somewhat	To a Great Extent	Not at All	To a Great Extent	17
	Emotional Connection	To a Great Extent	Somewhat	Not at All	To a Great Extent	Not at All	Somewhat	16
	Story	Somewhat	Not at All	Not at All	Very Little	Somewhat	Very Little	12
External Factor	**Safe Environment**	Very Little	To a Great Extent	Not at All	To a Great Extent	To a Great Extent	To a Great Extent	19
Visual Principles	**Low Fidelity Graphics**	Very Little	Very Little	Very Little	To a Great Extent	Not at All	To a Great Extent	15
	High Fidelity Graphics	Very Little	To a Great Extent	To a Great Extent	Very Little	To a Great Extent	Very Little	18
	First-Person View	Somewhat	To a Great Extent	To a Great Extent	To a Great Extent	Somewhat	To a Great Extent	22
	Third-Person View	To A Great Extent	To a Great Extent	Somewhat	Not at all	Not at all	Somewhat	16
Sound Principles	**Feedback Sounds**	Somewhat	To a Great Extent	Somewhat	To a Great Extent	Very Little	To a Great Extent	20
	Ambient Sounds	Somewhat	Somewhat	Very Little	To a Great Extent	Very Little	Very Little	16
Music Principles	**Feedback Music**	To a Great Extent	Somewhat	Not at All	Very Little	Not at All	Somewhat	14
	Ambient Music	To a Great Extent	Somewhat	Not at All	To a Great Extent	Not at All	Somewhat	16

The total scores were then ranked and grouped based on the importance groupings described in Table 4. The results are shown in Table 6, with "pts." standing for "points."

Table 6. Game Design Principle Rankings

Warrant the Focus of Further Investigation (24 pts.)	Also Important to a Great Extent (21 – 23 pts.)	High Importance (18 – 20 pts.)	Somewhat Important (12 – 17 pts.)	Little Importance (6 – 11 pts.)
• Awareness (24 pts.) • Feedback (24 pts.) • Interactivity (24 pts.) • Flow (24 pts.) • Challenge (24 pts.)	• Attention (23 pts.) • Involvement (23 pts.) • Motivation (23 pts.) • Effort (23 pts.) • Clear Instructions (23 pts.) • Usability (23 pts.) • Interest (22 pts.) • Psychological Absorption (22 pts.) • Purpose (22 pts.) • First-Person View (22 pts.)	• Arousal (20 pts.) • Perceived Control (20 pts.) • Feedback Sounds (20 pts.) • Presence (19 pts.) • Enjoyment (19 pts.) • Choice (19 pts.) • Fun (19 pts.) • Reward (19 pts.) • Safe Environment (19 pts.) • Immersion (18 pts.) • High Fidelity Graphics (18 pts.)	• Socialisation (17 pts.) • Identification (17 pts.) • Delight (16 pts.) • Emotional Connection (16 pts.) • Third Person View (16 pts.) • Ambient Sounds (16 pts.) • Ambient Music (16 pts.) • Novelty (15 pts.) • Low Fidelity Graphics (15 pts.) • Improvisation (14 pts.) • Feedback Music (14 pts.) • Story (12 pts.)	• Coolness (10 pts.)

VR Intervention Improvements

Participant 1 requested more informative feedback on performance during gameplay and that this could be supported by more sound and music cues. For the web portal's feedback, he requested greater detail on how to self-analyse the scores and a more in-depth breakdown of the meaning of scores to be given, with trends being displayed. This would be so his performance can be better understood, and he can therefore define his own goals on how to progress during his rehabilitation. He also suggested that players could compare their performance with other players for competitive reasons while also providing feedback. For variety, he suggested more variation in how rings are placed along the in-game track, the possibility of having a single game speed up and slow down for increased difficulty and the addition of more game options (courses, game speeds, etc.).

Participant 2 expressed a desire for better feedback in the form of a graph showing performance over a day, week or month. She also requested the use of sound and music cues for feedback during a game, including a special sound cue for when achieving a perfect score on a given ring. She also said that showing a comparison between current ability and predicted ability would assist the player with understanding their improvement. For variety, she also suggested adding more exercises, courses and game options, including making some courses secret and unlockable with achievements (such as a specific score or goal).

Participant 3, like 1 and 2, also wanted more detail on what graphs on the web portal mean to better understand his performance and how to improve. He was a big proponent of a first-person view, saying that the game would become very novel and interesting. He described the elevation gauge as "too broad" and should be made clearer and "definite". He suggested that the gauge could have different coloured regions to help show how far the player's arm angle is from the threshold. He also said that the black bar on the gauge could be made thinner to make it clearer how the player's arm angle relates to the threshold.

He also suggested that the centre of rings could have a bullseye for clarity. Finally, he said that being able to move the Wingman horizontally could be an interesting addition.

Participant 4 said that the game should give more informative feedback on how well a player did on a given ring, including how far away they were from the ring's centre. Overall feedback should tell the player which aspect of the game they should focus on to increase their score while also going into more detail on a player's overall performance. The web portal's graphs need a more in-depth explanation to clarify what they mean in relation to player performance. Finally, she indicated her preference for a first-person view since the Wingman blocks the rings in the game view, making her feel frustrated, thereby decreasing her engagement.

Participant 5 stressed that the game needs more complexity, variety and exercises. Since he felt the game was rather simple, the game became very unengaging after many weeks with the NRS. He was also frustrated by having to request increases to the angle threshold from the clinician, feeling that it would be better if the threshold increased automatically, with the criteria for an increase being clearly described. He also noted that the web portal would give inconsistent scores with the game itself and that those shown on the portal did not reflect his performance. He also noted that the Kinect sensor would sometimes act jerky, negatively affecting his engagement. Sometimes the game would not allow him to play more than two games in a session, even though three were explicitly allowed.

Participant 6 emphasised that a more substantial explanation of what the web portal graphs mean, including what he should focus upon in the game to improve, should be given. He also felt that the in-game feedback was distracting and should be simplified for clarity. He said that some of this feedback could be replaced with sounds. He indicated that a gradient should be added to the threshold bar (becoming lighter at the centre) to make it easier to see where the black line should be (and therefore how the arm should be angled) for a perfect score to be achieved. He also felt that a bullseye should be added to each ring's centre to make it clearer where the player should be positioned to get a perfect score. He did not find the metres to the next ring counter useful and said that a second to the next ring counter would be more useful in preparing for the next ring. He also found that the sensor would misbehave, giving him poor control over the game, impacting his engagement. Finally, he requested a first-person view to have a clear view of the rings.

Analysis and Discussion

"Game Design Principles Responses" analyses and discusses the results from "Results" — "Game Design Principles Responses", while "VR Intervention Feedback" analyses and discusses the results from "Results" — "VR Intervention Feedback".

Game Design Principles Responses

Warranting the focus of further investigation (with a full 24 points each, meaning all 6 stroke survivors agreed they were important "to a great extent") are *awareness, feedback, interactivity, flow* and *challenge*. Lohse et al. (2013) found that *feedback, interactivity* and *challenge* have an empirical basis for increasing user engagement and motivation with a rehabilitation tool. Having 24 points gives them a basis for likely increasing user engagement with VR-based upper limb rehabilitation post-stroke. Burke et al. (2009) also identified *challenge* as important for engaging stroke survivors with Serious Game-based upper limb rehabilitation. The use of Serious Game-based upper limb rehabilitation in a desktop

VR setting further highlights its importance. The large emphasis on *flow* and *challenge* together makes sense since *flow* is a balance between challenge and skill, with *flow* being highlighted as important by Brockmyer et al. (2009), Rabin (2010) and Whitton (2011). O'Brien and Toms (2008) recognised the importance of *awareness* for engagement, and the results further support this.

Lohse et al. (2013) also identified *reward* and *choice* (both with 19 points) as important engagement principles, and here they were still reasonably well supported. Burke et al. (2009) also placed a large emphasis on meaningful play and split it into five principles: *novelty*, *purpose*, *fun*, *reward* and *socialisation*. *Purpose* was also identified as important to a great extend with 22 points, while *fun* and *reward* were also recognised as important with 19 points. *Novelty* was only recognised as somewhat important with 15 points. Of note, the only principle of little importance was *coolness* with 10 points, suggested by Desurvire and Wixon (2013) within the principles of "PLAY".

VR Intervention Improvements

Better feedback, larger gameplay variety and use of a first-person view were the most common requests for the NRS to better support engagement. For better feedback, the participants requested reducing the amount of in-game feedback so that visual cues are kept to a minimum (potentially replacing them with sound) to increase focus on performing the exercise. Another request included modifying the arm angle gauge's black bar to be thinner and adding a gradient to the arm angle threshold bar (that gets lighter closer to the middle). The black bar could then be slotted into the middle of the gradient, making it easier to find where to angle the arm for a perfect score. Two final requests were adding bullseyes to the centre of rings (so where the player needs to hit is shown) and changing the metres to the next ring to seconds to the next ring (as this is more informative in telling a player how long they have to prepare for the next ring).

Regarding external feedback, the participants wanted more informative breakdowns on what the scores and the graphs on the web portal mean in terms of performance. Such information would include how to self-analyse scores and trends in performance outcomes. One request was to also show a graph at the conclusion of a day, week or month and show outcomes for that timespan to visualise improvements in performance (including displaying trends). Players should also be told which area they should focus upon to improve (i.e. playing more often, increasing their score, or having their angle threshold increased). This feedback will provide players with an improved understanding of how they are performing and how to improve. More courses, game speed options and exercises were requested for a larger variety within the NRS.

Improved feedback (with the increased understanding of prior performance and how to perform better in the future that it brings) will support the principles of *feedback*, *clear instructions*, *usability* and *purpose*, while also improving player *awareness*, *attention*, *involvement*, *motivation*, *effort*, *interest* and *psychological absorption*. Because a player will better understand how to perform, the balance between challenge and control will be improved, supporting *flow* and making the player more likely to go for increased *challenge*. A first-person view will make a player feel like the Wingman because they will be looking through his eyes. This will make the game feel more *interactive* and increase player *awareness*, *attention*, *involvement*, *interest* and *psychological absorption* since they will see the game world without obstruction.

FUTURE RESEARCH DIRECTIONS

Further research would be required to determine which game design principles engage stroke survivors with the NRS, but these game design principles provide a strong basis for orienting that research. Once the NRS is updated by taking the stroke survivor feedback into account, the NRS can be used to determine whether the 13 game design principles that were determined as likely to engage do engage the stroke survivors that participated in this study. However, stroke survivors will be asked whether they feel the NRS adequately supports a given game design principle before being asked how much that game design principle supports their engagement. This would be to ensure that their opinion of how well that game design principle engages is informed.

This study evaluated which of the 39 game design principles are likely to engage with a Desktop VR-based upper-limb rehabilitation tool. However, applying the same theory, further research could evaluate which game design principles are likely to engage with other types of rehabilitation using VR. These other types of rehabilitation may include other types of physical rehabilitation, including lower limb, balance and motor skills. The 39 game design principles may also be applied in similar research related to cognitive rehabilitation, such as rehabilitation of cognitive speed, memory, orientation, attention, language skills, visuospatial ability and abstracted reasoning. This future work will help further develop the gamification of stroke rehabilitation to make it more engaging.

CONCLUSION

Stroke is a debilitating condition that impairs one's ability to live independently, while also greatly decreasing quality of life. For these reasons, stroke rehabilitation is important. Engagement is a crucial part of rehabilitation, increasing a stroke survivor's recovery rate and positive outcomes of their rehabilitation. For this reason, VR has been very widely used to gamify stroke rehabilitation to support engagement. While VR-based therapy may or may not be more beneficial than conventional therapy on its own (as there is no consensus on this), the engagement and accessibility of in-home VR therapy aspects will likely have a positive effect on the rehabilitation overall.

Given that VR and the Serious Games that form their base may not necessarily be engaging in themselves, ensuring the game design is engaging is important. This chapter discussed 39 game design principles that may be useful for engaging stroke survivors with VR-based rehabilitation post-stroke:

1. **General Engagement Principles — Initial:** *Arousal, attention* and *interest.*
2. **General Engagement Principles — Keeping:** *Immersion, presence, involvement* and *psychological absorption.*
3. **General Engagement Principles — Further:** *Motivation* and *effort.*
4. **General Engagement Principles — User Response:** *Delight, enjoyment* and *coolness.*
5. **User Awareness Principles:** *Awareness, feedback, clear instructions, improvisational* and *usability.*
6. **Interactivity Principles:** *Interactivity, choice* and *perceived control.*
7. **Flow Principles:** *Flow* and *optimal challenge.*
8. **Meaningful Play Principles:** *Novelty, purpose, fun, rewards* and *socialisation.*
9. **User Involvement Principles:** *Identification, emotional connection* and *story.*
10. **External Factors:** *Safe environment.*

11. **Visual Principles:** *Low* and *high-fidelity graphics*; *first-person* and *third-person view*.
12. **Sound Principles:** *Ambient* and *feedback sounds*.
13. **Music Principles:** *Ambient* and *feedback music*.

This chapter then demonstrated their application in VR-based upper limb rehabilitation post-stroke for optimising engagement. For this application, this subset, i.e. 5, of the 39 game design principles were found to warrant further investigation: *awareness, feedback, interactivity, flow, challenge*; another subset, i.e. 10 out of 39, was found to also be important to a great extent for engaging: *attention, involvement, motivation, effort, clear instructions, usability, interest, psychological absorption, purpose* and a *first-person view* (Table 6). This demonstrates that the methodology utilised here may be applied to research into what engages stroke survivors with other types of VR-based rehabilitation. Such rehabilitation may be physical or cognitive to optimise their engagement level as well. This work demonstrates the importance of gamification to enable engagement with stroke rehabilitation using VR and Serious Games.

ACKNOWLEDGMENT

This research was supported by an Australian Government Research Training Program (RTP) scholarship.

REFERENCES

Aminov, A., Rogers, J. M., Middleton, S., Caeyenberghs, K., & Wilson, P. H. (2018). What do randomized controlled trials say about virtual rehabilitation in stroke? A systematic literature review and meta-analysis of upper-limb and cognitive outcomes. *Journal of Neuroengineering and Rehabilitation*, *15*(1), 29–24. doi:10.118612984-018-0370-2 PMID:29587853

Brockmyer, J. H., Fox, C. M., Curtiss, K. A., McBroom, E., Burkhart, K. M., & Pidruzny, J. N. (2009). The development of the Game Engagement Questionnaire: A measure of engagement in video game-playing. *Journal of Experimental Social Psychology*, *45*(4), 624–634. doi:10.1016/j.jesp.2009.02.016

Brown, S. (2010). *Likert Scale Examples for Surveys*. Iowa State University Extension. https://www.extension.iastate.edu/Documents/ANR/LikertScaleExamplesforSurveys.pdf

Bruno, M. A., & Griffiths, L. (2014). Serious games: supporting occupational engagement of people aged 50+ based on intelligent tutoring systems/Juegos serios: apoyo a la participación ocupacional de personas mayores de 50 años basado en sistemas de tutoría inteligente. *Ingeniare. Revista Chilena de Ingeniería*, *22*(1), 125. doi:10.4067/S0718-33052014000100012

Buijs-Spanjers, K. R., Hegge, H. H. M., Cnossen, F., Hoogendoorn, E., Jaarsma, D. A. D. C., & de Rooij, S. E. (2019). Dark Play of Serious Games: Effectiveness and Features (G4HE2018). *Games for Health Journal*, *8*(4), 301–306. doi:10.1089/g4h.2018.0126 PMID:30964340

Burke, J. W., McNeill, M. D. J., Charles, D. K., Morrow, P. J., Crosbie, J. H., & McDonough, S. M. (2009). Optimising engagement for stroke rehabilitation using serious games. *The Visual Computer*, *25*(12), 1085–1099. doi:10.100700371-009-0387-4

Connolly, T. M., Hainley, T., Boyle, E., Baxter, G., & Moreno-Ger, P. (2014). *Psychology, Pedagogy, and Assessment in Serious Games*. Information Science Reference. doi:10.4018/978-1-4666-4773-2

Dele-Ajayi, O., Sanderson, J., Strachan, R., & Pickard, A. (2016). *Learning mathematics through serious games: An engagement framework*. Academic Press.

Desurvire, H., & Wixon, D. (2013). Game principles: choice, change & creativity: making better games. CHI '13 Extended Abstracts on Human Factors in Computing Systems, Paris, France.

Fluet, G. G., Qiu, Q., Patel, J., Cronce, A., Merians, A. S., & Adamovich, S. V. (2019). Autonomous Use of the Home Virtual Rehabilitation System: A Feasibility and Pilot Study. *Games for Health Journal*, *8*(6), 432–438. doi:10.1089/g4h.2019.0012 PMID:31769724

Garcia-Agundez, A., Reuter, C., Becker, H., Konrad, R., Caserman, P., Miede, A., & Göbel, S. (2019). Development of a Classifier to Determine Factors Causing Cybersickness in Virtual Reality Environments. *Games for Health Journal, 8*(6), 439–444. doi:10.1089/g4h.2019.0045 PMID:31295007

Henderson, A., Korner-Bitensky, N., & Levin, M. (2007). Virtual reality in stroke rehabilitation: A systematic review of its effectiveness for upper limb motor recovery. *Topics in Stroke Rehabilitation*, *14*(2), 52–61. doi:10.1310/tsr1402-52 PMID:17517575

Herne, R., Shiratuddin, M. F., Rai, S., Laga, H., Dixon, J., & Blacker, D. (2019). *Game design principles influencing stroke survivor engagement for VR-Based upper limb rehabilitation*. 31st Australian Conference on Human-Computer-Interaction (OzCHI), Esplanade Hotel, Fremantle, Australia.

Howard, M. C. (2017). A meta-analysis and systematic literature review of virtual reality rehabilitation programs. *Computers in Human Behavior*, *70*, 317–327. doi:10.1016/j.chb.2017.01.013

Ishak, N. M., Bakar, A., & Yazid, A. (2014). Developing Sampling Frame for Case Study: Challenges and Conditions. *World Journal of Education*, *4*(3), 29–35.

Jeong, S., & Kim, M. T. (2007). Effects of a theory-driven music and movement program for stroke survivors in a community setting. *Applied Nursing Research*, *20*(3), 125–131. doi:10.1016/j.apnr.2007.04.005 PMID:17693215

Kalawsky, R. S. (1993). *The Science of Virtual Reality and Virtual Environments: A Technical, Scientific and Engineering Reference on Virtual Environments*. Addison-Wesley Longman Publishing Co., Inc.

Kourtesis, P., Collina, S., Doumas, L. A. A., & MacPherson, S. E. (2019). Validation of the Virtual Reality Neuroscience Questionnaire: Maximum Duration of Immersive Virtual Reality Sessions Without the Presence of Pertinent Adverse Symptomatology. *Frontiers in Human Neuroscience*, *13*, 417–417. doi:10.3389/fnhum.2019.00417 PMID:31849627

Langstaff, C., Martin, C., Brown, G., McGuinness, D., Mather, J., Loshaw, J., Jones, N., Fletcher, K., & Paterson, J. (2014). Enhancing community-based rehabilitation for stroke survivors: Creating a discharge link. *Topics in Stroke Rehabilitation*, *21*(6), 510–519. doi:10.1310/tsr2106-510 PMID:25467399

Laver, K. E., Lange, B., George, S., Deutsch, J. E., Saposnik, G., Crotty, M., & Laver, K. E. (2017). Virtual reality for stroke rehabilitation. *Cochrane Database of Systematic Reviews*, *2018*(1), CD008349. doi:10.1002/14651858.CD008349.pub4 PMID:29156493

Lee, H. S., Park, Y. J., & Park, S. W. (2019). The Effects of Virtual Reality Training on Function in Chronic Stroke Patients: A Systematic Review and Meta-Analysis. *BioMed Research International*, *2019*, 1–12. doi:10.1155/2019/7595639 PMID:31317037

Lohse, K., Shirzad, N., Verster, A., Hodges, N., & Van der Loos, H. F. M. (2013). Video Games and Rehabilitation: Using Design Principles to Enhance Engagement in Physical Therapy. *Journal of Neurologic Physical Therapy; JNPT*, *37*(4), 166–175. doi:10.1097/NPT.0000000000000017 PMID:24232363

Lyons, E. J. (2015). Cultivating Engagement and Enjoyment in Exergames Using Feedback, Challenge, and Rewards. *Games for Health Journal*, *4*(1), 12–18. doi:10.1089/g4h.2014.0072 PMID:26181675

MacDonald, G. A., Kayes, N. M., & Bright, F. (2013). Barriers and facilitators to engagement in rehabilitation for people with stroke: A review of the literature. *New Zealand Journal of Physiotherapy*, *41*(3), 112.

Martey, R. M., Kenski, K., Folkestad, J., Feldman, L., Gordis, E., Shaw, A., Stromer-Galley, J., Clegg, B., Zhang, H., Kaufman, N., Rabkin, A. N., Shaikh, S., & Strzalkowski, T. (2014). Measuring Game Engagement: Multiple Methods and Construct Complexity. *Simulation & Gaming*, *45*(4-5), 528–547. doi:10.1177/1046878114553575

Martin, M. W. (2012). *Serious game design principles: The impact of game design on learning outcomes*. ProQuest Dissertations Publishing.

McDaniel, R., Fiore, S. M., & Nicholson, D. (2010). Serious Storytelling: Narrative Considerations for Serious Games Researchers and Developers. In Serious Game Design and Development: Technologies for Training and Learning (pp. 13-30). IGI Global. doi:10.4018/978-1-61520-739-8.ch002

Murdoch University. (2015). *Virtual Reality software brings hope to stroke survivors*. Murdoch University. Retrieved 6/3/2019 from http://web.archive.org/web/20180331035704/http://media.murdoch.edu. au/virtual-reality-software-brings-hope-to-stroke-survivors

Norman, L. (2014). Stroke rehabilitation: Promoting physical recovery. *Nursing And Residential Care*, *16*(12), 699–702. doi:10.12968/nrec.2014.16.12.699

O'Brien, H. L., & Toms, E. G. (2008). What is user engagement? A conceptual framework for defining user engagement with technology. *Journal of the American Society for Information Science and Technology*, *59*(6), 938–955. doi:10.1002/asi.20801

Oates, B. J. (2006). *Researching information systems and computing*. SAGE Publications Ltd.

Oxarart, A., Weaver, J., Al-Bataineh, A., & Mohamed, T. A. B. (2014). Game Design Principles and Motivation. *The International Journal of the Arts in Society*, *7*(2), 347.

Oxford Dictionary of English (3rd ed.). (2010). Oxford University Press.

Patricio, R., Moreira, A., Zurlo, F., & Melazzini, M. (2020). Co-creation of new solutions through gamification: A collaborative innovation practice. *Creativity and Innovation Management*, *29*(1), 146–160. doi:10.1111/caim.12356

Patrício, R., Moreira, A. C., & Zurlo, F. (2018). Gamification approaches to the early stage of innovation. *Creativity and Innovation Management, 27*(4), 499–511. doi:10.1111/caim.12284

Pimentel, K., & Teixeira, K. (1995). *Virtual Reality: Through the New Looking Glass* (2nd ed.). Intel/McGraw-Hill.

Ploderer, B., Stuart, J., Tran, V., Green, T., & Muller, J. (2017). *The transition of stroke survivors from hospital to home: understanding work and design opportunities.* OZCHI. doi:10.1145/3152771.3152772

Rabin, S. (2010). *Introduction to game development* (2nd ed.). Course Technology, Cengage Learning.

Simões-Silva, V., Duarte Mesquita, A. F., Santos Da Silva, K. L., Arouca Quental, V. S., & Marques, A. (2021). Gamification as Upper Limb Rehabilitation Process. In R. A. Peixoto de Queirós & A. J. Marques (Eds.), *Handbook of Research on Solving Modern Healthcare Challenges With Gamification* (pp. 243–257). IGI Global. doi:10.4018/978-1-7998-7472-0.ch013

Viñas-Diz, S., & Sobrido-Prieto, M. (2016). Virtual reality for therapeutic purposes in stroke: A systematic review. *Neurologia (Barcelona, Spain), 31*(4), 255–277. PMID:26321468

Warlow, C., Sudlow, C., Dennis, M., Wardlaw, J., & Sandercock, P. (2003). Stroke. *Lancet, 362*(9391), 1211–1224. doi:10.1016/S0140-6736(03)14544-8 PMID:14568745

What is a stroke. (2021). *Stroke Foundation.* Retrieved 4/8/2021 from https://strokefoundation.org.au/About-Stroke/Learn/Types-of-stroke

Whitton, N. (2011). Game Engagement Theory and Adult Learning. *Simulation & Gaming, 42*(5), 596–609. doi:10.1177/1046878110378587

ADDITIONAL READING

Burke, J. W., McNeill, M. D. J., Charles, D. K., Morrow, P. J., Crosbie, J. H., & McDonough, S. M. (2009). Optimising engagement for stroke rehabilitation using serious games. *The Visual Computer, 25*(12), 1085–1099. doi:10.100700371-009-0387-4

Deloitte Access Economics. (2020). *The economic impact of stroke in Australia, 2020.* https://www2.deloitte.com/content/dam/Deloitte/au/Documents/Economics/deloitte-au-dae-economic-impact-stroke-report-061120.pdf

Herne, R., Shiratuddin, M. F., Rai, S., Laga, H., Dixon, J., & Blacker, D. (2019). *Game design principles influencing stroke survivor engagement for VR-Based upper limb rehabilitation.* 31st Australian Conference on Human-Computer-Interaction (OzCHI), Esplanade Hotel, Fremantle, Australia.

Lohse, K., Shirzad, N., Verster, A., Hodges, N., & Van der Loos, H. F. M. (2013). Video Games and Rehabilitation: Using Design Principles to Enhance Engagement in Physical Therapy. *Journal of Neurologic Physical Therapy; JNPT, 37*(4), 166–175. doi:10.1097/NPT.0000000000000017 PMID:24232363

Rabin, S. (2010). *Introduction to game development* (2nd ed.). Course Technology, Cengage Learning.

Simões-Silva, V., Duarte Mesquita, A. F., Santos Da Silva, K. L., Arouca Quental, V. S., & Marques, A. (2021). Gamification as Upper Limb Rehabilitation Process. In R. A. Peixoto de Queirós & A. J. Marques (Eds.), *Handbook of Research on Solving Modern Healthcare Challenges With Gamification* (pp. 243–257). IGI Global. doi:10.4018/978-1-7998-7472-0.ch013

Whitton, N. (2011). Game Engagement Theory and Adult Learning. *Simulation & Gaming*, *42*(5), 596–609. doi:10.1177/1046878110378587

KEY TERMS AND DEFINITIONS

Engagement: Having one's attention or interest attracted or occupied (*Oxford Dictionary of English*, 2010).

Game Design Principle: A single concept that can inform a segment or the entirety of the specifications of a game.

Non-Serious Game: A game designed purely for entertainment.

Rehabilitation: "The action of restoring someone to health or normal life through training and therapy after imprisonment, addiction, or illness" (*Oxford Dictionary of English*, 2010).

Serious Game: Games with greater aims than entertainment, intended for learning and behavioural alteration (Connolly et al., 2014).

Stroke: "The clinical syndrome of rapid onset of focal (or global, as in subarachnoid haemorrhage) cerebral deficit, lasting more than 24 hours or leading to death, with no apparent cause other than a vascular one" (Warlow et al., 2003).

Virtual Reality (VR): "A computer-based, interactive, multisensory simulation environment that occurs in real-time. VR presents users with opportunities to engage in activities within environments that appear, to various extents, similar to real-world objects and events" (Henderson et al., 2007).

Chapter 12
The Effects of Gamification on Nurse Work Motivation

Jaana-Maija Koivisto
iD https://orcid.org/0000-0001-5846-9360
Häme University of Applied Sciences, Finland

Ira H. Saarinen
iD https://orcid.org/0000-0001-8631-2897
Etelä-Pohjanmaa District Hospital, Finland

Elina Haavisto
iD https://orcid.org/0000-0002-9747-1428
Tampere University, Finland

Jari Multisilta
iD https://orcid.org/0000-0002-5636-6365
Satakunta University of Applied Sciences, Finland

Antti J. Kaipia
Pirkanmaa Hospital District, Finland

ABSTRACT

A current concern in the medical field is that nurses leave their careers due to low work motivation. Intrinsic motivation is a key factor that influences satisfaction in the workplace. This study aimed to develop a gamification intervention for implementation in a hospital setting and evaluate its effects on nurses' work motivation. It was hypothesized that nurses' work motivation would improve by the end of the intervention. The study was conducted in a surgical ward at a hospital in Finland. The design was descriptive and quasi-experimental. The study found that continuous feedback from gamification interventions influenced nurses' work motivation. The gamified group offered more positive feedback than the non-gamified group. These findings add to our understanding of the effects of gamification interventions on nurses' work motivation in hospital settings. However, more research is needed to demonstrate the potential of gamification to increase the retention of much-needed human resources.

DOI: 10.4018/978-1-7998-9223-6.ch012

INTRODUCTION

A key factor that influences well-being in the workplace is the intrinsic motivation experienced by employees (Deci & Ryan, 2008; Vansteenkiste et al., 2007). Intrinsically motivated employees are enthusiastic about the work itself, not just the external rewards that their job gives them (Gagne & Deci, 2005). According to the literature, a good work environment and workplace culture in hospitals are associated with good patient care (Aiken et al., 2012; Friese & Aiken, 2008; Hahtela et al., 2015). Nursing is the largest occupational group in the health sector (World Health Organization, 2020). However, concerns that nurses leave their careers due to low job satisfaction, lack of affective professional commitment, and poor opportunities for professional advancement (Flinkman et al., 2008; Tzeng, 2002) have arisen. There is an urgent need to improve the capacity to employ and retain nurses (World Health Organization, 2020). Nursing shortages are a global problem with serious consequences for the quality of care provided, as well as patient safety (Eckerson, 2018; Marć et al., 2019; World Health Organization, 2020). For example, in hospitals in Europe, many nurses are concerned with issues such as patient safety and quality of care, as adverse events, including healthcare-associated infections, often occur (Aiken et al., 2013). Thus, it is important that nurses experience intrinsic motivation, as this ensures high-quality patient care (Toode et al., 2015).

In this study, gamification was implemented by applying a four-phase framework (Blohm & Leimeister, 2013; Khaleel et al., 2016). First, the authors identified the main objective and reasons behind the use of gamification in a hospital setting. Second, the authors identified the factors that motivate nurses in their work. Third, the authors determined the game design elements of the intervention. Fourth, the authors evaluated the effects of the gamification intervention.

BACKGROUND

Gamification can be used to increase both the motivation and productivity of workers (Huotari & Hamari, 2011). Increased motivation typically leads to better results and more enjoyable work (Hamari et al., 2014). According to a study by Huotari and Hamari (2012), work-related intrinsic motivation and the reward of work can be promoted by applying gamification to workers' everyday work processes. Deterding et al. (2011) define "gamification" as the use of game design elements in non-game contexts. It can also be understood as the process of making activities more game-like (Werbach, 2014). In addition, gamification can comprise a process of enhancing a service with affordances for "gameful" experiences to support the user's overall value creation (Huotari & Hamari, 2012). Gamification is often based on the use of intrinsic motivation. Deci and Ryan (2004) developed a theory of self-determination that examines the choices people make without external influences (e.g., external rewards). According to Ryan (2009) "self-determination theory (SDT) is a macro-theory of human motivation, personality development, and well-being. The theory focuses especially on volitional or self-determined behaviour and the social and cultural conditions that promote it. SDT also postulates a set of basic and universal psychological needs, namely those for autonomy, competence and relatedness, the fulfilment of which is considered necessary and essential to vital, healthy human functioning regardless of culture or stage of development". Traditionally, different reward systems, such as financial rewards, non-monetary rewards and recognition have been used to influence employee motivation. However, rewards comprise external sources of motivation, and intrinsic motivation is more effective than external motivation at engaging employees. For example, Deci et al. (2001) stated that when a reward is taken away, an employee's motivation becomes even lower than it was before the reward was given.

In the healthcare field, gamification has been used to train people with Alzheimer's disease and their caregivers (Arambarri et al., 2014). It has also been used in in-home rehabilitation for stroke survivors (Tamayo-Serrano et al., 2018). Based on Tamayo-Serrano et al.'s (2018, p.1) review, "gamified systems are used to increase user motivation, hence gamified elements have been implemented into stroke rehabilitation therapies in order to improve patients' engagement and adherence." In addition, Roy-Burman et al. (2013, p. A23) aimed to support communication among hospital staff and improve peer recognition using social gamification, and the results of their study showed that "social gamification can enhance nursing engagement."

Game design elements include both game mechanics and dynamics (Deterding et al., 2011; Nicholson, 2012). Game mechanics cover the diverse features of games (e.g., scoring systems and badges), while game dynamics refer to the effects of those mechanics on the subjective user (Huotari & Hamari, 2012). Dynamics also correspond to users' motives (Blohm & Leimeister, 2013). Hamari et al. (2014) discussed the motivational affordances and psychological and behavioral outcomes of gamification. These affordances include points, leaderboards, achievements/badges, levels, stories/themes, clear goals, feedback, rewards, progress, and challenges. By utilizing motivational affordances, psychological outcomes such as motivation, a positive attitude, and enjoyment can be achieved. Behavioral outcomes, on the other hand, may be related to achieving goals and increasing knowledge, task performance, intention to use, and the quality of the completed tasks. To achieve permanent behavioral changes, the design elements used in the game should be meaningful, rewarding, and relevant to the user without the need for external rewards (Nicholson, 2012).

Different things motivate different people; thus, the gamified experience can vary. As a result, it is vital to understand the target group when gamifying work processes (Morschheuser et al., 2017) to increase motivation. Many published studies have described the factors related to nurses' work motivation. Motivational factors include appreciation (Kantek et al., 2015; Okello & Gilson, 2015), personal values and characteristics (Koch et al., 2014; Perreira et al., 2016), education (Perreira et al., 2016), salary (Negussie, 2012; Perreira et al., 2016), good cooperation (Perreira et al., 2016; Toode et al., 2011), high autonomy (Galletta et al., 2016; Perreira et al., 2016; Toode et al., 2011), appropriate working hours (Toode et al., 2011), opportunities to help others (Koch et al., 2014; Toode et al., 2011), rewards (Okello & Gilson, 2015), and meaningful work (Perreira et al., 2016; Toode et al., 2011). In addition to knowing the target group, it is important to understand the organizational context in which the gamification is being applied (Hamari et al., 2014; Morschheuser et al., 2017). Implementing gamification in a hospital setting can be challenging, as hospital workers deal with serious issues. Using the term "gamification" in this context can be misunderstood as "having fun at the patients' expense" or "playing with patients' lives" (Koivisto et al., 2017). Thus, it is vital for the success of the gamification project that the target group be involved in its ideation and design phases (Nicholson, 2012; Morschheuser et al., 2017). Involving the target group ensures that meaningful game design elements and goals that are in the interest of the target group are developed (Nicholson, 2012).

Although gamification might improve nurses' experiences of motivation in their work (Hamari et al., 2014; Khaleel et al., 2016) and therefore present a method of reducing nursing shortages, it has not yet been added to nurses' daily work routines. That is why the authors have chosen to develop a gamification intervention and evaluate its effect on nurses' work motivation.

Gamification Intervention

Objectives

The aim of this study was to develop a gamification intervention and evaluate its effects on nurses' work motivation. In this regard, the following research questions were addressed:

What game design elements will be applied to the gamification intervention?

1. Is there a difference in work motivation between the gamified and non-gamified groups in relation to
   a. how they perceive positive feedback?
   b. how they perceive the utilization of expertise?
   c. how they perceive the atmosphere in the workplace?
2. Upon discharge, is there a difference in patients' levels of knowledge of the postoperative instructions given to them by a nurse from the gamified group versus the non-gamified group?

It was hypothesized that, by using the gamification intervention, nurses' work motivation would be improved by the end of the intervention. In addition, it was hypothesized that a patient's knowledge of the postoperative instructions given to them by a nurse in the gamified group would be better than the instructions provided by a nurse in the non-gamified group.

Method and Design

This study was conducted in a single surgical ward at a central hospital in Finland. This hospital serves an area with a population of 230,000. Roughly 8,000 surgical operations are performed there annually. The study's design was descriptive and quasi-experimental. It consisted of a development phase and an evaluation phase.

Participants in the Development Phase

In this study, purposive sampling (Burns & Grove, 2005) was used mainly because of the limitations set up by the surgical ward. The entire staff body of the surgical ward was to participate in the intervention; thus, a ward with a small number of patients and staff members was selected for the study. All the nurses who worked in the ward participated in the focus group interviews (N = 12) and workshops (N = 18) in January 2018. More nurses participated in the workshops than in the interviews, as the ward had hired more staff following the interviews due to changes in its operations (specifically due to its opening hours changing).

Participants in the Evaluation Phase

In total, 18 nurses participated in the evaluation phase. The nurses who had cared for urologic patients participated in the data collection. Urologic patients and patients with ear, nose, throat, or eye diseases were treated in the surgical ward that participated in this study. Only urologic patients participated in the study (N = 55). Patients who met the following inclusion criteria were asked to participate in the study: a urologic patient who was co-operative upon their discharge, could speak Finnish, had certain physical and mental conditions that enabled their participation, and gave consent to participate. The exclusion criteria comprised patients with a dementia diagnosis (disorientation with regard to time and place), long-term patients, ambulatory patients, and patients with a rare diagnosis, the basis of which they were able to identify.

Ethical Considerations

This study was conducted in accordance with the Responsible Conduct of Research and Procedures for Handling Allegations of Misconduct in Finland (Finnish Advisory Board on Research Integrity, 2012). Permission to conduct the study was obtained from a chief physician at the central hospital. Ethical approval was received from the ethics committee of the higher education institution of Satakunta on December 27, 2017. The participants gave their informed consent to participate after they were informed of the research procedure and the duration of participation. They were told that participation was confidential and voluntary and that refusal to participate would not result in any consequences or affect their work or treatment in any way. Furthermore, they were informed that they could withdraw from the study at any time without consequence.

Development of the Gamification Intervention

The purpose of the development phase was to determine which game design elements would be applied in the intervention and to involve nurses in the ideation and design phases of the gamification intervention.

Phase 1

Previous studies suggest that gamification can have positive effects on motivation, and since it is important to involve the target group in defining game elements, the authors explored nurses' experiences regarding what motivates them in their everyday work. To determine the game design elements, focus group interviews and workshops were organized (Koivisto et al., 2021). This resulted in a gamification intervention that included game mechanics and game dynamics in the form of two online survey tools: nurses' Daily Experience of Work Motivation survey and Patient Education Knowledge Test (PEKTpat).

In December 2017, three focus group interviews were conducted. The nurses were asked to describe their perceptions of intrinsic work motivation in their everyday work. Then, in January 2018, three similar workshops were held in which the nurses were asked to describe the conditions that elicited and sustained intrinsic work motivation from the perspectives of autonomy, competence, and relatedness. One of the main results was that getting feedback was a key factor in the nurses' experience of competence (Koivisto et al., 2021). Another important finding was that collecting points, having leaderboards, competing against others, and comparing staff (good nurses vs. bad nurses) were not desired because they were not perceived to add value from the point of view of motivation—rather, they did the opposite. The results of the interviews and workshops were utilized in the development of a survey called nurses' Daily Experience of Work Motivation (DEWMnur).

During the workshops, the nurses participated in the development of a Patient Education Knowledge Test (PEKTpat), which was to be used as part of the gamification intervention. The PEKTpat was selected as part of the intervention due to the importance of patient education for patient recovery and the prevention of postoperative complications (Koivisto et al., 2020). The test was developed using existing patient instructions for urologic patients at a central hospital in Finland (N = 10). The patient instructions were based on the best available research evidence and clinicians' clinical expertise (Jordan et al., 2019). By analyzing patient instructions, similarities and differences in self-care instructions after surgery were identified. Similar instructions were selected for further consideration, as the goal was to create a generic knowledge test suitable for all urologic patients, regardless of the diagnosis or treatment procedure. The clinical experience of nurses in patient education was of great importance when analyzing the patient instructions and in determining the similarities in the self-care instructions. The nurses had valuable tacit knowledge of their patients' ability to receive information after their surgical procedures and to utilize it in their self-care after their discharge.

Phase 2

In the second development phase of the gamification intervention, the DEWMnur and the PEKTpat were further developed and finalized. During this phase, a multidisciplinary research team consisting of two medical doctors, one registered nurse specialized in urological nursing, one senior researcher of nursing science and multimedia, and one postdoctoral researcher with expertise in the gamification of education and nursing, participated. In the focus group interviews and workshops, the factors that were considered to influence nurses' work motivation were positive feedback, utilization of expertise, and a good workplace atmosphere (Koivisto et al., 2021). Since each nurse was supposed to complete the survey after each shift, the goal was to develop short and quick queries. Behind the development of the PEKTpat was evidence that over 30% of postoperative complications occur at home within 30 days following hospital discharge (Bilimoria et al., 2010; Wanzel et al., 2000) and that patient education may affect the occurrence of postoperative complications (Koivisto et al., 2020). As a result of this evidence, the items selected for the knowledge test were related to 1) knowing how to prevent complications, 2) identifying the most common symptoms associated with complications, and 3) knowing what to do when these symptoms occur.

Description of the Game Design Elements

Game design elements comprise game mechanics and game dynamics (Blohm & Leimeister, 2013; Deterding et al., 2011). The game mechanics of the intervention in this study included two gamification elements: PEKTpat and DEWMnur (Table 1). These elements enabled nurses to receive immediate and continuous feedback on their work motivation and the outcomes of their work (game dynamics), which, in turn, could correspond to the nurses' motivation in their work.

Table 1. Game design elements of the intervention

Game mechanics	Game dynamics
Gamification element: PEKTpat Patient scores in PEKTpat Weekly chart of the PEKTpat results	Immediate feedback was received from PEKTpat so that the nurses in the experimental group could see each patient's score in the test. This indicated the outcome of the nurses' own work (result of patient education = patient has understood their postoperative instructions). Continuous feedback from PEKTpat was presented to the nurses in the experimental group every Monday as a chart showing the results of the previous week.
Gamification element: DEWMnur Weekly chart of the DEWMnur results	Continuous feedback from the nurses' DEWMnur was presented to the nurses in the experimental group every Monday as a chart showing the results of previous week.

Game Mechanics

The PEKTpat gamification element consisted of 10 multiple-choice items and two items measured using a four-point Likert scale. The multiple-choice items included correct and incorrect answer options. However, the research team did not want patients to be misled; thus, the correct answer and justification for it were given for each question. In addition to the knowledge test, the patients were asked to rate their satisfaction with the education they received. This rating used a four-point Likert scale. The DEWMnur gamification element consisted of 10 items measured using a five-point Likert scale. These items are presented in Table 2.

Table 2. Sum of the variables and items in the DEWMnur element

POSITIVE FEEDBACK	Cronbach's alpha = .85
I have experienced that my competence is valued.	
I have received positive feedback from patients.	
I have received positive feedback from colleagues.	
I have received positive feedback from my manager.	
I have given positive feedback.	
UTILIZATION OF EXPERTISE	Cronbach's alpha = .83
I have coped with a challenging situation.	
I have shared my expertise with colleagues.	
I have used my expertise in decision-making related to patient care.	
I have received support from my colleagues in my decision-making.	
POSITIVE WORK ATMOSPHERE	
It was nice at work.	

Game Dynamics

During the nine-week intervention, all patients (N = 55) completed the PEKTpat upon discharge, and all nurses working in the ward (N = 18) completed the DEWMnur following each shift. The nurses were divided into two groups: gamified and non-gamified. Each patient who had consented to participate in the study received the same patient education and completed the PEKTpat upon discharge. The PEKTpat offered immediate feedback on their level of knowledge, after which they were able to ask the nurses questions if they felt they needed more information. This was done to ensure that the patients fully understood their postoperative instructions. All patients were treated in the same way; however, during the analysis of the results, they were divided into two groups, determined by the nurses' group (gamified vs. non-gamified). The nurses in the gamified group received immediate feedback on patient performance in the PEKTpat at the individual level (immediately after the patient completed the test) and weekly feedback on patient performance in the PEKTpat at the group level. Immediate and continuous feedback informed the nurses of how well their patients had internalized their postoperative instructions (see Table 1). Additionally, the nurses in the gamified group received weekly feedback on the DEWMnur at the group level. This provided them with information on work motivation at the ward level (see Table 1). The nurses in the non-gamified group did not receive any feedback during the nine-week intervention.

Evaluation of the Gamification Intervention

Data Collection

The data in the evaluation phase were collected daily by a research assistant during the nine-week intervention. These data included the PEKTpat and DEWMnur surveys. During the intervention, the workload and patient cases varied extensively. The number of respondents (patients and nurses) varied weekly in both groups because only those nurses who had treated urologic patients completed the DEWMnur survey, and the number of urologic patients varied daily during the intervention.

Data Analysis

Each patient was categorized into either the gamified or non-gamified group, depending on the group in which their nurse was categorized. A one-way analysis of variance (ANOVA) was used to test whether a difference between the PEKTpat test results existed between the two groups.

The data from the DEWMnur surveys conducted during the nine-week period were compiled into a single data matrix. These data were analyzed using a one-way ANOVA. Two sum variables were formed: "positive feedback" (Cronbach's alpha: 0.85) and "utilization of expertise" (Cronbach's alpha: 0.83) (Table 2).

RESULTS

There were 252 responses in the DEWMnur; these consisted of 132 responses from the gamified group, and 120 responses from the non-gamified group. Statistically significant differences were observed with regard to how the different groups experienced positive feedback ($F[1,250] = 7.04$, $P = .008$). The gamified group received more positive feedback (M = 2.62, SD = .99, N = 132) than the non-gamified group (M = 2.31, SD = .82, N = 120). When analyzed at the item level, it was found that positive feedback from a manager correlated with the item "It was nice at work" at a significance level of P < .005, while feedback from patients and colleagues had a significance level of P < .001 (Table 3). The item "I have received positive feedback from my manager" correlated less with patient experience and peer feedback. When compared with positive feedback on a weekly basis, there was no statistical difference in how the participants experienced positive feedback.

There were no differences in the utilization of expertise (F[1,250] = .21, P = .649) between the gamified group (M = 2.87, N = 132), and the non-gamified group (M = 2.82, N = 120). However, the data revealed that, on a weekly basis, the utilization of expertise varied statistically at a high significance level (F[9,242] = 3.82, P < .001).

Table 3. Correlation matrix, N = 252, P < .001

	Positive feedback	Utilization of expertise	Positive work atmosphere
Positive feedback	1	0.67	0.51
Utilization of expertise	0.67	1	0.48
Positive work atmosphere	0.51	0.48	1

The patients were also divided into two groups. In the gamified group, the nurses received weekly feedback from each patient's PEKTpat test, and in the non-gamified group, the nurses did not receive any feedback from their patients' PEKTpat tests. A one-way ANOVA was used to test whether a difference exists between the PEKTpat test results in the two groups.

In the PEKTpat test, 55 test results were successfully submitted. The maximum score for each patient's test was 10; however, no patient achieved it, as the scores varied between 3 and 9 in both the gamified group (M = 6.76, SD = 1.5, N = 33) and the non-gamified group (M = 7.14, SD = 1.42, N = 22). There were no statistical differences between the groups (F[1,53] = .88, P < .358).

SOLUTIONS AND RECOMMENDATIONS

In this pilot study, a gamification intervention was developed and implemented over a nine-week period in a surgical ward. The utilization of gamification in a hospital setting is novel, and in this study, the authors tested the possibility of gamification over a nine-week period in a surgical ward from the perspective of nurses' work motivation. The involvement of nurses in the development phase played a major role in terms of the success of the intervention, as it committed the nurses to the implementation of the intervention. The nurses' involvement also played a significant role in defining the content of the gamification elements. This is in line with evidence from previous observations (Morschheuser et al., 2017; Nicholson, 2012) regarding the importance of involving the target group in the ideation and design phases of an intervention.

Based on our study, the first recommendation is to involve the target group members when designing a gamification intervention in an organization. This is a key concept in user-centered design, where users communicate with the design team during the design process.

It was hypothesized that nurses' work motivation would improve by the end of the gamification intervention. Based on the results, receiving continuous feedback had an effect on the work motivation of nurses. The most significant difference was found in how the two groups experienced positive feedback: The gamified group experienced more positive feedback than the non-gamified group. Positive feedback from patients and colleagues correlated more with the experience of enjoying the work that was done. Obtaining positive feedback from a manager also had a positive effect, but it was not as significant. This reflects intrinsically motivated individuals. The nurses seemed to be enthusiastic about the work itself (e.g., providing good care to patients), not just the external rewards (e.g., manager feedback) (Deci & Ryan, 2008; Gagne & Deci, 200; Vansteenkiste et al., 2007). However, the generalizability of these results is subject to certain limitations. For instance, only 18 nurses and 55 patients participated in the study, which was based in one surgical ward in one hospital district. Furthermore, during the intervention, the workload and patient cases varied significantly. The number of respondents varied weekly in both groups because only the nurses who had treated urologic patients filled out the DEWMnur survey, and the number of urologic patients varied daily during the intervention.

The second recommendation is to implement game elements that provide positive feedback to workers. In addition, receiving positive feedback from clients is more significant to workers than receiving positive feedback from managers.

Regarding the impact of the PEKTpat test on patients' knowledge of their postoperative instructions, the effects of the intervention could not be demonstrated. A possible explanation for this might be the fact that certain challenges arose in matching the content of the knowledge test to the diverse needs of the patients. Although the knowledge test was designed by a multidisciplinary collaboration and addressed patients of one specialty (urology), their educational needs varied according to the procedures they underwent. The instruments used had not been validated prior to this study. This is clearly a significant limitation that must be considered. This challenge is present in individual patient education and thus presents further challenges in creating a knowledge test suitable for all patients. Notwithstanding this limitation, a knowledge test with gaming features could potentially educate patients, as it could provide objective information on how each patient has internalized their instructions. This in turn would have a major impact on complication prevention. This study has shown that the development of knowledge tests to meet patients' needs requires a great deal of time and financial resources. Therefore, the results of the pilot study are valuable in considering the type of patient education that will need to be developed in the future. Further work needs to be done with a larger dataset to establish the effects of the knowledge test in preventing complications.

Thus, the third recommendation is that all the gamification elements need to be tested and validated in the target group. Our results support the findings reported in the literature that different things motivate different people; thus, the gamified experience can vary.

Based on our intervention, the fourth finding would be that the nurses did not want to have leaderboard-type gamified elements that would show their personal measures to others. This finding supports Deci and Ryan's theory of relatedness. It is much more fruitful to belong to a group where each person's input contributes to the success of the group.

FUTURE RESEARCH DIRECTIONS

Considerably more work will need to be done to determine the ideal game design elements to be implemented in a hospital setting. Further research should be undertaken to investigate the effects of a gamification intervention with a larger dataset. In addition, gamification could be used to identify nurses who are at the risk of low motivation and job dissatisfaction.

Using gamification in work environments such as hospitals requires careful consideration of ethical issues. Patient privacy is extremely important. In addition, the most important thing someone in the nursing profession does is take care of patients; thus, if a nurse has too many tasks, such as filling out gamification intervention questionnaires, these tasks can take them away from their main duties and therefore contribute to low motivation at work.

CONCLUSION

Gamification has the potential to influence the work motivation of nurses, since it can help lead to a better work environment and workplace culture, both of which are associated with good patient care (Aiken et al., 2012; Aiken et al., 2013; Hahtela et al., 2015). Gamification can also help increase job satisfaction levels and professionalism, thereby reducing nurses' desires to leave their careers (Flinkman et al., 2008; Tzeng, 2002). In spite of the limitations of this study, developing feedback mechanisms using game design elements and making daily feedback visible in workplaces is recommended. There is already a shortage of nurses globally (World Health Organization, 2020); to reduce this shortage, it is important for nurses to be motivated in their work tasks. It is also important for nursing to be an attractive profession for future generations who are accustomed to receiving continuous feedback (e.g., through social media). This study found that receiving feedback is important for the utilization of expertise and in the creation of a positive work atmosphere. The study also found that the workplace atmosphere is important for the utilization of knowledge. This leads us to conclude that a positive workplace atmosphere encourages employees to perform more effectively, thus improving the quality of the work done.

This study adds to our understanding of the effects of gamification on nurses' work motivation. It suggests that the use of gamification could sustain nurses' work motivation and thus be used in a hospital setting.

ACKNOWLEDGMENT

This research was supported by the Regional Council of Satakunta [SL/93/04.03.00.04.00/2017]; the Finnish Cultural Foundation, Satakunta Regional Fund [11.04.2017]; the TTY Foundation – Tampere University of Technology; and the Satakunta Central Hospital.

REFERENCES

Aiken, L. H., Sermeus, W., Van den Heede, K., Sloane, D. M., Busse, R., McKee, M., Bruyneel, L., Rafferty, A. M., Griffiths, P., Moreno-Casbas, M. T., Tishelman, C., Scott, A., Brzostek, T., Kinnunen, J., Schwendimann, R., Heinen, M., Zikos, D., Sjetne, I. S., Smith, H. L., & Kutney-Lee, A. (2012). Patient safety, satisfaction, and quality of hospital care: Cross sectional surveys of nurses and patients in 12 countries in Europe and the United States. *BMJ (Clinical Research Ed.)*, *344*(2), e1717. doi:10.1136/bmj.e1717 PMID:22434089

Aiken, L. H., Sloane, D. M., Bruyneel, L., Van der Heede, K., & Sermeus, W. (2013). Nurses' reports of working conditions and hospital quality of care in 12 countries in Europe. *International Journal of Nursing Studies*, *50*(2), 143–153. doi:10.1016/j.ijnurstu.2012.11.009 PMID:23254247

Arambarri Basañez, J., De la Torre-Díez, I., Lopez-Coronado, M., & Álvarez-Lombardía, I. (2014). Investigating the potential market of a serious game for training of Alzheimer's caregivers in a northern Spain region. *International Journal of Serious Games, 1*(4), 75.79.

Bilimoria, K. Y., Cohen, M. E., Ingraham, A. M., Bentrem, D. J., Richards, K., Hall, B. L., & Ko, C. Y. (2010). Effect of postdischarge morbidity and mortality on comparisons of hospital surgical quality. *Annals of Surgery*, *252*(1), 183–190. doi:10.1097/SLA.0b013e3181e4846e PMID:20531000

Blohm, I., & Leimeister, J. M. (2013). Gamification - Design of IT-based enhancing services for motivational support and behavioral change. *Business & Information Systems Engineering*, *5*(4), 275–278. doi:10.100712599-013-0273-5

Burns, N., & Grove, S. K. (2005). *The practice of nursing research: Conduct, critique, and utilization.* Elsevier Saunders.

Deci, E., Koestner, R., & Ryan, R. (2001). Extrinsic rewards and intrinsic motivations in education: Reconsidered once again. *Review of Educational Research*, *71*(1), 1–27. doi:10.3102/00346543071001001

Deci, E., & Ryan, R. (2004). *Handbook of self-determination research.* University of Rochester Press.

Deci, E. L., & Ryan, R. M. (2008). Facilitating optimal motivation and psychological well-being across life's domains. *Canadian Psychology*, *49*(1), 14–23. doi:10.1037/0708-5591.49.1.14

Deterding, S., Dixon, D., Khaled, R., & Nacke, L. (2011). From game design elements to gamefulness: Defining "gamification." *Proceedings of MindTrek*, *11*, 9–15. doi:10.1145/2181037.2181040

Eckerson, C. M. (2018). The impact of nurse residency programs in the United States on improving retention and satisfaction of new nurse hires: An evidence-based literature review. *Nurse Education Today*, *71*, 84–90. doi:10.1016/j.nedt.2018.09.003 PMID:30268073

Finnish Advisory Board on Research Integrity. (2012). *Responsible conduct of research and procedures for handling allegations of misconduct in Finland.* https://www.tenk.fi/sites/tenk.fi/files/HTK_ohje_2012.pdf

Flinkman, M., Laine, M., Leino-Kilpi, H., Hasselhorn, H.-M., & Salanterä, S. (2008). Explaining young registered Finnish nurses' intention to leave the profession: A questionnaire survey. *International Journal of Nursing Studies*, *45*(5), 727–739. doi:10.1016/j.ijnurstu.2006.12.006 PMID:17280674

Friese, C. R., & Aiken, L. H. (2008). Failure to rescue in the surgical oncology population: Implications for nursing and quality improvement. *Oncology Nursing Forum, 35*(5), 779–785. doi:10.1188/08. ONF.779-785 PMID:18765323

Gagne, M., & Deci, E. (2005). Self-determination theory and work motivation. *Journal of Organizational Behavior, 26*(4), 331–362. doi:10.1002/job.322

Galletta, M., Portoghese, I., Pili, S., Piazza, M. F., & Campagna, M. (2016). The effect of work motivation on a sample of nurses in an Italian healthcare setting. *Work (Reading, Mass.), 54*(2), 451–460. doi:10.3233/WOR-162327 PMID:27286081

Hahtela, N., Paavilainen, E., McCormack, B., Slater, P., Helminen, M., & Suominen, T. (2015). Influence of workplace culture on nursing-sensitive nurse outcomes in municipal primary health care. *Journal of Nursing Management, 23*(7), 931–939. doi:10.1111/jonm.12237 PMID:24848308

Hamari, J., Koivisto, J., & Sarsa, H. (2014). Does gamification work? A literature review of empirical studies on gamification. In *Proceedings of the 47th Annual Hawaii International Conference on System Sciences, HICSS 2014* (pp. 3025-3034). IEEE Computer Society Press. 10.1109/HICSS.2014.377

Huotari, K., & Hamari, J. (2011). "Gamification" from the perspective of service marketing. *ACM Conference on Human Factors in Computing Systems (Gamification Workshop)*.

Huotari, K., & Hamari, J. (2012). Defining gamification - A service marketing perspective. In *Proceeding of the 16th International Academic MindTrek Conference (MindTrek '12)*. Association for Computing Machinery. 10.1145/2393132.2393137

Jordan, Z., Lockwood, C., & Aromataris, E. M. Z. (2019). The updated Joanna Briggs Institute model of evidence-based healthcare. *International Journal of Evidence-Based Healthcare, 17*(1), 58–71. doi:10.1097/XEB.0000000000000155 PMID:30256247

Kantek, F., Yildirim, N., & Kavla, İ. (2015). Nurses' perceptions of motivational factors: A case study in a Turkish university hospital. *Journal of Nursing Management, 23*(5), 674–681. doi:10.1111/jonm.12195 PMID:24372763

Khaleel, F. L., Tengku Wook, T., Ashaari, S. A., Wook, T. S. M. T., & Ismail, A. (2016). Gamification elements for learning applications. *International Journal on Advanced Science, Engineering and Information Technology, 6*(6), 868–874. doi:10.18517/ijaseit.6.6.1379

Koch, S. H., Proynova, R., Paech, B., & Wetter, T. (2014). The perfectly motivated nurse and the others: Workplace and personal characteristics impact preference of nursing tasks. *Journal of Nursing Management, 22*(8), 1054–1064. doi:10.1111/jonm.12083 PMID:24033771

Koivisto, J.-M., Multisilta, J., & Haavisto, E. (2017). Possible benefits of gamification for improving surgical patients' quality of care. *Proceedings of the 1st International GamiFIN Conference*.

Koivisto, J. -M., Multisilta, J., & Haavisto, E. (2021). Surgical nurses' experiences with intrinsic work motivation: A focus on autonomy, competence and relatedness. *Hoitotiede, 33*(2), 102–111.

Koivisto, J.-M., Saarinen, I., Kaipia, A., Puukka, P., Kivinen, K., Laine, K.-M., & Haavisto, E. (2020). Patient education in relation to informational needs and postoperative complications in surgical patients. *International Journal for Quality in Health Care, 32*(1), 35–40. doi:10.1093/intqhc/mzz032 PMID:31016323

Marć, M., Bartosiewicz, A., Burzyńska, J., Chmiel, Z., & Januszewicz, P. (2019). A nursing shortage - A prospect of global and local policies. *International Nursing Review, 66*(1), 9–16. doi:10.1111/inr.12473 PMID:30039849

Morschheuser, B., Werder, K., Hamari, J., & Abe, J. (2017). How to gamify? Development of a method for gamification. *Proceedings of the 50th Annual Hawaii International Conference on System Sciences (HICSS)*, 1298-1307.

Negussie, N. (2012). Relationship between rewards and nurses' work motivation in Addis Ababa hospitals. *Ethiopian Journal of Health Sciences, 22*(2), 107–112. PMID:22876074

Nicholson, S. A. (2012). *User-centered theoretical framework for meaningful gamification* [Paper presentation]. Games+Learning+Society 8.0, Madison, WI.

Okello, D., & Gilson, L. (2015). Exploring the influence of trust relationships on motivation in the health sector: A systematic review. *Human Resources for Health, 13*(1), 16. doi:10.118612960-015-0007-5 PMID:25889952

Perreira, T. A., Innis, J., & Berta, W. (2016). Work motivation in health care: A scoping literature review. *International Journal of Evidence-Based Healthcare, 14*(4), 175–182. doi:10.1097/XEB.0000000000000093 PMID:27552534

Roy-Burman, A., Lightbody, L., Henry, D., Huey, R. E., Lynch, M., & Martin, E. (2013). 118: Engaging nurses through social gamification. *Critical Care Medicine, 41*(12), A23. doi:10.1097/01.ccm.0000439267.10865.08

Ryan, R. M. (2009). Self-determination theory and wellbeing. *Wellbeing in Developing Countries Research Review, 1*(June), 1–2.

Tamayo-Serrano, P., Garbaya, S., & Blazevic, P. (2018). Gamified in-home rehabilitation for stroke survivors: Analytical review. *International Journal of Serious Games, 5*(1), 1–26. doi:10.17083/ijsg.v5i1.224

Toode, K., Routasalo, P., Helminen, M., & Suominen, T. (2015). Hospital nurses' working conditions in relation to motivation and patient safety. *Nursing Management, 21*(10), 31–41. doi:10.7748/nm.21.10.31. e1293 PMID:25727441

Toode, K., Routasalo, R., & Suominen, S. (2011). Work motivation of nurses: A literature review. *International Journal of Nursing Studies, 48*(2), 246–257. doi:10.1016/j.ijnurstu.2010.09.013 PMID:20947085

Tzeng, H. M. (2002). The influence of nurses' working motivation and job satisfaction on intention to quit: An empirical investigation in Taiwan. *International Journal of Nursing Studies, 39*(8), 867–878. doi:10.1016/S0020-7489(02)00027-5 PMID:12379304

Vansteenkiste, M., Neyrinck, B., Niemiec, C. P., Soenens, B., De Witte, H., & Van den Broeck, A. (2007). On the relations among work value orientations, psychological need satisfaction and job outcomes: A self-determination theory approach. *Journal of Occupational and Organizational Psychology, 80*(2), 251–277. doi:10.1348/096317906X111024

Wanzel, K. R., Jamieson, C. G., & Bohnen, J. M. (2000). Complications on a general surgery service: Incidence and reporting. *Canadian Journal of Surgery, 43*(2), 113–117. PMID:10812345

Werbach, K. (2014). (Re)Defining gamification: A process approach. In A. Spagnolli, L. Chittaro, & L. Gamberini (Eds.), *Persuasive Technology. 9th International Conference, PERSUASIVE 2014, Padua, Italy, May 21-23, 2014. Proceedings.* Springer International Publishers.

World Health Organization. (2020). *State of the world's nursing 2020: Investing in education, jobs and leadership.* https://www.who.int/publications-detail/nursing-report-2020

ADDITIONAL READING

Ahlstedt, C., Eriksson Lindvall, C., Holmström, I., & Muntlin Athlin, Å. (2019). What makes registered nurses remain in work? An ethnographic study. *International Journal of Nursing Studies, 89*, 32–38. doi:10.1016/j.ijnurstu.2018.09.008 PMID:30339953

Koivisto, J.-M., Multisilta, J., Niemi, H., Katajisto, J., & Eriksson, E. (2016). Learning by playing: A cross-sectional descriptive study of nursing students' experiences of learning clinical reasoning. *Nurse Education Today, 60*, 22–28. doi:10.1016/j.nedt.2016.06.009 PMID:27429399

KEY TERMS AND DEFINITIONS

Daily Experience of Work Motivation: DEWMnur is a questionnaire related to work motivation that the participating nurses filled out after each work shift. The nurses in the gamified group received weekly feedback based on this questionnaire (summarized at the group level), while the nurses in the non-gamified group did not receive any feedback.

Intrinsic Motivation: Employees who experience intrinsic motivation are enthusiastic about the work itself, not just the external rewards that the job gives them.

Patient Education Knowledge Test: PEKTpat is a multiple-choice test used to evaluate patients' level of understanding of their self-care instructions after their discharge.

Purposive Sampling: A sampling method in which the researchers select the participants of a study using their own expert knowledge of the population from which the study participants are being chosen.

Self-Determination Theory (SDT): A theory of human motivation, personality development, and well-being. It focuses on self-determined behaviour and basic psychological needs, namely autonomy, competence, and relatedness, that are in the core of human functioning.

Chapter 13
Collaborative Learning:
Increasing Work Motivation
Through Game–Based Learning

Jessica Reuter
GOVCOPP, University of Aveiro, Portugal

Marta Ferreira Dias
ⓘD https://orcid.org/0000-0002-6695-8479
GOVCOPP, DEGEIT, University of Aveiro, Portugal

Maria José Sousa
Business Research Unit, Instituto Universitário de Lisboa, Portugal

ABSTRACT

Organisations always seek to maximize the effectiveness of their internal systems. Gamification is a growing trend in work contexts, with employers realizing that many of the elements associated with it can be transferred to a business environment. Understanding the main concepts that make games appealing to society allows us to understand how they can be adapted and used in the professional environment, as well as in organizations. Therefore, besides gamification, game-based learning and serious games can be used in organizations for training and skills development. Understanding how gamification activities affect both extrinsic and intrinsic motivation is critical to understanding how they affect workers and how they can be used to their full potential. This study provides a critical analysis of the use of these tools to increase the motivation and collaboration of individuals in organizations. Playing in groups to learn is a practice that still needs more incentives and diffusion to be widely used in the company context.

INTRODUCTION

Organisations regardless the business in which they operate, need to engage, and motivate all their stakeholders to achieve good results. In a business context, motivating behavioural changes in employees, through inspiring affective responses from individuals, is often the key to success in achieving greater

DOI: 10.4018/978-1-7998-9223-6.ch013

collaboration and productivity among employees (Gruman & Saks, 2011). Motivation may emerge from different perspectives, including extrinsic rewards such as money and premiums, and intrinsic rewards, which occurs when a task is very interesting and enjoyable (Mekler et al., 2017).

Gamification and game-based learning (GBL) emerge as a proposal to achieve such goal. Different studies clearly suggest that games and gamified systems have the motivational potential for workplaces (Reiners & Wood, 2015). According to Mitchell et al (2017), harnessing rewards and emotions, an effective gamification experience will motivate changes in individuals' behaviour in business environments and promote the maximisation and effectiveness of their systems. Gamification at work consists of applying gaming features in the work context to direct and energise desired worker behaviour, with the ultimate aim of improving performance (Cardador et al., 2017). The use of GBL, on the other hand, aims to encourage learning through different types of serious games that have specific learning objectives and outcomes (Tercanli et al., 2021).

In this sense, a holistic view of GBL and serious games can be incorporated within organisations through elements of gamification. These elements when incorporated, lead to changes in behaviours that will facilitate learning within companies (Oprescu et al., 2014). This strategy involves the repetition of desired results. Through the motivational mechanisms of reinforcement and emotions, the desired results become automatic behavioural processes or habits. Habits are formed through hints that prompt behaviour and then this behaviour, if repeated several times, is automatically assumed by the individuals. This information loop is maintained without great cognitive effort, as this knowledge is obtained gradually throughout the gamification process (Mitchell et al., 2017).

Thus, the main features of games that are relevant to the workplace involve learning, rewards, and individual and group performance, with motivation to achieve certain goals at its core. Thus, gamification combines two types of essential motivations for the individual; on the one side, it uses extrinsic rewards such as levels, points, and premiums, while, on the other side, it uses intrinsic motivation using emotions to enhance the individual's sense of autonomy and sense of being part of the team (Robson et al., 2015). In other words, by using a points and awards system gamification provides a sense of quick reward in the people involved and improves the speed of feedback on their work. Scoreboards may provide real-time feedback to workers and provides them with the ability to access and analyse how their own work is being assessed. The score may be awarded by achieving a specific daily, weekly, or monthly goal, motivating the worker to do their best (Cardador et al., 2017). Intrinsic motivation arises from the proposal to borrow resources from games, to create an activity in the work environment that is more enjoyable and increases their motivation to perform certain actions. This is the affective and emotional way of motivation provided by gamification in the workplace.

However, this process within companies must be driven by a specific goal to be achieved. Just as activities developed through GBL, to be successful, must be created with specific learning goals, gamified activities within companies must be driven by long-term organisational goals, which may be financial, social or environmental (Friedrich et al., 2020). Focusing on a specific goal reduces complexity and ensures that dynamics and emotions are conducted in a manner that achieves specific goals. Furthermore, having a long-term goal encourages the autonomy of the worker who may manage how they will achieve this goal, also considering their personal development goals, purpose and individual motivations (Gruman & Saks, 2011).

In this context, an important concern emerges in this type of strategy, the competition. In gamified systems in the business environment this strategy will be more effective to promote motivation, by emphasizing cooperation to achieve certain goals. Working as a team will generate a healthy competition and social connection among the work group (Dale, 2014). Furthermore, the fact that the individual does not want to be a weak link in the work environment will encourage him to contribute. Another important factor in this connection is the synergy of diverse skills and experiences for the team, while promoting a social dimension to the work through relationships with colleagues (Ke et al., 2016). This cooperation between employees helps to improve the culture of an organisation and the working environment, promoting social wellbeing. Social wellbeing is intrinsically associated with better performance in the work environment (Mekler et al., 2017)

The basis of any game involves working within a set of pre-defined rules to achieve a goal; this will involve the engagement, collaboration, critical analysis, and problem-solving skills of those involved (Perryer et al., 2016). Thus, promoting cooperation among employees through gamification and serious games seems to be a good strategy to improve the motivation of individuals. Learning in the workplace, through games, and gamified systems, may play an important role for the development of individuals within organisations and for their performance (Ruhi, 2015). Games may provide greater benefits in problem solving for companies and facilitate and improve individuals' mastery and memory. In addition, sharing knowledge, through team play is a synergistic process between colleagues that may improve the work environment and promote joint problem solving (Oprescu et al., 2014).

In the synthesis of research on gamification and the use of GBL resources in the workplace, research suggests that the success of this strategy varies considerably and depends greatly on the response of employees and their attitude towards the purpose, relevance, type of game and individual motivators and drivers (Reiners & Wood, 2015). Thus, more research is needed into the different methods by which game principles may be applied in the workplace for motivation of workers in teams (Mekler et al., 2017). If the aims and game mechanics are not well developed, engaging in games may be a waste of time for the organisation, or lead to learning outcomes that are totally unrelated to the organisational goals. It is also necessary to understand the different psychological and motivational components at individual level. Each individual has different learning rhythms and the organisation's task is to understand and implement this strategy in order to take advantage of each individual's skills, motivating them to develop their abilities to solve problems and achieve strategic results in the organisation. Due to these particularities the games and gamified activities need to be combined with feedback during and after the games, i.e. it is necessary to promote reflection of the activities and discussion of the strategies to allow individuals to understand and develop skills (Mitchell et al., 2017).

This chapter explores and develops, through a critical literature review, the importance of collaborative games to increase the motivation of individuals in the workplace. The importance of cooperation in gamified systems is also emphasised. Workplaces, with the use of games and gamification resources, may be seen as self-learning environments in which behaviour change is created, developed, and maintained. Through the analysis of theoretical and empirical studies, we seek to understand how the social factors of working in groups, in pursuit of common goals, generate a sense of belonging and increase the motivation for cooperation, self-development and performance of individuals inside an organisation.

The Chapter is organised as follows: Initially, a theorical contextualization on the relevance the aspects intrinsic and extrinsic for motivation, the use of GBL, serious games and gamification in a company context. Followed by the importance of collaboration and teamwork for the development of knowledge in the workplace and discussion on their relevance to the scientific community. Finally, the main conclusions of the study are listed and some items for future work are suggested.

THE SYNERGY BETWEEM GBL AND GAMIFICATION IN THE WORK CONTEXT FOR INCREASE MOTIVATION

Intrinsic and Extrinsic Motivation

Motivation is the intention to perform an action. This intention can arise through extrinsic or intrinsic factors. According to self-determination theory, the author Perryer et al. (2016), explains that there are three necessary (but not sufficient) preconditions that influence intrinsic motivation: autonomy, competence, and relatedness. Intrinsic motivation occurs when a task is inherently interesting or enjoyable, while extrinsic motivation occurs when performing the task is a means to achieve a desirable outcome (Cardador et al., 2017).

An intrinsically motivated person will work hard by nature, genuinely dedicated to the activity they are doing, driven by their own personal reasons or beliefs. On the other hand, a person with extrinsic motivation will work hard to achieve a certain goal, such as a pay rise, and once that goal is achieved, the motivation may cease to exist. In extrinsic motivation, the focus is on the anticipation of compensation or achievement that is subject to direct or indirect external influences (Mekler et al., 2017). In the business context, external incentives can be tangible in monetary and non-monetary forms, these incentives are usually associated with financial rewards, performance bonuses or time off work. Or they can be intangible individual or social rewards, such as points and ratings for future promotions, or instant feedback and recognition. This expectation of financial and social reward is a small part of extrinsic motivation (Friedrich et al., 2020; Gruman & Saks, 2011).

In companies, the aim of using incentives is to motivate employees to show a certain desired behaviour. Workplace incentives can be a factor to increase motivation, but they cannot create the motivation; they must serve to reinforce the desired behaviour (Ruhi, 2015).

To increase employee motivation in organisations, different methodologies and strategies seek to influence the behaviour of individuals to achieve a specific goal, with greater motivation and engagement (Bardon et al., 2006). GBL and gamification emerge in the business context. These different methodologies have different concepts and are used in different roles in organisations. However, both are used to increase motivation and collaboration among employees (Allal-Chérif & Bidan, 2017; Ke et al., 2016). Let us proceed with the analysis of these methodologies.

The Use of Game-Based Learning

GBL has been used in recent years as a creative and innovative way to enrich the teaching and learning process. GBL a pedagogical methodology that focuses on the design, development and application of games in education (Almeida, 2020). New learning methodologies and strategies have been adopted in different contexts. The development of social and transversal skills such as critical thinking, team work, collaboration, self-management and communication are mentioned as the main contributions of games (Madani et al., 2017). GBL refers to a multiplicity of games used in formal and informal settings that provide different challenges to different audiences to increase the engagement and development of individuals in technical and transversal skills. In this strategy a mix of surprise and fun occurs which can result in effective learning in the short term, as well as behavioural changes over time, sustaining the mindset and practices of the individuals involved (Hoffmann & Matysiak, 2019).

In the literature, the concept of serious games is also widely used. As defined by Marsh (2011) serious games can constitute digital games, simulations, virtual environments and mixed gamified strategies that offer participants opportunities to engage in activities through narrative and gameplay. Serious games can be used to inform, influence, promote well-being, or to convey meaning through a learning experience. The quality or success of serious games will be characterised by the degree to which they achieve their purpose.

In the literature both concepts are used similarly, to designate the process and practice of learning with the use of games. The difference between GBL and a serious game is that GBL is more a method, the way of learning, and a serious game is a product in which GBL is possible. Just as there is no consensus on their definition, there is no agreement on which games can be classified as serious. The following terms describe serious games and are widely used in academia and in business context: educational games, simulation, virtual reality, alternative purpose games, edutainment, digital game-based learning, immersive learning, simulations, social impact games, persuasive games, games for change, game-based learning and/or training (Ulicsak & Wright, 2010). Thus, GBL is part of the general concept of serious games and has been used successfully in various fields such as health, management, tourism and psychology (Chetouani et al., 2018; Carenys & Moya, 2016; Xu et al., 2017; Almeida, 2020).

One of the most remarkable abilities of the human brain is recognising patterns. Filed away in our memories, the stories we know provide patterns that we can use to compare with our own experiences. They become a kind of reference library. Even unconsciously, we relate events to our past experience of the subject. GBL seeks to explore these memories through an immersive experience and active learning, to engage an audience and aid in important acts of remembrance. In fact, studies show that through active learning, it is easier to remember a specific topic (Ballance, 2013).

In organisations, by working as a team whit a games, employees are able to cooperate, confront ideas and acquire a deeper understanding of the content they are working on, which increases their confidence (Yi et al., 2020). In addition, the competitiveness between teams creates the need to learn how to optimise time and resources, thus dividing activities to solve challenges more quickly and effectively (Ballance, 2013). Sharing information is beneficial for both the organisation and the employees, but often this exchange does not occur naturally in organisations. However, during GBL activities, this exchange can occur gradually among participants. To achieve a common goal, participants tend to share their knowledge, either to show leadership, or to help their team in achieving such a goal (Greco et al., 2011). In a game environment, feedback has a key function for the user. It is through this feedback that he is kept informed about his choices (Coleman & Money, 2020). If feedback during the game is poorly managed and there are no real-time reactions to diminish user doubts as they happen, this can generate demotivation and lead the strategy to failure (Madani et al., 2017).

Often work over time can become repetitive and almost mechanical for some functions. Through GBL the concepts and objectives of each function performed can be conveyed lightly and effectively to employees (Allal-Chérif & Bidan, 2017). With a well-structured understanding of these factors it is possible to increase employees' confidence and motivation in performing certain functions. To obtain better results with the use of GBL, the game design should be well constructed, the tool should promote motivation, social interaction, and competition among participants (Henriksen & Borgesen, 2016). The mechanics, design, and components of games, as well as the learning objectives and guidance in instructional design have a great influence on the motivation, performance, and success of this tool (Uukkivi & Labanova, 2018).

In view of these factors, GBL activities can be used for training in specific areas in companies; for example to develop technical skills, to build leadership skills, to conduct sales training, for product training and to increase productivity (Ballance, 2013). These activities become motivational because it is possible for participants to quickly see and understand the connection between the experience and everyday situations at work. Researchers Xu et al. (2017); Carenys et al. (2016), shows that the results of games can be more effective than traditional training, in which the individual passively receives the content.

Among the different games used, we can mention games on mobile platforms that incorporate surveys, discussions, and quizzes in the form of games. Many of these platforms incorporate questions in a fun way to assess and improve users' knowledge on a particular subject (Brooks et al., 2017). Games that simulate virtual reality are used more frequently in recent years with the advancement of technology and digital systems (Carenys & Moya, 2016). In this type of game, the individual can make decisions simulating real life. This will require them to analyse situations to make appropriate decisions which will encourage active learning and increase their confidence.

A GBL methodology is broadly applicable because it can be fully customized, in accordance with the objectives targeted by the organisation. Because serious games motivate the players intrinsically, they can also be used for behavioural change. However, the development of a serious game is more complex and therefore often more expensive than, for example, gamification (Mitchell et al., 2020).One of the big problems encountered by organisations for its use, is the lack of evidence that attests to its benefits in similar companies, and demonstrations of return on investment (Larson, 2020). Many initiatives are not reported in scientific articles or shared so that a large mass can have access to the results.

There is also a great concern about the design and mechanics of the games, which in many cases are created without the theoretical basis on flipped learning and more specifically, game-based learning. In this way, the games may not achieve the desired goal (Larson, 2020; Yi et al., 2020). Some empirical evidence of the use of serious games in training is reported in large companies, such as L'Oreal, Siemens, IBM, Cisco, Deloitte, and McDonald's. However, most studies report evidence of the use of game elements in gamification (Larson, 2020). We will explore their differences in the next topic.

Using Game Elements in Gamification

Gamification is the process of implementing game elements to increase the motivation of individuals (Mitchell et al., 2017). Greco et al. (2013), defines gamification as the application of lessons from the game domain to change behaviour in non-game situations, and suggests that the growing interest in this issue stems from three different factors: the growth of the games industry and the understanding of what makes a computer game engaging, the amount of data available about people's preferences that has become useful for producing gamified experiences, and the fact that companies are always trying to find new and impactful ways to influence individuals' behaviour. As for organisations, the adoption of work gamification - applying principles of digital and computer games to work contexts - arises from the assumption that such incentives increase workers' motivation, effectiveness and performance (Friedrich et al., 2020). The different concepts addressed are clearly and succinctly set out in Figure 1.

According to the empirical study conducted by Patrício et al. (2020), gamification ensures close interaction between different actors, encourages contributions from all participants and supports high quality knowledge creation in an open and creative environment. Although actors may be involved in the process because it is playful and more relaxed, coordination is needed to maintain focus on the previously outlined objectives, which ensures the quality of solutions.

This method combines two types of motivation. On the one hand, it uses extrinsic rewards such as levels, points, badges to improve engagement, while striving to elicit feelings of mastery, autonomy, sense of belonging. In theory, three important aspects can be distinguished: dynamics, mechanics and game components (Mitchell et al., 2017). The most common game mechanics in the business world include achievements (experience points, bonuses); exercises (challenges, puzzles); community synchronisation (leaderboards); transparency of results (continuous feedback); time (counting) and luck (lottery, random events). These types of activities do not need to be integrated as a whole; a company can choose those that can best fit its system and apply them. Moreover, there is no need to impose them in a continuous context: a company can occasionally promote a gamified experience, simply as a reward system (Bardon et al., 2006). For example, in call centers, the gamification is used to transforms customer requests (e.g., telephone calls and comments posted on Twitter and Facebook) into virtual tickets randomly assigned to players (i.e., customer service employees). In the resulting realtime competitive environment, compete to improve their performance and better serve their clients (Hammedi et al., 2021).

Regarding game components, several aspects can be highlighted such as levels, points and teamwork. The game dynamics will be supported with the implementation of the game mechanics. The rewards, feedbacks, performance graphics and levels will determine all the dynamics to be executed. Through this well executed alignment the internal dynamics expected from the participants will occur. Among these dynamics are challenge, competition and cooperation, which cannot be managed or implemented directly and depend on the involvement and participation of each participant. These elements have a decisive impact on the motivation of those involved (Robson et al., 2015). After these general elements, more specific aspects should be considered such as the emotions, relationships and limitations of individuals. For game elements to be positively accepted by employees, they need to be properly accompanied by other organisational efforts so as not to bring frustration and pressure and lead the efforts to the opposite effect than expected (Henriksen & Borgesen, 2016).

In a study conducted by Hammedi et al. (2021), the results show that a low level of motivation in participating in the gamification challenge, is generated when participants focus their attention on the potential rewards or punishments they may receive if they achieve or fail to achieve their goals. However, in contrast, participants who accepted this challenge and focused on the experience they could have, achieved their goal without being concerned about their performance. In this sense, immediate feedback is another essential element for the player to feel in control of the game. Promote flow between participants with assertive motivational measures such as immediate feedback, verbal rewards or tangible rewards, and a clear and continuous process of evaluation is encouraged (Almeida, 2020).

Challenges provide the opportunity for members to work as a team to achieve certain goals. Time pressure, in some cases, can contribute to finding a collaborative solution. Competition is also an interesting and attractive strategy in gamified systems. Competition in general, can have a positive impact on employee performance (Algashami et al., 2018). The integration of quizzes and puzzles can be used in training or used to assess knowledge on a certain subject. The scoring and ranking system also generates competition, since employees can compare their results with the rest of the group. In both cases, competition can be appreciated, and can encourage engagement, especially for ambitious employees (Larson, 2020). The social comparison theory, proposes that information about others' performance compared to one's own can motivate people to improve their own performance. This theory, can help explain the importance of gamified elements in the work environment, such as scoreboards, which will not only help the worker to track their own score, but also to compare it with those achieved by others (Kiili et al., 2014).

Gamification provides different forms of feedback for users. On the one hand, feedback can be done through performance measured by points and ranking position. On the other hand, feedback can be motivated through a social incentive to create mutual opportunities between employees (Dale, 2014). When positive feedbacks are given in a public environment, this can generate recognition and increase the confidence of individuals. Furthermore, with the point and reward system it is possible to provide an opportunity for participants to demonstrate their skills and knowledge and to increase their social reputation within the group (Cardador et al., 2017). A good reputation has a great influence on a group, company or other social environment. This is because knowledge transfer creates trust between individuals and generates comparisons, so that everyone is engaged in improving their (Friedrich et al., 2020).

In contrast, negative feedback in front of the group can cause feelings of pressure and fear to participate in these activities and share knowledge as a team (Kiili et al., 2014). Lack of trust from the organisation and ineffective communication of gamification rules and objectives can decrease engagement in these activities. Therefore, there is a need for support from the organisation in encouraging the use of this strategy and ensuring fairness and error tolerance among employees (Algashami et al., 2018).

In a business context it is plausible to convert virtual rewards into tangible incentives such as pay or days off (Robson et al., 2015). However, it is important to bear in mind that monetary rewards are unsustainable in the long term, and it also undermines the intrinsic motivation of individuals. Applying gamified elements as a reward can be dangerous. According to Yi et al. (2020), when rewards cease, the behaviour is likely to cease as well, unless the subject has found some other reason to continue the behaviour.

For these reasons Oprescu et al. (2014), points out some principles when adopting gamification in a work environment. Firstly, the orientation of the gamification process should be aimed at employees, with appropriate conditions for operation, control and effectiveness. Persuasive elements also need to be included based on behavioural and psychological theories, these elements are fundamental to attract the attention of those involved and enable engagement. In gamification, a fundamental principle is learning orientation. In other words, it is necessary to define what knowledge is to be acquired or improved, or what skills and motivational goals are to be achieved through gamification. Finally, the author stresses that rewards or incentives, which must be clear and justifiable to all employees.

For Patricio et al. (2020), gamification has shown positive results, which reinforces the notion that it works particularly well when applied by a diverse team, i.e. multi-actors with different roles, backgrounds and knowledge. Dialogue, mutual understanding, goal alignment, creative experimentation, sharing and concept development are some of the core competencies of this strategy. Obaid and Farooq (2020) proposes that work gamification improves work motivation, and subsequently performance, by providing workers with greater access to visible, comparable, and immediate feedback and performance measures. Yu-Kai Chou lists over 90 examples of gamification in companies, including statistics on Return on Investment (A Comprehensive List of 90 Gamification Cases with ROI Stats, 2016).

However, as Hammedi et al. (2021), points out, despite the benefits and widespread popularity, of using gamification in organisations, care must be taken when implementing gamified experiences. Gamification is not a magic solution and needs to be incorporated with balance according to the culture and strategy of each company. This strategy should bring the benefits of increased motivation, group work and learning to employees, but without adding more stress to their work. In particular, if dissatisfaction is widespread in the workplace, then using these practices will probably aggravate the situation and evoke even more negative emotions and decrease commitment and performance at work. Thus, gamification needs to be implemented gradually, in an enjoyable way, for example by making it voluntary, first considering the structural and organisational aspects for its implementation.

Figure 1. Key terms and Definitions

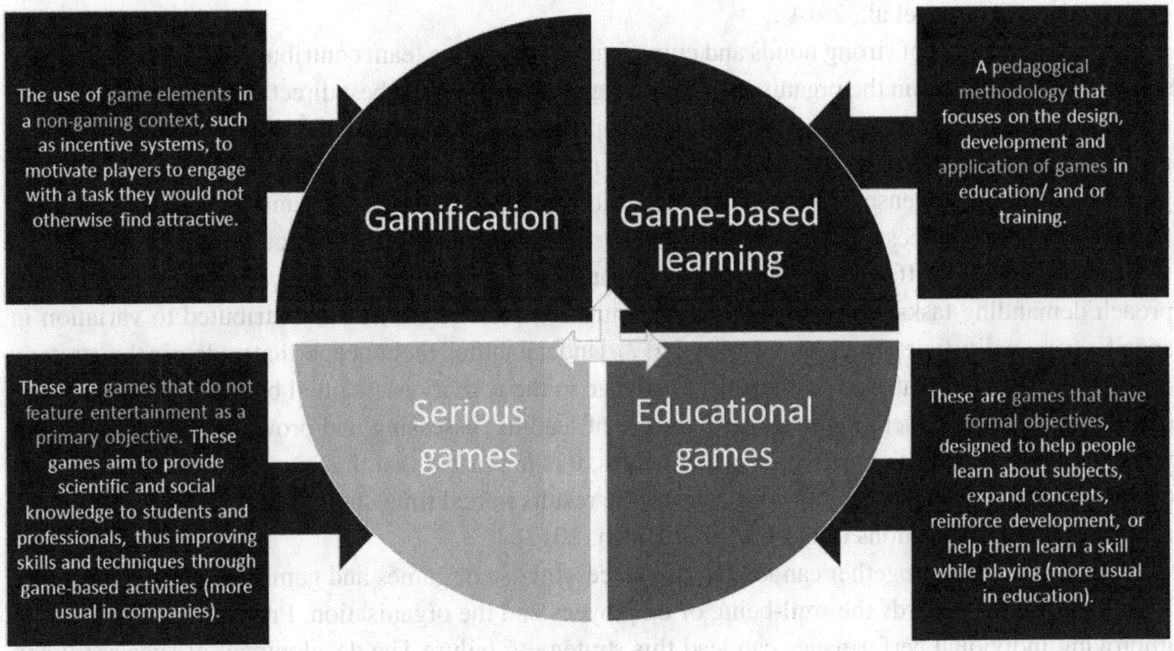

The use of game elements in a non-gaming context, such as incentive systems, to motivate players to engage with a task they would not otherwise find attractive.

Gamification

Game-based learning

A pedagogical methodology that focuses on the design, development and application of games in education/ and or training.

These are games that do not feature entertainment as a primary objective. These games aim to provide scientific and social knowledge to students and professionals, thus improving skills and techniques through game-based activities (more usual in companies).

Serious games

Educational games

These are games that have formal objectives, designed to help people learn about subjects, expand concepts, reinforce development, or help them learn a skill while playing (more usual in education).

THE IMPORTANCE OF COLLABORATION AND TEAMWORK FOR LEARNING

The insertion of GBL and gamification activities in companies, can bring advantages to the organisation and improve cooperation among employees. The combination of healthy competition and collaboration through teamwork, can be beneficial from the moment, that processes can be improved in organisations.

The formation of groups and teams to solve games will provide collaboration, critical thinking, quality dialogue and exchange of information between employees. In addition, this process sharpens participants' creativity, develops initiative, problem-solving skills, decision-making. Besides the technical knowledge that can be learned with the games, the transversal skills are of great importance for the well-being of the organisation and for better results in the individual performance of each employee. Encouraging the exchange of ideas, experiences and opinions between participants depends on a strong bond developed during the activity. This connection also improves employees' confidence and can increase their social circle. These emotional characteristics are also important, so that the employee feels a welcoming environment in which to develop and feel useful and recognised among colleagues and the company (Mekler et al., 2017).

In summary, some arguments can be put forward to explain the reasoning behind why GBL and gamification should increase workers' motivation. The fact that workers can earn points and badges by being first on the leaderboard. This can be motivating as workers have access to feedback and even get a sense of comparability - explained by social comparison theory. Countdowns can encourage workers to be more effective in their time management - however, schedules should not be tight, or the worker may instead feel pressured and demotivated. Activities such as puzzles and team quizzes can have a positive effect on community morale, and even develop soft skills such as leadership and collaboration among those involved. A well-designed gaming experience, with the right mix of rewards and emotions, can induce the desired behavioural changes, so that workers repeat the behavioural outcome desired by the organisation (Oprescu et al., 2014).

The establishment of strong bonds and commitment among the team contribute to the formation of a supportive culture within the organisation. Building consensus on the best direction to take is one of the most important social outcomes of gamification approaches (Patrício et al., 2018). As mentioned earlier gamification is not a magic formula and therefore needs to be properly aligned with the organisation's goals. Promoting this sense of inclusion and decision-making among participants is crucial for them to feel included in the process and consequently increase their motivation in the task (Hammedi et al., 2021).

However, people differ in how they behave in any given situation and in how they perceive and approach demanding tasks, conflicts and opportunities. These Differences are attributed to variation in specific personality traits (Buckley & Doyle, 2017). Understanding the concepts that underpin this strategy and the mechanisms that lead participants to engage in the activity is essential before it is applied. The game master in GBL methodologies has the role of leading, assessing and providing feedback during the activity. In gamification activities in companies, it is important that this immediate feedback occurs during the activities, and that everyone can see the results in real time and manage or adjust their work according to the evaluations (Allal-Chérif & Bidan, 2017).

All these practices together can lead to the successful use of games and gamification in companies, if they are geared towards the well-being of employees and the organisation. Practices aimed solely at improving individual performance can lead this strategy to failure.The development of successful and meaningful GBL and gamification experiences involves both the application of design principles and psychological, social and behavioural theories, ensuring that the experience provided to users is enjoyable and challenging. The process itself, cannot just be the application of point systems, reward graphics, colours and animation. The application of GBL can be developed in companies for training on specific topics, leadership development and to increase collaboration between employees. This strategy can be used in any business area of the organisation, but needs to be adapted according to specific objectives to be achieved (Mekler et al., 2017).

These same principles can be used in gamification in routine workplace activities to influence employees - provoking affective responses, and, unlike other activities, stimulating their intrinsic motivation. When we talk about incentives and rewards, the focus should be on the long-term effects. Then it is necessary to monitor these incentives, adjust them if necessary, and prevent the effects of incentives from fading over time. A holistic approach is also needed to avoid failure in this process. Inserting these strategies without concern for the dynamics, mechanics and components of the game can result in failures in the use of this approach (Cardador et al., 2017).

Gamification and GBL activities can be successful in the long term if combined with company culture and an organisational climate that promotes knowledge exchange between employees and reward systems. Game elements such as challenges, competition, feedbacks, rewards and status can create, in addition to extrinsic motivations, intrinsic motivations if well managed (Friedrich et al., 2020).

Figure 2. Proposed framework: "playing together to learn"

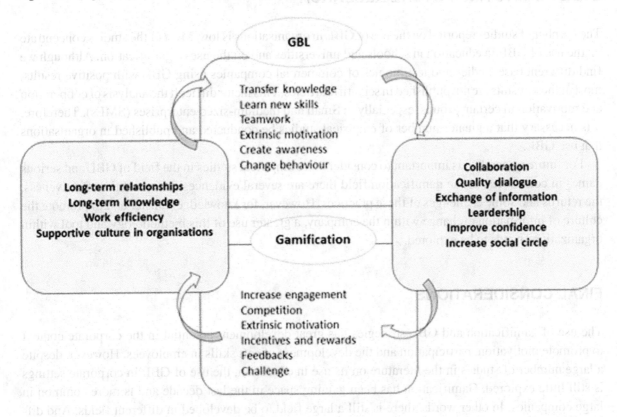

The results of different studies show that the gamification and GBL approach supports the engagement and coordination of the individual and encourages continuous dialogue, interaction and learning. These interactions and knowledge sharing are the basis for driving long-term relationships that will build lasting knowledge in organisations and for making work more efficient and faster with the exchange of information between individuals in organisations. This is why we reinforce that playing in groups to learn is a useful and efficient strategy in organisations (if well developed and managed). Inserting serious games for training and specific learning, and then using some game elements in the company's activities, to increase motivation and collaboration among employees is an alternative with great chances of success for organisations.

According to the studies reported and the arguments proposed, in Figure 2 is reported a summary of the main components and objectives of GBL and gamification. In addition to the components that are widely recognised, we highlight the factor of group work, collaboration and information sharing with the incentive to increase the social circle and dialogue between employees. Through this sharing of information within organisations it is expected that relationships and knowledge will increase in the long term and the company can promote a culture of exchange so that knowledge can be shared and the efficiency of services will increase.

STUDY LIMITS AND FUTURE RESEARCH

The number of studies reported on the use of GBL in organisations is low. Most of the studies concentrate on the use of GBL in education in schools and universities and on the use of gamification. Although we find different case studies and testimonies of commercial companies using GBL with positive results, most of these results are not published in scientific articles. This factor difficult the analysis of cooperation and motivation in certain groups, especially in Small and medium-sized enterprises (SMEs). Therefore, it is necessary that a greater number of empirical studies be conducted and published in organisations that use GBL.

For future research, it is important to consider more empirical studies in the field of GBL and serious games in companies. In the gamification field there are several evidences that attest the effectiveness, the returns and some challenges of these practices. However, for knowledge transfer and to promote the culture of information exchange within the company, a greater use of this methodology and tool within organizations needs to be explored.

FINAL CONSIDERATIONS

The use of gamification and GBL strategies has great development potential in the corporate context to promote motivation, participation and the development of soft skills in employees. However, despite a large number of studies in the literature on its use in education, the use of GBL in corporate settings is still little explored. Gamification has been gaining space in the last decade and is more common in large companies. In other words, there is still a large field to be developed in different fields. And different sizes of companies can be investigated. Understanding how and why this methodology is used is fundamental for the success and sustainability of both strategies.

As the subject matter has grown in recent years, we can conclude that as the interest in this subject grows, organisations are also becoming more aware of the benefits of using these practices. There is a wide range of gamification and GBL activities to be used, and companies only need to use the ones that best fit their model, their culture and the organisation's goals. Keeping these objectives in mind can help decision-makers choose how best to apply these tools and make the most of them.

This study sought to analyse through a critical literature review the importance of gamification and GBL in increasing motivation and collaboration among individuals in a company context. Existing studies suggest that these strategies have a positive impact on dialogue, knowledge sharing and collaboration between employees. The combination of these factors allows an improvement in motivation and performance of individuals in the long term. However, the literature on the subject still needs a greater number of experimental and empirical studies directly in organisations with the use of GBL and gamification tools to prove these results in different sectors and in different company sizes. For companies to be motivated to use this strategy, they need to know this tool, have easy access to the content and have greater proof of these results. Thus, it is also necessary that public agents encourage research on the subject, that companies receive support from public institutions such as universities and training centres to start implementing these tools in their companies and test the benefits of their use.

ACKNOWLEDGMENT

This work was co-funded by Erasmus+ Programme of the European Union Policy (Project Number:612645-EPP-1-2019-1-PT-EPPKA2-KA).

This work was supported by the research unit on Governance, Competitiveness and Public Policy (UIDB/04058/2020), funded by national funds through FCT -Fundação para a Ciência e a Tecnologia.

REFERENCES

A Comprehensive List of 90 Gamification Cases with ROI Stats. (2016). Retrieved October 10, 2021, from https://yukaichou.com/gamification-examples/gamification-stats-figures

Algashami, A., Cham, S., Vuillier, L., Stefanidis, A., Phalp, K., & Ali, R. (2018). *Conceptualising Gamification Risks to Teamwork within Enterprise*. Springer International Publishing. doi:10.1007/978-3-030-02302-7_7

Allal-Chérif, O., & Bidan, M. (2017). Collaborative open training with serious games: Relations, culture, knowledge, innovation, and desire. *Journal of Innovation and Knowledge*, 2(1), 31–38. doi:10.1016/j.jik.2016.06.003

Almeida, F. (2020). Adoption of a Serious Game in the Developing of Emotional Intelligence Skills. *European Journal of Investigation in Health, Psychology and Education*, 10(1), 30–43. doi:10.3390/ejihpe10010004 PMID:34542467

Ballance, C. (2013). Use of games in training : Interactive experiences that engage us to learn. *Industrial and Commercial Training*, 45(4), 218–221. doi:10.1108/00197851311323501

Bardon, T., Dauphine, P., & Josserand, E. (2006). *Why do we play the games ? Exploring institutional and political motivations*. doi:10.1108/00400910910987255

Brooks, A. L., Brooks, E., & Vidakis, N. (2017). Interactivity, Game Creation, Design, Learning, and Innovation. In *6th International Conference, ArtsIT* (*Vol. 2*). Springer International Publishing. 10.1007/978-3-319-55834-9

Buckley, P., & Doyle, E. (2017). Individualising gamification: An investigation of the impact of learning styles and personality traits on the efficacy of gamification using a prediction market. *Computers & Education*, 106, 43–55. doi:10.1016/j.compedu.2016.11.009

Cardador, M. T., Northcraft, G. B., & Whicker, J. (2017). A theory of work gamification: Something old, something new, something borrowed, something cool? *Human Resource Management Review*, 27(2), 353–365. doi:10.1016/j.hrmr.2016.09.014

Carenys, J., & Moya, S. (2016). Digital game-based learning in accounting and business education. *Accounting Education*, 25(6), 598–651. doi:10.1080/09639284.2016.1241951

Carenys, J., Moya, S., & Perramon, J. (2017). Is it worth it to consider videogames in accounting education? A comparison of a simulation and a videogame in attributes, motivation and learning outcomes. *Revista de Contabilidad-Spanish Accouting Review*, 20(2), 118-130. doi:10.1016/j.rcsar.2016.07.003

Chetouani, M., Vanden Abeele, V., Leuven, K., Carmen Moret-Tatay, B., Lopes, S., Magalhães, P., Pereira, A., Martins, J., Magalhães, C., Chaleta, E., & Rosário, P. (2018). Games Used With Serious Purposes: A Systematic Review of Interventions in Patients With Cerebral Palsy. *Frontiers in Psychology*, 9, 1712. doi:10.3389/fpsyg.2018.01712 PMID:30283377

Coleman, T. E., & Money, A. G. (2020). Student-centred digital game – based learning : A conceptual framework and survey of the state of the art. *Higher Education*, 79, 415–457. https://doi.org/10.1007/s10734-019-00417-0

Dale, S. (2014). Gamification: Making work fun, or making fun of work? *Business Information Review*, 31(2), 82–90. https://doi.org/10.1177/0266382114538350

Friedrich, J., Becker, M., Kramer, F., Wirth, M., & Schneider, M. (2020). Incentive design and gamification for knowledge management. . *Journal of Business Research*, 106, 341–352. doi:10.1016/j.jbusres.2019.02.009

Greco, M., Baldissin, N., & Nonino, F. (2013). An Exploratory Taxonomy of Business Games. *Simulation & Gaming*, 44(5), 645–682. https://doi.org/10.1177/1046878113501464

Greco, M., Branca, A. M., & Morena, G. (2011). An Experimental Study of the Reputation Mechanism in a Business Game. *Simulation & Gaming*, 42(1), 27–42. https://doi.org/10.1177/1046878110376793

Gruman, J. A., & Saks, A. M. (2011). Performance management and employee engagement. *Human Resource Management Review*, 21(2), 123–136. https://doi.org/10.1016/j.hrmr.2010.09.004

Hammedi, W., Leclercq, T., Poncin, I., & Alkire, L. (2021). Uncovering the Dark Side of Gamification at Work: Impacts on Engagement and Well-Being. *Journal of Business Research*, 122, 256–269. https://doi.org/https://doi.org/10.1016/j.jbusres.2020.08.032

Henriksen, T. D., & Borgesen, K. (2016). Can good leadership be learned through business games. *Human Resource Development International*, 19(5), 388-405. doi:10.1080/13678868

Hoffmann, G., & Matysiak, L. (2019). *Exploring Game Design for the Financial Education of Millenials* (Vol. 0–1). IEEE Xplore.

Ke, F., Xie, K., & Xie, Y. (2016). Game-based learning engagement: A theory- and data-driven exploration. *British Journal of Educational Technology*, 47(6), 1183–1201. https://doi.org/10.1111/bjet.12314

Kiili, K., Lainema, T., De Freitas, S., & Arnab, S. (2014). Flow framework for analyzing the quality of educational games q. *Entertainment Computing*, 5(4), 367–377. https://doi.org/10.1016/j.entcom.2014.08.002

Larson, K. (2020). Serious Games and Gamification in the Corporate Training Environment: A Literature Review.). . *TechTrends*, 64(2), 319–328. doi:10.100711528-019-00446-7

Madani, K., Pierce, T. W., & Mirchi, A. (2017). Serious games on environmental management.). . *Sustainable Cities and Society*, 29, 1–11. doi:10.1016/j.scs.2016.11.007

Marsh, T. (2011). Serious games continuum : Between games for purpose and experiential environments for purpose. *Entertainment Computing*, 2(2), 61–68. https://doi.org/10.1016/j.entcom.2010.12.004

Mekler, E. D., Brühlmann, F., Tuch, A. N., & Opwis, K. (2017). Towards understanding the effects of individual gamification elements on intrinsic motivation and performance.). . *Computers in Human Behavior, 71*, 525–534. doi:10.1016/j.chb.2015.08.048

Mitchell, R., Schuster, L., & Drennan, J. (2017). Understanding how gamification influences behaviour in social marketing. *Australasian Marketing Journal, 25*(1), 12–19. https://doi.org/10.1016/j.ausmj.2016.12.001

Mitchell, R., Schuster, L., & Jin, H. S. (2020). Gamification and the impact of extrinsic motivation on needs satisfaction : Making work fun? *Journal of Business Research, 106*, 323–330. https://doi.org/10.1016/j.jbusres.2018.11.022

Obaid, I., & Farooq, M. S. (2020). Gamification for Recruitment and Job Training : Model, Taxonomy, and Challenges. *IEEE Access: Practical Innovations, Open Solutions, 8*, 65164–65178. https://doi.org/10.1109/ACCESS.2020.2984178

Oprescu, F., Jones, C., & Katsikitis, M. (2014). I Play at Work. Ten principles for transforming work processes through gamification.). . *Frontiers in Psychology, 5*(JAN). doi:10.3389/fpsyg.2014.00014

Patricio, R., Moreira, A., Zurlo, F., & Melazzini, M. (2020). Co-creation of new solutions through gamification: A collaborative innovation practice. *Creativity and Innovation Management,* 146–160. doi:10.1111/caim.12356

Patrício, R., Moreira, A. C., & Zurlo, F. (2018). Gamification approaches to the early stage of innovation. *Creativity and Innovation Management, 27*(4), 499–511. https://doi.org/10.1111/caim.12284

Perryer, C., Celestine, N. A., Scott-Ladd, B., & Leighton, C. (2016). Enhancing workplace motivation through gamification: Transferrable lessons from pedagogy. *International Journal of Management Education, 14*(3), 327–335. https://doi.org/10.1016/j.ijme.2016.07.001

Reiners, T., & Wood, L. C. (2015). Gamification in education and business. *Gamification in Education and Business.* doi:10.1007/978-3-319-10208-5

Robson, K., Plangger, K., Kietzmann, J. H., McCarthy, I., & Pitt, L. (2015). Is it all a game? Understanding the principles of gamification. *Business Horizons, 58*(4), 411–420. https://doi.org/10.1016/j.bushor.2015.03.006

Ruhi, U. (2015). Level Up Your Strategy: Towards a Descriptive Framework for Meaningful Entruerprise Gamification. *Technology Innovation Management Review, 5*(8), 5–16. doi:10.22215/timreview918

Tercanli, H., Martina, R., Dias, M. F., Wakkee, I., Reuter, J., Amorim, M., Madaleno, M., Magueta, D., Vieira, E., Veloso, C., Figueiredo, C., Vitória, A., Gomes, I., Meireles, G., Daubariene, A., Daunoriene, A., Mortensen, A. K., Zinovyeva, A., Trigueros, I. R., … Gutiérrez-Pérez, J. (2021). *Educational Escape Room in Practice: Research, experiences and recommendations.* doi:https://doi.org/10.34624/rpxk-hc6

Uukkivi, A., & Labanova, O. (2018). How we have motivated students in sciences. *4th International Conference on Higher Education Advances (HEAd'18),* 769–776. doi:https://doi.org/10.4995/HEAd18.2018.8082

Xu, F., Buhalis, D., & Weber, J. (2017). Serious games and the gamification of tourism.). . *Tourism Management, 60*, 244–256. doi:10.1016/j.tourman.2016.11.020

Yi, L., Zhou, Q., Xiao, T., Qing, G., & Mayer, I. (2020). Conscientiousness in Game-Based Learning. *Simulation & Gaming*, *51*(5), 712–734. https://doi.org/10.1177/1046878120927061

ADDITIONAL READING

Grivokostopoulou, F., Kovas, K., & Perikos, I. (2019). Examining the impact of a gamified entrepreneurship education framework in higher education. *Sustainability (Switzerland)*, *11*(20), 5623. Advance online publication. doi:10.3390u11205623

Hosseini, H., & Mostafapour, W. M. (2019). Learning IS Child's Play: Game-Based Learning in Computer Science Education. *Computer Science Education. ACM Trans. Comput. Educ*, *19*(3), 1–18. Advance online publication. doi:10.1145/3282844

Nicholson, S. (2018). Creating engaging escape rooms for the classroom. *Childhood Education*, *94*(1), 44–49. doi:10.1080/00094056.2018.1420363

Patrício, R., Moreira, A. C., & Zurlo, F. (2020). Enhancing design thinking approaches to innovation through gamification. *European Journal of Innovation Management*, *24*(5), 1569–1594. doi:10.1108/EJIM-06-2020-0239

Chapter 14
Applying Gamification Strategies to Create Training in Lean Methodologies:
A Practical Case

Victor Neto

Centre for Mechanical Technology and Automation (TEMA), Department of Mechanical Engineering, University of Aveiro, Portugal

Henrique Bessa

Centre for Mechanical Technology and Automation (TEMA), Department of Mechanical Engineering, University of Aveiro, Portugal

Ricardo Ferreira de Mascarenhas

RM Consulting, Portugal

ABSTRACT

It is more important than ever that organizations make the most of their resources, reduce costs, optimize processes, and engage in continuous improvement. A lean philosophy presents itself as a management model that guides companies in this direction, but for the successful implementation of lean methodologies, human resources at all levels need to learn what it is and be engaged with it. Thus, there is a need to develop tools that would transmit the lean theoretical concepts in a practical and involved way. This chapter proposes the development of a tool that is the result of merging gamification and lean philosophy, developing a game for people without knowledge in this area, serving as an introduction to it, and demonstrating some applications of this philosophy. The practical result of the synergy created between strategies of gamification and training in lean methodologies is described.

DOI: 10.4018/978-1-7998-9223-6.ch014

INTRODUCTION

In an increasingly competitive, dynamic, and demanding labor market, training must be a strategy for professional and personal growth. Professional training allows the increase and/or adjustment of workers' knowledge and skills throughout life. Constant training depends very much on the commitment of the recipient, but also on how the information is exposed or communicated by the trainer (Allen & Poteet, 1999; Alsawaier, 2018; ILLERIS, 2003; Majuri et al., 2018; Mestrado & Vers, 2018; Pereira et al., 2018).

Gamification is the application of game design techniques and mechanics (Hunicke et al., 2004), to non-game problems, such as engineering, business, or social impact challenges (Markopoulos et al., 2015; Patrício et al., 2020). It is a method that can be used to achieve training goals using playable elements to arouse interest, increase participation, develop creativity and autonomy, promote dialogue, and engage learners to solve problematic situations. Ozelkan & Galambosi (Ozelkan & Galambosi, 2009) emphasize that there are different ways to teach production principles and strategies like 'lean', for instance, using some of the traditional approaches such as industry projects, case studies, computer simulations, class projects, or company visits. On the other hand, it is possible to make the learning process even more effective by using classroom games (or simulation exercises), since they provide a mechanism for active discovery learning (Blicblau et al., 2016).

Thus, this chapter intends to contribute with knowledge about how to apply the concept of gamification to business training in lean methodologies, giving a practical example. The result was the creation and development of a game, from theoretical aspects that were chained until arriving at a final physical form, a board game in which the main object is a *moliceiro* (a typical boat from the city of Aveiro, Portugal) that can be manipulated and played in lean vocational training actions. The chapter briefly introduces lean and gamification, where a canvas framework that guides the game design is presented, following the proposal by Jansons, Mediawake (Latvia) (Jansons, 2016). The material board game and playing rounds are then idealizes and prototyped. Preliminary testing to the prototyped game was made, which validate the overall proposal.

Lean

Lean is a practical and thinking philosophy that is based on the Toyota Production System principles and methods to make an entire organization work. It's a holistic business system that starts from understanding the goal (value to the customer), from designing and managing processes to efficiently, and from getting the most out of people. Its three main underlying principles are: act according to outlined objectives; respect all people; and continuous improvement. (Belhadi et al., 2018; Bhamu & Singh Sangwan, 2014; Cherrafi et al., 2016; Gould & Colwill, 2015)

The concept of Lean Manufacturing emerged in the 1950s, in Japan, within Toyota Motors Company. Today it is one of the most competitive production systems with high-quality indices (Kehr & Proctor, 2017; Rüttimann & Stöckli, 2016). The company was one of the most successful overpassing the 1973 oil crisis. This success aroused the interest of other car manufacturers worldwide and led the Toyota Production System to be considered on a global scale as a viable and profitable production philosophy at that time (Black†, 2007). At present, lean production principles are implemented not only in the automotive industry but also in operations and services such as hospitals, insurance agencies, government agencies, high technology products, oil production facilities, or information technology (Bhamu & Singh Sangwan, 2014; Blicblau et al., 2016; Leite et al., 2015; Rüttimann & Stöckli, 2016). This is valid because lean principles can adapt to any type of organization, since its focus is to improve the performance of companies, relying on employees and their knowledge, eliminating all the waste, and adapting to the realities of specific environments (Corbett, 2007; Habidin et al., 2016; Pinto, 2014).

Lean is defined as a process that includes five steps. The first step is defining customer value, then defining the value stream, making it 'flow', establish pull, and the last step is striving for excellence. In this way, lean-based strategies are intended to guide an organization to be able to produce the right things, in the right place, at the right time, and in the desired quantities, abolishing activities that do not add value to the product. However, there is still tolerance and flexibility to accommodate possible changes, considering customers customization. Figure 1 outlines the 5 principles of the lean philosophy. The market is becoming more volatile day by day, so understanding market dynamics is a crucial factor if one wants to design manufacturing systems better. Lean manufacturing believes in the simple fact that customers will pay for the value of services they receive but will not pay for mistakes. Thus, the search for continuous improvement and the reduction of waste are the main ways to increase efficiency and make a business profitable. (Bhamu & Singh Sangwan, 2014; Cherrafi et al., 2016; Rüttimann & Stöckli, 2016)

Figure 1. The 5 principles of lean philosophy

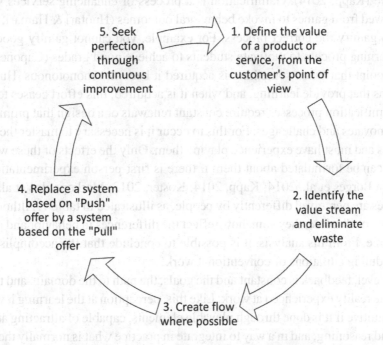

It is important to understand that lean thinking is not just a set of practices that are usually found on the shop floor but rather a profound cultural shift in the way people and organizations think and behave. The results are achieved through practices sustained by a set of beliefs and principles that are understood and adopted. In a lean organization, everyone is focused on identifying and eliminating all sources of waste and inefficiencies. The organization must look to the world through the eyes of the client and attempts to satisfy its expectations (and even surpasses them). The true power to transform lean thinking is only achieved if it is applied throughout the organization and subsequently throughout the supply chain. (Pinto, 2014)

Gamification

"Gamification" is an awkward word: a neologism that smacks frivolity and provisional terminology. The definition most employ is some version of the use of game design elements in non-game contexts, a concept that turns out not at all as flip as it sounds. Game dynamics in nongame tasks can make those tasks more engaging and encourage desirable behaviors in customers, users or students, unquestionably an effect worthy of exploration (Caponetto et al., 2014; Deterding, Dixon, et al., 2011; Deterding, Sicart, et al., 2011; Groh, 2012).

The word "gamification" was first typed in the early 2000s, but just become popular in the research and industry community about ten years later (Groh, 2012), therefore a concept that, despite the great curiosity that it arouses, still needs to be clarified and deepened, so that it is not confused with game design, the development of the concept of the game system that can be for an educational end, but, most often, it is intended the development of ludic games. It is important to recognize what gamification can and cannot achieve (Kapp, 2014). Gamification is a process of enhancing services with motivational affordances borrowed from games to invoke behavioral outcomes (Huotari & Hamari, 2012). It is therefore imperative to gamify the correct process. For example, you cannot gamify good grades, but you can gamify the learning process to motivate students to achieve good grades (Caponetto et al., 2014).

The literature point that when something is acquired it becomes monotonous. Humans invest their energy in situations that provide learning, and when it is acquired, this effort ceases to make sense. For this reason, the gamification processes require constant renewals or a design that promotes a continuous experience that innovates and challenges. For this to occur it is necessary to master the mechanisms that make up the games and must have experience playing them. Only the effects of these will be known, and a critical opinion can be formulated about them if there is first-person experimentation. (Caponetto et al., 2014; de Sousa Borges et al., 2014; Kapp, 2014; Koster, 2013; Markopoulos et al., 2015)

Work and games are perceived differently by people, as illustrated in table 1. Although the characteristics displayed are not absolute, they somehow reflect the differences in behavior and people's reactions to the type of source. From his analysis, it is possible to conclude that the accomplishment of tasks is fun in games and dull in situations of conventional work.

At the gaming level, feedback is constant and the goals, the path to the domain, and the rules are clear, contrasting with the reality experienced at work. Like this, perception at the learning level becomes much easier and more intuitive if it is done through playable elements, capable of attracting attention, allowing rapid responses and reasoning, and in a way to integrate in practice what is normally theoretical learning.

Gamification provides a range of acceptable actions, rules, time requirements, feedback mechanisms, and desired behaviors while providing opportunities for students to direct their experiences. This range of opportunities allows instructors to facilitate and guide (as opposed to dictating) the learning environment. (Armier et al., 2016; Caponetto et al., 2014)

Table 1. The human perception of work and games [adapted from (Jansons, 2016)]

Source	Work	Game
Tasks	repetitive, dull	repetitive, fun
Feedback	once a year	constantly
Goals	contradictory, vague	clear
Path to Mastery	unclear	clear
Rules	unclear, opaque	clear, transparent
Information	too much and not enough	the right amount at the right time
Failure	forbidden, punished, don't talk about it	expected, encouraged, spectacular, about it
Status of users	hidden	transparent, timely
Promotion	suck-up the boss	meritocracy
Collaboration	yes	yes
Speed/Risk	low/high	high/low

As far as gamification is concerned the construction of the game can be divided into six steps/ questions, which is represented in a canvas framework in table 2, adapted from the work of Jansons, Mediawake (Latvia) (Jansons, 2016). The first question is to realize what the real objective is or what is the problem that needs to be solved. Secondly, the type of behavior to be adopted to achieve the goal must be identified by defining the sequence of steps to be taken. Thirdly, who are the players, what is their personality, and what are their goals; it is important to realize from game to game what the target audience is, to provide the best learning methodology possible. Fourthly, define the dynamics of the game, it means defining how players will participate. The mechanics of how the game unfolds, what are its constituents, whether they are attractive or not to the touch, if the colors are desirable, if the game attracts attention and captivates the player, constitute the fifth-stage. Finally, define the success indicators of the game, that is, create a set of measures that allow classifying/quantify the outcome of the game.

Table 2. Guide for the development of gamified training elements [adapted from (Jansons, 2016)]

1. A REAL GOAL OR PROBLEM?	2. BEHAVIOR	3. PLAYERS
Study process, productivity, teamwork, leisure time, loyalty, altruism, etc.	How to reach the goal? A. Behavior guide towards the goal? B. What is their sequence?	Personality & Roles A. Who are they? B. What do they like or want? e.g. students, colleagues, partners, ...
4. DYNAMICS	**5. MECHANICS**	**6. SUCCESS**
Why will they participate? A. What is the player motivation? B. What will they gain? C. What created fun? e.g. events, points, money, prizes, …	What will trigger the actions? Actions, behaviors, and control mechanisms afforded to the player within a game context. e.g. apps, website, social media, leaflets, events, meetings, calls, recommendations.	How do we measure success? A. What are the indicators? B. How measurements will be taken? C Who will be responsible?

Gamification in a Business Context

Currently, technological advances are permanently transforming societal patterns, giving rise to obstacles that have never been seen before. An exhaustive routine, formed by new trends, scenarios in constant transformation, and new demands, where the capacity of companies to innovate represents a competitive advantage and is a strategic factor for the sustainability of the business. (Bartunek & Woodman, 2015)

People motivation is of crucial importance for organizational development; however, it is not an easy problem to solve in corporative environments. Maintaining high-performance teams is not a simple task for companies, especially given the great competitiveness and immediacy of the current society (Caroline Ngonyo Njoroge, 2014). Gamification is achieving an increased number of adepts in the marketing area, leading many companies to invest in this way to enthrall customers (Sailer et al., 2017).Each year, more organizations are driving innovation processes by gamifying processes. Gartner Consulting (USA) stated, in a 2014 report (Brian Burke, 2014), that scalable service in consumer goods marketing and customer retention will become as important as Facebook, eBay, or Amazon, with more than 70% of Global 2000 organizations having at least one gamified application. This means that large global business organizations are using gamification to captivate their target audience. Since 2010, the time from which gamification has resurfaced with the concept that is currently used, many companies have launched gamification projects. (Hamari & Koivisto, 2015)

Gamification of Lean

The "lean thinking" term as a concept of leadership and business management was first used in the form of a reference literary work by Womack *et al.* in 1990 (Womack et al., 1990). Since then, the term has been used as a reference to the management and leadership philosophy that aims to systematically eliminate waste and create value - one of the most successful management paradigms ever.

A set of practical tools and methods has been developed at the operational level to support lean thinking. Examples of such tools are the 5S, batch reduction, U layout, value flow analysis, supermarket, or poka-yoke.

In terms of gamification and to ensure the adoption by stakeholders of continuous improvement systems, the system should include a broader objective and constitutive rules to promote a fun attitude among users (voluntary overcoming of unnecessary obstacles).

Analyzing potential players is also essential for gamification design. Instructors should identify student motivations, cultural and generational norms, and prior content knowledge regarding topics of interest (Dignan, 2011). Instructors should also evaluate student tendencies toward cooperation and competition. Gaining information about player characteristics helps instructors use game elements that maintain attention and interest (Armier et al., 2016).

Lean laboratory exercises that were developed based on a physical simulation of a clock assembly called TIME WISE are described in the work of Johnson *et al.* (Johnson et al., 2003) where the students have a chance to be assembly personnel, production planners, material handlers, quality inspectors, warehouse clerks, and inspectors. While both traditional topics and lean principles are covered in the course, it is in a way where they have an opportunity to `discover' theory for themselves. Prusak (Prusak, 2004) studied the teaching of lean principles employing classroom simulations based on some lean efficiency factors to evaluate a production environment for improvements. His focus is on the move from qualification to the quantification of waste. After the simulation, he concludes that learning was very stimulating not only because of the hands-on activities and the freedom in designing improvement measures but also because of peer interaction (Ozelkan & Galambosi, 2009).

Currently, there is a wide range of games about lean. However, almost none has a high level of personalization nor is it able to introduce several theoretical concepts, being focused only on the teaching of only one concept. Most use Lego parts as the main object, or even sheets of paper to build boats or paper airplanes. Although there are some games about lean training, there was a need to create a new and unique tool that combines gamification with theoretical lean concepts (the concepts described above). It was essential that the game was attractive and could convey as much knowledge as possible. This game will be shown in the next section.

New Game Proposal

The game design follows procedures that align with traditional instructional design processes. These include conducting audience analyses to identify learner needs and desires, developing game rules, rewards, and punishments, and determining feedback mechanisms to indicate progress (Dichev et al., 2014; Dignan, 2011; Kelle et al., 2012; Patrício et al., 2018).

The first step of the developing process of the game was the product definition. It was defined that the game would simulate a boat production unit, in which the players will be productive elements where they will have to assemble the constituents of the boat - in this case, the boat is a *moliceiro*, a typical boat of Aveiro. It will have several rounds, among which there will be the introduction of concepts of lean and that will have a degree of difficulty increasing progressively through the introduction of new orders by customers.

Defining the design was the second step of the development of the game. This stage includes the definition of the number of pieces, the number of rounds, the number of lean concepts to incorporate, the requests that will be made in each round, and the entire learning process that will be the game. Table 2 shows the guide for the development of training elements through gamification that served as the basis for the development of the game. In Table 3 it can be seen the base used for the development of the game, as a result of completing the guide, and having in mind each stage:

1. The whole game should be focused on its main objective, which is to enable the trainees to learn on lean philosophies training context.
2. Through the successive introduction of lean theoretical concepts, in a weighted way and with a predefined succession of them, so that we never lose the thread of the game; the increasing difficult degree corresponding to new successive requests from the clients is also a way to keep the trainees focused on the main objective.
3. The main users of the game will be trainees in lean methodologies; during the course, the trainees will be placed in positions of work in which they will have the responsibility to fulfill the tasks that are proposed to them. Whenever there is a request from a customer, there will be tasks distribution - quantity and definition of parts to be assembled in each job - that will lead to each person having to take responsibility for the execution of their work.
4. Player's motivation is given by continuous learning and by the opportunity to see in practice, in an illustrated and simplified way, the application of theoretical concepts, allowing them to gain knowledge about these concepts and experience in their application; what will create fun in the

game will be the continuous learning allied to the interpersonal interaction and the group dynamics that it is intended to be generated.

5. The actions chain comes with the rounds succession and requests that are being made and added.

Table 3. Filled guide for the development of gamified training elements

1. A REAL GOAL OR PROBLEM?	2. BEHAVIOR	3. PLAYERS
A well-defined objective, to facilitate the learning of theoretical concepts about Lean methodologies	How to reach the goal? A. Successive introduction of theoretical concepts B. Increase the level of difficulty by changing the satisfaction of customers	Personality & Roles A. Lean methodologies trainees B. Learning theoretical concepts in a practical way
4. DYNAMICS	5. MECHANICS	6. SUCCESS
Why will they participate? A. Learn more, see practical applications B. Knowledge and experience C. Interaction and learning	What will trigger the actions? Set of *moliceiro* parts, that will be used as a puzzle. Successive rounds, level of difficulty increasing progressively, new orders appearance	How do we measure success? A. Acquired knowledge B. Trainees' satisfaction C. Trainer

6. Measured through the satisfaction of the trainees to the extent that they can recognize their importance, the acquisition of new skills, and the understanding of the importance of the applicability of theoretical concepts in practice.

The following two sections will present the game dynamics and materialization. These sections, although they are sequenced, should be considered parallel since both constitute the game construction process.

Game Materialization

Deterding *et al.* (Deterding, Dixon, et al., 2011) state that good game design is hard to obtain and that it cannot be performed by adding magical game mechanics. It is warned that game-based incentive method could only work with careful design and addressed that designers should consider the whole system than adding a gamified component and desired game-like user behavior requires comprehensive game-like experience that is supported by not only a "game structure" but also a "game-look" surface (Chee & Wong, 2017; Seaborn & Fels, 2015). It requires not just adoption, but also a creation of emotion, feeling, and sensation. It is easy to understand that how essential the emotional aspect in gamification but designing it to satisfy users' feelings, emotions, and experience states is more difficult to achieve as its emotional aspect involves multifaceted considerations (Chee & Wong, 2017). The constituents of this game were all created from scratch and based on the literature indications. An attempt was made to create a set of harmonious and attractive pieces that allowed to correspond to the dynamics of the game mentioned previously. Figure 2 presents different assemblies of the *moliceiro* and the pieces that constitute the 3D printing parts.

Figure 2. Examples of assemblies of the moliceiro (top) and the set of 3D printing game parts (bottom)

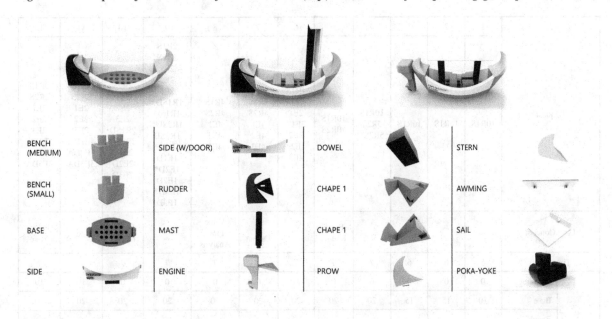

All parts were built through 3D printing by FFF (Fused Filament Fabrication), with a resolution of 200 microns and a 10% internal fill. The game is still constituted by a transport box, in which there are compartments for each type of piece; these box components aid in the introduction of the lean supermarket concept. There is also the technical documentation of the game divided into two parts, an instruction booklet (reduced size, only with indications to sequence the game), and a user manual (more complete, with suggestions of how to introduce theoretical concepts).

Game Dynamics

This game is intended for people without knowledge in lean, serving as an introduction and to simply demonstrate some of the advantages of this philosophy. There is sometimes some difficulty in understanding the connection between the various lean tools used and one of the goals of this game is to make this connection visible and easy; so, a threaded introduction of each methodology is made as new customer requests emerge.

The game is to be used in a teaching environment, by a Lean methodology's trainer, that will serve as the facilitator of the vocational training actions.

To demonstrate in a reduced and practical way the game dynamics, Table 4, contains the number of pieces, the times of each round, the type of order (decoded later in Table 5), and the timings which lean theoretical concepts should be introduced. In this table, it is possible to see the number of pieces used in each round, and the maximum values to be used throughout the game for each type of part. The time for each round ranges from 5 to 7 minutes and there is space for six lean concept's introduction: 5S, Batch Reduction, U Layout, Value Flow Analysis, Supermarket, and Poka-Yoke.

Each request (simulation of a request by a customer) is identified and coded according to the rules described in Table 5. A detailed explanation of each round is given later.

Table 4. Summary game board - number of pieces, concepts introduced, time per round.

		1	2	3	4	5	6	7	8	9	10	11	12
Request		10R1S	16R1S	16R1S	10R1S 5R2S 5R2S*	10R1S 10R2S	4R1S 4R2S 2E1 2E1* 2E2 2E2* 4E3	4R1S 4R2S 4E1 4E2 4E3	4R1S 4R2S 4E1 4E2 4E3	2R1S 2R2S 2E1 2E2 2E3 1R1SD* 1R1SD 1R2SD* 1R2SD 1E1D* 1E1D 1E2D* 1E2D 1E3D* 1E3D	2R1S 2R2S 2E1 2E2 2E3 2R1SD 2R2SD 2E1D 2E2D 2E3D	2R1S 2R2S 2E1 2E2 2E3 4E1DA 3E2DA 3E3DA	2R1S 2R2S 2E1 2E2 2E3 4E1DA 3E2DA 3E3DA
Lean Concept				5S		Batch Reduc.		U Layout	Value Flow Analysis		Super-market		Poka-Yoke
Time (min)		5	6	6	7	7	7	7	7	7	7	7	7
Number of pieces	Awming	0	0	0	0	0	0	0	0	0	0	10	10
	Base	10	15	15	20	20	20	20	20	20	20	20	20
	Bench (medium)	0	0	0	20	20	24	24	24	24	24	24	24
	Bench (small)	20	30	30	20	20	20	20	20	20	20	21	21
	Chape 1	20	30	30	40	40	40	40	40	40	40	40	40
	Chape 2	20	30	30	40	40	40	40	40	40	40	40	40
	Dowel	20	30	30	40	40	40	40	40	40	40	40	40
	Engine	0	0	0	0	0	12	12	12	12	12	16	16
	Mast	20	30	30	40	40	16	16	16	16	16	28	28
	Prow	10	15	15	20	20	20	20	20	20	20	20	20
	Rudder	10	15	15	20	20	8	8	8	8	8	4	4
	Sail	10	15	15	15	20	8	8	8	8	8	4	4
	Side	20	30	30	40	40	40	40	40	30	30	30	30
	Side (w/ door)	0	0	0	0	0	0	0	0	10	10	10	10
	Stern	10	15	15	20	20	20	20	20	20	20	20	20

Table 5 serves as a guide for coding and decoding orders. In the rest position of the code appears the way the boat moves - whether it is the rudder or the engine. In the second, the number of seats that constitute it, if it is only one (two small seats together), if are two (two middle seats placed parallel) or three (two small seats placed parallel and a medium seat perpendicular to the small ones). In position 3 are the accessories, this is if the *moliceiro* has a sail, a door (notch on the side), or an awning. Finally, in the last position and with a binary response, either it is a boat reused/adapted from another model or not.

Table 5. Order coding guide

Position #1	Position #2	Position #3	Position #4
Locomotion	**No. of seats**	**Accessories**	**Reutilization**
R - Rudder		S - Sail	* - Yes
E - Engine		D - Door	
		A - Awning	

All boats must have a type of locomotion and at least one seat. If the *moliceiro* is ruddered it must contain a sail as well. To add to the positions there is the number of *moliceiros*, thus, an example code 10R1S, the order is 10 boats driven to the rudder (R), with 1 seat and with sail (S). This is not a reused boat. Another example is 1LR2SD*, 1 *moliceiro*, driven at the rudder with 2 seats, a sail, and a door (lateral with notch) that is reused.

It is added that the same must be played by at least five people and can be played for more if they are rotated. Of these five players, four should be allocated to the operation of the jobs and one should be the process manager.

To use the game as intended, it is suggested that it should be divided into 12 rounds which are described below. The first rounds are elementary round, to create relationship between the trainees and the *moliceiros* parts and creating on them the desire to win. As the round increase, the level of complexity is increased, and different Lean concepted are addressed.

First-Round

This round is free, 4 people should try to produce without indication or external references, 10 *moliceiros* in 5 minutes (the goal is not expected to be reached) of the type R1S - rudder, a large seat, and a sail. The pieces must be scattered in such a way that the search for them will be disorganized.

This round purpose is to create a close relationship between the trainees and the pieces of the game, make them want to fulfill the customer's request, and let them organize and structure the production in the way they think is most convenient.

In the end, all the boats must be disassembled, and all the pieces placed inside the box (in a disorganized way) or scattered on the table, as previously chosen.

Second-Round

This round has exactly the same type of *moliceiros* from the previous round (Round 1), giving another minute of available time. There is also an increase in the quantity requested (sixteen) and the imposition of batch manufacture (batches of 4 *moliceiros*, which must be used in all rounds until contrary orders emerge). Employees should be disposed in a line (simulating the conventional assembly line of mass production), and divided into 4 jobs; each station will have its parts to fit in, and Station No. 1 will be in charge of fitting the base and two shapes, Station No. 2 the remaining two shapes and the two sides, Station No. 3 the rudder, the dowel, the prow, and the stern; and finally, Station No. 4 will have to fit the accessories, this is, the mast (two, one above the other), the sail and the two small seats - which together will form what is considered the single, large seat. Figure 3 illustrates the assembly sequence requested. It is still plausible that trainees fail to achieve the goal.

Figure 3. Sequence of the assembly stations requested in round two

The pieces should be at the end, just like in the previous round, scattered on a table or all mixed inside the box.

Third-Round

This round works in the same way as the previous round (Round 2), it has the same type of order, and the only difference to register is the use of the lean tool introduced - 5S.

The procedure for implementing the 5S tool is as follows:

- **Seiri (Sort)**: ask a volunteer to sort out the obvious garbage (remove unused parts like engine, awning, etc.) from the material needed to assemble the product. Note that these parts do not necessarily go to the garbage, but to temporary storage.
- **Seiton (Set)**: Select the required parts for each job. Separate them and put them in the best position possible so that they can be assembled. Visual management referral.
- **Seiso (Shine)**: depending on the location, clean something (example: carry dust cloth, throw away the trash, etc). If it is not possible to demonstrate in practice, just mention the importance of cleaning in an industrial environment and in the service area (e.g., health sector or office).
- **Seiketsu (Standardise)**: place a copy of the corresponding assembly next to each workstation. Refer to the importance of standardization for continuous improvement. Refer that allows staff turnover and facilitates the last S (sustain).
- **Shitsuke (Sustain)**: note that the 5S must be sustainable so there is no retreat to the previous state. Refer importance of audits and verifications.

In this way, it is intended that:

- Realize the importance of standardization - the unused pieces are stored in the box leaving the rest scattered on the table; the parts used are separated by type of part and placed in an organized way in each workstation to facilitate assembly.
- Remove from the tables anything that is too much or does not add value.
- Rotate people (the operators).
- Realize the importance of audits and inspections to ensure that all previous steps are guaranteed.

It will be necessary to store 5 *moliceiros* at the end of the round without being disassembled so that they can be reused in the next round.

Fourth-Round

In this round there is the introduction of coding request; from there, all requests will be made by code identification, which is explained in Table 5.

In addition, there is a new request from a customer who thinks that only a long seat is not enough, so it intends to have two middle seats arranged perpendicular to the movement of the boat.

The time of the round becomes 7 minutes for the production of 20 *moliceiros*. The number of the batch, the number of jobs, and the use of the 5S tool are to be maintained.

The reused *moliceiros* should be the result of the removal of the small seats in line and the placement of the middle seats in the correct position. For the next round, it will not be necessary to store any type of *moliceiro*, all of which must be disassembled.*Fifth-round*

This round works the same way as the previous round, including the same type of order (except for the boats reused), and the only difference to register is the use of the lean tool introduced – Batch Reduction.

In this way, it is intended that it is no longer necessary to produce batches of 4 *moliceiros* before passing between workstations, for the production of batches of two vessels. Thus, each time an employee completes two assemblies, he/she must proceed immediately to the delivery of these parts to the next station.

It is also important to highlight the need for standardization since its use allows the reduction of product and production costs while maintaining or increasing quality.

It will be necessary to store 4 *moliceiros* at the end of the round without being disassembled so that they can be reused in the next round. Within these, 2 will be of L1V and another two of type L2V.

Sixth-Round

In this round, there is a client who thinks that only moving the *moliceiro* with the sail is not enough, because in little wind days the locomotion becomes impossible. Let them then go on to produce boats with engines.

In addition, the same customer also intends to add a new configuration of the seats - in this case, a layout with 3 seats in which two small parallels with each other and with a movement of the boat and a medium seat perpendicular to the other seats.

In this application, as shown in figure 4, there is then the production of *moliceiros* with an engine and with 3 different provisions of seats. Two *moliceiros* (R1S) are reused and it is necessary to remove the rudder and to install the engine and also with the same procedure two R2S, which will pass to E1 and E2 in succession.

All previously introduced theoretical concepts are to be retained.

It will not be necessary to store any type of *moliceiro* for the next round, and therefore all parts must be separated piece by piece.

Figure 4. Moliceiros order in round six

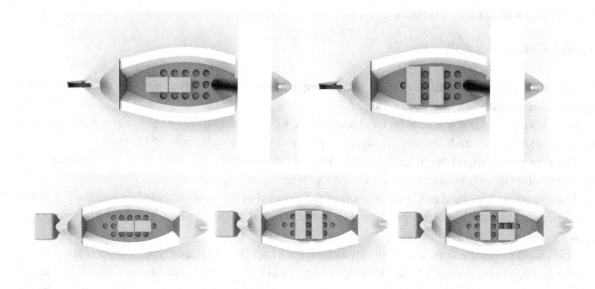

Seventh-Round

This round works the same way as the previous round, including the same type of order, this time without using reconfigured boats, and the difference to register is the use of the introduced lean tool – U Layout.

The procedure for implementing the U Layout tool is: refer to the advantages of a U-line in relation to a line in I or L (Figure 5 a); proceed to the elimination of one of the jobs and place the remaining ones according to Figure 5 b).

Figure 5. a) Line Layout - initial; b) U Layout - final

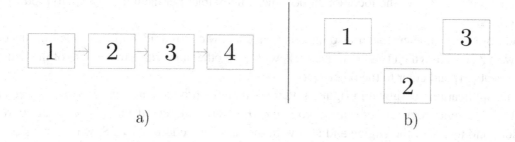

Production will cease to be done in a line layout, with the provision of jobs as U – 3 jobs. The surplus operator must be regarded as an unsatisfied operator and as such can be changed to logistics or quality departments (at the theoretical level, since in practice he is momentarily unemployed, and later on he will be called back to collaborate).

At the distribution level of pieces per workstation, it is done as follows: the first is now in charge of assembling the base and the shapes; the second, add the dowels, the locomotion ways (engine or rudder), the prow, and the stern; finally, the third station assembles the accessories.

Eighth-Round

This round works in the same way as the previous two rounds, including the same type of order, and the only difference to note is the use of the lean tool introduced – Value Flow Analysis.

In this round, a value flow analysis should be carried out. As a suggestion, you can use the Value Stream Mapping (VSM) tool with the following procedure:

1. Explain what VSM is, and its advantages.
2. Draw the old VSM (sheet or board).
3. Identify the flows and place the inventory.
4. Draw the current map.

This round must keep an assembled boat of each type of *moliceiro*, without disassembling, in a total of five *moliceiros*, so that they can be reused in the next round.

Ninth-Round

In this round, there are in addition to all the different previous orders, a new customer who is interested in buying *moliceiros* who take into consideration the entry for the same. On the sides of the current, no notch/no door facilitates the entrance to the boat. Thus, there is a need to make all the models so far mounted but add half of the twenty to make the side with a door.

In this application, there is then the production of *moliceiros* with an engine and with 3 different provisions of seats. Two *moliceiros* (R1S) are reused and it is necessary to remove the rudder and to install the engine and also with the same procedure two R2S, which will pass to E1 and E2 in succession.

Tenth-Round

This round works the same way as the previous round, even has the same type of order, and the only difference is the use of the lean tool introduced – Supermarket.

The procedure for implementing the Supermarket tool is as follows:

- Build a supermarket on an adjacent table to the U-line, with the various types of pieces divided by type-
- Place at each workstation two identical small containers for each type of workpiece-
- Organize the pieces that have been scattered so far, placing them inside their compartment.

It should be noted that it is not necessary to lay off staff although in Round 5 a staff member has been asked to cease to perform his duties; this employee will become the logistic operator, transporting the parts from the supermarket to each job.

Practical examples of everyday life should be added to this lean tool (e.g., explaining that the super-market in an industrial environment functions in the same way as a real supermarket).

For the next round, it will not be necessary to store any kind of *moliceiro*, and all of them must be disassembled.

Eleventh-Round

Following the growing use of the *moliceiros* in the tourism sector, there was a need by a customer to implement in engine boats an awning able to refresh in the summer (avoiding the sun) and to protect from the rain in the winter. Thus, order number 11 consists of the 5 *moliceiros* made up to that date (without a door), plus 4 E1DA (door and awning), 3 E2DA and 3 E3DA, none of which is reused.

The awning assembly is made by the inclusion of 2 masts (separate) into the hole's furthest from the base, into which the piece corresponding to the awning is fitted.

Twelfth-Round

This round works the same way as the previous round, even has the same type of order, and the only difference is the use of the introduced lean tool – Poka-Yoke. This will be the last round of the game. Figure 6 shows the 3 Poka-Yoke pieces and the respective *moliceiros*.

The implementing process for this tool is as follows:

- Introduce and explain the Poka-Yoke concept.
- Ask them to check out the 3 pieces of Poka-Yoke that are in the game box.
- Put these pieces on the table of the last workstation, so that the *moliceiros* can be tested – each piece corresponds to a type of boat.

Figure 6. Poka-Yoke pieces and the respective moliceiros

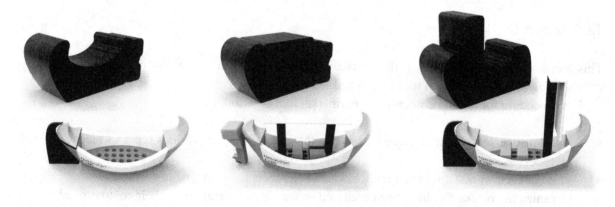

DISCUSSION

The use of games to transmit and share knowledge is always a challenge. So much for the one who manages the dynamics as for whoever plays it. Yet there are differences. If it is a simple game, like the paper airplane, it is easier to be committed to higher levels of decision than to the shop floor teams. The seconds lose interest after a short time. Already with a structured game, the level of involvement of the players is similar regardless of their hierarchical position.

With these dynamics, it was verified that even operators without any knowledge of the lean tools perceived the dynamics and managed to reach the objective of the game: what they had to change in their tasks, what they were going to gain with that, what was at stake in the reality of the company. There was even an interesting aspect that showed the importance of games: during the introduction and theoretical framework the operators show disinterest and boredom, something that changes radically with the beginning of the game and grows to the point that people lose the notion of the passage of time such is their involvement with the process and the results.

The fact that the game has a well-defined theme, with little industrial expression but very culturally present, allows the creation of involvement with the game and abstraction of the routine reality, managing throughout the game to make parallels between them, in order to transfer knowledge and to induce a new methodology. There is dynamism and emotion present. This shows that the choice was made in terms of the theme and that the decision-making process (through brainstorming, analysis of minimal activity, and high impact and ease of involvement) is a valid option. at this stage, there were, for the application of the table tools and lean concepts, several options of the game under discussion before opting for the *moliceiros*.

The game helps to understand concepts such as flow, customer, replacement, decision making, gain and loss, management of operation time, production leveling among others. Although, the developed game is still a prototype, its testing revealed that there was, on the part of those who have played, a good acceptance.

Yet everything is not perfect. Some parts and components need to be optimized because they are small and/or fragile, with repeated handling being damaged and this has an impact on the course of the game. The number of parts has also been presented as a conditioning factor.

CONCLUSION

Concerning this game, it is to emphasize its capacity to allow the learning experience in a practical way. It is a unique tool since all its development was done from scratch. It is simple but effective and versatile since anyone who uses it can use it in any way they can (you can follow the round-to-round guide above, or create your own way of using it, adding or removing concepts and rounds). Another factor that creates attraction to the game is the ability to see results on demand, and it can be verified that with lean concepts introduction there are productivity increases.

Ozelkan & Galambosi (Ozelkan & Galambosi, 2009) states that in an industrial setting, playing the game before a lean implementation would be recommended in the initial training phase of the project team. Thus, this game should be used as an introduction tool to lean philosophy giving the trainees a fun, satisfying, and practical way to learn lean concepts.

Looking at the product as a whole, there is a fusion of gamification and lean concepts. Observing the completed guide for the development of gamified training elements it is possible to see how gamification strategies are used in the design of this game. Regarding lean methodologies, there is the introduction of six theoretical concepts during the game.

A well-defined guideline made it possible to carry out all the pre-defined tasks, namely in addition to the introduction and fusion of theoretical concepts, a complete game strategy was drawn up, and the objectives, behavior, dynamic, and the success measure. The suggested rounds are fluid and allow through your thread to have room for the introduction of theoretical concepts, have a demonstration of results, and allow freedom for changes or suggestions.

The game consists of 15 different pieces, making a total of about 300 pieces. Due to its versatility, it allows assembling more than 15 different configurations of *moliceiros*. Moreover, it has in addition to the explicit theoretical concepts, some implicit such as pull systems, quality at the source, zero defects, and logistics operator. It also has space for the addition of other concepts such as Kanban.

ACKNOWLEDGMENT

The authors greatly acknowledge the people who participated in the game development as users. The analysis of their behavior and their feedback was of great value to the final result. Part of the research presented in this paper received the support of projects UIDB/00481/2020 and UIDP/00481/2020 - FCT - Fundação para a Ciencia e a Tecnologia; and CENTRO-01-0145-FEDER-022083 - Centro Portugal Regional Operational Program (Centro2020), under the PORTUGAL 2020 Partnership Agreement, through the European Regional Development Fund.

REFERENCES

Allen, T. D., & Poteet, M. L. (1999). Developing Effective Mentoring Relationships: Strategies From the Mentor's Viewpoint. *The Career Development Quarterly, 48*(1), 59–73. doi:10.1002/j.2161-0045.1999. tb00275.x

Alsawaier, R. S. (2018). The effect of gamification on motivation and engagement. *International Journal of Information and Learning Technology, 35*(1), 56–79. doi:10.1108/IJILT-02-2017-0009

Bartunek, J. M., & Woodman, R. W. (2015). Beyond Lewin: Toward a Temporal Approximation of Organization Development and Change. *Annual Review of Organizational Psychology and Organizational Behavior, 2*(1), 157–182. doi:10.1146/annurev-orgpsych-032414-111353

Belhadi, A., Sha'ri, Y. B. M., Touriki, F. E., & El Fezazi, S. (2018). Lean production in SMEs: Literature review and reflection on future challenges. *Journal of Industrial and Production Engineering, 35*(6), 368–382. doi:10.1080/21681015.2018.1508081

Bhamu, J., & Singh Sangwan, K. (2014). Lean manufacturing: Literature review and research issues. *International Journal of Operations & Production Management, 34*(7), 876–940. doi:10.1108/IJOPM-08-2012-0315

Black, J. (2007). Design rules for implementing the Toyota Production System. *International Journal of Production Research, 45*(16), 3639–3664. https://doi.org/10.1080/00207540701223469

Blicblau, A., Bruwer, M., & Dini, K. (2016). Do engineering students perceive that different learning and teaching modes improve their referencing and citation skills? *International Journal of Mechanical Engineering Education, 44*(1), 3–15. https://doi.org/10.1177/0306419015624186

Brian Burke. (2014). *Redefine Gamification to Understand Its Opportunities and Limitations.* https://www.gartner.com/en/documents/2699119-redefine-gamification-to-understand-its-opportunities-an

Caponetto, I., Earp, J., & Ott, M. (2014). Gamification and Education: A Literature Review. *Proceedings of the European Conference on Games Based Learning, 1*(2009), 50–57. doi:10.13140/RG.2.1.1181.8080

Caroline Ngonyo Njoroge, R. Y. (2014). The Impact of Social and Emotional Intelligence on Employee Motivation in a Multigenerational Workplace. *Global Journal of Management and Business Research.*

Chee, C.-M., & Wong, D. H.-T. (2017). Affluent Gaming Experience Could Fail Gamification in Education: A Review. *IETE Technical Review, 34*(6), 593–597. https://doi.org/10.1080/02564602.2017.1315965

Cherrafi, A., Elfezazi, S., Chiarini, A., Mokhlis, A., & Benhida, K. (2016). The integration of lean manufacturing, Six Sigma and sustainability: A literature review and future research directions for developing a specific model. *Journal of Cleaner Production, 139*, 828–846. https://doi.org/10.1016/J.JCLEPRO.2016.08.101

Corbett, S. (2007). *Beyond manufacturing: The evolution of lean production.* Academic Press.

de Sousa Borges, S., Durelli, V. H. S., Reis, H. M., & Isotani, S. (2014). A systematic mapping on gamification applied to education. *Proceedings of the 29th Annual ACM Symposium on Applied Computing - SAC '14*, 216–222. doi:10.1145/2554850.2554956

Des Armier, D., Shepherd, C. E., & Skrabut, S. (2016). Using Game Elements to Increase Student Engagement in Course Assignments. *College Teaching, 64*(2), 64–72. doi:10.1080/87567555.2015.1094439

Deterding, S., Dixon, D., Khaled, R., & Nacke, L. (2011). From game design elements to gamefulness. *Proceedings of the 15th International Academic MindTrek Conference on Envisioning Future Media Environments - MindTrek '11*, 9. doi:10.1145/2181037.2181040

Deterding, S., Sicart, M., Nacke, L., O'Hara, K., & Dixon, D. (2011). Using Game Design Elements in Non-Gaming Contexts. *Sociology: The Journal of the British Sociological Association*, 4–7. doi:10.1145/1979742.1979575

Dichev, C., Dicheva, D., Angelova, G., & Agre, G. (2014). From gamification to gameful design and gameful experience in learning. *Cybernetics and Information Technologies, 14*(4), 80–100. https://doi.org/10.1515/cait-2014-0007

Dignan, A. (2011). *Game Frame: Using Games as a Strategy for Success* (1st ed.). Free Press - Simon & Schuster.

Gould, O., & Colwill, J. (2015). A framework for material flow assessment in manufacturing systems. *Journal of Industrial and Production Engineering, 32*(1), 55–66. https://doi.org/10.1080/21681015.2014.1000403

Groh, F. (2012). Gamification: State of the Art Definition and Utilization. *Research Trends in Media Informatics*, 39–46. doi:10.1145/1979742.1979575

Habidin, N. F., Salleh, M. I., Md Latip, N. A., Azman, M. N. A., & Mohd Fuzi, N. (2016). Lean six sigma performance improvement tool for automotive suppliers. *Journal of Industrial and Production Engineering, 33*(4), 215–235. https://doi.org/10.1080/21681015.2015.1136966

Hamari, J., & Koivisto, J. (2015). Why do people use gamification services? *International Journal of Information Management, 35*(4), 419–431. https://doi.org/10.1016/J.IJINFOMGT.2015.04.006

Hunicke, R., Leblanc, M., & Zubek, R. (2004). MDA: A Formal Approach to Game Design and Game Research. *Proceedings AAAI Workshop on Challenges in Game.*

Huotari, K., & Hamari, J. (2012). Defining gamification. *Proceeding of the 16th International Academic MindTrek Conference on - MindTrek '12*, 17. doi:10.1145/2393132.2393137

Illeris, K. (2003). Towards a contemporary and comprehensive theory of learning. *International Journal of Lifelong Education, 22*(4), 396–406. doi:10.1080/02601370304837

Jansons, M. (2016). *Gamification Workshop.* EuropeHome Erasmus Project Intensive Programme - Entrepreneurship Skill Teaching and Training Programme, Riga, Latvia.

Johnson, S. A., Gerstenfeld, A., Zeng, A. Z., Ramos, B., & Mishra, S. (2003). Teaching lean process design using a discovery approach. *2003 ASEE Annual Conference and Exposition: Staying in Tune with Engineering Education, 3*, 7881–7892.

Kapp, K. (2014, March). Gamification: Separating Fact From Fiction. *Chief Learning Officer, 13*(3), 42–46. https://doi.org/10.2304/elea.2005.2.1.5

Kehr, T. W., & Proctor, M. D. (2017). People Pillars: Re-structuring the Toyota Production System (TPS) House Based on Inadequacies Revealed During the Automotive Recall Crisis. *Quality and Reliability Engineering International, 33*(4), 921–930. https://doi.org/10.1002/qre.2059

Kelle, S., Klemke, R., & Specht, M. (2012). Design patterns for learning games. *International Journal of Technology Enhanced Learning, 3*(6), 555. https://doi.org/10.1504/ijtel.2011.045452

Koster, R. (2013). *Theory of Fun for Game Design* (2nd ed.). O'Reilly Media.

Leite, H. dos R., Vieira, G. E., Leite, H. dos R., & Vieira, G. E. (2015). Lean philosophy and its applications in the service industry: A review of the current knowledge. *Production, 25*(3), 529–541. https://doi.org/10.1590/0103-6513.079012

Majuri, J., Koivisto, J., & Hamari, J. (2018). Gamification of education and learning: A review of empirical literature. *CEUR Workshop Proceedings, 2186*(GamiFIN), 11–19.

Markopoulos, A. P., Fragkou, A., Kasidiaris, P. D., & Davim, J. P. (2015). Gamification in engineering education and professional training. *International Journal of Mechanical Engineering Education, 43*(2), 118–131. https://doi.org/10.1177/0306419015591324

Mestrado, M., & Vers, R. H. (2018). *A Gamification como Ferramenta de Gestão de Recursos Humanos Raquel Filipa Almeida de Sousa.* Academic Press.

Ozelkan, E., & Galambosi, A. (2009). Lampshade Game for lean manufacturing. *Production Planning and Control, 20*(5), 385–402. https://doi.org/10.1080/09537280902875419

Patrício, R., Moreira, A. C., & Zurlo, F. (2018). Gamification approaches to the early stage of innovation. *Creativity and Innovation Management, 27*(4), 499–511. https://doi.org/https://doi.org/10.1111/caim.12284

Patrício, R., Moreira, A. C., & Zurlo, F. (2020). Enhancing design thinking approaches to innovation through gamification. *European Journal of Innovation Management.* doi:10.1108/EJIM-06-2020-0239

Pereira, M., Oliveira, M., Vieira, A., Lima, R. M., & Paes, L. (2018). The gamification as a tool to increase employee skills through interactives work instructions training. *Procedia Computer Science, 138,* 630–637. https://doi.org/10.1016/j.procs.2018.10.084

Pinto, J. L. (2014). Pensamento Lean - A filosofia das organizações vencedoras (6th ed.). Lidel.

Prusak, Z. (2004). Problem definition and problem solving in lean manufacturing environment. *ASEE Annual Conference Proceedings,* 11343–11353.

Rüttimann, B. G., & Stöckli, M. T. (2016). Going beyond Triviality: The Toyota Production System—Lean Manufacturing beyond Muda and Kaizen. *Journal of Service Science and Management, 09*(02), 140–149. https://doi.org/10.4236/jssm.2016.92018

Sailer, M., Hense, J. U., Mayr, S. K., & Mandl, H. (2017). How gamification motivates: An experimental study of the effects of specific game design elements on psychological need satisfaction. *Computers in Human Behavior, 69,* 371–380. https://doi.org/10.1016/J.CHB.2016.12.033

Seaborn, K., & Fels, D. I. (2015). Gamification in theory and action: A survey. *International Journal of Human-Computer Studies, 74,* 14–31. https://doi.org/10.1016/J.IJHCS.2014.09.006

Womack, J. P., Jones, D. T., & Roos, D. (1990). *The Machine That Changed the World.* Simon & Schuster.

KEY TERMS AND DEFINITIONS

Game Design: The development of the concept of the game system in a multidisciplinary and holistic approach, with close similarity to conventional product development.

Gamification: Application of game design techniques and mechanics to non-game problems, such as engineering, business, or social impact challenges, for educational proposes.

Lean Methodologies: Holistic organization practices, based on the Toyota Production System principles and methods, that aims to provide a new way to think about how to organize human activities to deliver more benefits to society and value to individuals while eliminating waste.

Chapter 15
Gamification or How to Make a "Green" Behavior Become a Habit

Lidia Aguiar-Castillo
Universidad de Las Palmas de Gran Canaria, Spain

Rafael Perez-Jimenez
Universidad de Las Palmas de Gran Canaria, Spain

ABSTRACT

One of the main challenges faced by tourist destinations is waste management. A poor waste collection and management policy is an additional factor affecting the tourist destination's sustainability within this general problem. These situations are trying to be solved with incentives derived from gamification tools that motivate people to recycle. This study, within the scope of a European project called UrbanWaste, found significant results that suggested that this tool can promote recycling behavior, but what happens when customers come back home? Gamification even makes a habit take root in the people who use it by activating external motivators. This recycling habit emanates from an altruistic feeling and aims to leave a better world for future generations (intrinsic motivation). However, they also recommend the app to show a benevolent image by making the behavior visible (internalized extrinsic motivation) and improving destination branding.

INTRODUCTION

Waste management is a crucial issue in tourist destinations (Shamshiry et al., 2011). Its management is a significant concern in those destinations with a high concentration of seasonal tourism with a relatively small resident population. A poor waste collection and management policy is an additional factor affecting the tourist destination's sustainability within this general problem. Thus, this factor is relevant to maintain the natural environment and has a significant impact on the perceived quality of the tourist destination. Moreover, the situation has been aggravated by the emergence of accommodation models

DOI: 10.4018/978-1-7998-9223-6.ch015

based on the collaborative economy. The traveler should interact directly with the waste collection and processing services at the destination (Mendes et al., 2013).

Recycling behavior is fundamental in the context of sustainability. Although waste sorting is critical for environmental and economic reasons, its effectiveness can be conditioned by the travelers' lack of information regarding regulations differentiated by municipalities (Gaggi et al., 2020). These problematic situations challenge administrations as they need to improve recycling rates as a part of their sustainability policies and improve their image as an environmentally aware municipality. These situations can be solved with incentives derived from gamification tools that motivate people to recycle. Among the gamification-specific elements that effectively support this behavior are feedback, prizes, and other collaborative and competitive factors (Helmefalk & Rosenlund, 2020).

Gamification has proven its potential to promote green behavior, convey comprehensive information through entertainment, reward users for good practices, improve engagement and help avoid problems arising from overtourism (Souza et al., 2020). This study used open data from the UrbanWaste project (2016) within the European H2020 framework program, which sought gamification to provide solutions to the sustainability problems of tourist destinations with a seasonal floating population far exceeding the resident one. One of the solutions provided by the project was the design and implementation of a gamified mobile application, WasteApp, to encourage recycling behavior in tourists since it has been seen that linking gamification with technology makes it extremely attractive to citizens (Guillen, Hamari, & Quist, 2021). In this research, an attempt was made to see if the application encourages the desired behavior and its effect on the tourist destination image (Aguiar-Castillo et al., 2019).

This chapter is organized as follows: a short state of the art on gamification and sustainable tourism is presented, followed by a description of the work based on user satisfaction and the habit cycle (Urban Waste, 2016, European Project), followed by solutions and recommendations for marketers and designers. Finally, future research directions and the conclusion where a new gamification concept are explained.

GAMIFICATION AND SUSTAINABLE TOURISM

Sustainability is defined as the ability or capacity to maintain or sustain itself (Goodland, 1995). Sustainable organizations are self-sufficient and engaged in the process of permanent evolution. In this context, creating habits of "green" behavior in employees and customers is a challenge. Sustainability can be considered the awareness of human beings' interconnectivity and ecosystems (Dunphy, 2011). According to Foley (2001), the organizations will achieve their sustainability goals if they act to maximize the utility of their products for customers and meet the expectations of non-customer stakeholders. Organizational sustainability has three distinct parts, popularized as Triple Bottom Line (TBL) by Elikington (1998). It is based on balancing social, environmental, and economic subsystems. Gamification can help organizations retain and motivate employees while improving employee loyalty. Its use is more likely to encourage employees to think and act beyond private interests and work towards broader goals, thus contributing to organizational sustainability. The ability of organizations to sustain themselves is driven by the three areas mentioned above, social, environmental, and economic, where gamification emerges as an aid to elicit behaviors. These behaviors ultimately transcend themselves and are presented to obtain from both employees and customers ultimate goals. The feeling of altruism can receive a substantial boost with these strategies. Individuals reproduce the behavior because they bring benefits, not only from pure altruism, a good for humanity, but they also obtain personal benefits of their own, impure altruism, such as exposing an excellent image to their fellow human beings (Andreoni, 1990; Benebou & Tirole, 2006).

Gamification helps to create an ecosystem where individuals are motivated to participate in a specific topic as they assume the need to change a behavior (Wee & Choong, 2019) to reflect on that conduct (Cheng et al., 2020). Gamification seems to be an effective way to educate people about sustainability and biodiversity by increasing (Tsai et al., 2019) young people's sense of personal responsibility in international cooperation to find solutions to climate change (Meya & Eisenack, 2018). Hamari, Sjoklint, and Ukkonen (2016) establish premises for collaborative consumption and sustainability finds in gamification a suitable tool to increase intrinsic motivation and track sustainable behaviors. Another relevant research in this double theme of sustainable tourism and its relationship with gamification is that of Negruşa et al. (2015), who established that gamification could help to make tourists aware of the need for stability in the use and consumption of resources and to provide education in responsible consumption habits. Among the proposals made by these researchers on gamification are improving efficiency in using local resources through information and preventing environmental degradation. The most important aspects of being achieved with gamification of the relationship between the organization and the community would be:

- The main objective would be to achieve social interaction, cultural understanding, sustainable habits, and improved quality of life for visitors and locals. The engagement encouraged by gamification should motivate tourists to develop new activities or visit alternative destinations and acquire new habits.
- The improvements that gamification would add would focus on marketing, where the aim would be to increase traveler engagement before, during, and after the experience. This fact would increase the reputation of the destination and the number of tourists and produce greater visibility of this destination, faster feedback, and presence in social networks, increasing visitor loyalty.
- Gamification would focus on intrinsic incentives that involve tourists in activities that bring them self-esteem and social recognition: recycling behavior that maintains a clean image of the environment. Extrinsic incentives would be complemented by intrinsic incentives, supporting the desired behavior.
- For cultural heritage organizations such as museums, gamification would have the opportunity to attract new visitors by offering learning experiences.

Gamification takes on its whole meaning through reward systems. These reward systems achieve user satisfaction through obtaining something especially valued by them. In this sense, Zichermann and Cunningham (2011) present the SAPS model that differentiates between status, access, power, and "stuff".

- Status refers to the position of a person within a community or group. Badges or leaderboards can give this position.
- Access, is a system that opens new routes to the user or unlocks new levels after reaching specific objectives.
- Power would be when users acquire special rights within a community.
- "Stuff" consists of material elements of the real world, for example, tangible prizes in exchange for points.

According to Zichermann and Cunningham (2011), status rewards are the most effective in the long term and are the most valued by users.

Paharia (2013) adds new previous categories: recognition and appreciation, as well as prosocial incentives. The first two can be feedback through badges and levels; however, the latter focuses on social interaction and recognition within colleagues.

Related Works and Contributions

The field of knowledge that concerns us shows precedents of this work listed below, where this research contributes are also shown.

For example, Lee et al. (2012) present a game engine that motivates players to learn about energy problems. As can be seen below, the exposed work delves into the same factors that these researchers have found (feedback, identification of winners, and incentives) and adds the success of recycling behavior and the effect on the image of the gamified environment.

Kiilumen (2013) inquired about the possibility of using mobile applications to improve sustainable behavior among tourists of generation Y. Faced with this research; the presented work provides an application and real experimentation supported by gamification tools.

The work of Negruşa et al. (2015) attempted to position the role of gamification in tourism and the hotel industry in the context of sustainable development. These researchers conclude that tourists should be motivated to engage in sustainable activities and encourage them to change their behaviors during the trip. In this sense, the base experimentation of the study shown in this book tried to encourage recycling behavior and make pro-environmental behavior visible on social networks by promoting feelings of self-esteem and social recognition.

In their work, Hsu et al. (2017) emphasize the need for research that examines the factors and characteristics that involve gamification in the environment of the commitment to recycling for sustainable development, a question that this work has tried to answer.

Yoon (2018) proposed a TAM for "green" technologies; however, it focused on energy-saving products and visualization systems, not on behavior change tools such as the one described in this work.

Dastjerdi et al. (2019) investigated the intention to use applications that report in real-time on traffic and the different means of transport to reach the destination. The work exhibited here provides the connection between user satisfaction and the reputation of the gamified environment.

USER SATISFACTION AND HABIT CYCLE

The leading theory on which the research has been based is self-determination (SDT). SDT research concerns human motivation, particularly autonomous motivation, characterized by people's complete and willing engagement in an activity. SDT researchers have focused on factors in social and cultural contexts that enhance or diminish people's autonomous motivation, such as variations in reward contingencies, leadership styles, types of feedback, and rationales for acting. These elements make up a theory of self-regulation where factors external to the person affect motivation, but also in how intrapersonal factors mobilize self-motivation. SDT specifically proposes motives characterized by a sense of volition and self-endorsement (Ryan & Deci, 2017).

SDT states that human propensities are fundamentally eudaimonic, tending toward growth, cooperation, and altruism, in the absence of social factors that thwart such tendencies. When autonomously motivated, individuals are more likely to internalize adaptive social values and norms, which tend to be prosocial and holistic.

This work has used gamification as an interface between tourists, organizations, and local communities to promote responsible and ethical behavior (Negruşa et al., 2015). Even though most tourists have declared themselves in favor of sustainable tourism, the percentage of them who have maintained pro-environmental behavior during their vacations is low. The cause may lie in the fact that tourists, in general, intend to lead a more comfortable life during their holidays than during their daily life, so it is difficult to convince them to adopt behaviors that involve obligations that take them out of their comfort zone (Negruşa et al., 2015). Therefore, the importance of introducing a substantial incentive that leads them to seek out and use waste recycling areas has been suggested. In light of this idea, a mobile application based on gamification has been developed.

WasteApp

WasteApp is an application for mobile devices aimed at tourists in which a triple objective was pursued. Firstly, it was sought to raise awareness among tourists about the correct use of infrastructure for separate waste collection. Secondly, it was intended to use the platform to collect data for a more detailed analysis of tourists' waste separation behavior. Finally, it was designed to provide tourist information and visibility to the local organizations involved in the application as award providers. The design of the application followed a paradigm based on gamification to achieve the objectives mentioned above. The proposal was based on obtaining points that could be redeemed for prizes in the pilot cities of the UrbanWaste consortium (2016). The mechanisms for obtaining rewards were reading QR codes located on rubbish bins in the recycling areas of the towns and posting comments on social networks using the project hashtag. These dumpsters appeared on a map provided by the application (see Figure 1). In addition, some organizations presented an offer of prizes in each city that tourists could redeem for the corresponding points.

Regarding privacy, no personal data was requested in this application to comply with European data protection regulations. The way to access was done through a login ID and password, with a skip encoding (encrypted coding) to improve security.

The application design was developed using the MDA (mechanics, dynamics, and aesthetics) paradigm (Hunicke, Leblanc & Zubeck, 2004). According to the definition of the framework, the following stratification was established:

- Mechanical. It was mainly established on a SQL (Structured Query Language) database in which both the positions of the selective waste collection areas and the QR code programming and point gain and exchange algorithm were stored.
- Dynamics. It was the process of obtaining points through the reading of QR codes and the subsequent exchange of rewards.
- Aesthetics (sensations). The ultimate goal of the game was to evoke an emotional response from the user. In this case, the objective was directly related to the three main mechanisms: the implicit reward of knowledge that contributes to the sustainability of the place visited, the obtaining of points, and finally, the tangible reward received (see Figure 2).

Figure 1. WasteApp presentation screen and a map of the Ponta Delgada city area showing sponsors and recycling areas

Figure 2. Process for exchanging point awards

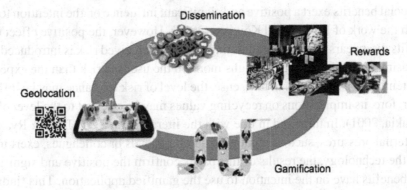

The sensations to be evoked in the user included the following:

- Usefulness. The application was intended to provide a valuable tool for users.
- Challenge. Users were encouraged to continue using the application in search of rewards.
- Social/ecological awareness. The background of the project was to try to convey this awareness to users.
- To fulfill the above aesthetics, the simple mechanics proposed first was that users would:

- ◦ Have information about the waste collection infrastructure on an interactive map.
- ◦ Earn points by reading QR codes on trash containers. Each city had its catalog of prizes, and the scores needed to exchange prizes were set to seek ease and not discourage users.
- ◦ Some eco-tips (ecological tips related to waste) were displayed on users' screens after reading the QR codes. In addition, some points were provided in exchange for tweeting using the project hashtag.

The game must run on cell phones' most distributed operating systems, and each city was studied independently. The game philosophy is based on a points-reward strategy in which the users obtain points by reading QR codes located on waste bins.

The application had a mobile-based interface, a relational database, and a server-side backend at a lower description level. Under this framework, the programmer and end-user sides address the design since MDA flow is bidirectional.

A total of 3325 people downloaded the application; most of the downloads were in the pilot cities, Lisbon and Punta Delgada had 1817 downloads; Santander and Tenerife had 497; Florence and Syracuse had 353 downloads, and the rest of the regions had a more uneven follow-up of the application (See Aguiar-Castillo et al., 2018; for technical details and http://www.urban-waste.eu/wp-content/uploads/2017/12/User-guide.pdf to the user guide).

Factors Influencing the Intention to use WasteApp

There was a first phase, where the factors (expected benefits, expected threats, and user characteristics) that could have influenced the intention to use the WasteApp to promote recycling behavior were analyzed (Aguiar-Castillo et al., 2018).

The results achieved show that within the expected benefits (functional, hedonic, and social), the functional and social benefits exert a positive and significant influence on the intention to use the Waste-App, in line with the work of Hamari and Koivisto (2015). However, the positive effect of the expected functional benefits disappears when the moderating effect of perceived risk is introduced, with the app's functionality ceasing to be significant. It weighs more on the user the risk than the expected functional benefit on the intention to use the app. In this sense, the level of risk tolerance may be influenced by user motivation. Therefore, its implications on recycling values may be relevant to the level of perceived risk tolerance (Dholakia, 2001). In turn, and in line with the literature on SDT (Deci & Ryan, 1985), which suggests that external pressures, such as reputation among friends or colleagues, exert influence on the intention to use the technology, the results of this paper confirm the positive and significant effect that expected social benefits have on the intention to use the gamified application. This finding reveals that users are willing to use WasteApp to promote recycling as long as it is disseminated among their social contacts. Visibility on social networks is relevant for these individuals, as they seem to want to present a specific image with which they can identify. As stated by the theory of planned behavior (Ajzen, 1991), there are situations in which people are willing to convey a favorable image of themselves through the projection of a positive attitude towards a specific topic, such as recycling. Finally, and concerning the expected hedonic benefits, the results show that they do not significantly influence the intention to use WasteApp. This result seems to indicate that the user does not expect a game with high-level attributes and, therefore, not many emotional stimuli are required to encourage the use of an app whose ultimate goal is to promote recycling (Yoo et al., 2017).

Concerning the expected threats, the findings of this research revealed that, although trust in the application provider is not a relevant factor, the expected risks do seem to be a determining aspect in the intention to use the WasteApp application, but in the opposite direction to that expected. Thus, the relationship between trust in WasteApp providers and the intention to use technology is not confirmed in this study. This fact could be explained by the very purpose of the app, which involves promoting recycling as a common good, regardless of who supports the app. Another explanation could be because of the context of the application with strict rules for the use of private data.

As for the expected risks, the results indicate that potential users do not seem to be very cautious about providing the required information when downloading a mobile application. Thus, a significant factor that could affect the intention to use the application is the request for geolocation data, which could accentuate the user's fear of losing their privacy. However, contrary to expectations, the results reveal that, even though users' expected risks are high, they still intend to use the app, which could be because they place a higher value on the geolocation of the recycling area (without the loss of privacy inherent in the user's geolocation the app makes no sense). In other words, users accept the risk of using WasteApp to achieve the goal of using the application and finding the nearest dumpster.

In terms of user characteristics, the analyzed personal environmental values also do not seem to have a significant influence in explaining the intention to use WasteApp. Thus, according to the findings found, it cannot be confirmed whether the importance of recycling rewards play a relevant role in the intention to use the technology, which could be explained by the fact that the users are willing to recycle regardless of the use of the application (Figure 3) (See Aguiar-Castillo et al., 2018; for details about methodology and analysis description).

Figure 3. Factors affecting the intention to use WasteApp

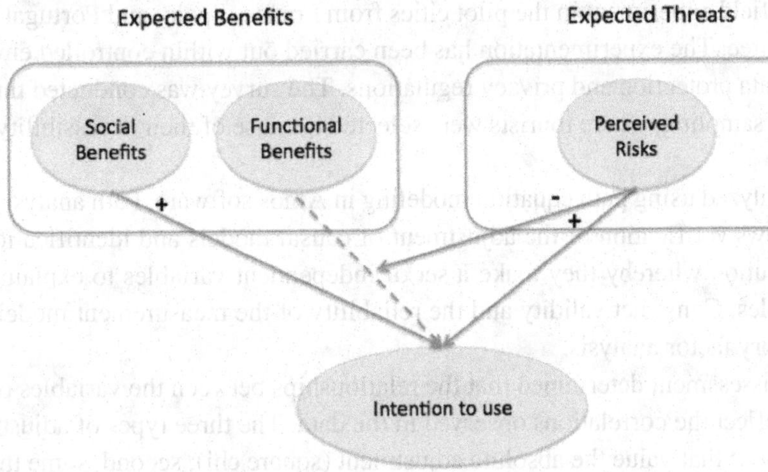

Consequences of Using WasteApp

The second phase of the study analyzes whether WasteApp can become a successful tool to promote recycling and improve the reputation of the tourist destination (Aguiar-Castillo et al., 2019). It is shown that, in line with the postulates of the TAM, the ease of use and perceived usefulness of the application positively and significantly influence user satisfaction, although the former indirectly through perceived usefulness (Kim & Chang, 2007). However, the game components of the app were not considered since, as concluded in the first study, the visitor does not expect the WasteApp to have significant elements with game functions (Yoo et al., 2017).

Regarding the expectations about the rewards, the results show that they positively influence the perceived usefulness of the app, but not the recycling behavior. This result could be explained because, according to specific authors, as soon as the relationship between WasteApp and travelers ends, the commitment to the promoted recycling behavior may also disappear. Therefore, rewards must allow for internalizing extrinsic motivation, such as making gifts that boost the destination's sustainability or are perceived as helpful to environmentally conscious tourists. In addition, and contrary to what was stated, this dimension significantly and negatively influences user satisfaction with the application. This fact may be due to the users' belief that pro-environmental recycling behavior is a must. Consequently, their satisfaction emanates from intrinsic motivation, making them perceive physical rewards and extrinsic incentives contrary to their conscience (Ryan & Deci, 2000; Werbach & Hunter, 2012).

Results reveal that both user satisfaction and recycling behavior positively influence the intention to recommend the app. This fact is probably due to two related reasons, firstly, that it is because the traveler sees the app as an aid to pro-environmental recycling behavior and, secondly, because of the tourist's desire to expose himself to his acquaintances and friends with generally private actions, for the sake of giving a favorable image among his acquaintances (McKenzie-Mohr, 2011). This recommendation made by the WasteApp traveler in their posts will improve their visibility in the social networks in which they are immersed. Finally, the reputation of the tourist destination will be improved as a consequence of this pro-environmental behavior derived from the use and satisfaction with the gamified technological application (Figure 4).

Survey data were collected from participants who were asked to answer a questionnaire after using the application in a field experiment in the pilot cities from France, Spain, and Portugal selected by the UrbanWaste committee. The experimentation has been carried out within controlled environments due to strict European data protection and privacy regulations. The survey was conducted throughout 2018. It used convenience sampling, where tourists were selected because of their accessibility and proximity to the researcher.

All data were analyzed using path equation modeling in Amos software. Path analysis is a multivariate method that allows verification of the adjustment of causal models and identification of the direct and indirect contribution whereby they make a set of independent variables to explain the variability of dependent variables. Construct validity and the reliability of the measurement model were assessed based on confirmatory factor analysis.

The adjustment assessment determined that the relationships between the variables of the estimated model adequately reflect the correlations observed in the data. The three types of adjustment goodness statisticians: first, those that value the absolute adjustment (square chi); second, some that compare the adjustment concerning another model, relative adjustment (comparative fit index, CFI); and finally, those using parsimonious adjustment that evaluates the fitting according to the number of used parameters (normed-fit index, NFI) provide all the necessary information to evaluate the model. Furthermore, the variance-covariance matrix was used to test the research model. Before verifying the hypotheses, it was confirmed the fit of the path model. All the fitness signaled a good model fit. (Aguiar-Castillo et al., 2019).

Figure 4. Consequences of using WasteApp

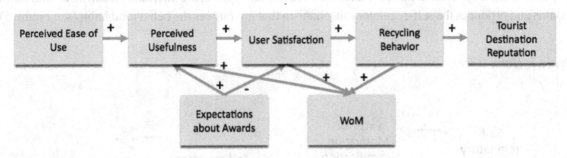

Habit Cycle

An interesting finding of the initial study was the connection between student satisfaction and creating a behavioral habit, since the more satisfied people are, and the more they want to recommend the application, the more recycling behavior is promoted. The relationship between satisfaction and recycling behavior has been found to occur recurrently. To begin with, the game tools used by gamified applications provoke a flow state in the user that intrinsically motivates the user to repeat pro-environmental behaviors, i.e., a habit is created as a consequence of gamification. This flow state can be consistent with user satisfaction since flow is closely related to user satisfaction (Ghani & Deshpande, 1994). This process occurs because the extrinsic motivators of gamification provide feedback on the evolution of their behaviors to the user, reinforcing the recycling behavior and promoting the self-esteem that makes this user want to expose their behavior to their networks of acquaintances. In addition to this, gamification enhances user satisfaction when regularly informed about their progress; continuous feedback is sent about the objectives they are achieving, as happens with the constant valuation of the contributions in a gamified application of accomplished goals. This fact favors a feeling of high individual performance that reinforces the promoted behavior (Park & Kim, 2003), i.e., an internalized extrinsic motivation is generated. The person ends up perceiving as a self-regulatory component rather than through external impositions. This behavior is close to internal motivation, so these actions repeated over time will ensure that the promoted behaviors will be maintained when the extrinsic motivation elements from gamification disappear. According to Von Krogh et al. (2012), internalized extrinsic motivation ends up making the reward unnecessary.

Additionally, it has been shown that new behaviors become a habit through reiteration. It is suggested that the frequency of this new behavior is significant, so it ends up engaging people in practice (Phillips & Gardner, 2016), and more importantly, the development of this habit leads people to maintain the behavior permanently, even without the need to use gamification as a motivational element. The long-term behavioral change will only appear if people execute a pro-environmental behavior many times and end up internalizing it (Judah, Gardner, & Aunger, 2013). In other words, the ultimate goal of the application is achieved, that when the application disappears, the user reproduces the recycling behaviors, in this case, by him. This chain of actions can succeed in its behavioral goal because satisfaction with the app comes from a combination of user motivations. The result is a good and beneficial habit for the users who present that excellent image to their acquaintances, and the promoter's reputation will be reinforced. The ultimate goal of the experimentation would be for the promoted behavior to become a habit, that is, to remain over time by internalizing the extrinsic motivation. The underlying idea is that, once the extrinsic motivation that promotes the behavior disappears, the internalized extrinsic motivation remains and produces the self-regulatory mechanism that guarantees the behavioral habit (see Figure 5).

Figure 5. Habit Cycle

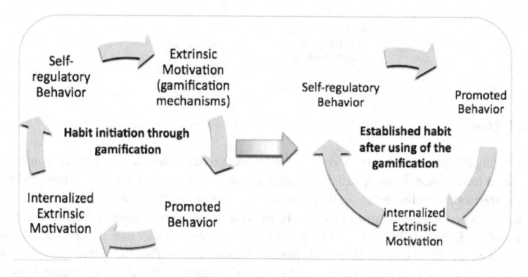

SOLUTIONS AND RECOMMENDATIONS

The increase in novel collaborative accommodation is causing a pressing problem in sustainability within tourist destinations. Visitors coming from different environments and customs have to be redirected towards pro-environmental behaviors. Since they tend to think that, being away from their usual environment, they should not respect the social norms of environmental coexistence until they return to their regular home. In this context, the solution provided in this work was an application based on gamification to promote appropriate recycling behavior. In the first phase, this research studied the characteristics that the design of this type of application should have to be adopted by travelers and, in a second phase, whether this application promoted pro-environmental behavior and whether it had consequences on the image of the destination that implemented this solution. This study showed that the social visibility factor is the most critical factor for individuals when adopting this application. A second factor is a usefulness in its use, although this is no longer appreciated if it presents a risk or threat to their privacy.

On the other hand, once they are using the application, this utility will produce satisfaction in the user that will promote recycling behavior in the traveler and cause them to recommend the application to their acquaintances. Finally, the last consequence of the satisfaction-behavior chain will lead to an improvement in the reputation of the tourist destination.

Several practical implications can be inferred from this research. The empirical results show that practitioners need to work on some critical aspects to increase the intention to use a gamification-based application that promotes recycling. The design of these applications should focus on functional elements useful to the user, emphasizing social diffusion, making visible the user to his contacts, and producing applications with low-emotional gamification tools. This social network diffusion of recycling activities covering the social recognition factor (subjective rules) (Ajzen, 1991) causes recycling behavior to move from private to public.

Another practical implication of this study is that application designers must consider user safety concerning technology use to balance the expected risk with the functional benefits provided by the application. Designers should warn potential users of the low risk that comes from using the application.

In a second phase, this work wanted to promote WasteApp to encourage users to engage in pro-environmental recycling behavior during their stays in several European cities. The UrbanWaste project, among other initiatives, aimed to correct the poor image of over-saturated destinations and help travelers use the means available to them to recycle waste, thereby improving the reputation of the destination city. Through the efficient use of resources, smart tourism was intended to positively affect the sustainability of the destination, taking advantage of the intensive use that travelers make of smartphones during their visit; in other words, it used this circumstance as a tool to promote pro-environmental behavior.

The WasteApp application, based on gamification, aimed to encourage and activate mechanisms that would produce a habit of recycling behavior in visitors. However, given that expectations about rewards influence the user's perception of the usefulness of the application, and, in line with recent studies proposing a design focused on the preferences of individuals, it would be pertinent for organizations implementing gamified applications to take into account these preferences among visitors. However, perhaps the most striking finding is detected in the fact that, although specific physical rewards should be given in this type of application, they should not be perceived as excessive-quality, although they should be considered valuable and help the promoted behavior. Interestingly, tourist satisfaction will come from other channels, originating more from intrinsic motivations than extrinsic ones. Although small doses of extrinsic motivation are favorable to promote the target behavior of the application, it is intrinsic motivation that weighs more in the visitor's mind.

In conclusion, according to the findings of our study, this type of initiative seems to be helpful, and the institutions should promote it to improve some behaviors of individuals and develop a more desirable reputation for the organizations that promote the application.

In short, for a gamified application to be successful and for tourists to adopt it, it must give visibility to the individual among their networks of acquaintances and friends, so that they will use it and recognize it as beneficial for their recycling behavior, will be satisfied with it, will promote this behavior and will have a favorable impact on the destination's image.

Finally, gamification tools have not been exempt from critical voices. They have been accused of manipulating behaviors, which has been called gamipulation, which is nothing more than game tools whose purpose is to direct certain habits to where the designer of these tools wants, regardless of the player's conscience. The power of gamification in creating conducts highlights the danger of these tools falling into the hands of unscrupulous people whose objective is not as benevolent as promoting green attitudes. Therefore, the relationship between the user and the tool provider must be based on ethics and trust. Regulations must be developed to control these possible situations.

FUTURE RESEARCH DIRECTIONS

From the above-described research, some new lines have been opened as a frame for future work. It is proposed to explore modifications of the already contrasted model (Aguiar-Castillo et al., 2019), as has been explained in this chapter. This new modified model will try to demonstrate that the habit cycle is fulfilled using gamification in smart tourism environments. The idea focuses on the need that arises in the individuals to give visibility to their behavior, disseminating private activities such as pro-environmental practices, and make their acquaintances aware of their good practices, which otherwise belong to the private sphere remain out of reach of other eyes. In fields such as sustainability and marketing, it has been shown that the visibility of personal behaviors affects the "intention to recommend" (Salvi, 2015).

On the other hand, the reason for sharing a positive recommendation may be due to the desire to improve them, and in other cases, to the hope of gaining social status. The recycling behavior derived from user satisfaction arouses a feeling of altruism that makes the person recommend the application as a kind of display in front of friends and acquaintances (Kim, Kim, & Kim, 2009). Thus pro-environmental practices will positively and directly influence the intention to recommend the app.

On the other hand, the visibility of the behavior produced by the users' recommendation of the app can affect the functional benefits, in the sense that the positive self-image users propagate is helpful to them since, immediately they obtain a reward, and in the long term, they improve the environment in which They live as a form of altruism (Song, & Kim, 2019; Salvi, 2015). Thus, it is proposed that the intention to recommend the application, which causes the visibility of the behavior, positively and directly influences the perceived usefulness of the gamified application (H1 in Figure 6).

Figure 6. Study Proposal

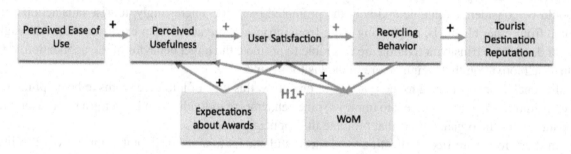

Future research in this field could also investigate factors affecting the success and failure of a gamified application, as some achieve the desired behavioral change and others do not. It would also be interesting to find out what balance is necessary for a gamified application encouraging green behavior between the "information" and "fun and game." The future of these tools for improving social awareness on recycling, as a part of the global fight against climate change, seems promising. (Douglas, & Brauer, 2021).

Regarding big data tools, it is possible to take advantage of the integration of gamification in different areas of society. Organizations could use this imbrication to discover certain behaviors of individuals while extracting location information and tracking their movements. It would be necessary to use data analysis and data scientists to identify which gamification strategies become helpful in making companies' decisions based on in-depth study and data monitoring. Thus, it would be essential to study the opinions of the vast number of large companies' customers through big data tools. Leading marketers are beginning to realize that they cannot change a behavior while they don't have measurements of its results. however, understanding the data is not enough; it is necessary to be behavioral scientists and game designers; in this framework, it is imperative both big data and the use of a strategy that understands cognitive science.

As for gamification and its integration into the circular economy, it can support a future line of research because, although studies have been developed on education in this area, there have been no experiments and studies where it intervenes in the circuit to encourage behaviors not only of customers but of human resources and suppliers that are integrated into the chain of the circular economy.

CONCLUSION

After analyzing the different principles established by researchers on the fundamentals of gamification, in this paper, and based on the research developed, it is considered that what lies behind these principles are the following:

- Motivation is attempted through gamification to generate habits through extrinsic motivators that move to internalize extrinsic motivation (Von Krogh et al., 2012).
- Feedback/interaction. In this foundation, we can encompass the elements that other researchers separate as goals and rules. They are fundamental for the interaction between the system and the individual and achieve effective feedback and an orientation towards learning specific behaviors. In addition, it makes it possible to contemplate progress on the path ahead. Even the interaction provides freedom of choice.
- In line with the idea put forward by Volkova (2013) on the importance of recognition among the media, visibility to personal networks is introduced as an essential element in gamification. The use of social networks to disclose a behavior can be central as an element of gamification in inducing a behavior.
- Oprescu, Jones, and Katsikitis (2014) posited that there is a transformative element in gamification that causes it to influence the image and reputation of the gamified environment.

This study attempts to focus a new definition of gamification towards motivation, supported by authors such as Kapp (2012) and Zichermann and Linder (2013), as will be discussed below.

Based on the assumption that motivation is the key driver of user behavior, the justification for a new definition based on the distinction made by Von Krog et al. (2012) of three types of motivation: extrinsic, intrinsic, and internalized extrinsic is presented below. Intrinsic motivation is based on intrinsic benefits such as personal values, self-actualization, altruism (Kankanhalli et al., 2005; Ray et al., 2014). However, extrinsic motivations are driven by tangible rewards. In the field of gamification, it is found mechanisms such as scores, leaderboards, or badges that can materialize in a good image in front of other individuals, and economic reward or simply fun (Huang & Zhang, 2013; Roberts et al., 2006). Finally, internalized extrinsic motivation is unique. It arises from external influences initially, but the individual may assimilate these influences and perceive them as self-regulatory behavior rather than coming from external impositions (Chen, Wei, & Zhu, 2017; Ryan & Deci, 2002).

By analyzing these theories and studying the research that led to this work, a new definition has been determined. In this definition, in addition to motivators, the time element is included. In general, studies contemplate gamification from a static point of view, but we propose to define it as a process that repeats itself. It is seen as a dynamic process that develops over time; it is not played only once. It is intended to obtain a commitment from players to continue with the behavior, and that behavior, as it is repeated, is getting the individual's commitment who converts the behavior into a habit.

In conclusion, this chain of actions may result because satisfaction with the application comes from a combination of intrinsic and extrinsic motivations of the users. Thus, individuals are satisfied with the application because it helps them to improve their behavior. This recycling habit emanates from an altruistic feeling and aims to leave a better world for future generations (intrinsic motivation). However, they also recommend the app to people in their environment to present themselves with a benevolent image by making the behavior visible (internalized extrinsic motivation). This theory translates into the following definition of gamification:

Gamification is a strategy based on the use of extrinsic motivators, game elements such as badges, leaderboards, and scores, which aim to convert, over time, a behavior into a habit, transforming those extrinsic motivators into internalized extrinsic ones. In essence, it would be a strategy that uses game elements that aim to convert, over time, a behavior into a habit.

ACKNOWLEDGMENT

This work was funded in part the Canary Islands Regional Government, through a Catalina Ruiz Grant and the ROIBOS Research project. This work was supported by a EU H2020 research project (URBAN WASTE). Authors wish to thank CVUT-Praha where Lidia Aguiar is currently following a research secondment under the advice of Prof. Zvanovec.

REFERENCES

Aguiar-Castillo, L., Clavijo-Rodriguez, A., Saa-Perez, D., & Perez-Jimenez, R. (2019). Gamification as an approach to promote tourist recycling behavior. *Sustainability*, *11*(8), 2201. doi:10.3390u11082201

Aguiar Castillo, L., Rufo Torres, J., De Saa Pérez, P., & Pérez Jiménez, R. (2018). *How to encourage recycling behaviour? The case of WasteApp: a gamified mobile application*. Sustainability.

Ajzen, I. (1985). From intentions to actions: A theory of planned behavior. In *Action control* (pp. 11–39). Springer. doi:10.1007/978-3-642-69746-3_2

Andreoni, J. (1990). Impure altruism and donations to public goods: A theory of warm-glow giving. *Economic Journal (London)*, *100*(401), 464–477. doi:10.2307/2234133

Bénabou, R., & Tirole, J. (2006). Incentives and Prosocial Behavior. *American Economic Review*, *96*(5), 1652–1678.

Chen, W., Wei, X., & Zhu, K. (2017). Engaging voluntary contributions in online communities: A hidden markov model. *Management Information Systems Quarterly*, *42*(1), 83–100. doi:10.25300/MISQ/2018/14196

Cheng, P. H., Yeh, T. K., Chao, Y. K., Lin, J., & Chang, C. Y. (2020). Design ideas for an issue-situation-based board game involving multirole scenarios. *Sustainability*, *12*(5), 2139. doi:10.3390u12052139

Dastjerdi, A. M., Kaplan, S., Silva, J. D. A., Nielsen, O. A., & Pereira, F. C. (2019). Participating in environmental loyalty program with a real-time multimodal travel app: User needs, environmental and privacy motivators. *Transportation Research Part D, Transport and Environment, 67*, 223–243. doi:10.1016/j.trd.2018.11.013

Deci, E. L., & Ryan, R. M. (2013). *Intrinsic motivation and self-determination in human behavior.* Springer Science & Business Media.

Dholakia, U. M. (2001). A motivational process model of product involvement and consumer risk perception. *European Journal of Marketing, 35*(11/12), 1340–1362. doi:10.1108/EUM0000000006479

Douglas, B. D., & Brauer, M. (2021). Gamification to Prevent Climate Change: A Review of Games and Apps for Sustainability. *Current Opinion in Psychology, 42*, 89–94. doi:10.1016/j.copsyc.2021.04.008 PMID:34052619

Dunphy, D. (2011). Conceptualizing sustainability: The business opportunity. In *Business and sustainability: Concepts, strategies and changes*. Emerald Group Publishing Limited. doi:10.1108/S2043-9059(2011)0000003009

Elkington, J. (1998). Partnerships from cannibals with forks: The triple bottom line of 21st-century business. *Environmental Quality Management, 8*(1), 37–51. doi:10.1002/tqem.3310080106

Foley, K. J. (2001). *Meta management: A stakeholder/quality management approach to whole-of-enterprise management*. Standards Australia.

Gaggi, O., Meneghello, F., Palazzi, C. E., & Pante, G. (2020, September). Learning how to recycle waste using a game. In *Proceedings of the 6th EAI International Conference on Smart Objects and Technologies for Social Good* (pp. 144-149). 10.1145/3411170.3411251

Ghani, J. A., & Deshpande, S. P. (1994). Task characteristics and the experience of optimal flow in human—Computer interaction. *The Journal of Psychology, 128*(4), 381–391. doi:10.1080/00223980.1994.9712742

Goodland, R. (1995). The concept of environmental sustainability. *Annual Review of Ecology and Systematics, 26*(1), 1–24. doi:10.1146/annurev.es.26.110195.000245

Guillen, M. G., Hamari, J., & Quist, J. (2021, January). Gamification of Sustainable Consumption: a systematic literature review. In *Proceedings of the 54th Hawaii International Conference on System Sciences* (p. 1345). 10.24251/HICSS.2021.163

Hamari, J., & Koivisto, J. (2015). Why do people use gamification services? *International Journal of Information Management, 35*(4), 419–431. doi:10.1016/j.ijinfomgt.2015.04.006

Hamari, J., Sjöklint, M., & Ukkonen, A. (2016). The sharing economy: Why people participate in collaborative consumption. *Journal of the Association for Information Science and Technology, 67*(9), 2047–2059. doi:10.1002/asi.23552

Helmefalk, M., & Rosenlund, J. (2020). Hedonic recycling: Using gamification and sensory stimuli to enhance the recycling experience. *EAI Endorsed Transactions on Serious Games*, (18), 1–12.

Hsu, C. L., Chen, Y. C., Yang, T. N., & Lin, W. K. (2017). Do website features matter in an online gamification context? Focusing on the mediating roles of user experience and attitude. *Telematics and Informatics*, *34*(4), 196–205. doi:10.1016/j.tele.2017.01.009

Huang, P., & Zhang, Z. (2013). (Forthcoming). Participation in open knowledge communities and job-hopping: Evidence from enterprise software. *Management Information Systems Quarterly*.

Hunicke, R., LeBlanc, M., & Zubek, R. (2004, July). MDA: A formal approach to game design and game research. In *Proceedings of the AAAI Workshop on Challenges in Game AI* (*Vol. 4*, No. 1, p. 1722). Academic Press.

Judah, G., Gardner, B., & Aunger, R. (2013). Forming a flossing habit: An exploratory study of the psychological determinants of habit formation. *British Journal of Health Psychology*, *18*(2), 338–353. doi:10.1111/j.2044-8287.2012.02086.x PMID:22989272

Kankanhalli, A., Tan, B. C., & Wei, K. K. (2005). Contributing knowledge to electronic knowledge repositories: An empirical investigation. *Management Information Systems Quarterly*, *29*(1), 113–143. doi:10.2307/25148670

Kapp, K. M. (2012). *The gamification of learning and instruction: game-based methods and strategies for training and education*. John Wiley & Sons.

Kiilunen, O. (2013). *Mobile applications as solutions to enhance sustainable travel behaviour among Generation Y. HAAGA-HELIA*. University of Applied Science.

Kim, D., & Chang, H. (2007). Key functional characteristics in designing and operating health information websites for user satisfaction: An application of the extended technology acceptance model. *International Journal of Medical Informatics*, *76*(11-12), 790–800. doi:10.1016/j.ijmedinf.2006.09.001 PMID:17049917

Kim, T. T., Kim, W. G., & Kim, H. B. (2009). The effects of perceived justice on recovery satisfaction, trust, word-of-mouth, and revisit intention in upscale hotels. *Tourism Management*, *30*(1), 51–62. doi:10.1016/j.tourman.2008.04.003

Lee, G. E., Xu, Y., Brewer, R. S., & Johnson, P. M. (2012). Makahiki: An open source game engine for energy education and conservation. Department of Information and Computer Sciences, University of Hawaii.

McKenzie-Mohr, D. (2011). *Fostering sustainable behavior: An introduction to community-based social marketing*. New society publishers.

Mendes, P., Santos, A. C., Nunes, L. M., & Teixeira, M. R. (2013). Evaluating municipal solid waste management performance in regions with strong seasonal variability. *Ecological Indicators*, *30*, 170–177. doi:10.1016/j.ecolind.2013.02.017

Meya, J. N., & Eisenack, K. (2018). Effectiveness of gaming for communicating and teaching climate change. *Climatic Change*, *149*(3), 319–333. doi:10.100710584-018-2254-7

Negruşa, A. L., Toader, V., Sofică, A., Tutunea, M. F., & Rus, R. V. (2015). Exploring gamification techniques and applications for sustainable tourism. *Sustainability*, *7*(8), 11160–11189. doi:10.3390u70811160

Oprescu, F., Jones, C., & Katsikitis, M. (2014). I play at work—Ten principles for transforming work processes through gamification. *Frontiers in Psychology, 5*, 14. doi:10.3389/fpsyg.2014.00014 PMID:24523704

Paharia, R. (2013). *Loyalty 3.0: How to revoluzionize Customer and Employee Engagement with Big Data and Gamification*. McGraw-Hill Book.

Park, C. H., & Kim, Y. G. (2003). Identifying key factors affecting consumer purchase behavior in an online shopping context. *International Journal of Retail & Distribution Management, 31*(1), 16–29. doi:10.1108/09590550310457818

Phillips, L. A., & Gardner, B. (2016). Habitual exercise instigation (vs. execution) predicts healthy adults' exercise frequency. *Health Psychology, 35*(1), 69–77. doi:10.1037/hea0000249 PMID:26148187

Ray, S., Kim, S. S., & Morris, J. G. (2014). The central role of engagement in online communities. *Information Systems Research, 25*(3), 528–546. doi:10.1287/isre.2014.0525

Roberts, J. A., Hann, I. H., & Slaughter, S. A. (2006). Understanding the motivations, participation, and performance of open source software developers: A longitudinal study of the Apache projects. *Management Science, 52*(7), 984–999. doi:10.1287/mnsc.1060.0554

Ryan, R. M., & Deci, E. L. (2000). Intrinsic and extrinsic motivations: Classic definitions and new directions. *Contemporary Educational Psychology, 25*(1), 54–67. doi:10.1006/ceps.1999.1020 PMID:10620381

Ryan, R. M., & Deci, E. L. (2002). Overview of self-determination theory: An organismic dialectical perspective. Handbook of Self-Determination Research, 2, 3-33.

Ryan, R. M., & Deci, E. L. (2017). *Self-determination theory: Basic psychological needs in motivation, development, and wellness*. Guilford Publications. doi:10.1521/978.14625/28806

Salvi, F. (2015). *Nuevo comportamiento del consumidor: la influencia del eWOM (electronic Word-of-Mouth) en relación a la lealtad de los clientes en el sector hotelero* (Doctoral dissertation). Universitat de les Illes Balears.

Shamshiry, E., Nadi, B., Bin Mokhtar, M., Komoo, I., Saadiah Hashim, H., & Yahaya, N. (2011). Integrated models for solid waste management in tourism regions: Langkawi Island, Malaysia. *Journal of Environmental and Public Health, 2011*, 2011. doi:10.1155/2011/709549 PMID:21904559

Song, S. Y., & Kim, Y. K. (2019). Doing good better: Impure altruism in green apparel advertising. *Sustainability, 11*(20), 5762. doi:10.3390u11205762

Souza, V. S., de Vasconcelos Marques, S. R. B., & Veríssimo, M. (2020). How can gamification contribute to achieve SDGs?: Exploring the opportunities and challenges of ecogamification for tourism. *Journal of Hospitality and Tourism Technology, 11*(2), 255–276. doi:10.1108/JHTT-05-2019-0081

Tsai, J. C., Cheng, P. H., Liu, S. Y., & Chang, C. Y. (2019). Using board games to teach socioscientific issues on biological conservation and economic development in Taiwan. *Journal of Baltic Science Education, 18*(4), 634–645. doi:10.33225/jbse/19.18.634

UrbanWaste. (2016). Available online: www.urban-waste.eu

Volkova, I. I. (2013). Four pillars of gamification. *Middle East Journal of Scientific Research, 13*, 149–152.

Von Krogh, G., Haefliger, S., Spaeth, S., & Wallin, M. W. (2012). Carrots and rainbows: Motivation and social practice in open source software development. *Management Information Systems Quarterly, 36*(2), 649–676. doi:10.2307/41703471

Wee, S. C., & Choong, W. W. (2019). Gamification: Predicting the effectiveness of variety game design elements to intrinsically motivate users' energy conservation behaviour. *Journal of Environmental Management, 233*, 97–106. doi:10.1016/j.jenvman.2018.11.127 PMID:30572268

Werbach, K., & Hunter, D. (2012). *For the win: How game thinking can revolutionize your business.* Wharton Digital Press.

Yoo, C., Kwon, S., Na, H., & Chang, B. (2017). Factors affecting the adoption of gamified smart tourism applications: An integrative approach. *Sustainability, 9*(12), 2162. doi:10.3390u9122162

Yoon, C. (2018). Extending the TAM for Green IT: A normative perspective. *Computers in Human Behavior, 83*, 129–139. doi:10.1016/j.chb.2018.01.032

Zichermann, G., & Cunningham, C. (2011). *Gamification by Design. Implementing Game Mechanics in Web and Mobile Apps.* O'Reilly Media.

Zichermann, G., & Linder, J. (2013). *Gamification revolution.* Academic Press.

ADDITIONAL READING

Gatti, L., Ulrich, M., & Seele, P. (2019). Education for sustainable development through business simulation games: An exploratory study of sustainability gamification and its effects on students' learning outcomes. *Journal of Cleaner Production, 207*, 667–678. doi:10.1016/j.jclepro.2018.09.130

Lee, J. J., Matamoros, E., Kern, R., Marks, J., de Luna, C., & Jordan-Cooley, W. (2013). Greenify: fostering sustainable communities via gamification. In CHI'13 Extended Abstracts on Human Factors in Computing Systems (pp. 1497-1502). doi:10.1145/2468356.2468623

Mitchell, R., Schuster, L., & Jin, H. S. (2020). Gamification and the impact of extrinsic motivation on needs satisfaction: Making work fun? *Journal of Business Research, 106*, 323–330. doi:10.1016/j.jbusres.2018.11.022

Paravizo, E., Chaim, O. C., Braatz, D., Muschard, B., & Rozenfeld, H. (2018). Exploring gamification to support manufacturing education on industry 4.0 as an enabler for innovation and sustainability. *Procedia Manufacturing, 21*, 438–445. doi:10.1016/j.promfg.2018.02.142

Raftopoulos, M. (2014). Towards gamification transparency: A conceptual framework for the development of responsible gamified enterprise systems. *Journal of Gaming & Virtual Worlds, 6*(2), 159–178. doi:10.1386/jgvw.6.2.159_1

Scurati, G. W., Ferrise, F., & Bertoni, M. (2020). Sustainability awareness in organizations through gamification and serious games: a systematic mapping. *DS 101: Proceedings of NordDesign 2020, Lyngby, Denmark*, 12th-14th August 2020, 1-10. 10.35199/NORDDESIGN2020.1

Walz, S. P., & Deterding, S. (Eds.). (2014). *The gameful world: Approaches, issues, applications*. MIT Press.

Warmelink, H., Koivisto, J., Mayer, I., Vesa, M., & Hamari, J. (2020). Gamification of production and logistics operations: Status quo and future directions. *Journal of Business Research*, *106*, 331–340. doi:10.1016/j.jbusres.2018.09.011

KEY TERMS AND DEFINITIONS

Altruist Behavior: It is a behavior that decreases the vulnerabilities and increases the chances of survival of others even if it means reducing their well-being.

Destination Reputation: Destination reputation is the intangible value or reputation of a location through its multiple dimensions, such as its culture, sports, companies, organizations, tourism.

Extrinsic Motivation: This motivation refers to the type of motivation in which the motives that lead a person to perform a certain job or activity are subject to contingencies or external factors.

Habit Cycle: It is a strategy that uses game elements that aim to convert, over time, a behavior into a habit.

Internalized Extrinsic Motivation: It is a motivation that begins as extrinsic and, with time, ends up being internalized, generating a perception of self-regulation, and ceasing to depend on the external factor.

Intrinsic Motivation: It is the motivation that drives us to do things for the simple pleasure of doing them. The execution of the task itself is the reward.

Recycling Behavior: It is defined as actions that the consumer carries out to deposit garbage in differentiated areas by type of waste.

Word of Mouth: It is the passing of information from person to person.

Chapter 16

Review Bomb:
On the Gamification of the Ideological Conflict

Venera Tomaselli

https://orcid.org/0000-0002-2287-7343
University of Catania, Italy

Giulio Giacomo Cantone
University of Catania, Italy

Valeria Mazzeo
University of Catania, Italy

ABSTRACT

This chapter provides a comprehensive overview of the phenomenon of review bomb, which occurs when an abnormally large amount of information is submitted to a rating system in a very short period of time by an overtly anonymous mass of accounts, with the overall goal of sabotaging the system's proper functioning. Because review bombs are frequently outbursts of social distress from gaming communities, gamification theories have proven useful for understanding the behavioral traits and conflict dynamics associated with such a phenomenon. A prominent case is analysed quantitatively. The methodology is discussed and proposed as a generalized framework for descriptive quantification of review bombs. As a result of the study, considerations for technological improvements in the collection of rating data in systems are proposed too.

INTRODUCTION

The Last of Us Part II (TLOU2) is the sequel of The Last of Us (TLOU), a video game originally published by Sony in 2013. Both TLOU and TLOU2 are works of fiction classified as only-for-adults because of the presence of violence and horror scenes. They have been commercial successes for Sony. The main character of TLOU is Joel, who protects his adoptive daughter Ellie. In TLOU2, the new character Abigail,

DOI: 10.4018/978-1-7998-9223-6.ch016

whose father was killed by Joel himself in TLOU, kills Joel. Ellie and Abigail are both main characters of TLOU2, and they share a fierce rivalry fuelled by a common sentiment of vengeance. Through the marketing campaign started in 2018, Sony revealed that:

- Joel would have not been the protagonist and he would have been killed in TLOU2.
- Ellie would experience a homosexual relationship with a person of Jewish ethnicity.

It became also of public knowledge that Sony was working into producing a TV series adaptation of the video game. This news was received with contempt from some communities of video game players. Major topics of criticism regarded LGBTQ and feminism-related issues. The presence of these elements in the narrative was perceived by someone as an attack against the cultural identity of the typical player of violent horror video games. This was also strongly linked with the Internet hashtag #GamerGate, an anger campaign against the mainstream artistic direction of video games (Ferguson and Glasgow 2020). #GamerGate is associated with social media activity and Internet communities (e.g., *4Chan*) where there is a presence of American far-right supporters and other political extremists.

After being postponed for reasons related to Covid-19 pandemic, TLOU2 was released for worldwide retail on June 19th, 2020. Even if the median time to have a full experience of the video game can be estimated between 15 and 30 hours, after few hours from the publication date, the website *metacritic. com* (*Metacritic*) received a peak of thousands of negative ratings and sour reviews.

On Metacritic, a user with a registered account can secretly submit a score (from 0 to 10), or a whole public rating (score plus text, also generating more metadata), of an item. This mechanism is part of a rating system, or a system devoted to collection of data in the form of ratings. When a user submits a rating, this is publicly displayed on the webpage of the item and on the webpage of the user's account. In the first days of ratings, the users' rating metric of TLOU2 on Metacritic felt into a value slightly above 3/10, making The Last of Us Part II the worst first-day performer video game in Metacritic's history.

This was immediately seen as a case of Review Bomb (RB). RB is a jargon expression, mostly adopted in journalism (PC Gamer, 2020), to refer to a phenomenon where a crowd of people performs an explicit, perceptible, sabotage of a website, showing public ratings or reviews. The result of the low rating metric on Metacritic was achieved through the socio-political mobilization of a mass of accounts that rated the video game with strategically low scores (0 or 1).

Expert reviewers question the legitimacy of such extreme ratings. Indeed, the expert assessment of TLOU2 on Metacritic (METASCORE, which is also the primary business of the website) was extremely high (97/100). Ratings from buyers on Amazon were ranging around extremely high scores, too. Differently from Amazon, Metacritic does not verify who purchased the item (Anderson and Simester, 2014).

After noticing the case for an RB, Metacritic changed its internal rules to avoid rating submissions by 48h after the publication date of an item (Yahoo!Finance, 2020). It is possible that while in the first days extremely low ratings were submitted mostly as a subtle attack against the video game and the website Metacritic, this attack had the effect to influence the ratings of other users in the days after.

This is surely true in a case: the occurrence of the bomb of negative scores against TLOU2 made more radical the judgement of other users. These become ideological defenders of the item in the following days. Users who would have rated the item with a generic positive score (e.g., 8/10) felt the ideological push to rate it as a 10, the maximum score to balance the rating metric and bring 'justice'. This push for positive reviews is, for the original review bombers, a 'boomerang effect' that needs to be balanced with injection to even more negative reviews until one of two parties desists. This is in accord with the formal theory of escalation of conflicts (Saperstein, 2004).

But this notion of influence likely goes in the other direction, too: it could be possible that a user, who would have regarded TLOU2 as a mediocre product, felt propelled to rate it as extremely bad, instead. This is true especially if the second user (the follower) regards the first one (the original bomber) as a friend or if he or she self-identifies with the general message of the RB, producing an effect of crowd mentality, or *herding* (Lee et al., 2015; Wang et al., 2018).

Escalation of conflict *plus* herding set for a valid theory of polarised conflict that self-propagates. If these concepts could be made operative with method, such hypotheses can be discussed with the public data of the public ratings (score and text) as empirical basis.

Objectives of the Research

The ideal objective of a scientific research on public opinion dynamics (conflict *vs.* herding) would be to observe and quantify effects at individual level. For example, to infer what is the (complex) effect of the mediatic exposition to a Review Bomb in terms of behaviour for a user of a website like Metacritic. Unfortunately, lacking any experimental data on the exact opinion on the item before the exposition to RB of those users who gave extreme scores, this task seems not approachable, at least directly.

A key point is that the video game was bombed since the publication date, which means that the opinion on it was pre-formed already through advertising trailers. A net impact evaluation that quantifies how much RB distorted the rating metric, if possible, would be misleading.

It is worth to consider the flux of reviews to Metacritic as a population of statistical events, instead. These events are characterised by some features that can be employed to stratify the population into groups. The prevalence across the time of these groups describes in detail the dynamics internal to this statistical population, mapping the conflict between users who attacked the item, users who defended it and neutral reviewers. For these reasons, the objective of the research is to perform an analysis on the dynamics of these groups in conflict rather than to infer effects at individual level.

Core Features

- Since scores were submitted with a strategic intent (to push the rating metric), scores are the stronger identifiers of the conflict among groups.
- Users who wanted to influence others had to write a review. Reviews may differ hugely from each other, and techniques of text mining can be employed to cluster reviews according to their content. There are three concepts that can be detected in a review:
  - if a review brings a judgement over elements within the product (e.g., a technical benchmarking if the graphics are at the state-of-the-art), which is the normal function of a review;
  - if the text of a review is ideologically charged;
  - finally, one of the typical contents of a 'bombing' review is a reference to a situation that is external to the item under judgement. All ideological reviews are judging something that is external to the technical merits of TLOU2 and that reflects, for example, the normative values of the reviewer. However, there could be reviews that reflect a judgement over the behaviour of other users without an explicit ideological criticism. For example, user u_2 could say: "people like user u_1 are rude", without explicating an ideological position about those.

This is a reflexive act of communication. This communication is, again, not about the virtual experience of the video game itself, which should be the focus of a user's review, instead. This concept is referred to as Metatalk (Tomaselli et al., 2021).

- Users have a history on Metacritic. Some of them have rated a lot of items, others only a few. But the most important distinction should be between users that reviewed only TLOU2 and users that reviewed other items on Metacritic (Tomaselli et al., 2021).

A combination of scores, textual clusters, and number of past reviews can stratify the population of users that rated TLOU2 on Metacritic to catch and describe its internal dynamics.

BACKGROUND

In order to help online users and customers in filtering items, recommender systems are being used to try to get predictions accordingly to users' preferences. Specifically, a recommender system (RS) is a system of tasks aimed to nudge a user (a generic person that interacts with it) to take one or more decision, or to call the user for some actions. In recommender systems, the nudges are determined with data collected through a rating system.

With the aim to 'recommend the best', a RS suggests what to do to their users sorting and filtering (Jannach et al., 2010) the options in a catalogue of the system ('items'). These functions of sorting and filtering are evidence-based, which means that a RS needs evaluative data (i.e., the 'ratings') about the items in the catalogue in an explicit (e.g., explicit votes or declarations) or implicit (e.g., counts of observed actions or facts) format.

The most common format to collect explicit ratings is user's score, i.e., a numerical value in multi-point scale. The score quantifies both the user's opinion and sentiment on an item. Sometimes, a textual declaration ('review' or 'comment') is also provided with the score, as explicit data.

Rating aggregators (RAs) are online platforms that, functioning as rating systems, collect ratings to provide a RS-like service to the public. Differently from the personalised variant of RS, RAs are less invasive of privacy. Personalised RS perform a normative function towards individuals, RAs hold this function for a generic public.

While personalised RS are focused on filtering items tailored for what the rating system knows about the user, RAs focus on the construction of ratings metrics. These metrics are sometimes presented as statistics descriptive of a population, but the correct way to interpret such statistics is like estimations of a latent central value of the quality of item (Tomaselli and Cantone, 2020). However, since items in the same category can be ranked according to these estimates, they have an important function of filtering items: best values determine 'tops of the charts' and most of users will only look at items topping their charts of interest.

Statistical Distributions of Scores and Fake Reviews

While scores collected in experimental settings (i.e., Randomized Clinical Trials) respect methodological assumptions or normality (i.e., independence of observations), scores collected in online (open) platforms are subject to two biases:

- Purchasing bias: people review what they purchase but they purchase what is already reviewed or at least already popular (a case of "Matthew Effect");
- Under-reporting bias: people review when they are extremely satisfied or unsatisfied.

The consequence of these biases is a *J*-shaped distribution of scores in online ratings (Hu et al., 2009; Schoenmuller et al., 2020; Smirnova et al., 2020). *J*-shaped distributions fit Beta-binomial models when α and β parameters are both < 1 (Figure 1).

Figure 1. The Probability Mass Functions of a Beta-Binomial distribution with α = .6 and β =.3, compared to a corresponding Binomial distribution with $p = \alpha / (\alpha + \beta) = .66$. The two distributions have the same mean, but the mass of the Beta-Binomial is shifted towards the extremes, not the centre.

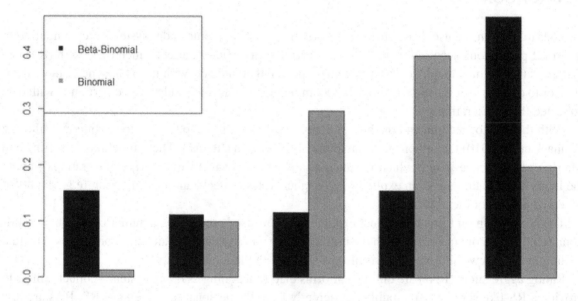

These biases make easier to fraud the RS. Fake reviews with extreme scores can be injected:

- through the so-called 'sock puppet' accounts, when there is only one physical person that secretly operates through different accounts and identities. If these identities are managed by an automated system, sometimes it can be referred as a *botnet* of fake accounts;
- or by 'shills', that are people persuaded or bribed to report insincere or misleading reviews.

Experimental results confirm that positive fake reviews have an impact on the success of online business: according to van de Rijt et al. (2014), fake success breeds real success. This is predicted by the basic formulation of Thomas's Theorem of the self-fulfilling prophecy: situations defined as real in their premises (a fake considered genuine), became real in their consequences (induce a cognition of quality). A consensus on the impact of negative fake reviews has not been reached, yet.

An RS having the information that the reviewer purchased the item (e.g., Amazon has this knowledge) can weight the relevance and the authenticity of a rating through this information (Anderson and Simester, 2014).

However, usually RAs do not know how much the user is experienced about the item (e.g., how much time spent interacting with the item). Shilling is an easy job on a RA: one could ask an uninterested friend with an account in the system to rig a review (Ong et al., 2014).

To overcome such ambiguities, researchers have adopted the broader perspective of 'attacks of spam reviews' (Hussain et al., 2019). Spam is not necessarily fake but it is an excess of information, which is undesired or harmful for the purposes of the system. The operative shift from the categories of 'fake reviews' or 'shilling intents' to the broader 'review spam' is both methodological and conceptual. The questions around illegitimacy of the content are not searched in the subjective disposition of the reviewer (e.g., "are they good guys, well informed, who want to provide useful data to our system … or bad guys who want to corrupt our metrics?") but in objective features (e.g., "are these data harmful for our system?").

Review Bomb: Spam Attack or Cyber-Mob?

Aggarwal (2016) devotes entire Chapter 12 (pp. 385-408) on the topic of spam attacks. To make a spam attack harder to detect, fake ratings must be deployed slowly in the time. The goal is to mimicry the behaviour of a regular user. The consequence of this precautionary mechanism is that systems that collect a lot of ratings are general robust against mainstream spam attacks. Indeed, one of the first public statements on RB came in September 2017 from Steam, a digital online market and social network for video game players, and it says:

"Review bombing is where players post a large number of reviews in a very compressed time frame, aimed at lowering the Review Score of a game. [...] Players doing the bombing are fulfilling the goal of User Reviews - they're voicing their opinion [...]. But one thing we've noticed is that the issue players are concerned about can often be outside the game itself. It might be that they're unhappy with something the developer has said online, or about choices the developer has made in the Steam version of their game relative to other platforms, or simply that they don't like the developer's political convictions. Many of these out-of-game issues aren't very relevant when it comes to the value of the game itself, but some of them are real reasons why a player may be unhappy with their purchase. [...] we believe the issue behind the review bomb genuinely did affect the happiness of future purchasers of the game, and ended up being accurately reflected in the regular ongoing reviews submitted by new purchasers. In some review bomb cases, the developers made changes in response to the community dissatisfaction, and in others they didn't - but there didn't seem to be much correlation between whether they did and what happened to their Review Score afterwards" (Steam, 2017).

In the words of Steam, RB is seen just as an anomaly: "there didn't seem to be much correlation between whether they did and what happened to their Review Score afterwards". The system cannot precisely assert the correct rating of an item. At the same time, Steam is well guarded against fake reviews because by its own mixed nature of both marketplace and performance-enhancer, Steam has a lot of information about its user base. In particular, Steam knows the exact amount of time the user interacted with the reviewed item.

The case of RB of TLOU2 on Metacritic is an exception in regard of all the mentioned 'roles' of spam attacks. The bombing was organised as attack before the actual publishing of the video game. It is also unclear how many accounts are sock puppets (same user, different accounts) and how many are the more ambiguous category of shills (liars).

However, accounts involved in RB usually lack a history of previous reviews or ratings in the system (because they are spammers or because they just people herding into it). This is an important point, because it links the theory of RB as a spam attack to a more general issue in RS, the problem of cold-start.

Review Bomb as a Problem of Cold-Start

The phenomenon of Review Bomb can be seen as a particular case of spam attack where users publish, in a short time span, fake or misleading reviews on specific products, brands or services, with the aim of discrediting or promoting these.

Recommendations are reliable by profiling the accounts through their past statistics (preferences, ratings, reviews) and demographic information (e.g., location, age, gender). In the case of review spamming, generally it can be observed that spammers are new accounts, i.e., accounts lacking past interactions with the system. Any new account is, therefore, hard to identify correctly as malicious.

This scenario is known as a "cold start problem" and refers to the case where new user data is limited, or historical information is not available. (Revathy and Anitha, 2018).

A possible way to address this issue is through the construction of effective behavioural features from pre-existing data, looking for similarities: this involves checking out complex characteristics as linguistic style. Generally, linguistic features can be employed in spam review detection, but these might result ineffective as review spammers easily can change their writing style (Wang et al., 2017; Tang et al., 2020).

There is another issue: detection algorithms are geared towards a conservative approach. In facts, RS cannot exceed in flagging reviews as spam in absence of robust evidence, because this will make it a hostile environment for new users with strong or divergent opinions, but definitely genuine and not malicious ones.

All these elements make RAs perfect targets for review bombers: RAs are not very optimized at tracking information about their own accounts. A high percentage of reviews is published by users who try the service once and, unbound by any payment for access or perceived benefit, will never review anymore. In this context, it is easy for a sock-puppet or a shill to disguise as someone who just tried to make a review. During an RB, illegitimate account can disguise for people genuinely engaged in the controversy.

Sock-puppets are more common in reviewing experience goods, i.e., goods which value is only loosely tied to their technical characteristics, like food or books) because these goods are the most influenced by word-of-mouth.

A difference between review spam and sock-puppetry is represented by the fact that sock-puppets usually dilute the trend of their malicious and non-legitimate reviews through time, making difficult to spot the fake accounts.

Review Bomb as a Gamified Conflict

From a gamified perspective, users in social platforms can be seen as real/virtual players that can compete, cooperate or engage in conflict (Sailer et al., 2017). Social Media, for instance, enable e-participation (Khan and Krishnan, 2017), motivating user participation and content consumption (Laeeq Khan, 2017).

Looking at the phenomenon from another perspective, the organisation of the bombing could pursue the symbolic goal to trigger a broader discussion about issues as the integrity of the reputational systems (i.e., journalism, RAs like Metacritic, etc.), or other (someway) ideologically driven issues. Quoting Steam (2017), again: "they're voicing their opinion [...]. But one thing we have noticed is that the issue players are concerned about can often be outside the game itself. It might be that they're unhappy with something the developer has said online, or about choices the developer has made in the Steam version of their game relative to other platforms, or simply that they do not like the developer's political convictions". Those "issues outside the game itself" (Steam, 2017) constitute the Metatalk of the review (Tomaselli et al., 2021). It is evident that political discussions are frequent in cases of RB.

Social platforms, including Metacritic, have gamification elements embedded into their systems; for example, the number of likes/dislikes is a gamification element. This aspect can be extended also to items, where the number of scores assigned to it represents another gamification element, making gamification easily to be applied to marketing and sales on a business level (Patrício et al., 2018). The link between RB and gamification is that RB is becoming a typical strategy of conflict among self-identified gamers or 'fanatics of video games'. Figure 2 displays peaks of the argument "Review Bomb" on Google Trends across the year 2020: most of them are video games.

Figure 2. Events associated with peaks in popularity of the research on Google on the argument 'Review Bomb'.
Source: Tomaselli et al., 2021.

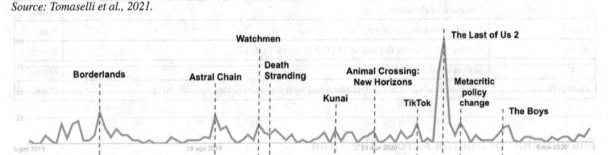

The proposition here is that, in the mindset of the bomber, the RB is a gamified social and political conflict in a gamified environment, too.
According to the 'scheme of gamification' in Robson et al. (2015):

- The mechanics of the game: the rating metric is like a global score and users can move it towards 0 or 10 with their 'votes', one vote for each account. The rating metric does not reflect anymore a latent feature of the item but the strength of the leading faction.
- The dynamics of the game: users will call for help as much as possible. Among the tactics of the players, they can try to gamble the game with spam reviews, or they can try to persuade the undecided with their rhetorical skills.
- The emotions in play: gamification approaches attempt to encourage participants' engagement, giving the opportunity to actively interact with a specific service, e.g., a brand (Alsawaier, 2018; Kujur and Singh, 2016), and leading users to experience different emotions and motivations (Papanaoum, 2019). In the RB context, users have strong motivations to think they are on the right side. Negative bombers (low scores) can think that they are fighting against a corrupted system, while Positive bombers (high scores) can think that they are fighting for social justice.

Finally, it can be said that these emotions involve so many people with a *gamified mind-set* in a tug-of-war game.

DATA ANALYSIS

Features of the Dataset

The dataset is a corpus of 59,687 English reviews. 70k reviews were extracted from Metacritic with R package *rvest* on April 1st, 2021. Packages *cld3* and *rlang* were used to identify reviews written in English. The dataset has 5 variables, listed in Table 1.

Table 1. Variables in the corpus dataset

Variable	Description	Type
ID	Username of the account	String
Date	Day of submission of the review	Date
Score	A value submitted by the user to TLOU2 in the range [0:10]	Integer
Text	Textual comment of the review	String
Past Ratings (k)	Number of ratings submitted on Metacritic by the account before April 1st, 2021	Count

Distribution of Scores Across the Time

As displayed in Figure 3, most of the reviews were submitted before August, with a time distribution that can be approximated by an exponential decay over time.

Figure 3. The 11 classes of scores are represented as different shades. Absolute frequencies are represented as continuously distributed across the period from July 19th, 2020, to August 19th, 2020. After this date, the numbers of new reviews falls into a trivial entity.

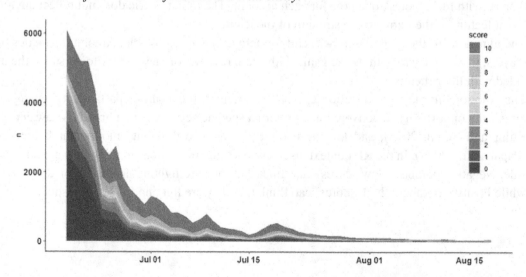

In Figure 3 and Figure 4 can be noticed that 0 and 10 are the two values of the score variable with the largest number of reviews (n). On April 1st, 2021, these two still have the largest *n* but more users rated the item as 10 than 0, resulting into an inversion of the *J*-shape (Figure 4).

Figure 4. A representation of how all the scores submitted to TLOU2 were distributed at the end of the first day vs. at the end of April 1st, 2021.

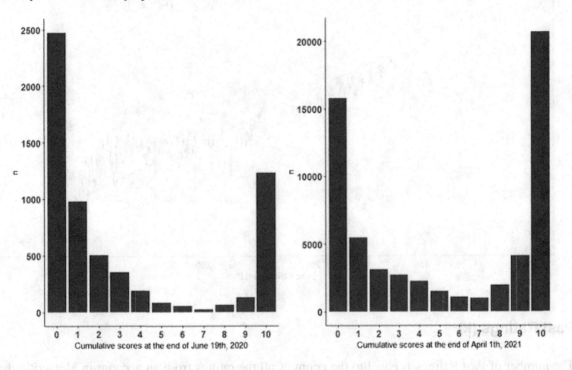

Lexical Diversity (LD) in the Text

Lexical diversity (LD) is the number of unique unigram tokens (the text between two spaces) in a text. Conceptually, it is the number of unique words of a document (Zhou and Zafarani, 2019). This measure provides information that is similar to the count of characters (*n-char*) in the text of review. Indeed, in the dataset the R^2 of the linear fit is .9619 and these quantities grow in a similar trend, aside few exceptions. These exceptions are cases where the text contains a long nonsense sequence of characters. Therefore, LD is a marginally more robust indicator of the user's effort than *n-char*.

The distribution of LD in the corpus fits a log-linear model of decay (Figure 5). With exception of reviews with less than 15 words (right side of Figure 5, before the peak in y-axis), there is a statistical regularity between the effort put in the review and the likelihood to write a review, with the reviews with 15 words being the most frequent in the corpus, and the frequency decreasing at the increase of the number of words.

Figure 5. Lexical diversity is the number of different words. The number of reviews (y-axis) is represented in the log-scale. The exponential decay model fits well ($R^2 > .9$) the distribution of LD.

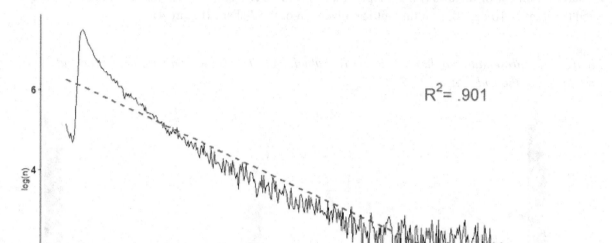

Past Ratings (k)

The number of Past Ratings is equal to the count of all the ratings from an account in Metacritic that are not TLOU2, and it is denoted by k. Since TLOU2 was published in June 2020 but k is collected in April 2020, there may be ratings that have been submitted to Metacritic after TLOU2. In the dataset, this variable has an extremely skewed distribution, with more than 68% of accounts having been signed up on the website to only review TLOU2 (Table 2).

Table 2. Distribution among users of the number of ratings (i.e., reviews to another item).

	Number of Ratings (k)					
	k = 0	k = 1	k = 2	k = 3	k = 4	k => 5
n	40961	7613	3003	1720	1105	6390
f	.686	.128	.050	.023	.018	.107

The major discriminant in k is between k = 0 and k > 1, indeed. There is no dependence between the value assumed in the score variable and this binary classification (*p*-value of Chi-Square test is .232, see Table 3), neither there is correlation (Pearson: 0.002, Kendall: -0.032) between k and the value of score.

Table 3. Cross-distribution between two classes of users (with and without reviews to other items) and scores.

	Score										
	0	**1**	**2**	**3**	**4**	**5**	**6**	**7**	**8**	**9**	**10**
n(k = 0)	10791	3661	2057	1748	1328	883	582	530	1345	2976	15060
f(k = 0)	.263	.089	.05	.042	.032	.021	.014	.013	.038	.072	.367
n(k > 0)	4982	1805	1060	968	927	602	483	456	625	1172	5646
f(k > 0)	.266	.096	.056	.052	.049	.032	.026	.24	.033	.062	.301

The interpretation of statistics in Table 3 is that the quota of accounts k=0 has been influenced by pushes towards both very positive and very negative reviews. Scores that Metacritic considers neutral (5, 6, 7) are proportionally overrepresented among in the class k > 0. Score = 10 is underrepresented for k > 0.

Method of Detection of Clusters of Reviews

To label the text variable, the corpus is processed according to an approach that mixed pre-processing text vectorisation into tokens and Bag-of-words (BoW) counting techniques (Silge and Robinson, 2017). Each comment from each user is represented as a vector of tokens, i.e. sequences of symbols (alphanumeric, or also blank spaces, etc.). Stop words (e.g., " the ", " not ", " do ", etc.) are then removed (i.e., replaced with a blank space) in the vector.

After counting the frequencies of singular tokens between two blank spaces (unigrams) and token combining 2 words separated by a blank space (bigrams) in the whole corpus, peculiar tokens are labelled as elements of a Vocabulary (see, Table 4). Each comment with at least a labelled word is then excluded from the observed corpus for next iterations of BoW counting. The process is iterated until at least ~50,000k comments had at least a token within labelled in a meaningful way. Iteration after iteration, by counting frequencies only of tokens in comments incrementally harder to label, is possible to discover very meaningful 'niches' of linguistic patterns as slurs and jargon which are both meaningful and statistically relevant in the corpus.

On the construction of Vocabularies, the concept of Metatalk was regarded as relevant for reviews in RB. Metatalk is opposed to technical topics of reviews, which focuses on the criticism of contents within the reviewed item (and not outside of it). Two vocabularies of words associated with Metatalk and Technical jargon are displayed in Table 4. Tokens are 'truncated' because, through this feature, misclassification due to typos by the users is reduced. In some cases, typos (e.g., "grafic" instead of "graphics") were directly included in the Vocabulary, instead.

Table 4. Vocabularies for two classes: Technical and Metatalk (including LGBTQ, Politics)

Vocabulary	Tokens
Technical Jargon	abbi, abby, actin, actor, ai, animat, antagonist, atmospher, boss, bugs, character, cinematic, clich, collectibl, combat, cut scene, cutscen, design, dialog, dina, dinah, ebby, ell, environment, execut, fireflies, flashbac, flaw, frame rat, framerat, game play, gamebreak, gameplay, gaming exp, gampl, glitc, golf, gore, goty, grafic, graphic, hero, improvemen, innovative, jess, jj, joe, killer, lev, linear, loot, manni, mechani, melee, motion blu, murderer, music, narrat, open world, openworl, pathin, performa, platin, plot, protagonist, puzzle, realistic, sandbox, script, sideque, storyl, storytell, structur, technic, tomm, villain, visual, worldbuild, writin, yara
Metatalk (LGBTQ)	androge, bigot, bisex, cis, degenerate, dyke, erotic, fag, femenin, gay, gender, hetero, homo, homophob, homophon, homosex, hulk, inclusi, intersex, kiss, lbgt, lesb, lezb, lezz, lgbt, masculin, musc, non-binary, nonbinary, pedo, porn, queer, same sex, sex scene, sexual, shemale, sodom, stereotyp, taboo, trann, virgin
Metatalk (Politics)	activis, agenda, anita, asian, censor, far-right, fascis, feminis, freedom of, gamerga, globoho, idealo, idelo, ideol, jew, justice war, kike, lectur, moral, nazi, nazis, pc, politc, politic, progressiv, propagan, propogan, racis, religio, retcon, sanders, shill, sjw, social, socialis, sponsor, trump, virtue sign, white man, white men, woke
Metatalk (Other)	0s, 10s, 19th, are mad, balanc, bandwag, bann, bias, bigot, blind, bomb, bots, bottin, boycot, brigad, comment, communit, complai, controvers, criticis, criticiz, critics, critiq, crybab, divisiv, downvot, fake, first day, frustrat, grade, hater, hating, ignore the, immature, incel, industry, jedi, journal, leak, metacri, moron, overreac, people, people who, polar, propaganda, ratin, review, sabotag, salty, scor, star war, statisti, stats, streame, the 0, troll, user, who hate, who say, whoever say

The two labels are not mutually exclusive (or: they are fuzzy), with:

1. 6,497 reviews labelled as Metatalk but not Technical, with a median LD equal to 26;
2. 21,102 reviews labelled as Technical but not Metatalk, with a median LD equal to 31;
3. 21,572 reviews with both labels, with a median LD equal to 80;
4. 10,516 with no label, with a median LD equal to 18.

The higher the effort to in writing the review (i.e., the longer the review), the more users felt appropriate to both judge technical features of the item and to take part in the external debate.

There is an open debate if fuzzy clustering (or soft clustering) is appropriate for short texts (not only reviews, but also comments, tweets, etc.) instead of hard clusters (i.e., mutually exclusive clusters). The general issue with fuzzy clustering is that it lacks statistical reliability and meaningfulness due to the low frequencies of word occurrences (Qiang et al., 2020). The implication of adoption of hard clustering for short texts is that the short text could discuss different topics, but there is always only one core topic that characterize short text.

The Technical label is characteristic of content for reviews of a video game, while Metatalk is the characteristic content expected when a Review Bomb occurs (Steam, 2017). The second is a specific case of the first, which is the general case. So, while is not peculiar that many reviews (42,674, sum of group 2 and 3) discussed technical features of the video game, it is of interest that, giving that the bombing happened, there are 21,572 users (group 2) that reviewed 'correctly' the video game without referencing features associate to RB. Merging groups 1 and 3, there are three hard clusters that characterise:

- reviews explicitly engaged in the discussion of RB (group 1 plus group 3)
- reviews from users that ignored RB and focused only on the video game (group 2)
- reviews avoiding both the two characteristic topics of the case (group 4)

RESULTS OF ANALYSIS

Combining the three hard clusters with the information scores, the dataset is partitioned into 7 archetypes of users (Table 5).

Table 5. How descriptive groups of users (archetypes) are constructed combing labels and scores.

Archetype	Condition	Description	n	%(n | k = 0)	Median LD
Attacker	Metatalk = T, score < 5	Willing to boycott TLOU2	11,916	.662	52
Defender	Metatalk = T, score > 7	Hinder attempts to boycott TLOU2.	13,156	.722	63
Disappointed	Metatalk = F, Technical = T, score < 5	Disliked TLOU2 but tries to explain the reasons in an objective way.	8,606	.717	30
Enthusiast	Metatalk = F, Technical = T, score > 7	Liked very much TLOU2 but tries to explain the reasons in an objective way.	10,026	.674	30
Neutral	5 < score < 7	Less interested in taking a side, more in providing their opinions.	5,791	.574	70
No Label (Negative)	Metatalk = F, Technical = F, score < 5	Likely Disappointed but did not provide a sufficient explanation.	5,130	.703	18
No Label (Positive)	Metatalk = F, Technical = F, score > 7	Likely Enthusiast but did not provide a sufficient explanation.	5,062	.733	19

From the statistics in Table 5, it can be noticed that, while Defenders have a higher propensity to recruit accounts in the k=0 group than Attackers, this relationship is inverted between Disappointed and Enthusiasts. There are two possible explanations for this empirical observation:

- Negative review bombers (i.e., Attackers) influenced the cognition of the item. A distaste in elements outside the video game induced a more critical reception of the technical elements of the video game.
- Disappointed accounts are dissimulating their real motivations behind the low score.

In absence of more accurate relational data (at individual level), the second explanation seems tempting, but the first one has an empirical validation in the actual dynamics of the distribution of the archetypes across the time. In Figure 6, the daily proportion Archetype displays prevalence of Attackers in the first 10 days. While Attackers progressively retreat until stabilizing in July, the quota of negative reviews does not really decrease a lot. Their role is taken from Disappointed users, who stop to mention topics like Politics or LGTBQ and focus on technical criticism of the video game. A possibility is that, as a collective strategy, negative review bombers they gave up on discussing political/ethical issues after realizing that they were unable to boycott sales (indeed, they sparked interest for it!). By this time, too involved in the tug-of-war game, they may have collectively realized they had to send a different message to be credible.

Figure 6. The continuous day-per-day relative frequencies of the 7 archetypes are represented as different shades in the period from July 19th, 2020 to August 1st, 2020.

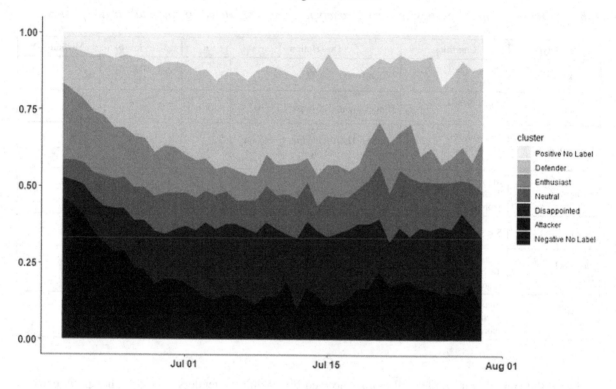

As a relevant note, the Neutral Archetype is particularly important because, since it has no power to pull the rating metric (which is general dynamic that users are plying in this gamified environment), it represents a baseline value to measure the interest of k=0 in the case of TLOU2 on Metacritic. Since Neutrals lack intentions to boycott TLOU2 or 'game' Metacritic, the relatively high value of % (k = 0) means that it is plausible that a not trivial portion of users that rated only TLOU2 on Metacritic where genuinely and not necessarily maliciously interested into contribution with their own opinion, regardless of whether it was positive or negative.

The paradox here is that, exactly how described by Steam, the final effect of RB over TLOU2 was to trigger a very large discussion over its own and flaws.

SOLUTIONS AND RECOMMENDATIONS

The problem presented here can be approached from various perspectives. From the point of view of the technology of measuring consumer opinion, the main interest is to allow the rating structure (be it a recommendation system or even a simpler technology) to better identify legitimate contributions and spam. One of the problems with multipoint scales in measuring satisfaction is that it is difficult to differentiate cases in which there is a genuine distaste for the item from cases of strategically oriented voting. In this case, any increase in the number of scoring classes helps make this distinction less ambiguous.

Scales with more than 11 classes (e.g., 0 to 10) are, however, very atypical and can present serious problems of interface. Put simply, they are very confusing for the user experience. With the transition to digital technologies, it is possible that slider tools, which make it easier to allocate preferences, will replace multipoint scales. The underlying theory is based on a fundamental principle: on a slider scale from 0 to 100, identifying the satisfaction of an item at 0 should be a much rarer event than voting 1 out of 5. Systematic inflations of some values in a slider could be an important alarm of a spam voting. Unfortunately, this solution is effective only outside cold-start conditions.

The type of analysis proposed in this paper has resulted in a decomposition of the corpus into archetypes. Although this decomposition is essentially descriptive in nature, it can represent a good starting point for the development of spam detection techniques.

Beyond the technical problem of identification, there is the topic of the gamified conflict. Much has been said about the conflict between groups of individuals, but this research leads to another latent dimension of the conflict: that between one's past and present opinions. In other words, the conflict among groups may be the result of unfulfilled expectations in individuals. The researcher's task here is not to judge the validity of these expectations or the choices of the producer, but to increase the knowledge and the possibilities of quantifying opinion's dynamics. Recalling Steam (2017) words: "Players doing the bombing are fulfilling the goal of User Reviews - they're voicing their opinion".

Most of RSs do not sufficiently consider the possibilities of quantifying an individual expectation before experiencing the item. Here it is proposed to allow users of sites such as Metacritic to express one, or even more than one, expectation of the score towards a future object. The system can compare this expected score with the final score after having experimented the item.

In this regard, it can be very useful to collect open data on the impact of a new advertising trailer. How many people got interested after a specific event, like the release of a trailer? And how has the global expectation changed?

Applied to our case study, it would have been crucial to know to what extent the ideological conflict arises from the impact of the advertising campaign versus the cognitive manipulation effects of the bombers. It is worth noticing that similar gamified phenomena and impacts can be also found in relation to other fields, for example in political debates, during election campaigns, where gamification strategy may be promoted by leaders, affecting users'- then electors - behaviours (Loh, 2019; Grisolia and Martella, 2019).

FUTURE RESEARCH DIRECTIONS

Studies on political polarization in social media would welcome the topic of the manifestation of latent social or political conflict through reputation systems and/or gamified environments (e.g., video games themselves but also gamified apps…). Political polarization as a period of increase of radicalization of political beliefs is a topic covered all along the 20th century. The sociodemographic phenomenon has been linked to the individual mechanism of group polarization as originally formulated after the experimental results of Moscovici and Zavalloni (1969): the exposition to debates does not promote convergence towards common grounds, instead it radicalises pre-existing beliefs in subjects. Bail et al. (2018) demonstrated that this is the effect of social media on political beliefs.

On the technical side, of great relevance is the topic of detection of spam reviews. While there is a growing stock of knowledge on the approaches for the automation of this process, from empirical research it seems that the new possibilities of misinformation are going at least as fast as the technical innovations in detection. Surely a solid approach is based on the identification of distinct topological structures in the possible relational schemes of reviews (Varol et al., 2018).

The dataset under consideration, while revealing many things about the trend of the population of reviews as a stratified agglomeration, lacks both a relational structure and the exact temporal order in which the reviews have been submitted, since the time variable is approximated per day, not per second.

The research over Archetypes (hard clusters) of users in Review Bomb has a value on its own. Five Archetypes (plus two residual Archetypes) haven been individuated after recognition of the general metalinguistic patterns of Review Bombing as expressed in the Steam's statement (2017). While the 'how' Metatalking can be identified in reviews can be context-dependent, the validity of this construct and its contraposition with the Technical label can be generalized as a standard approach to measure the influence of persuasive intents over items typically attacked by review bombers. In other words, while there are many sub-topics associated with Metatalking and Technical-talking and there are many methods for assigning the labels, the method of stratification of the population of reviews into Archetypes has the potential to become a standard for analysis of misinformation in gamified environments.

CONCLUSION

This chapter has developed a consistent and generalizable methodological approach to empirical research on the problem of Review Bomb. This has been possible through the study of relevant theoretical concepts taken from the field of information studies and decision systems, and through the insights from quantitative data analysis of a relevant and complex case study.

It is evident that the Review Bomb can not be considered neither only a technical problem, nor a mere manifestation of social distress. In this regard, the framework of gamification provides key insights to understand the dynamics of the phenomenon. Of particular relevance in this study is the concept of archetypes: these are stratifying (or "clustering") variables for the population of users. They constitute the link between theory and method, since archetypes as labels far data actually reflect the theoretical role that users decided to 'play' in the gamified conflict. Hopefully, this scheme can be generalized for virtually all the cases of Review Bomb, with a use for inferential methodology, too. For example, arguably the most relevant archetype is the neutral: since neutral users are people who refuse to play the game of distorting the rating metric, their statistics likely represent the best natural control (or baseline) to infer quantitative effects of Review Bomb, e.g., in quantifying the presence of illegitimate accounts, fake reviews, etc.

It is also important the construct validity of the Metatalk category. Presumably, the best theoretical framework to refine what exactly 'metatalking' is the distinction between judgements of merit (or technical inferences, objective valuation) and ideological judgement (or judgement according individual or societal norms, customs, ideas, and social values). However, Metatalk as a label overcomes this naive division and it welcomes a feature of increasing importance in the 'society of information': namely the role of the communication of these ideological positions. When a user expresses a judgment as herding or in opposition to another user, plausibly this decision is still following an ideological justification, or at least is motivated by social values, although this is not necessarily clearly expressed in the text.

The ability to identify sentences referencing to a socialized behaviour (i.e., an ideological position) as a kind of judgment that differs from the request for an evaluation of merit can represent a fruitful development of detection algorithms, overcoming the cold-start problem.

REFERENCES

Aggarwal, C. C. (2016). *Recommender Systems: The Textbook. Charm.* Springer.

Alsawaier, R. (2018). The Effect of Gamification on Motivation and Engagement. *International Journal of Information and Learning Technology, 35*(1), 56-79. doi:10.1108/IJILT-02-2017-0009

Anderson, E. T., & Simester, D. I. (2014). Reviews without a Purchase: Low Ratings, Loyal Customers, and Deception. *JMR, Journal of Marketing Research, 51*(3), 249–269.

Bail, C. A., Argyle, L. P., Brown, T. W., Bumpus, J. P., Chen, H., Hunzaker, M. B. F., Lee, J., Mann, M., Merhout, F., & Volfovsky, A. (2018). Exposure to opposing views on social media can increase political polarization. *Proceedings of the National Academy of Sciences of the United States of America, 115*(37), 9216–9221. doi:10.1073/pnas.1804840115 PMID:30154168

Ferguson, C. J., & Glasgow, B. (2021). Who are GamerGate? A descriptive study of individuals involved in the GamerGate controversy. *Psychology of Popular Media, 10*(2), 243–247. doi:10.1037/ppm0000280

Gamer, P. C. (2020). *Getting a bunch of negative user reviews is not automatically a 'review bomb'.* https://www.pcgamer.com/getting-a-bunch-of-negative-user-reviews-is-not-automatically-a-review-bomb/

Grisolia, F., & Martella, A. (2019). *Devoted users: EU elections and gamification on Twitter.* https://ocean.sagepub.com/blog/devoted-users-eu-elections-and-gamification-on-twitter

Hu, N., Zhang, J., & Pavlou, P. A. (2009). Overcoming the J-shaped distribution of product reviews. *Communications of the ACM, 52*(10), 144–147.

Hussain, M., Zhu, W., Zhang, W., & Abidi, R. (2018). Student Engagement Predictions in an e-Learning System and Their Impact on Student Course Assessment Scores. *Computational Intelligence and Neuroscience*, 1–21. doi:10.1155/2018/6347186 PMID:30369946

Jannach, D., Zanker, M., Felfernig, A., & Friedrich, G. (2010). *Recommender Systems - An Introduction.* Cambridge University Press.

Khan, A., & Krishnan, S. (2017). Social Media Enabled E-Participation: Review and Agenda for Future Research. *e-Service Journal, 10*(2), 45–75. doi:10.2979/eservicej.10.2.03

Kujur, F., & Singh, S. (2016). Engaging customers through online participation in social networking sites. *Asia Pacific Management Review, 22.* Advance online publication. doi:10.1016/j.apmrv.2016.10.006

Laeeq Khan, M. (2017). Social Media Engagement: What motivates User Participation and Consumption on YouTube? *Computers in Human Behavior, 66*, 236–247. doi:10.1016/j.chb.2016.09.024

Lee, Y. J., Hosanagar, K., & Tan, Y. (2015). Do I follow my friends or the crowd? Information cascades in online movie ratings. *Management Science, 61*(9), 2241–2258.

Loh, W. (2019). The Gamification of Political Participation. *Moral Philosophy and Politics, 6*(2). Advance online publication. doi:10.1515/mopp-2018-0037

Moscovici, S., & Zavalloni, M. (1969). The group as a polarizer of attitudes. *Journal of Personality and Social Psychology, 12*(2), 125–135.

Ong, T., Mannino, M., & Gregg, D. (2014). Linguistic characteristics of shill reviews. *Electronic Commerce Research and Applications, 13*(2), 69–78.

Papanaoum, E. (2019). *Effect of Gamification on the emotions of users of an online advertising platform.* Kth Royal Institute of Technology School of Electrical Engineering and Computer Science.

Patricio, R., Moreira, A., & Zurlo, F. (2018). Gamification approaches to the early stage of innovation. *Creativity and Innovation Management, 27*, 499–511. doi:10.1111/caim.12284

Qiang, J., Qian, Z., Li, Y., Yuan, Y., & Wu, X. (2020). Short Text Topic Modeling Techniques, Applications, and Performance: A Survey. *IEEE Transactions on Knowledge and Data Engineering*. Advance online publication. doi:10.1109/TKDE.2020.2992485

Revathy, V. R., & Anitha, S. P. (2018). Cold Start Problem in Social Recommender Systems: State-of-the-Art Review. In S. K. Bhatia, S. Tiwari, K. K. Mishra, & M. C. Trivedi (Eds.), *Advances in Computer Communication and Computational Sciences* (pp. 105–115). Springer.

Robson, K., Plangger, K., Kietzmann, J. H., McCarthy, I., & Pitt, L. (2015). Is it all a game? Understanding the principles of gamification. *Business Horizons, 58*(4), 411–420.

Sailer, M., Hense, J., Mayr, S., & Mandl, H. (2017). How gamification motivates: An experimental study of the effects of specific game design elements on psychological need satisfaction. *Computers in Human Behavior, 69*, 371–380. doi:10.1016/j.chb.2016.12.033

Saperstein, A. M. (2004). "The Enemy of My Enemy Is My Friend" Is the Enemy: Dealing with the War-Provoking Rules of Intent. *Conflict Management and Peace Science, 21*(4), 287–296.

Schoenmueller, V., Netzer, O., & Stahl, F. (2020). The Polarity of Online Reviews: Prevalence, Drivers and Implications. *JMR, Journal of Marketing Research, 57*(5), 853–877.

Silge, J., & Robinson, D. (2017). *Text mining with R: A tidy approach.* O'Reilly Media, Inc.

Smironva, E., Kiatkawsin, K., Lee, S. K., Kim, J., & Lee, C.-H. (2020). Self-selection and non-response biases in customers' hotel ratings – a comparison of online and offline ratings. *Current Issues in Tourism, 23*(10), 1191–1204.

Steam. (2017). *User Reviews.* https://steamcommunity.com/games/593110/announcements/detail/1448326897426987372

Tang, X., Qian, T., & You, Z. (2020). Generating Behavior Features for Cold-Start Spam Review Detection with Adversarial Learning. *Information Sciences, 526*, 274–288. doi:10.1016/j.ins.2020.03.063

Tomaselli, V., & Cantone, G. G. (2020). *Evaluating Rank-Coherence of Crowd Rating in Customer Satisfaction*. Social Indicator Research. doi:10.100711205-020-02581-8

Tomaselli, V., Cantone, G. G., & Mazzeo, V. (2021). *The polarising effect of Review Bomb*. arXiv:2104.01140.

van de Rijt, A., Kang, S. M., Restivo, M., & Patil, A. (2014). Field experiments of success-breeds-success dynamics. *Proceedings of the National Academy of Sciences of the United States of America*, *111*(19), 6934–6939. PMID:24778230

Varol, O., Ferrara, E., Davis, C., Menczer, F., & Flammini, A. (2017). Online Human-Bot Interactions: Detection, Estimation, and Characterization. *Proceedings of the International AAAI Conference on Web and Social Media*, *11*(1), 280-289.

Wang, C., Zhang, X., & Hann, I. H. (2018). Socially nudged: A quasi-experimental study of friends' social influence in online product ratings. *Information Systems Research*, *29*(3), 641–655.

Wang, X., Liu, K., & Zhao, J. (2017). Handling cold-start problem in review spam detection by jointly embedding texts and behaviors. In *Proceedings of the 55th Annual Meeting of the Association for Computational Linguistics* (vol. 1, pp. 366–376). Association for Computational Linguistics.

Yahoo. Finance. (2020). *Metacritic changes its user review policy to combat score bombing*. https://au.finance.yahoo.com/news/metacritic-score-bombing-game-review-changes-150200740.html

Zhou, X., & Zafarani, R. (2020). A Survey of Fake News: Fundamental Theories, Detection Methods, and Opportunities. *ACM Computing Surveys*, *53*(5), 1–40. doi:10.1145/3395046

ADDITIONAL READING

Carman, M., Koerber, M., Li, J., Choo, K. R., & Ashman, H. (2018). Manipulating Visibility of Political and Apolitical Threads on Reddit via Score Boosting. In *Proceedings of 17th IEEE International Conference On Trust, Security And Privacy In Computing And Communications/ 12th IEEE International Conference On Big Data Science And Engineering* (pp. 184-190). doi: 10.1109/TrustCom/BigDataSE.2018.00037

Érdi, P. (2019). *Ranking: The unwritten rules of the social game we all play*. Oxford University Press.

Geiger, D. (2016). *Personalized Task Recommendation in Crowdsourcing Systems*. Springer.

Hassan, L., & Hamari, J. (2020). Gameful civic engagement: A review of the literature on gamification of e-participation. *Government Information Quarterly*, *37*(3), 1–21.

Kasper, P., Koncar, P., Santos, T., & Gutl, C. (2019). On the Role of Score, Genre and Text in Helpfulness of Video Game Reviews on Metacritic. In *Proceedings of Sixth International Conference on Social Net-works Analysis, Management and Security* (pp. 75-82). doi:10.1109nams.2019.8931866

King, R. A., Racherla, P., & Bush, V. D. (2014). What we know and don't know about online word–of–mouth: A review and synthesis of the literature. *Journal of Interactive Marketing*, *28*(3), 167–183.

Kumar, S., Cheng, J., Leskovec, J., & Subrahmanian, V. S. (2017). An army of me: Sockpuppets in online discussion communities. In *Proceedings of the 26th International Conference on World Wide Web* (pp. 857-866).

Lumsden, K., & Harmer, E. (2019). *Online Othering. Palgrave Studies in Cybercrime and Cybersecurity.* Palgrave Macmillan.

Shi, Y., Larson, M., & Hanjalic, A. (2014). Collaborative filtering beyond the user-item matrix: A survey of the state of the art and future challenges. *ACM Computing Surveys, 47*(1), 1–45.

Tuzzi, A. (2010). What to put in the bag? Comparing and contrasting procedures for text clustering. *Italian Journal of Applied Statistics, 22*(1), 77–94.

KEY TERMS AND DEFINITIONS

Cold-Start: A terminology to refer the difficulty to make algorithmic inferences for new uses or items about because there is not sufficient information. In some algorithmic application, this difficulty is not temporary but permanent, due a majority of illegitimate accounts, e.g., detection of sock-puppets.

Gamified Conflict: A social situation defined as a real conflict (i.e., not a play) but that, even without the parties noticing, follow the structure of a game. For example, in a gamified conflict, people can always get quantitative information of how the side are scoring a performance regarding the conflict.

Illegitimate Accounts (Shills and Sock-Puppets): Accounts made for sabotaging the correct functioning of a rating system. Shills are users who trade their rating rights submitting reviews or ratings of items they have not experience with, while sock-puppets are accounts controlled by the same physical person.

J-Shape: A name for a two-dimensional distribution of values that fits well a convex shape. When the two extremes of the distribution are equal in value, it can be referred as U-shape, too.

Metatalk: When someone is requested to provide a justification on a judgment of merit over an item, and the justification mentions elements that are expressed as partially or totally disjointed to the merit proprieties of the item. Not only ideological judgements are considered metatalking in this context ("The use of this item goes against my moral ideas"), but also any expression of dependency to judgements provided by others ("I value this like that because a third party valued it like that").

Rating Systems, Recommender Systems (RSs), and Rating Aggregators: Rating systems are those systems devoted to the collection of ratings data from users. A recommender system is any system whose state of existence is tied to predictions about the future ratings or the propensity of satisfactory response from a population of users towards a catalogue of items. Such predictions are usually inferred from past ratings from users in the systems. It could be said that the rating system is an important sub-system of the recommender system. Rating aggregators are platforms aimed at algorithmic measurement of public estimates of collective ratings on items. These measurements can be ranked into charts, and items topping the charts are considered the best or the most recommendable items in their group or typology.

Chapter 17
Game–Based Learning for the Acquisition of Transversal Skills:
Preventing and Addressing Hate Speech

Eva Ordóñez-Olmedo

https://orcid.org/0000-0003-3608-8262

Universidad Internacional de La Rioja, Spain

Sergio Albaladejo-Ortega

Universidad Católica de Murcia, Spain

Marta Pérez-Escolar

https://orcid.org/0000-0003-2575-7993

Universidad Loyola Andalucía, Spain

ABSTRACT

Hate speech is increasingly hindering the possibility of raising collective understanding as well as the values of democracy based on mutual respect, tolerance, and equality. For that reason, the main objective of this chapter is to determine how game-based learning favors the acquisition of transversal competences within the framework of 21st century skills for tackling and addressing hate speech. In doing so, a total of four serious games—Bury Me, My Love; Another Lost Phone: Laura's Story; Never Alone; and Life is Strange: Episode 2 "Out of Time"—have been selected to analyze their potential as a learning tool for combating hate speech. To this end, the Octalysis framework serves as a methodology for identifying transversal competences in matters of justice, equity, and emotional intelligence. The main results show that serious games are helpful assets in promoting empathy and other social values and skills that are necessary to combat hate speech in young people.

DOI: 10.4018/978-1-7998-9223-6.ch017

INTRODUCTION

Hate speech is not an isolated phenomenon nowadays, but a menace that breeds and increases evil attitudes that are prohibited under international law, like discrimination, hostility, and violence (United Nations, 2019). Hate speech is increasingly hindering the possibilities for raising a collective understanding, as well as weakening the values of democracy based on mutual respect, tolerance, and equality. For that reason, combating hate speech does not imply limiting freedom of speech, but stamping out dangerous incitement that jeopardizes democratic values, social stability, and peace. Freedom of speech is a prized asset in democratic societies, but "it is not the only one" (Parekh, 2012, p.45). As a matter of principle, the urgent debate nowadays is tackling incendiary rhetoric that stigmatizes and dehumanizes vulnerable people, minorities, and any so-called *other*. Drawing upon this context, the main objective of this chapter is to determine how game-based learning favors the acquisition of transversal competences, within the framework of 21st century skills, in the Communication Degree, for preventing and addressing hate speech.

The nature of any game accomplishes to connects with the individual from an emotional, physical, or mental perspective. Moreover, the human being is, by nature, a "*homo ludens*" (Huizinga, 1949) who feels devotion to play and playful contents.

Nowadays, gamification goes beyond incorporating elements of fun or competition into a narrative, as there are currently numerous examples in which gamification could be implemented across various sectors of society, so much so that it implies technological, economic, cultural, and societal developments in which reality is becoming more gameful and, consequently, publics increase their loyalty through ludological practices (Hamari, 2019; Fernández Galeote & Hamari, 2021). As Zichermann and Cunningham (2011) define the term, it is a process that takes place, essentially, in non-game contexts where "serious games, advergaming, and games-for-change" (p.14) are employed. Therefore, gamification uses the logic and tools of the game –game thinking and game mechanics– to engage users and solve problems (Zichermann & Cunningham, 2011). Similarly, Werbach and Hunter (2012, p.26) agree with Zichermann and Cunningham (2011) that gamification relates to the use of game techniques, elements, and designs in non-game contexts. Along these lines, Kapp (2012) offers a broader definition and explains that gamification involves "using game-based mechanics, aesthetics and game thinking to engage people, motivate action, promote learning, and solve problems" (p.10). Consequently, far from being a strategy limited to the instructional processes that serious games comprise (Deterding et al., 2011), gamification aspires to change society and its members, especially in teaching contexts, "as the goal of gamification is to alter a contextual learner behavior or attitude" (Landers, 2014, p. 579).

Thus, considering that gamification "can afford the accruing of skills, motivational benefits, creativity, playfulness, engagement, and overall positive growth and happiness" (Hamari 2019, p. 3), gamification can be summarized as the integration of game dynamics and elements in non-game scenarios, such as learning processes –which is the case we are concerned with in this study– to solve problems, like hate speech among students and young people.

This chapter is organized as follows. First, we propose a theoretical background to understand hate speech as an informational disorder. Second, we propose the necessary transversal competences in the 21st century that Communication Degree students should acquire for solving real-world problems nowadays. Third, we develop the concept of serious game. Fourth, we explain our method –the Octalysis framework (Chou, 2014a)– to approach the main objective of this research. Fifth, we discuss the results relating to the necessary skills students should acquire through serious games to tackle hate speech. Finally, we present some solutions, recommendations and concluding remarks, as well as further research topics.

A BENCHMARK FOR GRASPING HATE SPEECH

According to Wardle and Derakhshan (2018), hate speech is a type of information disorder that belongs to the category termed mal-information –that refers to "information that is based on reality, but used to inflict harm on a person, organisation or country" (p.44), such as some leaks or harassment. These malicious narratives become increasingly powerful as they are fueled by new technologies and digital platforms that favor the sharing of information more rapidly than ever before. The digital realm is a space for participation, including new possibilities for human interaction, but also ways for spreading intolerance and hate against other people due to a range of reasons: skin color, race, social class, ethnicity, political ideology, among others. In other words, hate speech is "any kind of communication in speech, writing or behaviour, that attacks or uses pejorative or discriminatory language with reference to a person or group on the basis of who they are, in other words, based on their religion, ethnicity, nationality, race, colour, descent, gender or other identity factor" (United Nations, 2019, p.2).

Notwithstanding offline hate speech is already a dangerous phenomenon, since any kind of public manifestation of hate speech involves undermining minorities (Greenberg & Pyszczynski, 1985), the effect of hate speech in digital spaces is of particular concern (Olteanu et al. 2018). For that reason, Mathew et al. (2020) suggest that online hate speech results in a "crime against minorities" (Mathew et al., 2020, p.2). Online hate speech represents the "perfect storm" (Posetti, 2018, p.55), since the digital landscape feeds information disorders and enables the emergence of other pernicious environments, like ideological polarization. Soral, Bilewicz and Winiewski (2018) state that a repetitive exposure to hate speech could strengthen an individual's outgroup prejudice. Thus, hateful rhetoric leads to more polarized societies, mainly when politicians use hate speech, and can even lead to a violent movement (Piazza, 2020).

One of the most representative and recent examples of this reality was the attack on the US Capitol at the beginning of January 2021. Donald Trump's political strategy was based on promoting widespread violence and delegitimizing his opponents (Blade, 2021). For that reason, after the 2020 presidential election, this hateful rhetoric (Conklin, 2021) pushed thousands of pro-Trump extremists to carry out a violent invasion of one of the most iconic American buildings, seeking to fight against the election of Joe Biden –seen as the main enemy of Trump (Fuchs, 2021). The mob of Donald Trump's supporters was mainly comprised by members of different right-wing nationalist extremist groups, like the Proud Boys, Qanon, among others, who firmly believed Trump's hate speeches and rejected evidence or proofs that challenged their existing convictions outright (Smith, Ballard & Sanders, 2021).

For that reason, when polarized ideological ghettos magnify information disorder and reinforce outrageous behaviors, like the assault on the US Capitol, it is essential to counterattack hate speech, break up social segregation and political fragmentation which emerge due to the echo chamber effect, cyber-balkanization or enclave deliberation, among other radical behaviors.

Therefore, addressing hate speech requires a coordinated response that tackles the drivers of hate speech and its impact on vulnerable people or victims of abuse by malicious actors who use online and offline channels to spread hateful. Only then we could protect the basic assurance of inclusion in the society for all members.

WITHIN THE CONTEXT OF 21ST CENTURY SKILLS

After clarifying the risks and threats of hate speech to society, it is important to propose a series of transversal competences –which serve as a basis for lifelong learning - that are common to all students and must be acquired by all graduates of the same university, regardless of the degree they take and represent the seal that identifies each institution.

They are skills necessary for students to face real problems nowadays, e.g. hate speech or other informational disorders (Wardle & Derakhshan, 2018). The recommended transversal competences emerge within the framework of the necessary 21st century skills (UNESCO, 2005; Ananiadou & Magdalean, 2009; Silva et al., 2016) for solving real problems (INTEF, 2019; Pérez-Escolar, Ordóñez-Olmedo & Alcaide-Pulido, 2021). This is the reason why its inclusion in the curriculum of the Degree in Communication is emphasized with the intention of reducing hate speech.

The 21st century digital skills stem from the premise that these are linked to interpersonal, social, and competitive skills –soft skills– that are required to achieve a technological culture –when individuals successfully face the challenges of this time– in order to improve pedagogical practices and reformulate the main aspirations in terms of learning (Valencia-Molina, et al. 2016).

Table 1. Proposal for 21st century skills.

21ST CENTURY SKILLS	DEFINITION AND DESCRIPTION
Information literacy	It requires a process that allows to recognize and contextualize the essential information to respond to a demand for information, technology and the media. UNESCO (2016) considers it essential to train citizens in media and information literacy, to guarantee their development in society.
Media literacy	It "is the ability to access and process information from any kind of transmission" (Potter, 2018). Buckingham (2005) points to production, language, representation, and audience as key concepts in media literacy.
Critical thinking	It is the process of intentional, self-regulated judgment. This process considers evidence, context, conceptualizations, methods, and criteria (Butterworth & Thwaites, 2013).
Communications and collaboration	They are intended to enable the expression of thoughts and ideas to responsibly, efficiently, and effectively solve the problems encountered (Triana, Anggraito, & Ridlo, 2020). Promote clarity and efficiency in the articulation of ideas and thoughts, through speech and writing; as well as the responsibility of collaborative work and the flexibility and willingness to assume commitments with a common goal (Romero & Turpo, 2015).
ICT literacy	It is a set of abilities to locate, evaluate and use needed information effectively (Shivakumaraswamy & Narendra, 2021).
Problem-solving	First the task is related to previous knowledge (monitoring and conducting a subjective evaluation of the correct answers), then, it establishes goals for the correct execution, and later it analyzes the given answer (reflection about the action) and a decision about whether it is necessary to modify it (answer proposal). Monitoring has a retrospective and prospective function in the resolution algorithm. The retrospective function refers to the analysis of previous responses and the prospective function includes feelings and value judgments about one's own learning (Sáiz-Manzares & Pérez, 2016).
Creativity and innovation	Creative thinking, knowledge construction and development of products and processes using technology. Loveless (2002) shows that to foster creativity in the classroom, teachers need to create a social atmosphere where children feel secure enough to play with ideas (innovation) and to take risks.
Productivity and Accountability	They are focused on three interrelated elements, namely, efficiency, effectiveness and high-quality goods and services, or as stated by Trilling and Fadel (2009), "producing results" (p. 83). Teaching students to maximize productivity, to plan well and to allocate and manage time according to the demand imposed by the task to be completed.
Initiative and self-direction	Learners must be ready to take initiative to learn new ideas, concepts, processes, and applications, which increase their efficiency and effectiveness. Self-direction is necessary to cope with change and to discover how organizational effectiveness and productivity can be improved has become an essential skill for success and continued employability (Kivunja, 2015).
Social interaction	Students need to be taught social skills to communicate effectively with each other, and to interact with one another using words, or non-verbal cues such as gestures, facial expressions, body language or personal appearance. Kagan (1994) says: "it is hard to imagine a job today which does not involve some cooperative interaction with others. The most frequent reason individuals are fired from a job is not lack of job-related skills, but rather a lack of interpersonal skills" (p. 1).
Flexibility and adaptability	Future graduates must adapt to changing circumstances and environments and to welcome new ideas, and new ways of completing tasks. These characteristics lead to success whereas the lack of these skills leads to stagnation and failure (Kivunja, 2015).
Cross-cultural interaction	Workplaces require people to be able to interact effectively with coworkers or people they meet, and to work in various teams, not only in their own physical workplace, but also in the virtual community, for example, within the serious game in which they can be immersed.

Source: The authors.

There are differences between the delimitation of competency and the rest of the processes within information literacy, as they often lead to confusion (Ruiz & Chapman, 2017). To this end, it is considered necessary to clearly establish that information competences are determined by three constituent elements, which are: knowledge, skills and attitudes (Alonso & Saraiva, 2020). Drawing upon these precepts and previous experts' proposals, (table 1) we suggest the following set of necessary 21st century skills:

In this context, serious games represent valuable assets for students to acquire the necessary 21st century skills. For that reason, we have selected a set of serious games that favors the acquisition of these skills. 21st century skills also favor the acquisition of other transversal competences (table 2). The transversal components of knowledge in all areas are developed through a teaching-learning process based on competences, as explained above, which is characterized by its dynamism, its comprehensive nature, and its gamification, which makes this transfer process more attractive. Therefore, the serious games selected in this research will not only address the acquisition of the 21st century skills, but also the acquisition of the following transversal competences in the Degree of Communication:

Table 2. Transversal competences within the context of the 21st century skills.

TRANSVERSAL COMPETENCES	DEFINITION AND DESCRIPTION
TC1. Ability to make judgments using scientific knowledge	Ability to integrate knowledge and face the complexity of making judgments from information that, incomplete or limited, includes reflection and decision-making based on evidence and arguments linked to the application of knowledge and judgments. This is done while respecting the data, its truthfulness and ethical criteria associated with science; and being responsible for one's own acts, excluding expressions of hatred, incitement to violence and hostility.
TC2. Ability to communicate and social skills	Ability to communicate knowledge in all fields of study, in a clear and unambiguous way, showing interest in interacting with others. It also involves the ability to maintain a critical and constructive dialogue and speak in public, if necessary. It involves the ability to understand and express oneself freely in written and/or spoken form, respecting democratic values.
TC3. Skills in the use of Information and Communication Technologies (ICTs)	Ability to use ICTs as tools for expression and communication, to access information sources, as tools to archive data and documents to create content, for presentation tasks, for learning, research and cooperative work. Students should know their rights and risks in the digital world and respect relevant ethical principles during their use without creating prejudices or stereotypes.
TC4. Critical skills, initiative and entrepreneurship	Ability to demonstrate a cognitive behavior that questions things and is interested in the foundations upon which individual and collective ideas, values, actions, and judgments, including society, trade unions and business organizations. Foster initiative in analysis, planning, organization, and management. It involves acting creatively and proactively, with an entrepreneurial and innovative approach at the private, social and professional levels. This enables opening borders to cooperation and a commitment to peace.
TC5. Ethical commitment and respect for cultural diversity	Ability to think and act according to universal principles related to the value of a person, cultural heritage, among others. It is directed to the full personal, social, and professional development of the student body. It involves respect for the right to cultural and multicultural diversity, dialogue between different races, sexes and minority groups in society, including the value of freedom of expression. It includes ability to integrate and collaborate actively and assertively in a team to achieve common goals with other people, areas, and organizations in national and international contexts.
TC6. Social skills and global citizenship	Respect the fundamental rights of justice and equality between men and women, regardless of their culture or country of origin. Ensure human rights, values of a culture of peace and democracy, environmental principles, and development cooperation that promote ethical commitment in a global, intercultural, socio-economic, free, and fair society.

Source: authors' own elaboration.

To sum up, these transversal competences will be worked on in the classroom through game-based learning to decrease hate speech. Serious games are interdependent and, for each of them, although not specified as such, emphasis is placed on critical reflection on skills for teamwork, creativity, initiative, motivation, autonomy, resolution of problems, mastery of oral and written expression in different languages, risk assessment, decision making skills, and a positive attitude towards learning and constructive management of feelings.

SERIOUS GAMES FOR SERIOUS ISSUES

In 1970, Clark C. Abt coined the term 'serious games' in his work Serious Games, applying it to board, card and role-playing games, and describing education, industrial and governmental training, planning, research, analysis and evaluation as rich fields for the use of games able "to create dramatic representations of the real problem being studied", offering "a rich field for a risk-free, active exploration of serious intellectual and social problems" (Abt, 1987, p. 13). Since then, serious games have grown in popularity, taking advantage of new digital and interactive media to adapt their mechanics for very different purposes.

Considering the large number of existing proposals today, serious games could be described as "(digital) games used for purposes other than mere entertainment" (Susi, Johannesson, & Backlund., 2007). Therefore, it is very important to think about the value that resides in serious games from the following two perspectives: the game as an experience with educational value and the game as an educational product with playful value. Regarding these purposes, bringing the definition closer to the areas where games exert a great influence at present, a generic but valuable definition could be the following: "A serious game is a digital game created with the intention to entertain and to achieve at least one additional goal (e.g., learning or health)" (Dörner et al., 2016, p. 3). These additional goals, which the authors name 'characterizing goals', allow training in cognitive, emotional, sensory-motor, social, learning or media competences.

These different competences are especially interesting in educational environments insofar as not only the transmission of knowledge stands out as basic but also the development of emotional intelligence, media literacy or social interaction skills. According to Mitgutsch (2011), "from an educational and learning theoretical perspective, it can be argued that serious games, compared to entertainment-oriented games, aim at teaching something beyond the game play experience itself" (p.46). This declaration, collected in the collective volume Serious Games and Edutainment Applications (2011), connects directly with the main statement expressed by its editors Minhua Ma, Andreas Oikonomou and Lakhmi C. Jain, professors of Games Technology, Computer Sciences and Electronic Engineering respectively, who recognize that serious games require the combination of both pedagogic and game design principles (Ma, Oikonomou, & Jain, 2011), in order to reach their ludo-literacy nature (Grace, 2020), enabling the achievement of serious goals through play and, therefore, offering added motivation to students.

In this sense, it is inevitable not to think about the way in which these different aspects are related by Djaouti et al. (2011) through the G/P/S model, whose initials already indicate the relationship of its fundamental components: *gameplay*, *purpose* and *scope*. For these expert professors in serious games, this model allows classifying games "according to both their 'serious-related' and 'game-related' characteristics" (p. 118), considering the structure of the game, its rules (*gameplay*); its specific goal, apart from entertainment (*purpose*); and the kind of audience to which it is targeted, in formal, informal, and non-formal contexts (*scope*). However, taking into account the preponderance of serious purposes that, in many cases, make sense of the kind of video games proposed, the order of the acronyms could be reversed, going from G/P/S to S/P/G, to the extent that the first consideration is the area in which to use the game; next, the purpose to be achieved with it; and, lastly, the game mechanics that will make it attractive from a ludological point of view. Although the motivating nature of serious games is an advantage in awakening the interest of students, it must be supplemented with other instruction methods in order to transfer its content and educational skills. In the specific case of games that deal with issues of great social importance and, in many cases, of a certain ideological and moral complexity, it is especially necessary to promote a dialogue between those involved in these game dynamics. Authors such as Wouters, van Nimwegen et al. (2013) propose the class discussion as an exceptional opportunity for students to go beyond reflection about serious issues addressed by serious games but so that, based on them, "verbalize this knowledge and anchor it more profoundly in their knowledge base" (Wouters, Paas, & van Merriënboer, 2008).

In order to achieve the objectives described, it is essential to resort to a gamification-based model. Marin, Lee and Landers (2021) define "gamification" as a design strategy where game mechanics and/or game attributes are used within non-game contexts to make users' experience within that context more gameful, boosting engagement and learner motivation with the purpose of promoting better learning outcomes. For this type of process to reach its full meaning, the so-called Octalysis framework (Chou, 2014a) is proposed below for approaching the video games that comprise the object of study.

METHODOLOGY

Objective and Sample

The main objective of this chapter is to determine how game-based learning favors the acquisition of transversal competences, within the framework of the 21ˢᵗ century skills, in the Communication Degree, for preventing and addressing hate speech. This specific degree is especially indicated for the implementation of the proposed methodology because, in its different categories (Associate, Bachelor, Master or Doctoral), it offers training related to Journalism, Audiovisual Communication and Advertising and Public Relations, involving culture, technology and media management. Taking into account that the degree seeks to train students so that they are capable of responding to the communication challenges of the current media ecosystem, it presents great potential to prepare professionals of the future in content, skills and values. Therefore, the transmission of competences aimed at professional integrity and social responsibility is essential in its different forms, both those linked to the use of each medium and to the interrelationships between media, as well as those others related to interactive and ludic possibilities that they offer more and more frequently.

These transversal competences are expected to help students to develop empathy and social skills through gamification practices. To this end, we have selected a total of 4 serious games to analyze their potential as a learning tool to help students, from the Communication Degree, to acquire the 21st century skills –see Table 1– and the transversal competences –see Table 2– described above. Consequently, the study sample consisted of the following two serious games that addresses transcendent issues such as hate speech and social exclusion: *Bury me, My Love* (The Pixel Hunt, 2017) and *Another Lost Phone: Laura's Story* (Accidental Queens, 2017); and two fun games that also raises these topics of interest for the study and others such as cooperation and multiculturality: *Never Alone* (Upper One Games, 2016) and *Life is Strange: Episode 2 'Out of Time'* (Dontnod Entertainment, 2017).

In doing so, we have decided to use the Octalysis framework (Chou, 2014a) as a methodology for identifying transversal competences, within the context of to the 21st century skills, in matters of justice, equity and emotional intelligence. This method consists of 8 core drives that can be taken advantage of when playing video games to increase engagement and motivation.

Method: the Octalysis Framework

Octalysis, whose name derives from the octagonal shape of its graphic representation, is a framework for gamification and behavioral design proposed by the Taiwanese American pioneer Yu-Kai Chou. This model allows to conceptualize, design and implement gamified systems in order to identify and define the best solution for a specific challenge with resources for motivational design. (Teixes-Argilés, 2016). To do this, it features 8 Core Drives, each one assisting the different motivational aspects that the playful experience of interactive products implies, promoting the involvement of its users and increasing the significance of the issues addressed. This last question is so relevant that the author introduces the model as follows on his website:

If life is a game, then we can't just stand by passively like NPCs (non-playable characters); instead, we need to be proactive, gain knowledge and experience, team up with other motivated players, obtain mentors, and have fun doing it! (Chou, 2014b).

The processes mentioned in this definition, such as rewards, interaction with peers or motivation, are found in the different core drives, which are described below following Chou (2014a, pp. 25-28):

- **Core drive 1: Epic Meaning & Calling**. It happens "when a person believes they are doing something greater than themselves and/or were 'chosen' to take that action".
- **Core drive 2: Development & Accomplishment**. This corresponds to the "internal drive for making progress, developing skills, achieving mastery, and eventually overcoming challenges".
- **Core drive 3: Empowerment of Creativity & Feedback**. This drive takes shape "when users are engaged in a creative process where they repeatedly figure new things out and try different combinations".
- **Core drive 4: Ownership & Possession.** It is located "where users are motivated because they feel like they own or control something. When a person feels ownership over something, they innately want to increase and improve what they own".
- **Core drive 5: Social Influence & Relatedness**. This one "incorporates all the social elements that motivate people, including: mentorship, social acceptance, social feedback, companionship, and even competition and envy".
- **Core drive 6: Scarcity & Impatience**. It translates into "wanting something simply because it is extremely rare, exclusive, or immediately unattainable".
- **Core drive 7: Unpredictability & Curiosity**. For this drive, it is necessary to be constantly engaged because of the impossibility "to know what is going to happen next".
- **Core drive 8: Loss & Avoidance**. Its importance lies in "the motivation to avoid something negative from happening".

Figure 1. Octalysis tool
Source: Chou, 2014b

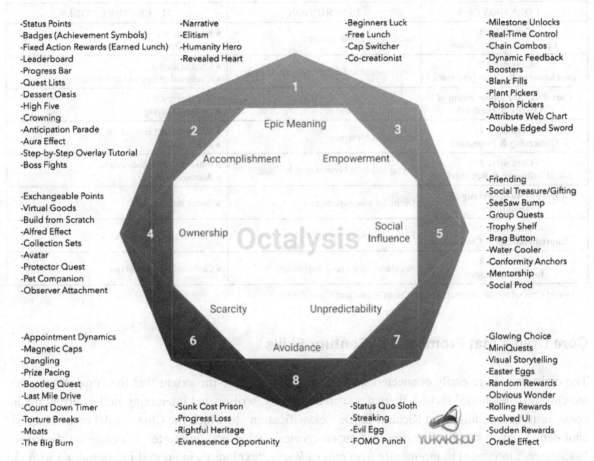

- Status Points
- Badges (Achievement Symbols)
- Fixed Action Rewards (Earned Lunch)
- Leaderboard
- Progress Bar
- Quest Lists
- Dessert Oasis
- High Five
- Crowning
- Anticipation Parade
- Aura Effect
- Step-by-Step Overlay Tutorial
- Boss Fights

- Exchangeable Points
- Virtual Goods
- Build from Scratch
- Alfred Effect
- Collection Sets
- Avatar
- Protector Quest
- Pet Companion
- Observer Attachment

- Appointment Dynamics
- Magnetic Caps
- Dangling
- Prize Pacing
- Bootleg Quest
- Last Mile Drive
- Count Down Timer
- Torture Breaks
- Moats
- The Big Burn

- Narrative
- Elitism
- Humanity Hero
- Revealed Heart

- Sunk Cost Prison
- Progress Loss
- Rightful Heritage
- Evanescence Opportunity

- Beginners Luck
- Free Lunch
- Cap Switcher
- Co-creationist

- Status Quo Sloth
- Streaking
- Evil Egg
- FOMO Punch

- Milestone Unlocks
- Real-Time Control
- Chain Combos
- Dynamic Feedback
- Boosters
- Blank Fills
- Plant Pickers
- Poison Pickers
- Attribute Web Chart
- Double Edged Sword

- Friending
- Social Treasure/Gifting
- SeeSaw Bump
- Group Quests
- Trophy Shelf
- Brag Button
- Water Cooler
- Conformity Anchors
- Mentorship
- Social Prod

- Glowing Choice
- MiniQuests
- Visual Storytelling
- Easter Eggs
- Random Rewards
- Obvious Wonder
- Rolling Rewards
- Evolved UI
- Sudden Rewards
- Oracle Effect

All these core drives are essential for the correct functioning of the gamified product, since "if there are none of these Core Drives behind a Desired Action, there is no motivation, and no behavior happens" (Chou, 2014a, p. 25). In this regard, it should be noted that there is a ninth Core Drive called 'Sensation', which is the physical pleasure one obtains from taking an action. Despite not being expressly included in the model by Chou (2014a), it underlies the entire framework and conditions the different behaviors that the 8 Core Drives lead to. For these reasons, in this paper this methodology is considered as relevant to 21st century skills, will lead to the implementation and acquisition of transversal skills able to prevent and address hate speech.

Table 3. Core drives and 21ˢᵗ century skills.

CORE DRIVES	DESCRIPTION	21ST CENTURY SKILLS
Core drive 1: **Epic Meaning & Calling**	Meaningful call-to-action	• Information literacy • Media literacy
Core drive 2: **Development & Accomplishment**	Development and overcoming challenges	• Critical thinking • Communications and collaboration
Core drive 3: Empowerment of **Creativity & Feedback**	Co-creation combining different skills	• ICT literacy • Problem-solving
Core drive 4: **Ownership & Possession**	Personal achievement	• Creativity and innovation • Productivity
Core drive 5: **Social Influence & Relatedness**	Socialization and community building	• Initiative and self-direction • Accountability
Core drive 6: Scarcity & **Impatience**	Desire for new experiences	• Social interaction
Core drive 7: **Unpredictability & Curiosity**	Forward-looking attitude	• Flexibility and adaptability
Core drive 8: **Loss & Avoidance**	Avoidance of negative happenings	• Cross-cultural interaction

Source: Created by the authors based on Chou (2014a) and Care (2018).

Core Drives that Promote 21ˢᵗ Century Skills

The eight drives are easily connected with 21ˢᵗ century skills to the extent that the competences that are currently demanded involve literacies such as reading, writing and interacting in the current media ecosystem. In fact, following Richard Bartle's classification –to which the Chou model owes a significant debt– players can be classified in four categories: 'achievers', interested in *acting on the world*; 'socializers', interested in *interacting with other players*; 'explorers', interested in *interacting with the world*; and 'killers', interested in *acting on other players* (Bartle, 1996). These categories demonstrate the different attitudes that viewers/users/players (Dinehart, 2006) have towards narratives, *storyworlds* and characters. Therefore, associating them with well-known fictions such as those that follow, can shed light on their importance.

- **Core drive 1: Epic Meaning & Calling.** It resembles Joseph Campbell's monomyth or hero's journey -adapted to cinema by Christopher Vogler (2002), and to video games by James Plyler (2013)– and it coincides with the second stage, "The Call to Adventure" (Campbell, 2004), which corresponds to the trigger that changes the status quo of the 'ordinary world'. It is a significant event, usually linked to a situation of injustice or danger, which moves the hero, who is nothing more than an ordinary person, to action. It must be the engine of change in society, within the represented fiction. A good example of how this drive works is the video game *Death Stranding* (Kojima Productions, 2019), whose protagonist Sam Porter makes sense of that kind of heroism.
- **Core drive 2: Development & Accomplishment.** This type of change is associated with the hero's growth, who develops new capacities and grows internally (sense of justice, courage, empathy ...). It can be exemplified, above all, by *The Lord of the Rings* character Frodo, who empathizes

with Gollum's agony. What makes him heroic is his imperfection, his mistakes, and conflicts, which humanize him, without making him deviate from his noble intentions.

- **Core drive 3: Empowerment of Creativity & Feedback.** It can be associated, especially, with problem solving and, above all, with being proactive when it comes to being an important part of the solution. In a way, it implies the deployment of strategies that enable the achievement of goals in the most efficient and beneficial way. The choice of the path to follow is important, so that it not only offers "on rail" interactivity, but multidirectional interactivity or, in the best of cases, an open world. *Death Stranding* (Kojima Productions, 2019) is an example of this, due to the behavior of players during its week of release, when many of them decided to help others instead of simply progressing individually and selfishly.

- **Core drive 4: Ownership and possession.** Possession does not necessarily have to involve something material, although it is sometimes materialized in an object (for example, the ring of power in *The Lord of the Rings*). Ideally, possessions should be associated with values, which are often represented in statistics and characters' roles. It can also be interesting to connect them with the inventory: things that the hero has acquired thanks to actions carried out that, in the end, define him. In many video games, the values of the characters are represented in their configuration and/ or in equipment/accessories/skins/abilities...

- **Core drive 5: Social influence and relatedness.** This type of change is also associated with the hero's growth, but externally (allies, support...), it involves being a model to follow and favoring understanding among others. It can also be exemplified with the character Frodo, from *The Lord of the Rings*, who is valued by everyone: from his friends and the Fellowship of the Ring to all the pro-Gondor side of the Middle-earth that knows him, who end up considering him a hero even if he is not named king, as shown when they exclaim: *"For Frodo!"*.

- **Core drive 6: Scarcity & Impatience.** Following the scheme of the hero's journey, it would be the elixir with which the protagonist returns after living countless experiences that mold him and make him a more complete person. The hero wants to see the world, to enter the unknown, and that pushes him to accept an adventure with risks and difficulties. However, when he returns home, he understands that everything he has done has been worthwhile and has given him a lot: experiences, memories and, above all, resources for what will come. The resolution of this type of story becomes a recapitulation of what has been lived and an enjoyment of what said experiences have provided. The experience provided to the player by the video game *Journey* (Thatgamecompany, 2012) gives a good example of this positive recall.

- **Core drive 7: Unpredictability & Curiosity.** Continuing with the previous idea, this drive welcomes the desire to embark on the next adventure, being able to take advantage of the previous ones to reach greater achievements and carry out better feats. Thinking about it in relation to stories that have a continuity or are structured in chapters, it is especially evident that everything that has been lived allows to reach knowledge and restore order. The famous *Zelda* video games, following the model of other monomythic stories such as *Star Wars: Episode IV – A New Hope* (George Lucas, 1977), repeat this scheme but, each time, renew the formula.

- **Core drive 8: Loss & Avoidance.** All the previous drives have an impact on reducing fear of the other that leads to othering behaviors and structures, due to knowledge and experience. However, there is a risk that, by wanting to avoid negative situations, a "loss" and an "avoidance" of the encounter with the other will be generated, erecting barriers and a fear of the outside, of the alien, of the different. In order to avoid this causing a problem, the key is to show that non-involvement triggers negative consequences and that, therefore, it is necessary to tend towards the common project instead of small separate and confronting worlds. In the *Metro* video game series, for example, this fear of otherness is perfectly represented. The population does not want to abandon the subway stations for fear of what is outside; however, the only way to get ahead is to try to redirect the critical state the world is in.

The connection of the core drives with the Campbellian monomyth, far from being casual, seeks to correspond the adventurous nature of the Octalysis framework. This relationship aims to promote diversity, positive interaction between equals and the fight against stereotypes of any nature, since what is intended is that, like the protagonists of the different fictions involved, the players can fulfill the solemn task indicated by Campbell (2004): "to return then to us, transfigured, and teach the lesson he has learned of life renewed" (p. 18).

Core Drives that Connect to Transversal Competences

Video games, like other types of literary and cinematographic fictions of undisputable scope in the present, allow working on values such as justice, equality and emotional intelligence, as well as phenomena such as cooperation and multiculturalism. However, their particular characteristics -mainly interactivity, multidirectionality and agency- give them greater potential to motivate and retain their consumers, instilling in them transversal skills and, consequently, leading to valuable outcomes.

Working in accordance with the transversal competences and the core drives already explained, can give rise to an interconnection such as that described in Table 4, making it possible to obtain a series of outcomes that prepare young people today to face future challenges on the management and reduction of hate speech. We have considered that the outcomes that could be obtained with this relationship are as follows:

a)   Embolden access to knowledge.
b)   Inspire fellowship.
c)   Increase intercultural experiences.
d)   Boost active participation.
e)   Encourage social change.
f)   Reduce fear of the other.
g)   Enhance fair citizenship.
h)   Strengthen human values.

Table 4. Transversal competences, drives and outcomes for preventing and addressing hate speech

CORE DRIVES	OUTCOMES	TRANSVERSAL COMPETENCES
Core drive 1: **Epic Meaning & Calling**	a) Embolden access to knowledge	TC1. Ability to make judgments and scientific knowledge
Core drive 2: **Development & Accomplishment**	b) Inspire fellowship c) Increase intercultural experiences	TC2. Ability to communicate and social skills
Core drive 3: **Empowerment of Creativity & Feedback**	d) Boost active participation	TC3. Skills in the use of Information and Communication Technologies (ICTs)
Core drive 4: **Ownership & Possession**	a) Embolden access to knowledge	
Core drive 5: **Social Influence & Relatedness**	d) Boost active participation	TC4. Critical skills, initiative, and entrepreneurship
Core drive 6: Scarcity & Impatience	e) Encourage social change	TC5. Ethical commitment and respect for cultural diversity
Core drive 7: **Unpredictability & Curiosity**	f) Reduce fear of the other	
Core drive 8: **Loss & Avoidance**	g) Enhance fair citizenship h) Strengthen human values	TC6. Social skills and global citizenship

Source: Created by the authors based on Chou (2014a) and Ordóñez-Olmedo (2017).

RESULTS AND DISCUSSION

Considering the relationships between transversal skills and core drives that have been explained and established, the results obtained after applying the Octalysis model to the four games that make up the object of study are presented below.

In order to present them as clearly as possible, the aspects that stand out with respect to the different core drives and based on this, the outcomes that can be generated by those other aspects of the game linked to the six transversal competences.

Bury me, My Love (2017)

Bury me, my Love tells the story of a Syrian couple, Nour and Majd, who are forced to separate because she decides to leave their country and travel to Europe to get a safer life while Majd has to stay and take care of older relatives. The only way they can communicate is through a chat app on their smartphones, hence the player must assume the role of Majd to give Nour the best possible advice and support (Games-4sustainability.com, 2018). Following this plot, this game motivates players and configures their behavior through the following core drives:

- Core drive 1. Help the protagonists to overcome their odyssey.
- Core drive 2. Use the mobile phone efficiently so as not to lose contact and hope.
- Core drive 3. Find solutions to unforeseen events.
- Core drive 4. Obtain and produce resources to continue progressing.
- Core drive 5. Interact with equals to achieve a goal.
- Core drive 6. Do not cease in the effort to achieve the desired change.

- Core drive 7. Avoid losing motivation to keep moving forward.
- Core drive 8. Prevent negative events for oneself and others.

Figure 2. Octalysis design for 'Bury me, my love'.
Source: Created by the authors based on Chou (2014b)

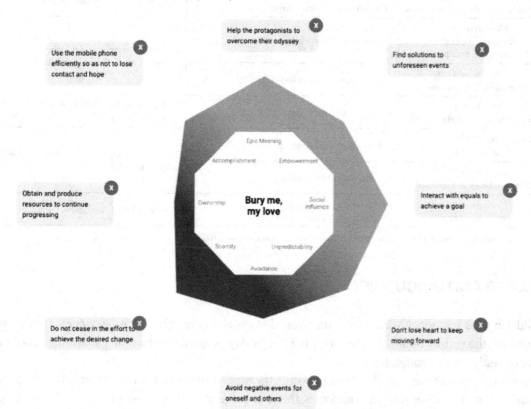

The resulting design shows the great capacity of the game to make the players empathize with the problems of the protagonist couple. Involving them in the particular odyssey that Nour and Majd live when they are separated and conveying the constant fear that they will not survive the consequences of the migratory crisis, the game manages to make players live this reality and understand its consequences. This becomes especially relevant if the players decide to play it in real time, receiving the messages in the least expected moments and experiencing waiting and uncertainty.

The linearity of the proposal, in which the players are limited to interactions through mobile messaging, not only does not harm the experience but also increases it, since it makes them aware of the very barriers that these people face because of the risk of social exclusion. The conscientious nature of the game is not strange considering that it was created in collaboration with ARTE France, famous for producing audiovisual content in which multicultural values are promoted. Also in this case, the players are encouraged to achieve positive goals and it becomes possible to work on them while activating the following actions and attitudes through transversal skills:

- TC1. Search for information on the migration crisis.

- TC2. Awareness of the importance of communication (mobile phone as a *transitional object*).
- TC3. Access to network communication: pros and cons.
- TC4. Problem solving in crisis scenarios.
- TC5. Empathy with the other and blurring differences.
- TC6. Risks of being excluded from citizenship.

Regarding its potential to prevent hate speech, this video game informs about a current and very important problem, allowing players to experience the particular journey of refugees and understand the reasons for their displacement and consequent search for a better life in a country capable of offering them new opportunities. The visibility not only of the causes but, above all, of the consequences of the situation experienced by the protagonists, offers in this sense an indisputable opportunity for public awareness and mobilization.

Another Lost Phone: Laura's Story (2017)

Another Lost Phone: Laura's Story is a game that, simulating the player's discovery of a young woman's mobile phone, explores the social life of a young woman in distress. Designed as a narrative investigation, the player must scroll through the phone's content and piece together elements from the different applications, messages and pictures to progress. This way, players will find out everything about Laura: her friendships, her professional life and the events that led to her mysterious disappearance and the loss of this phone (Anotherlostphone.com, 2017). Based on this premise, which once again gives vital importance to the mobile phone, the game encourages the following core drives:

- Core drive 1. Find out what happened to the owner of the phone.
- Core drive 2. Communicate with other users to move forward.
- Core drive 3. Use the different apps to find answers.
- Core drive 4. Make good use of the telephone and the information it contains.
- Core drive 5. Gain the trust of contacts to discover the truth.
- Core drive 6. Initiate or resume relationships that may be helpful.
- Core drive 7. Adapt interactions to unfolding events.
- Core drive 8. Stop abusive situations and alerting others about them.

Figure 3. Octalysis design for 'Another Lost Phone: Laura's Story'.
Source: Created by the authors based on Chou (2014b).

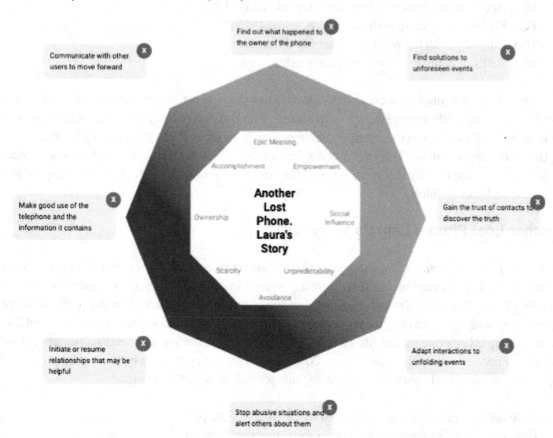

Despite the controversial game mechanics, in which players have to access someone else's mobile phone, the message that emerges is positive and raises awareness of such important problems as bullying and abuse. And, in this case, unlike what happened in *Bury me, my love*, players can feel a greater degree of interactivity, which can lead them to feel a greater degree of responsibility, thus promoting a greater balance in the different core drives.

The interactivity the game fosters has a special impact on the way in which the mobile device is navigated, managing the information obtained through the different apps, and the relationships that are established with its owner's contacts, seeking to clarify the events. All this leads to a fairly strong emotional and moral implication, since the game ends up leading to the discovery that situations of abuse were taking place and the final message ends up being revealing, especially in the messages offered in the credits, from which players are encouraged to stop this type of situations. Therefore, through this kind of conversational adventure, the game allows working on transversal competences and give sense to the following aspects:

- TC1. Relevance of knowing the background of a situation.
- TC2. Right to communicate ideas, feelings and emotions.
- TC3. Threats to privacy in digital media.

- TC4. Importance of judging based on evidence.
- TC5. Protecting the integrity of minorities.
- TC6. Consequences of isolation and bullying.

This video game addresses situations of hatred and discrimination, showing how they perpetuate and even normalize hate speech. In this way, exposing the players to complex and unwanted scenarios, it shows the fatal consequences that trigger reprehensible attitudes and punish them from an ethical and moral perspective. In addition, the fact that the player becomes aware of the problems exposed and acquires responsibility in managing them through the use of a mobile phone, allows a greater connection of young audiences with a reality that concerns them on a daily basis through this device and the practices in which they participate through it.

Never Alone (2016)

Never Alone was the first game developed in collaboration with the Alaskan native community Iñupiat. It is a puzzle platform that offers the players the possibility to explore awe-inspiring environments, perform heroic deeds, and meet legendary characters from this indigenous community. Its game mechanics allow to play alternately (in single-player mode) or cooperatively (in multi-player mode) as a young Iñupiat girl or as her arctic fox companion to find the source of the eternal blizzard which threatens the survival of their civilization (Neveralonegame.com, 2016). This game, despite not being a *serious game* but just a fun game, is especially relevant because it deals with serious issues through the following core drives:

- Core drive1. Avoid the extinction of civilization.
- Core drive 2. Progress taking advantage of the laws that govern the system.
- Core drive 3. Solve challenges with lateral thinking.
- Core drive 4. Achieve successes that have a global impact.
- Core drive 5. Connect with other communities.
- Core drive 6. Live experiences cooperatively.
- Core drive 7. Not giving up in the effort to reach the end.
- Core drive 8. Prevent a valuable culture from being lost.

Figure 4. Octalysis design for 'Never Alone'.
Source: Created by the authors from Chou (2014b).

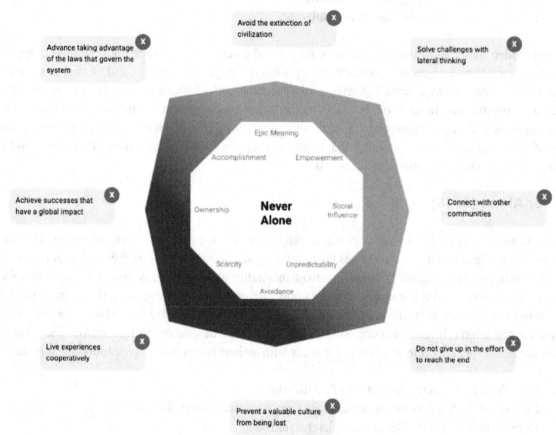

The main motivation of this game is to advance through the different levels, overcoming the puzzles and enjoying the challenges that its platformed nature implies. However, the storytelling that sustains the playful proposal makes it possible to deal with serious issues such as respect for diverse cultures and their protection against the threats to which their people are exposed. In fact, despite being customized to a specific town, and starring a single girl and her arctic fox, it represents a global situation that can be extrapolated to many other regions of the world. Thus, due to that connection with an easily recognizable situation, the projection and empathy of the players can be such that it leads them to want to know more about those people that they embody in the game.

On the other hand, the cooperation that takes place between the two characters that the players control, as well as between them and the other characters they meet in their adventure, is an essential aspect of the game. Its defense of the spirit of service, sacrifice, solidarity and multiculturalism, lead to a valuable message compared to other video games that use similar mechanics but do not offer values like these and even defend countervalues. Therefore, the game allows working on these aspects through transversal competences which drive to the following results:

- TC1. Encouraging research about other cultures.
- TC2. Claiming the value of collaboration and cooperation.

- TC3. Using of technology to achieve objectives.
- TC4. Taking the initiative in solving problems.
- TC5. Knowing and valuing the communities at risk of disappearing.
- TC6. Promoting global citizenship.

Being, of the four video games analyzed, the one that less obviously addresses hate speech, its message has such a global and necessary value that it is essential to underline the great message it conveys regarding global citizenship, respect and protection of minority cultures. Therefore, despite being the least adult-oriented, it represents a great opportunity to remember fundamental values that concern us all and that, once the innocence of childhood is lost, they tend to be forgotten.

Life is Strange: Episode 2 'Out of Time' (2015)

Life is Strange is an episodic game saga based on a choice-and-consequence narrative which, in the case of this second episode, allows players to take on the role of high school student Max Caulfield with the power to rewind time. As Max, players navigate school life through a linear path, interacting with classmates, teachers and friends through choice-driven dialogue, but these decisions can be modified because of the "rewind" time power. This option allows you to relive a scenario several times and observe the consequences associated with the decisions made (Polygon.com, 2015). This episode of the famous *Life is Strange* saga is not, as *Never Alone* was, a *serious game*, but it has enormous potential to address necessary issues in today's world through the following core drives:

- Core drive 1. Restore order, welfare and justice.
- Core drive 2. Make progress through communication.
- Core drive 3. Use technology to change the state of things.
- Core drive 4. Be responsible for major changes.
- Core drive 5. Lead the desire for change and help to achieve it.
- Core drive 6. Intervene positively in unwanted situations.
- Core drive 7. Find ways to improve the sphere of influence.
- Core drive 8. Promote positive peer interaction.

Figure 5. Octalysis design for 'Life is Strange: Episode 2 «Out of Time»'.
Source: Created by the authors from Chou (2014b).

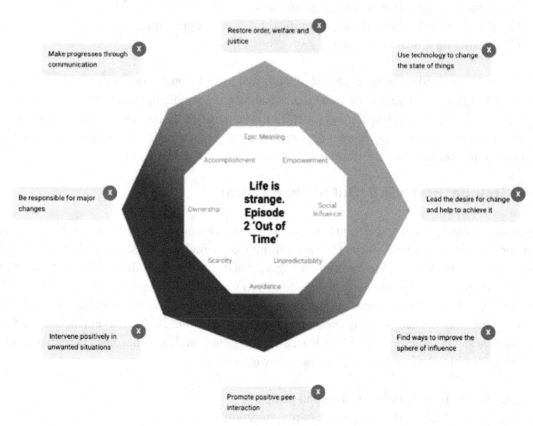

By relating the storytelling of the serial narratives with some mechanics of the graphic adventures, this game offers a complete and complex game experience that welcomes adult themes of great importance and supposes a notable emotional impact on those who play it. As the Octalysis design created shows, the high degree of interaction it allows has an equally high awareness of situations witnessed in the third person or experienced in the first person. This is essential to the understanding of the game to the extent that it is heavily committed to transferring a sense of presence in that fictional world to the players.

Regarding this last idea, it should be noted that, although it is obviously a game, it deals with real situations and offers a representation of their causes and consequences through simulation. However, sadly, there is an essential difference between the game and reality: in reality, rewinding is not an option. This fact gives the playful proposal a great almost philosophical background and increases the potential of the game to make players aware of the implications of those acts that threaten the integrity of minorities or people at risk of exclusion. In this sense, it is possible to include transversal competences in order to reach significant outcomes:

- TC1. Investigating the implications of choosing in a decision tree schema.
- TC2. Importance of expressing yourself freely.
- TC3. Getting involved in life using technology.
- TC4. Supporting others in managing their problems.

- TC5. Encouraging respect for diversity.
- TC6. Risks of being excluded by any condition.

In a similar way to *Another Lost Phone: Laura's Story* (2017), it defends diversity and warns about the threats that both its lack of protection and permissiveness entail in situations of discrimination and mistreatment of those groups that are at greater risk of social exclusion. It is not surprising that the *Life is Strange* saga has tackled these issues in a more notable way, becoming a celebrated and vindicated example of the ability of video games to reflect on these types of social realities and offer ways of dealing with the hateful speeches that emanate from them.

In the end, the four games -both the two serious games and the two fun games that address serious issues- offer an exceptional opportunity to work on these transcendent issues in the classroom through a medium that can increase the motivation of students and encourage their involvement in the resolution of negative situations related to hate speech. Furthermore, since all of them are carried out by women, it is especially interesting to approach these situations while taking into account the question of gender, since this is undoubtedly connected to many of those serious issues that affect the contemporary world.

SOLUTIONS AND RECOMMENDATIONS

The recommendation that the authors provide in this chapter is to organize didactic planning for students of the Degree in Communication. By using the serious games that have been proposed in previous sections. In this way, the 21st century skills that facilitate the acquisition of transversal competences are worked indirectly. These competences will train future graduates in Communication in ethical professionals against hate speech, mainly. According to Defaz (2020) gamification favors the achievement of competences through the ERCA learning cycle (Concrete Experience, Reflection, Abstract Conceptualization and Application).

The first intention in the learning cycle is concrete experience through serious games, students can start game-based learning by resorting to gamified experiences.

The second phase intends to unite the experience and the conceptualization with the core drivers proposed in the Octalysis framework. Students must reflect on the experience, analyze it and relate it to 21st century skills and their own experiences.

In the third phase, the teacher raises questions that make the ideas contrast with the learning experiences, in order to conceptualize the drives and outcomes for preventing and addressing hate speech.

The fourth phase, called application, is the closing of the cycle, where students interact to link the new knowledge with the transversal competences that they have acquired to put into practice in future real situations. Teachers must integrate ICTs so that their students can achieve a better use of the contents in the concretion of general and specific skills of each area of study; if the learning sessions are carried out in a dynamic and participatory manner, as proposed, the students will achieve better results.

CONCLUSION

Hate speech is a social problem nowadays that affects, principally, young people. Social networks, forums and other online spaces are a reflection of the worrying proliferation of radical attitudes, unfounded prejudices and harmful stereotypes. However, the real threat lies not only in the online arena, but in the offline world, since online hate speech is usually transformed into violent and criminal behaviors in real life.

During the sample selection phase of this study, it was found that there are a significant number of video games that seek to placate the prejudices that have traditionally existed in video games on gender issues. In this way, it is inferred that player have been able to assume and internalize, involuntarily, a series of conventionalisms and stereotypes that, in the worst cases, have led to hate speech against women and even sexist violence.

It is, therefore, crucial to instruct students not only to identify hate speech, but also to know how to combat it and to promote more empathetic, humane, fair and social behaviors in online and offline scenarios. To achieve this, it is essential to redefine the competences that students acquire throughout their academic training. In this sense, future information professionals acquire a transcendental role. For this reason, Communication Degree syllabi at all universities should include a series of transversal competences, inspired by the 21st century skills, to reinforce future communicators to professionally fight against hate speech and prevent extreme and radical behavior.

FUTURE RESEARCH DIRECTIONS

Future works could experiment with this methodology –the Octalysis framework– with other hate speech and serious games. Hate speech is based on aspects such as: skin color, race, social class, ethnicity, political ideology, etc. Therefore, there are different sorts of hate speech depending on the victims of hatred. Then, it is crucial to tackle the diverse expressions of hate speech throughout other serious games. In this sense, further studies are required to apply the Octalysis framework in analyzing the potential of various games to help combat the different types of hate speech emerging in society.

Regarding the education context, and given the wide variety of hate speech, it is particularly significant to identify the types of hate speech that are most frequently verbalized by young people. In doing so, it is important to design a pre-test to identify the main prejudices and stereotypes of the students. This way, it is easier for teachers or instructors to focus on tackling the most prevalent types of hate speech among students, throughout certain serious games, thus improving the effect of the game-based learning process.

Clearly, further studies are required to test all these proposals. Serious games favor the acquisition of transversal competences and the 21st skills, but there is no guarantee that students will actually acquire the knowledge, skills and competences necessary for tackling hate speech. Then, teachers and instructors also need to design a post-test in order to assess the effectiveness of the selected serious games regarding the different types of hate speech.

REFERENCES

Abt, C. C. (1987). *Serious games*. University Press of America.

Accidental Queens. (2017). Another Lost Phone: Laura's Story (iOS Version) [Video game]. France.

Alonso Varela, L., & Saraiva Cruz, I. (2020). Búsqueda y evaluación de información: Dos competencias necesarias en el contexto de las fake news. *Palabra Clave (La Plata)*, 9(2), e090. doi:10.24215/18539912e090

Ananiadou, K., & Magdalean, C. (2009). *21st Century Skills & Competences for New Millennium Learners in OECD Countries*. OECD. doi:10.1787/19939019

Bartle, R. (1996). Hearts, clubs, diamonds, spades: Players who suit MUDs. *Journal of MUD Research, 1*(1), 19.

Blake, S. (2021, June 11). What Trump said before his supporters stormed the Capitol, annotated. *The Washington Post.* https://wapo.st/3mbpDzb

Buckingham, D. (2005). *Educación en medios: Alfabetización, aprendizaje y cultura contemporánea.* Paidós.

Butterworth, J., & Thwaites, G. (2013). *Thinking skills: Critical thinking and problem solving.* Cambridge University Press.

Campbell, J. (2003). *The hero's journey: Joseph Campbell on his life and work.* New World Library.

Care, E. (2018). Twenty-First Century Skills: From Theory to Action. In Assessment and Teaching of 21st Century Skills: Research and Application (pp. 3-17). Springer.

Chou, Y. (2014a). *Actionable gamification: Beyond points, badges, and leaderboards.* Octalysis Media.

Chou, Y. (2014b). *Gamification & Behavioral Design. Learn how to use Gamification to make a positive impact on your work and life.* https://yukaichou.com/start-here/

ConklinM. (2021, January 15). Capitol Offense: Is Donald Trump Guilty of Inciting a Riot at the Capitol? *J.L. & Pub. Pol'y.* doi:10.2139/ssrn.3767085

Defaz, M. (2020). Metodologías activas en el proceso enseñanza-aprendizaje. *Revista Científico-Educacional, 16*(1), 463–472.

Dinehart, S. (2006). *Transmedial Play: Cognitive and Cross-Platform Narrative* [Blog post]. Available at http://narrativedesign.org/2008/05/trans-medial-playcognitive-and-cross-platform-narrative/

Djaouti, D., Alvarez, J., Jessel, J. P., & Rampnoux, O. (2011). Origins of serious games. In Serious games and edutainment applications (pp. 25-43). Springer. doi:10.1007/978-1-4471-2161-9_3

Dontnod Entertainment. (2017). Life is Strange: Episode 2 'Out of Time' (PS4 Version) [Video Game]. France.

Dörner, R., Göbel, S., Effelsberg, W., & Wiemeyer, J. (2016). Introduction. In R. Dörner, S. Göbel, W. Effelsberg, & J. Wiemeyer (Eds.), Serious Games. Foundations, Concepts and Practice (pp. 1-34). Springer.

Fuchs, C. (2021). How Did Donald Trump Incite a Coup Attempt? *tripleC: Communication, Capitalism & Critique Open Access Journal for a Global Sustainable Information Society, 19*(1), 246–251.

Grace, L. D. (2020). *Doing things with games: social impact through play.* CRC Press.

Greenberg, J., & Pyszczynski, T. (1985). The effect of an overheard ethnic slur on evaluations of the target: How to spread a social disease. *Journal of Experimental Social Psychology, 21*(1), 61–72. doi:10.1016/0022-1031(85)90006-X

Huizinga, J. (1949). *Homo ludens. A study of the play-element in culture.* Routledge & Kegan Pau.

INTEF. (2019, September 19). *Resumen del Informe Horizon 2019.* https://bit.ly/3ieYycM

Kagan, S. (1994). *Cooperative Learning. Resources for Teachers* Inc.

Kapp, K. M. (2012). The gamification of learning and instruction: case-based methods and strategies for training and education. Pfieffer: An Imprint of John Wiley & Sons.

Kivunja, C. (2015). Teaching students to learn and to work well with 21st century skills: Unpacking the career and life skills domain of the new learning paradigm. *International Journal of Higher Education, 4*(1), 1–11.

Kojima Productions. (2019). Death Stranding (PS4 Version) [Video game]. Japan.

Loveless, A. M. (2002). *Literature review in creativity, new technologies and learning.* Futurelab Series Report, 4. Futurelab. https://hal.inria.fr/docs/00/19/04/39/PDF/loveless-a-2002-r4.pdf

Lucas, G. (Director). (1977). *Star Wars: Episode IV – A New Hope* [Film]. 20ᵗʰ Century Fox.

Ma, M., Oikonomou, A., & Jain, L. C. (2011). Innovations in serious games for future learning. In M. Ma, A. Oikonomou, & L. C. Jain (Eds.), Serious games and edutainment applications (pp. 3-7). Springer. doi:10.1007/978-1-4471-2161-9_1

Marin, S., Lee, V., & Landers, R. N. (2021). Gamified Active Learning and Its Potential for Social Change. In A. Spanellis & J. T. Harviainen (Eds.), *Transforming Society and Organizations through Gamification: From the Sustainable Development Goals to Inclusive Workplaces* (pp. 205–223). Palgrave Macmillan. doi:10.1007/978-3-030-68207-1_11

Mathew, B., Saha, P., Yimam, S. M., Biemann, C., Goyal, P., & Mukherjee, A. (2020). *Hatexplain: A benchmark dataset for explainable hate speech detection.* https://bit.ly/3AmrHc1

Mitgutsch, K. (2011). Serious learning in serious games. Learning In, Through, and Beyond Serious Games. In M. Ma, A. Oikonomou, & L. C. Jain (Eds.), Serious games and edutainment applications (pp. 45-58). Springer. doi:10.1007/978-1-4471-2161-9_4

Olteanu, A., Castillo, C., Boy, J., & Varshney, K. R. (2018). The Effect of Extremist Violence on Hateful Speech Online. In *Proceedings of the Twelfth International Conference on Web and Social Media* (pp.221–230). AAAI Press.

Ordóñez-Olmedo, E. (2017). Teaching Innovation Proposal: The Inclusion of Transversal Competences in Official University Studies of Master's degrees and the Strengthening of Democratic Values. *IJERI: International Journal of Educational Research and Innovation, 8*, 148–162.

Parekh, B. (2012). Is there a case for banning hate speech? In M. Herz & P. Molnar (Eds.), *The Content and Context of Hate Speech: Rethinking Regulation and Responses* (pp. 37–56). Cambridge University Press. doi:10.1017/CBO9781139042871.006

Pérez-Escolar, M., Ordóñez-Olmedo, E., & Alcaide-Pulido, P. (2021). Fact-checking skills and project-based learning about infodemic and disinformation. *Thinking Skills and Creativity, 41*, 100887. Advance online publication. doi:10.1016/j.tsc.2021.100887

Piazza, J. (2020, September 28). When politicians use hate speech, political violence increases. *The Conversation*. Available at https://cutt.ly/ZbGE7cx

Plyler, J. (2013). *Video Games and the Hero's Journey*. Available at https://bit.ly/3xpRhux

Posetti, J. (2018). News industry transformation: digital technology, social platforms and the spread of misinformation and disinformation. In C. Ireton & J. Posetti (Eds.), *Journalism, fake news & disinformation: handbook for journalism education and training* (pp. 55–69). UNESCO.

Potter, W. J. (2018). *Media literacy*. Sage Publications.

Romero, M., & Turpo, O. (2015). Serious Games para el desarrollo de las competencias del siglo XXI. *Revista de Educación a Distancia (RED)*, (34). https://bit.ly/3xuL0xN

Ruiz, M. E. P., & Chapman, M. C. S. (2017). Las competencias informacionales en las ciencias médicas. *Revista de la Facultad de Ciencias Médicas de la Universidad de Guayaquil*. https://bit.ly/3fGSVSK

Sáiz-Manzares, M. C., & Pérez, M. I. (2016). Autorregulación y mejora del autoconocimiento en resolución de problemas. *Psicologia desde el Caribe*, *33*(1), 14–30.

Shivakumaraswamy, K. N., & Narendra, B. K. (2021). Assessing Information Communication Technology (ICT) Literacy Skills: A Study of Students of BGS Institute of Technology. Academic Press.

Silva, M., García, T., Guzmán, T., & Chaparro, R. (2016). Study of Moodle tools to develop 21st century skills. *Virtual Campus*, *5*(2), 58–69.

Smith, M., Ballard, J., & Sanders, L. (2021). Most voters say the events at the US Capitol are a threat to democracy. *YouGov Politics & Current Affairs*. https://bit.ly/3pAsALT

Soral, W., Bilewicz, M., & Winiewski, M. (2018). Exposure to hate speech increases prejudice through desensitization. *Aggressive Behavior*, *44*(2), 136–146. doi:10.1002/ab.21737 PMID:29094365

Susi, T., Johannesson, M., & Backlund, P. (2007). *Serious Games—An Overview* (Technical report: HIS-IKI-TR-07-001). University of Skövde. Available at http:// www.his.se/iki/ingame/publications

Teixes-Argilés, F. (2016). *Gamificación: motivar jugando*. UOC.

Thatgamecompany. (2012). *Journey* (PS4 Version) [Video game]. USA.

The Pixel Hunt. (2017). Bury me, My Love (iOS Version) [Video game]. France.

Triana, D., Anggraito, Y. U., & Ridlo, S. (2020). Effectiveness Environmental Change Learning Tools Based on STEM-PjBL Towards Students' Collaboration and Communications Skills. *Journal of Innovative Science Education*, *9*(3), 244–249.

Trilling, B., & Fadel, C. (2009). *21st Century Skills: Learning for Life in Our Times*. Jossey-Bass.

UNESCO. (2005). *Towards the Knowledge Society*. United Nations Educational, Scientific and Cultural Organization. https://bit.ly/3kVa381

UNESCO. (2016). *Marco de avaliação global da alfabetização midiática e informacional: disposição e competências do país*. Brasilia: UNESCO. https://bit.ly/2VqHqHI

United Nations. (2019, June 18). *United Nations strategy and plan of action on hate speech.* Available at https://cutt.ly/ObF7sf7

Upper One Games. (2016). Never Alone (iOS Version) [Video game]. USA.

Valencia-Molina, T., Serna-Collazos, A., Ochoa-Angrino, S., Caicedo-Tamayo, A. M., Montes-González, J. A., & Chávez-Vescance, J. D. (2016). *Competencias y estándares TIC desde la dimensión pedagógica: Una perspectiva desde los niveles de apropiación de las TIC en la práctica educativa docente.* Pontificia Universidad Javeriana – Cali.

Vogler, C. (2002). *El viaje del escritor. Las estructuras míticas para escritores, guionistas, dramaturgos y novelistas.* Ediciones Robinbook.

Wardle, C., & Derakhshan, H. (2018). Journalism, fake news & disinformation: handbook for journalism education and training. In C. Ireton & J. Posetti (Eds.), *Journalism, fake news & disinformation: handbook for journalism education and training* (pp. 43–52). UNESCO.

Werbach, K., & Hunter, D. (2012). *For the Win: How Game Thinking Can Revolutionize Your Business.* Wharton Digital Press.

Wouters, P., Paas, F., & van Merriënboer, J. J. (2008). How to optimize learning from animated models: A review of guidelines base on cognitive load. *Review of Educational Research, 78*(3), 645–675. doi:10.3102/0034654308320320

Wouters, P., van Nimwegen, C., van Oostendorp, H., & van der Spek, E. D. (2013). A meta-analysis of the cognitive and motivational effects of serious games. *Journal of Educational Psychology, 105*(2), 249–265. doi:10.1037/a0031311

Zichermann, G., & Cunningham, C. (2011). *Gamification by Design: Implementing Game Mechanics in Web and Mobile Apps.* O'Reilly Media.

Chapter 18
The Potential of Gamification for Humanitarian Organizations to Support Integration in Migration Contexts

Marvin Jammermann
Carl von Ossietzky Universität Oldenburg, Germany

Beybin Elvin Tunc
Carl von Ossietzky Universität Oldenburg, Germany

ABSTRACT

The aim of this chapter is to explore the connections between the inherent characteristics of gamification and the current need for sustainable integration activities that are based on meaningful social interactions. By highlighting the potential of gamification for creating democratic spaces of social interaction and engaging diverse actors in joyful encounters, it is possible to underline the notion of social change that gamification can induce. In the area of integration, humanitarian organizations can harness the potential of gamification in their integration activities in order to ensure increased social cohesion. Through a critical analysis of existing gamification and integration approaches, the chapter provides arguments for why gamification is perfectly suited to improve integration processes by highlighting the manifold applications of gamification experience in the humanitarian field.

INTRODUCTION

Games can be an effective tool to motivate people, based on its attractive play and fun elements. Besides being inherently fun-oriented, games are far more complex and include various elements that might have the potential to address pivotal social, political and economic issues in society (Stewart et al., 2013). Games´ ultimate purpose of having fun, its strong mechanics that encourages a continuous engagement and its elements that provide a safe-to-fail space can have a drastic impact on social processes by using

DOI: 10.4018/978-1-7998-9223-6.ch018

people's motivation. This applies in particular to integration activities bringing together migrants and members of the host society.

This chapter will outline the inherent potential of games, and gamification more precisely, by highlighting that gamification offers valuable solutions to complex problems of current integration approaches. In this context, humanitarian organisations play a leading role when it comes to supporting integration efforts. It is their operations that could widely profit from applying gamification approaches to their integration activities. Games apply simple rules of equality as the rules are equal for everyone. In the beginning the materials are distributed equally, while the rest is the responsibility of the players. When playing games together, all the players agree on the conditions of winning, and, more importantly, everyone has equal chances to win. In this logic games already apply the notion of fairness between diverse actors that interact with each other, which is correlating with the principle of integration. People have already invested considerable time in entertainment and gaming, which can be used to make them aware of specific topics in society or to even change their perceptions on controversial issues. Games are on the search for meaning and constantly solve problems in a virtual world which can be used to solve certain challenges and to induce social change in the real world (Hassan & Leigh, 2021). Research shows that "[...] games-based approaches provide adaptable, motivating and engaging techniques that can be used to empower individuals and communities in ways that lead to social inclusion." (Stewart et al., 2013, p. 11). In this context, games are defined as game-based joyful interactions between players, while gamification refers to the innovative application of typical game elements (e.g. point scoring, competition with others, rules of play) to non-game contexts such as integration. As such, gamification can be understood as a transformational practice itself, as the underlying idea strives to revolutionize certain fields and to change procedures making them more engaging and fun (Thibault & Hamari, 2021). Moreover, games and the mechanisms of gamification are perfectly equipped to support various groups in society as e.g. migrants to achieve certain education goals (Stewart et al., 2013). This crossroad between the potential for increased learning outcomes for members of society and the pursuit for enjoyment as transformational potential makes gamification a considerable tool for social change. Furthermore, unlike in life, in games everyone has the same starting point and moves according to their own choices. For certain groups in society life is often characterized by inequality, but games provide a space to gain the autonomy and responsibility of their responses towards circumstances. Games establish a feeling of equal opportunity and creates a convivial space to perform agency throughout the game. Either in front of a screen or at the table, players gain a new identity that they define with their own choices within the game and during the process of playing. When they finish playing a game, people turn back to the in-world reality. The *magic circle* is an arranged space for a certain duration of time. As Huizinga (1955) describes, the *magic circle* works like a door where players are passing through both in entering and leaving. It separates real and alternate worlds, as it separates ascribed and achieved identities. In this context, Nguyen (2017) claims "Inside the magic circle, players take on new roles, follow different rules, and actions have different meanings. Actions inside the magic circle do not have their usual consequences for the rest of life" (p. 2).

Even though the magic circle can refer to the real-world, gamification breaks in the magic circle by reducing the barriers between fiction and reality (Salen et al., 2004). Therefore, the magic circle in gamification does not have borders and is embedded in reality and virtual reality. Eventually, embeddedness is crucial to contribute to the democratic values of equality and respect that empower dialogue between different actors (Maraffi & Sacerdoti, 2018). Hence, in the context of supporting migrants and refugees, gamification is an excellent tool to empower and build resilience. Furthermore its underlying element of fun drives encounters with distinct and distant lives and identities. By bringing diverse groups together through playing and by creating learning experiences, gamification contains a crucial potential to positively influence society. This makes gamification a valuable approach to support integration processes. Based on the research conducted by Patricio et al. (2018), proposing an analytical framework on usage of gamification in early innovation processes, their research proves gamification has significant social outcomes. Rather than focussing on hedonic outcomes, gamification is impacting players´ social behaviors. Accordingly, it helps to create team-building upon common aims. By bringing people together, gamification reduces the social barriers and facilitates interaction in between, the game-likeness leads people to collaborate to succeed (Patricio et al., 2018). Gamification is simplifying the complex processes, enlarging necessary steps and distributing the responsibilities to achieve a constructive solution. Its structure is accessible, inclusive and collaborative. It is exactly this unique structure of gamification that is directly aligning to the process of integration.

In this chapter, the authors theoretically discuss the strong conceptual interconnection between gamification and integration from a humanitarian perspective to answer the research question: In how far are the concepts of integration and gamification linked and why should humanitarian organisations apply gamification for their integration practices? The chapter will start with introducing aspects of humanitarian work, and the development of humanitarian organizations in the migration field. Based on humanitarian responses towards assisting integration, the concept of gamification will be conceptualized by concentrating on the differences between games and gamification. After defining the interrelations between humanitarian work and gamification, the concept of integration will be introduced. In this context, the concept of integration will be considered as an action and as a practice. Therefore, the chapter will touch upon three main practices of integration: building commonalities while embracing diversities, understanding and taking an action, and its process oriented nature. Each practice will be compared with the gamification approaches to underline the promising application in the area of integration activities. Based on the knowledge gained during this discussion, limitations and suggestions for further applications will be discussed. With this fruitful debate around the use of gamification for integration and social cohesion practices, the present contribution calls for more recognition of gamification as a tool for social change in humanitarian organisations. With the outlined idea to use gamification approaches for integration and social cohesion activities, it will be possible to capitalize from their potential and to use the human desire for joyful interaction for social interventions. The ongoing trend of applying gamification approaches in various contexts and the increasing recognition of gamification as change-bringing concepts already hint to the positive effects that gamification can have to create more democratic and cohesive societies.

BACKGROUND

Humanitarian organizations can have a great impact on social transformations. What they all have in common is their dedication to humanitarian principles such as *humanity, impartiality,* and *independence* (Macrea & Harmer, 2004). Based on the research by Gomez et al. (2020), the development of humanitarian organizations after the Cold War era was progressively organized and professionalized. During the 1990s, humanitarian work started to resolve the hidden reasons for struggle by involving different stakeholders into the process. This development and institutional construction is more perceived and drawn positively by numerous donors who, in return, requested responsibility, viability, and particular requirements for their staff. The financial benefits increased and more expertise specialized interventions in the field based on principles for mediation, and instruments for monitoring and evaluation evolved (Gomez et al., 2020).

As a guiding principle, humanitarian organizations are saving lives and livelihood and uphold international standards through protection activities (Studer & Fox, 2002). In addition to humanitarian interventions in crisis situations, humanitarian organizations are also involved in post-conflict, social-engagement and psycho-social wellbeing activities (Rogers et al., 2010). Dia'a Al Masry (2015), a humantarian workers from Mercy Corps, is characterizing the scope of humanitarian organizations as following: "[...] humanitarian work requires being responsible, conscious of the circumstances of other people's lives, and helping them on the basis of need, without discrimination" (para. 7). This definition comprehensively lays down why humanitarian organizations are mainly engaged in post-crises protection and emergency response. However, in the last decade, humanitarian organizations increased their activities in providing services to prevent the occurence (or recurrence) of crises.

One important political topic that is often framed as a crisis is migration, which is best described in an historic turning point in 2007 (Linde, 2009). In the 30th International Conference of the Red Cross and Red Crescent, migration was framed as the topic of the high-level agendas and was defined as one of the major upcoming global challenges that requires effective "solutions". As a response, the humanitarian dimension of *solving* migration is covered as a crucial responsibility of humanitarian organizations. The needs and vulnerabilities of migrants are considered a high priority, while forgetting the reality of many migrants who struggle for legal statuses and their rights (Linde, 2009). As a consequence of depicting migration as having various effects on society, the impact of migration has been taken into consideration more seriously and the responses towards these impacts have become wider. Therefore, the humanitarian responsibilities are shared between organizations that act on the local (civil society, initiatives), national (governmental and non-governmental organizations), and international level (international organisations). These structural actors can have a great impact on transformation processes in society - which particularly applies to integration - due to access to resources and social influence (Hassan & Leigh, 2021). For this reason, humanitarian organizations play an important role in coordinating, implementing and monitoring integration processes. As providing basic needs, safety and security conditions and emergency responses, humanitarian organizations´ are working for migrants with the goal of reducing discrimination, anti-racism and xenophobia through improving integration activities (Greene et al., 2017). However, there is a very important pitfall of humanitarian work. According to the research about the relation between dependency and humanitarian relief, Harvey and Lind (2005) outlines this relation as:

Relief risks creating a dependency mentality or syndrome, in which people expect continued assistance. This undermines initiative, at individual or community levels. Relief undermines local economies, creating a continuing need for relief assistance and trapping people into ongoing or chronic dependency on outside assistance (p. 3).

Therefore, it is important to be critical of the sustainability of these activities. Humanitarian organizations are giving assistance to people, communities or governments for a limited time and amount. The main work of humanitarian organizations is assisting the process of establishing or recovering self-sufficient structures with and for locals until they can maintain their lives without any assistance. In this regard, a crucial issue on migration revolves around the question of how to promote and sustain integration in society. This guiding question correlates with Deci and Flaste´s (1996) essential posing about self-motivation: "Instead of asking 'How can I motivate people?' we should be asking 'How can I create the conditions within which people will motivate themselves?' "(p. 10).To seek an answer to this question in the field of integration, it might be time for humanitarian organizations to utilize gamification in order to achieve a sustainable, cohesive and inclusive integration process.

The Real Potential: Games or Gamification

Games have the potential to connect people in joyful and convivial interactions and they can increase learning experiences based on their interactive and comprehensive nature. In this light, many people might already connect positive feelings with the concept of gaming and the principle of playing together. As an expected result of this effective, and natural devotion to games, more and more companies and organizations have explored the potential of games to raise profits or to increase their impact. Figueroa-Flores (2016) discusses these positive feelings within the motivational aspects of games by highlighting that the variety of motivational mechanisms exist in games. According to him, even though the possibility of losing in the game is equal to the possibility of winning, the game mechanisms exist to compel people to engage with games just for the sake of enjoyment. However, considering the sustainability of the linear relation between joy and engagement, creating such a game requires economic, social, and mental resources (Figueroa-Flores, 2016). In addition, games construct an alternative world for the sake of fun. To achieve a fun-engagement consistency, this world needs to become the main action which requires detachment and full commitment (Azawi et al., 2016). Games have a magic that holds an immersive power on increasing motivation and engagement through game design elements. In this context, Game mechanics relate to sustaining motivation and providing engagement. It is the mechanics that helps participants to approach the obstacles and overcome challenges (Sicart, 2008). Game mechanics keep the participant in the game for the hope of success. It promotes "challenges, chance, competition, cooperation, feedback, resource acquisition, rewards, transactions, turns and win states" (Németh, 2015, p.1). The use of games has the potential to also address issues of policy concerns such as ageing, education and employability (Stewart et al., 2013). The evolving research field on games is a remarkable signal that the true value of games for sustainable social transformation is more and more recognized (Spanellis & Harviainen, 2021). Nevertheless, most practical approaches on gamification focus on reinforcing organizations´ visibility through increasing the commitment and consumptions of the potential clients (Kotler et al., 2017; Shen et al., 2020). However, the inherent nature of gamification to contribute to social change remains widely unexplored in all of these contributions.

Despite the fact that games are engaging, they are considered as "Escapism" (Deleuze et al., 2019, p. 1028) interpreted as a desire to escape the real world. Its pleasure-centered leisure time activity, detached from reality, and too amusing for worldly-matters structure, is more preferred than coping with real-world problems (Deleuze et al., 2019). Gamification is a concept that emerges from this segregation between an alternative world and the real-world. It carries game-design elements into non-game contexts (Deterding et al., 2011). Similar to games, gamification still needs a structure defined by definite rules and regulations, certain challenges to pursue engagement and a goal to keep players motivated (Patrício et al., 2018). Separately, gamification is settled in reality, it is built-up as a process. Its main goal is to change non-game contexts. Obviously, gamification is being implemented to solve, to approach or to act towards a certain desired and planned goal. While games are played consciously and voluntarily to have fun, where players are accepting to step into a magic circle (Huizinga, 1955). Gamification is embedded into a specific context in order to reinforce a motivation for a while, until the motivation dissolves into behavior. Ceker and Ozdamli (2017) draw the interrelation between these concepts as "[…]

in gamification, game is only a tool, an element to accomplish specific targets in any area, which usually is not game oriented" (p. 223). Rather than centralizing the game and the fun that emerges, gamification has a substantial goal outside the game (Patrício et al. 2018). This goal outside the game is defined as "performing desired behaviors", "overcoming difficulties" or "developing possible solutions" (Patrício et al., 2018, p. 2). Therefore, it is important to highlight this distinction between games and gamification. Lending from Patricio et al. (2018): "In fact, the benefits of gamification go beyond the hedonic elements as they also include utilitarian and social benefits." (p. 4) Though, through utilizing the value of hedonic instincts and the appeal of fun, gamification can harness a great potential of social transformation. It is this promising dynamic that makes gamification an unique area of study with the full potential to use the intrinsic human desires for playing for the social benefit of society. Consequently, gamification is positively satisfying certain inherent needs such as immersion, autonomy, achievements and social interactions by game mechanics and game elements (Xi & Hamari, 2019). Gamification makes it possible to use the aspect of triggering motivation, to create social impact and worthwhile learning outcomes. This makes the gamification approach a perfect tool for social change - understood as a transformation of behaviour, social institutions, and social structures - especially in relation to contested and controversial areas of society such as migration and integration (Tunc & Jammermann, 2021).

THE SYNERGIES BETWEEN INTEGRATION AND GAMIFICATION

By discussing certain aspects of integration theory and their connection to the principles of gamification, it will be possible to demonstrate how gamification is perfectly equipped to support integration efforts in society. Games are not completely new in the work of humanitarian organizations and there are various examples how games can be used to improve field interventions (Guardiola, 2019). For example, organizations such as *Save the Children* or *UNESCO* have already used games in their interventions to improve their impact and to make actions more effective and comprehensive (Hassan & Leigh, 2021; Papathanasiou-Zuhrt et al., 2017). Nevertheless, especially in digital projects, the use of games remains merely a tool for self-reflection and/or awareness rising, and game-based approaches rarely go beyond the layer of understanding a certain issue (Mäyrä, 2007). However, serving humans and acknowledging their needs and interests should also encompass natural desires for joyful learning and motivational mediation. In that respect, many humanitarian organizations are not harnessing the potential of games and have not fully utilized gamification to create valuable spaces of social interaction in which meaningful encounters and exchanges can take place. These specific exchanges can turn into concrete outcomes such as successful integration activities and increased social cohesion. Hence, extending existing gamification approaches can lead to a valuable change in integration practices.

To begin with the word *integration*, it has usually stood upon a thin line between being the problem and being the solution. The vicious circle of needing integration for integration. An endless loop of problematizing integration and trying to solve this ´problem´ with the problem itself. To put it simpler, the absence of integration is depicted as the core of migration related conflicts, while public discourses are constructed to underpin the lack of integration and the need for integration (Agirdag et al., 2016). Mainly, this discourse is reinforcing a wrong sense of *togetherness*. During the integration process, certain motivations are apparently not being covered (which will be discussed below) and the 'togetherness' turns into *they* are not integrated (Agirdag et al., 2016). Namely, during this strict differentiation between us versus them, *the other* is becoming the problem. As an outcome, migrants are actively excluded and become framed as *the other* who was created in the first place without an option to become part of society. After all, the solution creates the problem again. This contradictory debate is not related to the supposedly lack of integration. It is related to how integration has been practiced. The following section will further elaborate on this paradigm based on three essential conceptual pinpoints that define a sustainable, inclusive, and comprehensive practice of integration: integration is build-upon commonalities while embracing differences, integration is an action of understanding and challenging, integration is a two-way process and always in transformation. In this context, gamification can be understood as a supporting and comprehending approach that aligns to this definition.

Integration is Built Upon Commonalities While Embracing Diversities

The process of including newcomers through reciprocal relations and the reflection of interactions in a social system can be defined as *social integration* (Lockwood, 1964). According to Heckmann (2005) "Social integration refers to the conscious and motivated interaction and cooperation of individual actors and groups." (p. 9) In comparison to assimilation, which is based on proximity of acceptance and openness of host communities towards migrants, social integration is based on reciprocity of interaction and cooperation. Whereas, in order to interact, certain commonness is needed. As Esser (2010) claims "Interaction is a case of social action characterized by mutual orientations of actors and the formation of relations and networks" (p. 272). This implies that integration is a dynamic process, focusing on actions between actors towards a common goal.

Integration defined as the relation between two different parts evolves into equal interactions between individuals. Therefore, practices such as a coming together space where diverse people can have meaningful exchanges gain prominence. As OHCHR (n.d.) promotes in its teaching material Stand Up 4 Migrants: "[…] we stopped and listened to one other, we realized we had much more in common than what divided us" (01:09). Gamification can provide this "stopping and listening" moment through providing a common ground with equal rules and regulations that are the same for everyone. This game element can be useful to start from a common ground. In this way, gamification approaches are prepared for equal exchange between diverse participants and encourage social interaction between actors that might not meet otherwise. Using gamification for integration processes is not only reducing the fear from differences, but also preventing a one-dimensional belonging into a certain group (Jones & Krzyzanowski, 2008). In other words, gamification constructs a space of commonness where distant groups can interact and develop understanding for each other. As Patricio et al. (2019) outlines:

Gamification can motivate people to change their behaviors and achieve the desired states when it taps into key motivational drivers of human behavior through a balanced mix of reinforcements that can be both extrinsic (i.e. prizes, money, status or fame, points and badges, trophies, fear of failure or punishment, penalties and even progress bars) and intrinsic (i.e. sense of fun and enjoyment, belonging to a group, mastery, purpose in the work carried out, learning from an activity, personal achievement or more responsibility, autonomy and power) (p. 3).

In the same way, this beginning will be defined with equal rules, approached with different positionalities for a common goal. Despite the previous interactions based on negative discourses; this new narrative in gamification, which is sharing the circumstances and consequences all together, can open a way for more positive interactions under this commonness. Through gamification approaches, the recognition of the possibility (or discovery) of another narration is possible. "By shifting from the negative (what we do not want) to the positive (the world we want to create) we are better positioned to motivate and inspire others to take action" (OHCHR, n.d.). Gamification can create inspiration through motivating all players to be part of constructing new equal starting points (Marin et al., 2021).

Besides applying common rules, gamification has a pre-defined agenda to take actions towards a common goal. In other words, gamification can unite diverse groups on the same ground, not only based on structured and equal rules of the game, but also on the same ground of being humans. This will lead to a level beyond being a migrant, refugee, threat, crises, problem, victim but towards being humans who can be afraid, hesitate, fail, struggle etc.. Through this connection, humans can work together to shift negative connotations into positive affirmations. Griffin (2007) argues that the adjustments in the vocabularies and their meanings around migration is a result of political and economic agendas of certain macro level structures. Mainly, the discourse in policies, the political attitude and approaches towards migration can benefit some ideologies, political or economic interests (Griffin, 2007). Based on this, this constructed barrier in front of coming together needs to be reduced. Apparently, gamification has a power to shift this narration of division and distinction into realization of commonness. Through playing under common rules and for a common goal.

Lastly, the most critical point of integration is defining two parts: the one who is integrating and the one to integrate into an entity. In brief, to play the integration game you need two or more unequal players of society to start, with the goal of equality. Heckmann (2005) clarifies the parts as:

For the migrants, integration refers to a process of learning a new culture, an acquisition of rights, access to positions and statuses, a building of personal relations to members of the receiving society and a formation of feelings of belonging and identification towards [that] society. Integration is an interactive process between migrants and the receiving society, in which, however, the receiving society has much more power and prestige (p.18).

Accordingly, the integration process should not be structured as migrants learning the dominant culture and the institutions make it easier and quicker for them. In other words, integration should not be limited to institutional support such as providing language courses or putting extra cultural courses for migrants. Concretely, integration needs to be understood as a mutual learning process, and not solely relying on the responsibility of migrants (Penninx & Garcés-Mascareñas, 2016). On the contrary, to transform integration as an equal process, both sides of the integration paradigm should support each other to create a space to exchange. In this context, integration needs to be understood as a two-way process that establishes cooperation and interaction between these different parts of society, to recognize and become recognized by the others (Penninx & Garcés-Mascareñas, 2016).

Obviously, games can be used in various environments for diverse actors and proved to be very efficient for supporting minority groups (Stewart et al., 2013), however, the major challenge of using games for the integration process lies in the limits of games. The (social) interaction component that characterizes integration is largely missing in conventional games. Following the common approach of integration activities, they are mainly based on a one-sided narration of educating migrants about society. As such, education concepts on integration reach their limits by overlooking the key component of integration and inclusion processes: *social interaction*. When humanitarian organizations work for migrants and contribute to integration activities, they need to ensure that social interactions are actually taking place between migrants and the host society. Consequently, it is crucial to further discuss the limited concept and narration of integration as it holds manifold implications for the various players and for the understanding of who is playing the game. When practicing integration activities, humanitarian organizations do not only serve these needs and interests of migrants, but they also ensure that diversity is enshrined in valuable interactions and encounters between migrants and the host society. In this way, the very logic of using gamification approaches for integration activities should be recognized and put into practice more effectively. In this regard, gamification uses game design elements by virtue of changing behaviors. Its purpose is more than educating or simulating, it is more related with motivations, behaviors, engagements rather than knowledge building (Patricio et al., 2018). That is why, gamification is embedded in life. It is like a public space where people are coming and leaving. It does not differentiate or select its participants, participants can (sometimes) select to be involved or not. It is accessible, and inclusive for any volunteer participant. This might lead to a wider perspective and incorporation with real-life while enhancing more outcomes, such as strengthening relations and belongings (Patricio et al., 2018). Accordingly, as mentioned in the previous section, gamification has the power to empower people and give back the agency in a world characterized by inequality. Moreover, through creating commonness, it invites the host society to realize their part in the integration process through involving them directly or indirectly. Discovering interest in a distant subject through gamification can increase learning outcomes of learners and can, in turn, encourage marginalized groups in their learning effort (Marin et al., 2021). Consequently, new sets of relations are being constructed. With the use of game elements and mechanics, participants are engaged in interaction. However, different from games, gamification is applied in non-game contexts. This makes everyone exposed to gamification as persons rather than players. The participants are being part of the experience with their differences, authentic selves and positionalities. With this provocative and activist structure, gamification proves that it can also indirectly combat xenophobic, discriminatory, and segregating discourses in a peaceful and substantial way by creating a new picture between diverse actors. Gamification provides a co-existing experience, not despite differences but with differences.

Integration is an Action of Understanding and Challenging

Humanitarian organizations are uniting theory and practice of integration, mainly through knowledge management, education and awareness raising activities. These components are significant steps towards a trustful dialogue between various actors and institutions as stakeholders. Besides playing a crucial role in creating encounters between partners, beneficiaries, and civil society, one pivotal pillar of the work of humanitarian organizations represents awareness raising for certain topics and the training of relevant actors. In this context, they have a special status and owe certain responsibilities and opportunities to lead important processes and to inspire new angles of intervention to serve societies. This makes large organizations specifically relevant for adapting innovative approaches to better produce and disseminate knowledge.

Education has a crucial role in sensitizing learners and to make them aware of different traditions and cultures (UNICEF, 2020). Education is a powerful tool for migrants to be included in social life. Not only based on certification of skills or knowledge development, but also including informal learning through *encounters*. Socializing, meeting with local people and building common experiences are all important indicators of integration, which makes it more effective and sustainable for society. The *power of contact* between host society and migrants is an essential mechanism to increase social cohesion and to build more inclusive societies (IOM, 2021). Creating purposeful encounters and engaging a great portion of the local population are key for successful integration activities. For example, so-called ´social mixing´ activities correlate with this desire and demonstrate the power of contact, in which games can play a major role for the interaction between migrants and local communities under the principle of equality and social connections (IOM, 2021). Humanitarian organizations have a great potential to provide spaces of meaningful interaction. However, making these crucial encounters of social interaction meaningful for host society and migrants remains a major challenge for many integration activities.

As Clark Abt (1987) explains: "The autonomy of human wills and the diversity of human motives result in game-like forms in all human interactions, and in this sense all human history can be regarded as game-like in nature" (p. 7). Therefore, to benefit from the game-like nature of human interaction, *serious games* and *simulations* are significant for providing a space to practice ´real-life´ in a ´safe-to-fail´ environment. Simulations, serious games, and role plays have an important effect on decreasing the comfort zone through inviting participants into a ´magic circle´ (Huizinga, 1955). By including roles that may be contradicting participants´ own identity and actions, forcing them to act differently in order to win the game, can have a great impact. Encountering a real-life problem through a fictional play enables simulated decision-making processes and helps solving serious socio-historical issues which can be very important to increase democratic values in society. Similarly, it can be a worthwhile learning effect to recognize the diversity of opinions and actors, putting oneself into somebody else's position, preparing strategies according to *a simulated identity*. In contrast, these *simulated identities* belong to the magic circle, which causes real-life identities to slip away. The cultural-religious-economic backgrounds are losing their meanings as persons are dissolving under the identity of the player´s pre-defined role. However, the integration concept is not a game in itself, and it carries a purpose to change the society into an inclusive, equal and cohesive space for everyone. In society, a variety of personalities, backgrounds, beliefs, etc exist. The complexity and multiplicity of integration needs to be experienced with intersectional identities, different responses, and genuine feelings. Therefore, it is important to keep the identities, positionalities and the context needed to exist. That is why, gamification is a better approach to integration rather than simulations or serious games. In this context, gamification might represent a valuable bridge between theory and practice within knowledge management context. According to the findings of Patricia et al.´s (2018) research:

Gamification approaches play an effective role in managing the knowledge exchange process across different phases. It supports the identification of knowledge gaps, new actors with whom to interact and collaborate, as well as information flow between key innovation stakeholders. The fact that participants dive into different concepts without knowing the final results in advance removes relevant knowledge yet it discloses relevance in irrelevant knowledge [...] Besides fostering knowledge transfer, gamification supports new ways of thinking and learning while playing (p. 9).

Furthermore, according to Mäyrä (2007), "the role of ludic challenge is central, and the model is at its strongest in describing player experiences that occur among games that require time, dedication and skill to master" (p. 810). Through gamification this ludic engagement, will also lead to flexibility and fluidity of ideas in real life. Gamification is creating a learning experience where the participants are becoming students who would like to improve their skills and form strategies constantly to overcome challenges. Al-Azawi et al. (2016) characterizes gamification´s effects on pupils in schools. Gamification is not only changing the end-behavior, during the process as a side-effect, it also creates new perspectives. As the experience is fun, students are becoming more courageous to choose other pathways as they are also less concerned about being wrong (Al-Azawi et al., 2016). For this reason, despite the fact that they are rigid roles and clusters that are socially constructed, putting oneself into the position of another person or situation becomes easier through the motivation of winning (Werbach & Hunter, 2015).

By improving services and increasing their impact in the field of integration, humanitarian organizations can profit from gamification approaches to combine theory and practice. Therefore, being provident for this side of the process is crucial. Despite the use of passive voice, gamification is addressing the actors directly as the agents of the actions during the process. It is practicing a holistic and comprehensive analysis of the complexity of the situation by simplifying it through game elements and urges participants to respond. According to Blackmore (2006), the public discourse has been reproduced through adults many times, in media or in family etc.. Consequently, starting from childhood, people are occupied by prejudices, biased information, and stereotypes. As a consequence, there is an action needed to become aware of one's own bias and then proceed on working on them through exchanges. Gamification is making these exchanges meaningful by using game mechanics as a tool to shift participants from passive thinkers and pull them to input themselves into the situation. Through mechanics, the nouns become verbs, passive encounters turn into actions (Németh, 2015). This implies integration is a dynamic process, focusing on actions. The correlation of terms in the application of the concepts can reduce the distance between people through exposing many diverse individuals in this exchange and interaction. Penninx and Garcés-Mascareñas (2016) explain the integration process as establishing cooperation and interaction in between to recognize and become recognized by the others. It even starts with the migrant taking the responsibility and starting to use the institutions, accessing the public spaces and interacting, which will gradually change relations in the community. The host society will certainly react to this interaction, creating valuable encounters. Therefore, a social transformation will be inevitable (Penninx & Garcés-Mascareñas, 2016). Gamification is based on reciprocity of interactions either for cooperation or competition. In the context of integration, this reciprocity can start with understanding. According to Singleton (2015), understanding means listening with one's heart, thinking with one's head, and acting with one's hands. Therefore, being provident for this side of the process is crucial. Moreover, it is essential to address the actors directly as the agents of the actions during the process. Correspondingly, Patricio et. al (2018) outlines, " [...] the open and collaborative environment provided by gamification also allows for greater flexibility on the part of participants to think, listen, and share ideas" (p. 11). Throughout the meaningful exchanges fed by actions and reactions, gamification has potential to transform social conflicts into social bonds. As Freire (1972) says, "Only human beings are praxis—the praxis which, as the reflection and action which truly transform reality, is the source of knowledge and creation. Animal activity, which occurs without a praxis, is not creative; peoples transforming activity is" (p. 101).

Integration is a Two-Way Process, Always in Transformation

As society is a heterogeneous group of diverse people with various motivations and interests, thus, inequalities can also be very diverse. It is essential to acknowledge that integration is a shifting and shrinking space for all the members and groups involved in the process. For those reasons, there is not a linear integration process for everyone. The integration process depends on the unit of analysis. It depends on the relations between actors, who they are, and where and when encounters occur. Considering integration as a one-way process is a misleading conception. Migration itself is not a linear process from the country A to B and might take many turns. Rather than a desirable end to achieve, integration is continuous. Penninx and Garcés-Mascareñas (2016) claim "Integration is the process of becoming an accepted part of society" (p. 14). It is essential to distance from classical concepts of static integration, in which the host country is the dominant part that sets the rules of inclusion and accepts certain efforts while disregarding others (King & Lulle, 2016). Integration only works by recognizing the others by equally engaging all parts of society. For these reasons, addressing the determinants of xenophobic attitudes in societies is necessary to provide sustainable, and inclusive solutions in integration activities and it is only possible through tailored responses (King & Lulle, 2016).

It would be wrong to assume that gamification approaches and, conversely, integration processes are conflict free spaces. In fact, the premise of integration itself might be based on a very conflictual relation as "in a modern globalized and multicultural world, it is difficult and problematic to cultivate a similarity of mind. It might actually be in direct conflict with the idea to ensure non-discrimination, tolerance [and] respect for diversity" (Larsen, 2014, p. 4). Migrants are heterogeneous actors and engage with diverse members of society, which makes conflicts inevitable. However, gamification allows to resolve these conflicts in a safe environment that is characterized by fun, engagement and a democratic process (Lerner, 2011). In this way, gamification can reduce conflict potential in society revolving around migration by projecting these conflicts in a game-like democratic space that can be shaped by different needs, interests, and perceptions without escalating the boundaries and norms of society. It can provide worthwhile solutions to this diversity of integration needs and responses by providing versatile nature in its development. Al-Azawi et al. (2016) describes gamification as the entire process, rather than a task or a segment: "Gamification turns the entire learning process into a game. It takes game mechanics and gameplay elements and applies them to existing learning courses and content in order to better motivate and engage learners" (p.134). Since it is a continuous and intimate process, it is tailored according to different needs and interests. Furthermore, gamification is participant centered. As the situation of the participants changes, so can the gamification approach. It is possible to jointly adapt new rules and, if necessary, change the game mechanics to create more suitable approaches. This is an important aspect in which gamification presents a *democratic space* where ideas are shared and debated to find a way to achieve something together.

As much as integration can be a powerful and empowering outcome, the process itself takes time. Social transformation (or adaptation) needs time and so does creating meaningful encounters. Despite having supporting regulations and effective policies in place; there will be obstacles along the way. To put it simply, as much as some soceites are chararcterised by welcoming strucutres, prejudices and discrimination remain. According to Heckmann (2005) "This is where the receiving society has to learn in the mutual process of integration." (p. 15) Following that integration is also a learning process for every member, Becker (2021) differentiates gamification in learning processes focussing on "how things are taught and administered rather than what is taught" (p. 2). With this kind of innovative and creative approach towards knowledge building and sharing, not only the responsibility of teaching, but also the responsibility of learning is becoming a shared project. Therefore, engagement and participation are essential in this learning process. Patricio et al. (2018) explains this process in gamification as "the transfer of more explicit knowledge to others, in a more collaborative and open environment, overcomes the limitations of tacit knowledge mechanisms, and conflict is managed with consensus building that fundamentally encourages interaction and reduces the social distance between participants.'' (p. 9) As such, gamification resembles a vivid space for conflict creation, but also a mutual learning space that motivates participants to engage with these conflicts in a cohesive way.

SOLUTIONS AND RECOMMENDATIONS

Working in the humanitarian sector, the authors have developed a workshop concept to seek the possibilities of utilizing the synergies between gamification and integration. From 2016 to 2020, this workshop concept "Gamification for Social Change" has been facilitated in six different countries with participants from more than 20 countries. Its goal is to provide a space to investigate the possibilities of gamification as a solution to approach controversial topics. The target participants have been education practitioners, humanitarian workers, social workers, and youth workers mainly engaged with migrants and refugees. The workshop structure is using non-formal learning methods to provide a peer to peer learning space. After introducing basic concepts around migration and gamification, possibilities, advantageous and disadvantageous, have been discussed. As a last step, participants have selected a theme that they see as a problem trying to apply game elements around it.

In order to apply gamification approaches to integration practices, humanitarian organizations need to be alerted to the needs and risks of participants. As gamification needs engagement, humanitarian organizations should know the field well and consider the potential conflicts arising to design game elements accordingly. Based on the experiences from this workshop, there can be three recommendations formulated:

First of all, the non-game context needs to be analyzed in the sense of its readiness. For example, some non-game contexts in the humanitarian field may not be proper to apply to game elements. If there are emergency responses, severe protection cases, or apparent violence between groups, it is problematic to expose people into a fun process. Again, similar to the integration interventions, gamification can only be applicable after some needs are covered and some risks are reduced in the humanitarian field.

Secondly, as targeting a controversial topic (e.g. migration), cross-disciplinary approaches are essential. Gamification approaches should be more deeper than applying game design elements. Since migration is politically highly charged and very sensitive as it is always connected to personal stories, the encounters and interactions can lead to conflicts. As discussed before, the magic circle is less rigid than games which can lead to more personalized, triggering discussions. Therefore, getting support from specialized experts such as sociologists, psychologists, or social workers can offer a safer environment. Moreover, in the design process, migrants themselves or members of different groups in host societies can contribute to the process.

Thirdly, cross-sectoral co-operations are valuable. Despite humanitarian organizations having the best knowledge and practice in the field, they may not be aware of innovative and creative methods such as gamification. That is why it is important to disseminate knowledge, work together for co-creative processes. Sectors like marketing, communications, and computer sciences have an immense gamification application that can be adapted to the humanitarian field. Eventually, communities of practices, research projects and network organizations have a crucial impact on sharing, developing and multiplying knowledge and practice.

CONCLUSION

Gamification is inviting, proactive and transformative. It is these characteristics that integration activities need to include to be effective and sustainable. The connections between the concepts of gamification and integration should encourage humanitarian organisations to adapt gamification approaches in their integration activities. The idea of using gamification as a central approach to increase self-reliant integration processes is an untapped potential especially for humanitarian organisations. In this context, the links between the principles of gamification and the requirements of successful integration activities have been debated in this work, underlining the powerful link for creating motivation to increase social cohesion. Gamification has the capacity to safely and confidently approach a controversial topic such as migration through integration practices. Accordingly, approachability can result in a pleasing process of social interaction and exchange which will eventually improve equality and democracy in societies.

Humanitarian organisations can play a creditable part for social change processes by placing the inherent human desire for joyful and convivial interaction at the core of their operation. With the outlined correlations between integration and gamification approaches, a democratic space of real togetherness can be created contributing to more understanding and unity in diverse societies. Hence, both sides are supporting each other to co-create a democratic space in which social cohesion prevails. When engaging diverse parts of society in integration activities, it might be possible to create encounters that transforms stereotypes, prejudices and discrimination drastically into a diversity appreciating all parts of society. By doing so, a democratic space for social interaction can be created in which conflicts can be resolved and experiences exchanged. Finally, when using gamification for social change, it is possible to not only stress the idea that gamification can make a motivational difference, but also that this difference can lead to a valuable transformation; valuable for receiving societies and migrants alike, but also for the common understanding that we are all united in the passion for playing.

REFERENCES

Abt, C. C. (1987). *Serious games*. University Press of America.

Agirdag, O., Merry, M. S., & Van Houtte, M. (2016). Teachers' understanding of multicultural education and the correlates of multicultural content integration in Flanders. *Education and Urban Society*, *48*(6), 556–582. doi:10.1177/0013124514536610

Al-Azawi, R., Al-Faliti, F., & Al-Blushi, M. (2016). Educational gamification vs. game based learning: Comparative study. *International Journal of Innovation, Management and Technology*, *7*(4), 132–136. doi:10.18178/ijimt.2016.7.4.659

Becker, K. (2021). What's the difference between gamification, serious games, educational games, and game-based learning. *Academia Letters*. Advance online publication. doi:10.20935/AL209

Blackmore, J. (2006). Deconstructing diversity discourses in the field of educational management and leadership. *Educational Management Administration & Leadership*, *34*(2), 181–199. doi:10.1177/1741143206062492

Çeker, E., & Özdamla, F. (2017). What " Gamification" Is and What It's Not. *European Journal of Contemporary Education*, *6*(2), 221–228.

Deci, E. L., & Flaste, R. (1996). *Why we do what we do: Understanding self-motivation*. Penguin books.

Deleuze, J., Maurage, P., Schimmenti, A., Nuyens, F., Melzer, A., & Billieux, J. (2019). Escaping reality through video games is linked to an implicit preference for virtual over real-life stimuli. *Journal of Affective Disorders*, *245*, 1024–1031. doi:10.1016/j.jad.2018.11.078 PMID:30699844

Deterding, S., Dixon, D., Khaled, R., & Nacke, L. (2011). From game design elements to gamefulness: defining "gamification". *Proceedings of the 15th international academic MindTrek conference: Envisioning future media environments*, 9-15. 10.1145/2181037.2181040

Esser, H. (2010). Assimilation, ethnic stratification, or selective acculturation? Recent theories of the integration of immigrants and the model of intergenerational integration. *Sociologica*, *4*(1), 1–29.

Figueroa-Flores, J. F. (2016). Gamification and game-based learning: Two strategies for the 21st century learner. *WORLD (Oakland, Calif.)*, *3*(2), 507. Advance online publication. doi:10.22158/wjer.v3n2p507

Freire, P. (1972). *Pedagogy of the Oppressed* (M. B. Ramos, Trans.). Herder.

Greene, M. C., Jordans, M. J., Kohrt, B. A., Ventevogel, P., Kirmayer, L. J., Hassan, G., & Tol, W. A. (2017). Addressing culture and context in humanitarian response: Preparing desk reviews to inform mental health and psychosocial support. *Conflict and Health*, *11*(1), 1–10. doi:10.118613031-017-0123-z PMID:29163666

Griffin, G. (2007). *The uses of discourse analysis in the study of gender and migration. Research Paper.* The University of York.

Guardiola, E. (2019). Game and Humanitarian: From Awareness to Field Intervention. *Proceedings of the Game On Conference.*

Hassan, L., & Leigh, E. (2021). Do you have a moment to increase the world awesome? Game-based engagement with social change. In A. Spanelli & J. T. Harviainen (Eds.), *Transforming Society and Organizations through Gamification: From the Sustainable Development Goals to Inclusive Workplaces* (pp. 49–65). Palgrave Macmillan. doi:10.1007/978-3-030-68207-1_4

Heckmann, F. (2005). *Integration and integration policies.* IMISCOE Network Feasibility Study.

Huizinga, J. (1955). *Homo Ludens–A Study of the Play-Element in Culture.* Beacon Press.

International Organization for Migration (IOM). (2021). *The Power of Contact: Designing, Facilitating and Evaluating Social Mixing Activities to Strengthen Migrant Integration and Social Cohesion Between Migrants and Local Communities - A Review of Lessons Learned.* Retrieved from: https://eea.iom.int/publications/power-contact-designing-facilitating-and-evaluating-social-mixing-activities-strengthen

Jones, P. R., & Krzyzanowski, M. (2008). Identity, Belonging and Migration: Beyond Describing 'Others. In G. Delanty, R. Wodak, & P. R. Jones (Eds.), *Identity, Belonging, Migration* (pp. 38–53). Liverpool University Press. doi:10.5949/liverpool/9781846311185.003.0003

King, R., & Lulle, A. (2016). *Research on migration facing realities and maximising opportunities: a policy review.* European Commission.

Larsen, C. A. (2014). *Social cohesion: Definition, measurement and developments.* Working Paper. Faculty of Social Science. Aalborg University.

Lerner, J. (2012). *Making democracy fun? Games as a Tool for Democratic Participation.* New School University.

Lockwood, D. (1964). Social integration and system integration. *Explorations in Social Change, 244*, 53-57.

Macrae, J., & Harmer, A. (2004). *Good humanitarian donorship and the European Union: Issues and options*. Overseas Development Institute.

Maraffi, S., & Sacerdoti, F. M. (2018). Innovative Digital Games to Improve Science Education through Storytelling, Mystery and Myth. *Proceedings of the British DiGRA 14 Conference.*

Marin, S., Lee, V., & Landers, N. (2021). Gamified Active Learning and Its Potential for Social Change. In A. Spanellis & J. T. Harviainen (Eds.), *Transforming Society and Organizations through Gamification: From the Sustainable Development Goals to Inclusive Workplaces* (pp. 205–224). Plagrave Macmillian. doi:10.1007/978-3-030-68207-1_11

Mäyrä, F. (2007). The Contextual Game Experience: On the Socio-Cultural Contexts for Meaning in Digital Play. In *Proceedings of the 2007 DiGRA International Conference: Situated Play*. University of Tokyo.

Mercy Corps. (2015, August 18). *We asked our staff: What does being a humanitarian mean to you?* Retrieved from: https://www.mercycorps.org/blog/what-does-being-humanitarian-mean

Németh, T. (2015). *English Knight: Gamifying the EFL Classroom* [Unpublished master's thesis]. Pázmány Péter Katolikus Egyetem Bölcsészet- és Társadalomtudományi Kar, Piliscsaba, Hungary. Retrieved from: https://ludus.hu/gamification/

Nguyen, C. T. (2017). Philosophy of games. *Philosophy Compass, 12*(8), e12426. doi:10.1111/phc3.12426

Papathanasiou-Zuhrt, D., Weiss-Ibanez, D. F., & Di Russo, A. (2017). The gamification of heritage in the UNESCO enlisted the medieval town of Rhodes. In *Proceedings of GamiFIN Conference* (pp. 60-70). Academic Press.

Patrício, R., Moreira, A. C., & Zurlo, F. (2018). Gamification Approaches to the Early Stage of Innovation. *Creativity and Innovation Management, 27*(4), 499–511. doi:10.1111/caim.12284

Penninx, R., & Garcés-Mascareñas, B. (2016). The Concept of Integration as an Analytical Tool and as a Policy Concept. In R. Penninx & B. Garcés-Mascareñas (Eds.), *Integration Processes and Policies in Europe: Contexts, Levels and Actors* (pp. 11–29). Springer Open. doi:10.1007/978-3-319-21674-4_2

Rogers, M., Chassy, A., & Bamat, T. (2010). *Integrating Peacebuilding into Humanitarian and Development Programming*. Catholic Relief Services.

Salen, K., Tekinbaş, K. S., & Zimmerman, E. (2004). *Rules of play: Game design fundamentals*. MIT Press.

Sicart, M. (2008). Defining game mechanics. *Game Studies, 8*(2), 1–14.

Singleton, J. (2015). Head, heart and hands model for transformative learning: Place as context for changing sustainability values. *Journal of Sustainability Education, 9*(3), 171–187.

Spanellis, A., & Harviainen, J. T. (Eds.). (2021). *Transforming Society and Organizations through Gamification: From the Sustainable Development Goals to Inclusive Workplaces*. Plagrave Macmillian., doi:10.1007/978-3-030-68207-1

Stewart, J., Bleumers, L., Van Looy, J., Mariën, I., All, A., Schurmans, D., & Misuraca, G. (2013). *The potential of digital games for empowerment and social inclusion of groups at risk of social and economic exclusion: evidence and opportunity for policy*. Joint Research Centre, European Commission.

Studer, M., & Fox, O. (2002). The Role of Humanitarian and Development Organisations in Relation to the Security Sector in Transition Situations. In A. H. Ebnöther & P. H. Fluri (Eds.), *After Intervention: Public Security Management in Post-Conflict Societies - From Intervention to Sustainable Local Ownership* (pp. 357–375). National Defense Academy.

The Office of the High Commissioner for Human Rights (OHCHR). (n.d.). *Migration*. Retrieved from: https://www.standup4humanrights.org/migration/en/toolbox.html

Thibault, M., & Hamari, J. (2021). Seven points to reappropriate gamification. In A. Spanelli & J. T. Harviainen (Eds.), *Transforming Society and Organizations through Gamification: From the Sustainable Development Goals to Inclusive Workplaces* (pp. 11–28). Palgrave Macmillan. doi:10.1007/978-3-030-68207-1_2

Tunc, B. E., & Jammermann, M. (2021). Games and Gamification as a tool for Social Change. *Ludogogy Online Magazine*. Retrieved from: https://www.ludogogy.co.uk/article/games-and-gamification-as-a-tool-for-social-change

United Nations Children's Fund (UNICEF). (2020). *Education Solutions for Migrant and Displaced Children And Their Host Communities*. Working Paper. Retrieved from: https://www.unicef.org/documents/education-solutions-migrant-and-displaced-children-and-their-host-communities

Werbach, K., & Hunter, D. (2015). *The gamification toolkit: dynamics, mechanics, and components for the win*. Wharton School Press.

Xi, N., & Hamari, J. (2019). Does gamification satisfy needs? A study on the relationship between gamification features and intrinsic need satisfaction. *International Journal of Information Management*, *46*, 210–221. doi:10.1016/j.ijinfomgt.2018.12.002

KEY TERMS AND DEFINITIONS

Democracy: A decision-making process that provides space to hear minorities' voices despite the majority´s will.

Diversity: Recognizing and accepting different social categories and together co-existing with differences.

Equality: A mutual agreement that every individual embraces the same natural value as human beings and holds the same rights being able to benefit from the same opportunities.

Humanitarian Work: An action to facilitate equity for humans to be treated with dignity.

Migration: The movement of people over borders either willingly or compulsory.

Social Change: Transformative action through interactions in order to challenge the existing status-quo.

Social Cohesion: Strength of togetherness including the sense of belonging and trust as well as reciprocity between members of the society.

Chapter 19
The Dehumanising Consequences of Gamification:
Recognising Coercion and Exploitation in Gamified Systems

Sean Fitzpatrick
Griffith University, Australia

Timothy Marsh
Griffith University, Australia

ABSTRACT

While gamification represents one of the largest technology trends of the last decade, only a limited selection of literature exists that explores the negative outcomes of contemporary gamified services, applications, and systems. This chapter explores the consequences of gamified systems and services, investigating contemporary implementations of gamification and acknowledging the ethical concerns raised by researchers towards contemporary gamified services. This chapter further explores these ethical concerns through a critical instance case study of China's Social Credit System and arrives at informed observations on the potential for gamified cycles of reward and punishment to encourage unethical activity within organisations as well as legitimise ideological objectives that violate fundamental human rights. Recommendations are then made for researchers to explore this potential further, while recognising how gamification may justify the authority and practices of organisations, particularly those engaged in unethical and dehumanising behaviour.

INTRODUCTION

In recent years, attention to gamification has risen dramatically among both scholars and practitioners (Huotari & Hamari, 2017), and the principles of game design have been successfully applied to fields as diverse as business, crowd-sourcing, healthcare, and education (Legaki et al., 2020). However, while gamification represents one of the largest technology trends of the last decade (Xi & Hamari, 2020), there

DOI: 10.4018/978-1-7998-9223-6.ch019

exists only a limited selection of literature that explores the negative contemporary consequences of applying game principles to non-game contexts. While foundational, comprehensive texts on game design ethics (Sicart, 2009, 2013), as well as research which more specifically explores the negative consequences of gamification (Hyrynsalmi et al., 2017; Kim & Werbach, 2016), offer informative perspectives on the potential effects of gamification, these perspectives also may not accurately reflect the current trends and societal consequences that have been facilitated by the meteoric rise of gamification. This chapter will therefore explore the possible detrimental, coercive – and potentially, unethical – circumstances that have arisen out of the contemporary acceptance of gamification among organisations, sectors, and societies. This chapter will achieve this by first exploring cautionary recommendations in gamification, with an aim toward understanding the potential disadvantages of gamified systems. The disadvantages and effects reflected within contemporary gamified services will then be methodly examined, with a particular focus towards recognising any detrimental human consequences that have gone unreported. Lastly, the authors will make evidence-based recommendations towards guidelines and principles that may inform the ethical and responsible development of gamification moving forward. This chapter aims to facilitate a deeper understanding of the unethical potential of contemporary gamified systems, while also challenging the presumption that gamification effectively satisfies the intrinsic, essential needs of individuals (Xi & Hamari, 2019). This chapter will build on the observations and concerns of other researchers, acknowledging that, rather than fulfilling an individual's need for mastery, self-expression and connectivity (Thibault & Hamari, 2021; Tobon et al., 2020), gamification may instead be used to legitimise unethical actions that *exploit* these needs.

BACKGROUND

Positive Potential of Gamification

Much has been written on the positive effects of gamification, particularly in regards to private industry. The principles of gamification – defined in this context as "the use of game design elements in non-game contexts" (Deterding, Dixon, et al., 2011) – may be employed strategically to "engage customers, stimulate employee performance, encourage health and wellness activity, motivate students, [or] achieve public policy objectives" (Kim & Werbach, 2016, p. 1). The gamification of serious work environments may have the potential to increase worker's task motivation, engagement, and enjoyment; which, in turn, may lead to a "higher willingness to contribute, higher quality of work and long-term engagement" (Lichtenberg et al., 2020), and it has been argued that gamification is perceived to have mass appeal among learners and students for "stimulating motivation, learner engagement, and social influence" (Zainuddin et al., 2020). Likewise, Patrício et al (2018) note that "effective gamification approaches attempt to encourage users' engagement, amusement, and enjoyment toward various activities".

Furthermore, Oxarart & Houghton note that important individual and organisational outcomes may be affected by gamification through the "mediating mechanisms of self-leadership and self-concordance" – the mechanics and elements of games, such as choices, avatars, leader-boards, points and levels, badges, themes and narratives, and competition and cooperation may encourage and develop valuable self-leadership skills, such as self-observation, self-goal-setting, and self-rewards, while offering feelings of competence, self-control, and purpose (Oxarart & Houghton, 2021). As noted in Andrade et al. (2016), the incorporation of these kinds of game mechanics and elements into non-game contexts has offered the opportunity for companies and research groups to increase learners' performance, communication between different groups of people, and to promote better health care and healthy habits.

Negative Potential of Gamification

However, as Deterding notes, video games have also long been studied for their potential to instil embedded values or "shape user behaviour intended by the system designer" (Deterding, Sicart, et al., 2011, p. 1), and historically, the application of game design principles into non-game environments has raised a number of concerns among game researchers. Researchers have argued that gamification vendors show little concern for the ethical consequences of end users (Walz & Deterding, 2014, p. 6), ignoring the complex, risky, skill-based, situation-bound processes that define games, and commodifying "the cultural cachet of games" into easily marketable business opportunities (Bogost, 2015; Walz & Deterding, 2014, p. 5). More condemnatory arguments have also been made to suggest that gamification exists as a design objective which prioritises corporate interests over the needs and behaviours of individuals or employees (Chaplin, 2011; Rey, 2014).

Other researchers have argued that gamification fails to appreciate play as an intrinsically motivating activity (Walz & Deterding, 2014, p. 6); though gamification may entice or coerce engagement through punishment or rewards (Benson, 2014), these systems may not sustain engagement (Rigby, 2014), and may instead obstruct the motivational characteristics of game play (Stenros, 2014). Furthermore, Stenros notes that the kind of "game play" encouraged by gamification may not always be "creative, emancipating, and liberating", and may instead encourage game play that is unexpectedly "disruptive and destructive" (2014, p. 207). Deterding has also noted that the framing of activities around the singular pursuit of reaching goals through metrics and targets may "crowd out wider concerns for any factor not captured in the metrics" (Walz & Deterding, 2014, p. 6), such as exceptions for moral conduct or human interactions (Deterding, 2012).

Yet, while these concerns remain pressing, Trang & Weiger (2021) note that contemporary research into gamification has neglected to address the potential drawbacks of more modern gamified services, applications and systems, and has instead fixated on favourable outcomes. As such, a growing collection of contemporary researchers have begun to explore these drawbacks more directly, challenging the uncritical acceptance and proliferation of gamification, and emphasising the specific risks associated with contemporary gamified services. The concerns raised by these researchers include, but are not limited to: issues of privacy and the potential for gamification to encourage the sharing of private information with private interests (Trang & Weiger, 2021); the potential for gamification to promote manipulative behavioural changes, such as an increase in commercial consumption (Tobon et al., 2020); the lowering of content knowledge, satisfaction, and course experience in educational environments (Kwon & Özpolat, 2020); and the potential for gamification to facilitate "dangerous" or "manipulative" organisational approaches that may encourage asymmetrical power relations (Thibault & Hamari, 2021, pp. 20, 21). Some researchers have even gone as far as to suggest that gamification may act as a humiliating medium of suppression, imposing the interests of managers over the needs and interests of employees (Goethe & Palmquist, 2020, p. 691). In this context, Goethe & Palmquist liken gamification to a socio-technical "Panopticon" – a prison concept that allows a single guard to observe all convicts within an institution, without those inmates being aware of when they are being watched, and motivating them to act as though they are being watched at all times (2020, p. 691).

Lived Experiences of Coercion and Exploitation Through Gamification

The concerns raised by Goethe & Palmquist, though dire, remain significant as they accurately reflect the lived accounts of workers within gamified occupational systems. In a now infamous example of poor gamification implementation, Disney incorporated a number of changes to the union contracts of their Disneyland and Paradise Pier hotel staff in Anaheim and Florida, in 2008 (Gabrielle, 2018). One of these changes was the implementation of a mandatory electronic tracking system which allowed managers to monitor worker productivity in real time; the staff would accumulate points by completing their daily tasks, such as cleaning hotel rooms, or washing and folding linen, and the points of each employee would then be displayed numerically and competitively on a public scoreboard (Gabrielle, 2018; Goethe & Palmquist, 2020; Lopez, 2011). If employees kept up with the goals of management, their names would be displayed in green, and if not, they would be displayed in red; the laundry machines themselves would also flash red and yellow lights directly at workers if they slowed down (Gabrielle, 2018). Employees of these locations begun referring to this system as "the electronic whip" (Barrera, in Lopez, 2011), as employees began to skip lunch and bathroom breaks, fearing the repercussions of not climbing the leaderboard continuously (Goethe & Palmquist, 2020).

The gamification practices implemented in the Disney Anaheim and Florida workplaces are not unique – US retail chain Target has drawn attention for their implementation of The Checkout Game, in which checkout clerks are tracked and scored by the speed of their transactions, and in which their scores are displayed in real-time on their point-of-sale computers (Gabrielle, 2018; Kim, 2018). Amazon and Uber, likewise, have dramatically increased their adoption of gamified systems in recent years, encouraging their workers to engage with their occupational responsibilities through "ludic loops" (Gabrielle, 2018; Martineau & Stefano, 2021; Scheiber, 2017). Amazon in particular is notable for expanding their incorporation of gamification in the workplace through the FC Games program, in which workers pick from arcade-style mini-games, and earn points by picking items in the warehouse, stowing them on shelves, and accomplishing other tasks (Martineau & Stefano, 2021).

However, it has been argued that these practices may not necessarily constitute "exploitation" or "manipulation". As Kim argues, these practices may not be exploitative if the designer acknowledges the hermeneutical dimension, carefully considers feedback, and deliberates directly with those engaged with the system; likewise, these practices may not be manipulative, if players are offered time to learn about their jobs and the outcomes of their jobs, such as "helping others, contributing to society, or enhancing important moral goods such as friendship or sustainability", allowing players to develop their own intrinsic motivation for their actions (Kim, 2015, pp. 2, 4). Furthermore, as Tobon et al. notes, the value and growing ubiquity of gamification is often justified through a concept known as Self-Determination Theory (SDT) (2020). Within SDT, individuals are assumed to have "an inherent growth tendency and innate psychological need that is the basis of their self-motivation and personality integration" (Tobon et al., 2020, p. 5), and are understood to hold three basic psychological needs: competence (the capacity to make changes to environments, and arrive at intended outcomes); relatedness (a sense of belonging and community to a persons, group, or culture disseminating a goal); and autonomy (a perceived internal locus of causality) (Deci & Ryan, in Tobon et al., 2020). It could therefore be argued that gamified systems of Disney or Amazon appeal to these needs, facilitating the individual worker's fundamental desire to feel competent, connected, and autonomous.

However, this justification is also not without criticism, as it has been argued that gamification may not build meaningful experiences, or convey feelings of autonomy and mastery, as previously thought

(Thibault & Hamari, 2021, p. 14). Rather than satisfying an individual's need for mastery, self-expression and social connectivity, gamification may instead promote narrow goals, encourage unreasonable levels of activity, encourage addictive and off-task behaviour, and reorient efforts towards "chasing metrics rather than substantive outcomes" (Andrade et al., 2016; Moldon et al., 2021, p. 1). In competitive environments, the expectation to "play well" can lead to overwork and interpersonal conflict (Moldon et al., 2021), and encourage behavioural practices that are physically and psychologically harmful (Goethe & Palmquist, 2020). Following the implementation of gamification within the Disneyland and Paradise Pier hotel workplaces, a higher number of workplace injuries were recorded, as employees began to prioritise productivity over safety, and as one union organiser noted, the formerly collegial workplace devolved into a race, where employees completed with each other, hostility grew, and pregnant employees couldn't keep up (Topete, in Gabrielle, 2018). As Kim & Werbach note, the competitive hierarchies that games are often innocuously based on "can be expressively pernicious in some social contexts" (Kim & Werbach, 2016, p. 167). Gamification has also prompted concern for its potential to encourage workers to internalise company goals (Howe, in Scheiber, 2017), with Massimo criticising gamification practices within Amazon as nothing more than "rituals" intended to "foster workplace identity and workers' investment to their job", individualising employment relations and breaking worker's associational power (Massimo, 2020, p. 135). In the case of Amazon Mechanical Turk (a crowd-sourcing platform for businesses to hire discrete on-demand tasks), it has been argued that gamification may notably improve productivity and participation, without increased economic compensation (Feyisetan et al., 2015; Lellis, 2020), leading workers to perform more work than what they are paid for (Lichtenberg et al., 2020). These observations align with criticisms from game studies, which argue that gamification may simply mask economic and political disenfranchisement through playful mechanisms, potentially disempowering workers, threatening worker solidarity through competition, and promoting the exploitation of labour (Bogost, 2015; Rey, 2014; Walz & Deterding, 2014).

Gamification, Ideology and "Gamified Rhetoric"

The capacity for gamification to encourage the internalisation of organisational goals or foster the formation of identities intrinsically linked to organisations also calls into question the potential for gamified systems to motivate and incentivise forms of moral or ethical behaviour that these organisations would deem preferable. This consideration becomes particularly ethically alarming when one considers the increasing incorporation of gamification into military activity and recruitment initiatives (Gabrielle, 2018; Goethe & Palmquist, 2020; Kim & Werbach, 2016; Noh, 2020). While Kim & Werbach note the complexity of discussing and evaluating moral character, they also, drawing on Grant (2012), note the capacity for incentives in gamified systems to motivate individuals to "cultivate and express unjustifiable moral indifference to fundamental human values, like the sanctity of innocent life" (Kim & Werbach, 2016, p. 168). Kim & Werbach therefore note that extreme care should be taken around the use of gamification in military organisations and "other business activities that involve fundamental human values" (2016, p. 168). Within the contemporary discourse surrounding gamification, much debate can be observed around the use of gamification in propaganda and recruitment initiatives, with particular concern directed towards the ethicality of gamification practices that have already been extensively adopted by organisations like the United States Army (Bjelajac & Filipović, 2020; Gabrielle, 2018; Goethe & Palmquist, 2020; Kim & Werbach, 2016), the Israel Defense Force (Dwyer & Silomon, 2019; Goethe & Palmquist, 2020; Kim & Werbach, 2016), al-Qaeda (Dikken, 2020), and the Islamic State

(ISIS/ISIL) (Schlegel, 2020). In the case of the United States Army, games have long been incorporated into military activity for a number of explicit purposes: the recruitment of new soldiers and officers; the practical training of soldiers and security agency officers; and the psychological preparation of soldiers and security officers for stress and desensitisation in stressful combat situations (Bjelajac & Filipović, 2020). However, as Goethe & Palmquist note, gamification has also been used in training simulations that reward participants with points and achievements for tapping colleagues' emails or finding contraband – a practice that may raise questions about how gamification facilitates and encourages particular actions surrounding privacy (Goethe & Palmquist, 2020, p. 692).

Goethe & Palmquist also acknowledge the use of gamification in the Israel Defense Force (Goethe & Palmquist, 2020), and the gamification practices that have long drawn objections from other observers (Mitchell, 2012). The Israel Defense Force (IDF) distinguishes itself in this context, for not only using gamification in military training simulations, but also for incorporating gamification into civilian society, previously through a blog where readers would acquire badges and points for reading, searching and sharing information produced by the IDF on popular social media sites (Goethe & Palmquist, 2020). As Kim & Werbach note, this "war blog" was specifically developed as a propaganda tool – it served as a "fully transparent effort to engage and motivate supporters" of the IDF (Kim & Werbach, 2016, p. 167). For this reason, both Goethe & Palmquist (2020) and Kim & Werbach (2016) question whether gamification of this kind would encourage participants to approach moral choices (in this case, the sharing of propaganda) not as serious ethical considerations, but as playful ones – participants may be incentivised by gamified systems and reward structures to consider important moral decisions humourously or irreverently (Palmquist & Linderoth, 2020).

However, Dwyer & Silomon note that more recently, the IDF has begun to incorporate "gamified logic" into their public correspondences; rather than simply adopting the principles, practices and techniques that are more commonly associated with gamification, the IDF has adopted the logical, rhetorical, linguistic and visual cues of games, advertising their on-going conflict with Hamas through gamified language (Dwyer & Silomon, 2019). Dwyer & Silomon draw particular attention to the phrases and rhetoric employed by the IDF on Twitter, noting that public statements, such as the acknowledgement of a drone strike performed against the centre of an alleged cyber-attack, frame the on-going conflict as play or competition; the lives, environments and behaviours that comprise the space of conflict are reduced to something not unlike a strategy computer game – conflict becomes stylised, time and space become compressed and distorted, and distantiation and detachment are generated between players and the subjects of "game-play" (Dwyer & Silomon, 2019). This form of "gamified logic" challenges conventional forms of state communication, as it goes beyond simply "conveying facts"; instead, gamified rhetoric is used through social media to deliver carefully constructed messages that justify actions by the state, offer insight into their strategic thinking, and as Dwyer & Solimon note, may be intended by the IDF to "merely provoke" (2019). By adopting the visual and linguistic cues of games, rather than just the features and reward patterns of games, organisations like the IDF may sidestep "inevitable operational and political complexities that are prevalent in assessing cyber-attacks" (Egloff & Wenger, in Dwyer & Silomon, 2019), and may once again prompt reflection on the concerns illustrated by Kim & Werbach – that being, the capacity for gamification to motivate individuals to cultivate and express inexcusable moral indifference to fundamental human values (Kim & Werbach, 2016).

Background Summary

Ethical questions surround all of the concerns that have been outlined above: the potential for gamification to act as a humiliating form of suppression or surveillance; the harm and exploitation that gamification may facilitate in workplaces; the occupational arrangements and power structures that make engaging with gamified systems mandatory; the capacity for gamification to encourage the internalisation of occupational or organisational goals; and the contemporary implementation of gamification in military activity to encourage and promote particular moral actions through playful or gamified framing. However, while these concerns are all significant individually, nowhere do they more dramatically coalesce than in the evolving policies and gamified systems that form the Social Credit System, a "state surveillance infrastructure" (Liang et al., 2018) currently in development by the government of the People's Republic of China – an ecosystem of gamified initiatives (Thibault & Hamari, 2021, p. 11), which, through "a fusion of state power", "existing corporate data platforms" and "incentives for citizens" aim to "embed gamified surveillance into society as a whole" (Benjamin, 2019, p. 702).

CASE STUDY: SOCIAL CREDIT SYSTEM

The Social Credit System represents a situation that contemporary, optimistic examinations of gamification have not adequately taken into consideration; it reflects an informative example of gamification taken to its extreme – where even social interactions and personal expression may be monitored, gamified, incentivised, and analysed. As Kim & Werbach recommend, questions involving moral or ethical concerns within gamification should be engaged with on a case-by-case basis (2016, p. 168), and the Social Credit System offers a compelling opportunity to holistically and contextually demonstrate many of the severe ethical concerns of gamification that this chapter has already raised (i.e. the use of ludic loops to encourage desired behaviour; economic and political disenfranchisement through playful mechanisms; gamified logic, aimed at motivating individuals to cultivate and express inexcusable moral indifference to fundamental human values). As this case study will demonstrate, the outcomes and consequences of the Social Credit System are substantially more severe than those traditionally anticipated within ethics research into gamification, such as game addiction, undesired competition, and off-task behaviour (Andrade et al., 2016); and instead, illuminate the potential for gamification to facilitate human rights abuses, and political and religious suppression.

As such, this chapter will comprehensively analyse the mechanisms and systems that comprise the Social Credit System, while acknowledging the ethical recommendations raised by Kim & Werbach - that generally, researchers, practitioners, and designers should be cautious of gamified services that take unfair advantage of participants; that infringe upon participants' autonomy; that harm involved parties, whether intentionally or unintentionally; or that have a negative effect on the moral character of involved parties (Kim & Werbach, 2016). In doing so, this chapter will offer a disruptive perspective that recognises the dehumanising potential of pervasive, contemporary gamification practices, particularly those that, in pursuit of uncompromising corporate, organisational or political goals (Liang et al., 2021; Scheiber, 2017; Zhang, 2020), do not incorporate appropriate ethical boundaries for participants and individuals.

What is the Social Credit System?

To examine the ethical concerns presented by the Social Credit System, one must first acknowledge that the Social Credit System is not a single system, but rather "a heterogeneous ensemble of fragmented and decentralised systems" (Adelmant, 2021). As Adelmant notes, the significant attention that the Social Credit System has received from Western media and human rights organisations has often characterised the program as a "comprehensive, nation-wide system in which every action is monitored and a single score is assigned to each individual" (Adelmant, 2021), with inevitable comparisons drawn to the work of George Orwell, or to an episode of the dystopian science fiction series, *Black Mirror* (Nguyen, 2016). The objectives of the system, as Creemers writes, have led observers to portray the Social Credit System as an "omnipotent behemoth", "relentlessly carrying out a long-prepared scheme for complete control", and facilitating "the totalitarian impulses of China's autocratic leaders" (Creemers, 2018, p. 3). While such concerns may not be misplaced, these conceptualisations also ignore the far more complex reality of the Social Credit System; as Daum argues, such caricatures misrepresent the real and more subtle human rights crises that may be associated with the Social Credit System, and may distract researchers from acknowledging similar technological developments in the West – those that may be deemed more acceptable by comparison (Daum, 2019). Adelmant recommends that a nuanced understanding of the Social Credit System is required to more accurately recognise and acknowledge the specific human rights concerns that are raised by the program (Adelmant, 2021) – a maxim that is reflected in the work of other researchers (Creemers, 2018; Daum, 2019; Liang et al., 2021; Pabisiak, 2020; Zhang, 2020), and a position that will be supported in this chapter.

Zhang clarifies that, beyond the Orwellian caricatures, the Social Credit System is far more complex, "involving an extremely diverse range of decentralised, experimental and fragmented programs across social, economic and legal fields" (Zhang, 2020, p. 566), and despite misrepresentations, the Social Credit System does not include a numerical scoring system for individuals and companies (Daum, 2019); this misconception potentially arising from the adoption of numerical scoring systems for monitoring and ranking trust among local governments and private financial credit agencies (Creemers, 2018; Liang et al., 2021). Rather, as Daum observes, the system is primarily concerned with the use of existing public and government records to ensure compliance with legal and contractual obligations in social and economic activity (Daum, 2019), and Zhang notes that the Social Credit System itself is intended to be constituted through a "number of programs aiming to govern social and economic activities through problematising, assessing, and utilising the trustworthiness of individuals, enterprises, organisations, and government agencies" (Zhang, 2020, p. 1). This "ecology of initiatives" (Creemers, 2018, p. 25) would be facilitated by an underlying informational infrastructure; systematically providing a standardised means of recording "credit-related information in different sections of the administration", as well as supporting "databases to store credit information at central and local levels" and "credit reporting mechanisms to enable public access to the information" (2018, p. 13). Due to this complexity of this system, it is therefore almost impossible to directly point to a singular system that represents the concerns presented by the Social Credit System as a whole, despite the adoption of numerical "social credit" by firms such as Sesame Credit and Qianhai Credit (Dai, 2018, p. 24).

However, while no actual quantitative score is awarded to those engaged with it, the Social Credit System still makes heavy use of gamified design; and Creemers notes that a supporting pillar of the program would be a system of rewards and punishments based on blacklists and "redlists" (public records of conspicuous merit), implemented through governmental means, "market mechanisms", and "self-regulatory regimes" (2018, p. 13); this is reinforced by Adelmant, who writes that the Social Credit System would rely on information-sharing, restrictive lists, and the publicisation of both "good" and "shameful" personal records, to encourage or discourage particular forms of behaviour (Adelmant, 2021). This aim – to encourage "acceptable" forms of behaviour through gamified structures of reward and punishment – is indisputable; Creemers cites official planning documentation from 2014, which directly states that the Social Credit System is designed to establish "the idea of a sincerity culture", promote "honesty and traditional virtues", and utilise "encouragement for trust, and constraints against breaking trust as incentive mechanisms" (Creemers, 2015, 2018, p. 2). These aims are only further reinforced in more recent official correspondence, as a report from the Chinese Communist Party's Central Committee indicated that the Social Credit System would be expanding on these initial goals, with the purported intention of promoting financial trustworthiness, law-abiding behaviour, self-governance, and moral values such as honesty and integrity (Drinhausen & Brussee, 2021); compliance to these goals would continue to be ensured through a series of blacklists, public "naming and shaming", legal repercussions, administrative and personal sanctions, and rewards distributed by public and private organisations, operating among a number of different jurisdictions (Drinhausen & Brussee, 2021; Zhang, 2020, p. 579). Dai points to the incentives introduced in Guizhou Province as an example of the more specific systems that may fall under the Social Credit System, in which local authorities have sought to evaluate individual rural residents and households through community monitoring and peer review mechanisms; the scores generated through this process, evaluated according to a set of "publicised village norms", then form the basis for the local government's distribution of agricultural loans, subsidies and multiple types of local and residential benefits (Dai, 2018, p. 30). Cook also identifies a number of specific examples of incentive systems that contribute to the Social Credit System as a whole (Cook, 2017, 2019). These may include digital gamified incentive systems, such as the mobile app Xué Xí Qiáng Guó and the English-language state newspaper China Daily, as both platforms offer points for reading and sharing articles, which may then be used to make purchases from an online store (Cook, 2019). These incentives may also be offered physically: Cook points to manual scoring systems being incorporated in the Aksu Prefecture of Xinjiang, Rongcheng in Shandong, and Qingzhen in Guizhou (2019), and notes that within the current system, "promotions and bonuses are available to officers who effectively crack down on targeted religious groups and behaviours" (Cook, 2017, p. 21).

Creemers argues that these objectives and incentives frame the Social Credit System as a set of mechanisms intended to provide rewards or punishments as feedback to actors, based not just on lawfulness, but also on the morality of their actions, including economic, social and political conduct (Creemers, 2018, p. 2). Creemers continues, noting that this "maximalist objective" (2018, p. 2), when combined with China's increasing technological capabilities, the absence of strong constitutions for individual citizens, and move toward stricter governmental control under the Xi Jinping administration would undoubtedly have a significant effect on people's lives; and such objectives reflect an ideology that fundamentally believes in "social engineering on the basis of system science", on "the malleability and transformability of the individual", and one that is explicitly expanding the use of automated, data-based system for social control (2018, p. 26). The utilisation of mechanisms to reward or punishment moral conduct may immediately raise ethical questions regarding manipulation and the violation of moral character (Kim & Werbach, 2016); however, the implementation of gamified mechanisms to facilitate social control may have far deeper moral implications, reflected in their ideological and political justifications.

Legitimising Exploitation through Gamification

Knight explains that, in its inception, China's credit infrastructure was established with the aim of "mitigating risk in the country's increasingly market-driven economy", not unlike other financial credit systems in the world (Knight, 2021, p. 254). However, what began as a plan for the provision of financial credit (*zhengxin* 征信) evolved into a "highly decentralised collective of thousands of different initiatives, unified by an abstract ideological goal", that being the promotion of honesty and credibility, or "social credit" (*chengxin* 诚信) (2021, p. 237). As such, the initial provision of financial services developed into a "disciplinary technology of regulation", that served a role in "the enforcement of judicial decisions" and the "pursuit of a state-arbitered moral ideal" (2021, p. 237). For this reason, Knight argues that the expansion of the Social Credit System must be viewed not just as a means of judicial enforcement or "as a narrow financial tool" or even as a singular, gamified program, but as a reinsertion of a moralising ideology in the political landscape of China under Xi Jinping (2021, p. 245). This transition is partially seen by Knight as a response to the discourse of perceived "moral decay" in China that preceded Jinping's rise to power (2021, p. 245); a response that both legitimises the creators of the Social Credit System as "moral saviours", while also "positioning them as absolute arbiters of moral authority" (2021, p. 246). In this sense, Knight argues that the rhetoric of *chengxin* legitimises a system that arguably benefits the state more than the individual citizen, while ensuring that serious ethical questions surrounding privacy, data protection and access to justice are more easily avoided – circumvented through the collective understanding that initiatives like the Social Credit System are the supposed answer to the "lack of trust and moral decay" in society (2021, p. 247).

Knight's potent observations allow one to recognise that the reward and punishment cycles of the Social Credit System may not just impact the individual citizen, but may also "manufacture consent" towards the moral authority, political ideals and "paternalistic aspirations" of the state (2021, p. 255). Such systems disregard every recommendation made by ethicists like Kim & Werbach (2016), and ideologically perpetuate further unethical situations – if the state is accused of causing harm (Drinhausen & Brussee, 2021), but the Social Credit System legitimises the authority of the state to commit that harm in the name of civil and moral stability, then by extension, the gamified mechanisms of the Social Credit System contribute to the legitimisation of harm. Likewise, if the state is accused of exploiting and dehumanising minorities, or committing severe human rights violations (Adelmant, 2021; Roth, 2020), but the Social Credit System supports, rewards and justifies engagement with the state's ideological and social objectives (including the objectives that contribute to exploitation), then by extension, those gamified mechanisms legitimise and contribute to these violations, as well as the exploitation of human beings.

This is an observation supported by Adelmant, who notes that the Social Credit System exists within an already repressive context – an individual can be arrested for protesting labour conditions or for speaking about certain issues on social media – and as such, the gamified mechanisms that seek to increase legal compliance within this context may be deeply problematic, amplifying legal consequences and worsening already severe issues surrounding privacy, discrimination, and disproportionate punishment (Adelmant, 2021). Furthermore, Adelmant notes that the Social Credit System exhibits a kind of "technological solutionism"; digital solutions are promised to "fix" systemic problems, which, in the process, only serve to obscure and perpetuate structural inequalities (2021). These concerns are only further reinforced by Drinhausen & Brussee, who note that the Social Credit System is simply an extension of the current legal and administrative systems in place; as such, the Social Credit System exists to enforce laws and regulations, including repressive laws aimed at "tackling anti-social conduct", or restricting behaviour in line with state-proclaimed "socialist core values" (Drinhausen & Brussee, 2021). Furthermore, Drinhausen & Brussee note that the Social Credit System facilitates administrative abuse, as it allows officials to punish individuals for unrelated behaviours, and use credit assessment beyond its defined purposes – as in the cases of children excluded from schools or blacklisted, due to their parent's financial conduct (Drinhausen & Brussee, 2021).

DISCUSSION

The intention of this chapter has been to provide a disruptive perspective that emphasises the negative potential of gamification, through a critical examination of the Social Credit System. This negative potential can be observed in the past implementations of gamification that encourage employees to fearfully work beyond their limits; in the ways gamification may encourage worker disempowerment and the exploitation of labour; and in the ways that gamification may be used for propaganda, intentionally promoting an indifference to human life. However, an examination into the Social Credit System has demonstrated that gamification may also be incorporated into regulation and governance to legitimise the moral authority and expectations of government institutions, through processes that do not resemble more recognisable and superficial mechanics and elements of gamification, i.e. points, leader-boards, badges, etc. (Oxarart & Houghton, 2021). Instead, gamification may take the form of "gamified logic"; in this instance, policy initiatives that incorporate traditional cycles of reward and punishment in order to incentivise and justify particular forms of moral behaviour. These policy initiatives facilitate the ideological objectives of the state through gamified mechanisms of reward and punishment, and consequentially, playing these "games" contributes to social and political objectives – particularly objectives that Knight observes justify the legal and moral authority of officials and government bodies to continue producing gamified initiatives (Knight, 2021). This is a broad practice that contributes to Bogost's declaration of gamification as "bullshit", as he argues that gamification is primarily concerned with the "establishment and continuance of the practice itself" – to Bogost, gamification fundamentally begets more gamification (Bogost, 2015, pp. 70, 76). The concerning dimension to this however, is that in the context of the Social Credit System, the continuation of gamified initiatives begets the continued legitimisation of unethical action perpetuated by the state against individuals and minority groups. As Cook writes, some incentive systems that comprise the Social Credit System are quite explicit about encouraging private citizens to inform on one another – scoring tables produced by party-based security forces include incentives for reporting Falan Gong, Uighur and Hui Muslims, Tibetan Buddhists, and Protestant Christians, among others, to authorities (Cook, 2017).

In the case of the Social Credit System, a question remains: how exactly might one demonstrate and quantify the potential for gamified mechanisms to facilitate this kind of harm? What systems specifically contribute to the exploitation or dehumanisation of individuals? A concise answer to this question is complicated by the fact that implementations of gamification *may not directly* cause harm or exploit individuals – instead, the unethical potential of gamified systems lies in their capacity to legitimise the actions of organisations and states that adopt them, and which do directly cause harm or violate human rights. While it may be tempting to conceptualise the Social Credit System as a single monolithic scoring system, to do so would be to ignore the complex manner in which gamification has been more realistically integrated into the fundamental structures of ethics and governance in the People's Republic of China, and how those structures, through systems of reward and punishment, may perpetuate instances of dehumanisation and exploitation. Furthermore, while the dehumanising and exploitative potential of gamification can be identified through these case studies, an effective means of quantifying and assessing the ethicality of these practices would need to acknowledge the complicated role that responsibility and organisational moral authority play in justifying these cases.

RECOMMENDATIONS AND FUTURE RESEARCH

Though the four concerns that were raised by Kim & Werbach (2016) provide a compelling foundation for discussing the ethics of gamification, a deeper examination into the Social Credit System has illuminated how cultural paradigms, policy goals, and ideological motivations may complicate the identification and discussion of unethical gamification systems. If appropriate, informed research is to be produced that further explores the role that gamification plays in perpetuating and justifying exploitation, dehumanisation and harm, then important clarifications need to be made that acknowledge the negative potential and severity of gamification, as well as the evolving and ambiguous application of gamification in contemporary ethics and governance. For this reason, the authors propose three important recommendations for further ethical discussion – clarifications that future researchers may need to recognise, in order to evaluate and assess the exploitative or coercive potential of gamification.

Recommendation One

The first is that researchers must recognise the growing incorporation of less conventional forms of gamification into existing power structures. As gamification becomes an essential component of everyday services, software and systems (Xi & Hamari, 2019), it only becomes more necessary for researchers to analyse how gamification is being incorporated into organisations and governments through "gamified logic", rather than through more superficial indicators of gamification, such as points, badges, levels, and leaderboards (Deterding, Sicart, et al., 2011).

Though the Social Credit System does incorporate cycles of reward and punishment, one may also observe how gamification is being incorporated into the foundational structures of ethical and judicial systems, in ways that are unlike traditional forms of gamification, and in ways that are difficult to identify *as gamification*. As such, an evaluation of the dehumanising potential of gamification may not be based solely on traditional indicators of gamification; and instead must recognise how gamification can be incorporated into organisational structures in ways that are complex, decentralised, or unlike prior implementations of gamification.

In the Social Credit System, researchers must recognise that these unconventional, complicated forms of gamification are becoming indistinguishable from judicial and administrative practices. This presents a severe challenge for researchers who wish to analyse the consequences of gamification specifically, and presents a notable obstacle to those wishing to explore how gamification may be contributing to the exploitation and dehumanisation of individuals within those systems – while one may wish to condemn gamification practices that cause "harm", the complexity and unconventional nature of contemporary gamification may make it difficult to identify and qualify what specifically is causing "harm" or violating moral "character".

The complexity and indistinguishability of gamification in this context, as well as the consequences of being unable to identify unethical gamification, aligns with observations made by Daum, who argues that researchers must be aware of how subtle, or even comfortable, a "control-based model" of "surveillance capitalism" can be, and how such models may lead to complacency around the threats to freedom and autonomy that technology may bring to western societies and organisations (Daum, 2019). Such systems may hold an immense capacity for harm and exploitation, particularly if researchers and ethicists lack the tools to appropriately identify and assess harmful gamification practices, due to their unconventionality and complexity.

Recommendation Two

The second recommendation is that researchers must observe the ways in which gamified systems have begun to occupy functional roles within the social, legal and political systems of states and organisations, and incorporate these observations into ethical assessments of gamification.

As the gamification practices of the Israel Defence Force demonstrate, the use of gamification is no longer limited to badges or points on public forums; instead, military organisations are adopting the aesthetic, rhetoric and logic of games to deliver official correspondence. This is notable in the Social Credit System as well, where diverse gamified systems form an integral component of the state's legal, judicial and financial systems. This is reflective of not only the increasing unconventionality of gamification, but also the growing incorporation of gamification into the fundamental operational structures of organisations. The role that gamification plays in facilitating the operations of these organisations must therefore be taken into consideration when performing ethical evaluations; drawing once again from Adelmant (2021), one must consider: if the Social Credit System exists to support the operation of a state, and that state is accused of exploiting minority communities or committing human rights violations, then one must consider the role that the Social Credit System occupies in supporting those violations through its gamified functions. As such, the authors recommend that researchers acknowledge both the ways that gamification is incorporated into the processes of organisations, and the ways gamification may permit unethical practices within these structures, for future ethical assessments.

Recommendation Three

The third and final recommendation is that researchers and ethicists should be mindful of the ways in which gamification is being utilised to rhetorically justify unethical behaviour. While gamification may not always directly cause harm, some implementations of gamification may instead legitimise the ideological goals and behaviours that *do* cause harm. As such, the potential for gamification to indirectly contribute to or justify harm remains an area that requires further exploration.

Discussions into contemporary uses of gamification have demonstrated the capacity for gamification to incentivise the internalisation of organisational goals, while legitimising the moral authority of organisations and governments. In the case of Amazon, one can observe the ways in which gamification may be used to individualise workplace relationships and break worker's associational power (Massimo, 2020); in the case of Disneyland and Paradise Pier hotels, gamification incentivised the internalisation of productivity goals, to the point of facilitating physical harm among employees (Gabrielle, 2018); and, one may argue that the gamified legal and regulatory structures of the Social Credit System are intended to legitimise the moral authority of the state, justifying threats to privacy, data protection and justice as "necessary" protections within society (Knight, 2021). Just as gamification may support the operational procedures of unethical organisations or governments, gamification may likewise be used to justify the ideological goals of authoritative bodies – further validating any potentially harmful behaviours and policies that those bodies engage in. The authors therefore recommend that further research be performed, specifically focused on the potential for gamification to legitimise harm or violations to moral character, and ideologically validate exploitative or coercive practices.

CONCLUSION

This chapter has predominately explored the negative ethical consequences of gamification, with the aim of identifying the exploitative, dehumanising implications of gamified design. To consider these implications, this chapter first examined ethical concerns that have raised by existing implementations of gamification in organisations – including the gamified practices adopted by Disneyland and Paradise Pier hotels, Target, Amazon, Uber, the United States military, and the Israel Defense Force. Cautionary ethical recommendations for gamification were introduced in this context, and the work of Kim & Werbach (2016), Goethe & Palmquist (2020), and Dwyer & Solimon (2019) facilitated the analysis of these practices.

This chapter then explored the ethical implications of gamification through a critical instance case study of China's Social Credit System, and clarified some misconceptions on the program to more accurately recognise the human rights violations and unethical gamified design that is notable within the system. Through the work of Zhang (2020), Liang (2018, 2021), Creemers (2018), Adelmant (2021), Daum (2019), and Drinhausen & Brussee (2021), this chapter was able to make observations on not just the relative obscurity and complexity of the Social Credit System as a series of gamified practices, but also on how inseparably the Social Credit System is linked with social, legal, economic, and administrative fields.

This relationship was further explored by engaging with the work of Knight (2021), and observations were made on the role of the Social Credit System in ideologically validating the authority and sovereignty of the state. These observations supported further arguments that the gamified reward and punishment cycles that comprise the Social Credit System are presented as a "necessary" response to a supposed moral decline in China – a response that both legitimises the state as moral saviours, while also positions those that created the Social Credit System as the arbiters of moral authority. As a consequence, the purported "necessary" nature of the Social Credit System justifies and legitimises unethical activity, including exploitation, harm, behavioural manipulation, and disproportionate legal consequences, as well as the organisational and ideological goals of the state, in the name of good moral intentions – all facilitated through gamified structures of reward and punishment.

Lastly, the authors have made three recommendations based on these observations, proposing that researchers must recognise the growing incorporation of less-overt gamification into existing power structures; that gamification must understood, not just as simple techniques or patterns of design, but as complex tools that facilitate the potentially unethical operational processes of organisations that adopt them; and lastly, that researchers must recognise how gamification may rhetorically justify the practices, behaviours, and policies of institutions that directly cause harm. These recommendations reflect a broader recommendation for future research – that a means of assessing and quantifying the complex exploitative potential of gamification should be pursued further, with these three recommendations in mind.

Through the observations made in this chapter, it can be acknowledged that contemporary gamified systems, particularly those such as the Social Credit System, hold severe unethical potential, and may legitimise the authority of organisations engaged in unethical, dehumanising behaviour. Moving forward, researchers, ethicists, and designers must recognise the role that gamification may play in justifying and incentivising potentially unethical organisational goals and ideological objectives, particularly taking note of how these forms of gamification may not appear as superficially simple point and badge systems, or even as traditional feedback cycles of reward and punishment. Instead these forms of gamification may become fundamental to justifying the ethical sovereignty of organisations through gamified rhetoric, or through gamified systems of ethics and governance. Though implementations such as these may seem overly exaggerated, the increasing ubiquity of gamification, and its use as a means of incentivising preferable behaviour in both private interests and government policy, may demonstrate how gamification is already becoming inextricably linked to the operational and ideological objectives of organisations. It is in the capacity for gamification to facilitate these objectives – which may include exploitation, dehumanisation, social control, and occupational, legal, and political injustices – where the unethical potential of gamification truly lies.

REFERENCES

Adelmant, V. (2021, April 20). *Social Credit in China: Looking Beyond the "Black Mirror" Nightmare.* Centre for Human Rights and Global Justice. https://chrgj.org/2021/04/20/social-credit-in-china-looking-beyond-the-black-mirror-nightmare/

Andrade, F., Mizoguchi, R., & Isotani, S. (2016). The Bright and Dark Sides of Gamification. *The Bright and Dark Sides of Gamification.*, *9684*, 1–11. doi:10.1007/978-3-319-39583-8_17

Benjamin, G. (2019). Playing at Control: Writing Surveillance in/for Gamified Society. *Surveillance & Society*, *17*(5), 699–713. doi:10.24908s.v17i5.13204

Benson, B. (2014). The Gameful Mind. In The Gameful World: Approaches, Issues, Applications (pp. 223–224). MIT Press.

Bjelajac, Ž., & Filipović, A. (2020). Gamification as an Innovative Approach in Security Systems. Academic Press.

Bogost, I. (2015). Why Gamification is Bullshit. In The Gameful World: Approaches, Issues, Applications (pp. 65–79). MIT Press.

Chaplin, H. (2011, March 29). Gamification: Ditching reality for a game isn't as fun as it sounds. *Slate Magazine.* https://slate.com/technology/2011/03/gamification-ditching-reality-for-a-game-isn-t-as-fun-as-it-sounds.html

Cook, S. (2017). *The Battle for China's Spirit.* Freedom House. https://freedomhouse.org/report/special-report/2017/battle-chinas-spirit

Cook, S. (2019, February 27). *"Social credit" scoring: How China's Communist Party is incentivising repression.* Hong Kong Free Press HKFP. https://hongkongfp.com/2019/02/27/social-credit-scoring-chinas-communist-party-incentivising-repression/

Creemers, R. (2015, April 25). Planning Outline for the Construction of a Social Credit System (2014-2020). *China Copyright and Media*. https://chinacopyrightandmedia.wordpress.com/2014/06/14/planning-outline-for-the-construction-of-a-social-credit-system-2014-2020/

Creemers, R. (2018). *China's Social Credit System: An Evolving Practice of Control* (*SSRN* Scholarly Paper No. 3175792). Social Science Research Network. doi:10.2139/ssrn.3175792

Dai, X. (2018). *Toward a Reputation State: The Social Credit System Project of China* (*SSRN* Scholarly Paper ID 3193577). Social Science Research Network. doi:10.2139/ssrn.3193577

Daum, J. (2019, June 27). Untrustworthy: Social Credit Isn't What You Think It Is. *Verfassungsblog*. https://verfassungsblog.de/untrustworthy-social-credit-isnt-what-you-think-it-is/

Deterding, S. (2012, February 23). *Ruling the World: When Life Gets Gamed*. Lift Conference 2012, Geneva, Switzerland. https://www.slideshare.net/dings/ruling-the-world-when-life-gets-gamed/39-But_if_you_put_a

Deterding, S., Dixon, D., Khaled, R., & Nacke, L. (2011). From game design elements to gamefulness: Defining "gamification." *Proceedings of the 15th International Academic MindTrek Conference: Envisioning Future Media Environments*, 9–15. 10.1145/2181037.2181040

Deterding, S., Sicart, M., Nacke, L., O'Hara, K., & Dixon, D. (2011). Gamification. Using game-design elements in non-gaming contexts. *CHI '11 Extended Abstracts on Human Factors in Computing Systems*, 2425–2428. doi:10.1145/1979742.1979575

Dikken, M. (2020). *Game over: Gamification in Al-Qaeda's Magazine Inspire To address lone-wolf terrorists*. Leiden University. https://hdl.handle.net/1887/136052

Drinhausen, K., & Brussee, V. (2021). *China's Social Credit System in 2021: From fragmentation towards integration*. Mercator Institute for China Studies. https://merics.org/en/report/chinas-social-credit-system-2021-fragmentation-towards-integration

Dwyer, A., & Silomon, J. (2019, September 23). Dangerous Gaming: Cyber-Attacks, Air-Strikes and Twitter. *E-International Relations*. https://www.e-ir.info/2019/09/23/dangerous-gaming-cyber-attacks-air-strikes-and-twitter/

Feyisetan, O., Simperl, E., Van Kleek, M., & Shadbolt, N. (2015). Improving Paid Microtasks through Gamification and Adaptive Furtherance Incentives. *Proceedings of the 24th International Conference on World Wide Web*, 333–343. 10.1145/2736277.2741639

Gabrielle, V. (2018, October 10). *How employers have gamified work for maximum profit*. Aeon. https://aeon.co/essays/how-employers-have-gamified-work-for-maximum-profit

Goethe, O., & Palmquist, A. (2020). Broader Understanding of Gamification by Addressing Ethics and Diversity. In C. Stephanidis, D. Harris, W.-C. Li, D. D. Schmorrow, C. M. Fidopiastis, P. Zaphiris, A. Ioannou, X. Fang, R. A. Sottilare, & J. Schwarz (Eds.), *HCI International 2020 – Late Breaking Papers: Cognition, Learning and Games* (pp. 688–699). Springer International Publishing. doi:10.1007/978-3-030-60128-7_50

Grant, R. W. (2012). *Strings attached: Untangling the ethics of incentives*. Princeton University Press.

Huotari, K., & Hamari, J. (2017). A definition for gamification: Anchoring gamification in the service marketing literature. *Electronic Markets*, *27*(1), 21–31. doi:10.100712525-015-0212-z

Hyrynsalmi, S., Smed, J., & Kimppa, K. (2017). The Dark Side of Gamification: How We Should Stop Worrying and Study also the Negative Impacts of Bringing Game Design Elements to Everywhere. *GamiFIN*. /paper/The-Dark-Side-of-Gamification%3A-How-We-Should-Stop-Hyrynsalmi-Smed/048a 43b5059ffc16a30124be3bbf5e1a8f0b7702

Kim, T. W. (2015, January). *Gamification Ethics: Exploitation and Manipulation.* Gamifying Research Workshop Papers. CHI 2015, Seoul, South Korea.

Kim, T. W. (2018). Gamification of Labor and the Charge of Exploitation. *Journal of Business Ethics*, *152*(1), 27–39. doi:10.100710551-016-3304-6

Kim, T. W., & Werbach, K. (2016). More than Just a Game: Ethical Issues in Gamification. *Ethics and Information Technology*, *18*(2), 157–173. doi:10.100710676-016-9401-5

Knight, A. (2021). Technologies of Risk and Discipline in China's Social Credit System. In R. Creemers & S. Trevaskes (Eds.), *Law and the Party in China: Ideology and Organisation* (pp. 237–262). Cambridge University Press.

Kwon, H. Y., & Özpolat, K. (2020). The Dark Side of Narrow Gamification: Negative Impact of Assessment Gamification on Student Perceptions and Content Knowledge. *INFORMS Transactions on Education*, *21*(2), 67–81. doi:10.1287/ited.2019.0227

Legaki, N.-Z., Xi, N., Hamari, J., Karpouzis, K., & Assimakopoulos, V. (2020). The effect of challenge-based gamification on learning: An experiment in the context of statistics education. *International Journal of Human-Computer Studies*, *144*, 102496. Advance online publication. doi:10.1016/j.ijhcs.2020.102496 PMID:32565668

Lellis, L. D. (2020). How Gamification Affects Crowdsourcing: The Case of Amazon Mechanical Turk. *Eludamos (Göttingen)*, *10*(1), 27–37.

Liang, F., Chen, Y., & Zhao, F. (2021). The Platformization of Propaganda: How Xuexi Qiangguo Expands Persuasion and Assesses Citizens in China. *International Journal of Communication*, *15*, 20.

Liang, F., Das, V., Kostyuk, N., & Hussain, M. M. (2018). Constructing a Data-Driven Society: China's Social Credit System as a State Surveillance Infrastructure. *Policy and Internet*, *10*(4), 415–453. doi:10.1002/poi3.183

Lichtenberg, S., Lembcke, T.-B., Brenig, M., Brendel, A., & Trang, S. (2020, March 8). *Can Gamification lead to Increase Paid Crowdworkers Output?* Academic Press.

Lopez, S. (2011, October 19). Steve Lopez: Disneyland workers answer to "electronic whip." *Los Angeles Times*. https://www.latimes.com/health/la-xpm-2011-oct-19-la-me-1019-lopez-disney-20111018-story. html

Martineau, P., & Stefano, M. D. (2021, March 15). *Amazon Expands Effort to 'Gamify' Warehouse Work.* The Information. https://www.theinformation.com/articles/amazon-expands-effort-to-gamify-warehouse-work

Massimo, F. (2020). A Struggle for Bodies and Souls: Amazon Management and Union Strategies in France and Italy. In J. Alimahomed-Wilson & E. Reese (Eds.), *The Cost of Free Shipping: Amazon in the Global Economy* (pp. 129–144). Pluto Press. doi:10.2307/j.ctv16zjhcj.15

Mitchell, J. (2012, November 15). Unbelievable! The IDF Has Gamified Its War Blog. *ReadWrite*. https://readwrite.com/2012/11/15/unbelievable-the-idf-has-gamified-its-war-blog/

Moldon, L., Strohmaier, M., & Wachs, J. (2021). How Gamification Affects Software Developers: Cautionary Evidence from a Natural Experiment on GitHub. *2021 IEEE/ACM 43rd International Conference on Software Engineering (ICSE)*, 549–561. 10.1109/ICSE43902.2021.00058

Nguyen, C. (2016, October 27). *China might create a Black Mirror-like score for each citizen based on how trustworthy they are*. Business Insider Australia. https://www.businessinsider.com.au/china-social-credit-score-like-black-mirror-2016-10

Noh, D. (2020). *The Gamification Framework of Military Flight Simulator for Effective Learning and Training Environment*. University of Central Florida. https://stars.library.ucf.edu/etd2020/259

Oxarart, R. A., & Houghton, J. D. (2021). A Spoonful of Sugar: Gamification as Means for Enhancing Employee Self-Leadership and Self-Concordance at Work. *Administrative Sciences*, *11*(2), 35. doi:10.3390/admsci11020035

Pabisiak, J. (2020). Dangerous, Yet Not So Unique. Characteristics of the Chinese Social Credit System. *Polish Political Science Yearbook*, *49*(3), 30–53. doi:10.15804/ppsy2020303

Palmquist, A., & Linderoth, J. (2020). Gamification Does Not Belong at a University. *Proceedings of the 2020 DiGRA Conference*, 21.

Patrício, R., Moreira, A. C., & Zurlo, F. (2018). Gamification approaches to the early stage of innovation. *Creativity and Innovation Management*, *27*(4), 499–511. doi:10.1111/caim.12284

Rey, P. (2014). Gamification and post-Fordist Capitalism. In The Gameful World: Approaches, Issues, Applications (pp. 277–295). MIT Press.

Rigby, S. C. (2014). Gamification and Motivation. In The Gameful World: Approaches, Issues, Applications (pp. 113–137). MIT Press.

Roth, K. (2020, January 3). *China's Global Threat to Human Rights*. Human Rights Watch. https://www.hrw.org/world-report/2020/country-chapters/global

Scheiber, N. (2017, April 2). How Uber Uses Psychological Tricks to Push Its Drivers' Buttons. *The New York Times*. https://www.nytimes.com/interactive/2017/04/02/technology/uber-drivers-psychological-tricks.html

Schlegel, L. (2020). Jumanji Extremism? How games and gamification could facilitate radicalization processes. *Journal for Deradicalization*, *23*, 1–44.

Sicart, M. (2009). *The Ethics of Computer Games* (1st ed.). MIT Press. doi:10.7551/mitpress/9780262012652.001.0001

Sicart, M. (2013). *Beyond Choices: The Design of Ethical Gameplay*. MIT Press. doi:10.7551/mitpress/9052.001.0001

Stenros, J. (2014). Behind Games: Playful Mindsets and Transformative Practices. In The Gameful World: Approaches, Issues, Applications (pp. 201–222). MIT Press.

Thibault, M., & Hamari, J. (2021). Seven Points to Reappropriate Gamification. In A. Spanellis & J. T. Harviainen (Eds.), *Transforming Society and Organizations through Gamification: From the Sustainable Development Goals to Inclusive Workplaces* (pp. 11–29). Springer Nature. doi:10.1007/978-3-030-68207-1_2

Tobon, S., Ruiz-Alba, J. L., & García-Madariaga, J. (2020). Gamification and online consumer decisions: Is the game over? *Decision Support Systems, 128*.

Trang, S., & Weiger, W. H. (2021). The perils of gamification: Does engaging with gamified services increase users' willingness to disclose personal information? *Computers in Human Behaviour, 116*.

Walz, S. P., & Deterding, S. (2014). An Introduction to The Gameful World. In The Gameful World: Approaches, Issues, Applications (pp. 1–13). MIT Press.

Xi, N., & Hamari, J. (2019). Does gamification satisfy needs? A study on the relationship between gamification features and intrinsic need satisfaction. *International Journal of Information Management, 46*, 210–221. doi:10.1016/j.ijinfomgt.2018.12.002

Xi, N., & Hamari, J. (2020). Does gamification affect brand engagement and equity? A study in online brand communities. *Journal of Business Research, 109*, 449–460. doi:10.1016/j.jbusres.2019.11.058

Zainuddin, Z., Chu, S. K. W., Shujahat, M., & Perera, C. J. (2020). The impact of gamification on learning and instruction: A systematic review of empirical evidence. *Educational Research Review, 30*, 100326. doi:10.1016/j.edurev.2020.100326

Zhang, C. (2020). Governing (through) trustworthiness: Technologies of power and subjectification in China's social credit system. *Critical Asian Studies, 52*(4), 565–588. doi:10.1080/14672715.2020.1822194

ADDITIONAL READING

Kim, T. W. (2015, January). Gamification Ethics: Exploitation and Manipulation. *Gamifying Research Workshop Papers*. CHI 2015, Seoul, South Korea.

Kim, T. W. (2018). Gamification of Labor and the Charge of Exploitation. *Journal of Business Ethics, 152*(1), 27–39. doi:10.100710551-016-3304-6

Knight, A., & Creemers, R. (2021). *Going Viral: The Social Credit System and COVID-19* (SSRN Scholarly Paper ID 3770208). Social Science Research Network. doi:10.2139/ssrn.3770208

Koivisto, J., & Hamari, J. (2019). The rise of motivational information systems: A review of gamification research. *International Journal of Information Management, 45*, 191–210. doi:10.1016/j.ijinfomgt.2018.10.013

Kostka, G. (2019). China's social credit systems and public opinion: Explaining high levels of approval. *New Media & Society, 21*(7), 1565–1593. doi:10.1177/1461444819826402

Langer, P. F. (2020, June). Lessons from China - The Formation of a Social Credit System: Profiling, Reputation Scoring, Social Engineering. *21st Annual International Conference on Digital Government Research.* 10.1145/3396956.3396962

Toda, A., Valle, P. H., & Isotani, S. (2018). *The Dark Side of Gamification: An Overview of Negative Effects of Gamification in Education.* doi:10.1007/978-3-319-97934-2_9

Vieira dos Reis, A., & Press, L. T. (2019, October 29). Sesame Credit and the Social Compliance Gamification in China. In *Proceedings of SBGames 2019.* Brazilian Symposium on Computer Games and Digital Entertainment. https://www.sbgames.org/sbgames2019/files/papers/ArtesDesignFull/196937.pdf

Chapter 20
Gamifying Cultural Heritage. Education, Tourism Development, and Territory Promotion:
Two Italian Examples

Samanta Mariotti
(iD) https://orcid.org/0000-0001-8958-9293
University of Siena, Italy

ABSTRACT

In recent years, communication and digital technologies have widely affected the cultural heritage sector, offering incredible opportunities to enhance the experiential value of heritage assets and improve cultural activities. Furthermore, another trend has gained significant attention: increasing users' engagement through gamification. Several studies have shown the efficacy of gamification for learning achievements, and gaming is also emerging as a useful tool for touristic objectives such as marketing, dynamic engagement with users, and audience development. This chapter aims at presenting two Italian game projects for mobile devices, created to enhance and promote the cultural offer of two peculiar territories. Game design choices, objectives, and outcomes will be discussed to highlight the benefits and limits of these tools and point out the changing practices of cultural institutions and local administrations, which are showing an increasing interest in the exploitation of video games, considering them as strategic marketing tools to promote cultural heritage and tourism.

INTRODUCTION

In recent years, information and communication technologies have widely affected the cultural heritage sector, offering incredible opportunities to enhance the experiential value of heritage assets. The relationship between the cultural heritage domain and new technologies has always been complex and dialectical,

DOI: 10.4018/978-1-7998-9223-6.ch020

often characterized by the pursuit of technologies that can become a "deadweight" during users' cultural experiences (Cameron & Kenderdine, 2007), especially if they propose non-sustainable solutions, they are too invasive and they are not designed with a specific attention to the context and to users' needs.

In the last decades, with the increasingly widespread use of advanced personal devices technology such as smartphones and tablets and thanks to broadband internet access, the number of multimedia products developed within the cultural heritage community has certainly increased (Economou, 2015). Researchers have witnessed how innovative applications and services can shorten the distance between cultural spaces, such as museums, art exhibitions, historical centres archaeological parks, and citizens: technology can become a facilitator of interactions and connections between all involved actors, and create that common (digital) space where interventions can be sustainable, where enjoyment can be enhanced and where people can discover new places and learn more effectively about culture.

Digital tools have proved to be powerful instruments for improving cultural activities, and at the same time, they represent new paradigms for enhancing the diffusion and acquisition of the cultural message. Techniques like augmented reality, virtual reality, and, more broadly, all multimedia technologies are providing visitors with new ways to interact with cultural activities.

Furthermore, another trend has gained significant attention: increasing users' engagement through gaming and gamification. Several studies have shown the efficacy of gamification and serious games in dissemination and education, revealing improvements in learning achievements (Faiella & Ricciardi, 2015; Mortara et al., 2014; Read, 2015), public outreach activities (Mariotti 2021) and touristic outcomes (Dubois & Gibbs, 2018; Sajid et al., 2018).

The progress of human-machine interfaces, virtual reality, 3D, computer graphics and animation allowed to transfer the gamification approach and game-thinking in more serious contexts, including the cultural sector.

Gaming (or electronic games) provide players with an immersive and interactive entertainment experience often through dynamic and real-time interaction with their context, local organisations and fellow players (Doughty & O'Coill, 2005). With the rapid development of mobile devices, such as smartphones and tablets, gaming becomes mobile and allows dynamic interaction at the location of the user. Smartphones enable players to interact with their real-world environment in real-time. Researchers suggest that mobile games have changed the game players' experiences in many ways. One of the fundamental changes is that gaming experiences have been extended into the real world, and are potentially available at any place and at any time.

Gaming, as a cutting-edge concept, is emerging as a useful tool and has also been used by many tourism organisations for marketing, for dynamic engagement with users, and in general, for audience development (Xu et al., 2015). As a new approach to promote tourism destinations, gaming provides tourism organisations, cultural institutions and destination marketers an opportunity to create informative and entertaining settings for successful brand awareness, interaction and communication.

This chapter aims at presenting the potential of digital gamification applied to the heritage sector through the presentation of two Italian case studies regarding two different digital games projects for mobile devices developed by Entertainment Game Apps, Ltd. (EGA), a serious game company whose mission is to create historical-archaeological videogames enhancing cultural heritage thanks to contents accurately conceived and designed in collaboration with researchers and experts in the specific fields.

Game design choices, objectives and outcomes will be discussed to highlight the benefits and limits of these tools and point out the changing practices of cultural institutions and local administrations, which are showing increasing interest in the exploitation of gamification practices and video games, considering them as strategic marketing tools to promote cultural heritage, territories and tourism.

BACKGROUND

Recently, persuasive technologies such as gaming and the application of game elements have been used in non-gaming contexts, such as business, health and education (Xu et al., 2014): a very fortunate trend that is now widely known as gamification.

The term gamification was coined in 2002 (Marczewski, 2012) and has made its appearance in 2008 in education technology literature (Deterding et al., 2011). In 2010 the term began to be used more frequently, but still, there are not many systematic studies that have dealt with this subject and for this reason reference to games and video games is inevitable. By analyzing the different definitions of gamification in the international literature (Deterding et al., 2011; Marczewski, 2012; Perrotta et al., 2013; Simões et al., 2013; de Sousa Borges et al., 2014), a substantial agreement among contributors who consider gamification as an approach that uses game features (elements, mechanics, frameworks, aesthetics, thinking, metaphors) into non-game settings can be noticed. The term gamification is used in relation to many issues - the pervasiveness and ubiquity of computer games and video games in everyday life; the need to arouse and maintain students' interest in learning – to involve users and encourage them to achieve more ambitious goals, following rules and having fun. Therefore gamification is recommended for applications in the areas of daily life where boredom, repetition and passivity are prevalent to encourage a desired type of behaviour.

The core of its concept is the idea that the use of games, both as an applied subset of design elements or as models for simulating whole activities, can imbue non-game contexts of positive values associated with games. These "gameful" values would, then, foster a change of behaviour and perception about the non-game activity being gamified. This persuasive capacity of gamification operates in two dimensions, one related to cultural and societal framing of games and gamification and the other to the systemic persuasive characteristics of these systems to foster a change of behaviour and perception in users-players (Llagostera, 2012). Persuasive technology is broadly defined as technology that is designed to change attitudes or behaviour of users through persuasion and social influence (Bogost, 2007). Persuasive applications are often computerized software or information systems designed to reinforce, change or shape attitudes or behaviours or both, without using coercion or deception (Oinas-Kukkonen & Harjumaa, 2008).

Gaming is regarded as a closed system in which guidelines and rules have to be clearly stated beforehand (Salen & Zimmermann, 2004). McGonigal (2011) suggests that goals, rules, feedback systems and voluntary participation are important characteristics of gaming. Crawford (2011) states that a game is a subset of reality in which the players dive in while playing. Juul (2003) adds emotional attachment of a player assigned to the game itself and its specific outcome.

Moreover, with the popularity of smartphones and tablets, gaming experiences have become much more mobile and context plays a critical role in the gaming experience. In this paper, gaming is intended as a digital game played on mobile devices and smartphones and dedicated to a well-defined context. Mobile games emphasize mobility and positioning, often using the context of their location as the background for the game. Klopfer & Squire (2008) observe that mobile gaming is expanding to more context-sensitive, supporting game apps that relate the player to his physical location and encourage users to complete local tasks, as well as connect with and compete against other players. The technological features of the latest generation of smart devices has been introducing gaming experiences into entirely new solutions (Garcia et al., 2018). In addition, from smartphone game apps to online social interaction, technology and social media has made gaming rapidly acceptable for both males and females, young and old as well as people who have never played games before.

Heritage institutions have been experimenting with these tools for quite some time as part of their efforts at greater democratization, opening up to diverse communities and inviting different viewpoints and interpretations of their sites and collections. In the last decades, researchers have witnessed the increasing use of games to support cultural heritage promotion, such as historical knowledge learning and teaching, or promoting museums and sites tourism (Anderson et al., 2010). The majority of architectural and cultural heritage awareness games either offer an immersive, realistic reconstruction of reallocation to appreciate and learn the artistic, architectural, or values of cultural heritage sites or provides an engaging method to persuade users into the real experience (Mortara & Catalano, 2018). As Khan et al. (2020) state, museums, as well as highly cultural heritage attractions, are multi-functional services whose mandates commonly comprise a variety of objectives and are usually considered as being informal education and training sites and have been broadly recognized for their ability to promote the development of interest, motivation, enthusiasm, general openness, alertness and eagerness to learn and cultural awareness.

As many scholars state, video games are an acknowledged tool for several purposes (Granic et al., 2014) and from cultural perspective, among this range of possibilities, they can meet cultural institutions aims and so, represent an extraordinary medium for heritage enhancement. First of all, they are a potential for public outreach and education, because they can strongly motivate learners and create awareness about a topic. They can also provide immersive environments where a large variety of users can practice knowledge and skills, and finally, they can be used as an asset to promote tourism and sustainable cultural heritage development.

Video games for cultural heritage seem particularly suited for the affective domain. Empathy with a game character and plot may be very helpful to understand historical events, different ancient cultures, other people's feelings, problems, and behaviours, on the one hand, and the beauty and value of the past, architecture, art, and heritage, on the other one. This persuasive approach should be combined with the rigour of the scientific method, which is a balance not easy to achieve, not only in games. As pointed out by Mortara et al. (2014), games are particularly suited to implement the "learning by doing" approach (Dewey, 1938), which is related to the constructivism theory, where the player learns by constructing knowledge while doing a meaningful activity. In this approach to education, the learner does not passively receive information – as in a simple explanation, a panel or a virtual reconstruction although accompanied by a description – but rather actively constructs new knowledge by finding information in the game, understanding it, and then applying the new knowledge to fulfil tasks (Boyan & Sherry, 2011). As underlined in Froschauer (2012), players remember more the knowledge related to task completion than information directly provided by the game, not to mention that simply responding to direct instructions would not be fun at all.

On the public engagement side, video games are a form of new media, whose novel affordances facilitate active participation and agency through player interaction with both content and digital systems, thus providing the player with the ability to direct or alter the course and outcome of the game as it progresses. The thrill of discovery and exploration combined with the opportunity to engage in a challenge or an adventure is something that appeals both on an instinctive and emotional level. Video games have played into this desire in several ways (Mariotti, 2021). One above all, because they allow players to immerse themselves in the experience. Games, in fact, engage people psychologically – they can be very emotional experiences – and they also engage people physiologically. A compelling experience develops memory hooks and means that learners not only remember what happened but also why it happened.

At the same time, and in a similar manner, the use of games offers a variety of benefits for cultural tourism marketing too and can increase brand awareness, attract potential customers, enhance tourists' on-site experiences and increase engagement (Mariotti, 2021). The use of games in the tourism industry may potentially provide great marketing opportunities (Bulencea & Egger, 2015). Tourism is an experience industry (Pine & Gilmore, 2011) that is increasingly based on co-creating customizable services. New technologies such as social media, smartphones, and gaming provide technological tools for developing such experiences.

The importance of using experiential information in promoting stimuli for cultural tourism marketing has been recognized by many academics (Huang et al., 2013). Williams (2006) recommends the use of immersive virtual environments as a new approach to promote tourism sites, offers destination marketers an opportunity to create informative and entertaining settings for successful interaction and communication between the destination and the tourists (Bogdanovych et al. 2007) but also between territories and local citizens who can have the opportunity to discover new things about their surroundings. In addition, gaming provides a good opportunity to build an online community as often a sense of community is identified (Fong & Frost, 2009).

The tourism industry provides multidimensional and multifaceted experiences. Researchers suggest that leisure experiences are about feeling, fantasy and fun (Holbrook & Hirschman, 1982), escape and relaxation (Beard & Ragheb, 1983), entertainment (Farber & Hall, 2007), and novelty and surprise (Duman & Mattila, 2005). The research on tourist experiences could benefit from gaming and gamification research since game features can be considered a tool to engage people in tasks (Nicholson, 2015), promote relationships (Caporarello et al., 2017), or improve motivation (Sailer et al., 2017), the enjoyment of playing (Klimmt, 2003) and the desire to continue playing to challenge one's own abilities (Brown & Vaughn, 2011). The different types of emotion, such as hope, fear, excitement (Zichermann & Cunningham, 2011), the experiences of fantasy, fun, discovery and challenges, all contribute to a deep engagement and the addiction to gameplay and engaging with tourism organizations, local administrations and territories. So, gamification as well as digital games aim at adding new driving components that can draw the attention of users, pushing them to participate and fulfil achievements, encouraging them to invest their time in cultural activities, modifying, in fact, their behaviour. Gamification strategies appear consistent with cultural heritage institutions' goals to promote territories, museums, and encourage touristic experiences.

TWO GAMES FOR TWO TERRITORIES

In this section, the two culture-centric games (Majewski, 2017) – *Memories* and *The Umbrian Chronicles* – developed by Entertainment Game Apps Ltd. will be discussed and analyzed. Even if the two study cases have very different objectives and backgrounds (which obviously depend on the content, the context, and the potential public), still a general common line can be detected. In both cases, projects' objectives, game design choices, and outcomes will be illustrated and collaboration between local cultural institutions, gamification experts, and the above-mentioned serious game company will be examined.

Case Study I: *Memories*

Project Overview

The video game *Memories* was developed as part of the Abruzzi regional project LAB8, winner of the tender "Restart: development of cultural potential for the tourist attraction of the Crater" that involved the 11 municipalities of the province of L'Aquila (Acciano, Barisciano, Fagnano Alto, Fontecchio, Fossa, Ocre, Poggio Picenze, San Demetrio ne' Vestini, Sant'Eusanio Forconese, Tione Degli Abruzzi, Villa Sant'Angelo) strongly affected by the 2009 earthquake. The objective of the project, which also involved the University of L'Aquila, the Soprintendenza Archeologia, Belle Arti e Paesaggio of L'Aquila, and The Academy of Fine Arts in L'Aquila, was to take stock of the state of the art and share a vision and perspective of future development for this area, that would last after the effort on physical reconstruction would be concluded. Twelve years later, in fact, this territory is still deeply affected by the earthquake's consequences: many areas, houses, and monuments are still highly damaged and inaccessible and, in some cases, the rubble has not yet been cleared due to the danger of further collapsing. The physiognomy of these villages has changed as the lives of their inhabitants. A future perspective has to be taken into serious consideration since the risk of abandonment is very high. According to the last census (data updated to May 2019 and August 2020), only four municipalities out of eleven show a population between 1.000 and 2.000 inhabitants. In the other seven cases, the average population is only 400 residents.

The revitalization of small towns that have lost their identity also goes through the reconstruction of places, people and stories which represent the backbone, the more intimate and at the same time more exposed part marked by profound changes. So, the main challenge for the LAB8 project was twofold and vital: revitalize the territory in fact, also means giving a future to those people who still live there. There can be no innovation that strives for economic improvement that does not also provide special attention to the well-being of the people who live in and represent those places. The LAB8 project stems from the desire to combine the enhancement of cultural material and immaterial assets of the 11 Municipalities of the so-called "Homogeneous Area 8 of L'Aquila Crater" with the development of infrastructures that can make the villages accessible, welcoming, and able to prepare a coordinated and modern tourist offer.

In this context, the video game *Memories* stands as an original tool to promote the rich local heritage, as it involves the player in the rediscovery of landscapes, monuments and artistic beauties scattered around the small towns of this part of Abruzzo and as it was specifically designed to enhance and promote the territories of the 11 municipalities involved in the project. To do so, a careful photographic survey was conducted over several weeks, information about villages, monuments, and cultural attractions was collected (together with their actual state of preservation and accessibility), and the game design was carefully adapted to the main project's objective. From a general perspective, all the core features of the game are conceived to give the players a feeling of presence (Riva et al., 2003) in the real places; to do so, every single spot (even those that are currently inaccessible), for a total of 117 sites, has been drawn with total accuracy starting from thousands of photographs (1604 to be exact) taken throughout the territory.

The next step regarded the systematization and organization of the collected material for each municipality to organize information around three main topics: history, buildings/landscapes, and synthesis. For each municipality, an in-depth analysis of the buildings and landscapes of cultural interest, studying their relationship with the territory, the typology, the history, their accessibility and possible geolocation was conducted. Among this material, 90 points of interest to be included in the game have been selected. Next, they have been divided into five main categories: church, monument, historic building, tower, and landscape. For each spot, a set of information has been collected to let players get a general idea of the context.

The Game

The game develops from a map representing the Abruzzi territory of the 11 municipalities and their relative hamlets (Figure 1). Each player's objective is to unlock all the "photographic" polaroid cards illustrating the 90 points of interest and by doing so, collect their own set of memories. To do so, the player has to walk a precise number of steps for each card (Figure 2). The basic mechanics of the game take advantage of the step counter incorporated in the majority of smart and mobile devices. The related objective is to promote physical activity and possibly stimulate players' curiosity to encourage them to visit those places.

Figure 1. Map of the game representing the 11 municipalities territory

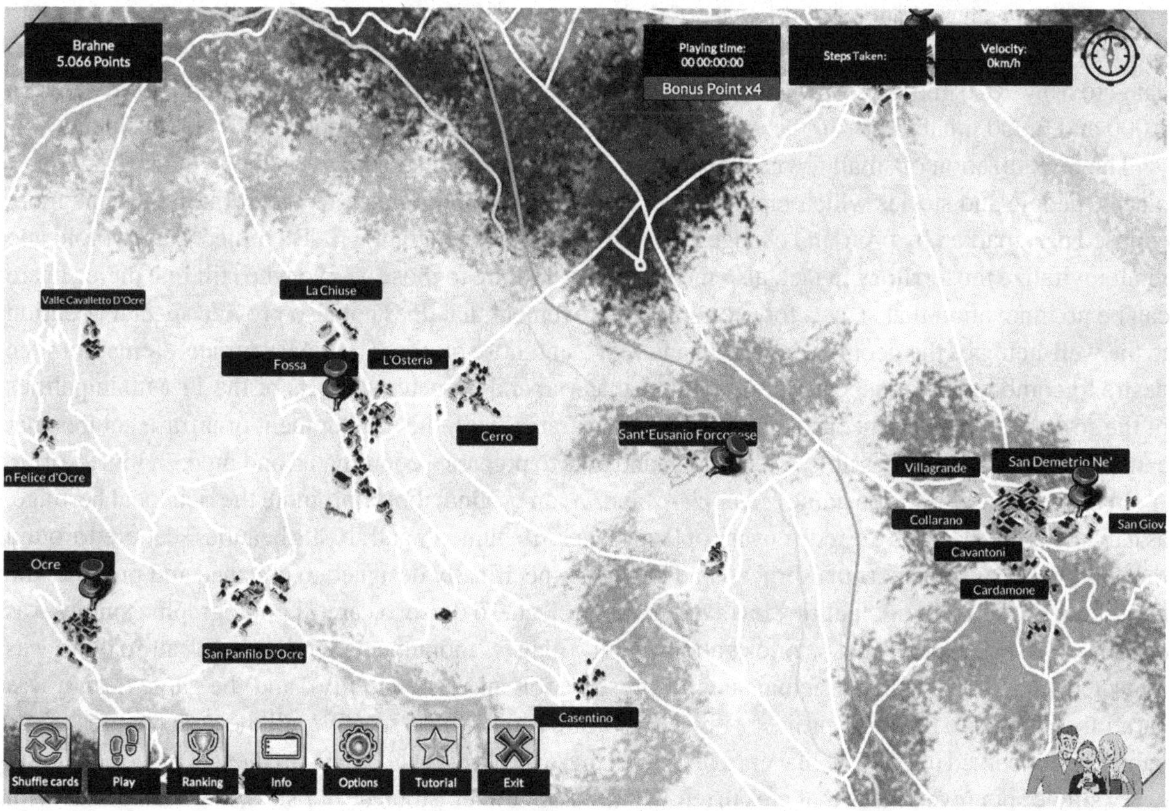

Figure 2. Indication of steps to be taken to unlock the cards

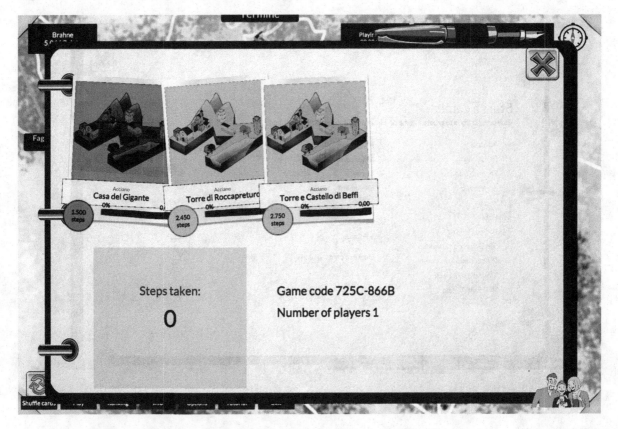

The game offers the user different cards randomly, based on specific criteria that he/she decides to apply: the player can decide the number of cards for each game; he/she can choose on the basis of their type (monument, historical building, church, tower or landscape) or he/she can select a specific municipal area (Figure 3). Once unlocked, the card will give access to extra content regarding the illustrated spot (Figure 4). The game also provides a multiplayer mode called "tournament" that gives the player the chance to challenge other users by playing with the same set of cards (Figure 5).

Figure 3. Game customization and selection of criteria

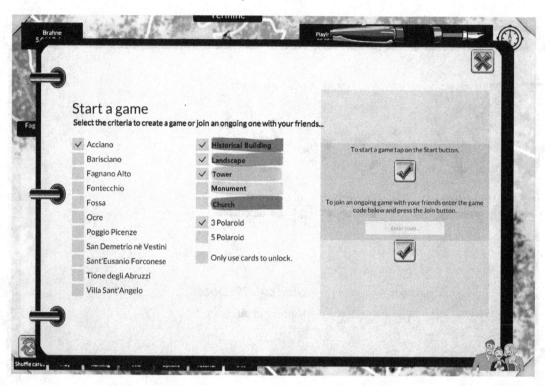

Figure 4. Card content unlocked and indication for accessibility

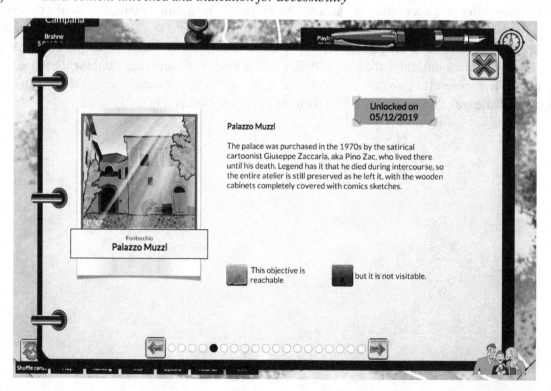

Figure 5. Multiplayer mode

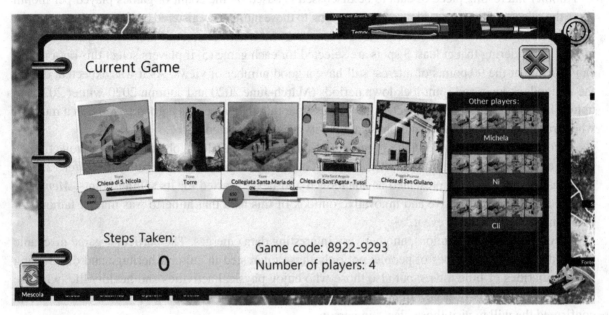

Numbers and Outcomes

Memories was released in the Italian and English language at the end of 2019 for Android and iOS devices. As already mentioned, the objectives of the game were very specific and ambitious: contribute to the revitalization of a damaged and very little-known territory.

Table 1. Memories, number of downloads per country

Country	Downloads	Incidence (%)
Italy	3.481	97,89%
USA	4	0,11%
United Kingdom	2	0,06%
Albania	1	0,03%
unknown	68	1,91%
TOTAL	3.556	

As it is clear from Table 1, so far data (updated to the end of July 2021 and collected through the game server) indicate 3.556 downloads, the vast majority of cases regarding Italian players. A more precise provenance could not be established, but the feedback on the app stores show a large number of users coming from all over Italy. The users' comments show that the game mechanic was highly appreciated, even if, unfortunately, due to the inaccessibility of some places involved in the game, the number of steps couldn't be associated with the location-based smartphone system. The data available so far, show a total amount of 2.455.050 registered steps taken (about 1870 km).

Another interesting piece of data to be discussed is based on the count of games played per month since the release of the game (Figure 6). According to these numbers registered by the game server, even if a physiological deflection can be observed, one year and a half later, a fair amount of games are still played. Considering that at least 3 spots are selected for each game (5, if players select this option), we can affirm that the 90 points of interest still have a good number of views. As it was expected, during the Italian lockdown and semi-lockdown periods (March-June 2020 and autumn 2020-winter 2021) an upturn in the numbers can be detected: we can assume that the game was a good pastime in a moment when travelling was forbidden and physical activity was very limited.

According to the feedback on the stores, people also valued the global objective of the project. They openly congratulated and admired Entertainment Game Apps tribute to this territory that after 12 years is almost neglected, often presented as abandoned and never praised for its selling points. *Memories* contributed to give a positive and innovative outlook of this area that hitherto was mainly famous for being the scene of a tragic event.

According to users' opinions, another very interesting data emerges. The particular game mechanic engaged very different types of people: not only those interested in cultural heritage and discovering the peculiarities of little towns, but also those who enjoy physical activities and healthy life, who use the video game to discover new things and new places while doing something they like. Many of them confirmed the will to visit those places in person.

Figure 6. Memories, number of games played per month

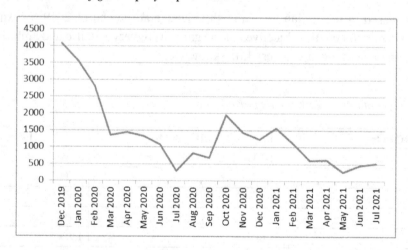

Case Study II: *The Umbrian Chronicles*

Project Overview

The video game *The Umbrian Chronicles* was developed as part of the project "Museum Connections: between valleys and mountains, villages and cities" promoted and funded by the Umbria Region, to enhance the cultural and environmental heritage of 11 museums (Collicola Palace, the Roman House, the Museum of Textile and Costume, the Museum of the Former Spoleto-Norcia Railway, the Morgnano Mines Museum, the Earthly Sciences Lab, the Hemp Museum, the Chariot Museum, The House of Tales, the Museum of Mummies, the Museum of the Charlatan) located in 5 municipalities (Spoleto, Sant'Anatolia di Narco, Monteleone di Spoleto, Vallo di Nera, Cerreto di Spoleto) in the territory of Spoleto and Valnerina. The game was developed for smartphones and tablets and it can be used as a playful, promotional and educational tool, for the institutions and territories involved in the project.

Figure 7. Game setting and interface: 3D low poly reconstructions of the main points of interest

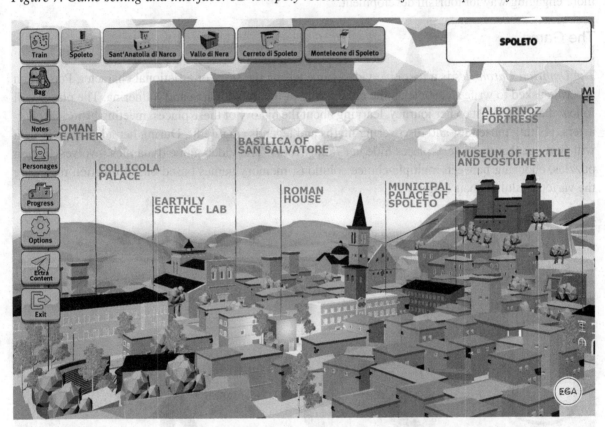

For each municipality involved, useful information to conceive the video game was collected: famous characters, buildings, historical details, legends/myths, and more. For the development of the video game, Entertainment Game Apps planned a series of inspections, supervised by the cultural association Italian Videogame Program. Later, the most suitable information for the development of the video game, such as historical characters linked to places or institutions, was selected from each municipality file record. As it is easy to imagine, the objective of the project required the design of the video game to allow the inclusion of a large variety of points of interest. The cultural institutions involved in the project, in fact, are museums of very different types: they span from classical archaeological museums to documentation centres, from ethnographic museums to historical palaces. Moreover, many other very important spots throughout the territory were selected such as the Roman Theatre, the Albornoz Fortress and the Basilica of San Salvatore in Spoleto; the Abbey of San Felice and Mauro in Sant'Anatolia di Narco; the ancient Convent of Saint Caterina in Monteleone di Spoleto.

The game environment involves the 5 Umbrian municipalities territory: from the photographic material collected, Spoleto and its surroundings were reconstructed in 3D. The game setting highlights the main sites in the municipalities involved: with a low poly aesthetic able to make them, in a stylized but realistic way, immediately recognizable to the player, 3D models of the identified points of interest (museums, fortresses, palaces, and churches) have been reproduced (Figure 7). In this way, the video game becomes a didactic tool that can be used both on-site and off-site, and a touristic asset that can be exploited by local administrations and cultural institutions to promote the local cultural heritage in a more engaging way for tourism development.

The Game

The Umbrian Chronicles is a narrative video game telling the story of a fictional character, Ponzia, an art critic asked to write an article on the cultural life of the Spoleto area and Valnerina. The player will follow the protagonist on her journey, learning about the history of these places, meeting historical characters, visiting museums, and discovering myths and legends (Figure 8). During her adventure, Ponzia will find out that those very places hide her family roots. The video game dynamics involves solving puzzles, choosing between multiple-choice solutions, memory games based on information regarding the various cultural spots (Figure 9).

Figure 8. Cover of the game and main characters

Figure 9. Game screen with indication of game progress

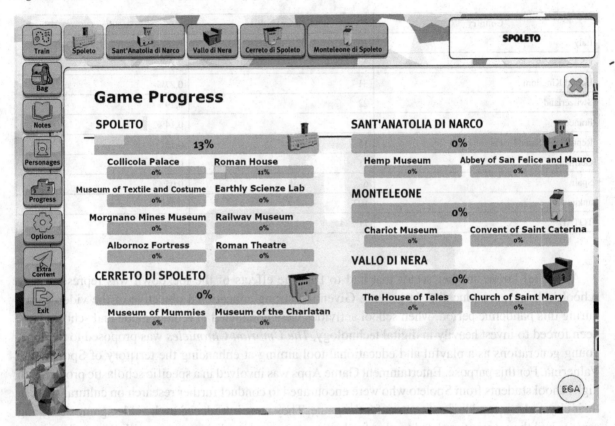

Numbers and Outcomes

The Umbrian Chronicles was released in the Italian and English language at the end of 2020 for Android and iOS devices, in a very difficult time for the tourism industry. This territory, like Italy in general, has suffered greatly from the consequences of the COVID-19 pandemic.

So far data (updated to the end of July 2021 and collected through the game server) indicate 11.524 downloads. The majority of players are Italian but other nationalities are attested, mostly European and 3,19% from the USA (Table 2).

Table 2. The Umbrian Chronicles, number of downloads per country

Country	Downloads	Incidence (%)
Italy	10.948	95%
USA	368	3,19%
United Kingdom	31	0,27%
Switzerland	22	0,19%
France	16	0,14%
Republic of San Marino	15	0,13%
Germany	11	0,10%
Spain	6	0,05%
unknown	107	0,93%
TOTAL	11.524	

As we all know, another sector that had to face the effects of the lockdown was represented by schools' classes and education in general. Given the strong educational objective of the video game, during this pandemic period, when school activities were conducted in remote mode and schools have been forced to invest heavily in digital technology, *The Umbrian Chronicles* was proposed to the local young generations as a playful and educational tool aiming at enhancing the territory of Spoleto and Valnerina. For this purpose, Entertainment Game Apps was involved in a specific scholastic project with high school students from Spoleto who were encouraged to conduct further research on cultural spots in their city and create additional content for the game. They were introduced to the video game designing aspects and they were stimulated to plan further steps to promote their territory with the precise aim to transform them into the main curators and promoters of the cultural attractions of the Spoleto area. They created new mini-games, they added information and some of them also collaborated on the illustration's aspects. The project was considered and presented as a project of excellence during the Literally Classical Lyceum National Night and on the TV program *Tg2 Weekend*, a column of the Italian news Tg2. On these occasions, the features and the benefits of such an educational program developed in collaboration with a video game company and through the use of digital technologies were underlined by both students and teachers.

Furthermore, a specific monitoring activity has been set by submitting two questionnaires to the local junior high schools' classes. The first survey involved 152 students. They were first asked if they had already played a game related to a museum. 86,8% of them answered "no", only 5,9% answered "yes" and 7,2% said they didn't remember. When asked if they would have liked to play a game dedicated to the museums on their territory, the majority (78,3%) said "yes", 10,5% were undecided while 11,2% said "no". They were also asked to indicate those museums (among those included in the video game) they already heard about (Figure 10) or visited (Figure 11). The most famous ones (the Albornoz Fortress, the Roman House, Collicola Palace, the Archaeological Museum of Spoleto, the Museum of the Former Spoleto-Norcia Railway known by more than half of the students) correspond to the most visited ones (with an average of 5% discrepancy). It is noteworthy that almost 4% of the students had never heard about any of these museums.

During this first survey, students were also asked if they thought video games could be a good tool to encourage them to better understand their region. 48,7% answered positively, 27% of them was not sure, and 24,3% said "no".

Figure 10. Responses to the question "Which museums have you heard of?"

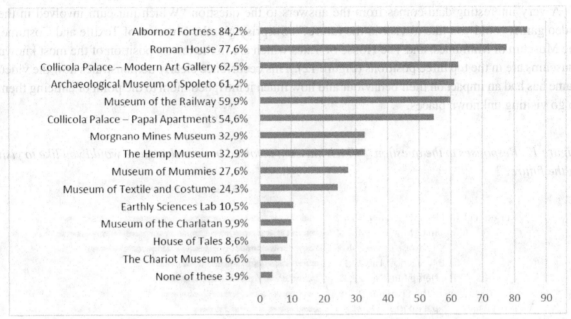

Figure 11. Responses to the question "Which museums have you visited?"

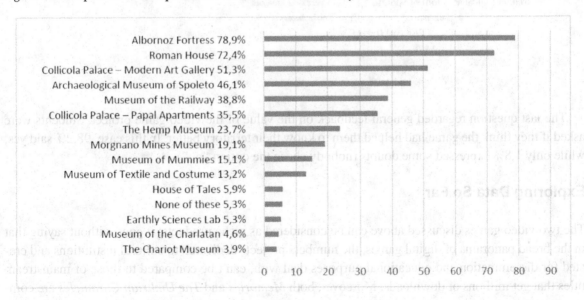

The second survey was administered to those students who had played *The Umbrian Chronicles* (55 players so far, but the study is still ongoing) to evaluate the actual impact of the game on their approaches to cultural heritage and their responses. Thus, the assessment is still partial, the earliest data show positive feedback and allow some reflection on the opportunity and the benefits of these digital tools. First of all, they were asked if they liked the game: 56,4% said they liked it "very much", 41,8% "enough", 1,8% "so and so", while no one chose the two other options "a little" and "at all".

A very interesting data comes from the answers to the question "Which museum involved in the video game would you like to visit in the future?". Surprisingly, the Museum of Textile and Costume, the Museum of Mummies, and The House of Tales which are in the lowest position of the most known museums are in the top three positions (Figure 12). This occurrence clearly demonstrates how the video game has had an impact on their behaviour and how much it intrigued them to the point of enticing them to go visiting unknown places.

Figure 12. Responses to the question "Which museum involved in the video game would you like to visit in the future?"

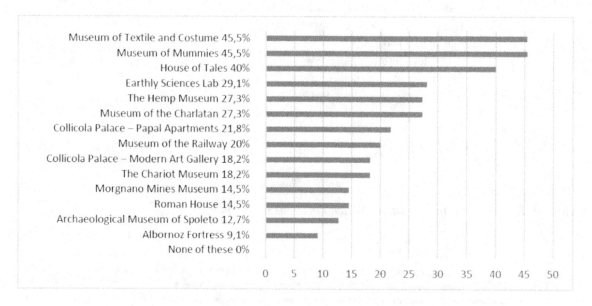

The last question regarded general feedback on the value of the video game project. Students were asked if they think the game had helped them to know their territory better. In this case, 98,2% said yes, while only 1,8% expressed some doubts (nobody chose the option "no").

Exploring Data So Far

The two video games discussed above can be considered as niche products: it goes without saying that in the broad panorama of digital games, the numbers projects dedicated to cultural institutions and created for dissemination and educational purposes deal with, can't be compared to those of mainstream titles that get millions of downloads. Moreover, both *Memories* and *The Umbrian Chronicles* are commissioned projects which have a very specific target based on two very defined territories and their promotion: in the first case, it is a very damaged area that, from a touristic point of view, is still suffering the consequences of the earthquake; in the second case, the Valnerina territory is the destination of a particular type of tourism - green, sustainable, and slow - far from the large numbers of the most famous art cities and their mass tourism. Despite these premises, the download numbers of the two games suggest an undeniable curiosity both for the video game project per se and for the territorial game content. Another interesting finding is represented by the nationality of users: while, as it is predictable, the majority of players comes from Italy, a certain variety of other provenances is also attested. Obviously, it doesn't mean necessarily that all those users were spending their time in those territories, nor that the game has encouraged all of them to go visiting those places (the pandemic made it impossible to have data available for analysis). However, it is a fact that many different users from the USA and the main European countries had the opportunity to get to know better the cultural offer of two little known, yet culturally rich and beautiful, territories. Besides, video game-induced tourism is already a recognized phenomenon (Dubois & Gibbs, 2018). A recent survey of 827 Italian gamers carried out by the project Italian Videogame Program (2019) confirmed that the majority of them (79.9%) are willing to visit a place they got to know through a video game and that 47,9% already have done so.

Moreover, the close collaboration between a private video game company, cultural institutions, and local administrations is a very crucial and significant occurrence that deserved to be considered more in detail. First of all, it shows the growing interest of cultural institutions and administrations in exploiting digital game and gamification in general for the promotion of museums, sites and territories; secondarily, it underlines the benefits of the collaboration between the public and the private spheres represented by those organizations that are in charge of the conservation and the promotion of cultural heritage and, in this case, a private company that can offer its professionalism in designing a game able to meet the needs of commissioners (Bonacini & Giaccone, 2021). Entertainment Game Apps took charge not only of the technical and programming sides, but also of the research part, the content creation, and the narrative aspects.

Furthermore, in 2020, the unexpected COVID-19 pandemic forced the governments of many countries, among them Italy, to enforce the total closure of all non-essential structures and activities, museums included. Museums unable to open their doors to a visiting public have had to take the only option of spreading culture and knowledge through online and digital means (Agostino et al., 2020). At the same time, also tourism suffered the consequences of the closed borders and isolation, and it continues to be one of the sectors hit hardest by the COVID-19 pandemic. It appears quite obvious that, also due to the particular situation, 2020 marked a record in the use of digital content. A very recent survey (Creative Keys 2020) shows that, during the lockdown, video games were amongst the tools cultural institutions used to engage with their public. According to the survey, people who played serious games linked to a cultural institution stated that: they have the perception of having learnt something (78%), they enjoyed that time (85.8%), they were encouraged to try other digital games with cultural content (81.1%), and more than half of them (54.4%) confirmed their willingness to visit those sites or museums in the future.

The analysis conducted so far shows that both video games are successful examples of the application of gaming experiences to cultural heritage (Mortara et al., 2014). This is confirmed by the very positive feedback from players, particularly appreciating: the quality of historical-cultural content and the resulting learning opportunity; the playful game experience itself allowing players to explore unknown places and museums; the challenges faced to unlock game levels as well as the engaging prize mechanisms. This is consistent with previous studies assessing the relevance of game design on learning and engagement of players (Paliokas & Sylaiou, 2016; Rowe et al., 2017; Rubino et al., 2015). Players' feedback also shed light on the opportunity to promote developers-players interaction encouraging player involvement in co-designing some elements of the game, so to improve the game features and strengthen the relationship with users.

Finally, we cannot fail to mention the excellent educational outcomes of *The Umbrian Chronicles*, which gave teachers and students the uncommon opportunity to exploit and experiment with video games mechanics to promote but also create culture and value.

SOLUTIONS AND RECOMMENDATIONS

Researchers agree that digital games are an acknowledged tool for several purposes and while previously welcoming gamification as an educational tool for accessing their exhibitions (in particular in scientific museums, where interaction gaming is a typical approach), cultural institutions are now proactively also engaged in producing video games, as well as in managing them as digital marketing tools to implement new specific strategies of cultural dissemination, audience development and engagement through a gamified approach. The growing active involvement of cultural institutions in producing and using video games (Bonacini & Giaccone, 2021) shows a promising and long-term evolutionary path of their role in cultural heritage management, as well as audience development strategies.

However, all that glitters is not gold and the risks that digital tools might be just the "must-have current trend" should also be considered to avoid a meaningless rush in order to keep up with cutting-edge technologies. As Economou (2015) argues, even if heritage digitization programs have been creating digital resources which constitute the building blocks of research, learning, management, cultural tourism, the general understanding and appreciation of heritage, and even if these resources are often used to create interpretative and "edutainment" applications related to heritage, it is not the tools or the digital assets themselves which are causing concerns, but rather the use that these are being put to. Who is producing them and towards what means? In what way are these being used and by whom? Are they actually effective and engaging? These are amongst the most important questions researchers and professionals should give an answer before diving into a digital cultural project to avoid the risk of pursuing the mere digitalization of the existent and its simple presentation in a different form (just more eye catching). Additionally, in a good digital cultural project, the context and the users have to be carefully assessed: what is good in one case, may be totally wrong for another. The challenge for the future in this field is the exploitation of tools (such as digital games) that can promote the creation of awareness, lasting engagement, and critical knowledge starting from a specific and scientifically validated cultural content that should be maintained as the main focus of the project (Mariotti, 2021).

Finally, a last consideration about the opportunity of promoting tourism through digital games. Being one of the world's largest and most pervasive industries, the travel and tourism sector is as exposed as any other to the forces of change that are at work in the rapid developments in the information and communication technologies arena. That's why it is possible to foresee a growing number of digital gamification projects applied to this sector. In the future, it is to be expected that the combination of heritage and gaming becomes one of the main assets in cultural promotion strategies and also a sector capable of employing many people.

FUTURE RESEARCH DIRECTIONS

According to Black (2012), one of the main challenges museums face as cultural institutions is renewing their approach to their visitors in order to transform them from one-time users into visitors who perceive themselves as active participants engaging with the museum's collections and works. The same practice can be broadly applied to any site or monument considered as cultural heritage if we want people to care about it and take care of it. This process is quite slow and discontinuous if we consider the Italian panorama. However, in the last years, some adjustments can be detected and a growing number of cultural institutions have been slowly changing their attitude toward their public. The gradual transformation of the public from being "visitors" to being "participants" guarantees that their experience is enjoyable and interactive. Nevertheless, as new museums and institutions are seeking to be more engaging in their approaches, new communications technologies and, more particularly, gaming and gamification have become remarkable tools owing to their enjoyable and engaging natures. To further emphasize the significance of a gamified approach as a way for enhancing the attraction of sites and museums from the viewpoint of visitors, the term "prosumers" can be utilized. Coşkun and Yılmaz (2016) point out the evolution of consumers in the tourism industry and state that the developments in communication technologies have increased the rate of the transformation of consumers into prosumers. Laconically, prosumer refers to the dedifferentiation between the producer and consumer. Having said that gamification can blur the relationship between producers (museums) and consumers (visitors) and create meaningful interactivity. For example, visitors can play games offered by museums for cultural purposes to complete the levels and get rewards such as discounts or free admission tickets; by playing the game, or consuming the experience that is offered, they are, however, producing new products for themselves.

Gamification and video game design for cultural heritage promotion should definitely follow this approach. The cooperation between cultural institutions, gaming and gamification professionals, and content experts is the main ingredient to certify the validity of a project and to create valuable game experiences capable of engaging users and promoting territories touristic offers.

The tourism industry as well as all kinds of cultural experiences in the future will be based heavily on customization. Game mechanisms and the game elements if applied in cultural tourism can bring excitement, fun, arousal, pleasure and a sense of achievement and can help engage a greater number of tourists (Xu et al., 2014). Additionally, the increasing convenience of 3D and interactive digital technologies will give further opportunities to explore the potential of these means for touristic outcomes. Future scenarios suggest a diffusion of a play-centric approach to life and wider use of gamification in the fields of knowledge management and social learning, and this trend will accelerate the social innovation processes. In fact, the "virality" (typical mechanism of content diffusion on the Net) generates imitative behaviours and helps to spread more and more the game thinking and game dynamics in our society.

Moreover, as Mariotti (2021) and Sailer et al. (2017) mention, while several video games and gamification projects involving cultural heritage and territories promotion have been developed in the last years, and despite the consensus that they have as a tool for education and users' engagement, still the literature stresses a lack of significant, extensive user tests. 11 years ago, Bellotti et al. (2010) affirmed that further research was necessary to investigate in greater detail the real effectiveness of the various types of video games, to define a methodology based on metrics and evaluation tools. This still remains valid for video games aiming at enhancing cultural content.

In this sense, the evaluation project developed on *The Umbrian Chronicles* can be a first step in this direction. Further assessment must be carried out to implement data, build a wider case history, compare data with other similar projects, and plan future improvements for gaming projects applied to cultural heritage.

CONCLUSION

As Robson et al. (2015) affirm, gaming and gamification can change stakeholder behaviour because it taps into motivational drivers of human behaviour in two connected ways: reinforcements and emotions. Through the motivational mechanisms of reinforcements and emotions, desired outcomes become automatic behavioural processes or habits. Gamification can produce desired behaviour change through the formation of habits by reinforcing the reward and emotional response of the individuals participating in the experience, thus requiring fewer cognitive resources each time the desired activity is reproduced.

Based on the recent systematic review by Khan and colleagues (2020), over the past five years, researchers and producers are using a gamified approach as a comprehensive tool to develop innovative systems and applications for the promotion of cultural heritage. Moreover, gamified tools can motivate tourists to visit cultural heritage and explore historical sites by playing video games. Furthermore, the systematic review highlights the importance of the gamification method and how we can develop gamification not only with AR and VR tools but through various approaches. The review studies describes that gamification does not only offer entertainment platforms but also offers tourists the means to enhance their knowledge level by playing serious games.

Applying digital technologies to gamification means broadening the effects and the possibilities of creating engagement and motivation around a specific topic.

The two projects presented are two examples of an increasing phenomenon that is affecting the cultural heritage sector in the last decades. Moreover, in the Italian panorama, they represent a successful model of the positive collaboration between cultural institutions, local administrations and a video game company: an occurrence that is more and more evident and that will get even more remarkable in the future. The data presented, even if limited at two projects and in some cases, partial, provide insights into the potential of games and their nature to facilitate engagement and knowledge enhancement. Future studies should be conducted to assess more in detail the positive (and the critical) effects of this approach. However, the cases study presented in the paper suggests that, by using the theoretical framework of motivational factors related to digital gamification together with the benefits of cooperation between different actors, and accurate research on the territory, it is possible to envision how a previously less ludic tourism context might be gamified by creating a dedicated video game and to offer the users not only a "game board", but a whole playground where both competitive and creative play can flourish and where cultural engagement, territories enhancement and touristic outcomes can be promoted.

REFERENCES

Agostino, D., Arnaboldi, M., & Lampis, A. (2020). Italian state museums during the COVID-19 crisis: From onsite closure to online openness. *Museum Management and Curatorship*, *35*(4), 362–372. doi: 10.1080/09647775.2020.1790029

Anderson, E. F., McLoughlin, L., Liarokapis, F., Peters, C., Petridis, P., & de Freitas, S. (2010). Developing serious games for cultural heritage: A state-of-the-art review. *Virtual Reality (Waltham Cross)*, *14*(4), 255–275. doi:10.100710055-010-0177-3

Beard, J., & Ragheb, M. G. (1983). Measuring leisure motivation. *Journal of Leisure Research*, *15*(3), 219–228. doi:10.1080/00222216.1983.11969557

Bellotti, F., Berta, R., & De Gloria, A. (2010). Designing Effective Serious Games: Opportunities and Challenges for Research. *International Journal of Emerging Technologies in Learning*, *5*(3), 22–35. doi:10.3991/ijet.v5s3.1500

Black, G. (2012). *Transforming museums in the twenty-first century*. Routledge. doi:10.4324/9780203150061

Bogdanovych, A., Esteva, N., Gu, M., Simoff, S., Maher, M. L., & Smith, G. (2007). The role of online travel agents in the experience economy. In *Proceedings of the 14th international conference on information technology in tourism ENTER*. Academic Press.

Bogost, I. (2007). *Persuasive games: The expressive power of videogames*. MIT Press. doi:10.7551/mitpress/5334.001.0001

Bonacini, E., & Giaccone, S. C. (2021). Gamification and cultural institutions in cultural heritage promotion: A successful example from Italy. *Cultural Trends*, 1–20. doi:10.1080/09548963.2021.1910490

Boyan, A., & Sherry, J. (2011). The Challenge in Creating Games for Education: Aligning Mental Models With Game Models. *Child Development Perspectives*, *5*(2), 82–87. doi:10.1111/j.1750-8606.2011.00160.x

Brown, V. R., & Vaughn, E. D. (2011). The writing on the (Facebook) wall: The use of social networking sites in hiring decisions. *Journal of Business and Psychology*, *26*(2), 219–225. doi:10.100710869-011-9221-x

Bulencea, P., & Egger, R. (2015). *Gamification in tourism: Designing memorable experiences*. BoD-Books on Demand.

Cameron, F., & Kenderdine, S. (Eds.). (2007). *Theorizing Digital Cultural Heritage: A Critical Discourse*. MIT Press. doi:10.7551/mitpress/9780262033534.001.0001

Caporarello, L., Magni, M., & Pennarola, F. (2017). Learning and gamification: A possible relationship? *EAI Endorsed Transactions on E-Learning*, *4*(16), 1–8. doi:10.4108/eai.19-12-2017.153488

Coşkun, İ. O., & Yılmaz, H. (2016). An Introduction to Consumer Metamorphosis in the Digital Age. In E. Sezgin (Ed.), *e-Consumers in the era of new tourism* (pp. 1–12). Springer. doi:10.1007/978-981-10-0087-4_1

Crawford, C. (2011). *The art of computer game design*. Osborne/McGraw-Hill.

Creative Keys. (2020). *Fruizione culturale in un click? Come il pubblico ha reagito alle proposte di fruizione culturale durante il lockdown e quali prospettive future*. https://bit.ly/3nmaj0a

de Sousa Borges, S., Durelli, V. H. S., Macedo Reis, H., & Isotani, S. (2014). A Systematic Mapping on Gamification Applied to Education. In *Proceedings of the 29th Annual ACM Symposium on Applied Computing (SAC '14)* (216-222). Association for Computing Machinery. 10.1145/2554850.2554956

Deterding, S., Dixon, D., Khaled, R., & Nacke, L. (2011). From Game Design Elements to Gamefulness: Defining 'Gamification'. In Lugmayr, A., Franssila, H., Safran, C., & Hammouda, I., (Eds.), *Proceedings of the 15th International Academic MindTrek Conference: Envisioning Future Media Environments* (9-15). The Association of Computing Machinery. 10.1145/2181037.2181040

Dewey, J. (1938). *Experience and Education*. MacMillan.

Doughty, M., & O'Coill, C. (2005). Collaborative software environments and participatory design. In *Proceedings of IADIS international conference on web based communities* (303–306). IADIS.

Dubois, L.-E., & Gibbs, C. (2018). Video game–induced tourism: A new frontier for destination marketers. *Tourism Review*, *73*(2), 186–198. doi:10.1108/TR-07-2017-0115

Duman, T., & Mattila, A. S. (2005). The role of affective factors on perceived cruise vacation value. *Tourism Management*, *26*(3), 311–323. doi:10.1016/j.tourman.2003.11.014

Economou, M. (2015). Heritage in the Digital Age. In W. Logan, M. N. Craith, U. Kockel (Eds.), A Companion to Heritage Studies (pp. 215-228). Wiley Blackwell. doi:10.1002/9781118486634.ch15

Faiella F., Ricciardi M. (2015), Gamification and learning: a review of issues and research. *Journal of e-Learning and Knowledge Society*, *11*(3), 13-21.

Farber, M. E., & Hall, T. E. (2007). Emotion and environment: Visitors extraordinary experiences along the Dalton highway in Alaska. *Journal of Leisure Research*, *39*(2), 248–270. doi:10.1080/00222216.2007.11950107

Fong, P., & Frost, P. M. (2009). The social benefits of computer games. In *Proceedings of the 44th Annual APS conference* (62–65). The Australian Psychological Society Ltd.

Froschauer, J. (2012). *Serious Heritage Games: Playful Approaches to Address Cultural Heritage* [Unpublished doctoral dissertation]. Wien University of Technology.

Garcia, A., Linaza, M. T., Gutierrez, A., & Garcia, E. (2018). Gamified mobile experiences: Smart technologies for tourism destinations. *Tourism Review*, *74*(1), 30–49. doi:10.1108/TR-08-2017-0131

Granic, I., Lobel, A., & Engels, R. C. M. E. (2014). The benefits of playing video games. *The American Psychologist*, *69*(1), 66–78. doi:10.1037/a0034857

Holbrook, M. B., & Hirschman, E. C. (1982). The experiential aspects of consumption: Consumer fantasies, feelings, and fun. *The Journal of Consumer Research*, *9*(2), 132–139. doi:10.1086/208906

Huang, Y., Backman, S. J., Backman, K. F., & Moore, D. (2013). Exploring user acceptance of 3d virtual worlds in travel and tourism marketing. *Tourism Management*, *36*, 490–501. doi:10.1016/j.tourman.2012.09.009

Italian Videogame Program. (2019). *Videogiochi e luoghi reali: analisi del questionario IVIPRO*. https://bit.ly/38noqOv

Juul, J. (2003). The game, the player, the world: Looking for a heart of gameness. In M. Copier & J. Raessens (Eds.), *Level Up: Digital Games Research Conference, 4-6 November 2003, Utrecht University* (pp. 30–45). Universiteit Utrecht.

Khan, I., Melro, A., Amaro, A. C., & Oliveira, L. (2020). Systematic Review on Gamification and Cultural Heritage Dissemination. *Journal of Digital Media & Interaction*, *3*(8), 19–41. doi:10.34624/jdmi.v3i8.21934

Klimmt, C. (2003). Dimensions and determinants of the enjoyment of playing digital games: A three-level model. In M. Copier & J. Raessens (Eds.), *Level up: Digital games research conference* (pp. 246–257). Faculty of Arts, Utrecht University.

Klopfer, E., & Squire, K. (2008). Environmental detectives—The development of an augmented reality platform for environmental simulations. *Educational Technology Research and Development*, *56*(2), 203–228. doi:10.100711423-007-9037-6

Llagostera, E. (2012). On Gamification and Persuasion. *Proceedings of SBGames*, *2012*, 12–21.

Majewski, J. (2017). The Potential for Modding Communities in Cultural Heritage. In A. Mol, C. Ariese-Andemeulebroucke, K. Boom, & A. Politopoulos (Eds.), *The Interactive Past: Archaeology, Heritage, and Video Games* (pp. 185–205). Sidestone Press.

Marczewski, A. (2012). *Gamification: A Simple Introduction. Tips, advice and thoughts on gamification*. Lulu.

Mariotti, S. (2021). The Use of Serious Games as an Educational and Dissemination Tool for Archaeological Heritage. Potential and Challenges for the Future. *Magazén*, *2*(1), 119-138. . doi:10.30687/mag/2724-3923/2021/03/005

McGonigal, J. (2011). *Reality is broken: Why games make us better and how they can change the world*. Vintage.

Mortara, M., & Catalano, C. E. (2018). 3D Virtual environments as effective learning contexts for cultural heritage. *Italian Journal of Educational Technology*, *26*(2), 5–21. doi:10.17471/2499-4324/1026

Mortara, M., Catalano, C. E., Bellotti, F., Fiucci, G., Houry-Panchetti, M., & Petridis, P. (2014). Learning cultural heritage by serious games. *Journal of Cultural Heritage*, *15*(3), 318–325. doi:10.1016/j.culher.2013.04.004

Nicholson, S. (2015). A recipe for meaningful gamification. *Gamification in Education and Business*, *2015*, 1–20. doi:10.1007/978-3-319-10208-5_1

Oinas-Kukkonen, H., & Harjumaa, M. (2008). Towards deeper understanding of persuasion in software and information systems. In *Proceedings of The First International Conference on Advances in Human-Computer Interaction (ACHI 2008)* (pp. 200–205). IEEE Computer Society. 10.1109/ACHI.2008.31

Paliokas, I., & Sylaiou, S. (2016). The use of serious games in Museum visits and exhibitions: A systematic mapping study. In *2016 8th International Conference on Games and Virtual Words for Serious Applications Barcelona* (pp. 1-8). Institute of Electrical and Electronics Engineers. 10.1109/VS-GAMES.2016.7590371

Perrotta, C., Featherstone, G., Aston, H., & Houghton, E. (2013). *Game-based Learning: Latest Evidence and Future Directions*. National Foundation for Educational Research.

Pine, B. J., & Gilmore, J. H. (2011). *The Experience Economy*. Harvard Business School Press.

Read, J. C. (2015). Serious games in education. *EAI Endorsed Transactions on Serious Games*, 2(6), 1–5. doi:10.4108/eai.5-11-2015.150614

Riva, G., Davide, F., & Ijsselsteijn, W. (Eds.). (2003). *Being there: concepts, effects and measurement of user presence in synthetic environments*. Ios Press.

Robson, K., Plangger, K., Kietzmann, J. H., McCarthy, I., & Pitt, L. (2015). Is it all a game? Understanding the principles of gamification. *Business Horizons*, 58(4), 411–420. doi:10.1016/j.bushor.2015.03.006

Rowe, J. P., Lobene, E. V., Mott, B. W., & Lester, J. C. (2017). Play in the museum: Design and development of a game-based learning exhibit for informal science education. *International Journal of Gaming and Computer-Mediated Simulations*, 9(3), 96–113. doi:10.4018/IJGCMS.2017070104

Rubino, I., Barberis, C., Xhembulla, J., & Malnati, G. (2015). Integrating a location-based mobile game in the museum visit: Evaluating visitors' behaviour and learning. *Journal on Computing and Cultural Heritage*, 8(3), 1–18. doi:10.1145/2724723

Sailer, M., Hense, J. U., Mayr, S. K., & Mandl, H. (2017). How gamification motivates: An experimental study of the effects of specific game design elements on psychological need satisfaction. *Computers in Human Behavior*, 69, 371–380. doi:10.1016/j.chb.2016.12.033

Sajid, M. J., Cao, Q., Xinchun, L., Brohi, M. A., & Sajid, M. F. (2018). Video Gaming a New Face of Inducement Tourism: Main Attractors for Juvenile Gamers. *International Journal of Scientific Study*, 4(5), 52–56.

Salen, K., & Zimmerman, E. (2004). *Rules of play: Game design fundamentals*. MIT Press.

Simões, J., Díaz Redondo, R., & Vilas, A. F. (2013). A social gamification framework for a K-6 learning platform. *Computers in Human Behavior*, 29(2), 345–353. doi:10.1016/j.chb.2012.06.007

Williams, A. (2006). Tourism and hospitality marketing: Fantasy, feeling and fun. *International Journal of Contemporary Hospitality Management*, 18(6), 482–495. doi:10.1108/09596110610681520

Xu, F., Webber, J., & Buhalis, D. (2014). The gamification of tourism. In Z. Xiang & I. Tussyadiah (Eds.), *Information and communication technologies in tourism 2014. Proceedings of the International Conference in Dublin, Ireland, (January 21-24 2014)* (pp. 525–537). Springer.

Xu, F., Tian, F., Buhalis, D., Weber, J., & Zhang, H. (2015). Tourists as Mobile Gamers: Gamification for Tourism Marketing. *Journal of Travel & Tourism Marketing*, 33(8), 1124–1142. doi:10.1080/10548408.2015.1093999

Zichermann, G., & Cunningham, C. (2011). *Gamification by design: Implementing game mechanics in web and mobile apps*. O'Reilly Media.

ADDITIONAL READING

Araújo, N., Barroso, B., Azevedo Gomes, R., & Cardoso, L. (2019). La Gamificación aplicada al Sector Turístico: Análisis sistemático sobre la base de datos Scopus. *International Journal of Marketing. Communication and New Media*, 7(12), 5–23.

Bellotti, F., Berta, R., De Gloria A., D'Ursi A. & Fiore V. (2012). A Serious Game Model for Cultural Heritage. *Journal on Computing and Cultural heritage*, 5(4), 1-27. . doi:10.1145/2399180.2399185

Boom, K. H. J., Ariese, C. E., van den Hout, B., Mol, A. A. A., & Politopoulos, A. (2020). Teaching through Play: Using Video Games as a Platform to Teach about the Past. In Hageneuer, S. (Ed.) *Communicating the Past in the Digital Age: Proceedings of the International Conference on Digital Methods in Teaching and Learning in Archaeology* (27–44). Ubiquity Press. 10.5334/bch.c

Bozkurt, A., & Durak, G. (2018). A Systematic Review of Gamification Research: In Pursuit of Homo Ludens. *International Journal of Game-Based Learning*, 8(3), 15–33. doi:10.4018/IJGBL.2018070102

Konstantinov, O., Kovatcheva, E., & Palikova, N. (2018). Gamification in Cultural and Historical Heritage Education. In L. Gómez Chova, A. López Martínez, I. Candel Torres (Eds.), *Proceedings of 12th International Technology, Education and Development Conference* (8443-8451). IATED Academy. 10.21125/inted.2018.2043

Metzger, S. A., & Paxton, R. J. (2016). Gaming History: A Framework for What Video Games Teach About the Past. *Theory and Research in Social Education*, 44(4), 532–564. doi:10.1080/00933104.2016.1208596

Orji, R., Tondello, G. F., & Nacke, L. E. (2018). Personalizing Persuasive Strategies in Gameful Systems to Gamification User Types. In *Proceedings of the 2018 CHI Conference on Human Factors in Computing Systems* (1-14). Association for Computing Machinery. 10.1145/3173574.3174009

Salen, K. (Ed.). (2008). *The Ecology of Games: Connecting Youth, Games, and Learning*. Massachusetts Institute of Technology.

KEY TERMS AND DEFINITIONS

Cultural Institutions: Organization within a culture/subculture that work for the preservation or promotion of culture. Examples of cultural institutions in modern society are museums, libraries, and archives, but also, in the case of Italy, local Soprintendenze centered around the Ministry of Culture.

Entertainment Game Apps, Ltd.: A serious game company whose mission is to create historical-archaeological videogames enhancing cultural heritage thanks to contents accurately conceived and designed in collaboration with researchers and experts in the specific fields.

Memories: Video game conceived within the Abruzzi regional project LAB8, which aim was to revitalize and promote the 11 municipalities in the province of L'Aquila strongly affected by the 2009 destructive earthquake.

Mobile Applications: Computer programs or software applications designed to run on a mobile device such as a phone, tablet, or watch.

Prosumers: Consumers who becomes involved with designing or customizing products for their own needs.

Serious Games: Games that have an explicit and carefully thought-out educational purposes and are not intended to be played primarily for amusement. However, this does not mean that serious games are not, or should not be, entertaining.

The Umbrian Chronicles: Video game developed as part of the project "Museum Connections: between valleys and mountains, villages and cities" promoted and funded by the Umbria Region, to enhance the cultural and environmental heritage of 11 museums located in 5 municipalities in the territory of Spoleto and Valnerina.

Video Games: Games played by interacting with a user interface or input device and electronically manipulating images produced by a computer program on a monitor or other display.

Chapter 21
Studying Thracian Civilization Through Serious Games and Storytelling

Desislava Paneva-Marinova
Institute of Mathematics and Informatics, Bulgarian Academy of Sciences, Bulgaria

Maxim Goynov
Institute of Mathematics and Informatics, Bulgarian Academy of Sciences, Bulgaria

Detelin Luchev
Institute of Mathematics and Informatics, Bulgarian Academy of Sciences, Bulgaria

Lilia Pavlova
Laboratory of Telematics, Bulgarian Academy of Sciences, Bulgaria

Zsolt László Márkus
Institute for Computer Science and Control, Hungary

Miklós Veres
Institute for Computer Science and Control, Hungary

Zsolt Weisz
Institute for Computer Science and Control, Hungary

György Szántó
Institute for Computer Science and Control, Hungary

Tibor Szkaliczki
https://orcid.org/0000-0002-7699-8132
Institute for Computer Science and Control, Hungary

ABSTRACT

This chapter presents a novel learning approach for studying ancient Bulgarian history, civilization, and their cultural heritage, namely the Thracian civilization, through storytelling and serious game combinations. The chapter also provides an overview of serious educational games, digital storytelling, and game development tools that can be used to present ancient history and their cultural heritage. The combination of storytelling and serious games successfully helps instructors to motivate student learning, stimulate their curiosity, and make them interested. The authors developed a game editor and a game portal that facilitated the game's development by applying game templates, layout styles, and question pools.

DOI: 10.4018/978-1-7998-9223-6.ch021

INTRODUCTION

The knowledge society and knowledge-based economy signifies a new era for education and training, aiming at replacing old-fashioned time / place / content-predetermined learning with a just-in-time / at work-place / customized / on-demand process of learning by new ICT-based tools (Bontchev et al., 2016; Pavlov et al., 2007). Ubiquitous learning is aimed to provide learners with content and interaction anytime and anywhere (Hwang et al., 2008; Nussli & Oh, 2021). Current technology-enhanced learning points to the investigation and the deployment of practical learning methods and scenarios for creative thinking, learning-by-doing and learning-by-authoring, engaging learners in more active participation during the perception of knowledge (Draganov et al., 2015). The main challenges during the training material development imply the following questions:

- How to increase motivation, engagement, and improved learning outcomes?
- What learning methods can be used to attract learners in more active participation in the learning process?
- What tasks could be interesting and attractive and could stimulate learners' desire to work?

Serious games become an important modern-day educational method, which reflects both the current state of technology and the learners' social profiles. Serious educational games provide a novel way to transfer knowledge, which can especially attract young people by using interactive multimedia technology. They could provide tools for better understanding, creative thinking and engaging young people in more active participation during the perceiving of knowledge. The technological revolution gives innovative learning tools to the teachers and the possibility to deploy new learning approaches for deeper understanding and better demonstration of the learning content. Serious games represent a power tool to seek creative and logical thought, problem-solving, as well as develop a variety of skills and competencies to the learner.

Digital storytelling learning method successfully helps instructors to motivate students learning, stimulate curiosity, and to make them interested. Combination of storytelling and serious game represents a novel learning approach. The new strategies for teaching and learning point to the investigation and the deployment of workable learning methods and scenarios for better understanding of the learning content and engagement learners in more active participation during the perception of knowledge (Slavova-Petkova et al., 2016).

The serious game development requires a flexible tool for developing, managing, and presenting games. We developed a game editor and a game portal for creating various games (Connolly et al., 2012). The server-based solution can facilitate the game development by applying game templates, layout styles and question pools. It also supports the development of game packages for multiple languages and multiple platforms (Web and mobile). The games can easily be customized for various learning domains. Complex games can be composed from several so-called mini-games and the tool also supports the evaluation of the user answers and organizing competitions (Georgieva-Tsaneva et al., 2018).

The main objective of the chapter is to present how serious games can be applied in teaching humanities in primary school. This chapter presents a novel learning approach for studying the ancient Bulgarian history, civilization and their cultural heritage and the Thracian civilization in particular by storytelling and serious game combination.

The rest of the book chapter is organized as follows. The background section provides an overview of serious educational games and digital storytelling. Then factors related to the learner experience and content understanding issues are presented. The subsequent sections introduce the applied game development tools and the games transferring knowledge on ancient civilizations lived on the area of present Bulgaria. Future research directions are also shown. Finally, the chapter is summarized in the last section.

BACKGROUND

Serious Games/Gamification

Serious games represent an intensively studied topic in the literature (Hamari et al., 2014; Marzullo & Oliveira, 2021). The literature review of the empirical experiences related to computer games shows that the game-based approach is being used for learning in many different areas, the players like to use it to acquire new knowledge and find it motivating and enjoyable (Connolly et al., 2012).

Serious games represent an innovative way in technology-enhanced learning to perceive new knowledge in an entertaining and engaging way (Mortara et al., 2014). Abt introduced the term "serious game" for the first time and described the utilization of situations in and outside the class room in his book "Serious games" (Abt, 1970). He described "serious game" as a "game having explicit and carefully crystalized educational purpose, as the main goal is not entertainment". Although computer games were originally developed for entertainment, the primary goal of a serious game is something else (Michael & Chen, 2005; Djaouti et al., 2011).

Games created for educational purposes can attract attention, support learning-by-doing and learning-by-authoring, inspire creative thinking and engage users in an active participation during the perception of knowledge. Games with educational purposes can provide the same psychological experiences as other games do. The intrinsic motivation for learning plays a key role in "making learning fun". The motivation can be encouraged by seven factors: challenge, curiosity, control, fantasy, competition, co-operation and recognition, which are all present in the games (Malone & Lepper, 1987). The serious games can successfully assist, facilitate and support to achieve the effective goal of the learning process while the users acquire new knowledge, skills, and/or attitudes (Huotari & Hamari, 2012). A literature overview of computer games and serious games illustrates the increased interest in the positive impacts and outcomes of these games, furthermore, the term "serious games" has become mainstream during the last ten years, and it is used interchangeably with "games for learning" (Boyle et al., 2016). The modern education can be characterized as personal, fun, collaborative, relevant, multimodal, technical and open-minded, where gamification can be treated like a tool to provide the above features (Guzik et al., 2015). In this context, the educational games are effective both in transferring knowledge and in entertainment. Learning experiences based on games have unique particularities such as fun or engagement due to their game-based nature (Caballero-Hernández et al., 2017). Serious games can elicit significant engagement from learners and further to the effectiveness of the learning process. Education based on serious games generates good levels of comprehension and unconscious processing of content of relatively great difficulty.

Serious games are widely applied in cultural heritage and history domain as well (Mortara et al., 2014; Draganov et al., 2015; D. Paneva-Marinova et al., 2017). In a maze game, the students use different skills, competences, and experience to solve the mini games and reach the target (Bontchev et al., 2016). The integration of information and communication technology (ICT) in the ancient history curriculum by means of game playing, interactive interface, visualization, video, and animation allows to present the material in a fun and accessible way (Slavova-Petkova et al., 2016). This integration will make it easier to explain connections, relationships, and influences among ancient civilizations; to demonstrate the continuity of ideas, despite the demise of entire nations, and will improve the students understanding of the evolution of civilization. Serious games play an important role in providing the young learners with orientational literacy and an ability to apply their knowledge in activities different from those practiced at school (D Luchev et al., 2016).

Although gamification approach also applies game elements in non-gaming contexts it can be differentiated from serious games (Deterding et al., 2011; Galetta, 2013; Patrício et al., 2018). Gamification refers to the use of parts of game design elements while serious games represent complete games with educational purpose. Gamification applies game elements to encourage users' enjoyment and engagement while performing jobs or solving problems (Robson et al., 2015). Gamification can enhance various skills including co-creation (Ind & Coates, 2013), collaborative innovation (Patricio et al., 2020a), design thinking (Patrício et al., 2020b), etc.

Storytelling

Digital storytelling is the practice of using digital technologies to tell a short story (Robin B.R, 2008). Like traditional narratives, digital stories focus on a subject and feature from a particular point of view. What distinguishes digital storytelling is the inclusion of digital images, text, audio narration, moving image (video), and music. These multimedia narratives tend to be short (2–10 min), personalized reflections which use still pictures or videos of personal artefacts to create short evocative stories/plots. Such digital narratives are an extension of traditional storytelling, providing engaging stories, which can be shared within social/leaning communities.

Digital Storytelling is employed in a range of contexts and for a variety of purposes: self-awareness or discovery; narrative (knowledge management) in businesses; facilitating group understanding; engagement of marginalized sections of society; subject learning and development of subject, cultural or societal resources (Benmayor, 2008; Petrucco & De Rossi, 2009; Roby, 2010). The digital story genre is perhaps most frequently associated with the telling of personal stories, often of cultural or historical importance to the author (Lambert, 2010). Such stories often focus on interesting experiences, memories of some past event or person or personal journeys to overcome challenges or achieve goals (Gunter & Kenny, 2008). Robin (Robin B.R, 2008) identifies two other types of digital story – one that informs or instructs and one which examines historical events. We will focus on a story based on historical facts aiming to improve knowledge understanding and to make and educational application of digital storytelling.

Kenny (2007) argues that classroom practice that combines use of digital media with the art of story – leveraging both the skills and preferences of digital age students and the inherent human interest in story – is a potentially powerful pedagogy. Digital storytelling can be used to engage, inform, explore and transform, and thereby lends itself to educational contexts. Indeed, as shown by (Yuksel et al., 2010) world-wide survey investigating the use of digital storytelling to support learning. The digital storytelling is used in educational contexts not only to develop subject area knowledge, writing skills, technical skills, and presentation skills, but additionally reflection, language, higher level thinking, social, and artistic skills are also developed.

Digital storytelling, when well-conceived and executed, provides an engaging and powerful account of a 'story' – be it informative, imaginative or reflective. While any well-formed story should achieve this, the integrated visual and audio nature of digital storytelling is particularly potent to generations who have grown up in a social and multi-media world. The nature of the engagement goes beyond mere entertainment, although the value of fun in educational contexts is not to be underrated; using digital storytelling in the curriculum can afford real educational advantages (Roby, 2010). Firstly, the multi-media nature makes the content of the digital narrative more accessible to technology-centric students, many of whom are alienated from traditional textual forms (Gunter & Kenny, 2008). Secondly, as researchers such as (Burmark, 2004) have shown, the combination of text integrated with visual images enhances student understanding. The visual component, especially where of a personal nature, helps situate the story within a recognizable context. According to Bruner's theory of situated cognition, this increases the time that students can retain and understand information (Kenny, 2007) as well as enabling students to better organize information into manageable chunks. Thirdly, the multimedia nature of digital stories encourages active listening.

The stronger educational benefits could arise when students become involved as active learners in the authorship of digital stories. Creating their own digital stories, whether personal, informative or imaginative, requires the student to engage with the structure of storytelling. In developing the story, students must understand the basics of narrative structure as well as grammar. For example, students will need to consider dramatic tension, pacing and narrative flow. Further, as (Ohler, 2005) advocates, authoring of digital stories provides a powerful opportunity for students to develop critical media skills.

Appropriate combination storytelling with game can make the learning content interesting and desirable for the students (Slavova-Petkova et al., 2016; Vasileva et al., 2014).

The chapter presents below several serious educational games for improved understanding of history, habits and culture of the ancient civilizations on the Balkan Peninsula. The learners' engagement with these methods and tools is pursued, aiming to provide more active knowledge perception and understanding.

SERIOUS GAMES, LEARNER EXPERIENCE AND CONTENT UNDERSTANDING

Factors Related to the Learner Experience in Serious Game: Content Understanding Issues

Computer games are attractive for the wide public. When the gamer is a learner, or has learning purposes in the environment, "one size fits all" solutions are not enough to satisfy his/her needs. Different learners have different learning needs and preferences that (should) affect the learning function outcome. Learners expect from the game to play, "personal game facilitator/instructor" and not a "classroom" behavior, where their personality and needs are known and taken into account.

There are several benefits of thinking about and trying to understand learning preferences:

- People learn most effectively when the strategies used are closely matched with their preferred learning style.
- Sometimes we can improve our learning by knowing what our strengths are and then doing more of what we're good at.

- Often we can improve our learning by knowing what our weakness are and trying to enhance our skills in these areas.
- Different situations and learning environments require different learning strategies, so it's best to have a large repertoire from which to draw.

The authors' research practices point to some factors that should affect even more the learning activities in a serious game, such as:

- The space in which learning takes place, its aesthetics and mood, user interfaces, visual elements, input devices, interaction with other learners / mentors, possibility of dynamic changing of the learning place, even its realism.
- Interactivity and the learner immersion in the learning place.
- The "interplay" between the learner and the learning's narrative or the learning place as a whole.
- The learnativity content model - the concept of assembling content into higher-level objects, as it is defined by (Wagner, 2008).
- The set of challenges the learner will face within the learning space; Synchronization of the challenges with the ability of the learner.
- Keeping interests by:
  - Implementation of multiple difficulty settings for the different learners.
  - Usage of non-trivial learning objects – applied games, puzzles, stories, conundrums, *etc.*
- Transforming the boring learning activities in a fun and adventures. The quality of the learner experience – whether learner enjoy working with the e-system, or whether they find it frustrating.
- Setting awards for the efforts – Reward the learners for skill, imagination, intelligence and dedication.
- Enhancing the motivation by encouragement, diversity, and extended curiosity.
- Eventually, conscious awareness of the learning as a key engine for the future success.

It could be also mentioned the provision of creative experiences, learning-by-doing and role-playing scenarios.

The key issues that developers had to take into full consideration concerned the game architectural design and the methodology. One of the larger challenges could be faced is how to select and present only the most salient information so as not to overwhelm students with too many facts, names, and dates, as textbooks tend to do. Furthermore, the creators need to relate historical data by means of both text and image, used on equal terms as sources of information. They must aim to train students to view visual images analytically and understand that architecture and objects (such as the archeological finds featured in the game) also communicate about the history, religion, and daily lives of the people of the past, often revealing information not otherwise accessible (Rousseva, 2018).

Challenges During the Game Developments

Major problems appeared during the design of the game software solutions, closely capturing the above discussed factors. Some of them concern the communication between the learner and the game environment. Other are related with the formal presentation of the subjective issues such as learner' skill, imagination, motivation, intelligence, dedication, *etc.* Moreover, in order to provide effective forms of personalized learner experiences the focus must be on the design of the interaction per se as an integral part of the whole system. There is a need to develop multi-modal mixed initiative interfaces that draw on a range of user information seeking models. The requirement is thus for research to develop theories of interaction which underpin the design of applications and vice versa and which go beyond issues of simple elicitation, presentation and feedback.

Developing a computer game is a time-consuming task and requires large amount of resources. It is a challenge to shorten the development time and reduce the costs by applying proper tools and methodology. High-level learning content is also crucial for the success of the project and the content developers should be motivated to timely deliver it.

GAME DEVELOPMENT

This section presents game development tools we applied to create serious educational games.

Game Development Tools

The games target a large set of devices – PCs, notebooks, mobile phones and tablets, smart TVs and VR devices. This is the reason for choosing a web technology for its implementation. One of the most popular, well developed and documented libraries for 3D in the web – THREE.JS – was used for the development of our game engine. Open source, based on WebGL (a technology, which utilizes the graphic card of the devices) and HTML Canvas, it is powerful and its performance offers close resemblance to the feel of the native games for the particular device.

THREE.JS supports most of the 3D elements needed for the development of a game: scenes, cameras, meshes, animations, loaders (imported from variety of 3D object file standards), player controls (first person, device orientation – for VR, orbit, point, *etc*.), a large set of lights and shadows, material types, shaders, access to the OpenGL using GLSL language, *etc*.

Most of the objects and meshes for the game (rooms, walls, mini-game elements) were designed using Blender, and exported to GLTF format - (GL Transmission Format) – the most efficient format for loading 3D objects in a web environment.

As a result, the game becomes very lightweight. Additionally, all textures and graphics are optimized for web and for devices with limited network bandwidth.

Apart from classic 3D representation of the games, we have added the ability to play the game using VR glasses (*e.g.*, cardboard ones with mobile phones, along with some pointing device like a Bluetooth mouse, a keyboard or a joystick) and anaglyph glasses (red/cyan filter glasses, usable with any standard display) in order to make the game more immersive and more realistic.

Several tools were implemented to accelerate the game development process:

- Game Template Developer. A game template consists of the mini-game logic files and the list of necessary parameters with their types.
- Game Editor. The editors can select game templates, question-answer combinations and styles to create a mini-game by using the Game Editor.
- Game Publisher. A game package containing multiple mini-games can be created by using the Game Publisher.

- Game Portal. The players can select game packages, play any of them and see their scores on Game Portal.
- User Management. In the user management area, the administrator of the system can see and manage the user.
- Question pool. Question pools contain questions along with the correct answers. The questions are randomly selected from the pool when the user plays the game.

The layout of the games can be easily customized by using style sheets. The application of HTML5 together with CSS3 technology have made it possible to set up various style sheets containing layout parameters which can be used to display the games in an appropriate form (color, fonts, background, etc.). The implementation of the games supports using multiple languages by applying translation keys. The games development is accomplished in HTML5 and JavaScript. The games can run on multiple platforms (Web and mobile). For more details on the implemented game server, see (Márkus et al., 2018).

Main Educational Mini-Games

Complex games can be composed from several so-called mini-games (e.g., puzzle, multiple choice, memory game, crossword etc.) The interactive game types we applied in serious educational games. are as follows:

Multiple-Choice Question

The well-known multiple-choice questions represent the simplest mini-games which can be used to check the knowledge of the player in an easy way. An example is depicted on Fig. 1 from the "Thracians" serious game (Márkus et al., 2018).

Figure 1. Multiple-choice question Source: "Thracians" serious game

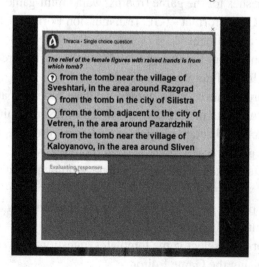

Sliding Puzzle

A picture is cut into small square tiles. The starting screen of the puzzle contains the tiles arranged in random order with one tile missing. The objective of the puzzle is to move the tiles to their right position thereby restoring the original picture. Tiles can be moved by using the empty space. The puzzle exists in two sizes with different difficulty levels. The easier version has 3×3 tiles, whereas the more difficult version has 4×4 tiles (Fig. 2).

Figure 2. Sliding puzzle Source: "Thracians" serious game

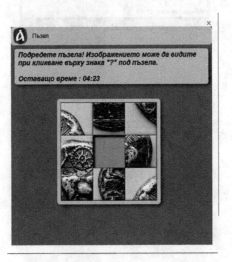

Memory Game

Cards containing pictures are located along a grid. Initially, the cards are laid face down and two cards are flipped face up over each turn. The objective of the game is to turn over pairs of matching pictures (Fig.3).

Figure 3. Memory game Source: "Thracians" serious game

Matching

Given the names of some terms, locations and persons. The aim is to match pairs of the predefined items (Fig.4).

Figure 4. Matching Source: "Thracians" serious game

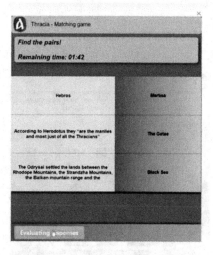

Crossword

The word puzzle contains definitions related to the life of the poet (Fig.5).

Figure 5. Crossword Source: "Thracians" serious game

Word Search

The user has to find meaningful words in a square of letters (Fig. 6).

Figure 6. Word search Source: "Thracians" serious game

Blind Map

The user should find locations on a blind map containing no names (Fig. 7).

Figure 7. Blind map Source: "Thracians" serious game

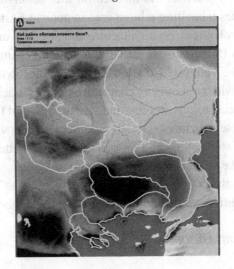

Ordering

Events are given in random order. The objective of the game is to put them in chronological order (Fig. 8).

Figure 8. Ordering Source: "Attila József" literature walk

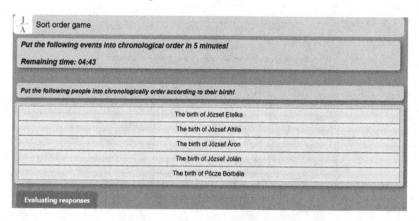

SERIOUS EDUCATIONAL GAMES

This section presents serious educational games with the purpose of transferring knowledge on ancient civilizations lived on the area of present Bulgaria.

Thracians Serious Game

The serious educational game *"Thracians"* is focused on life, beliefs and traditions of the Thracians (a group of Indo-European tribes inhabiting a large area in ancient Eastern and South-eastern Europe) and is drawn on ancient primary sources, on architecture and artefacts unearthed during archaeological excavations and on research by Bulgarian scholars. Exploring the chambers of the structure excavated beneath Ostrousha mound (in the Valley of Thracian Kinds near the town of Kazanlak, Bulgaria), learners will discover and retain knowledge about key characteristics of Thracian culture as known to us from the excavated and studied Thracian tombs, heroes, and sanctuaries, and from the weapons and treasures uncovered inside or outside these structures (Desislava Paneva-Marinova et al., 2018).

The proposed combining of storytelling and serious games for a better study of the Thracian history and civilization is *the base of the following learning scenario:*

Established Goals: To learn the concepts, facts and specifics for the Thracian civilization, focusing on the lifestyle, beliefs and traditions of this ancient people living on the Balkan Peninsula.

The Content of the Thracian Story

The first part of the story is related to the Thracian tribes, their nature and costumes, traditions, manners, different areas of high achievements, place of habitation, *etc.*

The second part of the story presents Tomb traditions and rituals of the Thracians and their beliefs for the life after death.

The third part presents the military power of these glorious ancient wars.

The fourth part is dedicated to the Heroon building that honors the memory of a deity ruler, a prophet hero, who restores harmony in the tribe when an annual ritual is performed in his honor. This is the very key for the Thracians because some of their tribes used to immortalize their rulers, priests and heroes and worshiped them as demigods.

The fifth part of the story presents treasures, feasts and abundance that accompany the everyday life of the Thracian kings and their deputies. This ancient civilization was glorified with its vast handmade and unique riches.

The last part of the story reveals the mysteries around the Thracian gods that were worshiped at that time.

The data and facts provided in the story derive from ancient documents, architecture, artefacts found during archaeological excavations, and from scholarly research by Bulgarian specialists.

The story is told through a serious game representing a labyrinth of rooms. The game will take you through the rooms of the building uncovered beneath the Ostrusha Mound, located in the Valley of the Thracian Kings near the city of Kazanlak. All of the objects, drawings and reliefs are real and were discovered at the time of the archaeological excavations made by scientists. Their position in the building's rooms is the creative decision of the team who prepared the story and the game, but the main purpose is to tell the Thracian story in the most realistic way. A great number of educational mini-games are available; completing them successfully will allow you to visit the next chamber of the building.

The Thracian game scenario: There are six rooms through which you need to pass: "Thrace", "Tomb", "Armory", "Heroon" (a temple to an immortalized tribal chief, priest, or hero), "Treasury" and "Sanctuary". In order to enter the sixth and final room, "Sanctuary," you need to visit the other five, successfully complete all of the games and receive pieces of Thracian treasure as prizes.

Implementation

The first version of the game is available in Bulgarian and the multilingual version is under development. The player can play in a virtual 360° panorama environment consisting of seven scenes, one of them is external the others are internal. The rooms include Thrace, Treasury, Heroon, Armory, Sanctuary and Tomb.

The technological implementation of the storytelling&game solution was done by the team from the Institute for Computer Science and Control, Hungarian Academy of Sciences (MTA SZTAKI) under the joint project "Development of Software Systems for Multimedia and Language Technologies" of Institute of Mathematics and Informatics, Bulgarian Academy of Sciences and MTA SZTAKI. MTA SZTAKI team developed a special tool for multilingual and multi-platform game development, management, and presentation (Márkus et al., 2018).

The starting point of the game is outside of the tomb and the player can enter through a door. The player can move and turn in the virtual environment and look around. Each room has several pictures, descriptions, games and doors, see Figs. 9 and 10 for a sample room. The pictures and descriptions help to solve the interactive minigames. The doors are initially closed and they can be opened by solving the minigames assigned to them. The colors of the symbols indicate the status (solved, unsolved) of the minigame in the given room. The players can see the next room through the open door. The goal of the game is to solve all minigames and get into the Sanctuary.

Figure 9. The Thrace room Source: "Thracians" serious game

Figure 10. The Heroon room Source: "Thracians" serious game

Aquae Calidae Serious Game

Aquae Calidae is situated in the ancient region of Thrace, near the Black Sea. The history of Aquae Calidae (Therma, Thermopolis) is related to the famous hot mineral springs at the site and covers a long period of time from the 1st millennium BCE to the 16th century CE. It is linked with events from the history of Ancient Greece, the Roman and the Byzantine empires, the Medieval Bulgarian state, the

Crusades and the Ottoman empire, and was visited by famous historical figures. The rich history of the place makes it possible to develop related educational games (Detelin Luchev et al., 2020).

The "Aquae Calidae" serious game is an inspiring and entertaining way for primary-school students to meet the ancient civilizations on the Balkan Peninsula, offering active participation during the learning process and encouragement for creative thinking. This learning resource combines a number of digital tools for serious game development including virtual reality, 3D of archaeological excavations, interactive gaming components for effective knowledge acquisition, etc.(Zlatkov et al., 2019).

Through immersion in the virtual 3D reality of the complex, learners are able to play intuitive mini-games and improve their historical knowledge and understanding of the ancient inhabitants and civilizations of the Balkan peninsula. In the game, the player initially encounters the Thracian ruler Rhoemetalces II, king of the Sapaeans and the Odrysian Kingdom from 18 to 38 CE, who presents the story of how the temple of the goddess Demeter was built near the magical springs of Aqua Calidae. The player visits a hall with artefacts of Thracian treasures from the period, and, in gaming mode, acquires crucial aspects of the Thracian culture and civilization. The game is mostly centered on the heyday of Aqua Calidae under the rule of the Roman emperors. In the beginning of 1st century CE, Emperor Nero issues a decree for the initiation of the construction of the Roman thermae at Aqua Calidae, where the water was thought to have magical powers. The Nero's decree for the building of the thermae is presented

Figure 11. Thracian Sanctuary screen A Source: "Aquae Calidae" serious game

in the game in its authentic form – engraved on stone. The game follows the development of the thermae into a desirable place for the subjects of the Roman Empire thanks to its healing hot springs. Later emperor Trajan builds a big thermae complex with an area of 5000 m². The Roman emperor Septimius Severus (293-211 CE) organizes in Aqua Calidae the athletic games Severia Nymphea, in honor of the Three nymphs. Justinian the Great, the emperor of the Eastern Roman Empire (527-565 CE) reinforces the thermae with massive, fortified walls. This is part of the centuries-old history of the archaeological complex Aqua Calidae and the region, and subsequent versions of the game are planned to present its history during the Middle Ages and the Ottoman period.

The first part named "Thracian Sanctuary" tells the story of the hot mineral spring near to the ancient city of Aquae Calidae as a sacred place for Thracians in the first millennium BCE. The historical information on the Thracian tribes in the area, as well as their lifestyle, traditions and customs are illustrated. Screens from the first part of the game are depicted on figures 11-13.

Figure 12. Thracian Sanctuary screen B Source: "Aquae Calidae" serious game

The second room is called "Severa Nimphaea", named after the celebrations and sport games, organized by Roman emperor Septimius Severus (209-211) in the town of Aquae Calidae. The room explains the

Figure 13. Thracian Sanctuary screen C Source: "Aquae Calidae" serious game

important role of the mineral springs and the surrounding settlements as places for building the Roman towns in the conquered new province. During the reign of Emperor Trajan (98-117), the crucial Roman Road Via Pontica was built and Aquae Calidae became an important stop on that route. Its location was marked on the very first Roman maps of the region.

FUTURE RESEARCH DIRECTIONS

The further investigations in the above-discussed domain point to a wide variety of directions:

- To create of workable methods and tools, aiming to increase and generalize the learner experience in the digital culture educational platforms (*incl.* digital games). Moreover, creative learner experiences will support the effective on-line learning through the game.
- Contextual techniques for personalizing learners' experience in the educational gaming platform.
- Wider context-dependent use of digital cultural resources in the game.

- To develop of new digital and transmedia storytelling solutions for learning purposes, creation of interactive virtual exhibitions, gaming and gamification, virtual worlds, live simulations, animations, interactive media previews.
- Multimodal interfaces and intelligent visualization of complex information relying on enhanced learner experience and usability (*incl.* user-centric visualization and analytics, real-time adaptable and interactive visualization, real-time and collaborative 3D visualization, dynamic clustering of information, *etc.*), *etc.*

Moreover, the serious game design and improvement of the learner' experience in the changing cases would not be restricted by the available technologies, platforms and tools. The field has great potential for innovations especially in our world of active imposition of e-devices, e-literacy, and e-content. The focus will be in the research and exploitation of new or emerging technologies (*e.g.,* 3D, augmented and virtual reality, visual computing, smart world, environments and devices, media convergence, social media, *etc.*) for the development of innovative products, tools, applications, and services for creative digital content production, usage and management. The aims are to transform and customize the valuable parts of mankind's cultural and historical ancestry into digital assets, whose integration and reuse through research-lead methods has high commercial and non-commercial potential for learning and cultural institutions, tourism, creative and media industries.

CONCLUSION

A key factor of developing games in the domain of cultural heritage is to preserve valuable historical knowledge and share it with the next generation in a suitable way (Georgieva-Tsaneva, 2019). The integration of ICT in the primary school ancient history curriculum allows – by means of game playing, interactive interface, visualization, video, and animation – presentation of the material in a fun and accessible way. It makes it easier to explain connections, relationships, and influences among ancient people, events, and history. It could improve the students' understanding of the evolution of a civilization. The virtual panoramic tour of historical place mimics the feel of the actual tour of the site. The user interface could be personalized. The first-person point-of-view interface and the high-quality textures and graphic images, used for the creation of the game, offer an authentic and exciting exploration experience. The basic mapping of the site is augmented with realistic interactive 3D objects, avatars and light shade effects. The mini-games' graphic outlook is designed to be smoothly incorporated in the environment. The user experience is enhanced by adequate in-game media effects.

ACKNOWLEDGMENT

This research is partially supported by the Bulgarian Ministry of Education and Science under the National Research Programme "Cultural heritage, national memory and development of society" approved by DCM N°577/17.08.2018.

REFERENCES

Abt, C. (1970). *Serious games: The art and science of games that simulate life.* Viking Compass Book.

Benmayor, R. (2008). Digital storytelling as a signature pedagogy for the new humanities. *Arts and Humanities in Higher Education, 7*(2), 188–204. doi:10.1177/1474022208088648

Bontchev, B., Paneva-Marinova, D., & Draganov, L. (2016). Educational Video Games for Bulgarian Orthodox Iconography. *ICERI2016 Proceedings, 1,* 1679–1688.

Boyle, E. A., Hainey, T., Connolly, T. M., Gray, G., Earp, J., Ott, M., Lim, T., Ninaus, M., Ribeiro, C., & Pereira, J. (2016). An update to the systematic literature review of empirical evidence of the impacts and outcomes of computer games and serious games. *Computers & Education, 94,* 178–192. doi:10.1016/j.compedu.2015.11.003

Burmark, L. (2004). Visual Presentations that Prompt, flash & transform. *Media and Methods, 40*(6), 4–5.

Caballero-Hernández, J. A., Palomo-Duarte, M., & Dodero, J. M. (2017). Skill assessment in learning experiences based on serious games: A Systematic Mapping Study. *Computers & Education, 113,* 42–60. doi:10.1016/j.compedu.2017.05.008

Connolly, T. M., Boyle, E. A., MacArthur, E., Hainey, T., & Boyle, J. M. (2012). A systematic literature review of empirical evidence on computer games and serious games. *Computers & Education, 59*(2), 661–686. doi:10.1016/j.compedu.2012.03.004

Deterding, S., Dixon, D., Khaled, R., & Nacke, L. (2011). From game design elements to gamefulness: Defining "gamification." *Proceedings of the 15th International Academic MindTrek Conference: Envisioning Future Media Environments, MindTrek 2011,* 9–15. 10.1145/2181037.2181040

Djaouti, D., Alvarez, J., & Jessel, J.-P. (2011). Classifying serious games: The G/P/S model. Handbook of Research on Improving Learning and Motivation through Educational Games: Multidisciplinary Approaches, 2005, 118–136.

Draganov, L., Paneva-Marinova, D., Pavlova, L., Luchev, D., Márkus, Z. L., Szántó, G., & Szkaliczki, T. (2015). Technology-enhanced learning for cultural heritage. *Digital Presentation and Preservation of Cultural and Scientific Heritage, 5,* 293–301.

Galetta, G. (2013). *The Gamification: Applications and Developments for Creativity and Education.* Creative Personality. Collection of Scientific Papers.

Georgieva-Tsaneva, G. (2019). Serious games and innovative technologies in medical education in Bulgaria. *TEM Journal, 8*(4), 1398–1403.

Georgieva-Tsaneva, G., Noev, N., & Bogdanova, G. (2018). Serious educational games and the study of the military historical heritage. *Digital Presentation and Preservation of Cultural and Scientific Heritage, 8,* 133–140.

Gunter, G., & Kenny, R. (2008). Digital Booktalk: Digital Media for Reluctant Readers. *Contemporary Issues in Technology & Teacher Education, 8*(1), 84–99.

Guzik, A., Nerc, O., Zalewska, M., Gałecka, J., Chyrk, P., Milewski, P., Mizerska, M., Siekierska, E., Wiśniowski, W., & Żylińska, M. (2015). *The Book of Trends in Education*. Academic Press.

Hamari, J., Koivisto, J., & Sarsa, H. (2014). Does gamification work? - A literature review of empirical studies on gamification. *Proceedings of the Annual Hawaii International Conference on System Sciences*, 3025–3034. 10.1109/HICSS.2014.377

Huotari, K., & Hamari, J. (2012). Defining gamification - A service marketing perspective. *Proceedings of the 16th International Academic MindTrek Conference 2012: "Envisioning Future Media Environments", MindTrek 2012*, 17–22.

Hwang, G. J., Tsai, C. C., & Yang, S. J. H. (2008). Criteria, strategies and research issues of context-aware ubiquitous learning. *Journal of Educational Technology & Society*, *11*(2), 81–91.

Ind, N., & Coates, N. (2013). The meanings of co-creation. *European Business Review*, *25*(1), 86–95. doi:10.1108/09555341311287754

Kenny, R. F. (2007). *Digital Narrative as a Change Agent to Teach Reading to Media-Centric Students*. Academic Press.

Lambert, J. (2010). Digital storytelling cookbook. Handbook of Research on Transformative Online Education and Liberation: Models for Social Equality, 408–423.

Luchev, D., Paneva-Marinova, D., Pavlova, L., Zlatkov, L., & Pavlov, R. (2020). Development of a Serious Game "Aquae Calidae" for Studying the Ancient History and Civilizations in Primary School. *INTED2020 Proceedings*, *1*, 5253–5258.

Luchev, D, Paneva-Marinova, D., Pavlov, R., & Kaposi, G. (2016). *Game-based learning of Bulgarian iconographical art on smart phone application*. Academic Press.

Malone, T. W., & Lepper, M. R. (1987). Making learning fun: A taxonomy of intrinsic motivations for learning. *Aptitude. Learning and Instruction III: Conative and Affective Process Analyses*, *98*(3), 223–253.

Márkus, Z. L., Kaposi, G., Veres, M., Weisz, Z., Szántó, G., Szkaliczki, T., Paneva-Marinova, D., Pavlov, R., Luchev, D., Goynov, M., & Pavlova, L. (2018). *Interactive game development to assist cultural heritage*. Academic Press.

Marzullo, F. P., & de Oliveira, F. A. (Eds.). (2021). *Practical Perspectives on Educational Theory and Game Development*. IGI Global. doi:10.4018/978-1-7998-5021-2

Michael, D. R., & Chen, S. L. (2005). *Serious games: Games that educate, train, and inform*. Academic Press.

Mortara, M., Catalano, C. E., Bellotti, F., Fiucci, G., Houry-Panchetti, M., & Petridis, P. (2014). Learning cultural heritage by serious games. *Journal of Cultural Heritage*, *15*(3), 318–325. doi:10.1016/j.culher.2013.04.004

Nussli, N., & Oh, K. (2021). Culturally Responsive Pedagogy, Universal Design for Learning, ubiquitous learning, and seamless learning: How these paradigms inform the intentional design of learner-centered online learning environments. In G. Panconesi & M. Guida (Eds.), *Handbook of Research on Teaching With Virtual Environments and AI* (pp. 163–188). IGI Global. doi:10.4018/978-1-7998-7638-0.ch008

Ohler, J. (2005). The world of digital storytelling. *Educational Leadership, 63*(4), 44–47.

Paneva-Marinova, D., Pavlov, R., & Kotuzov, N. (2017). Approach for analysis and improved usage of digital cultural assets for learning purposes. *Cybernetics and Information Technologies, 17*(3), 140–151. doi:10.1515/cait-2017-0035

Paneva-Marinova, D., Rousseva, M., Dimova, M., & Pavlova, L. (2018). Tell the Story of Ancient Thracians Through Serious Game. *Lecture Notes in Computer Science, 11196,* 509–517.

Patricio, R., Moreira, A., Zurlo, F., & Melazzini, M. (2020). Co-creation of new solutions through gamification: A collaborative innovation practice. *Creativity and Innovation Management, 29*(1), 146–160. doi:10.1111/caim.12356

Patrício, R., Moreira, A. C., & Zurlo, F. (2018). Gamification approaches to the early stage of innovation. *Creativity and Innovation Management, 27*(4), 499–511. doi:10.1111/caim.12284

Patrício, R., Moreira, A. C., & Zurlo, F. (2020). Enhancing design thinking approaches to innovation through gamification. *European Journal of Innovation Management.*

Pavlov, R., Paneva, D., Pavlova-Draganova, L., & Draganov, L. (2007). Ubiquitous learning applications on top of iconographic digital library. *The Proceedings of the International Conference on Mathematical and Computational Linguistics, 6,* 107–118.

Petrucco, C., & De Rossi, M. (2009). *Narrare con il digital storytelling a scuola e nelle organizzazioni.* Academic Press.

Robin, B. R. (2008). Digital storytelling: A powerful technology tool for the 21st century classroom. *Theory into Practice, 47*(3), 220–228. doi:10.1080/00405840802153916

Robson, K., Plangger, K., Kietzmann, J. H., McCarthy, I., & Pitt, L. (2015). Is it all a game? Understanding the principles of gamification. *Business Horizons, 58*(4), 411–420. doi:10.1016/j.bushor.2015.03.006

Roby, T. (2010). Opus in the Classroom: Striking CoRDS with Content-Related Digital Storytelling. *Contemporary Issues in Technology & Teacher Education, 10,* 133–144.

Rousseva, M. (2018). Challenges in the design and the development of the educational serious game "The Thracians." *Digital Presentation and Preservation of Cultural and Scientific Heritage, 8,* 83–85.

Slavova-Petkova, S., Dimova, M., & Luchev, D. (2016). *Learning Scenario for Better Understanding of Fairy Tales Using Role-playing and Serious Games Methods.* Academic Press.

Vasileva, M., Bakeva, V., Vasileva-Stojanovska, T., Malinovski, T., & Trajkovik, V. (2014). Grandma's Games Project: Bridging Tradition and Technology Mediated Education. *TEM Journal, 3*(1), 13–21.

Wagner, E. (2008). Steps to creating a content strategy for your organization. *The ELearning Developers,* 103–117.

Yuksel, P., Robin, B. B. R., & McNeil, S. (2010). Educational Uses of Digital Storytelling Around the World. *Elements*, *1*, 1264–1271.

Zlatkov, L., Paneva-Marinova, D., Luchev, D., Pavlova, L., & Pavlov, R. (2019). Aquae Calidae - Towards a Serious Game Attracting Students to Ancient Civilizations. *Proceedings of the 2019 2nd International Conference on Education Technology Management*, 14–18. 10.1145/3375900.3375919

KEY TERMS AND DEFINITIONS

Learning Service: A functional unit that refers to the management of training activities and/or processes in the software platform.

Learning-by-Authoring: A learning approach, which lays down on experiences resulting directly from the learner' authoring actions.

Learning-by-Doing: A learning approach, which lays down on experiences resulting directly from the learner' own actions.

Mini-Game: A short computer game contained in a more complex game.

Personalized Content Observation: A technique for customizing the user content exploration and usage in a software environment.

Serious Game: Computer game with educational purpose.

Technology-Enhanced Learning: Application of electronic communication and computer-based technology in education.

Chapter 22
Is the Gamification of Scientific Work a Good Idea?
"Little Lies Between Friends" at MT180®

Stéphane Le Lay
Institut de Psychodynamique du Travail, France

Jean Frances
ENSTA-Bretagne, France

ABSTRACT

This chapter shows that, contrary to what some researchers claim, setting up the conditions for a "playful environment" is not so simple, in particular when it comes to organizing a new competition for the popularization of science (MT180®). In fact, we will see that popularization does not fit so easily into the "playful environment" desired by the organizers due to the gamified nature of the approach, which gradually colonizes the initial desire to present one's scientific work and pushes some participants to exaggerate their results in order to go as far as possible in the competition. It is therefore feared that the gamification of scientific work, while compatible with neoliberal expectations, will in fact lead to the production of bad science. The question then arises as to whether the need to turn researchers into effective communicators with a view to building the "knowledge society" advocated by international institutions can be achieved through gamified approaches, with the risk of creating an ever-greater distance between (real) scientific knowledge and citizens.

INTRODUCTION

In recent years, there has been an intense scientific production devoted to the "gamification" of society in general[1] and of work in particular[2], and to an older phenomenon, known as "fun at work[3]" (Le Lay, 2020). While, due to their many limitations[4], these two notions are primarily descriptive and strictly situated from a socio-historical perspective, and cannot be considered as sociological concepts, they nevertheless make it possible to empirically identify managerial devices that use various fun mecha-

DOI: 10.4018/978-1-7998-9223-6.ch022

nisms to encourage workers to become subjectively involved in their activities. In this way, they make it possible to question the social and subjective effects of the unbridled use of fun mechanisms in various professional configurations, in the public and private sectors.

This is in particular the case for Ma Thèse en 180 secondes®[5] (MT180®), a science communication competition that has been open to French-speaking doctoral students and PhDs since 2013. In the eyes of its proponents, this tournament combines the concern to improve the life of doctoral students, by complementing it with festive and entertaining events, with a political desire to make the postgraduate degree curriculum more professional. This professionalization, which has been written into European texts since the 1990s, involves access to communication training that is supposed to provide "tricks" and soft skills aimed at increasing the performance level of MT180® candidates, and that are useful for adapting to the expectations of employment markets.

With its competition format, its precise and non-negotiable framework and rules of the game, its succession of encounters with referees (the jury and the public) and its rewards, MT180® offers doctoral students mindful to communicate about their thesis work, within the framework of a gamified apparatus, the possibility of putting on a show, and therefore resorting to both stand-up comedy and scientific popularization codes, with a view to winning votes and supplanting their competitors. This tournament can thus be considered as a spectacular scheme for expressive challenges, i.e. a set of discourses, knowledge and material and symbolic means oriented towards the use of public theatrical performances, based on showmanship and scientific discourse in a competitive and fun configuration.

Based on the results of our long-term collective field survey (2014-2017) using a number of varied empirical elements (observations, individual interviews, group interviews, questionnaires - see Table 1)[6], this article will show that, contrary to what some Human Resources researchers claim, setting up the conditions for a "playful environment" is not so simple, in particular when it comes to organizing a new competition for the *popularization* of science. In fact, we will see that popularization does not fit so easily into the "playful environment" desired by the organizers, due to the gamified nature of the approach, which gradually colonizes the initial desire to present one's scientific work and pushes some participants to exaggerate their results, or even "lie just a little bit", in order to go as far as possible in the competition. It is therefore to be feared that the gamification of scientific work (in this case in its popularized communicative dimension), while compatible with neoliberal expectations, will in fact lead to the production of bad science. The question then arises as to whether the need to turn researchers into effective communicators with a view to building the "knowledge society" advocated by international institutions can be achieved through gamified approaches, with the risk of creating an ever greater distance between (real) scientific knowledge and citizens.

Table 1. Data corpus

Survey preparation	Ethnographic observations	Interviews	Questionnaires
- Viewing of performances on the Internet - E-mail contacts of participants in the 2014 national final - E-mail contacts of participants (2015 and 2016 competitions) - E-mail contacts of institutional representatives	13 observations (local, national and international challenges)	- 22 institutional representatives (including jury) - 20 participants (local, national and international challenges)	420 usable questionnaires (2014, 2015 and 2016 competitions)

Background: Ma Thèse en 180 Secondes®, An Unknown Competition From a Sociological Point of View

One point should be emphasized at the outset: the sociological literature devoted to the MT180® is non-existent in France, because we are for the moment the only researchers to have carried out a precise empirical survey, immediately after the launch of the competition (Frances, Le Lay & Pizzinat, 2016). One of the dimensions that interested us was the gamification of the academic field, a trend that we had already pointed out through the increasingly frequent use of apparatus like serious games in doctoral studies (Frances & Le Lay, 2017). In our opinion, the term gamification is not a concept, because of the vagueness of its definition[7]. As Seaborn and Fels indeed remind us, "games are subject to the elephant test: instantly recognizable, they are nonetheless hard to define" (2014, p. 16). However, this difficulty has not prevented many researchers in marketing or business studies from proposing more or less convergent definitions. "A standard definition of gamification is emerging: the intentional use of game elements for a gameful experience of non-game tasks and contexts. Game elements are patterns, objects, principles, models, and methods directly inspired by games." (Seaborn & Fels, 2014, p. 17). However, there is not necessarily agreement on what exactly the game elements are (Dicheva *et al.*, 2015, p. 77), and furthermore in this definition, one element is not clearly announced, the competition principle, which is central to distinguish game from other forms of playing situations (Bogost, 2011; Hamayon, 2015). Indeed, currently, the essential objective assigned to the gamified apparatus is to obtain the best possible performance and productivity from its users.

If the MT180® has not been discussed in the French literature, its Australian "ancestor", The Three Minute Thesis Competition (3MT®), has been the subject of a few articles. Invented in Australia at the University of Queensland, this competition was set up in 2008, following the idea put forward by Professor Alan Lawson, a philosopher and specialist in post-colonial studies (Corsi, Frances & Le Lay, 2021, pp. 44-47). In line with the issue of "employability" via soft skills and "transferable skills" to support the "adaptability" of jobseekers and workers in increasingly competitive labor markets, several "modules" were introduced into Queensland's higher education curricula to teach students to communicate in formats different from those used in the academic field, emphasizing orality over the written word (authors' email exchange with Alan Lawson, April 2018). This was the context in which the 3MT® competition was conceived and developed based on precise rules: requirement for a presentation lasting not longer than three minutes in spoken form (no poems or songs) with no interruption after the start is given[8]. In fact, as researchers in the field of microwave technologies write, the "3MT aimed to buck the tradition of densely detailed and unengaging technical talks and instead reward presenters for brevity, clarity, and, above all, understandability, engagement, and capturing a general audience's imagination." (Bandler & Kiley, 2018, p. 117).

The major difficulty, for our purposes, lies in the fact that the rare research on the 3MT® does not at all take into consideration the question of work in general, and its gamification in particular. Indeed, these works are conducted by linguists, who focus primarily on the discursive content of the contest, in particular the rhetorical structure of 3MT® presentations, using quantitative approaches (Hu & Liu, 2018), in order to provide future participants with a sort of vade mecum on rhetorical strategy, because "a key aspect of contemporary academic literacy is the ability to establish the usefulness and immediacy of research topics to real-life concerns" (Jiang & Qiu, 2021, p. 3). In fact, all these articles seem to take for granted that "3MT is not an exercise in trivialising or 'dumping-down' research but encourages students to consolidate their ideas and crystallise their research discoveries to engage a non-specialist audience[9]". For example, Jiang and Qiu emphasize the efforts made in the presentations to popularize complex scientific topics, which they argue follow a well-known rhetorical pattern:

"Sharing the features of science popularizations, such as TED talks, 3MT presentations start with a rhetorical orientation of the presented research topics to the general audience, typically by establishing a common ground, while discussing research methods and results as academic speeches. This argumentative organization of discourse extends what is known about other recontextualization strategies used by presenters to engage with the lay audience" (2021, p. 16-17).

The two authors thus conclude that 3MT® and popularization in the strongest sense of the term are actually close, without ever accounting for the actual content of the presentations. This approach neglects all the more the question of the intrinsic quality of the "scientific content" as some authors use the stance model, which "refers to the ways that writers project themselves into their texts to communicate their integrity, credibility, involvement and a relationship to their subject matter and audiences" (Hyland & Zou, 2021, p. 3), which eliminates from the outset the question of the potential use of promise and deception in the competition. Yet, results would have allowed to ask the question, in particular when the expression "promising application" appears in a presentation extract (Hyland & Zou, 2021, p. 9). The authors do not take the time to ask what "promising" means, and simply explain that it illustrates what they call "attitude markers", which "indicate the writer's affective perspectives and include evaluations and personal feelings as he or she comments on the material under discussion or on the communication itself" (Hyland & Zou, 2021, p. 8); at no time do they ask the question of the PhD student's position on the scientific credibility of his promise.

Moreover, the authors using the stance model never consider the fact that it is in order to perform well in the gamified apparatus that the candidates favor "a heavily stance-laden discourse" (Hyland & Zou, 2021, p. 11). Yet, "when discussing results, 3MT presenters in all disciplines attach more importance to what can be gained from research findings than how they are arrived at, anticipating what a wide audience expect to see as 'glamorizing material'" (Jiang & Qiu, 2021, p. 16). The reader will not know more. This lack of analysis of the effects of competition on the form of presentations[10] must be put in perspective with the absence of a link between 3MT® and gamification, except incidentally in the article by Carter-Thomas and Rowley-Jolivet (2020, p. 32), who unfortunately ignore the French literature on this precise point (Le Lay, Pizzinat & Frances, 2017). This is probably due to the methodological choices made in these different studies. For example, Carter-Thomas and Rowley-Jolivet only carried out a small textual analysis of the presentations compared to the thesis summaries (a narrowness also pointed out by

Hyland & Zou, 2021, p. 11), without ever raising the question of the potential exaggerations, promises and/or lies of the candidates, and only mentioning the fact that one of the discursive strategies is "the use of scenarios" (Carter-Thomas and Rowley-Jolivet, 2020, p. 20), a vague expression that allows for many different specific cases. Perhaps to explore these issues, it would have been necessary to meet with the participants to ask them to explain how and why they went about this discursive elaboration. While Hyland and Zou (2021, p. 11) also note this limitation in their own work analyzing presentations, with a brief mention of the issue of the body in performance (particularly the potential influence of non-verbal cues), ultimately, we see that these studies are relatively disembodied.

Our investigation is therefore original in two ways, as it allows us to explore, from a sociological point of view, the effects of a gamified apparatus on the work of doctoral scientific communication, based on what the participants try *to embody* during the whole process of competition in order to win the different rounds of the tournament (and not only on what they say during the show).

MAIN FOCUS

The Organization of a New Science Popularization Competition: A Not So Simple Organizational Challenge

Since its inception, the 3MT® competition has been a great success, which has never dwindled[11]. Its "area of influence" went beyond the English-speaking academic world. In 2012, after seeing the Australian competition on the Internet, the management team of the Association francophone pour le savoir (French-speaking association for knowledge - ACFAS), a Quebec-based non-profit organization founded in 1923 to further progress in science, decided to contact the organizers of the Australian tournament to ask them for permission to adopt their scheme, in preparation for its 80th annual conference. In line with one of the areas of its strategic plan, the association promotes a number of activities aimed at the "next generation of researchers" (young researchers in MSc, doctoral and post-doctoral studies), including the "Votre soutenance en 180 secondes" ("Your 180-second presentation") competition (the final took place in May 2012), a French-language adaptation of 3MT®. Indeed, the implementation of the "Your 180-second presentation" competition is precisely in line with ACFAS' twofold role: to protect, enhance and support the research community on the one hand, and to relate to society by disseminating scientific culture on the other. But the format and tone adopted make the competition "a kind of mini-show" (interview with ACFAS manager, April 2015), with a host, music, and the participation of members of the "Ligue nationale d'improvisation" (National Improv League). Here, elements specific to the fun work environment are thus mixed with elements relating to the gamification of work, with the aim of developing a pleasant and friendly atmosphere during the competition.

After the first edition of the "Your 180-second presentation" in Quebec, ACFAS repeated the experience in 2013. That year, during a study trip to Canada, a member of the Scientific and Technical Culture Department[12] of the University of Lorraine attended the final of the competition with one of his colleagues. Both were keen to further the training of doctoral students in communication. Identified by the Communication departments of Centre National de la Recherche Scientifique (CNRS) and Conférence des Présidents d'Université (Conference of University Chairs) (CPU), in particular for their relations with ACFAS, they were encouraged to explore possible ways of improving the curricula in this area. They then decided to adapt the scheme to import it into France. CNRS and CPU became involved in

2014 with the support of the University of Lorraine, which then acted as a relay to ensure that the system could be rolled out as easily as possible at the national level (interview with a member of the Scientific and Technical Culture Department of the University of Lorraine, December 2014). The competition then became known as Ma thèse en 180 secondes®.

During this competition, apprentice researchers have to make their results or questions known to various audiences and summarize their expression, and are in a position to control, on their own, the channels of scientific information for the "general public". Candidates are therefore *normally* invited to try their hand at a form of communication that meets the common criteria of popularization. Things seem simple. However, if you listen carefully to the organizers, you will notice the wide variety of words with which "popularization" is conjugated. While it is primarily associated with education and the dissemination of knowledge, it is also qualified by entertainment and promotion. The recurrent nature of the usage thus goes hand in hand with the instability of the associated meanings, which, from an organizational perspective, is useful. Indeed, if the organizers were to refer in an orthodox way to a strict definition of popularization (Hilgartner, 1990), it would be harder for the scheme to be entertaining: schematic statements that accurately reflect the progress of given knowledge without lapsing into science-fictional anticipation tend to attract a smaller audience than more or less mythological accounts of heroic scientific epics heralding bright technological futures. Therefore, to demand a certain popularization rectitude would limit recourse to metaphorical or dreamlike registers and, in this light, it would undoubtedly be difficult to make MT180® an event for the promotion of doctoral students. In using a malleable definition of popularization, however, the institutional leaders of the competition do not stand in the way of future candidates using more oracular registers, or using the right words and theatrics, in other words, of entertaining and "putting on a show".

While the competition was immediately heralded as a success by the general public and the media (many regional and national press articles have been published about the candidates, and regional and national television channels have reported on the competition[13]), it came in for much more criticism from the researchers themselves. For example, voices were raised to denounce a distressing form of "happening management[14]", even though the instigators of the scheme were concerned to make MT180® a quality event for the dissemination of scientific culture. In the academic field, fun and entertainment cannot be sought at just any cost. Whatever the case, this aim alone would not be enough to gain the support of university and CNRS researchers nor communication departments alone. The first two editions of the competition (2014 and 2015) thus encountered a number of difficulties during their implementation (reluctance of teacher-researchers, selection of "good" candidates[15], insufficient material resources), in particular during the local and regional phases of the competition.

The tension is therefore palpable: on the one hand, the sciences, their producers and their dissemination, and on the other, the show, its entertainers and its promotion. This tension may not be felt as such by candidates due to the dynamics of the fun mechanisms used through the gamification of work (timed competition, successive stages of the competition, prizes to be won) and fun at work (relaxed atmosphere, fun training): the immersive power inherent in the game makes it possible not to think about certain potentially undesirable aspects of mixing games and work (Le Lay, 2020). However, this tension between putting on a show and science has undoubtedly given rise to misunderstandings, or even mistrust, in laboratories. Even more so, the tension between the desire to disseminate science and the spectacularization of research seems difficult to contain. The dual aim of disseminating knowledge and putting on a show puts the organizers of MT180® on a slippery slope, as one aspect may at any time take precedence over the other.

With "Your 180-second presentation", ACFAS managers wanted to mix some fun with the 3MT® original version in particular to avoid the TED (Technology, Entertainment and Design) conference format, which in their eyes made the exercise too formal. In contrast to this restrictive exercise - which Alan Lawson in fact wanted - a format and tone that made the competition a kind of mini-show was preferred. To achieve this, aspects of the fun work environment[16], a managerial policy aimed at creating a pleasant, friendly atmosphere in the workplace, were used. For their part, the French promoters of MT180® have kept the Quebec spirit of sharing, play and theater. While the spirit of fun reigns at MT180®, just *wanting to be fun* is not enough to avoid the limits of the "mini industry of prescribed fun in the workplace" (Warren & Fineman, 2007). However, the people for whom these pleasurable aspects are intended would have to actually enjoy them, which is far from always being the case. So what about MT180®? In fact, its organizers are unanimous on both sides of the Atlantic: the feedback from the participants was positive and highlighted the friendly and convivial atmosphere[17]. There is, however, a competition and the candidates cannot get away from this.

When Gamification Takes Precedence Over Fun at Work: Making Promises to Win

In taking the form of a tournament in which the candidates attempt to go as far as possible in a series of knockout rounds, MT180® refers to an agonal form of play (game), in the service of which is deployed the expressive dimension (play) of the games played, namely the aspects of speech and theatrics, which are extremely important in the context of the competition, and which are the subject of specific training during the competition. This training curriculum and the advice gleaned from friends and family lead candidates to prefer writing a spectacular speech and putting on a fun show to precise writing (logical rigor of statements, concern for demonstration) and a professorial tone. The ambitions in terms of disseminating scientific knowledge called for at the outset are moreover progressively revised downwards as the training courses and tests progress, in the course of the *"shortcuts"* (Valentin, agronomy) to which the candidates consent - a systematic comparison with the 3MT® competition would be interesting in this respect. These successive recompositions lead doctoral students to conceive and act out performances that are much more akin to the dissemination of promises than to *popularization*. It is a well-known fact: the promise involves writing and putting on a show with the aim of articulating the researchers' projects, on the one hand, and stimulating the commitments of their funders, assessors and supporters, on the other (Fujimura, 1987). Unlike the prospective approach and the effort of *popularization* that it requires, the narratives involving making promises proposed by scientists and technologists are based on the writing of speeches where often contradictory writing requirements have to hang together: announcing the irreversible arrival of a "radical novelty" while trying to establish its "credibility" as a scientist (Joly, 2015, p. 37). In this case, you have to be both (very) serious and make people dream at the same time. The work of convincing and getting people on board often pays little attention to the scientific precision and accuracy of the publicized statements, since their "recipients have few means of assessing their validity" (Joly, 2015, p. 38): after all, content is only a means to an end. Indeed, according to Arie Rip (2006), the pedagogical casualness of scientists and technologists making promises towards their audiences is explained by their "fears of public fear", i.e. their adherence to the "myth of an audience with irrational fears" about science and technology, which thus needs to be "reassured" (Joly, 2015, p. 40) and made to dream (Durand, 2018).

Scientific promise thus refers to a form of communication aimed at financial and institutional supporters of research (who need to be made to dream and be reassured), often theatrically presented during auditions, competitions and contests. During the latter, those who engage in them announce future results and applications, without necessarily referring intelligibly to created knowledge, thereby preventing their audience from being able to make a rational assessment as to the probability of them happening in the future, without for all that attracting the disapproval of their peers. This is because scientists making promises could not make a career without their counterparts also agreeing to make promises - even if it means legitimizing these activities through rationalizations. This definition seems to us to be a valid description of the activity of the MT180 ®candidates, with the proviso, in our case, that the promises made are in a "competitive game" configuration involving playing at promising and not promising and assuming the consequences in a professional context. Some candidates do not hesitate to say that they *"oversell"* (Alexis, physics) the imminence of a discovery by overestimating the progress of the knowledge from which it is supposed to result and by draping the statements made in esoteric-sounding formulations, while others predict with a well-played certainty the rapid transformation of scientific proposals into innovative products... Rather than opening up possible futures, they promise certain futures by colonizing the present with their promises thereby opposing the enunciation of alternative futures (Joly, 2015, p. 31).

At MT180®, participants adopt these rhetorical, theatrical options in deference to two major competitive mechanisms. The first mechanism involves "rallying the public to the cause". This term refers to the propensity of candidates to base their reasons for making a fun, spectacular presentation of their thesis work on the audience's (supposed) expectations and ignorance. The second mechanism refers to "the influence of the competition": the imminence of going on stage, the ambition to shine in front of the spectators and the members of the jury, and to be worthy of one's peers, finally convince the participants that announcing applications and discoveries with certainty is much more decisive, from the perspective of going forward in the tournament, than explaining the phenomena and questions actually dealt with in the thesis: this approach is impressive as it places its author alongside the most important scientific advances and the most "disruptive" innovations. Seeking to entertain and impress thereby leads candidates to relegate adhering to the principle of truthfulness and embrace the perspective of promise.

"Clearly I don't get up in the morning and say 'I'm going to improve telecommunications'. I would like to. I say to myself maybe in ten years, if it works [...]. But that's not what I'm presenting at all. Obviously, I'm saying it's already done, it's working and it's too good [laughs]." (Mélanie, physics)

Not all candidates have the same narrative resources to successfully engage the audience. In this case, disciplines are discriminating. While historians and astronomers can only claim to explain phenomena that are far away in time and space, biotechnologists and energy specialists are much more able to announce new therapies or technical solutions to climate change. As they enter the competition, however, the majority of them see and are convinced of the need to rouse the audience's interest and make themselves memorable. Once they have made these spectacular objectives their own, participants rewrite their speeches adding various rhetorical gimmicks which, from humor to staggering analogy (Bouveresse, 1999), from ellipsis to applicative exaggerations and even various shortcuts, aim to increase the entertaining or impressive character of their performance, and lead inexorably to making promises.

The imperative of spectacular writing and theatrics is all the more compelling as the competition approaches and doctoral students try to tailor their performance to the expectations and knowledge they credit the audience with. While doctoral students offer a glimpse of their desire to actually talk about their research to a non-specialist audience, they quickly close this door in deference to, or because of, the audience's perceived lack of knowledge about science.

"I think it's more to get people curious about certain things because in three minutes there's not much you can really say. The audience comes in, they don't know anything about... They may have some knowledge about one thing or another because they're interested in it. [...] But they're not going to retain more than that." (Nina, history)

Because they still hope to disseminate knowledge related to their thesis, but consider the public's inability to understand and memorize it - the famous fears of fear evoked by Arie Rip -, doctoral students may end up justifying various exaggerations, anachronisms or shortcuts in order to *"impress"*. One young physicist said that he was afraid that his performance would be *"nice but forgettable"*. Even though his presentation explained *"the scientific background"* of his thesis topic *"not too badly"*, it was not sufficiently *"lively"* and lacked *"a pinch of madness"* (Alexis, physics) to hope for any success. With the national final just around the corner, the solution to these drawbacks was quickly found. He rewrote his speech so as to make promises and while he did not announce any revolutionary discoveries or radical innovations, he nevertheless managed to *"sell"* his work as generating innovative uses of well-controlled techniques and knowledge. In a way, he partly abandoned the observance of the principle of truthfulness and the corollary concern for *popularization*, and attempted to promise a technological future before justifying this rhetorical option of exaggeration on the basis of reducing the *"forgettable"* character of his performance.

Moreover, baffling people by using specialist vocabulary and common words in a specific way can impress audiences far removed from the research field: this is a resource that scientists making promises use to establish their "credibility" with their mixed audiences (Joly, 2015). In front of audiences who are not scientists, professing rhetoric with an abstruse, scientific sounding construction, can sometimes confer a certain aura to its enunciator. As one another physicist explained, making reference to *"quantum computers"* or *"ultrafine transistors"* (Clément, physics) is to use adjectives that are both scientific and heralding of radical innovation. "Upgrading" these banal technical entities - almost everyone has a computer and listens to the radio - with these scientific words is an effective, easily achievable discursive ploy for those who want to impress their audience and make them believe in their close proximity with the most innovative, revolutionary research fields and investigations. Without enough time to rationally prove their "competence", impressing an audience is therefore an effective, if not inescapable way, of making them believe in promises (Colonomos, 2014): it is a way of "putting the audience in a position to recognize the validity of a number of ideas" (Scarantino, 2007, p. 24). In this context, trying to anticipate by extrapolating uses for one's work is an effective discursive technique. Finally, having been urged to present *"memorable"* performances and compare them for weeks on end against those of their counterparts, MT180® candidates put pressure on each other to make hollow promises, right up to the end.

DISCUSSION AND CONCLUSION: IS GAMIFICATION OF RESEARCH WORK GOOD FOR THE "KNOWLEDGE SOCIETY"?

In the course of our analyses, we have seen that in the MT180®, candidates and jurors together establish an assessment framework where giving the impression of sharing knowledge ensures a good ranking. In this context, saying that one's own work has a promising potential for applications is undeniably effective. The promise becomes a tool for promoting and connecting scientists and audiences in such a way that the uninitiated think they understand the meaning of the speech: it gives the audience and the assessors the misleading impression that they can raise their real level of knowledge to that delivered superficially and with promises made in the brief. It seems that both sides agree to produce and congratulate a "manipulative speech". Indeed, as notes Philippe Breton, discursive manipulation often begins where the speakers' ambition is to "win support at any cost" (Breton, 2015, p. 26) without opening dialogue, and where the rhetorical techniques used aim to make highly uncertain facts or phenomena appear to true and verified. It therefore seems to us to be perfectly fair to say that MT180® congratulates "manipulative" capabilities, whose promise is the most appropriate embodiment of the requirements of a communication competition for scientists, but whose deployment may be accompanied by a feeling of "disqualification" (Breton, 2015, pp. 23-25) and "dishonor" which may raise concerns about the emergence of a lasting form of ethical suffering[18] in a number of actors in the academic field.

This problem is not insignificant, in an institutional configuration where researchers have to increasingly seek support and budgets to undertake research projects. Admittedly, the resources obtained through promises can be used to commit investigations and researchers. If financing institutions do not hold anyone to account, the operation is likely to be beneficial: indeed, cases of instrumental promises are legion. Scientists agree to this as long as the potential benefits are high and the risks remain low of having to assume its unrealistic nature. However, since promises have to be kept (faced with funding agencies demanding progress reports, or venture capitalists demanding a "return on investment"), they also narrow the paths of science: they are thus likely to generate "path dependency effects", forcing scientists to produce the predicted futures at all costs. This is also noted by Arie Rip, when he states that "there have been cases of fraud motivated by the need to fulfill promises of excellence and social relevance, from the rigged mouse [...] to the Korean stem cell scientist Hwang Woo-Suk and the German nanotechnology scientist Jan-Hendrik Schön" (2006, p. 302).

Beyond these spectacular promise "pathologies", the promise is in fact very much an instrument for bringing together scientists, the general public and the financial and institutional supporters of research. The link then established between researchers making promises, on the one hand, and assessors and funders, on the other, certainly contributes to strengthening the organization of research through projects and contracts, but above all it helps to speed up the pace and to vary the ways (and tricks) of winning the various races for budgets and resources. In making promises, researchers are stating goals they know are unrealistic and agreeing to submit to less than skeptical assessments; in making hollows promises, commissioners ensure the deployment of science workers and protect themselves from their potential critics by not giving too much credit to those who have won contracts on the strength of promises but have never come close to delivering the results they promise.

In this game where researchers and funders support each other mutually (but where ethical suffering is more on the researchers' side), the public and "civil society" are the main losers: they are confined to being impressed by the oracles of science, without being able to ask them questions or hold them to account, and then realize how great the gap is between what the sciences say they can do, in particular through their funding institutions (which are themselves led to make promises to their central administration), and what they actually do. Finally, it should be noted that research has long been organized around contracts and that this is not a problem in itself. It becomes one if budgets are allocated to projects in disregard of an assessment where peers have a decisive voice, if this method of financing is the only way to "survive" (at the expense of more recurrent funding methods), if contracts become so scarce and shortened as to require scientists to spend more time working to obtain the resources to do research than actually doing it. Learning how to win contracts and projects is therefore not a problem in itself. What it is, however, is learning how to make promises, as this means learning how to chase contracts with a stopwatch in the hand, to obtain the resources needed to do research in a world of science that structurally lacks such resources, and to consent to resources being directed through channels whose scientific legitimacy seems questionable.

This speeding up of project-based science thus stimulates the making of promises and encourages researchers to become professional in the activity of making promises. In so doing, a desynchronization occurs between the ability of scientists to obtain budgets and support, on the one hand, and their ability to effectively produce original knowledge and to direct their work in a more democratic way, on the other. Analyzing the similarity between the race for contracts and MT180®, the members of a doctoral student association committed to popularization, and responsible for the local organization of an edition of the competition, regretted during an interview that the mechanism did not allow the public to become involved and ask questions. They saw how such an organization of the tournament prevented any dialogue between science and society and ultimately kept young researchers on a sort of symbolic pedestal - since in practice the social position of doctoral students remains unstable - distancing them from any possibility of *popularizing*, of effectively passing on any knowledge and of dialoguing on the advisability or otherwise of pursuing a particular research project. Finally, MT180® influences the *hexis* of doctoral students before changing their *ethos* and aligning their specificities with the requirements of races for contracts and projects. In so doing, the (question of the) morality of scientists resurfaces where competition used to excuse its repression. Indeed, while the struggles for publication, positions and scholarships are increasingly competitive, they are also increasingly permeable to the institutionalization of various forms of fraud[19] - like an apprenticeship in the cycling profession, which often involves an apprenticeship in how to get away with doping or "getting the job done", as the saying goes (Buisine, 2009) - which, ultimately, requires recipients to acquaint themselves with mutual ethical arrangements... which are not very ethical.

It is therefore problematic to institutionalize training courses, such as those proposed in the MT180® course[20], which aim to equip apprentice researchers with skills in communicative distortion. All the more so since it is the doctoral students who accumulate the most guarantees of academic "excellence", i.e. those whose chances of a career in higher education and research institutions are the highest (Frances, 2017), who play the competition game best and easily excuse themselves from making promises. The problem of the institutionalization of learning how to make promises and the potential disruptions then brought about in the normal functioning of the scientific field thus seem increasingly pressing. And if apprentice researchers find, within the latter, having to justify themselves in taking part in such communication competitions, their commitment is strengthened by the public image they gain. Once again, spectators play a key role in this curriculum: that of stimulating the pleasures of the candidates' oracle, with the narcissistic implications that this can have. Indeed, succeeding in making promises with brilliance and being applauded for one's performance leads doctoral students, for the time of a theatrical scene, to incarnate an ideal or dreamed of figure of a scientist: making promises, in general, and at MT180®

in particular, offers a moment making it possible to bridge, through fiction, the wide gap between the stories about the heroes of science and the arid everydayness of research work.

Admittedly, MT180® is only a "game". But does winning the competition by deliberately distorting the state of given knowledge in order to make people believe that a scientific enigma will be solved very soon and that radical innovations will be produced come down to depriving one's peers making fewer promises from access to public or jury awards? And would this not ultimately come down to taking a certain degree of liberty with regard to professional standards and values - seeking of truth, concern for accuracy and precision, contribution to the opening up of probable futures, etc. - called for by scientists (Shinn & Ragouet, 2005)? And even here, is it not a question of fraud with regard to the rules (including that of truthfulness) which, in the course of the normal working of the scientific field, govern the competition for access to the resources needed for research (Bourdieu, 1976; Gingras, 2002)? Thus, while it is illusory to imagine a world of science without promises, its inflation accentuates "the separation between those who make the promise and those who are supposed to accept it" (Joly, 2015, p. 44), and thus contributes to further desynchronizing what science can do from what scientists say they can do.

FUNDING

This research was supported by a financial contribution from the "Groupement d'intérêt scientifique Jeux et société" and from Christophe Dejours's research team, in the Conservatoire National des Arts et Métiers. We thank them for it.

REFERENCES

Bandler, J. W., & Kiley, E. M. (2018). The Clarity of Hindsight: The First-Ever IMS Three Minute Thesis Competition. *IEEE Microwave Magazine*, 116-123.

Bogost, I. (2011). *Gamification is bullshit*. http://bogost.com/writing/blog/gamification_is_bullshit

Bourdieu, P. (1976). Le champ scientifique. *Actes de la Recherche en Sciences Sociales, 2-3*(2), 88–104. doi:10.3406/arss.1976.3454

Bouveresse, J. (1999). *Prodiges et vertiges de l'analogie*. Raison d'agir.

Breton, P. (2015). *La parole manipulée*. La Découverte. (Original work published 1997)

Buisine, S. (2009). *"Faire le métier" de cycliste: une sociologie pragmatique du travail dans le domaine sportif*. Thèse de doctorat en STAPS, Université Paris X.

Carter-Thomas, S., & Rowley-Jolivet, E. (2020). Three minute thesis presentations: Recontextualisation strategies in doctoral research. *Journal of English for Academic Purposes*. doi:10.1016/j.jeap.2020.100897

Colonomos, A. (2014). *La politique des oracles. Raconter le futur aujourd'hui*. Albin Michel.

Corsi, J.-M., Frances, J., & Le Lay, S. (2021). *Ma Thèse en 180 secondes®. Quand la science devient spectacle*. Éditions du Croquant.

Darde, J.-N. (2012). Enseignants-chercheurs, recherche et plagiat. *Mouvements (Paris)*, *71*(3), 128–137. doi:10.3917/mouv.071.0128

Dejours, C. (1998). *Souffrance en France. La banalisation de l'injustice sociale*. Seuil.

Deterding, S., Dixon, D., Khaled, R., & Nacke, L. (2011). From Game Design Elements to Gameful-ness: Defining "Gamification". In *Proceedings of the 15th International academic MindTrek conference "Envisioning future media environments"*. ACM. 10.1145/2181037.2181040

Dicheva, D., Dichev, C., Agre, G., & Angelova, G. (2015). Gamification in education: A systematic mapping study. *Journal of Educational Technology & Society*, *18*(3), 75–88.

Duarte, A. (2017). *Défenses et résistance en psychodynamique du travail*. Thèse de doctorat en psy-chologie, Université Paris Descartes.

Durand, R. (2018). *L'évangélisme technologique. De la révolte hippie au capitalisme high-tech de la Silicon Valley*. Fyp.

Frances, J. (2017). "Employabilité" doctorale et lutte des places dans le monde académique. In J.-P. Durand, D. Glaymann, F. Moatty, & G. Tiffon (Eds.), L'employabilité et ses usages sociaux (pp. 81-92). Presses Universitaires de Rennes.

Frances, J., & Le Lay, S. (2017). L'usage des *business games* dans le cursus doctoral. "Esprit d'entreprendre" et "esprit d'entreprise" dans la formation à la recherche. *Formation Emploi*, *140*(140), 67–86. doi:10.4000/formationemploi.5217

Frances, J., Le Lay, S., & Pizzinat, B. (2016). Des chercheurs en liberté. Le MT180 sur l'établi de la "sociologie (de) garage". *Carnet Zilsel*. https://zilsel.hypotheses.org/2608

Fujimura, J. H. (1987). Constructing "Do-able" Problems in Cancer Research: Articulating Alignment. *Social Studies of Science*, *17*(2), 257–293. doi:10.1177/030631287017002003

Gingras, Y. (2002). Les formes spécifiques de l'internationalité du champ scientifique. *Actes de la Re-cherche en Sciences Sociales*, *141-142*(1), 31–45. doi:10.3917/arss.141.0031

Hamayon, R. (2015). Petit pas de côté. *La Revue du MAUSS*, *45*(1), 75–90. doi:10.3917/rdm.045.0075

Hammarfelt, B., de Rijcke, S., & Rushforth, A. D. (2016). Quantified academic selves: The gamification of research through social networking services. *Information Research*, *20*(2). http://www.informationr.net/ir/21-2/SM1.html

Hilgartner, S. (1990). The Dominant View of Popularization: Conceptual Problems, Political Uses. *Social Studies of Science*, *20*(3), 519–539. doi:10.1177/030631290020003006

Hu, G., & Liu, Y. (2018). Three Minute Thesis Presentations as an Academic Genre: A Cross-disciplinary Study of Genre Move. *Journal of English for Academic Purposes*. doi:10.1016/j.jeap.2018.06.004

Hyland, K., & Zou, H. (2021). "I believe the findings are fascinating": Stance in three-minute theses. *Journal of English for Academic Purposes*, *50*, 100973. Advance online publication. doi:10.1016/j.jeap.2021.100973

Jiang, F., & Qiu, X. (2021). Communicating disciplinary knowledge to a wide audience in 3MT presentations: How students engage with popularization of science. *Discourse Studies*. Advance online publication. doi:10.1177/14614456211037438

Joly, P.-B. (2015). Le régime des promesses technoscientifiques. In M. Audétat (Ed.), *Sciences et technologies émergentes: pourquoi tant de promesses?* (pp. 31–47). Éditions Hermann.

Le Lay S. (2020). *Destin du jouer et du travail à l'ère du management distractif*. Habilitation à diriger des recherches en sociologie, Université Aix-Marseille.

Le Lay, S., Pizzinat, B., & Frances, J. (2017). *"Candidats du MT180®, Soyez fun et sexy"*. Un "dispositif spectaculaire" au service de la gamification du champ académique. In E. Savignac, Y. Andonova, P. Lénel, A. Monjaret, & A. Seurrat (Eds.), *Le travail de la gamification. Enjeux, modalités et rhétoriques de la translation du jeu au travail* (pp. 73–91). Peter Lang.

Le Lay, S., Savignac, E., Frances, J., & Lénel, P. (Eds.). (2021). *The gamification of society*. Iste-Wiley. doi:10.1002/9781119821557

Michel, J. W., Tews, M. J., & Allen, D. G. (2019). Fun in the Workplace: A Review and Expanded Theoretical Perspective. *Human Resource Management Review*, *29*(1), 98–110. doi:10.1016/j.hrmr.2018.03.001

Owler, K., Morrison, R., & Plester, B. (2010). Does Fun Work? The Complexity of Promoting Fun at Work. *Journal of Management & Organization*, *16*(3), 338–352. doi:10.5172/jmo.16.3.338

Rip, A. (2006). Folks Theories of Nanotechnologists. *Science as Culture*, *15*(4), 349–365. doi:10.1080/09505430601022676

Robertson, M. (2010). *Can't play, won't play*. https://web.archive.org/web/20110521091044/http://www.hideandseek.net/2010/10/06/cant-play-wont-play

Rolo, D. (2015). *Mentir au travail*. Presses universitaires de France. doi:10.3917/puf.rolod.2015.03

Rossette-Crake, F. (2020). 'The new oratory': Public speaking practice in the digital, neoliberal age. *Discourse Studies*, *22*(5), 571–589. doi:10.1177/1461445620916363

Savignac, E., Andonova, Y., Lénel, P., Monjaret, A., & Seurrat, A. (Eds.). (2017). *Le travail de la gamification. Enjeux, modalités et rhétoriques de la translation du jeu au travail*. Peter Lang. doi:10.3726/b11612

Scarantino, L. M. (2007). Persuasion, rhétorique et autorité. *Diogène*, *217*, 22–38.

Seaborn, K., & Fels, D. I. (2014). Gamification in Theory and Action: A Survey. *International Journal of Human-Computer Studies*, *74*, 14–31. doi:10.1016/j.ijhcs.2014.09.006

Shinn, T., & Ragouet, P. (2005). *Controverses sur la science. Pour une sociologie transversaliste de l'activité scientifique*. Raisons d'agir.

Warren, S., & Fineman, S. (2007). 'Don't get me wrong, it's fun here, but…' Ambivalence and paradox in a 'fun' work environment. In R. Westwood & C. Rhodes (Eds.), Humour, Work and Organization (pp. 92-112). Routledge.

ENDNOTES

1   For a recent summary of work written in English and French in particular in the educational, political and health fields, see Le Lay et al. (2021).

2   For a recent summary of work written in English and French, see Savignac et al. (2017).

3   For a recent summary of work written in English, see Michel, Tews & Allen (2019).

4   For a criticism of the normative assumptions of fun at work, see Owler, Morrison & Plester (2010). For a criticism of the theoretical limitations of gamification, see in particular Deterding et al. (2011) and Seborn & Fels (2014).

5   My Thesis in 180 seconds.

6   For further details on the survey methodology and a detailed analysis of the empirical evidence which allow us to develop our subject here, see Corsi, Frances & Le Lay (2021).

7   An example can be found in the article by Hammarfelt, de Rijcke & Rushforth (2016) dedicated to the relationship between quantified-self, gamification and the academic field. Indeed, the authors tend to reduce gamification to what Robertson (2010) calls "poinstification" (points, badges, scores). Moreover, they use the term "play" in a metaphorical sense that does not necessarily refer to the playful world.

8   For further details on the formal operation of 3MT®: https://threeminutethesis.org/rules-judging-criteria.

9   https://www.ke.hku.hk/hku3mt/index.php/about-3mt/about-the-competition.

10 Hu and Liu note in passing, however, that "the 3MT presentations are more promotional than other academic genres. This finding could be accounted for by the competition nature of 3MT presentations" (2018, p. 25). This trend towards self-branding is also pointed out by Rossette-Crake, when she analyses the New Oratory, "a new face for public speaking" (2020, p. 572) in digital communication in the age of neoliberalism.

11 This competition is currently taking place in more than 900 universities in 85 different countries (Oceania, Asia-Pacific, North America and Europe), in particular in networks that aim to be at the forefront of international scientific research, such as the Universitas 21 Network.

12 In 2015, this Directorate offered "the general public, as well as its students and staff, a complete panorama of exact, human or social sciences in society" based on "meetings, debates, exhibitions, animations, screenings and thematic visits": https://www.univ-lorraine.fr/CultureSci.

13 For a discussion of this phenomenon, see Corsi, Frances and Le Lay (2021, pp. 175-186).

14 Source: https://affordance.typepad.com/mon_weblog/2018/06/ma-these-en-180-secondes.html.

15 Our statistical analysis shows, however, that the participants in the first three sessions of the competition were characterized by social properties linking them to the dominant fractions of doctoral students (social origins, quality of professional inclusion during the doctoral program, etc.). Thus, 27% of the respondents to our survey have at least one family member in higher education and research, while 39.5% of them have a professional title (lawyer, pharmacist) or an engineering level at the time of their enrolment in a thesis. Moreover, 87% of them benefit from a research grant or contract (the national average is about 70%).

16 For a critical review of the North American managerial and practitioner literature on this aspect, see Owler, Morrison & Plester (2010).

[17]   Our quantitative and qualitative data support this view. For 91.2% of the doctoral students surveyed, the atmosphere of the MT180® is pleasant and, for 67%, it is recreational. Only 7.1% considered it as difficult.

[18]   In psychodynamics of work, "*ethical suffering* is characterized by an intrapsychic conflict caused by an opposition between the subject's moral values and their tangible action in the work situation." (Duarte, 2017, p. 54). Clinical research conducted in a number of professional fields (health care institutions, judicial institutions, commercial enterprises, research institutions, etc.) has shown that "participating in, or assisting with, actions that a subject finds morally reprehensible is a painful affective experience" (Duarte, 2017, p. 26). This conflict between thought and action, between what we think we should do and what we end up doing, represents a serious narcissistic threat (self-love). To avoid decompensation and to sinking into pathology, workers establish individual or collective defense strategies, designed precisely to deny ethical suffering (Dejours, 1998; Rolo, 2015).

[19]   This institutionalization is all the more problematic when the dominant actors in the scientific field concerned play a direct role in the political field. On this point, see Leonid Schneider's analysis of Frédérique Vidal, the current Minister of Higher Education, Research and Innovation (https://academia.hypotheses.org/24479). Fraud is not limited to the more or less manifest manipulation of empirical materials. It also increasingly takes the form of plagiarism (Darde, 2012). On this point, the International Institute for research and action on academic fraud and plagiarism created in 2016 by Michelle Bergadaà is a useful source of information to refer to: https://irafpa.org.

[20]   That's why we don't share Jiang and Qiu's enthusiasm about the 3MT®: "we would recommend that teachers introduce 3MT presentations to learners, especially research students, to raise their awareness of both professional research genres and popularization discourse and develop their abilities to communicate scientific knowledge to audiences with different levels of expertise. Moreover, teachers can adopt 3MT award-winning presentations as materials to teach English as a second language learners how to engage the audience and how to prepare academic speeches" (2021, p. 17).

Chapter 23
Introducing Serious Games as a Master Course in Information Security Management Programs:
Moving Towards Socio–Technical Incident Response Learning

Grethe Østby

https://orcid.org/0000-0002-7541-6233

Norwegian University of Science and Technology, Norway

Stewart James Kowalski

https://orcid.org/0000-0003-3601-8387

Research Institutes of Sweden, Sweden

ABSTRACT

In this chapter, the authors outline their process for introducing serious games as a course in an Information Security Master Course Program at the Norwegian University of Science and Technology. The process is built on the author's experiences from both participating, coaching, judging, and even arranging serious games and cyber security challenges. With the lack of cultural recipes (or shared experiences) in information and cyber security from previous generations, these recipes must be learned in other environments. Given the efficiency of using exercises for incident response training, the authors suggest that information and cyber security incident response can be learned efficiently through serious games as one type of exercise. The authors suggest that serious games give relevant learning experiences from both developing them and participating in them, and they suggest these learning experiences as part of the course, in addition to necessary instructions.

DOI: 10.4018/978-1-7998-9223-6.ch023

INTRODUCTION

There is a large skill shortage in the information- and cyber security area around the world and a number of universities have and are developing courses and programs to bring information- and cyber security into the standard curriculum (Bogolea & Wijekumar, 2004; Whitman & Mattord, 2004; Woodward, Imboden, & Martin, 2013). However, the authors suggest that curriculums are often traditional in design, and the instruction material is insufficient to understand and act on real life implications in the area of the socio-technical incident response challenges facing society today (Beuran et al., 2018; Fredette, 2019).

Learning from information security incidents are often limited only to those participating in the incident response teams (IRT) (Ahmad, Maynard, & Shanks, 2015), and "the purpose of the follow-up phase is to reflect on the incident handling experience and identify 'lessons learned' that can be incorporated into standard operating procedures". Sharing information along the security system value chain about the lessons learned from the incidents and thereby consequences to e.g. other parts of the organization, business-partners, and competence to other stakeholders like governance and academia, is however not necessarily a motivation in the IRT (Ahmad et al., 2015; Tøndel, Line, & Jaatun, 2014). Accordingly, the socio-technical response system (Davis, Challenger, Jayewardene, & Clegg, 2014; Kowalski, 1994) will be unbalanced and unaligned, and necessary competence might be lost. To meet these challenges of filling and aligning the information- and cyber security incident response skill gap in Norway, the concept of serious games and cyber ranges have been introduced at the Norwegian University of Science and Technology (Kianpour, Kowalski, Zoto, Frantz, & Overby, 2019).

In this chapter the authors suggest conceptualizing the experiences from serious games to meet the socio-technical incident response challenges by introducing serious games as a course in an information security master program at the Norwegian University of Science and Technology (NTNU). To implement a new course at NTNU, several measures must be considered. The course must be applicable to the program, and must contain academic content, learning outcomes, learning methods etc. (NTNU, 2019c), which also include the UN sustainable development goals (UN, 2021).

After the introduction the authors present the background in the second section and discuss some theoretical concepts of learning adaptable for learning from games in the third section, before presenting the research approach in the fourth section. In the fifth section, the authors present how to establish the course, based on desired results, acceptable evidence from relevant academic literature, relevant serious games existing today, experiences from past participations in serious games, and finally how to plan for instructions and learning experiences in the course. Finally, in the sixth section the authors conclude and suggest future research to help improve the development of the course.

BACKGROUND

For the last 5 years students in bachelor, masters, and doctoral programs in information security at the department of information security and communication (NTNU, 2021) have been offered the opportunity to participate in extracurricular activities that included different technical security competitions (ECSC, 2021) and societal focus' (Atlantic Council, 2021; Sikkerhetsfestivalen, 2019). When preparing for the student's train sessions the preparation is executed outside regularly scheduled course programs. Coaches gather relevant support from a team of expertise and prepare the students "as best as they can". The goal is often to win the game, and desired learning experiences to understand and meet the incident response challenges is often left behind (Lacruz & Américo, 2018).

The authors of this chapter have collected data from various approaches (and judging sessions) during these years, and when implementing the course, both experiences from these challenges, but also tested academic approaches and learning methods used will be implemented. In addition, the desired learning outcomes will be aligned with the UN Sustainability goals (UN, 2021) considering information- and cyber security, to give the students a more reflective learning situation like outlined by A. Y. Kolb & Kolb (2009).

Serious games have been introduced (amongst others) as innovation tools (Hannula & Harviainen, 2016; Patrício, Moreira, & Zurlo, 2020), business games (Lacruz & Américo, 2018), to train operators of critical infrastructure (Bartnes, Moe, & Heegaard, 2016; Gustafsson & Swedish Defence, 2020), and to serious games platforms in cyber ranges (Yamin, Katt, & Nowostawski, 2021). Serious games are a form of experiential learning by simulation to meet specific learning goals (Kianpour, Kowalski, et al., 2019), but also a form of training/exercise used to improve incident response techniques (DSB, 2016a; HSEEP, 2006; Kirk, 2019). HSEEP has introduced a ladder of training/exercises, where the next step of exercise includes elements of all the previous. Consequently, a serious game in this approach has the capacity to include elements from both seminars, workshops, and table-top exercises. The HSEEP approach is presented in figure 1.

Figure 1. Exercise Types and Capacity Levels (HSEEP, 2006)

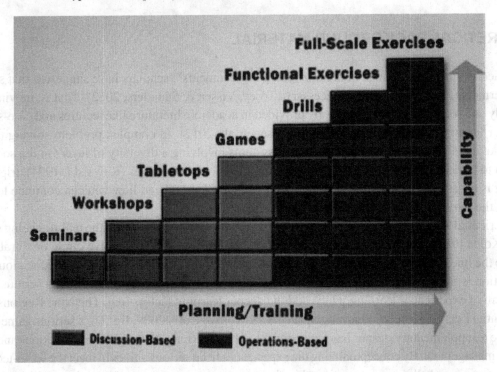

Using games for educational purposes has previously been criticized for being "highly susceptible to a muddle of approaches, methodologies, and descriptions of gaming for educational purposes"

(Vandercruysse, Vandewaetere, & Clarebout, 2012). However, given the efficiency of exercises for incident response training (Fimreite, Lango, Lægreid, & Rykkja, 2014, chap 8) the authors suggests that information- and cyber security incident response can be learned efficient through serious games if the HSEEP-approach is used in the design process so as to permit reuse of learning material between the different steps used.

In addition, game based learning often has some fundamental foundations, and may have their own place of learning (Plass, Homer, & Kinzer, 2015). That is: "treating game design elements as strategies to achieve this engagement based on established cognitive, affective, motivational, and sociocultural foundations ... can contribute to a more systematic process of conceptualizing and designing games." (Plass et al., 2015)

Transacting concepts from abstract theories into games, may also give the students the necessary expansive learning needed to grasp the more practical part of the theories.

"The theory of expansive learning is a process that erupts from a set of contradictions that are overcome as abstract concepts become concrete by being expressed as practice." (Engeström, 2019)

The key outcome of an expansive learning process is for the students to be able to negotiate and make decisions based on competence and skills (Gross & Ho, 2021), which could be fully adapted into games, and whereas the students would thereby consider themselves prepared to "participate in cyber defense" (Gross & Ho, 2021).

THEORETICAL BACKGROUND MATERIAL

In the face of "profound change in organizational environments", scholars have suggested that secondary (alternative) form of learning is necessary (Tosey, Visser, & Saunders, 2012). That is, moving from primarily and secondarily learning mostly provided in academic literature like lectures and case-studies, to deeper learning like triple loop learning (Tosey et al., 2012). In complex problem solving (Funke, 2010) like incident response in socio-technical systems involving a diversity of layers in the society in addition to socio-technical problems within the organizations themselves (Kowalski, 1994), triple loop learning is necessary to be able to consider what you have learned and how you can continue learning to make the most informed and hopefully optimal decisions.

Experiential learning is often provided in courses to introduce the learner to the realities being studied (D. A. Kolb, 1984). The learning cycle in experimental learning "is a recursive circle or spiral as opposed to the linear, traditional information transmission model of learning used in most education where information is transferred from the teacher to the learner" (A. Kolb & Kolb, 2018). As serious games are a form of experiential learning which add the deeper learning factors (e.g. The Nine Regions of the Experiential Learning Theory Learning Space (A. Y. Kolb & Kolb, 2009, fig. 7)), a serious game course would be a supplementary deeper learning course to other learning materials in information- and cyber security management. By conceptualizing the experiences from serious games to meet the socio-technical incident response challenges as mentioned in the introduction, as a form of experimental learning, the authors suggest that shared awareness and expertise distribution (like presented in Nyre-Yu, Gutzwiller and Caldwell (2019)), can contribute to more efficient triage decisions in a real life context.

When some form of decision (internal or in teams) must be taken that create difficulties prioritizing societal crisis responsibilities vs. cyber security (that is: e.g. sharing secure information to save people's lives – when would it be appropriate and when not), it can be referred to as polytelic situations (Funke, 2010). Management scenarios presented in cyber security challenges and serious games often involve such challenges. Traditional crisis management decisions for example, are based on analyzing the situation (risk-analysis about the situation before making decisions), interrogation, personnel, operations, supply- and logistics needed (Fimreite et al., 2014), and of course, from relevant information (both internal and media).

In a comparative qualitative analysis of 17 games Czaurdena & Budke examined how strategy- and management games "can facilitate the practice of dynamic decision-making" (Czauderna & Budke, 2020). More specific, how one applies to "complication not found in static situations". They found that 1) "the core gameplay loop of strategy and management games implies dynamic decision-making as players must take over the role of a decider and solve polytelic conflicts" and that 2) "structural features of strategy and management games foster processes of learning where players' practice of decision-making is structured by typical features of games that make the process of decision-making more transparent and digestible", which is what the authors will apply in the course as a triple loop learning to adapt incident management.

To make an informed action "decision-making is a central element of all forms of gameplay and of the gameplay loop in general" (Czauderna & Budke, 2020). A Gameplay is:

"All actions performed by the player, influencing negatively or positively the outcome of the uncertain game situation in which he is engaged in." (Guardiola, 2016)

The game itself must be able to apply to the decision and action in some various ways and give the participant new challenges to consider. This loop may be referred to as Game loop learning (Guardiola, 2016), and is presented in figure 2.

Figure 2. Interaction between a player and a game/Gameplay loop (Guardiola, 2016; Tenkinbas & Zimmerman, 2003)

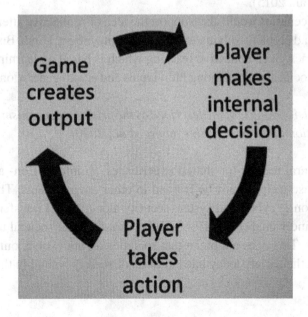

The game output/injects/scenarios, however, play an important role to meet the learning goals. To bring a course to the triple loop of learning, participatory modelling will be introduced in the course. For example using a GAMA-model as presented in Taillandier et al. (2019), which could meet the request for new and not known injects, or unknown scenarios as presented in Hove, Tarnes, Line and Bernsmed (2014), instead of more static cases provided in traditional primarily academic courses (Tosey et al., 2012), seminars, discussion and table-top exercises (DSB, 2016b; FEMA, 2020; HSEEP, 2006).

To create scenarios for information- and cyber incident response management (- and crisis decisions) games, root-cause analysis of previous incidents and socio-technical models can be used to "cover" necessary stakeholders, systems-stacks, and regulations in a specific exercise/game (Nyblom, Wangen, Kianpour, & Østby, 2020; Østby, Berg, Kianpour, Katt, & Kowalski, 2019). An important part of the course will be to introduce these necessary socio-technical models, both to understand the concept of socio-technical thinking, but also for future managers to understand the novelty of using serious games for training in their organizations.

In addition, the scenarios must cover a semiotic framework to evolve the triple-loop learning technique from only handling the data, to further understand the necessity of information and thereby gain knowledge (and at some point, wisdom) of societal impacts. In the area of information security, the FRISCO Semiotic Framework for IT communication cover the different layers from physical/empirical data, via syntaxes, semantics, pragmatics and finally the social understanding (Hesse & Verrijn-Stuart, 2001; Kowalski, 1994, chap 1). The games themselves must therefore be applicable to the same framework to meet the goal of learning from them.

The scenarios should also be developed to cover the subject, object and community, combined with activities, rules and division of labor, more known as the basis for analysis in Activity theory (Engeström, 2019; Gross & Ho, 2021). Using the Activity theory approach to develop the scenarios, the relationships amongst the different elements in the scenario can be all tested for each participant, targeting collective learning which Gross and Ho (2021) suggest that "as a result, the subject takes actions to mature in problem-solving and technical trouble-shooting ability, reaching the consciousness of cyber defense as an intended outcome". In three evaluation studies testing activity theory for educational serious games, Carvalho et al. found that the theory "helped participants, particularly those with gaming experience, identify and understand the roles of each component in the game and recognize the game's educational objectives" (Carvalho et al., 2015).

This approach to the scenarios would also support the idea of "collective attention facilitates communication, remembering, and problem-solving in the team" (Shteynberg, Hirsh, Bentley, & Garthoff, 2020) attending the serious games. Such collective learning which is based on learning *with* others instead of from others, is based on social learning among individuals and across generations from the dawn of time.

"Observational, or social, learning is often described as the primary mechanism for transmitting cultural recipes from one generation to the next." (Shteynberg et al., 2020)

With the lack of cultural recipes (or shared experiences) in information- and cyber security from previous generations, these recipes must be learned in other environments. These (teaching) environments are often focused on 1) cyber- and system security alone, and 2) transfer of knowledge from the educator to the learning individual (Eder, 1999), and do not consider societal understanding (learning) as a place of evolvement. This does not mean that societies do not evolve, only that the technological determinism going on in the society today has left parts of society behind in the evolvement.

This can be compared to other "incidents" happening/being presented in the public sphere, like amongst other "the power of rhetoric in politically effective communication, of the power of group identities, and of the related problem of what motivates loyalty to a polity and participation in democratic politics" (Garnham, 2007).

"Public communication acts as a hinge between informal opinion-formation and the institutionalized processes of will formation – a general election or a cabinet meeting, for example. For this reason, the discursive constitution of the public sphere is important." (Habermas, 2006)

The trouble of using only a collective learning approach in serious games, would be that "experimental groups learn through deliberation on political issues (such as affirmative action, gays in the military, or the distributive justice of flat tax schemes)" (Habermas, 2006). Thereby, the course would need a section of reflection upon responsibilities, not only learning from collective understanding in information- and cyber security, but also from societal incident response responsibilities (Fimreite et al., 2014). To understand and select the necessary information from both public newspapers and social media communication would however be an important part of the scenario-building for the games.

More specific, reflective assessment and critique of society and culture to reveal and challenge power structures, especially technological control and domination as described by Marcuse (1941) would be a necessity in the "media-communication" in the scenarios to understand and discuss critical theory.

"Critical Theory in the narrow sense designates several generations of German philosophers and social theorists in the Western European Marxist tradition known as the Frankfurt School. According to these theorists, a "critical" theory may be distinguished from a "traditional" theory according to a specific practical purpose: a theory is critical to the extent that it seeks human "emancipation from slavery", acts as a "liberating ... influence", and works "to create a world which satisfies the needs and powers of" human beings." (Horkheimer, 2002; Stanford, 2005)

Similar to the Frankfurt School Critical Theory, socio-technical approaches seek to improve workers (at times) poor work environments (Davis et al., 2014; Kowalski, 1994; Mumford, 2006), and the complementary work of Critical Theory and socio-technical approaches mentioned in this section would build the foundation for creation of the serious games and reflections in the student groups participating in and creating games.

RESEARCH APPROACH

The authors propose to address the skill shortage in information- and cyber security by establishing a course on serious games for incident management. To be able to establish a course at NTNU, the authors plan the work by using a deductive inference approach as suggested by Sturm (2011). First, the authors have adapted the regulations from NTNU before they investigated cases of curriculum activities in information- and cyber security, and searched to find best possible facts to meet the course criteria's (NTNU, 2019a, 2019c).

Additionally, the authors approach the development of the course by using a backward design model proposed by Yale (2019). The backward design model first starts by identifying desired results, second by determining acceptable evidence, and third by planning for learning experiences and instructions. In Østby and Kowalski (2020), a modified version, including both socio and technical considerations/ actions, was suggested for use when preparing for exercises. The authors will use the same approach when preparing course material.

The desired result of the course is for the students to better understand information- and cyber security incident response, and thereby to be able to create and use games to better make informed decisions in an incident response situation. Evidence is collected from the authors several years of both working with crisis management (both being crisis managers and from training/lecturing), societal incident response, information- and cyber security incident response, and from both participating, coaching, judging, and arranging serious games. Finally, learning experiences and instructions are planned based on mentioned triple-loop-learning and game-loop-learning activities as presented in the theoretical background section.

ESTABLISHING THE COURSE "INCIDENT RESPONSE MANAGEMENT - SERIOUS GAMES"

To meet the requirements at NTNU (2019b) relevance to society, to the discipline, internationalization and internal collaborations are considered. Additionally, curriculum used in comparable programs are evaluated to separate the genuineness of the course. Basic requirements like funding are also considered but will not be discussed in this chapter. Initially in this chapter, however, the authors present the desired results, some evidence and plan for learning experiences and instructions, to support a decision to move forward with the requirements.

Desired Results

In the Information security MSc program at NTNU, an introductory course to management in information security[1] is mandatory. Incident response is introduced in the course (Whitman & Mattord, 2018), and a digital incident response discussion exercise is mandatory to be able to take the exam. The goal (and thereby tasks) in the discussion exercise is to learn and deliver a situational top-down brief[2] (traditional), a BLUF[3], a management summary[4], and finally a draft for a press-brief[5]. For the authors suggested incident response management – serious games course, a deeper understanding of incident response, and efficient communication beyond mentioned deliveries in the introduction course's discussion exercise will be provided. Added academic literature on socio-technical incident response, introduction to societal regulations and legislations, and practice from participating in and creating serious games will be the core elements of the course.

In traditional games there are winners and losers – that is the very basic of most games (Ansoms & Geenen, 2012). However, in a university course the learning goals and experiences are in focus not winning or losing the game. The desired result of the course would be for the students to learn how to learn from games, and to gain exceeded knowledge of incident response management.

To learn how to learn from games, one must understand the experimental learning space like presented in Kolb and Kolb (A. Y. Kolb & Kolb, 2009), semiotic frameworks like the FRISCO framework (Kowalski, 1994), and understanding how a society can learn (Eder, 1999). By introducing reflection activities suggested by Sloan and College (2015) in the early stage of the course, the students can reflect upon both preparation and participation in a (or several) selected game(s).

Finally, the students will be required to create a game for the Norwegian Cyber Range (NCR)[6], based on 1) critical theory and socio-technical approaches to create scenarios from the information security landscape, 2) social learning and 3) sustainable goals for information security. The goal of creating a game, is for the students to understand and challenge the gameplay loop (Guardiola, 2016) in an information security incident response context, and understanding the value of using serious games in future training with colleagues.

Determining Acceptable Evidence

In developing the course, acceptable evidence from 1) relevant academic literature, 2) surveys on what serious games already existing today, and 3) experiences from planning and participating in serious games, is considered (Yale, 2019).

Relevant Academic Literature

The American National Institute of Standards and Technology (NIST) and other national institute bodies provide organizations with a structure for "assessing and improving their ability to prevent, detect and respond to cyber incidents" (Scarfone, Grance, & Masone, 2008). The NIST framework consists of 5 stages, 1) identify, 2) protect, 3) detect, 4) respond and 5) recover. The framework is presented in figure 3.

Figure 3. NIST Cyber security framework (NIST, 2020)

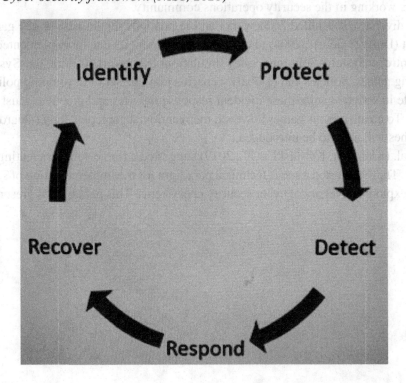

How to apply the NIST framework is described by Anderson (Anderson, 2017) and should make the students capable of preparing for the game-play loop. In addition the FEMA framework (FEMA, 2017), NATO incident response frameworks (NATO Public Diplomacy Division, 2016) and EU security, defense and crisis response measures (EEAS, 2020) are incident response policies and frameworks which in addition to a variety of national incident response systems would need to be presented and discussed in the course.

Fundamental regulations and legislations like the regulations of war, the Tallin manual, national information security laws, the ISO 27000 series certifications, and the NIST SP-800 series, would be a necessity in the course material to understand information- and cyber security incident response responsibilities. Thereby, also the variety of international, European, and national bodies and community roles responsible for executing the incident response (e.g. European Commission (2017)) will be presented.

In recent years, many states have begun enacting "data localization laws" that prevent certain kinds of information from leaving a state's jurisdiction (Chander & Le, 2014). In Norway a new law on national security was established in 2019 (Norwegian Government, 2019). Understanding the consequences and the effect this has on who to collaborate with during an attack, and what classification and authorization one might need to establish routines for such collaboration will in the course be approached with an hierarchical management framework established by Eloff and Solms (2000). Thereby also classification of information leakage prevention (Hauer, 2015) and especially access (or not) to communication channels for response teams like relevant SOC, CSIRT and CERT where the communication is protected by PGP-keys (Karra, 2010) and generally regulated by RF 2350 (The_Internet_Society, 1998). National laws on data exchange and jurisdiction also impact the formal sharing of data with colleagues in response teams and others working in the security operations community.

To meet the diversity of detailed frameworks and regulations the holistic policy gaming paradigm should be taught (Duke & Geurts, 2004) to understand how policies can be implemented. It can also be taught by the Centre for Systems Solutions policy simulations framework (Centre_for_System_Solutions, 2021), combining games, policies and (global) scenarios into one set of developing policies.

To participate in serious games these incident response theories and practices must be well known for the students. To create serious games however, the mentioned gameplay loop (Guardiola, 2016) and similar approaches will need to be introduced.

Kianpour et al. (Kianpour, Kowalski, et al., 2019) suggested a framework for creating serious games for cyber ranges. They suggested a socio-technical paradigm for the implementation of serious games in cyber ranges to explore a diversity of cyber security ecosystems. This paradigm is presented in figure 4.

Figure 4. Socio-technical paradigm for the implementation of serious games (Kowalski, 1994)

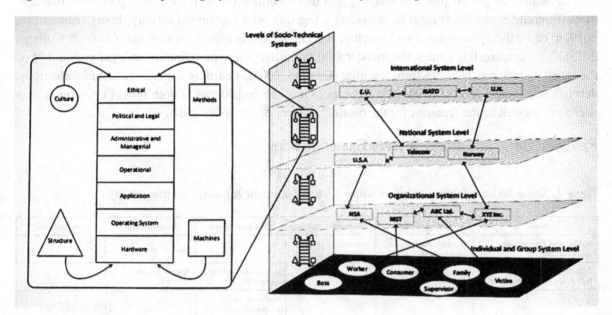

Socio-technical approaches like Kowalski's SBC model on the left side in figure 4, and also Davis et al. hexagon model (Davis et al., 2014), are the foundation for socio-technical considerations on each structures in the game, to meet the mentioned Activity theory approach (Engeström, 2019) when creating the scenarios.

The suggested framework of Kianpour et al. (2019) creating serious games is based on the Hunicke et al. MDA-framework (Hunicke, Leblanc, & Zubek, 2004), consisting of mechanics, dynamics, and aesthetics. Adapting situational leadership and preliminary analysis into mechanics, socio-technical systems and deployment into dynamics, and finally experimental learning and concluding analysis into aesthetics, combined with reflection processes, Kianpour et al. (2019) suggest this as a systematic approach to create games. Their final suggestion is presented in figure 5.

Figure 5. Framework for creating serious games (Kianpour, Kowalski, et al., 2019)

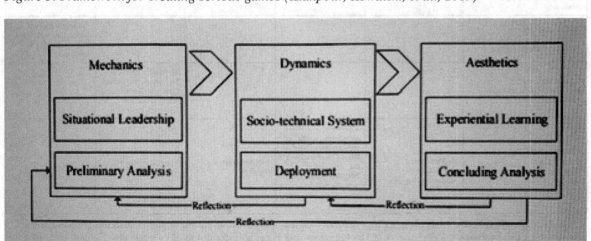

The authors of this chapter however, suggest that mentioned roles for leadership in crisis management (Fimreite et al., 2014) must be considered, together with mentioned activity theory (Engeström, 2019) to cover the dynamics in a socio-technical scenario. Using reflection activities (Sloan & College, 2015) also when creating games, the transferability of reflection to participating in a game would be of the same character as learning from teaching (Cortese, 2005). Learning experiences from reflections, debriefs and other scientific evaluation techniques must be considered to both reflect upon one's own decisions, as well as the "reasons for the results" (Lacruz & Américo, 2018).

Relevant Serious Games Already Existing Today

Table 1. Some serious games for information security incident response existing today

Game	Incident response	Information security	Crisis management	Crisis decisions	Communication
RANGEFORCE https://www.rangeforce.com/	Both individual and team-based scenarios	Real world attack scenarios		Team decisions	
IMMERSIVE LABS https://www.immersivelabs.com/	Stress-test for incident response	Cyber security	Organizational respond Apply skills	Range of possible decisions	
The SRE Incident Response game https://medium.com/@bruce_25864/the-sre-incident-response-game-db242fff391c	Incident response		Incident response commander and Site Reliability Engineers (SRE) training https://sre.google/sre-book/accelerating-sre-on-call/		
Cyber Nations https://www.cybernations.net/default.asp			Nation simulation game		
Stone Paper Scissors https://www.stonepaperscissors.co.uk/			Societal board game		Communication between actors/ roles taking part in the game
Zero escape https://zeroescape.fandom.com/wiki/Decision_Game				Player's decisions can affect life and death	
DREAD https://dreadthegame.wordpress.com/about-dread-the-game/				Making difficult decisions	
gamelearn https://www.game-learn.com/game-based-learning-corporate-training/serious-game-for-internal-communication-training-and-onboarding/					Communication training and onboarding
Serious game store https://www.seriousgamestore.com/en/collection/communication					Training to give and receive information and develop effective work relations
Games 4 Sustainability https://games4sustainability.org/gamepedia/discoord/				No Poverty, Reduced Inequalities, Sustainable Cities and Communities, Peace, Justice and Strong Institutions	
Adam Shoestack* Tabletop Security Games & Cards https://adam.shostack.org/games.html	https://www.blackhillsinfosec.com/projects/backdoorsandbreaches/	http://www.controlalthack.com/ http://cryptorpg.com/ https://cias.utsa.edu/ctd_cards.php http://d0x3d.com/d0x3d/welcome.html https://www.riskio.co.uk/	https://emergynt.com/risk-deck/	https://diegeticgames.com/cia-collect-it-all/	

*The last row in the table (the Adam Shoestack page) gave an overview of n=29 serious games, varying from incident response, via information security awareness, risk-perpetration, and hacker-games. n=8 games are presented based on where they "belong" in the table-row, but even more games presented on the webpage could be relevant for the course.

The field of serious games are crossdisciplinarity in nature, and there is an overload of games to be found online today. Meeting the goal of learning incident response management in the field of information security through relevant serious games, the authors searched for games online limited to covering incident response, information- and cyber security, crisis management, crisis decisions and crisis communication, relevant to be discussed in the course, and selected a few games to be presented in this section. The purpose of the search was not to get a full overview of relevant games and select from those, but mainly to establish a fact that there are games relevant to use in the course. A onetime search for sustainability-games was also executed. The selected games are presented in table 1.

The heuristic search was executed in the period of 01.08.2021 – 05.08.2021, and considering the limited time spent on search, the authors believe a search over an extended period of time would be preferable. In the search however, the authors could not find any gaming platforms/games covering all the necessary information security fields described in the previous paragraph and in the relevant academic literature section. Especially communication was a "field of its own", and not well implemented into the other games presented (except Stone Paper Scissors). No games were tested as the primary goal of the search was to find relevant games to meet the mentioned learning goals. The authors information came from game-rule descriptions, so there is a possibility that communication is better established than what the authors have found.

The overview gives an implication that there would be possibilities for the students to create more serious games applicable to the total content of socio-technical information - and cyber security incident response.

Experiences From Planning for and Participating in Serious Games

The authors have vast experience on planning for most types of exercises presented in the HSEEP-framework (HSEEP, 2006). For exercises in general an exercise-directive (where, who and what to be trained) and a scenario meeting the directive is the foundation for executing the exercise. Such framework are established for seminars, discussion exercises (e.g. ovelse.no (NSM, DSB, Digitaliseringsdirektoratet, NTNU, & NorSIS, 2020)), and table-top exercises at NTNU/Norwegian Cyber Range (NCR), and plans for full-scaled exercises are in the early stages of being established.

A few serious games have been planned for and executed so far at NTNU/NCR, these being the European Cyber Security Challenge (ECSC) (2021) and Lillehammer megagame (Sikkerhetsfestivalen, 2019). A megagame may have a content of

"attacking forces alarming the world's governments, where multiple teams of three-to-six players represent various nations, and teams take on roles like diplomats or military leaders. Each team plays its own straightforward game of economics to balance a country's budget, fund the military, and direct scientific research." (Dean, 2016)

In addition, students have been given the possibility to participate in the Atlantic council 9/12 cyber security strategy challenge (Atlantic Council, 2021a).

The authors themselves were responsible for Lillehammer megagame, a societal game provided by Stone Paper Scissors (stonepaperscissors.co.uk, 2019). In this game students from different colleges and universities were invited to participate, and proximately 60 students attended the game. The students were divided into teams, playing different stakeholders in the society, varying from scientists to national leaders. The game was based on a scenario, and the scenario developed in a static form with relevant injects over a set period of time.

The authors experienced that the scenario-injects in the game could have been more dynamic, however, that would have required a more advanced game, and a better prepared game-master-team, this being a board-game. In addition, the lack of information- and cyber security in the game have been a good motivation for writing this book-chapter, trying to seek solutions and education to create better serious games for information- and cyber security challenges.

The authors have also participated as team-member, coaches, and judges in the Atlantic council's 9/12 cyber security strategy challenge. The 9/12 challenge is designed as a competition and the learning goals are not primary objectives. Establishing this course, however, would meet the need for learning goals, and the authors suggest that the learning materials used to prepare for the 9/12 challenge can be used as learning materials also in the suggested course. The preparations for the 9/12 challenge are therefore presented in the next section of this chapter.

A final remark to the 9/12 challenge is that it was difficult to participate in the challenge after several years as a crisis manager, experiencing that the traditional approaches in crisis management did not give the desired results. Thereby, after evaluating that required information- and cyber incident response have a different content, the combination of traditional crisis management with information- and cyber security incident response will be implemented as the "next level" of crisis incident response knowledge required.

Planning for Instructions and Learning Experiences in the Course

The three main goals of the course are to learn incident response – in both a societal and an information security context, and to learn how to prepare for participation in serious games, but also how to build and execute a serious game.

Instructions

The very nature of the course is to learn information security incident response from serious games. There will, however, be introductory lectures based on literature in the Relevant academic literature section in this chapter. Both from the information- and cyber security incident response theories and the creation of games theories. In addition, literature on argumentation theory, including language philosophy and ethics, values and norms will be provided as preparation for participation in a serious game.

Prepare for Participation in a Serious Game

Often, serious games reflect a societal context (scenario) where you play a part in this context. The mentioned Atlantic council 9/12 cyber security strategy challenge (Atlantic Council, 2021) is one such game, where an European cyber security incident scenario is developed to challenge the participants. The authors are in this section presenting how it has been planned for instructions and learning experiences to prepare for the participation. It will be a goal in the course to give the students possibility to participate and/or observe this or similar serious game at the end of the semester.

In the Atlantic Council 9/12 Cyber security strategy challenge (Atlantic Council, 2021a), teams consisting of 4 team-members (and one reserve) compete against each other. The first part of the competition consists of three main deliveries: 1) a 500-word policy suggestion, 2) a one-page decision document, and 3) a 10 min oral presentation. The 500-word policy is to be delivered 14 days before the competition, and the one-page decision document is to be delivered to the judges just before executing the oral presentation (Atlantic Council, 2021b). Two critical thinking seminars were thereby prepared to meet these challenges.

To prepare for the seminars, the focus for the first seminar was on how to use argumentation theory in the written material, whereas the focus for the second seminar was on how to use argumentation theory in decision making and oral presentations. The authors prepared the first seminar based on the Føllesdal, Walløe and Elster book (1984), to meet the need for written argumentation when writing the 500-word policy suggestion. The selected context from the book is presented in red in figure 6.

Figure 6. Ethics and language philosophy in argumentation theory (Føllesdal et al., 1984)

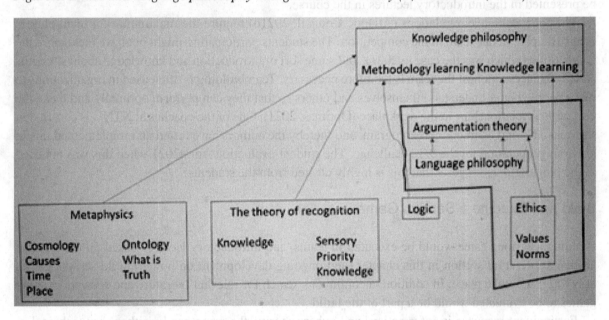

The ethics presented in the book addresses differences in teleology and deontology, whereas the language philosophy addresses the concept of "sender and receiver" in syntaxes, semantics, pragmatics, and interpretation. To support the learning outcome, the authors prepared a case once provided for students in a rhetoric's exam. The issue of clarification from the book was also prepared for discussion.

By the time of the second seminar preparing for oral presentations (specifically rhetoric), the students had already delivered their 500-word policy document and had a first draft of a decision document. Thereby, it was possible to use their deliveries to discuss the theories in the seminar. For this seminar, the authors prepared theories from a variety of literature. For the strength in arguments part of the seminar the authors used van den Brink-Budgen (2010) pervasiveness, rhetoric's and functional analysis. However, the rhetoric's section of the van den Brink-Budgen book (2010) did not cover the preparations needed for the game, and the literature was supplemented with Weston rules of arguments (Weston, 1987).

Additionally, Chalmers (1999) theory of inductivist vs sophisticated falsificationist approach to research was presented and discussed, and so was Sturm's (2011) differences in abduction, deduction and induction. The seminar also covered ethos, pathos and logos where the authors prepared a case based on what van den Brink-Budgen (2010) suggested as non-arguments, in addition to logos, ethos and pathos variables in courts (Braet, 1992). Finally, at the end of the second seminar, the authors presented the analysis of President Obama's speech after the killing of Osama Bin Laden (Gilbert, 2013) for the students to get a real-life perspective on the terms from the seminar.

An important factor in argumentation theory is the fallacies of argumentation (Weston, 1987). Unfortunately, this was forgotten in the preparations, but the authors suggest to implement these into the course, both by using Weston (1987) but also by using Shulman (1951) as a good and humoristic example of how one can understand and use fallacies.

In addition to the seminars, introduction to relevant cyber-security EU-bodies were introduced (European Commission, 2017), but not necessary according to the specific suggested approach in the Relevant academic literature section in this chapter. As mentioned in the Instruction section, this will be presented in the introductory lectures in the course.

The 9/12 challenge regulations (Atlantic Council, 2021b) require the maximum of 4 team players can participate in one team in the competition. The students participating might not have met before the competition (which was the case in 2021), and some sort of introduction and knowledge about strengths and preferences amongst the team is therefore necessary. Teambuilding is often used in organizations to make people better understand themselves and others so that they can perform optimally and make the best of their relationships in the workplace (Optimas, 2021). One of the coaches at NTNU is certified in Optimas JTI- and team-compass program, and thereby the authors have tested and implemented this in previous preparation for the 9/12 challenge. The student-evaluation from 2021 when this was not used in the preparations, suggests that this is highly desired from the students.

Build and Execute a Serious Game

Building a serious game would be executed in teams, and introductory lectures based on the relevant academic literature section in this chapter (and ongoing development on how to build serious games at NTNU) will take place. In addition, a continuous search for relevant literature and relevant existing games to be evaluated would be a part of the build.

For incident response in information- and cyber security, the game can be either very technical or non- technical. On the technical side, an example of a dynamic serious game can be found in Yamin et al. (2021). The game presented in Yamin et al. (2021) however, only targets the traditional system-security environment of 1) white team, 2) blue team, and 3) red team, and is missing other parts of an organization and other societal participants affected in an information- and cyber security incident. The game also does not include non-technical aspects like collaboration with business-partners or business measures to meet the sustainability goals. The development-phase of the game took 5 months (2 persons/bachelor thesis), which can be too extensive for a regular master-course. However, the NCR system platform at NTNU being finalized autumn 2021, will provide a necessary basic structure to start to develop other similar technical serious games.

In contrast to dynamic technical serious games, a megagame is often more of a non-technical (social) game (Brynen, 2021; Crisis-games.co.uk, 2021; stonepaperscissors.co.uk, 2019), and building a traditional megagame could have more social learning outcomes and also entertainment goals. As these types of games focus on many types of crises and drama (Arciuli, Carroll, & Cameron, 2008), it is important to scope the game development in the course to only consider information- and cyber security incident response. The range of impact can be vast, and it might be necessary to downsize the scope for a specific scenario (Østby et al., 2019). In terms of the scenario build, it should be scoped to model several relationships and control layers in a society. Cassano-Piché et al. in their analysis of the bovine spongiform encephalopathy epidemic suggest a 6 level model (Cassano-Piché, Vicente, & Jamieson, 2006), and Østby et al., have adapted this 6 level model to cyber security exercises planning to cover full scaled socio-technical exercises (Østby et al., 2019). When building a serious game, it is not always necessary to meet the full-scaled scope but more important to focus on meeting the intended learning outcomes. The impact mentioned in the previous paragraphs would however be important to consider, and especially third parties (Kianpour, Øverby, Kowalski, & Frantz, 2019) and sustainability goals (UN, 2021) need to be scoped due to NTNU course requirements and also to consider impact on complex information systems (Hasan & Kazlauskas, 2009; NTNU, 2019a).

Level of technical development, scoping of scenario and impacts on third parties and sustainability goals are presented in figure 7. On the left side of the figure, one finds the multi-level societal stack representing the Y-axis, and the need for technical development on the X-axis. The two types of serious games discussed, the megagame and the dynamic technical scenario game, are presented in the model on where it would be scoped and how much they would impact learning goals presented.

Figure 7. Scoping development of serious games in information- and cyber security incident response in a master study course

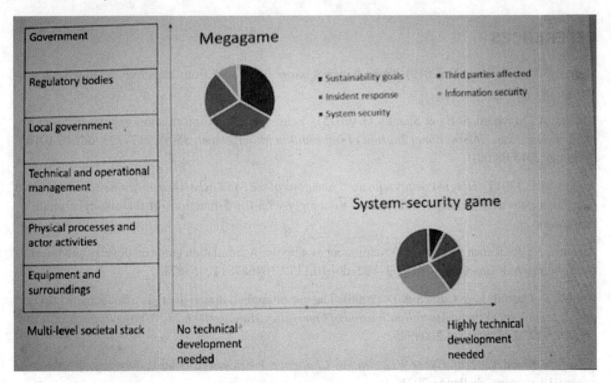

The authors of this chapter suggest that a variety of serious games can be developed based on these terms, and as new information- and cyber security vulnerabilities, threats and attacks emerge, new games can be developed to meet such.

CONCLUSION AND FUTURE RESEARCH DIRECTIONS

In this chapter the authors have outlined how to develop suggested conceptualizing of serious games to train for information- and cyber incident management response in a university master level course. The authors have outlined how to use the incident management process from standard crisis management and integrated them with a focus on information- and cyber security incident response.

The work is also a part of the proposed exercises for the NTNU/NCR based on the HSEEP approach (HSEEP, 2006), serious games being one step on the ladder. The research goal is shared scenarios in the different stages of exercises and shared output amongst the students and in the society. Necessary collaboration with the NCR is therefore required to meet these goals, and developed games will be provided for further research upon and (if necessary) further development in collaboration with the developers (students) and the NCR.

Broader research on serious games, to understand how teams (Coovert, Winner, Bennett, & Howard, 2017), organizations (Riedel, Feng, & Azadegan, 2013) and societies can adapt the information- and cyber security challenges through the games will be a continuous work, both in the course (together with the students), but also as a part of the expected evaluation of the course which is a part of the information security master-program (NTNU, 2019b). In addition, continuous search for relevant existing games to meet the learning goals and thereby to participate in such games, must be considered.

REFERENCES

StonePaperScissors.co.uk. (2019). *Stone Paper Scissors*. Retrieved from https://www.stonepaperscissors.co.uk/

Ahmad, A., Maynard, S. B., & Shanks, G. (2015). A case analysis of information systems and security incident responses. *International Journal of Information Management*, 35(6), 717–723. doi:10.1016/j.ijinfomgt.2015.08.001

Anderson, E. (2017). *How to comply with the 5 functions of the NIST cybersecurity framework*. Retrieved from https://www.secmatters.com/blog/how-to-comply-with-the-5-functions-of-the-nist-cybersecurity-framework

Ansoms, A., & Geenen, S. (2012). Development monopoly: A simulation game on poverty and inequality. *Simulation & Gaming*, 43(6), 853–862. doi:10.1177/1046878112451877

Arciuli, J., Carroll, J., & Cameron, D. (2008). The use of applied drama in crisis management: An empirical psycological study. *Australian Journal of Emergency Management*, 23(3). https://search.informit.org/doi/pdf/10.3316/agispt.20083952

Atlantic Council. (2021a). *Cyber 9/12 Strategy Challenge*. Retrieved from https://www.gcsp.ch/events/cyber-912-strategy-challenge-2021

Atlantic Council. (2021b). *Description and rules*. Author.

Bartnes, M., Moe, N. B., & Heegaard, P. E. (2016). The future of information security incident management training: A case study of electrical power companies. *Computers & Security, 61*(217528), 32–45. https://doi.org/10.1016/j.cose.2016.05.004

Beuran, R., Tang, D., Pham, C., & Chinen, K. 2018). Integrated framework for hands-on cybersecurity training: CyTrONE. *Computers and Security, 78*, 43–59. doi:10.1016/j.cose.2018.06.001

Bogolea, B., & Wijekumar, K. (2004). Information security curriculum creation: A case study. *2004 Information Security Curriculum Development Conference, InfoSecCD 2004*, 59–65. doi:10.1145/1059524.1059537

Braet, A. C. (1992). Ethos, pathos and logos in Aristotle's Rhetoric: A re-examination. *Argumentation, 6*(3), 307–320. https://doi.org/10.1007/BF00154696

Brynen, R. (2021). *How I learned to stop worrying and love climate change and geo-politics*. Retrieved from https://paxsims.wordpress.com/tag/climate-change/

Carvalho, M. B., Bellotti, F., Berta, R., De Gloria, A., Sedano, C. I., Hauge, J. B., ... Rauterberg, M. (2015). An activity theory-based model for serious games analysis and conceptual design. *Computers and Education, 87*, 166–181. doi:10.1016/j.compedu.2015.03.023

Cassano-Piché, A., Vicente, K. J., & Jamieson, G. A. (2006). A sociotechnical systems analysis of the BSE epidemic in the UK through case study. In Proceedings of the 50th Annual Meeting of the Human Factors and Ergonomics Society (pp. 386–390). SAGE Publications Inc. https://doi.org/https://journals.sagepub.com/doi/10.1177/154193120605000337.

Centre for System Solutions. (2021). *Policy simulations*. Retrieved from https://drive.google.com/file/d/19nn0mnujnggKA2Ti7jGlMWEP990aPVsF/view

Chalmers, A. (1999). *What Is This Thing Called Science. Hackett Publishing Company* (3rd ed.). Hackett Publishing. Retrieved from https://mycourses.aalto.fi/pluginfile.php/1139027/mod_resource/content/1/WhatIsThisThingCalledScience-Chalmers-1999.pdf

Chander, A., & Le, U. P. (2014). Breaking the Web: Data Localization vs. The Global Internet. *SSRN Electronic Journal*. doi:10.2139/ssrn.2407858

Coovert, M. D., Winner, J., Bennett, W., & Howard, D. J. (2017). Serious Games are a Serious Tool for Team Research. *International Journal of Serious Games, 4*(1), 41–55. https://doi.org/10.17083/ijsg.v4i1.141

Cortese, C. G. (2005). Learning through teaching. *Management Learning, 36*(1), 87–115. https://doi.org/10.1177/1350507605049905

Crisis-games.co.uk. (2021). *Crisis games*. Retrieved from http://crisis-games.co.uk/

Czauderna, A., & Budke, A. (2020). How digital strategy and management games can facilitate the practice of dynamic decision-making. *Education in Science, 10*(4). https://doi.org/10.3390/educsci10040099

Davis, M. C., Challenger, R., Jayewardene, D. N. W., & Clegg, C. W. (2014). Advancing socio-technical systems thinking: A call for bravery. *Applied Ergonomics, 45*(2 Part A), 171–180. https://doi.org/10.1016/j.apergo.2013.02.009

Dean, P. (2016). *The explosive growth of the 300-person "megagame."* Retrieved from https://arstechnica. com/gaming/2016/09/the-explosive-growth-of-the-300-person-megagame/

DSB. (2016a). *Spilløvelser.* Retrieved from https://www.dsb.no/veiledere-handboker-og-informasjons-materiell/metodehefte-spillovelse/

DSB. (2016b). *Veileder i planlegging, gjennomføring og evaluering av øvelser Metodehefte: Fullska-laøvelse.* DSB.

Duke, R. D., & Geurts, J. (2004). *Policy Games for Strategic Management.* Retrieved from http://books. google.com/books?id=XGUdoRPFx30C&pgis=1

ECSC. (2021). *European cyber security challenge.* Retrieved from https://europeancybersecuritychal-lenge.eu/

Eder, K. (1999). Societies Learn and Yet the World is Hard to Change. *European Journal of Social Theory, 2*(2), 195–215.

EEAS. (2020). *EU Security, Defense and Crisis response.* Retrieved from https://eeas.europa.eu/topics/ security-defence-crisis-response/43281/security-defence-crisis-response_en

Eloff, M. M., & Von Solms, S. H. (2000). Information security management: A hierarchical frame-work for various approaches. *Computers & Security, 19*(3), 243–256. https://doi.org/10.1016/S0167-4048(00)88613-7

Engeström, Y. (2019). *Learning by expanding - An activity theoretical approach to developmental re-search* (2nd ed.). Cambridge University Press. Retrieved from Learningfromexperience.com/downloads/ research-library/eight-important-things-to-know-about-the-experiential-learning-cycle.pdf

European Commission. (2017). *Annex to "Coordinated Response to Large Scale Cybersecurity Incidents and Crises".* Commission Recommendation. COM(2017) 6100 final. 13.09.2017.

FEMA. (2017). *National Incident Management System.* Retrieved from www.dhs.gov

FEMA. (2020). *Exercises.* Retrieved from https://www.fema.gov/emergency-managers/national-pre-paredness/exercises

Fimreite, A. L., Lango, P., Lægreid, P., & Rykkja, L. H. (2014). *Organisering, krisehåndtering og sam-funnssikkerhet.* Universitetsforlaget. Retrieved from https://www.universitetsforlaget.no/organisering-samfunnssikkerhet-og-krisehandtering-1

Føllesdal, D., Walløe, L., & Elster, J. (1984). Argumentasjonsteori, språk og vitenskapsfilosofi (3rd ed.). Universitetsforlaget.

Fredette, C. (2019). *Cybersecurity Education: Why Universities are Missing the Mark.* Retrieved from https://www.cybintsolutions.com/cybersecurity-education-why-universities-are-missing-the-mark/

Funke, J. (2010). Complex problem solving: A case for complex cognition? *Cognitive Processing, 11*(2), 133–142. https://doi.org/10.1007/s10339-009-0345-0

Garnham, N. (2007). Habermas and the public sphere. *Global Media and Communication*, *3*(2), 201–214. https://doi.org/10.1177/1742766507078417

Gross, M., & Ho, S. M. (2021). Collective Learning for Developing Cyber Defense Consciousness: An Activity System Analysis. *Journal of Information Systems Education*, *32*(1), 65–77.

Guardiola, E. (2016). The gameplay loop: A player activity model for game design and analysis. *ACM International Conference Proceeding Series*. doi:10.1145/3001773.3001791

Gustafsson, T., & Defence, S. (2020). *Using serious gaming to train operators of critical infrastructure : an Industry/Experience report*. Retrieved from https://www.researchgate.net/profile/Tommy-Gustafsson-3/publication/341287480_Using_serious_gaming_to_train_operators_of_critical_infrastructure_an_In-dustryExperience_report/links/5eb93a3a299bf1287f7cb072/Using-serious-gaming-to-train-operators-of-critical-infrastructure-an-Industry-Experience-report.pdf

Habermas, J. (2006). Political communication in media society: Does democracy still enjoy an epistemic dimension? The impact of normative theory on empirical research. *Communication Theory*, *16*(4), 411–426. https://doi.org/10.1111/j.1468-2885.2006.00280.x

Hannula, O., & Harviainen, J. T. (2016). Efficiently Inefficient: Service Design Games as Innovation Tools. ServDes. *2016 Service Design Geographies; Proceedings from the Fifth Conference on Service Design and Service Innovation*, (125), 241–252. Retrieved from http://www.ep.liu.se/ecp/article.asp?issue=125&article=020&volume=%0Ahttp://www.ep.liu.se/ecp/125/020/ecp16125020.pdf

Hasan, H., & Kazlauskas, A. (2009). Making sense of IS with the Cynefin framework. *PACIS 2009 - 13th Pacific Asia Conference on Information Systems: IT Services in a Global Environment*.

Hauer, B. (2015). Data and information leakage prevention within the scope of information security. *IEEE Access: Practical Innovations, Open Solutions*, *3*, 2554–2565. https://doi.org/10.1109/ACCESS.2015.2506185

Hesse, W., & Verrijn-Stuart, A. (2001). Towards a theory of information systems: The FRISCO approach. *Frontiers in Artificial*, 1–12. Retrieved from http://citeseerx.ist.psu.edu/viewdoc/download?doi=10.1.1.68.7598&rep=rep1&type=pdf

Horkheimer, M. (2002). *Critical theory - selected essays*. The Continuum Publishing Company. Retrieved from https://books.google.no/books?hl=no&lr=&id=YiXUAwAAQBAJ&oi=fnd&pg=PR3&dq=horkheimer+1972+critical+theory&ots=uxQGfrftw1&sig=eL2AGBZIqa-qktynN6oD1Nrotas&redir_esc=y#v=onepage&q=horkheimer1972criticaltheory&f=false

Hove, C., Tarnes, M., Line, M. B., & Bernsmed, K. (2014). Information security incident management: Identified practice in large organizations. *Proceedings - 8th International Conference on IT Security Incident Management and IT Forensics, IMF 2014*, 27–46. doi:10.1109/IMF.2014.9

HSEEP. (2006). *Homeland Security Exercise and Evaluation Program Volume 1: HSEEP Overview and Exercise Program Management*. Retrieved from http://hseep.dhs.gov

Hunicke, R., Leblanc, M., & Zubek, R. (2004). MDA: A formal approach to game design and game research. *AAAI Workshop - Technical Report, WS-04-04*, 1–5.

Karra, M. (2010). *Key Distribution in PGP*. Academic Press.

Kianpour, M., Kowalski, S., Zoto, E., Frantz, C., & Overby, H. (2019). Designing Serious Games for Cyber Ranges: A Socio-Technical Approach. *Proceedings - 4th IEEE European Symposium on Security and Privacy Workshops, EUROS and PW 2019*, 85–93. doi:10.1109/EuroSPW.2019.00016

Kianpour, M., Øverby, H., Kowalski, S. J., & Frantz, C. (2019). Social Preferences in Decision Making Under Cybersecurity Risks and Uncertainties. *Lecture Notes in Computer Science, 11594*, 149–163. doi:10.1007/978-3-030-22351-9_10

Kirk, P. (2019). *Teach Incident Response with Games*. Retrieved from https://medium.com/slalom-build/teach-incident-response-with-games-5a69cf19fa88

Kolb, A., & Kolb, D. (2018). Eight Important Things to Know About The Experiential Learning Cycle. *Australian Educational Leader, 40*(3), 8–14. https://www.acel.org.au/ACEL/ACELWEB/Publications/AEL/2018/3/Lead_Article_1.aspx

Kolb, A. Y., & Kolb, D. A. (2009). The learning way: Meta-cognitive aspects of experiential learning. *Simulation & Gaming, 40*(3), 297–327. https://doi.org/10.1177/1046878108325713

Kolb, D. A. (1984). *Experiential Learning: Experience as The Source of Learning and Development*. Prentice Hall, Inc. doi:10.1016/B978-0-7506-7223-8.50017-4

Kowalski, S. (1994). *IT Insecurity: A Multi-disiplinary Inquiry*. Stockholm University.

Lacruz, A. J., & Américo, B. L. (2018). Debriefing's influence on learning in business game: An experimental design. *Brazilian Business Review, 15*(2), 192–208. doi:10.15728/bbr.2018.15.2.6

Marcuse, H. (1941). Some Social Implications of Modern Technology. *Studies in Philosophy and Social Sciences, 9*, 138–162. Retrieved from https://courses.cs.washington.edu/courses/cse490e/19wi/readings/marcuse_social_implications_1941.pdf

Mumford, E. (2006). The story of socio-technical design: Reflections on its successes, failures and potential. *Information Systems Journal*. doi:10.1111/j.1365-2575.2006.00221.x

NATO Public Diplomacy Division. (2016). *NATO Cyber Defence Fact Sheet*. Fact Sheet. Retrieved from https://www.nato.int/nato_static_fl2014/assets/pdf/pdf_2016_07/20160627_1607-factsheet-cyber-defence-eng.pdf

NIST. (2020). *Uses and Benefits of the Framework*. Retrieved from https://www.nist.gov/cyberframework/online-learning/uses-and-benefits-framework?campaignid=70161000001Cs1OAAS&vid=2117383

Norwegian Government. (2019). *Lov om nasjonal sikkerhet*. Retrieved from https://lovdata.no/dokument/NL/lov/2018-06-01-24?q=sikkerhetsloven

NSM, DSB, Digitaliseringsdirektoratet, NTNU, & NorSIS. (2020). Retrieved from https://ovelse.no/

NTNU. (2019a). *Guide for design of study programmes and courses at NTNU (the programme description guide)*. NTNU.

NTNU. (2019b). *Guide to periodic evaluation of programmes of study*. NTNU.

NTNU. (2019c). *Requirements for the academic portfolio at NTNU*. NTNU.

Nyblom, P., Wangen, G., Kianpour, M., & Østby, G. (2020). The root causes of compromised accounts at the university. *ICISSP 2020 - Proceedings of the 6th International Conference on Information Systems Security and Privacy*, (July), 540–551. doi:10.5220/0008972305400551

Nyre-Yu, M., Gutzwiller, R. S., & Caldwell, B. S. (2019). Observing Cyber Security Incident Response: Qualitative Themes From Field Research. *Proceedings of the Human Factors and Ergonomics Society Annual Meeting*, *63*(1), 437–441. https://doi.org/10.1177/1071181319631016

Optimas. (2021). *JTI personality and teamcompass*. Retrieved from https://optimas.no/jti/

Østby, G., Berg, L., Kianpour, M., Katt, B., & Kowalski, S. (2019). A Socio-Technical Framework to Improve cyber security training. *Work*. https://ntnuopen.ntnu.no/ntnu-xmlui/handle/11250/2624957

Østby, G., & Kowalski, S. (2020). Preparing for Cyber Crisis Management Exercises. *Augmented Cognition*. doi:https://doi.org/10.1007/978-3-030-50439-7_19

Patrício, R., Moreira, A. C., & Zurlo, F. (2020). Enhancing design thinking approaches to innovation through gamification. *European Journal of Innovation Management*. doi:10.1108/EJIM-06-2020-0239

Plass, J. L., Homer, B. D., & Kinzer, C. K. (2015). Foundations of Game-Based Learning. *Educational Psychologist*, *50*(4), 258–283. https://doi.org/10.1080/00461520.2015.1122533

Riedel, J., Feng, Y., & Azadegan, A. (2013). Serious Games Adoption in Organizations – An Exploratory Analysis. In EC-TEL 2013 (Vol. 8095, pp. 508–513). Springer Verlag. https://doi.org/10.1007/978-3-642-40814-4.

Shteynberg, G., Hirsh, J. B., Bentley, R. A., & Garthoff, J. (2020). Shared worlds and shared minds: A theory of collective learning and a psychology of common knowledge. *Psychological Review*, *127*(5), 918–931. https://doi.org/10.1037/rev0000200

Shulman, M. (1951). Max Shulman: Love is a Fallacy. *Love Is a Fallacy*, 6.

Sikkerhetsfestivalen. (2019). *Megagame*. Retrieved from https://sikkerhetsfestivalen.no/bidrag2019/megagame

Sloan, D., & College, M. (2015). *Tried and True Teaching Methods to Enhance Students' Service-Learning Experience*. Retrieved from https://www.usf.edu/engagement/documents/s-l-reflection-activities.pdf

Stanford. (2005). *Critical Theory*. Retrieved from https://plato.stanford.edu/entries/critical-theory/

Sturm, S. K. (2011). *Deduction, induction and abduction in academic writing*. Retrieved from https://seansturm.wordpress.com/2011/05/23/deduction-induction-and-abduction/

Taillandier, P., Grignard, A., Marilleau, N., Philippon, D., Huynh, Q. N., Gaudou, B., & Drogoul, A. (2019). Participatory modeling and simulation with the gama platform. *JASSS*, *22*(2). doi:10.18564/jasss.3964

Tenkinbas, K. S., & Zimmerman, E. (2003). *Rules of play*. Massachusetts Institute of Technology. Retrieved from https://mitpress.mit.edu/books/rules-play

The Internet Society. (1998). *RFC 2350*. Retrieved from https://www.ietf.org/rfc/rfc2350.txt

Tøndel, I. A., Line, M. B., & Jaatun, M. G. (2014). Information security incident management: Current practice as reported in the literature. *Computers & Security, 45*, 42–57. https://doi.org/10.1016/j.cose.2014.05.003

Tosey, P., Visser, M., & Saunders, M. N. K. (2012). The origins and conceptualizations of "triple-loop" learning: A critical review. *Management Learning, 43*(3), 291–307. https://doi.org/10.1177/1350507611426239

UN. (2021). *UN Sustainable development goals*. Retrieved from https://www.un.org/sustainabledevelopment/sustainable-development-goals/

van den Brink-Budgen, R. (2011). *Advanced Critical Thinking*. Hachette. Retrieved from https://books.google.no/books?hl=no&lr=&id=KoOeBAAAQBAJ&oi=fnd&pg=PT5&dq=roy+van+den+brink+budgen&ots=23RXDoCOKo&sig=l4x62t3RRzbyfiII4dZ6T8JWQvA&redir_esc=y#v=onepage&q=roy van den brink budgen&f=false

Vandercruysse, S., Vandewaetere, M., & Clarebout, G. (2012). Game-based learning: A review on the effectiveness of educational games. *Handbook of Research on Serious Games as Educational, Business and Research Tools*, 628–647. doi:10.4018/978-1-4666-0149-9.ch032

Weston, A. (1987). *A Rulebook for Arguments. Teaching Philosophy* (Vol. 10). doi:10.5840/teachphil198710235

Whitman, M. E., & Mattord, H. J. (2004). Designing and teaching information security curriculum. *2004 Information Security Curriculum Development Conference, InfoSecCD 2004*, 1–7. doi:10.1145/1059524.1059526

Whitman, M. E., & Mattord, H. J. (2018). *Management of Information Security*. Cengage. Retrieved from https://www.adlibris.com/no/bok/management-of-information-security-9781337405713?gclid=CjwKCAjwo4mIBhBsEiwAKgzXONCA2b5KlFWEPgb7kC7L6GGT8O-nUzmz0Y3Mx4YJ0IinwIxJrGs6WRoCE5QQAvD_BwE

Woodward, B., Imboden, T., & Martin, N. L. (2013). An undergraduate information security program: More than a curriculum. *Journal of Information Systems Education, 24*(1), 63–70.

Yale. (2019). *Intendent learning outcomes*. Retrieved from https://poorvucenter.yale.edu/IntendedLearningOutcomes

Yamin, M. M., Katt, B., & Nowostawski, M. (2021). Serious games as a tool to model attack and defense scenarios for cyber-security exercises. *Computers and Security, 110*. doi:10.1016/j.cose.2021.102450

ENDNOTES

[1]   https://www.ntnu.edu/studies/courses/IMT4115/2021/1#tab=omEmnet

[2]   https://www.fema.gov/sites/default/files/2020-07/fema_nims_doctrine-2017.pdf

[3]   https://www.urbandictionary.com/define.php?term=BLUF

[4]   https://dictionary.cambridge.org/dictionary/english/management-summary

[5]   https://dictionary.cambridge.org/dictionary/english/press-briefing

[6]   https://www.ntnu.no/ncr

Chapter 24
Enablers and Barriers of Integrating Game–Based Learning in Professional Development Programmes:
Case Study of Child Witness Interview Simulation in the Police Sector

Nashwa Ismail
Durham University, UK

Anne Adams
The Open University, UK

ABSTRACT

This study investigates the enablers and barriers of embedding technology for continuing professional development (CPD) of staff in the police sector. The research team developed an online game called "Child Witness Interview Simulation" (CWIS) to complement existing interview training for police officers and help them gain competency in interviewing children. Within the game design, development, and commercializing phases, the research team came across key themes that define the opportunities and challenges of implementing GBL through a police-based learning approach to CPD. The study identified that the successful implantation of Technology-Enhanced learning (TEL) in CPD falls into two broad categories: organizational, which considers learning outcomes, and individual, which considers learning aims and competency. Therefore, for successful implementation of TEL in CPD, ongoing supportive organizational culture that encourages employees and managers to be committed and motivated to implement TEL in CPD is necessary.

DOI: 10.4018/978-1-7998-9223-6.ch024

INTRODUCTION AND STUDY CONTEXT

Police training is traditionally based on empirical and experiential knowledge (HMIC 2015; HMCPSI/ HMIC, 2014). Whilst there is empirical evidence and procedural guidance for the topic of taking a first account from children, there is no direct training provided. In addition, evaluations of existing training only broadly relate to police practice e.g., training in taking accounts from vulnerable witnesses. These limitations were reported nationally as an 'area of concern' (HMIC, 2015) and identified the need for all police officers to improve their ability to listen and communicate with children, especially when taking an 'initial response' witness account upon their first arrival to a scene. The report (HMIC. 2015) went on to highlight the current reliance on simplistic online training that was deemed 'ineffective', as it 'does not provide any opportunity for reflection' (p.67, HMIC. 2015). Further insights for the evaluation of this project were provided by internal police reports, such as the 'Achieving Best Practice' (ABP) guidelines, which provided procedural direction on safeguarding children's welfare whilst collecting high-quality evidence (Binsubaih, *et al.,* 2006., Blandford, 2013, HMIC. 2015, HMCPSI/HMIC, 2014).

The proposed solution by the team of researchers is to embed the gamed-based learning (GBL) module "Child Witness Interview Simulation" (CWIS) in the Learning and Development (L&D) programme for police officers in order to develop the newly recruited police officers' skills in interviewing a child that has witnessed a crime. With a GBL module, learners are expected to make decisions and problem solve in increasingly difficult circumstances (Backlund and Hendrix, 2013; Boyle *et al.,* 2016). CWIS is a solution to complement existing interview training for new recruits and early career front-line police officers (Adams *et al.,* 2019). This simulation/ game addresses gaps in the knowledge and skills of new recruits and serving officers when interviewing child witnesses to develop their communication skills (HMIC, 2015). CWIS incorporates triggers for emotional recognition to support the training of rapport building of police officers when interviewing children.

Prior to the implementation of CWIS in L&D, development and dissemination of CWIS went through 3 stages: (1) co-design, (2) co-evaluation and, (3) commercialisation. Within these stages (which will be explained later in this chapter), the team of researchers explored the opportunities and barriers to implementing gamification in Continuing Professional Development (CPD) programmes to enhance the provision of appropriate and effective Technology-Enhanced Learning (TEL) learning through CPD initiatives.

This book chapter starts with introduction and study context to explain the background behind the research study and the main terminology used. Then, the literature review focuses on the main discussed topics about the study includes, TEL, GBL, CPD and police organisational culture. Next, the methodology section includes the design and evaluation of CWIS, followed by findings and analysis of commercialising the CWIS. The discussion section highlights the significant issues in embedding GBL in the police sector (enablers and barriers). The study concludes with recommendations and future work.

LITERATURE REVIEW

CPD and Technology in Policing

Continuing Professional Development (CPD)

Professional development is the acquisition of skills and development both formally and informally and has been improved through staff development, continuing education, or in-service training (Penuel *et al.*, 2007). This wide range of notions for CPD reflects the diversity of gained competencies by CPD. Therefore, professional development, when presented in a variety of forms, allows practitioners and employees to gain various competencies to overcome barriers, change beliefs, learn new skills, and practice implementation in their specific content area.

Gusky (2000) focused on the strong standing of social perspective in CPD and the importance of embedding collaboration and communication in it. As for Vygotsky (1978), social constructivism, where knowledge is socially situated and constructed through interaction with others, is a social interaction that has fundamental role in the development of cognition. Within the social perspective, Darling-Hammond and McLaughlin (1995) emphasised that traditional CPD needs to be replaced by opportunities for "knowledge sharing" based on real situations. They added that individuals should be provided with opportunities to share and discuss what they know and connect new concepts and strategies to their own unique contexts. Therefore, in CPD designing and planning, culture of sharing and knowledge exchange needs to be considered on an organisational level. In the study context of policing, we identified this culture and highlighted the motivations, benefits and sharing individuals' needs within the police (See more details about culture and organisational culture in later section).

Jones and Dexter (2014) suggested a variety of forms of professional development to be considered for the effective integration of instructional technology.

Formal or traditional professional development are activities arranged by the organisation's management and leadership team. These activities are aligned to the organisational goals therefore, covered topics are predetermined. Examples of such activities include workshops, conferences, in-service trainings and training courses (Jones and Dexter, 2014). Therefore, if CPD is highly prioritising the organisation's strategic goals and decision making is taking the top-bottom approach, the CPD plan will be rigid and place the employees' individual goals and learning objectives at a lower priority.

Informal Professional Development (IPD) is collaboration in the Community of Practice (COP) (a group of people who share a craft or a profession (Wenger, 2006)). Examples of IPD practices include: talking during lunch, internships, and mentoring relationships with technology proficient staff members (Jones and Dexter, 2014). IPD as type of CPD is well associated with TEL, as it is classified as "just in time" activities as they happen at the moment of embedding technology in Teaching & Learning (T&L). For example, sharing a technical topic, which is directly associated with the daily job practice, and discussing with colleagues, is IPD. Moreover, IPD tackles different perspectives other than learning, such as social collaboration and linking with the social construction of knowledge (Vygotsky, 1978). Furthermore, IPD's flexibility, can be pursued not only in the workplace but anywhere and anytime. However, Bauer (2010) condemned IPD for giving too much control to learners and raised the concern that learners might get overwhelmed because they get unplanned information from different sources of knowledge. Therefore, establishing the culture of pervasive learning within the organisation and facilitating structured learning resources (i.e., online micro teaching resources on the organisation intranet) can help to avoid the potential chaos in learning.

Personal Professional Development (PPD) includes activities that allow for individualised learning through the management and selection of content, co-construction of knowledge, demonstration of competencies, and generation of networks for ongoing learning outside of the school day and on the teacher's own time (Ross *et al.,* 2015). Forms of PPD include Google searches, reading wikis and blogs, and other applications of social network (Jones and Dexter, 2014). PPD is essential in order to develop staff's technical and soft skills, plan which areas need more work and develop their needs. For PPD, the role lies on both individuals and the organisation. For the organisation, its role is to set out long-term aims, priorities and action plans that break the PPD work into stages and address the details of the action to be taken. For individuals, their role is to identify and acknowledge their skills, learning intentions and outcomes. Based on this knowledge, the organisation can setup a CPD plan that can be responsive to the individuals' needs. Table 1 below summarises the characteristics of the three types of CPD (Formal, IPD and PPD). The comparison looks at each type according to its planning, benefits and features.

Table 1. Comparison between different types of professional training programmes

Point of comparison	Formal or traditional professional development	Informal professional development (IPD)	Personal professional development (PPD)
Planning and management	organisation and leadership team management	• Individuals • CoP	Individuals
Features	Pre-scheduled	• Just in time • Flexible	• When training is unavailable • Area of improvement is highlighted
Examples	workshops, conferences	Google searches	Any
Benefits	Achieving organisational objectives	Achieving individual objectives	Focusing on the area of improvement
Drawback	Top-bottom approach only is considered	Learning overwhelming Too much learner's control	Guidance is needed
Best practice	Considering individual learning goals (bottom-top approach)	Organisational culture of pervasive learning	Personal development plan

This section summarises that in order to design a CPD plan, each one of the three types is essential for improving the individual's and organisation's job performance. Moreover, for each type, there is a role for individuals, and/or organisation, and/ or both. It is worth noting that, learning is one of the main objectives in any training program. However, one of the basic characteristics in any learning process is the depth of study that it involves with the two extremes in the spectrum being Surface Learning (SL) and Deep Learning (DL). Biggs (1991) and Ramsden (1992) differentiated between DL and SL in a way by breaking the cognitive dimensions into two methods of processing information: surface processing and in-depth processing. This differentiation informs with examples of indicators of surface processing. For example: duplicating previous information without putting forward inferences, supporting the opinions of others without expanding on the ideas, critiquing with no substantiation, asking irrelevant questions, presenting multiple solutions without prioritising, and disjointed postings. These are all examples of SL and this highlights the worries around embedding TEL in CPD. This needs to be validated and evaluated, otherwise it would highlight the concern of SL not DL.

Ramsden (1992) directly related between DL and the availability of time to learn. In details, with SL, when learners lack the positive motivation to learn and become disengaged with the studies course, they feel overwhelmed and they find that there is not enough time to grasp the knowledge. In the study context, workload and limited time are common limitations for CPD and one of the barriers of learning within CPD (Wood and Tong, 2009). On the other hand, DL gives the learner positive experience of education leading to confidence in doing work which is also aligned with having time to pursue interests through good time management. Finally, for professional practice, when deep learning occurs, practitioners' self-confidence and gained knowledge increase. For police officers, being confident in what they learn will reflect positively in what they do due to the gained confidence. Consequently, whilst using this collaborative approach, learners were actively engaged and motivated to learn and the potential for improved job practice to be transferable to impact upon practice, is augmented.

Technology- Enhanced Learning (TEL)

According to Alexander (2018), the benefit of embedding TEL in CPD is to support the organisation and staff to design, reflect, experiment and share best practice in their professional training. However, both CPD and TEL have their own levels of complexity (see the section above about CPD). For TEL, despite the breadth of technology knowledge, technology users may have no depth in how to use the technologies to support pedagogical goals in CPD (Alexander, 2018). In other words, irrational use of TEL may lead to SL - see 2.2 Deep Learning Versus Surface Learning.

Kirkwood and Price (2013) attempt to draw a clearer definition of TEL where they synthesise the various conceptions of enhancement in learning such as: operationally (i.e., spatial mobility and travel while learning), quantitively (i.e., attainment of student's assessment score) and qualitatively (i.e.TEL improves students' online communication via social network).

From a social view, Vygotsky (1978) introduced the Zone of Proximal Development (ZPD) as the difference between what a learner can do with help (within the prescribed zone), and what they can do without help (outside the prescribed zone). TEL helps learners to be able to extend their learning/ acquisition beyond the prescribed zone with the advancement of internet technology. However, TEL has been critiqued in literature because of the absence of social elements and social practice from teaching and learning. For Irwin (2018), social isolation is one of the pitfalls in the excessive embedding of technology in learning and the absence of the social assets in teaching and learning (book, teacher, class, etc).

Czaja *et al.,* 2017; TELRP 2013:5; cf. Kirkwood and Price 2014:1, advocated the claim of TEL's social isolation, as they see TEL with its connection with teaching and learning – found in programmes like Blackboard Learn, Moodle and Socrative. TEL could also include social media as learning and teaching tools. It is a complex system, involving 'communities, technologies and practices that are informed by pedagogy. Therefore, TEL induces the social aspects of learning and social network applications and their revolutionary spread can be a significant to this claim.

Bayne (2015) listed different scopes for enhancement that are to be considered. Firstly, a social scope with enhancement value of social technologies which promotes and enables collaboration and connection among groups. Then, a technological scope which has improved hardware and software for an efficient computer interface. Finally, an educational scope which, from teachers' view, can enhance their productivity with new tools for designing teaching and learning about how computers are able to help learners better shape the world around them (Sclater and Lally, 2016). The use of technology in service of education must be driven by pedagogical, research and community-directed needs and not by technological determinism.

In conclusion, literature shows that TEL has various characteristics where it is flexible (increasing flexibility in the requirements, time, and location of study, teaching and assessment), interactive (considering the interaction catalysts of the learning process i.e., student – teacher – content) through promoting social practices and engaging. TEL is also able to stimulate attention, curiosity, interest, optimism, and passion that students show when they are learning or being taught, which extends to the level of motivation they have to learn and progress in their education. Moreover, in each scope in TEL, the characteristics (flexible, interactive, engaging….) have to be met.

Table 2. Enablers and barriers to embed TEL in CPD

Enablers	Barriers
• Usability of technology	• Cultural
• Improved engagement	• Knowledge sharing
• Game visual appeal (rapport bar)	• Misconception about TEL
• Increased Learning	• Professional
• Improved attention span	• CPD provided
• Instant feedback	• Limited time
• Improved job performance	• Technical
• Developing interviewing skills	• Security and confidentiality
• Increased confidence in interviewing a child	• Limited IT resources
• Improved training	• Institutional
	• Police hierarchy
	• Top-bottom approach

Regarding organisational support to TEL for work practice and provided training, literature concludes that a lack of organisational support to TEL leads to barriers in its adoption. Birch and Burnett (2009) carried out a literature review into the barriers related to the adoption of TEL and asserted that institutions should identify their own definitions and develop a clear vision of TEL in order to address the lack of common understanding. Barriers include lack of institutional direction towards TEL and supporting it and examples may include limited access to suitable educational software and ICT equipment (Buabeng-Andoh, 2012). Although time has consistently been cited as the biggest barrier to TEL development (Walker *et al.*, 2016), it is believed that, if organisational culture supports TEL, more time can be dedicated to facilitating the understanding of TEL and embedding it in CPD. On the other hand, when organisational culture supports implementation of TEL, all stakeholders (practitioners, academic technology innovators developers…), should work together and make the best use of technology to improve teaching and learning. See table 2 above.

In the police sector, digital transformation is central to the 2030 digital policing ambition to drive improvements in data, technology and, most importantly, the skills of the people that lead, manage and use it. To do this, there is an ongoing call to prioritise and focus efforts across professional development service to equip police staff with innovative technologies.

Games-Based Learning (GBL)

GBL has gained increased popularity over recent years and has been advocated as a promising piece of technology for supporting training within sectors such as, education, healthcare and the military (Adams *et al.*, 2019). For Sugahara (2018), GBL fosters employees' decision-making and develops design thinking skills (Patrıcio *et al.*, 2020) when embedding in CPD programmes. Rivera (2016) confirmed that GBL enhances learner's motivation for learning because of their engaging nature and challenging the players where the challenge usually increases if the game goes on and engagement is augmented. The perceived engagement allows them to freely define and modify their strategies according to their learning objectives and goals. Therefore, players keep on improving their skills and learning new strategies until the game is completed.

The following section references other games which identify the impact of GBL in supporting CPD and qualitative impact on individual and/or organisational context

Examples of GBL transferability to job practice

Example 1

Beer Distribution Game is a simulation exercise developed at MIT's Sloan School of Management to teach systems concepts and systems thinking to managers. The game has been effectively employed to identify how management behaviours commonly found in complex business systems lead to dysfunctional management practices as well as poor performance and suggests how alternative ways of thinking. (Jacks *et al.*, 1994)

Example 2

Sukhov, A. (2018), designed "Total War: Medieval II" (TWM2). The game could identify "external educational aspects that represent innovative educational opportunities of TWM2 for both personal and professional development. TWM2 can form professional competences in the sphere of administrative management, economic management and even crisis management in extreme conditions of limited resources (on the strategic turn-based world map level) as well as army management (on the tactical real-time level).

Example 3

Cubic Global Defence (2015) is a 3D training game developed by GBL for on-the-job training. Cubic defence, UK recently showcased a selection of the live, virtual and constructive training solutions it provides for the UK ministry of defence, including its use during a British army training exercise. This CPD training is public safety job training, including high-risk jobs such as firefighting, using virtual training environments. According to (Anderson *et al.*, 2016), this can be viewed live and is also recorded for analysis after the event in an after-action review so trainees can better understand what they did right and wrong and ensure training objectives and performance standards are met. This increases participants' readiness, so they can best perform in a real-world setting.

In the police sector, CPD requires simulating a task in a risk-free and controlled environment and allows an easy transition of players through its virtual reality training into the real world. That real world otherwise might prove risky for staff and public whom they are servicing. In the study context, policing has a high-risk nature to be repeated in real life practice. Therefore, with GBL, police officers and staff members will have the opportunity to practice learning (such as child interview) in a free risk, unlimited trials and authentic learning environment. Besides, this learning environment offers flexibility, so anyone can try the game, anywhere and anytime. Therefore, we found GBL can provide the free-risk, unlimited trials that is around a real-life scenario and includes photo-realistic portrayals of environments and characters and this is an element of TEL that can be embedded into the CPD of police.

Ordering Factors in the Implementation of TEL in CPD

In terms of the implementation of TEL in CPD, there are factors that influence this implementation. Ertmer (1999) classified these factors into enablers and barriers; we argue this classification, as both are influential factors where mismanagement of an enabler can shift it to be a barrier. The following section details literature that looks at these factors. For the consistency with literature, we would keep referring to these factors as barriers.

According to Ertmer (1999), barriers can be sorted as either first-, or second-order. First-order barriers are extrinsic to the practitioner, whereas second-order barriers are more intrinsic. Table 2 below compares between the two types of barriers.

Table 3.

Type	Example
First Order Barriers/external: barriers that are extrinsic to the staff and imposed by external forces	• Availability of resources: time, technical support, access to technology, budget • Institutional and administrative support, • Organisational expectations • Policies and leadership
Second Order Barriers/internal: barriers that are intrinsic to teachers and involve changing beliefs about technology and teaching with technology	• Content knowledge and its delivery • Technological knowledge benefit of technology Pedagogical knowledge to address individual and group learning. • Training, skills and experience
✓ Beliefs and knowledge about : • Content and its delivery • Technologies and their benefits to learning, • Effective pedagogy to address individual and group learning. • Personal beliefs (i.e., self-esteem) • Social Engagement	

The researchers argue the sequence of order of these barriers as first and second order, as this order means that one group has higher priority than the other and this higher priority implies that overcoming first order barriers would resolve the second order barriers. The following section gives different scenarios where the first and second order priorities can be positioned differently depending on the situational context.

Second Order Resolves First Order

For example, facilitating resources improves the development of staff personal skills. This hypothesis might narrow down the reasons that are behind the poor enhancement of professional skills to facilitating resources exclusively, as self-esteem and self-actualisation motivate individuals to getting engaged with others and using their utmost abilities to pursue objectives (Dweck, 1999). Therefore, hypothetically, facilitating staff training, that helps them to do their job, would improve their self-esteem and reflect on their positive determination to achieve organisational objectives.

However, other causes such as (low self-esteem, technophobia) can be leading reasons. In the latter case, for the implementation of TEL in CPD, the start will be considering the second-order barrier which can then lead into planning the first-order barrier.

Different Position for the Same Barrier in the Two Orders

The other argument is that some barriers can fall under both internal and external groups. For example, limited time can occur due to a lack of the individual's belief in the usefulness of technology that leads to the negative attitude to its implementation. In this scenario, limited time will fall under the internal barrier. Besides, on the organisational level, if lack of time is caused by the organisation and enterprise work plan towards achieving objectives, in this scenario, limited time will fall under the external barrier.

Intra-Relationship Between the Two Orders

The third argument at this point is the intra-relationship between all barriers and how one barrier can interfere with the other. For example, looking at staff resistance to change to adopt technology, Prochaska and Prochaska (1999) listed four main reasons behind our difficulties in changing our behaviour: (1) 'I can't change'; (2) 'I don't want to change'; (3) 'I don't know how to change'; and (4) 'I don't know what to change'. Although they are so-called internal barriers, according to (GLC 2015) and (TELRP 2013), the key reasons for this resistance are: *Training provided* (first-order factors) *Understanding and contextualisation of learning* (second-order factors) *Time constraints* (first-order factors), *Personal experience* (first-order factors) social interaction with colleagues (first-order factors). Some of these factors can combine both factors (i.e., first- and second-order). Therefore, intervention from the external barriers at different stages can help to overcome these barriers. At some points, both groups need to work collaboratively and not isolated from each other.

The fourth argument refers to the decision makers who resolve these barriers Table 3 shows that first-order reflects organisational priorities and second-order reflects individual priorities. Therefore, the distinctive separation and ordering between the two groups gives the impression of a top-bottom management approach. In this approach, top level reaches independent conclusions that change or improve the workplace. These conclusions are then handed down to employees, who work to accomplish the goals on their own or with other employees (Geisler, 2012). Some lower-level managers add inputs into how to accomplish the end goal, but they may not have much authority to change policies without approval from the highest level of management. This approach is well situated in the study context in with Policing, as according to Adams *et al.* (2019), sharing of views and visions is much easier for officers and staff in higher ranks. However, for lower ranks, it is often felt that sharing decisions needed to be deferred up the hierarchy. Ertmer and Ottenbreit-Leftwich (2010), explain the consequences of the lack of sharing in CPD plan when there is a lack of collaboration with external bodies (i.e. technology developers) and a lack of co-working in TEL. Therefore, CPD provided may not consider the beneficiaries' need or isolate the learning outcomes from the TEL. This can be a reason of poor implementing of TEL in CPD. In other words, grouping and prioritising of barriers is not a "one size fits all". Understanding the extent to which these barriers affect individuals and institutions can help deciding how to tackle them (Becta, 2004). This understanding requires implementing a top-bottom-top approach to combine both groups of orders.

Police Organisational Culture

Organisational Culture

This section highlights Organisational culture (OC) and correlates it with individual/person culture. According to Schredt (2002), in business terms, different phrases are often used to refer to OC interchangeably, including "corporate culture," "workplace culture," and "business culture." The term "culture" itself is a system of knowledge, beliefs, procedures and attitudes that is shared within a group (Needle, 2004). For Gill (2013), culture influences the whole organisation as it exerts a strong influence on individuals' behaviours beyond dispute.

Handy (1999), in defining OC, denoted to four aspects (see figure 1): Power (control is centred with few people to make decisions), Role (emphasis on organisation structure with roles and responsibilities), Task (functional and project oriented) and Person (culture is structured to be individualistic rather that organisational). In our context, in defining OC, we would focus on a person's culture (as in CPD individual is the focus). Moreover, we highlight the influence of the person's culture on the achievement of the holistic OC and whether they are overlapping/conflicting fully/partially.

Figure 1. Model of Organisational Culture (Handy, 1999)

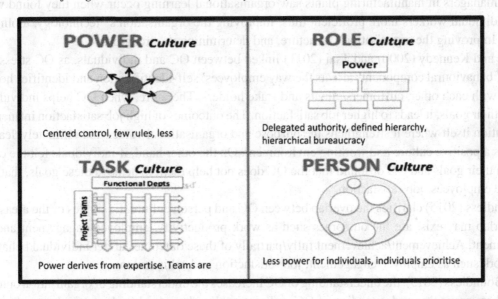

Literature defines OC from different perspectives; Chartered Management Institute (2015), explains that OC includes the organization's vision, values, norms, systems, symbols, language, assumptions, beliefs, and habits. Needle (2004) expands OC to people as the underlying beliefs, assumptions, values and ways of interacting contribute to how people should behave and interact, how decisions should be made and how work activities should be carried out. Consequence of these shared assumptions guide to what happens in organisations by defining appropriate behaviour for various situations (Ravasi and Schultz, 2006). In summary, for Deal and Kennedy (2000), OC is the way things are done around here. In other words, key factors in an organisation's culture include its history and environment as well as the people who lead and work for it, as what is happening in the organisation and ways things are done define the organisational behaviour and this behaviour in turn identifies the OC.

With respect to a person's culture, according to Handy (1999), each individual is seen as more valuable than the organisation itself, where the individual is the focal point of this culture and there is no organisational structure, control mechanism, management hierarchy or overriding objective. The high priority of a person's culture and individual's objectives raises a concern for Boundless (2015), as the organisation may suffer due to competing people and priorities and it can be difficult to sustain if priorities between person and organisation are conflicting.

In terms of learning, we claim that there is a strong link between OC that considers individuals and CPD provided that supports DL. However, it is for the organisation to take fundamental prospective on whether SL or DL is the adopted learning approach. Researchers recommend revisiting which learning objective has higher priority, when planning CPD. Either CPD is provided for staff to get a certificate in an area of their practice and the organisation gets 100% completion while relevance knowledge obtained is less important, or the CPD enables staff to do their work and positively change their job practices.

Learning in the organisational context creates and organizes knowledge relating to their functions and culture. Organisational learning occurs in all the organisation's activities, and it happens at different speeds. The goal of organisational learning is to successfully adapt to changing environments, to adjust under uncertain conditions, and to increase efficiency (Tucker, *et al.,* 2007). According to Argote (1993), managers in manufacturing plants saw organisational learning occur when they found ways to make individual workers more proficient thus, improving the organisation's "technology, tooling, and layout," improving the organisation's structure, and determining its strengths.

Deal and Kennedy (2000) and Tsai (2011) linked between OC and individuals, as OC stresses employees' behavioural components affects the way employees' self-identification and identifies how they interact with each other, customers/clients and stake holders. Therefore, when OC helps individuals to achieve their goals, it leads to higher job satisfaction. The outcomes of high job satisfaction influence the organisation itself where it strengthens the purpose and organisational values and ultimately, leads and develops a positive culture and working environment. On the other hand, if individuals felt the conflict between their goals and OC or found that the OC does not help them to achieve these goals, that would decrease employees' job satisfaction.

Boundless (2015) clarifies the overlap between OC and person culture. Examples of the areas where this overlap may exist are the outcomes such as work productivity, employee engagement and work commitment. Achievement/achievement fully/partially of these outcomes affect individual behavioural framework such as employee engagement, job satisfaction and achievement.

For Boundless (2015), the understanding of OC increases the understanding of organisation outcomes. Researchers argue that understanding of OC and a person's culture leads to better understanding of the organisation and personal outcomes. When designing a CPD model, a debate arises on the different order and priority settings of CPD aims and objectives between the start (individuals) and the end (organisation). Specially that, junior employees reside at the bottom layer of the organisation hierarchy structure, whilst seniors, decision makers and strategic planners reside in the top hierarchical level. The researchers developed the below figure (figure 2) to explain this debate.

Figure 2. Interrelationship between organisation and culture

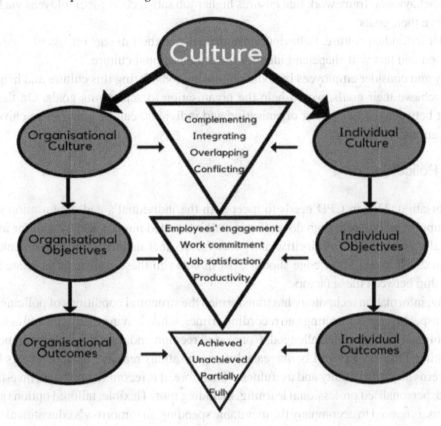

The above diagram illustrates the interrelationship between person/ individual and organisational culture and how they might have been defined and approached differently between the person and the organisation. It is worth noting that, there are links that need to be acknowledged and identified. Examples of these links are the interdependency between OC and culture/ individual culture, whether they are complementary/ integrating/ conflicting/ overlapping as well as the prioritisation of both OC and person culture and the status of achieved outcomes for both OC and person culture partially/ fully/ unachieved. Referring Dweck (1999 regarding the improving of employees' self-esteem and the reflection on their positive determination to achieve organisational objectives, we assume that the achieved/ unachieved outcomes will influence organisational behaviour positively/ negatively respectively.

Thus, the benefit of illustrating the model organisation (OC) and individual (IC) cultures (Figure 3) is that when designing and planning CPD, visiting the OC, IC and objectives and outcomes of each need to be considered. The reason behind considered both cultures is that if there is a conflict between the culture of each, different objectives' priorities of each, that would influence the behavioural framework and ultimately the achievement of their outcomes.

In summary, organisational culture is made up of shared values, beliefs and assumptions about how people should behave and interact. So, the focus point is to build and share these views is the people. Worth to mention that, a conflict between the objectives of OC and PC, would negatively influence the behavioural framework and ultimately the achievement of their outcomes. Therefore, to design effective CPD, it needs to:

- Ensure behavioural framework that ensures higher job satisfaction for employees via helping them to achieve their goals
- Consider individual culture, Behavioural framework and their impact on organisational outcomes, as by then end that will shape and identify the organisational culture.
- Identify and consider employees induvial culture, as considering this culture and helping employees to achieve their goals, would help the organisation to achieve its goals. On the other hand, conflict between the two goals; organisation and individual can be a barrier to chive the holistic organisational goals.

Culture of Police Sector

For an organisation, TEL in CPD needs to meet both the individual's and organisation's needs. TEL design can support learning through doing if it is well integrated into a wider system for individual and organisational development. To prioritise and order factors that influence the implementation of TEL in CPD, shared vision and knowledge should exist in between these factors to facilitate the flow and interrelationship between these factors.

In policing, information technology has transformed the structural conditions of policing in important professional aspects such as detecting and recording crimes, while leaving many cultural assumptions and traditional policing practices unchallenged. Concluded recommendation that, the likelihood of success in implementing TEL in CPD will be increased if organisations reassure users about its benefits, and address concerns about its validity and usefulness. Therefore, it is recommended that, investment in carefully planned, personalised professional learning, including more flexible, tailored options such as action learning teams, is needed to accompany the inevitable spending on tomorrow's educational technologies, and guide pedagogically diverse applications of these ICTs and dissemination of exemplary practices.

Specific benefit of this study concluded results in the police context is about the preparation for Initial Police Learning and Development Programme (IPLDP). IPLDP is a two-year programme with approximately 35 weeks of supporting learning materials. According to the college of policing (2018), the main call in the new curriculum that there is need to update it to embed content on vulnerability and digitally facilitated crime, to operate with a high degree of autonomy, solve complex problems, exercise personal judgement and apply their skills to a wide range of situations understand their impact and refine approaches to ensure getting the best possible outcomes. Therefore, the findings of this study can help the college of policing is working to understand the difficulties they face, offer support and explore their options.

In summary, when planning to implant TEL in CPD, ordering and prioritising the factors that influence this implementation need to be considered and assessed, as these factors are not "one size fits all", what can be a barrier in an organisation, can be an enabler in another. What can be first order priority in an organisation, can be second order priority in another. For TEL implementation within CPD, learning scope needs to be clearly articulated and adhered within existing programmes and activities. Also, key stakeholders (i.e., trainers and trainees) need to be identified and appropriately consulted to have the necessary skills to improve the likelihood of success. To achieve the later recommendation, encouraging co-working and sharing between colleagues to continue developing an effective user community enabling to learn from the experts within job practice, is highly recommended.

Risk Averse Culture

According to Hayward (2018), risk adverse culture is a culture of caution that can inhibit progress and it is the barrier to agility. For risk averse people, attempting to mitigate all risk out of an action eliminates any possibility that action will result in substantive change. Therefore, traditionality and resistance to change can reduce the risk. Consequently, for adverse culture seekers, CPD, that develops skills to overcome barriers, change beliefs, learn new skills, and practice implementation in their specific content area, raises a concern for risk. For active learning, motivation, engagement and curiosity of knowledge, that are aligned with DL (Biggs, 1999), raises a concern for risk too. Therefore, surface learning that exists in the lower level of Bloom's Taxonomy (1956) that is based on memorising and understanding, can secure risk averse culture's positions and minimise risk.

Adams *et al.* (2018), focused on the adverse culture in Policing and explained that there perpetuated a risk-adverse culture to data sharing beyond personal information into institutional procedures and policy. This also resulted in an increased perception of security risks from breaching data protection and an elevated perception of fines that could be received from sharing. Moreover, Adams *et al.* (2018), explained that across forces interviewed it was noted that often external organisations used the Data Protection Act as a barrier preventing sharing and thus the development of work-based learning approaches.

The negative implications of police work practice that constraining data sharing highlights not only a cost for police time and effort but also as impeding investigations. This is confirmed by Hayward (2018), the concern here is it inhibits experimentation and risk-taking and it slows down innovation and improvement. If we fear making mistakes, the only thing we will learn is how to avoid them. In showcasing the game phase, referring to the findings in phase 2, the team confronted the risk averse culture, this culture of caution can inhibit the organisation progress.

In risk averse culture, CPD objectives are to achieve learning outcomes rather than competency and learning aims. In this culture, the prioritising of needs is towards organisation rather than individuals' needs. Therefore, for effective CPD, organisations need to shift a risk-averse culture to adopt new and innovative thinking approach.

METHODOLOGY

Child Witness Interview Simulation (CWIS)

According to Adams *et al.* (2018), police sharing is key enabler in the police context, regardless of police rank and role, they all have a strong collaborative nature, through a deep motivation to share, that benefits the wider social community. On the other hand, police strong hierarchical culture is a key barrier to police sharing that does not encourage the independent nature of sharing. Whilst police officers and staff act independently within the confines of their prescribed roles, they rarely independently share beyond this. Therefore, study design of CWIS has been informed by the aforementioned enablers and barriers to conduct its design and developing in a collaborative approach.

Phase 1: Co-Designing and Co-Evaluation of CWIS

In this phase of the study, we detail a novel co-creation method that can specifically evaluate how technology enhances learning based on educational threshold concept theories in this tricky topic. Before interacting with the game, we used Tricky Topic Tool (TTT) to support the co-creating knowledge-based evaluation questionnaires and identify the gaps and training needs. TTT is underpinned as pedagogical threshold concept theories (Meyer and Land, 2006) that provide a unique opportunity to test the applicability of the co-design approach to evaluating learning technologies such as serious games. This tool was previously co-created with teachers, and subject matter and educational experts to facilitate the development of appropriate evaluation questions. Tricky topic tool shows the gaps in the practitioners' practice in interviewing children such as asking limited questions and attracting the child's attention.

116 new recruit police officers from three UK forces participated in a randomised control trial and tested the CWIS. The evaluation method provided insights of how the game increased police officers' understanding against face-to-face training. This was based on statistically significant results with p < 0.001 (large effect size) (see figure 3).

Figure 3. Pre/post F2F and games (simulation) training

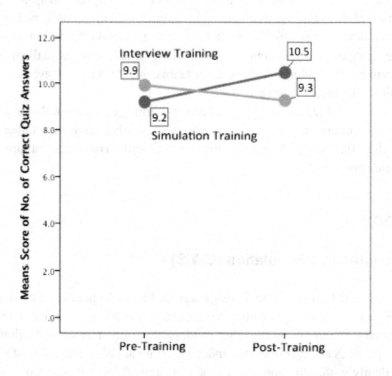

Figure 3 above clearly indicates that the games training increased (Pre-Post Training), compared to the decrease with Interview training (Pre-Post Training). The feedback from these evaluations (TTT and questionnaire) addresses: game usability, game mechanics, learning and training needs and preferences. Moreover, the outcomes of this phase confirm that the game can shift from a pre-production to production stage and then to saleable and scalable developing stage.

Phase 2: Commercialisation of CWIS

The commercialisation of CWIS progressed into a full programme in April 2018 based upon research and development work being conducted for several years prior to this date. Within the commercialisation process, after developing the prototype of CWIS into saleable and scalable product, we planned a series of workshops, seminars and online video sessions for launching and selling (Parker, 2018). At this stage, participants consisted of police officers and individuals occupying different job roles in their police force such as; front line police officers, senior police officers, trainers, different job roles in the IT department, strategic planners and finance team members. This diversity of professional backgrounds helps the case study to be reflective and willing to see others' views. Within this period, commercialisation activities carried out included:

- Interviews and emails with L&D leaders and trainers
- Events and brainstorming discussions in these events
- Document reviews, training agenda/reports

Reports from the above activities have been thematically analysed for identifying, analysing, organising, describing, and reporting themes found within a data set (Clarke and Braun, 2013). The researchers started by: (1) Data familiarisation, (2) Generating initial codes, (3) Searching for themes, (4) Reviewing themes, (5) Defining and naming themes and, (6) Generating reports.

FINDINGS

Findings from phase 2 entailed different factors that influence the implementation of TEL in CPD where some of the factors are barriers and others are enablers. Findings from showcasing and commercialising CWIS are summarised in table 1 below which shows the enablers and barriers in implementing CWIS in policing.

Two emerging super themes have been thematically emerged from data analysis; *"What"* and *"Who"*. "WHAT", explaining the factors that influence the implementation of CWIS in CPD. This explanation leads on to another important point in the research: "WHO" is a decision maker in the implementation of technology in the police sector? Therefore, the team grouped and classified police staff members who took part in the commercialising activities where participants who took part in phases; (1) co-design, (2) co-evaluate and, (3) commercialisation were classified into two groups; see table 3 below.

Table 4. Comparison between Group 1 and Group 2 of CWIS participants

Point of comparison	Group 1	Group 2
Audience affiliation/department	• Trainers • Early recruits of police forces • Experts	• Trainers' leaders • Strategic planners and L&D decision makers • IT staff members
Audience objectives	Learning aims and competency	Learning outcomes
Aspired learning type	• Deep learning • Personalized learning • Navigating the learning journey • Learning needs	• Surface learning • Organisational learning
Feedback summary	Engaging, interactive, improved job performance	• The game may not achieve learning • Technical concerns about security

From Table 4 above, it is noted that there are two different views between the two groups: end-users and leadership for L&D within the police. The suggested explanation behind this difference is that each group has different motivations and goals behind using the game where one is more practice impact-orientated and one more organisational objective-focused. For example, users from the IT department were mainly considering issues related to security and technical infrastructure, while users from early recruits were considering aspects that were related to their job practice such as building rapport with the child witness. Enhancement of these aspects would have a positive impact on their job practice.

Moreover, there is clear variation between the targeted training outcomes and objectives for each group. For group 1, learners aspired to achieve the learning aims through completing the training and being engaged by making links between ideas to achieve deep learning. Deep learning is learning through a set of learning outcomes that includes thinking critically and solving complex problems, working collaboratively and communicating effectively (Gee, 2003, Kirriemuir and McFarlane, 2004). On the other hand, group 2 learners, who are strategic planners and decision makers, tried the game to assess its efficacy from different angels (i.e., technically, and financially). From the educational point, participants in group 2 accepted new facts and learned ideas uncritically and this is known as surface learning. The variance between findings from both groups in table 2 demonstrated differences between the perspectives of end-users (i.e., bottom-up) and leadership (i.e., top-bottom) for learning and development within the police force. There appear to be contrasting motivations and goals behind using the game in phase 1 and 2 and the decision of implementing the game in phase 3. The next section discusses the influential factors in embedding technology (CWIS in the study context) in organisations (police sector in the study context) for CPD.

DISCUSSION

Significant Issues in Embedding GBL in the Police Sector

Sharing of Knowledge in the Policing Context

The following section addresses sharing knowledge as one of the most pervasive barriers in the organisational culture according to the literature and study findings.

Within an organisation, there is a need for an effective infrastructure to manage knowledge effectively and support the processes of knowledge sharing, transfer and use (Abrahamson *et al.*, 2014). For CPD, according to Michalski (2014), changing organisational culture and structures have weakened the legitimacy of using technology in CPD and ultimately its ability to effectively engage and enrol a significant mass of professionals. Referring to Ertmer (1999) around first and second barriers in imbedding TEL in training, we claim that sharing knowledge can inform a cross disciplinary CPD (Top-Bottom-Top) approach. In detail, intra-sharing of knowledge and vision within an organisation can help to prioritise and order these barriers and respond to them in accordance with the individual and organisational needs and objectives.

In the policing context, police practices and procedures are governed by laws and departmental rules that are enforced by the courts and the police hierarchies respectively (Wall, 2017). In response to the technological which encouraged more online communication and collaboration using web 2.0 technology (O'Reilly, 1995), the threat from cybercrime grows - whether it's fraud, data theft, grooming and exploitation of children or stalking and harassment. However, IT infrastructure is required to be able to support shared online learning including webinars, virtual classrooms and e-conferences to meet national and force training requirements. According to the study findings, for the IT department in Policing, in order to comply with security precautions and confidential protection procedures, sharing of knowledge has to be limited.

There are two poles of sharing knowledge through technology in Policing. Firstly, policing has to focus on protecting people from this type of harm through the development of new tactics and capabilities (NPCC, vision of 2025). However, new devices, such as driverless cars and virtual reality, pose new risks and opportunities for the police service.

Moreover, according to the College of Policing (2017), technology that is based on a co-sharing culture considers the new technical learning development through retiring legacy courses which are no longer valid or used. Therefore, according to the College of Policing, this will take some time as it involves making important decisions on the future of some existing national systems.

The Policing Vision 2025 report (APCC and NPCC, 2016) identifies sharing intermediaries as facilitating greater indirect benefits (such as changing roles and responsibilities and improved social interaction) rather than direct benefits (such as cost and time saving). These intermediaries have been argued to be "Boundary creators" (Adams *et al.*, 2013). It was noted that the people who cross these boundaries bring new ideas and practices into the domain. According to Adams *et al.* (2019), a sharing barrier is identified based on the parity of value given to different types of knowledge (i.e., between professional judgement and research evidence knowledge). Consequently, the result is perceived to be poor cultural ability to learn from mistakes and likelihood to repeat errors.

The link between lack of poor sharing of knowledge within the organisation and the implementation of TEL is explained by Ertmer and Ottenbreit-Leftwich (2010), where poor sharing is addressed in lack of collaboration with external bodies and lack of co-working. In TEL, this isolates between recipients of learning in the organisation and technology providers and separates learning outcomes from technology. Consequences of this separation influences CPD plans leading to "tick box" training where security and limited sharing of knowledge outweigh the importance and benefits of achieving learning objectives.

As a proposed practice for sharing of knowledge in the study findings, intra-sharing between police forces was addressed strongly as one of the prioritised gaps in police professional practices. However, to bridge this gap, within the Randomised Controlled Trial (RCT) and commercialisation of CWIS, some engaging activities have been conducted which could facilitate the concept of sharing between participants. The researchers argue that these engaging activities introduced and facilitated the concept of sharing of knowledge when implementing the game in training. CWIS design approach was a participatory design approach and this helped in the co-creation of evaluation methods for practice-based learning. Through co-creating game designs, we can provide a more effective solution for practice needs and customers. Examples of evidence-based practice include Evidence café and tricky topics. These events gathered Community of Practice (CoP) (Wenger, 2006) as a group of people (police staff members) who share a concern for something they do and want to learn how to do it better as they interact regularly through creating channels of communication between designers (i.e., academics, developers) and end users. According to Meloncon and Oswal (2014), CoPs can facilitate meetings, events and broadcasts in order to demonstrate the benefits, share success stories and connect relevant people. Moreover, CoPs alleviate many of the curricular and institutional challenges which online instructors face.

For the organisation role, in order to implement TEL in CPD, there are requirements to establish a culture of pervasive learning:

1. Pedagogically, it is important to create a learning experience that is more cognisant of a learner's needs, preferences, and location whilst aligning the e-learning training to their work. (Roy and Raymond, 2008). This learning environment aims to adopt a personalised approach.
2. Technically, systems are improved and their costs reduced through utilising technology systems - design e-learning for emerging web standards and adopt standard web technologies.

In summary, from a CPD perspective, lack of sharing views does not give a clear view for the CPD needs and would lead to designing and planning training programs that are not responsive to the staff needs. Moreover, it will result in a "Tick Box" training and learning as an outcome of this training can be surface learning instead of deep learning. The benefit of sharing knowledge in CPD is that training programs are strategically aligned to organisational needs. Furthermore, within the co-construction of knowledge, training evaluation can reflect the individual's needs and their learning objectives. On the other hand, lack of a sharing culture results in a CPD top-bottom approach consisting of tick box training and focusing on learning pouches solely.

Top-Bottom Approach

In this section, we focus on the difference between top-bottom and bottom-top approaches in organisations and the subsequent impact on CPD planning. "Top-Bottom" means giving the roles at the top of the organisation where there is more control over key decisions than those lower in the hierarchy. "Bottom-up" means having little to no centralised control so that those doing the work are free to organise, make decisions, and perform as they best see fit.

Within the CWIS project, it is worth mentioning that the game project reviewed both individual concepts and organisational needs. The difference between both approaches was clear when comparing between the participants' hierarchy based on phase 1 (bottom) and those in phase 2 (top and bottom). However, the voice in decision making was for the top-level management in the organisation (phase 2 in the project).

According to the objectives of each group of participants (see table 2), there was a clear difference between the two groups. In phase 1, participants were educators and practitioners who discussed topics between them around features of deep learning such as engagement and self confidence in job practices. In phase 2, participants' background and jobs were different so their outcomes were different. For example, a dominant topic of discussion was about security and data sharing, while the archived learning was not an emerging topic.

According to (Sisney, 2012), the top-bottom extremist approach believes that an autocratic, hierarchical style of command-and-control decision-making is necessary for an organisation to be successful, whilst the bottom-up extremist approach believes that most forms of hierarchy are unnecessary and inefficient. This finding agrees with Adams *et al.* (2018), they explain that hierarchical culture means that innovations in sharing are often initiated or approved top-down and tied to leadership. The hierarchical culture is also perceived as providing poor clarity on what is of value to share and how to effectively share.

To overcome the barrier of the centralised control of top-bottom approach, McChrystal (2015) explains that rather than relying on authority, the design-centric leader almost exclusively depends on feedback, communication, relationships, and influence on sense and respond to environmental signals occurring from within and outside the organisation. In CWIS, we found that the co-design approach facilitates participants to communicate, discuss, identify challenges and find solutions collaboratively. However, in commercialisation and decision-making process, aspects such as shared feedback, cross organisation communication were not evident and each group (IT, finance, etc) was communication individually.

CONCLUSION AND RECOMMENDATIONS

In the police sector, equipping police staff members with innovative technologies has high priority to keep pace with changing technology and develop professional skills. In Policing, where work practice has its high-risk nature to be repeated in real life practice, GBL simulates a task in a risk-free and controlled environment and allows an easy transition of players through its virtual reality training into the real world. Consequently, embedding GBL in CPD for staff in the police sector develops making decisions, critical thinking and problem-solving skills in increasingly difficult circumstances.

From this study, TEL design in general GBL in particular can enhance learning if it is well-integrated into a wider system for individual and organisational development. Therefore, there are two points which have been concluded around organisational culture. *Firstly*, when embedding GBL in L&D, further consideration is required around the organisational and individuals' culture towards the adoption and implementation of technology. Furthermore, sharing of knowledge and encouraging collaboration between hierarchical levels within the organisation when embedding technology in work practice are enablers. However, limited sharing and collaboration between individuals is a barrier as this is a hindrance to bridge the gap between both individual and organisational views and expectations. *Secondly*, when planning to implant TEL in CPD, ordering and prioritising the factors that influence this implementation is not a "one size fits all" approach as it can be a barrier in an organisation and an enabler in another.

This could also be an aspect that is first order priority in one organisation and a second order priority in another. Finally, key stakeholders (i.e., trainers and trainees) need to be identified and appropriately consulted to have the necessary skills in order to improve the likelihood of success. To achieve the latter recommendation, we recommend creating the Community of Practice (CoP) and encourage knowledge exchange between members of this community. This will seek to develop an understanding of learning that fulfils practice changes (deep learning) whilst also supporting the achievement of organisational strategic objectives (surface learning). This approach would then support a CPD plan that would consider and acknowledge the objectives, needs and preferences of the TEL beneficiaries (end-user stakeholders) rather than simply providing learning that is a simple "tick box" CPD process.

Finally, as a reflection of the successful implementation of CWIS and in order to give the full picture to the audience, we recommend a follow-on research where participants from police forces will be divided into two groups, controlled group that does not experience CWIS in their training followed by interviewing children as part of their routine daily work. Experiment group that experiences the simulation and completed the training followed by interviewee children. Then, comparing and measuring the impact of this training on the efficacy of police officers' job practice.

REFERENCES

Abrahamson, D. E., & Goodman-Delahunty, J. (2014). Impediments to Information and Knowledge Sharing Within Policing: A Study of Three Canadian Policing Organizations. *SAGE Open*, *4*(January). Advance online publication. doi:10.1177/2158244013519363

Adams, A., Clough, G., & FitzGerald, E. (2018). *Police Knowledge Exchange: Summary Report*. The Open University.

Adams, A., Clough, G., & FitzGerald, E. (2018). *Police Knowledge Exchange: Full Report 2018*. The Open University.

Adams, A., FitzGerald, E., & Priestnall, G. (2013). Of catwalk technologies and boundary creatures. *ACM Transactions on Computer-Human Interaction*, *20*(3), 15. doi:10.1145/2491500.2491503

Adams, A., Hart, J., Iacovides, I., Beavers, S., Olivera, M., & Margoudi, M. (2019). Co-created Evaluation: Identifying how games support police learning. *International Journal of Human-Computer Studies*, *132*, 34–44. doi:10.1016/j.ijhcs.2019.03.009

Alexander, C. (2018). *A Technology Enhanced Learning (TEL) Framework À La Hierarchy Of Needs*. Educational Technology. Online at: https://elearningindustry.com/technology-enhanced-learning-tel-framework-hierarchy-needs

Andersen, J. P., & Gustafsberg, H. (2016, April). A Training Method to Improve Police Use of Force Decision Making: A Randomized Controlled Trial. *SAGE Open*, *6*(2). Advance online publication. doi:10.1177/2158244016638708

Backlund, P., & Hendrix, M. (2013). Educational games-are they worth the effort? A literature survey of the effectiveness of serious games. In *Games and virtual worlds for serious applications (VS-GAMES), 2013 5th international conference on* (pp. 1-8). IEEE.

Bauer, W. I. (2010). Your Personal Learning Network: Professional Development on Demand. *Music Educators Journal*, *97*(2), 37–42. doi:10.1177/0027432110386383

Bayne, S. (2015). What's the matter with 'technology-enhanced learning'? *Learning, Media and Technology*, *40*(1), 1, 5–20. doi:10.1080/17439884.2014.915851

Biggs, J. (1999). *Teaching for Quality Learning at University*. SHRE and Open University Press.

Binsubaih, A., Maddock, S., & Romano, D. (2006). A serious game for traffic accident investigators. *Interactive Technology and Smart Education*, *3*(4), 329–346. doi:10.1108/17415650680000071

Blandford, A. (2013). Semi-structured qualitative studies. In M. Soegaard & R. F. Dam (Eds.), *The Encyclopedia of Human-Computer Interaction* (2nd ed.). The Interaction Design Foundation. http://www.interaction-design.org/ encyclopedia/semi-structured_qualitative_studies.html

Boyle, E. A., Hainey, T., Connolly, T. M., Gray, G., Earp, J., Ott, M., Lim, T., Ninaus, M., Ribeiro, C., & Pereira, J. (2016). An update to the systematic literature review of empirical evidence of the impacts and outcomes of computer games and serious games. *Computers & Education*, *94*, 178–192. doi:10.1016/j.compedu.2015.11.003

Buabeng-Andoh, C. (2012). 'Factors influencing teachers' adoption and integration of information and communication technology into teaching: A review of the literature'. *International Journal of Education and Development Using Information and Communication Technology*, *8*(1), 136–155.

Clarke, V., & Braun, V. (2013). Teaching thematic analysis: Overcoming challenges and developing strategies for effective learning. *The Psychologist*, *26*(2), 120–123.

Czaja, J. S. (2017). PhD, The Role of Technology in Supporting Social Engagement Among Older Adults. *The Public Policy and Aging Report*, *27*(4), 145–148. doi:10.1093/ppar/prx034

Darling-Hammond, L., & McLaughlin, M. W. (1995). Policies that support professional development in an era of reform. *Phi Delta Kappan*, *76*(8), 597–604.

DeVries, I. (2018) The Student Experience of Distance Education over Time – A Research Challenge. *Distances et médiations des savoirs*. doi:10.4000/dms.2739

Ertmer, P. A. (1999). Addressing first- and second-order barriers to change: Strategies for technology integration. *ETR&D*, *47*(4), 47–61. doi:10.1007/BF02299597

Gee, J. P. (2003). *What video games have to teach us about literacy and learning*. Academic Press.

Gill, G. (2013). Culture, Complexity, and Informing: How Shared Beliefs Can Enhance Our Search for Fitness. *Informing Science: The International Journal of an Emerging Transdiscipline*, *16*.

Gordon, N. (2014). *Flexible Pedagogies: Technology-Enhanced Learning*. The Higher Education Academy (HEA). Available at: https://www.heacademy.ac.uk/flexible-pedagogies-technology-enhanced-learning

Gusky, T. (2000). *Evaluating Professional Development*. Corwin.

Handy, C. B. (1999). *Gods of management: The changing work of organizations*. Oxford University Press.

HMCPSI Her Majesty's Crown Prosecution Service Inspectorate / HMIC. (2014). *Achieving Best Evidence in Child Sexual Abuse Cases – A Joint Inspection, December 2014*. Available from: www.justiceinspectorates.gov.uk/cjji/wp-content/uploads/sites/2/ 2014/12/CJJI_ABE_Dec14_rpt.pdf

HMIC. (2015). *In harm's way: the role of the police in keeping children safe HM Crown Prosecution Service Inspectorate (HMCPSI) and HM Inspectorate of Constabulary (HMIC)*. https://www.justiceinspectorates.gov.uk/hmic/wpcontent/uploads/in-harms-way.pdf

Jones, W. M., & Dexter, S. (2014). How teachers learn: The roles of formal, informal, and independent learning. *Educational Technology Research and Development, 62*(3), 367–384. doi:10.100711423-014-9337-6

Kirkwood, A., & Price, L. (2014). Technology-enhanced learning and teaching in higher education: What is "enhanced" and how do we know? A critical literature review. *Learning, Media and Technology, 39*(1), 1–44. http://oro.open.ac.uk/36675/1/TEL%20in%20Higher%20Education-What%20is%20enhanced%20and%20how%20do%20we%20 know.pdf

Kirriemuir, J., & McFarlane, A. E. (2004). *Literature Review in Games and Learning*. Futurelab. Available http://www.futurelab.org.uk/resources/documents/lit_reviews/Games_Review.pdf

McChrystal, S. (2015). *Team of Teams: New Rules of Engagement in a Complex World*. https://organizationalphysics.com/2016/10/13/top-down-vs-bottom-up-hierarchy-or-how-to-build-a-self-managed-organization/

Meyer, J., & Land, R. (2006). Overcoming barriers to student understanding: Threshold concepts and Troublesome Knowledge. In J. Meyer & R. Land (Eds.), *Overcoming Barriers to Student Understanding: Threshold concepts and Toublesome Knowledge* (pp. 19–32). Routledge.

Michalski, M. P. (2014). Symbolic meanings and e-learning in the workplace: The case of an intranet-based training tool. *Management Learning, 45*(2), 145–166. doi:10.1177/1350507612468419

NPCC (National Police Chiefs' Council). (2016). *Policing Vision 2025*. London: APCC and NPCC. Available at: www.npcc.police.uk/documents/ Policing%20Vision.pdf

O'Reilly, T. (2005) *What is Web 2.0: Design patterns and business models for the next generation of software*. Available at: http://www.oreillynet.com/pub/a/oreilly/tim/news/2005/09/30/what-is-web-20.html

Oswal, S. K., & Meloncon, L. (2014). Paying Attention to Accessibility When Designing Online Courses in Technical and Professional Communication. *Journal of Business and Technical Communication, 28*(3), 271–300. doi:10.1177/1050651914524780

Parker, K. (2018). Impact and Knowledge Exchange for STEM Disciplines. *The Open University Workshop*.

Penuel, W., Fishman, B., Yamaguchi, R., & Gallagher, L. (2007). What Makes Professional Development Effective? Strategies That Foster Curriculum Implementation. *American Educational Research Journal, 44*, 921-958. . doi:10.3102/0002831207308221

Ramsden, P. (1992). *Learning to Teach in Higher Education*. Routledge.

Ross, C. R., Maninger, R. M., LaPrairie, K. N., & Sullivan, S. (2015). The use of Twitter in the creation of educational professional learning opportunities. *Administrative Issues Journal, 5*(1), 55–76. doi:10.5929/2015.5.1.7

Roy, A., & Raymond, L. (2008). *E-Learning as a Solution to the Training Problems of SMEs - A Multiple Case Study*. WEBIST.

Sclater, M., & Lally, V. (2016) Critical TEL: The importance of theory and theorisation. In *Proceedings of the 10th international conference on networked learning 2016*. University of Lancaster.

Sisney, L. (2012). Organizational Physics: The Science of Growing a Business. Academic Press.

Vygotsky, L. S. (1978). *Mind in Society*. Harvard University Press.

Walker, R. (2016). *Survey of technology enhanced learning for higher education in the UK*. Universities and Colleges Information Systems Association.

Wall, D. S. (2017). *Cyberspace Crime*. Routledge. doi:10.4324/9781315199627

Wenger, E. C. (2006). *Communities of Practice: A brief introduction*. Available at: http://www.ewenger.com/theory/index.htm

Wood, D., & Tong, S. (2009). The future of initial police training: A university perspective. *International Journal of Police Science and Management, 11*(3), 294-305.

KEY TERMS AND DEFINITIONS

CPD: Continuing Professional Development refers to the process of tracking and documenting the skills, knowledge, and experience that you gain both formally and informally as you work, beyond any initial training.

CWIS: Child Witness Interview Simulation is a developed online simulation for learning and development in the Police sector to address gaps in the knowledge and skills when interviewing child witnesses.

GBL: Games-Based Learning is the integration of gaming into learning experiences to increase engagement and motivation.

HMIC (Her Majesty's Inspectorate of Constabulary and Fire & Rescue Services): Has statutory responsibility for the inspection of the police forces.

L&D (Learning and Development): Term used to describe everything a business does to encourage professional development among its employees.

NPCC (National Police Chiefs' Council): Is a national coordination body for law enforcement in the United Kingdom and the representative body for British police chief officers.

TEL (Technology-Enhanced Learning): The application of technology to teaching and learning.

APPENDIX

CWIS Screenshots

CWIS provides an interactive scenario where one takes on the role of an officer that needs to interview a nine-year-old boy, who allegedly witnessed a woman being attacked on his way home from school. The first episode requires the trainee to take an 'initial response' account from the child at their home whilst the second episode requires the trainee to conduct a full ABE (Achieving Best Evidence) interview for the purposes of gathering evidence.

Figure 4. Episode 1(interviewing a child at home) & Episode 2 (interviewing a child in the police station)

Chapter 25
Embracing Simulations and Problem–Based Learning to Effectively Pair Concepts of Aeronautics With Flight Safety Training

Ioanna K. Lekea
Hellenic Air Force Academy, Greece

Dimitrios G. Stamatelos
Hellenic Air Force Academy, Greece

ABSTRACT

Cadets, in order to become pilots, apart from successfully passing their flight training program, need to also complete their academic education, where many technical subjects, such as aeronautics, exist. Cadets often face difficulties in comprehending certain concepts in the subject "aeronautics" as well as the applied link between aeronautics and flight safety. To this end, at the Hellenic Air Force Academy, an innovative educational tool is under development so as to facilitate students' understanding of the practical use of aeronautics and its impact on aircraft safety. An important aspect of the proposed educational tool is that it can be easily adopted into the pilots' flight training program and offer a complimentary training experience regarding mid-air crisis scenarios. The new educational tool is based on introducing in-class simulation and problem-based learning, thus combining theory and practice. The aim of this chapter is to describe the development of this educational tool and to demonstrate the way that it can be employed for academic and flight training purposes.

DOI: 10.4018/978-1-7998-9223-6.ch025

INTRODUCTION

Trainee pilots who study the subject of 'Aeronautics', as part of their academic education, have difficulties in comprehending certain fundamental concepts. Moreover, they struggle to understand the applied link between Aeronautics and flight safety, which is of great importance. Therefore, in HAFA, an innovative educational tool that simulates cases of flight crisis and relates them to aeronautics and physics is under development with the purpose of facilitating students to deeply realise the practical use of Aeronautics to the modern aircraft design, as well as the impact of it to aircraft's safety. Furthermore, the proposed educational simulation is suitably developed to allow its utilization to the pilots' flight training program offering them a complimentary training experience regarding mid-air crisis incidences. Consequently, the tool can be used in both academic training (Aeronautics) and flight training in a targeted interdisciplinary case-study analysis for in-flight risk management and for the discussion of flight safety issues. Thus, the ultimate aim of the educational tool is to assist trainee pilots to comprehend in an applied manner fundamental concepts, such as: loading conditions, stresses, critical structural areas, safety issues etc.

The aim of this chapter is to firstly demonstrate the approach followed for developing the educational tool and to present the changes occurred in the teaching methodology of the subject of Aeronautics in HAFA and, secondly, to describe the way that it can be part of the flight training program. The new educational approach is based on introducing in class simulation, serious games and problem based learning. To this end, the teaching methodology on the aforementioned subject will be briefly documented; accordingly, the difference between the teaching approach before and after the utilization of the simulations and simulators, as part of the Laboratory of Aeronautics, will be evident. A detailed discussion will highlight the changes that the simulation and simulators brought to the teaching process from the point of view of the educational personnel, as well as of the trainee pilots.

Consequently, the educational tool is presented in detail, while currently is in the trial phase. This tool aims to assist trainee pilots to visualize and comprehend among other, the way the forces exerted on the aircraft at critical events or in critical phases of the flight (e.g. during take-off or landing and can create flight hazards. In this context, in flight crises are categorized according to the type of hazard they pose (structural, aerodynamic etc.) and the degree of risk they cause to the flight.

In the following steps the conformed design process is described;

1. The concept stage was completed by defining the objectives and the expected educational outcomes of our tool.
2. We then moved to the elaboration stage concerning the parameters (e.g. height of flying, aircraft speed, geometry of structural components, configuration, forces exerted etc.) that are related to flight safety and could pair well with an interdisciplinary approach to aeronautical decision making. Preliminary investigation of whether fundamental concepts of Aeronautics are well and clearly understood by the trainee pilots in relation to their effects on flight (HAFA, Courses: Aeronautics II & III for the Stream of Pilots). To this end, field research took place with questionnaires that were specifically formulated to serve the research questions and that were distributed to both trainee pilots and flight instructors.
3. Development and testing of the scenarios that are simulated and visualized, in order to cover a range of incidents. The scenarios' specifications, along with their parameters and the technical elements are analysed and are fully justified.

4.   Development of an educational tool in order to visualize the behaviour of the aircraft in a selected scenario and to analyse the risks posed to the flight.

The aforementioned procedure led to the development of a prototype educational tool that was tested through its pilot application in class. A field research followed with the purpose of providing us input on the satisfaction of the students and the amount of help the simulation actually provided to them in terms of relating the academic education with the flight training; let us not forget that using the simulation tool cadets are supposed to get help in understanding the aeronautics and physics behind the emergency procedures.

HOW ARE PILOTS CURRENTLY TAUGHT AERONAUTICS

The Aeronautics II & III Modules, according to the HAFA's Students' Guide are to be dealt in a theoretical manner. However, cadets seem to have difficulties in understanding fundamental concepts and their relation to flight. So, a more applied approach is clearly needed in order to help future pilots understand the interrelation between Aeronautics and flight safety, especially in relation to mid-air crises. To this end, academic education and flight training need to come together in a Module, which will make cadets realize the implications of physics and aeronautics, but in an applied way (Ören 2017).

When we come to think how to effectively prepare pilots involved in a potential crisis management in mid-air, the first think that strikes our minds is to extensively train and educate them well and in depth, so those, who could find themselves in critical situations, to be able to understand and describe what is happening, and, also, to make decisions or act or both. Therefore, given the differences between a theoretical education and a realist training, the second point needs to be effectively and fully addressed (Ouyang, Sun & Li 2021). One thing is certain: we need to prepare pilots before the crisis comes around, so we must start discussing the safety issues as early as possible and as in much depth as possible (Boyd 2017, Casner, Geven & Williams 2013).

Trainee pilots usually start discussing flight safety issues (Federal Aviation Administration 2011) on a theoretical level during the first semester of their studies. Modules like Aeronautics are not linked to flight safety and cadets learn how to deal with mid-air crises at the practical level, without understanding how a crisis evolves and why they need to follow the particular steps described in their check list. However, can a theoretical approach be considered as a successful way of training on safety procedures? Apparently not, trainees definitely need to know how things work in theory (physics and mechanics), but they also need to practice on decision making and taking actions when there is no time to lose. Therefore, we need to provide pilots both with the theoretical background and the hands-on training, if we want them to be able to effectively deal with emergencies.

Given the aforementioned and the educational scope of HAFA, in order to enhance trainee pilots' knowledge on flight safety and emergency procedures, we thought it is extremely important to plan, design and develop the Aeronautics II & III Modules in an interactive, problem based learning experience for educational purposes (Petroski 2012, Brodeur 2002, Mohd et al. 2004), designed to provide pilots with an in depth academic experience on dealing with critical situations related to flight safety. The idea is that using real-life and hypothetical case studies, trainee pilots will have the opportunity to practice their theoretical knowledge and think by themselves how to best handle difficult situations in mid-air. Also, they will be able to consider different options and think about their actions in risky situations, when there is no time to lose. Consequently, a new educational tool for teaching Aeronautics, which would take into account flight safety and in-flight risk management, was created.

DO WE NEED A CHANGE? GAMIFICATION AND PROBLEM BASED LEARNING FOR EFFECTIVE EDUCATION

The innovation of our approach, to teaching Aeronautics with specific reference to flight safety, is that it truly brings problem based learning as an applied, yet academic, element in flight training. Nowadays, the main educational approach to flight safety training is a mixture of providing totally theoretical knowledge in class (Aeronautics) and hand-on-training either by a real flight either with the use of a flight simulation (Blow 2012, Schank et al. 2002). As it can be seen from Table 1 each educational approach has an essential limitation that doesn't promote a holistic educational approach, as it doesn't lead students to link theory (as in Aeronautics courses) to practice (ensuring conscious flight safety during flight training and during all flights after successful completion of studies). That leads to the conclusion that a change, in a fundamental level, is required to overcome the difficulties that the current methodology possess.

Table 1. Methodological approaches to combine academic education on Aeronautics and flight training on safety and emergency procedures

Solution 1	Provide trainee pilots with the theoretical aeronautical background in class, then by the use of appropriate documentaries or educational films give them a view of a critical situation and, finally, by role-playing put them in the shoes of those who had to deal with a flight emergency.
Limitation 1	But while studying and analysing flight manuals, rules and safety regulations may help trainees to think of the appropriate action one should take in a critical situation, this educational approach cannot prepare pilots to deal with complex situation in limited real time while being under stress. This is because they learn and discuss various approaches to deal with emergencies, but mainly in theory. One needs a more systematic approach to handle real life emergencies effectively.
Solution 2	Discuss safety regulations before or after a real or simulated flight takes place during briefing or debriefing are also used in order to provide pilots with a useful framework, so as to reflect on emergencies in a more organized context.
Limitation 2	The applied approach is not missing, since a discussion and analysis of applied issues takes place and theory is combined with practice (even when the flight simulator is used). However, trainee pilots have no access to specially developed educational materials that will help them understand the reason (Aeronautics) behind the actions.
Solution 3	Use of approved and tested scenarios with limited risk for the trainee pilots involved during real or simulated flight to make trainees get the real feeling of an emergency situation.
Limitation 3	It is not advisable to train pilots in dangerous situations in order to show them how to deal with mid-air crises no matter how limited the danger might be. In mid-air any additional unforeseen factor might put the flight in real danger. As far as the flight simulator (Kozuba & Bondaruk 2014, Landman et al 2018) is concerned, this may be a better option (Byrnes 2017, Taylor 2014), but we should not forget that for the use of flight simulator, a flight officer always must be available. Therefore, trainees cannot even practice virtually as frequently as they would wish.

Problem based learning, as well as games and simulations (Clarke 2017, Doskow 2012, Newman 2002), on the other hand, allow us to cater for these aspects. Employing the proposed educational tool everything will be put to the test: theoretical knowledge, different approaches, and hard choices (Korteling, Helsdingen & Sluimer 2017, Hays 2005, Helmreich 2000). A number of developed scenarios and cases will allow trainee pilots to work together and test how they would cooperate in difficult situations (Sun 2007, Veldkamp et al. 2020, Westrum et al. 2017). Using simulations and games to introduce the applied element in the module has a number of advantages (Nistor 2018). Gamification (Welbers, Konijn, Burgers et al. 2019) is an educational approach that can increase learners' motivation and engagement by incorporating game design elements in educational environments (Dichev & Dicheva 2017). Students, through the use of educational games, improve their particular skills and optimize their learning (Smiderle, Rigo, Marques et al. 2020), but also enhance their critical thinking and decision making (Patrício, Moreira & Zurlo 2020, Patrício, Moreira, Zurlo & Melazzini 2020, Patrício, Moreira & Zurlo 2018). Of course, gamification and game-based learning does not fit all educational environments and not all learning can be gamified, which means that other educational approaches should balance the ratio between the theoretical and the applied elements of our Modules (Hernández-Fernández, Olmedo-Torre, Peña 2020).

Regarding the students' evaluation of the Aeronautics II & III Modules (before the introduction of our educational tool in class), we designed a questionnaire (Lavrakas 2008) using a 5-point Likert scale to assess trainee pilots' knowledge after completing the aforementioned Modules. The questionnaire was distributed to 2nd and 3rd year cadets (Stream of pilots) at the Hellenic Air Force Academy who had completed the Modules during the academic years: 2017-18, 2018-19 and 2019-20. In total, 146 students participated (98% of the total population, who attended the Modules). The results of our field research showed that even cadets who succeeded both Courses could discuss fundamental concepts of Aeronautics in a theoretical manner (88%), but those concepts were not well and clearly understood in relation to flight (63%) for the majority of the trainees. More specifically, cadets stated that they only MODERATELY understand how the following parameters affect aircraft's safety and performance: the permissible stress (35%), the safety factor (37%), the angle of the wing or the curvature of the airfoil (44%), the elastic center (27%) or the aeroelasticity (32%), the reversal effect of the rudders (42%) or the effect of flutter (20%). Furthermore, cadets stated that because of the (mainly) theoretical approach of the Modules, they could only MODERATELY:

- understand how the design, the technical and construction components affect the speed, the maneuverability and the limits of the aircraft (32%),
- relate how the design and the technical elements could help them effectively react to potential critical in-flight incidents (35%),
- comprehensively understand the limits of the aircraft (32%),
- fully understand the safety issues that the aircraft limits set to the flight (32%),
- interrelate plane crashes to limitations of the aircraft design and/or specific technical issues (17%),
- discuss in detail with technological argumentation and examples how the design and the technical/construction component can ensure flight safety (32%),
- debate on whether specific types of air accidents could be prevented (29%), and,
- discuss with technological argumentation if and how specific types of in-flight crises could be handled (35%).

It is no surprise that 92% of the cadets requested that the two Modules had a more applied approach and discuss flight with specific case studies. Cadets stated the two Modules would be more interesting if they were related to flight (structure limitations and aircraft stability, maneuvers, design and its effects on control). Among the hypothetical scenarios and real-life cases trainee pilots sought to be examined were mid-air crises (66%), human error combined with mechanical failure (18%), mechanical failure combined with harsh weather (14%) and others (12%) (Wiegmann & Shappell 2003, National Transportation Safety Board 2021, Federal Aviation Administration 2021, Air Accidents Investigation Branch 2021, Australian Transport Safety Bureau 2021, The Judge Advocate General's Corps 2021, Embry-Riddle Aeronautical University/Hunt Library 2021).

Taking those results into consideration, our proposed educational tool aims, firstly, to holistically educate (Virovac 2017) trainee pilots on flight safety from day one they enter the Academy. Secondly, to enhance the use of traditional techniques and role playing to teach the theoretical background. Thirdly, to use our interactive, educational scenarios to further test the theoretical background, but also to make trainees to put to test their knowledge, their ability for critical thinking and cooperation with other trainees (if the scenario has to do with flight in formation). Finally, to benefit from the mixed method of testing the theoretical knowledge per se, as well as its application in a virtual practice platform.

The benefits of our proposed method will help us provide future pilots with well-rounded training. Traditional techniques can still be used in order to provide an effective education (on the theoretical background of physics and mechanics) and applied training experience (briefing/debriefing, analysis of flight emergencies, role playing etc.), but trainees will also be able to use our virtual escape room in order to:

a)   test the level of their theoretical knowledge,
b)   check how stress and time limitations affect how knowledge is applied in practice, and,
c)   get virtual hands-on training, and, the most complete possible education, in terms of theory and practice.

Trainees will also get the best possible training, in terms of both theory and practice, whenever they feel like using our educational tool on their Personal Computer (PC) or smartphone.

Trainee pilots' evaluation will be based on their choices, decisions and actions within the simulated emergency situation. At the end of the game, trainees will be presented with the list of options they made and how it rated against the different flight parameters that determined its payoff. Module moderators will be able to use the evaluation in a de-briefing class after the game.

The first step for our educational tool was to develop emergency scenarios to virtually train future pilots in a variety of situations of graduated difficulty with time constraints. For each scenario we made sure to prepare tables that relate principles of aeronautics to emergency flight management, so that trainees will understand how important physics are to flight safety and why every time we need to take the steps we take. We used the T-6A Texan II aircraft, which is an aircraft that trainee pilots fly in our Academy, as the aircraft of our case-studies.

In order to develop and test our scenarios we followed the following procedure, which is schematically presented in Figure 1.

Figure 1. The development of our scenarios

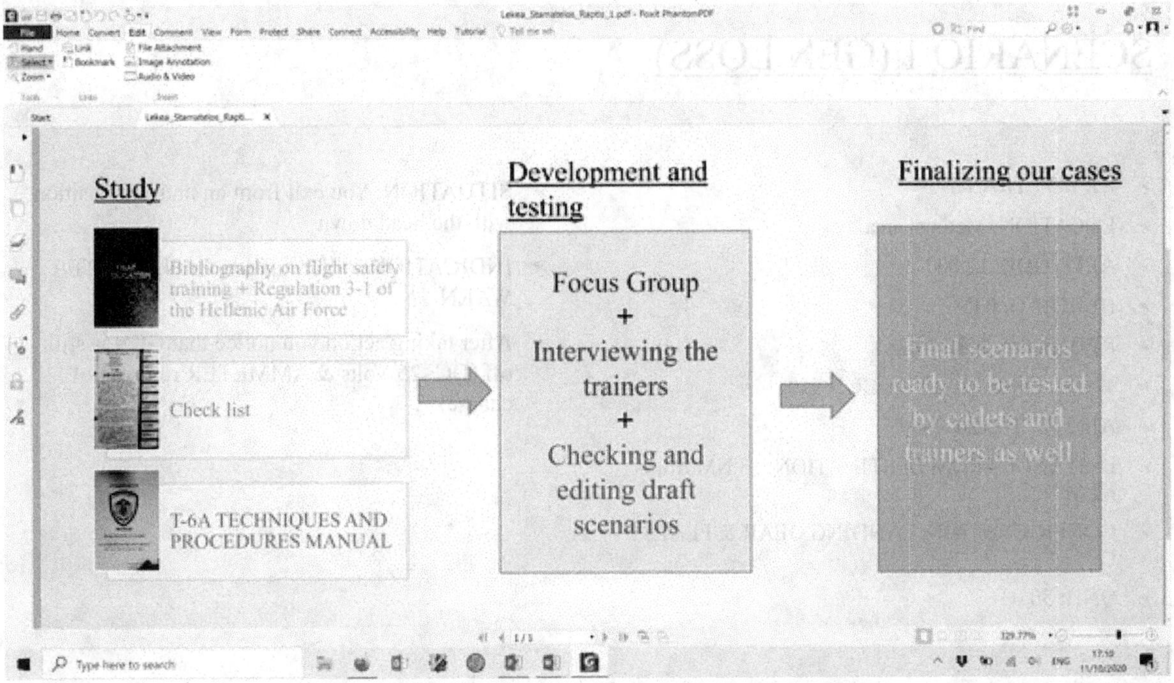

We studied paying particular importance to the Check List and the T-6A Techniques and Proceedings Manual and then, we used focus groups and interviews with the flight officers in order to test our scenarios and edit them or change any parameter that wasn't right.

Each scenario has a different level of difficulty and needs specific knowledge of aeronautics in order to be dealt with. Also, the time frame for the trainee to handle each critical situation is different, depending on the issues that he/she has to face and the phase of the flight (limited time is available during take-off and landing for obvious reasons).

A short presentation of the parameters of each scenario is available in Figures 2-5, starting from the most manageable one to the most difficult.

Figure 2. Level of Difficulty 1. Scenario on Generator Failure

SCENARIO 1 (GEN LOSS)

- ID: MYSTRAS 69
- LOCATION: Methoni area
- ALTITUDE: 12.000′
- HEADING: 045°
- RWY in use: 35L
- WEATHER: FEW 020, BKN 080
- AIRSPEED: 120 Kts
- DISTANCE FROM DESTINATION: 18 NM from KLM
- CONFIGURATION: LANDING GEAR & FLAPS UP
- QNH: 30.03

- SITUATION: You exit from an unusual position with the head down
- INDICATIONS: illumination GEN, MASTER WARN
- After taking action you notice that GEN is still off (DC<25 Volts & AMMETER runs out of charge).

Figure 3. Level of Difficulty 2. Scenario: Smoke in the cockpit

SCENARIO 2 (SMOKE IN THE COCKPIT)

- ID: MYSTRAS 69
- LOCATION: FILIATRA
- ALTITUDE: 15.000′
- HEADING: 270°
- AIRSPEED: 110 Kts
- DISTANCE FROM DESTINATION: 15 NM from KLM
- CONFIGURATION: LANDING GEAR & FLAPS UP
- RWY in use : 35L
- QNH: 29.92
- WEATHER: OVC 080, SCT 030

- SITUATION: You perform an unusual position with the head up
- INDICATIONS: Smoke in the cockpit (smell of plastic). Smoke remains even after taking action.

Figure 4. Level of Difficulty 3. Scenario: Engine Stall/Failure

SCENARIO 3 (ENGINE STALL/FAILURE)

- ID: MYSTRAS 69
- LOCATION: Pylos area
- ALTITUDE: 15.000´
- HEADING: 120°
- AIRSPEED: 140 Kts
- DISTANCE FROM DESTINATION: 22 NM from KLM
- CONFIGURATION: LANDING GEAR & FLAPS UP
- RWY in use : 17R
- QNH: 29.80
- WEATHER: CAVOK

- SITUATION:
  • Manoeuvre: Loop, shortly after the reverse
  • Loss of power and accompanied by a noticeable change in engine noise
- INDICATIONS:

1. Complete loss of power
2. Speed reduction
3. Lower N1, torque, ITT
4. Lower oil pressure, lower propeller movement, low fuel flow, low hydraulic pressure
5. INDICATIONS: Gen, Fuel PX, OIL PX, OBOGS Fail, PMU Fail, CKPT PX

Figure 5. Level of Difficulty 4. Scenario: Low Hydraulic Pressure and Uncommanded Propeller Feather

SCENARIO 4 (LOW HYDRAULIC PRESSURE AND UNCOMMANDED PROPELLER FEATHER)

- ID: MYSTRAS 69
- MANEUVER: TAKE OFF
- ALTITUDE: 700´
- HEADING: 350°
- AIRSPEED: 140 Kts
- DISTANCE FROM DESTINATION: 2 NM from KLM
- CONFIGURATION: LANDING GEAR & FLAPS UP
- RWY in use : 35L
- QNH: 29.88
- WEATHER: CAVOK

- INDICATIONS:
1. Loss of power
2. LowerNp
3. Increased torque
4. Master Warn, PMU FAIL
5. CHIP
- During landing configuration the following indications appear:
I. Master Caution
II. HYDR FL LO

A short presentation of the difficulty parameters for each scenario can be found in Table 2, starting from the most manageable one (Scenario 1) to the most difficult (Scenario 4). Please, note that each situation needs specific actions to be dealt with, so:

i.   trainees have to both think and use the information provided to them in the aircraft's manual and the check list, but

ii. they also have to explain in terms of physics and aeronautics why these choices will help manage the situation and bring the aircraft to safe flight conditions.

Table 2. Levels of Difficulty to Different Scenarios

Scenario	Level of difficulty	Type of emergency	Parameters to exceed difficulty	Situation	Indications	Narratives
1	I	Generator Failure	**Weather**, Distance from destination, configuration	Trainee exits from an unusual position with the head down.	Illumination GEN, MASTER WARN	After taking off trainee notices that GEN is still off (DC<25 Volts & AMMETER runs out of charge)
2	II	Smoke in the Cockpit	**Weather**, Distance from destination, configuration	Trainee exits from an unusual position with the head up.	Smoke in the cockpit and smell of plastic.	Smoke remains even after taking action.
3	III	Engine Stall/ Failure	**Altitude, Distance from destination**	Manoeuvre: loop, shortly after the reverse. Loss of power, accompanied by a noticeable change in engine noise.	Gen. Fuel PX. OIL PX. OBOGS FAIL. PMU FAIL. CKTP PX.	Complete loss of power. Speed reduction. Lower N1, torque, ITT. Lower oil pressure. Lower propeller movement. Low fuel flow. Low hydraulic pressure.
4	IV	Low Hydraulic Pressure and Uncommanded Propeller Feather	**Manoeuvre**: take off	Loss of power. Lower Np. Increased torque.	Master Warn. PMU FAIL. CHIP.	During landing configuration, the following indications appear Master Caution & HYDR FL LO.

Our simulation is played via an e-tool that students can use in class or in their free time, in order to test their knowledge. First of all, they have to identify the problem that causes the crisis and deal with it. Critical parameters and flight data, e.g. height, speed, distance from the airport, flight area, flight course and the corridor in use are displayed on screen at the beginning of the simulation.

After identifying the emergency, the trainee pilot / student must deal with it in the most appropriate way, succeeding in the following tasks:

1) **Classification of actions:** In this section the student has to put some steps in the correct order. These steps consist of the actions that he must follow in order to escape the dangerous situation that he previously recognized. The actions are displayed in the form of cards and the student needs to

sort them in the right order. Depending on the scenario and the level of difficulty, the student will have to classify all the available options that are provided by the game story, or at a more difficult level, he/she will have to classify additional tabs with similar actions that appear as part of the game story with the sole purpose of confusing the student's judgment. At this point, the student must ignore any extra, unneeded actions. And of course, he/she must also identify the principles of aeronautics and physics that support the choices made. This is a critical educational parameter of the simulation, because the student must link theory (academic education) to practice (flight training), in order to gain a better and deeper understanding of the steps identified in the emergency check lists as necessary in order to maintain the safety of the flight.

2) **Analysis of Actions:** This is the largest part of our simulation e-tool, and it is divided into several smaller sections, which correspond to the analysis and examination of each of the actions that the student put in the correct order in the previous part. In each of these sections the student is asked to provide justification based on the material of the Aeronautics' courses.

Getting to the final part of the simulation, the student is asked to answer some multiple-choice questions, which are related to the particular scenario he/she dealt with. These questions may refer to details of the respective checklist, boldface, or in-flight guide and test the respective student's knowledge, which is necessary to address the emergency in hand.

Upon completion of these answers the educational game ends and the player score is displayed. The batch results are automatically displayed on the screen, and they consist of a list of all the parts of the game, next to which it is written whether the player succeeded or failed. At the same time, if:

- the game was part of a test in class or a course prerequisite the results will be automatically sent to the academic tutor,
- the student chooses to play the game individually, just to test his/her knowledge, if he/she provided the email of his/her academic tutor and/or flight trainer at the beginning of the game, then the results will be automatically sent to the them as well, along with the date and time, the game difficulty level and the scenario played.

This will complete the evaluation of the student/player.

PRELIMINARY ASSESSMENT OF OUR EDUCATIONAL APPROACH

A briefing on the scenarios was initially held for the trainee pilots and then, they were prompted to run the simulation. After using the e-tool (simulation), we asked them to evaluate it by answering specifically developed questionnaires (Creswell & Poth 2018) using a 5-point Likert scale to measure satisfaction (Table 3). So, through the questionnaires each trainee could express his/her point of view regarding the scenario he/she played and the factors that influence his/her choices. We chose to begin our testing phase with pilot trainees, because for them it is extremely important to understand a critical situation for the flight and bring their knowledge together in order to deal with it effectively.

Table 3. The 5-point Likert scale

Very satisfied	Satisfied	Neither satisfied nor dissatisfied	Dissatisfied	Very dissatisfied

We were particularly interested in the evaluation of the realism and the educational validity of our scenarios, but, also, wanted to see whether the amount of time given to the trainees was sufficient for them to run the simulation in as close to real life terms as possible, and, finally, to ensure that the appropriate recommended steps to deal with each critical situation had been taken into account.

The questionnaires were distributed to 4th year cadets (Stream of pilots) at the Hellenic Air Force Academy (academic year 2020-21). In total, 46 questionnaires were collected (a trustworthy research sample covering the 95% of the target population) for the first assessment of the scenarios of our simulation. Additionally, 28 trainees, who graduated the previous academic year (2019-2020) and are now completing their flight training at the 120 Air Training Wing (which is located in the area of Kalamata), participated in our research, covering the 60% of the targeted population of the particular Air Training Wing. All of them had previously successfully completed the courses of Aeronautics, therefore they were able to answer the relevant questions and fill in the sections needed. The results from the field research and the simulation trials are compared with trainee pilots' theoretical knowledge and the findings are highlighted below.

The results we received were extremely encouraging, as the vast majority of the targeted population was satisfied with:

- the realism of the game (40% & 40% identified themselves in the scales VERY SATISFIED & SATISFIED respectively),
- the response to the theory (48% & 32% chose the scales VERY SATISFIED & SATISFIED respectively), and,
- its contribution in maintaining the interest of the player / trainee (32% & 52% chose the scales VERY SATISFIED & NEITHER SATISFIED NOR DISSATISFIED respectively).

Trainees (76%) expressed the view that the simulation helped them realize the importance of theoretical understanding of the flight and its elements. They, also, stated (89%) that the questions in our educational tool / simulation that asked them to relate the application of theory to real life, made them link the information provided in the manual of the aircraft and the emergency procedures checklists to the materials they studied as part of the Aeronautics courses. Documentaries that were played in the courses, case studies and briefing and de-briefings before and after each of their flight came together for the 74% of the trainees who played the simulation.

Regarding the technical elements of our educational tool, such as the choice of colors (Table 4) and the clarity of displaying the information, the vast majority of respondents chose the scales VERY SATISFIED & SATISFIED in percentages of 52 & 28% and 52 & 36% respectively. The satisfaction from the sound as a mean to show the severity of the crisis was high (52% & 12% on the scales VERY SATISFIED & SATISFIED and NEITHER SATISFIED NOR DISSATISFIED respectively), but we were concerned about the appearance of 28% of the respondents who stated that they were DISSATISFIED with the stress caused through the sound. However, 20 & 32% of the sample considered the stress challenge VERY SATISFIED & SATISFIED respectively.

Table 4. Satisfaction of the trainees in relation to certain technical aspects of the simulation

	Very satisfied	Satisfied	Neither satisfied nor dissatisfied	Dissatisfied	Very dissatisfied
Realism of the game	40	40	12	8	Ø
Maintaining the trainee's interest	32	52	12	4	Ø
Response of the game to theory	48	32	16	4	Ø
Colors on the screen	52	28	4	12	4
Sound as a means to simulate stress	20	32	12	28	8

In terms of keeping the trainees' interest, the sound seems to help significantly, as the vast majority of the sample population chose the scales VERY SATISFIED & SATISFIED at a rate of 44 & 40% respectively, while for the sound as a precursor to the plot the scales VERY SATISFIED & SATISFIED were chosen at a percentage of 24 & 32% respectively.

The vast majority of the sample population was VERY SATISFIED & SATISFIED by the transmission of data and information, as those parameters were rated at 35% & 46% respectively.

According to the vast majority of our sample there was sufficient time for thought (76%) and action (80%).

In total:

- ° 54% of those, who participated in the trial of the e-tool simulation and filled in our questionnaire, stated that they felt stressed during the game process,
- ° 91% stated that they felt they were being examined (which is a reality, since the e-tool is developed to be used as an evaluation tool both in academic education and in flight training, however, we still have to deal with this issue and make the e-tool as pleasant as possible),
- ° 89% stated that they received real virtual experience and appeared VERY SATISFIED with the evaluation and understanding of their mistakes (72%) and VERY SATISFIED with the objectivity of the results (60%).

Furthermore, 60% of the sample stated that they prefer to receive the results of the game automatically through the platform compared to the remaining 40% who would like to be informed by their instructor. De-briefing the results of the simulation, either individually (with each student than has completed it), either collectively (but in an anonymous manner) in class (during the Aeronautics courses) or in flight safety lectures, is a great element for the tutor or the flight instructor as well. And this is because both the tutor and the flight instructor can get crucial information about the level, extent and depth of their students' knowledge, as well as their ability to critical think and interrelate all available information that students receive as a result of both their academic education and flight training.

FUTURE RESEARCH DIRECTIONS

Scenarios and our e-tool simulation will be further developed so as to cover new areas and dilemmas related to aeronautics and mid-air crises. In the future, other types of mid-air crisis will be also included in the simulation options such as overload/metal fatigue, pilot error and design flaw, loss of vertical stabilizer, propeller manufacturing defect, roof separated from fuselage, in-flight wing failure due to fatigue etc.

From both our field research and interviews (Lekea, Stamatelos & Raptis 2021) it appears that games and simulations are deemed necessary for trainees' education and training on flight safety. An extension of our e-tool to a full virtual escape room with an educational focus, which can be remotely accessed and runs in a full digital mode, as well as any new methodology of training on emergencies, would be helpful as a complimentary approach to study (theoretical approach), actually flying and using the flight simulation along with briefing and debriefing. But there are specific parameters that need to be in effect in order to make sure that the education purpose is served. On the future extended digital platform, trainees should feel the amount of stress they would feel, if they had to deal with a real in-flight emergency. Therefore, 3D graphics, time and sound warnings should be as realistic as possible.

In this paper we have described the salient points of our simulation e-tool, briefly discussed the scenarios that are so far included in it, and presented the evaluation of the pilot testing of our e-tool simulation. In the future, we need to reflect on the challenge, i.e., how we can introduce an educational method that will cover both the theoretical background, but also fully digitally and remotely provide with the much-needed training in realistic situations without compromising the safety of the flight trainees.

Our scenarios are part of a currently under development and testing virtual simulation, accessed digitally through a platform, available for smartphones, tablets and/or PCs. Our goal is to further develop and use those scenarios for a completely virtual, digitally supported, 3D experience, where trainees will have to use their knowledge of the aircraft and flight safety procedures, but also test their ability to critical examine flight parameters and prioritize their thoughts over the problem they face. In addition, we have to make sure that trainees receive a valid, straightforward assessment of their choices, because otherwise they might be tempted to think that everything is relevant and even excusable in times of danger, which is not true. Scenario, storytelling, narratives and the visuals of the simulation must be evaluated and confirmed as educationally valid.

Therefore, the main objectives of our future VR digital simulation on flight safety (that will replace our currently in trial use simulation e-tool) are:

a) to facilitate the transition between theoretical education on the subjects of flight safety and emergency procedures to applied hands-on training,

b) to provide trainees –through a simulated environment– with the analytic tools, in order to understand why safety rules and emergency procedures are mandatory and how to effectively use their knowledge to face possible critical situations that could arise during the flight, but, also,

c) to make education and training on emergency procedures and flight safety, easily and remotely accessible to the trainees even from their room and when flight instructors are not around.

Consequently, the evolution of the e-tool presented in this paper and the design of our future VR simulation game based on it will refer to real-life flight emergencies, and trainees will definitely need to study the theoretical framework before playing the game. At the end of the game and after their choices are evaluated, they will receive a full report of how they applied the acquired knowledge of aeronautics and the safety rules. In this way trainees will fully understand the connection between theory and practice.

On the technical level, our future goal is that our scenarios will be supported by a fully digital simulation that can be played by one or multiple players, who will have the opportunity to fly alone or in formation. State of the art machine learning and artificial intelligence methods are currently tested, in order to automate processes in the game play.

The first prototype of our simulation e-tool was out for testing and use during flight training on May 4, 2021 at 120 Air Training Wing of the Hellenic Air Force. More scenarios are prepared and are currently tested; they are further enhanced by additional reading and supporting bibliography that can be found at the end of each scenario. Also, some short tests follow each emergency scenario consisting of multiple choice questions, true or false (T/F) questions and multiple choice questions for the trainees to answer. The schedule is to incorporate and use the tool in class as a way of both educating and evaluating cadets (implementation period of about 12 months). We expect to use our simulation for the 2nd and 3rd year cadets in the spring term of 2022. As far as the VR simulation is concerned, we are also working on its development with the goal of testing its prototype in the spring term of 2023.

CONCLUSION

The main educational objectives of our simulation e-tool and the scenarios incorporated in it are:

a) to make students use the knowledge they acquainted during Aeronautics courses in a practical way in order to facilitate the transition between theoretical education on the subjects of flight safety and emergency procedures,

b) to enhance education and training on emergency procedures and flight safety with the application of problem based learning techniques.

Therefore, the design of our simulation was based on real-life fight emergencies, and trainee pilots need to study the theoretical framework (Aeronautics, flight manual and check list) before playing the game. This way they will fully understand the connection between theory and practice from the beginning of their studies, as cadets.

From the field research we conducted we received important information about the educational gains of our approach. Participants admitted that applying their knowledge on Aeronautics in order to virtually cope with scenarios of in-flight crisis helped them to better understand the emergency procedures and feel more confident in dealing with possible real life incidents.

The e-tool used for our simulation provided trainee pilots with some sort of virtual experience related to aircraft construction and safety issues and gave them the opportunity to both play and understand the role of Aeronautics to flight engineering and flight safety. Additional reading and supporting bibliography that can be found at the end of each scenario further enhance the educational experience.

Trainees, who used our simulation e-tool at the testing phase, admitted that their understanding of how aeronautics influence the flight and the treatment of mid-air crises was improved with the use of a synthetic educational approach and the use of problem based learning. The simulation provided them with virtual experience on how to deal with mid-air emergencies and how to make informed choices, when they had no piecemeal solutions to choose from; in other words, they had to:

a)   combine their knowledge,
b)   apply critical thinking to solve the problem they had to face,
c)   resolve practical issues, and,
d)   fully justify their choices.

In terms of educational gain, our e-tool didn't just help trainee pilots better understand flight safety and their choices when dealing with an emergency situation, which is great benefit of course, but it has another important element as well: it can be also used by tutors and flight instructors as a means to get crucial information about the level, extent and depth of their students' knowledge, their ability to critical think and combine everything they know in order to escape a flight disaster.

ACKNOWLEDGMENT

We would like to cordially thank the flight officers of the 120 Air Training Wing for participating in our research and for providing us with valuable information that helped us develop and correct the scenarios that form the basis of our simulation.

This research received no specific grant from any funding agency in the public, commercial, or not-for-profit sectors, however it was supported by the Hellenic Air Force Academy, and in particularly the War Games Laboratory and the Laboratory of Strength of Materials.

REFERENCES

Abu Hassan. (2004). A review and survey of Problem-Based Learning application in Engineering Education. *Proceedings of the Conference on Engineering Education.*

Air Accidents Investigation Branch. (2021). *Air Accidents Investigation Branch reports.* Available online: https://www.gov.uk/aaib-reports

Australian Transport Safety Bureau. (2021). *Aviation safety investigations & reports.* Available online: https://www.atsb.gov.au/publications/safety-investigation-reports/?mode=Aviation

Blow, C. (2012). *Flight school in the virtual environment: Capabilities and risks of executing a simulations-based flight training program.* School of Advanced Military Studies.

Boyd, D. D. (2017). A review of general aviation safety (1984–2017). *Aerospace Medicine and Human Performance, 88*(7), 657–664. doi:10.3357/AMHP.4862.2017 PMID:28641683

Brodeur, D., Young, P. W., & Blair, K. B. (2002). Problem Based Learning in Aerospace Engineering Education. *Proceedings of the 2002 American Society for Engineering Education Annual Conference & Exposition.*

Byrnes, K. P. (2017). Employing flight simulation in the classroom to improve the understanding of the fundamentals of instruction among flight instructor applicants. *Journal of Aviation/Aerospace Education Research*, *26*(1), 49–63. doi:10.15394/jaaer.2017.1623

Casner, St., Geven, R., & Williams, K. (2013). The Effectiveness of Airline Pilot Training for Abnormal Events. *Human Factors*, *55*(3), 477–485. doi:10.1177/0018720812466893 PMID:23829023

Clarke, S., Peel, D., Arnab, S., Morini, L., Keegan, H., & Wood, O. (2017). EscapED: A Framework for Creating Educational Escape Rooms and Interactive Games to For Higher/Further Education. *International Journal of Serious Games*, *4*(3), 73–86. doi:10.17083/ijsg.v4i3.180

Creswell, J.W. & Poth, C. N. (2018). Qualitative Inquiry & Research Design: Choosing Among Five Approaches. *Sage (Atlanta, Ga.).*

Dichev, C., & Dicheva, D. (2017). Gamifying education: what is known, what is believed and what remains uncertain: a critical review. *International Journal of Educational Technology in Higher Education*, *14*(9), 9. Advance online publication. doi:10.118641239-017-0042-5

Doskow, M. G. (2012). *Analysis of the Impact of Scenario-Based Training on the Aeronautical Decision Making of Collegiate Flight Students*. Embry-Riddle Aeronautical University.

Embry-Riddle Aeronautical University/Hunt Library. (2021). *NTSB Aircraft Accident Reports (AAR)*. Available online: https://huntlibrary.erau.edu/collections/aerospace-and-aviation-reports/ntsb/aircraft-accident-reports

Federal Aviation Administration. (2011). *Aviation Instructor's Handbook (FAA-H-8083-9)*. FAA Publications. https://www.faa.gov/regulations_policies/handbooks_manuals/aviation/aviation_instructors_handbook/media/11_aih_chapter_9.pdf

Federal Aviation Administration. (2021). *Accident and Incident Data*. Available online: https://www.faa.gov/data_research/accident_incident/

Fotaris, P., & Mastoras, T. (2019). Escape Rooms for Learning: A Systematic Review. In *Proceeding of the 13th European Conference on Games Based Learning* (pp. 235-243). Academic Press.

Hays, R. T. (2005). *The effectiveness of instructional games: A literature review and discussion. Technical Report*. Naval Air Warfare Center. doi:10.21236/ADA441935

Helmreich, R. L. (2000). On error management: Lessons from aviation. *BMJ (Clinical Research Ed.)*, *320*(7237), 781–785. doi:10.1136/bmj.320.7237.781 PMID:10720367

Hernández-Fernández, A., Olmedo-Torre, N., & Peña, M. (2020). Is Classroom Gamification Opposed to Performance? *Sustainability*, *12*(23), 9958. doi:10.3390u12239958

Korteling, H. J. E., Helsdingen, A. S., & Sluimer, R. R. (2017). An Empirical Evaluation of Transfer-of-Training of Two Flight Simulation Games. *Simulation & Gaming*, *48*(1), 8–35. doi:10.1177/1046878116671057

Kozuba, J., & Bondaruk, A. (2014). Flight simulator as an essential device supporting the process of shaping pilot's situational awareness. *AFOSR*, *1*, 41–60.

Landman, A., van Oorschot, P., van Paassen, M. M., Groen, E. L., Bronkhorst, A. W., & Mulder, M. (2018). Training pilots for unexpected events: A simulator study on the advantage of unpredictable and variable scenarios. *Human Factors*, *60*(6), 793–805. doi:10.1177/0018720818779928 PMID:29913086

Lavrakas, P. J. (2008). *Encyclopedia of survey research methods* (Vol. 1-0). Sage Publications, Inc. doi:10.4135/9781412963947

Lekea, I. K., Stamatelos, D. G., & Raptis, P. (2021). Learning how to escape the unthinkable with virtual reality: the case of pilots' training on emergency procedures. In *IOP Conference Series: Materials Science and Engineering, 10th EASN International Conference on Innovation in Aviation & Space to the Satisfaction of the European Citizens (10th EASN 2020)* (vol. 1024, Issue 1, pp. 012098). 10.1088/1757-899X/1024/1/012098

National Transportation Safety Board. (2021). *Investigation Reports. Aviation.* Available online: https://www.ntsb.gov/investigations/AccidentReports/Pages/Reports.aspx?mode=Aviation

Newman, D. (2002). *Interactive Aerospace Engineering and Design.* McGraw Hill.

Nistor, G. (2018). The Advantages of Gamification and Game-Based Learning. *The International Scientific Conference eLearning and Software for Education, 1*, 308-312.

Ören, T., Turnitsa, C., Mittal, S., & Diallo, S. Y. (2017). *Simulation-based learning and education.* Springer.

Ouyang, T., Sun, H., & Li, F. (2021). Researches on the Education Reform for the Core Competencies-oriented Flight Training of Civil Aviation Pilots. In *Proceedings of the 6th International Conference on Education Reform and Modern Management (ERMM 2021).* Atlantis Press. 10.2991/assehr.k.210513.088

Patrício, R., Moreira, A. C., & Zurlo, F. (2018). Gamification Approaches to the Early Stage of Innovation. *Creativity and Innovation Management, 27*(4), 499–511. doi:10.1111/caim.12284

Patrício, R., Moreira, A. C., & Zurlo, F. (2020). Enhancing design thinking approaches to innovation through gamification. *European Journal of Innovation Management.* Advance online publication. doi:10.1108/EJIM-06-2020-0239

Patrício, R., Moreira, A. C., Zurlo, F., & Melazzini, M. (2020). Co-Creation of New Solutions through Gamification: A Collaborative Innovation Practice. *Creativity and Innovation Management, 29*(1), 146–160. doi:10.1111/caim.12356

Petroski, A. (2012). Games vs. Simulations: When Simulations May Be a Better Approach. *T+D Magazine, 66*(2), 27.

Schank, J. F., Thie, H. J., Graff, C. M. II, Beel, J., & Sollinger, J. (2002). *Finding the right balance: Simulator and live training for navy units.* RAND.

Smiderle, R., Rigo, S. J., Marques, L. B., Peçanha de Miranda Coelho, J. A., & Jaques, P. A. (2020). The impact of gamification on students' learning, engagement and behavior based on their personality traits. *Smart Learning Environments, 7*(3), 3. Advance online publication. doi:10.118640561-019-0098-x

Sun, R., Lei, W., & Zhang, L. (2007). Analysis of Human Factors Integration Aspects for Aviation Accidents and Incidents. In *Proceedings of 7th Engineering Psychology and Cognitive Ergonomics International Conference (EPCE 2007)* (pp. 834-841). Academic Press.

Taylor, A., Dixon-Hardy, D. W., & Wright, S. J. (2014). Simulation training in UK general aviation: An undervalued aid to reducing loss of control accidents. *The International Journal of Aviation Psychology*, *24*(2), 141–152. doi:10.1080/10508414.2014.892762

The Judge Advocate General's Corps. (2021). *AIB Reports*. Available online: https://www.afjag.af.mil/AIB-Reports/

Veldkamp, A., Grint, L., Knippels, M.-C., & van Joolingen, W. (2020). Escape Education: A Systematic Review on Escape Rooms in Education. *Educational Research Review*, *31*, 1–18. doi:10.1016/j.edurev.2020.100364

Virovac, D., Domitrovic, A., & Bazijanac, E. E. (2017). The Influence of Human Factor in Aircraft Maintenance. *PROMET – Traffic & Transportation, 29*(3), 257.

Welbers, K., Konijn, E. A., Burgers, C., de Vaate, A. B., Eden, A., & Brugman, B. C. (2019). Gamification as a tool for engaging student learning: A field experiment with a gamified app. *E-Learning and Digital Media*, *16*(2), 92–109. doi:10.1177/2042753018818342

Westrum, R. & Adamski, A. J. (2017). Organizational factors associated with safety and mission success in aviation environments. *Human Error in Aviation*, 475–512.

Wiegmann, D. A., & Shappell, S. A. (2003). *A Human Error Approach to Aviation Accident Analysis: The Human Factors Analysis and Classification System*. Routledge. doi:10.4324/9781315263878

KEY TERMS AND DEFINITIONS

Aeronautics: The study of the science of flight.

Aircraft Flight Manual (AFM): A manual, associated with the Certificate of Airworthiness, containing limitations within which the aircraft is to be considered airworthy, and instructions and information necessary to the flight crew members for the safe operation of the aircraft.

Crisis Management: Identification of a threat to an organization and its stakeholders in order to respond effectively to the threat.

Educational Simulation: A simulation created to facilitate learning on the part of students or trainees.

Emergency and Abnormal Checklist (EAC): A handbook containing checklists of actions which are the initial response element of Emergency and Abnormal procedures.

Flight Safety: The state of the aviation system or organization in which the risks associated with aviation activities related to the operation of aircraft or directly providing such operation are reduced to an acceptable level and monitored.

In-Flight Emergency Procedures: A plan of actions to be conducted in a certain order or manner, in response to a specific class of reasonably foreseeable emergency, a situation that poses an immediate risk to the flight.

Game-Based Learning: The design and development of learning activities that can incrementally introduce concepts and guide students towards an educational goal.

Problem-Based Learning: A student-centered educational approach in which students learn about a given subject through the experience of solving an open-ended problem found in trigger material.

VR: A simulated experience that can be similar to or completely different from the real world, developed for entertainment or educational purposes.

Compilation of References

A Comprehensive List of 90 Gamification Cases with ROI Stats. (2016). Retrieved October 10, 2021, from https://yukaichou.com/gamification-examples/gamification-stats-figures

Aboujaoude, E., Gega, L., Parish, M. B., & Hilty, D. M. (2020). Editorial: Digital Interventions in Mental Health: Current Status and Future Directions. *Frontiers in Psychiatry*, *11*(February), 10–12. doi:10.3389/fpsyt.2020.00111 PMID:32174858

Abou-Shouk, M., & Soliman, M. (2021). The impact of gamification adoption intention on brand awareness and loyalty in tourism: The mediating effect of customer engagement. *Journal of Destination Marketing & Management*, *20*, 100559. doi:10.1016/j.jdmm.2021.100559

Abrahamson, D. E., & Goodman-Delahunty, J. (2014). Impediments to Information and Knowledge Sharing Within Policing: A Study of Three Canadian Policing Organizations. *SAGE Open*, *4*(January). Advance online publication. doi:10.1177/2158244013519363

Abt, C. (1970). *Serious games: The art and science of games that simulate life*. Viking Compass Book.

Abt, C. C. (1987). *Serious games*. University Press of America.

Abu Hassan. (2004). A review and survey of Problem-Based Learning application in Engineering Education. *Proceedings of the Conference on Engineering Education*.

Abu-Shanab, E. A., & Al-Sayed, M. R. (2019). Can Gamification Concepts Work With E-Government? *Journal of Information Technology Research*, *12*(3), 44–59. doi:10.4018/JITR.2019070103

Accidental Queens. (2017). Another Lost Phone: Laura's Story (iOS Version) [Video game]. France.

Açikgöz, Ö., & Günay, A. (2020). The early impact of the Covid-19 pandemic on the global and Turkish economy. *Turkish Journal of Medical Sciences*, *50*(SI-1), 520–526. doi:10.3906ag-2004-6 PMID:32283904

Adams, A., Clough, G., & FitzGerald, E. (2018). *Police Knowledge Exchange: Full Report 2018*. The Open University.

Adams, A., Clough, G., & FitzGerald, E. (2018). *Police Knowledge Exchange: Summary Report*. The Open University.

Adams, A., FitzGerald, E., & Priestnall, G. (2013). Of catwalk technologies and boundary creatures. *ACM Transactions on Computer-Human Interaction*, *20*(3), 15. doi:10.1145/2491500.2491503

Adams, A., Hart, J., Iacovides, I., Beavers, S., Olivera, M., & Margoudi, M. (2019). Co-created Evaluation: Identifying how games support police learning. *International Journal of Human-Computer Studies*, *132*, 34–44. doi:10.1016/j.ijhcs.2019.03.009

Adams, J. S. (1965). Inequity in social exchange. *Advances in Experimental Social Psychology*, *2*, 267–299. doi:10.1016/S0065-2601(08)60108-2

Adelmant, V. (2021, April 20). *Social Credit in China: Looking Beyond the "Black Mirror" Nightmare*. Centre for Human Rights and Global Justice. https://chrgj.org/2021/04/20/social-credit-in-china-looking-beyond-the-black-mirror-nightmare/

Adukaite, A., van Zyl, I., & Cantoni, L. (2016). The role of digital technology in tourism education: A case study of South African secondary schools. *Journal of Hospitality, Leisure, Sport and Tourism Education*, *19*, 54–65. doi:10.1016/j.jhlste.2016.08.003

Aggarwal, C. C. (2016). *Recommender Systems: The Textbook. Charm*. Springer.

Agirdag, O., Merry, M. S., & Van Houtte, M. (2016). Teachers' understanding of multicultural education and the correlates of multicultural content integration in Flanders. *Education and Urban Society*, *48*(6), 556–582. doi:10.1177/0013124514536610

Agnieszka, W. S. (2014). Gamification as a new trend in marketing. *Marketing and Management of Innovations*, *4*, 57–64.

Agostino, D., Arnaboldi, M., & Lampis, A. (2020). Italian state museums during the COVID-19 crisis: From onsite closure to online openness. *Museum Management and Curatorship*, *35*(4), 362–372. doi:10.1080/09647775.2020.1790029

Agrawal, V., Duggirala, M., & Chanda, S. (2018). Journey: A game on positive affect. *CHI PLAY 2018 - Proceedings of the 2018 Annual Symposium on Computer-Human Interaction in Play Companion Extended Abstracts*, 373–379. 10.1145/3270316.3271532

Aguiar Castillo, L., Rufo Torres, J., De Saa Pérez, P., & Pérez Jiménez, R. (2018). *How to encourage recycling behaviour? The case of WasteApp: a gamified mobile application*. Sustainability.

Aguiar-Castillo, L., Clavijo-Rodriguez, A., Saa-Perez, D., & Perez-Jimenez, R. (2019). Gamification as an approach to promote tourist recycling behavior. *Sustainability*, *11*(8), 2201. doi:10.3390u11082201

Aguilar, J., Díaz, F., Altamiranda, J., Cordero, J., Chavez, D., & Gutierrez, J. (2020). Metropolis: Emergence in a Serious Game to Enhance the Participation in Smart City Urban Planning. *Journal of the Knowledge Economy*. Advance online publication. doi:10.100713132-020-00679-5

Ahmad, A., Maynard, S. B., & Shanks, G. (2015). A case analysis of information systems and security incident responses. *International Journal of Information Management*, *35*(6), 717–723. doi:10.1016/j.ijinfomgt.2015.08.001

Ahn, S. J., Johnsen, K., & Ball, C. (2019). Points-based reward systems in gamification impact children's physical activity strategies and psychological needs. *Health Education & Behavior*, *46*(3), 417–425. doi:10.1177/1090198118818241 PMID:30678507

Ahtinen, A., Mattila, E., Välkkynen, P., Kaipainen, K., Vanhala, T., Ermes, M., Sairanen, E., Myllymäki, T., & Lappalainen, R. (2013). Mobile mental wellness training for stress management: Feasibility and design implications based on a one-month field study. *JMIR mHealth and uHealth*, *1*(2), e11. doi:10.2196/mhealth.2596 PMID:25100683

Aiken, L. H., Sermeus, W., Van den Heede, K., Sloane, D. M., Busse, R., McKee, M., Bruyneel, L., Rafferty, A. M., Griffiths, P., Moreno-Casbas, M. T., Tishelman, C., Scott, A., Brzostek, T., Kinnunen, J., Schwendimann, R., Heinen, M., Zikos, D., Sjetne, I. S., Smith, H. L., & Kutney-Lee, A. (2012). Patient safety, satisfaction, and quality of hospital care: Cross sectional surveys of nurses and patients in 12 countries in Europe and the United States. *BMJ (Clinical Research Ed.)*, *344*(2), e1717. doi:10.1136/bmj.e1717 PMID:22434089

Aiken, L. H., Sloane, D. M., Bruyneel, L., Van der Heede, K., & Sermeus, W. (2013). Nurses' reports of working conditions and hospital quality of care in 12 countries in Europe. *International Journal of Nursing Studies*, *50*(2), 143–153. doi:10.1016/j.ijnurstu.2012.11.009 PMID:23254247

Air Accidents Investigation Branch. (2021). *Air Accidents Investigation Branch reports*. Available online: https://www.gov.uk/aaib-reports

Ajzen, I. (1985). From intentions to actions: A theory of planned behavior. In *Action control* (pp. 11–39). Springer. doi:10.1007/978-3-642-69746-3_2

Ajzen, I. (1991). The theory of planned behavior. *Organizational Behavior and Human Decision Processes, 50*(2), 179–211. doi:10.1016/0749-5978(91)90020-T

Alahäivälä, T., & Oinas-Kukkonen, H. (2016). Understanding persuasion contexts in health gamification: A systematic analysis of gamified health behavior change support systems literature. *International Journal of Medical Informatics, 96*, 62–70. doi:10.1016/j.ijmedinf.2016.02.006 PMID:26944611

Al-Azawi, R., Al-Faliti, F., & Al-Blushi, M. (2016). Educational gamification vs. game based learning: Comparative study. *International Journal of Innovation, Management and Technology, 7*(4), 132–136. doi:10.18178/ijimt.2016.7.4.659

Albertazzi, D., Ferreira, M. G. G., & Forcelli, F. A. (2019). A Wide View on Gamification. *Technology. Knowledge and Learning, 24*(2), 191–202. doi:10.100710758-018-9374-z

Aldemir, T., Celik, B., & Kaplan, G. (2018). A qualitative investigation of student perceptions of game elements in a gamified course. *Computers in Human Behavior, 78*, 235–254. doi:10.1016/j.chb.2017.10.001

Alderfer, C. P. (1969). An empirical test of a new theory of human needs. *Organizational Behavior and Human Performance, 4*(2), 142–175. doi:10.1016/0030-5073(69)90004-X

Aleem, S., Capretz, L. F., & Ahmed, F. (2016). Game development software engineering process life cycle: A systematic review. *Journal of Software Engineering Research and Development, 4*(1), 6. Advance online publication. doi:10.118640411-016-0032-7

Aleksandrovna, M. S. (2020). *Impact of gamification in marketing on consumer behavioural intentions* [Doctoral dissertation]. St. Petersburg University.

Alexander, C. (2018). *A Technology Enhanced Learning (TEL) Framework À La Hierarchy Of Needs*. Educational Technology. Online at: https://elearningindustry.com/technology-enhanced-learning-tel-framework-hierarchy-needs

Algashami, A., Cham, S., Vuillier, L., Stefanidis, A., Phalp, K., & Ali, R. (2018). *Conceptualising Gamification Risks to Teamwork within Enterprise*. Springer International Publishing. doi:10.1007/978-3-030-02302-7_7

Allal-Chérif, O., & Bidan, M. (2017). Collaborative open training with serious games: Relations, culture, knowledge, innovation, and desire. *Journal of Innovation and Knowledge, 2*(1), 31–38. doi:10.1016/j.jik.2016.06.003

Allam, A., Kostova, Z., Nakamoto, K., & Schulz, P. J. (2015). The effect of social support features and gamification on a Web-based intervention for rheumatoid arthritis patients: Randomized controlled trial. *Journal of Medical Internet Research, 17*(1), e3510. doi:10.2196/jmir.3510 PMID:25574939

Allen, T. D., & Poteet, M. L. (1999). Developing Effective Mentoring Relationships: Strategies From the Mentor's Viewpoint. *The Career Development Quarterly, 48*(1), 59–73. doi:10.1002/j.2161-0045.1999.tb00275.x

AlMarshedi, A., Wills, G. B., & Ranchhod, A. (2015). The Wheel of Sukr: A Framework for Gamifying Diabetes Self-Management in Saudi Arabia. *Procedia Computer Science, 63*, 475–480. doi:10.1016/j.procs.2015.08.370

AlMarshedi, A., Wills, G., & Ranchhod, A. (2016). Gamifying self-management of chronic illnesses: A mixed-methods study. *JMIR Serious Games, 4*(2), e5943. doi:10.2196/games.5943 PMID:27612632

Almarzooq, Z. I., Lopes, M., & Kochar, A. (2020). Virtual Learning During the COVID-19 Pandemic. *Journal of the American College of Cardiology, 75*(20), 2635–2638. doi:10.1016/j.jacc.2020.04.015 PMID:32304797

Almeida, F. (2020). Adoption of a Serious Game in the Developing of Emotional Intelligence Skills. *European Journal of Investigation in Health, Psychology and Education, 10*(1), 30–43. doi:10.3390/ejihpe10010004 PMID:34542467

Alonso Varela, L., & Saraiva Cruz, I. (2020). Búsqueda y evaluación de información: Dos competencias necesarias en el contexto de las fake news. *Palabra Clave (La Plata), 9*(2), e090. doi:10.24215/18539912e090

Alqithami, S., Alzahrani, M., Alzahrani, A., & Mostafa, A. (2019). Modeling an augmented reality game environment to enhance behavior of adhd patients. In *International conference on brain informatics* (pp. 179-188). Springer. 10.1007/978-3-030-37078-7_18

Al-Ramahi, M., El-Gayar, O., & Liu, J. (2016). Discovering Design Principles for Persuasive Systems: A Grounded Theory and Text Mining Approach. *2016 49th Hawaii International Conference on System Sciences (HICSS)*, 3074–3083. 10.1109/HICSS.2016.387

Alsalman, D., Ali, Z. M. B., Alnosaier, Z. F., Alotaibi, N. A., & Alanzi, T. M. (2020). Gamification for diabetes type 1 management: A review of the features of free Apps in Google Play and App Stores. *Journal of Multidisciplinary Healthcare, 13*, 425–432. doi:10.2147/JMDH.S249664 PMID:32523349

Alsawaier, R. S. (2018). The effect of gamification on motivation and engagement. *International Journal of Information and Learning Technology, 35*(1), 56–79. doi:10.1108/IJILT-02-2017-0009

AlSkaif, T., Lampropoulos, I., Van Den Broek, M., & Van Sark, W. (2018). Gamification-based framework for engagement of residential customers in energy applications. *Energy Research & Social Science, 44*, 187–195. doi:10.1016/j.erss.2018.04.043

Altarriba, F. (2014). The revolution of fun. *Documento de trabajo. Disponible en.*

Al-Yafi, K., & El-Masri, M. (2016). Gamification of e-Government Services: A Discussion of Potential Transformation. In *Proceedings of the Twenty-second Americas Conference on Information Systems* (pp. 1-9). Academic Press.

Al-Zaidi, Z. (2012). Gamification's march to ubiquity. *The Guardian*. https://www.theguardian.com/media-network/media-network-blog/2012/apr/26/gamification-ubiquity

Amaro, S., & Duarte, P. (2015). An integrative model of consumers' intentions to purchase travel online. *Tourism Management, 46*, 64–79. doi:10.1016/j.tourman.2014.06.006

Aminov, A., Rogers, J. M., Middleton, S., Caeyenberghs, K., & Wilson, P. H. (2018). What do randomized controlled trials say about virtual rehabilitation in stroke? A systematic literature review and meta-analysis of upper-limb and cognitive outcomes. *Journal of Neuroengineering and Rehabilitation, 15*(1), 29–24. doi:10.118612984-018-0370-2 PMID:29587853

Ammar, A., Bouaziz, B., Trabelsi, K., Glenn, J. M., Zmijewski, P., Müller, P., Chtourou, H., Jmaiel, M., Chamari, K., Driss, T., & Hökelmann, A. (2021). Applying digital technology to promote active and healthy confinement lifestyle during pandemics in the elderly. *Biology of Sport, 38*(3), 391–396. doi:10.5114/biolsport.2021.100149 PMID:34475622

Ananiadou, K., & Magdalean, C. (2009). *21st Century Skills & Competences for New Millennium Learners in OECD Countries.* OECD. doi:10.1787/19939019

Andersen, E., Liu, Y.-E., Snider, R., Szeto, R., & Popovic, Z. (2011). Placing a value on aesthetics in online casual games. *Proceedings of the 2011 annual conference on Human factors in computing systems*, 1275–1278. 10.1145/1978942.1979131

Andersen, J. P., & Gustafsberg, H. (2016, April). A Training Method to Improve Police Use of Force Decision Making: A Randomized Controlled Trial. *SAGE Open, 6*(2). Advance online publication. doi:10.1177/2158244016638708

Anderson, E. (2017). *How to comply with the 5 functions of the NIST cybersecurity framework*. Retrieved from https://www.secmatters.com/blog/how-to-comply-with-the-5-functions-of-the-nist-cybersecurity-framework

Anderson, M. (2020, August). Prescription-strength gaming: ADHD treatment now comes in the form of a first-person racing game. *IEEE Spectrum, 57*, 9–10. doi:10.1109/MSPEC.2020.9150542

Anderson, E. F., McLoughlin, L., Liarokapis, F., Peters, C., Petridis, P., & de Freitas, S. (2010). Developing serious games for cultural heritage: A state-of-the-art review. *Virtual Reality (Waltham Cross), 14*(4), 255–275. doi:10.100710055-010-0177-3

Anderson, E. T., & Simester, D. I. (2014). Reviews without a Purchase: Low Ratings, Loyal Customers, and Deception. *JMR, Journal of Marketing Research, 51*(3), 249–269.

Andrade, F., Mizoguchi, R., & Isotani, S. (2016). The Bright and Dark Sides of Gamification. *The Bright and Dark Sides of Gamification., 9684*, 1–11. doi:10.1007/978-3-319-39583-8_17

Andreoni, J. (1990). Impure altruism and donations to public goods: A theory of warm-glow giving. *Economic Journal (London), 100*(401), 464–477. doi:10.2307/2234133

Ansoms, A., & Geenen, S. (2012). Development monopoly: A simulation game on poverty and inequality. *Simulation & Gaming, 43*(6), 853–862. doi:10.1177/1046878112451877

Antonaci, A., Klemke, R., & Specht, M. (2019). The effects of gamification in online learning environments: A systematic literature review. *Informatics (MDPI), 6*(3), 32. doi:10.3390/informatics6030032

Antunes, J., & Santana, P. (2018). A study on the use of eye tracking to adapt gameplay and procedural content generation in first-person shooter games. *Multimodal Technologies and Interaction, 2*(2), 23. Advance online publication. doi:10.3390/mti2020023

Aparicio, A. F., Vela, F. L. G., Sánchez, J. L. G., & Montes, J. L. I. (2012, October). Analysis and application of gamification. In *Proceedings of the 13th International Conference on Interacción Persona-Ordenador - INTERACCION '12, Elche, Spain* (pp. 3-5). 10.1145/2379636.2379653

App Store Preview. (2021). *Starbucks iPhone screenshots*. Retrieved October 10, 2021, from https: //apps.apple.com/us/app/starbucks/id331177714?_branch_match_id=981323254902129837&utm_source=Web&utm_medium=marketing

Arambarri Basañez, J., De la Torre-Díez, I., Lopez-Coronado, M., & Álvarez-Lombardía, I. (2014). Investigating the potential market of a serious game for training of Alzheimer's caregivers in a northern Spain region. *International Journal of Serious Games, 1*(4), 75.79.

Arciuli, J., Carroll, J., & Cameron, D. (2008). The use of applied drama in crisis management: An empirical psycological study. *Australian Journal of Emergency Management, 23*(3). https://search.informit.org/doi/pdf/10.3316/agispt.20083952

Armier, D. D. Jr, Shepherd, C. E., & Skrabut, S. (2016). Using game elements to increase student engagement in course assignments. *College Teaching, 64*(2), 64–72. doi:10.1080/87567555.2015.1094439

Arrasvuori, J., Boberg, M., Holopainen, J., Korhonen, H., Lucero, A., & Montola, M. (2011). Applying the PLEX framework in designing for playfulness. In *Proceedings of the 2011 Conference on Designing Pleasurable Products and Interfaces* (pp. 1-8). 10.1145/2347504.2347531

Asociación Española de Videojuegos. (2021). *Anuario de la Industria del Videojuego*. http://www.aevi.org.es/web/wpcontent/uploads/2021/04/AEVI_Anuario_2020.pdf

Asociación Española de Videojuegos. (2021). *Las Mujeres Juegan, Consumen, Participan*. http://www.aevi.org.es/descargables/informe-las-mujeres-juegan-consumen-participan/

Atlantic Council. (2021a). *Cyber 9/12 Strategy Challenge*. Retrieved from https://www.gcsp.ch/events/cyber-912-strategy-challenge-2021

Atlantic Council. (2021b). *Description and rules*. Author.

Attig, C., & Franke, T. (2019). I track, therefore I walk–Exploring the motivational costs of wearing activity trackers in actual users. *International Journal of Human-Computer Studies*, *127*, 211–224. doi:10.1016/j.ijhcs.2018.04.007

Augustin, K., Thiebes, S., Lins, S., Linden, R., & Basten, D. (2016). Are we playing yet? A review of gamified enterprise systems. In PACIS (p. 2). Academic Press.

Australian Transport Safety Bureau. (2021). *Aviation safety investigations & reports*. Available online: https://www.atsb.gov.au/publications/safety-investigation-reports/?mode=Aviation

Azevedo, J., Padrão, P., Gregório, M. J., Almeida, C., Moutinho, N., Lien, N., & Barros, R. (2019). A web-based gamification program to improve nutrition literacy in families of 3-to 5-year-old children: The nutriscience project. *Journal of Nutrition Education and Behavior*, *51*(3), 326–334. doi:10.1016/j.jneb.2018.10.008 PMID:30579894

Babin, B. J., Darden, W. R., & Griffin, M. (1994). Work and/or fun: Measuring hedonic and utilitarian shopping value. *The Journal of Consumer Research*, *20*(4), 644–656. doi:10.1086/209376

Backlund, P., & Hendrix, M. (2013). Educational games-are they worth the effort? A literature survey of the effectiveness of serious games. In *Games and virtual worlds for serious applications (VS-GAMES), 2013 5th international conference on* (pp. 1-8). IEEE.

Bail, C. A., Argyle, L. P., Brown, T. W., Bumpus, J. P., Chen, H., Hunzaker, M. B. F., Lee, J., Mann, M., Merhout, F., & Volfovsky, A. (2018). Exposure to opposing views on social media can increase political polarization. *Proceedings of the National Academy of Sciences of the United States of America*, *115*(37), 9216–9221. doi:10.1073/pnas.1804840115 PMID:30154168

Bai, S., Hew, K. F., & Huang, B. (2020). Does gamification improve student learning outcome? Evidence from a meta-analysis and synthesis of qualitative data in educational contexts. *Educational Research Review*, *30*, 100322. doi:10.1016/j.edurev.2020.100322

Ballance, C. (2013). Use of games in training : Interactive experiences that engage us to learn. *Industrial and Commercial Training*, *45*(4), 218–221. doi:10.1108/00197851311323501

Bandler, J. W., & Kiley, E. M. (2018). The Clarity of Hindsight: The First-Ever IMS Three Minute Thesis Competition. *IEEE Microwave Magazine*, 116-123.

Bandura, A. (1997). *Self-efficacy: The exercise of control*. W. H. Freeman and Company.

Baptista, G., & Oliveira, T. (2019). Gamification and serious games: A literature meta-analysis and integrative model. *Computers in Human Behavior*, *92*, 306–315. doi:10.1016/j.chb.2018.11.030

Barata, G., Gama, S., Jorge, J., & Gonçalves, D. (2014). Identifying student types in a gamified learning experience. *International Journal of Game-Based Learning*, *4*(4), 19–36. doi:10.4018/ijgbl.2014100102

Barata, G., Gama, S., Jorge, J., & Gonçalves, D. (2017). Studying student differentiation in gamified education: A long-term study. *Computers in Human Behavior*, *71*, 550–585. doi:10.1016/j.chb.2016.08.049

Bardon, T., Dauphine, P., & Josserand, E. (2006). *Why do we play the games ? Exploring institutional and political motivations.* doi:10.1108/00400910910987255

Bartle, R. (1996). Hearts, clubs, diamonds, spades: Players who suit MUDs. *Journal of MUD Research, 1*(1), 19.

Bartle, A. R. (2004). *Designing virtual worlds.* New Riders Publishing.

Bartle, R. (1996). Hearts, clubs, diamonds, spades: Players who suit MUDs. *Journal of MUD Research, 1*(1), 19.

Bartle, R. (2011). *Gamification: Too much of a good thing.* Digital Shoreditch.

Bartnes, M., Moe, N. B., & Heegaard, P. E. (2016). The future of information security incident management training: A case study of electrical power companies. *Computers & Security, 61*(217528), 32–45. https://doi.org/10.1016/j.cose.2016.05.004

Bartunek, J. M., & Woodman, R. W. (2015). Beyond Lewin: Toward a Temporal Approximation of Organization Development and Change. *Annual Review of Organizational Psychology and Organizational Behavior, 2*(1), 157–182. doi:10.1146/annurev-orgpsych-032414-111353

Bateman, C., & Boon, R. (2005). *21st century game design (game development series).* Charles River Media.

Bauer, W. I. (2010). Your Personal Learning Network: Professional Development on Demand. *Music Educators Journal, 97*(2), 37–42. doi:10.1177/0027432110386383

Bayne, S. (2015). What's the matter with 'technology-enhanced learning'? *Learning, Media and Technology, 40*(1), 1, 5–20. doi:10.1080/17439884.2014.915851

Beard, J., & Ragheb, M. G. (1983). Measuring leisure motivation. *Journal of Leisure Research, 15*(3), 219–228. doi:10.1080/00222216.1983.11969557

Becker, K. (2021). What's the difference between gamification, serious games, educational games, and game-based learning. *Academia Letters.* Advance online publication. doi:10.20935/AL209

Belhadi, A., Sha'ri, Y. B. M., Touriki, F. E., & El Fezazi, S. (2018). Lean production in SMEs: Literature review and reflection on future challenges. *Journal of Industrial and Production Engineering, 35*(6), 368–382. doi:10.1080/21681015.2018.1508081

Bellotti, F., Berta, R., & De Gloria, A. (2010). Designing Effective Serious Games: Opportunities and Challenges for Research. *International Journal of Emerging Technologies in Learning, 5*(3), 22–35. doi:10.3991/ijet.v5s3.1500

Belogianni, K., Ooms, A., Ahmed, H., Nikoletou, D., Grant, R., Makris, D., & Moir, H. J. (2019). Rationale and design of an Online educational program using game-based learning to improve nutrition and physical activity outcomes among university students in the United Kingdom. *Journal of the American College of Nutrition, 38*(1), 23–30. doi:10.1080/07315724.2018.1476929 PMID:30071183

Bénabou, R., & Tirole, J. (2006). Incentives and Prosocial Behavior. *American Economic Review, 96*(5), 1652–1678.

Benjamin, G. (2019). Playing at Control: Writing Surveillance in/for Gamified Society. *Surveillance & Society, 17*(5), 699–713. doi:10.24908s.v17i5.13204

Benmayor, R. (2008). Digital storytelling as a signature pedagogy for the new humanities. *Arts and Humanities in Higher Education, 7*(2), 188–204. doi:10.1177/1474022208088648

Benson, B. (2014). The Gameful Mind. In The Gameful World: Approaches, Issues, Applications (pp. 223–224). MIT Press.

Berber, A. (2018). *Oyunlaştırma: Oynayarak başarmak.* Seçkin Yayıncılık.

Berger, V., & Schrader, U. (2016). Fostering sustainable nutrition behavior through gamification. *Sustainability*, *8*(1), 67. doi:10.3390u8010067

Beuran, R., Tang, D., Pham, C., & Chinen, K. 2018). Integrated framework for hands-on cybersecurity training: Cy-TrONE. *Computers and Security, 78*, 43–59. doi:10.1016/j.cose.2018.06.001

Bhamu, J., & Singh Sangwan, K. (2014). Lean manufacturing: Literature review and research issues. *International Journal of Operations & Production Management, 34*(7), 876–940. doi:10.1108/IJOPM-08-2012-0315

Bianchini, D., Fogli, D., & Ragazzi, D. (2016). TAB sharing: A gamified tool for e-participation. In *Proceedings of the International Working Conference on Advanced Visual Interfaces - AVI '16* (pp. 294–295). ACM Press. 10.1145/2909132.2926071

Biggs, J. (1999). *Teaching for Quality Learning at University*. SHRE and Open University Press.

Bilimoria, K. Y., Cohen, M. E., Ingraham, A. M., Bentrem, D. J., Richards, K., Hall, B. L., & Ko, C. Y. (2010). Effect of postdischarge morbidity and mortality on comparisons of hospital surgical quality. *Annals of Surgery, 252*(1), 183–190. doi:10.1097/SLA.0b013e3181e4846e PMID:20531000

Binsubaih, A., Maddock, S., & Romano, D. (2006). A serious game for traffic accident investigators. *Interactive Technology and Smart Education, 3*(4), 329–346. doi:10.1108/17415650680000071

Biro, G. I. (2014). Didactics 2.0: A pedagogical analysis of gamification theory from a comparative perspective with special view to the components of learning. *Procedia: Social and Behavioral Sciences, 141*, 148–151. doi:10.1016/j.sbspro.2014.05.027

Bista, S. K., Nepal, S., & Paris, C. (2013). Data abstraction and visualisation in next step: Experiences from a government services delivery trial. In *Proceedings International Congress on Big Data* (pp. 263–270). IEEE. 10.1109/BigData.Congress.2013.42

Bittner, J. V., & Shipper, J. (2014). Motivational effects and age differences of gamification in product advertising. *Journal of Consumer Marketing, 31*(5), 391–400. doi:10.1108/JCM-04-2014-0945

Bjelajac, Ž., & Filipović, A. (2020). Gamification as an Innovative Approach in Security Systems. Academic Press.

Black, G. (2012). *Transforming museums in the twenty-first century*. Routledge. doi:10.4324/9780203150061

Black, J. (2007). Design rules for implementing the Toyota Production System. *International Journal of Production Research, 45*(16), 3639–3664. https://doi.org/10.1080/00207540701223469

Blackmore, J. (2006). Deconstructing diversity discourses in the field of educational management and leadership. *Educational Management Administration & Leadership, 34*(2), 181–199. doi:10.1177/1741143206062492

Blake, S. (2021, June 11). What Trump said before his supporters stormed the Capitol, annotated. *The Washington Post*. https://wapo.st/3mbpDzb

Blake, J. (2012). *Natural User Interfaces in. NET*. Manning Publications Company.

Blandford, A. (2013). Semi-structured qualitative studies. In M. Soegaard & R. F. Dam (Eds.), *The Encyclopedia of Human-Computer Interaction* (2nd ed.). The Interaction Design Foundation. http://www.interaction-design.org/ encyclopedia/semi-structured_qualitative_studies.html

Blazhko, O., Luhova, T., Melnik, S., & Ruvinska, V. (2017). Communication model of open government data gamification based on Ukrainian websites. In *Proceedings of 2017 4th Experiment at International Conference: Online Experimentation* (pp. 181–186). IEEE. 10.1109/EXPAT.2017.7984367

Blicblau, A., Bruwer, M., & Dini, K. (2016). Do engineering students perceive that different learning and teaching modes improve their referencing and citation skills? *International Journal of Mechanical Engineering Education, 44*(1), 3–15. https://doi.org/10.1177/0306419015624186

Block, G., Azar, K. M., Block, T. J., Romanelli, R. J., Carpenter, H., Hopkins, D., Palaniappan, L., & Block, C. H. (2015). A fully automated diabetes prevention program, Alive-PD: Program design and randomized controlled trial protocol. *JMIR Research Protocols, 4*(1), e3. doi:10.2196/resprot.4046 PMID:25608692

Blohm, I., & Leimeister, J. M. (2013). Gamification: Design of IT-based enhancing services for motivational support and behavioral change. *Business & Information Systems Engineering, 5*(4), 275–278. doi:10.100712599-013-0273-5

Blok, A. C., Valley, T. S., & Abbott, P. (2021). Gamification for family engagement in lifestyle interventions: A systematic review. *Prevention Science, 22*(7), 1–14. doi:10.100711121-021-01214-x PMID:33786746

Blow, C. (2012). *Flight school in the virtual environment: Capabilities and risks of executing a simulations-based flight training program.* School of Advanced Military Studies.

Bock, B. C., Dunsiger, S. I., Ciccolo, J. T., Serber, E. R., Wu, W. C., Tilkemeier, P., Walaska, K. A., & Marcus, B. H. (2019). Exercise videogames, physical activity, and health: wii heart fitness: A randomized clinical trial. *American Journal of Preventive Medicine, 56*(4), 501–511. doi:10.1016/j.amepre.2018.11.026 PMID:30777705

Boendermaker, W. J., Boffo, M., & Wiers, R. W. (2015). Exploring elements of fun to motivate youth to do cognitive bias modification. *Games for Health Journal, 4*(6), 434–443. doi:10.1089/g4h.2015.0053 PMID:26421349

Bogdanovych, A., Esteva, N., Gu, M., Simoff, S., Maher, M. L., & Smith, G. (2007). The role of online travel agents in the experience economy. In *Proceedings of the 14th international conference on information technology in tourism ENTER.* Academic Press.

Bogolea, B., & Wijekumar, K. (2004). Information security curriculum creation: A case study. *2004 Information Security Curriculum Development Conference, InfoSecCD 2004*, 59–65. doi:10.1145/1059524.1059537

Bogost, I. (2011). *Gamification is bullshit.* http://bogost.com/writing/blog/gamification_is_bullshit

Bogost, I. (2011). Gamification is bullshit. *The Atlantic.* Retrieved from https://www.theatlantic.com/technology/archive/2011/08/gamification-is-bullshit/243338

Bogost, I. (2015). Why Gamification is Bullshit. In The Gameful World: Approaches, Issues, Applications (pp. 65–79). MIT Press.

Bogost, I. (2007). *Persuasive games. The expressive power of videogames.* MIT Pr. doi:10.7551/mitpress/5334.001.0001

Bohøj, M., Borchorst, N. G., Bødker, S., Korn, M., & Zander, P. (2011). Public deliberation in municipal planning: Supporting Action and Reflection with Mobile Technology. In *Proceedings of the 5th International Conference on Communities and Technologies - C&T '11* (pp. 88–97). ACM Press. 10.1145/2103354.2103367

Bonacini, E., & Giaccone, S. C. (2021). Gamification and cultural institutions in cultural heritage promotion: A successful example from Italy. *Cultural Trends,* 1–20. doi:10.1080/09548963.2021.1910490

Bontchev, B., Paneva-Marinova, D., & Draganov, L. (2016). Educational Video Games for Bulgarian Orthodox Iconography. *ICERI2016 Proceedings, 1,* 1679–1688.

Bourdieu, P. (1976). Le champ scientifique. *Actes de la Recherche en Sciences Sociales, 2-3*(2), 88–104. doi:10.3406/arss.1976.3454

Bouveresse, J. (1999). *Prodiges et vertiges de l'analogie.* Raison d'agir.

Bowman, N. D., Kowert, R., & Cohen, E. (2015). When the ball stops, the fun stops too: The impact of social inclusion on video game enjoyment. *Computers in Human Behavior, 53*, 131–139. doi:10.1016/j.chb.2015.06.036

Bowman, N. D., Pietschmann, D., & Liebold, B. (2017). The golden (hands) rule: Exploring user experiences with game-pad and natural-user interfaces in popular video games. *Journal of Gaming and Virtual Worlds, 9*(1), 71–85. Advance online publication. doi:10.1386/jgvw.9.1.71_1

Bowser, A., Hansen, D., He, Y., Boston, C., Reid, M., Gunnell, L., & Preece, J. (2013, October). Using gamification to inspire new citizen science volunteers. In *Proceedings of the first international conference on gameful design, research, and applications*, (pp. 18-25). 10.1145/2583008.2583011

Boyan, A., & Sherry, J. (2011). The Challenge in Creating Games for Education: Aligning Mental Models With Game Models. *Child Development Perspectives, 5*(2), 82–87. doi:10.1111/j.1750-8606.2011.00160.x

Boyd, D. D. (2017). A review of general aviation safety (1984–2017). *Aerospace Medicine and Human Performance, 88*(7), 657–664. doi:10.3357/AMHP.4862.2017 PMID:28641683

Boyle, E. A., Hainey, T., Connolly, T. M., Gray, G., Earp, J., Ott, M., Lim, T., Ninaus, M., Ribeiro, C., & Pereira, J. (2016). An update to the systematic literature review of empirical evidence of the impacts and outcomes of computer games and serious games. *Computers & Education, 94*, 178–192. doi:10.1016/j.compedu.2015.11.003

Brabham, D. C. (2013). *Crowdsourcing*. The MIT Press. doi:10.7551/mitpress/9693.001.0001

Brady, H. (1999). Political Participation. In J. P. Robinson, P. R. Shaver, & L. S. Wrightsman (Eds.), *Measures of Political Attitudes* (pp. 737–801). Academic Press.

Braet, A. C. (1992). Ethos, pathos and logos in Aristotle's Rhetoric: A re-examination. *Argumentation, 6*(3), 307–320. https://doi.org/10.1007/BF00154696

Brahma, A., & Dutta, R. (2018). Cashless Transactions and Its Impact-A Wise Move Towards Digital India. *International Journal of Scientific Research in Computer Science, Engineering and Information Technology, 3*(3), 14–28.

Branch, R. M., & Kopcha, T. J. (2014). Instructional design models. In J. Spector, M. Merrill, J. Elen, & M. Bishop (Eds.), *Handbook of research on educational communications and technology*. Springer. doi:10.1007/978-1-4614-3185-5_7

Breton, P. (2015). *La parole manipulée*. La Découverte. (Original work published 1997)

Brian Burke. (2014). *Redefine Gamification to Understand Its Opportunities and Limitations*. https://www.gartner.com/en/documents/2699119-redefine-gamification-to-understand-its-opportunities-an

Briffa, M., Jaftha, N., Loreto, G., Pinto, F. C. M., & Chircop, T. (2020). Improved students' performance within gamified learning environment: A meta-analysis study. *International Journal of Education and Research, 8*(1), 223–244.

Brockmyer, J. H., Fox, C. M., Curtiss, K. A., McBroom, E., Burkhart, K. M., & Pidruzny, J. N. (2009). The development of the Game Engagement Questionnaire: A measure of engagement in video game-playing. *Journal of Experimental Social Psychology, 45*(4), 624–634. doi:10.1016/j.jesp.2009.02.016

Brodeur, D., Young, P. W., & Blair, K. B. (2002). Problem Based Learning in Aerospace Engineering Education. *Proceedings of the 2002 American Society for Engineering Education Annual Conference & Exposition*.

Brodie, R. J., Hollebeek, L. D., Juric, B., & Ilic, A. (2011). Customer engagement: Conceptual domain, fundamental propositions, and implications for research. *Journal of Service Research, 14*(3), 252–271. doi:10.1177/1094670511411703

Brooks, A. L., Brooks, E., & Vidakis, N. (2017). Interactivity, Game Creation, Design, Learning, and Innovation. In *6th International Conference, ArtsIT (Vol. 2)*. Springer International Publishing. 10.1007/978-3-319-55834-9

Brown, S. (2010). *Likert Scale Examples for Surveys*. Iowa State University Extension. https://www.extension.iastate.edu/Documents/ANR/LikertScaleExamplesforSurveys.pdf

Brown, M., O'Neill, N., van Woerden, H., Eslambolchilar, P., Jones, M., & John, A. (2016). Gamification and adherence to web-based mental health interventions: A systematic review. *JMIR Mental Health, 3*(3), e39. doi:10.2196/mental.5710 PMID:27558893

Brown, V. R., & Vaughn, E. D. (2011). The writing on the (Facebook) wall: The use of social networking sites in hiring decisions. *Journal of Business and Psychology, 26*(2), 219–225. doi:10.100710869-011-9221-x

Brühlmann, F. (2018). *Gamification From the Perspective of Self-Determination Theory and Flow*. 10.31237/ doi:osf.io/6kauv

Bruno, M. A., & Griffiths, L. (2014). Serious games: supporting occupational engagement of people aged 50+ based on intelligent tutoring systems/Juegos serios: apoyo a la participación ocupacional de personas mayores de 50 años basado en sistemas de tutoría inteligente. *Ingeniare. Revista Chilena de Ingeniería, 22*(1), 125. doi:10.4067/S0718-33052014000100012

Brynen, R. (2021). *How I learned to stop worrying and love climate change and geo-politics*. Retrieved from https://paxsims.wordpress.com/tag/climate-change/

Buabeng-Andoh, C. (2012). 'Factors influencing teachers' adoption and integration of information and communication technology into teaching: A review of the literature'. *International Journal of Education and Development Using Information and Communication Technology, 8*(1), 136–155.

Buckingham, D. (2005). *Educación en medios: Alfabetización, aprendizaje y cultura contemporánea*. Paidós.

Buckley, P., & Doyle, E. (2017). Individualising gamification: An investigation of the impact of learning styles and personality traits on the efficacy of gamification using a prediction market. *Computers & Education, 106*, 43–55. doi:10.1016/j.compedu.2016.11.009

Buijs-Spanjers, K. R., Hegge, H. H. M., Cnossen, F., Hoogendoorn, E., Jaarsma, D. A. D. C., & de Rooij, S. E. (2019). Dark Play of Serious Games: Effectiveness and Features (G4HE2018). *Games for Health Journal, 8*(4), 301–306. doi:10.1089/g4h.2018.0126 PMID:30964340

Buisine, S. (2009). *"Faire le métier" de cycliste: une sociologie pragmatique du travail dans le domaine sportif*. Thèse de doctorat en STAPS, Université Paris X.

Bulencea, P., & Egger, R. (2015). *Gamification in tourism: Designing memorable experiences*. BoD- Books on Demand.

Buller, M. K., Kane, I. L., Dunn, A. L., Edwards, E. J., Buller, D. B., & Liu, X. (2009). Marketing fruit and vegetable intake with interactive games on the internet. *Social Marketing Quarterly, 15*(1), 136–154. doi:10.1080/15245000903038316

Bunchball. (2010). *Gamification 101: An introduction to the use of game dynamics to influence behavior*. https://www.bunchball.com/sites/default/files/downloads/gamification101.pdf

Bunchball. (2010). *Gamification 101: An introduction to the use of game dynamics to influence behavior*. Retrieved from June 20, 2021, from http://jndglobal.com/wp-content/uploads/2011/05/gamification1011.pdf

Burke, B. (2013). How Gamification Motivates the Masses. *Forbes*. https://www.forbes.com/sites/gartnergroup/2014/04/10/how-gamification-motivates-the-masses/?sh=6f613665c047

Burke, B. (2014). *Gamify: How gamification motivates people to do extraordinary things*. Gartner, Inc.

Burke, J. W., McNeill, M. D. J., Charles, D. K., Morrow, P. J., Crosbie, J. H., & McDonough, S. M. (2009). Optimising engagement for stroke rehabilitation using serious games. *The Visual Computer, 25*(12), 1085–1099. doi:10.100700371-009-0387-4

Burmark, L. (2004). Visual Presentations that Prompt, flash & transform. *Media and Methods, 40*(6), 4–5.

Burns, N., & Grove, S. K. (2005). *The practice of nursing research: Conduct, critique, and utilization.* Elsevier Saunders.

Busch, M., Mattheiss, E. E., Hochleitner, W., Hochleitner, C., Lankes, M., Fröhlich, P., & Tscheligi, M. (2016). Using player type models for personalized game design an empirical investigation. *Interaction Design and Architecture, 28,* 145–163. http://www.mifav.uniroma2.it/inevent/events/idea2010/doc/28_8.pdf

Butterworth, J., & Thwaites, G. (2013). *Thinking skills: Critical thinking and problem solving.* Cambridge University Press.

Byrnes, K. P. (2017). Employing flight simulation in the classroom to improve the understanding of the fundamentals of instruction among flight instructor applicants. *Journal of Aviation/Aerospace Education Research, 26*(1), 49–63. doi:10.15394/jaaer.2017.1623

Caballero-Hernández, J. A., Palomo-Duarte, M., & Dodero, J. M. (2017). Skill assessment in learning experiences based on serious games: A Systematic Mapping Study. *Computers & Education, 113,* 42–60. doi:10.1016/j.compedu.2017.05.008

Cafazzo, J. A., Casselman, M., Hamming, N., Katzman, D. K., & Palmert, M. R. (2012). Design of an mHealth App for the Self-management of Adolescent Type 1 Diabetes: A Pilot Study. *Journal of Medical Internet Research, 14*(3), e70. doi:10.2196/jmir.2058 PMID:22564332

Cameron, F., & Kenderdine, S. (Eds.). (2007). *Theorizing Digital Cultural Heritage: A Critical Discourse.* MIT Press. doi:10.7551/mitpress/9780262033534.001.0001

Cameron, J., Pierce, W. D., Banko, K. M., & Gear, A. (2005). Achievement-based rewards and intrinsic motivation: A test of cognitive mediators. *Journal of Educational Psychology, 97*(4), 641–655. doi:10.1037/0022-0663.97.4.641

Campbell, J. (2003). *The hero's journey: Joseph Campbell on his life and work.* New World Library.

Cao, X., & Sun, J. (2018). Exploring the effect of overload on the discontinuous intention of social media users: An SOR perspective. *Computers in Human Behavior, 81,* 10–18. doi:10.1016/j.chb.2017.11.035

Caponetto, I., Earp, J., & Ott, M. (2014). Gamification and Education: A Literature Review. *Proceedings of the European Conference on Games Based Learning, 1*(2009), 50–57. doi:10.13140/RG.2.1.1181.8080

Caporarello, L., Magni, M., & Pennarola, F. (2017). Learning and gamification: A possible relationship? *EAI Endorsed Transactions on E-Learning, 4*(16), 1–8. doi:10.4108/eai.19-12-2017.153488

Cardador, M. T., Northcraft, G. B., & Whicker, J. (2017). A theory of work gamification: Something old, something new, something borrowed, something cool? *Human Resource Management Review, 27*(2), 353–365. doi:10.1016/j.hrmr.2016.09.014

Care, E. (2018). Twenty-First Century Skills: From Theory to Action. In Assessment and Teaching of 21st Century Skills: Research and Application (pp. 3-17). Springer.

Carenys, J., Moya, S., & Perramon, J. (2017). Is it worth it to consider videogames in accounting education? A comparison of a simulation and a videogame in attributes, motivation and learning outcomes. *Revista de Contabilidad-Spanish Accouting Review, 20*(2), 118-130. doi:10.1016/j.rcsar.2016.07.003

Carenys, J., & Moya, S. (2016). Digital game-based learning in accounting and business education. *Accounting Education, 25*(6), 598–651. doi:10.1080/09639284.2016.1241951

Caroline Ngonyo Njoroge, R. Y. (2014). The Impact of Social and Emotional Intelligence on Employee Motivation in a Multigenerational Workplace. *Global Journal of Management and Business Research*.

Carras, M. C., Van Rooij, A. J., Spruijt-Metz, D., Kvedar, J., Griffiths, M. D., Carabas, Y., & Labrique, A. (2018). Commercial video games as therapy: A new research agenda to unlock the potential of a global pastime. *Frontiers in Psychiatry*, 8(JAN), 1–7. doi:10.3389/fpsyt.2017.00300 PMID:29403398

Carter-Thomas, S., & Rowley-Jolivet, E. (2020). Three minute thesis presentations: Recontextualisation strategies in doctoral research. *Journal of English for Academic Purposes*. doi:10.1016/j.jeap.2020.100897

Carvalho, M. B., Bellotti, F., Berta, R., De Gloria, A., Sedano, C. I., Hauge, J. B., … Rauterberg, M. (2015). An activity theory-based model for serious games analysis and conceptual design. *Computers and Education, 87*, 166–181. doi:10.1016/j.compedu.2015.03.023

Casner, St., Geven, R., & Williams, K. (2013). The Effectiveness of Airline Pilot Training for Abnormal Events. *Human Factors, 55*(3), 477–485. doi:10.1177/0018720812466893 PMID:23829023

Cassano-Piché, A., Vicente, K. J., & Jamieson, G. A. (2006). A sociotechnical systems analysis of the BSE epidemic in the UK through case study. In Proceedings of the 50th Annual Meeting of the Human Factors and Ergonomics Society (pp. 386–390). SAGE Publications Inc. https://doi.org/https://journals.sagepub.com/doi/10.1177/154193120605000337.

Castells, M. (1997). *La era de la información, Vol. Nº 1 La sociedad Red*. Alianza Editorial.

Castells, M. (2001). *La Galaxia Internet*. Plaza & Janes. doi:10.1007/978-3-322-89613-1

Castro, K. A. C., Sibo, Í. P. H., & Ting, I.-h. (2018). Assessing gamification effects on e-learning platforms: An experimental case. In L. Uden, D. Liberona & J. Ristvej (Eds.), *Learning technology for education challenges* (pp. 3-14). Springer. 10.1007/978-3-319-95522-3_1

Cechetti, N. P., Bellei, E. A., Biduski, D., Rodriguez, J. P. M., Roman, M. K., & De Marchi, A. C. B. (2019). Developing and implementing a gamification method to improve user engagement: A case study with an m-Health application for hypertension monitoring. *Telematics and Informatics, 41*, 126–138. doi:10.1016/j.tele.2019.04.007

Çeker, E., & Özdamla, F. (2017). What " Gamification" Is and What It's Not. *European Journal of Contemporary Education, 6*(2), 221–228.

Centre for System Solutions. (2021). *Policy simulations*. Retrieved from https://drive.google.com/file/d/19nn0mnujng gKA2Ti7jGlMWEP990aPVsF/view

Cermak-Sassenrath, D. (2015). Playful computer interaction. In V. Frissen, S. Lammes, M. de Lange, J. de Mul & J. Raessens (Eds.), Playful Identities: The ludification of digital media cultures (pp. 93–110). Amsterdam Univ. Pr. doi:10.1515/9789048523030-005

Cermak-Sassenrath, D. (2019). Current challenges in gamification identified in empirical studies. In R. Ørngreen, M. Buhl, & B. Meyer (Eds.), Proceedings of the 18th European Conference on e-Learning (ECEL 2019) (pp. 119–127). Academic Conferences and Publishing International Limited.

Chalmers, A. (1999). *What Is This Thing Called Science. Hackett Publishing Company* (3rd ed.). Hackett Publishing. Retrieved from https://mycourses.aalto.fi/pluginfile.php/1139027/mod_resource/content/1/WhatIsThisThingCalled-Science-Chalmers-1999.pdf

Chander, A., & Le, U. P. (2014). Breaking the Web: Data Localization vs. The Global Internet. *SSRN Electronic Journal*. doi:10.2139/ssrn.2407858

Chang, A. Y.Alenda Y. Chang. (2011). Games as Environmental Texts. *Qui Parle*, *19*(2), 56. Advance online publication. doi:10.5250/quiparle.19.2.0057

Chang, C.-T., Hajiyev, J., & Su, C.-R. (2017). Examining the students' behavioral intention to use e-learning in Azerbaijan? The General Extended Technology Acceptance Model for E-learning approach. *Computers & Education*, *111*, 128–143. doi:10.1016/j.compedu.2017.04.010

Chang, Y.-W., Hsu, P.-Y., & Wu, Z.-Y. (2015). Exploring managers' intention to use business intelligence: The role of motivations. *Behaviour & Information Technology*, *34*(3), 273–285. doi:10.1080/0144929X.2014.968208

Chaplin, H. (2011, March 29). Gamification: Ditching reality for a game isn't as fun as it sounds. *Slate Magazine*. https://slate.com/technology/2011/03/gamification-ditching-reality-for-a-game-isn-t-as-fun-as-it-sounds.html

Chatfield, T. (2011). *Fun Inc. Why gaming will dominate the twenty-first century*. Pegasus Communications.

Chee, C.-M., & Wong, D. H.-T. (2017). Affluent Gaming Experience Could Fail Gamification in Education: A Review. *IETE Technical Review*, *34*(6), 593–597. https://doi.org/10.1080/02564602.2017.1315965

Chemingui, H., & Ben lallouna, H. (2013). Resistance, motivations, trust and intention to use mobile financial services. *International Journal of Bank Marketing*, *31*(7), 574–592. doi:10.1108/IJBM-12-2012-0124

Cheng, P. H., Yeh, T. K., Chao, Y. K., Lin, J., & Chang, C. Y. (2020). Design ideas for an issue-situation-based board game involving multirole scenarios. *Sustainability*, *12*(5), 2139. doi:10.3390u12052139

Chen, J. (2007). Flow in Games. *Communications of the ACM*, *50*(4), 31–34. doi:10.1145/1232743.1232769

Chen, L., & Nath, R. (2008). Determinants of mobile payments: An empirical analysis. *Journal of International Technology and Information*, *17*(1), 9–20.

Chen, S. C., Yen, D. C., & Hwang, M. I. (2012). Factors influencing the continuance intention to the usage of Web 2.0: An empirical study. *Computers in Human Behavior*, *28*(3), 933–941. doi:10.1016/j.chb.2011.12.014

Chen, W., Wei, X., & Zhu, K. (2017). Engaging voluntary contributions in online communities: A hidden markov model. *Management Information Systems Quarterly*, *42*(1), 83–100. doi:10.25300/MISQ/2018/14196

Cherrafi, A., Elfezazi, S., Chiarini, A., Mokhlis, A., & Benhida, K. (2016). The integration of lean manufacturing, Six Sigma and sustainability: A literature review and future research directions for developing a specific model. *Journal of Cleaner Production*, *139*, 828–846. https://doi.org/10.1016/J.JCLEPRO.2016.08.101

Chetouani, M., Vanden Abeele, V., Leuven, K., Carmen Moret-Tatay, B., Lopes, S., Magalhães, P., Pereira, A., Martins, J., Magalhães, C., Chaleta, E., & Rosário, P. (2018). Games Used With Serious Purposes: A Systematic Review of Interventions in Patients With Cerebral Palsy. *Frontiers in Psychology*, *9*, 1712. doi:10.3389/fpsyg.2018.01712 PMID:30283377

Chiu, C.-M., Lin, H.-Y., Sun, S.-Y., & Hsu, M.-H. (2009). Understanding customers' loyalty intentions towards online shopping: An integration of technology acceptance model and fairness theory. *Behaviour & Information Technology*, *28*(4), 347–360. doi:10.1080/01449290801892492

Chon, S.-H., Timmermann, F., Dratsch, T., Schuelper, N., Plum, P., Berlth, F., Datta, R. R., Schramm, C., Haneder, S., Späth, M. R., Dübbers, M., Kleinert, J., Raupach, T., Bruns, C., & Kleinert, R. (2019). Serious Games in Surgical Medical Education: A Virtual Emergency Department as a Tool for Teaching Clinical Reasoning to Medical Students. *JMIR Serious Games*, *7*(1), e13028. doi:10.2196/13028 PMID:30835239

Choo, Y.-K. (2015). The Octalysis Framework for Gamification & Behavioral Design. *Yu-kai Chou: Gamification & Behavioral Design*. https://yukaichou.com/gamification-examples/octalysis-complete-gamification-framework/

Chorney, A. I. (2012). Taking the game out of gamification. *Dalhousie Journal of Interdisciplinary Management*, 8(1), 1–14. doi:10.5931/djim.v8i1.242

Chou, Y. (2014b). *Gamification & Behavioral Design. Learn how to use Gamification to make a positive impact on your work and life.* https://yukaichou.com/start-here/

Chou, Y. K. (2015). *Gamification & Behavioral Design.* Available at: https://yukaichou.com/gamification-examples/octalysis-complete-gamification-framework/

Chou, Y.-K. (2016). *Actionable gamification: Beyond points, badges, and leaderboards.* Octalysis Media.

Chow, C. Y., Riantiningtyas, R. R., Kanstrup, M. B., Papavasileiou, M., Liem, G. D., & Olsen, A. (2020). Can games change children's eating behaviour? A review of gamification and serious games. *Food Quality and Preference*, 80, 103823. doi:10.1016/j.foodqual.2019.103823

Christiansen, K. R., & Shalamov, A. (2017). *Motion Sensors Explainer.* Retrieved June 20, 2020, from https://www.w3.org/TR/motion-sensors/

Chung, A. E., Skinner, A. C., Hasty, S. E., & Perrin, E. M. (2017). Tweeting to health: A novel mHealth intervention using Fitbits and Twitter to foster healthy lifestyles. *Clinical Pediatrics*, 56(1), 26–32. doi:10.1177/0009922816653385 PMID:27317609

Clarke, S., Peel, D., Arnab, S., Morini, L., Keegan, H., & Wood, O. (2017). EscapED: A Framework for Creating Educational Escape Rooms and Interactive Games to For Higher/Further Education. *International Journal of Serious Games*, 4(3), 73–86. doi:10.17083/ijsg.v4i3.180

Clarke, V., & Braun, V. (2013). Teaching thematic analysis: Overcoming challenges and developing strategies for effective learning. *The Psychologist*, 26(2), 120–123.

Cobo, C., & Pardo, H. (2007). *Planeta Web 2.0. Inteligencia colectiva o medios fast food.* Grup de Recerca d'Interaccions Digitals, Universitat de Vic.

Cohen, K. A., Stiles-Shields, C., Winquist, N., & Lattie, E. G. (2021). Traditional and Nontraditional Mental Healthcare Services: Usage and Preferences Among Adolescents and Younger Adults. *The Journal of Behavioral Health Services & Research*, 48(4), 537–553. Advance online publication. doi:10.100711414-020-09746-w PMID:33474642

Coleman, T. E., & Money, A. G. (2020). Student-centred digital game – based learning : A conceptual framework and survey of the state of the art. *Higher Education*, 79, 415–457. https://doi.org/10.1007/s10734-019-00417-0

Colonomos, A. (2014). *La politique des oracles. Raconter le futur aujourd'hui.* Albin Michel.

Cömert, Z., & Samur, Y. (2021). A comprehensive player types model: Player head. *Interactive Learning Environments*, 1–17. doi:10.1080/10494820.2021.1914113

Conaway, R., & Garay, M. C. (2014). Gamification and service marketing. *SpringerPlus*, 3(1), 1–11. doi:10.1186/2193-1801-3-653 PMID:25392812

Conejo, G. G., Gasparini, I., & da Silva Hounsell, M. (2019). Detailing motivation in a gamification process. In *Proceedings of 19th International Conference on Advanced Learning Technologies* (pp. 89-91). Washington, DC: IEEE Computer Society.

ConklinM. (2021, January 15). Capitol Offense: Is Donald Trump Guilty of Inciting a Riot at the Capitol? *J.L. & Pub. Pol'y*. doi:10.2139/ssrn.3767085

Connolly, T. M., Boyle, E. A., MacArthur, E., Hainey, T., & Boyle, J. M. (2012). A systematic literature review of empirical evidence on computer games and serious games. *Computers & Education*, *59*(2), 661–686. doi:10.1016/j.compedu.2012.03.004

Connolly, T. M., Hainley, T., Boyle, E., Baxter, G., & Moreno-Ger, P. (2014). *Psychology, Pedagogy, and Assessment in Serious Games*. Information Science Reference. doi:10.4018/978-1-4666-4773-2

Consalvo, M. (2009). *Cheating: Gaining advantage in videogames*. MIT Press.

Contreras-Espinosa, R. S., & Blanco-M, A. (2021). A Literature Review of E-government Services with Gamification Elements. *International Journal of Public Administration*, 1–17. Advance online publication. doi:10.1080/01900692.2021.1930042

Contreras-Espinosa, R. S., Blanco-M, A., & Eguía-Gómez, J. L. (2021). Implementation Barriers to Augmented Reality Technology in Public Services. *International Journal of Interactive Mobile Technologies*, *15*(3), 43–56. doi:10.3991/ijim.v15i13.22667

Cook, S. (2019, February 27). *"Social credit" scoring: How China's Communist Party is incentivising repression*. Hong Kong Free Press HKFP. https://hongkongfp.com/2019/02/27/social-credit-scoring-chinas-communist-party-incentivising-repression/

Cook, S. (2017). *The Battle for China's Spirit*. Freedom House. https://freedomhouse.org/report/special-report/2017/battle-chinas-spirit

Coovert, M. D., Winner, J., Bennett, W., & Howard, D. J. (2017). Serious Games are a Serious Tool for Team Research. *International Journal of Serious Games*, *4*(1), 41–55. https://doi.org/10.17083/ijsg.v4i1.141

Corbett, S. (2007). *Beyond manufacturing: The evolution of lean production*. Academic Press.

Cornellá, A., & Rucabado, S. (2006). *Futuro presente: 101 Ideas-Fuerza para entender las próximas décadas*. Deusto.

Coronado Escobar, J. E., & Vasquez Urriago, A. R. (2014). Gamification: an effective mechanism to promote civic engagement and generate trust? In *ICEGOV '14: Proceedings of the 8th International Conference on Theory and Practice of Electronic Governance* (pp. 514-515). ACM Press. 10.1145/2691195.2691307

Corsi, J.-M., Frances, J., & Le Lay, S. (2021). *Ma Thèse en 180 secondes®. Quand la science devient spectacle*. Éditions du Croquant.

Cortese, C. G. (2005). Learning through teaching. *Management Learning*, *36*(1), 87–115. https://doi.org/10.1177/1350507605049905

Cortizo, J. C., Carrero García, F., Monsalve Piqueras, B., Velasco Collado, A., Díaz del Dedo, L. I., & Pérez Martín, J. (2011). Gamificación y docencia: Lo que la Universidad tiene que aprender de los videojuegos [Paper presentation]. VII jornadas internacionales de innovación universitaria, España.

Coşkun, İ. O., & Yılmaz, H. (2016). An Introduction to Consumer Metamorphosis in the Digital Age. In E. Sezgin (Ed.), *e-Consumers in the era of new tourism* (pp. 1–12). Springer. doi:10.1007/978-981-10-0087-4_1

Cothrel, J., & Williams, R. (1999). Understanding on line communities. *Strategic Communication Management*, (Feb), 16–21.

COVID-19 spurring impulse spending, reveals survey. (2020). *Retail Customer Experience*. https://www.retailcustomer-experience.com/news/covid-19-spurring-impulse-spendingreveals-survey/

Cowley, B., Charles, D., Black, M., & Hickey, R. (2013). Real-time rule-based classification of player types in computer games. *User Modeling and User-Adapted Interaction*, *23*(5), 489–526. doi:10.100711257-012-9126-z

Cox, A. L., Cairns, P., Berthouze, N., & Jennett, C. (2006). The Use of Eyetracking for Measuring Immersion. *CogSci 2006 Workshop: What Have Eye Movements Told Us so Far, and What Is Next*.

Cox, J. (2014). What Makes a Blockbuster Video Game? An Empirical Analysis of US Sales Data. *Managerial and Decision Economics*, *35*(3), 189–198. doi:10.1002/mde.2608

Cózar-Gutiérrez, R., & Sáez-López, J. M. (2016). Game-based learning and gamification in initial teacher training in the social sciences: An experiment with MinecraftEdu. *International Journal of Educational Technology in Higher Education*, *13*(2), 2. Advance online publication. doi:10.118641239-016-0003-4

Crawford, C. (2011). *The art of computer game design*. Osborne/McGraw-Hill.

Creative Keys. (2020). *Fruizione culturale in un click? Come il pubblico ha reagito alle proposte di fruizione culturale durante il lockdown e quali prospettive future*. https://bit.ly/3nmaj0a

Creemers, R. (2015, April 25). Planning Outline for the Construction of a Social Credit System (2014-2020). *China Copyright and Media*. https://chinacopyrightandmedia.wordpress.com/2014/06/14/planning-outline-for-the-construction-of-a-social-credit-system-2014-2020/

Creemers, R. (2018). *China's Social Credit System: An Evolving Practice of Control* (*SSRN* Scholarly Paper No. 3175792). Social Science Research Network. doi:10.2139/ssrn.3175792

Creswell, J.W. & Poth, C. N. (2018). Qualitative Inquiry & Research Design: Choosing Among Five Approaches. *Sage (Atlanta, Ga.)*.

Crisis-games.co.uk. (2021). *Crisis games*. Retrieved from http://crisis-games.co.uk/

Crowley, D. N., Breslin, J. G., & Corcoran, P. (2012). Gamification of Citizen Sensing through Mobile Social Reporting, In *Proceedings of the 2012 IEEE International Games Innovation Conference* (pp.1–5). IEEE. 10.1109/IGIC.2012.6329849

Cruea, M. D. (2020). Gaming the Mind and Minding the Game: Mindfulness and Flow in Video Games. In Video Games and Well-being. doi:10.1007/978-3-030-32770-5_7

Csikszentmihalyi, M. (1990). Flow: The Psychology of Optimal Experience. New York: Harper Collins.

Csikszentmihalyi, M. (2014). Flow and the Foundations of Positive Psychology. In Flow and the Foundations of Positive Psychology. doi:10.1007/978-94-017-9088-8

Csikszentmihalyi, M. (1975). Play and intrinsic rewards. *Journal of Humanistic Psychology*, *15*(3), 41–63. doi:10.1177/002216787501500306

Csikszentmihalyi, M. (1990). *Flow: The psychology of optimal experience*. Harper & Row Publishers, Inc.

Csikszentmihalyi, M. (2007). *Aprender a fluir*. Editorial Kairós.

Cugelman, B. (2013). Gamification: What it is and why it matters to digital health behavior change developers. *JMIR Serious Games*, *1*(1), e3139. doi:10.2196/games.3139 PMID:25658754

Currier, J. (2008). *Gamification Game Mechanics is the new marketing*. https://blog.oogalabs.com/2008/11/05/gamification-game-mechanics-is-the-newmarketing/

Czaja, J. S. (2017). PhD, The Role of Technology in Supporting Social Engagement Among Older Adults. *The Public Policy and Aging Report*, *27*(4), 145–148. doi:10.1093/ppar/prx034

Czauderna, A., & Budke, A. (2020). How digital strategy and management games can facilitate the practice of dynamic decision-making. *Education in Science, 10*(4). https://doi.org/10.3390/educsci10040099

D'arc da Silva Brito, R., Hernan Contreras Pinochet, L., Luiz Lopes, E., & Aparecido de Oliveira, M. (2018). Development of a gamification characteristics measurement scale for mobile application users. *Internext, 13*(1), 1–16. doi:10.18568/1980-4865.1311-16

Da Rocha Seixas, L., Gomes, A. S., & De Melo Filho, I. J. (2016). Effectiveness of gamification in the engagement of students. *Computers in Human Behavior, 58*, 48–63. doi:10.1016/j.chb.2015.11.021

da Silva Júnior, J. N., de Sousa Oliveira, J. M., Winum, J.-Y., Melo Leite, A. J. Junior, Alexandre, F. S. O., do Nascimento, D. M., Silva de Sousa, U., Pimenta, A. T. Á., & Monteiro, A. J. (2020). Interactions 500: Design, Implementation, and Evaluation of a Hybrid Board Game for Aiding Students in the Review of Intermolecular Forces During the COVID-19 Pandemic. *Journal of Chemical Education, 97*(11), 4049–4054. https://doi.org/10.1021/acs.jchemed.0c01025

da Silva, R. J. R., Rodrigues, R. G., & Leal, C. T. P. (2019). Gamification in management education: A systematic literature review. *BAR – Brazilian Administration Review, 16*(2), art. 3.

da Silva, T. P. (2021). Why Gamification Is Not the Solution for Everything. In *Handbook of research on solving modern healthcare challenges with gamification* (pp. 20–33). IGI Global. doi:10.4018/978-1-7998-7472-0.ch002

Dai, X. (2018). *Toward a Reputation State: The Social Credit System Project of China* (SSRN Scholarly Paper ID 3193577). Social Science Research Network. doi:10.2139/ssrn.3193577

Dale, S. (2014). Gamification: Making work fun, or making fun of work? *Business Information Review, 31*(2), 82–90. doi:10.1177/0266382114538350

Darde, J.-N. (2012). Enseignants-chercheurs, recherche et plagiat. *Mouvements (Paris), 71*(3), 128–137. doi:10.3917/mouv.071.0128

Darejeh, A., & Salim, S. S. (2016). Gamification solutions to enhance software user engagement–A systematic review. *International Journal of Human-Computer Interaction, 32*(8), 618–642. doi:10.1080/10447318.2016.1183330

Darling-Hammond, L., & McLaughlin, M. W. (1995). Policies that support professional development in an era of reform. *Phi Delta Kappan, 76*(8), 597–604.

Dassen, F. C., Houben, K., Van Breukelen, G. J., & Jansen, A. (2018). Gamified working memory training in overweight individuals reduces food intake but not body weight. *Appetite, 124*, 89–98. doi:10.1016/j.appet.2017.05.009 PMID:28479405

Dastjerdi, A. M., Kaplan, S., Silva, J. D. A., Nielsen, O. A., & Pereira, F. C. (2019). Participating in environmental loyalty program with a real-time multimodal travel app: User needs, environmental and privacy motivators. *Transportation Research Part D, Transport and Environment, 67*, 223–243. doi:10.1016/j.trd.2018.11.013

Daum, J. (2019, June 27). Untrustworthy: Social Credit Isn't What You Think It Is. *Verfassungsblog.* https://verfassungsblog.de/untrustworthy-social-credit-isnt-what-you-think-it-is/

Davaris, M. T., Bunzli, S., Dowsey, M. M., & Choong, P. F. (2021). Gamifying health literacy: How can digital technology optimize patient outcomes in surgery? *ANZ Journal of Surgery, 91*(10), 2008–2013. doi:10.1111/ans.16753 PMID:33825300

Davies, D., Jindal-Snape, D., Collier, C., Digby, R., Hay, P., & Howe, A. (2013). Creative learning environments in education-A systematic literature review. *Thinking Skills and Creativity, 8*(1), 80–91. doi:10.1016/j.tsc.2012.07.004

Davis, A. J., Parker, H. M., & Gallagher, R. (2021). Gamified applications for secondary prevention in patients with high cardiovascular disease risk: A systematic review of effectiveness and acceptability. *Journal of Clinical Nursing*, *30*(19-20), 3001–3010. doi:10.1111/jocn.15808 PMID:33872436

Davis, F. D. (1989). Perceived Usefulness, Perceived Ease of Use, and User Acceptance of Information Technology. *Management Information Systems Quarterly*, *13*(3), 319–340. doi:10.2307/249008

Davis, M. C., Challenger, R., Jayewardene, D. N. W., & Clegg, C. W. (2014). Advancing socio-technical systems thinking: A call for bravery. *Applied Ergonomics*, *45*(2 Part A), 171–180. https://doi.org/10.1016/j.apergo.2013.02.009

Davis, S. B. (2014). *Constructing a Players-Centred Definition of Fun for Video Games Design*. ResearchGate.

de Araújo, F. M. A., Fonseca Ferreira, N. M., Mascarenhas, V. T. O. C., Adad Filho, J. A., & Viana Filho, P. R. F. (2020). *Eye Tracking in Framework for the Development of Games for People with Motor Disabilities*. doi:10.1007/978-981-15-1465-4_25

de Kort, Y. A. W., IJsselsteijn, W. A., & Poels, K. (2007). Digital games as social presence technology: development of the Social Presence in Gaming Questionnaire. PRESENCE 2007 Proceedings, 195–203.

de Ribaupierre, S., Kapralos, B., Haji, F., Stroulia, E., Dubrowski, A., & Eagleson, R. (2014). Healthcare Training Enhancement Through Virtual Reality and Serious Games. In M. Ma, L. C. Jain, & P. Anderson (Eds.), *Virtual, Augmented Reality and Serious Games for Healthcare 1* (pp. 9–27). Springer. doi:10.1007/978-3-642-54816-1_2

de Sousa Borges, S., Durelli, V. H. S., Reis, H. M., & Isotani, S. (2014). A systematic mapping on gamification applied to education. *Proceedings of the 29th Annual ACM Symposium on Applied Computing - SAC '14*, 216–222. doi:10.1145/2554850.2554956

Dean, P. (2016). *The explosive growth of the 300-person "megagame."* Retrieved from https://arstechnica.com/gaming/2016/09/the-explosive-growth-of-the-300-person-megagame/

Deci, E. L., & Flaste, R. (1996). *Why we do what we do: Understanding self-motivation*. Penguin books.

Deci, E. L., Koestner, R., & Ryan, R. M. (2001). Extrinsic rewards and intrinsic motivation in education: Reconsidered once again. *Review of Educational Research*, *71*(1), 1–27. doi:10.3102/00346543071001001

Deci, E. L., & Porac, J. (1978). Cognitive evaluation theory and the study of human motivation. In M. R. Lepper & D. Greene (Eds.), *The hidden costs of reward: new perspectives on the psychology of human motivation* (pp. 149–176). Lawrence Erlbaum Associates.

Deci, E. L., & Ryan, R. M. (1985). *Instrinsic motivation and self-determination in human behavior*. Springer. doi:10.1007/978-1-4899-2271-7

Deci, E. L., & Ryan, R. M. (2008). Facilitating optimal motivation and psychological well-being across life's domains. *Canadian Psychology*, *49*(1), 14–23. doi:10.1037/0708-5591.49.1.14

Deci, E. L., & Ryan, R. M. (2013). *Intrinsic motivation and self-determination in human behavior*. Springer Science & Business Media.

Deci, E., & Ryan, R. (2004). *Handbook of self-determination research*. University of Rochester Press.

Defaz, M. (2020). Metodologías activas en el proceso enseñanza-aprendizaje. *Revista Científico-Educacional*, *16*(1), 463–472.

Dehghanzadeh, H., Fardanesh, H., Hatami, J., Talaee, E., & Noroozi, O. (2019). Using gamification to support learning English as a second language: A systematic review. *Computer Assisted Language Learning*, 1–24. doi:10.1080/09588 221.2019.1648298

Dejours, C. (1998). *Souffrance en France. La banalisation de l'injustice sociale*. Seuil.

dela Cruz, C. S., & Palaoag, T. D. (2019). An empirical study of gamified learning application engagement to exceptional learners. *Proceedings IEEA, 2019*, 263–267. doi:10.1145/3323716.3323762

Dele-Ajayi, O., Sanderson, J., Strachan, R., & Pickard, A. (2016). *Learning mathematics through serious games: An engagement framework*. Academic Press.

Deleuze, J., Maurage, P., Schimmenti, A., Nuyens, F., Melzer, A., & Billieux, J. (2019). Escaping reality through video games is linked to an implicit preference for virtual over real-life stimuli. *Journal of Affective Disorders, 245*, 1024–1031. doi:10.1016/j.jad.2018.11.078 PMID:30699844

De-Marcos, L., Domínguez, A., Saenz-de-Navarrete, J., & Pagés, C. (2014). An empirical study comparing gamification and social networking on e-learning. *Computers & Education, 75*, 82–91. doi:10.1016/j.compedu.2014.01.012

Denny, P., McDonald, F., Empson, R., Kelly, P., & Petersen, A. (2018). Empirical Support for a Causal Relationship Between Gamification and Learning Outcomes. *Proceedings CHI 2018*, paper 331. 10.1145/3173574.3173885

Denny, P. (2013). The effect of virtual achievements on student engagement. *Proceedings of the SIGCHI Conference on Human Factors in Computing Systems*, 763–72. 10.1145/2470654.2470763

DeSmet, A., Van Ryckeghem, D., Compernolle, S., Baranowski, T., Thompson, D., Crombez, G., Poels, K., Van Lippevelde, W., Bastiaensens, S., Van Cleemput, K., Vandebosch, H., & De Bourdeaudhuij, I. (2014). A meta-analysis of serious digital games for healthy lifestyle promotion. *Preventive Medicine, 69*, 95–107. https://doi.org/10.1016/j.ypmed.2014.08.026

Desurvire, H., & Wixon, D. (2013). Game principles: choice, change & creativity: making better games. CHI '13 Extended Abstracts on Human Factors in Computing Systems, Paris, France.

Deterding, S. (2012, February 23). *Ruling the World: When Life Gets Gamed*. Lift Conference 2012, Geneva, Switzerland. https://www.slideshare.net/dings/ruling-the-world-when-life-gets-gamed/39-But_if_you_put_a

Deterding, S., Dixon, D., Khaled, R., & Nacke, L. (2011). *From game design elements to gamefulness: Defining gamification* [Paper presentation]. 15th International Academic MindTrek Conference: Envisioning Future media Environments, Finland.

Deterding, S., Sicart, M., Nacke, L., O'Hara, K., & Dixon, D. (2011). Gamification. using game-design elements in non-gaming contexts. In CHI'11 extended abstracts on human factors in computing systems, (pp. 2425-2428). ACM.

Deterding, S., Sicart, M., Nacke, L., O'Hara, K., & Dixon, D. (2011). Gamification. Using game-design elements in non-gaming contexts. *CHI'11 Extended Abstracts on Human Factors in Computing Systems*, 2425–8.

Deterding, S., Sicart, M., Nacke, L., O'Hara, K., & Dixon, D. (2011b). Gamification. using game-design elements in non-gaming contexts. *CHI '11 Extended Abstracts on Human Factors in Computing Systems*, 2425-2428. doi:10.1145/1979742.1979575

Deterding, S. (2011). Situated motivational affordances of game elements: A conceptual model. In *CHI 2011* (pp. 1–4). ACM Press.

Deterding, S. (2015). The lens of intrinsic skill atoms: A method for gameful design. *Human-Computer Interaction, 30*(3–4), 294–335. doi:10.1080/07370024.2014.993471

Deterding, S., Dixon, D., Khaled, R., & Nacke, L. (2011). From game design elements to gamefulness: defining gamification. In *Proceedings of the 15th International AcademicMindTrek Conference* (pp. 9–15). 10.1145/2181037.2181040

Deterding, S., Dixon, D., Khaled, R., & Nacke, L. (2011b). Gamification: Toward a definition. In *Proceedings of CHI 2011 Gamification Workshop* (pp. 12-15). New York, NY: Association for Computing Machinery.

Devaraj, S., Easley, R. F., & Crant, J. M. (2008). How does personality matter?: Relating the five-factor model to technology acceptance and use. *Information Systems Research*, *19*(1), 93–105. doi:10.1287/isre.1070.0153

Devisch, O., Poplin, A., & Sofronie, S. (2016). The Gamification of Civic Participation: Two Experiments in Improving the Skills of Citizens to Reflect Collectively on Spatial Issues. *Journal of Urban Technology*, *23*(2), 81–102. doi:10.10 80/10630732.2015.1102419

DeVries, I. (2018) The Student Experience of Distance Education over Time – A Research Challenge. *Distances et médiations des savoirs*. doi:10.4000/dms.2739

Dewey, J. (1938). *Experience and Education*. MacMillan.

Dholakia, U. M. (2001). A motivational process model of product involvement and consumer risk perception. *European Journal of Marketing*, *35*(11/12), 1340–1362. doi:10.1108/EUM0000000006479

Díaz-García, A., González-Robles, A., Mor, S., Mira, A., Quero, S., García-Palacios, A., ... Botella, C. (2020). Positive and negative affect schedule (Panas): Psychometric properties of a venezuelan Spanish version in medical students. *BMC Psychiatry*, *20*(56), 301–315. doi:10.118612888-020-2472-1 PMID:32039720

Díaz-Ramírez, J. (2020). Gamification in engineering education – An empirical assessment on learning and game performance. *Heliyon*, *6*(9, e04972), 1–10. doi:10.1016/j.heliyon.2020.e04972 PMID:32995639

Dicheva, D., Dichev, C., Agre, G., & Angelova, G. (2015). Gamification in education: A systematic mapping study. *Journal of Educational Technology & Society*, *18*(3), 75–88. https://scinapse.io/papers/2187022131

Dichev, C., & Dicheva, D. (2017). Gamifying education: What is known, what is believed and what remains uncertain: A critical review. *International Journal of Educational Technology in Higher Education*, *14*(9), 9. doi:10.118641239-017-0042-5

Dichev, C., Dicheva, D., Angelova, G., & Agre, G. (2014). From gamification to gameful design and gameful experience in learning. *Cybernetics and Information Technologies*, *14*(4), 80–100. https://doi.org/10.1515/cait-2014-0007

Dickey, M. D. (2005). Engaging by Design: How Engagement Strategies in Popular Computer and Video Games Can Inform Instructional Design. *Educational Technology Research and Development*, *53*(2), 67–83. doi:10.1007/BF02504866

Dignan, A. (2011). *Game Frame. Using games as a strategy for success*. Free Press.

Dignan, A. (2011). *Game Frame: Using Games as a Strategy for Success* (1st ed.). Free Press - Simon & Schuster.

Dikken, M. (2020). *Game over: Gamification in Al-Qaeda's Magazine Inspire To address lone-wolf terrorists*. Leiden University. https://hdl.handle.net/1887/136052

Dinehart, S. (2006). *Transmedial Play: Cognitive and Cross-Platform Narrative* [Blog post]. Available at http://narrativedesign.org/2008/05/trans-medial-playcognitive-and-cross-platform-narrative/

Djaouti, D., Alvarez, J., & Jessel, J.-P. (2011). Classifying serious games: The G/P/S model. Handbook of Research on Improving Learning and Motivation through Educational Games: Multidisciplinary Approaches, 2005, 118–136.

Djaouti, D., Alvarez, J., Jessel, J. P., & Rampnoux, O. (2011). Origins of serious games. In Serious games and edutainment applications (pp. 25-43). Springer. doi:10.1007/978-1-4471-2161-9_3

Domínguez, A., Saenz-De-Navarrete, J., De-Marcos, L., Fernández-Sanz, L., Pagés, C., & Martínez-Herráiz, J.-J. (2013). Gamifying learning experiences: Practical implications and outcomes. *Computers & Education*, *63*, 380–392. doi:10.1016/j.compedu.2012.12.020

Donthu, N., & Gustafsson, A. (2020). Effects of COVID-19 on business and research. *Journal of Business Research*, *117*(January), 284–289. https://doi.org/10.1016/j.jbusres.2020.06.008

Dontnod Entertainment. (2017). Life is Strange: Episode 2 'Out of Time' (PS4 Version) [Video Game]. France.

Dörner, R., Göbel, S., Effelsberg, W., & Wiemeyer, J. (2016). Introduction. In R. Dörner, S. Göbel, W. Effelsberg, & J. Wiemeyer (Eds.), Serious Games. Foundations, Concepts and Practice (pp. 1-34). Springer.

Doskow, M. G. (2012). *Analysis of the Impact of Scenario-Based Training on the Aeronautical Decision Making of Collegiate Flight Students*. Embry-Riddle Aeronautical University.

Doughty, M., & O'Coill, C. (2005). Collaborative software environments and participatory design. In *Proceedings of IADIS international conference on web based communities* (303–306). IADIS.

Douglas, B. D., & Brauer, M. (2021). Gamification to Prevent Climate Change: A Review of Games and Apps for Sustainability. *Current Opinion in Psychology*, *42*, 89–94. doi:10.1016/j.copsyc.2021.04.008 PMID:34052619

Draganov, L., Paneva-Marinova, D., Pavlova, L., Luchev, D., Márkus, Z. L., Szántó, G., & Szkaliczki, T. (2015). Technology-enhanced learning for cultural heritage. *Digital Presentation and Preservation of Cultural and Scientific Heritage*, *5*, 293–301.

Drinhausen, K., & Brussee, V. (2021). *China's Social Credit System in 2021: From fragmentation towards integration*. Mercator Institute for China Studies. https://merics.org/en/report/chinas-social-credit-system-2021-fragmentation-towards-integration

DSB. (2016a). *Spilløvelser*. Retrieved from https://www.dsb.no/veiledere-handboker-og-informasjonsmateriell/metodehefte-spillovelse/

DSB. (2016b). *Veileder i planlegging, gjennomføring og evaluering av øvelser Metodehefte: Fullskalaøvelse*. DSB.

Duarte, A. (2017). *Défenses et résistance en psychodynamique du travail*. Thèse de doctorat en psychologie, Université Paris Descartes.

Dubois, L.-E., & Gibbs, C. (2018). Video game–induced tourism: A new frontier for destination marketers. *Tourism Review*, *73*(2), 186–198. doi:10.1108/TR-07-2017-0115

Duchowski, A. T. (2017). Eye Tracking Techniques. In *Eye Tracking Methodology*. Springer International Publishing., doi:10.1007/978-3-319-57883-5_5

Du, H. S., Ke, X., & Wagner, C. (2020). Inducing individuals to engage in a gamified platform for environmental conservation. *Industrial Management & Data Systems*, *120*(4), 692–713. doi:10.1108/IMDS-09-2019-0517

Duke, R. D., & Geurts, J. (2004). *Policy Games for Strategic Management*. Retrieved from http://books.google.com/books?id=XGUdoRPFx30C&pgis=1

Duman, T., & Mattila, A. S. (2005). The role of affective factors on perceived cruise vacation value. *Tourism Management*, *26*(3), 311–323. doi:10.1016/j.tourman.2003.11.014

Dunniway, T., & Novak, J. (2008). *Game Development Essentials: Gameplay mechanics*. Delmar Cengage Learning.

Dunphy, D. (2011). Conceptualizing sustainability: The business opportunity. In *Business and sustainability: Concepts, strategies and changes*. Emerald Group Publishing Limited. doi:10.1108/S2043-9059(2011)0000003009

Durand, R. (2018). *L'évangélisme technologique. De la révolte hippie au capitalisme high-tech de la Silicon Valley*. Fyp.

Dwyer, A., & Silomon, J. (2019, September 23). Dangerous Gaming: Cyber-Attacks, Air-Strikes and Twitter. *E-International Relations*. https://www.e-ir.info/2019/09/23/dangerous-gaming-cyber-attacks-air-strikes-and-twitter/

Ebert, D. D., Cuijpers, P., Muñoz, R. F., & Baumeister, H. (2017). Prevention of mental health disorders using internet- and mobile-based interventions: A narrative review and recommendations for future research. *Frontiers in Psychiatry*, *8*, 116. doi:10.3389/fpsyt.2017.00116 PMID:28848454

Eccles, J. S., Adler, T. F., Futterman, R., Goff, S. B., Kaczala, C. M., Meece, J. L., & Midgley, C. (1983). Expectancies, values, and academic behaviors. In J. T. Spence (Ed.), *Achievement and achievement motivation: Psychological and sociological approaches* (pp. 75–146). W. H. Freeman and Company.

Eckerson, C. M. (2018). The impact of nurse residency programs in the United States on improving retention and satisfaction of new nurse hires: An evidence-based literature review. *Nurse Education Today*, *71*, 84–90. doi:10.1016/j.nedt.2018.09.003 PMID:30268073

Economou, M. (2015). Heritage in the Digital Age. In W. Logan, M. N. Craith, U. Kockel (Eds.), A Companion to Heritage Studies (pp. 215-228). Wiley Blackwell. doi:10.1002/9781118486634.ch15

ECSC. (2021). *European cyber security challenge*. Retrieved from https://europeancybersecuritychallenge.eu/

Eder, K. (1999). Societies Learn and Yet the World is Hard to Change. *European Journal of Social Theory*, *2*(2), 195–215.

Edney, S., Ryan, J. C., Olds, T., Monroe, C., Fraysse, F., Vandelanotte, C., Plotnikoff, R., Curtis, R., & Maher, C. (2019). User engagement and attrition in an app-based physical activity intervention: Secondary analysis of a randomized controlled trial. *Journal of Medical Internet Research*, *21*(11), e14645. doi:10.2196/14645 PMID:31774402

EEAS. (2020). *EU Security, Defense and Crisis response*. Retrieved from https://eeas.europa.eu/topics/security-defence-crisis-response/43281/security-defence-crisis-response_en

Eisingerich, A. B., Marchand, A., Fritze, M. P., & Dong, L. (2019). Hook vs. hope: How to enhance customer engagement through gamification. *International Journal of Research in Marketing*, *36*(2), 200–215. doi:10.1016/j.ijresmar.2019.02.003

Ekici, M. (2021). A systematic review of the use of gamification in flipped learning. *Education and Information Technologies*, *26*(3), 3327–3346. doi:10.100710639-020-10394-y

El-Adly, M. I. (2019). Modelling the relationship between hotel perceived value, customer satisfaction, and customer loyalty. *Journal of Retailing and Consumer Services*, *50*, 322–332. doi:10.1016/j.jretconser.2018.07.007

Elkington, J. (1998). Partnerships from cannibals with forks: The triple bottom line of 21st-century business. *Environmental Quality Management*, *8*(1), 37–51. doi:10.1002/tqem.3310080106

Elliott, C. (2015). 'Big Food' and 'gamified' products: Promotion, packaging, and the promise of fun. *Critical Public Health*, *25*(3), 348–360. doi:10.1080/09581596.2014.953034

Eloff, M. M., & Von Solms, S. H. (2000). Information security management: A hierarchical framework for various approaches. *Computers & Security*, *19*(3), 243–256. https://doi.org/10.1016/S0167-4048(00)88613-7

Emarketer. (2021). *How the Starbucks app is energizing mobile payment use*. Retrieved October, 6, 2021, from https://www.emarketer.com/content/how-starbucks-app-energizing-mobile-payment-use

Embry-Riddle Aeronautical University/Hunt Library. (2021). *NTSB Aircraft Accident Reports (AAR)*. Available online: https://huntlibrary.erau.edu/collections/aerospace-and-aviation-reports/ntsb/aircraft-accident-reports

Engeström, Y. (2019). *Learning by expanding - An activity theoretical approach to developmental research* (2nd ed.). Cambridge University Press. Retrieved from Learningfromexperience.com/downloads/research-library/eight-important-things-to-know-about-the-experiential-learning-cycle.pdf

Eppmann, R., Bekk, M., & Klein, K. (2018). Gameful experience in gamification: Construction and validation of a gameful experience scale. *Journal of Interactive Marketing*, *43*, 98–115. doi:10.1016/j.intmar.2018.03.002

Epstein, D. S., Zemski, A., Enticott, J., & Barton, C. (2021). Tabletop board game elements and gamification interventions for health behavior change: Realist review and proposal of a game design framework. *JMIR Serious Games*, *9*(1), e23302. doi:10.2196/23302 PMID:33787502

Erdoğdu, F., & Karatas, F. O. (2016). *Examining the effects of gamification on different variables in science education.* Identifying Turkish Society's Level of Scientific Literacy View Project Identifing Turkish Society's Level of Scientific Literacy View Project. Available online: https://www.researchgate.net/publication/312164266_Examining_the_Effects_of_Gamification_on_Different_Variables_in_Science_Education

Ertmer, P. A. (1999). Addressing first- and second-order barriers to change: Strategies for technology integration. *ETR&D*, *47*(4), 47–61. doi:10.1007/BF02299597

Esnaola, G. (2009). Videojuegos en redes sociales: Aprender desde experiencias óptimas. *Comunicación (Cartago)*, *1*(7), 265–279.

Esser, H. (2010). Assimilation, ethnic stratification, or selective acculturation? Recent theories of the integration of immigrants and the model of intergenerational integration. *Sociologica*, *4*(1), 1–29.

European Commission. (2017). *Annex to "Coordinated Response to Large Scale Cybersecurity Incidents and Crises".* Commission Recommendation. COM(2017) 6100 final. 13.09.2017.

Everymind. (n.d.). *Understanding mental health and wellbeing*. Retrieved August 4, 2021, from https://everymind.org.au/mental-health/understanding-mental-health/understanding-mental-health-and-wellbeing#:~:text=Mental health is a positive,a state of overall wellbeing.

Fadhli, M., Brick, B., Setyosari, P., Ulfa, S., & Kuswandi, D. (2020). A meta-analysis of selected studies on the effectiveness of gamification method for children. *International Journal of Instruction*, *13*(1), 845–854. doi:10.29333/iji.2020.13154a

Faiella F., Ricciardi M. (2015), Gamification and learning: a review of issues and research. *Journal of e-Learning and Knowledge Society*, *11*(3), 13-21.

Fang, Y., Ma, Y., Mo, D., Zhang, S., Xiang, M., & Zhang, Z. (2019). Methodology of an exercise intervention program using social incentives and gamification for obese children. *BMC Public Health*, *19*(1), 1–10. doi:10.118612889-019-6992-x PMID:31159776

Farber, M. E., & Hall, T. E. (2007). Emotion and environment: Visitors extraordinary experiences along the Dalton highway in Alaska. *Journal of Leisure Research*, *39*(2), 248–270. doi:10.1080/00222216.2007.11950107

Farzan, R., DiMicco, J. M., Millen, D. R., Brownholtz, B., Geyer, W., & Dugan, C. (2008). Results from deploying a participation incentive mechanism within the enterprise. *Proceedings of the Twenty-Sixth Annual SIGCHI Conference on Human Factors in Computing Systems*, 563–72. 10.1145/1357054.1357145

Federal Aviation Administration. (2011). *Aviation Instructor's Handbook (FAA-H-8083-9)*. FAA Publications. https://www.faa.gov/regulations_policies/handbooks_manuals/aviation/aviation_instructors_handbook/media/11_aih_chapter_9.pdf

Federal Aviation Administration. (2021). *Accident and Incident Data*. Available online: https://www.faa.gov/data_research/accident_incident/

Feijoo, C., Gómez-Barroso, J.-L., Aguado, J.-M., & Ramos, S. (2012). Mobile gaming: Industry challenges and policy implications. *Telecommunications Policy, 36*(3), 212–221. doi:10.1016/j.telpol.2011.12.004

FEMA. (2017). *National Incident Management System*. Retrieved from www.dhs.gov

FEMA. (2020). *Exercises*. Retrieved from https://www.fema.gov/emergency-managers/national-preparedness/exercises

Feng, W., Tu, R., & Hsieh, P. (2020). Can gamification increases consumers' engagement in fitness apps? The moderating role of commensurability of the game elements. *Journal of Retailing and Consumer Services, 57*, 102229. doi:10.1016/j.jretconser.2020.102229

Fenu, G., & Pau, P. L. (2015). An analysis of features and tendencies in mobile banking apps. *Procedia Computer Science, 56*(1), 26–33. doi:10.1016/j.procs.2015.07.177

Ferguson, C. J., & Glasgow, B. (2021). Who are GamerGate? A descriptive study of individuals involved in the GamerGate controversy. *Psychology of Popular Media, 10*(2), 243–247. doi:10.1037/ppm0000280

Fernández-Gómez, J. D., & Gordillo-Rodríguez, M. T. (2015). Aproximación teórica al branding relacional: De las teorías de Fournier a las brand communities. *Revista Mediterranea de Comunicación, 6*(1), 131–152. doi:10.14198/MEDCOM2015.6.1.08

Fernández, J. D. (2013). *Principios de estrategia publicitaria y gestión de marcas. Nuevas tendencias de Brand Management*. McGraw-Hill.

Ferro, L. S., Walz, S. P., & Greuter, S. (2013). Towards personalised, gamified systems: an investigation into game design, personality and player typologies. In *Proceedings of The 9th Australasian Conference on Interactive Entertainment: Matters of Life and Death* (p. 7). ACM. 10.1145/2513002.2513024

Festinger, L. (1954). A theory of social comparison processes. *Human Relations, 7*(2), 117–140. doi:10.1177/001872675400700202

Feyisetan, O., Simperl, E., Van Kleek, M., & Shadbolt, N. (2015). Improving Paid Microtasks through Gamification and Adaptive Furtherance Incentives. *Proceedings of the 24th International Conference on World Wide Web*, 333–343. 10.1145/2736277.2741639

Figueroa-Flores, J. F. (2016). Gamification and game-based learning: Two strategies for the 21st century learner. *WORLD (Oakland, Calif.), 3*(2), 507. Advance online publication. doi:10.22158/wjer.v3n2p507

Filsecker, M., & Hickey, D. T. (2014). A multilevel analysis of the effects of external rewards on elementary students' motivation, engagement and learning in an educational game. *Computers & Education, 75*, 136–148. doi:10.1016/j.compedu.2014.02.008

Fimreite, A. L., Lango, P., Lægreid, P., & Rykkja, L. H. (2014). *Organisering, krisehåndtering og samfunnssikkerhet*. Universitetsforlaget. Retrieved from https://www.universitetsforlaget.no/organisering-samfunnssikkerhet-og-krisehandtering-1

Finnish Advisory Board on Research Integrity. (2012). *Responsible conduct of research and procedures for handling allegations of misconduct in Finland*. https://www.tenk.fi/sites/tenk.fi/files/HTK_ohje_2012.pdf

Fiş Erümit, S., Şılbır, L., Erümit, A. K., & Karal, H. (2021). Determination of player types according to digital game playing preferences: Scale development and validation study. *International Journal of Human-Computer Interaction, 37*(11), 991–1002. doi:10.1080/10447318.2020.1861765

Fish, M. T., Russoniello, C. V., & O'Brien, K. (2018). Zombies vs. Anxiety: An Augmentation Study of Prescribed Video Game Play Compared to Medication in Reducing Anxiety Symptoms. *Simulation & Gaming, 49*(5), 553–566. doi:10.1177/1046878118773126

Fitzgerald, M., & Ratcliffe, G. (2020). Serious games, gamification, and serious mental illness: A scoping review. *Psychiatric Services (Washington, D.C.), 71*(2), 170–183. doi:10.1176/appi.ps.201800567 PMID:31640521

Fitz-Walter, Z., Johnson, D., Wyeth, P., Tjondronegoro, D., & Scott-Parker, B. (2017). Driven to drive? Investigating the effect of gamification on learner driver behavior, perceived motivation and user experience. *Computers in Human Behavior, 71*, 586–595. doi:10.1016/j.chb.2016.08.050

Fizek, S. (2014). Why fun matters: In search for emergent playful experiences. In Rethinking Gamification. Meson Pr.

Flatla, D. R., Gutwin, C., Nacke, L. E., Bateman, S., & Mandryk, R. L. (2011). Calibration games: Making calibration tasks enjoyable by adding motivating game elements. In *Proceedings of the 24th Annual ACM Symposium on User Interface Software and Technology* (pp. 403-412). 10.1145/2047196.2047248

Fleming, T. M., Bavin, L., Stasiak, K., Hermansson-Webb, E., Merry, S. N., Cheek, C., Lucassen, M., Lau, H. M., Pollmuller, B., & Hetrick, S. (2017). Serious games and gamification for mental health: Current status and promising directions. *Frontiers in Psychiatry, 7*, 215. doi:10.3389/fpsyt.2016.00215 PMID:28119636

Flett, J. A. M., Hayne, H., Riordan, B. C., Thompson, L. M., & Conner, T. S. (2019). Mobile Mindfulness Meditation: A Randomised Controlled Trial of the Effect of Two Popular Apps on Mental Health. *Mindfulness, 10*(5), 863–876. doi:10.100712671-018-1050-9

Flinkman, M., Laine, M., Leino-Kilpi, H., Hasselhorn, H.-M., & Salanterä, S. (2008). Explaining young registered Finnish nurses' intention to leave the profession: A questionnaire survey. *International Journal of Nursing Studies, 45*(5), 727–739. doi:10.1016/j.ijnurstu.2006.12.006 PMID:17280674

Fluet, G. G., Qiu, Q., Patel, J., Cronce, A., Merians, A. S., & Adamovich, S. V. (2019). Autonomous Use of the Home Virtual Rehabilitation System: A Feasibility and Pilot Study. *Games for Health Journal, 8*(6), 432–438. doi:10.1089/g4h.2019.0012 PMID:31769724

Foley, K. J. (2001). *Meta management: A stakeholder/quality management approach to whole-of-enterprise management.* Standards Australia.

Føllesdal, D., Walløe, L., & Elster, J. (1984). Argumentasjonsteori, språk og vitenskapsfilosofi (3rd ed.). Universitetsforlaget.

Fong, P., & Frost, P. M. (2009). The social benefits of computer games. In *Proceedings of the 44th Annual APS conference* (62–65). The Australian Psychological Society Ltd.

Fontana, M. T. (2020). Gamification of ChemDraw during the COVID-19 Pandemic: Investigating how a serious, educational-game tournament (molecule madness) impacts student wellness and organic chemistry skills while distance learning. *Journal of Chemical Education, 97*(9), 3358–3368. doi:10.1021/acs.jchemed.0c00722

Fontana, M. T. (2020). Gamification of ChemDraw during the COVID-19 Pandemic: Investigating How a Serious, Educational-Game Tournament (Molecule Madness) Impacts Student Wellness and Organic Chemistry Skills while Distance Learning. *Journal of Chemical Education, 97*(9), 3358–3368. https://doi.org/10.1021/acs.jchemed.0c00722

Fortunato, M., Harrison, J., Oon, A. L., Small, D., Hilbert, V., Rareshide, C., & Patel, M. (2019). Remotely monitored gamification and social incentives to improve glycemic control among adults with uncontrolled type 2 diabetes (idiabetes): Protocol for a randomized controlled trial. *JMIR Research Protocols, 8*(11), e14180. doi:10.2196/14180 PMID:31746765

Fotaris, P., & Mastoras, T. (2019). Escape Rooms for Learning: A Systematic Review. In *Proceeding of the 13th European Conference on Games Based Learning* (pp. 235-243). Academic Press.

Fournier, S. (1998). Consumers and their brands: Developing relationship theory in consumer research. *The Journal of Consumer Research, 24*(4), 343–353. doi:10.1086/209515

Foxman, M., & Forelle, M. (2014). Electing to Play: MTV's Fantasy Election and Changes in Political Engagement Through Gameplay. *Games and Culture, 9*(6), 454–467. doi:10.1177/1555412014549804

Frances, J. (2017). "Employabilité" doctorale et lutte des places dans le monde académique. In J.-P. Durand, D. Glaymann, F. Moatty, & G. Tiffon (Eds.), L'employabilité et ses usages sociaux (pp. 81-92). Presses Universitaires de Rennes.

Frances, J., Le Lay, S., & Pizzinat, B. (2016). Des chercheurs en liberté. Le MT180 sur l'établi de la "sociologie (de) garage". *Carnet Zilsel.* https://zilsel.hypotheses.org/2608

Frances, J., & Le Lay, S. (2017). L'usage des *business games* dans le cursus doctoral. "Esprit d'entreprendre" et "esprit d'entreprise" dans la formation à la recherche. *Formation Emploi, 140*(140), 67–86. doi:10.4000/formationemploi.5217

Fredette, C. (2019). *Cybersecurity Education: Why Universities are Missing the Mark.* Retrieved from https://www.cybintsolutions.com/cybersecurity-education-why-universities-are-missing-the-mark/

Fredricks, J. A., Blumenfeld, P. C., & Paris, A. H. (2004). School engagement: Potential of the concept, state of the evidence. *Review of Educational Research, 74*(1), 59–109. doi:10.3102/00346543074001059

Freire, P. (1972). *Pedagogy of the Oppressed* (M. B. Ramos, Trans.). Herder.

Friedrich, J., Becker, M., Kramer, F., Wirth, M., & Schneider, M. (2020). Incentive design and gamification for knowledge management. *Journal of Business Research, 106*, 341–352. doi:10.1016/j.jbusres.2019.02.009

Friedrich, M. J. (2017). Depression Is the Leading Cause of Disability Around the World. *Journal of the American Medical Association, 317*(15), 1517. doi:10.1001/jama.2017.3826 PMID:28418490

Friese, C. R., & Aiken, L. H. (2008). Failure to rescue in the surgical oncology population: Implications for nursing and quality improvement. *Oncology Nursing Forum, 35*(5), 779–785. doi:10.1188/08.ONF.779-785 PMID:18765323

Frisiello, A., Nhu Nguyen, Q., Chiesa, M., Contreras-Espinosa, R. S., & Blanco-M., A. (in press). Conceptual design of a Gamification strategy applied to Commoning. In *XII Congress of the Italian Society of Ergonomics "Gentle Ergonomics".* Academic Press.

Froschauer, J. (2012). *Serious Heritage Games: Playful Approaches to Address Cultural Heritage* [Unpublished doctoral dissertation]. Wien University of Technology.

Fuchs, M. (2014). Predigital Precursors of Gamification. In Rethinking Gamification. Meson Pr.

Fuchs, C. (2021). How Did Donald Trump Incite a Coup Attempt? *tripleC: Communication, Capitalism & Critique Open Access Journal for a Global Sustainable Information Society, 19*(1), 246–251.

Fu, F.-L., Su, R.-C., & Yu, S.-C. (2009). EGameFlow: A scale to measure learners' enjoyment of e-learning games. *Computers & Education, 52*(1), 101–112. https://doi.org/10.1016/j.compedu.2008.07.004

Fujimura, J. H. (1987). Constructing "Do-able" Problems in Cancer Research: Articulating Alignment. *Social Studies of Science*, *17*(2), 257–293. doi:10.1177/030631287017002003

Fullerton, T. (2008). Working with dramatic elements. In *Game Design Workshop: A playcentric approach to creating innovative games* (pp. 97-128). CRC Press.

Fullerton, T. (2019). *Game design workshop: A playcentric approach to creating innovative games*. AK Peters/CRC Press.

Fumero, A., Roca, G., & Sáez, F. (2007). *Web 2.0*. Fundación Orange España.

Funke, J. (2010). Complex problem solving: A case for complex cognition? *Cognitive Processing*, *11*(2), 133–142. https://doi.org/10.1007/s10339-009-0345-0

Gabrielle, V. (2018, October 10). *How employers have gamified work for maximum profit*. Aeon. https://aeon.co/essays/how-employers-have-gamified-work-for-maximum-profit

Gaggi, O., Meneghello, F., Palazzi, C. E., & Pante, G. (2020, September). Learning how to recycle waste using a game. In *Proceedings of the 6th EAI International Conference on Smart Objects and Technologies for Social Good* (pp. 144-149). 10.1145/3411170.3411251

Gagne, M., & Deci, E. (2005). Self-determination theory and work motivation. *Journal of Organizational Behavior*, *26*(4), 331–362. doi:10.1002/job.322

Galetta, G. (2013). *The Gamification: Applications and Developments for Creativity and Education*. Creative Personality. Collection of Scientific Papers.

Gallarza, M. G., & Saura, I. G. (2006). Value dimensions, perceived value, satisfaction and loyalty: An investigation of university students' travel behaviour. *Tourism Management*, *27*(3), 437–452. doi:10.1016/j.tourman.2004.12.002

Galletta, M., Portoghese, I., Pili, S., Piazza, M. F., & Campagna, M. (2016). The effect of work motivation on a sample of nurses in an Italian healthcare setting. *Work (Reading, Mass.)*, *54*(2), 451–460. doi:10.3233/WOR-162327 PMID:27286081

Gamer, P. C. (2020). *Getting a bunch of negative user reviews is not automatically a 'review bomb'*. https://www.pcgamer.com/getting-a-bunch-of-negative-user-reviews-is-not-automatically-a-review-bomb/

Gan, C., & Wang, W. (2017). The influence of perceived value on purchase intention in social commerce context. *Internet Research*, *27*(4), 772–785. doi:10.1108/IntR-06-2016-0164

Gao, Z., Chen, S., Pasco, D., & Pope, Z. (2015). A meta-analysis of active video games on health outcomes among children and adolescents: A meta-analysis of active video games. *Obesity Reviews*, *16*(9), 783–794. https://doi.org/10.1111/obr.12287

Garcia, A., Linaza, M. T., Gutierrez, A., & Garcia, E. (2018). Gamified mobile experiences: Smart technologies for tourism destinations. *Tourism Review*, *74*(1), 30–49. doi:10.1108/TR-08-2017-0131

Garcia-Agundez, A., Reuter, C., Becker, H., Konrad, R., Caserman, P., Miede, A., & Göbel, S. (2019). Development of a Classifier to Determine Factors Causing Cybersickness in Virtual Reality Environments. *Games for Health Journal*, *8*(6), 439–444. doi:10.1089/g4h.2019.0045 PMID:31295007

García, F., Pedreira, O., Piattini, M., Cerdeira-Pena, A., & Penabad, M. (2017). A framework for gamification in software engineering. *Journal of Systems and Software*, *132*, 21–40. doi:10.1016/j.jss.2017.06.021

García-Jurado, A., Castro-González, P., Torres-Jiménez, M., & Leal-Rodríguez, A. L. (2019). Evaluating the role of gamification and flow in e-consumers: Millennials versus generation X. *Kybernetes*, *48*(6), 1278–1300. https://doi.org/10.1108/K-07-2018-0350

García, P. (2005). Comunidades de marca. El consumo como relación social. *Política y Sociedad*, *42*(1), 257–272.

Garnham, N. (2007). Habermas and the public sphere. *Global Media and Communication*, *3*(2), 201–214. https://doi.org/10.1177/1742766507078417

Garris, R., Ahlers, R., & Driskell, J. E. (2002). Games, motivation, and learning: A research and practice model. *Simulation & Gaming*, *33*(4), 441–467. doi:10.1177/1046878102238607

Gartner Group. (2011). *More Than 50 Percent of Organizations That Manage Innovation Processes Will Gamify Those Processes*. Retrieved from https://www.gartner.com/newsroom/id/1629214

Gartner. (2014). *Gartner's 2014 hypecycle for emerging technologies maps out evolving relationship between humans and machines*. https://www.gartner.com/newsroom/id/2819918

Gee, J. P. (2003). *What video games have to teach us about literacy and learning*. Academic Press.

Gelder, A., & Kovenock, D. (2017). Dynamic behavior and player types in majoritarian multi-battle contests. *Games and Economic Behavior*, *104*, 444–455. doi:10.1016/j.geb.2017.05.008

Gennari, R., Melonio, A., & Torello, S. (2016). Gamified probes for cooperative learning: A case study. *Multimedia Tools and Applications*, *76*(4), 4925–4949. doi:10.100711042-016-3543-7

Georgieva-Tsaneva, G. (2019). Serious games and innovative technologies in medical education in Bulgaria. *TEM Journal*, *8*(4), 1398–1403.

Georgieva-Tsaneva, G., Noev, N., & Bogdanova, G. (2018). Serious educational games and the study of the military historical heritage. *Digital Presentation and Preservation of Cultural and Scientific Heritage*, *8*, 133–140.

Ghani, J. A., & Deshpande, S. P. (1994). Task characteristics and the experience of optimal flow in human—Computer interaction. *The Journal of Psychology*, *128*(4), 381–391. doi:10.1080/00223980.1994.9712742

Ghassemlou, S., Marini, C., Chemi, C., Ranjit, Y. S., & Tofighi, B. (2020). Harmful smartphone applications promoting alcohol and illicit substance use: A review and content analysis in the United States. *Translational Behavioral Medicine*, *10*(5), 1233–1242. doi:10.1093/tbm/ibz135 PMID:33044528

Gil, B., Cantador, I., & Marczewski, A. (2015). Validating gamification mechanics and player types in an e-learning environment. In *Design for teaching and learning in a networked world* (pp. 568–572). Springer. doi:10.1007/978-3-319-24258-3_61

Gill, G. (2013). Culture, Complexity, and Informing: How Shared Beliefs Can Enhance Our Search for Fitness. *Informing Science: The International Journal of an Emerging Transdiscipline, 16*.

Gingras, Y. (2002). Les formes spécifiques de l'internationalité du champ scientifique. *Actes de la Recherche en Sciences Sociales*, *141-142*(1), 31–45. doi:10.3917/arss.141.0031

Glover, I. (2013). *Play as you learn: Gamification as a technique for motivating learners*. In J. Herrington, A. Couros & V. Irvine (Eds.), *Proceedings of EdMedia 2013--World conference on educational media and technology* (pp. 1999-2008). Association for the Advancement of Computing in Education (AACE). https://www.learntechlib.org/primary/p/112246/

Gnat, M., Leszek, K., & Olszewski, R. (2016). The Use of Geoinformation Technology, Augmented Reality and Gamification in the Urban Modeling Process. In O. Gervasi & ... (Eds.), Lecture Notes in Computer Science: Vol. 9787. *Computational Science and Its Applications. ICCSA 2016.* Springer. doi:10.1007/978-3-319-42108-7_37

Gochman, D. S. (1982). Labels, systems and motives: Some perspectives for future research and programs. *Health Education Quarterly*, *9*(2-3), 167–174. doi:10.1177/109019818200900213 PMID:7188305

Gode, B., Manthiou, A., Pederzoli, D., Rokka, J., Aiello, G., Donvito, R., & Singh, R. (2016). Social media marketing efforts of luxury brands: Influence on brand equity and consumer behavior. *Journal of Business Research, 69*(12), 5833–5841. doi:10.1016/j.jbusres.2016.04.181

Goehle, G., & Wagaman, J. (2016). The impact of gamification in web based homework. *PRIMUS (Terre Haute, Ind.), 26*(6), 557–569. doi:10.1080/10511970.2015.1122690

Goethe, O., & Palmquist, A. (2020). Broader Understanding of Gamification by Addressing Ethics and Diversity. In C. Stephanidis, D. Harris, W.-C. Li, D. D. Schmorrow, C. M. Fidopiastis, P. Zaphiris, A. Ioannou, X. Fang, R. A. Sottilare, & J. Schwarz (Eds.), *HCI International 2020 – Late Breaking Papers: Cognition, Learning and Games* (pp. 688–699). Springer International Publishing. doi:10.1007/978-3-030-60128-7_50

Gómez-Carreño, E., & Palacios-Alvarado, W. (2021). Revisión de literatura sobre Marketing en Redes Sociales. *Revista de Ingenierías Interfaces, 4*(1), 1–16.

González, C. S., Gómez, N., Navarro, V., Cairós, M., Quirce, C., Toledo, P., & Marrero-Gordillo, N. (2016). Learning healthy lifestyles through active videogames, motor games and the gamification of educational activities. *Computers in Human Behavior, 55*, 529–551. doi:10.1016/j.chb.2015.08.052

Goodland, R. (1995). The concept of environmental sustainability. *Annual Review of Ecology and Systematics, 26*(1), 1–24. doi:10.1146/annurev.es.26.110195.000245

Goodyear, V. A., Wood, G., Skinner, B., & Thompson, J. L. (2021). The effect of social media interventions on physical activity and dietary behaviours in young people and adults: A systematic review. *The International Journal of Behavioral Nutrition and Physical Activity, 18*(1), 1–18. doi:10.118612966-021-01138-3 PMID:34090469

Gordon, N. (2014). *Flexible Pedagogies: Technology-Enhanced Learning*. The Higher Education Academy (HEA). Available at: https://www.heacademy.ac.uk/flexible-pedagogies-technology-enhanced-learning

Gordon, R., Dibb, S., Magee, C., Cooper, P., & Waitt, G. (2018). Empirically testing the concept of value-in-behavior and its relevance for social marketing. *Journal of Business Research, 82*, 56–67. doi:10.1016/j.jbusres.2017.08.035

Götzenbrucker, G., & Köhl, M. (2009). Ten years later. Towards the careers of long-term gamers in Austria. *Eludamos (Göttingen), 3*(2), 309–324. https://www.eludamos.org/index.php/eludamos/article/view/vol3no2-12/143

Gould, O., & Colwill, J. (2015). A framework for material flow assessment in manufacturing systems. *Journal of Industrial and Production Engineering, 32*(1), 55–66. https://doi.org/10.1080/21681015.2014.1000403

Grace, L. D. (2020). *Doing things with games: social impact through play*. CRC Press.

Granic, I., Lobel, A., & Engels, R. C. M. E. (2014). The benefits of playing video games. *The American Psychologist, 69*(1), 66–78. doi:10.1037/a0034857

Grant, R. W. (2012). *Strings attached: Untangling the ethics of incentives*. Princeton University Press.

Gray, L. (2014). *How Does a Touch Screen Work?* Gareth Stevens Publishing.

Greco, M., Baldissin, N., & Nonino, F. (2013). An Exploratory Taxonomy of Business Games. *Simulation & Gaming, 44*(5), 645–682. https://doi.org/10.1177/1046878113501464

Greco, M., Branca, A. M., & Morena, G. (2011). An Experimental Study of the Reputation Mechanism in a Business Game. *Simulation & Gaming, 42*(1), 27–42. https://doi.org/10.1177/1046878110376793

Greenberg, J., & Pyszczynski, T. (1985). The effect of an overheard ethnic slur on evaluations of the target: How to spread a social disease. *Journal of Experimental Social Psychology, 21*(1), 61–72. doi:10.1016/0022-1031(85)90006-X

Greene, M. C., Jordans, M. J., Kohrt, B. A., Ventevogel, P., Kirmayer, L. J., Hassan, G., & Tol, W. A. (2017). Addressing culture and context in humanitarian response: Preparing desk reviews to inform mental health and psychosocial support. *Conflict and Health*, *11*(1), 1–10. doi:10.118613031-017-0123-z PMID:29163666

Griffin, G. (2007). *The uses of discourse analysis in the study of gender and migration. Research Paper.* The University of York.

Griffiths, M. (2005, July). Video games and health. *British Medical Journal*, *331*, 122–123. doi:10.1136/bmj.331.7509.122

Grisolia, F., & Martella, A. (2019). *Devoted users: EU elections and gamification on Twitter*. https://ocean.sagepub.com/blog/devoted-users-eu-elections-and-gamification-on-twitter

Gross, M., & Ho, S. M. (2021). Collective Learning for Developing Cyber Defense Consciousness: An Activity System Analysis. *Journal of Information Systems Education*, *32*(1), 65–77.

Gruman, J. A., & Saks, A. M. (2011). Performance management and employee engagement. *Human Resource Management Review*, *21*(2), 123–136. https://doi.org/10.1016/j.hrmr.2010.09.004

Guardiola, E. (2016). The gameplay loop: A player activity model for game design and analysis. *ACM International Conference Proceeding Series*. doi:10.1145/3001773.3001791

Guardiola, E. (2019). Game and Humanitarian: From Awareness to Field Intervention. *Proceedings of the Game On Conference*.

Guillen, M. G., Hamari, J., & Quist, J. (2021, January). Gamification of Sustainable Consumption: a systematic literature review. In *Proceedings of the 54th Hawaii International Conference on System Sciences* (p. 1345). 10.24251/HICSS.2021.163

Gunter, G., & Kenny, R. (2008). Digital Booktalk: Digital Media for Reluctant Readers. *Contemporary Issues in Technology & Teacher Education*, *8*(1), 84–99.

Gupta, A., Lawendy, B., Goldenberg, M. G., Grober, E., Lee, J. Y., & Perlis, N. (2021). Can video games enhance surgical skills acquisition for medical students? A systematic review. *Surgery*, *169*(4), 821–829. https://doi.org/10.1016/j.surg.2020.11.034

Gusky, T. (2000). *Evaluating Professional Development*. Corwin.

Gustafsson, T., & Defence, S. (2020). *Using serious gaming to train operators of critical infrastructure : an Industry / Experience report*. Retrieved from https://www.researchgate.net/profile/Tommy-Gustafsson-3/publication/341287480_Using_serious_gaming_to_train_operators_of_critical_infrastructure_an_IndustryExperience_report/links/5eb93a3a299bf1287f7cb072/Using-serious-gaming-to-train-operators-of-critical-infrastructure-an-Industry-Experience-report.pdf

Guzik, A., Nerc, O., Zalewska, M., Gałecka, J., Chyrk, P., Milewski, P., Mizerska, M., Siekierska, E., Wiśniowski, W., & Żylińska, M. (2015). *The Book of Trends in Education*. Academic Press.

Habermas, J. (2006). Political communication in media society: Does democracy still enjoy an epistemic dimension? The impact of normative theory on empirical research. *Communication Theory*, *16*(4), 411–426. https://doi.org/10.1111/j.1468-2885.2006.00280.x

Habidin, N. F., Salleh, M. I., Md Latip, N. A., Azman, M. N. A., & Mohd Fuzi, N. (2016). Lean six sigma performance improvement tool for automotive suppliers. *Journal of Industrial and Production Engineering*, *33*(4), 215–235. https://doi.org/10.1080/21681015.2015.1136966

Hägglund, P. (2012). *Taking gamification to the next level – A detailed overview of the past, the present and a possible future of gamification* (Master's thesis). Umeå University.

Hahtela, N., Paavilainen, E., McCormack, B., Slater, P., Helminen, M., & Suominen, T. (2015). Influence of workplace culture on nursing-sensitive nurse outcomes in municipal primary health care. *Journal of Nursing Management, 23*(7), 931–939. doi:10.1111/jonm.12237 PMID:24848308

Hakulinen, L., Auvinen, T., & Korhonen, A. (2015). The effect of achievement badges on students' behavior: An empirical study in a university-level computer science course. *International Journal of Emerging Technologies in Learning, 10*(1), 18–29. doi:10.3991/ijet.v10i1.4221

Hall, M., Caton, S., & Weinhardt, C. (2013, July). Well-being's predictive value. In *International Conference on Online Communities and Social Computing* (pp. 13-22). Springer. 10.1007/978-3-642-39371-6_2

Hamari, J., & Tuunanen, J. (2014). Player types: A meta-synthesis. *Transactions of the Digital Games Research Association, 1*(2).

Hamari, J., Koivisto, J., & Sarsa, H. (2014, January). Does gamification work?--A literature review of empirical studies on gamification. In *2014 47th Hawaii International Conference on System Sciences* (pp. 3025-3034). IEEE.

Hamari, J. (2013). Transforming homo economicus into homo ludens: A field experiment on gamification in a utilitarian peer-to-peer trading service. *Electronic Commerce Research and Applications, 12*(4), 236–245. doi:10.1016/j.elerap.2013.01.004

Hamari, J. (2015). Do badges increase user activity? A field experiment on the effects of gamification. *Computers in Human Behavior*, 1–10.

Hamari, J., & Koivisto, J. (2014). Measuring flow in gamification: Dispositional Flow Scale-2.). . *Computers in Human Behavior, 40*, 133–143. doi:10.1016/j.chb.2014.07.048

Hamari, J., & Koivisto, J. (2015). Why do people use gamification services? *International Journal of Information Management, 35*(4), 419–431. doi:10.1016/j.ijinfomgt.2015.04.006

Hamari, J., Koivisto, J., & Sarsa, H. (2014). Does gamification *work? – A* literature review of empirical studies on gamification. *Proceedings of the 47th Hawaii International Conference on System Sciences*, 3025–34. 10.1109/HICSS.2014.377

Hamari, J., & Lehdonvirta, V. (2010). Game design as marketing: How game mechanics create demand for virtual goods. *International Journal of Business Science and Applied Management, 5*(1), 14–29.

Hamari, J., Sjöklint, M., & Ukkonen, A. (2016). The sharing economy: Why people participate in collaborative consumption. *Journal of the Association for Information Science and Technology, 67*(9), 2047–2059. doi:10.1002/asi.23552

Hamari, J., & Tuunanen, J. (2014). Player types: A meta-synthesis. *Transactions of the Digital Games Research Association, 1*(2), 29–53. doi:10.26503/todigra.v1i2.13

Hamayon, R. (2015). Petit pas de côté. *La Revue du MAUSS, 45*(1), 75–90. doi:10.3917/rdm.045.0075

Hamid, M., & Kuppusamy, M. (2017). Gamification implementation in service marketing: A literature review. *Electronic Journal of Business & Management, 2*(1), 38–50.

Hamid, M., & Kuppusamy, M. (2017). Gamification implementation in service marketing: A literature. *Electronic Journal of Business & Management, 2*(1), 38–50.

Hammarfelt, B., de Rijcke, S., & Rushforth, A. D. (2016). Quantified academic selves: The gamification of research through social networking services. *Information Research, 20*(2). http://www.informationr.net/ir/21-2/SM1.html

Hammedi, W., Leclercq, T., & Poncin, I. (2019). Customer engagement: The role of gamification. In *Handbook of research on customer engagement* (pp. 164–185). Edward Elgar Publishing. doi:10.4337/9781788114899.00014

Hammedi, W., Leclercq, T., Poncin, I., & Alkire, L. (2021). Uncovering the Dark Side of Gamification at Work: Impacts on Engagement and Well-Being. *Journal of Business Research*, *122*, 256–269. https://doi.org/https://doi.org/10.1016/j.jbusres.2020.08.032

Hammedi, W., Leclerq, T., & Van Riel, A. C. R. (2017). The use of gamification mechanics to increase employee and user engagement in participative healthcare services: A study of two cases. *Journal of Service Management*, *28*(4), 640–661. doi:10.1108/JOSM-04-2016-0116

Handy, C. B. (1999). *Gods of management: The changing work of organizations*. Oxford University Press.

Hannula, O., & Harviainen, J. T. (2016). Efficiently Inefficient: Service Design Games as Innovation Tools. ServDes. *2016 Service Design Geographies; Proceedings from the Fifth Conference on Service Design and Service Innovation*, (125), 241–252. Retrieved from http://www.ep.liu.se/ecp/article.asp?issue=125&article=020&volume=%0Ahttp://www.ep.liu.se/ecp/125/020/ecp16125020.pdf

Hansen, J. M., & Levin, M. A. (2016). The effect of apathetic motivation on employees' intentions to use social media for businesses. *Journal of Business Research*, *69*(12), 6058–6066. doi:10.1016/j.jbusres.2016.06.009

Hansen, J. M., Saridakis, G., & Benson, V. (2018). Risk, trust, and the interaction of perceived ease of use and behavioral control in predicting consumers' use of social media for transactions. *Computers in Human Behavior*, *80*, 197–206. doi:10.1016/j.chb.2017.11.010

Hanus, M. D., & Fox, J. (2015). Assessing the effects of gamification in the classroom: A longitudinal study on intrinsic motivation, social comparison, satisfaction, effort, and academic performance. *Computers & Education*, *80*, 152–161. doi:10.1016/j.compedu.2014.08.019

Harris, M. A. (2019). Maintenance of behaviour change following a community-wide gamification based physical activity intervention. *Preventive Medicine Reports*, *13*, 37–40. doi:10.1016/j.pmedr.2018.11.009 PMID:30510892

Harrison, J. D., Jones, J. M., Small, D. S., Rareshide, C. A., Szwartz, G., Steier, D., Guszcza, J., Kalra, P., Torio, B., Reh, G., Hilbert, V., & Patel, M. S. (2019). Social incentives to encourage physical activity and understand predictors (STEP UP): Design and rationale of a randomized trial among overweight and obese adults across the United States. *Contemporary Clinical Trials*, *80*, 55–60. doi:10.1016/j.cct.2019.04.001 PMID:30954675

Harwood, T., & Garry, T. (2015). An investigation into gamification as a customer engagement experience environment. *Journal of Services Marketing*, *29*(6–7), 533–546. doi:10.1108/JSM-01-2015-0045

Hasan, H., & Kazlauskas, A. (2009). Making sense of IS with the Cynefin framework. *PACIS 2009 - 13th Pacific Asia Conference on Information Systems: IT Services in a Global Environment*.

Hashem, T. N. (2020). Examining the Influence of COVID 19 Pandemic in Changing Customers' Orientation towards E-Shopping. *Modern Applied Science*, *14*(8), 59. https://doi.org/10.5539/mas.v14n8p59

Hassan, L. (2016). Governments Should Play Games: Towards a Framework for the Gamification of Civic Engagement Platforms. *Simulation & Gaming*, *48*(2), 249–267. doi:10.1177/1046878116683581

Hassan, L., & Hamari, J. (2020). Gameful civic engagement: A review of the literature on gamification of e-participation. *Government Information Quarterly*, *37*(3), 1–21. doi:10.1016/j.giq.2020.101461

Hassan, L., & Leigh, E. (2021). Do you have a moment to increase the world awesome? Game-based engagement with social change. In A. Spanelli & J. T. Harviainen (Eds.), *Transforming Society and Organizations through Gamification: From the Sustainable Development Goals to Inclusive Workplaces* (pp. 49–65). Palgrave Macmillan. doi:10.1007/978-3-030-68207-1_4

Hauer, B. (2015). Data and information leakage prevention within the scope of information security. *IEEE Access: Practical Innovations, Open Solutions, 3*, 2554–2565. https://doi.org/10.1109/ACCESS.2015.2506185

Hays, R. T. (2005). *The effectiveness of instructional games: A literature review and discussion. Technical Report.* Naval Air Warfare Center. doi:10.21236/ADA441935

Heckmann, F. (2005). *Integration and integration policies.* IMISCOE Network Feasibility Study.

Helmefalk, M., & Marcusson, L. (2019). Gamification in a servicescape context: A conceptual framework. *International Journal of Internet Marketing and Advertising, 13*(1), 22–46. doi:10.1504/IJIMA.2019.097894

Helmefalk, M., & Rosenlund, J. (2020). Hedonic recycling: Using gamification and sensory stimuli to enhance the recycling experience. *EAI Endorsed Transactions on Serious Games*, (18), 1–12.

Helmreich, R. L. (2000). On error management: Lessons from aviation. *BMJ (Clinical Research Ed.), 320*(7237), 781–785. doi:10.1136/bmj.320.7237.781 PMID:10720367

Hemovich, V. (2021). It Does Matter If You Win or Lose, and How You Play the (Video) Game. *Games and Culture, 16*(4), 481–493. doi:10.1177/1555412020913760

Henderson, A., Korner-Bitensky, N., & Levin, M. (2007). Virtual reality in stroke rehabilitation: A systematic review of its effectiveness for upper limb motor recovery. *Topics in Stroke Rehabilitation, 14*(2), 52–61. doi:10.1310/tsr1402-52 PMID:17517575

Henriksen, T. D., & Borgesen, K. (2016). Can good leadership be learned through business games. *Human Resource Development International, 19*(5), 388-405. doi:10.1080/13678868

Herbert, B., Charles, D., Moore, A., & Charles, T. (2014). An Investigation of Gamification Typologies for Enhancing Learner Motivation. *2014 International Conference on Interactive Technologies and Games*, 71-78. 10.1109/iTAG.2014.17

Hernández-Fernández, A., Olmedo-Torre, N., & Peña, M. (2020). Is Classroom Gamification Opposed to Performance? *Sustainability, 12*(23), 9958. doi:10.3390u12239958

Herne, R., Shiratuddin, M. F., Rai, S., Laga, H., Dixon, J., & Blacker, D. (2019). *Game design principles influencing stroke survivor engagement for VR-Based upper limb rehabilitation.* 31st Australian Conference on Human-Computer-Interaction (OzCHI), Esplanade Hotel, Fremantle, Australia.

Herrero, A., & Martin, H. S. (2012). Developing and testing a global model to explain the adoption of websites by users in rural tourism accommodations. *International Journal of Hospitality Management, 31*(4), 1178–1186. doi:10.1016/j.ijhm.2012.02.005

Hesse, W., & Verrijn-Stuart, A. (2001). Towards a theory of information systems: The FRISCO approach. *Frontiers in Artificial*, 1–12. Retrieved from http://citeseerx.ist.psu.edu/viewdoc/download?doi=10.1.1.68.7598&rep=rep1&type=pdf

Hew, K. F., Huang, B., Chu, K. W. S., & Chiu, D. K. (2016). Engaging Asian students through game mechanics: Findings from two experiment studies. *Computers & Education, 92*, 221–236. doi:10.1016/j.compedu.2015.10.010

Hilgartner, S. (1990). The Dominant View of Popularization: Conceptual Problems, Political Uses. *Social Studies of Science, 20*(3), 519–539. doi:10.1177/030631290020003006

Himanen, P. (2004). *La ética del hacker y el espíritu de la era de la información*. Destino.

HMCPSI Her Majesty's Crown Prosecution Service Inspectorate / HMIC. (2014). *Achieving Best Evidence in Child Sexual Abuse Cases – A Joint Inspection, December 2014*. Available from: www.justiceinspectorates.gov.uk/cjji/wp-content/uploads/sites/2/ 2014/12/CJJI_ABE_Dec14_rpt.pdf

HMIC. (2015). *In harm's way: the role of the police in keeping children safe HM Crown Prosecution Service Inspectorate (HMCPSI) and HM Inspectorate of Constabulary (HMIC)*. https://www.justiceinspectorates.gov.uk/hmic/wpcontent/uploads/in-harms-way.pdf

Hofacker, C. F., de Ruyter, K., Lurie, N. H., Manchanda, P., & Donaldson, J. (2016). Gamification and Mobile Marketing Effectiveness. *Journal of Interactive Marketing, 34*, 25–36. doi:10.1016/j.intmar.2016.03.001

Hoffman, B., & Nadelson, L. (2010). Motivational engagement and video gaming: A mixed methods study. *Educational Technology Research and Development, 58*(3), 245–270. doi:10.100711423-009-9134-9

Hoffmann, G., & Matysiak, L. (2019). *Exploring Game Design for the Financial Education of Millenials* (Vol. 0–1). IEEE Xplore.

Holbrook, M. B. (1996). Customer value - A framework for analysis and research. *Advances in Consumer Research. Association for Consumer Research (U. S.), 23*, 138–142.

Holbrook, M. B., & Hirschman, E. C. (1982). The experiential aspects of consumption: Consumer fantasies, feelings, and fun. *The Journal of Consumer Research, 9*(2), 132–139. doi:10.1086/208906

Hollebeek, L. (2011). Exploring customer brand engagement: Definition and themes. *Journal of Strategic Marketing, 19*(7), 555–573. doi:10.1080/0965254X.2011.599493

Holzmann, S. L., Schäfer, H., Groh, G., Plecher, D. A., Klinker, G., Schauberger, G., Hauner, H., & Holzapfel, C. (2019). Short-term effects of the serious game "fit, food, fun" on nutritional knowledge: A pilot study among children and adolescents. *Nutrients, 11*(9), 2031. doi:10.3390/nu11092031 PMID:31480257

Horkheimer, M. (2002). *Critical theory - selected essays*. The Continuum Publishing Company. Retrieved from https://books.google.no/books?hl=no&lr=&id=YiXUAwAAQBAJ&oi=fnd&pg=PR3&dq=horkheimer+1972+critical+theory&ots=uxQGfrftw1&sig=eL2AGBZIqa-qktynN6oD1Nrotas&redir_esc=y#v=onepage&q=horkheimer1972criticaltheory&f=false

Hove, C., Tarnes, M., Line, M. B., & Bernsmed, K. (2014). Information security incident management: Identified practice in large organizations. *Proceedings - 8th International Conference on IT Security Incident Management and IT Forensics, IMF 2014*, 27–46. doi:10.1109/IMF.2014.9

Howard, M. C. (2017). A meta-analysis and systematic literature review of virtual reality rehabilitation programs. *Computers in Human Behavior, 70*, 317–327. doi:10.1016/j.chb.2017.01.013

Howe, J. (2008). *Crowdsourcing, How the Power of the Crowd is Driving the Future of Business*. Random House Business Books.

HSEEP. (2006). *Homeland Security Exercise and Evaluation Program Volume 1: HSEEP Overview and Exercise Program Management*. Retrieved from http://hseep.dhs.gov

Hsu, C. L., & Chen, M. C. (2018a). How does gamification improve user experience? An empirical investigation on the antecedences and consequences of user experience and its mediating role. *Technological Forecasting and Social Change, 132*, 118–129. doi:10.1016/j.techfore.2018.01.023

Hsu, C. L., & Chen, M. C. (2018b). How gamification marketing activities motivate desirable consumer behaviors: Focusing on the role of brand love. *Computers in Human Behavior*, *88*, 121–133. doi:10.1016/j.chb.2018.06.037

Hsu, C. L., Chen, Y. C., Yang, T. N., & Lin, W. K. (2017). Do website features matter in an online gamification context? Focusing on the mediating roles of user experience and attitude. *Telematics and Informatics*, *34*(4), 196–205. doi:10.1016/j.tele.2017.01.009

Hsu, C. L., & Lin, C. C. (2016). Effect of perceived value and social influences on mobile app stickiness and in-app purchase intention. *Technological Forecasting and Social Change*, *108*, 42–53. doi:10.1016/j.techfore.2016.04.012

Hu, G., & Liu, Y. (2018). Three Minute Thesis Presentations as an Academic Genre: A Cross-disciplinary Study of Genre Move. *Journal of English for Academic Purposes*. doi:10.1016/j.jeap.2018.06.004

Huang, B., & Hew, K. F. (2018). Implementing a theory-driven gamification model in higher education flipped courses: Effects on out-of-class activity completion and quality of artifacts. *Computers & Education*, *125*, 254–272. doi:10.1016/j.compedu.2018.06.018

Huang, C. K., Chen, C. D., & Liu, Y. T. (2019). To stay or not to stay? Discontinuance intention of gamification apps. *Information Technology & People*, *32*(6), 1423–1445. doi:10.1108/ITP-08-2017-0271

Huang, P., & Zhang, Z. (2013). (Forthcoming). Participation in open knowledge communities and job-hopping: Evidence from enterprise software. *Management Information Systems Quarterly*.

Huang, R., Ritzhaupt, A. D., Sommer, M., Zhu, J., Stephen, A., Valle, N., Hampton, J., & Li, J. (2020). The impact of gamification in educational settings on student learning outcomes: A meta analysis. *Educational Technology Research and Development*, *68*(4), 1875–1901. doi:10.100711423-020-09807-z

Huang, Y., Backman, S. J., Backman, K. F., & Moore, D. (2013). Exploring user acceptance of 3d virtual worlds in travel and tourism marketing. *Tourism Management*, *36*, 490–501. doi:10.1016/j.tourman.2012.09.009

Hubspot. (2021). *Tendencias en Redes Sociales*. https://offers.hubspot.es/tendencias-redes-sociales-2021

Huizinga, J. (1949). *Homo ludens. A study of the play-element in culture*. Routledge & Kegan Pau.

Huizinga, J. (1955). *Homo ludens. A study of the play element in culture*. Beacon Pr.

Huizinga, J. (1955). *Homo Ludens–A Study of the Play-Element in Culture*. Beacon Press.

Huizinga, J. (2008). *Homo Ludens*. Alianza Editorial.

Huizinga, J. (2014). *Homo ludens ils 86*. Routledge. doi:10.4324/9781315824161

Hu, N., Zhang, J., & Pavlou, P. A. (2009). Overcoming the J-shaped distribution of product reviews. *Communications of the ACM*, *52*(10), 144–147.

Hung, A. C. Y. (2017). A Critique and Defense of Gamification. *Journal of Interactive Online Learning*, *15*(1), 57–72.

Hung, S.-Y., Durcikova, A., Lai, H.-M., & Lin, W.-M. (2011). The influence of intrinsic and extrinsic motivation on individuals' knowledge sharing behavior. *International Journal of Human-Computer Studies*, *69*(6), 415–427. doi:10.1016/j.ijhcs.2011.02.004

Hung, S.-Y., Lai, H.-M., & Chang, W.-W. (2011). Knowledge-sharing motivations affecting R&D employees' acceptance of electronic knowledge repository. *Behaviour & Information Technology*, *30*(2), 213–230. doi:10.1080/0144929X.2010.545146

Hunicke, R., LeBlanc, M., & Zubek, R. (2004). MDA: A formal approach to game design and game research. In *Proceedings of the Challenges in Games AI Workshop, Nineteenth National Conference of Artificial Intelligence* (vol. 4, pp. 1-9). Academic Press.

Hunicke, R., LeBlanc, M., & Zubek, R. (2004, July). MDA: A formal approach to game design and game research. In *Proceedings of the AAAI Workshop on Challenges in Game AI* (Vol. 4, No. 1, p. 1722). Academic Press.

Hunicke, R., Leblanc, M., & Zubek, R. (2004). MDA: A formal approach to game design and game research. *AAAI Workshop - Technical Report, WS-04-04*, 1–5.

Hunicke, R., Leblanc, M., & Zubek, R. (2004). MDA: A Formal Approach to Game Design and Game Research. *Proceedings AAAI Workshop on Challenges in Game.*

Huotari, K., & Hamari, J. (2011). "Gamification" from the perspective of service marketing. *ACM Conference on Human Factors in Computing Systems (Gamification Workshop).*

Huotari, K., & Hamari, J. (2011). "Gamification" from the perspective of service marketing. *Proc. CHI 2011 Workshop Gamification.*

Huotari, K., & Hamari, J. (2012). Defining gamification - A service marketing perspective. *Proceedings of the 16th International Academic MindTrek Conference 2012: "Envisioning Future Media Environments", MindTrek 2012*, 17–22.

Huotari, K., & Hamari, J. (2012). Defining gamification – A service marketing perspective. *Proceedings of the 16th International Academic MindTrek Conference*, 17–22. 10.1145/2393132.2393137

Huotari, K., & Hamari, J. (2017). A definition for gamification: Anchoring gamification in the service marketing literature. *Electronic Markets*, *27*(1), 21–31. doi:10.100712525-015-0212-z

Hussain, M., Zhu, W., Zhang, W., & Abidi, R. (2018). Student Engagement Predictions in an e-Learning System and Their Impact on Student Course Assessment Scores. *Computational Intelligence and Neuroscience*, 1–21. doi:10.1155/2018/6347186 PMID:30369946

Hwang, G. J., Tsai, C. C., & Yang, S. J. H. (2008). Criteria, strategies and research issues of context-aware ubiquitous learning. *Journal of Educational Technology & Society*, *11*(2), 81–91.

Hwang, J., & Choi, L. (2020). Having fun while receiving rewards?: Exploration of gamification in loyalty programs for consumer loyalty. *Journal of Business Research*, *106*, 365–376. doi:10.1016/j.jbusres.2019.01.031

Hyeuk, C. (2016). Consumer brand engagement by virtue of using Starbucks's branded mobile app based on grounded theory methodology. *International Journal of Asia Digital Art and Design*, *19*, 91–97.

Hyland, K., & Zou, H. (2021). "I believe the findings are fascinating": Stance in three-minute theses. *Journal of English for Academic Purposes*, *50*, 100973. Advance online publication. doi:10.1016/j.jeap.2021.100973

Hyrynsalmi, S., Smed, J., & Kimppa, K. (2017). The Dark Side of Gamification: How We Should Stop Worrying and Study also the Negative Impacts of Bringing Game Design Elements to Everywhere. *GamiFIN*. /paper/The-Dark-Side-of-Gamification%3A-How-We-Should-Stop-Hyrynsalmi-Smed/048a43b5059ffc16a30124be3bbf5e1a8f0b7702

Hyrynsalmi, S., Smed, J., & Kimppa, K. (2017, May). The dark side of gamification: How we should stop worrying and study also the negative impacts of bringing game design elements to everywhere. In GamiFIN (pp. 96-104). Academic Press.

Ibáñez, M.-B., Di-Serio, A., & Delgado-Kloos, C. (2014). Gamification for engaging computer science students in learning activities: A case study. *IEEE Transactions on Learning Technologies*, *7*(3), 291–301. doi:10.1109/TLT.2014.2329293

Ibrahim, E. N. M., Jamali, N., & Suhaimi, A. I. H. (2021). Exploring gamification design elements for mental health support. *International Journal of Advanced Technology and Engineering Exploration*, 8(74), 114–125. doi:10.19101/IJATEE.2020.S1762123

Iglesias-Pradas, S., Hernández-García, Á., & Fernández-Cardador, P. (2017). Acceptance of Corporate Blogs for Collaboration and Knowledge Sharing. *Information Systems Management*, 34(3), 220–237. doi:10.1080/10580530.2017.1329998

Illeris, K. (2003). Towards a contemporary and comprehensive theory of learning. *International Journal of Lifelong Education*, 22(4), 396–406. doi:10.1080/02601370304837

Imbeault, F., Bouchard, B., & Bouzouane, A. (2011). Serious games in cognitive training for Alzheimer's patients. *2011 IEEE 1st International Conference on Serious Games and Applications for Health (SeGAH)*. doi:10.1109/SeGAH.2011.6165447

Ind, N., & Coates, N. (2013). The meanings of co-creation. *European Business Review*, 25(1), 86–95. doi:10.1108/09555341311287754

Insley, V., & Nunan, D. (2014). Gamification and the online retail experience. *International Journal of Retail & Distribution Management*, 42(5), 340–351. doi:10.1108/IJRDM-01-2013-0030

INTEF. (2019, September 19). *Resumen del Informe Horizon 2019*. https://bit.ly/3ieYycM

International Organization for Migration (IOM). (2021). *The Power of Contact: Designing, Facilitating and Evaluating Social Mixing Activities to Strengthen Migrant Integration and Social Cohesion Between Migrants and Local Communities - A Review of Lessons Learned*. Retrieved from: https://eea.iom.int/publications/power-contact-designing-facilitating-and-evaluating-social-mixing-activities-strengthen

Ip, B., & Jacobs, G. (2005). Segmentation of the games market using multivariate analysis. Journal of Targeting. *Measurement and Analysis for Marketing*, 13(3), 275–287. doi:10.1057/palgrave.jt.5740154

Ishak, N. M., Bakar, A., & Yazid, A. (2014). Developing Sampling Frame for Case Study: Challenges and Conditions. *World Journal of Education*, 4(3), 29–35.

Italian Videogame Program. (2019). *Videogiochi e luoghi reali: analisi del questionario IVIPRO*. https://bit.ly/38noqOv

Itani, O. S., Kassar, A. N., & Loureiro, S. M. C. (2019). Value get, value give: The relationships among perceived value, relationship quality, customer engagement, and value consciousness. *International Journal of Hospitality Management*, 80, 78–90. doi:10.1016/j.ijhm.2019.01.014

Jagoda, P., & McDonald, P. (2019). Game Mechanics, Experience Design, and Affective Play. In The Routledge Companion to Media Studies and Digital Humanities (pp. 174–182). Routledge. doi:10.4324/9781315730479-17

Jain, A., & Dutta, D. (2019). Millennials and gamification: Guerilla tactics for making learning fun. *SA Journal of Human Resource Management*, 6(1), 29–44.

Jang, S., Kitchen, P. J., & Kim, J. (2018). The effects of gamified customer benefits and characteristics on behavioral engagement and purchase: Evidence from mobile exercise application uses. *Journal of Business Research*, 92, 250–259. doi:10.1016/j.jbusres.2018.07.056

Jannach, D., Zanker, M., Felfernig, A., & Friedrich, G. (2010). *Recommender Systems - An Introduction*. Cambridge University Press.

Jansons, M. (2016). *Gamification Workshop*. EuropeHome Erasmus Project Intensive Programme - Entrepreneurship Skill Teaching and Training Programme, Riga, Latvia.

Javed, B., Sarwer, A., Soto, E. B., & Mashwani, Z. (2020). The coronavirus (COVID-19) pandemic's impact on mental health. *The International Journal of Health Planning and Management*, 35(5), 993–996. doi:10.1002/hpm.3008 PMID:32567725

Jennett, C., Cox, A. L., Cairns, P., Dhoparee, S., Epps, A., Tijs, T., & Walton, A. (2008). Measuring and defining the experience of immersion in games. *International Journal of Human-Computer Studies*, 66(9), 641–661. doi:10.1016/j. ijhcs.2008.04.004

Jeong, S., & Kim, M. T. (2007). Effects of a theory-driven music and movement program for stroke survivors in a community setting. *Applied Nursing Research*, 20(3), 125–131. doi:10.1016/j.apnr.2007.04.005 PMID:17693215

Jiang, F., & Qiu, X. (2021). Communicating disciplinary knowledge to a wide audience in 3MT presentations: How students engage with popularization of science. *Discourse Studies*. Advance online publication. doi:10.1177/14614456211037438

Jia, Y., Xu, B., Karanam, Y., & Voida, S. (2016). Personality-targeted gamification: a survey study on personality traits and motivational affordances. *CHI '16: Proceedings of the 2016 CHI Conference on Human Factors in Computing Systems*, 2001-2013. 10.1145/2858036.2858515

Jiménez, S. (2013). *Gamification Model Canvas*. Available at: https://gecon.es/wp-content/uploads/2017/07/GMC-Evolution_vDef.pdf

Johannes, N., Vuorre, M., & Przybylski, A. K. (2021). Video game play is positively correlated with well-being. *Royal Society Open Science*, 8(2), 202049. Advance online publication. doi:10.1098/rsos.202049 PMID:33972879

Johnson, D., Deterding, S., Kuhn, K.-A., Staneva, A., Stoyanov, S., & Hides, L. (2016). Gamification for health and wellbeing: A systematic review of the literature. *Internet Interventions: the Application of Information Technology in Mental and Behavioural Health*, 6, 89–106. doi:10.1016/j.invent.2016.10.002 PMID:30135818

Johnson, M. R. (2018). How to talk about videogames. *Information Communication and Society*, 21(12), 1862–1865. Advance online publication. doi:10.1080/1369118X.2017.1409787

Johnson, S. A., Gerstenfeld, A., Zeng, A. Z., Ramos, B., & Mishra, S. (2003). Teaching lean process design using a discovery approach. *2003 ASEE Annual Conference and Exposition: Staying in Tune with Engineering Education*, 3, 7881–7892.

Joly, P.-B. (2015). Le régime des promesses technoscientifiques. In M. Audétat (Ed.), *Sciences et technologies émergentes: pourquoi tant de promesses?* (pp. 31–47). Éditions Hermann.

Jonassen, D. H., & Grabowski, B. L. (1993). *Handbook of individual differences, learning, and instruction*. Routledge., doi:10.4324/9780203052860

Jones, B. A., Madden, G. J., Wengreen, H. J., Aguilar, S. S., & Desjardins, E. A. (2014). Gamification of dietary decision-making in an elementary-school cafeteria. *PLoS One*, 9(4), e93872. doi:10.1371/journal.pone.0093872 PMID:24718587

Jones, C. M., Scholes, L., Johnson, D., Katsikitis, M., & Carras, M. C. (2014). Gaming well: Links between videogames and flourishing mental health. *Frontiers in Psychology*, 5(MAR), 1–8. doi:10.3389/fpsyg.2014.00260 PMID:24744743

Jones, P. R., & Krzyzanowski, M. (2008). Identity, Belonging and Migration: Beyond Describing 'Others. In G. Delanty, R. Wodak, & P. R. Jones (Eds.), *Identity, Belonging, Migration* (pp. 38–53). Liverpool University Press. doi:10.5949/ liverpool/9781846311185.003.0003

Jones, W. M., & Dexter, S. (2014). How teachers learn: The roles of formal, informal, and independent learning. *Educational Technology Research and Development*, 62(3), 367–384. doi:10.100711423-014-9337-6

Jordan, Z., Lockwood, C., & Aromataris, E. M. Z. (2019). The updated Joanna Briggs Institute model of evidence-based healthcare. *International Journal of Evidence-Based Healthcare*, *17*(1), 58–71. doi:10.1097/XEB.0000000000000155 PMID:30256247

Judah, G., Gardner, B., & Aunger, R. (2013). Forming a flossing habit: An exploratory study of the psychological determinants of habit formation. *British Journal of Health Psychology*, *18*(2), 338–353. doi:10.1111/j.2044-8287.2012.02086.x PMID:22989272

Juul, J. (2003). The game, the player, the world: Looking for a heart of gameness. In M. Copier & J. Raessens (Eds.), *Level Up: Digital Games Research Conference, 4-6 November 2003, Utrecht University* (pp. 30–45). Universiteit Utrecht.

Kafai, Y. B., & Burke, Q. (2015). Constructionist Gaming: Understanding the Benefits of Making Games for Learning. *Educational Psychologist*, *50*(4), 313–334. doi:10.1080/00461520.2015.1124022 PMID:27019536

Kagan, S. (1994). *Cooperative Learning. Resources for Teachers* Inc.

Kalawsky, R. S. (1993). *The Science of Virtual Reality and Virtual Environments: A Technical, Scientific and Engineering Reference on Virtual Environments*. Addison-Wesley Longman Publishing Co., Inc.

Kallio, K. P., Mäyrä, F., & Kaipainen, K. (2011). At least nine ways to play: Approaching gamer mentalities. *Games and Culture*, *6*(4), 327–353. doi:10.1177/1555412010391089

Kalogiannakis, M., Papadakis, S., & Zourmpakis, A.-I. (2021). Gamification in science education. A systematic review of the literature. *Education in Science*, *11*(1), 22. doi:10.3390/educsci11010022

Kamel, M. M., Watfa, M. K., Lobo, B., & Sobh, D. (2017). Is enterprise gamification being cannibalized by its own brand? *IEEE Transactions on Professional Communication*, *60*(2), 147–164. doi:10.1109/TPC.2017.2656598

Kankanhalli, A., Taher, M., Cavusoglu, H., & Kim, S. H. (2012). *Gamification: A new paradigm for online user engagement*. Academic Press.

Kankanhalli, A., Tan, B. C., & Wei, K. K. (2005). Contributing knowledge to electronic knowledge repositories: An empirical investigation. *Management Information Systems Quarterly*, *29*(1), 113–143. doi:10.2307/25148670

Kantek, F., Yildirim, N., & Kavla, İ. (2015). Nurses' perceptions of motivational factors: A case study in a Turkish university hospital. *Journal of Nursing Management*, *23*(5), 674–681. doi:10.1111/jonm.12195 PMID:24372763

Kaplan, A. M., & Haenlein, M. (2010). Users of the world, unite! The challenges and opportunities of Social Media. *Business Horizons*, *53*(1), 59–68. doi:10.1016/j.bushor.2009.09.003

Kapp, K. M. (2012). The gamification of learning and instruction: case-based methods and strategies for training and education. Pfieffer: An Imprint of John Wiley & Sons.

Kapp, K. (2012). *The Gamification of Learning and Instruction: Game-based Methods and Strategies for Training and Education*. John Wiley & sons, Inc.

Kapp, K. (2014, March). Gamification: Separating Fact From Fiction. *Chief Learning Officer*, *13*(3), 42–46. https://doi.org/10.2304/elea.2005.2.1.5

Kapp, K. M. (2012). *The gamification of learning and instruction: game-based methods and strategies for training and education*. John Wiley & Sons.

Kapp, K. M. (2012). *The gamification of learning and instruction: Game-based methods and strategies for training and education*. Pfeiffer.

Kapur, M. (n.d.). An Octalysis Analysis of WhatsApp. Retrieved May 28, 2021, from https://yukaichou.com/gamification-guest-posts/octalysis-analysis-whatsapp/

Karać, J., & Stabauer, M. (2017). Gamification in e-commerce a survey based on the octalysis framework. *Lecture Notes in Computer Science, 10294*, 41–54. doi:10.1007/978-3-319-58484-3_4

Karahanna, E., Xu, S. X., Xu, Y., & Zhang, N. A. (2018). The needs–affordances–features perspective for the use of social media. *Management Information Systems Quarterly, 42*(3), 737–756. doi:10.25300/MISQ/2018/11492

Karra, M. (2010). *Key Distribution in PGP*. Academic Press.

Kato, P. M. (2010). *Video Games in Health Care: Closing the Gap*. doi:10.1037/a0019441

Kaye, L. K., & Bryce, J. (2012). Putting the "Fun Factor" into gaming: The influence of social contexts on experiences of playing video games. *International Journal of Internet Science, 7*(1), 23–37.

Kazhamiakin, R., Marconi, A., Martinelli, A., Pistore, M., Fondazione, G. V., & Kessler-Trento, B. (2016). A Gamification Framework for the Long–term Engagement of Smart Citizens. In *Proceedings of the IEEE 2nd International Smart Cities Conference: Improving the Citizens Quality of Life, ISC2 2016* (pp. 1–7). IEEE. 10.1109/ISC2.2016.7580746

Ke, F. (2014). An implementation of design-based learning through creating educational computer games: A case study on mathematics learning during design and computing. *Computers & Education, 73*(1), 26–39. doi:10.1016/j.compedu.2013.12.010

Ke, F., Xie, K., & Xie, Y. (2016). Game-based learning engagement: A theory- and data-driven exploration. *British Journal of Educational Technology, 47*(6), 1183–1201. https://doi.org/10.1111/bjet.12314

Kehr, T. W., & Proctor, M. D. (2017). People Pillars: Re-structuring the Toyota Production System (TPS) House Based on Inadequacies Revealed During the Automotive Recall Crisis. *Quality and Reliability Engineering International, 33*(4), 921–930. https://doi.org/10.1002/qre.2059

Kelle, S., Klemke, R., & Specht, M. (2012). Design patterns for learning games. *International Journal of Technology Enhanced Learning, 3*(6), 555. https://doi.org/10.1504/ijtel.2011.045452

Kenny, R. F. (2007). *Digital Narrative as a Change Agent to Teach Reading to Media-Centric Students*. Academic Press.

Khaleel, F. L., Tengku Wook, T., Ashaari, S. A., Wook, T. S. M. T., & Ismail, A. (2016). Gamification elements for learning applications. *International Journal on Advanced Science, Engineering and Information Technology, 6*(6), 868–874. doi:10.18517/ijaseit.6.6.1379

Khalil, M., Wong, J., de Koning, B., Ebner, M., & Paas, F. (2018). Gamification in MOOCs: A review of the state of the art. *Proceedings IEEE Global Engineering Education Conference (EDUCON2018)*. 10.1109/EDUCON.2018.8363430

Khan, A., & Krishnan, S. (2017). Social Media Enabled E-Participation: Review and Agenda for Future Research. *e-Service Journal, 10*(2), 45–75. doi:10.2979/eservicej.10.2.03

Khan, I., Melro, A., Amaro, A. C., & Oliveira, L. (2020). Systematic Review on Gamification and Cultural Heritage Dissemination. *Journal of Digital Media & Interaction, 3*(8), 19–41. doi:10.34624/jdmi.v3i8.21934

Kianpour, M., Kowalski, S., Zoto, E., Frantz, C., & Overby, H. (2019). Designing Serious Games for Cyber Ranges: A Socio-Technical Approach. *Proceedings - 4th IEEE European Symposium on Security and Privacy Workshops, EUROS and PW 2019*, 85–93. doi:10.1109/EuroSPW.2019.00016

Kianpour, M., Øverby, H., Kowalski, S. J., & Frantz, C. (2019). Social Preferences in Decision Making Under Cybersecurity Risks and Uncertainties. *Lecture Notes in Computer Science, 11594*, 149–163. doi:10.1007/978-3-030-22351-9_10

Kiili, K., de Freitas, S., Arnab, S., & Lainema, T. (2012). The Design Principles for Flow Experience in Educational Games. *Procedia Computer Science, 15,* 78–91. doi:10.1016/j.procs.2012.10.060

Kiili, K., Lainema, T., De Freitas, S., & Arnab, S. (2014). Flow framework for analyzing the quality of educational games q. *Entertainment Computing, 5*(4), 367–377. https://doi.org/10.1016/j.entcom.2014.08.002

Kiilunen, O. (2013). *Mobile applications as solutions to enhance sustainable travel behaviour among Generation Y. HAAGA-HELIA.* University of Applied Science.

Kim, M. J., Lee, C.-K., & Bonn, M. (2016). The effect of social capital and altruism on seniors' revisit intention to social network sites for tourism-related purposes. *Tourism Management, 53,* 96–107. doi:10.1016/j.tourman.2015.09.007

Kim, T. W. (2015, January). *Gamification Ethics: Exploitation and Manipulation.* Gamifying Research Workshop Papers. CHI 2015, Seoul, South Korea.

Kim, A. W., Nyengerai, T., & Mendenhall, E. (2020). Evaluating the Mental Health Impacts of the COVID-19 Pandemic in Urban South Africa: Perceived Risk of COVID-19 Infection and Childhood Trauma Predict Adult Depressive Symptoms. *Psychological Medicine,* 1–13. doi:10.1017/S0033291720003414 PMID:32895082

Kim, B. (2015). Understanding Gamification. *ALA TechSource, 51*(2). Advance online publication. doi:10.5860/ltr.51n2

Kim, C., Kim, C., Mirusmonov, M., & Lee, I. (2010). An empirical examination of factors influencing the intention to use mobile payment. *Computers in Human Behavior, 26*(3), 310–322. doi:10.1016/j.chb.2009.10.013

Kim, C.-S., Oh, E.-H., Yang, K. H., & Kim, J. K. (2010). The appealing characteristics of download type mobile games. *Service Business, 4*(3), 253–269. doi:10.100711628-009-0088-0

Kim, D., & Chang, H. (2007). Key functional characteristics in designing and operating health information websites for user satisfaction: An application of the extended technology acceptance model. *International Journal of Medical Informatics, 76*(11-12), 790–800. doi:10.1016/j.ijmedinf.2006.09.001 PMID:17049917

Kim, J., & Castelli, D. M. (2021). Effects of gamification on behavioral change in education: A meta-analysis. *International Journal of Environmental Research and Public Health, 18*(7), 3550. doi:10.3390/ijerph18073550 PMID:33805530

Kim, K., & Ahn, S. J. (2017). Rewards that undermine customer loyalty? A motivational approach to loyalty programs. *Psychology and Marketing, 34*(9), 842–852. doi:10.1002/mar.21026

Kim, K., & Ahn, S. J. G. (2017). The role of gamification in enhancing intrinsic motivation to use a loyalty program. *Journal of Interactive Marketing, 40,* 41–51. doi:10.1016/j.intmar.2017.07.001

Kim, M. J., Lee, C.-K., & Bonn, M. (2017). Obtaining a better understanding about travel-related purchase intentions among senior users of mobile social network sites. *International Journal of Information Management, 37*(5), 484–496. doi:10.1016/j.ijinfomgt.2017.04.006

Kim, M. J., & Preis, M. W. (2016). Why Seniors use Mobile Devices: Applying an Extended Model of Goal-Directed Behavior. *Journal of Travel & Tourism Marketing, 33*(3), 404–423. doi:10.1080/10548408.2015.1064058

Kim, M., & Qu, H. (2014). Travelers' behavioral intention toward hotel self-service kiosks usage. *International Journal of Contemporary Hospitality Management, 26*(2), 225–245. doi:10.1108/IJCHM-09-2012-0165

Kim, S. Y., Prestopnik, N., & Biocca, F. A. (2014). Body in the interactive game: How interface embodiment affects physical activity and health behavior change. *Computers in Human Behavior, 36,* 376–384. doi:10.1016/j.chb.2014.03.067

Kim, T. T., Kim, W. G., & Kim, H. B. (2009). The effects of perceived justice on recovery satisfaction, trust, word-of-mouth, and revisit intention in upscale hotels. *Tourism Management, 30*(1), 51–62. doi:10.1016/j.tourman.2008.04.003

Kim, T. W. (2018). Gamification of Labor and the Charge of Exploitation. *Journal of Business Ethics*, *152*(1), 27–39. doi:10.100710551-016-3304-6

Kim, T. W., & Werbach, K. (2016). More than just a game: Ethical issues in gamification. *Ethics and Information Technology*, *18*(2), 157–173. doi:10.100710676-016-9401-5

Kim, Y. H., Kim, D. J., & Wachter, K. (2013). A study of mobile user engagement (MoEN): Engagement motivations, perceived value, satisfaction, and continued engagement intention. *Decision Support Systems*, *56*(1), 361–370. doi:10.1016/j.dss.2013.07.002

King, R., & Lulle, A. (2016). *Research on migration facing realities and maximising opportunities: a policy review*. European Commission.

Király, O., Urbán, R., Griffiths, M. D., Ágoston, C., Nagygyörgy, K., Kökönyei, G., & Demetrovics, Z. (2015). The mediating effect of gaming motivation between psychiatric symptoms and problematic online gaming: An online survey. *Journal of Medical Internet Research*, *17*(4), e88. doi:10.2196/jmir.3515 PMID:25855558

Kirillov, A. V., Vinichenko, M. V., Melnichuk, A. V., Melnichuk, Y. A., & Vinogradova, M. V. (2016). Improvement in the learning environment through gamification of the educational process. *International Electronic Journal of Mathematics Education*, *11*(7), 2071–2085.

Kirk, P. (2019). *Teach Incident Response with Games*. Retrieved from https://medium.com/slalom-build/teach-incident-response-with-games-5a69cf19fa88

Kirkwood, A., & Price, L. (2014). Technology-enhanced learning and teaching in higher education: What is "enhanced" and how do we know? A critical literature review. *Learning, Media and Technology*, *39*(1), 1–44. http://oro.open.ac.uk/36675/1/TEL%20in%20Higher%20Education-What%20is%20enhanced%20and%20how%20do%20we%20 know.pdf

Kirriemuir, J., & McFarlane, A. E. (2004). *Literature Review in Games and Learning*. Futurelab. Available http://www.futurelab.org.uk/resources/documents/lit_reviews/Games_Review.pdf

Kirsh, B. A. (2014). *Game in Libraries: Essays on using play to connect and instruct*. McFarland & Company Inc. Publishers.

Kivunja, C. (2015). Teaching students to learn and to work well with 21st century skills: Unpacking the career and life skills domain of the new learning paradigm. *International Journal of Higher Education*, *4*(1), 1–11.

Klabbers, J. H. G. (2018). On the architecture of game science. *Simulation & Gaming*, *49*(3), 207–245. doi:10.1177/1046878118762534

Klimmt, C. (2003). Dimensions and determinants of the enjoyment of playing digital games: A three-level model. In M. Copier & J. Raessens (Eds.), *Level up: Digital games research conference* (pp. 246–257). Faculty of Arts, Utrecht University.

Klock, A. C., Hamari, J., Gasparini, I., & Pimenta, M. S. (2020). Tailored gamification: A review of literature. *International Journal of Human-Computer Studies*, *144*.

Klopfer, E., & Squire, K. (2008). Environmental detectives—The development of an augmented reality platform for environmental simulations. *Educational Technology Research and Development*, *56*(2), 203–228. doi:10.100711423-007-9037-6

Klug, G. C., & Schell, J. (2006). *Playing video games: Motives, Responses and Consequences*. Routledge Taylor and Francis Group.

Knaving, K., & Björk, S. (2013). Designing for fun and play: Exploring possibilities in design for gamification. In *Proceedings of The First International Conference on Gameful Design, Research, and Applications* (pp. 131-134). 10.1145/2583008.2583032

Knight, A. (2021). Technologies of Risk and Discipline in China's Social Credit System. In R. Creemers & S. Trevaskes (Eds.), *Law and the Party in China: Ideology and Organisation* (pp. 237–262). Cambridge University Press.

Koch, S. H., Proynova, R., Paech, B., & Wetter, T. (2014). The perfectly motivated nurse and the others: Workplace and personal characteristics impact preference of nursing tasks. *Journal of Nursing Management*, *22*(8), 1054–1064. doi:10.1111/jonm.12083 PMID:24033771

Koivisto, J. -M., Multisilta, J., & Haavisto, E. (2021). Surgical nurses' experiences with intrinsic work motivation: A focus on autonomy, competence and relatedness. *Hoitotiede*, *33*(2), 102–111.

Koivisto, J., & Hamari, J. (2014). Demographic differences in perceived benefits from gamification. *Computers in Human Behavior*, *35*, 179–188. doi:10.1016/j.chb.2014.03.007

Koivisto, J., & Hamari, J. (2019). The rise of motivational information systems: A review of gamification research. *International Journal of Information Management*, *45*, 191–210. doi:10.1016/j.ijinfomgt.2018.10.013

Koivisto, J.-M., Multisilta, J., & Haavisto, E. (2017). Possible benefits of gamification for improving surgical patients' quality of care. *Proceedings of the 1st International GamiFIN Conference.*

Koivisto, J.-M., Saarinen, I., Kaipia, A., Puukka, P., Kivinen, K., Laine, K.-M., & Haavisto, E. (2020). Patient education in relation to informational needs and postoperative complications in surgical patients. *International Journal for Quality in Health Care*, *32*(1), 35–40. doi:10.1093/intqhc/mzz032 PMID:31016323

Koivisto, J., & Malik, A. (2020). Gamification for older adults: A systematic literature review. *The Gerontologist*, 1–13. PMID:32530026

Kojima Productions. (2019). Death Stranding (PS4 Version) [Video game]. Japan.

Kolb, D. A. (1984). *Experiential Learning: Experience as The Source of Learning and Development.* Prentice Hall, Inc. doi:10.1016/B978-0-7506-7223-8.50017-4

Kolb, A. Y., & Kolb, D. A. (2009). The learning way: Meta-cognitive aspects of experiential learning. *Simulation & Gaming*, *40*(3), 297–327. https://doi.org/10.1177/1046878108325713

Kolb, A., & Kolb, D. (2018). Eight Important Things to Know About The Experiential Learning Cycle. *Australian Educational Leader*, *40*(3), 8–14. https://www.acel.org.au/ACEL/ACELWEB/Publications/AEL/2018/3/Lead_Article_1.aspx

Kopcha, T. J., Ding, L., Neumann, K. L., & Choi, I. (2016). Teaching technology integration to K-12 educators: A 'gamified' approach. *TechTrends*, *60*(1), 62–69. doi:10.100711528-015-0018-z

Korn, O., Schmidt, A., & Hörz, T. (2012). Assistive systems in production environments: Exploring motion recognition and gamification. In *Proceedings of the 5th International Conference on Pervasive Technologies Related to Assistive Environments* (pp. 1-5). 10.1145/2413097.2413109

Korteling, H. J. E., Helsdingen, A. S., & Sluimer, R. R. (2017). An Empirical Evaluation of Transfer-of-Training of Two Flight Simulation Games. *Simulation & Gaming*, *48*(1), 8–35. doi:10.1177/1046878116671057

Koster, R. (2013). *Theory of Fun for Game Design* (2nd ed.). O'Reilly Media.

Kotsios, A. (2015). Privacy in an augmented reality. *International Journal of Law and Information Technology*, *23*(2), 157–185. doi:10.1093/ijlit/eav003

Kourtesis, P., Collina, S., Doumas, L. A. A., & MacPherson, S. E. (2019). Validation of the Virtual Reality Neuroscience Questionnaire: Maximum Duration of Immersive Virtual Reality Sessions Without the Presence of Pertinent Adverse Symptomatology. *Frontiers in Human Neuroscience, 13,* 417–417. doi:10.3389/fnhum.2019.00417 PMID:31849627

Kovacevic, I., Zecevic, G., & Veljkovic, S. (2014). "Gamification" concept: Theoretical framework and destination marketing management practice. *Ekonomika Preduzeca., 62*(5-6), 315–322. doi:10.5937/ekopre1406315K

Kowal, J., & Fortier, M. S. (1999). Motivational Determinants of Flow: Contributions From Self-Determination Theory. *The Journal of Social Psychology, 139*(3), 355–368. doi:10.1080/00224549909598391

Kowal, M., Conroy, E., Ramsbottom, N., Smithies, T., Toth, A., & Campbell, M. (2021). Gaming Your Mental Health: A Narrative Review on Mitigating Symptoms of Depression and Anxiety Using Commercial Video Games. *JMIR Serious Games, 9*(2). Advance online publication. doi:10.2196/26575

Kowalski, S. (1994). *IT Insecurity: A Multi-disiplinary Inquiry.* Stockholm University.

Kozuba, J., & Bondaruk, A. (2014). Flight simulator as an essential device supporting the process of shaping pilot's situational awareness. *AFOSR, 1,* 41–60.

Kujur, F., & Singh, S. (2016). Engaging customers through online participation in social networking sites. *Asia Pacific Management Review, 22.* Advance online publication. doi:10.1016/j.apmrv.2016.10.006

Kumar, H., & Raghavendran, S. (2015). Gamification, the finer art: Fostering creativity and employee engagement. *The Journal of Business Strategy, 36*(6), 3–12. doi:10.1108/JBS-10-2014-0119

Kumar, J., & Herger, M. (2013). *Gamification at work: Designing engaging business software.* The Interaction Design Foundation. doi:10.1145/2468356.2468793

Kuo, M.-S., & Chuang, T.-Y. (2016). How gamification motivates visits and engagement for online academic dissemination – An empirical study. *Computers in Human Behavior, 55,* 16–27. doi:10.1016/j.chb.2015.08.025

Kurbalija, J. (2014). *An Introduction to Internet Governance* (6th ed.). Diplo Foundation.

Kurtzman, G. W., Day, S. C., Small, D. S., Lynch, M., Zhu, J., Wang, W., Rareshide, C. A. L., & Patel, M. S. (2018). Social incentives and gamification to promote weight loss: The LOSE IT randomized, controlled trial. *Journal of General Internal Medicine, 33*(10), 1669–1675. doi:10.100711606-018-4552-1 PMID:30003481

Kwon, H. Y., & Özpolat, K. (2020). The Dark Side of Narrow Gamification: Negative Impact of Assessment Gamification on Student Perceptions and Content Knowledge. *INFORMS Transactions on Education, 21*(2), 67–81. doi:10.1287/ited.2019.0227

Kyewski, E., & Krämer, N. C. (2018). To gamify or not to gamify? An experimental field study of the influence of badges on motivation, activity, and performance in an online learning course. *Computers & Education, 118,* 25–37. doi:10.1016/j.compedu.2017.11.006

Laato, S., Islam, A. K. M. N., Farooq, A., & Dhir, A. (2020). Unusual purchasing behavior during the early stages of the COVID-19 pandemic: The stimulus-organism-response approach. *Journal of Retailing and Consumer Services, 57*(July), 102224. https://doi.org/10.1016/j.jretconser.2020.102224

Lacruz, A. J., & Américo, B. L. (2018). Debriefing's influence on learning in business game: An experimental design. *Brazilian Business Review, 15*(2), 192–208. doi:10.15728/bbr.2018.15.2.6

Laeeq Khan, M. (2017). Social Media Engagement: What motivates User Participation and Consumption on YouTube? *Computers in Human Behavior, 66,* 236–247. doi:10.1016/j.chb.2016.09.024

Lambert, J. (2010). Digital storytelling cookbook. Handbook of Research on Transformative Online Education and Liberation: Models for Social Equality, 408–423.

Landers, R. N., & Callan, R. C. (2011). Casual social games as serious games: The psychology of gamification in undergraduate education and employee training. *Serious Games and Edutainment Applications*, 399–423.

Landers, R. N. (2014). Developing a Theory of Gamified Learning: Linking Serious Games and Gamification of Learning. *Simulation & Gaming*, *45*(6), 752–768. https://doi.org/10.1177/1046878114563660

Landers, R. N. (2019). Gamification misunderstood: How badly executed and rhetorical gamification obscures its transformative potential. *Journal of Management Inquiry*, *28*(2), 137–140. doi:10.1177/1056492618790913

Landers, R. N., Auer, E. M., Collmus, A. B., & Armstrong, M. B. (2018). Gamification science, its history and future: Definitions and a research agenda. *Simulation & Gaming*, *49*(3), 315–337. doi:10.1177/1046878118774385

Landers, R. N., Bauer, K. N., Callan, R. C., & Armstrong, M. B. (2015). Psychological theory and the gamification of learning. In T. Reiners & L. Wood (Eds.), *Gamification in education and business* (pp. 165–186). Springer., doi:10.1007/978-3-319-10208-5_9

Landers, R. N., & Landers, A. K. (2014). An empirical test of the theory of gamified learning: The effect of leaderboards on time-on-task and academic performance. *Simulation & Gaming*, *45*(6), 769–785. doi:10.1177/1046878114563662

Landman, A., van Oorschot, P., van Paassen, M. M., Groen, E. L., Bronkhorst, A. W., & Mulder, M. (2018). Training pilots for unexpected events: A simulator study on the advantage of unpredictable and variable scenarios. *Human Factors*, *60*(6), 793–805. doi:10.1177/0018720818779928 PMID:29913086

Langstaff, C., Martin, C., Brown, G., McGuinness, D., Mather, J., Loshaw, J., Jones, N., Fletcher, K., & Paterson, J. (2014). Enhancing community-based rehabilitation for stroke survivors: Creating a discharge link. *Topics in Stroke Rehabilitation*, *21*(6), 510–519. doi:10.1310/tsr2106-510 PMID:25467399

Larsen, C. A. (2014). *Social cohesion: Definition, measurement and developments*. Working Paper. Faculty of Social Science. Aalborg University.

Larson, K. (2020). Serious Games and Gamification in the Corporate Training Environment: A Literature Review.). . *TechTrends*, *64*(2), 319–328. doi:10.100711528-019-00446-7

Lasén, A. (2014). *Las mediaciones digitales de la educación sentimental de los y las jóvenes. Jóvenes y comunicación. La impronta de lo virtual*. Fundación de Ayuda contra la Drogadicción.

Lau, H. M., Smit, J. H., Fleming, T. M., & Riper, H. (2017). Serious games for mental health: Are they accessible, feasible, and effective? A systematic review and meta-analysis. *Frontiers in Psychiatry*, *7*, 209. doi:10.3389/fpsyt.2016.00209 PMID:28149281

Laver, K. E., Lange, B., George, S., Deutsch, J. E., Saposnik, G., Crotty, M., & Laver, K. E. (2017). Virtual reality for stroke rehabilitation. *Cochrane Database of Systematic Reviews*, *2018*(1), CD008349. doi:10.1002/14651858.CD008349.pub4 PMID:29156493

Lavoué, E., Monterrat, B., Desmarais, M., & George, S. (2018). Adaptive gamification for learning environments. *IEEE Transactions on Learning Technologies*, *12*(1), 16–28. doi:10.1109/TLT.2018.2823710

Lavrakas, P. J. (2008). *Encyclopedia of survey research methods* (Vol. 1-0). Sage Publications, Inc. doi:10.4135/9781412963947

Lazzaro, N. (2009). Why we play: affect and the fun of games. In A. Sears & L. A. Jacko (Eds.), Human-computer interaction: Designing for diverse users and domains (pp. 156-175). CRC Press, Taylor & Francis Group. doi:10.1201/9781420088885. ch10

Lazzaro, M. (2008). *Game usability: Advice from the experts for advancing the player experience.* Morgan Kaufmann.

Le Lay S. (2020). *Destin du jouer et du travail à l'ère du management distractif.* Habilitation à diriger des recherches en sociologie, Université Aix-Marseille.

Le Lay, S., Pizzinat, B., & Frances, J. (2017). *"Candidats du MT180®, Soyez fun et sexy".* Un "dispositif spectaculaire" au service de la gamification du champ académique. In E. Savignac, Y. Andonova, P. Lénel, A. Monjaret, & A. Seurrat (Eds.), *Le travail de la gamification. Enjeux, modalités et rhétoriques de la translation du jeu au travail* (pp. 73–91). Peter Lang.

Le Lay, S., Savignac, E., Frances, J., & Lénel, P. (Eds.). (2021). *The gamification of society.* Iste-Wiley. doi:10.1002/9781119821557

Lee Son, T., Wesson, J., & Vogts, D. (2018). Designing a Natural User Interface to Support Information Sharing among Co-Located Mobile Devices. *South African Computer Journal, 30*(2). Advance online publication. doi:10.18489acj. v30i2.440

Lee, G. E., Xu, Y., Brewer, R. S., & Johnson, P. M. (2012). Makahiki: An open source game engine for energy education and conservation. Department of Information and Computer Sciences, University of Hawaii.

Lee, D. (2021). Knowledge gaps in mobile health research for promoting physical activity in adults with autism spectrum disorder. *Frontiers in Psychology, 12,* 12. doi:10.3389/fpsyg.2021.635105 PMID:33841267

Lee, H. E., & Cho, J. (2017). What motivates users to continue using diet and fitness apps? Application of the uses and gratifications approach. *Health Communication, 32*(12), 1445–1453. doi:10.1080/10410236.2016.1167998 PMID:27356103

Lee, H. S., Park, Y. J., & Park, S. W. (2019). The Effects of Virtual Reality Training on Function in Chronic Stroke Patients: A Systematic Review and Meta-Analysis. *BioMed Research International, 2019,* 1–12. doi:10.1155/2019/7595639 PMID:31317037

Lee, J. J., & Hammer, J. (2011). Gamification in education: What, how, why bother? *Academic Exchange Quarterly, 15*(2), 146. https://mybrainware.com/wp-content/uploads/2017/11/Gamification_in_Education_What_How_Why.pdf

Lee, J. J., & Hammer, J. (2011). Gamification in education: What, how, why Bother? *Academic Exchange Quarterly, 15*(2), 1–5.

Lee, J. J., & Hammer, J. (2011). Gamification in education: What, How, Why bother? *Academic Exchange Quarterly, 15*(2), 1–5.

Lee, J. Y., & Jin, C. H. (2019). The role of gamification in brand app experience: The moderating effects of the 4Rs of app marketing. *Cogent Psychology, 6*(1), 1576388. doi:10.1080/23311908.2019.1576388

Lee, M. R., Yen, D. C., & Hsiao, C. Y. (2014). Understanding the perceived community value of Facebook users. *Computers in Human Behavior, 35,* 350–358. doi:10.1016/j.chb.2014.03.018

Lee, P. C., & Mao, Z. (2016). The relation among self-efficacy, learning approaches, and academic performance: An exploratory study. *Journal of Teaching in Travel & Tourism, 16*(3), 178–194. doi:10.1080/15313220.2015.1136581

Lee, Y. J., Hosanagar, K., & Tan, Y. (2015). Do I follow my friends or the crowd? Information cascades in online movie ratings. *Management Science, 61*(9), 2241–2258.

Legaki, N.-Z., Xi, N., Hamari, J., Karpouzis, K., & Assimakopoulos, V. (2020). The effect of challenge-based gamification on learning: An experiment in the context of statistics education. *International Journal of Human-Computer Studies*, *144*, 102496. Advance online publication. doi:10.1016/j.ijhcs.2020.102496 PMID:32565668

Leite, H. dos R., Vieira, G. E., Leite, H. dos R., & Vieira, G. E. (2015). Lean philosophy and its applications in the service industry: A review of the current knowledge. *Production*, *25*(3), 529–541. https://doi.org/10.1590/0103-6513.079012

Lekea, I. K., Stamatelos, D. G., & Raptis, P. (2021). Learning how to escape the unthinkable with virtual reality: the case of pilots' training on emergency procedures. In *IOP Conference Series: Materials Science and Engineering, 10th EASN International Conference on Innovation in Aviation & Space to the Satisfaction of the European Citizens (10th EASN 2020)* (vol. 1024, Issue 1, pp. 012098). 10.1088/1757-899X/1024/1/012098

Lellis, L. D. (2020). How Gamification Affects Crowdsourcing: The Case of Amazon Mechanical Turk. *Eludamos (Göttingen)*, *10*(1), 27–37.

Lenihan, D. (2012). Health games: A key component for the evolution of wellness programs. *Games for Health Journal*, *1*(3), 233–235. doi:10.1089/g4h.2012.0022 PMID:26193441

Lenihan, D. (2012). Health Games: A Key Component for the Evolution of Wellness Programs. *Games for Health Journal*, *1*(3), 233–235. https://doi.org/10.1089/g4h.2012.0022

Lepper, M. R., Greene, D., & Nisbett, R. E. (1973). Undermining children's intrinsic interest with extrinsic reward: A test of the 'overjustification' hypothesis. *Journal of Personality and Social Psychology*, *28*(1), 129–137. doi:10.1037/h0035519

Lerner, J. (2012). *Making democracy fun? Games as a Tool for Democratic Participation*. New School University.

Lévy, P. (1994). *Inteligencia colectiva: por una antropología del ciberespacio*. Centro Nacional de Información de Ciencias Médicas.

Liang, F., Chen, Y., & Zhao, F. (2021). The Platformization of Propaganda: How Xuexi Qiangguo Expands Persuasion and Assesses Citizens in China. *International Journal of Communication*, *15*, 20.

Liang, F., Das, V., Kostyuk, N., & Hussain, M. M. (2018). Constructing a Data-Driven Society: China's Social Credit System as a State Surveillance Infrastructure. *Policy and Internet*, *10*(4), 415–453. doi:10.1002/poi3.183

Li, C. Y. (2018). Consumer behavior in switching between membership cards and mobile applications: The case of Starbucks. *Computers in Human Behavior*, *84*, 171–184. doi:10.1016/j.chb.2017.12.042

Lichtenberg, S., Lembcke, T.-B., Brenig, M., Brendel, A., & Trang, S. (2020, March 8). *Can Gamification lead to Increase Paid Crowdworkers Output?* Academic Press.

Lieberoth, A. (2014). Shallow gamification: Testing psychological effects of framing an activity as a game. *Games and Culture*, 1–20.

Li, J., Theng, Y. L., & Foo, S. (2016). Exergames for older adults with subthreshold depression: Does higher playfulness lead to better improvement in depression? *Games for Health Journal*, *5*(3), 175–182. doi:10.1089/g4h.2015.0100 PMID:27135146

Li, M., Xu, D., Ma, G., & Guo, Q. (2021). Strong tie or weak tie? Exploring the impact of group-formation gamification mechanisms on user emotional anxiety in social commerce. *Behaviour & Information Technology*, 1–30. doi:10.1080/0144929X.2021.1917661

Lindley, J., & Coulton, P. (2015). Game of Drones. In *Proceedings of the 2015 Annual Symposium on Computer-Human Interaction in Play - CHI PLAY '15* (pp.613–618). ACM Press. 10.1145/2793107.2810300

Linehan, C., Kirman, B., & Roche, B. (2015). Gamification as behavioral psychology. In *The gameful world: Approaches, issues, applications* (pp. 81–105). MIT Press.

Liu, L., Zhao, Y.-Y., Yang, C., & Chan, H. Y.-L. (2021). Gamification for promoting advance care planning: A mixed-method systematic review and meta-analysis. *Palliative Medicine, 35*(6), 1005–1019. doi:10.1177/02692163211005343 PMID:33775174

Llagostera, E. (2012). On Gamification and Persuasion. *Proceedings of SBGames, 2012*, 12–21.

Locke, E. A., & Latham, G. P. (1990). *A theory of goal setting & task performance*. Prentice-Hall, Inc.

Locke, E. A., & Latham, G. P. (2006). New Directions in Goal-Setting Theory. *Current Directions in Psychological Science, 15*(5), 265–268. https://doi.org/10.1111/j.1467-8721.2006.00449.x

Lockwood, D. (1964). Social integration and system integration. *Explorations in Social Change, 244*, 53-57.

Lohse, K., Shirzad, N., Verster, A., Hodges, N., & Van der Loos, H. F. M. (2013). Video Games and Rehabilitation: Using Design Principles to Enhance Engagement in Physical Therapy. *Journal of Neurologic Physical Therapy; JNPT, 37*(4), 166–175. doi:10.1097/NPT.0000000000000017 PMID:24232363

Loh, W. (2019). The Gamification of Political Participation. *Moral Philosophy and Politics, 6*(2). Advance online publication. doi:10.1515/mopp-2018-0037

Lombriser, P., & van der Valk, R. (2011). *Improving the Quality of the Software Development Lifecycle with Gamification*. Springer-Verlag.

Looyestyn, J., Kernot, J., Boshoff, K., Ryan, J., Edney, S., & Maher, C. (2017). Does gamification increase engagement with online programs? A systematic review. *PLoS One, 12*(3), e0173403. Advance online publication. doi:10.1371/journal.pone.0173403 PMID:28362821

Lopez, S. (2011, October 19). Steve Lopez: Disneyland workers answer to "electronic whip." *Los Angeles Times*. https://www.latimes.com/health/la-xpm-2011-oct-19-la-me-1019-lopez-disney-20111018-story.html

Lopez, S. J., & Snyder, C. R. (2012). The Oxford Handbook of Positive Psychology. In The Oxford Handbook of Positive Psychology (2nd ed.). doi:10.1093/oxfordhb/9780195187243.001.0001

Lopez, C. E., & Tucker, C. S. (2019). The effects of player type on performance: A gamification case study. *Computers in Human Behavior, 91*, 333–345. doi:10.1016/j.chb.2018.10.005

Loveless, A. M. (2002). *Literature review in creativity, new technologies and learning*. Futurelab Series Report, 4. Futurelab. https://hal.inria.fr/docs/00/19/04/39/PDF/loveless-a-2002-r4.pdf

Lovelock, C., & Wright, L. (2002). *Principles of service marketing and management*. Pearson Education Inc.

Lucas, G. (Director). (1977). *Star Wars: Episode IV – A New Hope* [Film]. 20th Century Fox.

Lucassen, G., & Jansen, S. (2014). Gamification in consumer marketing – Future or fallacy? *Procedia: Social and Behavioral Sciences, 148*, 194–202. doi:10.1016/j.sbspro.2014.07.034

Luchev, D, Paneva-Marinova, D., Pavlov, R., & Kaposi, G. (2016). *Game-based learning of Bulgarian iconographical art on smart phone application*. Academic Press.

Luchev, D., Paneva-Marinova, D., Pavlova, L., Zlatkov, L., & Pavlov, R. (2020). Development of a Serious Game "Aquae Calidae" for Studying the Ancient History and Civilizations in Primary School. *INTED2020 Proceedings, 1*, 5253–5258.

Lu, J., Mao, Z., Wang, M., & Hu, L. (2015). Goodbye maps, hello apps? Exploring the influential determinants of travel app adoption. *Current Issues in Tourism*, *18*(11), 1059–1079. doi:10.1080/13683500.2015.1043248

Lyons, E. J. (2015). Cultivating Engagement and Enjoyment in Exergames Using Feedback, Challenge, and Rewards. *Games for Health Journal*, *4*(1), 12–18. doi:10.1089/g4h.2014.0072 PMID:26181675

Ma, M., Oikonomou, A., & Jain, L. C. (2011). Innovations in serious games for future learning. In M. Ma, A. Oikonomou, & L. C. Jain (Eds.), Serious games and edutainment applications (pp. 3-7). Springer. doi:10.1007/978-1-4471-2161-9_1

MacDonald, G. A., Kayes, N. M., & Bright, F. (2013). Barriers and facilitators to engagement in rehabilitation for people with stroke: A review of the literature. *New Zealand Journal of Physiotherapy*, *41*(3), 112.

Macrae, J., & Harmer, A. (2004). *Good humanitarian donorship and the European Union: Issues and options*. Overseas Development Institute.

Madani, K., Pierce, T. W., & Mirchi, A. (2017). Serious games on environmental management.). . *Sustainable Cities and Society*, *29*, 1–11. doi:10.1016/j.scs.2016.11.007

Maedche, A., Botzenhardt, A., & Neer, L. (2012). *Software for people: Fundamentals, trends and best practices*. Springer. doi:10.1007/978-3-642-31371-4

Maehr, M. L., & Braskamp, L. A. (1986). *The motivation factor: A theory of personal investment*. Lexington Books.

Magazine, I. O. T. (2017). *Four Essential Elements for Smart City Success*. Available at: https://www.iotnow.com/2017/10/05/68412-four-essential-elementssmart-city-success/

Maher, C., Ferguson, M., Vandelanotte, C., Plotnikoff, R., De Bourdeaudhuij, I., Thomas, S., Nelson-Field, K., & Olds, T. (2015). A web-based, social networking physical activity intervention for insufficiently active adults delivered via Facebook app: Randomized controlled trial. *Journal of Medical Internet Research*, *17*(7), e4086. doi:10.2196/jmir.4086 PMID:26169067

Maican, C., Lixandroiu, R., & Constantin, C. (2016). Computers in Human Behavior Interactivia. ro e A study of a gami fi cation framework using zero-cost tools. *Computers in Human Behavior*, *61*, 186–197. doi:10.1016/j.chb.2016.03.023

Maier, C., Laumer, S., Weinert, C., & Weitzel, T. (2015). The effects of technostress and switching stress on discontinued use of social networking services: A study of Facebook use. *Information Systems Journal*, *25*(3), 275–308. doi:10.1111/isj.12068

Maitland, C., Granich, J., Braham, R., Thornton, A., Teal, R., Stratton, G., & Rosenberg, M. (2018). Measuring the capacity of active video games for social interaction: The Social Interaction Potential Assessment tool. *Computers in Human Behavior*, *87*, 308–316. doi:10.1016/j.chb.2018.05.036

Majewski, J. (2017). The Potential for Modding Communities in Cultural Heritage. In A. Mol, C. Ariese-Andemeule-broucke, K. Boom, & A. Politopoulos (Eds.), *The Interactive Past: Archaeology, Heritage, and Video Games* (pp. 185–205). Sidestone Press.

Majuri, J., Koivisto, J., & Hamari, J. (2018). Gamification of education and learning: A review of empirical literature. *CEUR Workshop Proceedings*, *2186*(GamiFIN), 11–19.

Majuri, J., Koivisto, J., & Hamari, J. (2018a). Gamification of education and learning: A review of empirical literature. *CEUR Workshop Proceedings*, *2186*(GamiFIN), 11–19.

Majuri, J., Koivisto, J., & Hamari, J. (2018b). *Gamification of education and learning: A review of empirical literature*. Academic Press.

Majuri, J., Koivisto, J., & Hamari, J. (2018). Gamification of education and learning: A review of empirical literature. *Proceedings of the 2nd International GamiFIN Conference (GamiFIN 2018)*, 11–9.

Malone, T. W., & Lepper, M. R. (1987). Making learning fun: A taxonomy of intrinsic motivations for learning. *Aptitude. Learning and Instruction III: Conative and Affective Process Analyses*, *98*(3), 223–253.

Marache-Francisco, C., & Brangier, E. (2013, October). Process of Gamification. From the Consideration of Gamification to its Practical Implementation. In *CENTRIC 2013, The Sixth International Conference on Advances in Human oriented and Personalized Mechanisms, Technologies, and Services, Venice, Italy* (pp. 126–131). Academic Press.

Maraffi, S., & Sacerdoti, F. M. (2018). Innovative Digital Games to Improve Science Education through Storytelling, Mystery and Myth. *Proceedings of the British DiGRA 14 Conference.*

Marć, M., Bartosiewicz, A., Burzyńska, J., Chmiel, Z., & Januszewicz, P. (2019). A nursing shortage - A prospect of global and local policies. *International Nursing Review*, *66*(1), 9–16. doi:10.1111/inr.12473 PMID:30039849

Marcuse, H. (1941). Some Social Implications of Modern Technology. *Studies in Philosophy and Social Sciences, 9*, 138–162. Retrieved from https://courses.cs.washington.edu/courses/cse490e/19wi/readings/marcuse_social_implications_1941.pdf

Marczewski, A. (2014). *Marczewski's Gamification User Types.* E-Learning Industry. https://elearningindustry.com/marczewski-gamification-user-types

Marczewski, A. (2015). Even Ninja Monkeys Like to Play: Gamification, game thinking and motivational design. Gamified UK.

Marczewski, A. (2017). *A revised gamification design framework.* Gamified UK: Thoughts on gamification and more. https://www.gamified.uk/2017/04/06/revised-gamification-design-framework/

Marczewski, A. (2012). *Gamification: A Simple Introduction. Tips, advice and thoughts on gamification.* Lulu.

Marczewski, A. (2013). *Gamification: a simple introduction. Tips, advice and thoughts on gamification.* Andrzej Marczewski.

Marín, B., Frez, J., Cruz-Lemus, J., & Genero, M. (2018). An empirical investigation on the benefits of gamification in programming courses. *ACM Trans. Comput. Educ.*, *19*(1), 4:1–4:22.

Marin, S., Lee, V., & Landers, R. N. (2021). Gamified Active Learning and Its Potential for Social Change. In A. Spanellis & J. T. Harviainen (Eds.), *Transforming Society and Organizations through Gamification: From the Sustainable Development Goals to Inclusive Workplaces* (pp. 205–223). Palgrave Macmillan. doi:10.1007/978-3-030-68207-1_11

Mariotti, S. (2021). The Use of Serious Games as an Educational and Dissemination Tool for Archaeological Heritage. Potential and Challenges for the Future. *Magazén*, *2*(1), 119-138. . doi:10.30687/mag/2724-3923/2021/03/005

Markopoulos, A. P., Fragkou, A., Kasidiaris, P. D., & Davim, J. P. (2015). Gamification in engineering education and professional training. *International Journal of Mechanical Engineering Education*, *43*(2), 118–131. https://doi.org/10.1177/0306419015591324

Márkus, Z. L., Kaposi, G., Veres, M., Weisz, Z., Szántó, G., Szkaliczki, T., Paneva-Marinova, D., Pavlov, R., Luchev, D., Goynov, M., & Pavlova, L. (2018). *Interactive game development to assist cultural heritage.* Academic Press.

Marlow, S. L., Salas, E., Landon, L. B., & Presnell, B. (2016). Eliciting teamwork with game attributes: A systematic review and research agenda. *Computers in Human Behavior*, *55*, 413–423. doi:10.1016/j.chb.2015.09.028

Marsh, T. (2011). Serious games continuum : Between games for purpose and experiential environments for purpose. *Entertainment Computing, 2*(2), 61–68. https://doi.org/10.1016/j.entcom.2010.12.004

Martey, R. M., Kenski, K., Folkestad, J., Feldman, L., Gordis, E., Shaw, A., Stromer-Galley, J., Clegg, B., Zhang, H., Kaufman, N., Rabkin, A. N., Shaikh, S., & Strzalkowski, T. (2014). Measuring Game Engagement: Multiple Methods and Construct Complexity. *Simulation & Gaming, 45*(4-5), 528–547. doi:10.1177/1046878114553575

Martineau, P., & Stefano, M. D. (2021, March 15). *Amazon Expands Effort to 'Gamify' Warehouse Work.* The Information. https://www.theinformation.com/articles/amazon-expands-effort-to-gamify-warehouse-work

Martínez-Pérez, B., de la Torre-Díez, I., & López-Coronado, M. (2013). Mobile Health Applications for the Most Prevalent Conditions by the World Health Organization: Review and Analysis. *Journal of Medical Internet Research, 15*(6), e2600. https://doi.org/10.2196/jmir.2600

Martinho, D., Carneiro, J., Corchado, J. M., & Marreiros, G. (2020). A systematic review of gamification techniques applied to elderly care. *Artificial Intelligence Review, 53*(7), 4863–4901. doi:10.100710462-020-09809-6

Martin, M. W. (2012). *Serious game design principles: The impact of game design on learning outcomes.* ProQuest Dissertations Publishing.

Marzullo, F. P., & de Oliveira, F. A. (Eds.). (2021). *Practical Perspectives on Educational Theory and Game Development.* IGI Global. doi:10.4018/978-1-7998-5021-2

Maslow, A. H. (1943). A theory of human motivation. *Psychological Review, 50*(4), 370–396. doi:10.1037/h0054346

Massimo, F. (2020). A Struggle for Bodies and Souls: Amazon Management and Union Strategies in France and Italy. In J. Alimahomed-Wilson & E. Reese (Eds.), *The Cost of Free Shipping: Amazon in the Global Economy* (pp. 129–144). Pluto Press. doi:10.2307/j.ctv16zjhcj.15

Mat Zain, N. H. (2020). GAMEBC Model: Gamification in Health Awareness Campaigns to Drive Behaviour Change in Defeating COVID-19 Pandemic. *International Journal of Advanced Trends in Computer Science and Engineering, 9*(1.4), 229–236. doi:10.30534/ijatcse/2020/3491.42020

Mat Zain, N. H., Johari, S. N., Abdul Aziz, S. R., Ibrahim Teo, N. H., Ishak, N. H., & Othman, Z. (2021). Winning the Needs of the Gen Z: Gamified Health Awareness Campaign in Defeating COVID-19 Pandemic. *Procedia Computer Science, 179*, 974–981. https://doi.org/10.1016/j.procs.2021.01.087

Matallaoui, A., Koivisto, J., Hamari, J., & Zarnekow, R. (2017). How effective is "exergamification"? A systematic review on the effectiveness of gamification features in exergames. *Proceedings of the 50th Hawaii International Conference on System Sciences.* 10.24251/HICSS.2017.402

Mathew, B., Saha, P., Yimam, S. M., Biemann, C., Goyal, P., & Mukherjee, A. (2020). *Hatexplain: A benchmark dataset for explainable hate speech detection.* https://bit.ly/3AmrHc1

Mathwick, C., Malhotra, N., & Rigdon, E. (2001). Experiential value: Conceptualization, measurement and application in the catalog and internet shopping environment. *Journal of Retailing, 77*(1), 39–56. doi:10.1016/S0022-4359(00)00045-2

Maturo, A., & Setiffi, F. (2016). The gamification of risk: How health apps foster self-confidence and why this is not enough. *Health Risk & Society, 17*(7-8), 477–494. doi:10.1080/13698575.2015.1136599

May Saßmannshausen, S., Radtke, J., Bohn, N., Hussein, H., Randall, D., & Pipek, V. (2021). Citizen-Centered Design in Urban Planning: How Augmented Reality can be used in Citizen Participation Processes. In *Designing Interactive Systems Conference 2021 (DIS '21),* (pp.250-265). ACM Press. 10.1145/3461778.3462130

Mäyrä, F. (2007). The Contextual Game Experience: On the Socio-Cultural Contexts for Meaning in Digital Play. In *Proceedings of the 2007 DiGRA International Conference: Situated Play*. University of Tokyo.

McChrystal, S. (2015). *Team of Teams: New Rules of Engagement in a Complex World*. https://organizationalphysics.com/2016/10/13/top-down-vs-bottom-up-hierarchy-or-how-to-build-a-self-managed-organization/

McClelland, D. C. (1965). Toward a theory of motive acquisition. *The American Psychologist, 20*(5), 321–333. doi:10.1037/h0022225 PMID:14323512

McDaniel, R., Fiore, S. M., & Nicholson, D. (2010). Serious Storytelling: Narrative Considerations for Serious Games Researchers and Developers. In Serious Game Design and Development: Technologies for Training and Learning (pp. 13-30). IGI Global. doi:10.4018/978-1-61520-739-8.ch002

McDougall, G. H. G., & Leveque, T. (2000). Customer satisfaction with services: Putting perceived value into the equation. *Journal of Services Marketing, 14*(5), 392–410. doi:10.1108/08876040010340937

McGonigal, J. (2011). *Reality is broken. Why games make us better and how they can change the world*. Random House.

McGonigal, J. (2011). *Reality is broken: Why games make us better and how they can change the world*. Vintage.

McGuire, M., & Jenkins, O. C. (2009). *Creating Games: Mechanics*. Content and Technology. A K Peters, Ltd.

McKenzie-Mohr, D. (2011). *Fostering sustainable behavior: An introduction to community-based social marketing*. New society publishers.

Meditation. (2020). In *APA Dictionary of Psychology*. Retrieved from https://dictionary.apa.org/meditation

Mekler, E. D., Brühlmann, F., Opwis, K., & Tuch, A. N. (2013). Do points, levels and leaderboards harm intrinsic motivation? *Proceedings of the First International Conference on Gameful Design, Research, and Applications (Gamification '13)*, 66–73. 10.1145/2583008.2583017

Mekler, E. D., Brühlmann, F., Tuch, A. N., & Opwis, K. (2017). Towards understanding the effects of individual gamification elements on intrinsic motivation and performance. *Computers in Human Behavior, 71*, 525–534. doi:10.1016/j.chb.2015.08.048

Mendes, P., Santos, A. C., Nunes, L. M., & Teixeira, M. R. (2013). Evaluating municipal solid waste management performance in regions with strong seasonal variability. *Ecological Indicators, 30*, 170–177. doi:10.1016/j.ecolind.2013.02.017

Mercy Corps. (2015, August 18). *We asked our staff: What does being a humanitarian mean to you?* Retrieved from: https://www.mercycorps.org/blog/what-does-being-humanitarian-mean

Mestrado, M., & Vers, R. H. (2018). *A Gamification como Ferramenta de Gestão de Recursos Humanos Raquel Filipa Almeida de Sousa*. Academic Press.

Mettler, T. (2015). Health Behaviour Change Support Systems: Past Research and Future Challenges. *Management Research*, 12.

Meya, J. N., & Eisenack, K. (2018). Effectiveness of gaming for communicating and teaching climate change. *Climatic Change, 149*(3), 319–333. doi:10.100710584-018-2254-7

Meyer, J., & Land, R. (2006). Overcoming barriers to student understanding: Threshold concepts and Troublesome Knowledge. In J. Meyer & R. Land (Eds.), *Overcoming Barriers to Student Understanding: Threshold concepts and Toublesome Knowledge* (pp. 19–32). Routledge.

Michael, D. R., & Chen, S. L. (2005). *Serious games: Games that educate, train, and inform*. Academic Press.

Michael, D. R., & Chen, S. L. (2005). *Serious games: Games that educate, train, and inform* (1st ed.). Thomson Course Technology.

Michaelidou, N., Siamagka, N. T., & Christodoulides, G. (2011). Usage, barriers and measurement of social media marketing: An exploratory investigation of small and medium B2B brands. *Industrial Marketing Management*, *40*(7), 1153–1159. doi:10.1016/j.indmarman.2011.09.009

Michalski, M. P. (2014). Symbolic meanings and e-learning in the workplace: The case of an intranet-based training tool. *Management Learning*, *45*(2), 145–166. doi:10.1177/1350507612468419

Michel, H. (2005). e-Administration, e-Government, e-Governance and the Learning City: A typology of Citizenship management using ICTs. *The Electronic Journal of E-Government*, *3*(4), 213–218.

Michel, J. W., Tews, M. J., & Allen, D. G. (2019). Fun in the Workplace: A Review and Expanded Theoretical Perspective. *Human Resource Management Review*, *29*(1), 98–110. doi:10.1016/j.hrmr.2018.03.001

Michie, S., Johnston, M., Abraham, C., Lawton, R., Parker, D., & Walker, A. (2005). Making psychological theory useful for implementing evidence based practice: A consensus approach. *BMJ Quality & Safety*, *14*(1), 26–33. doi:10.1136/qshc.2004.011155 PMID:15692000

Middelweerd, A., Mollee, J. S., van der Wal, C. N., Brug, J., & te Velde, S. J. (2014). Apps to promote physical activity among adults: A review and content analysis. *The International Journal of Behavioral Nutrition and Physical Activity*, *11*(1), 97. https://doi.org/10.1186/s12966-014-0097-9

Miller, A. S., Cafazzo, J. A., & Seto, E. (2016). A game plan: Gamification design principles in mHealth applications for chronic disease management. *Health Informatics Journal*, *22*(2), 184–193. doi:10.1177/1460458214537511 PMID:24986104

Mills, D. J., Milyavskaya, M., Mettler, J., & Heath, N. L. (2018). Exploring the pull and push underlying problem video game use: A Self-Determination Theory approach. *Personality and Individual Differences*, *135*, 176–181. doi:10.1016/j.paid.2018.07.007

Mindfulness. (2020). In *APA Dictionary of Psychology*. Retrieved from https://dictionary.apa.org/mindfulness

Mintel. (2020). *Lifestyles of Gamers - China - October 2020*. Mintel. https://reports.mintel.com/display/1046705/?fromSearch=%3Ffreetext%3Dvideo%2520gamers%2520demographics

Mitchell, J. (2012, November 15). Unbelievable! The IDF Has Gamified Its War Blog. *ReadWrite*. https://readwrite.com/2012/11/15/unbelievable-the-idf-has-gamified-its-war-blog/

Mitchell, R., Schuster, L., & Drennan, J. (2017). Understanding how gamification influences behaviour in social marketing. *Australasian Marketing Journal*, *25*(1), 12–19. doi:10.1016/j.ausmj.2016.12.001

Mitchell, R., Schuster, L., & Jin, H. S. (2020). Gamification and the impact of extrinsic motivation on needs satisfaction : Making work fun? *Journal of Business Research*, *106*, 323–330. https://doi.org/10.1016/j.jbusres.2018.11.022

Mitgutsch, K. (2011). Serious learning in serious games. Learning In, Through, and Beyond Serious Games. In M. Ma, A. Oikonomou, & L. C. Jain (Eds.), Serious games and edutainment applications (pp. 45-58). Springer. doi:10.1007/978-1-4471-2161-9_4

Mochocki, M. (2011). Reality is Broken: Why Games Make Us Better and How They Can Change the World. Jane McGonigal. 2011. New York: Penguin Press, ss. 388. Czasopismo ludologiczne Polskiego Towarzystwa Badania Gier, 239.

Moin, M. T., & Rahman, M. A. U. (2019). *Eliminating laundering of virtual currency*. Academic Press.

Moise, D. (2013). Gamification-The new game in marketing. *Romanian Journal of Marketing*, (2).

Moise, D., & Cruceru, A. F. (2014). The use of gamification in events marketing. *International Journal of Economic Practices and Theories*, *4*(2), 185–190.

Moldon, L., Strohmaier, M., & Wachs, J. (2021). How Gamification Affects Software Developers: Cautionary Evidence from a Natural Experiment on GitHub. *2021 IEEE/ACM 43rd International Conference on Software Engineering (ICSE)*, 549–561. 10.1109/ICSE43902.2021.00058

Molinillo, S., Japutra, A., & Liebana-Cabanillas, F. (2020). Impact of perceived value on casual mobile game loyalty: The moderating effect of intensity of playing. *Journal of Consumer Behaviour*, *19*(5), 493–504. doi:10.1002/cb.1831

Montagni, I., Mabchour, I., & Tzourio, C. (2020). Digital gamification to enhance vaccine knowledge and uptake: Scoping review. *JMIR Serious Games*, *8*(2), e16983. doi:10.2196/16983 PMID:32348271

Monteiro-Guerra, F., Rivera-Romero, O., Fernandez-Luque, L., & Caulfield, B. (2019). Personalization in real-time physical activity coaching using mobile applications: A scoping review. *IEEE Journal of Biomedical and Health Informatics*, *24*(6), 1738–1751. doi:10.1109/JBHI.2019.2947243 PMID:31751254

Moore, M. E. (2011). *Basics of game design*. Taylor and Francis Group.

Mora, A., Riera, D., Gonzalez, C., & Arnedo-Moreno, J. (2015). A literature review of Gamification design frameworks. In *7th International Conference on Games and Virtual Worlds for Serious Applications (VS-Games)* (pp.1–8). IEEE. 10.1109/VS-GAMES.2015.7295760

Mora, A., Tondello, G. F., Nacke, L., & Arnedo-Moreno, J. (2018). Effect of personalized gameful design on student engagement. *2018 IEEE Global Engineering Education Conference (EDUCON)*, 1925-1933. 10.1109/EDUCON.2018.8363471

Morrison, G. R., Ross, S. J., Morrison, J. R., & Kalman, H. K. (2019). *Designing effective instruction*. John Wiley & Sons.

Morschheuser, B., Werder, K., Hamari, J., & Abe, J. (2017). How to gamify? Development of a method for gamification. *Proceedings of the 50th Annual Hawaii International Conference on System Sciences (HICSS)*, 1298-1307.

Morschheuser, B., Hassan, L., Werder, K., & Hamari, J. (2018). How to design gamification? A method for engineering gamified software. *Information and Software Technology*, *95*, 219–237. doi:10.1016/j.infsof.2017.10.015

Mortara, M., & Catalano, C. E. (2018). 3D Virtual environments as effective learning contexts for cultural heritage. *Italian Journal of Educational Technology*, *26*(2), 5–21. doi:10.17471/2499-4324/1026

Mortara, M., Catalano, C. E., Bellotti, F., Fiucci, G., Houry-Panchetti, M., & Petridis, P. (2014). Learning cultural heritage by serious games. *Journal of Cultural Heritage*, *15*(3), 318–325. doi:10.1016/j.culher.2013.04.004

Mortensen, D. H. (2020). *Natural User Interfaces – What are they and how do you design user interfaces that feel natural?* Retrieved July 20, 2021, from Interaction Design Foundation website: https://www.interaction-design.org/literature/article/natural-user-interfaces-what-are-they-and-how-do-you-design-user-interfaces-that-feel-natural

Moscovici, S., & Zavalloni, M. (1969). The group as a polarizer of attitudes. *Journal of Personality and Social Psychology*, *12*(2), 125–135.

Mulcahy, R. F., Russell-Bennett, R., Zainuddin, N., & Kuhn, K. A. (2018). Designing gamified transformative and social marketing services: An investigation of serious m-games. *Journal of Service Theory and Practice*, *28*(1), 26–51. doi:10.1108/JSTP-02-2017-0034

Mulcahy, R. F., Zainuddin, N., & Russell-Bennett, R. (2021). Transformative value and the role of involvement in gamification and serious games for well-being. *Journal of Service Management*, *32*(2), 218–245. doi:10.1108/JOSM-05-2019-0137

Mulcahy, R., Russell-Bennett, R., & Iacobucci, D. (2020). Designing gamified apps for sustainable consumption: A field study. *Journal of Business Research*, *106*, 377–387. doi:10.1016/j.jbusres.2018.10.026

Mulcahy, R., Russell-Bennett, R., & Rundle-Thiele, S. (2015). Electronic games: Can they create value for the moderate drinking brand? *Journal of Social Marketing*, *5*(3), 258–278. doi:10.1108/JSOCM-06-2014-0043

Mumford, E. (2006). The story of socio-technical design: Reflections on its successes, failures and potential. *Information Systems Journal*. doi:10.1111/j.1365-2575.2006.00221.x

Muniz, A. M. Jr, & O'Guinn, T. C. (2001). Brand community. *The Journal of Consumer Research*, *27*(4), 412–432. doi:10.1086/319618

Muntean, C. I. (2011). Raising engagement in e-learning through gamification. In *Proceedings 6th International Conference on Virtual Learning ICVL* (pp. 323-329). Bucharest: Bucharest University Press.

Murdoch University. (2015). *Virtual Reality software brings hope to stroke survivors*. Murdoch University. Retrieved 6/3/2019 from http://web.archive.org/web/20180331035704/http://media.murdoch.edu.au/virtual-reality-software-brings-hope-to-stroke-survivors

Murray, J. H. (1999). *Hamlet en la Holocubierta. El futuro de la narrativa en el ciberespacio*. Paidos.

Myneni, S., & Iyengar, S. (2016). Socially Influencing Technologies for Health Promotion: Translating Social Media Analytics into Consumer-facing Health Solutions. *2016 49th Hawaii International Conference on System Sciences (HICSS)*, 3084–3093. doi:10.1109/HICSS.2016.388

Nabavi, N. (2021). Covid-19: Pandemic will cast "a long shadow" on mental health, warns England's CMO. *BMJ (Clinical Research Ed.)*, (June), n1655. Advance online publication. doi:10.1136/bmj.n1655 PMID:34183352

Nacke, L. E., Bateman, C., & Mandryk, R. L. (2014). BrainHex: A neurobiological gamer typology survey. *Entertainment Computing*, *5*(1), 55–62. doi:10.1016/j.entcom.2013.06.002

Nacke, L. E., & Deterding, S. (2017). Editorial: The Maturing of Gamification Research. *Computers in Human Behavior*, *71*, 450–454. doi:10.1016/j.chb.2016.11.062

Nah, F. F. H., Zeng, Q., Telaprolu, V. R., Ayyappa, A. P., & Eschenbrenner, B. (2014). Gamification of Education: A Review of Literature. In F. F.-H. Nah (Ed.), Lecture Notes in Computer Science: Vol. 8527. *HCI in Business. HCIB 2014*. Springer. doi:10.1007/978-3-319-07293-7_39

Naqvi, M. H., Guoyan, S., & Naqvi, M. H. A. (2021). Measuring the Influence of Web Features in the Online Gamification Environment: A Multimediation Approach. *Wireless Communications and Mobile Computing*, *2021*, 2021. doi:10.1155/2021/3213981

Naslund, J. A., Aschbrenner, K. A., Araya, R., Marsch, L. A., Unützer, J., Patel, V., & Bartels, S. J. (2017). Digital technology for treating and preventing mental disorders in low-income and middle-income countries: A narrative review of the literature. *The Lancet. Psychiatry*, *4*(6), 486–500. doi:10.1016/S2215-0366(17)30096-2 PMID:28433615

Natarajan, T., Balasubramanian, S. A., & Kasilingam, D. L. (2017). Understanding the intention to use mobile shopping applications and its influence on price sensitivity. *Journal of Retailing and Consumer Services*, *37*, 8–22. doi:10.1016/j.jretconser.2017.02.010

National Transportation Safety Board. (2021). *Investigation Reports. Aviation*. Available online: https://www.ntsb.gov/investigations/AccidentReports/Pages/Reports.aspx?mode=Aviation

NATO Public Diplomacy Division. (2016). *NATO Cyber Defence Fact Sheet.* Fact Sheet. Retrieved from https://www.nato.int/nato_static_fl2014/assets/pdf/pdf_2016_07/20160627_1607-factsheet-cyber-defence-eng.pdf

Negruşa, A. L., Toader, V., Sofică, A., Tutunea, M. F., & Rus, R. V. (2015). Exploring gamification techniques and applications for sustainable tourism. *Sustainability*, *7*(8), 11160–11189. doi:10.3390u70811160

Negussie, N. (2012). Relationship between rewards and nurses' work motivation in Addis Ababa hospitals. *Ethiopian Journal of Health Sciences*, *22*(2), 107–112. PMID:22876074

Németh, T. (2015). *English Knight: Gamifying the EFL Classroom* [Unpublished master's thesis]. Pázmány Péter Katolikus Egyetem Bölcsészet- és Társadalomtudományi Kar, Piliscsaba, Hungary. Retrieved from: https://ludus.hu/gamification/

Neupane, A., Hansen, D., Fails, J. A., & Sharma, A. (2021). The role of steps and game elements in gamified fitness tracker apps: A systematic review. *Multimodal Technologies and Interaction*, *5*(2), 5. doi:10.3390/mti5020005

Newman, D. (2002). *Interactive Aerospace Engineering and Design.* McGraw Hill.

Nguse, S., & Wassenaar, D. (2021). Mental health and COVID-19 in South Africa. *South African Journal of Psychology. Suid-Afrikaanse Tydskrif vir Sielkunde*, *51*(2), 304–313. doi:10.1177/00812463211001543

Nguyen, C. (2016, October 27). *China might create a Black Mirror-like score for each citizen based on how trustworthy they are.* Business Insider Australia. https://www.businessinsider.com.au/china-social-credit-score-like-black-mirror-2016-10

Nguyen, C. T. (2017). Philosophy of games. *Philosophy Compass*, *12*(8), e12426. doi:10.1111/phc3.12426

Nicholson, S. (2012). A User-Centered Theoretical Framework for Meaningful Gamification. *Games+Learning+Society*, *8*(1), 223–230.

Nicholson, S. (2012). A user-centered theoretical framework for meaningful gamification. *Proceedings Games+Learning+Society*, 223–30.

Nicholson, S. (2015). A recipe for meaningful gamification. In *Gamification in education and business* (pp. 1–20). Springer. https://scottnicholson.com/pubs/recipepreprint.pdf

Nicholson, S. A. (2012). *User-centered theoretical framework for meaningful gamification* [Paper presentation]. Games+Learning+Society 8.0, Madison, WI.

Nicholson, S. (2015). A recipe for meaningful gamification. *Gamification in Education and Business*, *2015*, 1–20. doi:10.1007/978-3-319-10208-5_1

Nieto-Escamez, F. A., & Roldán-Tapia, M. D. (2021). Gamification as Online Teaching Strategy During COVID-19: A Mini-Review. *Frontiers in Psychology*, *12*, 648552. https://doi.org/10.3389/fpsyg.2021.648552

NIST. (2020). *Uses and Benefits of the Framework.* Retrieved from https://www.nist.gov/cyberframework/online-learning/uses-and-benefits-framework?campaignid=70161000001Cs1OAAS&vid=2117383

Nistor, G. (2018). The Advantages of Gamification and Game-Based Learning. *The International Scientific Conference eLearning and Software for Education*, *1*, 308-312.

Nobre, H., & Ferreira, A. (2017). Gamification as a platform for brand co-creation experiences. *Journal of Brand Management*, *24*(4), 349–361. doi:10.105741262-017-0055-3

Noh, D. (2020). *The Gamification Framework of Military Flight Simulator for Effective Learning and Training Environment.* University of Central Florida. https://stars.library.ucf.edu/etd2020/259

Noorbehbahani, F., Salehi, F., & Zadeh, R. J. (2019). A systematic mapping study on gamification applied to e-marketing. *Journal of Research in Interactive Marketing, 13*(3), 392–410. doi:10.1108/JRIM-08-2018-0103

Norman, D. A. (2004). *Emotional design: Why we love (or hate) everyday things.* Basic Civitas Books.

Norman, L. (2014). Stroke rehabilitation: Promoting physical recovery. *Nursing And Residential Care, 16*(12), 699–702. doi:10.12968/nrec.2014.16.12.699

Norwegian Government. (2019). *Lov om nasjonal sikkerhet.* Retrieved from https://lovdata.no/dokument/NL/lov/2018-06-01-24?q=sikkerhetsloven

Nour, M. M., Rouf, A. S., & Allman-Farinelli, M. (2018). Exploring young adult perspectives on the use of gamification and social media in a smartphone platform for improving vegetable intake. *Appetite, 120,* 547–556. doi:10.1016/j.appet.2017.10.016 PMID:29032184

Nowland, R., A. Necka, E., & Cacioppo, J. T. (2017). Loneliness and social internet use: Pathways to reconnection in a digital world? *Perspectives in Psychological Science, 13*(1,2), 70–87.

NPCC (National Police Chiefs' Council). (2016). *Policing Vision 2025.* London: APCC and NPCC. Available at: www.npcc.police.uk/documents/ Policing%20Vision.pdf

NSM, DSB, Digitaliseringsdirektoratet, NTNU, & NorSIS. (2020). Retrieved from https://ovelse.no/

NTNU. (2019a). *Guide for design of study programmes and courses at NTNU (the programme description guide).* NTNU.

NTNU. (2019b). *Guide to periodic evaluation of programmes of study.* NTNU.

NTNU. (2019c). *Requirements for the academic portfolio at NTNU.* NTNU.

Nussli, N., & Oh, K. (2021). Culturally Responsive Pedagogy, Universal Design for Learning, ubiquitous learning, and seamless learning: How these paradigms inform the intentional design of learner-centered online learning environments. In G. Panconesi & M. Guida (Eds.), *Handbook of Research on Teaching With Virtual Environments and AI* (pp. 163–188). IGI Global. doi:10.4018/978-1-7998-7638-0.ch008

Nyblom, P., Wangen, G., Kianpour, M., & Østby, G. (2020). The root causes of compromised accounts at the university. *ICISSP 2020 - Proceedings of the 6th International Conference on Information Systems Security and Privacy,* (July), 540–551. doi:10.5220/0008972305400551

Nyre-Yu, M., Gutzwiller, R. S., & Caldwell, B. S. (2019). Observing Cyber Security Incident Response: Qualitative Themes From Field Research. *Proceedings of the Human Factors and Ergonomics Society Annual Meeting, 63*(1), 437–441. https://doi.org/10.1177/1071181319631016

O'Brien, H. L., & Toms, E. G. (2008). What is user engagement? A conceptual framework for defining user engagement with technology. *Journal of the American Society for Information Science and Technology, 59*(6), 938–955. doi:10.1002/asi.20801

O'Connell, A., Tomaselli, P. J., & Stobart-Gallagher, M. (2020). Effective Use of Virtual Gamification During COVID-19 to Deliver the OB-GYN Core Curriculum in an Emergency Medicine Resident Conference. *Cureus, 12*(6), e8397. https://doi.org/10.7759/cureus.8397

O'Donovan, S., Gain, J., & Marais, P. (2013). A case study in the gamification of a university-level games development course. In *Proceedings of the South African Institute for Computer Scientists and Information Technologists Conference* (pp. 242-251). 10.1145/2513456.2513469

O'Reilly, T. (2005) *What is Web 2.0: Design patterns and business models for the next generation of software*. Available at: http://www.oreillynet.com/pub/a/oreilly/tim/news/2005/09/30/what-is-web-20.html

O'Reilly, T. (2007). What is Web 2.0: Design Patterns and Business Models for the Next Generation of Software. *Communications & Stratégies*, *1*, 17–37.

Oates, B. J. (2006). *Researching information systems and computing*. SAGE Publications Ltd.

Obaid, I., & Farooq, M. S. (2020). Gamification for Recruitment and Job Training : Model, Taxonomy, and Challenges. *IEEE Access: Practical Innovations, Open Solutions*, *8*, 65164–65178. https://doi.org/10.1109/ACCESS.2020.2984178

Oe, H., Takemoto, T., & Ridwan, M. (2020). Is Gamification a Magic Tool?: Illusion, Remedy, and Future Opportunities in Enhancing Learning Outcomes during and beyond the COVID-19. *Budapest International Research and Critics in Linguistics and Education (BirLE) Journal*, *3*(3), 1401–1414.

Ohler, J. (2005). The world of digital storytelling. *Educational Leadership*, *63*(4), 44–47.

Oinas-Kukkonen, H., & Harjumaa, M. (2009). Persuasive Systems Design: Key Issues, Process Model, and System Features. *Communications of the Association for Information Systems, 24*. doi:10.17705/1CAIS.02428

Oinas-Kukkonen, H. (2013). A foundation for the study of behavior change support systems. *Personal and Ubiquitous Computing*, *17*(6), 1223–1235. https://doi.org/10.1007/s00779-012-0591-5

Oinas-Kukkonen, H., & Harjumaa, M. (2008). Towards deeper understanding of persuasion in software and information systems. In *Proceedings of The First International Conference on Advances in Human-Computer Interaction (ACHI 2008)* (pp. 200–205). IEEE Computer Society. 10.1109/ACHI.2008.31

Okello, D., & Gilson, L. (2015). Exploring the influence of trust relationships on motivation in the health sector: A systematic review. *Human Resources for Health*, *13*(1), 16. doi:10.118612960-015-0007-5 PMID:25889952

Oliveira, W., Pastushenko, O., Rodrigues, L., Toda, A. M., Palomino, P. T., & Hamari, J. (2021). Does gamification affect Flow experience? A systematic literature review. *Proceedings of the 5th International GamiFIN Conference 2021 (GamiFIN 2021)*.

Olsson, M., Hogberg, J., Wastlund, E., & Gustafsson, A. (2016). In-store gamification: Testing a location-based treasure hunt app in a real retailing environment. *Proceedings 49th Annu. Hawaii Int. Conf. Syst. Sci. (HICSS) 2016*, 1634–41. 10.1109/HICSS.2016.206

Olszewski, R., Turek, A., & Łączyński, M. (2016). Urban Gamification as a Source of Information for Spatial Data Analysis and Predictive Participatory Modelling of a City's Development. In *Proceedings of the 5th International Conference on Data Management Technologies and Applications – DATA* (pp. 176-181). 10.5220/0006005201760181

Olteanu, A., Castillo, C., Boy, J., & Varshney, K. R. (2018). The Effect of Extremist Violence on Hateful Speech Online. In *Proceedings of the Twelfth International Conference on Web and Social Media* (pp.221–230). AAAI Press.

Ong, T., Mannino, M., & Gregg, D. (2014). Linguistic characteristics of shill reviews. *Electronic Commerce Research and Applications*, *13*(2), 69–78.

Oprescu, F., Jones, C., & Katsikitis, M. (2014). I Play at Work. Ten principles for transforming work processes through gamification.). . *Frontiers in Psychology*, *5*(JAN). doi:10.3389/fpsyg.2014.00014

Opromolla, A., Ingrosso, A., Volpi, V., Medaglia, C. M., Palatucci, M., & Pazzola, M. (2015). Gamification in a Smart City context. An analysis and a proposal for its application in co-design processes. In *Proceedings of the international conference on games and learning alliance* (pp. 73-82). 10.1007/978-3-319-22960-7_8

Optimas. (2021). *JTI personality and teamcompass*. Retrieved from https://optimas.no/jti/

Ordóñez-Olmedo, E. (2017). Teaching Innovation Proposal: The Inclusion of Transversal Competences in Official University Studies of Master's degrees and the Strengthening of Democratic Values. *IJERI: International Journal of Educational Research and Innovation, 8*, 148–162.

Ören, T., Turnitsa, C., Mittal, S., & Diallo, S. Y. (2017). *Simulation-based learning and education*. Springer.

Orji, R., Tondello, G. F., & Nacke, L. E. (2018). Personalizing persuasive srategies in gameful systems to gamification user types. *CHI '18: Proceedings of the 2018 CHI Conference on Human Factors in Computing Systems, 435*, 1-14. 10.1145/3173574.3174009

Ortiz-Rojas, M., Chiluiza, K., & Valcke, M. (2017). Gamification and learning performance: A systematic review of the literature. *Proceedings ECGBL17*.

Østby, G., & Kowalski, S. (2020). Preparing for Cyber Crisis Management Exercises. *Augmented Cognition*. doi:https://doi.org/10.1007/978-3-030-50439-7_19

Østby, G., Berg, L., Kianpour, M., Katt, B., & Kowalski, S. (2019). A Socio-Technical Framework to Improve cyber security training. *Work*. https://ntnuopen.ntnu.no/ntnu-xmlui/handle/11250/2624957

Oswal, S. K., & Meloncon, L. (2014). Paying Attention to Accessibility When Designing Online Courses in Technical and Professional Communication. *Journal of Business and Technical Communication, 28*(3), 271–300. doi:10.1177/1050651914524780

Ouyang, T., Sun, H., & Li, F. (2021). Researches on the Education Reform for the Core Competencies-oriented Flight Training of Civil Aviation Pilots. In *Proceedings of the 6th International Conference on Education Reform and Modern Management (ERMM 2021)*. Atlantis Press. 10.2991/assehr.k.210513.088

Owler, K., Morrison, R., & Plester, B. (2010). Does Fun Work? The Complexity of Promoting Fun at Work. *Journal of Management & Organization, 16*(3), 338–352. doi:10.5172/jmo.16.3.338

Oxarart, A., Weaver, J., Al-Bataineh, A., & Mohamed, T. A. B. (2014). Game Design Principles and Motivation. *The International Journal of the Arts in Society, 7*(2), 347.

Oxarart, R. A., & Houghton, J. D. (2021). A Spoonful of Sugar: Gamification as Means for Enhancing Employee Self-Leadership and Self-Concordance at Work. *Administrative Sciences, 11*(2), 35. doi:10.3390/admsci11020035

Oxford Dictionary of English (3rd ed.). (2010). Oxford University Press.

Ozelkan, E., & Galambosi, A. (2009). Lampshade Game for lean manufacturing. *Production Planning and Control, 20*(5), 385–402. https://doi.org/10.1080/09537280902875419

Pabisiak, J. (2020). Dangerous, Yet Not So Unique. Characteristics of the Chinese Social Credit System. *Polish Political Science Yearbook, 49*(3), 30–53. doi:10.15804/ppsy2020303

Paharia, R. (2013). *Loyalty 3.0: How to revoluzionize Customer and Employee Engagement with Big Data and Gamification*. McGraw-Hill Book.

Pakinee, A., & Puritat, K. (2021). Designing a gamified e-learning environment for teaching undergraduate ERP course based on big five personality traits. *Education and Information Technologies, 26*(4), 4049–4067. https://doi.org/10.1007/s10639-021-10456-9

Paliokas, I., & Sylaiou, S. (2016). The use of serious games in Museum visits and exhibitions: A systematic mapping study. In *2016 8th International Conference on Games and Virtual Words for Serious Applications Barcelona* (pp. 1-8). Institute of Electrical and Electronics Engineers. 10.1109/VS-GAMES.2016.7590371

Palmquist, A., & Linderoth, J. (2020). Gamification Does Not Belong at a University. *Proceedings of the 2020 DiGRA Conference*, 21.

Pandian, G. S. B., Jain, A., Raza, Q., & Sahu, K. K. (2021). Digital health interventions (DHI) for the treatment of attention deficit hyperactivity disorder (ADHD) in children - a comparative review of literature among various treatment and DHI. *Psychiatry Research*, *297*, 113742. doi:10.1016/j.psychres.2021.113742 PMID:33515870

Paneva-Marinova, D., Rousseva, M., Dimova, M., & Pavlova, L. (2018). Tell the Story of Ancient Thracians Through Serious Game. *Lecture Notes in Computer Science, 11196*, 509–517.

Paneva-Marinova, D., Pavlov, R., & Kotuzov, N. (2017). Approach for analysis and improved usage of digital cultural assets for learning purposes. *Cybernetics and Information Technologies*, *17*(3), 140–151. doi:10.1515/cait-2017-0035

Papadopoulos, P. M., Lagkas, T., & Demetriadis, S. N. (2016). How revealing rankings affects student attitude and performance in a peer review learning environment. In *Communications in Computer and Information Science* (pp. 225–240). Springer International Publishing. doi:10.1007/978-3-319-29585-5_13

Papanaoum, E. (2019). *Effect of Gamification on the emotions of users of an online advertising platform.* Kth Royal Institute of Technology School of Electrical Engineering and Computer Science.

Papathanasiou-Zuhrt, D., Weiss-Ibanez, D. F., & Di Russo, A. (2017). The gamification of heritage in the UNESCO enlisted the medieval town of Rhodes. In *Proceedings of GamiFIN Conference* (pp. 60-70). Academic Press.

Parekh, B. (2012). Is there a case for banning hate speech? In M. Herz & P. Molnar (Eds.), *The Content and Context of Hate Speech: Rethinking Regulation and Responses* (pp. 37–56). Cambridge University Press. doi:10.1017/CBO9781139042871.006

Park, C. H., & Kim, Y. G. (2003). Identifying key factors affecting consumer purchase behavior in an online shopping context. *International Journal of Retail & Distribution Management*, *31*(1), 16–29. doi:10.1108/09590550310457818

Parker, K. (2018). Impact and Knowledge Exchange for STEM Disciplines. *The Open University Workshop*.

Park, H. J., & Bae, J. H. (2014). Study and research of gamification design. *International Journal of Software Engineering and Its Applications*, *8*(8), 19–28.

Park, J., Snell, W., Ha, S., & Chung, T. L. (2011). Consumers' post-adoption of m-services: Interest in future m-services based on consumer evaluations of current m-services. *Journal of Electronic Commerce Research*, *12*(3), 165–175.

Parra-López, E., Bulchand-Gidumal, J., Gutiérrez-Taño, D., & Díaz-Armas, R. (2011). Intentions to use social media in organizing and taking vacation trips. *Computers in Human Behavior*, *27*(2), 640–654. doi:10.1016/j.chb.2010.05.022

Patrício, R., Moreira, A. C., & Zurlo, F. (2020). Enhancing design thinking approaches to innovation through gamification. *European Journal of Innovation Management.* doi:10.1108/EJIM-06-2020-0239

Patricio, R., Moreira, A., Zurlo, F., & Melazzini, M. (2020). Co-creation of new solutions through gamification: A collaborative innovation practice. *Creativity and Innovation Management,* 146–160. doi:10.1111/caim.12356

Patrício, R., Moreira, A. C., & Zurlo, F. (2018). Gamification approaches to the early stage of innovation. *Creativity and Innovation Management*, *27*(4), 499–511. doi:10.1111/caim.12284

Patrício, R., Moreira, A. C., & Zurlo, F. (2020). Enhancing design thinking approaches to innovation through gamification. *European Journal of Innovation Management.*

Patricio, R., Moreira, A., Zurlo, F., & Melazzini, M. (2020). Co-creation of new solutions through gamification: A collaborative innovation practice. *Creativity and Innovation Management, 29*(1), 146–160. https://doi.org/10.1111/caim.12356

Pautasso, E., Frisiello, A., Chiesa, M., Ferro, E., Dominici, F., Tsardanidis, G., Efthymiou, I., Zgeras, G., & Vlachokyriakos, V. (2021). The Outreach of Participatory Methods in Smart Cities, From the Co-Design of Public Services to the Evaluation: Insights From the Athens Case Study. *International Journal of Urban Planning and Smart Cities, 2*(1), 59–83. doi:10.4018/IJUPSC.2021010105

Pavlov, R., Paneva, D., Pavlova-Draganova, L., & Draganov, L. (2007). Ubiquitous learning applications on top of iconographic digital library. *The Proceedings of the International Conference on Mathematical and Computational Linguistics, 6,* 107–118.

Peng, W., Lin, J. H., Pfeiffer, K. A., & Winn, B. (2012). Need satisfaction supportive game features as motivational determinants: An experimental study of a self-determination theory guided exergame. *Media Psychology, 15*(2), 175–196. doi:10.1080/15213269.2012.673850

Penninx, R., & Garcés-Mascareñas, B. (2016). The Concept of Integration as an Analytical Tool and as a Policy Concept. In R. Penninx & B. Garcés-Mascareñas (Eds.), *Integration Processes and Policies in Europe: Contexts, Levels and Actors* (pp. 11–29). Springer Open. doi:10.1007/978-3-319-21674-4_2

Penuel, W., Fishman, B., Yamaguchi, R., & Gallagher, L. (2007). What Makes Professional Development Effective? Strategies That Foster Curriculum Implementation. *American Educational Research Journal, 44,* 921-958. . doi:10.3102/0002831207308221

Pereira, M., Oliveira, M., Vieira, A., Lima, R. M., & Paes, L. (2018). The gamification as a tool to increase employee skills through interactives work instructions training. *Procedia Computer Science, 138,* 630–637. https://doi.org/10.1016/j.procs.2018.10.084

Pereira, P., Duarte, E., Rebelo, F., & Noriega, P. (2014). A review of gamification for health-related contexts. In *International Conference of Design, User Experience, and Usability* (pp. 742-753). Springer. 10.1007/978-3-319-07626-3_70

Perera, C., McCormick, C., Bandara, A. K., Price, B. A., & Nuseibeh, B. (2016). Privacy-by-Design Framework for Assessing Internet of Things Applications and Platforms. In *Proceedings of the 6th International Conference on the Internet of Things.* 10.1145/2991561.2991566

Pérez-Escolar, M., Ordóñez-Olmedo, E., & Alcaide-Pulido, P. (2021). Fact-checking skills and project-based learning about infodemic and disinformation. *Thinking Skills and Creativity, 41,* 100887. Advance online publication. doi:10.1016/j.tsc.2021.100887

Perreira, T. A., Innis, J., & Berta, W. (2016). Work motivation in health care: A scoping literature review. *International Journal of Evidence-Based Healthcare, 14*(4), 175–182. doi:10.1097/XEB.0000000000000093 PMID:27552534

Perrotta, C., Featherstone, G., Aston, H., & Houghton, E. (2013). *Game-based Learning: Latest Evidence and Future Directions.* National Foundation for Educational Research.

Perryer, C., Celestine, N. A., Scott-Ladd, B., & Leighton, C. (2016). Enhancing workplace motivation through gamification: Transferrable lessons from pedagogy. *International Journal of Management Education, 14*(3), 327–335. doi:10.1016/j.ijme.2016.07.001

Petroski, A. (2012). Games vs. Simulations: When Simulations May Be a Better Approach. *T+D Magazine, 66*(2), 27.

Petrucco, C., & De Rossi, M. (2009). *Narrare con il digital storytelling a scuola e nelle organizzazioni*. Academic Press.

Phillips, L. A., & Gardner, B. (2016). Habitual exercise instigation (vs. execution) predicts healthy adults' exercise frequency. *Health Psychology*, *35*(1), 69–77. doi:10.1037/hea0000249 PMID:26148187

Piazza, J. (2020, September 28). When politicians use hate speech, political violence increases. *The Conversation*. Available at https://cutt.ly/ZbGE7cx

Pierce, W. D., Cameron, J., Banko, K. M., & So, S. (2003). Positive effects of rewards and performance standards on intrinsic motivation. *The Psychological Record*, *53*(4), 561–578. doi:10.1007/BF03395453

Pimentel, K., & Teixeira, K. (1995). *Virtual Reality: Through the New Looking Glass* (2nd ed.). Intel/McGraw-Hill.

Pine, B. J., & Gilmore, J. H. (2011). *The Experience Economy*. Harvard Business School Press.

Pine, R., Fleming, T., McCallum, S., & Sutcliffe, K. (2020). The effects of casual videogames on anxiety, depression, stress, and low mood: A systematic review. *Games for Health Journal*, *9*(4), 255–264. doi:10.1089/g4h.2019.0132 PMID:32053021

Pine, R., Sutcliffe, K., McCallum, S., & Fleming, T. (2020). Young adolescents' interest in a mental health casual video game. *Digital Health*, *6*, 1–7. doi:10.1177/2055207620949391 PMID:32944270

Pink, D. H. (2009). *Drive: The surprising truth about what motivates us*. Penguin Group, Inc.

Pinto, J. L. (2014). Pensamento Lean - A filosofia das organizações vencedoras (6th ed.). Lidel.

Plangger, K., Kietzmann, J., Robson, K., Pitt, L., & McCarthy, I. (2016). Experiences with gamification: The MDE framework. In *Marketing Challenges in a Turbulent Business Environment* (pp. 491–491). Springer. doi:10.1007/978-3-319-19428-8_125

Plass, J. L., Homer, B. D., & Kinzer, C. K. (2015). Foundations of Game-Based Learning. *Educational Psychologist*, *50*(4), 258–283. https://doi.org/10.1080/00461520.2015.1122533

Ploderer, B., Stuart, J., Tran, V., Green, T., & Muller, J. (2017). *The transition of stroke survivors from hospital to home: understanding work and design opportunities*. OZCHI. doi:10.1145/3152771.3152772

Plyler, J. (2013). *Video Games and the Hero's Journey*. Available at https://bit.ly/3xpRhux

Poncin, I., Garnier, M., Mimoun, M. S. B., & Leclercq, T. (2017). Smart technologies and shopping experience: Are gamification interfaces effective? The case of the Smartstore. *Technological Forecasting and Social Change*, *124*, 320–331. doi:10.1016/j.techfore.2017.01.025

Poppelaars, M., Lichtwarck-Aschoff, A., Otten, R., & Granic, I. (2021). Can a Commercial Video Game Prevent Depression? Null Results and Whole Sample Action Mechanisms in a Randomized Controlled Trial. *Frontiers in Psychology*, *11*(January), 1–17. doi:10.3389/fpsyg.2020.575962 PMID:33510666

Posetti, J. (2018). News industry transformation: digital technology, social platforms and the spread of misinformation and disinformation. In C. Ireton & J. Posetti (Eds.), *Journalism, fake news & disinformation: handbook for journalism education and training* (pp. 55–69). UNESCO.

Potter, W. J. (2018). *Media literacy*. Sage Publications.

Prensky, M. (2001). Digital Natives, Digital Immigrants. *On the Horizon*, *9*(5), 1–6.

Prensky, M. (2016). *Education to better their world: Unleashing the power of 21st-century kids*. Teachers College Press.

Primack, B. A., Carroll, M. V., McNamara, M., Klem, M., King, B., Rich, M., Chan, C. W., & Nayak, S. (2012). Role of video games in improving health-related outcomes: A systematic review. *American Journal of Preventive Medicine*, *42*(6), 630–638. doi:10.1016/j.amepre.2012.02.023 PMID:22608382

PRISMA. (2021). *PRISMA- Transparent reporting of systematic reviews and meta-analyses.* http://prisma-statement.org/PRISMAStatement/PRISMAStatement

Prusak, Z. (2004). Problem definition and problem solving in lean manufacturing environment. *ASEE Annual Conference Proceedings*, 11343–11353.

Przybylski, A. K., Rigby, C. S., & Ryan, R. M. (2010). A motivational model of video game engagement. *Review of General Psychology*, *14*(2), 154–166. doi:10.1037/a0019440

Qiang, J., Qian, Z., Li, Y., Yuan, Y., & Wu, X. (2020). Short Text Topic Modeling Techniques, Applications, and Performance: A Survey. *IEEE Transactions on Knowledge and Data Engineering*. Advance online publication. doi:10.1109/TKDE.2020.2992485

Rabin, S. (2010). *Introduction to game development* (2nd ed.). Course Technology, Cengage Learning.

Raczkowski, F. (2014). Making points the point: Towards a history of ideas of gamification. In Rethinking Gamification. Meson Pr.

Raitskaya, L., & Tikhonova, E. (2019). Gamification as a field landmark in educational research. *Journal of Language & Education*, *5*(3), 4–10. doi:10.17323/jle.2019.10688

Raj, B., & Gupta, D. (2018, September). Factors Influencing Consumer Responses to Marketing Gamification. In *2018 International Conference on Advances in Computing, Communications and Informatics (ICACCI)* (pp. 1538-1542). IEEE. 10.1109/ICACCI.2018.8554922

Ramírez, J. L. (2014). *Gamificación. Mecánicas de juegos en tu vida personal y profesional.* SCLibro.

Ramsden, P. (1992). *Learning to Teach in Higher Education.* Routledge.

Rapp, A., Hopfgartner, F., Hamari, J., Linehan, C., & Cena, F. (2019). Strengthening gamification studies: Current trends and future opportunities of gamification research. *International Journal of Human Computer Studies, 127*(November), 1–6. doi:10.1016/j.ijhcs.2018.11.007

Rapp, A. (2017). Drawing inspiration from World of Warcraft: Gamification design elements for behavior change technologies. *Interacting with Computers*, *29*(5), 648–678. doi:10.1093/iwc/iwx001

Rapp, A. (2018). Social Game Elements in World of Warcraft: Interpersonal Relations, Groups, and Organizations for Gamification Design. *International Journal of Human-Computer Interaction*, *34*(8), 759–773. doi:10.1080/10447318.2018.1461760

Ray, S., Kim, S. S., & Morris, J. G. (2014). The central role of engagement in online communities. *Information Systems Research*, *25*(3), 528–546. doi:10.1287/isre.2014.0525

Read, J. C. (2015). Serious games in education. *EAI Endorsed Transactions on Serious Games*, *2*(6), 1–5. doi:10.4108/eai.5-11-2015.150614

Reich, J., & Ruipérez-Valiente, J. A. (2019). The MOOC pivot. *Science*, *363*(6423), 130–131. doi:10.1126cience.aav7958 PMID:30630920

Reiners, T., & Wood, L. C. (2015). *Gamification in education and business.* Springer International Publishing, School of Information Systems, Curtin University. doi:10.1007/978-3-319-10208-5

Revathy, V. R., & Anitha, S. P. (2018). Cold Start Problem in Social Recommender Systems: State-of-the-Art Review. In S. K. Bhatia, S. Tiwari, K. K. Mishra, & M. C. Trivedi (Eds.), *Advances in Computer Communication and Computational Sciences* (pp. 105–115). Springer.

Rey, P. (2014). Gamification and post-Fordist Capitalism. In The Gameful World: Approaches, Issues, Applications (pp. 277–295). MIT Press.

Reynolds, L., Sosik, V. S., & Cosley, D. (2013). When Wii doesn't fit: How non-beginners react to Wii fit's gamification. In *Proceedings of the First International Conference on Gameful Design, Research, and Applications* (pp. 111-114). 10.1145/2583008.2583027

Ricciardi, F., & Paolis, L. T. D. (2014). A comprehensive review of serious games in health professions. *International Journal of Computer Games Technology, 2014*(9), 9. https://doi.org/10.1155/2014/787968

Richter, G., Raban, D. R., & Rafaeli, S. (2015) Studying gamification: The effect of rewards and incentives on motivation. In Gamification in Education and Business. Springer.

Richter, G., Raban, D. R., & Rafaeli, S. (2015). Studying gamification: The effect of rewards and incentives on motivation. In T. Reiners & L. C. Wood (Eds.), *Gamification in education and business* (pp. 21–46). Springer. doi:10.1007/978-3-319-10208-5_2

Riedel, J., Feng, Y., & Azadegan, A. (2013). Serious Games Adoption in Organizations – An Exploratory Analysis. In EC-TEL 2013 (Vol. 8095, pp. 508–513). Springer Verlag. https://doi.org/10.1007/978-3-642-40814-4.

Rigby, S. C. (2014). Gamification and Motivation. In The Gameful World: Approaches, Issues, Applications (pp. 113–137). MIT Press.

Rigby, C. S. (2015). Gamification and motivation 4. In S. P. Walz & S. Deterding (Eds.), *Gameful world: Approaches, issues, applications* (pp. 113–138). The MIT Press.

Rip, A. (2006). Folks Theories of Nanotechnologists. *Science as Culture, 15*(4), 349–365. doi:10.1080/09505430601022676

Riva, G., Davide, F., & Ijsselsteijn, W. (Eds.). (2003). *Being there: concepts, effects and measurement of user presence in synthetic environments*. Ios Press.

Roberts, J. A., Hann, I. H., & Slaughter, S. A. (2006). Understanding the motivations, participation, and performance of open source software developers: A longitudinal study of the Apache projects. *Management Science, 52*(7), 984–999. doi:10.1287/mnsc.1060.0554

Robertson, M. (2010). *Can't play, won't play*. https://web.archive.org/web/20110521091044/http://www.hideandseek.net/2010/10/06/cant-play-wont-play

Robin, B. R. (2008). Digital storytelling: A powerful technology tool for the 21st century classroom. *Theory into Practice, 47*(3), 220–228. doi:10.1080/00405840802153916

Robson, K., Plangger, K., Kietzmann, J. H., McCarthy, I., & Pitt, L. (2015). Is it all a game? Understanding the principles of gamification. *Business Horizons, 58*(4), 411–420. doi:10.1016/j.bushor.2015.03.006

Robson, K., Plangger, K., Kietzmann, J. H., McCarthy, I., & Pitt, L. (2016). Game on: Engaging customers and employees through gamification. *Business Horizons, 59*(1), 29–36. doi:10.1016/j.bushor.2015.08.002

Roby, T. (2010). Opus in the Classroom: Striking CoRDS with Content-Related Digital Storytelling. *Contemporary Issues in Technology & Teacher Education, 10*, 133–144.

Rodrigues, M., Monteiro, V., Novais, P., & Analide, C. (2019). Getting Residents Closer to Public Institutions Through Gamification. In *Ambient Intelligence – Software and Applications –, 9th International Symposium on Ambient Intelligence. ISAmI2018 2018* (pp. 33-39). Springer. 10.1007/978-3-030-01746-0_4

Rodrigues, L. F., Oliveira, A., & Costa, C. J. (2016). Does ease-of-use contributes to the perception of enjoyment? A case of gamification in e-banking. *Computers in Human Behavior, 61*, 114–126. doi:10.1016/j.chb.2016.03.015

Rodrigues, L. F., Oliveira, A., & Costa, C. J. (2016b). Playing seriously - How gamification and social cues influence bank customers to use gamified e-business applications. *Computers in Human Behavior, 63*, 392–407. doi:10.1016/j.chb.2016.05.063

Rodrigues, L., Costa, C., & Oliveira, A. (2017). How does the web game design influence the behavior of e-banking users? *Computers in Human Behavior, 74*, 163–174. doi:10.1016/j.chb.2017.04.034

Rogers, M., Chassy, A., & Bamat, T. (2010). *Integrating Peacebuilding into Humanitarian and Development Programming*. Catholic Relief Services.

Rogers, R. (2017). The motivational pull of video game feedback, rules, and social interaction: Another self-determination theory approach. *Computers in Human Behavior, 73*, 446–450. doi:10.1016/j.chb.2017.03.048

Roggeveen, A. L., & Sethuraman, R. (2020). Customer-Interfacing Retail Technologies in 2020 & Beyond: An Integrative Framework and Research Directions. . *Journal of Retailing, 96*(3), 299–309. doi:10.1016/j.jretai.2020.08.001

Rolo, D. (2015). *Mentir au travail*. Presses universitaires de France. doi:10.3917/puf.rolod.2015.03

Romano, M., Díaz, P., & Aedo, I. (2021). Gamification-less: May gamification really foster civic participation? A controlled field experiment. *Journal of Ambient Intelligence and Humanized Computing*. Advance online publication. doi:10.100712652-021-03322-6

Romero, M., & Turpo, O. (2015). Serious Games para el desarrollo de las competencias del siglo XXI. *Revista de Educación a Distancia (RED)*, (34). https://bit.ly/3xuL0xN

Roohi, S., & Forouzandeh, A. (2019). Regarding color psychology principles in adventure games to enhance the sense of immersion. *Entertainment Computing, 30*, 100298. doi:10.1016/j.entcom.2019.100298

Ross, C. R., Maninger, R. M., LaPrairie, K. N., & Sullivan, S. (2015). The use of Twitter in the creation of educational professional learning opportunities. *Administrative Issues Journal, 5*(1), 55–76. doi:10.5929/2015.5.1.7

Rossette-Crake, F. (2020). 'The new oratory': Public speaking practice in the digital, neoliberal age. *Discourse Studies, 22*(5), 571–589. doi:10.1177/1461445620916363

Roth, K. (2020, January 3). *China's Global Threat to Human Rights*. Human Rights Watch. https://www.hrw.org/world-report/2020/country-chapters/global

Rousseva, M. (2018). Challenges in the design and the development of the educational serious game "The Thracians." *Digital Presentation and Preservation of Cultural and Scientific Heritage, 8*, 83–85.

Rowe, J. P., Lobene, E. V., Mott, B. W., & Lester, J. C. (2017). Play in the museum: Design and development of a game-based learning exhibit for informal science education. *International Journal of Gaming and Computer-Mediated Simulations, 9*(3), 96–113. doi:10.4018/IJGCMS.2017070104

Roy, A., & Raymond, L. (2008). *E-Learning as a Solution to the Training Problems of SMEs - A Multiple Case Study*. WEBIST.

Roy-Burman, A., Lightbody, L., Henry, D., Huey, R. E., Lynch, M., & Martin, E. (2013). 118: Engaging nurses through social gamification. *Critical Care Medicine*, *41*(12), A23. doi:10.1097/01.ccm.0000439267.10865.08

Rozman, T., & Donath, L. (2019). The current state of the gemification in e-learning: A literature review of literature reviews. *Journal of Innovative Business and Management*, *11*(3), 5–19.

Rubin, D. S., Severin, R., Arena, R., & Bond, S. (2020). Leveraging technology to move more and sit less. *Progress in Cardiovascular Diseases*. PMID:33129794

Rubino, I., Barberis, C., Xhembulla, J., & Malnati, G. (2015). Integrating a location-based mobile game in the museum visit: Evaluating visitors' behaviour and learning. *Journal on Computing and Cultural Heritage*, *8*(3), 1–18. doi:10.1145/2724723

Rubio-Romero, J., & Barón-Dulce, G. (2019). Actitudes de los jóvenes hacia las comunidades virtuales y su vínculo con las marcas. Una aproximación a través de los estudiantes universitarios de comunicación y de marketing de la Universidad Nebrija. adComunica. *Revista Científica de Estrategias. Tendencias e Innovación en Comunicación*, (18), 41–62.

Rubio-Romero, J., Jiménez, J. M., & Barón-Dulce, G. (2019). Digital social networks as spaces for sociability among adolescents. Case study: Escolapios school in Aluche. *Mediterranean Journal of Communication*, *10*(2), 85–99.

Ruhi, U. (2015). Level Up Your Strategy: Towards a Descriptive Framework for Meaningful Entruerprise Gamification. *Technology Innovation Management Review*, *5*(8), 5–16. doi:10.22215/timreview918

Ruhi, U. (2015). Level Up Your Strategy: Towards a Descriptive Framework for Meaningful Enterprise Gamification. *Technology Innovation Management Review*, *5*(8), 5–16. doi:10.22215/timreview/918

Ruiz, M. E. P., & Chapman, M. C. S. (2017). Las competencias informacionales en las ciencias médicas. *Revista de la Facultad de Ciencias Médicas de la Universidad de Guayaquil*. https://bit.ly/3fGSVSK

Rüttimann, B. G., & Stöckli, M. T. (2016). Going beyond Triviality: The Toyota Production System—Lean Manufacturing beyond Muda and Kaizen. *Journal of Service Science and Management*, *09*(02), 140–149. https://doi.org/10.4236/jssm.2016.92018

Ryan, R. M., & Deci, E. L. (2002). Overview of self-determination theory: An organismic dialectial perspective. Handbook of self-determination research, 3-33.

Ryan, R. M., & Deci, E. L. (2002). Overview of self-determination theory: An organismic dialectical perspective. Handbook of Self-Determination Research, 2, 3-33.

Ryan, R. M. (2009). Self-determination theory and wellbeing. *Wellbeing in Developing Countries Research Review*, *1*(June), 1–2.

Ryan, R. M., & Deci, E. L. (2000). Self-Determination Theory and the Facilitation of Intrinsic Motivation, Social Development, and Well-Being. *The American Psychologist*, *55*(1), 68–78. doi:10.1037/0003-066X.55.1.68 PMID:11392867

Ryan, R. M., & Deci, E. L. (2000). The darker and brighter sides of human existence: Basic psychological needs as a unifying concept. *Psychological Inquiry*, *11*(4), 319–338. doi:10.1207/S15327965PLI1104_03

Ryan, R. M., & Deci, E. L. (2017). *Self-determination theory: Basic psychological needs in motivation, development, and wellness*. The Guilford Press. doi:10.1521/978.14625/28806

Ryan, R. M., & Deci, E. L. (2020). Intrinsic and extrinsic motivation from a self-determination theory perspective: Definitions, theory, practices, and future directions. *Contemporary Educational Psychology*, *61*, 101860. doi:10.1016/j.cedpsych.2020.101860

Ryan, R. M., & Deci, L. E. (2000a). Intrinsic and Extrinsic Motivations: Classic Definitions and New Directions. *Contemporary Educational Psychology*, *25*(1), 54–67. doi:10.1006/ceps.1999.1020 PMID:10620381

Ryan, R. M., Rigby, C. S., & Przybylski, A. (2006). The Motivational Pull of Video Games: A Self-Determination Theory Approach. *Motivation and Emotion*, *30*(4), 344–360. doi:10.100711031-006-9051-8

Rybak, C. (2013). Nurturing Positive Mental Health: Mindfulness for Wellbeing in Counseling. *International Journal for the Advancement of Counseling*, *35*(2), 110–119. doi:10.100710447-012-9171-7

Sailer, M., Hense, J. U., Mayr, S. K., & Mandl, H. (2017). How gamification motivates: An experimental study of the effects of specific game design elements on psychological need satisfaction. *Computers in Human Behavior*, *69*, 371–380. doi:10.1016/j.chb.2016.12.033

Sailer, M., & Homner, L. (2020). The gamification of learning: A meta-analysis. *Educational Psychology Review*, *32*(1), 77–112. doi:10.100710648-019-09498-w

Sáiz-Manzares, M. C., & Pérez, M. I. (2016). Autorregulación y mejora del autoconocimiento en resolución de problemas. *Psicologia desde el Caribe*, *33*(1), 14–30.

Sajid, M. J., Cao, Q., Xinchun, L., Brohi, M. A., & Sajid, M. F. (2018). Video gaming a new face of inducement tourism: Main attractors for juvenile gamers. *International Journal of Scientific Study*, *4*(5), 52–56.

Sajid, M. J., Cao, Q., Xinchun, L., Brohi, M. A., & Sajid, M. F. (2018). Video Gaming a New Face of Inducement Tourism: Main Attractors for Juvenile Gamers. *International Journal of Scientific Study*, *4*(5), 52–56.

Sakamoto, M., Nakajima, T., & Alexandrova, T. (2012). Value-based design for gamifying daily activities. In M. Errlich, R. Malaka, & M. Masuch (Eds.), *Entertainment Computing – ICEC 2012* (pp. 421–424). Springer. doi:10.1007/978-3-642-33542-6_43

Salen, K., Tekinbaş, K. S., & Zimmerman, E. (2004). *Rules of play: Game design fundamentals*. MIT Press.

Salvi, F. (2015). *Nuevo comportamiento del consumidor: la influencia del eWOM (electronic Word-of-Mouth) en relación a la lealtad de los clientes en el sector hotelero* (Doctoral dissertation). Universitat de les Illes Balears.

Sanders, I., Short, C. E., Bogomolova, S., Stanford, T., Plotnikoff, R., Vandelanotte, C., Olds, T., Edney, S., Ryan, J., Curtis, R. G., & Maher, C. (2019). Characteristics of adopters of an online social networking physical activity mobile phone app: Cluster analysis. *JMIR mHealth and uHealth*, *7*(6), e12484. doi:10.2196/12484 PMID:31162130

Santos, A. C. G., Oliveira, W., Hamari, J., Rodrigues, L., Toda, A. M., Palomino, P. T., & Isotani, S. (2021). The relationship between user types and gamification designs. *User Modeling and User-Adapted Interaction*, *31*(5), 907–940. Advance online publication. doi:10.100711257-021-09300-z

Saperstein, A. M. (2004). "The Enemy of My Enemy Is My Friend" Is the Enemy: Dealing with the War-Provoking Rules of Intent. *Conflict Management and Peace Science*, *21*(4), 287–296.

Sardi, L., Idri, A., & Fernández-Alemán, J. L. (2017). A systematic review of gamification in e-Health. *Journal of Biomedical Informatics*, *71*, 31–48. doi:10.1016/j.jbi.2017.05.011 PMID:28536062

Saucedo-Araujo, R. G., Chillón, P., Pérez-López, I. J., & Barranco-Ruiz, Y. (2020). School-based interventions for promoting physical activity using games and gamification: A systematic review protocol. *International Journal of Environmental Research and Public Health*, *17*(14), 5186. doi:10.3390/ijerph17145186 PMID:32709132

Savignac, E. (2017). *Gamification of Work: The Use of Games in the Workplace*. Wiley Publishing. doi:10.1002/9781119384564

Savignac, E., Andonova, Y., Lénel, P., Monjaret, A., & Seurrat, A. (Eds.). (2017). *Le travail de la gamification. Enjeux, modalités et rhétoriques de la translation du jeu au travail*. Peter Lang. doi:10.3726/b11612

Savulich, G., Piercy, T., Fox, C., Suckling, J., Rowe, J. B., O'Brien, J. T., & Sahakian, B. J. (2017). Cognitive training using a novel memory game on an iPad in patients with amnestic mild cognitive impairment (aMCI). *The International Journal of Neuropsychopharmacology*, *20*(8), 624–633. doi:10.1093/ijnp/pyx040 PMID:28898959

Scarantino, L. M. (2007). Persuasion, rhétorique et autorité. *Diogène*, *217*, 22–38.

Schank, J. F., Thie, H. J., Graff, C. M. II, Beel, J., & Sollinger, J. (2002). *Finding the right balance: Simulator and live training for navy units*. RAND.

Scheiber, N. (2017, April 2). How Uber Uses Psychological Tricks to Push Its Drivers' Buttons. *The New York Times*. https://www.nytimes.com/interactive/2017/04/02/technology/uber-drivers-psychological-tricks.html

Schell, J. (2010). *The art of game design: A book of lenses*. Morgan Kaufmann Publishers.

Schlegel, L. (2020). Jumanji Extremism? How games and gamification could facilitate radicalization processes. *Journal for Deradicalization*, *23*, 1–44.

Schöbel, S. M., Janson, A., & Söllner, M. (2020). Capturing the complexity of gamification elements: A holistic approach for analysing existing and deriving novel gamification designs. *European Journal of Information Systems*, *29*(6), 641–668. doi:10.1080/0960085X.2020.1796531

Schoenmueller, V., Netzer, O., & Stahl, F. (2020). The Polarity of Online Reviews: Prevalence, Drivers and Implications. *JMR, Journal of Marketing Research*, *57*(5), 853–877.

Schunk, D. H. (2014). *Learning theories – An educational perspective* (6th ed.). Pearson.

Schuurman, D., De Moor, K., De Marez, L., & Van Looy, J. (2008). Fanboys, competers, escapists and time-killers: a typology based on gamers' motivations for playing video games. *DIMEA '08: Proceedings of the 3rd international conference on Digital Interactive Media in Entertainment and Arts*, 46-50. 10.1145/1413634.1413647

Sclater, M., & Lally, V. (2016) Critical TEL: The importance of theory and theorisation. In *Proceedings of the 10th international conference on networked learning 2016*. University of Lancaster.

Scolari, C. A. (2013). *Homo Videoludens 2.0. De Pacman a la gamification*. Laboratori de Mitjans Interactius (Universitat de Barcelona).

Seaborn, K., & Fels, D. I. (2015). Gamification in theory and action: A survey. *International Journal of Human-Computer Studies*, *74*, 14–31. doi:10.1016/j.ijhcs.2014.09.006

Seels, B., & Glasgow, Z. (1990). *Exercises in instructional design*. Merrill Pub.

Şenocak & Bozkurt, A. (2020). Oyunlaştırma, oyuncu türleri ve oyunlaştırma tasarım çerçeveleri. *Açıköğretim Uygulamaları ve Araştırmaları Dergisi*, *6*(1), 78-96. https://hdl.handle.net/11421/24971

Sever, N. S., Sever, G. N., & Kuhzady, S. (2015). The evaluation of potentials of gamification in tourism marketing communication. *International Journal of Academic Research in Business & Social Sciences*, *5*(10), 188–202. doi:10.6007/IJARBSS/v5-i10/1867

Sezgin, S. (2020). Digital player typologies in gamification and game-based learning approaches: a meta-synthesis. *Bartın University Journal of Faculty of Education*, *9*(1), 49-68. https://dergipark.org.tr/en/pub/buefad/issue/51796/610524

Sgueo, G. (2017). *Gamification, participatory democracy and engaged public (S)*. University of Vienna. https://papers.ssrn.com/sol3/papers.cfm?abstract_id=3045361

Shah, A. (2012). Gamification: It's all about Processes. *Cognizant 20-20 Insights*, 1-4.

Shamshiry, E., Nadi, B., Bin Mokhtar, M., Komoo, I., Saadiah Hashim, H., & Yahaya, N. (2011). Integrated models for solid waste management in tourism regions: Langkawi Island, Malaysia. *Journal of Environmental and Public Health*, *2011*, 2011. doi:10.1155/2011/709549 PMID:21904559

Shen, C. W., Luong, T. H., Ho, J. T., & Djailani, I. (2020). Social media marketing of IT service companies: Analysis using a concept-linking mining approach. *Industrial Marketing Management*, *90*, 593–604.

Sheth, J. (2020). *Impact of Covid-19 on consumer behavior: Will the old habits return or die?* doi:10.1016/j.jbusres.2020.05.059

Sheth, J. N., Newman, B. I., & Gross, B. L. (1991). Why we buy what we buy: A theory of consumption values. *Journal of Business Research*, *22*(2), 159–170. doi:10.1016/0148-2963(91)90050-8

Shinn, T., & Ragouet, P. (2005). *Controverses sur la science. Pour une sociologie transversaliste de l'activité scientifique*. Raisons d'agir.

Shivakumaraswamy, K. N., & Narendra, B. K. (2021). Assessing Information Communication Technology (ICT) Literacy Skills: A Study of Students of BGS Institute of Technology. Academic Press.

Shrikumar, K. (2018). *PLAYNE – The Meditation Game*. Vismaya.

Shteynberg, G., Hirsh, J. B., Bentley, R. A., & Garthoff, J. (2020). Shared worlds and shared minds: A theory of collective learning and a psychology of common knowledge. *Psychological Review*, *127*(5), 918–931. https://doi.org/10.1037/rev0000200

Shulman, M. (1951). Max Shulman: Love is a Fallacy. *Love Is a Fallacy*, 6.

Sicart, M. (2008). Defining game mechanics. *Game Studies*, *8*(2), 1–14.

Sicart, M. (2009). *The Ethics of Computer Games* (1st ed.). MIT Press. doi:10.7551/mitpress/9780262012652.001.0001

Sicart, M. (2013). *Beyond Choices: The Design of Ethical Gameplay*. MIT Press. doi:10.7551/mitpress/9052.001.0001

Siegel, R. D., Germer, C. K., & Olendzki, A. (2009). Mindfulness: What is it? where did it come from? In Clinical Handbook of Mindfulness (pp. 17–35). New York, NY: Springer New York. doi:10.1007/978-0-387-09593-6_2

Siemens, J. C., Smith, S., Fisher, D., Thyroff, A., & Killian, G. (2015). Level Up! The Role of Progress Feedback Type for Encouraging Intrinsic Motivation and Positive Brand Attitudes in Public Versus Private Gaming Contexts. *Journal of Interactive Marketing*, *32*, 1–12. doi:10.1016/j.intmar.2015.07.001

Sigala, M. (2015). Gamification for crowdsourcing marketing practices: Applications and benefits in tourism. Advances in crowdsourcing, 129-145.

Sigala, M. (2015a). Gamification for crowdsourcing marketing practices: Applications and benefits in tourism. In F. J. Garrigos-Simon, I. Gil-Pechuan, & S. Estelles-Miguel (Eds.), *Advances in crowdsourcing* (pp. 129–145). Springer. doi:10.1007/978-3-319-18341-1_11

Sigala, M. (2015b). The application and impact of gamification funware on trip planning and experiences: The case of TripAdvisor's funware. *Electronic Markets*, *25*(3), 189–209. doi:10.100712525-014-0179-1

Sikkerhetsfestivalen. (2019). *Megagame*. Retrieved from https://sikkerhetsfestivalen.no/bidrag2019/megagame

Silge, J., & Robinson, D. (2017). *Text mining with R: A tidy approach*. O'Reilly Media, Inc.

Silpasuwanchai, C., Ma, X., Shigemasu, H., & Ren, X. (2016). Developing a comprehensive engagement framework of gamification for reflective learning. In *Proceedings of the 2016 ACM Conference on Designing Interactive Systems* (pp. 459-472). 10.1145/2901790.2901836

Silva, M., García, T., Guzmán, T., & Chaparro, R. (2016). Study of Moodle tools to develop 21st century skills. *Virtual Campus*, *5*(2), 58–69.

Silva, R. J. R., Rodrigues, R. G., & Leal, C. T. P. (2019). Gamification in management education: A systematic literature review. *BAR - Brazilian Administration Review*, *16*(2), e180103. Advance online publication. doi:10.1590/1807-7692bar2019180103

Simões, J., Redondo, R. D., & Vilas, A. F. (2013). A social gamification framework for a K-6 learning platform. *Computers in Human Behavior*, *29*(2), 345–353. doi:10.1016/j.chb.2012.06.007

Simões-Silva, V., Duarte Mesquita, A. F., Santos Da Silva, K. L., Arouca Quental, V. S., & Marques, A. (2021). Gamification as Upper Limb Rehabilitation Process. In R. A. Peixoto de Queirós & A. J. Marques (Eds.), *Handbook of Research on Solving Modern Healthcare Challenges With Gamification* (pp. 243–257). IGI Global. doi:10.4018/978-1-7998-7472-0.ch013

Simon, C. R., & Durand-Bush, N. (2014). Differences in psychological and affective well-being between physicians and resident physicians: Does high and low self-regulation capacity matter? *Psychology of Well-Being*, *4*(1), 1–19. doi:10.118613612-014-0019-2

Singleton, J. (2015). Head, heart and hands model for transformative learning: Place as context for changing sustainability values. *Journal of Sustainability Education*, *9*(3), 171–187.

Sisney, L. (2012). Organizational Physics: The Science of Growing a Business. Academic Press.

Sitra, O., Katsigiannakis, V., Karagiannidis, C., & Mavropoulou, S. (2017). The effect of badges on the engagement of students with special educational needs: A case study. *Education and Information Technologies*, *22*(6), 3037–3046. doi:10.100710639-016-9550-5

Skinner, B. F. (1969). *Contingencies of reinforcement: A theoretical analysis*. Appleton-Century-Crofts.

Skinner, B. F. (1974). *About behaviorism*. Knopf.

Slavova-Petkova, S., Dimova, M., & Luchev, D. (2016). *Learning Scenario for Better Understanding of Fairy Tales Using Role-playing and Serious Games Methods*. Academic Press.

Sliwinski, J., Katsikitis, M., & Jones, C. M. (2015). Mindful gaming: How digital games can improve mindfulness. Lecture Notes in Computer Science, 9298, 167–184. doi:10.1007/978-3-319-22698-9_12

Sloan, D., & College, M. (2015). *Tried and True Teaching Methods to Enhance Students' Service-Learning Experience*. Retrieved from https://www.usf.edu/engagement/documents/s-l-reflection-activities.pdf

Smiderle, R., Rigo, S. J., Marques, L. B., Peçanha de Miranda Coelho, J. A., & Jaques, P. A. (2020). The impact of gamification on students' learning, engagement and behavior based on their personality traits. *Smart Learning Environments*, *7*(3), 3. Advance online publication. doi:10.118640561-019-0098-x

Smironva, E., Kiatkawsin, K., Lee, S. K., Kim, J., & Lee, C.-H. (2020). Self-selection and non-response biases in customers' hotel ratings – a comparison of online and offline ratings. *Current Issues in Tourism*, *23*(10), 1191–1204.

Smith, J. D., & Graham, T. C. N. (2006). Use of eye movements for video game control. *International Conference on Advances in Computer Entertainment Technology 2006*. 10.1145/1178823.1178847

Smith, M., Ballard, J., & Sanders, L. (2021). Most voters say the events at the US Capitol are a threat to democracy. *YouGov Politics & Current Affairs*. https://bit.ly/3pAsALT

Smith, L. J., Gradisar, M., & King, D. L. (2015). Parental Influences on Adolescent Video Game Play: A Study of Accessibility, Rules, Limit Setting, Monitoring, and Cybersafety. *Cyberpsychology, Behavior, and Social Networking, 18*(5), 273–279. doi:10.1089/cyber.2014.0611 PMID:25965861

Snow, S., Bernardi, N. F. N. S.-K., Moran, D., & Lehmann, A. (2018). Exploring the Experience and Effects of Vocal Toning. *Journal of Music Therapy, 55*(3), 381. doi:10.1093/jmt/thy003 PMID:29800304

Soengas, X., Vivar, H., & Abuin, N. (2015). Del consumidor analógico al digital. Nuevas estrategias de publicidad y marketing para una sociedad hiperconectada. *Revista Telos, 101*, 115–124.

Song, S. Y., & Kim, Y. K. (2019). Doing good better: Impure altruism in green apparel advertising. *Sustainability, 11*(20), 5762. doi:10.3390u11205762

Sooksatit, K. (2016). Customer Decisions on Hotel Booking via Mobile Phone and Tablet Applications: A Case Study of Luxury Hotels in Bangkok. In e-Consumers in the Era of New Tourism. Managing the Asian Century. Springer. doi:10.1007/978-981-10-0087-4_6

Soral, W., Bilewicz, M., & Winiewski, M. (2018). Exposure to hate speech increases prejudice through desensitization. *Aggressive Behavior, 44*(2), 136–146. doi:10.1002/ab.21737 PMID:29094365

Sorenson, N., Pasquier, P., & DiPaola, S. (2011). A generic approach to challenge modelling for the procedural creation of video game levels. *IEEE Transactions on Computational Intelligence and AI in Games, 3*(3), 229–244. doi:10.1109/TCIAIG.2011.2161310

Sousa, P., Martinho, R., Reis, C. I., Dias, S. S., Gaspar, P. J., Dixe, M. D. A., Luis, L. S., & Ferreira, R. (2020). Controlled trial of an mHealth intervention to promote healthy behaviours in adolescence (TeenPower): Effectiveness analysis. *Journal of Advanced Nursing, 76*(4), 1057–1068. doi:10.1111/jan.14301 PMID:31880009

Souza, V. S., de Vasconcelos Marques, S. R. B., & Veríssimo, M. (2020). How can gamification contribute to achieve SDGs?: Exploring the opportunities and challenges of ecogamification for tourism. *Journal of Hospitality and Tourism Technology, 11*(2), 255–276. doi:10.1108/JHTT-05-2019-0081

Spanellis, A., & Harviainen, J. T. (Eds.). (2021). *Transforming Society and Organizations through Gamification: From the Sustainable Development Goals to Inclusive Workplaces*. Plagrave Macmillian., doi:10.1007/978-3-030-68207-1

Stanford. (2005). *Critical Theory*. Retrieved from https://plato.stanford.edu/entries/critical-theory/

Starbucks Rewards. (2020). *Starbucks rewards terms of use*. Retrieved October 16, 2021, from https://www.starbucks.com/rewards/terms#about-starbucks-rewards

Starbucks Rewards. (2021). *Cash or card, you earn stars*. Retrieved October 16, 2021, from https://www.starbucks.com/rewards

Starbucks Stories & News. (2021). *Celebrate 50 years of Starbucks with the Starland: 50th anniversary edition game*. Retrieved October 17, 2021, from https://stories.starbucks.com/press/2021/starbucks-starland-50th-anniversary-edition/

Statista. (2019a). *Frequency of visits to Starbucks by those who use the app in the United States as of October 2019*. Retrieved October 17, 2021, from https://www.statista.com/statistics/1083426/starbucks-app-users-visit-frequency/

Statista. (2019b). *Frequency of visits to Starbucks by those who do not use the app in the United States as of October 2019.* Retrieved October 17, 2021, from https://www.statista.com/statistics/1083461/starbucks-non-app-users-visit-frequency/

Steam. (2017). *User Reviews.* https://steamcommunity.com/games/593110/announcements/detail/1448326897426987372

Stenros, J. (2014). Behind Games: Playful Mindsets and Transformative Practices. In The Gameful World: Approaches, Issues, Applications (pp. 201–222). MIT Press.

Stepanovic, S., & Mettler, T. (2018). Gamification applied for health promotion: Does it really foster long-term engagement? A scoping review. In *Proceedings of the 26th European Conference on Information Systems* (pp. 1-16). AIS.

Stevens, K. (2009). Developing a descriptive system for a new preference-based measure of health-related quality of life for children. *Quality of Life Research: An International Journal of Quality of Life Aspects of Treatment, Care and Rehabilitation, 18*(8), 1105–1113. doi:10.100711136-009-9524-9 PMID:19693703

Stewart, J., Bleumers, L., Van Looy, J., Mariën, I., All, A., Schurmans, D., & Misuraca, G. (2013). *The potential of digital games for empowerment and social inclusion of groups at risk of social and economic exclusion: evidence and opportunity for policy.* Joint Research Centre, European Commission.

StonePaperScissors.co.uk. (2019). *Stone Paper Scissors.* Retrieved from https://www.stonepaperscissors.co.uk/

Studer, M., & Fox, O. (2002). The Role of Humanitarian and Development Organisations in Relation to the Security Sector in Transition Situations. In A. H. Ebnöther & P. H. Fluri (Eds.), *After Intervention: Public Security Management in Post-Conflict Societies - From Intervention to Sustainable Local Ownership* (pp. 357–375). National Defense Academy.

Sturm, S. K. (2011). *Deduction, induction and abduction in academic writing.* Retrieved from https://seansturm.wordpress.com/2011/05/23/deduction-induction-and-abduction/

Suh, A., & Wagner, C. (2017). How gamification of an enterprise collaboration system increases knowledge contribution: An affordance approach. *Journal of Knowledge Management, 21*(2), 416–431. doi:10.1108/JKM-10-2016-0429

Sun, R., Lei, W., & Zhang, L. (2007). Analysis of Human Factors Integration Aspects for Aviation Accidents and Incidents. In *Proceedings of 7th Engineering Psychology and Cognitive Ergonomics International Conference (EPCE 2007)* (pp. 834-841). Academic Press.

Surendeleg, G., Murwa, V., Yun, H. K., & Kim, Y. S. (2014). The role of gamification in education - a literature review. *Contemporary Engineering Sciences, 7*(29-32), 1609–1616. doi:10.12988/ces.2014.411217

Susi, T., Johannesson, M., & Backlund, P. (2007). *Serious games: An overview.* Academic Press.

Susi, T., Johannesson, M., & Backlund, P. (2007). *Serious Games—An Overview* (Technical report: HIS-IKI-TR-07-001). University of Skövde. Available at http:// www.his.se/iki/ingame/publications

Sweeney, J. C., & Soutar, G. N. (2001). Consumer perceived value: The development of a multiple item scale. *Journal of Retailing, 77*(2), 203–220. doi:10.1016/S0022-4359(01)00041-0

Syakur, A., Susilo, T. A. B., Wike, W., & Ahmadi, R. (2020). Sustainability of Communication, Organizational Culture, Cooperation, Trust and Leadership Style for Lecturer Commitments in Higher Education. *Budapest International Research and Critics Institute (BIRCI-Journal): Humanities and Social Sciences, 3*(2), 1325–1335. doi:10.33258/birci.v3i2.980

Taggart, F., & Stewart-brown, S. (2015). *A Review of Questionnaires Designed to Measure Mental Wellbeing.* Retrieved July 27, 2021, from - website: https://warwick.ac.uk/fac/sci/med/research/platform/wemwbs/research/validation/frances_taggart_%0Aresearch.pdf%0D

Taherdoost, H. (2018). A review of technology acceptance and adoption models and theories. *Procedia Manufacturing*, *22*, 960–967. doi:10.1016/j.promfg.2018.03.137

Taillandier, P., Grignard, A., Marilleau, N., Philippon, D., Huynh, Q. N., Gaudou, B., & Drogoul, A. (2019). Participatory modeling and simulation with the gama platform. *JASSS, 22*(2). doi:10.18564/jasss.3964

Taiminen, H., & Taiminen, K. (2016). Usage of Facebook-and Anonymous Forum – Based Peer Support Groups Online and Their Influence on Perceived Social Support Types in Weight Loss. *2016 49th Hawaii International Conference on System Sciences (HICSS)*, 3094–3103. doi:10.1109/HICSS.2016.389

Tamayo-Serrano, P., Garbaya, S., & Blazevic, P. (2018). Gamified in-home rehabilitation for stroke survivors: Analytical review. *International Journal of Serious Games*, *5*(1), 1–26. doi:10.17083/ijsg.v5i1.224

Tan, G. W.-H., Ooi, K.-B., Leong, L.-Y., & Lin, B. (2014). Predicting the drivers of behavioral intention to use mobile learning: A hybrid SEM-Neural Networks approach. *Computers in Human Behavior*, *36*, 198–213. doi:10.1016/j.chb.2014.03.052

Tang, J., & Zhang, P. (2019). Exploring the relationships between gamification and motivational needs in technology design. *International Journal of Crowd Science*, *3*(1), 87–103. doi:10.1108/IJCS-09-2018-0025

Tang, S. H., & Hall, V. C. (1995). The overjustification effect: A meta-analysis. *Applied Cognitive Psychology*, *9*(5), 365–404. doi:10.1002/acp.2350090502

Tang, X., Qian, T., & You, Z. (2020). Generating Behavior Features for Cold-Start Spam Review Detection with Adversarial Learning. *Information Sciences*, *526*, 274–288. doi:10.1016/j.ins.2020.03.063

Tanouri, A., Mulcahy, R., & Russell-Bennett, R. (2019). Transformative gamification services for social behavior brand equity: A hierarchical model. *Journal of Service Theory and Practice*, *29*(2), 122–141. doi:10.1108/JSTP-06-2018-0140

Tarute, A., Nikou, S., & Gatautis, R. (2017). Mobile application driven consumer engagement. *Telematics and Informatics*, *34*(4), 145–156. doi:10.1016/j.tele.2017.01.006

Taşkın, N., & Kılıç Çakmak, E. (2017). Öğrenci Merkezli Öğrenme Ortamlarında Oyunlaştırmanın Alternatif Değerlendirme Amaçlı Kullanımı. *Bartın Üniversitesi Eğitim Fakültesi Dergisi*, *6*(3), 1227–1248. doi:10.14686/buefad.333286

Taylor, A., Dixon-Hardy, D. W., & Wright, S. J. (2014). Simulation training in UK general aviation: An undervalued aid to reducing loss of control accidents. *The International Journal of Aviation Psychology*, *24*(2), 141–152. doi:10.1080/10508414.2014.892762

Teixes-Argilés, F. (2016). *Gamificación: motivar jugando*. UOC.

Teixes, F. (2015). *Gamificación. Motivar jugando*. Editorial UOC.

Tenkinbas, K. S., & Zimmerman, E. (2003). *Rules of play*. Massachusetts Institute of Technology. Retrieved from https://mitpress.mit.edu/books/rules-play

Tenório, T., Bittencourt, I. I., Isotani, S., Pedro, A., & Ospina, P. (2016). A gamified peer assessment model for on-line learning environments in a competitive context. *Computers in Human Behavior, 64*, 247–263. doi:10.1016/j.chb.2016.06.049

Tercanli, H., Martina, R., Dias, M. F., Wakkee, I., Reuter, J., Amorim, M., Madaleno, M., Magueta, D., Vieira, E., Veloso, C., Figueiredo, C., Vitória, A., Gomes, I., Meireles, G., Daubariene, A., Daunoriene, A., Mortensen, A. K., Zinovyeva, A., Trigueros, I. R., … Gutiérrez-Pérez, J. (2021). *Educational Escape Room in Practice: Research, experiences and recommendations*. doi:https://doi.org/10.34624/rpxk-hc6

Thakur, R., & Srivastava, M. (2014). Adoption readiness, personal innovativeness, perceived risk and usage intention across customer groups for mobile payment services in India. *Internet Research*, *24*(3), 369–392. doi:10.1108/IntR-12-2012-0244

Thatgamecompany. (2012). *Journey* (PS4 Version) [Video game]. USA.

The Internet Society. (1998). *RFC 2350*. Retrieved from https://www.ietf.org/rfc/rfc2350.txt

The Judge Advocate General's Corps. (2021). *AIB Reports*. Available online: https://www.afjag.af.mil/AIB-Reports/

The Office of the High Commissioner for Human Rights (OHCHR). (n.d.). *Migration*. Retrieved from: https://www.standup4humanrights.org/migration/en/toolbox.html

The Pixel Hunt. (2017). Bury me, My Love (iOS Version) [Video game]. France.

Theng, Y.-L., Lee, J. W. Y., Patinadan, P. V., & Foo, S. S. B. (2015). The Use of Videogames, Gamification, and Virtual Environments in the Self-Management of Diabetes: A Systematic Review of Evidence. *Games for Health Journal*, *4*(5), 352–361. https://doi.org/10.1089/g4h.2014.0114

Thibault, M., & Hamari, J. (2021). Seven points to reappropriate gamification. In A. Spanelli & J. T. Harviainen (Eds.), *Transforming Society and Organizations through Gamification: From the Sustainable Development Goals to Inclusive Workplaces* (pp. 11–28). Palgrave Macmillan. doi:10.1007/978-3-030-68207-1_2

Thiebes, S., Lins, S., & Basten, D. (2014). Gamifying information systems-a synthesis of gamification mechanics and dynamics. In *Proceedings of the 20th European Conference on Information Systems*. AIS.

Thiel, S-K. (2017). Let's play Urban Planner: The use of Game Elements in Public Participation Platforms. *PlaNext - Next Generation Planning*, *4*, 58–75. doi:10.24306/plnxt.2017.04.005

Thiel, S-K., Reisinger, M., Röderer, K., & Fröhlich, P. (2016). Playing (with) Democracy: A Review of Gamified Participation Approaches. *eJournal of eDemocracy and Open Government*, *8*(3), 32-60.

Thiel, S.-K., & Fröhlich, P. (2017). Gamification as Motivation to Engage in Location-Based Public Participation? In G. Gartner & H. Huang (Eds.), *Progress in Location-Based Services 2016*. Springer. doi:10.1007/978-3-319-47289-8_20

Thorndike, E. L. (1918). Individual differences. *Psychological Bulletin*, *15*(5), 148–159. doi:10.1037/h0070314

Thorpe, A. S., & Roper, S. (2019). The ethics of gamification in a marketing context. *Journal of Business Ethics*, *155*(2), 597–609. doi:10.100710551-017-3501-y

Tobon, S., Ruiz-Alba, J. L., & García-Madariaga, J. (2020). Gamification and online consumer decisions: Is the game over? *Decision Support Systems*, *128*.

Tobon, S., Ruiz-Alba, J. L., & García-Madariaga, J. (2020). Gamification and online consumer decisions: Is the game over? *Decision Support Systems*, *128*, 113167. doi:10.1016/j.dss.2019.113167

Toda, A. M., Klock, A. C. T., Oliveira, W., Palomino, P. T., Rodrigues, L., Shi, L., Bittencourt, I., Gasparini, I., Isotani, S., & Cristea, A. I. (2019). Analysing gamification elements in educational environments using an existing Gamification taxonomy. *Smart Learning Environments*, *6*(1), 16. Advance online publication. doi:10.118640561-019-0106-1

Toda, A. M., Valle, P. H., & Isotani, S. (2017). The dark side of gamification: An overview of negative effects of gamification in education. In *Researcher links workshop: higher education for all* (pp. 143–156). Springer.

Toda, A. M., Valle, P. H., & Isotani, S. (2017, March). The dark side of gamification: An overview of negative effects of gamification in education. In *Researcher Links Workshop: Higher Education for all* (pp. 143-156). Springer.

Tolks, D., Sailer, M., Dadaczynski, K., Lampert, C., Huberty, J., Paulus, P., & Horstmann, D. (2019). ONYA—The Wellbeing Game: How to Use Gamification to Promote Wellbeing. *Information, 10*(2), 58. doi:10.3390/info10020058

Tomaselli, V., Cantone, G. G., & Mazzeo, V. (2021). *The polarising effect of Review Bomb.* arXiv:2104.01140.

Tomaselli, V., & Cantone, G. G. (2020). *Evaluating Rank-Coherence of Crowd Rating in Customer Satisfaction.* Social Indicator Research. doi:10.100711205-020-02581-8

Tøndel, I. A., Line, M. B., & Jaatun, M. G. (2014). Information security incident management: Current practice as reported in the literature. *Computers & Security, 45*, 42–57. https://doi.org/10.1016/j.cose.2014.05.003

Tondello, G. F., Orji, R., & Nacke, L. E. (2017). Recommender systems for personalized gamification. In *Adjunct publication of the 25th conference on user modeling, adaptation, and personalization* (pp. 425-430). 10.1145/3099023.3099114

Tondello, G. F., Wehbe, R. R., Diamond, L., Busch, M., Marczewski, A., & Nacke, L. E. (2016). The gamification user types hexad scale. *CHI PLAY '16: Proceedings of the 2016 Annual Symposium on Computer-Human Interaction in Play,* 229-243. 10.1145/2967934.2968082

Toode, K., Routasalo, P., Helminen, M., & Suominen, T. (2015). Hospital nurses' working conditions in relation to motivation and patient safety. *Nursing Management, 21*(10), 31–41. doi:10.7748/nm.21.10.31.e1293 PMID:25727441

Toode, K., Routasalo, R., & Suominen, S. (2011). Work motivation of nurses: A literature review. *International Journal of Nursing Studies, 48*(2), 246–257. doi:10.1016/j.ijnurstu.2010.09.013 PMID:20947085

Tosey, P., Visser, M., & Saunders, M. N. K. (2012). The origins and conceptualizations of "triple-loop" learning: A critical review. *Management Learning, 43*(3), 291–307. https://doi.org/10.1177/1350507611426239

Trang, S., & Weiger, W. H. (2021). The perils of gamification: Does engaging with gamified services increase users' willingness to disclose personal information? *Computers in Human Behaviour, 116.*

Trees, L. (2015). Encouraging millennials to collaborate and learn on the job. *Strategic HR Review, 14*(4), 118–123. doi:10.1108/SHR-06-2015-0042

Triana, D., Anggraito, Y. U., & Ridlo, S. (2020). Effectiveness Environmental Change Learning Tools Based on STEM-PjBL Towards Students' Collaboration and Communications Skills. *Journal of Innovative Science Education, 9*(3), 244–249.

Trilling, B., & Fadel, C. (2009). *21st Century Skills: Learning for Life in Our Times.* Jossey-Bass.

Trucker, H. (2020). Coronavirus bankruptcy tracker: These major companies are failing amid the shutdown. *Fobes.* www.forbes.com/sites/hanktucker/2020/05/03/%0Acoronavirus-bankruptcy-tracker-these-major-companies-are-failing-amid-theshutdown/#%0A5649f95d3425

Tsai, J. C., Cheng, P. H., Liu, S. Y., & Chang, C. Y. (2019). Using board games to teach socioscientific issues on biological conservation and economic development in Taiwan. *Journal of Baltic Science Education, 18*(4), 634–645. doi:10.33225/jbse/19.18.634

Tsay, C. H.-H., Kofinas, A., & Luo, J. (2018). Enhancing student learning experience with technology-mediated gamification: An empirical study. *Computers & Education, 121*, 1–17. doi:10.1016/j.compedu.2018.01.009

Tseng, F.-C. (2011). Segmenting online gamers by motivation. *Expert Systems with Applications, 38*(6), 7693–7697. doi:10.1016/j.eswa.2010.12.142

Tuah, N. M., Ahmedy, F., Gani, A., & Yong, L. N. (2021). A survey on gamification for health rehabilitation care: Applications, opportunities, and open challenges. *Information (Basel), 12*(2), 91. doi:10.3390/info12020091

Tulloch, R. (2014). Reconceptualising gamification: Play and pedagogy. *Digital Culture & Education*, 6(4), 317–333.

Tulloch, R., & Randell-Moon, H. E. K. (2018). The Politics of Gamification: Education, Neoliberalism and the Knowledge Economy. *Review of Education, Pedagogy & Cultural Studies*, 40(3), 204–226. doi:10.1080/10714413.2018.1472484

Tunc, B. E., & Jammermann, M. (2021). Games and Gamification as a tool for Social Change. *Ludogogy Online Magazine*. Retrieved from: https://www.ludogogy.co.uk/article/games-and-gamification-as-a-tool-for-social-change

Turan, Z., Avinc, Z., Kara, K., & Goktas, Y. (2016). Gamification and education: Achievements, cognitive loads, and views of students. *International Journal of Emerging Technologies in Learning*, 11(7), 64-69. doi:10.3991/ijet.v11i07.5455

Tzeng, H. M. (2002). The influence of nurses' working motivation and job satisfaction on intention to quit: An empirical investigation in Taiwan. *International Journal of Nursing Studies*, 39(8), 867–878. doi:10.1016/S0020-7489(02)00027-5 PMID:12379304

UN. (2021). *UN Sustainable development goals*. Retrieved from https://www.un.org/sustainabledevelopment/sustainable-development-goals/

UNESCO. (2005). *Towards the Knowledge Society*. United Nations Educational, Scientific and Cultural Organization. https://bit.ly/3kVa381

UNESCO. (2016). *Marco de avaliação global da alfabetização midiática e informacional: disposição e competências do país*. Brasilia: UNESCO. https://bit.ly/2VqHqHI

United Nations Children's Fund (UNICEF). (2020). *Education Solutions for Migrant and Displaced Children And Their Host Communities*. Working Paper. Retrieved from: https://www.unicef.org/documents/education-solutions-migrant-and-displaced-children-and-their-host-communities

United Nations. (2015). *Transforming our world: the 2030 Agenda for Sustainable Development*. Retrieved April 4, 2019, from Sustainable Development Goals Knowledge Platform website: https://sustainabledevelopment.un.org/post2015/transformingourworld

United Nations. (2019, June 18). *United Nations strategy and plan of action on hate speech*. Available at https://cutt.ly/ObF7sf7

Unity. (n.d.). *Developer Tools*. Retrieved August 7, 2021, from https://unity.com/developer-tools

University of Melbourne. (n.d.). *Social play in immersive gaming environments*. Retrieved July 20, 2021, from https://cis.unimelb.edu.au/hci/projects/social-play/

Upper One Games. (2016). Never Alone (iOS Version) [Video game]. USA.

UrbanWaste. (2016). Available online: www.urban-waste.eu

Uukkivi, A., & Labanova, O. (2018). How we have motivated students in sciences. *4th International Conference on Higher Education Advances (HEAd'18)*, 769–776. doi:https://doi.org/10.4995/HEAd18.2018.8082

UW Human Photonics Lab. (n.d.). *Virtual Reality Pain Reduction*. Retrieved June 10, 2021, from https://depts.washington.edu/hplab/research/virtual-reality/

Vahlo, J., Kaakinen, J. K., Holm, S. K., & Koponen, A. (2017). Digital game dynamics preferences and player types. *Journal of Computer-Mediated Communication*, 22(2), 88–103. doi:10.1111/jcc4.12181

Vaishnavi, V., Kuechler, B., & Petter, S. (2017). *Design Science Research in Information Systems*. http://www.desrist.org/design-research-in-information-systems/

Vajawat, B., Varshney, P., & Banerjee, D. (2020). Digital gaming interventions in psychiatry: Evidence, applications and challenges. *Psychiatry Research*, 113585. PMID:33303223

Valencia-Molina, T., Serna-Collazos, A., Ochoa-Angrino, S., Caicedo-Tamayo, A. M., Montes-González, J. A., & Chávez-Vescance, J. D. (2016). *Competencias y estándares TIC desde la dimensión pedagógica: Una perspectiva desde los niveles de apropiación de las TIC en la práctica educativa docente*. Pontificia Universidad Javeriana – Cali.

van de Rijt, A., Kang, S. M., Restivo, M., & Patil, A. (2014). Field experiments of success-breeds-success dynamics. *Proceedings of the National Academy of Sciences of the United States of America*, *111*(19), 6934–6939. PMID:24778230

van den Brink-Budgen, R. (2011). *Advanced Critical Thinking*. Hachette. Retrieved from https://books.google.no/books?hl=no&lr=&id=KoOeBAAAQBAJ&oi=fnd&pg=PT5&dq=roy+van+den+brink+budgen&ots=23RXDoCOKo&sig=l4x62t3RRzbyfiII4dZ6T8JWQvA&redir_esc=y#v=onepage&q=roy van den brink budgen&f=false

van Gaalen, A. E. J., Brouwer, J., Schönrock-Adema, J., Bouwkamp-Timmer, T., Jaarsma, A. D. C., & Georgiadis, J. R. (2021). Gamification of health professions education: A systematic review. *Advances in Health Sciences Education: Theory and Practice*, *26*(2), 683–711. doi:10.100710459-020-10000-3 PMID:33128662

Van Lippevelde, W., Vangeel, J., De Cock, N., Lachat, C., Goossens, L., Beullens, K., Vervoort, L., Braet, C., Maes, L., Eggermont, S., Deforche, B., & Van Camp, J. (2016). Using a gamified monitoring app to change adolescents' snack intake: The development of the REWARD app and evaluation design. *BMC Public Health*, *16*(1), 1–11. doi:10.118612889-016-3286-4 PMID:27494932

van Reijmersdal, E. A., Rozendaal, E., & Buijzen, M. (2012). Effects of prominence, involvement, and persuasion knowledge on children's cognitive and affective responses to advergames. *Journal of Interactive Marketing*, *26*(1), 33–42. doi:10.1016/j.intmar.2011.04.005

Van Rooij, M., Lobel, A., Harris, O., Smit, N., & Granic, I. (2016). DEEP: A biofeedback virtual reality game for children at-risk for anxiety. In *Conference on Human Factors in Computing Systems – Proceedings*. Association for Computing Machinery. 10.1145/2851581.2892452

Vandercruysse, S., Vandewaetere, M., & Clarebout, G. (2012). Game-based learning: A review on the effectiveness of educational games. *Handbook of Research on Serious Games as Educational, Business and Research Tools*, 628–647. doi:10.4018/978-1-4666-0149-9.ch032

Vansteenkiste, M., Neyrinck, B., Niemiec, C. P., Soenens, B., De Witte, H., & Van den Broeck, A. (2007). On the relations among work value orientations, psychological need satisfaction and job outcomes: A self-determination theory approach. *Journal of Occupational and Organizational Psychology*, *80*(2), 251–277. doi:10.1348/096317906X111024

Vara, M. D., Baños, R. M., Rasal, P., Rodríguez, A., Rey, B., Wrzesien, M., & Alcañiz, M. (2016). A game for emotional regulation in adolescents: The (body) interface device matters. *Computers in Human Behavior*, *57*, 267–273. doi:10.1016/j.chb.2015.12.033

Varol, O., Ferrara, E., Davis, C., Menczer, F., & Flammini, A. (2017). Online Human-Bot Interactions: Detection, Estimation, and Characterization. *Proceedings of the International AAAI Conference on Web and Social Media*, *11*(1), 280-289.

Vasileva, M., Bakeva, V., Vasileva-Stojanovska, T., Malinovski, T., & Trajkovik, V. (2014). Grandma's Games Project: Bridging Tradition and Technology Mediated Education. *TEM Journal*, *3*(1), 13–21.

Vassileva, J. (2012). Motivating participation in social computing applications: A user modeling perspective. *User Modeling and User-Adapted Interaction*, *22*(1-2), 177–201. doi:10.100711257-011-9109-5

Veldkamp, A., Grint, L., Knippels, M.-C., & van Joolingen, W. (2020). Escape Education: A Systematic Review on Escape Rooms in Education. *Educational Research Review, 31*, 1–18. doi:10.1016/j.edurev.2020.100364

Venkatesh, V. (2000). Determinants of Perceived Ease of Use: Integrating Control, Intrinsic Motivation, and Emotion into the Technology Acceptance Model. *Information Systems Research, 11*(4), 342–365. doi:10.1287/isre.11.4.342.11872

Veretehina, S. V. (2015). Automated personnel evaluation system. *Personnel and Intellectual Resources Management in Russia, 4*(5), 72-77.

Villasana, M. V., Pires, I. M., Sá, J., Garcia, N. M., Zdravevski, E., Chorbev, I., Lameski, P., & Flórez-Revuelta, F. (2020). Promotion of healthy nutrition and physical activity lifestyles for teenagers: A systematic literature review of the current methodologies. *Journal of Personalized Medicine, 10*(1), 12. doi:10.3390/jpm10010012 PMID:32121555

Viñas-Diz, S., & Sobrido-Prieto, M. (2016). Virtual reality for therapeutic purposes in stroke: A systematic review. *Neurologia (Barcelona, Spain), 31*(4), 255–277. PMID:26321468

Vinichenko, M. V., Melnichuk, A. V., Kirillov, A. V., Makushkin, S. A., & Melnichuk, Y. A. (2016). Modern views on the gamification of business. *Journal of Internet Banking and Commerce.*

Virovac, D., Domitrovic, A., & Bazijanac, E. E. (2017). The Influence of Human Factor in Aircraft Maintenance. *PROMET – Traffic & Transportation, 29*(3), 257.

Vogler, C. (2002). *El viaje del escritor. Las estructuras míticas para escritores, guionistas, dramaturgos y novelistas.* Ediciones Robinbook.

Volkova, I. I. (2013). Four pillars of gamification. *Middle East Journal of Scientific Research, 13*, 149–152.

Von Ahn, L., & Dabbish, L. (2008). Designing games with a purpose. *Communications of the ACM, 51*(8), 58–67. doi:10.1145/1378704.1378719

Von Der Heiden, J. M., Braun, B., Müller, K. W., & Egloff, B. (2019). The association between video gaming and psychological functioning. *Frontiers in Psychology, 10*, 1731. doi:10.3389/fpsyg.2019.01731 PMID:31402891

Von Krogh, G., Haefliger, S., Spaeth, S., & Wallin, M. W. (2012). Carrots and rainbows: Motivation and social practice in open source software development. *Management Information Systems Quarterly, 36*(2), 649–676. doi:10.2307/41703471

Vygotsky, L. S. (1978). *Mind in Society.* Harvard University Press.

Wagner, E. (2008). Steps to creating a content strategy for your organization. *The ELearning Developers*, 103–117.

Wagner, I., & Minge, M. (2015). The gods play dice together: The influence of social elements of gamification on seniors' user experience. In *International Conference on Human-Computer Interaction* (pp. 334-339). Springer. 10.1007/978-3-319-21380-4_57

Walker, R. (2016). *Survey of technology enhanced learning for higher education in the UK.* Universities and Colleges Information Systems Association.

Wall, D. S. (2017). *Cyberspace Crime.* Routledge. doi:10.4324/9781315199627

Walz, S. P., & Deterding, S. (2014). An Introduction to The Gameful World. In The Gameful World: Approaches, Issues, Applications (pp. 1–13). MIT Press.

Wang, C., Zhang, X., & Hann, I. H. (2018). Socially nudged: A quasi-experimental study of friends' social influence in online product ratings. *Information Systems Research, 29*(3), 641–655.

Wang, R., DeMaria, S. J., Goldberg, A., & Katz, D. (2016). A Systematic Review of Serious Games in Training Health Care Professionals. *Simulation in Healthcare*, *11*(1), 41–51. https://doi.org/10.1097/SIH.0000000000000118

Wang, X., Liu, K., & Zhao, J. (2017). Handling cold-start problem in review spam detection by jointly embedding texts and behaviors. In *Proceedings of the 55th Annual Meeting of the Association for Computational Linguistics* (vol. 1, pp. 366–376). Association for Computational Linguistics.

Wanzel, K. R., Jamieson, C. G., & Bohnen, J. M. (2000). Complications on a general surgery service: Incidence and reporting. *Canadian Journal of Surgery*, *43*(2), 113–117. PMID:10812345

Wardle, C., & Derakhshan, H. (2018). Journalism, fake news & disinformation: handbook for journalism education and training. In C. Ireton & J. Posetti (Eds.), *Journalism, fake news & disinformation: handbook for journalism education and training* (pp. 43–52). UNESCO.

Warlow, C., Sudlow, C., Dennis, M., Wardlaw, J., & Sandercock, P. (2003). Stroke. *Lancet*, *362*(9391), 1211–1224. doi:10.1016/S0140-6736(03)14544-8 PMID:14568745

Warmelink, H. (2014). *Online Gaming and Playful Organization*. Routledge. doi:10.4324/9780203781920

Warmelink, H., Koivisto, J., Mayer, I., Vesa, M., & Hamari, J. (2020). Gamification of production and logistics operations: Status quo and future directions. *Journal of Business Research*, *106*, 331–340. doi:10.1016/j.jbusres.2018.09.011

Warren, S., & Fineman, S. (2007). 'Don't get me wrong, it's fun here, but…' Ambivalence and paradox in a 'fun' work environment. In R. Westwood & C. Rhodes (Eds.), Humour, Work and Organization (pp. 92-112). Routledge.

Watson, D., Clark, L. A., & Tellegen, A. (1988). Development and Validation of Brief Measures of Positive and Negative Affect: The PANAS Scales. *Journal of Personality and Social Psychology*, *54*(6), 1063–1070. doi:10.1037/0022-3514.54.6.1063 PMID:3397865

Wee, S.-C., & Choong, W.-W. (2019). Gamification: Predicting the effectiveness of variety game design elements to intrinsically motivate users' energy conservation behaviour. *Journal of Environmental Management*, *233*, 97–106. https://doi.org/10.1016/j.jenvman.2018.11.127

Welbers, K., Konijn, E. A., Burgers, C., de Vaate, A. B., Eden, A., & Brugman, B. C. (2019). Gamification as a tool for engaging student learning: A field experiment with a gamified app. *E-Learning and Digital Media*, *16*(2), 92–109. doi:10.1177/2042753018818342

Wen, D. M. H., Chang, D. J. W., Lin, Y. T., Liang, C. W., & Yang, S. Y. (2014, June). Gamification design for increasing customer purchase intention in a mobile marketing campaign app. In *International conference on HCI in business* (pp. 440-448). Springer. 10.1007/978-3-319-07293-7_43

Wenger, E. C. (2006). *Communities of Practice: A brief introduction*. Available at: http://www.ewenger.com/theory/index.htm

Werbach, K. (2014). (Re)Defining gamification: A process approach. In A. Spagnolli, L. Chittaro, & L. Gamberini (Eds.), *Persuasive Technology. 9th International Conference, PERSUASIVE 2014, Padua, Italy, May 21-23, 2014. Proceedings.* Springer International Publishers.

Werbach, K., & Hunter, D. (2012). *For the win: How game thinking can revolutionize your business*. Wharton Digital Press.

Werbach, K., & Hunter, D. (2012). *For the win: How game thinking can revolutionize your business*. Wharton Digital Press.

Werbach, K., & Hunter, D. (2012). *For the Win: How Game Thinking Can Revolutionize Your Business*. Wharton Digital Press.

Werbach, K., & Hunter, D. (2015). *The gamification toolkit: dynamics, mechanics, and components for the win.* Wharton School Press.

Werbach, K., & Hunter, D. (2015). *The gamification toolkit: Dynamics, mechanics, and components for the win.* Wharton School Press.

Weston, A. (1987). *A Rulebook for Arguments. Teaching Philosophy* (Vol. 10). doi:10.5840/teachphil198710235

Westrum, R. & Adamski, A. J. (2017). Organizational factors associated with safety and mission success in aviation environments. *Human Error in Aviation*, 475–512.

Whang, L. S.-M., & Chang, G. (2004). Lifestyles of virtual world residents: Living in the on-line game "Lineage". *Cyberpsychology & Behavior, 7*(5), 592–600. doi:10.1089/cpb.2004.7.592 PMID:15667054

What is a stroke. (2021). *Stroke Foundation.* Retrieved 4/8/2021 from https://strokefoundation.org.au/About-Stroke/Learn/Types-of-stroke

Whitman, M. E., & Mattord, H. J. (2004). Designing and teaching information security curriculum. *2004 Information Security Curriculum Development Conference, InfoSecCD 2004*, 1–7. doi:10.1145/1059524.1059526

Whitman, M. E., & Mattord, H. J. (2018). *Management of Information Security.* Cengage. Retrieved from https://www.adlibris.com/no/bok/management-of-information-security-9781337405713?gclid=CjwKCAjwo4mIBhBsEiwAKgzXONCA2b5KlFWEPgb7kC7L6GGT8O-nUzmz0Y3Mx4YJ0IinwIxJrGs6WRoCE5QQAvD_BwE

Whittaker, L., Mulcahy, R., & Russell-Bennett, R. (2021). 'Go with the flow' for gamification and sustainability marketing. *International Journal of Information Management, 61*, 102305. doi:10.1016/j.ijinfomgt.2020.102305

Whitton, N. (2011). Game Engagement Theory and Adult Learning. *Simulation & Gaming, 42*(5), 596–609. doi:10.1177/1046878110378587

Whitton, N., & Langan, M. (2019). Fun and games in higher education: An analysis of UK student perspectives. *Teaching in Higher Education, 24*(8), 1000–1013. https://doi.org/10.1080/13562517.2018.1541885

Wiegmann, D. A., & Shappell, S. A. (2003). *A Human Error Approach to Aviation Accident Analysis: The Human Factors Analysis and Classification System.* Routledge. doi:10.4324/9781315263878

Wigdor, D., & Wixon, D. (2011). Brave NUI World: Designing Natural User Interfaces for Touch and Gesture. In *Brave NUI World.* Morgan Kaufmann Publishers Inc. doi:10.1016/C2009-0-64091-5

Williams, A. (2006). Tourism and hospitality marketing: Fantasy, feeling and fun. *International Journal of Contemporary Hospitality Management, 18*(6), 482–495. doi:10.1108/09596110610681520

Wilson, S. (1993). *The Aesthetics and Practice of Designing Interactive Computer Events.* online.sfsu.edu/~swilson/papers/interactive2.html

Wolf, T., Weiger, W. H., & Hammerschmidt, M. (2020). Experiences that matter? The motivational experiences and business outcomes of gamified services. *Journal of Business Research, 106*, 353–364. doi:10.1016/j.jbusres.2018.12.058

Womack, J. P., Jones, D. T., & Roos, D. (1990). *The Machine That Changed the World.* Simon & Schuster.

Wood, D., & Tong, S. (2009). The future of initial police training: A university perspective. *International Journal of Police Science and Management, 11*(3), 294-305.

Woodward, B., Imboden, T., & Martin, N. L. (2013). An undergraduate information security program: More than a curriculum. *Journal of Information Systems Education, 24*(1), 63–70.

World Economic Outlook Update, July 2021: Fault Lines Widen in the Global Recovery. (2021, July). *IMF*. https://www.imf.org/en/Publications/WEO/Issues/2021/07/27/world-economic-outlook-update-july-2021

World Health Organisation. (2018). *Mental health: Strengthening our response*. Retrieved June 29, 2021, from https://www.who.int/news-room/fact-sheets/detail/mental-health-strengthening-our-response

World Health Organisation. (2019). *Mental Disorders*. Retrieved June 29, 2021, from https://www.who.int/news-room/fact-sheets/detail/mental-disorders

World Health Organisation. (2020). *Depression*. Retrieved June 29, 2021, from https://www.who.int/news-room/fact-sheets/detail/depression

World Health Organisation. (n.d.). *Mental Health*. Retrieved June 29, 2021, from https://www.who.int/health-topics/mental-health#tab=tab_2

World Health Organization. (2017). *Depression and Other Common Mental Disorders Global Health Estimates*. WHO.

World Health Organization. (2020). *State of the world's nursing 2020: Investing in education, jobs and leadership*. https://www.who.int/publications-detail/nursing-report-2020

Wouters, P., Paas, F., & van Merriënboer, J. J. (2008). How to optimize learning from animated models: A review of guidelines base on cognitive load. *Review of Educational Research*, 78(3), 645–675. doi:10.3102/0034654308320320

Wouters, P., van Nimwegen, C., van Oostendorp, H., & van der Spek, E. D. (2013). A meta-analysis of the cognitive and motivational effects of serious games. *Journal of Educational Psychology*, 105(2), 249–265. doi:10.1037/a0031311

Wróblewski, M., Klingemann, J. I., & Wieczorek, Ł. (2020). Review and analysis of the functionality of mobile applications in the field of alcohol consumption. *Alcohol Drug Addict*, 33(1), 1–18. doi:10.5114/ain.2020.95977

Wrona, K. (2012). Gamification and games, their potential for application in marketing strategies. *Transactions of the Institute of Aviation*, 227(6), 93–105. doi:10.5604/05096669.1076720

WTM. (2011). *World travel market global trends report 2011*. Retrieved September 20, 2021, from http://www.toposophy.com/files/1/files/onsite_global_trends_v3_lo.pdf

Wu, M. (2011). *The gamification backlash + two long term business strategies*. community.lithium.com/t5/Science-of-Social-Blog/The-Gamification-Backlash-Two-Long-Term-Business-Strategies/ba-p/30891

Wünderlich, N. V., Gustafsson, A., Hamari, J., Parvinen, P., & Haff, A. (2020). The great game of business: Advancing knowledge on gamification in business contexts. *Journal of Business Research*, 106, 273–276. doi:10.1016/j.jbusres.2019.10.062

Xiao, L., & Mou, J. (2019). Social media fatigue-Technological antecedents and the moderating roles of personality traits: The case of WeChat. *Computers in Human Behavior*, 101, 297–310. doi:10.1016/j.chb.2019.08.001

Xin, O. W., Zuo, L., Iida, H., & Aziz, N. (2018). Gamification effect of loyalty program and its assessment using game refinement measure: Case study on Starbucks. In Computational science and technology (pp. 161-171). Springer Nature Singapore Pte Ltd.

Xi, N., & Hamari, J. (2019). Does gamification satisfy needs? A study on the relationship between gamification features and intrinsic need satisfaction. *International Journal of Information Management*, 46, 210–221. doi:10.1016/j.ijinfomgt.2018.12.002

Xi, N., & Hamari, J. (2019, January). The relationship between gamification, brand engagement and brand equity. *Proceedings of the 52nd Hawaii International Conference on System Sciences*. 10.24251/HICSS.2019.099

Xi, N., & Hamari, J. (2020). Does gamification affect brand engagement and equity? A study in online brand communities. *Journal of Business Research*, *109*, 449–460. doi:10.1016/j.jbusres.2019.11.058

Xu, F., Buhalis, D., & Weber, J. (2017). Serious games and the gamification of tourism. *Tourism Management, 60*, 244–256. doi:10.1016/j.tourman.2016.11.020

Xu, F., Webber, J., & Buhalis, D. (2014). The gamification of tourism. In Z. Xiang & I. Tussyadiah (Eds.), *Information and communication technologies in tourism 2014. Proceedings of the International Conference in Dublin, Ireland, (January 21-24 2014)* (pp. 525–537). Springer.

Xu, F., Weber, J., & Buhalis, D. (2013). Gamification in tourism. In Information and communication technologies in tourism, (pp. 525-537). doi:10.1007/978-3-319-03973-2_38

Xu, F., Tian, F., Buhalis, D., Weber, J., & Zhang, H. (2016). Tourists as mobile gamers: Gamification for tourism marketing. *Journal of Travel & Tourism Marketing*, *33*(8), 1124–1142. doi:10.1080/10548408.2015.1093999

Xu, F., Weber, J., & Buhalis, D. (2014). Gamification in tourism. In Z. Xiang & I. Tussyadiah (Eds.), *Information and communication technologies in tourism 2014* (pp. 525–537). Springer.

Xu, Y., Poole, E. S., Miller, A. D., Eiriksdottir, E., Kestranek, D., Catrambone, R., & Mynatt, E. D. (2012). This is not a one-horse race: Understanding player types in multiplayer pervasive health games for youth. In *Proceedings of the ACM 2012 conference on computer supported cooperative work* (pp. 843-852). ACM.

Yahoo. Finance. (2020). *Metacritic changes its user review policy to combat score bombing*. https://au.finance.yahoo.com/news/metacritic-score-bombing-game-review-changes-150200740.html

Yale. (2019). *Intendent learning outcomes*. Retrieved from https://poorvucenter.yale.edu/IntendedLearningOutcomes

Yamin, M. M., Katt, B., & Nowostawski, M. (2021). Serious games as a tool to model attack and defense scenarios for cyber-security exercises. *Computers and Security, 110*. doi:10.1016/j.cose.2021.102450

Yang, H., & Li, D. (2021). Understanding the dark side of gamification health management: A stress perspective. *Information Processing & Management*, *58*(5), 102649. doi:10.1016/j.ipm.2021.102649

Yang, Y., Asaad, Y., & Dwivedi, Y. (2017). Examining the impact of gamification on intention of engagement and brand attitude in the marketing context. *Computers in Human Behavior*, *73*, 459–469. doi:10.1016/j.chb.2017.03.066

Yang, Y., & Koenigstorfer, J. (2020). Determinants of physical activity maintenance during the Covid-19 pandemic: A focus on fitness apps. *Translational Behavioral Medicine*, *10*(4), 835–842. doi:10.1093/tbm/ibaa086 PMID:32926160

Yee, N. (2006). Motivations for play in online games. *Cyberpsychology & Behavior*, *9*(6), 772–775. doi:10.1089/cpb.2006.9.772 PMID:17201605

Yee, N., Ducheneaut, N., & Nelson, L. (2012). Online gaming motivations scale: Development and validation. *CHI '12: Proceedings of the SIGCHI Conference on Human Factors in Computing Systems*, 2803-2806. 10.1145/2207676.2208681

Yen, B. T. H., Mulley, C., & Burke, M. (2019). Gamification in transport interventions: Another way to improve travel behavioural change. *Cities (London, England)*, *85*, 140–149. doi:10.1016/j.cities.2018.09.002

Yi, L., Zhou, Q., Xiao, T., Qing, G., & Mayer, I. (2020). Conscientiousness in Game-Based Learning. *Simulation & Gaming*, *51*(5), 712–734. https://doi.org/10.1177/1046878120927061

Yıldırım, İ., & Şen, S. (2019). The effects of gamification on students' academic achievement: A meta-analysis study. *Interactive Learning Environments*.

Yılmaz, H., & Coşkun, İ. O. (2016). New toy of marketing communication in tourism: Gamification. In e-Consumers in the Era of New Tourism (pp. 53-71). Springer.

Yi, M. Y., & Hwang, Y. (2003). Predicting the use of web-based information systems: Self-efficacy, enjoyment, learning goal orientation, and the technology acceptance model. *International Journal of Human-Computer Studies*, *59*(4), 431–449. doi:10.1016/S1071-5819(03)00114-9

Yoo, C., Kwon, S., & Chang, B. (2017). Factors Affecting the Adoption of Gamified Smart Tourism Applications: An Integrative Approach. *Sustainability, 9*(12), 2162. doi:10.3390/su9122162

Yoon, C. (2018). Extending the TAM for Green IT: A normative perspective. *Computers in Human Behavior, 83*, 129–139. doi:10.1016/j.chb.2018.01.032

Yuksel, P., Robin, B. B. R., & McNeil, S. (2010). Educational Uses of Digital Storytelling Around the World. *Elements, 1*, 1264–1271.

Zagal, J. P., Mateas, M., Fernández-Vara, C., Hochhalter, B., & Lichti, N. (2007). Towards an ontological language for game analysis. *Worlds in play: International perspectives on digital games research, 21*, 21.

Zain, N. H. M., Othman, Z., Noh, N. M., Teo, N. H. I., Zulkipli, N. H. B. N., & Yasin, A. M. (2020). GAMEBC model: Gamification in health awareness campaigns to drive behaviour change in defeating COVID-19 pandemic. *International Journal of Advanced Trends in Computer Science and Engineering, 9*(4).

Zainuddin, Z., Chu, S. K. W., Shujahat, M., & Perera, C. J. (2020). The impact of gamification on learning and instruction: A systematic review of empirical evidence. *Educational Research Review, 30*(100326), 1–23. doi:10.1016/j.edurev.2020.100326

Zaoui, I., Elmaghraoui, H., Benhlima, E., & Chiadmi, D. (2014). Towards a Personalized E-Government Platform. *International Journal of Computer Science: Theory and Application, 2*(2), 35–40.

Zatwarnicka-Madura, B. (2015). Gamification as a tool for influencing customers' behaviour. *International Journal of Economics and Management Engineering, 9*(5), 1461–1464.

Zeithaml, V. A. (1988). Consumer perceptions of price, quality, and value: A means-end model and synthesis of evidence. *Journal of Marketing, 52*(3), 2–22. doi:10.1177/002224298805200302

Zeithaml, V. A., Bitner, M. J., & Gremler, D. D. (2018). *Services marketing: Integrating customer focus across the firm.* Mc-Graw Hill Education.

Zeng, J., & Shang, J. (2018). A review of empirical studies on educational games: 2013–2017. *Proceedings of the 26th International Conference on Computers in Education*, 533-42.

Zhan, C., Li, B., Zhong, X., Min, H., & Wu, Z. (2020). A model for collective behaviour propagation: A case study of video game industry. *Neural Computing & Applications, 32*(9), 4507–4517. doi:10.100700521-018-3686-8

Zhang, C. (2020). Governing (through) trustworthiness: Technologies of power and subjectification in China's social credit system. *Critical Asian Studies, 52*(4), 565–588. doi:10.1080/14672715.2020.1822194

Zhang, C., Phang, C. W., Wu, Q., & Luo, X. (2017). Nonlinear effects of social connections and interactions on individual goal attainment and spending: Evidences from online gaming markets. *Journal of Marketing, 81*(6), 132–155. doi:10.1509/jm.16.0038

Zhang, P. (2008). Technical opinion Motivational affordances: Reasons for ICT design and use. *Communications of the ACM, 51*(11), 145–147. doi:10.1145/1400214.1400244

Zhou, T., Lu, Y., & Wang, B. (2010). Integrating TTF and UTAUT to explain mobile banking user adoption. *Computers in Human Behavior, 26*(4), 760–767. doi:10.1016/j.chb.2010.01.013

Zhou, X., & Zafarani, R. (2020). A Survey of Fake News: Fundamental Theories, Detection Methods, and Opportunities. *ACM Computing Surveys, 53*(5), 1–40. doi:10.1145/3395046

Zicherman, G., & Linder, J. (2010). *Game based marketing*. John Wiley & Sons.

Zichermann, G. (2011). *Intrinsic and extrinsic motivation in gamification*. Gamification Co. www.gamification.co/2011/10/27/intrinsic-and-extrinsic-motivation-in-gamification

Zichermann, G. (2011, January). *A long engagement and a shotgun wedding: Why engagement is the power metric of the decade*. Paper presented at The Gamification Summit, San Francisco, CA.

Zichermann, G., & Linder, J. (2013). *Gamification revolution*. Academic Press.

Zichermann, G., & Cunningham, C. (2011). *Gamification by design implementing game mechanics in web and mobile apps*. O'Reilly Media, Inc.

Zichermann, G., & Cunningham, C. (2011). *Gamification by Design. Implementing Game Mechanics in Web and Mobile Apps*. O'Reilly Media.

Zichermann, G., & Cunningham, C. (2011). *Gamification by Design: Implementing Game Mechanics in Web and Mobile Apps*. O'Reilly Media, Inc.

Zichermann, G., & Cunningham, C. (2011). *Gamification by design: Implementing game mechanics in web and mobile apps*. O'Reilly Media.

Zichermann, G., & Linder, J. (2010). *Game-based marketing. Inspire customer loyalty through rewards, challenges and contests*. John Wiley & Sons.

Zichermann, G., & Linder, J. (2010). *Game-based marketing: Inspire customer loyalty through rewards, challenges, and contests*. Wiley.

Zlatkov, L., Paneva-Marinova, D., Luchev, D., Pavlova, L., & Pavlov, R. (2019). Aquae Calidae - Towards a Serious Game Attracting Students to Ancient Civilizations. *Proceedings of the 2019 2nd International Conference on Education Technology Management*, 14–18. 10.1145/3375900.3375919

About the Contributors

Oscar Bernardes holds a Ph.D. in management, since 2013. He worked as management consultant for several years, in several organizations (social, profitable, and governmental). He is Invited Professor at Polytechnic Institute of Porto (P.Porto), Portugal, where he has been lecturing courses in the following areas: entrepreneurship, innovation, marketing and general management. His research interests include entrepreneurship, gamification, innovation, and marketing.

Vanessa Amorim is a Business and Economics Ph.D. student at the University of Aveiro - Portugal. She has a master's in Organizational Management - Specialization: Business Management and a Post-Graduation in Management Tools for Business Competitiveness from Institute Polytechnic of Porto - Portugal. She works in a multinational company and her main research interests are Gamification and Technologies, Marketing, and Business Management.

António Carrizo Moreira obtained a Bachelor's degree in Electrical Engineering and a Master's degree in Management, both from the University of Porto, Portugal. He received his Ph.D. in Management from the University of Manchester, England. He has a solid international background in industry leveraged working for a multinational company in Germany as well as in Portugal. He has also been involved in consultancy projects and research activities. He is an Associate Professor at the Department of Economics, Management, Industrial Engineering, and Tourism, University of Aveiro, Portugal, where he headed the Bachelor and Master Degrees in Management for five years. He is member of GOVCOPP research unit.

* * *

Anne Adams is a Professor of Engaged Practice and Research. From an initial acting career in theatre and film, she spent several years in Market Research. Her reputation as a researcher was then saved by a degree in Psychology with IT. It was here that she realised computers can do quite useful things, as long as they are designed for mere mortals to use them and people are supported in developing their use of these technologies. She continued with this notion by studying for an MSc in HCI (Human Computer Interaction) at the UCL interaction center [formerly known as the ergonomics group]. She furthered her knowledge with a PhD at UCL, CS & Psychology department, looking at security, privacy, and multimedia communication. After research fellow posts and consultancy work at Middlesex University & UCLmy quest to make computers work and support people's development through "elearning" took her into an academic position at Nottingham University. She now continues her "elearning" and professional development research in IET at the Open University.

Lidia Aguiar Castillo (BSc. 2014, Hon. MSc. 2016, Hon. PhD. 2020) is now a postdoctoral fellow at the Institute for Technological Development and Innovation in Communications at the University of Las Palmas de Gran Canaria, Spain. Currently, she is doing a secondment for two years at the CVUT in Prague (Catalina Ruiz grant). Her research interests include gamification, technology-enhanced learning, and sustainability education.

Sergio Albaladejo-Ortega is an assistant professor in the Department of Audiovisual Communication at the Universidad Católica de Murcia (Spain). PhD in Communication Management, his main research fields are transmedia narratives and, more specifically, transmedia literacy, topics on which he has publications, communications, and invited papers at international conferences. He belongs to the Asociación Española de Investigación de la Comunicación (AE-IC) and is a member of the research group Digital Audiovisual Communication (DIGITALAC).

Umit Basaran is an assistant professor of Marketing at Zonguldak Bulent Ecevit University. She received her PhD degree from Zonguldak Bulent Ecevit University, Marketing in 2014. She received her MSc degree from Zonguldak Bulent Ecevit University, Finance in 2008. She received her undergraduate degree from Marmara University, Business Administration, in 2006. She started her academic life as a research assistant in 2008 and was appointed as an assistant professor in 2015 at the same university. Her fields of study consist of consumer behavior, marketing strategy, and service marketing.

Henrique Bessa is a PhD student at the Centre for Mechanical Technology and Automation (TEMA) / Department of Mechanical Engineering of the University of Aveiro.

David Blacker trained as a neurologist in Perth before undertaking further training and a stroke fellowship at the Mayo Clinic, USA. He returned to Australia and commenced full-time hospital practice at Sir Charles Gairdner Hospital (SCGH) in 2003, establishing the acute stroke team and building one of the busiest interventional stroke services in Australia. He has been continuously active in stroke clinical trials, including acute intervention, secondary prevention, and rehabilitation. He received a Stroke Foundation of Australia Award for Excellence in Stroke Care Delivery in 2018. He has also worked with the experimental stroke group at the Perron Institute (where he has been the Medical Director since 2015), assisting with the development of neuroprotective agents for stroke. He is a Clinical Professor at the University of Western Australia and has a private neurology practice at the Hollywood Medical Centre. In 2020, he revealed publicly that he had Parkinson's Disease, and he has written and spoken about his experience. He has developed an exercise program for PD utilising non-contact boxing and is about to commence the first of several clinical trials in collaboration with a team including a professional boxing trainer and exercise physiologists.

Giulio Giacomo Cantone is a PhD student in Complex Systems for Physical, Socio-economic, and Life Sciences at the University of Catania. Cantone's interests include quantitative methods and statistical theory for the study of information systems for evaluative research. He is focusing on methods to infer the impact of online misinformation on online reviews and on information dynamics in complex networks. In Cantone's research, gamification, the theory of signaling, and game theory are among the theoretical tools to understand information dynamics.

Daniel Cermak-Sassenrath is an Associate Professor at the ITU, Copenhagen, and a member of the Center for Computer Games Research. Daniel is interested in artistic, analytic, explorative, critical, and subversive approaches to and practices of play.

Ruth S. Contreras-Espinosa is a professor at the University of Vic-Central University of Catalonia. Founder of the Observatory of Communication, Video Games, and Entertainment. UAB-UVIC.

Ifeoluwapo Fashoro is a lecturer at Nelson Mandela University, South Africa, where she attained her PhD. She has a Master's degree in Management Information Systems and a Bachelor's degree in Computing from the University of Surrey, UK and the University of Portsmouth, UK, respectively. Her research focus is in the area of Information Systems with an interest in social media, smart cities, and health informatics.

Ricardo Ferreira de Mascarenhas is the CEO of RM Consulting.

Marta Ferreira Dias has a PhD in Economics from the University of Warwick, UK, a MSc in Economics from the University of Coimbra and a degree in Economics from the University of Coimbra. She is an Assistant Professor at the University of Aveiro, in the Department of Economics, Management, Industrial Engineering, and Tourism. She lectures under graduated and graduated courses in Microeconomics, European Economics, Microeconomic Analysis, International Economics, and others, Energy Economics, and Energy Policy and Regulation. Presently, she is a member of the research unit on Competitiveness, Governance and Public Policies (GOVCOPP). She coordinates and she is a member of research teams at the University of Aveiro participating in several European sponsored projects in the fields of Social Economy and Competences for graduates.

Sean Fitzpatrick is a PhD candidate and researcher at Griffith University, Brisbane, Australia. Sean completed his Bachelor of Games Design with Honours in 2017, and currently lectures in game design and Honours research at the Griffith Film School. Sean's research interests include ethics and morality within interactive media; the impact of games on contemporary society; serious games; and diversity, fairness, and inclusion within game development. His upcoming dissertation, titled Restricted by Design: The Existential Consequences of Syntactic Restriction, explores the emerging and concerning ethical implications of interactive media from the perspective of existentialist philosophy.

Jean Frances is a French sociologist. He is currently a full professor at ENSTA-Bretagne.

Anoop George is a research scholar at the Cochin University of Science and Technology, School of Management Studies, in Cochin, India. He received his MBA Marketing degree from Amrita Business School, India. His formal education includes a Bachelor of Business Administration specializing in Jewelry Design and Management. He has work experience with reputable retail corporations such as Tata Group, Shoppers Stop, etc., and has academic experience. His field of research includes gamification, loyalty, marketing, and game mechanics in modern business management.

Jose Luis Gomez is a lecturer at the Polytechnic University of Catalonia.

Maxim Goynov is a member of the Mathematical Linguistics Department at the Institute of Mathematics and Informatics at the Bulgarian Academy of Sciences. Participant in many projects and activities, bringing innovations and technologies that help the presentation, preservation, and popularisation of cultural and historical heritage assets and artefacts.

Elina Haavisto is a registered nurse with a specialty in psychiatric nursing. She has a Master's degree in nursing science (healthcare administration), a teaching degree in nursing, and a PhD in health sciences. She has been a docent since 2002 at the University of Turku, Finland, and since 2019 at Tallinn Health Care College, Estonia. In August 2021, she was appointed Professor (Nursing Science) at Tampere University, Faculty of Social Sciences. Prior to that, from 2015–2021, she worked as a Professor (Nursing Science) at the University of Turku, Department of Nursing Science. For twelve years, she held the position of director at the Helsinki Metropolia University of Applied Sciences (the biggest University of Applied Sciences in Finland), in the faculty of healthcare and nursing. During these years, she has been a member of many official national committees on higher education. Since 2005, she has been a member of the Advisory Board of the Tallinn Health College in Estonia. Over her 30-year career, her research has concentrated on two fields. Seriously ill patients and their families consist of two research projects: 1) Evidence-based Palliative Care (including end-of-life care, EOL) and 2) Family Members of Cancer Patients in the Acute Care Phase. Healthcare education consists of two projects: 1) Learning Clinical Reasoning (CR) and 2) Reforming Student Selection in Nursing Education (ReSSNE). The projects employ three post-doc researchers, PhD students, and masters students.

Robert Herne completed his Bachelor of Computer Science (BSc) with First Class Honours at Murdoch University, Western Australia. He first began research into the benefits of utilising games and virtual reality in stroke rehabilitation in 2015. He is currently completing his Computer Science PhD on the optimisation of engagement in upper limb rehabilitation using VR. He co-coordinated a weekly stroke survivor support group at the Perron Institute at Sir Charles Gairdner Hospital from January 2016 until March 2020, when the group was put on indefinite hold due to the coronavirus pandemic.

Nashwa Ismail has an MSc and a PhD in Education from Southampton Education School, UK, and she is a Fellow of the Higher Education Academy (FHEA). Dr. Ismail is a lecturer in the School of Education at Durham University. In research, Dr. Ismail's area of expertise is Technology-Enhanced Learning (TEL). In this area, she takes part in different research projects in the UK and overseas countries such as Kenya, Nigeria, Indonesia, Malaysia, the Middle East (Egypt, Saudi Arabia), Myanmar, and Thailand. Furthermore, she teaches qualitative research methods and their application on Qualitative Data Analysis Software (QDAS) using NVivo and ATLAS.ti. She has a special focus on Games-Based Learning (GBL), Academic Professional Development (APD) and educational leadership. Her current role is as a Research Associate in the LEARN Cit Sci project, Institute for Educational Technology at the Open University. Dr. Ismail's role is to engage with youth online and evaluate online citizen science learning activities using mainly qualitative approaches (e.g., interviews). Besides, Dr. Ismail has a technical background as a Microsoft Certified Trainer (MCT), Microsoft Certified Educator (MCE) and a qualified Training Assessor Assessment and Quality Assurance (TAQA), since 2005. She has delivered a wide range of programs to technical audiences in an industry setting in the Gulf, the Middle East and the UK.

Marvin Jammermann received a bachelor's degree in Political Science from the University of Hamburg in 2018 and a master's degree from the Erasmus Munuds Joint Master Degree in the European Master of Migration and Intercultural Relations (EMMIR) program in 2021. He is specialised in the area of Labour Migration & Human Development and conducts research on citizenship regimes and the mechanisms of exploitation affecting migrant workers in the EU. Previously, he worked as a project coordinator on a refugee project in Hamburg from 2016-2018 and at the Eswatini National Commission for UNESCO in 2019. He is currently a project assistant at an international organisation working on a project to protect migrant workers in supply-chain contexts in Europe.

Jose M. Jimenez has a PhD in Communication Sciences. Professor at the Faculty of Languages and Education and at Professional Training of Escolapios Betania. Member of the research group "Teaching innovation in gamificated techniques, Playing Based Learning and storytelling fiction" (Rey Juan Carlos University). His research lines are focused on gamification, social networks, games, learning methodologies, and professional skills development.

Manu Melwin Joy is an assistant professor at the Cochin University of Science and Technology, School of Management Studies, in Cochin, India. He has a PhD degree and six Master's degrees from various verticals such as business administration, psychology, psychotherapy and counseling, and sociology, to name a few. He has worked at various reputed organizations as a corporate trainer. From the perspectives of gamification, consumer behavior, and customer loyalty, he has authored several seminal empirical, theoretical, and meta-analytical scholarly articles on several topics.

Antti Kaipia, M.D., Ph.D., is the chief physician in the department of urology at Tampere University Hospital, Finland. His former positions were as the head of the department of surgery in Satakunta central hospital in Pori and professor of surgery at the University of Turku. Dr. Kaipia started his research career and completed his Ph.D. in the field of andrology, after which he did a post-doctoral fellowship at Stanford University in the department of OB/GYN under the supervision of Prof. AJW Hsueh. After specialization in general surgery and urology, Dr. Kaipia's research interests have focused on the diagnostics and treatment of urological cancers as well as quality measurement in surgery.

Ebru Kılıç-Çakmak is a Professor in the Department of Computer Education and Instructional Technology, Gazi Faculty of Education, Gazi University. She undertook graduate studies at Ankara University, Turkey (MSc. Educational Technology) and at Ankara University, Turkey (Ph.D. Educational Technology). She has been the head of the Department of Computer Education and Instructional Technology at Gazi Education Faculty since September 2018. Her research interests include e-learning, designing online learning environments, instructional design for e-learning, technology integration into education, project management, and scale development. She has taught undergraduate and graduate courses in face-to-face and distance education. She has improved the course content for distance education. She attended many seminars, gave in-service training, and served as a member of the scientific committees at national and international meetings. Prof. Kılıç Çakmak has published many articles in international and national refereed journals, international book chapters, national books, national book chapters. There are a total of 68 citations from the indexed journals in the Web of Science database. She has more than 2000 citations for her articles, books, and book chapters published in national refereed journals. She has also worked as a researcher and consultant on several national and international projects. She has also been working as an instructor, researcher, consultant, and executor on EU projects and national (TUBITAK and BAP) projects.

Jaana-Maija Koivisto is a principal research scientist at the HAMK Smart research unit. She is a team leader in the research area of Digital Solutions in Pedagogy. She did her PhD at the University of Helsinki, Faculty of Educational Sciences. Dr. Koivisto is also a postdoctoral researcher at Tampere University. Her special expertise is in the development of pedagogical innovations, especially in relation to serious games, virtual reality, and gamification. Her strength is in the evidence-based development of new digital learning methods and digital services, the implementation of experiments by using design-based research methods, and educational product development in multidisciplinary research teams. She has very strong pedagogical competence. Previously, she worked as a postdoctoral researcher at the University of Turku, Tampere University of Technology, and Satakunta Hospital District. In addition, she has been working as a senior lecturer at Metropolia University of Applied Sciences and Diaconia University of Applied Sciences. She has a history of working as a registered nurse in Finland.

Stewart Kowalski has over 35 years of industry and academic experience in information security and has worked for a number of large international companies, including Ericsson, Telia Research, Huawei, Digital, and HP. He is currently Professor of Information Security at the Department of Information Security and Communication Technology, Norwegian University of Science and Technology, Norway. He is currently on a sabbatical from NTNU and is a visiting researcher at the Research Institutes of Sweden, Cyber Security unit, and a visiting professor at the University of Skövde School of Informatics, working with the Privacy Information and Cyber-Security platform (PICS).

Stéphane Le Lay is a French sociologist. He's currently a senior researcher, and he deals with studies regarding work precariousness and mental health.

Ioanna K. Lekea holds a BA (Hons) in Classics from the University of Athens, a MSc (with distinction) in History and Philosophy of Science and Technology, and a PhD (with distinction) in Military Ethics, awarded jointly by the University of Athens and the National Technical University of Athens. She currently works as an Assistant Professor at the Hellenic Air Force Academy and teaches Military Ethics and Just War Theory. She is also the Director of the War Games Lab of the Hellenic Air Force Academy, focusing on the development of simulation games and their application to teaching scientific areas such as military ethics, ethical leadership, aviation safety and security, crisis management, and the prediction and prevention of terrorism activities using computer-aided techniques.

Detelin Luchev is an Associate Professor in the Institute of Mathematics and Informatics at the Bulgarian Academy of Sciences, Sofia, Bulgaria.

Samanta Mariotti received her MSc in Byzantine Archaeology from the University of Siena in 2010. In 2016, she obtained a post-graduation degree at the University of Trieste. Over the years, she participated in many excavation campaigns in Italy and Greece as a supervisor and GIS expert, and she started dealing with public archaeology and communication. She's currently a research fellow at the Department of History and Cultural Heritage at the University of Siena, developing an educational and dissemination project for a video game dedicated to an archaeological site. Since 2018, she's been collaborating with a serious gaming society as an archaeological expert and narrative designer. She has published many contributions to scientific magazines and books and has participated in many international conferences presenting her research on the convergence between video games and cultural heritage.

Zsolt László Márkus is the head of the eLearning Department. He graduated from the Faculty of Science of Eötvös Loránd University (ELTE), Budapest, Hungary, in 1996 as a Teacher of Maths. He has more than 15 years of experience in eLearning course development and project management. He has managed national and international projects (LdV.: CHIRON - Reference material, JASON - Pilot project, OSTRICH - Pilot project; FP6.: LOGOS- STREP). He is a member of the professional bodies: APERTUS - Tender expert's group. His main interests are new information and communication technologies, systems, and their use for uLearning purposes. Besides conference publications, he also publishes his work on the Hungarian eLearning forums.

Timothy Marsh is currently with the Griffith Film School (GFS), Griffith University, Brisbane, Australia. His research-practice explores the design and development of new and emerging interactions, narratives, and experiences with interactive media, virtual and augmented reality, and digital games. He's previously held appointments across Europe, the US, Singapore, and Australia, including the University of Southern California in Los Angeles and the National University of Singapore. Past research projects include collaborations with the Massachusetts Institute of Technology's Comparative Media Studies ┃ Writing, Education Arcade, and GAMBIT Game Lab. As a consultant with Singapore's Ministry of Education, he advised on the introduction of game-based storyworlds and interactive storytelling/storybooks across Singapore schools. He has a PhD (2005) in Human-Computer Interaction from the University of York, UK.

Valeria Mazzeo is a PhD student in Complex Systems for Physical, Socio-economic, and Life Sciences at the University of Catania, where she got a Master's in Theoretical Physics. Valeria's research is focused on the study and identification of fake news and misinformation on the World Wide Web, including online Social Media and Web Search Engines. Her main research interests are: Graph and Network theory; Multi-Agent Modeling of Complex Systems (in particular social systems); identification of textual patterns and trends within data through the use of Machine Learning, Text Mining, and Text Analysis; fake news as a form of cyber attack (phishing, typosquatting).

Elina (Eleni) Michopoulou is an Associate Professor of Business Management at the University of Derby, UK. She holds a PhD in Accessible Tourism Information Systems from the University of Surrey, UK. Her research interests include technological applications and information systems in tourism, online consumer behaviour, and technology acceptance. She is particularly interested in the fields of accessible and wellness tourism, which she has actively been researching for over fifteen years. Elina has been involved in various research projects on these topics and worked with funding bodies such as the Wellness Tourism Initiative, the Tanzania Tourism Board, Africa Oracle, and the European Commission. Eleni has published over 60 academic journal articles, book chapters, and conference papers and is the co-founder of the THEINC International Conference. She often acts as guest editor for special issues in service sector journals and sits on the editorial board of over 10 high-impact academic journals. Elina is the Editor-in-Chief of the International Journal of Spa and Wellness, published by T&F, Routledge.

Jari Multisilta is the President and Managing Director of Satakunta University of Applied Sciences. In his former position, he was a professor of Multimedia at Tampere University of Technology and the director of the Pori University Consortium. He was a Visiting Fellow at Nokia Research Center in 2008-2009, a Nokia Visiting Professor in 2012 and a Visiting Scholar at Stanford University, H-STAR Institute from 2007-2014 (18 months). His research interests include mobile learning, mobile video storytelling, gamification and games, and teaching computer coding.

Sithembile Ncube received a BSc in Computer Science at Mathematics from Nelson Mandela University, South Africa, in 2020. She proceeded to study for a BSc Honours in Computer Science and Information Systems at Nelson Mandela University and received her degree in 2021. Her research interests include game design for mental health, the African game development ecosystem, and African women in games. Related to her interests in game design within Africa, in 2021, Sithembile was hired as a junior producer at an award-winning game development company in South Africa. Sithembile is currently independently documenting the experiences of African women involved in games through her initiative, prosearium.net.

Victor Neto is a researcher and teacher developing work on Product Development and Manufacturing Technologies, specially involving thermoplastics processing, eco-design and nanoengineering. His main professional activity is at the Department of Mechanical Engineering of the University of Aveiro (Portugal), where he has an assistant professor position. He is a researcher at the Centre for Mechanical Technology and Automation (TEMA) and a member of a number of scientific organizations. He has over 85 papers published in international refereed journals and over 100 conference communications. He has been involved in several research projects, on the management of scientific events and science dissemination activities. Victor Neto has a BSc degree in Physics Engineering (2001), an MSc in Applied Physics (2004), a PhD in Mechanical Engineering (2008), and an MSc in Management (2012).

Selin Ögel Aydın received her MSc in the Department of Business Administration, Marketing from Eskişehir Osmangazi University Social Sciences Institute in 2014. She started working as a lecturer at Faruk Saraç Vocational School of Design in 2016. She received her Ph.D. in the Department of Business Administration, Marketing from Anadolu University Social Sciences Institute in 2018. She is still working as a lecturer at the same institution, whose name was changed to Istanbul Vocational School of Health and Social Sciences in 2021.

Eva Ordóñez Olmedo is a university professor in Early Childhood and Primary Education Degrees at UNIR. Extraordinary Doctorate Award in the Social Sciences Program at Pablo de Olavide University, investigating curricula based on competencies and innovative methodologies. University Master's Degree in Education for Development, Social Awareness, and Culture of Peace. Graduate in Psychopedagogy. Graduated in Primary Education. Member of the research group HUM-971 INNOVAGOGÍA. Author of various publications in the line of competences at the Postgraduate level, linked to different stays both nationally at the Catholic University of Ávila and internationally at prestigious universities such as Suor Orsola Benincasa - Facoltà di Scienze della Formazione de Napoles (Italy) and at the University of Southampton (UK).

Grethe Østby is a PhD candidate at the Norwegian University of Science and Technology. Her research is being conducted within the Norwegian Cyber Range Innovation Project and focuses on information security awareness in society and cyber-and information security incident response in public emergency organizations. Grethe graduated as a Siviløkonom/Master of Science in Business in 1998, and she has been working for several years in sales and leading implementation and managing teams to operate sales systems, customer-service systems, and management systems in a number of private companies. She has also worked for several years as a crisis manager at the Norwegian Civil Defense national competence center. Grethe also has a short career from the Norwegian Army Signal Core officers' school, today the Norwegian Army Cyber Defense Academy. Her research interest is in combining crisis management and cyber security, and thereby socio-technical research in society and in public emergency organizations.

Sebastian Joy Panattil is a research scholar with the School of Management Studies at Cochin University of Science and Technology, Cochin, India. He has worked in the advertising industry, and his areas of interest include brand management, consumer behavior, and gamification. His field of research involves gamification and consumer engagement.

Desislava Paneva-Marinova is a professor at the Institute of Mathematics and Informatics at the Bulgarian Academy of Sciences (IMI-BAS), PhD (Informatics, 2008), Head of the Department of Mathematical Linguistics at IMI-BAS (2016-present), Secretary of the Scientific Council at IMI-BAS. Her major research interests are in the fields: Multimedia Digital Libraries, Knowledge and Semantic Web Technologies, eLearning, Personalization, Advance Gamification and Storytelling. Participant in more than 20 research projects of IMI-BAS. Author or co-author of two books and more than 130 journal and conference peer-reviewed papers; More than 350 citations.

Demos Parapanos, PhD, is a Lecturer in Tourism Management at the University of Cumbria. Demos's research interests include gamified systems and applications in the tourism and hospitality industry, and his field of research is focused on gamification and understanding hotel visitors' motives when using hotel gamified applications. Demos's background in the hospitality industry started in 2006 as a chef in hotels, restaurants, and pubs.

Lilia Pavlova is an Assistant Professor at the Laboratory of Telematics at the Bulgarian Academy of Sciences (LT-BAS), PhD (Informatics, 2013). Her major research interests are in the fields of Multimedia Digital Libraries, Knowledge and Semantic Web Technologies, eLearning, Serious Games, and Storytelling. Participant in more than 10 research projects. Author or co-author of more than 40 journal and conference peer-reviewed papers; More than 45 citations.

Marta Pérez-Escolar is an assistant professor in the Department of Communication at Loyola University (Sevilla, Spain). She received the Civic Participation, Transparency, and Good Governance PhD Extraordinary Award in 2018, awarded by the Region of Murcia (Spain). Her main lines of research are focused on civic participation, public opinion, political communication, and information disorders, such as hate speech or disinformation.

Rafael Pérez-Jiménez was born in Madrid in 1965. Eng & MSc (Tech. Univ. of Madrid 1991), PhD in Communications Engineering (ULPGC, 1995, Honors), and History (ULL, 2020). Full Professor at the

School of Telecommunication Engineering of the ULPGC (University of Las Palmas de Gran Canaria) from 2003, and from 2010 to 2020, he was chairperson of the Research Institute IDeTIC of ULPGC. Its main area of specialization corresponds to the development of wireless optical communication systems, especially for IoT sensor networks and medium/low speed links, including both the vehicular and domestic environment, and the characterization of optical channels in indoor and mobile systems. He is also working on applications of OWC and the internet of things in Smart Cities, especially those known as tourist destinations. He is also serving at the Spanish Research Agency in the ICT area.

Shri Rai is a lecturer and unit coordinator in the Computer Science and Games Technology majors at Murdoch University, Western Australia. His current research projects are in the use of technology (Games, Virtual Reality and Artificial Reality) for rehabilitation and training, and ML and predictive analytics. He also performs presentations and lectures for high school students on topics in Computer Science and Games Technology.

Jéssica Chaves Reuter has a Master's Degree in Finance from the University of Aveiro and a Degree in Management from the University of Santa Maria (Brazil). She is a PhD student in Business and Economics (University of Aveiro) and a Research Fellow of the project Erasmus +, UNLOCK - Creativity through game-based learning in higher education. Her research interests are related to game-based learning, gamification, financial literacy, financial investments, behavioural finance, and international finance.

Juana Rubio-Romero is a PhD in Philosophy (Complutense University of Madrid). Full-professor at the Faculty of Communication and Arts (Nebrija University). Member of the research group InnoMedia. Part of the RD+I project "Disability and Digital Competences in the Audiovisual Sector", financed by the Spanish Ministry of Science and Innovation. Her research lines are centered on gamification, social networks and the young, and professional communication competences and profiles. She has been a Research and Doctorate Coordinator. PI of the INNECOM research group, and Visiting Professor at the IEDE in Madrid and the TEC of Monterrey (Campus Puebla, Mexico).

Ira Saarinen has her M.D. degree from Helsinki University and completed her specialist training there in Plastic Surgery in 2010. Since then, she has worked as a senior consultant in Plastic Surgery in Satakunta and Etelä-Pohjanmaa District Hospitals. She is currently completing her PhD studies on different aspects of surgical quality and safety during the course of surgical care.

Mohd Fairuz Shiratuddin is a Senior Lecturer at Murdoch University, Australia. He holds a Bachelor of Engineering (BEng) in Electrical and Electronics from Northumbria University, UK, a Master of Science (MSc) in Information Technology (Virtual Reality) from University Utara, Malaysia, a Master of Science (MS) in Architecture (Construction Management) from Virginia Tech, USA, and a Doctor of Philosophy (PhD) in Environmental Design and Planning, also from Virginia Tech, USA. In his early career, he was trained in the United Kingdom and Malaysia as an Electrical and Electronics Engineer, mainly dealing with computers, high-speed internet communication technologies and their applications. He then decided to pursue a career in academia. His main areas of research and teaching are in eXtended Reality (XR = Virtual/Mixed/Augmented Reality), Human-Computer-Interaction, Games Design, Development, and Technologies; for research and practical real-world purposes. He is currently leading Project Neuromender: A Low-Cost Home-Based Stroke Rehabilitation System. In collaboration with other colleagues, he is also currently working on other projects for education, training and simulation, such as: [1] utilising Augmented Reality, image processing, facial recognition technologies and artificial intelligence for security-related applications; [2] design and development of core technologies utilising eXtended Reality for a Multi-User Collaborative and Interactive Virtual Environment (MUCIVE); [3] utilising MUCIVE for Urban Planning; [4] SimJection where VR is used to train nursing students to perform injections in a virtual environment; [5] design and development of a VR learning environment to learn cell biology. Dr. Shiratuddin has over one hundred publications in national and international conference proceedings, journals, books, book chapters, and technical reports.

Maria José Sousa (PhD in Management) is a University Professor and a research fellow at ISCTE/ Instituto Universitário de Lisboa. Her research interests currently are public policies, information science, innovation, and management issues. She is a best-selling author in ICT and People Management and has co-authored over 70 articles and book chapters and been published in several scientific journals (e.g., Journal of Business Research, Information Systems Frontiers, European Planning Studies, Systems Research, and Behavioral Science, Computational and Mathematical Organization Theory, Future Generation Computer Systems, and others). She has also organized and peer-reviewed international conferences and is the guest-editor of several Special Issues. She has participated in several European projects of innovation transfer and is also an External Expert of the COST Association - European Cooperation in Science and Technology, and President of the ISO/TC 260 – Human Resources Management, representing Portugal in the International Organization for Standardization.

Dimitris Stamatelos is a assistant professor at the Hellenic Air Force Academy in the Department of Aeronautical Sciences, Division of Aeronautics, Applied Mechanics, and Infrastructure. He teaches Mechanics of Materials, Aeronautics, Advanced Aeronautics, and Aeroelasticity. He graduated with a Bachelor Honors degree in Aeromechanical Systems Engineering and he holds a Master's Degree in Aerospace Vehicle Design from Cranfield University. He completed his PhD in unconventional aerostructures at the University of Patras. Most of his work is focused on simulation and numerical modelling using the Finite Element Method on large and small-scale structural problems. He has many scientific publications in the fields of aerospace, educational simulations, game development, strength of materials, and structural integrity. His research interests, in relation to the research program, include the following scientific areas: game modelling, game development, and realistic representation of game parameters (space, time, speed, etc.).

György Szántó works as project manager at the eLearning Department of the Institute of Computer Science and Control, Budapest, Hungary. He graduated from the Budapest Technical University (BME) as an electrical engineer (1973). His key activities covered hardware and software development, system design and project management. He has many years of experience in the fields of co-operating systems, multiprocessing, eHealth systems, computer-assisted and electronic training, web and mobile-based application development, as well as in managing international RTD projects.

Tibor Szkaliczki received the M.S. and Ph.D. degrees in electrical engineering from the Technical University of Budapest, Hungary, in 1992 and 1998, respectively. He joined the Computer and Automation Research Institute, Hungarian Academy of Sciences, Budapest, Hungary, in 1997 and is currently a research fellow at the eLearning Department. His research interests include optimization in multimedia systems, VLSI routing, combinatorial optimization, and eLearning.

Necati Taşkın graduated from the Karadeniz Technical University Faculty of Education Department of Computer Education and Instructional Technology in 2006. In 2012, he received his MSc. degree in the department of Computer Education and Instructional Technology at the Institute of Educational Science. He received his Ph.D. degree in the department of Computer Education and Instructional Technology at Gazi University in 2020. Between 2006 and 2011, he worked as an information technology teacher at a public school. In 2011, he started to work as an instructor at Ordu University's Department of Computer Technology. In 2021, he started to work as an assistant professor at Ordu University's Department of Computer Technology. He has also worked at the Distance Education Research and Application Center of Ordu University. He has improved the course content for distance education. His areas of research interest include online learning, blended learning, open and distance education, and gamification.

Venera Tomaselli has a PhD in Sociology and Methods of Social Sciences. Since 1993, she has been Associate Professor of Social Statistics at the Department of Political and Social Sciences at the University of Catania. She was a research fellow at Essex University (UK, 1992), a member of the European Research Group at Munich University (1996), and a visiting professor at the University of Salford (UK, 2015). She was a member of the editorial boards of specialised editions on tourism. She is a reviewer for scientific journals specializing in tourism research and statistics, such as Tourism Economics, Tourism Management, Current Issues in Tourism, Economics, Italian Journal of Applied Statistics (IJAS), Rivista Italiana di Economia, Demografia e Statistica (RIEDS). Her research interests are focused on Multivariate Statistical Models, Network Analysis, Tourism and Market Segmentation Analysis, Ecological Fallacy, Accuracy of Surveys and Opinion Polls, Meta-Analysis, and Clinical Research in Genetics. She has a rich profile of articles in peer-reviewed journals, book chapters, and volumes.

Beybin Elvin Tunc has experience in education, migration, and youth work. She holds a degree in sociology and an international master's degree in migration and intercultural relations. She has worked in child protection, psycho-social support, and social cohesion with refugees and migrants in different non-governmental organizations and UN agencies. Currently, she is working as an independent trainer, facilitator, and learning experience designer. She is designing and facilitating the learning and development processes of the organizations. She is mainly delivering international training and developing guidelines on capacity-building for education practitioners, youth organizations, and humanitarian workers. She is interested in developing and implementing innovative and creative pedagogical approaches in the field of migration. Besides her background, games have always been her passion. Therefore, she is trying to bring humanitarian approaches to game design and gamification.

Miklós Veres works as a project manager at the eLearning Department of the Institute of Computer Science and Control in Budapest, Hungary. He graduated from the Budapest Tech Polytechnical Institution (BMF) as an engineer in Information Technology (2003). He is an expert in electronic training material development and learning management systems. His activities include Web development, graphical interface design, and multimedia editing.

Zsolt Weisz works as a project coordinator at the eLearning Department of the Institute of Computer Science and Control in Hungary. He completed his master's degree in Informatics for Computer Programming at the Faculty of Informatics of Eötvös Loránd University (ELTE), Budapest, Hungary (1994). He is an expert in electronic training material development. His activities include testing, Web development, and multimedia editing.

Index

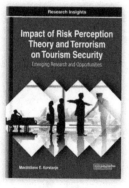

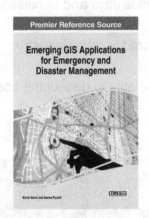
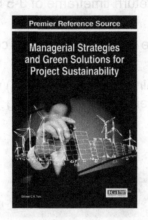

IGI Global Author Services

Providing a high-quality, affordable, and expeditious service, IGI Global's Author Services enable authors to streamline their publishing process, increase chance of acceptance, and adhere to IGI Global's publication standards.

Benefits of Author Services:

- **Professional Service:** All our editors, designers, and translators are experts in their field with years of experience and professional certifications.

- **Quality Guarantee & Certificate:** Each order is returned with a quality guarantee and certificate of professional completion.

- **Timeliness:** All editorial orders have a guaranteed return timeframe of 3-5 business days and translation orders are guaranteed in 7-10 business days.

- **Affordable Pricing:** IGI Global Author Services are competitively priced compared to other industry service providers.

- **APC Reimbursement:** IGI Global authors publishing Open Access (OA) will be able to deduct the cost of editing and other IGI Global author services from their OA APC publishing fee.

Author Services Offered:

 English Language Copy Editing
Professional, native English language copy editors improve your manuscript's grammar, spelling, punctuation, terminology, semantics, consistency, flow, formatting, and more.

 Scientific & Scholarly Editing
A Ph.D. level review for qualities such as originality and significance, interest to researchers, level of methodology and analysis, coverage of literature, organization, quality of writing, and strengths and weaknesses.

 Figure, Table, Chart & Equation Conversions
Work with IGI Global's graphic designers before submission to enhance and design all figures and charts to IGI Global's specific standards for clarity.

 Translation
Providing 70 language options, including Simplified and Traditional Chinese, Spanish, Arabic, German, French, and more.

Hear What the Experts Are Saying About IGI Global's Author Services

 "Publishing with IGI Global has been an amazing experience for me for sharing my research. The strong academic production support ensures quality and timely completion." – **Prof. Margaret Niess, Oregon State University, USA**

"The service was very fast, very thorough, and very helpful in ensuring our chapter meets the criteria and requirements of the book's editors. I was quite impressed and happy with your service." – **Prof. Tom Brinthaupt, Middle Tennessee State University, USA**

Learn More or Get Started Here: For Questions, Contact IGI Global's Customer Service Team at cust@igi-global.com or 717-533-8845

IGI Global
PUBLISHER of TIMELY KNOWLEDGE
www.igi-global.com

Printed in the United States
by Baker & Taylor Publisher Services